Machine Learning

Machine Learning

A Hands-on Approach

C R Rene Robin

Ph.D. (Computer Science and Engineering);
M.E. (Computer Science and Engineering)

Professor, Department of Computer Science and Engineering, and
Dean (Innovation), Sri Sairam Engineering College, Chennai, Tamil Nadu

Doreen Robin

Ph.D. (Computer Science and Engineering);
M.E. (Computer Science and Engineering); B.Tech. (Information Technology)

Founder and Director, Computational Intelligence Research Foundation (CIRF),
Chennai, Tamil Nadu

Chandra Mouli P V S S R

Ph.D. (Computer Science); M.C.A.

Professor, Department of Computer Science,
Central University of Tamil Nadu, Thiruvarur, Tamil Nadu

Universities Press

MACHINE LEARNING: A HANDS-ON APPROACH

UNIVERSITIES PRESS (INDIA) PRIVATE LIMITED

Registered Office
3-6-747/1/A & 3-6-754/1, Himayatnagar, Hyderabad 500 029, Telangana, India
info@universitiespress.com; www.universitiespress.com

Distributed by
Orient Blackswan Private Limited

Registered Office
3-6-752 Himayatnagar, Hyderabad 500 029 Telangana, India

Other Offices
Bengaluru / Chennai / Guwahati / Hyderabad / Kolkata
Mumbai / New Delhi / Noida / Patna

First published 2025

ISBN 978-81-974249-8-4

502159

Typeset in Adobe Garamond Pro 11 points *by*
Cameo Corporate Services Limited, Coimbatore

Printed in India by
B.B. Press, Tronica City, Ghaziabad 201 102

Published by
Universities Press (India) Private Limited
3-6-747/1/A & 3-6-754/1, Himayatnagar, Hyderabad 500 029, Telangana, India

About the Authors

C R Rene Robin received his M.E. and Ph.D. (both in Computer Science and Engineering) from the College of Engineering, Guindy, Anna University. He is currently working as Professor in the Department of Computer Science and Engineering, and as Dean (Innovation) at Sri Sairam Engineering College, Chennai. His areas of specialization are data science, ontological engineering, knowledge management, e-learning, and the semantic web. He is a recognized supervisor of Anna University to guide Ph.D. scholars in Computer Science and Engineering. He is also a doctoral committee member of Anna University and other universities and a senior member of IEEE, lifetime member of Indian Society for Technical Education (ISTE), and member of several professional bodies. He has published three books and has written over 100 articles in both national and international conferences and journals. He has created an innovation ecosystem that integrates with the UN's Sustainable Development Goals.

Doreen Robin is Founder and Director of Computational Intelligence Research Foundation (CIRF), Chennai. A skilled data scientist and an experienced trainer in Machine Learning and Deep Learning, she is also a renowned keynote speaker. She earned her B.Tech. in Information Technology from the University of Madras, M.E. in Computer Science and Engineering from Anna University, and Ph.D. in Computer Science and Engineering from the same institution. Her research interests encompass parallel and distributed computing, peer-to-peer computing, grid computing, cloud computing, cybersecurity, blockchain technology and big data analytics.

With over 500 keynote addresses, conference presentations, and hands-on training sessions delivered to corporations, faculty, and students, Doreen Robin has shared her expertise on topics such as data engineering, blockchain, software testing, cybersecurity, cloud computing, and digital educational tools for teaching and learning. She has published approximately 40 papers in both national and international journals and conferences and is a life member of the Indian Society for Technical Education (ISTE).

Chandra Mouli P V S S R has been associated with the Department of Computer Science, Central University of Tamil Nadu since 2019. Prior to that, he worked at the National Institute of Technology, Jamshedpur, and VIT University, Vellore. He received his M.C.A. from Osmania University, Hyderabad in 2000. He obtained his Ph.D. in Computer Science from the National Institute of Technology (NIT), Tiruchirappalli in 2010. His research interests include digital image processing, digital watermarking, pattern classification, machine learning and deep learning. He has around 35 papers published in SCI/SCIE/Scocpus-indexed journals and around 30 papers in international conferences. He is the resource person for various Faculty Development Programmes conducted under the ATAL scheme introduced by AICTE. He has given many talks and lectures on machine learning and deep learning with practical demonstration using Keras and TensorFlow.

Preface

Machine Learning is how computers learn from data and experience without being explicitly programmed. It is very important in the modern world because it can help us solve many problems that are too complex or too large for humans to handle. Machine learning is a fascinating and powerful technology that can improve our lives in many ways. However, it also has some challenges and limitations we must be aware of.

This book is a comprehensive guide to machine learning, covering the theoretical and practical aspects of the field. It is intended for students, researchers, and practitioners who want to learn the fundamentals and applications of machine learning. At the end of this book, you will have a deep understanding of machine learning and be ready to apply your knowledge to real-world problems.

The book is organized into 14 chapters, each covering a different topic or aspect of machine learning. This structure is designed to provide a comprehensive understanding of the field, starting from the basics and gradually progressing to more advanced topics. This approach allows readers to build a solid foundation and then apply their knowledge to real-world problems.

Chapter 1 introduces you to the basic definitions, types, and challenges of machine learning, as well as some examples and applications. Chapters 2, 3, and 4 provide the mathematical background and tools that you will need to understand and implement machine learning algorithms. They introduce the basic concepts and tools of probability theory and statistics, which are essential for understanding and analyzing data. The book also covers linear algebra, algorithms, and complex optimization, which are the foundation of many machine-learning algorithms and models.

Chapter 5 explores computational learning theory, which includes its definition, objects, history and importance as well as the main methods used. Chapter 6 discusses different machine learning model types and highlights different feature types. It also introduces concept learning in a detailed manner, briefly introduces artificial neural networks, multilayer perceptrons, and linear discriminant analysis, and introduces regression types and logistic regression.

Chapters 7, 8, and 9 cover two major machine learning categories: unsupervised and supervised learning. Unsupervised learning is the process of finding patterns and structures in unlabeled data, while supervised learning is the process of learning from labeled data. You will learn to discover patterns and structure in data without labels using clustering, dimensionality reduction, and association rules. You will also learn how to train models that can predict outcomes or labels from data using linear and non-linear regression, classification, and ensemble methods.

Chapter 10 introduces the most potent and popular of machine learning models: artificial neural networks. You will learn how to build and train neural networks using various architectures, activation functions, optimization algorithms, regularization techniques, and loss functions. You will also learn how to use neural networks for tasks such as image recognition, natural language processing, and reinforcement learning.

Chapter 11 discusses trends in machine learning, including reinforcement learning, multitasking learning, online learning, sequence learning, prediction, bagging, and boosting. Chapter 12 focuses on machine learning applications in various industries, such as Retail, Logistics, Manufacturing, Energy and Utilities, Travel, Banking, Finance, and Insurance.

Chapters 13 and 14 cover practical aspects of machine learning, including capstone projects in Python and R, Jupyter notebook-based programs, and various assignments.

This book is intended for anyone who wants to learn about machine learning, whether you are a student, a researcher, a developer, or a hobbyist. You do not need any prior knowledge or experience in machine learning, but you should have some basic familiarity with programming (preferably Python) and mathematics (especially algebra). The book is designed to be self-contained, but it also provides references and links to further reading for those who want to dig deeper into any topic. The book is also interactive, with exercises and questions at the end of each chapter to help you test your understanding and practice your skills.

We hope it inspires readers to explore machine learning's potential for solving real-world problems and creating value for society.

C R Rene Robin
Doreen Robin
Chandra Mouli P V S S R

Acknowledgements

Writing technical books is one of the desires of any teacher. It ensures the migration of a teacher's perspective from the teaching–learning process to the learning–teaching process. But it has not been possible without support from family members. My gratitude goes to my lovely wife, Dr. Doreen Robin. I extend my gratitude to my daughter, Geona, and my son, Joanez. I also thank Dr. Sai Prakash LeoMuthu, Chairman and CEO, Sairam Institutions, and my colleagues. My Ph.D. Research Scholars provide me with invaluable support and serve as a driving force to continuously update my knowledge. I am deeply grateful to the publisher for giving me this wonderful opportunity to participate.

C R Rene Robin

The successful delivery of this book stands as a testament to the power and impact of outcome-based education. Writing it has been both a journey of discovery and a labor of dedication, made possible by the invaluable support and encouragement of those closest to me.

First and foremost, I extend my deepest gratitude to my husband, Dr. C. R. Rene Robin, for his unwavering support, understanding, and motivation throughout this process. To my beloved parents, Dr. N. Durairaj and Dr. Mrs. Florance Durairaj, who have instilled in me the values of hard work and perseverance, I owe heartfelt thanks. Their lifelong guidance has been a cornerstone of my academic and personal endeavors. I am also incredibly grateful to my wonderful children, Geona and Joanez, whose patience, love, and understanding have been a source of strength and inspiration.

Additionally, I am profoundly thankful to my dedicated team at the Computational Intelligence Research Foundation (CIRF). Their collective commitment and hard work were instrumental in the preparation and completion of this project.

Lastly, I would like to thank everyone on the publishing team for their professionalism, attention to detail, and support in bringing this book to life. Each person's efforts have made a significant impact, and I am genuinely grateful to have had such a talented and dedicated team working alongside me. Thank you to all who contributed to making this book a reality.

Doreen Robin

I would like to express my sincere gratitude to my Vice-Chancellor, Prof. M. Krishnan, who is the inspiration and driving force for my taking up this assignment of contributing some chapters in my fascinating area of interest – Machine Learning. I thank my registrar, Prof. R. Thirumurugan, for encouraging me and provide a platform to contribute to this book. My heartful thanks to my colleagues, friends and well-wishers, Prof. V. Madhurima (Department of Physics, Central University of Tamil Nadu) and Dr. Sangeetha Sriraam (Department of Law, Central University of Tamil Nadu), who always provide strong support in all my endeavors.

Words are not sufficient to express my gratitude for the unconditional support extended by my wife, Santha Kumari, and my children, Sree Lalitha and Saatwik Sravan. The astonishing support rendered by my students, Uzra and Sai Ratna, was remarkable for making my job easier.

Chandra Mouli P V S S R

We are grateful to Universities Press, who came forward to publish this book. Thomas Mathew Rajesh, Kallol Das, and Madhavi Sethupathi of Universities Press were always kind and understanding. Madhavi reviewed this book with abundant patience and helped us say what we had wanted to, enhancing each page of this book with care.

C R Rene Robin
Doreen Robin
Chandra Mouli P V S S R

Contents

I am dedicating this book to God Almighty.

C R Rene Robin

To
My husband, Dr C R Rene Robin, for his steadfast support;
my parents, Dr N Durairaj and Dr Mrs Florance Durairaj, for their enduring guidance; and
my children, Geona and Joanez, who inspire me every day.
With heartfelt appreciation, I dedicate this work to each of you.

Doreen Robin

To
My parents, P V S Prasad and P Vara Lakshmi;
my wife, M C Santha Kumari;
my children, P V S Sree Lalitha and P Saatwik Sravan; and
my students, Uzra Rahman and Puppala Sai Ratna.

Chandra Mouli P V S S R

1 Introduction to Machine Learning

Learning Objectives

At the end of this chapter, you will be able to:

- Define the fundamental concepts of machine learning and explain its historical context
- Explain the significance of machine learning in computer science and its role in problem solving
- State the principles of supervised learning and its subcategories, regression and classification
- Elaborate on the concepts of unsupervised learning, including clustering and association
- Explain the process and objectives of reinforcement learning
- Elucidate the concepts of transfer learning and meta learning and their relevance in machine learning
- Recognize real-world problems that have been solved using machine learning
- Discuss the disadvantages and limitations of data-driven solutions
- Define well-posed machine learning problems
- Outline the life cycle of a machine learning system, from design to deployment

1.1 Introduction

In the real world, we are surrounded by people who can learn from their experiences, thanks to their capacity for learning; we also have computers or other machines that carry out our orders. However, can a machine learn from past data or experiences, like humans? The answer is "Yes," and it is called machine learning. Machine learning (ML) is a powerful tool in computer science and problem solving because it enables computers to learn from data and make predictions or decisions without being explicitly programmed. Complex problems that would be impossible or difficult for traditional algorithms to solve can be worked out using this type of learning. For instance, ML can determine the best route you can take to a destination, the best time to drive, and even provide updates as you drive. Numerous fields, such as robotics and natural language processing, use machine learning.

1.2 What is Machine Learning?

Machine learning is a branch of computer science and artificial intelligence (AI) that focuses on using statistical methods to create intelligent computer systems that can learn from databases that are already available. ML systems are designed with advanced algorithms that enable them to identify patterns and forecast outcomes with limited necessity for human intervention.

In addition, they can automatically learn from data, improve performance based on experience, and make predictions. This refers to devices that can comprehend a text written in natural language, identify a visual scene, or carry out a physical action. ML focuses on emulating human learning processes through data and algorithms, gradually increasing their accuracy.

Arthur Samuel coined the term 'machine learning' in 1959 and described it as, "the scientific field that enables computers/machines to learn without being explicitly programmed." Data such as numbers, images, or text is the foundation of machine learning. **Examples of data sources** include:

- Bank transactions
- Photos of people or specific objects
- Bank statements
- Profit and loss statements
- Time series data from sensors
- Sales reports

First, a machine learning model will be trained on the data (Fig. 1.1), which has been collected and prepared for use as training data. The next step is for programmers to choose a machine learning model to employ, provide the actual data, and then sit back and watch as the computer model learns to spot patterns or predict outcomes. Finally, the human programmer can adjust the model over time, including changing its parameters, to help it produce more accurate results.

A machine learning system's function can be **descriptive**, in which case it makes use of the data to explain what has happened; **predictive**, in which case it uses the data to forecast what will occur; or **prescriptive**, in which case it uses the data to suggest possible courses of action.

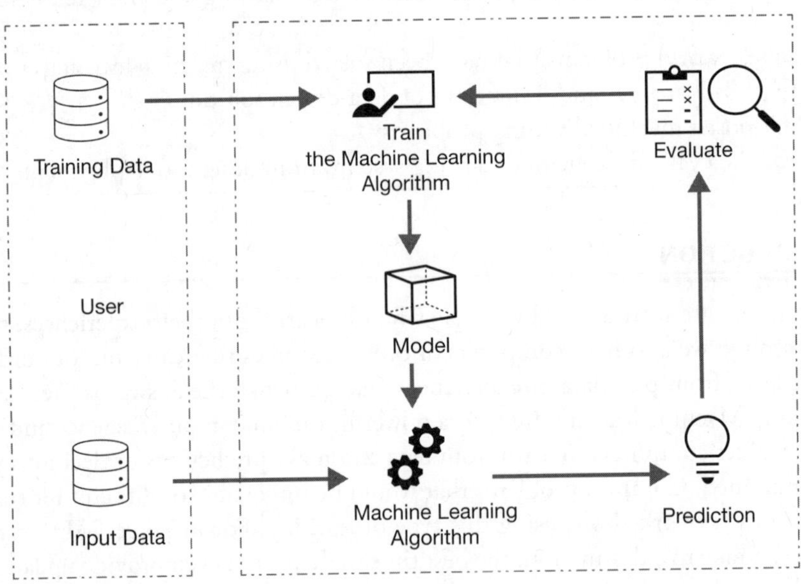

Figure 1.1 Simple flow of a machine learning program

A portion of the training data is stored and used as evaluation data to determine how accurate the ML model is when exposed to new data. The outcome is a model that can be applied in the future to analyze different data sets. Without being explicitly programmed, ML algorithms build a mathematical model using historical sample data, or 'training data,' to help with predictions or decisions.

Computer science and statistics are combined with machine learning to create predictive models. ML uses algorithms to go through vast amounts of data in search of patterns and learn in an iterative process. Ideally, decisions are made based on these insights that impact essential growth metrics in applications and businesses. Recent technological advancements in storage and processing power have made it possible for ML-based products like Netflix's recommendation engine and self-driving cars.

An advanced concept of ML, called deep learning, teaches computers to mimic natural human abilities, such as learning from examples. As a result, compared to traditional ML algorithms, it offers better performance parameters. While ML is not new – it was used in the Second World War to crack the Enigma code – the ability to automatically perform complex mathematical operations on the expanding quantities and diversity of available data is a more recent innovation. With the growth of big data, internet-of-things (IoT), and universal computing, ML is crucial for finding solutions to issues in various fields.

Normal programming involves writing code (the program) for a computer to execute instructions given by the programmer (Fig. 1.2). This code is often written to perform tasks such as sorting numbers, adding two values, or printing something on the screen. The instructions are written so that when they are followed, it will result in an expected outcome. For example, if you write code telling the computer to add two numbers and store them in memory, when the program is run, it will do that regardless of what those two numbers are.

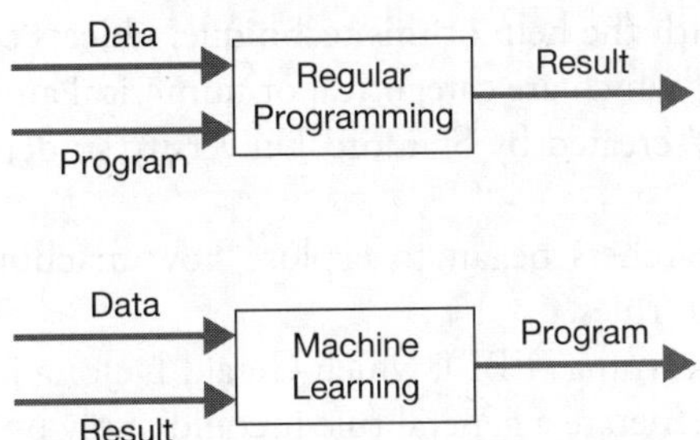

Figure 1.2 Normal programming versus machine learning programming

ML programming, on the other hand, works differently from regular programming. Instead of writing instructions in code for the computer to follow exactly, ML programs use algorithms that help teach the computer how to think and make decisions without being explicitly told what to do by a programmer – this is why we call it 'machine learning' and not 'programming.' For example, if you have a program designed with ML capabilities and give it an image with different colored shapes – circles and squares – then this program could be taught how to recognize which shapes are circles and which are squares without ever being explicitly told how many sides each shape has or what color each shape is supposed to be.

1.3 History of Machine Learning

Machine learning was once considered science fiction, but today it is a reality in our daily lives. Machine learning is aiding our daily lives, from self-driving cars to the Amazon virtual assistant Alexa. The concept behind ML, however, is ancient and has a long history.

The history of ML can be traced back to the mid-1950s, when researchers began to explore algorithms that could learn from data. In the 1950s and '60s, researchers developed algorithms that used numerical input and output data to learn to make predictions. By the late 1960s and early '70s, researchers began exploring algorithms that could learn from more complex data. Another significant milestone in ML's history was the development of the **backpropagation algorithm**. This algorithm allowed neural networks to process data and make predictions by adjusting the weights and bias values of the network. Backpropagation quickly became the standard for training neural networks.

Arthur Samuel's paper was the first significant turning point in machine learning history; Samuel proposed a computer program that could learn from its own experience to play checkers. In addition, his program was the first to use a feedback loop, allowing it to improve its play as it gained experience. Some significant events in the history of machine learning are listed below (Fig. 1.3):

- **1952**: This year saw the invention of a program by ML pioneer Arthur Samuel that assisted an IBM computer in a game of checkers. The more it played, the better it played.
- **1959**: Arthur Samuel first used the phrase 'machine learning.' Using an adaptive filter to eliminate echoes over phone lines, the first neural network came into use.
- **1967**: An article titled 'Nearest Neighbor Pattern Classification' was published by Cover and Hart. This article postulated that machine learning is a technique of inductive logic that divides input objects into two groups. The classification pattern assigns items to the same categories as their closest neighbors. With the help of this technique, objects can be categorized according to various attributes, many of which are categorical or numerical and may have values that overlap.
- **1979**: The 'Stanford Cart,' created by Stanford University students, could autonomously move around obstacles in space.
- As the **1980s** began, researchers began to explore how machines could learn without being explicitly programmed with rules.
- **1981**: Explanation-based learning (EBL), which Gerald DeJong introduced, used a computer to analyze training data and generate a general rule it could apply by ignoring irrelevant data.
- **1985**: Terry Sejnowski and Charles Rosenberg created NETtalk, a neural network that learned how to pronounce 20,000 words correctly in a single week.
- **1986**: Geoffrey Hinton and David Rumelhart proposed a new algorithm called the backpropagation algorithm. This was the first to use an artificial neural network to learn from input data.
- **1997**: A computer defeated a human chess expert for the first time when IBM's Deep Blue defeated chess master Garry Kasparov.
- **2006**: Geoffrey Hinton, a computer scientist, renamed neural network research 'deep learning.' Since then, it has emerged as one of the most popular technologies.
- **2010**: People could interact with computers by moving and making gestures, thanks to Microsoft Kinect's ability to track 20 human features at a rate of 30 times per second.
- **2011**: Watson from IBM defeated human opponents on Jeopardy.
- **2012**: Google developed a deep neural network that learned to identify images of people and cats in YouTube videos.
- **2014**: The chatbot Eugene Goostman passed the Turing test. About 33% of the event's judges thought that Goostman was human. Facebook developed a deep neural network called DeepFace that the company claimed could recognize people as precisely as humans.
- **2016**: Google's artificial intelligence algorithm defeated a professional Go player, in what is regarded as the world's most challenging board game that is many times more complex than chess. In the Go competition, the AlphaGo algorithm created by Google DeepMind won all five games.

- **2017**: Waymo began testing driverless vehicles in the US, but only with backup drivers in the back. They rolled out fully autonomous taxis in Phoenix later that year.
- **2017 to the present**: Building neural networks and deep learning algorithms has advanced many sectors from 2017 to 2024. The industry prioritized ethical AI and explainability in 2020 to improve algorithm fairness, transparency, and accountability. Generative models dominated content production and simulation by 2022, as the ML business grew. AI outperformed humans in image categorization, visual reasoning, and language interpretation. However, it lacked advanced cognitive skills like competitive mathematics and common sense logic. The ML market is predicted to reach $21 billion by 2024, illustrating its rapid growth and AI investment.

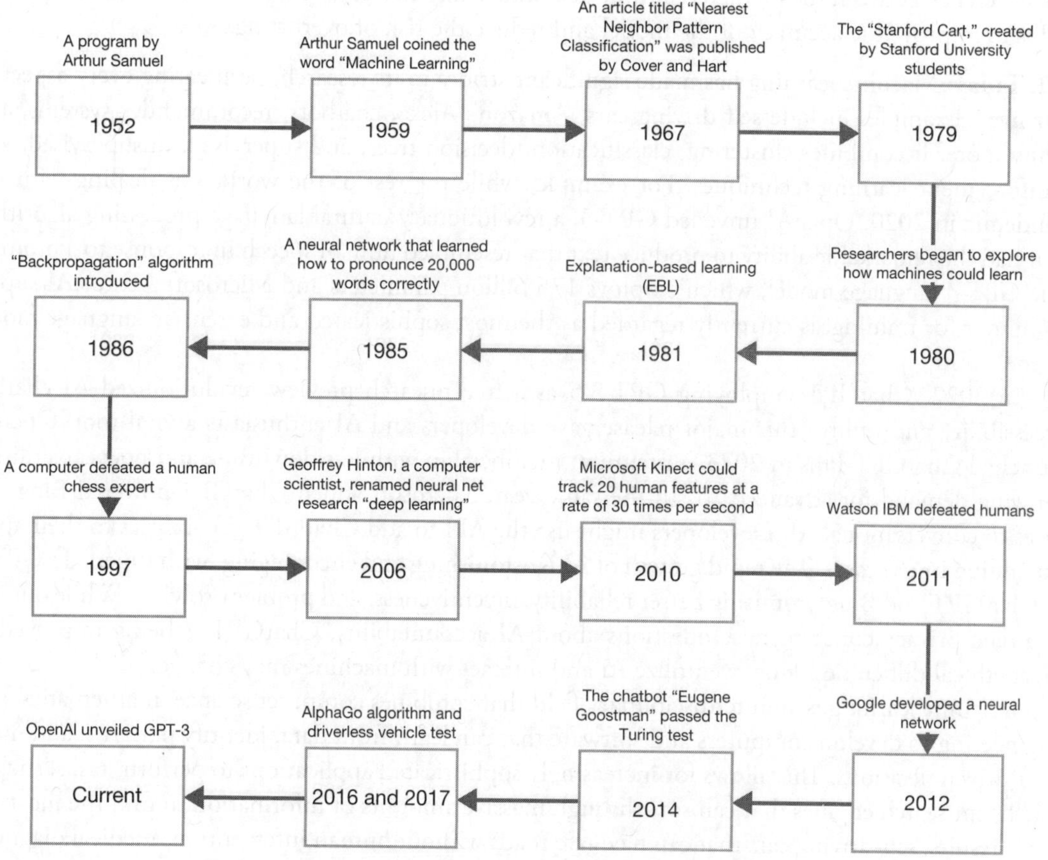

Figure 1.3 History of machine learning

The principles of learning observed in animals also inspired the development of ML algorithms. Experiments such as bait shyness and Skinner's pigeon superstition provide examples of how animal behavior can be related to machine learning concepts such as sampling data and empirical risk minimization. By understanding these principles, ML researchers can develop more effective algorithms that can learn from data and improve their accuracy over time.

The **bait shyness experiment** involved rats and their learning behavior. The experiment showed that rats tend to eat small quantities of food before consuming a full meal. This behavior is akin to the concept of sampling data in machine learning. In ML, sampling data involves selecting a subset of data from a larger data set to train a model. This process helps to reduce the computational complexity of the model and improve its accuracy.

Skinner's pigeon superstition experiment involved pigeons and their behavior in response to a reward. The experiment showed that pigeons developed superstitious behavior when they received a reward randomly, even if the reward was not related to their behavior. This behavior is like the concept of empirical risk minimization in machine learning. Empirical risk minimization involves minimizing the difference between the predicted output of a model and the actual output of the data. This process helps to improve the accuracy of the model and reduce the risk of overfitting.

ML Today: Machine learning has made significant strides in its research, permeating every aspect of our lives. Examples include self-driving cars, Amazon's Alexa, chatbots, recommender systems, and many more. It combines clustering, classification, decision trees, and supervised, unsupervised, and reinforcement learning techniques. For example, while the rest of the world was dealing with the pandemic in 2020, OpenAI unveiled GPT-3, a revolutionary natural language processing algorithm that had the remarkable ability to produce text that resembled human speech in response to a prompt. The GPT-3 language model, which employs 175 billion parameters and Microsoft Azure's AI supercomputer for training, is currently regarded as the most sophisticated and extensive language model in the world.

In 2022, ChatGPT employing GPT-3.5 as a free research preview revolutionized AI chatbot accessibility and utility. This major release gave developers and AI enthusiasts a vital tool. OpenAI launched ChatGPT Plus in 2023, a premium membership with less downtime and new capabilities, showing demand for advanced AI. In the same year, Microsoft added ChatGPT-powered Bing features to conversational AI. Developers might use the API to add ChatGPT capabilities to their apps, expanding its use cases. The rapid growth of AI is astonishing and encouraging, with OpenAI's GPT-4 in ChatGPT and Bing promising better reliability, inventiveness, and problem-solving. While outages and data privacy concerns raise questions about AI accountability, ChatGPT is being improved to meet ethical difficulties. How we utilize AI and interact with machines may change.

Machine learning is an interdisciplinary field that combines computer science, mathematics, and engineering to develop computers and software that can learn from data, identify patterns, and make data-driven decisions. This allows for increasingly sophisticated applications to perform tasks, such as intelligent search engines that can sort through massive amounts of information to find the most relevant results, self-driving cars that can navigate roads without human intervention, medical diagnosis systems that can diagnose diseases before they become too severe, and facial recognition systems that allow for secure access control in many settings.

1.4 Role of Machine Learning in Computer Science and Problem Solving

Computer science and machine learning have formidable problem-solving capabilities. ML enables computers to learn from data and make decisions without directly programming them. This form of technology aids in the resolution of a range of problems that are too complicated or time-consuming for people to handle alone.

ML employs techniques that may be used to solve various problems, including classification, grouping, prediction, and search optimization. These algorithms teach computers to recognize patterns in massive data sets and utilize them to make predictions or judgments.

ML is widely employed in computer science when dealing with massive data sets or issues that require substantial computational power, such as picture recognition or natural language processing (NLP). For example, suppose a group of photos requires labeling based on their content. An ML algorithm may be created to detect specific aspects within the images, such as color composition and texture.

This algorithmic technique is significantly faster than human labeling since it does not require human experience; it only requires training on relevant data sets to identify photos reliably based on their content. Furthermore, once trained on one type of data set, the same algorithm can frequently be reused for similar types of image recognition tasks without requiring additional training, leading to more efficient results.

Another example where ML shows its worth is in predicting user behavior by analyzing historic trends pointed out by big data analytics companies such as Google Analytics. This helps businesses better understand how users interact with their services/products so they can tailor their offerings to maximize user engagement while also minimizing the costs associated with development/marketing.

Due to its versatility and scalability, ML has been widely embraced by both industry professionals and academics alike. Although there remain challenges when developing these algorithms (ease of interpretability, avoiding overfitting), ML continues to revolutionize how we look at problem solving, provide more significant opportunities than ever before, analyze situations accurately, and arrive at meaningful conclusions.

1.5 Why Machine Learning?

One of the reasons why machines need to learn is to perform tasks that are beyond the capability of human beings. For example, machines can process and analyze large amounts of data that humans cannot, such as the results of thousands of scientific experiments. Machines can also learn from their own experiences and improve their performance over time, which is called **experiential learning**.

Let us consider an example of a scientific experiment that involves testing different combinations of chemicals to produce a desired reaction. A human scientist may conduct several trials and record the outcomes, but it would be very difficult and time-consuming for the scientist to analyze all the possible patterns and correlations among the variables. However, a machine can use data mining techniques to discover hidden insights and generate hypotheses from the data. The machine can also use ML algorithms to test and refine its hypotheses and optimize its results.

Another reason why machines need to learn is to emulate human abilities, such as voice recognition and image recognition. These tasks require machines to understand and interpret natural language and visual information, which are unstructured and complex forms of data.

Let us consider an example of a voice recognition system that can transcribe speech into text. A human listener may be able to understand what a speaker is saying, but it would be very challenging for them to write down every word accurately and quickly. However, a machine can use speech recognition techniques to convert the sound waves into digital signals and extract features from them. The machine can also use NLP techniques to parse the sentences and assign meanings to the words. The machine can learn from its own errors and feedback and improve its accuracy and speed over time.

The growth of ML has been fueled by the virtually infinite amount of accessible, affordable data storage options, accessibility and affordability of computational power, development of less expensive and more powerful processors, and accessibility of high-speed internet. Thanks to these digital transformation factors, one can quickly and automatically create models that can quickly and accurately analyze extensive and complex data sets (Fig. 1.4).

Another way ML enables companies to stay competitive is by automating complex processes such as manufacturing assembly lines or customer service chatbots. Automation can improve efficiency while also reducing costs related to labor expenses and improving time-to-market speeds for new products or services.

ML may be the key to unlocking the value of corporate and customer data and making decisions that keep a business ahead of the competition. Many industries are now creating more powerful models that can analyze more significant and complex data sets and produce faster, more precise results on a large scale. In addition, many of the largest organizations in the world today, including Facebook, Twitter, and Google, rely heavily on machine learning for their daily operations. As a result, it has become an essential competitive differentiator for many businesses worldwide.

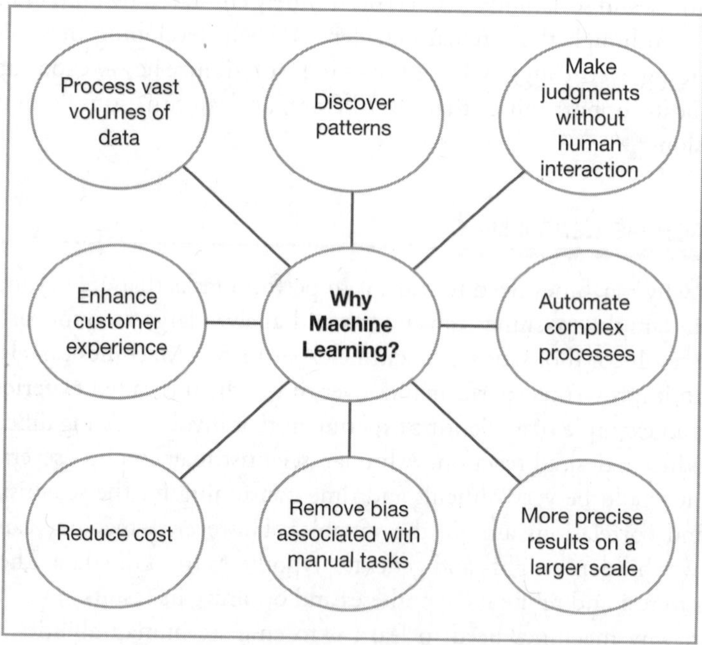

Figure 1.4 Why machine learning?

ML's practical applications use data to drive business outcomes, significantly impacting an organization's bottom line. Organizations have adopted ML as the best method for creating models, strategizing, and planning, and they need a system to analyze it effectively and accurately. It is significant because it helps companies develop new products and gives them insights into consumer behavior trends and business operating patterns. In addition, automation with machine learning capabilities helps remove the bias associated with manual tasks where human error may occur due to unintentional prejudices or oversight during decision-making processes involving subjective criteria such as hiring practices.

ML can quickly and accurately identify complex relationships in data quickly and accurately, whereas doing so manually would take a lot of time and effort. As a result, organizations can more quickly spot lucrative opportunities and potential risks, thanks to ML tools.

Finally, machine learning helps enable personalized experiences in sectors like retail by leveraging behavior analysis data collected from customers' interactions with websites and mobile apps so that companies can tailor their offerings based on individual preferences while at the same time providing more efficient customer service options through AI-driven automated conversations using chatbots; this provides customers with quick resolution times as they do not have to wait for a human representative's response which could take hours or even days.

1.6 Adaptivity of Machine Learning

Adaptivity is the ability of a machine learning system to adjust its decisions according to the current state of the environment, without requiring human intervention or retraining from scratch. For example, an adaptive machine learning system for spam detection may learn to identify new types of spam emails that emerge over time by updating its model based on feedback from users or the email server. Another example is self-driving cars, which may learn to cope with different road conditions, traffic patterns, or weather situations, by adapting its behavior based on sensory inputs and rewards from the environment.

Adaptivity of machine learning can be achieved in different ways, depending on the type and degree of change in the environment. Some of the common methods are as follows:

- **Online learning:** This is a form of incremental learning, where the ML system updates its model continuously as new data arrives, without storing or revisiting the previous data. Online learning can handle gradual or moderate changes in data distribution or the task, but may suffer from catastrophic forgetting if the change is abrupt or drastic.
- **Active learning**: This is a form of selective learning, where the ML system queries the most informative or uncertain data points from a pool of unlabeled data, and obtains their labels from an oracle (such as a human expert or a simulator). Active learning can reduce labeling cost and improve model accuracy, especially when the data is scarce or noisy. Active learning can also handle changes in data distribution or the task, by focusing on the most relevant or novel data points.
- **Reinforcement learning**: This is a form of interactive learning, where the ML system learns from its own actions and their consequences in an environment, without requiring explicit labels or supervision. Reinforcement learning can optimize a long-term goal or reward, which may depend on the state of the environment and the actions of other agents. Reinforcement learning can handle changes in feedback or the reward function, by exploring different actions and exploiting the best ones.

1.7 Designing versus Learning

Designing and learning are two different aspects of machine learning. The method used to solve problems is the main distinction. Developing predictive models that can precisely predict future outcomes by learning from historical data is the main focus of **learning**. Creating novel algorithms or architectures that can be used to address challenging real-world issues like image recognition, natural language processing, and autonomous driving, on the other hand, is the focus of **designing**.

Designing calls for originality and frequently entails the creation of new algorithms or architectural frameworks. This may entail modifying already-in-use algorithms or building entirely new models from scratch. Working with subject-matter experts to comprehend the issue being addressed and generate solutions may also be a part of the design process. Designing is creating models using algorithms or templates with specific parameters or assumptions about the input data. This includes designing a deep neural network (DNN), a type of AI model composed of multiple layers connected by neurons. Designers need to define what types of layers will be used in the network (such as convolutional layers), how those layers are connected (such as skip connections), and what values will be used for each layer's weights (which determine how strongly one neuron influences another).

Designing entails creating new methods or techniques for achieving a desired result. In contrast, learning can be thought of as applying current algorithms or architectures to data to infer a result.

Unsupervised learning and supervised learning are additional categories of learning. Labeled data is necessary for supervised learning, which means that the input data must have labels that specify the desired output before the model is created. The model is then trained using the labeled data to discover an input–output mapping. Unsupervised learning makes an effort to identify patterns directly from the data and does not require labeled data. In this process, algorithms refine their internal parameters to better model relationships between inputs/outputs to accurately predict future outcomes, given new inputs not seen during training sessions. Using techniques like backpropagation helps ensure accuracy when dealing with large amounts of data or complex problems where traditional approaches may fail due to their inability to optimize things like hyperparameters faster than manual optimization techniques like the hill climbing approach.

Designing and learning are closely related but distinct concepts in ML development projects. Designers create machines with appropriate architectures (design) while learners use those designs plus existing data sets to refine them further until accurate results are presented. By understanding both concepts, developers can build solutions quickly, adaptively, and efficiently since designers focus on constructing models while learners work on optimizing them over time. In conclusion, designing entails developing new algorithms or architectures, whereas learning is applying current algorithms or architectures to input data to make predictions.

1.8 Training versus Testing in Machine Learning

Training and testing are two vital components of the ML process that work together to produce reliable models. Training and testing are two distinct phases of the model building process. While testing involves assessing the model's performance on new data, training involves building a model from training data. In other words, testing is validating the model using data that has not been seen before, whereas training is learning from the data.

Training: Training is the process of providing the model with input data to learn how to recognize patterns or identify relationships among variables. This can be done using supervised or unsupervised methods, depending on the problem being solved. Different algorithms are applied to the input data during training, and parameters are adjusted until an optimal solution is found. The main goal of training is to make sure that the model performs well on unseen examples or test sets. Thus, it involves tweaking parameters such as weights and hyperparameters until satisfactory results are applied to a subset (training set) of the provided examples/data points/inputs.

The process of training a model involves several steps:

1. **Data preprocessing:** This involves transforming the raw data into a form the model can use. Techniques such as normalization, scaling, transformation, imputation, and encoding are applied to prepare the data for ML algorithms. Statistics and mathematics help us understand the properties and distributions of the data and to choose appropriate methods for data manipulation.
2. **Feature engineering:** This involves creating new features or variables from the existing data that can improve the performance of ML algorithms. Statistics and mathematics help to identify relevant features, measure their importance, and apply techniques such as dimensionality reduction, feature selection, feature extraction, and feature construction.
3. **Model selection:** This involves selecting the best model to use for the given data set. This requires understanding the type of data and the type of model that will best solve the problem. The best ML algorithm needs to be chosen for a given problem and data set. Statistics and mathematics help to compare different algorithms based on their assumptions, complexity, accuracy, generalization, and robustness. They also help to tune the hyperparameters of the algorithms using methods such as cross-validation, grid search, random search, and Bayesian optimization.
4. **Model fitting:** This involves optimizing the model parameters to fit the data. This is done using an optimization algorithm such as gradient descent, which adjusts the model parameters to minimize the prediction error. Gradient descent is a powerful optimization technique that can be used to find the optimal values of parameters that minimize a loss function. In ML, the loss function measures how well a model fits the data, and the goal is to minimize the error between the model's predictions and the actual outcomes. Gradient descent works by iteratively updating the parameters in the direction of the steepest descent of the loss function, using a learning rate that controls the size of each update. One of the challenges of gradient descent is choosing an appropriate learning rate. If the learning rate is too small, the algorithm will take a long time to converge to the optimal solution. The algorithm may overshoot the optimal solution and diverge if the learning rate is too large. Another challenge of gradient descent is that it may get stuck in a local minimum, where the loss function has a lower value than any nearby point but not necessarily the lowest value overall. To avoid this problem, some variants of gradient descent have been developed that use different strategies to explore the loss function landscape and escape from local minima. Some of the common types of gradient descent are given below:
   - **Batch gradient descent (BGD)**: This is the simplest form of gradient descent and it ensures that the algorithm converges to the global minimum, but it can be very slow and computationally expensive when the data set is large. BGD is an iterative optimization approach that involves moving in the direction of the steepest descent, which is determined by the negative gradient of the function. In ML, this function typically serves as the loss or error function,

which quantifies the degree of fit between the model and the data. The model parameters can be acquired from the data by minimizing the loss function. BGD involves calculating the gradient utilizing the complete data set at each iteration. An advantage of BGD is the assurance of convergence to the global minimum of the loss function, provided that the learning rate is sufficiently small. Another benefit is that BGD may be readily parallelized and dispersed across numerous machines or processors. A limitation of BGD arises when the data set is extensive since it can result in sluggish performance and high computing costs. In addition, in the event of data set modifications or the inclusion of new data points, the algorithm must recalculate the gradient by utilizing the complete data set, resulting in potential wastage and inefficiency. Another disadvantage is that BGD might be susceptible to outliers and noisy data points. This can result in inadequate performance and less-than-ideal solutions.

- **Stochastic gradient descent (SGD)**: SGD employs a modification whereby, instead of utilizing the entire data set, it randomly chooses a single data point (or a small group of data points) throughout each iteration and calculates the gradient based on it. This minimizes the computational expense and enables quicker updates. In addition, when the gradient is calculated from a random subset, the algorithm provides inherent variability and randomness. This characteristic prevents the algorithm from becoming trapped in suboptimal local minima or saddle points. SGD can adjust to varying data distributions and effectively manage noisy or redundant data, surpassing the performance of traditional gradient descent methods. Nevertheless, SGD also presents certain limitations and obstacles. One issue is that the gradient derived from a random sample might exhibit significant noise and inaccuracy, leading to fluctuations and instability in parameter updates. Another obstacle lies in the fact that SGD can be highly responsive to the arrangement and choice of data points, impacting its convergence and overall efficiency. Numerous variations and extensions of SGD have been developed to address these difficulties and to enhance its efficiency and resilience. One such technique is momentum, which incorporates a fraction of the previous parameter update into the current update to expedite convergence and mitigate oscillations. Another technique is adaptive learning rate methods, such as AdaGrad, RMSProp, and Adam, which dynamically adjust the learning rate for each parameter based on its historical gradients.
- **Mini-batch gradient descent**: This is a method that merges the benefits of BGD and SGD for optimizing the parameters of an ML model. Mini-batch gradient descent divides the training data set into smaller subsets, known as mini-batches. It then utilizes each mini-batch to calculate the gradient and modify the parameters during each iteration. Implementing this technique can mitigate the noise and variability inherent in SGD while enhancing the velocity and effectiveness of batch gradient descent. The ideal mini-batch size is contingent upon several aspects, including the data distribution, the model's architecture, and the hardware's setup. Mini-batch gradient descent can be enhanced by employing distinct learning rates for each parameter or by utilizing adaptive learning rates that dynamically adjust based on the prior gradients. These strategies can be used to prevent being stuck at local minima or saddle points and to achieve faster convergence towards the global minimum of the loss function. Several examples of these techniques are momentum, RMSProp, Adam, and AdaGrad.

- **Momentum-based gradient descent**: This is an alternative form of gradient descent that helps accelerate the optimization process and prevent it being trapped in local minima. This incorporates a momentum component that monitors and includes prior parameter adjustments into the current update using a scaling factor. By following this approach, the algorithm may effectively build up speed in areas where the gradient remains steady and smooth while decreasing speed in areas where the gradient frequently changes direction. This can facilitate the algorithm's escape from regions with low gradients or local minima more rapidly and mitigate oscillations around the optimal point. Momentum-based gradient descent is a prevalent optimization approach in machine learning and deep learning. It is widely utilized due to its ability to enhance the performance and efficiency of neural networks and other intricate models.
- **Adaptive gradient descent**: This is a family of algorithms that adaptively adjusts the learning rate for each parameter based on its historical gradients. This means that parameters with large and frequent updates will have a lower learning rate, while those with small and infrequent updates will have a higher learning rate. This way, the algorithm can avoid overshooting the optimal value or getting stuck in a local minimum. Some examples are AdaGrad, Adadelta, RMSProp, and Adam. AdaGrad is a learning rate scaling algorithm that is inversely proportional to the square root of the sum of squared gradients. This means that the learning rate decreases as the gradient accumulates over time. This can be beneficial for sparse features but can also cause the learning rate to become too small and stop the learning process. Adadelta is an extension of AdaGrad that addresses the problem of diminishing learning rates. Instead of a cumulative sum, it employs a moving average of squared gradients. In addition, it provides a decay rate parameter to regulate the speed at which the average diminishes. This way, the algorithm can adapt to changing gradients and maintain a more robust learning rate. RMSProp is another AdaGrad extension that uses a moving average of squared gradients but with a different formula. The average's square root splits the learning rate, and a momentum parameter is included to incorporate a percentage of the previous update into the current one. By employing this method, the algorithm can expedite the convergence process and overcome stagnant points in the optimization process. Adam is a popular algorithm that combines the ideas of Adadelta and RMSProp. It uses both moving averages of gradients and squared gradients, and it also introduces two parameters called beta1 and beta2 that control the decay rates of these averages. In addition, it performs bias correction to account for the initial values of these averages. This way, the algorithm can achieve fast and stable convergence with minimal hyperparameter tuning.

5. **Model evaluation:** This involves assessing how well the model performs on unseen data. This means assessing the quality and validity of the machine learning models using metrics such as accuracy, precision, recall, F1-score, ROC curve, AUC, confusion matrix, MSE, MAE, R2-score, etc. Statistics and mathematics help to interpret these metrics, test the significance of the results, and diagnose potential problems such as overfitting, underfitting, bias and variance.
6. **Model interpretation:** This involves explaining how the ML models work and why they make certain predictions or decisions. Statistics and mathematics help to understand the logic and mechanisms of the algorithms, and to visualize or quantify their outputs using methods such as feature importance, partial dependence plots, SHAP values and LIME.

7. **Testing:** Testing refers to assessing how well an ML algorithm performs on unseen data points or inputs compared to its performance when trained (estimation). This evaluation helps assess whether the predictions made by a given algorithm match up with those made by humans for similar inputs (validation). Testing typically consists of splitting available input into two subsets: one for training purposes and the other for testing purposes; this helps ensure unbiased results since both sets contain randomly distributed examples from the provided data set (cross-validation). The testing phase also allows us to measure performance metrics like accuracy rate, recall score, and precision score, which can then be compared against benchmark values or those achieved during earlier iterations while tuning parameters to improve them further, if needed. Moreover, it indicates overfitting/underfitting problems associated with our approach towards solving the given problem(s). In addition, some ML algorithms utilize cross-validation techniques wherein multiple tests are conducted using different combinations/splits between 'training' versus 'testing' data sets; this further assists in ensuring better estimates while making predictions about future outcomes/scenarios.

1.9 Machine Learning versus Automation

Machine learning and automation are two related but distinct concepts that are often used interchangeably in the context of artificial intelligence. However, they have different meanings and implications for various domains and applications.

ML is a branch of computer science that deals with creating systems or algorithms that can learn from data and improve their performance over time. It can be used for tasks such as classification, regression, clustering, recommendation, natural language processing and computer vision. It can also be seen as a form of automation, since it enables computers to perform tasks that would otherwise require human intelligence or intervention.

Automation, on the other hand, is a broader term that refers to the use of technology to control or operate processes or systems without human input. Automation can be applied to various fields such as manufacturing, transportation, agriculture and healthcare. Automation can also involve machine learning, but not necessarily.

The main difference between ML and automation is that ML involves learning from data, while automation involves executing predefined rules or instructions. Machine learning can enable automation to adapt to changing conditions or situations, while automation can enable machine learning to scale up or speed up its operations. ML and automation can also complement each other in various ways. For example, ML can be used to optimize or improve the performance of automated systems, while automation can be used to collect or label data for ML models.

ML and automation are both important and powerful technologies that have the potential to transform various industries and domains. However, they also pose some challenges and limitations that need to be addressed. For instance, ML may require large amounts of data or computational resources, while automation may require careful design or regulation. Moreover, ML and automation may have ethical or social implications that need to be considered, such as the impact on human jobs, privacy, security, and accountability. Therefore, it is essential to understand the differences and similarities between ML and automation and use them wisely and responsibly.

1.10 Predictive and Descriptive Tasks in Machine Learning

Predictive and descriptive tasks are two of the major types of tasks that are performed in machine learning. Predictive tasks involve predicting future events or behaviors based on data from the past, while descriptive tasks involve describing the characteristics of existing data.

Predictive tasks create a model that can predict future events or behavior based on prior data. For example, predictive models in financial forecasting may be used to estimate future stock prices or exchange rates. Forecasting client demand for certain products and services, anticipating fraudulent behavior before it occurs, and recommending content to social media platform users are some more examples.

Descriptive tasks entail using techniques like grouping or segmentation analysis to explain aspects of current data sets without making future predictions. Descriptive analysis can frequently uncover previously unknown or poorly understood correlations between elements.

Finally, it is vital to remember that ML algorithms may also be used for productive tasks, such as making new digital photographs, in which machines create something new rather than merely evaluating what already exists (as is seen with predictive and descriptive analytics). Such techniques enable machines to learn from previous experiences and develop new material with some degree of uniqueness – essential skills when used appropriately!

1.11 Some Terminology Related to Machine Learning

Let us use examples to explain the terminology. To buy good quality lady's fingers, one should look for the following:

- The color should be bright green, without any brown or black spots.
- The texture should be firm and crisp, not soft or mushy.
- The size should be medium, not too small or too large.
- The shape should be straight and slender, not curved or twisted.

These factors are examples of a domain set, which is a collection of possible values for a certain attribute or feature. A **domain set** defines the range and type of values that an attribute can take.

A **label** is a value that represents the category or class of an object or an observation. For example, in a classification problem, the label can be yes or no, positive or negative, spam or not spam, etc. A label is usually the output or the target variable that we want to predict or learn from the data.

A **domain point** is a specific value or instance of an attribute or feature. For example, if the attribute is color, then a domain point can be green, red, blue, etc. A domain point is usually the input or independent variable that we use to predict or learn the label.

A **mapping function** is a mathematical function that relates the domain points to the labels. For example, if we have a mapping function $f(x) = y$, then x is the domain point and y is the label. A mapping function describes how the input affects the output, or how the features influence the target.

A **learner** is an algorithm or a model that learns the mapping function from the data. For example, a learner can be a decision tree, a neural network, a logistic regression, etc. A learner tries to find the best mapping function that fits the data and minimizes error.

A **predictor** is a function that uses the learned mapping function to predict the label for a new domain point. For example, if we have a predictor $p(x) = f(x)$, then $p(x)$ is the predictor and $f(x)$ is the learned mapping function. A predictor applies the mapping function to a new input and outputs the predicted label.

1.12 Types of Machine Learning

The algorithms and techniques used in machine learning are used to build models that can learn from data and make predictions or decisions. Following are the types of machine learning: supervised learning, unsupervised learning, reinforcement learning, transfer learning, and meta learning (Fig. 1.5).

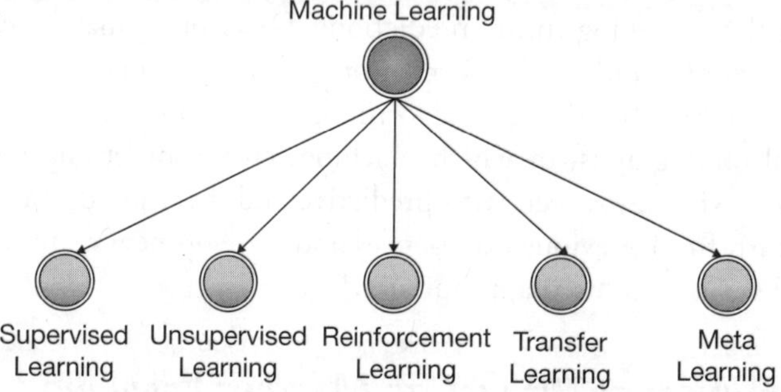

Figure 1.5 Types of machine learning

1.12.1 Supervised Learning

Supervised learning is ML in which machines are trained using well 'labeled' training data, and they predict the output based on that data. 'Labeled data' means some input data that is already tagged with the correct output. Although this method requires accurate data labeling, supervised learning is compelling and yields excellent results when applied appropriately. The supervisor instructs the machines to predict the output using the training data correctly.

The training data set provides the algorithm with the labeled parameters necessary for the problem and shares many characteristics with the final data set. It provides the algorithm with information about the issue, the solution, and the various data points to be handled. To establish a cause-and-effect relationship between the variables in the data set, the ML algorithm then finds relationships between the input parameters. For example, a supervised learning algorithm aims to find a mapping function to map the input variable (x) with the output variable (y). It applies the same concept as a student learning under a teacher's supervision.

When the training and processing are complete, we test the model by supplying sample data to see if it accurately predicts the output. The system builds a model using labeled data to understand the data sets and learn about each data. In the real world, supervised learning can also be used for risk assessment, image classification, fraud detection and spam filtering. When we play a film or episode on Amazon Prime Video, we are also informing the ML algorithm to find similar shows based on our preference.

Supervised learning can be further grouped into two categories of algorithms (Fig. 1.6): regression and classification. Classification and regression are two fundamental types of ML problems that are used to solve a wide range of real-world problems. In essence, classification is a type of problem where the goal is to predict a categorical outcome, while regression is a type of problem where the goal is to predict a continuous outcome. To illustrate this concept, let us consider the example of an average person's needs and how they can be grouped into classification and regression problems.

For instance, if a person is concerned about whether their son will get a job or not, this is a classification problem. The outcome is binary: either the son will get a job or he will not. Similarly, if a person is interested in knowing at what age their son will get married, this is a regression problem. The output will be a numerical value, such as 28 or 30. Another example of a regression problem is when a person wants to know which area the bride will come from. The answer will be in the form of a city or area name, which is a continuous variable.

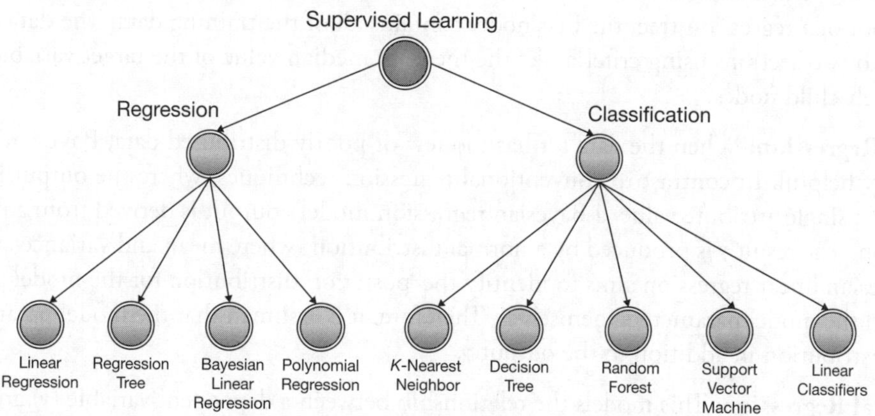

Figure 1.6 Types of supervised learning

1.12.1.1 Regression

Regression algorithms are used if there is a relationship between the input variable and the output variable. It is used for prediction of continuous variables, such as in weather forecasting, market trends and stock values. Some popular regression algorithms that come under supervised learning are linear regression, regression tree, Bayesian linear regression, and polynomial regression.

Linear Regression: Here, a mathematical equation describes the relationship between two or more variables. For example, the 'dependent variable' and additional variables ('independent variables') are investigated. Regression uses independent variables to model a target prediction value. These models vary according to the number of independent variables they use and the type of relationship they take into account between the dependent and independent variables.

Consider a scenario where you wish to forecast your monthly salary based on your years of experience and educational background. Monthly salary can be the dependent variable in linear regression, whereas years of experience and education can be considered as independent variables. A line that best matches these points is then estimated using the linear regression model.

To make predictions with fresh observations that fall within the range of values in our data set, we need to identify the mathematical equation that best captures the data. **Ordinary least squares (OLS)**, the most popular type of linear regression, determines the line with the fewest squared distances between each point and its corresponding value on our estimated line. This method provides us with an estimate for our model's unknown parameters, which we can use to make predictions with new data points outside the data set range using extrapolation techniques.

Regression Tree: A continuous target variable is predicted using a regression tree. Based on the values of the input features, it recursively divides the data into various branches, and the target variable is predicted using the mean or median of the values in each leaf node. Each internal node in a decision tree or regression tree represents a feature, and each leaf node in a tree-like structure represents a predicted value or class. The type of target variable that a regression tree and a decision tree are used to predict is their primary distinction.

The root of a regression tree, the first node, contains all of the training data. The data set is then divided into two sections using criteria like the mean or median value of the target variable, creating right and left child nodes.

Bayesian Regression: When the data set has too few or poorly distributed data, Bayesian regression can be very helpful. In contrast to conventional regression techniques, where the output is only derived from a single attribute value, a Bayesian regression model's output is derived from a probability distribution. The result y is produced by a normal distribution (where mean and variance are normalized). Bayesian linear regression aims to identify the 'posterior' distribution for the model parameters rather than the model parameters themselves. Therefore, it is assumed that the model parameters will follow a distribution in addition to the output y.

Polynomial Regression: This models the relationship between a dependent variable (y) and an independent variable (x) as an nth-degree polynomial. Like linear regression, polynomial regression seeks the optimal path through the data points by utilizing the relationship between the variables x and y. For instance, it is frequently used to forecast the rate at which COVID-19 and other infectious diseases will spread. Numerous varieties of polynomial regression exist because a polynomial equation's degree has no upper bound and can go up to the nth value. For instance, the second degree of a polynomial equation is typically expressed as a quadratic equation. As stated, this degree can reach the nth value, and you can create as many equations as you like.

1.12.1.2 Classification

The second category of supervised learning methods uses classification models to draw conclusions from observed categorical values. It predicts the likelihood that new data will fall into one of the predetermined categories using the input training data. Filtering emails into 'spam' or 'non-spam' is one of the most popular uses of classification.

In ML, there are two different classification types. When there are only two possible classes for a problem, it is said to be in the binary classification category (as in 'cat or dog,' 'yes or no'). If there are more than two potential classes, the problem is a multi-class classifier.

Some classification algorithms are *K*-nearest neighbor, decision tree, random forest, support vector machine (SVM), and linear classifiers.

***K*-Nearest Neighbor (KNN):** KNN is classified as a lazy learner because it does not create any predictive models. Instead, it stores all the training data and uses it to make predictions about new data points based on their similarity to stored points. This technique groups the closest objects in a data set and identifies the most common or average traits. It determines a data point's likelihood of joining any of the groups based on which group the data points closest to it belong to.

Decision Tree: A decision tree is best utilized to solve classification problems; it can also be used to tackle regression difficulties. It divides data points into two similar groups at a time, starting with the 'tree trunk,' moving through the 'branches,' and ending with the 'leaves,' until the groups are more closely related to one another. This method is similar to a flow chart. Internal nodes in a tree-structured classifier stand in for a data set's features, branches for the decision-making process, and each leaf node for the classification result. They do not require feature scaling and are simple to understand. In addition, compared to other algorithms, data cleaning requirements are lower. It also leaves out insignificant features.

Random Forest: A random forest is a collection of many decision trees drawn from randomly selected data subsets, and it may be able to predict outcomes more accurately than a single decision tree.

Support Vector Machine (SVM): This well-known ML algorithm is frequently used for classification and regression tasks. Specifically, it is employed to address classification issues. Finding the best decision boundaries in an *N*-dimensional space that can divide data points into classes is the primary goal of SVM, and the best decision boundary is referred to as a hyperplane. Support vectors are the extreme vectors that SVM chooses to locate the hyperplane. SVMs use a hyperplane to group objects based on shared characteristics and generate coordinates for each object in an *N*-dimensional space.

Linear Classifiers: These categorize objects based on the value of a linear combination of their attributes. The characteristics of an object are also referred to as feature values, and they are usually displayed to the machine in a feature vector. Such classifiers achieve accuracy levels comparable to non-linear classifiers while requiring less time to train and use, making them an excellent solution for real-world issues like document classification and, more generally, for issues with many variables (features).

1.12.2 Unsupervised Learning

Unsupervised learning, as the name suggests, has no data labels and is the process of learning patterns from unlabeled data without any supervision.

For example, suppose we have a data set of the sales transactions from a shop, and we want to find out which items are sold more frequently than others. We do not need to tell the computer what the items are. We can simply feed the data to an unsupervised learning algorithm, such as clustering or association rule mining, and let the computer discover the patterns and relationships among the items. The output of the unsupervised learning algorithm can help us understand customer behavior and preferences, and optimize the inventory and marketing strategies of the shop.

The training is provided to the machine with the set of data that has not been labeled, classified, or categorized, and the algorithm needs to act on that data without any supervision. The goal of unsupervised learning is to find the structure and patterns in the input data, group that data according to similarities, and represent that data set in a compressed format. Compared to supervised learning, unsupervised ML services are not very popular because they have fewer applications in day-to-day life. Unsupervised learning creates hidden structures. Relationships between data points are then perceived by the algorithm randomly or abstractly, with absolutely no input required from humans. Instead of a specific, defined, and set problem statement, unsupervised learning algorithms can adapt to the data.

Suppose the unsupervised learning algorithm is given an input data set containing images of different types of bulls and cows. The algorithm is not trained upon the given data set, which means it does not have any idea about the features of the data set. The task of the unsupervised learning algorithm is to identify the image features on it own. The unsupervised learning algorithm will perform this task by clustering the image data set into groups according to similarities between images.

In unsupervised learning, we do not have a predetermined result. The machine tries to find useful insights from the huge amount of data. It can be further classified into two categories: clustering and association (Fig. 1.7). Anomaly detection and dimension reduction are also other types. We will discuss these in detail in Chapter 6.

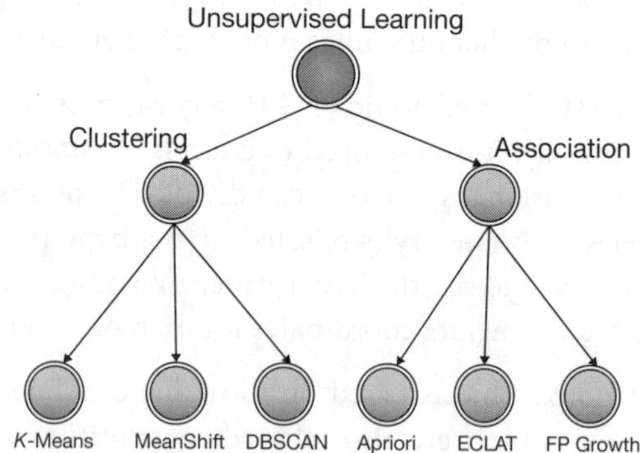

Figure 1.7 Types of unsupervised learning algorithms

1.12.2.1 Clustering

The process of grouping objects into clusters so that those with the most significant similarity stay together and share little to no similarities with those in other groups is called clustering. A **cluster** is a collection of related items or individuals that are situated or placed close to one another. Because every point in a cluster typically exhibits similarities in those characteristics, ML could be used to identify traits and distinguish between these clusters. Clustering serves as the foundation for numerous ML applications that address data issues in various industries. In a perfect world, machines would be able to recognize various objects and distinguish between them based on their physical characteristics. Therefore, clustering algorithms can be widely used in tasks such as image segmentation, statistical data analysis, classifying diseases in medical science, and customer classification in marketing research. Some commonly used clustering algorithms are *K*-means, MeanShift clustering, and DBSCAN.

***K*-Means Clustering:** This is a popular unsupervised machine learning technique for data exploration and analysis. It is used for grouping or clustering data points into distinct clusters or categories. It aims to divide the data set into meaningful subgroups based on specific characteristics. The algorithm examines each data point and assigns it to one of several groups based on attribute similarities.

The *K*-means algorithm can analyze data containing discrete, continuous, numerical entities. However, this algorithm has flaws, including difficulties with categorical data, outliers, and non-linear data. Furthermore, it would help if we decided how many data clusters we want. Finally, *K*-means is best applied to smaller data sets because it iterates over all the data points. As a result, if a data set contains many data points, it would take longer to classify them.

Consider the following example. Assume a company makes sports shoes and wants to divide its customers into two distinct groups: male and female. We would begin by gathering customer information such as age, gender, shopping preferences, and spending patterns, among other things, and then use *K*-means clustering to determine distinct criteria to determine who should go where!

For example, suppose the data indicates that consumers between 18 and 25 generally spend more on sports shoes. In that case, this specific age group may be grouped as a cluster, with a centroid representing the higher expenditure. In contrast, clients who are 30 years or older and may have distinct purchasing patterns would form a separate cluster characterized by a centroid representing reduced spending on footwear. This differentiation enables the organization to comprehend and anticipate client conduct by considering their age.

MeanShift Clustering: The MeanShift algorithm does not require us to specify the number of clusters, in contrast to the *K*-means algorithm. If we need clarification on the patterns in the data, the algorithm automatically determines the number of clusters, which is a significant advantage over *K*-means. Dense data point areas use a sliding window, centroid-based algorithm to locate the center group/class points. All center point candidates are the mean value of the sliding window points. Such windows are then sorted post-processing to remove duplicates and give the final group center points. Image segmentation tasks are where MeanShift clustering is most frequently used. Kernel density estimation is the foundation of the MeanShift algorithm.

MeanShift algorithms iteratively assign each data point to the closest cluster centroid, which is initialized arbitrarily. Then, each point is iteratively moved in the space based on where the most points are, that is, the mode. This is similar to the *K*-means algorithm. This method overcomes the selection of groups and cluster centers as the mean values are discovered automatically. The clusters also exhibit data sense due to convergence to the areas having maximum data points intuitively.

DBSCAN: Density-based spatial clustering of applications with noise is a prominent algorithm for identifying clusters in spatial data based on the density of data points. DBSCAN does not require the number of clusters to be specified in advance. It works on the principle that clusters are high-density areas separated by low-density regions. The clusters can therefore be found in any arbitrary shape.

1.12.2.2 Association

Association is the second type of unsupervised learning. Association rule mining finds associations based on co-occurrences. It determines the set of items that occur together in the data set.

The association rule makes marketing strategy more practical; for example, people who buy X items (say, a toothbrush) also tend to purchase Y items (say, toothpaste).

Association rule mining is used to identify new and exciting insights between different objects in a set and frequent patterns in transactional data or any relational database. The relationship is usually represented in the form of rules or frequent itemsets. It is used in market basket analysis (where items are bought together), web usage mining, and continuous production.

Market basket analysis examines consumer purchasing patterns by identifying relationships between the various items consumers place in their shopping baskets. Retailers create marketing strategies by analyzing which items users frequently purchase and discovering these associations. Web mining has the unique ability to support a variety of different data types. Many aspects of the web produce various mining methods. These include web pages, hyperlinks between web pages, and web server logs that can be used to track user activity.

Association rule learning can be divided into three algorithms: Apriori, ECLAT and FP Growth.

Apriori Algorithm: The Apriori algorithm uses relational databases to learn association rules and mine frequently occurring itemsets. It assists in identifying products that can be purchased in combination and is primarily used for market basket analysis.

This algorithm efficiently determines the itemset using a breadth-first search and a hash tree. Its 'join' and 'prune' steps condense the search space. It establishes the strength or weakness of the connection between two objects. Finding the frequent itemsets from a large data set involves an iterative process. The itemsets frequently used are those whose support is higher than the threshold value or the minimum support specified by the user. It means that if A and B together are frequent itemsets, then A and B should also be frequent itemsets separately.

This is the most simple and easy-to-understand algorithm among the association rule learning algorithms. The rules are intuitive and easy to communicate to an end user. However, the disadvantage of this algorithm is that when working with large data sets, it could be faster and more efficient. It uses a lot of resources to scan the database many times, generate many candidate sets, and check each of them.

ECLAT Algorithm: This stands for equivalence class transformation. It uses a depth-first search technique to find frequent itemsets in a transaction database. It performs faster than the Apriori algorithm. The ECLAT algorithm can be applied only to data sets in the vertical format. Since most data sets are in the horizontal format, to apply the ECLAT algorithm, we first have to convert them to the vertical format. Thus, the ECLAT algorithm works better with small and medium-sized data sets. The ECLAT algorithm has low memory requirements compared to Apriori as it uses a depth-first search approach. The result of the ECLAT algorithm is frequent itemsets with their support.

FP Growth Algorithm: The FP (frequent pattern) Growth algorithm is a better version of the Apriori algorithm. Instead of using candidate generations, this algorithm finds frequent itemsets which improve performance. It employs the divide-and-conquer tactic.

1.12.3 Reinforcement Learning

A significant drawback of ML is that vast volumes of data are needed to train models. The more complex a model, the more data it may require. The required data may not exist, or we may need access to the correct data. Further, the data collected might need to be more reliable. It may have false or missing values or need to be updated. Learning from a small subset of actions will not help expand the vast realm of solutions that may work for a particular problem. Machines must learn to perform actions alone rather than just learn from humans. These problems are overcome by reinforcement learning (RL).

Reinforcement learning is a sub-branch of ML that trains a model to return an optimum solution for a problem by taking a sequence of decisions. RL differs from supervised learning in that in the latter, the training data has the answer key, so the model is trained with the correct answer itself. In contrast, there is no answer key in reinforcement learning, but the reinforcement agent decides what to do to perform the given task. Without a training data set, it is bound to learn from experience. RL solves a specific type of problem where decision-making is sequential and the goal is long-term, such as game-playing, robotics, etc.

For example, a dog cannot be told directly what to do because he does not understand human language. So, instead, we adopt a different approach. For example, we will reward the dog with food if he behaves in the desired manner. Now, whenever the dog encounters the same circumstance, the dog performs a similar action even more eagerly, anticipating a greater reward (food). This is similar to discovering that a dog learns 'what to do' from satisfying experiences. At the same time, the dog also learns what not to do when faced with negative experiences. In this case, the dog is an agent exposed to the environment (house). For example, when your dog is sitting, you ask it to go for a walk using a particular word. The agent responds by moving from one 'state' to another through an action. For instance, your dog transitions from lying down to walking.

An agent's response is an action, and a policy is a way to choose an action given a state in the hopes of better results. After the transition, they may receive a reward or a punishment. Reinforcement comes in two varieties. **Positive reinforcement** is when a behavior increases in strength and frequency because of an external event. In other words, it influences behavior in a good way. **Negative reinforcement** is the strengthening of behavior because an adverse condition is stopped or avoided. The main elements of an RL system are:

- The agent or learner (the dog, in this case)
- The environment the agent interacts with (house)
- The policy that the agent follows to take actions
- The reward signal (food) that the agent observes upon taking actions

The agent gains knowledge through trial and error, and using its experience, it improves its performance. The agent keeps doing these three things – take action, alter his state or remain in it, and get feedback – which helps him learn about and explore his surroundings.

In RL, the agent must be instructed on the surroundings and the appropriate course of action. The agent then performs the subsequent action and modifies its state in response to feedback from the preceding action. The agent might, as a result, receive a postponed reward. To maximize positive rewards, the agent must explore the stochastic environment. In RL, we introduce a model to a controlled environment based on the problem statement to be solved, instead of using actual data to solve it. The model interacts with this environment and comes up with solutions independently, without human interference. To push it in the right direction, we give it a positive reward if it performs an action that brings it closer to its goal or a negative reward if it goes away from its goal.

There are three ways of implementing RL in ML:

- **Value-based approach**: Finding the best value function, or the most significant value possible at any given state under any policy, is the goal of the value-based approach. As a result, the agent anticipates a long-term return in any state covered by the policy.
- **Policy-based approach**: Without using the value function, the policy-based approach identifies the best course of action for the most significant potential rewards. In this method, the agent tries to implement a policy so that each action helps maximize the future reward. Two types of policy make up the bulk of the policy-based approach: deterministic, where any state's policy produces the same action, and stochastic, where the action produced in this policy is determined by probability.
- **Model-based approach**: The agent learns about the environment by interacting with a virtual model of it. This method lacks a specific solution or algorithm because each environment's model representation is unique.

Although both supervised learning and reinforcement learning use mapping between input and output, reinforcement learning uses rewards and punishments as signals for good and bad behavior, in contrast to supervised learning, which gives the agent feedback on the proper course of action for carrying out a task. Reinforcement learning has different objectives from unsupervised learning. In unsupervised learning, the objective is to identify similarities and differences among data points. In RL, the objective is to identify an appropriate action model to maximize the agent's overall cumulative reward.

1.12.4 Transfer Learning

Supervised ML models are developed and trained to carry out specific tasks using labeled data. The algorithm is fed with mapped input and desired output. The model can then use the recognized patterns and trends to analyze new data.

The models created in this manner will solve problems with high accuracy when used in the same environment as their training data. However, it will become much less accurate if the conditions or environment changes in real-world applications beyond the training data. A new model based on new training data may be required, even if the tasks are similar. Humans are very good at applying transfer of knowledge between tasks. This means that whenever we encounter a new problem or task, we recognize it and apply relevant knowledge from previous learning experiences. This makes our work easy and we finish it quickly. For instance, imagine being asked to learn the Python language which you do not know, even though you know how to write a program in Java. In this situation, Java language expertise will be used to manage learning of the Python language. This will make things more straightforward than they would be for a beginner. Such perspectives are beneficial in real life because they help us become more perfect and increase our experience.

The same methodology led to the coining of the phrase 'transfer learning' in ML. Here, information gleaned from a model used for one task can be applied again as the basis for another. It is uncommon to train a model from scratch for tasks related to image or NLP because transfer learning is widespread. Transfer learning uses the relevant parts of the model that have already been trained to address a distinct but connected issue. This is the fundamental knowledge required for the model to work. Programmers will need to determine which model components need to be retrained and which are relevant to the new task. In addition, because the model will have already picked up general features that are likely to be helpful in the second task, this can also aid in preventing overfitting.

Transfer learning is essential in any learning. Humans are only taught some tasks or problems to be successful at them. All of us get into situations that we have not encountered, and we still manage to solve problems in an ad-hoc manner. The ability to learn from many experiences and export 'knowledge' into new environments is precisely what transfer learning is all about.

Transfer learning is most likely to be successful with a machine learning model that recognizes a particular subject among a collection of images. The portion of the model that deals with subject recognition can be retained. The algorithmic component that highlights a particular subject for categorization will need to be retrained. In this case, rebuilding and retraining an ML algorithm from scratch is unnecessary. Researchers and data scientists prefer to start from a pre-trained model that knows how to classify objects and has learned general features like edges and shapes in images.

A **source task** is a task from which knowledge is transferred to a target task. A **target task** is when improved learning occurs due to transferring knowledge from a source task. During transfer learning, the knowledge leveraged and rapid progress from a source task is used to improve the learning and development to a new target task. However, if the transfer method decreases the performance of the new target task, it is called a **negative transfer**. One of the significant challenges when working with transfer learning methods is providing and ensuring **positive transfer** between related tasks while avoiding negative transfer. To understand which parts of the learned knowledge to transfer, we need to figure out which portions of knowledge best reflect both the source and target. Our goal is to improve the performance of the target task, not to make it worse.

Reasons for using transfer learning: The main advantages are not needing much data, saving training time, and improving the performance of neural networks (in most cases). Transfer learning can be used in a range of industries. Gaining access to data is always a hindrance due to its lack of availability. However, working with sufficient amounts of data can result in high performance.

Transfer learning can be helpful when access to large amounts of data is occasionally unavailable but necessary to train a neural network from scratch. Because the model has already been trained, transfer learning allows for the construction of robust ML models using relatively little training data. This is particularly useful in NLP because producing sizable labeled data sets requires expert knowledge. In addition, training time is reduced because ML models are challenging to train and can take up much time, leading to inefficiency. We begin the learning process using patterns discovered while completing a related task instead of starting from scratch. Generalized knowledge can be shared between two models if they are created to perform comparable tasks. This method of developing ML models requires fewer resources and less labeled data to train new models.

Disadvantages of transfer learning: Only when information is 'appropriate' can it be transferred. Defining what appropriate means in this context takes work, and experimentation is typically required. For example, it would be beneficial if you did not believe that a young child who rides around in a toy aeroplane can handle a real aeroplane. The same rule applies to transfer learning: despite being challenging to measure, transfer learning has a maximum level. It is only a solution that fits some problem cases. For example, the pre-trained model may not be well-suited to the second task, if the two tasks are vastly different or the data distribution between the two tasks is very different. Transfer learning can lead to overfitting if the model is fine-tuned too much on the second task, as it may learn task-specific features that do not generalize well to new data. Finally, the pre-trained model and fine-tuning process can be computationally expensive and require specialized hardware.

Freezing and Trainable Layers: How do we decide which layers to train and which to freeze now? The simple solution is to freeze layers more frequently, when there are more features you want to inherit from a pre-trained model. For example, if the pre-trained model identifies certain vegetable species, we must identify additional vegetable species. In this scenario, a new data set with fresh species has many characteristics in common with the trained model. Thus, we freeze more layers so that we can use most of its knowledge in a new model.

Consider another scenario where a pre-trained model can recognize cars in images, and we want to apply that knowledge to recognize humans. In this scenario, where the data set is entirely different, it is not a good idea to freeze many layers because doing so will produce high-level features like car model, tyre type, and other material features that are useless for the new data set (human detection). As a result, we train the entire network on a new data set while only copying the low-level features from the base network.

Let us consider all the scenarios where the target task's size and data set differ from that of the base network:

- **Target data set is small and similar to the base network data set**: We can fine-tune the pre-trained network with the target data set because the latter is small. However, this could result in overfitting. The target task's class count may also change in a few ways. Therefore, we add a new fully connected layer that satisfies the number of new classes in this situation and remove the fully connected layers from the end, possibly one or two. We now freeze the rest of the model and train only the most recent layers.
- **Target data set is large and similar to the base training data set**: In this situation, there is no chance of overfitting because the data set is large and can accommodate a pre-trained model. Here, the previous fully connected layer is removed, and a new fully connected layer with the appropriate number of classes is added. The entire model is now trained using a new data set. This ensures the model is tuned while maintaining the same model architecture on a new giant data set.
- **Target data set is small and different from the base network data set**: High-level features of the pre-trained model cannot be used because the target data set differs. Remove most of the layers from the end of a pre-trained model in this situation, and then add new layers with the appropriate number of classes in a new data set. In this manner, we can train the remaining layers to fit a new data set while using low-level features from the previously trained model. Sometimes training the entire network before adding a new layer at the end is advantageous.
- **Target data set is large and different from the base network data set**: The best method for training the entire network without freezing any layers is to remove the final layers from the pre-trained network and add new layers with a satisfying number of classes. This is because the target network is large and diverse.

1.12.5 Meta Learning

The term 'meta' usually refers to something comprehensive or abstract. For example, a metaverse is a virtual world or a world within our world; metadata is data that provides details about other data; and so on.

A good ML model frequently necessitates training with many samples. Humans, on the other hand, learn new concepts and skills much more quickly and efficiently. Children who have only seen cats and birds a few times can tell them apart. People who know how to ride a bike will likely discover how to ride a motorcycle quickly, with little or no demonstration. Is it possible to design a machine learning model with similar properties, that is, learning new concepts and skills quickly with a few training examples? That is essentially what meta learning aims to solve.

In computer science, meta learning, also known as 'learning to learn,' is a subset of ML that learns from the output of other ML algorithms. We frequently find which algorithms work best with our data in ML. These algorithms generate models by learning from historical data, and those models can then be used to predict outcomes for our tasks. Meta learning algorithms do not directly use historical data but instead learn from the outputs of ML models. Meta learning algorithms use the metadata of learning algorithms as input. They then make predictions and provide information about the performance of these learning algorithms as output. For example, ML models take images as input and predict classes if the goal is to classify images. On the other hand, meta learning models take the predictions of those ML models as input and predict image classes based on them.

Meta learning occurs one level above machine learning in this sense. It helps researchers understand which algorithms generate the best/better predictions from data sets. The performance of a learning model depends on its training data set, algorithm, and parameters. Many experiments are needed to find the best-performing algorithm and algorithm parameters. Meta learning approaches help them find and optimize the number of experiments. The result is better predictions in less time. An image's metadata in a learning model can include, for example, its size, resolution, style, creation date, and owner.

We expect an excellent meta learning model to be capable of adapting well or generalizing to new tasks and environments that have never been encountered during training. The adaptation process, essentially a mini-learning session, happens during a test but with limited exposure to new task configurations. Eventually, the adapted model can complete new tasks. For example, a classifier trained on non-dog images can tell whether a given image contains a dog after seeing a handful of dog pictures. A gamebot (for game 1) can quickly master a new game (called game 2).

1.13 Passive Learning versus Active Learning

Passive learning is a type of machine learning that does not use feedback from the environment to adjust the learner's behavior. Spamming is an example of passive learning, where the spammer sends out messages without knowing whether they are effective or not. The spammer relies on a fixed rule or hypothesis to generate the messages, such as using certain keywords or phrases. **Inductive bias** is the set of assumptions that a learner uses to make predictions or generalizations from a finite set of data. It is necessary for learning, because without it, the learner would not be able to choose from among the infinite possible hypotheses that are consistent with the data. The rule that the spammer uses to generate messages is an example of inductive bias. However, this inductive bias may not be optimal or accurate, because it may not reflect the true preferences or behavior of the recipients. A better inductive bias would be one that adapts to feedback from the environment, such as using reinforcement learning or active learning.

Active learning is a machine learning technique that aims to reduce the amount of labeled data required for training a model. It does so by selecting the most informative and relevant examples from a large pool of unlabeled data and asking a human expert to provide labels for them. This way, the model can learn more efficiently and effectively from fewer examples. **Anomaly detection** is a machine learning task that involves identifying instances that deviate significantly from the normal or expected behavior of a system or a process. Anomalies can indicate potential problems, such as fraud, intrusion, malfunction, or disease. Anomaly detection can be applied to various domains, such as cybersecurity, healthcare, finance, manufacturing, and more.

Active learning and anomaly detection can be combined to create a powerful and robust system that can detect and handle anomalies in complex and dynamic environments. For example, an active learning system can monitor the network traffic of an organization and raise questions to the network administrator whenever it encounters a suspicious or unusual pattern. The administrator can then label the pattern as normal or anomalous and provide feedback to the system. The system can then update its model and improve its performance over time. This way, the system can adapt to changing conditions and detect new types of anomalies that may arise.

1.14 Online versus Batch Machine Learning

Online and batch machine learning are two different approaches to train a machine learning model. Online machine learning, also known as incremental or online learning, is a method where the model learns from new data as it arrives, without having to retrain on the entire data set. Batch machine learning, also known as offline or batch learning, is a method where the model learns from a fixed and finite data set, and then applies the learned knowledge to new data. One of the main advantages of online machine learning is that it can adapt to changing data and environments, and handle large and streaming data efficiently. Online machine learning is suitable for applications such as recommender systems, spam filtering, fraud detection, and sentiment analysis, where the data is dynamic and evolving. One of the main challenges of online machine learning is that it requires careful tuning of the learning rate and the forgetting factor, which determine how much the model updates its parameters and forgets its previous knowledge.

One of the main advantages of batch machine learning is that it can optimize the model parameters using the entire data set, and achieve higher accuracy and stability. Batch machine learning is suitable for applications such as image recognition, natural language processing, and speech recognition, where the data is relatively static and of high quality. One of the main challenges of batch machine learning is that it can be computationally expensive and time-consuming, and may not be able to handle new data or concept drift.

1.15 Differences between Machine Learning Models and Algorithms

One of the most common areas of confusion among beginners is the distinction between ML models and algorithms. This is because, in various cases in ML and data science, these terms are used interchangeably.

An algorithm can be considered as instructions telling a computer how to execute a task. Algorithms can be written using any programming language, but they typically use high-level languages such as Python or R to define their inputs and outputs. Algorithms define the steps required to process data, including preprocessing (cleaning and normalizing), feature extraction (identifying valuable features), parameter estimation (determining the best values for parameters), training (building models), and evaluation (testing accuracy). Algorithms form the foundation of most ML applications by providing an effective means for quickly processing large amounts of data.

On the other hand, a model is a representation of data that can be used for prediction or classification tasks in ML. Models are generated from algorithms by applying them to input data sets containing known results or classifications; these trained models can then be applied to new data sets to make predictions about unknown results or classifications.

Models differ from algorithms in that they are not necessarily defined by code. Instead, they represent relationships between variables within a given data set which may not have been explicitly stated beforehand.

An algorithm defines how data should be processed while a model represents relationships within existing data sets which may provide insight into unknown outcomes when applied to new ones; both play critical roles in successful ML applications but do so through different techniques and approaches depending upon their purpose within each particular application context. The concept of algorithm versus model is also related closely to supervised versus unsupervised methods for dealing with large amounts of data. Supervised methods involve training an algorithm using labeled input samples. In contrast, unsupervised methods involve identifying patterns without requiring any labeled examples. For example, support vector machines (SVMs) utilize supervised learning, meaning it requires labeled inputs; here, one might describe an SVM as both an algorithm as well as a type of predictive model since it generates specific decision boundaries based upon those labels providing insight into future 'unknown' cases where labels may not yet exist. Conversely, *K*-means clustering would fall under unsupervised learning, meaning no labels are required before being applied; here, *K*-means would typically only be described as an algorithmic approach since its output reflects patterns without having access to any known labels, making its insights less grounded towards predicting future cases when compared SVM.

Ultimately understanding algorithms versus models allows us to make better decisions regarding choosing appropriate choices given our desired objective at hand – whether it is utilizing supervised/unsupervised approaches along with associated algorithmic/model structures towards making accurate predictions about real-world scenarios. In terms of implementation, ML models are often implemented using ML libraries such as TensorFlow or scikit-learn. In contrast, algorithms are often implemented using programming languages such as Python, Java, or C++.

1.16 Disadvantages of Data-driven Solutions

Although machine learning is being used in every industry and helps organizations make more informed and data-driven choices that are more effective than classical methodologies, it still has many problems that cannot be ignored.

Large quantity of data: One disadvantage is that it requires a large quantity of reliable and accurate data in order for it to be valuable. If the data used is incomplete or inaccurate, then the results and conclusions drawn will not be valid. Furthermore, companies must also have an understanding on how they should structure their data sets, so they are able to derive meaningful insights from them.

Finally, organizations need experienced personnel, who know how to interpret and utilize this information properly.

Updated data: These systems require frequent updating with new data sets, in order for them to remain relevant – just like any other type of technology system or business process, if you do not continually update it, you may begin seeing diminishing returns over time. In addition, if you rely too heavily on automated decision making, based solely upon predictive analytics, there could be potential concerns regarding bias being introduced into your models, which may lead inaccurate predictions/recommendations.

Privacy and security issues: Privacy and security issues should also be considered when implementing any form of digital solution. For example, failure to comply with General Data Protection Regulations (GDPR) can result in heavy fines along with tarnished reputations, negatively impacting business operations.

Inadequate training data: The quality of the output of any ML algorithm is highly dependent on the data it is trained on. If the training data is inadequate or contains a biased sample, the ML model will not be able to learn correctly, and its output will not be accurate. In addition, inadequate training data can lead to overfitting or underfitting, both of which can degrade the performance of a machine learning algorithm.

Poor data quality: Data is essential in ML and must also be of high quality. On the other hand, poor-quality data can lead to poor results and limit the effectiveness of algorithms. Poor quality data can come in many forms:

- **Noisy data:** Noisy or irrelevant information can have a significant detrimental influence on ML algorithm performance. More noise in training examples will mean that some authentic relationships between features may be overlooked by the model, leading to low predictive accuracy. This noisy information can also create overfitting problems since it is difficult for models to detect patterns from random noise. To reduce this effect, it is essential to identify and remove irrelevant features from the data set before training begins.
- **Incomplete data:** Incomplete data sets are another common problem encountered in ML projects due to missing or incorrectly recorded values in specific entries or columns. These missing values are known as 'holes' in the data set which will negatively affect a model's performance. In addition, they may lead to incorrect assumptions made by the model based on the incomplete input information, which reduces predictive accuracy and may even cause overfitting issues when too many holes exist within a data set. To prevent these problems from arising, it is essential that any missing values or abnormal entries be identified and removed before using them for training purposes; otherwise, their removal should be considered at an early stage of training so that their potential effects on accuracy can be minimized.
- **Inaccurate data:** Another issue with poor-quality data sets is inaccurate entries, which may have been caused during preprocessing stages or manual user input errors such as typos. These inaccuracies will reduce predictive accuracy levels and increase overfitting risks if noticed. Incorrect results may occur due to false assumptions being made by models based on corrupted samples during the training phases or inference operations.

- **Unclean data:** Unclean data sets refer primarily to those which contain inconsistencies, outliers, duplicated entries, and uncorrelated inputs. These anomalies pose serious risks when modeling systems since inaccurate predictions based on false assumptions could lead to costly mistakes. Furthermore, anomalies within large-scale databases could lead to paralysis where neither humans nor computer algorithms would know what action to follow once abnormal records have been encountered. Thus, it becomes highly essential that all such discrepancies be removed so as to minimize their impact on modeling operations and ultimately improve prediction accuracies while minimizing ethical lapses. Hence, having high-quality clean data sets free from errors and anomalies becomes one of the strongest pillars upon which ML infrastructures rely.

Non-representative training data: This is a term used to describe a data set that does not accurately reflect the population it is intended to represent. This can have significant implications for the accuracy of ML models which use this data as their input. Generally speaking, non-representative training data can lead to unfair model predictions, potential decision-making bias, and inaccurate estimates of the underlying population. If ML models are trained with data sets that are not representative of the underlying population, they may be unable to identify essential patterns unbiasedly.

In addition, non-representative training data will likely lead to inaccurate estimates of the characteristics and behaviors within a given population. This could be dangerous if used for predictive analytics such as market forecasts or economic policy decisions. It can also affect user experience and trustworthiness when put into production systems such as recommendation engines and chatbots. These problems can have severe implications for businesses relying on AI technology, making it essential for them to curate their data sets properly.

Overfitting: Overfitting is a common issue among ML engineers and data scientists. Here, a model learns and retains too much training data. Consequently, it performs well on training data but needs improvement on unknown test data. In addition, overfitting decreases a machine learning system's generalizability, resulting in an erroneous representation of reality when employed for predictions or classifications on new data sets. Using linear and parametric approaches, we may prevent overfitting in ML models.

To address overfitting issues, some techniques can be applied:

(a) **Cross-validation:** Before training your model, divide your data set into train and test sets to guarantee that it remembers its inputs. Then, using cross-validation methods such as *k*-fold or Leave One Out (LOO), you may determine how well a model performs when exposed to new data.

(b) **Regularization:** It involves imposing limits on parameters during the training process so they can be simple and begin remembering instead of generalizing from their inputs.

(c) **Feature selection:** Before feeding them into ML models for better generalizability across different data sets, feature selection methods are used to identify irrelevant features present in our data set, which can reduce complexity while increasing accuracy and reducing the overfitting risks associated with unnecessary features present in our data set. It entails using algorithms such as principal component analysis (PCA), stability selection, and others to identify essential features from large feature spaces with higher accuracy scores than traditional feature selection methodologies such as stepwise regression, which frequently struggle with the curse of dimensionality due to their linear nature within large feature spaces.

Feature selection is an essential and critical stage in the ML process since it substantially impacts the model's accuracy and effectiveness. By eliminating extra or inconsequential attributes, we can diminish the dimensionality of the data, resulting in several advantages, including:

- **Enhanced model performance and precision**: By exclusively utilizing the features that exhibit a significant correlation with the target variable, we may circumvent the issues of overfitting and data noise, augmenting the model's capacity for generalization.
- **Minimised computational expenditure and time**: By employing a reduced number of features, we may accelerate the training and inference procedures of the model while conserving memory and storage capacity.
- **Improved comprehensibility and clarity**: By reducing the number of features, we may enhance our knowledge of the model's functioning and the individual contributions of each feature to the prediction.

Various methodologies and approaches exist for feature selection, which vary depending on the nature of the data, the learning objective, and the criteria used for evaluation. Several prevalent techniques include:

- **Filter techniques/methods**: These approaches assess each feature individually using statistical measures such as correlation, variance, information gain, and chi-squared test. The features with high scores are chosen, while those with poor scores are eliminated. Filter approaches are efficient and uncomplicated, although they do not consider the interplay between features or the learning process.

  Filter methods are a category of feature selection approaches that employ statistical measures to assess the relevance and significance of each feature concerning the target variable. Filter techniques differ from wrapper methods because they do not rely on a particular classifier or predictor to identify the best subset of features. Instead, filter methods operate independently of any learning methodology. They can be a preliminary step before inputting the data into any ML algorithm. A key advantage of filter approaches is their computational efficiency and scalability, as they only need to process the data once to determine the scores for each characteristic. They also avoid the problem of overfitting, which can occur when employing wrapper approaches that seek the best subset of features based on the performance of a particular model. Several prevalent strategies employed in filter systems include:

  - **Information gain**: This metric measures how much a characteristic contributes valuable information or reduces uncertainty (entropy) regarding the target variable. Features that exhibit more significant information gain are more pertinent and enlightening for the classification endeavor.
  - **Chi-squared test**: This assesses the statistical significance of the relationship between a particular characteristic and the target variable. Features with higher chi-square values exhibit a more substantial likelihood of reliance on the target variable, making them more advantageous for classification.
  - **Fisher's score**: This score quantifies the proportion of the variance across different classes compared to the variance within each class for a specific attribute. Features having a higher Fisher's score exhibit greater discriminative power and are more effective at distinguishing across classes.

- **Missing value ratio**: This is a metric that quantifies the proportion of missing values in a specific characteristic. Features with a larger percentage of missing values are less dependable and can potentially add noise or bias to the model.

- **Wrapper approaches**: These methods assess the effectiveness of a particular learning algorithm by evaluating each feature or a subset of features individually. The algorithm's performance is enhanced by selecting favorable traits and eliminating those that hinder it. Wrapper methods exhibit higher accuracy and provide a more thorough analysis than filter approaches. However, they are also computationally intensive and susceptible to overfitting.
- **Embedded techniques**: These methods incorporate feature selection within the learning process. The algorithm selects the pertinent traits and eliminates the irrelevant ones. Embedded methods offer the benefits of both filter and wrapper methods while being algorithm specific.

(d) Model ensembling techniques: These include combining numerous independent models, which improves accuracy by reducing the likelihood of mistakes caused by any one component within the ensemble architecture. Bagging, boosting, stacking, and other techniques are used in these procedures. However, all of these approaches operate on the same principle: combining numerous 'weak' or low-accuracy individual models results in a strong learner with more predictive ability than any one component alone.

(e) Data augmentation: This is the process of artificially adding more examples to an existing data set by randomly altering existing examples within a given target data set until it reaches the desired size level while maintaining the same distribution pattern within target labels or classes as the original data set. This significantly increases the ability of ML algorithms to perform better at predicting unseen samples compared to no augmented data sets.

Overall, the methods listed above help reduce the risk posed by simple unregularized linear classifiers becoming overly complex and beginning to memorize instead of generalizing from their inputs when exposed to new types of inputted samples/data sets. This results in improved predictive power as well as robustness against unexpected types of future scenarios encountered during the deployment stage, giving better outcomes.

Underfitting: When a machine learning model is trained with fewer data points, it produces incomplete and erroneous results. This usually arises when we have a small data set and try to develop a linear model with non-linear data. In such scenarios, the model's complexity is destroyed, ML rules become too easy to apply to the data set, and the model makes wrong predictions. In addition, underfitting can lead to high bias, which means that the model tends to make similar mistakes in different data points. To avoid underfitting, ML engineers and practitioners need to understand how much flexibility should be built into a model and how much regularization should be used along with proper validation techniques such as cross-validation, *k*-fold validation and LOO validation.

In addition, feature engineering plays a vital role in avoiding underfitting by helping identify meaningful features from noisy data sets along with dimensionality reduction techniques like PCA, which help reduce the number of input variables while retaining most of its helpful information. Finally, boosting algorithms like AdaBoost may also be employed.

Monitoring and maintenance: Monitoring and maintaining the model is essential for achieving successful outcomes from ML applications. The model can be made reliable with proper maintenance, leading to accurate results. Monitoring allows us to detect when something goes wrong with the model. We use metrics like accuracy, recall, and precision to understand how well our system performs against existing data as new data enters the system due to changes in the environment or business needs. Furthermore, monitoring helps us track how different hyperparameters affect the performance of the models over time so we can adjust them when needed for optimal performance. By maintaining an ML model, we can ensure that it remains accurate and reliable throughout its lifetime of use by applying regular updates when needed.

Data drift: In ML, data drift occurs when the data distribution used to train the model shifts over time, either slowly or quickly. To avoid this problem, businesses must use technologies to have strategies that detect and address data drift as soon as it happens. There are numerous options for dealing with this problem.

Organizations should invest in monitoring tools that track changes in their data sets and alert them when those changes begin to affect the accuracy of their ML models. In addition, businesses should continuously retrain their algorithms using new data sets to keep up with changing patterns or trends. Regular testing should be conducted on any new models created so businesses can measure how well they are performing against existing benchmarks or performance standards before implementing them into production environments.

Secondly, companies must ensure that all input variables used in ML algorithms remain consistent across different versions of the same data set throughout its lifecycle; otherwise, inputs may change enough for output results generated by earlier versions of a given algorithm to become irrelevant.

Lack of skilled resources: Machine learning is a rapidly growing field transforming how we interact with technology and systems in our everyday lives. While the potential of ML is vast, it has yet to be fully realized due to a lack of skilled resources in the field. As a result, the demand for skilled ML professionals has skyrocketed as companies look for ways to leverage their capabilities and make their products more intelligent. Unfortunately, there need to be more qualified individuals with knowledge of both traditional software engineering practices and data science techniques necessary for successful product development using ML. In addition, building quality models requires expertise across numerous disciplines, including mathematics, computer science, software engineering fundamentals, and statistics – skills that many prospective candidates need to gain adequate experience.

Data scientists need an understanding of data modeling techniques such as supervised/unsupervised classification algorithms or deep neural networks; they also need an understanding of statistical analysis tools such as R or Python's scikit-learn library; finally, they need to understand how best to deploy their models into production environments so that they can scale effectively given different user behaviors in real-time conditions.

As a result, organizations must invest heavily in training existing staff and recruiting new talent from outside markets – both options being costly and time-consuming. This leads us to conclude that there needs to be a more significant focus on bridging the gap between current supply (qualified professionals) and demand (number of capable machines required by industries today).

Process complexity of machine learning: The degree of difficulty in understanding and working with an ML system is called process complexity. It is an issue because it adds time and cost to the development process and increases the risk of something going wrong.

In ML, process complexity is frequently caused by poor data management or poor algorithm or feature selection for training purposes. It is also directly related to run-time performance. Furthermore, without adequate knowledge of each component of an ML system, asn engineer is more likely to make mistakes when designing these components.

Another example of how processing complexity can cause problems with ML is deployment. Deployment in this context refers to putting already trained models into production environments to be used for real-world tasks such as image recognition and voice recognition. However, deploying ML systems necessitates complex environment architectures. Any error during this stage could break the entire system due to the lack of understanding processes involved, leading to low efficiency at best or complete failure in the worst-case scenario.

Data bias: Data biasing in ML is a phenomenon that occurs when a machine learning model produces inaccurate results due to the data used in its training. These errors exist when certain elements of the data set are heavily weighted or need more importance than others. It is often caused by incomplete or inaccurate data sets, uneven distribution of data points, incorrect categorization of data, or even by biased algorithms. Biased data leads to inaccurate results, skewed outcomes, and other analytical errors. However, we can resolve this error by determining where data is actually biased in the data set.

Another common form of bias involves incorrectly labeled or categorized data sets which can lead models astray as they try to 'learn' from these flawed data sets and produce inaccurate results due to relying on wrong information during their training process.

Finally, another primary source of bias comes from algorithms themselves – particularly those designed with pre-defined criteria such as age brackets or race/ethnicity profiles – which artificially restrict prediction outcomes based on predetermined parameters rather than actual evidence presented at hand, thus leading models astray depending on how limited those criteria might be (such as only taking into account young people rather than all ages).

Several techniques can be used to reduce or eliminate data bias in ML models:

- **Data balancing**: This involves ensuring that all classes are equally represented in a data set by oversampling minority classes and undersampling majority classes.
- **Data augmentation**: This involves creating synthetic training samples that represent real-world scenarios by generating new examples based on existing ones, using transformations such as rotations and noise injection.
- **Ensemble methods:** These are helpful in dealing with class imbalance issues and reducing biases caused by data sets with limited samples from specific subgroups or classes due to their ability to combine multiple models into one powerful prediction system that outperforms any individual model alone. The most famous ensemble method used for this purpose is boosting, where weak learners are combined into an ensemble where the strength of each learner increases with every round of prediction until an optimal result is achieved at test time.
- **Regularization techniques** such as dropout, weight decay, and early stopping can also be used to reduce overfitting when dealing with biased data sets by penalizing complex models, so they do

not learn irrelevant features or patterns from noise in training data that do not add value during testing stages;

- **Feature engineering**: This involves finding relevant features (attributes) within a data set through exploratory analysis then selecting those that best capture essential information about each class so they can be effectively used as input variables for modeling purposes while disregarding redundant ones since they may increase bias if left unchecked.

Lack of explainability: Explainability is critical in ML systems because it allows us to understand how and why the algorithm makes certain judgments. It is becoming increasingly important as more complicated models are utilized for predictive analytics and automated decision-making.

One strategy for tackling this issue is to increase system transparency. This might include showing the data used for training and information regarding which attributes are taken into account for generating predictions. Furthermore, allowing users to engage with a model through visualizations allows them to understand better how their input influences output and alter parameters accordingly. Another strategy is to employ interpretable models rather than complicated ones wherever feasible.

Finally, putting domain knowledge into our ML systems allows us to deliver unique interpretations depending on user context. Rather than relying exclusively on mathematical equations, we can employ human expertise to spot patterns inside data sets.

1.17 Well-posed Machine Learning Problems

A well-posed ML problem is a computer program that learns from experience E and produces performance measure P when faced with task T. The concept of well-posed learning problems is essential for AI research, as it allows us to understand how AI can learn from the given data to produce better results.

Well-posed learning problems are similar but involve computer programs instead of equations. In this case, experience E is data – usually stored in some form such as an array or database – describing how computers should respond when faced with input tasks T. This could take various forms, such as an image recognition or game-playing task. When presented with a specific task T and its associated experiences E, the computer program must use these inputs to perform on P – some performance measure – accurately and quickly. For example, this may involve calculating the accuracy rate of correctly classified images or the number of moves taken within a given time frame during game-playing tasks. If done successfully, the computer program will be upgraded to apply what it learned from experiences E to future tasks T based on similar inputs to achieve a higher accuracy rate/number of moves taken within shorter time frames.

This process brings up several attractive properties such as generalization ability, where AI can be applied beyond its training sets by using previous knowledge acquired during training sessions; scalability, which allows AI systems to scale up based on large amounts of data quickly; and robustness which makes AI systems fault tolerant even if there are significant variations in new data sets due changes in the environment.

Let us look at an example to better comprehend the topic. Chess Instructions: A computer's performance may improve as it gains the capacity to succeed at chess-related activities. By playing against itself, the performance improves over time. T -> Play a game of checkers. P -> Percentage of victories against the opponent. E -> Practicing games against itself.

1.18 Designing a Learning System (Life Cycle of Machine Learning)

Machine learning has enabled computer systems to learn on their own without being explicitly programmed. But how exactly does an ML system function? This may be defined using the machine learning life cycle. This is a cyclical approach to developing an effective ML project.

Generally, ML models are used to solve problems such as classification, clustering, or regression. To begin, the goal of the project must be clearly defined. This means that the expected outcome should be known in advance. For example, if the goal is to create a system that can recommend movies to users based on their past viewing history, it should be clear exactly how the output should be structured and what the criteria for recommending a movie should be. Once the goal of the project is known, it is important to have enough data to construct a model. If there is not enough data, it can be difficult to create an accurate model. The type and quantity of data needed will depend on the particular problem and the model being used.

The life cycle of a machine learning program consists of six stages. The success of any ML program depends on how well each stage is implemented.

1. **Understanding the Business Problem:** Before starting any ML project, it is essential to understand the expected outcome and goal. Gather all relevant information from stakeholders. Following that, comprehend the company challenge and what defines success. Before you can solve an issue, you must first comprehend it. Working with the project owner to identify the needs and objectives is part of this knowledge. Then, determine which aspects of the business require an ML solution and how you will know when you have succeeded.
2. **Gathering Data:** After understanding what needs to be done, the next step is collecting enough relevant data so that the model can be learned and applied in real-time scenarios. This involves gathering a large set of labeled data sets that are relevant to the problem being solved by the ML program. Depending upon your use case, you might have to collect data from different sources like web scrapping or purchasing third-party data sets, which help you kick-start your project with a sufficient amount of high-quality data sets. Learning ML algorithms requires clean, sufficient training data. You must also understand how and whether the ML model will operate with real-time data. For example, suppose you are training an image recognition system; in that case, you will need to collect images from multiple sources, different backgrounds, and lighting conditions to get accurate results during training. In addition, the format of this data must also be suitable for use by your ML program; this could include audio files, images, or text documents, depending on the task you are trying to complete.
3. **Data Preparation and Wrangling:** Now that you have identified your data sources, you must transform the information into something appropriate for ML training. This method involves gathering data from many sources, standardizing it, identifying and correcting erroneous information, deleting duplicate and unnecessary information, and segmenting the data into train, test, and validation sets. We also perform the feature engineering part, where we extract new features which will help us improve the accuracy of our models by making them more robust.
4. **Analyzing Data:** In this phase, we visualize relationships among different variables and correlations between them using various techniques so that meaningful insights can be extracted from it. It also helps us identify anomalies present within the data set if there are any. Finally, it will

also help us select suitable algorithms for modeling depending on the problem statement, such as classification versus regression.

5. **Training:** After collecting all relevant data sets, the training stage builds a model using those data sets as inputs. This model will contain parameters adjusted based on how accurately it can identify features in newly inputted data (usually called validation sets). During this step, some preprocessing may be done, such as normalizing values or converting them into another format better suited for learning algorithms like ANNs (artificial neural networks) or DTs (decision trees). Some popular ML frameworks like scikit-learn provide many easy-to-use tools for performing these types of preprocessing tasks quickly and easily.
6. **Testing and Deploying the Model:** After training has been completed, it is time to validate the model's performance by applying the test set against the trained one; after this, predictions could either be accepted or rejected depending on the results obtained while testing it against the test sets. This process is called cross-validation, wherein the trained model is tested against unseen instances by comparing predicted results with actual ones to measure the trained model's generalization power (accuracy) before deploying it in real-world applications. This stage is equivalent to the application development quality assurance process. The final step would include integrating created models in the form of applications, for example, web and mobile apps. Also, deploying these models online services like cloud servers makes the application available globally over the internet through API calls, allowing users to access them easily.

Continue to tweak and iterate on your model. Continue to monitor and improve it. After all, technology evolves and changes, business requirements alter, and the real world periodically throw a wrench in the works. Any of these variables might result in additional requirements. Consider your machine learning model to be a mobile app. The program will constantly need to be tweaked, updated, and improved. The same is true for your ML model.

SUMMARY

- Machine learning (ML), coined by Arthur Samuel in 1959, is a scientific field that enables computers to learn without being explicitly programmed. It combines clustering, classification, decision trees, supervised, unsupervised, and reinforcement learning techniques to solve complex problems. The growth of machine learning has been fueled by the availability of accessible, affordable data storage, computational power, less expensive processing, and high-speed internet.
- Designing and learning are two distinct aspects of ML. Learning focuses on developing predictive models that can predict future outcomes, while designing focuses on creating novel algorithms for real-world issues like image recognition and autonomous driving.
- ML is an iterative process that involves training, testing, and improving model accuracy. Predictive and descriptive tasks are two major types of machine learning tasks.
- Supervised learning involves machines training using well-labeled training data and predicting the output. It can be grouped into two categories: regression and classification. Regression algorithms are used for predicting continuous variables, while classification models predict the likelihood of new data falling into predetermined categories.

- Unsupervised learning, on the other hand, has no data labels and learns patterns from unlabeled data without supervision. It can be further classified into two categories: clustering and association. Clusters are collections of related items or individuals that exhibit similarities in characteristics, and machine learning can be used to identify traits and distinguish them.
- ML is a powerful tool that has numerous applications in various industries, including healthcare, logistics management, and natural language processing (NLP). It helps organizations make more informed and data-driven choices, but it also faces several challenges. These include large amounts of data, outdated data, privacy and security issues, inadequate training data, overfitting and underfitting, poor data quality, noisy data, incomplete data, inaccurate data, and unclean data.
- Reinforcement learning is a sub-branch of ML that trains a model to return an optimum solution for a problem by taking a sequence of decisions. Supervised ML models are developed and trained using labeled data, while transfer learning uses mapped input and desired output to analyze new data. Meta learning, or 'learning to learn', is a subset of ML that learns from the output of other algorithms.
- A model is a representation of data used for prediction or classification tasks in machine learning. Models are generated from algorithms by applying them to input data sets containing known results or classifications.
- In healthcare, NLP algorithms enable medical professionals to quickly and accurately process medical records for diagnoses, treatments, and prescriptions.
- In logistics management, AI-driven technologies like autonomous vehicles and drones can reduce costs associated with manual labor while improving delivery times and accuracy.
- ML still faces several problems, such as data bias, which occurs when a model produces inaccurate results due to the data used in its training.

EXERCISES

Part A (Objective Questions)

1. What is the main difference between normal programming and machine learning programming?
   a) Normal programming involves executing instructions given by the programmer, while machine learning programs teach computers how to think and make decisions without explicit instructions.
   b) Normal programming uses algorithms to teach computers how to think and make decisions, while machine learning programming follows precise instructions given by the programmer.
   c) Both normal programming and machine learning programming involve executing instructions given by the programmer.
   d) Normal programming is used for complex tasks, while machine learning programming is used for simple tasks.

2. How does machine learning programming differ from normal programming?
   a) Machine learning programming requires less computational power compared to normal programming.
   b) Machine learning programming uses algorithms to teach computers how to make decisions, while normal programming involves writing explicit instructions for the computer to follow.
   c) Machine learning programming is used for simple tasks, while normal programming is used for complex tasks.
   d) Machine learning programming involves executing instructions given by the programmer, while normal programming involves training the computer to make decisions.
3. What is the role of algorithms in machine learning programming?
   a) Algorithms are used to provide explicit instructions for the computer to follow.
   b) Algorithms help computers learn and make decisions without being explicitly told what to do.
   c) Algorithms are only used in normal programming, not in machine learning programming.
   d) Algorithms are used to speed up the execution of machine learning programs.
4. Which type of programming is more focused on teaching computers to think and make decisions?
   a) Normal programming
   b) Machine learning programming
   c) Both normal programming and machine learning programming
   d) None of the above
5. What is the primary purpose of normal programming?
   a) To teach computers how to think and make decisions.
   b) To execute instructions given by the programmer.
   c) To train computers to learn from data.
   d) To speed up the execution of machine learning programs.
6. What is the primary focus of learning in machine learning?
   a) Creating novel algorithms for real-world issues.
   b) Developing predictive models based on historical data.
   c) Designing architectures for image recognition.
   d) Solving challenging problems in natural language processing.
7. Which aspect of machine learning focuses on solving challenging real-world issues?
   a) Learning
   b) Designing
   c) Both learning and designing
   d) None of the above
8. What distinguishes learning from designing in machine learning?
   a) The focus on solving challenging real-world issues.
   b) The use of historical data for predictive modeling.
   c) The creation of novel algorithms and architectures.
   d) The application of machine learning in image recognition.

9. Which aspect of machine learning involves precise prediction based on historical data?
   a) Learning
   b) Designing
   c) Both learning and designing
   d) None of the above

10. What is the main purpose of designing in machine learning?
    a) To develop predictive models based on historical data.
    b) To solve challenging real-world issues with novel algorithms.
    c) To create architectures for image recognition.
    d) To address problems in natural language processing.

11. What is the main purpose of the training phase in machine learning?
    a) Assessing the model's performance on new data.
    b) Validating the model using unseen data.
    c) Building a model from the training data.
    d) Testing the model's predictions on training data.

12. What is the primary goal of the testing phase in machine learning?
    a) Assessing the model's performance on new data.
    b) Validating the model using unseen data.
    c) Building a model from the testing data.
    d) Testing the model's predictions on training data.

13. Which phase of the machine learning process involves using data that the model has not seen before?
    a) Training phase
    b) Testing phase
    c) Both training and testing phases
    d) None of the above

14. What is the purpose of training data in machine learning?
    a) To validate the model's predictions.
    b) To test the model's performance.
    c) To build a model.
    d) To assess the model's generalization.

15. What is the main objective of the testing phase in machine learning?
    a) To assess the model's accuracy on the training data.
    b) To evaluate the model's generalization on unseen data.
    c) To train the model using new instances.
    d) To validate the model's predictions on the testing data.

16. Which regression algorithm is suitable for modeling a linear relationship between the input features and the target variable?
    a) Linear Regression
    b) Regression Tree
    c) Bayesian Linear Regression
    d) Polynomial Regression

17. Which regression algorithm is capable of capturing non-linear relationships between the input features and the target variable?
    a) Linear Regression
    b) Regression Tree
    c) Bayesian Linear Regression
    d) Polynomial Regression

18. Which regression algorithm uses a tree-like structure to model the relationships between the input features and the target variable?
a) Linear Regression
b) Regression Tree
c) Bayesian Linear Regression
d) Polynomial Regression

19. Which regression algorithm incorporates prior knowledge or beliefs about the relationship between the input features and the target variable?
a) Linear Regression
b) Regression Tree
c) Bayesian Linear Regression
d) Polynomial Regression

20. Which regression algorithm can handle interactions and non-linearities by introducing polynomial terms and interaction terms?
a) Linear Regression
b) Regression Tree
c) Bayesian Linear Regression
d) Polynomial Regression

21. Which classification algorithm is based on finding the most similar instances to a given data point in order to make predictions?
a) *K*-nearest neighbor
b) Decision tree
c) Random forest
d) Support vector machines

22. Which classification algorithm uses a hierarchical structure of nodes to make decisions based on feature conditions?
a) *K*-nearest neighbor
b) Decision tree
c) Random forest
d) Support vector machines

23. Which classification algorithm combines multiple decision trees to make predictions?
a) *K*-nearest neighbor
b) Decision tree
c) Random forest
d) Support vector machines

24. Which classification algorithm aims to find an optimal hyperplane that separates different classes in the feature space?
a) *K*-nearest neighbor
b) Decision tree
c) Random forest
d) Support vector machines

25. Which classification algorithm uses linear decision boundaries to classify instances?
a) *K*-nearest neighbor
b) Decision tree
c) Random forest
d) Linear classifiers

26. Which type of learning does clustering belong to?
a) Supervised learning
b) Unsupervised learning
c) Reinforcement learning
d) Semi-supervised learning

27. What is the primary goal of clustering in machine learning?
a) Identifying outliers in the data
b) Predicting future outcomes
c) Grouping related items or individuals
d) Classifying data into predefined categories

28. In *K*-means clustering, what determines the number of clusters (*K*) that the algorithm generates?
a) The similarity measure between data points

b) The number of attributes in the data set
c) The available computing resources
d) The number of predefined clusters specified by the user

29. What is the main objective of *K*-means clustering??
a) To identify outliers in the data
b) To classify data into predefined categories
c) To explore and analyze the data
d) To group data points into distinct clusters based on similarity

30. What is one advantage of the MeanShift algorithm compared to the *K*-means algorithm?
a) It requires specifying the number of clusters in advance.
b) It is faster in terms of computation.
c) It automatically determines the number of clusters.
d) It is more suitable for image classification tasks.

31. In which type of task is MeanShift clustering commonly used?
a) Image segmentation
b) Text classification
c) Anomaly detection
d) Regression analysis

32. What is a notable advantage of the DBSCAN algorithm over *K*-means?
a) It can handle arbitrary-shaped clusters.
b) It is faster in terms of computation.
c) It requires a pre-set number of clusters.
d) It is more suitable for text classification tasks.

33. What is a requirement for a data point to be considered noise in the DBSCAN algorithm?
a) It should have a high density compared to its neighbors.
b) It should have a low density compared to its neighbors.
c) It should have a predefined label assigned.
d) It should be located at the center of a cluster.

34. What is the primary purpose of the Apriori algorithm?
a) Identifying outliers in a data set
b) Performing regression analysis
c) Discovering frequent item sets and association rules
d) Classifying text documents

35. Which type of analysis is commonly performed using the Apriori algorithm?
a) Sentiment analysis
b) Image recognition
c) Market basket analysis
d) Time series forecasting

36. In which type of data set does the ECLAT algorithm perform better than the Apriori algorithm?
a) Horizontal
b) Vertical
c) Time-series
d) Image

37. What search technique does the ECLAT algorithm utilize to find frequent item sets?
a) Breadth-first search
b) Depth-first search
c) Random search
d) Binary search

38. Which algorithm is considered an improved version of the Apriori Algorithm?
a) ECLAT algorithm
b) *K*-means algorithm
c) FP Growth algorithm
d) MeanShift algorithm

39. What is the key data structure used by the FP Growth algorithm?
a) Decision tree
b) Neural network
c) Frequent pattern (FP) tree
d) Support vector machine (SVM)

40. In which of the following scenarios would reinforcement learning be a suitable approach?
a) Sentiment analysis of customer reviews
b) Predicting stock market prices
c) Controlling the movements of a robot
d) Classifying images into different categories

41. How does reinforcement learning differ from supervised learning?
a) Supervised learning uses training data with answer keys, while reinforcement learning does not.
b) Reinforcement learning is used for image classification tasks, while supervised learning is used for game-playing.
c) Reinforcement learning relies on pre-trained models, while supervised learning trains models from scratch.
d) Supervised learning is suitable for solving problems where decision-making is sequential and long-term.

42. Which of the following scenarios is an example of transfer learning?
a) A model trained to classify images of cats is used to classify images of dogs.
b) A model trained to predict stock market prices is fine-tuned to predict cryptocurrency prices.
c) A model trained to play chess is used to play a completely different board game.
d) A model trained to recognize handwritten digits is used to recognize spoken words.

43. How does transfer learning relate to human problem-solving?
a) Humans rely on transfer learning to solve familiar problems but struggle with new situations.
b) Transfer learning allows humans to solve any problem without prior knowledge or experience.
c) Humans can only apply transfer learning in academic or educational settings.
d) Transfer learning is a concept exclusive to machine learning and has no connection to human problem-solving.

44. What is the primary focus of meta learning?
a) Learning from historical data
b) Generating models based on metadata

c) Learning from the outputs of other machine learning algorithms
d) Predicting outcomes for specific tasks

45. How do meta-learning algorithms differ from traditional machine learning algorithms?
a) Meta-learning algorithms directly use historical data to generate models.
b) Meta-learning algorithms rely solely on metadata for predictions.
c) Meta-learning algorithms learn from the outputs of other machine learning models.
d) Meta-learning algorithms are not used for prediction tasks.

46. What is the primary purpose of an algorithm in machine learning?
a) To define inputs and outputs for a model
b) To represent data for prediction or classification tasks
c) To provide high-level instructions for executing a task
d) To generate models from input data sets

47. What is the role of a model in machine learning?
a) To define inputs and outputs for an algorithm
b) To generate algorithms from input data sets
c) To represent data for prediction or classification tasks
d) To provide high-level instructions for executing a task

48. What happens when a machine learning model is trained with a small data set?
a) The model becomes more accurate due to limited data points.
b) The model produces incomplete and erroneous results.
c) The model captures all patterns in the data.
d) The model becomes more flexible to fit the data accurately.

49. What is data drift in machine learning?
a) The process of training a machine learning model with shifting data.
b) The shift in data distribution used to train the model over time.
c) The process of updating a machine learning model with new data.
d) The shift in customer expectations regarding recommendations.

50. What is the impact of data drift on a machine learning model?
a) The model becomes more accurate over time.
b) The model captures all customer requirements accurately.
c) The model remains unchanged regardless of shifting data.
d) The model provides recommendations that do not align with customer expectations.

51. What can cause incomplete and erroneous results in a machine learning model?
a) Training the model with a large data set.
b) Using a linear model for non-linear data.
c) Having a flexible model to fit the data accurately.
d) Capturing all patterns in the data during training.

52. How can training a machine learning model with a small data set affect its accuracy?
a) It improves the model's accuracy due to limited data points.
b) It has no impact on the model's accuracy.

c) It decreases the model's accuracy.
d) It makes the model more flexible in fitting the data accurately.

53. What is a well-posed learning problem?
a) A problem that has multiple solutions.
b) A problem that contains all necessary information and has a single solution or set of solutions.
c) A problem that lacks necessary information.
d) A problem that doesn't involve learning from experience.

54. How does a well-posed learning problem relate to artificial intelligence (AI) research?
a) It is not relevant to AI research.
b) It ensures that AI can learn from given data to produce better results.
c) It limits the capabilities of AI algorithms.
d) It focuses on solving equations in mathematics.

55. What is the key characteristic of a well-posed problem?
a) It has multiple possible solutions.
b) It lacks necessary information.
c) It contains all necessary information.
d) It does not involve learning from experience.

56. Which field often involves finding the value of an unknown variable to define a well-posed problem?
a) Mathematics. b) Physics.
c) Computer science. d) Linguistics.

57. What is the purpose of a well-posed learning problem in AI?
a) To limit the capabilities of learning algorithms.
b) To ensure that learning algorithms have multiple solutions.
c) To provide sufficient information for learning algorithms to produce better results.
d) To define learning problems that lack necessary information.

58. Which approach aims to find the best value function at any given state under any policy?
a) Value-based approach b) Policy-based approach
c) Model-based approach d) Supervised learning approach

59. Which approach identifies the best course of action for maximizing potential rewards without using the value function?
a) Value-based approach b) Policy-based approach
c) Model-based approach d) Supervised learning approach

60. In which approach does the agent learn about the environment through interaction with a virtual model?
a) Value-based approach b) Policy-based approach
c) Model-based approach d) Supervised learning approach

61. How does reinforcement learning differ from supervised learning in terms of feedback?
   a) Reinforcement learning uses rewards and punishments as signals, while supervised learning provides feedback on the proper course of action.
   b) Reinforcement learning uses unsupervised learning techniques, while supervised learning uses labeled data.
   c) Reinforcement learning focuses on maximizing cumulative reward, while supervised learning identifies similarities and differences among data points.
   d) Reinforcement learning and supervised learning have the same feedback mechanisms.

62. What is the objective of reinforcement learning compared to unsupervised learning?
   a) Reinforcement learning aims to identify similarities and differences among data points.
   b) Reinforcement learning focuses on maximizing the agent's overall cumulative reward.
   c) Reinforcement learning uses unsupervised learning techniques.
   d) Reinforcement learning and unsupervised learning have the same objective.

Part B (Short Answer Questions)

1. Differentiate between normal programming and machine learning.
2. Write about machine learning in the current scenario.
3. Machine learning is an interdisciplinary field. Explain. How it is useful?
4. Distinguish between designing and learning.
5. Differentiate between training and testing in machine learning.
6. Differentiate predictive versus descriptive tasks in machine learning.
7. Define supervised learning.
8. Define the regression algorithm in machine learning.
9. List some types of regression algorithm.
10. Define linear regression.
11. Define regression tree.
12. Define Bayesian linear regression.
13. Define polynomial regression.
14. Define the classification algorithm in supervised learning.
15. List the types of classification algorithms.
16. Define KNN.
17. What is a decision tree?
18. Define random forest.
19. What is a support vector machine?
20. Define linear classifiers.
21. Define unsupervised learning.
22. Define clustering.
23. What is *K*-means clustering?
24. What is MeanShift clustering?
25. Define DBSCAN.
26. What is association?
27. Define the Apriori algorithm.
28. Define the ECLAT algorithm.
29. Define the FP Growth algorithm.
30. What is reinforcement learning?
31. Define transfer learning.
32. What is meta learning?
33. Differentiate models and algorithms.
34. Define underfitting
35. Define data drift.
36. What is the meaning of well-posed machine learning problem?

Part C (Essay Questions)

1. Explain the role of machine learning in computer science and problem solving.
2. What is the need for machine learning?
3. Explain the differences between designing and learning.
4. Compare training and testing in machine learning.
5. Explain various types of regression algorithms in detail.
6. Explain linear regression in detail.
7. Explain the concept of KNN (*K*-nearest neighbor) with an example.
8. Explain the concept of decision tree with an example.
9. What is clustering? Explain the commonly used clustering algorithm.
10. What is association? Explain the commonly used association algorithm.
11. Explain reinforcement learning in detail along with its elements.
12. Explain the concepts of transfer learning in detail.
13. Explain meta learning in detail.
14. Explain some real-world problems solved by machine learning in healthcare.
15. Explain some real-world problems solved by machine learning in fraud detection in the finance industry.
16. Explain some real-world problems solved by machine learning in facial recognition technology.
17. Explain some real-world problems solved by machine learning in forecasting future market trends.
18. Explain some real-world problems solved by machine learning in email spam detection.
19. Explain some real-world problems solved by machine learning in speech recognition.
20. Explain some real-world problems solved by machine learning in product recommendation.
21. Explain some real-world problems solved by machine learning in customer segmentation.
22. Explain some real-world problems solved by machine learning in demand forecasting.
23. Explain some real-world problems solved by machine learning in virtual personal assistant.
24. Explain some real-world problems solved by machine learning in sentiment analysis.
25. Explain some real-world problems solved by machine learning in traffic prediction.
26. Explain some real-world problems solved by machine learning in automatic language translation.
27. Explain well posed machine learning problems in detail.
28. Write an essay on designing a learning system (life cycle of machine learning).

ANSWER KEY

Part A

1. (a)	**2.** (b)	**3.** (b)	**4.** (b)	**5.** (b)	**6.** (b)	**7.** (b)	**8.** (c)
9. (a)	**10.** (b)	**11.** (c)	**12.** (a)	**13.** (b)	**14.** (c)	**15.** (b)	**16.** (a)
17. (d)	**18.** (b)	**19.** (c)	**20.** (d)	**21.** (a)	**22.** (b)	**23.** (c)	**24.** (d)
25. (d)	**26.** (b)	**27.** (c)	**28.** (d)	**29.** (d)	**30.** (c)	**31.** (a)	**32.** (a)
33. (b)	**34.** (c)	**35.** (c)	**36.** (b)	**37.** (b)	**38.** (c)	**39.** (c)	**40.** (c)
41. (a)	**42.** (b)	**43.** (a)	**44.** (c)	**45.** (c)	**46.** (c)	**47.** (c)	**48.** (b)
49. (b)	**50.** (d)	**51.** (b)	**52.** (c)	**53.** (b)	**54.** (b)	**55.** (c)	**56.** (a)
57. (c)	**58.** (a)	**59.** (b)	**60.** (c)	**61.** (a)	**62.** (b)		

2 Probability Theory and Statistics in Machine Learning

Learning Objectives

At the end of this chapter, you will be able to:

- Explain the foundational concepts of probability and statistics
- Define and differentiate between joint, marginal, and conditional probabilities
- Identify the key concepts of probability distributions
- Analyze discrete probability distributions
- Explore continuous probability distributions, including the normal, exponential, and uniform distributions
- Use Bayes' theorem for updating the probability estimate for a hypothesis as additional evidence is acquired
- Implement moment generating function (MGF) to characterize probability distributions
- Use maximum likelihood estimation (MLE) to estimate the parameters of a probability distribution
- Utilize maximum posteriori estimation (MAP) for parameter estimation in Bayesian inference
- Interpret density functions and their role in probability and statistics

2.1 Introduction

Probability theory and statistics are foundational to the concepts of machine learning (ML) and data science. Data preprocessing, cleansing, and visualization depend heavily on probability theory and statistics. Therefore, it is crucial to comprehend the definitions of each phrase to know how they are connected.

A mathematical study of random phenomena with unknown outcomes is the subject of probability theory. Contrarily, the area of mathematics known as statistics is concerned with gathering, examining, interpreting, presenting, and organizing data. Statistics and probability theory have many applications in the social sciences, business, engineering, and other disciplines.

Supervised learning algorithms like linear regression and support vector machines (SVMs) employ probability distributions and statistical inference techniques to predict future values based on past values from a data set. For instance, a business wants to forecast the stock market using the linear regression algorithm. It will initially gather historical stock values for various periods before attempting to spot trends. However, this collected data contains inherent noise due to different circumstances, such as political difficulties. Therefore, we employ probability distribution functions (such as normal distribution) to remove outliers and reduce noise (data points far away from other points). Then, we run several statistical tests to evaluate how well our model fits our data set (such as the F-test).

Based on this, we assess the performance and make necessary parameter adjustments till the model is sufficiently tuned. After that, we use supervised learning to evaluate the model against actual market movements and make adjustments as necessary to obtain an appropriate degree of accuracy.

Another example is for utilizing convolutional neural networks (CNNS) to categorize photos. Before feeding the photos into the CNN training process, we would first need labeled images or pictures of objects that have been identified. We could obtain these by manually labeling them using programs like LabelImg, downloading them already labeled from online image collections like ImageNet, or even getting unlabeled pictures scraped off websites/social media pages and labeling them using crowdsourcing services like Amazon Mechanical Turk. Here, we would primarily be performing feature extraction operations using convolutional layers involving probability calculations based on input image pixels. We would then feed the extracted features through fully connected layers with perceptron neurons whose weights would be adjusted millions of times until the optimized probabilities come up, predicting the expected category labels beside each image correctly.

We will first discuss some important ML-related probability concepts before moving on to the related statistical concepts.

2.2 Probability

The study of random events and their likelihood of occurrence is known as probability. It measures the likelihood that a specific event will occur, expressed as a number between 0 and 1, with 0 denoting uncertainty (impossibility) and one denoting certainty (possibility).

Think about tossing a fair coin as an example. The likelihood of receiving heads and the likelihood of receiving tails is 0.5. As a result, if we flip the coin repeatedly, we anticipate getting heads and tails reasonably equally (Table 2.1).

Table 2.1 Tossing a coin and its possible outcomes and probability

Possible outcomes	Number of outcomes	Probability (Number of outcomes/Total outcomes)
Head	1	1/2 = 0.5
Tail	1	1/2 = 0.5
Total	2	

Another example is the roll of a six-sided die. Given that there are six possible outcomes and only one of it is 1, the likelihood of rolling a 1 is 1/6. There are three even numbers on the dice, so the likelihood of rolling an even number is 3/6 or ½ (Table 2.2).

Table 2.2 Tossing a dice and its possible outcomes and probability

Possible outcomes	Number of outcomes	Probability (Number of outcomes/Total outcomes)
Even number	3(2, 4, 6)	3/6 = 0.5
Odd number	3(1, 3, 5)	3/6 = 0.5
Total	6(1, 2, 3, 4, 5, 6)	

Moreover, probability is utilized in statistical inference, which is the process of inferring information about a population from sample data. For instance, if we wanted to know the percentage of people who like vanilla ice cream over chocolate, we could poll a random sample of people and use probability theory to draw conclusions about the entire population. Probability is a fundamental concept in mathematics and is widely used in ML and statistical analysis. It provides us with a framework to model and understand random events and make informed decisions based on the likelihood of their occurrence.

2.3 Probability Theory

Probability plays a crucial role in ML as it provides a solid foundation for modeling and reasoning about uncertainty in data, which is a fundamental aspect of many ML algorithms. Probability theory allows us to quantify uncertainty and make informed decisions based on probabilistic reasoning in the following ways:

- **Supervised learning**: Probability theory is used in techniques like naive Bayes and logistic regression to estimate the probability of an input belonging to a particular class.
- **Unsupervised learning**: In clustering algorithms like *K*-means and Gaussian mixture models, probability distributions are used to model the underlying structure of data.
- **Reinforcement learning**: Here, probabilities estimate the reward function based on the expected value of rewards for a particular action.
- **Bayesian networks:** Probabilistic graphical models are used to represent and reason about uncertain knowledge, a common feature in many real-world applications.

2.4 Joint, Marginal, and Conditional Probability

Probability is a way to gauge how likely it is that something will happen. We utilize probability to make decisions in daily life, such as what to wear depending on the likelihood of rain or which route to take based on the likelihood of traffic. Three different probability types, joint, marginal, and conditional, will be covered in this section.

The possibility of two or more occurrences happening simultaneously is known as **joint probability**. Consider rolling two dice to determine the likelihood of rolling a four on one die and a six on the other. You may calculate this probability, indicated as P(4 and 6), by dividing the total number of feasible scenarios by the potential alignments of the two events. The probability is 1/36 since there is only one way to roll a four on one die and a six on the other.

A single event's **marginal probability** is its likelihood that it will occur.

$$P\ (4 \text{ and } 6) = P\ (4) * P(6) = (1/6)* (1/6) = 1/36$$

Consider rolling two dice to determine the likelihood of rolling a four in total from both the dice. This probability, shown as P(4), is calculated by dividing the possible outcomes by the number of ways the event could occur. In order to obtain a total of 4, the combinations can be (1,3), (2,2) and (3,1), totaling 3 ways.

$$\text{Total number of events} = 6 * 6 = 36$$

So, the probability of getting a total of 4 from both the dice is 3/36 = 1/12.

Given that another event has already occurred, the likelihood of an event occurring is known as **conditional probability**. Usually, it is written as P(A|B), where A stands for the occurrence and B for the condition. Consider, for instance, the likelihood of rolling a number higher than two on a fair six-sided die if the outcome is an odd number. The event's sample space is 1, 3, 5, and the expected result is 3, 5. Rolling an odd number has a probability of 1/2, and getting a number greater than 2 has a probability of 4/6 or 2/3. Given that an outcome is an odd number, the probability of rolling a number greater than 2 is (2/3)/(1/2) or 4/3. Conditional probability, in general, aids in the improvement of probability calculation when some knowledge of the events is already known.

Example 1: Three red and two blue balls are placed in a bag. How likely is it that two balls drawn from the bag, without replacement, are red?

Solution: P(RR) = (3/5) × (2/4) = 3/10 is the joint probability of drawing two red balls. As the likelihood of drawing the first red ball is 3/5 and the likelihood of drawing a second red ball, given that the first ball was red, is 2/4, we multiply (3/5) by (2/4).

Example 2: There are 20 students in a class, 12 of whom are girls. What is the likelihood that a boy student will be chosen randomly from the class?

Solution: P(B) = 1 – P(G) = 1 – (12/20) = 8/20, which may be simplified to 2/5. This is the marginal probability of choosing a boy. As there are only two conceivable outcomes, that the pupil is either a boy or a girl, we deduct P(G) from 1.

Example 3: A and B are two different products that a corporation makes. Forty per cent of the products are type B, and 60% are type A. Ten per cent of type A items and 5% of type B products have flaws. What is the likelihood that a defective product, chosen randomly, is of type A?

Solution: P(A|D) = P(A and D) / P(D), where (D) is the probability of choosing a faulty product. This is the conditional probability that a defective product is of type A. P(A and D) = 0.6 × 0.1 = 0.06 is the joint probability of choosing a defective type A product, while P(B and D) = 0.4 × 0.05 = 0.02 is the joint likelihood of choosing a defective type B product. These two odds, 0.06 + 0.02 = 0.08, add to the probability of choosing a damaged product. As a result, P(A|D) = 0.06 / 0.08 = 0.75. Thus, there is a 75% chance that a damaged product will be of type A if chosen randomly.

The chance of developing a disease given a positive test result is one example of how conditional probability is frequently employed in medical testing.

It is significant to remember that these three probabilities are interconnected. Calculating conditional probability using joint probability and marginal probability using joint probability is possible. For instance, we may use conditional probability to determine the probability of one occurrence given the other, if we know the joint probability of the two events. We can use conditional probability to determine the likelihood of rolling a four on the second die provided that the first die rolled a three, if we know the joint probability of rolling a three on one die and a four on another die.

Probability theory is a tool statisticians use to evaluate data, forecast outcomes, and test theories. For instance, a statistician may use conditional probability to estimate the likelihood that a patient, given their age and medical history, would have a specific disease. Alternatively, they could compute the likelihood that two variables are related to one another using joint probability.

Finance is also a subject area where probability theory is significant. For instance, we could estimate the possibility of a company going bankrupt or compute the expected return of a stock portfolio using probability theory.

Probability theory is utilized in engineering to create dependable and durable systems and in physics to simulate the behavior of particles and systems. Finally, it is used in computer science to classify data and generate predictions in artificial intelligence (AI) and ML.

2.5 Statistics

Data collection, analysis, interpretation, presentation, and organization are all topics that fall under statistics, a subfield of mathematics. It offers a framework for comprehending and making choices based on data, and it is utilized in various sectors, including business, science, medical, and social sciences. For instance, a business might employ statistical analysis to forecast customer demand for a product based on historical sales information.

Statistics works by gathering and examining data sets to make inferences about them. It involves a variety of methods, including clustering (combining related parts), regression analysis (identifying correlations between variables), descriptive statistics (comparing averages), and inferential statistics (forming predictions). In addition, it is helpful in assessing the effectiveness of various ML models. It also offers strategies for validating models by comparing their accuracy to actual outcomes using t-tests and chi-squared tests. Finally, to improve models before they are tested against real-world data, statistics plays a crucial role by offering methods for analyzing data sets.

Statistics is integral to ML as it provides a framework for analysing and interpreting data. Statistical methods are used for understanding the relationships between variables and identifying patterns that can be used to build predictive models. Some examples of how statistics is used in ML include:

- **Data exploration and cleaning:** Before building a predictive model, the data needs to be analysed to identify patterns and remove errors or inconsistencies. Statistical methods such as descriptive statistics and graphical representations are used for this.
- **Data preprocessing:** Statistical techniques like feature scaling and normalization transform the data so that ML algorithms can better understand it.
- **Model selection:** Statistical methods are used to compare the performance of different models and select those that provide the best accuracy.
- **Model evaluation:** Statistical techniques such as cross-validation and hypothesis testing are used to evaluate a model's performance and determine its effectiveness.

In conclusion, statistics is an effective instrument for examining and drawing conclusions from data in various domains.

2.6 Key Concepts of Probability Distributions

When working with probability distributions, it is essential to understand certain key concepts and calculations.

2.6.1 Random Variables

Random variables are those that have varying values depending on the situation. They are a mathematical tool for understanding the irrationality of specific circumstances. In addition, they are used in ML to analyze data sets and estimate potential patterns and correlations.

Consider a data set with multiple variables, such as age, gender, etc. You can think of each variable as a separate random variable (RV). Using RV theory, you can determine the likelihood that a specific set of these variables will occur in the future. For example, you can use RV to compute the possibility that someone will be female and 25 years old next year.

Random variables are essential in ML since they represent data points in a probabilistic model. They can model uncertain or unknown values that may influence the outcome of a prediction, classification, or clustering task.

RVs can also be used in ML algorithms to test hypotheses and assist in making predictions about future events using historical data sets. For example, suppose we have a hypothesis that 'people who buy more expensive items tend to be older'. We could test this hypothesis by building an RV that captures age information and compare it against purchase records for expensive items versus cheaper ones. We could then deduce a statistic from these results that would tell us whether or not our hypothesis is true or false based on how closely related the two variables are when compared against each other's status.

2.6.2 Mean

A probability distribution's mean, or average, is calculated by adding all the possible outcomes and dividing the sum by the total number of outcomes. For instance, by adding all the students' heights and dividing that by the total number of students, the average height of the pupils in a class may be determined.

For a discrete distribution, this calculation looks like this:

$$\text{Mean} = (p_1 * x_1) + (p_2 * x_2) + \ldots + (p_n * x_n),$$

where $p_1, p_2, \ldots, p_n$ are the probabilities of each possible outcome, and $x_1, x_2, \ldots, x_n$ are the corresponding values.

For example, if X can take the values 1, 2, 3, and 4 with probabilities 0.2, 0.3, 0.4, 0.1, respectively, then the mean of X is:

$$\text{Mean} = 1*0.2 + 2*0.3 + 3*0.4 + 4*0.1 = 2.4$$

For a continuous distribution, the calculation is carried out using integration:

$$\text{Mean} = \int(xf(x)dx),$$

where $f(x)$ is the probability density function.

Mean is an essential measure of central tendency that helps us understand a distribution's 'typical' or expected outcome.

Probability Density Function (PDF): The chance of an event occurring within a specified range of values is expressed by the probability density function. It is used to calculate a continuous random variable's probability. Normal distribution, exponential distribution, and gamma distribution are a few examples of PDFs.

Cumulative Distribution Function (CDF): The likelihood that a random variable in a distribution will be less than or equal to a given value is described by the cumulative distribution function. It is a monotonically increasing function with a 0–1 range. Both discrete and continuous distributions can have their probability of events or ranges of values calculated using CDF.

For example, if we have a random variable X that follows a normal distribution with mean μ and standard deviation σ, then the CDF of X is given by:

$$F(x) = 1/2 * [1 + \mathrm{erf}((x - \mu)/(\sigma * \sqrt{2}))],$$

where erf is the error function.

Another example is the CDF of a uniform distribution, which is given by:

$$F(x) = (x - a)/(b - a),$$

where a and b represent the lower and upper limits of the uniform distribution.

2.6.3 Variance and Expectation

Variance and expectation serve as the foundation for analyzing random variables using mathematics, which is crucial for ML applications. They are crucial for understanding how well algorithms perform across various data sets, including test sets used for validation, and for identifying potential sources of bias within those algorithms that might affect results unexpectedly (for example, if one data set has significantly higher values than another). They also help evaluate how well algorithms perform in ML applications.

Expectation, which assesses the expected value of a random variable within a given set of values based on its probability distribution, is closely related to variance. The anticipated value indicates what should typically happen based on the sample data; it is essentially what you would expect to happen if you conducted the same experiment repeatedly under identical conditions.

For instance, if you flip two coins simultaneously 10 times, you will anticipate getting five heads and five tails (and your variance would show how close you came to this ideal result). Expectation is a measure of the central tendency of a random variable. It is calculated by multiplying each possible value of the variable by its probability of occurrence, and then summing the products. The result is the expected value of the variable. The formula for expectation can be expressed as:

$$E(X) = \Sigma\, x * P(X = x),$$

where X is the random variable, x is a possible value of X, and $P(X = x)$ is the probability of X taking the value x.

For example, consider a fair, six-sided die. The possible outcomes of rolling the die are 1, 2, 3, 4, 5, and 6, each with a probability of 1/6. The expected value of the die roll can be calculated as:

$$E(X) = (1 * 1/6) + (2 * 1/6) + (3 * 1/6) + (4 * 1/6) + (5 * 1/6) + (6 * 1/6) = 3.5$$

This means that if we were to roll the die many times, the average result would be 3.5.

Variance, on the other hand, measures how spread out the distribution of a random variable is. The difference between a collection of values, such as observations or samples drawn from a population, is measured as variance. It gauges the degree of dispersion between the data points and their mean or average value. It can be used to establish if an observed data point has a higher likelihood of being caused by an underlying factor driving its occurrence than it does being the result of pure chance.

It is calculated by taking the expected value of the squared deviations from the mean. The formula for variance can be expressed as:

$$Var(X) = E[(X - E(X))^2],$$

where X is the random variable and $E(X)$ is its expected value.

Continuing with the example of rolling a fair six-sided die, the variance of the die roll can be calculated as:

$$\begin{aligned} Var(X) &= E[(X - E(X))^2] \\ &= [(1 - 3.5)^2 * 1/6] + [(2 - 3.5)^2 * 1/6] + [(3 - 3.5)^2 * 1/6] + [(4 - 3.5)^2 * 1/6] + [(5 - 3.5)^2 * 1/6] + [(6 - 3.5)^2 * 1/6] = 35/12 \end{aligned}$$

The square root of variance is called **standard deviation**, which is a common measure of the spread of a distribution.

Let us imagine, for instance, that we intended to use linear regression with gradient descent optimization to forecast house prices based on local characteristics like pincode and median income level. Before training our model, we may perform both variance and expectation analysis. First, we would use variance analysis to identify the areas where house prices were significantly higher or lower than our target median, letting us know where more resources should be directed during training. Next, we would use expectation analysis to determine the magnitude of a house price increase or decrease given location-related factors like median income level or pincode changes, allowing us to adjust our model appropriately until it matches our expectations.

A high-variance model is susceptible to overfitting and performs well on the training set but poorly on test data. However, a low-variance model performs well on training and test data but may underfit the data. Kernel SVM and decision trees are examples of high-variance models, whereas linear regression is a low-variance model. **Mean squared error (MSE)** is an expectation that measures the difference between the actual value and predicted value in regression problems. For example, the expected value can be used to compute the accuracy of a clustering algorithm.

In conclusion, variance measures how well the model can predict new data after it has perceived the training data. Expectation is used to measure the performance of algorithms and models.

2.7 Probability Distributions

Sets of numbers, known as **standard distributions**, occur more frequently than would be predicted based on the average number of occurrences. Standard distributions, also called probability distributions, are frequently used in math, science, and economics to describe random variables, and to analyze data. In addition, these standard distributions can be used in ML to understand data trends and patterns or to group related objects.

Standard distributions are crucial in ML because they help reveal insights into data trends and patterns, enabling businesses and organizations to operate more effectively in response to changing business needs. As a result, businesses can maximize revenues while minimizing expenses by applying statistical modeling techniques like normal, Poisson, and exponential distributions, eventually leading to higher success!

Probability distributions, in general, have a wide range of practical uses. Probability distributions, for instance, are used by businesses to simulate the distribution of profits and losses and by insurance firms to simulate the distribution of claims. In addition, they are used by scientists to simulate the distribution of data in experiments as well as by weather forecasters to predict the possibility of specific weather patterns.

The testing of hypotheses is a typical use of probability distributions. Given a population mean or proportion, probability distributions determine the likelihood of attaining a specific sample mean or sample proportion.

Making assumptions or inferences about a population based on a sample from that group is known as statistical inference. For example, confidence intervals and p-values, which assist us in assessing the possibility that particular results ensue from chance, are computed using probability distributions.

Probability distributions can be discrete or continuous. Whereas continuous probability distributions are used to model events that can take on any value within a given range, discrete probability distributions are used to model occurrences that can only take on specific values. We shall now study these in greater detail.

2.7.1 Discrete Probability Distributions

Models of the probability of events that can only take particular values are called discrete probability distributions. Any probability distribution with countable and finite outcomes is said to be discrete. This indicates that the possible values for the random variable are different and independent.

The **probability mass function (PMF)**, which is used to characterize a discrete distribution, provides the likelihood of each possible result. For instance, because the possible outcomes are only the numbers 1 through 6, the probability distribution for the result of rolling a six-sided die is discrete.

Binomial, multinomial, Poisson, and Bernoulli are a few examples of discrete probability distributions.

2.7.1.1 Binomial Distribution

This is a type of discrete probability distribution that models the likelihood of a specific number of successes in a defined number of independent trials. A binomial distribution is used to model situations with only two possible outcomes, such as success or failure. The number of successes in a fixed number of independent trials is frequently modeled in statistics. For example, the number of heads in 10 coin flips can be modeled using a binomial distribution.

The PMF of a binomial distribution is given by:

$$P(X = k) = (n \text{ choose } k) * p\wedge k * (1 - p)\wedge(n - k)$$

The variables X, n, p, k, and (n select k) are all random. X is the random variable, p is the probability of success, n is the number of trials on each trial, and k is the number of successes. In ML, the binomial distribution is frequently used to simulate binary outcomes like click-through, conversion, and churn rates. For instance, we may have a data set of 1000 consumers and want to estimate how many of them will make a purchase based on their demographic and behavioral information. A binary logistic regression model with a binomial distribution can be used to predict the likelihood that a client will purchase the product.

A/B testing is another application of binomial distribution in ML. Here, we randomly divide consumers into two groups and present them with several iterations of a website or app. The probability of observing the conversion rate by chance is then modeled using binomial distribution after measuring the conversion rate for each group. This enables us to assess the statistical significance of the conversion rate difference between the two groups.

By knowing the binomial distribution, ML specialists can create more robust models and precise predictions. It is used for tasks such as binary classification, which involves predicting whether a given input belongs to one of two classes. In addition, it helps determine the probability of success or failure in each trial of a set of independent trials.

2.7.1.2 Multinomial Distribution

This is used to model data that has more than two probable outcomes. The binomial distribution, which describes data with two possible outcomes, is generalized in this way. For instance, multinomial distribution can be applied to natural language processing to simulate the frequency distribution of words in a document or corpus of documents. In this scenario, each word may be viewed as a category, and a multinomial distribution can be used to simulate the frequency of recurrence of each word in the document or corpus.

The classification of images is another application of the multinomial distribution in machine learning. A vector of characteristics, such as pixel values or color histograms, can represent a picture in this scenario. A multinomial distribution, in which each feature is associated with a category, can be used to simulate the distribution of these features.

Numerous characteristics of multinomial distribution make it valuable in ML. Since it is a discrete distribution, it can be used to model count data. It can be used as a prior distribution in Bayesian inference because it is also a conjugate before the multinomial likelihood function.

Let us say we have a data set of emails, and we want to categorize each email as spam or non-spam, depending on how often specific terms appear in the emails. Each email can be represented as a vector of word counts, where each item in the vector represents the frequency with which a specific word appears in an email. A multinomial distribution can be used to simulate the frequency of occurrence of each word, with each word denoting a specific category.

Another example is topic modeling, a popular technique for exploring large text data sets. It is predicated on the idea that each corpus document has a mixture of different themes, with each topic represented as a probability distribution over words. In this case, multinomial distribution estimates the likelihood of a word appearing in a particular topic and thereby aids in identifying the most relevant topics for a given corpus. Another application is sentiment analysis. It can be used, for instance, to simulate the distribution of positive, negative, or neutral attitudes in a corpus of text and assist in classifying new documents into one of these three groups depending on the sentiment that is most likely to exist in them.

2.7.1.3 Poisson Distribution

This is widely used to replicate sporadic events over time, such as the volume of cars going through a toll booth in an hour or the number of calls a call center receives daily. The Poisson distribution thus expresses the likelihood of an event occurring over time, given an average rate of occurrence, such as the number of times a week that store customers make purchases or the number of times a month that tourists arrive in a city. This enables us to estimate how likely such events are to occur during that time frame to make the necessary plans for inventory needs, etc.

Suppose we have an average of 10 customers who visit our store everyday. Using Poisson distribution and other variables like seasonality (such as during holidays), we can create scenarios where we might anticipate lower customer numbers on some days while experiencing higher numbers on other days. Based on these scenarios, we can adjust our staffing levels accordingly.

One everyday use case of the Poisson distribution in ML is in natural language processing, which can be used to model the frequency of specific words or phrases in a given document. By applying the Poisson distribution to this data, machine learning algorithms can examine and forecast the likelihood that specific words or phrases will appear in future texts. Another critical area where Poisson distributions are used in machine learning is in image processing, which can be applied to model the frequency and distribution of pixels in an image.

2.7.1.4 Bernoulli Distribution

This is frequently employed in the field of ML. As it is a discrete probability distribution, success or failure are the only two conceivable outcomes. Any binary event with two possible outcomes, such as a coin flip with two possible outcomes (heads or tails), can be modeled using the Bernoulli distribution. It can also be used to simulate more complex situations involving several independent binary variables, such as the combined result of two coin flips (heads or tails). The probability of success, or p, is the only parameter the distribution accepts. The likelihood of failure is $1-p$.

To assess whether a text is positive or negative, sentiment analysis uses Bernoulli distribution. For example, to categorize new reviews as positive or negative, we can estimate the likelihood that a word will appear in either positive or bad reviews.

Imagine a case when we have a data set of 100 coin tosses. The likelihood of getting a head or a tail can be modeled using the Bernoulli distribution. Imagine getting a head with a probability of 0.6. After that, we can predict the likelihood of receiving a head as:

$$P(X{=}1) = p = 0.6$$
$$P(X{=}0) = 1 - p = 0.4$$

We can use this information to predict the probability of getting heads or tails in future coin flips.

Another example is fraud detection, where we wish to categorize transactions as fraudulent or not. Using Bernoulli distribution, we can predict whether a transaction will be fraudulent. We can use this information to categorize future transactions as fraudulent or non-fraudulent if a particular transaction is more likely to be fraudulent than non-fraudulent.

Logistic regression models, which are frequently used for classification tasks where we have some data points that are labeled into one group (for example, cats) and others that are labeled into another group (for example, dogs), are an application of Bernoulli distribution in ML.

Finally, when experimenting with various methods for making decisions with uncertain information about some external events, we can also use Bayesian networks alongside Bernoulli distributions. For example, we could decide whether to purchase insurance against a potential event depending on certain factors related to its likelihood of occurring.

2.7.2 Continuous Probability Distributions

A continuous probability distribution, called a uniform distribution, represents random variables with an equal chance of happening within a specific range. When a random variable is anticipated to have a value within a range, and all values within that range are equally likely, it is frequently utilized in ML.

A continuous distribution is described by the **probability density function (PDF)**, which provides the relative likelihood that specific values will occur. The PDF is a non-negative function that integrates to 1 over the entire distribution's range.

For instance, because height can take on any value within a specified range, the probability distribution for the height of adult men in a specific population is continuous. The normal distribution, commonly called the Gaussian distribution, is a continuous probability distribution. Several real-world phenomena, like the distribution of IQ scores, are modeled using normal distribution.

2.7.2.1 Normal Distribution

A normal distribution, sometimes called a Gaussian distribution or bell curve due to its appearance in a histogram, is a popular type of standard distribution. With 50% of the values above the mean and 50% below it, it is symmetric about its mean. Because of the regular pattern it follows and the ease with which probability for particular outcomes can be predicted, this typeof distribution is frequently employed in statistics. A standard distribution model, for instance, can be used to calculate the number of students who will be able to receive an A grade on their exams, given that 70% of students scored between 80% and 90%. This is because most outcomes will likely fall within this range rather than at either end (over 90% or below 80%).

Machine learning frequently uses it to simulate real-world occurrences like measurements of physical quantities or noise in sensor readings. The Gaussian distribution can be used to simulate the return distribution on a stock in stock market analysis, with the mean reflecting the average return and the standard deviation representing the volatility of the stock. Uniform and Gaussian distributions are employed in a variety of ML applications, including:

- **Data generation**: To create synthetic data that may be utilized to train and test ML models. For instance, artificial images can be produced using a uniform distribution to mimic the pixel values in the case of image recognition.
- **Clustering**: To put similar data points together. A Gaussian distribution, for instance, can be used to cluster consumers with similar buying patterns and represent the distribution of client purchases in the context of customer segmentation.

- **Feature selection**: To assess the importance of features in a data set using feature selection approaches. For instance, the frequency of words in a document can be modeled using a multinomial distribution in the case of text classification, and only the words with the highest probability can be chosen as features for the model.

Normal distribution can represent a variety of real-world occurrences, including adult male height and fruit weight.

The PDF of a normal distribution is given by:

$$f(x) = (1 / (\sigma * \mathrm{sqrt}(2\pi))) * \exp(-((x - \mu)\^2) / (2\sigma\^2)),$$

where μ =mean and σ = standard deviation.

2.7.2.2 Exponential Distribution

The interval between events that occur randomly and independently over time is frequently modeled using exponential distribution. Consider that you are a call center employee who needs to know the time interval before the next customer calls. Exponential distribution can help determine the chance of a customer phoning in the next minute, five minutes, or at any other time.

In ML, it can be utilized, for example, to represent the intervals between events, such as the intervals between website user clicks. By examining this period, we may discover more about user behavior and modify the website's design to boost user engagement.

2.7.2.3 Uniform Distribution

This type of distribution assumes that all values falling inside a specific range are equally likely to occur. This implies that a flat, horizontal line would be produced if the likelihood of each value falling inside the range were plotted. Rolling a fair dice is an illustration of the uniform distribution in action. The uniform distribution can depict the likelihood that each number will appear because each side of the dice has an equal chance of being rolled. The probability of each value falling inside the range in this instance would be 1/6, and the range would be from 1 to 6.

Think about mimicking the performance of a stock portfolio, for instance. Uniform distribution can create random stock price values that fall within a specified range.

In ML, uniform distribution could be used, for instance, to produce random weight initializations for neural networks. We can ensure that each weight has an equal chance of being initialized to any value within a specified range by generating these values using the uniform distribution.

Making random samples from a data set is another way that ML uses uniform distribution. For example, you want to train a model to identify specific features in a data set of photos. You can ensure the training data is varied and representative of the complete data set by utilizing uniform distribution to randomly sample from it.

2.8 Examples of Probability Distributions

- *Flipping a coin*: When rolling a coin, there is an equal chance that head or tail appears. For example, head can appear with a probability of 1/2. Tail can appear with a probability of 1/2. This is an illustration of a discrete probability distribution.

- *Rolling a die*: When rolling a fair die, there is an equal chance that each number will appear. For example, any number between 1 and 6 can be rolled with a probability of 1/6. This is an illustration of a discrete probability distribution.
- *Height of students*: If the mean height is 5 feet and a student's height is within a 0.5-foot range, a normal distribution can determine the odds that the student will be that height.
- *Time taken to complete a task*: If, for example, the average time to complete a task is 10 minutes, we can use the exponential distribution to determine the likelihood that a task will be completed in that time.
- *Number of cars passing through a traffic light*: Poisson distribution can calculate the likelihood of a specific number of cars passing through the traffic light at a particular time if we know that the average number of vehicles passing through in a minute is 10.
- *Temperature*: For example, the likelihood that the temperature will be a particular value may be calculated using the normal distribution if the average temperature is 70 degrees Fahrenheit and the standard deviation is 5 degrees.
- *Sales of a product*: For example, the binomial distribution can be used to determine the likelihood of making five sales in a single day if we know that the probability of a sale is 0.2.
- *Number of defects in a product*: For example, the Poisson distribution can be used to calculate the likelihood that a particular product would have a specific number of flaws if we know that the average number of defects in a product is 2.
- *Arrival time of customers*: For example, if the standard deviation is 15 minutes and the average arrival time is 10 am, we can use the normal distribution to compute the probability that a client will arrive at that time.
- *Lifetime of a product*: For example, a product has an average lifespan of five years. In that case, we can use the exponential distribution to determine the likelihood that a product will fail within a given time frame.
- *Distance between two points*: If we know that the average distance is 100 meters, and the standard deviation is 10 meters, we can use the normal distribution to determine the probability that the distance is a specific value.
- *Stock prices*: If we know the mean and standard deviation of stock prices, we can use the lognormal distribution to determine the probability of the stock price being a specific value.
- *Reaction times*: If, for example, the average reaction time is 0.3 seconds, and the standard deviation is 0.05 seconds, we can use the normal distribution to determine the probability of a reaction time within a specific range.
- *Traffic flow*: If we know that the average number of cars passing through a particular intersection is 20 per minute, we can use the Poisson distribution to determine the probability of a certain number of cars passing through in a given period.
- *Temperature fluctuations*: If we know the average temperature and the standard deviation of temperature fluctuations, we can use the normal distribution to determine the probability of the temperature being within a specific range.
- *Duration of phone calls*: If we know the average duration of phone calls, we can use the exponential distribution to determine the probability of a phone call lasting for a specific time.

- *Rainfall*: If we know the average rainfall amount and gamma distribution's scale and shape parameters, we can use the gamma distribution to determine the probability of a certain amount of rainfall occurring.
- *Loan defaults*: A binomial distribution can calculate the likelihood that a specific number of loans in a portfolio will default if we know the likelihood that a loan will default and the total number of loans in the portfolio.
- *Customer arrivals*: A Poisson distribution can calculate the likelihood that a specific number of customers will arrive within a specified period if we know the average number of customers arriving per hour or day.
- *Test scores*: If we know the mean and standard deviation of the test scores, we can use the normal distribution to determine the probability of a specific score or range of scores.
- *Sales forecasting*: If we know the historical sales data and mean and standard deviation of sales, we can use normal distribution to determine the probability of sales being within a specific range in the future.
- *Website traffic*: If we know the average number of visitors to a website per day or hour, we can use a Poisson distribution to determine the probability of a certain number of visitors during a given period.

Probability distributions are essential for understanding and analyzing random events and phenomena. Discrete and continuous probability distributions have their characteristics and uses, and different types of probability distributions are suited to modeling different events.

2.9 Conditional Distribution

Conditional distribution describes the connection between two random variables. It displays the likelihood of one variable occurring, given the value of another. For instance, we could use a conditional distribution to explain how likely it is for Y to take on each value given X, if we had a random variable X that can only take on the values 0 or 1 and another random variable Y that can only take on the values A, B, or C. This kind of probability model aids our comprehension of the relationships between various variables and can be applied to predicting future data.

Depending on the kind of the relevant random variables, it may be discrete or continuous. The conditional distribution will be discrete if the relevant random variables are discrete in themselves. On the other hand, the conditional distribution will be continuous if the random variables are continuous. A person's height, for instance, can be a continuous random variable, and their gender, a discrete one.

Consider the straightforward case of flipping two coins. Assume that after the first coin has come up heads, we are also looking for the likelihood that the other one will. In this instance, the result of the first coin determines the conditional distribution of the second coin. The conditional distribution of the second coin would be different if the first coin lands tails.

For modeling and prediction, conditional distribution is frequently used in statistics and ML. For example, it is employed in natural language processing (NLP) to forecast the likelihood of a word given the words that came before it in a sentence. It is also used in image recognition, where the likelihood of a specific object is forecasted given a set of visual characteristics.

2.10 Joint Distribution

Like conditional distributions, joint distributions express the joint probability of two (or more) variables occurring simultaneously. These distributions assess the probability that our example variables, X and Y, will be 0 or 1 at any given moment. Using joint distributions, we may determine if two variables are correlated; for example, does a rise in X result in an increase in Y? Does a drop in one indicate a drop in the other? Examining joint distributions can provide an answer to these kinds of queries.

Joint distribution might be continuous or discontinuous. The joint distribution translates to particular values if the random variables are discrete (such as a coin flip). On the other hand, the joint distribution must be integrated to represent the probability density if the random variables are continuous (like temperatures on a thermometer). The joint distribution is helpful in both scenarios for comprehending correlations and interdependence between random variables.

For example, let us say we want to research the correlation between a student's study hours and grades on a particular topic. We can display this data as a table or matrix, where the rows correspond to the various study hours and the columns correspond to the various student grades (Table 2.3).

Table 2.3 Correlation between student's study hours and grades on a topic

Study hours	Grade A	Grade B	Grade C
1	0.05	0.10	0.05
2	0.10	0.20	0.10
3	0.05	0.10	0.05

The numbers in the cells represent the joint probability of a student getting a particular grade when they study for a specific number of hours. For instance, the joint probability of a student getting a grade of B when they study for two hours is 0.20.

In this scenario, we can also calculate the marginal distributions of the study hours and individual grades. Regardless of their grade, students can determine their likelihood of studying for a particular number of hours by looking at the marginal distribution of study hours. Similarly, regardless of the quantity of study time, the marginal distribution of grades gives the likelihood that a student will receive a particular grade.

Many statistical disciplines, such as regression analysis, hypothesis testing, and ML, might benefit from the concept of joint distribution. For instance, the joint distribution is used in ML to train probabilistic models like Bayesian networks and Markov models, which can predict future occurrences based on the connection between variables. Joint distribution offers a technique to comprehend the connection between two or more random variables and facilitates behavior predictions.

2.11 Combinatorics

Combinatorics is the study of counting or computing the potential outcomes of diverse situations in probability theory and statistics. Numerous disciplines use combinatorics, including game theory, probability theory, computer science, and ML.

Combinatorics is used in ML to uncover patterns in large data sets that may be too complex for more conventional approaches. It entails finding various data point combinations that reveal trends or correlations within a data set. Combinatorics is essential for determining the combination that best predicts a result, such as what kind of car a person will purchase based on location and age. It is concerned with systematically counting and arranging items and is essential for predicting potential outcomes in probability theory and statistics..

The idea of permutations is an example of combinatorics in probability theory. A **permutation** is a configuration of objects/items in a specific order. For instance, think about the word 'cat'. There are 3! (3 factorial) or six different ways the letters in the word 'cat' can be arranged. Six combinations can occur: cat, cat, atc, act, tca, and tac. Permutations are used in probability theory to determine the number of possible arrangements for a set of objects.

A **combination** is a selection of items made without regard to their order from a more extensive collection. For instance, let us say you wish to choose three marbles at random from a bag of five marbles (red, blue, green, yellow, and purple). Five different combinations are possible; choose 3, which equals 10. The 10 possible combinations are (red, blue, green), (red, blue, yellow), (red, blue, purple), (red, green, yellow), (red, green, purple), (red, yellow, purple), (blue, green, yellow), (blue, green, purple), (blue, yellow, purple), and (green, yellow, purple). In probability theory, combinations are used to calculate the number of ways that a subset of objects can be selected from a more extensive set.

Combinatorics is used in ML to determine the number of possible results for various algorithms. It can be used to determine the number of potential splits and the number of outcomes for each split in decision trees.

It can also assist in feature engineering, the process by which a researcher makes new variables from old ones by fusing them in novel ways. For example, a researcher might create a new gender variable by fusing data on age and occupation into a single variable. They could more precisely find patterns in the data by employing combinatorial techniques, which could result in better predictions from ML models.

2.12 Probability Rules and Axioms

Probability aids in our comprehension of the likelihood that an event will take place. It has axioms and rules that enable us to forecast the likelihood of an event. The primary axioms and rules that aid in our understanding of probability are as follows:

- **Law of Equality**: The likelihood that any given event will occur must lie within the range of 0 and 1; in other words, 0 P(A) 1, where 0 P(A) is the likelihood that event A will occur.
- **Law of Addition**: This rule helps in predicting the outcome when two separate events occur; if A and B are two independent events, then P (A or B) = P (A) + P (B). Therefore, we can calculate the likelihood of two separate events occurring concurrently by summing their individual probability.
- **Multiplication Rule**: This rule applies when two events are interdependent; for example, if occurrences A and B are interdependent, P(A and B) = P(A). P(B|A). What is the possibility of B also occurring if A occurs, as represented by the conditional probability B|A in this instance?
- **Rule of Conditional Probability**: This is a fundamental concept in probability and statistics, which deals with the likelihood of an event occurring given that another event has already taken place. The formula for conditional probability is expressed as $P(A|B) = P(A \cap B) / P(B)$, where

P(A|B) is the probability of event A occurring given that event B has occurred, P(A ∩ B) is the joint probability of both events A and B occurring, and P(B) is the probability of event B occurring. This formula is crucial in various real-world applications, such as medical diagnosis, where it helps in determining the probability of a disease given a positive test result, or in weather forecasting, where it might be used to calculate the likelihood of rain given certain atmospheric conditions. It is important to note that for the formula to be valid, the probability of the given event, P(B), must be non-zero, as you cannot have a condition on an event that has no chance of occurring. This concept is also closely related to Bayes' theorem, which is a way to update probabilities based on new information.

These principles and axioms are applied through ML in various methods, including decision trees, Bayesian networks, etc.

2.12.1 Bayes' Theorem

This is a mathematical formula for calculating conditional probabilities. Thomas Bayes was an 18th-century English mathematician. Based on prior knowledge of factors that might be related to the event, the Bayes theorem provides a way for calculating the likelihood of an event.

Bayes' theorem can be expressed as follows:

$$P(A|B) = P(B|A*P(A))/P(B)$$

The conditional probability, or probability of A given B, is denoted by P(A|B). P(A) and P(B) are prior probabilities, often known as unconditional probabilities, while P(B|A) stands for the probability of B given A.

Bayes' theorem makes it easier to update our knowledge when new evidence or information becomes available. It allows us to make more informed decisions. It is crucial in ML for tasks that require judgment, such as classification and regression analysis, where data-driven models have been trained using labeled data sets containing known results for each observation to predict unknown results on unobserved data points accurately. For instance, if you have a model that was developed using data from heart disease patients, you could use this model in conjunction with Bayesian inference techniques to predict whether or not a particular person is likely to have heart disease based on factors like age, gender, and other characteristics.

Compared to more straightforward techniques like linear regression or decision trees, which only consider one feature value at a time when performing prediction tasks, this type of predictive modeling achieves better results by utilizing both probabilistic distributions and features extracted from training examples.

2.13 Moment Generating Function

This is a mathematical concept frequently used to describe random variables in probability theory and statistics. It is an effective tool for comprehending a probability distribution's characteristics, including mean, variance, skewness, and kurtosis.

The expected value of the random variable's exponential function is called the moment generating function (MGF). As long as it exists in a range near zero, it is a function that distinguishes the probability distribution of the random variable. MGF is a method of producing distributional moments; hence the name.

The general formula for the MGF of a random variable X is given as follows:

$$M(t) = E(e^\wedge(tX)),$$

where E is the expected value operator, X is the random variable, t is a parameter, and e is the exponential function.

We can obtain the moments of distribution by obtaining the derivatives of MGF. The nth moment of the distribution is given explicitly by the nth derivative of MGF evaluated at time $t = 0$. The random variable's anticipated value is the MGF's first derivative, and variance is the second derivative.

Now let us explore some examples of how MGFs are used in ML.

Example 4: One of the probability distributions that is most frequently employed in ML is the Gaussian distribution, also referred to as normal distribution. The MGF of a Gaussian distribution is given by:

$$M(t) = e^\wedge(\mu t + (\sigma^\wedge 2t^\wedge 2)/2),$$

where μ is the mean, and $\sigma^\wedge 2$ is the variance. We can determine the expected value of the Gaussian distribution by taking the first derivative of MGF. We can obtain variance by taking the second derivative, which is $\sigma^\wedge 2$.

Example 5: Binomial distribution models the number of successes in a fixed number of independent trials. The MGF of a binomial distribution is given by:

$$M(t) = (1 - p + pe^\wedge t)^\wedge n,$$

where p = probability of success, n = number of trials, and t is the parameter. We can determine the expected value of the binomial distribution by taking the first derivative of MGF and evaluating it at t = 0. By taking the second derivative and evaluating it at $t = 0$, we can obtain variance, which is $np(1 - p)$.

Example 6: Exponential distribution models the time between events in a Poisson process. The MGF of an exponential distribution is given by:

$$M(t) = \lambda / (\lambda - t)$$

We may determine the expected value of the exponential distribution, which is $1//\lambda$, by taking (considering) the first derivative of MGF and evaluating it at $t = 0$. Likewise, we can obtain variance by taking the second derivative and evaluating it at $t = 0$, which is $1/\lambda^\wedge 2$.

Mean, variance, skewness, and kurtosis are examples of moments that can be understood by using MGFs. They are heavily utilized in ML to model data and estimate probability distribution parameters.

2.14 Maximum Likelihood Estimation

Maximum likelihood estimation (MLE) calculates the parameters of a probability distribution from a set of observations. Maximizing the likelihood of witnessing the data given the model's parameters is a common ML technique for model training. MLE can be used, for instance, in linear regression to estimate the coefficients that reduce the discrepancy between the response variable's expected and actual values. In addition, the parameters that maximize the likelihood of detecting the binary outcomes for a given set of predictors can also be estimated using MLE in logistic regression.

The Bayesian statistical framework, which employs probability distributions to model uncertainty, has a connection to prior and posterior distributions. In Bayesian statistics, prior distributions represent our preconceived notions regarding a model's parameters, while posterior distributions represent our revised notions from data observation.

The Bayesian technique known as maximum a posteriori (MAP) estimation uses prior distribution and the likelihood function to determine the parameter values that are most likely to occur. Since MAP aims to reconcile the data-driven method of MLE with the prior information of Bayesian estimate, it can be seen as a compromise between MLE and Bayesian estimation. MAP estimation is frequently used in ML to regularize models like logistic regression and neural networks.

Sampling techniques are utilized in ML to create samples from complex probability distributions, which are frequently found in Bayesian inference and probabilistic modeling. For example, a typical sampling technique called Markov Chain Monte Carlo (MCMC) creates samples from a target distribution by building a Markov chain with a stationary distribution identical to the target distribution. MCMC is frequently used in Bayesian inference in ML to approximate the posterior distribution of parameters.

MLE is frequently utilized to estimate the coefficients of a linear model that forecasts a continuous target variable in regression tasks. For instance, we want to estimate the cost of a new house depending on its size and number of bedrooms, and we have a data set of property prices. Then, a linear regression model's coefficient that relates the input features to the goal variable can be estimated using MLE.

The parameters of a probability distribution that models the class labels of the data are estimated using MLE in classification problems. For example, we want to categorize a data set of emails as spam or not spam. The parameters of a Bernoulli distribution that simulates the likelihood of seeing each word in the email given its class label can be estimated using MLE.

The purpose of density estimation, another application of MLE, is to determine the data's underlying probability distribution. For example, we have a stock price data set and we wish to estimate the probability distribution of the returns. The parameters of a normal distribution that simulates the probability distribution of the returns can be estimated using MLE.

2.15 Density Functions

Density functions are frequently used in anomaly detection in ML. Finding data points that are noticeably different from the rest of the data is known as anomaly detection. To accomplish this, we must comprehend the characteristics of the data's normal distribution. Then, we can calculate the probability of each data point being normal or an anomaly by modeling the data with a probability density function. We frequently employ this strategy in fraud detection to find anomalous patterns in financial transactions.

Clustering is a significant application of density functions in ML. Density-based clustering algorithms utilize PDF to find regions of the data with high density, which may then be used to construct clusters. Density functions are also used in regression analysis, where we try to predict a continuous outcome variable based on one or more predictor variables.

Density functions are utilized in various ML applications, such as classification, image processing, and natural language processing, in addition to these examples. For instance, consider a data set that details customer purchases at a retailer. The probability distribution of purchase quantities is calculated using a density function, and patterns in consumer behavior can then be found from this data. Density functions can also be utilized in generative models, which are used to generate new data points comparable to existing data points.

2.16 Density Estimation

Probability density estimation is a statistical technique used to estimate the probability density function of a random variable based on a set of data. The PDF describes the relative likelihood of different values of the variable occurring. For example, if we want to estimate the probability of a certain event happening, we can use probability density estimation to calculate the likelihood of that event occurring given the data that we have. This information can then be used to make decisions or to develop strategies based on the probabilities of certain outcomes. It is important to note that probability density estimation is not a perfect science, and there are limitations to the accuracy of the estimates. For example, the accuracy of the estimate may depend on the sample size and the distribution of the data. In addition, different estimation methods may have different biases and may produce different results for the same data. Probability density estimation is a useful tool in many fields, including finance, engineering, and biology. There are several methods for probability density estimation, including kernel density estimation, histogram, and parametric density estimation.

Kernel Density Estimation (KDE): Kernel density estimation is a non-parametric method for estimating the probability density function. It involves placing a kernel function at each data point and summing the kernel functions to obtain an estimate of the PDF. KDE works by estimating the PDF of a random variable by smoothing out the distribution of the observed data. It is commonly used in data science and ML applications.

Let us consider an example of estimating the probability density of a continuous variable, such as the height of students in a class. We start by collecting a sample of heights from the class and then choose a kernel function, such as the Gaussian function. We then place a Gaussian kernel at each data point and sum the kernels to obtain an estimate of the probability density function. The bandwidth of the Gaussian kernel can be chosen based on the sample size and the level of smoothing desired. The choice of kernel function and bandwidth can affect the estimate. Some applications of kernel density estimation include:

- Estimating the probability density of stock returns in finance
- Estimating the probability density of particle size in environmental engineering
- Estimating the probability density of gene expression levels in genomics

Histogram: Histograms work by dividing the range of the data into equal-sized intervals and counting the number of data points that fall in each interval. The height of each interval represents the estimated probability density for that range of values. Histograms are easy to compute and interpret but can be sensitive to the choice of bin size and the location of the bin boundaries. The height of each bin represents the density of data points in that range. Some applications of histogram include:

- Estimating the probability density of customer age in marketing
- Estimating the probability density of traffic volume on a road in transportation engineering
- Estimating the probability density of rainfall in hydrology

Parametric Density Estimation (PDE): This involves fitting a parametric distribution, such as the normal or exponential distribution, to the data and using the fitted distribution to estimate the PDF. The parametric approach can provide more precise estimates of the probability density function compared to non-parametric methods such as KDE and histograms. However, it assumes that the data follows a particular distribution, which may not always be the case. Some applications of parametric density estimation include:

- Estimating the probability density of interest rates in finance using normal distribution
- Estimating the probability density of reaction times in psychology using exponential distribution
- Estimating the probability density of species abundance in ecology using lognormal distribution

2.17 Challenges and Future Directions in Probability and Statistics for Machine Learning

It is crucial to remember that probability theory has drawbacks and objections. Its heavy reliance on presumptions and simplifications, which cannot adequately reflect the complexity of the natural world, is one complaint. For instance, the presumption of event independence may only hold sometimes in practical circumstances.

Another critique is that it occasionally produces incredible results. For instance, the well-known Monty Hall dilemma demonstrates how the host's behavior might impact the likelihood of receiving a prize even when the host has no control over the actual award.

Despite these drawbacks and criticisms, probability theory is a crucial and practical tool in many domains. We may make wise decisions and find solutions in a wide range of applications by comprehending the ideas of joint, marginal, and conditional probability.

It is also important to remember that probability theory is a topic that is continually developing and seeing new advancements. One such advancement is the Bayesian probability theory, which updates probabilities as new information becomes available using past knowledge and experience. Bayesian probability theory has been used in domains like genetics and epidemiology to generate predictions and analyze data.

Despite the significant progress made in applying probability and statistics in machine learning, several challenges still need to be addressed. One of the significant challenges is the interpretability of ML models. As models become more complex, it becomes harder to understand how they make decisions. Another challenge is the bias that can be introduced into the models due to the data used to train them.

Future directions in this field include:

- Developing more interpretable models
- Improving the fairness and transparency of ML algorithms
- Developing methods to deal with partial data

SUMMARY

- Probability theory and statistics are fundamental to machine learning and data science, guiding data preprocessing, cleansing, and visualization. Key concepts include joint, marginal, and conditional probability, probability distributions (discrete and continuous), density estimation, maximum likelihood estimation, regression with maximum likelihood, and Bayes' theorem.
- Statistics is a subfield of mathematics that helps understand and make decisions based on data in various sectors such as business, science, medical, and social sciences. It involves gathering and examining data sets to make inferences about them using methods like clustering, regression analysis, descriptive statistics, and inferential statistics.
- Random variables are mathematical tools used in ML to analyze data sets and estimate potential patterns and correlations. The probability density function (PDF) illustrates the probability of events or ranges of values in a continuous distribution. The cumulative distribution function (CDF) describes the likelihood that a random variable will be less than or equal to a given value.
- Expectation assesses the expected value of a random variable within a given set of values based on its probability distribution. Variance measures the degree of dispersion between data points and their mean or average value. Probability distributions have practical uses in businesses, insurance firms, scientists, and weather forecasters.
- Discrete probability distributions are models of the probability of events that can only take particular values, such as the binomial distribution, which models the likelihood of a specific number of successes in a defined number of independent trials. Multinomial distributions model data with more than two probable outcomes, while Poisson distributions replicate sporadic events over time. The Bernoulli distribution is a commonly used probability distribution in machine learning, as it has only two possible outcomes: success or failure.
- A uniform distribution is a continuous probability distribution that represents random variables with an equal chance of occurring within a specific range. It is commonly used in machine learning to describe the chance of a pixel having a specific value within a range of 0 to 255. Examples of continuous probability distributions include the normal distribution, exponential distribution, and uniform distribution.
- The normal distribution is used in statistics to simulate natural occurrences, while the exponential distribution is used to model the interval between events that occur randomly and independently over time. The uniform distribution assumes that all values falling inside a specific range are equally likely to occur, resulting in a flat, horizontal line.
- Combinatorics is the study of counting or computing potential outcomes of diverse situations in probability theory and statistics. It is used in machine learning to uncover patterns in large data sets that may be too complex for conventional approaches. Bayes' theorem is a mathematical formula for calculating conditional probabilities based on prior knowledge of factors related to an event.

- Moment generating functions (MGFs) are mathematical concepts used to describe random variables in probability theory and statistics. Maximum likelihood estimation (MLE) is a statistical technique used in ML to calculate the parameters of a probability distribution from observations.
- Density functions are crucial in data analysis and machine learning methods, particularly in unsupervised learning. They help estimate the probability distribution of a set of data, identifying patterns and structure. Probability density estimation is a statistical technique used to estimate the probability density function (PDF) of a random variable based on data. Kernel density estimation is a non-parametric method, while histograms divide data into equal-sized intervals and count the number of data points. Parametric density estimation uses a parametric distribution to estimate the PDF.
- Prior probability is the likelihood of an event occurring before accounting for new evidence, while posterior probability is the likelihood of an event occurring after accounting for new data. Bayesian learning uses the posterior probability method to improve understanding of a particular issue. However, probability theory has drawbacks, such as its heavy reliance on presumptions and simplifications, which may not accurately reflect the complexity of the natural world. In addition, it sometimes produces incredible results, such as the Monty Hall dilemma.

EXERCISES

Part A (Objective Questions)

1. In a machine learning model for sentiment analysis, which probability concept can be used to calculate the likelihood of a given sentence being positive or negative based on the occurrence of certain words?
   a) Joint probability b) Marginal probability
   c) Conditional probability d) None of the above
2. In a recommendation system, which probability concept can be used to calculate the probability of a user purchasing a specific item given their past purchase history?
   a) Joint probability b) Marginal probability
   c) Conditional probability d) None of the above
3. In a fraud detection system, which probability concept can be used to calculate the probability of a transaction being fraudulent based on certain transaction characteristics?
   a) Joint probability b) Marginal probability
   c) Conditional probability d) None of the above
4. In a weather prediction model, which probability concept can be used to calculate the probability of rain tomorrow given the current weather conditions?
   a) Joint probability b) Marginal probability
   c) Conditional probability d) None of the above
5. In a spam email classification system, which probability concept can be used to calculate the probability of an email being spam based on the occurrence of certain words and patterns?

a) Joint probability
b) Marginal probability
c) Conditional probability
d) None of the above

6. In order to identify and rectify errors or inconsistencies in a data set, which statistical method would be most appropriate?
a) Feature scaling
b) Cross-validation
c) Descriptive statistics
d) Model selection

7. Which statistical technique is commonly used to transform data in a way that makes it more suitable for machine learning algorithms?
a) Feature scaling
b) Model evaluation
c) Hypothesis testing
d) Data exploration

8. What statistical method can be employed to compare the performance of different models and select the most accurate one?
a) Feature scaling
b) Descriptive statistics
c) Model selection
d) Data preprocessing

9. Suppose you have a random variable X that follows a normal distribution with mean 50 and standard deviation 10. What does the cumulative distribution function (CDF) represent in this context?
a) The probability that X takes on a specific value.
b) The probability that X is greater than a given value.
c) The probability that X is less than or equal to a given value.
d) The probability that X is outside the range of a and b.

10. Consider a uniform distribution with lower limit a = 0 and upper limit b = 10. What is the cumulative distribution function (CDF) for this uniform distribution?
a) $F(x) = x/10$
b) $F(x) = (x - 0)/(10 - 0)$
c) $F(x) = 10/(x - 0)$
d) $F(x) = (x - 0)/10$

11. If the cumulative distribution function (CDF) for a random variable is given by $F(x) = 0.8$, what does this imply?
a) The random variable follows a uniform distribution.
b) The probability that the random variable is greater than x is 0.8.
c) The probability that the random variable is less than or equal to x is 0.8.
d) The random variable has a mean of 0.8.

12. In a machine learning model, if the expected value of a random variable is 0, what does this imply?
a) The model is overfitting the data.
b) The model is underfitting the data.
c) The model's predictions are unbiased.
d) The model's predictions are inconsistent.

13. You have a data set with house prices. Which statistical measure would you use to evaluate how spread out the prices are from the average value?
a) Expectation
b) Standard deviation
c) Variance
d) Mean squared error

14. In a linear regression model, if the variance of the residuals is very high, what does this indicate?
    a) The model is overfitting the data.
    b) The model is underfitting the data.
    c) The model's predictions are accurate.
    d) The model's predictions are inconsistent.
15. You are analyzing a data set of student scores in a mathematics test. Which statistical measure would you use to determine the average score achieved by the students?
    a) Expectation
    b) Standard deviation
    c) Variance
    d) Mean
16. You have two machine learning models, Model A and Model B, for predicting stock prices. Model A has a higher variance compared to Model B. What can you infer about the two models?
    a) Model A is likely to have lower prediction accuracy.
    b) Model A is likely to have higher prediction accuracy.
    c) Model B is likely to have lower prediction accuracy.
    d) No inference can be made solely based on variance.
17. Which type of probability distribution is most suitable for modeling occurrences that can only take on specific values, such as the number of customers arriving at a store per hour?
    a) Normal distribution
    b) Poisson distribution
    c) Exponential distribution
    d) Uniform distribution
18. In statistical inference, which probability distribution is often used to construct confidence intervals and compute p-values?
    a) Normal distribution
    b) Poisson distribution
    c) Exponential distribution
    d) Uniform distribution
19. A business wants to simulate the distribution of profits and losses for different scenarios. Which probability distribution would be most suitable for this purpose?
    a) Normal distribution
    b) Poisson distribution
    c) Exponential distribution
    d) Uniform distribution
20. A scientist is conducting an experiment and wants to simulate the distribution of data outcomes. Which probability distribution is commonly used for this purpose?
    a) Normal distribution
    b) Poisson distribution
    c) Exponential distribution
    d) Uniform distribution
21. An insurance company wants to simulate the distribution of insurance claims. Which probability distribution would be most appropriate for this simulation?
    a) Normal distribution
    b) Poisson distribution
    c) Exponential distribution
    d) Uniform distribution
22. A weather forecaster wants to predict the likelihood of specific weather patterns. Which probability distribution would be useful for this purpose?
    a) Normal distribution
    b) Poisson distribution
    c) Exponential distribution
    d) Uniform distribution
23. In a machine learning project, you want to model the likelihood of a customer making a purchase based on their demographic information. Which probability distribution is commonly used for this purpose?

a) Normal distribution
b) Poisson distribution
c) Exponential distribution
d) Binomial distribution

24. A data scientist is conducting A/B testing to compare the click-through rates of two different versions of a website. Which probability distribution can be used to model the probability of observing the observed click-through rates by chance?
a) Normal distribution
b) Poisson distribution
c) Exponential distribution
d) Binomial distribution

25. A machine learning model is trained to predict whether an email is spam or not based on certain criteria. Which probability distribution can be used to simulate the likelihood of an email being categorized as spam?
a) Normal distribution
b) Poisson distribution
c) Exponential distribution
d) Binomial distribution

26. In logistic regression, a popular machine learning algorithm, which probability distribution can be used to model the probability of an input belonging to a particular class?
a) Normal distribution
b) Poisson distribution
c) Exponential distribution
d) Binomial distribution

27. You want to simulate the likelihood of observing a specific number of successes in 20 independent trials. Which probability distribution is appropriate for this simulation?
a) Normal distribution
b) Poisson distribution
c) Exponential distribution
d) Binomial distribution

28. You are analyzing a data set of customer churn rates and want to predict the likelihood of a customer canceling their subscription. Which probability distribution is commonly used for modeling binary churn outcomes?
a) Normal distribution
b) Poisson distribution
c) Exponential distribution
d) Binomial distribution

29. In natural language processing, which probability distribution can be used to model the frequency distribution of words in a document or corpus of documents?
a) Normal distribution
b) Poisson distribution
c) Exponential distribution
d) Multinomial distribution

30. For image recognition tasks in machine learning, which probability distribution can be used to model the distribution of features represented by a vector of characteristics?
a) Normal distribution
b) Poisson distribution
c) Exponential distribution
d) Multinomial distribution

31. In which machine learning application is the multinomial distribution commonly used to explore large text data sets and identify relevant topics?
a) Sentiment analysis
b) Natural language processing
c) Image recognition
d) A/B testing

32. Which distribution can be used to simulate the distribution of positive, negative, or neutral attitudes in a corpus of text for sentiment analysis?

a) Normal distribution
b) Poisson distribution
c) Exponential distribution
d) Multinomial distribution

33. Which probability distribution is commonly used in machine learning for problems where the outcome can take on more than two values?
a) Normal distribution
b) Poisson distribution
c) Exponential distribution
d) Multinomial distribution

34. What distribution can be used as a prior distribution in Bayesian inference when the likelihood function follows the Multinomial distribution?
a) Normal distribution
b) Poisson distribution
c) Exponential distribution
d) Multinomial distribution

35. In which scenario can the Poisson distribution be used to estimate the likelihood of an event occurring over time given an average rate of occurrence?
a) Number of cars going through a toll booth in an hour
b) Number of products in a store's inventory
c) Number of employees in a company
d) Number of participants in a marathon

36. Which area of machine learning commonly utilizes the Poisson distribution to model the frequency of specific words or phrases in a given document?
a) Image recognition
b) Sentiment analysis
c) Natural language processing
d) Reinforcement learning

37. Which machine learning application can benefit from using the Poisson distribution to model the frequency and distribution of pixels in an image?
a) Object recognition
b) Speech recognition
c) Anomaly detection
d) Time series forecasting

38. Which type of data is commonly modeled using the Poisson distribution in machine learning?
a) Continuous data
b) Categorical data
c) Binary data
d) Count data

39. In which scenario can the Poisson distribution be applied to make staffing adjustments based on anticipated variations in customer numbers?
a) Predicting stock market trends
b) Analyzing social media sentiment
c) Managing call center operations
d) Optimizing search engine rankings

40. In which scenario can the Bernoulli distribution be used to predict the likelihood of a term appearing in a spam or non-spam email?
a) Predicting stock market trends
b) Analyzing sentiment in social media posts
c) Categorizing images based on content
d) Identifying fraudulent transactions

41. Which machine learning technique commonly utilizes the Bernoulli distribution for binary classification tasks?
a) *K*-means clustering
b) Decision tree regression
c) Logistic regression
d) Random forest classification

42. When would the Bernoulli distribution be useful in evaluating the reliability of a machine learning algorithm?
a) Determining image similarity b) Calculating feature importance
c) Tracking algorithm accuracy over time d) Identifying outliers in a data set

43. In which scenario can the Bernoulli distribution be applied alongside Bayesian networks for decision-making?
a) Predicting stock market trends b) Recommending personalized products
c) Evaluating sentiment in customer reviewsd) Purchasing insurance based on event likelihood

44. Which distribution is used to model the accuracy rate of a machine learning algorithm over time?
a) Bernoulli distribution b) Normal distribution
c) Poisson distribution d) Binomial distribution

45. Which probability distribution is commonly used to model the distribution of heights in a population?
a) Uniform distribution b) Exponential distribution
c) Normal distribution d) Poisson distribution

46. Which distribution is suitable for modeling the likelihood of a pixel having a specific value in an image recognition task?
a) Uniform distribution b) Exponential distribution
c) Normal distribution d) Poisson distribution

47. Which type of probability distribution has an unlimited number of continuous possible outcomes?
a) Uniform distribution b) Exponential distribution
c) Normal distribution d) Poisson distribution

48. Which probability distribution is described by the probability density function (PDF)?
a) Uniform distribution b) Exponential distribution
c) Normal distribution d) Poisson distribution

49. Which distribution is commonly used to model the distribution of arrival times between events?
a) Uniform distribution b) Exponential distribution
c) Normal distribution d) Poisson distribution

50. Which distribution is suitable for modeling the likelihood of a person's height within a specific population?
a) Uniform distribution b) Exponential distribution
c) Normal distribution d) Poisson distribution

51. Which distribution is commonly used to model the distribution of IQ scores?
a) Uniform distribution b) Exponential distribution
c) Normal distribution d) Poisson distribution

52. Which distribution is suitable for modeling the likelihood of the time required to complete a task?
a) Uniform distribution
b) Exponential distribution
c) Normal distribution
d) Poisson distribution

53. Which probability distribution is commonly used to model the intervals between events that occur randomly and independently over time, such as customer arrivals at a call center?
a) Uniform distribution
b) Exponential distribution
c) Normal distribution
d) Poisson distribution

54. In which machine learning application can the exponential distribution be used to analyze user behavior and optimize website design?
a) Data generation
b) Clustering
c) Feature selection
d) User engagement analysis

55. Which distribution can be used to predict the time it takes for a user to complete a task on a website or application?
a) Uniform distribution
b) Exponential distribution
c) Normal distribution
d) Poisson distribution

56. Which distribution is commonly used to model the intervals between customer calls in a call center?
a) Uniform distribution
b) Exponential distribution
c) Normal distribution
d) Poisson distribution

57. Which distribution is suitable for estimating the number of students who will receive an A grade on their exams, given that 70% of students scored between 80 and 90?
a) Uniform distribution
b) Exponential distribution
c) Normal distribution
d) Poisson distribution

58. In which machine learning application can the normal distribution be used to model the distribution of physical quantities or noise in sensor readings?
a) Data generation
b) Clustering
c) Feature selection
d) Sensor calibration

59. Which distribution can be used to generate synthetic data for training and testing machine learning models, such as artificial images for image recognition?
a) Uniform distribution
b) Exponential distribution
c) Normal distribution
d) Poisson distribution

60. In which application can the uniform distribution be used to generate random stock price values within a specified range?
a) Customer segmentation
b) Data generation for neural networks
c) Monte Carlo simulations
d) Image recognition

61. Which distribution is suitable for randomly sampling data from a data set to ensure varied and representative training data for a machine learning model?

a) Uniform distribution b) Exponential distribution
c) Normal distribution d) Poisson distribution

62. In which application can the uniform distribution be used to generate random weight initializations for neural networks?
a) Customer segmentation b) Data generation for neural networks
c) Monte Carlo simulations d) Image recognition

63. Which probability distribution can be used to simulate the number of vehicles passing through a traffic light in a given time period?
a) Uniform distribution b) Normal distribution
c) Exponential distribution d) Poisson distribution

64. Which probability distribution can be used to predict the likelihood of a specific number of flaws in a product, given the average number of defects is known?
a) Normal distribution b) Exponential distribution
c) Poisson distribution d) Binomial distribution

65. Which probability distribution is suitable for predicting the likelihood of a task being completed within a specific time frame?
a) Uniform distribution b) Exponential distribution
c) Normal distribution d) Binomial distribution

66. In which scenario can the normal distribution be used to model and predict outcomes?
a) Rolling a fair dice
b) Simulating stock price values
c) Predicting the number of defects in a product
d) Determining customer arrival times

67. Which probability distribution is appropriate for simulating product sales over a specific period?
a) Normal distribution b) Exponential distribution
c) Binomial distribution d) Poisson distribution

68. Which probability distribution can be used to simulate the height of a group of children?
a) Uniform distribution b) Normal distribution
c) Exponential distribution d) Poisson distribution

69. Which probability distribution can be used to generate random weight initializations for neural networks?
a) Uniform distribution b) Normal distribution
c) Exponential distribution d) Binomial distribution

70. In natural language processing (NLP), what does the conditional distribution help predict?
a) The likelihood of a word given the words that follow it in a sentence
b) The likelihood of a word given the words that came before it in a sentence
c) The likelihood of a word given its frequency in a corpus
d) The likelihood of a word given its part of speech

71. What kind of random variables determine the nature of a conditional distribution?
   a) The random variables involved in the conditional distribution
   b) The frequency of occurrence of the random variables
   c) The size of the data set used for modeling
   d) The type of machine learning algorithm employed

72. What does a conditional distribution describe?
   a) The relationship between two random variables
   b) The probability of an event occurring
   c) The mean value of a random variable
   d) The standard deviation of a random variable

73. When flipping two coins, what determines the conditional distribution of the second coin?
   a) The result of the first coin flip
   b) The total number of coin flips
   c) The weight of the coins
   d) The size of the coins

74. What does a conditional distribution help predict in image recognition?
   a) The likelihood of a specific object given a set of visual characteristics
   b) The likelihood of a specific object given its color
   c) The likelihood of a specific object given its size
   d) The likelihood of a specific object given its position

75. What serves as the conditioning variables in the likelihood of someone getting diabetes?
   a) Age and height
   b) Age and gender
   c) Weight and gender
   d) Weight and height

76. In which industry is the concept of conditional distribution frequently used?
   a) Banking
   b) Manufacturing
   c) Retail
   d) Transportation

77. In which field is conditional distribution commonly used for predicting future data?
   a) Machine learning
   b) Physics
   c) Sociology
   d) Music theory

78. Which type of random variables determines the character of the conditional distribution?
   a) Discrete random variables
   b) Continuous random variables
   c) Both discrete and continuous random variables
   d) None of the above

79. What does a conditional distribution describe?
   a) The likelihood of one variable occurring given the value of another
   b) The total number of outcomes in a probability experiment
   c) The average value of a random variable
   d) The standard deviation of a probability distribution

80. In what industry is conditional distribution used for natural language processing?
a) Banking
b) Biology
c) Machine learning
d) Music production

81. What is the purpose of using conditional distribution in image recognition?
a) To determine the color distribution of an image
b) To calculate the average brightness of an image
c) To forecast the likelihood of a specific object given visual characteristics
d) To measure the resolution of an image

82. Which concept in combinatorics is used to determine the number of possible arrangements for a set of objects?
a) Permutations
b) Combinations
c) Factorials
d) Probabilities

83. What does a combination represent in probability theory?
a) The number of possible arrangements for a set of objects
b) The likelihood of an event occurring
c) The total number of outcomes in an experiment
d) The selection of items made without regard to their order

84. How is combinatorics used in feature engineering?
a) To determine the probability of an event b) To count the potential outcomes in a data set
c) To identify patterns or correlations in datad) To calculate the average value of a variable

85. What does the Law of Addition state in probability theory?
a) The likelihood of any event lies within the range of 0 and 1
b) The probability of two independent events occurring simultaneously is the sum of their individual probabilities
c) The probability of two interdependent events occurring simultaneously is the product of their individual probabilities
d) The probability of an event occurring is equal to the conditional probability of another event

86. How is the Multiplication Rule used in probability theory?
a) To calculate the likelihood of two independent events occurring simultaneously
b) To calculate the likelihood of two interdependent events occurring simultaneously
c) To determine the conditional probability of one event given the occurrence of another event
d) To determine the average value of a random variable

87. What does the rule of conditional probability help determine?
a) The intersection or conjunction of two events
b) The likelihood of two independent events occurring together
c) The degree of influence one event has on another, dependent on whether it occurs or not
d) The average value of a random variable

88. How are probability rules and axioms applied in decision tree learning?
a) They determine the entropy-based information acquisition techniques
b) They calculate the conditional probabilities between different classes/events in the data set

c) They represent independence assumptions among variables/classes graphically
d) They estimate the likelihood of correct predictions in machine learning algorithms

89. What is the purpose of using Bayesian networks in machine learning?
a) To determine the entropy-based information acquisition techniques
b) To estimate the likelihood of correct predictions in algorithms
c) To represent independence assumptions among variables/classes graphically
d) To calculate the conditional probabilities in decision tree learning

90. What is the purpose of Bayes' theorem in machine learning?
a) To calculate the unconditional probabilities of events
b) To update beliefs based on new evidence or information
c) To perform linear regression analysis on data sets
d) To predict unknown results in decision trees

91. How is Bayes' theorem used in predictive modeling?
a) To analyze large amounts of data quickly and accurately
b) To combine different statistical methods with Bayesian inference techniques
c) To perform image recognition tasks using linear regression
d) To predict known results based on labeled data sets

92. In which scenarios can Bayes' theorem be applied in machine learning?
a) Predicting heart disease based on patient characteristics
b) Performing image recognition tasks using linear regression
c) Analyzing large data sets with decision trees
d) Calculating unconditional probabilities of events

93. How does Bayes' theorem contribute to achieving higher accuracy in machine learning?
a) By considering one feature value at a time in prediction tasks
b) By combining probabilistic distributions with extracted features from training examples
c) By calculating unconditional probabilities of events accurately
d) By analyzing large amounts of data quickly and accurately

94. What is the main advantage of using Bayes' theorem in machine learning?
a) It performs linear regression analysis on large data sets
b) It predicts unknown results accurately using decision trees
c) It allows for updating beliefs based on new evidence or information
d) It calculates unconditional probabilities without bias

95. Which statistical characteristics can be obtained from a moment generating function?
a) Mean and variance
b) Median and mode
c) Skewness and kurtosis
d) Standard deviation and range

96. In linear regression, what can the moment generating function be used for?
a) To estimate the distribution of random variables
b) To compute the odds ratio in logistic regression
c) To calculate the coefficients of the regression model
d) To evaluate the fit of two models using the likelihood ratio test statistic

97. Which distribution can be modeled using the moment generating function?
a) Poisson distribution
b) Uniform distribution
c) Exponential distribution
d) Chi-square distribution

98. What can be determined by evaluating the second derivative of the moment generating function at t=0?
a) Mean of the distribution
b) Variance of the distribution
c) Skewness of the distribution
d) Kurtosis of the distribution

99. Which application of moment generating functions is relevant to image processing?
a) Binary classification in logistic regression
b) Regression analysis in linear regression
c) Estimating the number of clusters in clustering
d) Finding image features using Fourier analysis

100. Which statistical technique is commonly used to estimate the coefficients in linear regression models?
a) Maximum Likelihood Estimation (MLE)
b) Maximum Posteriori Estimation (MAP)
c) Markov Chain Monte Carlo (MCMC)
d) Bayesian estimation

101. What type of distribution can be modeled using maximum posteriori estimation (MAP)?
a) Prior distribution
b) Bernoulli distribution
c) Gaussian mixture model
d) Posterior distribution

102. Which sampling technique is commonly used in Bayesian inference to approximate the posterior distribution of parameters?
a) Maximum Likelihood Estimation (MLE)
b) Maximum Posteriori Estimation (MAP)
c) Markov Chain Monte Carlo (MCMC)
d) Density estimation

103. In which machine learning problem is MLE commonly used to estimate the parameters of a probability distribution that models class labels?
a) Regression
b) Classification
c) Clustering
d) Density estimation

104. What is the purpose of density estimation in machine learning?
a) To estimate the coefficients of a linear model
b) To estimate the parameters of a probability distribution
c) To approximate the posterior distribution
d) To classify data points into clusters

105. In which scenario would maximum likelihood estimation (MLE) be used?
a) To estimate the number of clusters in clustering
b) To estimate the cost of a house in linear regression
c) To estimate the parameters of a Gaussian mixture model
d) To estimate the probability distribution of stock returns

106. What does maximum posteriori estimation (MAP) aim to reconcile?
   a) MLE with prior information
   b) MLE with Bayesian estimation
   c) MCMC with prior distribution
   d) Density estimation with the likelihood function

107. In which machine learning task are density functions commonly used to detect anomalies?
   a) Regression analysis
   b) Clustering
   c) Image classification
   d) Fraud detection

108. What is the main purpose of density-based clustering algorithms?
   a) To estimate the probability distribution of data
   b) To classify data into different categories
   c) To identify anomalies in the data
   d) To group related data points based on density

109. How can density functions be applied in regression analysis?
   a) To estimate the probability distribution of data
   b) To classify data into different categories
   c) To model the relationship between predictor variables and the outcome variable
   d) To detect anomalies in the data

110. What is the primary use of density functions in unsupervised learning?
   a) To estimate the probability distribution of data
   b) To classify data into different categories
   c) To identify anomalies in the data
   d) To detect patterns and structure in data

111. How can density functions be applied in generative modeling?
   a) To estimate the probability distribution of data
   b) To classify data into different categories
   c) To identify anomalies in the data
   d) To generate new data points similar to existing data

112. Which machine learning task involves estimating the probability distribution of a specific data set using density functions?
   a) Regression analysis
   b) Clustering
   c) Probability estimation
   d) Image classification

113. In which machine learning task are density functions used to model the distribution of pixel values in an image?
   a) Regression analysis
   b) Clustering
   c) Image processing
   d) Natural language processing

114. In machine learning, which probability is calculated before considering new evidence or data?
   a) Prior probability
   b) Posterior probability
   c) Conditional probability
   d) Joint probability

115. Which machine learning method uses both prior and posterior probabilities to classify data?
a) Naive Bayes classifier
b) Decision tree
c) Support Vector Machine
d) *K*-means clustering

116. What is the purpose of posterior probability in Bayesian learning?
a) To calculate the likelihood of an event before new evidence
b) To estimate the prior probability of an event
c) To update the probability of an event after considering new data
d) To classify data into different categories

117. In which machine learning scenario is the agent's decision-making guided by posterior probability distribution?
a) Reinforcement learning
b) Supervised learning
c) Unsupervised learning
d) Transfer learning

118. Which method is used to estimate the probability density function using kernel functions in machine learning?
a) Kernel density estimation
b) Naive Bayes classifier
c) *K*-means clustering
d) Decision tree

119. In which machine learning application can kernel density estimation be used?
a) Estimating stock returns in finance
b) Image classification
c) Speech recognition
d) Reinforcement learning

120. What determines the shape of the estimate in kernel density estimation?
a) Bandwidth of the kernel function
b) Number of data points
c) Type of kernel function
d) Dimensionality of the data

121. What is one criticism of probability theory mentioned in the text?
a) It relies too heavily on data
b) It assumes event independence in all practical situations
c) It is not applicable in real-world scenarios
d) It lacks mathematical rigor

122. Which famous probability problem demonstrates the impact of the host's behavior on the likelihood of receiving a prize?
a) Monty Hall dilemma
b) Gambler's fallacy
c) Birthday paradox
d) Simpson's paradox

123. What is the purpose of Bayesian probability theory?
a) To update probabilities based on new information
b) To challenge the assumptions of probability theory
c) To simplify complex real-world scenarios
d) To predict future events with high accuracy

124. What is one challenge in machine learning mentioned in the text?
a) Model interpretability
b) Data availability
c) Computing power limitations
d) Lack of training data

125. What is one future direction mentioned for machine learning?
a) Developing more interpretable models
b) Increasing the complexity of machine learning algorithms
c) Collecting larger data sets
d) Focusing on accuracy over interpretability

126. Which domain has utilized Bayesian probability theory for generating predictions and analyzing data?
a) Genetics
b) Robotics
c) Natural language processing
d) Image recognition

127. What does Bayesian probability theory rely on to update probabilities?
a) Past knowledge and experience
b) Real-time data
c) Expert opinions
d) Random chance

Part B (Short Answer Questions)

1. List some important machine learning related probability concepts.
2. List some important machine learning related statistics concepts.
3. What is probability?
4. Define probability theory.
5. What is joint probability? Give an example.
6. Three red and two blue balls are contained in a bag. How likely are two balls drawn from the bag, without replacement, red?
7. A and B are two different products a corporation makes. Forty per cent of the products are type B, 60% are type A. Ten per cent of type A items and 5% of type B products have flaws. What is the likelihood that a defective product, chosen randomly, is a type A product?
8. What is joint, marginal, and conditional probability?
9. How is joint probability used in machine learning?
10. How is marginal probability used in machine learning?
11. How is conditional probability used in machine learning?
12. How is statistics used in machine learning?
13. What is a random variable? How it is used in machine learning?
14. What is probability density function?
15. What is cumulative distribution function?
16. What is expectation in statistics?
17. What is variance in statistics?
18. What are the uses of probability distribution in business?
19. Define discrete probability distributions.
20. Give examples of discrete probability distributions.
21. What is binomial distribution?
22. What is multinomial distribution?
23. How are multinomial distributions used in machine learning?
24. How are Poisson distributions used in machine learning?
25. What is Bernoulli distribution?
26. What is continuous probability distribution?
27. What is normal distribution?
28. What is exponential distribution?
29. Give examples of an exponential distribution?
30. What is uniform distribution?
31. What is conditional distribution?

32. What is joint distribution?
33. Define combinatorics.
34. What is Bayes' theorem?
35. What is moment generating function (MGF)?
36. What is maximum likelihood estimation (MLE)?
37. What is maximum a posteriori estimation (MAP)?
38. Give a few applications of the density function.
39. What is kernel density estimation?
40. What is prior and posterior probability?

Part C (Essay Questions)

1. Give some examples of machine learning algorithms where probability plays a crucial role.
2. How are the concepts of joint, marginal, and conditional probability used in machine learning?
3. Explain cumulative distribution function (CDF).
4. Explain variance and expectation in detail.
5. Explain the concept of probability distribution and its usage.
6. Explain binomial distribution in detail.
7. Explain multinomial distribution in detail.
8. Explain Poisson distribution in detail.
9. Explain Bernoulli distribution in detail.
10. What are the applications of Bernoulli distribution in machine learning?
11. Explain the concept of continuous probability distributions.
12. Explain normal distribution in detail.
13. Explain exponential distribution.
14. Explain uniform distribution.
15. Give some examples of probability distributions in the real world.
16. Explain conditional distribution with examples.
17. Explain combinatorics in detail.
18. Explain the axioms of probability.
19. Write an essay on Bayes' theorem.
20. Write an essay on moment generating functions (MGF).
21. Explain maximum likelihood estimation (MLE).
22. Explain maximum posteriori estimation (MAP).
23. Explain density functions and its applications in machine learning.
24. Explain kernel density estimation.
25. Explain prior and posterior probability.
26. What are the challenges and future directions in probability and statistics for machine learning?

ANSWER KEY

Part A

1. (c)	**2.** (c)	**3.** (c)	**4.** (c)	**5.** (a)	**6.** (c)	**7.** (a)	**8.** (c)
9. (c)	**10.** (b)	**11.** (c)	**12.** (c)	**13.** (b)	**14.** (a)	**15.** (d)	**16.** (a)
17. (b)	**18.** (a)	**19.** (a)	**20.** (a)	**21.** (b)	**22.** (c)	**23.** (d)	**24.** (d)
25. (d)	**26.** (d)	**27.** (d)	**28.** (d)	**29.** (d)	**30.** (d)	**31.** (b)	**32.** (d)
33. (d)	**34.** (d)	**35.** (a)	**36.** (c)	**37.** (a)	**38.** (d)	**39.** (c)	**40.** (a)
41. (c)	**42.** (c)	**43.** (d)	**44.** (a)	**45.** (c)	**46.** (a)	**47.** (c)	**48.** (a)
49. (b)	**50.** (c)	**51.** (c)	**52.** (b)	**53.** (b)	**54.** (d)	**55.** (b)	**56.** (b)
57. (c)	**58.** (d)	**59.** (a)	**60.** (c)	**61.** (a)	**62.** (b)	**63.** (c)	**64.** (c)

65. (b) **66.** (d) **67.** (c) **68.** (b) **69.** (a) **70.** (b) **71.** (a) **72.** (a)
73. (a) **74.** (a) **75.** (c) **76.** (a) **77.** (a) **78.** (c) **79.** (a) **80.** (c)
81. (c) **82.** (a) **83.** (d) **84.** (c) **85.** (b) **86.** (b) **87.** (c) **88.** (b)
89. (c) **90.** (b) **91.** (b) **92.** (a) **93.** (b) **94.** (c) **95.** (a) **96.** (c)
97. (c) **98.** (b) **99.** (d) **100.** (a) **101.** (d) **102.** (c) **103.** (b) **104.** (b)
105. (b) **106.** (a) **107.** (d) **108.** (d) **109.** (c) **110.** (d) **111.** (d) **112.** (c)
113. (c) **114.** (a) **115.** (a) **116.** (c) **117.** (a) **118.** (a) **119.** (a) **120.** (c)
121. (b) **122.** (a) **123.** (a) **124.** (a) **125.** (a) **126.** (a) **127.** (a)

3 Linear Algebra

Learning Objectives

At the end of this chapter, you will be able to:

- Explain the fundamentals of linear algebra and its applications
- Apply linear regression techniques to model and analyze data
- Perform matrix operations, including multiplication, and understand their implications
- Calculate and interpret eigenvalues and eigenvectors
- Elaborate on the concepts of norms and vector spaces
- Implement Gaussian elimination for matrix solutions
- Explain LU decomposition and its use in matrix factorization
- Practice orthogonalization and explain its importance in linear algebra
- Integrate the principles of linear algebra in deep learning algorithms

3.1 Introduction

Many machine learning (ML) algorithms rely on linear algebra concepts as it is a crucial tool for problem resolution. This chapter will examine some of the most significant linear algebraic ideas and how they apply to ML.

Linear algebra is an essential mathematical tool used to represent and manipulate data in such a way that it can be used to make predictions and decisions. Examples of linear algebra in machine learning include linear regression, matrix decomposition, vectors and matrices, eigenvalues and eigenvectors, vector spaces, optimization, linear transformations, Cramer's rule, Gaussian elimination, matrix factorization, symmetric matrices, and orthogonalization.

3.2 Linear Regression

In ML, linear regression frequently uses matrices and vectors. Finding the relationship between a dependent variable and one or more independent variables is achieved statistically using linear regression. With this approach, the data points that most accurately depict the relationship between the variables are connected by a line. A straightforward linear regression equation looks like this:

$$y = mx + b,$$

where m is the line's slope, b is the y-intercept, y is the dependent variable, and x is the independent variable.

The values of *m* and *b* are determined using the least squares method. These values must be determined to minimize the sum of the squared discrepancies between the expected and actual values of *y*. Vectors and matrices can be used for this. Matrix X represents the independent variables, while vector Y represents the dependent ones. For example, the following equation can be used to find the coefficient vector, denoted as:

$$y = (XTX) - 1XTY,$$

where (XTX) – 1 is the inverse of the matrix product formed by XT and X, and XT is the transpose of matrix X. Then *m* and *b* can be ascertained once the coefficient vectors have been located.

Take a data set of house prices and their corresponding size, for instance. Each home's size can be modeled as an independent variable (*x*) and its price as a dependent variable (*y*). The size of each house can therefore be represented by a column of 1s in the matrix X, which will also contain the *y*-intercept. The dependent variable *y* can be shown as a vector. We can obtain the values of *m* and *b* that most accurately reflect the link between the size of the house and its price using the least squares method and the equation above.

Matrices and vectors are fundamental ideas in linear algebra and are frequently used in machine learning for various tasks, including data representation, linear regression, and more. Therefore, a solid understanding of these ideas is essential.

3.3 Matrix Decomposition

Matrix decomposition is a technique that breaks down a matrix into its constituent parts. It is used in ML to reduce the dimensionality of data, simplify calculations, and improve the accuracy of algorithms. Examples of matrix decomposition include principal component analysis (PCA) and singular value decomposition (SVD).

3.3.1 Principal Component Analysis

Here, the principal components that account for most of the variance in the data are identified and used to reduce the dimensionality of the data. Therefore, it is frequently employed in data visualization and analysis. PCA must find the eigenvalues and eigenvectors of the data's covariance matrix. This is because the eigenvectors represent the highest directions of variance in the data, and the amount of variance explained by each eigenvector is represented by the eigenvalues. The eigenvectors and eigenvalues of the covariance matrix are calculated using linear algebra. Finally, a lower-dimensional space is created for the data using the eigenvectors and eigenvalues.

PCA is utilized in various ML applications, including bioinformatics, text mining, and image and signal processing. For instance, PCA can be used in image processing to minimize the dimensionality of images while preserving the most crucial details, such as edges and textures. In addition, PCA can be used in bioinformatics to analyze gene expression data and find patterns connected to various phenotypes.

The detection of anomalies is another application of PCA in ML. For example, PCA can find outliers in a data set by comparing the distances between data points in the lower-dimensional space. Outliers are data points that are significantly different from most data points and may be eliminated from the data set.

PCA is used in natural language processing (NLP) to reduce the dimensionality of text data. For example, take a significant corpus of text data with millions of documents. A vector of word frequencies can represent each document, where each element in the vector represents the frequency of a particular word in the document. The processing of this high-dimensional representation, however, can be computationally expensive and can result in overfitting.

We can decrease the dimensionality of the data while retaining the most crucial information by using PCA on the word frequency vectors. This can shorten processing times, use less memory, and increase the precision of NLP models.

3.3.2 Singular Value Decomposition

Singular value decomposition (SVD) decomposes a matrix into three matrices. These matrices represent the original matrix's singular values, left singular vectors and right singular vectors, respectively. SVD has many applications, including data compression, image processing, and ML.

An example of SVD's application is image compression. It identifies the essential information in an image and discards the redundant information. This is achieved by reducing the number of singular values and truncating the left and right singular vectors.

For instance, an image of size 1000 × 1000 pixels can be represented by an SVD matrix of lower dimensionality, such as 100 × 100, without losing much of the image's essential structure. The lower-dimensional SVD matrix occupies less space, which makes it more manageable to store and transmit.

The relationship between the original picture's pixel values is represented by matrix U, whereas the relationship between the transformed image's pixel values is represented by matrix V. The SVD factors an image matrix into these three matrices: U, S, and V. The singular values, which represent the relative weights of the U and V matrices, are contained in the diagonal matrix S.

To achieve image compression, the singular values in the S matrix can be sorted in decreasing order, and only a few of them can be retained. This is because the final image will have fewer pixels and take up less memory if only the unique values with the most significant significance are kept.

Text data is represented using SVD in a lower-dimensional space for NLP. By using this method, the text data's dimensionality can be decreased while still retaining essential details. In addition, the text data can be converted into a matrix with a lower rank using SVD, making it better suited for ML techniques.

3.4 Vectors and Matrices

Matrix and vector representations of data are fundamental in ML. A two-dimensional collection of numbers set out in rows and columns is known as a two-dimensional matrix. Images, acoustic signals, and numerical data are some examples of the diverse data types represented by matrices.

A matrix is an array of numbers that is rectangular and is denoted by square brackets. For instance:

A = [1 2 3]
[4 5 6]

A is a 2 × 3 matrix, which means it has two rows and three columns. The elements of the matrix are the numbers. Matrices in ML frequently represent data types like pictures or numerical data. Matrix representations of linear transformations are also an option. A function known as a linear transformation translates one vector to another while maintaining specific characteristics. For instance, an image's rotation is a linear transformation that modifies its orientation while maintaining the image's size and shape.

Matrix representations of user-item interactions are also frequently used in recommender systems. In this method, each matrix element represents the interaction or rating of a user with an object, with the rows of the matrix representing users and the columns representing products. By examining this matrix, the recommender system can anticipate which products a user will likely be interested in based on their previous interactions.

A vector is a matrix with just one column or row. A single data point or feature is frequently represented using vectors. For instance, a vector could represent a single student's grade in a data set of student grades. Likewise, a feature of an image, such as its brightness or texture, can be represented by a vector in image recognition.

For instance:

b = [1 2 3]

As there is only one row and three columns, *b*, in this instance, is a 1 × 3 row vector.

In ML, data points are frequently represented using vectors. For example, consider a scenario where we wish to estimate a new home's cost using a property price data set. Each home can be represented as a vector, with each element denoting a characteristic of the home, such as the number of bedrooms, square footage, and location.

In addition, vectors can indicate magnitude and direction in space. ML frequently applies this idea to develop optimization algorithms determining the ideal model parameter values. For instance, we wish to identify the parameter values that reduce the discrepancy between the output's expected and actual values in linear regression. Finding the vector's direction and magnitude, which minimizes the mistake, can be used to illustrate this.

Vector embeddings are a popular method for representing words in NLP. According to this method, words are represented as high-dimensional vectors, where each dimension represents a distinct quality or feature of the word. As an illustration, the word 'king' may be visualized as a vector with high values for the attributes 'male', 'ruler', and 'powerful' and low values for the attributes 'female', 'weak', and 'poor'.

Data can be represented using matrices and vectors in various applications, including image recognition. A matrix with each element representing a pixel value can be used to represent a picture in image recognition.

For instance:

I = [255 0 255]
[0 255 0]
[255 0 255]

In this example, the 3 × 3 matrix displays a black-and-white image, where 255 denotes white and 0 denotes black. This matrix can be fed to an ML algorithm as input to identify patterns or items in the image.

Matrix addition is one of the simplest operations, where two matrices of identical dimensions are combined by adding the corresponding elements. For instance, if we have two 2 × 2 matrices, A and B, where A = [[1, 2], [3, 4]] and B = [[5, 6], [7, 8]], their sum, A + B, would be [[1 + 5, 2 + 6], [3 + 7, 4 + 8]] which results in [[6, 8], [10, 12]]. This operation is commutative, meaning that A + B equals B + A.

3.4.1 Multiplication of Matrices

The process of multiplying two matrices results in the creation of a new matrix. The final matrix has rows equal to the first matrix's number of rows and columns equal to the second matrix's number of columns. Matrix multiplication is a tool used in linear algebra to solve systems of linear equations and compute a matrix's inverse, among other tasks.

Matrix multiplication is a crucial component of many ML techniques. As an illustration, the objective of linear regression is to forecast a continuous output variable from one or more input variables. This can be shown as a matrix multiplication operation, with the coefficients as a matrix W and the input variables as a matrix X. The matrix product XW yields the anticipated result.

Let us say we have the following two matrices, A and B:

A =
[[1, 2],
[3, 4],
[5, 6]]

B =
[[7, 8],
[9, 10]]

We must ensure that the number of columns in matrix A and rows in matrix B is equal before multiplying these two matrices. Both matrices in this instance have two columns, so we can multiply them. Three rows and two columns will make up the output matrix.

We take the dot product of the first row of matrix A and the first column of matrix B to calculate the product of matrices A and B. This results in the following:

(1*7) + (2*9) = 25

Similarly, we can obtain the dot product of the first column of matrix B and the second row of matrix A:

(3*7) + (4*9) = 57

Adding the third row of matrix A's dot product and the first column of matrix B's dot product, we get:

(5*7) + (6*9) = 89

These values are subsequently added to the matrix's first column. Finally, to obtain the second column of the resulting matrix, we repeat this procedure for the second column of matrix B. For the example mentioned above, the resulting matrix would be:

C =
[[25, 28],
[57, 64],
[89, 100]]

ML methods like PCA and SVD employ matrix multiplication. In these algorithms, the data is multiplied into a matrix to reduce its dimension and make it easier to analyze or visualize.

Matrix multiplication is also employed in neural networks to carry out the forward propagation process. Each neuron in a neural network is linked to numerous neurons in the layer below it. To determine the neuron's output, the input is multiplied by a weight matrix, added together, and then the activation function is applied. This process is repeated for each neuron in the layer to obtain the output of the complete layer. The output of this layer then serves as the input for the following layer, and so on, until the desired outcome is achieved.

Consider a neural network with two input variables, and two hidden layers, each with three neurons and one output neuron, for instance. The matrix W1 of size (2,3), where 2 is the number of input variables and 3 is the number of neurons in the first hidden layer, can be used to represent the weights connecting the input layer to the first hidden layer. Likewise, a matrix W2 of size (3,3) can represent the weights connecting the first and second hidden layers. Finally, a matrix W3 of size (3,1) can represent the weights connecting the second hidden layer to the output neuron.
We carry out the following process to obtain the output of the first hidden layer:

H1 is equal to activation function (W1 * X + *b*1),

where *b*1 is the bias vector with a size of (3,1) and X is the input vector with a size of (2,1). H1's first hidden layer output is a vector with the size of (3,1). We repeat this process to obtain the outputs of the second hidden layer and the output neuron. A scalar value is the neural network's ultimate output.

In general, matrix multiplication is a critical operation in linear algebra and machine learning, enabling the efficient calculation of complex operations on massive data sets.

3.5 Eigenvalue and Eigenvectors

A non-zero vector that produces a scalar multiple of itself when multiplied by a matrix in linear algebra is known as an eigenvector. The scalar multiple is referred to as the matrix's eigenvalue. A fundamental idea in linear algebra, eigenvalues and eigenvectors are widely applied in many domains, including ML.

PCA and other dimensionality reduction approaches in ML frequently employ eigenvectors and eigenvalues. For example, the directions of the most significant variation in a data set are represented by the eigenvectors of a covariance matrix in PCA. Using these eigenvectors, the data set's most crucial properties can then be preserved while being projected onto a lower-dimensional space.

Take a data set with age and income as two attributes, for instance. We can determine the eigenvectors and eigenvalues of this data set by computing its covariance matrix. The direction of maximum variance in the data set is represented by the eigenvector with the highest eigenvalue, which in this case, is a direction that captures the most variation in both age and income. The data set can then be projected in this manner, thus condensing it to a single feature while retaining the most crucial data.

Clustering techniques like *K*-means also use eigenvectors and eigenvalues. Here, the clusters can be represented by the eigenvectors of a distance matrix, with each eigenvector standing for a different cluster.

Consider the scenario where we have a data set of client transactions with different variables, such as the price, date, and purchase location. This data can be represented as a matrix, and its eigenvectors and eigenvalues can be determined. These allow us to pinpoint the data directions with the highest variance, which may correspond to various customer segments. Then, we can use clustering algorithms like *K*-means to collect related transactions and spot patterns in consumer behavior.

3.6 Norms and Vector Spaces

Important linear algebraic ideas like vector spaces and norms are applied in ML to represent and quantify data.

A collection of vectors that may be multiplied by scalars and added together is known as a vector space. Vector spaces are used in ML to represent data points and characteristics. For instance, in NLP, the word embedding space, which has a high dimension, can represent each word in a phrase as a vector. Likewise, each pixel in an image can be represented as a vector in a high-dimensional space for image identification.

Conversely, norms are employed to quantify a vector's size or magnitude. In addition, they serve as a technique to measure the separation between two vector space points. In ML, norms are a crucial tool to measure the similarity between two data points or feature sets. For example, one everyday norm used in NLP is the **cosine similarity metric**. This metric compares the similarity of two phrases based on the angle between their word embedding vectors. For example, suppose we have two phrases: 'The cat sat on the mat' and 'The dog slept on the rug'. First, we can represent these phrases as vectors in a high-dimensional space, with each dimension corresponding to a particular word in the phrase. Then, using word embedding techniques, we can generate a set of real-valued numbers representing the meaning and context of each word in the phrase. Once we have these vectors, we can calculate their cosine similarity. This involves dividing the two vectors' dot product by the product of their magnitudes. If the two phrases are very similar in meaning, their vectors will be close together in this high-dimensional space, and their cosine similarity will be close to 1.

Conversely, if the two phrases differ in meaning, their vectors will be far apart in this space, and their cosine similarity will be close to 0. This technique is compelling in natural language processing, as it allows us to compare the similarity of two phrases without explicitly defining what we mean by similarity. Instead, we can rely on the inherent structure of the language itself to guide our comparisons.

Vector spaces and norms have several applications in ML. Regularization methods like L1 and L2, which use a penalty term to the loss function to prevent model overfitting, are examples of typical uses. Based on the norm of the model weights or coefficients, the penalty term is computed.

Distance computations involve the use of vector spaces and norms. The distance between data points is a crucial metric for assessing similarity and providing predictions in many machine learning algorithms. A popular distance metric is the Euclidean distance, based on the vector's norm.

In addition, vector spaces and norms are utilized in SVD and QR decomposition, two matrix factorization techniques. The norms of the vectors or matrices used in these procedures, which involve breaking down a matrix into a product of orthogonal matrices, are crucial in establishing the characteristics of the decomposition. For instance, the L2 norm is frequently employed in image processing to calculate the difference between two images. Using a set of basis images selected to minimize the L2 norm between the original image and the approximation, an image can be approximated to implement image compression techniques.

3.7 Optimization

Optimization algorithms play a crucial role in developing and training neural networks. These algorithms, like gradient descent, minimize the loss function by updating the network's parameters. Linear algebra is an essential tool used in this process, and vector calculus calculates the gradient of the loss function concerning the network's parameters.

Let us examine a straightforward linear regression problem to comprehend how optimization algorithms function. Suppose we have a data set containing the prices and sizes of homes. We intend to develop a model that can determine the price of a home based on its square footage. We begin by arbitrarily initializing the weights of our neural network. In this instance, the loss function would be the squared mean error between the predicted and actual prices. The network weights are then updated using gradient descent in the direction of the steepest descent of the loss function.

The update rule is given by:

$$w = w - \alpha \, \Delta L,$$

where w is the weight vector, α is the learning rate, and ΔL is the gradient of the loss function for the weights.

This procedure is repeated until the loss function is minimized and the network's weights are optimized. The optimized weights can then be applied to new data to make predictions. Optimization algorithms like gradient descent, vector calculus, and linear algebra are essential tools used in training and developing neural networks. These algorithms help us minimize the loss function and optimize the network weights. With the help of these optimization techniques, we can build accurate and efficient neural networks that can make predictions on new data with high accuracy.

3.8 Linear Transformation

Linear transformations have many applications in ML. One of the most common uses is in the representation of data. Matrix representations of linear transformations allow us to transform data into a new space where it is easier to work with. For example, PCA is a technique that uses linear transformations to reduce the dimensionality of a data set. By finding the most critical linear combinations of the original variables, we can create a new set of variables that captures most of the variation in the data.

Another application is in constructing neural networks, which consist of layers of interconnected nodes, each transforming its inputs linearly. By combining these linear transformations with non-linear activation functions, neural networks can learn complex, non-linear relationships between inputs and outputs.

Linear transformations can also be used in image processing. For example, a convolutional neural network uses a series of linear transformations to extract features from an image. Each layer of the network performs a linear transformation on the image, followed by a non-linear activation function. By stacking these layers, the network can learn to recognize patterns in the image, such as edges, corners, and shapes.

3.9 Cramer's Rule

When solving systems of linear equations, one of the most powerful tools in the mathematician's arsenal is Cramer's Rule. This formula is extremely versatile and can be used to solve problems in the areas of ML, physics, and engineering. In particular, it is often used to solve linear regression problems; that is, problems in which we try to find the best-fit line (or curve) that describes the relationship between two or more variables. By using Cramer's Rule to solve these equations, we can find the optimal values for the coefficients of our regression model, ensuring that our model is as accurate and efficient as possible.

For a system of linear equations in the form of $Ax = b$, where A is a square matrix of coefficients, x is the column vector of variables, and b is the column vector of constants, Cramer's Rule allows us to solve for the variables x by expressing them as ratios of determinants.

Cramer's Rule states that if the determinant of the coefficient matrix A is non-zero, then the system of equations has a unique solution, and this solution can be expressed as the ratio of the determinants of the matrices obtained by replacing one column of A with the column vector b in turn.

Cramer's Rule is not limited to ML; it can also be used in many other applications. For example, it is often used in physics and engineering to solve systems of equations that describe the behavior of complex systems. By using Cramer's Rule to find the solutions to these equations, scientists and engineers can better understand the behavior of these systems and design more efficient and effective solutions.

3.10 Gaussian Elimination

When solving linear regression problems in ML, Gaussian elimination is one of the most popular methods used. This is because linear regression aims to find the best-fit line for a set of data points, and Gaussian elimination helps to achieve this goal by reducing the problem to a more straightforward form.

The Gaussian elimination process involves transforming the data point matrix into an upper triangular matrix, which can then be easily solved. This method is beneficial when dealing with large data sets, as it helps to simplify the problem and reduce computational complexity.

In addition to linear regression, Gaussian elimination is also used in classification problems, where the objective is to find the best decision boundary for a given set of data points. By transforming the matrix into an upper triangular matrix, Gaussian elimination can help identify the optimal decision boundary that separates different classes in the data set.

Consider a bank's customer information data set as an example. The bank wants to use ML to forecast whether a customer will likely default on a loan. By applying Gaussian elimination to this data set, the bank can identify the best decision boundary that separates customers likely to default from those who are not.

3.11 LU Decomposition

This is a matrix factorization method for resolving systems of linear equations. This method divides a matrix into two matrices: an upper triangular matrix (U) and a lower triangular matrix (L). It is frequently used in numerical analysis and linear algebra and in machine learning to perform operations like regularization and matrix inversion.

For instance, consider the following matrices:

Matrix A = [2 –1 0] [4 –2 1]
[8 –5 –1] [9 –6 –2]

Using LU decomposition, we can decompose this into Matrix L and Matrix U.

Matrix L = [1 0 0] [2 1 0]
[4 3 1] [1 2 1]

Matrix U = [2 –1 0] [4 –2 1]
[0 –1 –1] [0 0 –1]

We can then use these matrices to resolve the system of linear equations.

LU decomposition can be applied to ML methods like least squares and linear regression. In linear regression, the standard equations are solved using LU decomposition to identify the coefficients that reduce the sum of the squared residuals. We first need to convert the standard equations into matrix form. This involves creating a matrix of independent variables (X) and a vector of dependent variables (y). We can then use LU decomposition to factorize the matrix X into L and U matrices. This involves first solving the lower triangular matrix equation $Ly = b$, where b is a vector of constants. Then, once we have solved for y, we can then solve the upper triangular matrix equation $Ux = y$, where x is a vector of coefficients. The resulting vector of coefficients represents the best-fit line and can be used to make predictions for new data.

Another instance is regularization, where LU decomposition can modify the objective function by including a penalty term to avoid overfitting. Ridge regression and LASSO regression frequently employ this. Ridge regression alters the objective function by adding a penalty term inversely proportional to the square of the coefficients' magnitude. This penalty term shrinks the coefficients towards zero, reducing the model's variance and improving its generalization performance. LASSO regression can help identify the most important features for making predictions.

One of the essential uses of LU decomposition in these fields is to determine a matrix's inverse, which is essential for 3D graphics to determine transformations and projections. Another important use of LU decomposition in ML is in image processing. LU decomposition is frequently used to break down an image into its component elements or various color channels. This can be useful for various applications, such as facial recognition, object detection, and medical imaging.

The covariance matrix of a data set can be computed using LU decomposition in PCA. By decomposing the covariance matrix, we can obtain the eigenvectors and eigenvalues necessary for identifying the primary components of the data. This technique can be beneficial for working with high-dimensional data sets, as it can reduce the dimensionality of the data and make it easier to visualize and analyze.

3.12 QR Decomposition

A matrix can be factored into an orthogonal matrix and an upper triangular matrix using the matrix decomposition method known as QR decomposition, sometimes referred to as QR factorization.

In ML, QR decomposition is frequently used to resolve the conventional equations in linear regression issues. For instance, we want to determine the coefficients w of a linear model where $y = w * x$, and we have a data set with input variables x and y. By breaking down the design matrix X into an orthogonal matrix Q and an upper triangular matrix R, with the result that X = QR, we may utilize QR decomposition to solve for the coefficients w. The standard equations $R * w = Q.T * y$ for the coefficients w can then be solved.

PCA can be carried out using QR decomposition. To perform this, we must first center the data matrix. This means subtracting the mean of each variable from all the data points. Then, we can apply QR decomposition to the centered data matrix to discover the eigenvectors of the covariance matrix. The covariance matrix and the eigenvector represent the primary components of the data. They stand for the axes where the data deviates the most. Each principal component's corresponding eigenvalues show how much variation that component explains. We can decrease the dimensionality of the data while maintaining the majority of the information by choosing a subset of the principal components with the highest eigenvalues.

3.13 Eigen Decomposition

Eigen decomposition is a technique for reducing the number of features in a data set; it is used in dimensionality reduction. PCA is frequently used to employ the eigenvectors of the data's covariance matrix to project the data onto a reduced dimensional space. Thus, the most crucial features that best capture the data's variation can be retained, while the less crucial ones can be eliminated.

Latent semantic analysis (LSA), a technique used in NLP, employs the eigenvectors of a term-document matrix to detect latent concepts in a vast corpus of text. As a result, it can be used to locate related papers, group related documents, or carry out topic modeling. LSA can detect relationships between words and documents that may not be immediately apparent. One of the most significant applications of LSA is in the field of information retrieval. By analyzing the underlying concepts within a collection of documents, LSA can identify and group related papers. As a result, LSA can streamline the search process and make it easier to find relevant papers quickly and efficiently.

Another application of LSA is in topic modeling. By identifying the underlying concepts within a text corpus, LSA can group similar documents together and identify common themes. This can be useful in various contexts, from analyzing customer feedback to conducting market research. By identifying key themes and topics, businesses can gain insights into their customer's needs and preferences and make more informed decisions about product development and marketing strategies.

Collaborative filtering is a powerful method used in recommendation systems to suggest items to users based on their prior interactions. One critical technique in collaborative filtering is eigen decomposition, a mathematical process used to break down complex data structures into simpler components. To illustrate how this works, imagine a user interacting with several items on a website or app. The user-item matrix contains information about these interactions, including the user's ratings for each item. By applying eigen decomposition to this matrix, the system can identify the underlying patterns in the data that are most relevant to the user. Using this information, the system can then make personalized recommendations to the user based on their preferences and behavior.

Spectral clustering is a powerful approach in ML that utilizes eigen decomposition to divide data into groups based on the eigenvectors of a graph's Laplacian matrix. The Laplacian matrix encapsulates the graph's structure, and its eigenvectors can be used to identify groups of connected points in the graph. For example, suppose we have a data set comprising fruit characteristics, including weight, color, and texture. Spectral clustering can divide the fruit into groups based on their similarities. The Laplacian matrix is constructed by considering each fruit as a node in a graph, with edges connecting similar fruits. The eigenvectors of the Laplacian matrix can then be used to identify clusters of similar fruits. Another example is image segmentation, where spectral clustering can be used to identify regions of an image that are similar. The image is represented as a graph, with each pixel as a node and edges connecting neighboring pixels. The Laplacian matrix of the graph is then computed, and its eigenvectors are used to identify regions of the image with similar pixel intensities.

One of the most significant advantages of eigen decomposition is that it helps to isolate the most crucial aspects of the input data, making it easier to analyze and understand. One example of how eigen decomposition is used in deep learning is through the first layer of convolutional neural networks (CNNs). This layer applies filters to the input image and produces a set of feature maps as its output. By conducting eigen decomposition analysis on these feature maps, it is possible to identify the most significant characteristics of the input image. For instance, let us say we have an image of a cat. When the first layer of the CNN applies filters to this image, it produces a set of feature maps highlighting different aspects of the cat, such as its fur, ears, and eyes.

3.14 Symmetric Matrices

A square matrix that is equal to its transpose is symmetric. In other words, a symmetric matrix equals the original matrix if you flip it across its diagonal. Due to this characteristic, symmetric matrices are extremely helpful in ML for several applications, such as graph theory and optimization issues.

For example, the following matrix is symmetric:

[1 2 3]
[2 4 6]
[3 6 9]

In this matrix, the entries in each row and column are the same, so it is symmetric. This is true for all symmetric matrices: the entries in each row and column are the same.

A **Hessian matrix** is a square matrix of second-order partial derivatives of a scalar-valued function or scalar field. It describes the local curvature of a function of many variables. For example, consider the function $f(x, y) = x^2 + 4xy + y^2$. The Hessian matrix of this function is given by:

[2 4]
[4 2]

This matrix describes the curvature of the function $f(x,y)$. The diagonal elements represent the curvature in the direction of the *x*-axis and *y*-axis, respectively. The off-diagonal elements represent the curvature in the direction of the *xy*-plane. In this example, the *x*-axis and *y*-axis have a positive curvature, while the *xy*-plane has a negative curvature.

In graph theory, symmetric matrices represent a graph's adjacency matrix. The **adjacency matrix** is a square matrix that contains information about the connections between nodes in a graph. For instance, if an edge connects nodes *i* and *j*, then the entry in row *i* and column *j* of the adjacency matrix will be 1. Otherwise, it will be 0. The adjacency matrix is symmetric in the case of an undirected graph, meaning entries in rows *i* and *j* are identical to entries in rows *j* and *i*. Due to this symmetry characteristic, the matrix can be diagonalized using eigenvalue decomposition. The process of eigenvalue decomposition entails determining the matrix's eigenvalues and eigenvectors. The eigenvalues are the scaling factors, whereas the eigenvectors are the directions in which the matrix maintains its structure. The eigenvectors represent the different communities or clusters inside the network in the case of the adjacency matrix. At the same time, the eigenvalues show the strength of the connections between these communities. For example, consider a graph with four nodes labeled A, B, C, and D. The adjacency matrix for this graph would be:

0 1 1 0
1 0 0 1
1 0 0 1
0 1 1 0

This matrix is symmetric, so we can diagonalize it using eigenvalue decomposition.The eigenvectors and eigenvalues for this matrix are:

Eigenvectors:

(1 1 −1 −1) with eigenvalue 2
(1 −1 1 −1) with eigenvalue 0
(1 0 1 0) with eigenvalue −1
(0 −1 0 1) with eigenvalue 2

These eigenvectors represent the four communities within the graph. The first and fourth eigenvectors indicate two different clusters, while the second and third eigenvectors represent two unrelated nodes that are not connected. The eigenvalues indicate the strength of the connections between these communities, with positive eigenvalues indicating strong connections and negative eigenvalues indicating weak connections. The nodes in the graph can then be grouped based on their connections using the eigenvectors of the adjacency matrix.

The covariance matrix, used to characterize the variability between multiple variables in a data set, is another example of how symmetric matrices are utilized in ML. For example, the covariance matrix is symmetric since the covariance between variable *i* and variable *j* is equal to the covariance between variable j and variable i. Therefore, PCA can be used to reduce dimensionality using the covariance matrix's eigenvectors.

Another use of symmetric matrices is in calculating the **Mahalanobis distance**. This metric measures the distance between two points in a multidimensional space. In addition, it considers the covariance between variables, which is calculated using a symmetric matrix. Symmetric matrices are also used in the calculation of the **Cholesky decomposition**. A symmetric positive-definite matrix is factorized using this technique into the sum of a smaller triangular matrix and its transpose. This factorization helps solve linear equations and generate random numbers with a specific distribution.

3.15 Orthogonalization

Orthogonalization and orthonormalization are two essential linear algebraic operations commonly used in feature engineering and data preparation in ML. These operations are crucial in eliminating feature correlations, providing fresh and independent features, and compressing data.

Orthogonalization is a mathematical technique that transforms a set of linearly dependent vectors into a set of orthogonal vectors. In other words, it converts a set of correlated features into uncorrelated features. This is accomplished by projecting the original data onto a new set of vectors perpendicular to each other. This technique is beneficial when dealing with high-dimensional data sets where the number of features is much larger than the number of observations.

Orthonormalization is a more advanced form of orthogonalization where the resulting vectors are not only orthogonal but also normalized to have a length of one. This technique is beneficial when dealing with data sets with many features or when the features have different scales. Normalizing the vectors ensures that each feature has equal weight, regardless of its scale.

One common application of orthogonalization and orthonormalization is in PCA. By applying orthogonalization or orthonormalization to the data, we can identify the most important features and use them to construct a new set of independent features that capture the most crucial information from the original data. Another application of these techniques is in image compression. By applying orthogonalization or orthonormalization to the pixel values of an image, we can identify the most critical features and eliminate the least important ones. This allows us to compress the image without losing too much information. By removing correlations between characteristics in a data set during data preprocessing, orthogonalization can enhance the effectiveness of ML models.

Machine learning can utilize orthonormalization to build orthonormal bases for vector spaces. This might be helpful in feature engineering, which involves combining existing features in a linear fashion to produce new features. The performance of machine learning models can be enhanced by guaranteeing that the new features are independent and uncorrelated by establishing an orthonormal basis for the feature space.

3.16 Deep Learning with Linear Algebra

Convolutional operations are carried out on input pictures in CNNs using linear algebra. First, a feature map is created by convolving the input image matrix with the convolutional filters' weights, represented as matrices. Then, matrix multiplication is also utilized in the pooling processes, where the highest or average value of a set of data is calculated.

The backpropagation algorithm uses vector calculus, which trains the neural network by altering the weights to minimize the error between expected and actual output. First, vector calculus is utilized to determine the error gradient concerning the weights, which is then used to update the weights.

In addition to CNNs, other kinds of neural networks also rely on linear algebra. For instance, using linear algebra, matrix multiplications that reflect the relationship between hidden states and input/output layers are carried out in recurrent neural networks (RNNs). The network can then learn the temporal dependencies in sequential input, including speech, music, and text.

Overall, applying linear algebra to deep learning has transformed the field of artificial intelligence by enabling the development of complex models that can learn from enormous amounts of data and carry out previously impossible tasks.

SUMMARY

- Linear algebra is a crucial mathematical tool used in machine learning to represent and manipulate data for making predictions and decisions. It is used in various algorithms such as linear regression, matrix decomposition, vectors and matrices, eigenvalues and eigenvectors, vector spaces, optimization algorithms like gradient descent, linear transformations, Cramer's Rule, Gaussian elimination, matrix factorization for recommendation systems, symmetric matrices, orthogonalization, and deep learning.
- Linear regression is a supervised learning algorithm that predicts continuous outcome variables based on predictor variables. Matrix decomposition reduces data dimensionality, simplifies calculations, and improves algorithm accuracy. Vectors and matrices are fundamental ideas in linear algebra, used to represent data points and characteristics. Eigenvalues and eigenvectors express a matrix's attributes, and are often employed in PCA and clustering.
- Vector spaces represent data points and characteristics, while optimization algorithms like gradient descent use linear algebra to update the weights of neural networks. Linear transformations are matrix representations of linear transformations, and Cramer's Rule is used to solve linear equation problems. Gaussian elimination is used in linear regression and classification problems. Matrix factorization for recommendation systems decomposes a matrix into smaller matrices, identifying user preferences and making recommendations.
- Symmetric matrices are useful in graph theory and optimization issues. Orthogonalization and orthonormalization processes are used in feature engineering and data preprocessing. Deep learning with linear algebra is crucial for neural network operations, such as convolutional and pooling operations in CNNs.

EXERCISES

Part A (Objective Questions)

1. What is the purpose of using the least squares method in linear regression?
   a) To maximize the sum of the squared discrepancies
   b) To minimize the sum of the squared discrepancies

c) To find the maximum value of the dependent variable
d) To find the minimum value of the dependent variable

2. What does the matrix X represent in linear regression?
   a) Independent variables b) Dependent variables
   c) Coefficients vector d) *y*-intercept
3. Which equation represents the linear regression model?
   a) $y = mx + b$ b) $x = my + b$
   c) $y = bx + m$ d) $x = by + m$
4. How are the values of *m* and *b* determined in linear regression?
   a) By finding the maximum value of the dependent variable
   b) By finding the minimum value of the dependent variable
   c) By minimizing the sum of the squared discrepancies
   d) By maximizing the sum of the squared discrepancies
5. What does the coefficients vector represent in linear regression?
   a) Independent variables b) Dependent variables
   c) Intercept d) Values of *m* and *b*
6. Which method is used to find the inverse of the matrix product XT and X?
   a) Least squares method b) Transpose method
   c) Inverse method d) Dot product method
7. What does the vector Y represent in linear regression?
   a) Independent variables b) Dependent variables
   c) Coefficients vector d) Intercept
8. In the given linear regression example, what does the size of each house represent?
   a) Independent variable b) Dependent variable
   c) Intercept d) Coefficients vector
9. Which technique is used to reduce the dimensionality of data by identifying the principal components that account for most of the variance?
   a) Principal component analysis (PCA) b) Singular value decomposition (SVD)
   c) Linear regression d) Data compression
10. In PCA, what do the eigenvalues represent?
    a) Principal components b) Covariance matrix
    c) Amount of variance explained d) Data dimensionality
11. Which application uses PCA to find outliers in a data set?
    a) Image processing b) Natural language processing (NLP)
    c) Anomaly detection d) Data compression
12. What is the purpose of singular value decomposition (SVD)?
    a) Image compression b) Data visualization
    c) Dimensionality reduction d) Matrix decomposition

13. Which matrix represents the relationship between the original and transformed pixel values in image compression using SVD?
a) U
b) S
c) V
d) Covariance matrix

14. What is the main benefit of using SVD for image compression?
a) Data visualization
b) Dimensionality reduction
c) Lossless compression
d) Reducing computational complexity

15. In PCA, what are the eigenvectors used for?
a) Data compression
b) Calculating eigenvalues
c) Reducing computational complexity
d) Projecting data onto lower-dimensional space

16. Which application of PCA involves reducing the dimensionality of text data in natural language processing?
a) Data compression
b) Image processing
c) Anomaly detection
d) Text data processing

17. Which data types can be represented using matrices in machine learning?
a) Images and acoustic signals
b) Textual data and numerical data
c) User-item interactions and linear transformations
d) All of the above

18. In a recommender system, how are user-item interactions represented using matrices?
a) Users as columns and products as rows
b) Users as rows and products as columns
c) Users as elements and products as rows
d) Users as rows and products as elements

19. What is the shape of the matrix A in the given example: A = [1 2 3; 4 5 6]?
a) 2×2
b) 2×3
c) 3×2
d) 3×3

20. How is a vector different from a matrix?
a) Vectors have more rows than columns
b) Vectors have more columns than rows
c) Vectors have only one column or row
d) Vectors have equal rows and columns

21. What can a vector represent in machine learning?
a) User-item interactions
b) Characteristics of a home in a property data set
c) Magnitude and direction in space
d) Images and acoustic signals

22. How is the brightness or texture of an image represented in image recognition?
a) Matrices
b) Vectors
c) Linear transformations
d) User-item interactions

23. What can be represented by matrix representations of linear transformations?
a) Images and acoustic signals
b) User-item interactions
c) Magnitude and direction in space
d) Textual data and numerical data

24. What is the result of multiplying matrix A with matrix B?
a) Matrix C with 2 rows and 3 columns
b) Matrix C with 3 rows and 2 columns
c) Matrix C with 2 rows and 2 columns
d) Matrix C with 3 rows and 3 columns

25. What process can matrix multiplication perform in neural networks?
a) Calculate the dot product of input and weight matrices
b) Compute the inverse of the weight matrix
c) Reduce the dimensionality of the input data
d) All of the above

26. How does matrix multiplication contribute to linear regression?
a) It helps compute the matrix inverse
b) It solves systems of linear equations
c) It predicts the output variable from input variables
d) It reduces the dimensionality of the data

27. Which dimensionality reduction techniques employ matrix multiplication?
a) Principal component analysis
b) Singular value decomposition
c) Both a and b
d) None of the above

28. In a neural network with multiple hidden layers, how are the weights between layers represented?
a) By a single weight matrix
b) By multiple weight matrices
c) By a weight vector
d) By a weight scalar

29. What is the size of matrix W1 in a neural network with two input variables and three neurons in the first hidden layer?
a) (2, 2)
b) (3, 2)
c) (2, 3)
d) (3, 3)

30. What are eigenvectors and eigenvalues commonly used for in dimensionality reduction techniques like PCA?
a) Represent the directions of maximum variance in a data set
b) Determine the number of dimensions in the reduced space
c) Identify outliers in the data
d) Measure the correlation between attributes

31. In clustering algorithms, what do the eigenvectors represent?
a) Cluster labels for each data point
b) Distances between clusters
c) Directions of the clusters
d) Variance within each cluster

32. How can eigenvectors and eigenvalues be used in understanding consumer behavior from transaction data?
a) Determine the number of customer segments
b) Identify patterns in consumer spending
c) Calculate the total revenue from transactions
d) Measure the customer satisfaction level

33. What is the role of eigenvectors and eigenvalues in picture compression?
a) They determine the image resolution
b) They identify the dominant colors in the image
c) They represent the image features with the most information
d) They determine the image file size

34. What does the eigenvector with the highest eigenvalue represent in PCA?
a) The average value of the data set
b) The direction of maximum variance in the data set
c) The smallest eigenvalue in the data set
d) The sum of all eigenvalues in the data set

35. What is the primary purpose of eigenvalues in linear algebra?
a) Determine the matrix's rank
b) Represent the matrix's scale
c) Measure the matrix's determinant
d) Calculate the matrix's inverse

36. In natural language processing, how are word embeddings represented in a machine learning model?
a) As vectors in a high-dimensional vector space
b) As scalar values representing word frequencies
c) As binary indicators for word presence
d) As strings of characters

37. What is the purpose of using norms in machine learning?
a) To represent word embeddings in natural language processing
b) To measure the similarity between two data points or feature sets
c) To classify and recognize images in computer vision
d) To generate recommendations in recommender systems

38. Which similarity metric is commonly used in natural language processing to compare the similarity of two phrases based on their word embeddings?
a) Cosine similarity
b) Euclidean distance
c) Jaccard similarity
d) Manhattan distance

39. How are norms utilized in regularization methods like L1 and L2 regularization in machine learning?
a) To compute the penalty term based on the norm of model weights or coefficients
b) To adjust the learning rate during model training
c) To determine the optimal number of iterations for convergence
d) To select the most relevant features for the model

40. Which distance metric is commonly used to assess similarity between data points in many machine learning algorithms?
a) Euclidean distance
b) Cosine similarity
c) Manhattan distance
d) Jaccard similarity

41. What is the role of vector spaces in computer vision?
a) Represent image features like edges and shapes in a high-dimensional space
b) Measure the similarity between images based on their pixel values
c) Generate recommendations for image content
d) Classify images based on their file size

42. How are vector spaces used in recommender systems?
a) To classify user preferences based on their item characteristics
b) To measure the distance between users and items
c) To represent user preferences and item characteristics in a shared space
d) To generate recommendations based on user demographics

43. In which field is Cramer's Rule commonly used to solve linear regression problems?
a) Machine learning b) Physics
c) Engineering d) Statistics

44. What is one of the main benefits of using Cramer's Rule in linear regression problems?
a) It guarantees an accurate solution
b) It provides a visual representation of the data
c) It handles non-linear relationships between variables
d) It optimizes the efficiency of the model

45. In addition to machine learning, where else is Cramer's Rule commonly applied?
a) Data visualization b) Financial analysis
c) Physics and engineering d) Image processing

46. What type of problems can be solved using Cramer's Rule?
a) Non-linear regression problems b) Classification problems
c) Optimization problems d) Systems of linear equations

47. How does Cramer's Rule contribute to solving linear regression problems?
a) By determining the significance of variables b) By finding the best-fit line or curve
c) By handling missing data points d) By computing statistical measures of dispersion

48. In which field is Cramer's Rule commonly used to understand the behavior of complex systems?
a) Machine learning b) Physics
c) Statistics d) Finance

49. What is the versatility of Cramer's Rule?
a) It can solve non-linear equations b) It can optimize machine learning models
c) It can be applied in various fields d) It can handle large data sets efficiently

50. How does Cramer's Rule contribute to optimization in machine learning?
a) By minimizing the loss function
b) By handling outliers in the data

c) By finding the optimal coefficients for the model
d) By improving the accuracy of predictions

51. Which method is commonly used in solving linear regression problems in machine learning?
a) Gaussian elimination b) Principal component analysis
c) Cramer's Rule d) Euclidean distance

52. What is the main advantage of using Gaussian elimination in linear regression?
a) It reduces the dimensionality of the data set
b) It guarantees accurate predictions
c) It simplifies the problem and reduces complexity
d) It handles non-linear relationships between variables

53. In addition to linear regression, where else is Gaussian elimination commonly used?
a) Image processing b) Natural language processing
c) Classification problems d) Time series analysis

54. Suppose you have a data set of customer information for a bank. Which problem could be solved using Gaussian elimination?
a) Customer segmentation b) Loan default prediction
c) Sentiment analysis d) Image recognition

55. What does Gaussian elimination transform the data matrix into?
a) A lower triangular matrix b) An identity matrix
c) A singular value decomposition d) An upper triangular matrix

56. What is the purpose of Gaussian elimination in classification problems?
a) To handle missing data points
b) To reduce overfitting
c) To identify the optimal decision boundary
d) To compute statistical measures of dispersion

57. How does Gaussian elimination contribute to solving complex problems in machine learning?
a) By reducing computational complexity b) By handling high-dimensional data
c) By improving feature selection d) By optimizing model parameters

58. What makes Gaussian elimination an essential technique in machine learning?
a) Its ability to handle non-linear relationships
b) Its effectiveness in handling missing data
c) Its simplicity and reduction of complexity
d) Its capability to handle large data sets efficiently

59. What is LU decomposition used for in machine learning?
a) Regularization b) Matrix factorization
c) Dimensionality reduction d) Non-linear regression

60. Which type of matrices are obtained through LU decomposition?
a) Square matrices b) Diagonal matrices
c) Symmetric matrices d) Lower and upper triangular matrices

61. In linear regression, LU decomposition is used to solve which equations?
 a) Eigenvalue equations b) Optimization equations
 c) Standard equations d) Quadratic equations

62. What is the benefit of applying LU decomposition to linear regression?
 a) Improved feature selection b) Reduced overfitting
 c) Simplified equation solving d) Non-linear relationship modeling

63. Which method is more numerically stable and effective for solving linear regression problems compared to matrix inversion?
 a) LU decomposition b) Principal component analysis
 c) Singular value decomposition d) Euclidean distance

64. What role does LU decomposition play in solving linear equations in machine learning?
 a) It handles missing data points
 b) It regularizes the model
 c) It factorizes the matrix into two triangular matrices
 d) It reduces computational complexity

65. Which technique does LU decomposition assist in machine learning?
 a) Image classification b) Clustering analysis
 c) Linear regression d) Natural language processing

66. What advantage does LU decomposition offer in analyzing larger data sets?
 a) Improved interpretability of results
 b) Reduced computational power required
 c) Ability to handle non-linear relationships
 d) Better handling of missing data

67. What is the purpose of QR decomposition in machine learning?
 a) Matrix inversion b) Dimensionality reduction
 c) Non-linear regression d) Eigenvalue computation

68. In linear regression, how does QR decomposition help determine the coefficients?
 a) By solving for eigenvalues b) By performing matrix inversion
 c) By decomposing the design matrix d) By minimizing the sum of squared residuals

69. Which matrix factorization technique is commonly used to perform principal component analysis (PCA)?
 a) LU decomposition b) QR decomposition
 c) Singular value decomposition d) Cholesky decomposition

70. What is the role of QR decomposition in dimensionality reduction with PCA?
 a) Computing eigenvalues b) Selecting the most significant features
 c) Centering the data matrix d) Performing matrix inversion

71. How can QR decomposition be used to reduce the dimensionality of a data set?
 a) By minimizing the sum of squared residuals
 b) By solving for eigenvalues iteratively

c) By selecting the top principal components
d) By performing matrix factorization

72. Which technique can QR decomposition be used iteratively to compute in a matrix?
a) Eigenvalues
b) Gradient descent
c) Covariance matrix
d) Optimal weights

73. What is the benefit of applying QR decomposition in numerical analysis?
a) Improved feature extraction
b) Reduced computational complexity
c) Enhanced model interpretability
d) Non-linear relationship modeling

74. How does QR decomposition assist in extracting essential features from high-dimensional data?
a) By maximizing the variance
b) By performing regularization
c) By minimizing the reconstruction error
d) By decomposing the data matrix

75. In which application is eigen decomposition commonly used to reduce the number of features in a data set?
a) Image processing
b) Natural language processing
c) Recommendation systems
d) Dimensionality reduction

76. How is eigen decomposition utilized in image processing?
a) To compress images
b) To enhance image quality
c) To remove image noise
d) To segment images into regions

77. Which mathematical process is commonly used in recommendation systems to suggest items to users based on their prior interactions?
a) Convolution
b) Eigen decomposition
c) Clustering
d) Regression

78. How does eigen decomposition assist in identifying relevant patterns in user-item interactions for recommendation systems?
a) By minimizing the error between predicted and actual ratings
b) By clustering users with similar preferences
c) By projecting data onto a reduced dimensional space
d) By performing matrix inversion

79. Which layer of convolutional neural networks (CNNs) utilizes eigen decomposition for identifying significant features in input images?
a) Output layer
b) Hidden layer
c) Pooling layer
d) First layer

80. How can eigen decomposition analysis on feature maps help improve image recognition in deep learning?
a) By increasing the training data set size
b) By enhancing the activation functions
c) By isolating the most critical features of the images
d) By reducing the learning rate

81. Which application benefits from eigen decomposition for isolating the most important aspects of input data?
a) Speech recognition
b) Image segmentation
c) Natural language processing
d) Clustering analysis

82. What is the primary advantage of eigen decomposition in deep learning?
a) Reducing computational complexity
b) Improving generalization capability
c) Isolating the most critical aspects of the data
d) Enhancing model interpretability

83. Which mathematical technique converts a set of correlated features into uncorrelated features?
a) Principal component analysis (PCA)
b) Orthogonalization
c) Orthonormalization
d) Regression analysis

84. What is the primary advantage of orthonormalization over orthogonalization?
a) It eliminates feature correlations entirely.
b) It reduces the computational cost of processing high-dimensional data sets.
c) It ensures each feature has equal weight, regardless of its scale.
d) It creates a set of normalized vectors with unit length.

85. In which scenario is orthogonalization beneficial in machine learning?
a) When dealing with high-dimensional data sets
b) When the features have different scales
c) When feature correlations need to be eliminated
d) When compressing image data

86. Which linear algebraic operation is commonly used in principal component analysis (PCA)?
a) Singular value decomposition (SVD)
b) Eigen decomposition
c) Orthogonalization
d) Matrix inversion

87. How can orthogonalization and orthonormalization benefit feature engineering?
a) By reducing the computational cost of processing high-dimensional data
b) By identifying the most important features and creating independent ones
c) By eliminating feature correlations entirely
d) By compressing data without losing too much information

88. Which technique is useful for data sets with many features or features of different scales?
a) Principal component analysis (PCA)
b) Singular value decomposition (SVD)
c) Orthonormalization
d) Regression analysis

89. In which application can orthogonalization and orthonormalization be used to compress data?
a) Natural language processing
b) Image recognition
c) Image compression
d) Clustering analysis

90. What is the main benefit of orthogonalization in data preprocessing?
a) It reduces the dimensionality of the data.
b) It improves the interpretability of machine learning models.
c) It eliminates feature correlations, enhancing model effectiveness.

d) It speeds up the training process of machine learning models.

91. Which operation is used in convolutional neural networks (CNNs) to create a feature map from the input image matrix?
a) Matrix multiplication
b) Matrix inversion
c) Convolution
d) Pooling

92. What is the role of matrix multiplication in the pooling process of CNNs?
a) Calculating the average value of a set of data
b) Determining the highest value in a set of data
c) Combining feature maps into a single matrix
d) None of the above

93. Which branch of mathematics is utilized by the backpropagation algorithm to update the weights of a neural network?
a) Linear algebra
b) Calculus
c) Probability theory
d) Set theory

94. In which type of neural network are matrix multiplications used to reflect the relationship between hidden states and input/output layers?
a) Convolutional neural networks (CNNs)
b) Recurrent neural networks (RNNs)
c) Feedforward neural networks (FNNs)
d) Generative adversarial networks (GANs)

95. How has the application of linear algebra transformed the field of artificial intelligence?
a) It enables the development of complex models.
b) It allows learning from large amounts of data.
c) It facilitates previously impossible tasks.
d) All of the above

96. Which operation is used in convolutional neural networks (CNNs) to determine the error gradient concerning the weights during backpropagation?
a) Matrix multiplication
b) Convolution
c) Pooling
d) Vector calculus

97. In which types of sequential data can recurrent neural networks (RNNs) learn temporal dependencies using linear algebra?
a) Images and videos
b) Speech and music
c) Text and numerical data
d) All of the above

98. What allows deep learning models to learn from enormous amounts of data?
a) Convolutional operations
b) Pooling processes
c) Backpropagation algorithm
d) Linear algebra

Part B (Short Answer Questions)

1. Give examples of the linear algebra concepts used in machine learning.
2. What is linear regression?
3. What is matrix decomposition? Give examples for matrix decomposition.
4. Explain PCA concept.

5. What is SVD? How is it used in machine learning?
6. What is a matrix? Give an example.
7. What is a vector? Give an example.
8. Multipy Matrix A and Matrix B to represent Matrix C.
9. What is eigenvector and eigenvalue?
10. What is vector space?
11. How is linear transformation used in machine learning?
12. How is Cramer's Rule used in machine learning?
13. Explain Gaussian elimination.
14. What is decomposition of LU?
15. What is QR decomposition?
16. Define eigen decomposition.
17. Define symmetric matrices.
18. What is orthogonalization and orthonormalization?

Part C (Essay Questions)

1. Explain linear regression.
2. Explain matrix decomposition in detail with examples.
3. Explain vectors and matrices.
4. Explain multiplication of matrices with an example and explain how it is used in machine learning.
5. Explain eigenvalue and eigenvectors in detail with its applications.
6. Write an essay on norms and vector spaces.
7. Explain linear transformation and its applications in machine learning.
8. Explain Cramer's Rule.
9. Explain Gaussian elimination.
10. Explain LU decomposition.
11. Explain QR decomposition.
12. Write an essay on eigen decomposition.
13. Write an essay on orthogonalization.
14. How can we apply linear algebra in deep learning?

ANSWER KEY

Part A

1. (b) **2.** (a) **3.** (a) **4.** (c) **5.** (d) **6.** (c) **7.** (b) **8.** (a)
9. (a) **10.** (c) **11.** (c) **12.** (d) **13.** (c) **14.** (b) **15.** (d) **16.** (d)
17. (d) **18.** (b) **19.** (b) **20.** (c) **21.** (b) **22.** (b) **23.** (c) **24.** (b)
25. (a) **26.** (c) **27.** (c) **28.** (b) **29.** (c) **30.** (a) **31.** (c) **32.** (b)
33. (c) **34.** (b) **35.** (b) **36.** (a) **37.** (b) **38.** (a) **39.** (a) **40.** (a)
41. (a) **42.** (c) **43.** (a) **44.** (a) **45.** (c) **46.** (d) **47.** (b) **48.** (b)
49. (c) **50.** (c) **51.** (a) **52.** (c) **53.** (c) **54.** (b) **55.** (d) **56.** (c)
57. (a) **58.** (c) **59.** (b) **60.** (d) **61.** (c) **62.** (c) **63.** (a) **64.** (c)
65. (c) **66.** (b) **67.** (b) **68.** (c) **69.** (b) **70.** (c) **71.** (c) **72.** (a)
73. (b) **74.** (d) **75.** (d) **76.** (a) **77.** (b) **78.** (c) **79.** (d) **80.** (c)
81. (a) **82.** (c) **83.** (b) **84.** (d) **85.** (c) **86.** (c) **87.** (b) **88.** (c)
89. (c) **90.** (c) **91.** (c) **92.** (d) **93.** (b) **94.** (b) **95.** (d) **96.** (d)
97. (b) **98.** (d)

4 Algorithms and Complex Optimizations

Learning Objectives

At the end of this chapter, you will be able to:

- Explain the fundamental concepts of sets, relations, and functions and their significance in optimization problems
- Differentiate between various types of optimization problems, including linear and non-linear, constrained and unconstrained, as well as discrete, continuous, and probabilistic models
- Elaborate on the complexities of constrained optimization and the formulation of dual optimization problems
- Utilize dynamic programming techniques and understand the principle of optimality for solving complex problems
- Explore sublinear algorithms and their applications in optimization and data processing
- Analyze the structure of graphs, including directed graphs and subgraphs, and their relevance in mathematical modeling
- Delve into the principles of information theory, including discrete and continuous random variables
- Calculate entropy and information gain to quantify uncertainty and information content in a data set

4.1 Sets, Relations, and Functions

Sets, relations, and functions are all related to machine learning (ML) in that they provide a way to represent data. For example, sets are collections of elements (objects) that can be used to classify data.

Sets: Georg Cantor, a German mathematician, developed set theory. A set is a well-defined collection of objects.

Example 1:

i. $A = \{1,2,3,4,5\}$

ii. $B = \{\}$

iii. $\mathbb{N}$: Set of natural numbers

iv. $\mathbb{Z}$: Set of all integers

v. $\mathbb{R}$: Set of all real numbers

Here, (i) is a set of five elements. The number of elements in this set is finite; hence, it is called a **finite set**. Finite sets are used in ML for various purposes, such as classification, clustering, and regression. In classification, finite sets can be used to separate data into different categories or labels (such as spam versus not spam). In clustering analysis, finite sets can be used to group similar data based on their characteristics (such as age group or gender). Finite sets can be used in regression analysis to build models that accurately predict outcomes based on input variables (such as housing prices or stock prices).

The set shown in (ii) has no elements; hence it is called an **empty set**. In mathematics, an empty set is a set with no elements and can be denoted using the symbol ∅. In ML, an empty set represents missing, unknown, or irrelevant data points. Another use for an empty ML set is in *K*-means clustering algorithms. These algorithms require an initial guess at which data set members belong in which clusters before training occurs. An empty set can be used as this initial guess while running the algorithm so that it can start from scratch instead of having some predetermined groupings already established by human input beforehand.

Finally, an empty set can also be used in anomaly detection algorithms to help identify outliers within large data sets. Individual observations could easily slip through undetected if not explicitly flagged as abnormal by the algorithm. By creating an explicit group containing no elements whatsoever, any observation whose features do not match those belonging in any other cluster will automatically become part of this particular 'outlier' category and thus more accessible for us humans to spot more quickly.

The sets in (iii)–(v) are infinite. An **infinite set** is one that contains an infinite number of elements. It is an abstract concept that can refer to objects like numbers, vectors, or any other data type. Infinite sets are used in ML when dealing with large data sets or continuous data such as images or text. These data sets often contain too much information for traditional ML algorithms to process efficiently. So using infinite sets helps to simplify the process by representing them as a single entity instead of an extensive collection of individual elements.

In addition, infinite sets can be used to construct more complex models, such as neural networks and deep learning systems, which require vast amounts of data to learn patterns and make accurate predictions. These models can use the properties and relationships between all elements within the set, allowing them to generalize across different data sources much better than traditional methods.

Consider two non-empty sets, A and B, having elements in each set, respectively. The Cartesian product of these two sets, denoted by A × B, is defined as the set of all ordered pairs of elements from A and B.

$$\mathrm{A} \times \mathrm{B} = \{(a1,b1),(a1,b2),(a1,b3),(a2,b1),(a2,b2),(a2,b3)\} \tag{4.1}$$

In ML, the Cartesian product is often used in data analysis. It can help identify relationships between variables in large data sets by creating an expanded data set with all possible combinations of the original variables. This can then be used to generate insights into correlations or patterns within the data that may not otherwise have been detected. It can also help reduce redundancy in data sets by providing more efficient storage solutions for large data sets than traditional methods, such as storing multiple copies of identical data points or columns. Using the Cartesian product also makes it easier to join multiple data sets together as each element becomes unique across all the different data sets when combined.

Relations: A relation R from a non-empty set A to a non-empty set B is a subset of the Cartesian product. A relationship between the first and second elements in the ordered pair can be derived. The set of all first elements in the ordered pair is called the **domain** of the relation R. The set of all second elements in the ordered pair is called the **range** of the relation R. The whole set B is called the **codomain** of the relation R. From this, it is inferred that

$$\text{Range} \subseteq \text{Codomain}$$

In ML, a relation is an ordered pair that expresses the relationship between two elements and is used to make predictions. This can be done with supervised learning algorithms such as decision trees, support vector machines (SVMs), and neural networks. Relations are identified by analyzing data sets containing input variables to identify their correlation. These correlations can then be used to develop models that generalize knowledge from existing training data sets and make predictions about unseen data points.

For example, a relationship may exist between a person's age, height, weight, and health condition. By utilizing ML techniques such as regression analysis or clustering techniques, it is possible to establish how these variables interact to make better predictions about future outcomes or trends in the examined data set.

In ML, the domain of the relation R is used to represent the input data for a model. The domain is an essential part of supervised learning, as it provides a set of values or attributes that can be used to make predictions from the given data. This set includes continuous and discrete values. The primary purpose of using a domain in ML is to provide training data for models. This also allows models to generalize across different scenarios since they are not trained on specific data sets but on more general parameters within their domains. Using domains in ML also helps reduce complexity in models by limiting potential inputs within specific ranges and restricting them from overfitting or underfitting when making predictions.

The range of the relation R is used in ML to determine how data values are related. For example, if an ML algorithm is analyzing data involving two variables, say *x* and *y*. The range of the relation R defines the range of values that *y* can take based on what value *x* takes. This helps us understand how our input variable (*x*) affects our output variable (*y*). It also helps us identify any patterns or correlations between these variables, which can help with prediction and classification tasks. The range of relations can be used in many ML tasks, such as neural networks, SVMs, decision trees, and regression analysis.

In ML, the codomain of a relation R is used to represent the output space of a function. That is, it is used to specify which values can be outputted by a given function. For example, if we have an AI-based system predicting stock prices, the codomain might include all possible future values for that stock price. The codomain will help determine what kind of prediction model should be used and how accurate it needs to be to predict future values accurately. This type of representation is commonly used in supervised learning models where an input data set is mapped onto some output space according to predetermined rules or algorithms.

Example 2: Let $Z = \{1,2,3,4,5,6\}$. Define a relation R1 (Fig. 4.1) from Z to Z as $R = \{(x, y) : y = x + 1\}$. Then $R = \{(1,2),(2,3),(3,4),(4,5),(5,6)\}$.

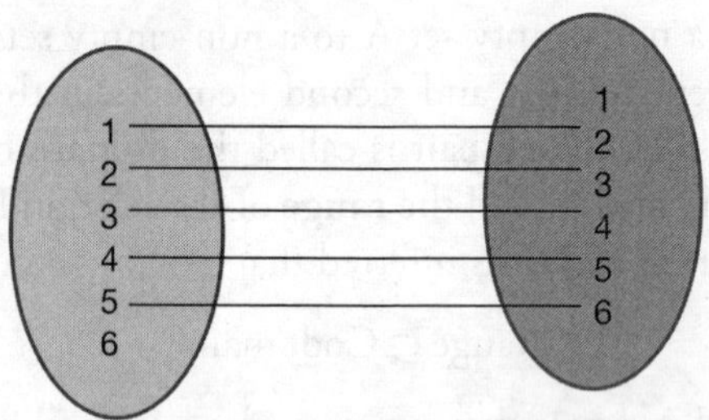

Figure 4.1 Venn diagram representation of the relation R1

Since the relation is defined from the set Z to itself and, by definition, a relation is a subset of the Cartesian product of two non-empty subsets, in this example, the Cartesian product of A with A should be calculated.

$$\begin{aligned} Z \times Z = \{&(1,1),(1,2),(1,3),(1,4),(1,5),(1,6),(2,1),(2,2),(2,3),(2,4),(2,5),(2,6),(3,1),(3,2),\\ &(3,3),(3,4),(3,5),(3,6),(4,1),(4,2),(4,3),(4,4),(4,5),(4,6),(5,1),(5,2),(5,3),(5,4),\\ &(5,5),(5,6),(6,1),(6,2),(6,3),(6,4),(6,5),(6,6)\} \end{aligned}$$

The relation defined in this example is a subset of the Cartesian product, that is, $R \subseteq Z \times Z$.

Functions: A function is a special type of relation. A function is a relation defined over a non-empty subset A to a non-empty subset B such that the domain of the function is A and no two distinct ordered pairs have the same first element.

If f is a function from A to B, and $(a,b) \in f$, then $f(a) = b$, where b is called the image of a under f and a is called the pre-image of b under f. The function is denoted as $f: A \to B$.

The relation R1 given in Example 2 is not a function because the element 6 has no image.

Example 3: A relation R = {(1,1), (2,1), (3, 2)} is a function because the domain of the function {1,2,3} has unique images.

Example 4: A relation R = {(1,1), (1,2), (2, 3)} is not a function because one of the elements in the domain of the function has two different images.

All three mathematical constructs (sets, relations, and functions) provide a way for ML algorithms to identify patterns in data and make predictions about future outcomes based on those patterns.

4.2 Convex Sets and Convex Functions

Convex sets and convex functions are fundamental concepts in ML. They are used in many optimization techniques employed in ML algorithms, such as gradient descent and stochastic gradient descent. In a nutshell, convex sets and functions allow us to determine the optimal solution to a given problem. Using convex sets and functions, we can calculate which point on our cost function will give us the minimum value or cost for our optimization problem.

In ML, most optimization problems are defined by an **objective function** with multiple variables (often called parameters). We want to optimize this objective function so that all parameters have set values that minimize or maximize some performance measure, such as accuracy or loss. We achieve this by finding the minimum or maximum point on the surface defined by our objective function; this process is known as minimization or maximization, respectively.

One major issue with this type of optimization is that it can often be challenging to find a **global optimum**; that is, a single point on the surface that represents an overall best result. This is because of non-convexity issues in many ML models (such as neural networks). An objective function is said to be convex when it has only one global optimum over its entire domain instead of multiple local optima spread across its surface. This makes it much easier for us to find that single global optimum. By using convex sets and applying additional constraints (that ensure all values stay within certain bounds), we can ensure that any optimization problem will yield only one global optimum value instead of several local ones.

Convex Set: A set CS is called a convex set if the line segment joining any two points in CS lies within the set. Mathematically, a convex set is defined as $\mathrm{CS} = \{s_1, s_2, \cdots s_n\}$ such that

$$\forall s_i, s_j \in \mathrm{CS}, \alpha s_i + (1-\alpha) s_j \in \mathrm{CS}, \text{ where } \alpha \in [0,1] \tag{4.2}$$

Example 5: $\mathrm{X} = \{x : x \geq 0\}$

For any two points $x_1, x_2 \in \mathrm{X}$, and for any $\alpha \in [0,1], \alpha x_1 + (1-\alpha) x_2 \in \mathrm{X}$.

Convex sets are widely used in ML as they provide an efficient way to optimize functions. In convex optimization, the goal is to minimize or maximize a function, subject to certain constraints. This can be used for many tasks, including classification, regression, and clustering. The critical advantage of convex optimization over other approaches is that it provides a global solution. Solving several linear or quadratic equations, given some constraints, can determine the optimal solution without searching all possible parameter values.

In addition, convex optimization ensures that the optimal solution remains valid even if the data set or parameters change over time. This means that models trained using this approach do not require constant retraining.

Convex Function: For a convex set $\mathrm{CS} \subseteq \mathbb{R}^n$, a function $f : \mathrm{CS} \to \mathbb{R}^n$ is convex on CS if for any two points $s_i, s_j \in \mathrm{CS}$, and for any $\alpha \in [0,1]$

$$f\left(\alpha s_i + (1-\alpha) s_j\right) \leq \alpha f(s_i) + (1-\alpha) f(s_j) \tag{4.3}$$

Strictly Convex Function: For a convex set $\mathrm{CS} \subseteq \mathbb{R}^n$, a function $f : \mathrm{CS} \to \mathbb{R}^n$ is strictly convex on CS if for any two points $s_i \neq s_j \in \mathrm{CS}$ and for any $\alpha \in (0,1)$

$$f\left(\alpha s_i + (1-\alpha) s_j\right) < \alpha f(s_i) + (1-\alpha) f(s_j) \tag{4.4}$$

Note: Notice the difference in the range of α.

$$\alpha \in [0,1] \Rightarrow 0 \leq \alpha \leq 1 \text{ whereas } \alpha \in (0,1) \Rightarrow 0 < \alpha < 1$$

Strictly convex functions are used in ML as part of the optimization process. Optimization helps to reduce the cost of a given task and improve its accuracy. Strictly convex functions can be used to find a global minimum by setting certain conditions, such as having a single local minimum for all points of the domain and being convex everywhere on the domain. This helps ML algorithms quickly learn from data sets, discover patterns and make predictions.

During optimization, strictly convex functions provide an advantage compared to other functions as they guarantee that any local minima are also global minima, meaning that there are no other minima values outside of what is found using this function. As such, this function can be used to accurately determine parameters needed for tasks in ML algorithms like SVMs, artificial neural networks (ANNs), and deep neural networks (DNNs).

Example 6: Prove that $f(x) = 2x + 3; x \in \mathbb{R}$ is convex (Fig. 4.2).

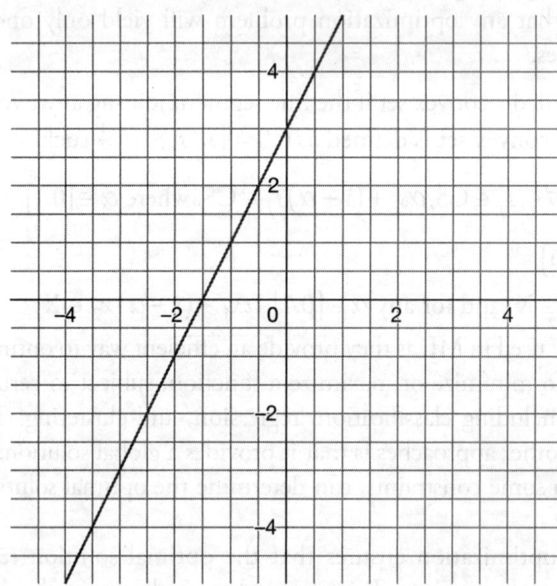

Figure 4.2 Graphical representation of the function $2x + 3$

Solution: To prove that a function is convex, we have to prove the inequality defined in Equation (4.2). We consider three different values of α. Let the two points in the set be 2 and 7.

Case 1: $\alpha = 0$

$$\Rightarrow f(0\times 2+(1-0)\times 7)\le 0\times f(2)+(1-0)\times f(7)$$

$$\Rightarrow f(7)\le f(7)$$

$$\Rightarrow 17\le 17$$

Case 2: $\alpha = 0.1$

$$\Rightarrow f(0.1\times 2+(1-0.1)\times 7)\le 0.1\times f(2)+(1-0.1)\times f(7)$$

$$\Rightarrow f(0.2+6.3)\le 0.1\times 7+0.9\times 17$$

$$\Rightarrow f(6.5)\le 0.7+15.3$$

$$\Rightarrow 16\le 16$$

Case 3: $\alpha = 0.5$

$$\Rightarrow f\left(0.5\times 2+(1-0.5)\times 7\right)\leq 0.5\times f(2)+(1-0.5)\times f(7)$$

$$\Rightarrow f(1.0+3.5)\leq 0.5\times 7+0.5\times 17$$

$$\Rightarrow f(4.5)\leq 3.5+8.5$$

$$\Rightarrow 12=12$$

Case 4: $\alpha = 1$

$$\Rightarrow f\left(1\times 2+(1-1)\times 7\right)\leq 1\times f(2)+(0)\times f(7)$$

$$\Rightarrow f(2)\leq 7+0$$

$$\Rightarrow 7=7$$

It has been shown that for any $\alpha \in [0,1]$, the inequality defined in Equation (4.3) is satisfied and turns out to be equality. Hence the function $f(x) = 2x+3; x \in \mathbb{R}$ is convex function.

Example 7: Prove that $f(x) = x^2; x \in \mathbb{R}$ is convex (Fig. 4.3).

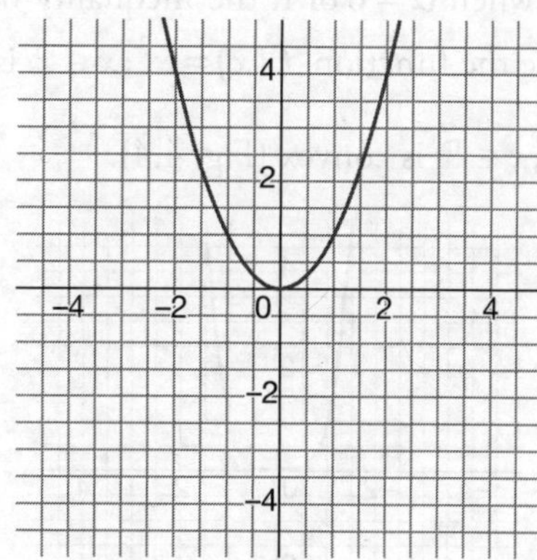

Figure 4.3 Graphical representation of the function x^2

Solution: We consider three different values of α. Let the two points in the set be 2 and 7.

Case 1: $\alpha = 0$

$$\Rightarrow f\left(0\times 2+(1-0)\times 7\right)\leq 0\times f(2)+(1-0)\times f(7)$$

$$\Rightarrow f(7)\leq 0\times 4+1\times 49$$

$$\Rightarrow 49\leq 49$$

Case 2: $\alpha = 0.1$

$$\Rightarrow f\left(0.1\times 2+(1-0.1)\times 7\right)\leq 0.1\times f(2)+(1-0.1)\times f(7)$$

$$\Rightarrow f(0.2+6.3)\leq 0.1\times 4+0.9\times 49$$

$$\Rightarrow f(6.5) \le 0.4 + 44.1$$

$$\Rightarrow 42.25 \le 44.5$$

Case 3: $\alpha = 0.5$

$$\Rightarrow f(0.5 \times 2 + (1-0.5) \times 7) \le 0.5 \times f(2) + (1-0.5) \times f(7)$$

$$\Rightarrow f(1.0 + 3.5) \le 0.5 \times 4 + 0.5 \times 289$$

$$\Rightarrow f(4.5) \le 2.0 + 144.5$$

$$\Rightarrow 20.25 \le 146.5$$

Case 4: $\alpha = 1$

$$\Rightarrow f(1 \times 2 + 0 \times 7) \le 1 \times f(2) + 0 \times f(7)$$

$$\Rightarrow f(2) \le 4 + 0$$

$$\Rightarrow 4 = 4$$

It has been shown that for any $\alpha \in [0,1]$, the inequality defined in Equation (4.3) is satisfied. At the boundary conditions, that is, when $\alpha = 0$ or 1, the inequality becomes equality and in all other cases, it is a strict inequality. Hence the function $f(x) = x^2; x \in \mathbb{R}$ is a strictly convex function.

Example 8: Prove that $f(x) = x^4; x \in \mathbb{R}$ is convex (Fig. 4.4).

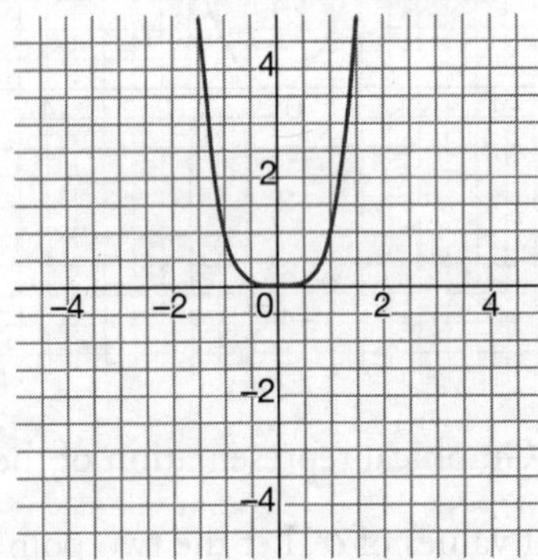

Figure 4.4 Graphical representation of the function x^4

Solution: We consider three different values of α. Let the two points in the set be 2 and 7.

Case 1: $\alpha = 0$

$$\Rightarrow f(0 \times 2 + (1-0) \times 7) \le 0 \times f(2) + (1-0) \times f(7)$$

$$\Rightarrow f(7) \le 0 + 1 \times 2401$$

$$\Rightarrow 2401 \le 2401$$

Case 2: $\alpha = 0.1$

$$\Rightarrow f\left(0.1\times 2+(1-0.1)\times 7\right)\le 0.1\times f(2)+(1-0.1)\times f(7)$$

$$\Rightarrow f(0.2+6.3)\le 0.1\times 16+0.9\times 2401$$

$$\Rightarrow 1785.0625\le 1.6+2160.9$$

$$\Rightarrow 1785.0625\le 1.6+2160.9$$

$$\Rightarrow 1785.0625\le 2162.5$$

Case 3: $\alpha = 0.5$

$$\Rightarrow f\left(0.5\times 2+(1-0.5)\times 7\right)\le 0.5\times f(2)+(1-0.5)\times f(7)$$

$$\Rightarrow f(1.0+3.5)\le 0.5\times 16+0.5\times 2401$$

$$\Rightarrow f(4.5)\le 8.0+1200.5$$

$$\Rightarrow 410.0625\le 1208.5$$

Case 4: $\alpha = 1$

$$\Rightarrow f(1\times 2+0\times 7)\le 1\times f(2)+0\times f(7)$$

$$\Rightarrow f(2)\le 16+0$$

$$\Rightarrow 16=16$$

It has been shown that for any $\alpha\in[0,1]$, the inequality defined in Equation (4.3) is satisfied. At the boundary conditions, that is, when $\alpha = 0$ or 1, the inequality becomes equality and in all other cases, it is a strict inequality. Hence the function $f(x)=x^4; x\in\mathbb{R}$ is a strictly convex function.

Example 9: Theoretically prove that $f(x)=|x|, x\in\mathbb{R}$ is convex.

Proof: $f\left(\alpha x_1+(1-\alpha)x_2\right)=\left|\alpha x_1+(1-\alpha)x_2\right|$

$$\Rightarrow\le\left|\alpha x_1\right|+\left|(1-\alpha)x_2\right| \text{ (by triangle inequality)}$$

$$=\alpha\left|x_1\right|+(1-\alpha)\left|x_2\right|$$

$$=\alpha f(x_1)+(1-\alpha)f(x_2)$$

Hence $|x|$ is a convex function. It is not strictly convex.

Given a plot of a function, one can easily determine whether the function is convex or not. For each pair of points $(s1, f(s1))$ and $(s2, f(s2))$ on the graph, the function is convex if the line segment stays above the plot. It is strictly convex if the connecting line segment stays strictly above the graph.

Readers can check the convexity or strong convexity for the function plots defined in Figs 4.2 to 4.4 by considering any pair of points.

4.2.1 Properties of Convex Functions

- Let $f_1, f_2, \cdots, f_p$ be p convex functions defined over $\mathbb{R}^n \rightarrow \mathbb{R}$, and let $\alpha_1, \alpha_2, \cdots, \alpha_p$ be p non-negative real values. Then the function g defined as $g(x) = \sum_{i=1}^{p} \alpha_i f_i(x)$ is also convex.
- If $f1$ is convex and $\alpha \geq 0$, then the function $\alpha f1$ is also convex.
- Every linear or affine function is convex.
- If $f(x)$ and $g(x)$ are convex functions, then $f \circ g$ is also convex.

Figure 4.5 shows the geometrical visualization of a convex function.

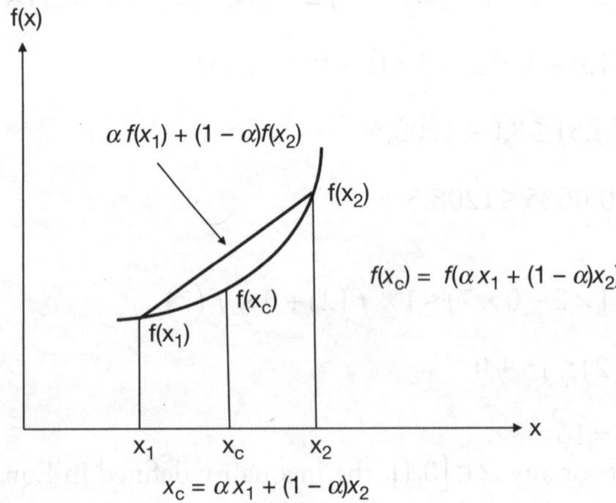

Figure 4.5 Geometrical visualization of a convex function

4.2.2 Other Definitions

Concave Function: A function $f : \mathbb{R}^n \rightarrow \mathbb{R}$ is concave if $\forall x, y$ and $\forall \alpha \in [0,1]$,

$$f(\alpha x + (1-\alpha) y) \geq \alpha f(x) + (1-\alpha) f(y) \tag{4.5}$$

A concave function is a mathematical function that takes a convex (upward-facing) shape when graphed. This function has several uses in ML. In supervised learning, where the model aims to predict a target variable based on input features, concave functions can help optimize by making it easier to detect local minima or maxima. When the cost function (which measures how accurate a model's predictions are) is plotted as a graph, its shape will be either convex or concave, depending on how well the model works. A shallow convex curve indicates that more training would be beneficial, whereas deep curves often indicate overfitting (where models fit too closely to their training data).

A concave cost curve typically indicates better performance than its convex counterpart, allowing for more efficient optimization by helping identify regions with lower values more easily. In addition, some unsupervised learning models (which do not use target variables) also rely on minimizing costs using concave functions.

Strictly Concave Function: A function $f:\mathbb{R}^n \to \mathbb{R}$ is concave if $\forall x, y, x \neq y$, and $\forall \alpha \in (0,1)$,

$$f(\alpha x+(1-\alpha)y)>\alpha f(x)+(1-\alpha)f(y) \tag{4.6}$$

Note: f is concave if and only if $-f$ is convex. Similarly f is strictly concave if and only if $-f$ is strictly convex.

Affine functions $f(x)=a^T x+b, \left(a\in\mathbb{R}^n, b\in\mathbb{R}\right)$ are functions that are both convex and concave.

When using strictly concave functions in ML, one usually looks at changes in objective function values (cost) and aims to reduce them gradually by considering small changes in inputs or parameters at each step. Strictly concave functions allow us to analyze how much impact any change has made on our overall cost quickly and efficiently without having to perform computations for every possible combination of inputs or parameters being tested. The ability of strictly concave functions to rapidly analyze complex data sets also allows them to be used as part of more sophisticated predictive models like neural networks where multiple layers of neurons can be trained simultaneously, with each layer receiving feedback from previous layers about how its output might affect performance downstream; this helps make training faster and more accurate than traditional methods which tend not require such insights into how one layer affects another during training.

Convex Combination: The convex combination of a set of points $x_1,\cdots x_k$ is defined as $\sum_{i=1}^{k}\alpha_i x_i$ such that $\alpha_i \geq 0 \forall i=1\cdots k$ and $\sum_{i=1}^{k}\alpha_i = 0$.

The convex combination method combines different models into one, taking a weighted average of all the individual models. The weights assigned to each model are based on how accurate each model is and how well they work together.

For example, suppose you have three different regression models that predict stock prices instead of choosing just one. In that case, you can combine them with convex combinations and get a more accurate prediction from the combined result. The same concept applies to other areas of ML, such as classification or clustering algorithms.

This technique helps create more robust and accurate systems by combining information from multiple sources rather than relying on just one source for all predictions or decisions made by an algorithm or system. In addition, this method allows for greater flexibility when making changes to optimize results since weights can be adjusted easily without having to rebuild the entire model from scratch.

Convex Hull: The convex hull of a set S is the set of all convex combinations of points in S.

$$conv(s)=\{\alpha_1 x_1+\cdots+\alpha_n x_n | x_i\in S, \alpha_i\geq 0, i=1\cdots n, \sum_{i=1}^{n}\alpha_i = 1\} \tag{4.7}$$

The convex hull of a set S is the smallest convex set which includes S.

The convex hull is a concept used in mathematics and computer science. It describes the shape of an object in terms of the boundary lines that can be drawn to enclose it. The idea is to find a set of points, called vertices, which form the convex hull such that any point inside the area enclosed by these points is also part of the convex hull.

Convex hulls have numerous applications in ML, as they can detect patterns and clusters in data sets. For example, if you want to identify specific areas with more concentrated clusters of data points, you could use a convex hull technique to draw boundaries around those areas, highlighting where those clusters are located. This type of analysis can be helpful in fraud detection since it helps identify clusters or outlying behavior that could indicate fraudulent activity. This technique can also improve accuracy when classifying new data sets since it allows us to quickly and easily group similar points into categories without having to examine each point individually.

Gradient: The gradient of a function $f:\mathbb{R}^n \to \mathbb{R}$ at a point $x \in \mathbb{R}^n$ is defined as

$$\nabla f(x) := \left[\frac{\partial f(x)}{\partial x_1}, \frac{\partial f(x)}{\partial x_2}, \ldots, \frac{\partial f(x)}{\partial x_n}\right]^T \tag{4.8}$$

In other words, for a function $f:\mathbb{R}^n \to \mathbb{R}$, the vector of first-order partial derivatives is called the **gradient vector** denoted by ∇.

A gradient vector is a mathematical tool that helps to calculate the direction and magnitude of change for certain variables. In ML, gradient vectors are used in optimization algorithms such as gradient descent. **Gradient descent** is an iterative approach to find the optimum value for specific parameters within a given function by calculating the derivative concerning those parameters. It allows us to find values of parameters that optimize our cost function and minimize errors in our ML models.

In practice, this means that when training complex models such ANNs, backpropagation can be used to calculate the derivative of each layer concerning each parameter (weights and bias) and use it in combination with gradient vectors to reduce errors during the training process. This encourages an efficient search process since we do not have to manually test thousands or millions of combinations before finding an optimal set of weights and bias values for our ANNs.

Properties of a gradient vector

- Orthogonal to the function contours
- Points in the direction of greatest increase of a function
- Negative gradient points in the direction of greatest decrease
- Dot product of a vector v orthogonal to the gradient vector is zero, that is, $v^T \nabla f(x) = 0$

Example 10: $f(x,y) = 4x^2 + 2y^2 - 5$ xy. Find the gradient at (2,3).

$$\nabla f(x,y) = \begin{bmatrix} 8x - 5y \\ -5x + 4y \end{bmatrix}$$

Evaluating the gradient at (2, 3),

$$\nabla f(x,y) = \begin{bmatrix} 1 \\ 2 \end{bmatrix}$$

Stationary Point: A point $\bar{x} \in \mathbb{R}^n$ for which $\nabla f(\bar{x}) = 0$ is called a stationary point.

Example 11: $f(x,y)=x^2+y^2$

$$\nabla f(x,y)=[2x,2y]^T=0 \Rightarrow (x,y)=(0,0)$$

That is, the origin is the stationary point.

Optimizing involves finding the optimal weights and hyperparameters that will provide the most accurate performance on unseen data. One way to achieve this is by using gradient descent, where we take small steps toward an optimum point, known as a stationary point or local minimum. In gradient descent, we start at an initial guess and iteratively move towards lower error rates until no further improvements can be made concerning that particular parameter set, known as converging at a stationary point.

The stationary points either have zero gradients because they are local minima (the lowest point in its vicinity) or equal gradients in all directions since they lie on flat surfaces (plateau regions). The primary purpose of optimizing ML models is to find the parameters which produce minimal errors when evaluated on unseen data; thus, identifying these stationary points help us optimize our models and produce more accurate results than before.

Hessian Matrix: For a function $f:\mathbb{R}^n \rightarrow \mathbb{R}$, the matrix of second-order partial derivatives is called the Hessian matrix, denoted by $\mathcal{H}$.

$$\mathcal{H}(x)=\nabla\left[\nabla f(x)\right]^T=\nabla^2 f(x)$$

$$\mathcal{H}(x)=\begin{bmatrix} \frac{\partial^2 f(x)}{\partial x_1^2} & \cdots & \frac{\partial^2 f(x)}{\partial x_1 x_n} \\ \vdots & \ddots & \vdots \\ \frac{\partial^2 f(x)}{\partial x_n x_1} & \cdots & \frac{\partial^2 f(x)}{\partial x_n^2} \end{bmatrix} \tag{4.9}$$

Example 12: $f(x,y)=4x^2+2y^2-5\,xy$. Find the Hessian matrix.

$$\nabla\left[\nabla f(x,y)\right]=\nabla\left[\begin{bmatrix} 8x-5y \\ -5x+4y \end{bmatrix}\right]=\begin{bmatrix} 8 & -5 \\ -5 & 4 \end{bmatrix}$$

The Hessian matrix is a matrix of a given function's second-order partial derivatives (derivatives of the derivatives). It is instrumental in ML to determine if a local maximum or minimum exists at a certain point by determining whether the underlying function is convex or concave. Moreover, it can help identify which parameters are essential for predicting output and how to improve them.

For example, we wish to determine the parameters leading us to the maximum global result for some ML problem. We can use the Hessian matrix to take partial derivatives of each parameter concerning the objective function and then compute its eigenvalues. If all the eigenvalues are positive, it implies that its corresponding parameter plays a vital role in predicting outputs as it contributes positively towards achieving better results; if any eigenvalue is negative, its corresponding parameter does not have much influence over predicting output and should be adjusted accordingly to achieve better results.

4.3 Optimization Problems

Optimization is defined informally as selecting the best choice about specific criteria from a set of alternatives or available choices. An optimization problem, in general, is defined as either a minimization or a maximization of a well-defined function of variables, subject to some constraints. Optimization problems are widely used in ML to help find a set of parameters that provide the best possible result. This is achieved by defining an objective function, which measures the performance of a given model, and then optimizing this function so that it is maximized or minimized.

For example, when dealing with supervised learning tasks such as classification or regression, an optimization problem is often used to determine the optimal parameters of the model that lead to maximum accuracy on unseen data. This can be done by minimizing some error metric such as mean squared error or log loss, and then finding parameters that minimize this metric.

Similarly, unsupervised learning algorithms also use optimization techniques such as clustering algorithms to identify data patterns without any associated labels. Optimization problems are also helpful for hyperparameter tuning when training a neural network model. They allow us to search through different combinations of hyperparameters (such as the number of layers and the number of neurons per layer) while maximizing our validation metrics (such as accuracy), thereby allowing us to achieve better performance from our models.

Optimization can be broadly classified into three categories: (a) linear and non-linear, (b) constrained and unconstrained, and (c) discrete, continuous, and probabilistic.

Linear optimization involves finding optimal solutions to problems, such as minimizing a cost function or maximizing a profit, to find the most efficient solution possible. It is often used when creating supervised ML models since it helps find best-fit solutions to linear problems. It can also be used in unsupervised models, where it can identify clusters or trends in data by optimizing parameters involved in clustering algorithms or principal component analysis.

Non-linear optimization looks for an optimal solution without requiring an exact mathematical formula. It helps with more general tasks, such as training neural networks and other deep learning architectures, where traditional linear methods cannot provide accurate results due to their limitations in dealing with non-linear mapping functions. Non-linear optimization algorithms work by looking at how different inputs affect outputs and then selecting those inputs which produce the best results given specific criteria, allowing for more accurate predictions from complex data sets.

Constrained and unconstrained optimization techniques enable us to create more accurate models by setting up certain boundaries or constraints that need to be met while optimizing an algorithm's performance. **Unconstrained optimization** refers to finding an optimal solution without imposing any restrictions or constraints on the parameters. It is used in many types of ML applications where all the parameters are unknown, such as supervised learning algorithms like decision tree and SVM, as well as deep learning techniques like backpropagation. This technique involves trying out different values for each parameter until the most optimal solution is achieved.

On the other hand, **constrained optimization** refers to finding an optimal value while imposing restrictions or constraints on the possible values that can be used for each parameter. This technique is often used in regression and classification problems where some general information (such as feature range) can be applied to narrow down possible solutions. Furthermore, constraints can also be imposed on objective functions (such as linearity or non-linearity constraint) to find better solutions with fewer iterations/steps compared to unconstrained optimization techniques; this reduces computational cost significantly while still achieving high accuracy.

Discrete, continuous, and probabilistic optimization helps us make decisions based on random probability distributions rather than predetermined values, such as step sizes in gradient descent methods. With **discrete optimizations**, we can make decisions based on discrete values representing categories in a data set rather than continuous values between two points; this enables us to understand better how each variable impacts the overall outcome being optimized for better accuracy for ML algorithms like decision trees or clustering methods like *K*-means.

Continuous optimization looks at continuous variables, where derivatives are taken into account when optimizing parameters; this helps identify global minima, which further boosts our model's performance even further through careful tuning from derivatives taken from mathematical equations used in calculus-related operations like gradient descent methods used heavily in deep learning applications such as convolutional neural networks (CNNs).

Lastly, **probabilistic optimization** attempts to make best guesses by approximating functions using probability distributions rather than set values; this helps us combine multiple pieces without having exact answers but still getting close enough results due to its ability to simulate different distributions allowing it to tackle uncertainty found within data sets more accurately. This makes it perfect for dealing with unstructured data sets produced from natural language processing (NLP) tasks like sentiment analysis applications.

4.3.1 Notations and Basic Terminology

$$\text{Minimize } f(x) \text{ subject to } f_i(x) \le 0, i = 1 \cdots m, h_j(x) = 0, j = 1 \cdots p \tag{4.10}$$

Equation (4.10) represents the basic notation of an optimization problem. The objective of the problem is to determine x such that x minimizes $f(x) \forall x$ that satisfies the conditions $f_i(x) \le 0, i = 1 \cdots m$ and $h_j(x) = 0, j = 1 \cdots p$.

- $x \in \mathbb{R}^n$ is called the **optimization variable.**
- The function $f : \mathbb{R}^n \to \mathbb{R}$ is known as the **objective function** or **cost function.**
- The inequalities $f_i(x) \le 0$ are called **inequality constraints** and the corresponding functions $f_i : \mathbb{R}^n \to \mathbb{R}$ are called **inequality constraint functions.**

  Inequality constraints can be applied to a problem to solve it. They determine the values of the solution's variables, thus providing the boundaries for a solution. In ML, inequality constraints can be used to solve problems such as optimization and feature selection. They can lead to more accurate predictions and better results when applied correctly.

  Inequality constraints are also helpful in improving the performance of supervised learning algorithms like classification and regression trees (CART). In CART models, an inequality constraint is used with cost-sensitive splitting rules, encouraging economically beneficial decisions rather than statistically optimal ones. Overall, using appropriate inequality constraints during model training ensures better generalizability of ML algorithms while avoiding potential performance issues caused by overly complex models.
- The equalities $h_j(x) = 0$ are called the **equality constraints** and the corresponding functions $h_j : \mathbb{R}^n \to \mathbb{R}$ are called **equality constraint functions.**

Equality constraints refer to any restriction that requires two values to be equal. In ML, equality constraints are helpful when optimizing complex models. By adding an equality constraint, the algorithm can use mathematical equations and/or other forms of logic to better convert data into information that can be used for predictive analysis or model optimization. This allows the algorithm to work more efficiently and accurately by accounting for all possible solutions within a given set of parameters.

- The set of points for which the objective function and all constraints are well defined is called the **domain** of the optimization problem. The domain of the optimization problem defined in Equation (4.10) is

$$D = \left(\bigcap_{i=1}^{m} f_i\right) \cap \left(\bigcap_{j=1}^{p} h_j\right) \tag{4.11}$$

The domain of optimization problems also helps machines identify patterns among large quantities of data more efficiently than humans can. For example, when dealing with unstructured data such as text documents or images, an optimization problem could determine which features are most important for predicting a specific outcome or classifying an item correctly from its contents. This type of approach is commonly used in deep learning applications where researchers rely on DNNs to extract meaningful information from vast amounts of data quickly and accurately without requiring too much manual work.

Optimization algorithms are essential in helping machines learn faster and make accurate predictions based on given inputs while reducing manual labor costs associated with traditional analysis approaches requiring significant human involvement at each step.

- A point $x \in D$ is called **feasible point** if it satisfies all the constraints defined in Equation (4.10).
- The problem defined in Equation (4.10) is said to be a **feasible problem** if there exists at least one feasible point. Otherwise it is called as **infeasible problem.**
- The set of all feasible points is called the **feasible set.**

  Feasible sets and problems are an essential part of ML. They help us understand the data and how it relates to each other. Feasible sets collect variables that can be used to solve a given problem. These variables can include categorization, clustering, classification, and regression, which help ML algorithms optimize results. Feasible problems, on the other hand, are mathematical equations or models used to obtain optimal solutions for a particular problem set. For example, when dealing with linear regression problems, we use the least-squares approach to find the best-fit line to predict future values based on past data points.

  Similarly, when dealing with classification problems, we use a logistic-regression approach. In both cases, the model is optimized using cost or loss functions, which help us get optimal solutions for our problems.
- The **optimal value** of the problem defined in Equation (4.10) is defined as

$$opt^* = \inf\{f(x) | f_i(x) \le 0, i = 1 \cdots m, h_i(x) = 0, i = 1 \cdots p\}, \tag{4.12}$$

  where inf represents the infimum value or minimum value
- For an infeasible problem, $opt^* = \infty$

- If there are feasible points x_k such that $f(x_k) \to -\infty ask \to \infty$, then such a problem is said to be **unbounded**.
- A point x^* is said to be an **optimal point** if it is a feasible point and solves the problem defined in Equation (4.10) such that $f(x^*) = opt^*$.
- If a point x is feasible and $f(x) \le opt^* + \epsilon$, then x is called $\epsilon -$**optimal**.
- If an optimal point exists, then the problem is **solvable.**
- An optimization problem can also be a **maximization problem**, by considering the negation of the objective function in the minimization problem.

4.3.2 Representation of Optimization Problems in Standard Form

The standard form of optimization is a mathematical method used to optimize an objective function by minimizing or maximizing the value of the function. This involves finding an equation's maximum or minimum values or inequality, subject to certain constraints. The standard form requires that all variables are non-negative and on the left side of all inequalities, while any values that constrain the solution must be on the right side.

For example, an inequality such as $x + 2 \le 4$ in its standard form can be written as $x \le 2$. In this case, 2 is a constraint because it must be subtracted from x to fit into the required format. All equality constraints must also be equal to zero for them to fit into this form. For instance, if we have $p = q + 3$, then in its standard form, this would become $p - q = 3$, and q would no longer appear on either side since it has been replaced by 0 (the right-hand side). This method lets us quickly identify which variables need adjustment to achieve our desired outcome and simplifies problem-solving.

Example 13: Consider the optimization problem

$$\text{Minimize } f(x)$$

$$\text{subject to low}_i \le x_i \le \text{high}_i,\ i = 1 \cdots n,\ x_i \in \mathbb{R}^n$$

This problem can be converted to the standard form as

$$\text{Minimize } f(x)$$

$$\text{subject to low}_i - x_i \le 0, i = 1 \cdots n$$

$$x_i - \text{high}_i \le 0, i = 1 \cdots n$$

4.3.3 Local Optima and Global Optima

A feasible point is said to be locally optimal if there are no other feasible points in its neighborhood with a lower objective value. A feasible point is said to be globally optimal if there are no other feasible points in its neighborhood with a lower objective value.

Formally they are defined as follows: A point x is called locally optimal if it is feasible and there exists some $R > 0$ such that all feasible points z with $x - z_2 \le R$ satisfy $f(x) \le f(z)$.

Note: $x - z_2$ represents the Euclidean norm.

A point x is called globally optimal if it is feasible and for all feasible points $z, f(x) \le f(z)$.

Local optima and global optima are concepts used in ML to determine the optimal solution to a problem. Local optima is the best solution within a particular region, while global optima is the best solution that could be achieved anywhere. Local optima can be seen as narrow valleys or hills in a landscape of possible solutions. Getting stuck in one of these local optima means that any changes made to improve one aspect of the solution will worsen other aspects, resulting in a worse outcome than staying at that optimum local state. The relative flatness and closeness of neighboring solutions mean that finding an even better solution than this local maximum requires big jumps across various parameters instead.

On the other hand, global optima are like being on top of a mountain peak from which every direction looks downwards – it is much easier to identify improvement areas and take steps towards them without risking getting stuck in another suboptimal state again. Furthermore, any changes will likely result in an improved overall outcome since all neighboring solutions look less attractive than this summit point.

ML algorithms use different techniques, such as gradient descent or simulated annealing, to search for local and global optima when solving problems involving multiple input variables (which can often yield thousands or even millions of possible combinations if left unchecked). This helps ensure they find both satisfactory and 'best' results by exploring all possible configurations before giving up on their search process – maximizing accuracy and effectiveness for tasks such as an image or speech recognition where solutions must be near perfect for successful completion.

For a convex optimization problem, all locally optimal points are globally optimal.

4.4 Convex Optimization

An optimization problem is convex if its objective function is a convex function, inequality constraints are convex and equality constraints are affine.

$$\text{Minimize } f(x) \text{ subject to } f_i(x) \le 0, h_j(x) = 0, i = 1 \cdots m, j = 1 \cdots p, \tag{4.13}$$

where $f_i(x) \le 0$ are convex sets and $h_j(x) = 0$ are affine functions.

The three main requirements for a convex optimization problem are:

- Objective function should be convex
- Inequality constraints should be convex
- Equality constraints are affine functions only

The feasible set of a convex optimization problem is convex since its domain is defined as

$$D = \text{domain}(f) \cap \left(\bigcap_{i=1}^{m} f_i \right) \cap \left(\bigcap_{j=1}^{p} h_j \right) \tag{4.14}$$

The inequality constraints defined in Equation (4.13) should always be less than or equal to zero because the zero-sublevel set of f_i is a convex set and hence the feasible region. If the constraints are greater than or equal to zero, it is no longer a convex set. The optimal value determined would no longer be a global optimum.

Convex optimization is preferred over general optimization due to the fundamental property that any locally optimal point is globally optimal.

Formally, if x is feasible and $x \in D$ and satisfies all constraints and minimizes f in a local neighborhood, then

$$f(x) \le f(y) \forall \text{ feasibly, } x - y_2 \le \rho \tag{4.15}$$

Linear programming (LP), quadratic programming (QP) and semi-definite programming (SDP) are special cases of convex optimization problems.

Example 14: Minimize $f(x) = x1^2 + x2^2$

$$\text{subject to } f1(x) = \frac{x1}{\left(1 + x2^2\right)} \le 0;\ h1(x) = (x1 + x2)^2 = 0$$

4.5 Unconstrained Optimization

Minimization/Maximization problems defined over $f : \mathbb{R}^n \to \mathbb{R}$ without any constraints on the input are called unconstrained problems. Optimizing such unconstrained problems is called unconstrained optimization.

Depending on specific criteria and variables, unconstrained optimization is used to find the optimal solution to a problem or task. By using unconstrained optimization, it becomes easier to train models in ML and make them more accurate. In ML, the goal is to minimize a cost function or error rate. This is where unconstrained optimization comes into play; it helps us find the best possible parameters for our model so that our cost function can be minimized as much as possible (or at least be as close to minimal as possible).

Unconstrained optimization algorithms such as gradient descent are used since they efficiently find local and global minima of functions with many variables. Using unconstrained optimization techniques, we can find an optimal set of parameters to give us a minimum error rate throughout our training process. This enables us to create better models which are more accurate and precise when presented with unknown data points.

Example 15: Find x that minimizes $f(x)$, where $x \in \mathbb{R}$, that is, x is a scalar.

Any local extremum will have the property $f'(x) = 0$. Such points are called **stationary points** or **critical points**. The stationary point may be (local) minimum, maximum or saddle point. The absolute lowest/highest level of $f(x)$ is called the global minimum/maximum.

$$Iff''(x) > 0 \to \text{the point is a local minimum}$$

$$Iff''(x) < 0 \to \text{the point is a local maximum}$$

$$Iff''(x) = 0 \to \text{the point is a saddle point}$$

The plot of the function looks like the one shown in Fig. 4.6.

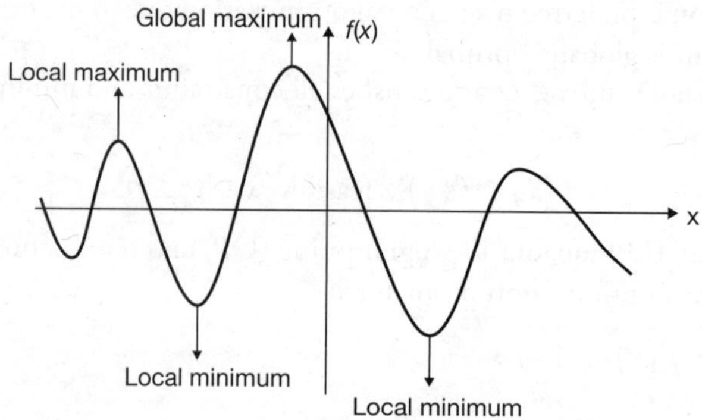

Figure 4.6 A one-dimensional function plot

Example 16: Find x that minimizes $f(x)$, where $x \in \mathbb{R}^n$, that is, x is a vector.

For a vector, gradient should be calculated. Any local extremum will have the property $\nabla f(x) = 0$. Such points are called stationary points or critical points. The stationary point may be (local) minimum, maximum or saddle point. The absolute lowest/highest level of $f(x)$ is called the global minimum/maximum.

$$\text{If } \mathcal{H} \text{ is positive definite} \rightarrow \text{the point is a local minimum}$$

$$\text{If } \mathcal{H} \text{ is negative definite} \rightarrow \text{the point is a local maximum}$$

$$\text{If } \mathcal{H} \text{ is indefinite}\left(\text{neither positve definite nor negative definite}\right) \rightarrow \text{the point is a saddle point}$$

If all the eigenvalues of the Hessian matrix $\mathcal{H}$ are positive, the matrix is said to be positive definite.
If all the eigenvalues of the Hessian matrix $\mathcal{H}$ are less than zero, the matrix is said to be negative definite.
If some eigenvalues of the Hessian matrix $\mathcal{H}$ are positive and some may be negative or zero, the matrix is said to be indefinite.

4.5.1 Solving an Unconstrained Optimization Problem when the Input is a Scalar

Newton's Method is a widely used optimization technique used to find the minimum of an unconstrained optimization problem in ML. It is an iterative method that can be used to solve non-linear equations and is applied to any function, regardless of its nature (linear, non-linear, convex, or non-convex).

In an unconstrained optimization problem in ML, it helps to understand derivatives and the concept of gradient descent. When dealing with an unconstrained problem, we usually aim to find the point at which the cost function has its lowest value. This point corresponds with the global minimum for that particular objective function. Gradient descent allows us to move towards this global minimum by taking small steps down our objective function until it reaches its local minima; that is, where our partial derivative equals 0. It tends to work well when we have small data sets; however, as data sets become larger and more complex, gradient descent can take quite some time before converging upon its best solution (as each step taken on the search space could be pretty significant). This is where Newton's Method comes into play.

Instead of attempting many small steps like gradient descent, Newton's Method takes one significant step per iteration towards finding a local minimum by using information from first- and second-order derivatives (or gradients) at each iteration in our search space. This also helps ensure we do not get stuck at any points on our search space due to flat areas or saddle points within the objective function – something that would cause problems with traditional methods such as gradient ascent/descent when trying to optimize for unconstrained problems in ML. Instead, Newton's Method can quickly identify potential optima points within its search space by using first- and second-order derivatives. This allows us to find better solutions faster than other techniques, such as gradient ascent/descent!

Assume that the function $f:\mathbb{R}\rightarrow\mathbb{R}$ is differentiable. Obtain the solution using $f(x)=0$. Starting from an initial estimate x_1, the next point can be approximated. In general,

$$x_{k+1}=x_k-\frac{f(x_k)}{f'(x_k)} \tag{4.16}$$

The process is repeated till convergence occurs.

Example 17: Find an approximate solution to $x^2-2=0$ starting with an initial estimate $x_1=2$.

k	x	$f(x)=x^2-2$	$f'(x)=2x$
1	2	2	4
2	1.5	0.25	3
3	1.416667	0.006944	2.833333
4	1.414216	0.000006	2.828431
5	1.414216	0	2.828427

The process gets converged and the approximate solution is $1.414216\approx\sqrt{2}$

Newton's method gives a good approximation to a function, but there are some drawbacks:

i. If $f'(x_k)=0$, the method fails.

ii. In some cases, the approximation may repeat the values.

iii. It is sensitive to the initial choice.

iv. In some cases, x_n may not be defined.

4.5.2 Gradient Descent Method (Solving an Unconstrained Optimization Problem when the Input is a Vector)

Gradient descent (GD) is a first-order optimization algorithm used to determine the local minimum/maximum of a given multivariate function. GD is a fundamental algorithm used in ML to update the parameters of a model based on an error/loss function. The algorithm works by calculating the gradient of the loss function concerning each parameter and then updating each parameter in such a way that it will reduce the value of the loss function. This process is repeated until we reach a point where further updates no longer improve the model's performance.

GD is usually used for supervised learning tasks, such as linear and logistic regression or neural networks, where you have labeled data that you can use to calculate errors/losses. By optimizing these parameters, we can make predictions more accurately and efficiently than if we had just used trial-and-error methods.

The requirements for GD are the function should be differentiable and convex. If a function is differentiable, it has a derivative for each point in its domain. For a univariate function to be convex, the line segment connecting any two points must lie on or above the curve. Another method to check whether a univariate function is convex or not is by calculating the second-order derivative and checking if it is greater than zero; that is, $f''(x) > 0$.

Example 18: $f(x) = x^2 + x - 5$

$$f'(x) = 2x + 1;\ f''(x) = 2$$

Since the second-order derivative is greater than zero, the given function is strictly convex.

Example 19: $f(x) = x^4 - 2x^3 + 2$

$$f'(x) = 4x^3 - 6x^2 = x^2(4x - 6)$$

$$f''(x) = 12x^2 - 12x = 12x(x - 1)$$

If $f'(x) = 0$, then $x = 0$ or 1.5.The slope at these points is zero and hence they are possible candidates for the function's extrema (minimum or maximum).

If $f''(x) = 0$, then $x = 0$ or 1.

The function is convex for $x < 0$ and $x > 1$. For values between 0 and 1, the function is concave since the second-order derivative is less than zero.

At the point $x = 0$, both the first-order derivative and the second-order derivative is zero, and hence it is a saddle point. At $x = 1.5$, the function has minimum value. Since the function is convex at certain points, the function is called **quasi-convex.**

For a multivariate function, the gradient is a vector of partial derivatives in each main direction.

Example 20: $f(x, y) = 2x^2 + y^2$

$$\frac{\partial f(x, y)}{\partial x} = 4x \quad \frac{\partial f(x, y)}{\partial y} = 2y$$

$$\nabla f(x, y) = \begin{bmatrix} 4x \\ 2y \end{bmatrix}$$

Gradient at point (1, 2) is

$$\nabla f(1,2) = \begin{bmatrix} 4 \\ 4 \end{bmatrix}$$

The gradient vector indicates that the slope is identical in both the *x*- and *y*-axes.

Working mechanism: We start with an arbitrary point and look for the next point to move to. The decision will be based on direction and step size. The direction will help us to move in a particular direction so that the function converges. The step size determines how quickly the function gets converged. The process is repeated until the function converges to a stationary point.

Start with an arbitrary point x^0 and at every step $k \geq 0$, move in a direction by step size t_k, the next point $x^{k+1} = x^k + \lambda \Delta f\left(x^k\right)$. The direction we move in is the negative gradient at that point. $\Delta f\left(x^k\right) = -\nabla f\left(x^k\right)$.

$$\Rightarrow x^{k+1} = x^k - \lambda \nabla f\left(x^k\right) \tag{4.17}$$

Since the objective is minimization of the given unconstrained function, a sensible approach is to choose the step size in such a way that it will minimize the value of the next point. A higher value of step size may not converge or diverge (shoot the point out of the region). A lower value of step size will proceed towards convergence slowly. A moderate value will move towards convergence.

Gradient Descent Algorithm
Step 1: Set $k = 0$.
Step 2: Choose the initial point x^0.
Step 3: Calculate the gradient at this point.
Step 4: Choose the next point in the negative or opposite direction of the gradient using Equation (4.17).
Step 5: Repeat steps 3 and 4 until the stopping criteria is met.

The stopping criteria can be either fixing the number of iterations or $\nabla f\left(x^k\right) \geq \varepsilon$.

Example 21: Minimize $f(x) = x_1^2 + x_2^2$. Choose the starting point as $[3,4]$.

$$\nabla f(x) = \begin{bmatrix} 2x_1 \\ 2x_2 \end{bmatrix}$$

Step-by-step process choosing $\lambda = 2$

Iteration #	Point	$\nabla f(x) = [2x_1, 2x_2]^T$	$f(x)$	New point $x^{k+1} = x^k - \lambda \nabla f\left(x^k\right)$
0	$[3,4]^T$	$[6,8]^T$	25	$[3,4]^T - 2[6,8]^T = [-9,-12]^T$
1	$[-9,-12]^T$	$[-18,-24]^T$	225	$[27,36]^T$
2	$[27,36]^T$	$[54,72]^T$	2025	$[-81,-108]^T$

The function is diverging

Step-by-step process choosing $\lambda = 1$

Iteration #	Point	$\nabla f(x) = [2x_1, 2x_2]^T$	$f(x)$	New point $x^{k+1} = x^k - \lambda \nabla f(x^k)$
0	$[3,4]^T$	$[6,8]^T$	25	$[3,4]^T - 1[6,8]^T = [-3,-4]^T$
1	$[-3,-4]^T$	$[-6,-8]^T$	25	$[3,4]^T$

The function does not converge at all

Step-by-step process choosing $\lambda = 0.5$

Iteration #	Point	$\nabla f(x) = [2x_1, 2x_2]^T$	$f(x)$	New point $x^{k+1} = x^k - \lambda \nabla f(x^k)$
0	$[3,4]^T$	$[6,8]^T$	25	$[3,4]^T - 0.5[6,8]^T = [0,0]^T$
1	$[0,0]^T$	$[0,0]^T$	0	$[0,0]^T$

The function has converged rapidly

Step-by-step process choosing $\lambda = 0.1$

Iteration #	Point	$\nabla f(x) = [2x_1, 2x_2]^T$	$f(x)$	New point $x^{k+1} = x^k - \lambda \nabla f(x^k)$
0	$[3,4]^T$	$[6,8]^T$	25	$[3,4]^T - 0.1[6,8]^T = [2.4,3.2]^T$
1	$[2.4,3.2]^T$	$[4.8,6.4]^T$	16	$[1.92,2.56]^T$
2	$[1.92,2.56]^T$	$[3.84,5.12]^T$	14.24	$[1.536,2.048]^T$
⋮	⋮	⋮	⋮	⋮
30	$[0.0031,^T$ 0.005]	⋮	0.000121	⋮

The function converges slowly

4.6 Constrained Optimization

An ML problem is an optimization problem where we seek the best possible outcome given certain conditions. Constrained optimization helps find this optimal solution by introducing constraints on how far away from the optimal point we can go. For example, a common constraint in neural networks is that weights cannot be too small or too large, which helps avoid overfitting and underfitting when training models. Constrained optimization can also help avoid bias during training by enforcing fairness constraints such as non-discrimination based on age or gender. This prevents models from making unfair or biased decisions against certain groups of people and ensures fairness in automated decision-making processes.

Constrained optimization techniques also allow us to solve complex problems by considering multiple objectives simultaneously, helping us quickly identify trade-offs between different goals and objectives when building our model architectures. Finally, constrained optimization helps with the interpretability of results, which is especially important with ML algorithms that produce complex outputs, such as deep learning models. By adding simple constraints like 'keep features related' or 'maximize model accuracy within a reasonable time,' we can improve our understanding of how individual parts contribute to overall performance without sacrificing the stability or accuracy of our model predictions.

A constrained optimization problem is of the form

$$\min f(x) s.t. g_i(x) \le 0, \forall i = 1 \cdots m h_j(x) = 0 \forall j = 1 \cdots p \tag{4.18}$$

The Lagrangian associated with this problem is

$$\min(x, \lambda, \upsilon) = f(x) + \sum_{i=1}^{m} \lambda_i g_i(x) + \sum_{j=1}^{p} \upsilon_j h_j(x) \tag{4.19}$$

The $\lambda_i^{'}$ and $\upsilon_j^{'}$ are called **Lagrangian multipliers**. The Lagrangian produces a family of lower bounds to the cost function at every feasible point.

Lagrangian multipliers are often used in ML to solve optimization problems. They are used to optimize the parameters of a system by employing constraints that limit and help shape the outcome of a function. For example, ML algorithms often employ regularization, which involves introducing penalty terms into an objective function to reduce overfitting and improve generalization. This penalty term can be expressed as a Lagrangian multiplier, where one can specify the regularization one desires for each parameter or feature set within the model. This technique can help keep models from overfitting while helping them perform better on unseen data.

Another example is when using neural networks for classification tasks; Lagrangian multipliers are commonly used to attempt to optimize decision boundaries between classes by adding constraints on specific parameters to try and increase accuracy or reduce misclassification errors. Introducing constraints through these penalty terms during optimization helps an algorithm find better decision boundaries between different classes.

Example 22: Minimize $x + y$ subject to $x^2 + y^2 = 1$.
The constraint is an external factor.
The Lagrangian associated with this problem is

$$L(x, y, \upsilon) = x + y + \upsilon\left(x^2 + y^2 - 1\right)$$

Calculate the gradient of this function to determine the stationary point.

$$\nabla L(x, y, \upsilon) = \begin{pmatrix} 1 + 2\upsilon x \\ 1 + 2\upsilon y \\ x^2 + y^2 - 1 \end{pmatrix}$$

$$\nabla L(x, y, \upsilon) = 0$$
$$\Rightarrow 1 + 2\upsilon x = 0; 1 + 2\upsilon y = 0; x^2 + y^2 - 1 = 0$$

Solving these, we get $x = y = \frac{-1}{2\upsilon}$ and $\upsilon = \pm\frac{1}{\sqrt{2}}$

The stationary points are $\left(\frac{1}{\sqrt{2}}, \frac{1}{\sqrt{2}}\right)$ and $\left(\frac{-1}{\sqrt{2}}, \frac{-1}{\sqrt{2}}\right)$

Example 23: Maximize $f(x, y) = xy$ subject to $x + y = 100$. Though it is a constrained optimization problem, the problem looks simple. For such simple problems, we can use the direct substitution method.

Direct substitution allows us to rewrite the constraints in a single variable.
Rewriting the given constraint, we get $y = 100 - x$.
Now the problem is transformed as $f(x, 100 - x) = x(100 - x) = 100x - x^2$
By differentiating *f*, we get $f'(x) = 100 - 2x$.
By equating $f'(x) = 0$, we get $100 - 2x = 0 \Rightarrow x = 50$ and hence $y = 50$
We determine the second-order derivative $f''(x) = -2 < 0$
Hence the function will be maximized at (50, 50).
The same problem can also be solved using Lagrangian multipliers.

$$L(x, y, \lambda) = f(x, y) + \lambda(x + y - 100) = xy + \lambda(x + y - 100)$$

$$L' = \begin{pmatrix} y + \lambda \\ x + \lambda \\ x + y - 100 \end{pmatrix}$$

$$L' = 0 \Rightarrow x = y = -\lambda,$$
$$x + y = 100 \Rightarrow -2\lambda = 100 \Rightarrow \lambda = -50 \Rightarrow x = y = 50$$

4.7 Dual Optimization Problems

Dual optimization is an ML technique that simultaneously optimizes two objectives. This can be useful when there are competing goals in the same optimization problem. For example, building a recommendation system for online shoppers might require optimizing for accuracy and speed of results or balancing between minimizing false positives and false negatives in fraud detection algorithms. In dual optimization techniques, one objective is seen as 'primary' and the other as 'secondary'. The primary objective is optimized first, followed by the secondary objective, which tries to improve the values found by optimizing the primary objective. To achieve this, each step of an optimal solution must satisfy both objectives. At any given time, either one may be slightly sacrificed (while still being above a certain threshold) so that they are both satisfied with mutually compatible solutions over time.

The optimal solution found using dual optimization will only sometimes be perfectly balanced between both objectives, but it should generally still provide satisfactory results. By using dual optimization instead of traditional single-objective methods, engineers can ensure that their systems are more robust and can take into account many different types of requirements simultaneously without sacrificing too much on any individual metric.

Duality Theorem: Every maximization problem (**primal**) defined in standard form in linear programming (LP) will have an LP minimization problem called **dual**. The primal and dual problems are linked. Every feasible solution of one problem gives a bound on the optimal value of the other. This is called duality theorem. Duality theorem is a powerful tool used in ML to make better decisions. It states that if two optimization problems are related, the solution to one problem will be related to the solution of the other.

In supervised learning, duality theorem is often used to solve LP problems such as regression or classification tasks. Suppose we have a set of data points with certain features (independent variables) and specific labels (dependent variables). We can use LP techniques to determine which features are more important for predicting the labels correctly. This allows us to identify which features have higher predictive power and improve our models accordingly. In unsupervised learning tasks such as clustering or anomaly detection, duality theorem can help us determine how two data sets might be related even though they may not contain identical labels or classes. This allows us to find patterns in data that would otherwise go unnoticed.

In reinforcement learning tasks such as game-playing algorithms, duality theorem helps us create strategies for minimizing loss by comparing scenarios based on their expected rewards for different actions an agent takes (such as a player). By calculating expected rewards from different states within a game-playing environment using LP techniques derived from this theorem, we can optimize strategies for different situations more efficiently than without its use. Finally, it has been found that neural networks also benefit from incorporating this theorem into their design process during optimization attempts, as it helps reduce overfitting and improves the accuracy of outputs when predicting unseen data points.

Primal and Dual Problems: Let the problem defined in Equation (4.20) be considered as primal.

$$\text{Maximize} \sum_{j=1}^{n} c_j x_j$$

$$\text{subject to} \sum_{j=1}^{n} a_{ij} x_j \leq b_i \forall i = 1 \cdots m$$

$$x_j \geq 0 \tag{4.20}$$

The dual of the primal is defined as

$$\text{Maximize} \sum_{i=1}^{m} (-b_j) y_i$$

$$\text{subject to} \sum_{j=1}^{m} (-a_{ij}) y_i \leq -c_j \forall j = 1 \cdots n$$

$$y_i \geq 0 \; \forall i = 1 \cdots m \tag{4.21}$$

Weak duality theorem states that any feasible solution to the dual problem is greater than any feasible solution to the primal problem. In other words, the optimal solution of a problem cannot be worse than the optimal solution of its dual problem. This means that even if an exact solution to a problem is hard to find, one can still get a good upper bound on the best possible value by solving its dual version instead. In ML, this theorem can solve optimization problems related to supervised and unsupervised learning algorithms. For example, minimizing the objective function (or cost function) in linear regression models requires finding the right combination of model parameters to minimize prediction error. Solving this problem's dual version may yield a different solution. However, it provides us with a lower bound on our minimum possible prediction error, which allows us to determine whether or not our current model parameters are sufficient for obtaining good predictions or if more fine-tuning is needed.

Similarly, in clustering applications such as *K*-means and Gaussian mixture models (GMM), weak duality theorem can be used to find approximate solutions when closed-form expressions for computing optimal cluster assignments are unavailable or too computationally costly. In GMM, for instance, it is usually impossible to obtain exact solutions since each data point must have its probability distribution associated with it; however, by using weak duality theorem, we can construct improved lower bounds on parameters for each data point without resorting to computationally expensive methods like Monte Carlo simulations/sampling-based algorithms. Finally, this theorem has been applied successfully in Markov decision processes (MDPs). In MDPs, we need to solve complicated optimization problems involving multiple variables and constraints; here, too, weak duality helps us obtain better estimates of optimal values by solving simpler versions of these problems, which results in better approximations than simply relying on heuristic search techniques like hill climbing.

Strong duality theorem states that if the primal problem has an optimal solution $\left(x_1^*, x_2^*, \cdots, x_n^*\right)$, the dual has an optimal solution $\left(y_1^*, y_2^*, \cdots, y_n^*\right)$ such that

$$\sum_{j=1}^{n} c_j x_j^* = \sum_{i=1}^{m} b_i y_i^* \tag{4.22}$$

Strong duality theorem is used in ML to provide mathematical proof for optimizing particular algorithms. The theorem states that for any given optimization problem, there exists a solution that maximizes the objective function and simultaneously meets the problem's constraints. In other words, if an algorithm has been designed to efficiently find a solution or set of solutions that meets specific criteria or objectives, then this solution can be proven optimal through solid duality. Strong duality is essential in specific ML algorithms such as SVMs. In these cases, it guarantees that any proposed solution will meet its specified objectives while providing insight into how this optimal solution was found and how to improve upon it. For example, SVM algorithms use strong duality to ensure they can accurately classify data points by finding an optimal hyperplane that maximizes its margin distance from each class boundary point.

Consider a constrained optimization problem

$$\text{Minimize } f(x)$$

$$\text{subject to } g_i(x) \le 0, \forall i = 1 \cdots m$$

$$h_j(x) = 0 \forall j = 1 \cdots p \tag{4.23}$$

This problem is also called a primal optimization problem.

The **primal optimization problem** is a mathematical problem that involves finding the optimal solution for a set of parameters. This problem can be used to optimize specific ML algorithms and processes. Primal optimization problems are beneficial in deep learning, where they are used to help create and improve neural networks. For example, many deep learning algorithms utilize primal optimization problems to identify the optimal combination of weights and biases within a network. This helps ensure the network can accurately recognize patterns, identify objects in images or videos, or perform other tasks with maximum accuracy. Primal optimization can also determine the best parameters for accurate predictions when using regression models or supervised ML approaches.

Primal optimization problems can also help reduce overfitting by helping researchers find an optimal model size and number of layers in a neural network. By using this technique, researchers can find an ideal balance between having too few layers leading to underfitting and too many layers leading to overfitting. Overall, primal optimization effectively allows researchers and engineers to optimize ML algorithms with minimal effort. It allows them to quickly identify an optimal solution from various possibilities without needing extensive trial-and-error testing methods that take up more time and resources than necessary.

Lagrangian Duality: Given a Lagrangian $L(x, \lambda, v)$ of some optimization problem, the Lagrangian dual is defined as a function:

$$F(\lambda, v) = \inf L(x, \lambda, v), \tag{4.24}$$

where $x \in$ domain D of the primal problem.

For the primal optimization problem defined above, the dual optimization problem is defined as

$$\text{Maximize } F(\lambda, v), \text{ subject to } \lambda \ge 0 \tag{4.25}$$

4.8 Dynamic Programming

Dynamic programming solves problems by combining solutions to sub-problems. A dynamic programming approach solves sub-problems or sub-sub-problems only once and store the results in a table-like structure. This approach is mostly used for solving optimization problems.

Principle of Optimality: A problem is said to satisfy the principle of optimality if the sub-solutions of an optimal solution of the problem are optimal solutions by itself for their sub-problems. The principle of optimality is widely used in ML for finding the best model structure through an iterative process. For example, it can be used to find the optimal set of parameters for a given model, determine a neural network's optimal size and complexity, or define the best hyperparameters for a given problem. In essence, this approach involves solving sub-problems within each iteration and then combining their solutions to arrive at a better solution than any individual sub-problem's solution.

This method has successfully tackled challenging problems such as feature selection, semi-supervised learning, reinforcement learning optimization, and deep learning optimization.

A Markov decision process (MDP) consists of states, actions, rewards, and descriptions of the effect of each action in each state. Reinforcement learning aims to learn an optimal policy and MDP provides the environment. Dynamic programming is employed in such cases to determine the optimal solutions.

4.9 Sublinear Algorithms

Sublinear algorithms are those that solve a given problem by reading a minute scale of the input and process the input in a sublinear time before the solution is given as output. These algorithms may give exact solutions or provide approximate solutions through randomization.

Sublinear algorithms are becoming increasingly popular in ML. These algorithms can be used for large data sets that are too big to process with traditional methods. The main idea of using sublinear algorithms is to reduce the number of calculations needed to get accurate results from a large data set. This helps improve performance, reduce time spent on processing, and minimize the resources required for the task at hand. In ML, sublinear algorithms can be used for various tasks such as feature selection, clustering, classification, and regression.

Example 27: Determine an odd number in a given array $A[1:n]$ consisting of a permutation of $\{1\cdots n\}$ for $n>1$ and which outputs an index i such that $A[i]$ is an odd number.

A deterministic approach outputs an exact solution in O(n) time. A randomized algorithm may produce an output in O(1) time. The idea is simple: randomly pick an element and check whether it is odd or not. Repeat until you find an odd number.

Streaming algorithms are those that solve a given problem by reading the input as it comes (streaming input) and give an exact solution or approximate solution with the help of randomization. These algorithms will not store the input sequence at all; they run 'on the fly'. They process the streaming input using only a sublinear amount of memory.

Like the concept of randomized algorithms and approximate algorithms, sublinear algorithms aim for some solution when there is no solution available in polynomial time.

4.10 Graphs

A graph is a non-linear data structure consisting of a non-empty set of vertices and a set of edges. It is represented as $G=(V,E)$. An example of a graph is shown in Fig. 4.7. with four vertices and seven edges.

$V=\{v_1,v_2,v_3,v_4\}$ $E=\{e_1,e_2,e_3,e_4,e_5,e_6,e_7\}$.

A graph is represented by an adjacency matrix or an adjacency list. For the graph shown in Fig. 4.7, the adjacency matrix (Table 4.1) is defined with dimensions $|V|\times|V|$.

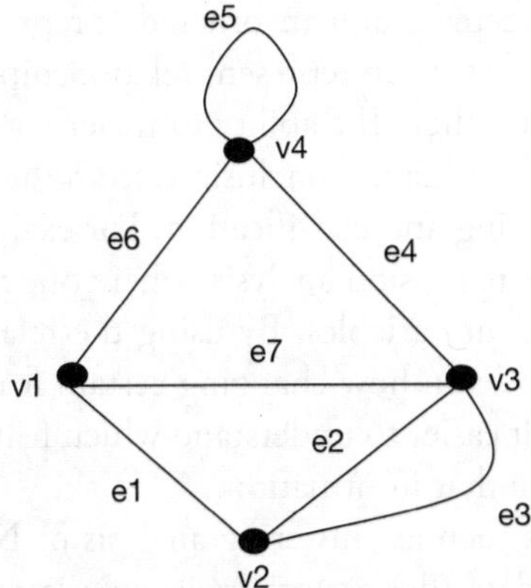

Figure 4.7 A graph with four vertices and seven edges

Table 4.1 Adjacency matrix for the graph given in Fig. 4.7.

	v_1	v_2	v_3	v_4
v_1	0	1	1	1
v_2	1	0	2	0
v_3	1	2	0	1
v_4	1	0	1	1

The entries in the adjacency matrix indicate the number of edges between the corresponding vertices. Between vertices v_2 and v_3, there are two edges; hence the number 2 in the adjacency matrix.

Undirected Graph: The edges in an undirected graph are unordered, that is, an edge between two vertices represented by (u, v) or (v, u) is the same.

Undirected graphs are useful in ML because they allow for the representation of data relationships. In particular, they can be used to identify patterns between different variables and help decide which ones should be used in the model. For example, an undirected graph could be used to understand how two variables interact; if one variable has a direct influence on another variable, these two variables will have a direct connection in the graph. This type of analysis can be helpful when building models as it can help determine which factors are most important for a given outcome.

Undirected graphs can also help analyze complex data sets by clustering similar data points together or identifying outliers that require further investigation or removal from the data set. Using network structures makes it possible to infer hidden connections between observations and uncover insightful information about the data set. This makes undirected graphs essential for exploratory analysis and feature selection during model building.

Directed Graph: The edges in a directed graph are ordered or represented by a directed pair. A directed graph is an essential tool for ML, as it can represent relationships between data points and explore different paths from one point to another. The ability to traverse a graph structure allows algorithms to identify patterns in data and draw valuable conclusions from them. In addition, the directed graph can be used for tasks such as clustering and classification. For example, a directed graph can be used in supervised learning tasks such as regression analysis, where one must predict the value of a dependent variable given some independent variables. By using the relationships represented by edges in the graph structure, algorithms can learn how changing certain features of an object or entity might affect its output value. This makes it easier to understand which features are essential when predicting values and deciding how best to use that information.

In unsupervised learning tasks such as clustering analysis or NLP, directed graphs help identify general patterns among pieces of data that are otherwise unrelated or difficult to classify manually. This helps machines learn how different pieces of information may correlate, allowing them to make more accurate predictions about unknown data points based on what they already know.

Here, the edge between the vertices u and v are represented as (u, v) in which the tail of the edge is at u and the head is at v. Hence (u, v) and (v, u) are different.

An edge from a vertex to itself is called a **self-loop**. Self-loops can be used to model situations where a node is somehow related to itself. For example, if one wanted to model the friendship between two people, one could have an edge with both ends pointing at the same vertex. If there is more than one edge between a pair of vertices, the edges are called **multiple edges**. Multiple edges are used in ML to capture and quantify the strength of relationships between different entities. For example, in a social network, multiple edges can be used to model how closely two people are connected or the likelihood that they will interact with each other. In a recommendation system, multiple edges can be used to score the affinity between items related by their category or context. This information can be used by algorithms such as collaborative filtering or matrix factorization to make recommendations. Multiple edges also enable algorithms such as neural graph networks, which help encode complex relationships among entities within a graph structure and use those complex interactions to make predictions more accurately than traditional methods.

For a graph with n vertices, the maximum number of distinct edges is $\dfrac{n(n-1)}{2}$.

Complete Graph: An undirected graph with exactly $n(n-1)/2$ edges is called a complete graph. In ML, complete graphs help identify patterns in data that are difficult to detect. For example, we want to identify which variables are related to each other. In this case, it is much easier to use a complete graph than to examine individual pairs of variables separately. A complete graph gives us an overview of the entire data set and makes it easier to see how different variables interact. Complete graphs also help machines make decisions based on large data sets or high-dimensional problems where multiple factors may be at play at any given time. By analyzing patterns within a complete graph, ML algorithms can more easily determine which factors contribute most towards specific outcomes or decisions and make predictions based on those findings. Finally, complete graphs offer an effective way of visualizing data so that humans can better understand its structure and meaning and identify outliers or anomalies more quickly than without this tool.

Subgraph: For a graph $G=(V,E)$, there exists a graph G' such that $V(G')\subseteq V(G)$ and $E(G')\subseteq E(G)$.

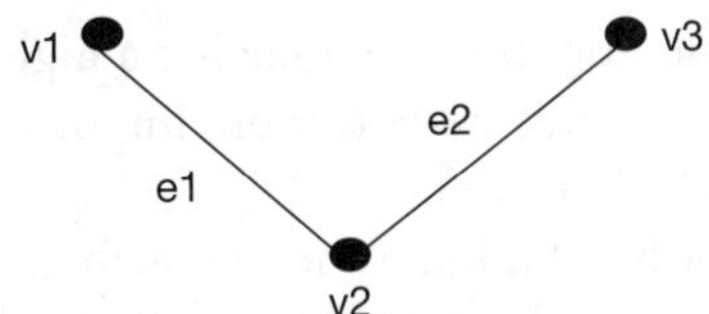

Figure 4.8 A subgraph of the graph given in Fig. 4.7

Subgraphs are helpful in ML because they allow the machine to identify patterns and relationships in the data. Subgraphs are subsets of graphs that contain all or part of an original graph's nodes and edges (Fig. 4.8). By breaking down the main graph into smaller components, subgraphs allow machines to find patterns in complex data sets easily. For example, suppose we were trying to predict credit card fraud using a data set of customer transactions. Here, we could create subgraphs by grouping customer transactions according to the date, merchant type, or location. This would allow us to understand customer spending patterns better and detect anomalies that may indicate fraudulent activity.

Subgraphs also enable machines to learn from previously learned models while still being able to recognize new relationships. By creating multiple subgraphs from similar but distinct data sets, machines can compare results from previous models with current ones and make better predictions about future data points more quickly and accurately than ever. In addition, subgraph algorithms can be used for dimensionality reduction, which helps reduce noise in large data sets so that the machine can focus on essential features instead of being overwhelmed by irrelevant information. This is especially helpful when working with unstructured data sets where it is difficult for computers to identify meaningful patterns from many available data points due to their sheer volume or complexity.

Path: A path from a vertex $v1$ to $v3$ is a sequence of vertices where any two adjacent vertices are connected by an edge.

Cycle: A cycle is a path where the initial vertex and the final vertex are the same. In other words, the sequence's starting and ending points are the same. The path can go through many vertices before returning to its beginning, never visiting any vertex twice (except for the start and end). This means that it forms a closed loop. Cycles are essential in graph theory because they can measure properties like connectivity or the distance between two points in a connected graph. They also solve specific problems like finding minimal spanning trees or identifying strongly connected components in directed graphs.

Connected Graph: An undirected graph is said to be connected if and only if there exists a path between every pair of distinct vertices. An undirected graph is connected if there is a path from any vertex to another vertex. This means that for any two distinct vertices in the graph, there is a way to get from one to the other without re-visiting previously visited nodes. In other words, every node in an undirected graph can be reached from every other node by some sequence of edges or steps. If there is no path between two distinct vertices, the undirected graph is not considered connected.

Degree of a Vertex: The number of edges incident on a vertex in an undirected graph is called the degree of the vertex. A vertex (also known as a node) is a point on a graph, and the degree of that vertex represents how many other nodes it is connected to. This number can be used to measure the strength of connections between nodes and understand how they relate. In ML, the degree of a vertex can help determine which connections are the most important in an algorithm and better understand the data being analyzed. For example, suppose one node has a high degree compared to others in the same network. This could indicate that this node is more important than others for making correct predictions or classifications with the algorithm.

This concept can also be used when building models such as neural networks or decision trees where understanding which features are the most important (and therefore should be given more weight) helps improve performance. In these cases, higher degrees may indicate features that are more predictive or meaningful than those with lower degrees, indicating they should not receive much attention from the model as they lack relevance for predictions/decisions made by it.

For a directed graph, the in-degree of a vertex v is the number of edges for which v is the head. The out-degree of a vertex v is the number of edges for which v is the tail.

4.11 Transforms

The **Fourier transform** of a continuous function $f(t)$ is defined as

$$F(\mu) = \int_{-\infty}^{+\infty} f(t) e^{-j2\pi\mu t} dt,$$

where t and μ are continuous variables.

The inverse Fourier transform is defined as

$$f(t) = \int_{-\infty}^{+\infty} f(t) e^{j2\pi\mu t} d\mu$$

These two equations represent a Fourier transform pair.

Euler's formula, $e^{-j2\pi\mu t} = \cos(2\pi\mu t) - j\sin(2\pi\mu t)$

Fourier transform is a mathematical technique to decompose any given function into a series of sine and cosine functions. It is an essential tool in ML because it allows us to analyze data more effectively and efficiently by changing it from the time domain into the frequency domain. In ML, Fourier transform can decompose complex signals (such as images) into simpler components that are easier for a computer to interpret and understand. By breaking down an image or sound clip into its essential elements, we can better decide what should be included in our model or program when using ML algorithms. For example, suppose we have a picture of someone's face. Fourier transform can help break this picture down into separate parts, such as eyes, nose, and lips, allowing us to give these different parts their weights when constructing our model or program for recognition purposes.

Fourier transform also helps reduce noise in data sets so that only relevant features remain, which can then be taken forward for further processing with various ML algorithms like SVMs and neural networks (NNs). This way, noise is eliminated while preserving meaningful information to improve the accuracy of predictions made with ML models built on such data sets.

Convolution: The convolution of two functions involves superimposing one function over the other about its origin and sliding it past the other. At every displacement location during the sliding, the computation includes the sum of products. It is defined as

$$(f * h)(t) = \int_{-\infty}^{+\infty} f(\tau)h(t-\tau)d\tau$$

Convolution is an ML technique that helps us identify patterns in data by performing mathematical operations on different inputs. It is commonly used in image recognition and classification tasks, where it helps to identify features within an image that can help distinguish one object from another. The basic is to take multiple small windows of data and apply a set of mathematical operations, such as multiplication, addition, or subtraction, across those windows to detect certain patterns or features. This process is repeated until a desired outcome is reached, resulting in a set of values that represent the image's features. The result can then be used for further analysis or prediction tasks.

In ML applications, convolution can help computers understand which parts of an image are important for classifying objects or predicting outcomes. For example, suppose we want to predict whether there will be rain tomorrow based on an array of weather images from the past week. We could use convolutional filters to identify which parts of each picture are most likely related to rainfall – like dark clouds or heavy rain – so that our algorithm can consider these patterns when making predictions about tomorrow's weather.

Properties of Convolution

- Convolution is commutative, that is, the order in which signals convolve has no effect on the result.

$$x(t) * y(t) = y(t) * x(t)$$

- Convolution is distributive over addition.

$$x(t) * [y(t) + z(t)] = [x(t) * y(t)] + [x(t) * z(t)]$$

- Convolution is associative.

$$x(t) * [y(t) * z(t)] = [x(t) * y(t)] * z(t)$$

- Shift property: Convolution of a signal with time shift results in a shift in the output signal.

$$\text{If } x(t) * y(t) = z(t), \text{ then } x(t) * y(t - t1) = z(t - t1)$$

Discrete Cosine Transform (DCT): Consider a sequence $p(n), 0 \le n \le N-1$. The one-dimensional DCT of this sequence is defined as

$$q(k) = \alpha(k) \sum_{n=0}^{N-1} p(n) \cos\left[\frac{\pi(2n+1)k}{2N}\right], 0 \le k \le N-1$$

$$\alpha(0) = \frac{1}{\sqrt{N}}$$

$$\alpha(k) = \sqrt{\frac{2}{N}} 1 \le k \le N-1$$

The inverse transform is given by

$$p(n) = \sum_{k=0}^{N-1} \alpha(k) q(k) \cos\left[\frac{\pi(2n+1)k}{2N}\right], 0 \le n \le N-1$$

Forward transform and inverse transform together form the DCT pair.

The $N \times N$ discrete cosine transform matrix is given by

$$c(k,n)=\begin{cases} \frac{1}{\sqrt{N}} & k=0, 0\le n\le N-1 \\ \sqrt{\frac{2}{N}}\cos\left[\frac{\pi(2n+1)k}{2N}\right] & 1\le k\le N-1, 0\le n\le N-1 \end{cases}$$

DCT is a commonly used ML technique that reduces the amount of data in an image or audio signal by removing less important information from it. This allows for more efficient storage and transmission of the data. In addition, DCT helps retain most of the essential features and reduces noise in the signal. In computer vision, DCT detects image features such as edges, shapes, and textures. It can be applied to grayscale and color images, allowing for faster processing since it focuses on only a few significant frequencies instead of all of those within an image. In addition, this technique can achieve more explicit object recognition with fewer parameters than with other methods like Fourier transforms or wavelets.

It can also be used to compress large data sets before they are transmitted over networks or stored on disk drives because reducing data size reduces transfer time and storage costs significantly. In addition to computer vision applications, DCT is popularly utilized in speech processing tasks like speech recognition systems and text-to-speech synthesizers due to its ability to extract salient characteristics from sound waves that are otherwise undetectable by human ears, such as pitch periodicity patterns and formant structure, among others. Furthermore, the extracted features help machines convert speech signals into meaningful words and sentences with better accuracy rates than other methods, such as Fourier transforms or wavelet analysis techniques. As a result, it is extremely popular among automatic speech recognition systems that use models trained using ML algorithms like DNNs, SVMs, and hidden Markov models (HMMs).

Discrete cosine transform (DCT) and discrete Fourier transform (DFT) are integral to signal processing. Yet, they serve different purposes and exhibit distinct characteristics, particularly in the context of optimization algorithms. DCT, utilizing only real numbers, is closely related to the Fourier series coefficients of a symmetrically extended sequence, which makes it highly suitable for applications that benefit from data compression, such as image and audio encoding. This is due to the DCT's ability to concentrate signal energy into a few coefficients, a property known as **spectral compaction**. On the other hand, DFT, employing complex numbers, is related to the Fourier series coefficients of periodically extended sequences and is widely used for spectral analysis across various fields.

Properties of DCT

- DCT is real and orthogonal.
- DCT is not the real part of DFT.
- DCT has excellent energy compaction for highly correlated data.
- DCT is a fast transform.

Discrete Sine Transform (DST): The sine transform pair for one-dimensional sequences is given as

$$q(k)=\sqrt{\frac{2}{N+1}}\sum_{n=0}^{N-1}p(n)\sin\frac{\pi(k+1)(n+1)}{N+1}\quad 0\le k\le N-1$$

$$p(n) = \sqrt{\frac{2}{N+1}} \sum_{k=0}^{N-1} q(k) \sin \frac{\pi(k+1)(n+1)}{N+1} \quad 0 \le n \le N-1$$

The $N \times N$ DST matrix is given by

$$\sqrt{\frac{2}{N+1}} \sin \frac{\pi(k+1)(n+1)}{N+1} \quad 0 \le k, n \le N-1$$

DST is a powerful mathematical tool used in ML and other areas of data science. It converts a signal or image into its frequency components, allowing for more efficient processing and analysis. In ML, DST is applied to data sets that are too large or complex to be processed quickly by traditional methods. Decomposing the data set into its frequency components allows for faster computation of patterns and correlations. This makes identifying clusters within the data possible, leading to better predictions or decisions from machine learning models. DST has also been applied successfully in image processing applications such as facial recognition and object detection algorithms.

Properties of DST

- Sine transform is real, symmetric and orthogonal.
- Sine transform is not the imaginary part of DFT.
- Sine transform is a fast transform.

4.12 Information Theory

Information theory is a branch of mathematics that deals with quantifying and manipulating information. It is primarily used to study communication systems and data compression. In recent years, information theory has also been applied to ML, where it can provide insights into learning algorithms and their performance. Claude Shannon first developed Information Theory in 1948 in his seminal paper "A Mathematical Theory of Communication." Shannon defined the fundamental concepts needed for a mathematical theory of information: entropy, mutual information, and channel capacity. These concepts were then used to study communication systems such as phone networks, radio broadcasting, and optical fiber cables.

In ML, applications of information theory are used to measure the complexity or uncertainty of a data set or task that an algorithm needs to learn from or solve, respectively; the more complex a task is thought to be, the higher its entropy value will be according to information theory metrics. In addition, ML researchers have been able to use these same metrics to evaluate performance on various problems as well as compare different learning algorithms based on their respective performances on those tasks at hand for both speed (training time) and accuracy (success rate).

Mutual information has been helpful for feature selection within data sets, meaning that rather than having all the features included within model input, engineers will select only relevant features, thus reducing noise in data while still preserving important relationships between variables.
The definitions of various terms related to information theory are given below:

Random variable: A real-valued function defined over a sample space of a random experiment is called a random variable. It can be either discrete or continuous. Random variables are a valuable tool in ML as they can quantify the uncertainty associated with predictions or results. For example, a random variable (like probability) can assign probabilities to different outcomes of a prediction algorithm. This allows the ML system to assign higher probabilities to more likely outcomes and lower probabilities to less likely ones. It also makes it easier for humans to interpret and make decisions based on the results of an algorithm. Random variables can also be used for decision-making in reinforcement learning algorithms. By applying a specific reward value or penalty value, the model can learn which action produces the highest expected return based on its understanding of random variables. This helps give better control over decisions by weighing pros and cons using values assigned by random variables rather than relying solely on intuition or pure trial-and-error methods. In addition, random variables provide insight into how different data sets interact when analyzing complex systems such as neural networks. They provide information about the correlations between input data points and their respective outputs from the ML models being trained with them. This further allows us to identify areas of improvement where we could tweak parameters to increase accuracy or efficiency when creating our models, which help in making better-informed decisions when developing ML algorithm.

- **Discrete random variable:** A random variable that takes a finite set of distinct values is called a discrete random variable. It is distinct in that it can only take whole numbers or specific values from a finite list, as opposed to continuous random variables, which can take any value within an interval. This means that the probability of a discrete random variable taking any value within its range must sum up to 1. For example, suppose you have an experiment where you roll two dice and count the total number of dots (dots being the possible values). The number of dots could be any whole number between 2 and 12, giving 11 possible outcomes (2–12). The probability for each outcome will vary depending on how many combinations are available for each number. For example, there are six different ways to obtain 7 by rolling two dice: (1 + 6), (2 + 5), (3 + 4), (4 + 3), (5 + 2), and (6 + 1). Therefore, the probability of rolling 7 equals 6/36, which is equal to 1/6. All in all, discrete random variables are useful for situations where we want to calculate probabilities about certain events with pre-defined outcomes, such as rolling dice or flipping coins.
- **Continuous random variable:** A random variable that takes infinite values defined over an interval is called a continuous random variable. It can take any value from an infinite set of numbers within a given interval. It is different from a discrete random variable, which has only limited possible values. Examples of continuous random variables include the temperature in degrees Celsius, the depth of water in oceans, and the diameter of a tree trunk. Continuous random variables are often used to describe probabilities related to physical phenomena such as time, space, or velocity. In addition, they are useful for modeling data that has smooth and gradual changes, such as stock prices or population growth. When dealing with continuous random variables, we typically use probability density functions (PDFs) instead of probability mass functions (PMFs). A PDF assigns probabilities to intervals rather than individual points on the number line and helps us determine the chance that a randomly chosen value falls within a certain range. To calculate probabilities related to continuous distributions, we can use integrals instead of sums since they are obtained by integrating over all possible values instead of simply summing up all possibilities, like discrete distributions do. Summation rules no longer apply when dealing with probability density functions since there is no fixed number of outcomes for them; this makes calculating probabilities much more difficult for this type of distribution

compared to discrete ones where we just have to add up all the possibilities associated with each outcome in order to obtain our desired result.

Probability distribution (PD): The possibility of each outcome of a random experiment or event can be measured by a probability distribution.

A random event E with a probability $P(E)$ contains $I(E) = \log \frac{1}{P(E)} = -\log P(E)$ units of information.

If $P(E) = 1$, then $I(E) = 0$, which indicates that no information is attributed to it, that is, there is no uncertainty associated with the event. PD is a critical concept in ML used to capture uncertainty and randomness. It allow us to estimate the likelihood of events happening or not happening and measure the strength of relationships between variables. PD can be instrumental in the decision-making processes, helping to determine which model architecture or hyperparameters will produce the best results. For example, when building models such as classification algorithms or neural networks, probability distributions can be used to select appropriate input features with the most predictive power and minimize overfitting. A PD can also help validate models by testing whether they are sensitive enough to changes in small amounts of data points. The prediction accuracy of a model is also influenced by prior knowledge about its expected performance, which can be obtained from studying probability distributions associated with different values for particular parameters like regularization coefficient lambdas and learning rates. Finally, probability distribution plays an important role when making predictions from models – it helps create estimates for what may happen in the future based on probabilities calculated from past data points rather than absolute values (such as Bayesian inference). This approach allows us to build more reliable prediction systems that are less prone to errors due to outliers or extreme cases where the output differs drastically from our expectations given a particular set of inputs.

Entropy: The entropy of a discrete random variable x with a probability distribution $p(x)$ is defined as

$$H_x = -\sum_{x \in \chi} p(x) \log_2 p(x)$$

Entropy gives a measure of the uncertainty of a random variable.

In information theory, entropy specifies the minimum number of bits needed to encode the class of an instance. In ML, entropy provides a measure of impurity in a collection of training data. Entropy is used to measure the amount of information contained in data. It can be used as an evaluation metric to assess the performance of a model and is also incorporated into many algorithms used for decision-making and optimization. The primary use of entropy in ML is related to decision trees. Decision trees are a type of algorithm that use hierarchical structures to classify data points. Entropy measures the uncertainty within each decision tree branch, allowing us to decide which branch requires further exploration and which should be discarded. This helps us evaluate how well our model performs against unseen data, making it an essential part of assessing the overall performance of a model.

Another common application of entropy in ML is feature selection or feature importance analysis. By calculating the entropy values for different features, we can better understand how much information they contain and determine which ones have more important contributions when predicting our target variables. When dealing with large data sets with many features, calculating entropies can help us reduce noise by selecting only relevant features that provide helpful information about our target variable. Finally, entropy plays an important role when it comes to optimization problems; this includes neural networks or other complex models built on data sets with multiple features that need some regularization methods (such as L1/L2) applied to them before being trained on unseen data points for better generalization performance and avoiding overfitting issues, thus ensuring better predictions. Entropy can help determine which weights should be assigned higher values to reduce computational complexity while still optimizing performance levels by choosing those weights with higher relevance (more predictive power).

For example, tossing a coin is a random event. The two possible outcomes are heads and tails with equal probability of 0.5. Entropy of this event is calculated as

$$H_x = -\sum_{x \in \chi} p(x) \log_2 p(x) = -\sum_{i=1}^{2} 0.5 * \log_2 (0.5)$$

$$= -\left(0.5 * (-1) + 0.5 * (-1)\right) = 1$$

Uniform probability of the outcomes of the event yields maximum uncertainty, and hence entropy is maximum.

Information gain: The expected reduction in entropy caused by partitioning the samples according to a particular attribute is called information gain. It is one of the most critical concepts in ML. It helps machines make decisions by evaluating the quality of data and providing insight into the amount of information held within a given set of data. In ML, information gain determines which attributes are most useful or relevant in making accurate predictions. This allows us to identify and focus on features that will impact our results most when making predictions. In essence, information gain measures how better off we are when a particular attribute (or split) is used versus not using it. For example, if splitting a data set based on an attribute would cause two different subsets to be created with distinct distributions for each subset (if there was an informational relationship between that attribute and class membership), this would be considered information gain because it would provide more information than what we had before splitting the data set. This would allow us to better learn from our data and make more accurate predictions down the line. To measure this information gain, metrics like entropy can be used, which calculate how much randomness or disorder there is within a given set of data. This enables us to quantify whether or not there is any real benefit in terms of increased accuracy when using different attributes or splits during the training phase of ML algorithms such as decision tree induction methods. For example, suppose a particular split/attribute provides no real benefit compared to another. In that case, it will have low information gain as opposed to one that does provide a benefit which might result in higher gains.

Let S be the set of training samples having many attributes represented by $A = \{A_1, A_2, \cdots, A_n\}$.

$$\text{Information Gain}(S, A_i) = \text{Entropy}(S) - \sum_{v \in \text{values of } A_i} \frac{|S_v|}{|S|} \text{Entropy}(S_v)$$

The second term represents the expected entropy after S is partitioned using attribute A_i.

4.13 MANIFOLDS

Machine learning deals with data pertaining to higher dimensions. Visualization of data in higher dimensions is difficult to plot. In order to plot the data for better understanding and visualization, the dimensions of the data should be reduced. There are many methods available for dimensionality reduction.

A manifold is a mathematical structure that describes a curved space. It is the generalization of ideas used in Euclidean geometry to describe objects moving in an environment with variable curvature. A manifold can be thought of as an abstract mathematical object that smoothly connects multiple points. To understand this better, think of it like a sheet of paper; if you bend one corner, the whole sheet will become curved, yet all the points on it are still somehow connected. This happens when we model our world using manifolds – even though space may be curving around us, we can still use mathematics to make sense of it by connecting all its points. Manifolds also allow us to describe how different shapes interact with each other and how they change over time and distance. In short, manifolds provide us with a powerful tool for understanding our universe from both a practical and theoretical perspective!

The process of modeling the manifold is called **manifold learning**. **Locally linear embedding (LLE)** is a manifold learning technique used for non-linear dimensionality reduction. LLE produces low-dimensional embedding of higher dimensional data by relating training instances to their close neighbors. LLE is a non-linear dimensionality reduction technique used to reduce data dimensions while preserving its original structure and information. This can be beneficial in cases where data has high dimensionality, which makes it challenging to visualize or analyze. The goal of the LLE technique is to find lower dimensional representations of the original data that are locally similar while preserving global structure. Local similarity means that similar points in the data set remain close together after performing dimensionality reduction. This can be achieved by having each point represented by its *K*-nearest neighbors, as these points are likely to be locally similar. To preserve the global structure and identify essential features, distances between faraway points cannot be ignored in this process.

To reduce the dimensions of a data set using LLE, first, each data point must find its *K*-nearest neighbors and form an n-dimensional vector with those data points (where n is equal to the number of samples). Next, it will calculate weights for each neighbor so that all n vectors are aligned with one another mostly along their local directions but still maintain distant correlations from one another; this is done by minimizing an objective function called **reconstruction error** which measures how well every point can be reconstructed from its neighbors using this weight matrix built up from *K*-nearest neighbors selection step. Finally, after weights have been found for each sample's corresponding neighbor, these weighted samples are projected onto a lower dimensional space using singular value decomposition (SVD) or other techniques such as PCA.

SVD is a powerful and versatile method used in many fields of mathematics, computer science, and engineering. SVD is an algorithm used to decompose a matrix into its constituent parts. It is also known as the matrix factorization process. This decomposition breaks down the original matrix into three smaller matrices: two unitary matrices and one diagonal matrix containing the singular values. The SVD algorithm has been used in various applications including image compression, signal processing, facial recognition systems and text mining. In image processing, for example, it can be used to reduce the size of a picture by discarding some of its information that is considered redundant or not useful for further analysis or display purposes. In terms of text mining applications, SVD may be used to analyze documents by capturing their semantic content through term-document matrices (TDMs). By combining words from different documents within these TDMs, we can properly analyze these documents' content by identifying topics discussed within them and whether or not those topics are well represented across all document samples; this allows us to group similar documents together based on their content or subject matter with greater accuracy than without using any form of clustering/grouping algorithm like KNN/*K*-means clustering methodology.

SVD can also be applied in reducing noise from audio signals as well as making data more compressible for storage purposes through reduction in dimensionality; this helps improve both memory efficiency as well as speed up computation times. The result will contain all the global information in the original sizeable dimensional space and also provide us with compressed representation reduced down into lower dimensional space without losing any essential local/global structures while being computationally efficient.

SUMMARY

- A set is a well-defined collection of objects, with finite sets used for classification, clustering, and regression. Empty sets, denoted by ∅, represent missing or irrelevant data points. Infinite sets, containing an infinite number of elements, are used in machine learning for large data sets or continuous data. The Cartesian product of sets is used in data analysis to identify relationships between variables. Relations, subsets of the Cartesian product, express relationships between elements and are used to make predictions using supervised learning algorithms like decision trees, SVM, and neural networks.
- Functions allow machines to make accurate predictions based on changing inputs, especially in complex tasks like stock price prediction or image recognition problems. Convex functions, such as strictly convex functions and convex combinations, minimize the total cost associated with performing tasks. Convex combination methods combine multiple models, reducing complexity and improving accuracy. The convex hull concept describes the shape of an object in terms of boundary lines, with vertices forming the convex hull.
- Gradient vectors are mathematical tools used in machine learning to calculate the direction and magnitude of change for variables. They are used in optimization algorithms like gradient descent to find the optimum value for specific parameters within a given function. The Hessian matrix is a matrix of a given function's second-order partial derivatives, helping to identify local maxima or minima. Optimization can be classified into three categories: linear and non-linear, constrained and unconstrained, and discrete, continuous, and probabilistic.
- Local and globally optimal points are considered locally and globally optimal. Constrained optimization helps find the best solution while accounting for specific constraints. Dual optimization optimizes two objectives simultaneously. The weak duality theorem states that any feasible solution to the dual problem is greater than any feasible solution to the primal problem. The strong duality theorem provides mathematical proof for optimizing algorithms.
- Dynamic programming solves problems by combining solutions to sub-problems. Sublinear algorithms solve problems by reading a minute scale of input and processing it in a sublinear

time. Complete graphs help identify difficult-to-detect patterns in data. Subgraphs help identify patterns and relationships in data. Fourier transforms decompose functions into sine and cosine functions, allowing for efficient data analysis. Information Theory, a branch of mathematics, has been applied to machine learning to provide insights into learning algorithms and performance.

EXERCISES

Part A (Objective Questions)

1. In machine learning, finite sets are commonly used for which of the following purposes?
   a) Classification b) Regression
   c) Clustering d) All of the above
2. An empty set is used in machine learning to represent which type of data points?
   a) Missing values b) Outliers
   c) Irrelevant data d) All of the above
3. Which type of set is commonly used in machine learning to deal with large data sets or continuous data?
   a) Finite set b) Infinite set
   c) Empty set d) Singleton set
4. When using finite sets for regression analysis, what are models aiming to predict?
   a) Categories or labels b) Similar data groups
   c) Outliers or anomalies d) Outcome based on input variables
5. Which mathematical concept is used to represent an empty set?
   a) Finite set b) Infinite set
   c) Singleton set d) None of the above
6. In machine learning, which algorithm can benefit from utilizing an empty set as an initial guess for data set grouping?
   a) Classification algorithms b) Regression algorithms
   c) Clustering algorithms d) Anomaly detection algorithms
7. Which type of set is a collection of elements with a finite number countable in machine learning?
   a) Empty set b) Finite set
   c) Infinite set d) Singleton set
8. How do infinite sets simplify the processing of large data sets in machine learning?
   a) They represent data sets as a single entity.
   b) They reduce the complexity of algorithms.
   c) They generalize patterns across different data sources.
   d) All of the above
9. Which type of set is used in recurrent neural networks (RNNs) to reflect the relationship between hidden states and input/output layers?
   a) Finite set b) Infinite set
   c) Empty set d) Singleton set

10. When using finite sets for clustering analysis, what is the goal of grouping similar data based on their characteristics?
    a) Regression
    b) Anomaly detection
    c) Pattern recognition
    d) All of the above
11. Which mathematical concept is used to represent a set that contains an infinite number of elements?
    a) Finite set
    b) Infinite set
    c) Empty set
    d) Singleton set
12. In CNNs, what operation is performed by convolving the input image matrix with the weights of convolutional filters?
    a) Classification
    b) Pooling
    c) Feature extraction
    d) Error minimization
13. What is the purpose of using an empty set in *K*-means clustering algorithms?
    a) Initializing the cluster centroids
    b) Handling missing values in the data set
    c) Identifying outliers within the data
    d) Allowing for parallel processing
14. Which type of set is commonly used in machine learning to represent missing, unknown, or irrelevant data points?
    a) Finite set
    b) Infinite set
    c) Empty set
    d) Singleton set
15. What mathematical concept is used to update the weights in the backpropagation algorithm?
    a) Linear algebra
    b) Vector calculus
    c) Set theory
    d) Matrix multiplication
16. How do finite sets contribute to the regression analysis in machine learning?
    a) By separating data into different categories or labels
    b) By grouping similar data based on characteristics
    c) By predicting outcomes based on input variables
    d) By identifying outliers within large data sets
17. In which type of neural network are matrix multiplications used to reflect the relationship between hidden states and input/output layers?
    a) Convolutional Neural Networks (CNNs)
    b) Recurrent Neural Networks (RNNs)
    c) Deep Neural Networks (DNNs)
    d) Generative Adversarial Networks (GANs)
18. Which type of set is used in machine learning to represent continuous data such as images or text?
    a) Finite set
    b) Infinite set
    c) Empty set
    d) Singleton set
19. How do finite sets contribute to the classification process in machine learning?
    a) By separating data into different categories or labels
    b) By grouping similar data based on characteristics
    c) By predicting outcomes based on input variables
    d) By identifying outliers within large data sets

20. Which mathematician developed the theory of sets?
a) Georg Cantor
b) Isaac Newton
c) Albert Einstein
d) Alan Turing

21. Which type of set is denoted using the symbol ∅ and represents a collection of elements with no members?
a) Finite set
b) Infinite set
c) Empty set
d) Singleton set

22. In machine learning, what can an empty set indicate when dealing with data sets containing missing values?
a) Irrelevant data points
b) Outliers within large data sets
c) Missing or unknown data points
d) Complex relationships between data points

23. How can an empty set be used in *K*-means clustering algorithms?
a) To identify outliers within large data sets
b) To group similar data based on characteristics
c) To initialize cluster assignments before training
d) To simplify the representation of continuous data

24. Which type of set is used in machine learning when dealing with large data sets or continuous data?
a) Finite set
b) Infinite set
c) Empty set
d) Singleton set

25. In machine learning, what does the domain of a relation represent?
a) The input data for a model
b) The set of possible outputs for a given input
c) The correlation between variables
d) The range of values that y can take based on x

26. What does the range of a relation represent in machine learning?
a) The input data for a model
b) The set of possible outputs for a given input
c) The correlation between variables
d) The range of values that y can take based on x

27. How is the codomain of a relation used in machine learning?
a) To represent the input data for a model
b) To specify the correlation between variables
c) To determine the range of values for the output variable
d) To map input data onto the output space of a function

28. Which type of machine learning algorithms can utilize relations to make predictions?
a) Decision trees and support vector machines
b) Neural networks and regression analysis
c) Clustering techniques and decision trees
d) Support vector machines and clustering techniques

29. What does the domain of a relation provide in supervised learning?
a) A set of values for clustering analysis
b) Training data for models
c) Input–output relationships
d) Correlations between variables

30. What is the primary purpose of using a domain in machine learning?
a) To establish correlations between variables
b) To generalize knowledge from existing training data
c) To handle missing values in data sets
d) To reduce complexity in models

31. Which type of machine learning algorithms can utilize relations to make predictions?
    a) Unsupervised learning algorithms
    b) Reinforcement learning algorithms
    c) Supervised learning algorithms
    d) Semi-supervised learning algorithms
32. How does the domain of a relation contribute to training data in machine learning?
    a) It provides attribute values for clustering analysis
    b) It represents the correlation between input and output variables
    c) It helps create accurate predictive models
    d) It reduces complexity in machine learning models
33. What is the purpose of using a domain in machine learning models?
    a) To handle missing values in data sets
    b) To identify correlations between input variables
    c) To restrict potential inputs within specific ranges
    d) To generalize knowledge from existing training data
34. Which type of relationship can be analyzed using relations in machine learning?
    a) Relationship between age and gender
    b) Relationship between input and output variables
    c) Relationship between salary and job title
    d) Relationship between discrete and continuous values
35. What can be inferred about the range and codomain of a relation?
    a) Range $\subseteq$ Codomain
    b) Range $\subset$ Codomain
    c) Range = Codomain
    d) Range $\cap$ Codomain = Ø
36. How can relations be used to improve predictive models in machine learning?
    a) By clustering input variables into groups
    b) By analyzing correlations between variables
    c) By increasing the complexity of machine learning algorithms
    d) By excluding certain input variables from the model
37. Why are convex sets and functions important in machine learning optimization?
    a) They guarantee global optima for any optimization problem.
    b) They increase the complexity of machine learning models.
    c) They allow for multiple local optima in the solution space.
    d) They improve the interpretability of machine learning algorithms.
38. What advantage does convex optimization offer over gradient descent in machine learning?
    a) Convex optimization provides a global solution.
    b) Convex optimization works better for non-convex functions.
    c) Gradient descent is faster than convex optimization.
    d) Gradient descent guarantees a global minimum.
39. How do convex sets contribute to efficient function optimization in machine learning?
    a) Convex sets provide bounds for the input variables.
    b) Convex sets allow for multiple global minima.
    c) Convex sets increase the complexity of optimization algorithms.
    d) Convex sets restrict the feasible solution space.
40. What property does a convex function have compared to a non-convex function?
    a) Convex functions have only one global minimum.

b) Convex functions have multiple local minima.
c) Non-convex functions guarantee a global minimum.
d) Non-convex functions are faster to optimize.

41. Why are strictly convex functions preferred in machine learning optimization?
a) Strictly convex functions are faster to compute.
b) Strictly convex functions allow for multiple local minima.
c) Strictly convex functions guarantee a global minimum.
d) Strictly convex functions handle non-linear data better.

42. How do convex sets and functions contribute to accuracy improvement in machine learning?
a) They improve the interpretability of machine learning models.
b) They handle outliers in the data set effectively.
c) They guarantee global optima for optimization problems.
d) They increase the complexity of machine learning algorithms.

43. Which machine learning algorithms can benefit from using strictly convex functions?
a) Linear regression and decision trees
b) Support Vector Machines (SVMs) and Neural Networks
c) Clustering algorithms and k-nearest neighbors
d) Reinforcement learning and unsupervised learning

44. What advantage does convex optimization offer in terms of stability and adaptability in machine learning?
a) Convex optimization guarantees a global solution regardless of parameter changes.
b) Convex optimization reduces computational time for training models.
c) Convex optimization handles outliers effectively during optimization.
d) Convex optimization provides a wider range of possible solutions.

45. How does a concave cost curve indicate the performance of a machine learning model?
a) A shallow convex curve indicates better performance.
b) A deep concave curve indicates overfitting.
c) A shallow concave curve indicates overfitting.
d) A deep convex curve indicates better performance.

46. In supervised learning, how can concave functions help optimize a model?
a) By detecting local minima or maxima more easily.
b) By increasing the complexity of the model.
c) By guaranteeing a global minimum.
d) By reducing the training time.

47. Which type of machine learning models can benefit from minimizing costs using concave functions?
a) Regression and decision trees.
b) Clustering and principal component analysis (PCA).
c) Reinforcement learning and unsupervised learning.
d) Support Vector Machines (SVMs) and Neural Networks.

48. What property does a strictly concave function have compared to a concave function?
a) Strictly concave functions have multiple local minima.
b) Strictly concave functions guarantee a global minimum.

c) Concave functions have a steeper curve than strictly concave functions.
d) Concave functions have a wider range of possible solutions.

49. How does using strictly concave functions benefit the training process of neural networks?
a) It increases the complexity of the training process.
b) It guarantees a global minimum for the neural network.
c) It reduces the training time for neural networks.
d) It improves the interpretability of the neural network.

50. How do strictly concave functions contribute to the accuracy improvement of machine learning models?
a) They handle outliers more effectively during optimization.
b) They guarantee a global minimum for the cost function.
c) They allow for multiple local minima in the solution space.
d) They increase the complexity of the machine learning algorithms.

51. Which type of cost curve indicates better performance for a machine learning model?
a) A shallow convex curve. b) A deep convex curve.
c) A shallow concave curve. d) A deep concave curve.

52. How does a concave cost function help in the optimization of unsupervised learning models?
a) It improves the interpretability of the unsupervised learning model.
b) It reduces the computational time for unsupervised learning.
c) It aids in identifying regions with lower values more easily.
d) It guarantees a global minimum for the unsupervised learning model.

53. What is the purpose of using convex combinations in machine learning?
a) To increase the complexity of the model.
b) To reduce the accuracy of the model.
c) To combine multiple models and improve accuracy.
d) To remove the need for model training.

54. How does the concept of convex hulls contribute to fraud detection in machine learning?
a) Convex hulls detect patterns and clusters in data sets.
b) Convex hulls can quickly group similar data points into categories.
c) Convex hulls can identify areas with concentrated clusters of data points.
d) Convex hulls enable machines to understand complex shapes and patterns in data.

55. What is the main purpose of the convex combination method in machine learning?
a) To increase the complexity of the model.
b) To reduce the accuracy of the model.
c) To combine information from multiple models and improve accuracy.
d) To speed up the training process of machine learning models.

56. In machine learning, how does the convex hull technique help with classification of new data sets?
a) It identifies areas with concentrated clusters of data points.
b) It groups similar data points into categories quickly and easily.
c) It helps detect fraudulent activity in data sets.
d) It enables machines to understand complex shapes and patterns in data.

57. What is the relationship between convex combinations and accuracy in machine learning?
a) Convex combinations reduce accuracy due to model complexity.
b) Convex combinations improve accuracy by combining multiple models.
c) Convex combinations have no impact on accuracy.
d) Convex combinations only improve accuracy in regression models.

58. How do convex hulls contribute to pattern and cluster detection in machine learning?
a) They help identify fraudulent activity within clusters.
b) They enable machines to understand complex shapes and patterns.
c) They group similar data points into categories efficiently.
d) They highlight areas with more concentrated clusters of data points.

59. What advantage does the convex combination method provide when making changes to machine learning models?
a) It reduces the need to rebuild the entire model from scratch.
b) It increases the complexity of the model with each change.
c) It guarantees a higher accuracy for the modified model.
d) It eliminates the need for weight adjustments during optimization.

60. How can the concept of convex hulls be applied to improve accuracy in clustering algorithms?
a) By reducing the complexity of the clustering model.
b) By grouping similar data points into distinct clusters.
c) By eliminating the need for iterative optimization.
d) By generating random clusters within the data set.

61. What is the main purpose of using gradient vectors in machine learning?
a) To calculate the direction and magnitude of change for variables.
b) To represent the contours of a function.
c) To optimize the cost function and minimize errors.
d) To perform backpropagation in neural networks.

62. In machine learning, which optimization algorithm utilizes gradient vectors?
a) Backpropagation.
b) Gradient descent.
c) Orthogonal regression.
d) Principal component analysis (PCA).

63. Which direction does a gradient vector point in relation to a function?
a) The direction of greatest increase of the function.
b) The direction of greatest decrease of the function.
c) Perpendicular to the function contours.
d) Parallel to the function contours.

64. What property holds true for the dot product of a vector orthogonal to a gradient vector?
a) It equals the magnitude of the gradient vector.
b) It equals zero.
c) It is parallel to the gradient vector.
d) It is perpendicular to the gradient vector.

65. Which algorithm uses backpropagation and gradient vectors to reduce errors during training?
a) *K*-means clustering.
b) Principal component analysis (PCA).
c) Support vector machines (SVM).
d) Artificial neural networks (ANNs).

66. What does gradient descent aim to find in machine learning?

a) The maximum value of the cost function.
b) The minimum value of the cost function.
c) The average value of the cost function.
d) The derivative of the cost function.

67. How does gradient descent contribute to training complex models like artificial neural networks?
a) It enables manual testing of thousands of parameter combinations.
b) It automates the process of adjusting model complexity.
c) It calculates derivatives using backpropagation and gradient vectors.
d) It simplifies the architecture of the neural network.

68. What information does the gradient vector provide in relation to a function's contours?
a) It represents the shape of the function's boundaries.
b) It indicates the areas of highest complexity in the function.
c) It identifies the regions of local minima and maxima.
d) It determines the average value of the function.

69. What is the main goal of optimization problems in machine learning?
a) To maximize the performance of a given model.
b) To minimize the complexity of the model.
c) To find the best set of parameters for a problem.
d) To determine the accuracy of the model.

70. How are optimization problems typically defined in machine learning?
a) As a search for the average value of a function.
b) As a maximization of an objective function.
c) As a minimization of an objective function.
d) As a maximization of the complexity of a model.

71. What role do optimization problems play in supervised learning?
a) Determining the number of layers in a neural network.
b) Calculating the accuracy of the model on unseen data.
c) Selecting the best set of hyperparameters for the model.
d) Identifying data patterns without labeled information.

72. Which type of error metric is commonly minimized in supervised learning optimization problems?
a) Mean squared error.
b) Log loss.
c) F1 score.
d) Precision.

73. What is the purpose of optimization in unsupervised learning?
a) To classify data into different categories.
b) To maximize the number of labeled data points.
c) To identify patterns and clusters in the data.
d) To calculate the precision and recall of the model.

74. How do optimization problems contribute to hyperparameter tuning in neural networks?
a) By reducing the complexity of the neural network model.
b) By automating the process of selecting hyperparameters.
c) By calculating the accuracy of the model on validation data.
d) By maximizing the number of hidden layers in the network.

75. What is the primary benefit of solving optimization problems in machine learning?
a) Maximizing the complexity of the model.
b) Minimizing the computational resources required.
c) Finding the global minimum of the objective function.
d) Achieving the best possible solution for a given problem.

76. Which of the following best describes the relationship between optimization problems and model reliability?
a) Optimization problems have no impact on model reliability.
b) Optimization problems can improve model reliability.
c) Optimization problems are only relevant for complex models.
d) Optimization problems decrease model reliability.

77. When is linear optimization commonly used in machine learning?
a) When dealing with highly complex problems.
b) When solving non-linear mapping functions.
c) When finding optimal solutions to linear problems.
d) When training neural networks.

78. In which types of machine learning models can linear optimization be applied?
a) Only in supervised learning models.
b) Only in unsupervised learning models.
c) In both supervised and unsupervised learning models.
d) Only in deep learning architectures.

79. What is the primary difference between linear and non-linear optimization?
a) Linear optimization requires an exact mathematical formula, while non-linear optimization does not.
b) Linear optimization is used for fine-tuning hyperparameters, while non-linear optimization is used for optimizing weights in neural networks.
c) Linear optimization solves complex problems, while non-linear optimization solves linear problems.
d) Linear optimization can handle interactions between multiple variables, while non-linear optimization cannot.

80. Which type of optimization is commonly used when training neural networks?
a) Linear optimization.
b) Non-linear optimization.
c) Both linear and non-linear optimization.
d) None of the above.

81. How does linear optimization contribute to unsupervised learning models?
a) By optimizing hyperparameters.
b) By identifying clusters and trends in data.
c) By fine-tuning weights in neural networks.
d) By minimizing cost functions.

82. What is the main purpose of non-linear optimization in machine learning?
a) To minimize complexity in machine learning models.
b) To maximize profits in linear problems.
c) To handle interactions between multiple variables.
d) To fine-tune hyperparameters in deep learning architectures.

83. What is the primary advantage of using non-linear optimization in machine learning?
a) It can provide accurate results for linear problems.
b) It can handle interactions between multiple variables.
c) It simplifies the optimization process in deep learning.
d) It is more computationally efficient than linear optimization.

84. What role does linear optimization play in supervised learning models?
a) It fine-tunes hyperparameters.
b) It optimizes weights in neural networks.
c) It minimizes error metrics.
d) It identifies clusters in data.

85. Which type of optimization allows for imposing restrictions or constraints on the parameters of a machine learning model?
a) Constrained optimization.
b) Unconstrained optimization.
c) Both constrained and unconstrained optimization.
d) Neither constrained nor unconstrained optimization.

86. In which type of machine learning applications is unconstrained optimization commonly used?
a) Regression and classification problems.
b) Supervised learning algorithms.
c) Deep learning techniques.
d) All of the above.

87. What is the primary goal of constrained optimization?
a) To achieve higher accuracy results in less time.
b) To impose restrictions on objective functions.
c) To remove constraints for flexible modeling.
d) To find an optimal solution within specific boundaries.

88. How does unconstrained optimization differ from constrained optimization?
a) Unconstrained optimization allows for imposing restrictions, while constrained optimization does not.
b) Unconstrained optimization requires fewer iterations/steps than constrained optimization.
c) Unconstrained optimization is used in supervised learning, while constrained optimization is used in unsupervised learning.
d) Unconstrained optimization finds optimal solutions without imposing constraints, while constrained optimization considers specific boundaries or restrictions.

89. In which type of machine learning problems can constrained optimization be particularly useful?
a) Problems where all parameters are unknown.
b) Problems involving clustering algorithms.
c) Problems requiring feature selection.
d) Problems with large search spaces.

90. How can constrained optimization reduce computational cost in machine learning?
a) By simplifying the optimization process.
b) By minimizing the number of iterations/steps.
c) By removing restrictions on the objective function.
d) By imposing linear constraints on the parameters.

91. What advantage does unconstrained optimization provide in machine learning?
a) It allows for imposing restrictions on the parameters.
b) It improves model flexibility without sacrificing accuracy.

c) It simplifies the optimization process for deep learning architectures.
d) It reduces computational cost compared to constrained optimization.

92. Which optimization technique is commonly used in decision trees and support vector machines (SVMs)?
a) Constrained optimization.
b) Unconstrained optimization.
c) Both constrained and unconstrained optimization.
d) Neither constrained nor unconstrained optimization.

93. Discrete optimization is particularly useful when dealing with which type of data?
a) Continuous data.
b) Categorical data.
c) Probabilistic data.
d) None of the above.

94. Which optimization technique takes derivatives into account and helps identify global minima?
a) Discrete optimization.
b) Continuous optimization.
c) Probabilistic optimization.
d) None of the above.

95. Which optimization method is suitable for dealing with uncertainty in data sets, such as those from natural language processing (NLP) tasks?
a) Discrete optimization.
b) Continuous optimization.
c) Probabilistic optimization.
d) None of the above.

96. Which optimization technique is commonly used in decision trees and *K*-means clustering?
a) Discrete optimization.
b) Continuous optimization.
c) Probabilistic optimization.
d) None of the above.

97. What type of optimization considers continuous variables and takes derivatives into account?
a) Discrete optimization.
b) Continuous optimization.
c) Probabilistic optimization.
d) None of the above.

98. Which optimization method approximates functions using probability distributions instead of set values?
a) Discrete optimization.
b) Continuous optimization.
c) Probabilistic optimization.
d) None of the above.

99. What type of optimization helps understand the impact of each variable in relation to the overall outcome in machine learning algorithms?
a) Discrete optimization.
b) Continuous optimization.
c) Probabilistic optimization.
d) None of the above.

100. Which optimization technique involves approximating functions using probability distributions, derivatives, and categorical decisions?
a) Discrete optimization.
b) Continuous optimization.
c) Probabilistic optimization.
d) None of the above.

101. A feasible point is called locally optimal if there are no other feasible points in its neighborhood with a __________ objective value.
a) Higher
b) Lower
c) Equal
d) None of the above

102. Which type of optima is the best solution that could be achieved anywhere?
a) Local optima
b) Global optima
c) Intermediate optima
d) None of the above

103. Local optima in machine learning can be compared to narrow valleys or hills because they:
 a) Have the highest objective value in the entire data set
 b) Represent the most common solution in the data set
 c) Are the best solution within a particular region
 d) None of the above

104. If an optimization problem is convex, what can be said about the relationship between local and global optima?
 a) Local optima are always better than global optima.
 b) Local optima are always worse than global optima.
 c) Local optima and global optima are the same.
 d) None of the above.

105. What makes it challenging to improve a solution when stuck in a local optimum?
 a) The complexity of the data set
 b) The flatness and closeness of neighboring solutions
 c) Lack of computing power
 d) None of the above

106. Which type of optima allows for easier identification of improvement areas and steps towards them without getting stuck?
 a) Local optima b) Global optima
 c) Intermediate optima d) None of the above

107. Which optimization techniques are commonly used to search for both local and global optima in machine learning?
 a) Gradient descent and simulated annealing
 b) Decision trees and random forests
 c) Principal component analysis (PCA) and clustering
 d) None of the above

108. Local and global optima are concepts used in machine learning to determine the ________ solution to a problem.
 a) Median b) Optimal
 c) Average d) None of the above

109. What is one of the requirements for a convex optimization problem?
 a) Linear objective function b) Convex inequality constraints
 c) Non-linear equality constraints d) None of the above

110. What type of functions should the equality constraints be in a convex optimization problem?
 a) Convex functions b) Concave functions
 c) Affine functions d) None of the above

111. Why should the inequality constraints in a convex optimization problem be less than or equal to zero?
 a) It ensures a convex feasible set
 b) It simplifies the optimization process
 c) It allows for greater flexibility in the solutions
 d) None of the above

112. What happens if the inequality constraints in a convex optimization problem are greater than or equal to zero?

a) The optimization problem becomes infeasible
b) The optimization problem becomes non-convex
c) The optimization problem becomes linear
d) None of the above

113. Why is convex optimization preferred over general optimization?
a) It guarantees a global optimum
b) It is faster to solve
c) It has fewer constraints
d) None of the above

114. Which type of programming is a special case of convex optimization?
a) Linear programming (LP)
b) Non-linear programming (NLP)
c) Genetic programming (GP)
d) None of the above

115. What is the feasible set of a convex optimization problem?
a) A set of all feasible solutions
b) A convex set defined by the domain of the objective function and constraints
c) A set of randomly generated solutions
d) None of the above

116. What property holds for a locally optimal point in convex optimization?
a) It is globally optimal
b) It is a unique solution
c) It is an infeasible solution
d) None of the above

117. What is an unconstrained problem in optimization?
a) A problem without any constraints on the input
b) A problem with unlimited variables
c) A problem that cannot be solved
d) None of the above

118. How does unconstrained optimization benefit machine learning?
a) It helps in feature selection
b) It improves accuracy of models
c) It reduces training time
d) None of the above

119. What is the goal of unconstrained optimization in machine learning?
a) To maximize the cost function
b) To minimize the error rate
c) To find all possible solutions
d) None of the above

120. Which optimization algorithm is commonly used for unconstrained optimization in machine learning?
a) Gradient descent
b) Simulated annealing
c) Genetic algorithm
d) None of the above

121. How does unconstrained optimization contribute to creating better machine learning models?
a) It reduces the number of training data samples required
b) It improves memory consumption during training
c) It helps find optimal parameters for minimizing error
d) None of the above

122. What is the role of unconstrained optimization in training machine learning models?
a) It finds global minima for the cost function
b) It helps in data preprocessing and feature engineering
c) It optimizes the model's architecture
d) None of the above

123. Why is unconstrained optimization important for resource consumption in machine learning?
a) It reduces the computational complexity of models
b) It minimizes the memory usage during training
c) It speeds up the training process
d) It allows us to remove these constraints to make our model more flexible while retaining accuracy

124. What is the purpose of Newton's Method in unconstrained optimization?
a) To find the global maximum of a function
b) To approximate the derivative of a function
c) To iteratively find the minimum of a function
d) None of the above

125. When is Newton's Method particularly useful in optimization problems?
a) When the objective function is linear
b) When the objective function is convex
c) When the objective function is non-linear
d) None of the above

126. What information does Newton's Method use to find a local minimum?
a) First-order derivatives b) Second-order derivatives
c) Both first- and second-order derivatives d) None of the above

127. How does Newton's Method differ from gradient descent in optimization?
a) Newton's Method takes smaller steps
b) Newton's Method uses second-order derivatives
c) Newton's Method converges faster
d) None of the above

128. What is the main advantage of Newton's Method over gradient descent?
a) It works well with large and complex data sets
b) It guarantees convergence to the global minimum
c) It requires fewer iterations to reach a solution
d) None of the above

129. What is the convergence criterion for Newton's Method?
a) The difference between consecutive estimates becomes zero
b) The objective function reaches the global minimum
c) The number of iterations exceeds a predefined limit
d) None of the above

130. In Newton's Method, what is the update equation for obtaining the next point?
a) $x\_(k+1) = x\_k - f(x\_k)$ b) $x\_(k+1) = x\_k - f'(x\_k)$
c) $x\_(k+1) = x\_k - f(x\_k)/f'(x\_k)$ d) None of the above

131. Which type of optimization problem is Newton's Method commonly used for in machine learning?
a) Constrained optimization b) Unconstrained optimization
c) Convex optimization d) None of the above

132. Which optimization algorithm is used to update the parameters of a model based on an error/loss function in machine learning?

a) Newton's Method
b) Gradient Descent
c) Both Newton's Method and Gradient Descent
d) None of the above

133. Which optimization algorithm can be applied to any function regardless of its nature in machine learning?
a) Newton's Method
b) Gradient Descent
c) Both Newton's Method and Gradient Descent
d) None of the above

134. What is the main difference between Newton's Method and Gradient Descent?
a) Newton's Method updates parameters based on the error/loss function, while Gradient Descent takes significant steps towards finding a local minimum.
b) Newton's Method is used for linear functions, while Gradient Descent is used for non-linear functions.
c) Newton's Method uses first- and second-order derivatives, while Gradient Descent uses only first-order derivatives.
d) None of the above

135. Which optimization algorithm is particularly useful for functions that are differentiable and convex?
a) Newton's Method
b) Gradient Descent
c) Both Newton's Method and Gradient Descent
d) None of the above

136. Which optimization algorithm iteratively improves the model's parameters to reduce the value of the loss function?
a) Newton's Method
b) Gradient Descent
c) Both Newton's Method and Gradient Descent
d) None of the above

137. What is the primary criterion for stopping the iterations in Gradient Descent?
a) The difference between consecutive parameter updates becomes zero.
b) The error/loss function reaches the global minimum.
c) The number of iterations exceeds a predefined limit.
d) None of the above

138. Which algorithm can handle large and complex data sets more efficiently in machine learning?
a) Newton's Method
b) Gradient Descent
c) Both Newton's Method and Gradient Descent
d) None of the above

139. How does Gradient Descent ensure faster training times while making accurate predictions?
a) By taking larger steps towards the global minimum.
b) By using second-order derivatives in the optimization process.

c) By iteratively improving model parameters based on the error/loss function.
d) None of the above

140. Constrained optimization is important in machine learning because it:
a) Helps avoid overfitting and underfitting
b) Ensures fairness in automated decision-making
c) Allows solving complex problems with multiple objectives
d) All of the above

141. Which type of constraint helps prevent models from making biased decisions based on characteristics like age or gender?
a) Regularization constraints
b) Fairness constraints
c) Accuracy constraints
d) None of the above

142. How does constrained optimization contribute to the interpretability of machine learning models?
a) By improving stability and accuracy
b) By introducing penalty terms into the objective function
c) By adding constraints related to feature relevance
d) None of the above

143. Which type of optimization problem involves simultaneously considering multiple objectives?
a) Unconstrained optimization
b) Convex optimization
c) Constrained optimization
d) None of the above

144. What role do Lagrangian multipliers play in machine learning optimization?
a) They introduce penalty terms for regularization
b) They help shape the outcome of a function
c) They enforce constraints on model parameters
d) None of the above

145. Which type of optimization problem is addressed by using Lagrangian multipliers in machine learning?
a) Unconstrained optimization
b) Convex optimization
c) Constrained optimization
d) None of the above

146. What purpose does regularization serve in machine learning?
a) To improve accuracy on training data
b) To reduce overfitting and improve generalization
c) To enforce fairness constraints
d) None of the above

147. How can Lagrangian multipliers help prevent overfitting in machine learning?
a) By introducing penalty terms for regularization
b) By adjusting the learning rate during training
c) By enforcing fairness constraints on the model
d) None of the above

148. Dual optimization is used in machine learning when:
a) Competing goals are present in the same optimization problem
b) Multiple objectives need to be optimized simultaneously
c) Trade-offs between different goals need to be made
d) All of the above

149. In dual optimization, which objective is optimized first?
a) Primary objective
b) Secondary objective
c) Both objectives are optimized simultaneously
d) None of the above

150. How does dual optimization handle trade-offs between competing objectives?
a) By sacrificing one objective for the other
b) By finding a perfectly balanced solution between objectives
c) By ensuring both objectives are satisfied above a certain threshold
d) None of the above

151. What is the role of the duality theorem in machine learning?
a) It links the primal and dual problems in linear programming
b) It provides a bound on the optimal value of one problem based on a feasible solution of the other
c) It helps make better decisions in various areas of machine learning
d) All of the above

152. How is the duality theorem used in supervised learning tasks?
a) To solve linear programming problems in regression or classification
b) To identify important features for predicting labels correctly
c) To improve models based on features' predictive power
d) All of the above

153. In unsupervised learning, how does the duality theorem help?
a) It allows finding patterns in data with similarities or differences
b) It relates data sets even without identical labels or classes
c) It assists in tasks such as clustering or anomaly detection
d) All of the above

154. What is the relationship between the primal and dual problems in the duality theorem?
a) They have identical solutions
b) They have similar objective functions
c) They are linked, and solutions in one problem provide bounds on the optimal value of the other
d) None of the above

155. Which type of optimization problems are commonly solved using the duality theorem in machine learning?
a) Linear programming problems
b) Non-linear programming problems
c) Convex optimization problems
d) All of the above

156. Dynamic programming is primarily used for solving which type of problems?
a) Optimization problems
b) Classification problems
c) Regression problems
d) All of the above

157. What is the principle of optimality in dynamic programming?
a) Sub-solutions of an optimal solution are also optimal for their sub-problems
b) Sub-solutions of an optimal solution are suboptimal for their sub-problems

c) Sub-solutions of an optimal solution are unrelated to their sub-problems
d) None of the above

158. How is the principle of optimality used in machine learning?
a) To find the best model structure through an iterative process
b) To determine the optimal set of parameters for a given model
c) To define the best hyperparameters for a given problem
d) All of the above

159. In which area of machine learning is dynamic programming commonly used?
a) Reinforcement learning b) Supervised learning
c) Unsupervised learning d) All of the above

160. What does a Markov Decision Process (MDP) consist of?
a) States, actions, rewards, and descriptions of action effects
b) States, rewards, and descriptions of action effects
c) Actions, rewards, and descriptions of action effects
d) None of the above

161. How does dynamic programming help in reinforcement learning?
a) It determines the optimal solutions for MDPs
b) It determines the best rewards and penalties for actions
c) It selects the best states for a given policy
d) None of the above

162. In dynamic programming, how are sub-problems solved?
a) Sub-problems are solved multiple times
b) Sub-problems are solved iteratively and their solutions are stored
c) Sub-problems are solved independently of each other
d) None of the above

163. Which type of problems can dynamic programming solve besides reinforcement learning?
a) Feature selection b) Semi-supervised learning
c) Deep learning optimization d) All of the above

164. Sublinear algorithms are designed to solve problems by processing only a small fraction of the input data, resulting in:
a) Exact solutions in sublinear time b) Approximate solutions in sublinear time
c) Exact solutions in linear time d) Approximate solutions in linear time

165. Sublinear algorithms are particularly useful in machine learning for:
a) Feature selection b) Image recognition
c) Natural language processing d) All of the above

166. Which aspect of traditional algorithms limits their effectiveness in processing massive data sets?
a) Linear time and space complexity b) Polynomial time and space complexity
c) Sublinear time and space complexity d) Exponential time and space complexity

167. What is the main advantage of using sublinear algorithms in machine learning?
a) Improved performance and reduced processing time
b) Exact solutions with higher accuracy
c) Reduction in the number of features in the data set
d) Minimization of computational models

168. In machine learning, feature selection using sublinear algorithms involves:
a) Selecting irrelevant features from the data set
b) Selecting the most important features from the data set
c) Selecting all features in the data set
d) None of the above

169. Which machine learning task involves grouping similar data points based on specific criteria?
a) Feature selection
b) Clustering
c) Classification
d) Regression

170. What does regression allow us to do in machine learning?
a) Predict future outcomes based on past trends
b) Classify data points into different categories
c) Select important features from the data set
d) Cluster similar data points together

171. Sublinear algorithms have applications beyond machine learning, such as:
a) Database search engines
b) Computer vision tasks
c) Natural language processing
d) All of the above

Part B (Short Answer Questions)

1. What is a set and what is a finite set?
2. How are finite sets used in machine learning?
3. What is an empty set?
4. How are empty sets used in machine learning?
5. What is an infinite set?
6. How are infinite are used in machine learning?
7. What is the Cartesian product of sets?
8. How is the Cartesian product of sets used in machine learning?
9. What is a relation in sets?
10. How are relations in sets used in machine learning?
11. What the primary purpose of using a domain in machine learning?
12. What is the range of R? How is it used in machine learning?
13. What is a function in a relation?
14. Define a convex set.
15. What is the use of convex sets?
16. What is the condition for an objective function to be called convex?
17. Define convex function.
18. What is concave function? How is it used in machine learning?
19. What is a strictly concave function? How is it used in machine learning?
20. What is a convex combination? How is it used in machine learning?
21. What is a convex hull? How is it used in machine learning?
22. What is a gradient vector? How is it used in machine learning?
23. Define the Hessian matrix.
24. What is optimization? How is it used in machine learning?
25. Explain the classification of optimization.
26. Define local optima and global optima.
27. What is constraint optimization?
28. What is dual optimization?
29. What is the weak duality theorem?
30. What is the strong duality theorem?
31. What is dynamic programming?
32. What is the use of sublinear algorithms?
33. Define a complete graph.
34. Define subgraph.

35. Define degree of a vertex.
36. Define Fourier transform
37. What is information theory?
38. What is entropy?

Part C (Essay Questions)

1. What is a set? What are the different types of sets? How are they useful in machine learning?
2. What is relation, domain of the relation, range of the relation, and codomain of the relation? How are they useful in machine learning?
3. Define convex sets and convex functions. How are they useful in machine learning?
4. Write an essay on concave function and strictly concave function. How is it useful in machine learning?
5. Write an essay on convex combination and convex hull. How they are useful in machine learning?
6. Write an essay on gradient vector.
7. What is optimization and how is it useful in machine learning?
8. Write an essay on linear and non-linear optimization.
9. Write an essay on constrained and unconstrained optimization.
10. Define discrete, continuous, and probabilistic optimization.
11. Explain local optima and global optima. How they are useful in machine learning?
12. Explain convex optimization.
13. Explain the unconstrained problem.
14. Explain Newton's method of optimization.
15. Explain the gradient descent (GD) method.
16. Write an essay on constrained optimization.
17. Explain dual optimization problem and how it is useful in machine learning.
18. Explain dynamic programming in detail.
19. Explain sublinear algorithms and its use in machine learning.

ANSWER KEY

Part A

1. (d)	**2.** (d)	**3.** (b)	**4.** (d)	**5.** (d)	**6.** (c)	**7.** (b)	**8.** (d)
9. (a)	**10.** (c)	**11.** (b)	**12.** (c)	**13.** (a)	**14.** (c)	**15.** (b)	**16.** (c)
17. (b)	**18.** (b)	**19.** (a)	**20.** (a)	**21.** (c)	**22.** (c)	**23.** (c)	**24.** (b)
25. (a)	**26.** (d)	**27.** (d)	**28.** (b)	**29.** (b)	**30.** (b)	**31.** (c)	**32.** (c)
33. (d)	**34.** (b)	**35.** (a)	**36.** (b)	**37.** (a)	**38.** (a)	**39.** (d)	**40.** (a)
41. (c)	**42.** (c)	**43.** (b)	**44.** (a)	**45.** (b)	**46.** (a)	**47.** (b)	**48.** (b)
49. (b)	**50.** (b)	**51.** (b)	**52.** (c)	**53.** (c)	**54.** (c)	**55.** (c)	**56.** (b)
57. (b)	**58.** (d)	**59.** (a)	**60.** (b)	**61.** (c)	**62.** (b)	**63.** (a)	**64.** (b)
65. (d)	**66.** (b)	**67.** (c)	**68.** (c)	**69.** (c)	**70.** (c)	**71.** (c)	**72.** (a)
73. (c)	**74.** (b)	**75.** (d)	**76.** (b)	**77.** (c)	**78.** (c)	**79.** (a)	**80.** (b)
81. (b)	**82.** (c)	**83.** (b)	**84.** (c)	**85.** (a)	**86.** (d)	**87.** (d)	**88.** (d)
89. (c)	**90.** (b)	**91.** (b)	**92.** (b)	**93.** (b)	**94.** (b)	**95.** (c)	**96.** (a)
97. (b)	**98.** (c)	**99.** (a)	**100.** (d)	**101.** (b)	**102.** (b)	**103.** (c)	**104.** (c)
105. (b)	**106.** (b)	**107.** (a)	**108.** (b)	**109.** (b)	**110.** (c)	**111.** (a)	**112.** (b)
113. (a)	**114.** (a)	**115.** (b)	**116.** (a)	**117.** (a)	**118.** (b)	**119.** (b)	**120.** (a)
121. (c)	**122.** (a)	**123.** (d)	**124.** (c)	**125.** (c)	**126.** (c)	**127.** (c)	**128.** (c)

129. (a)	**130.** (c)	**131.** (b)	**132.** (b)	**133.** (a)	**134.** (c)	**135.** (b)	**136.** (b)
137. (a)	**138.** (b)	**139.** (c)	**140.** (d)	**141.** (b)	**142.** (c)	**143.** (c)	**144.** (c)
145. (c)	**146.** (b)	**147.** (a)	**148.** (d)	**149.** (a)	**150.** (c)	**151.** (d)	**152.** (d)
153. (d)	**154.** (c)	**155.** (a)	**156.** (a)	**157.** (a)	**158.** (d)	**159.** (a)	**160.** (a)
161. (a)	**162.** (b)	**163.** (d)	**164.** (b)	**165.** (d)	**166.** (a)	**167.** (a)	**168.** (b)
169. (b)	**170.** (a)	**171.** (d)					

Computational Learning Theory

Learning Objectives

At the end of this chapter, you will be able to:

- Explain the fundamental concepts of computational learning theory
- Describe the objectives and historical development of computational learning theory
- Explain the significance and main methodologies of computational learning theory, including inductive, deductive, abductive, and reinforcement learning
- Explain the probably approximately correct (PAC) learning model and its relevance
- Analyze the complexity theory of machine learning, covering computational, space, and sample complexities
- Evaluate the time complexity of learning algorithms and the mistake-bound learning model
- Appreciate the principles of generative learning and contrast it with discriminative models
- Assess various evaluation metrics used in computational learning theory
- Anticipate future trends and directions in computational learning theory, including deep learning, explainable AI (XAI), and quantum machine learning

5.1 Introduction

Computational learning theory (CLT) is a branch of artificial intelligence (AI) that focuses on the design and analysis of algorithms that learn from data. It is a relatively new field of research, but it has already had a significant impact on the development of machine learning (ML) and AI. At its core, computational learning theory is concerned with understanding the principles that govern the learning process. It seeks to understand how machines can learn from data, how they can generalize from that data, and how they can use that knowledge to make decisions. It also seeks to understand how machines can learn from experience and how they can adapt to changing environments. CLT theory also focuses on the application of learning algorithms. This involves understanding how learning algorithms can be used in real-world applications, such as in robotics, natural language processing (NLP), and computer vision.

5.2 Objectives of Computational Learning Theory

CLT is closely related to the field of statistics, which also deals with the analysis of data. The main objective (goal) of computational learning theory is to develop algorithms that can learn from data and make predictions about future data.

The field of computational learning theory has been in existence since the 1950s and has seen tremendous growth in recent years. This is due to the increasing availability of large data sets, the development of powerful computational tools, and the emergence of powerful ML algorithms. At its core, computational learning theory is concerned with the development of algorithms that can learn from data. This involves the development of algorithms that can identify patterns in data and use those patterns to make predictions about future data. This is done by using a variety of techniques, such as supervised learning, unsupervised learning, reinforcement learning, and deep learning.

Supervised learning involves the use of labeled data, where the labels are known in advance. Unsupervised learning involves the use of unlabeled data, where the labels are not known. This type of learning is used to identify patterns in data and to cluster data points into groups.

Reinforcement learning is a type of learning where an agent interacts with an environment and receives rewards or punishments based on its actions. This type of learning is used to develop agents that can learn to perform tasks in an environment. Deep learning is a type of learning that uses artificial neural networks (ANNs) to learn from data. This type of learning is used to develop models that can identify patterns in data and make predictions about future data.

Another objective (goal) of CLT is in understanding the boundaries (limits) of what can be learned from data. This includes being aware of the learning algorithms' sample complexity. The quantity of data points a learning algorithm must encounter to learn a function is known as the **sample complexity**. The sample complexity indicates the amount of data an algorithm needs to learn a function. These metrics vary based on the characteristics of the learning challenges, such as the size or complexity of the hypothesis space the learner is considering, the degree of accuracy required to approach the target concept, and the probability that the learner will generate a reasonable hypothesis.

5.3 History

The history of CLT can be traced back to the 1950s, when Alan Turing proposed the Turing Test to measure a computer's ability to think like a human. Turing's work laid the foundation for the development of AI. In the 1960s, AI researchers began to explore the idea of using computers to learn from data. This led to the development of the first ML algorithms, such as decision trees and neural networks.

The 1970s saw the development of supervised learning algorithms, such as linear regression and logistic regression. These algorithms were able to learn from labeled data and make predictions about the future. In the 1980s, unsupervised learning algorithms, such as clustering and principal component analysis, were developed. These algorithms were able to learn from unlabeled data and make predictions about the future.

In the 1990s, the first deep learning algorithms, such as convolutional neural networks (CNNs) and recurrent neural networks (RNNs), were developed. These algorithms were able to learn from large amounts of data and make predictions about the future. Today, computational learning theory is an active area of research and is used in a variety of applications.

5.4 Importance of Computational Learning Theory

The importance of CLT lies in its ability to help us understand the underlying principles of ML and AI. By understanding these principles, we can develop algorithms that can learn from data and make predictions about future events. This is especially important in AI, where algorithms are used to make decisions and solve problems.

CLT also helps us understand the limitations of ML algorithms, so we can develop better algorithms that can learn from data more efficiently and accurately. This is useful in data mining, where algorithms are used to identify patterns and trends in large data sets.

Finally, using CLT, we can understand how to design algorithms that can learn from data more effectively and efficiently. This is of great value in robotics, where algorithms are used to control robots and make decisions.

Thus, the goal of CLT is to understand the following:

- What kind of tasks are learnable?
- What kind of data is required for learnability?
- What are the time and space requirements of the learning algorithm?

5.5 The Main Methods

At its core, CLT is concerned with understanding the process of learning from data (Fig. 5.1). This involves understanding the types of data that can be used to learn, the types of algorithms that can be used to learn from data, and the performance of these algorithms on different types of data. In particular, CLT focuses on understanding how algorithms can learn from data in a way that is both accurate and efficient.

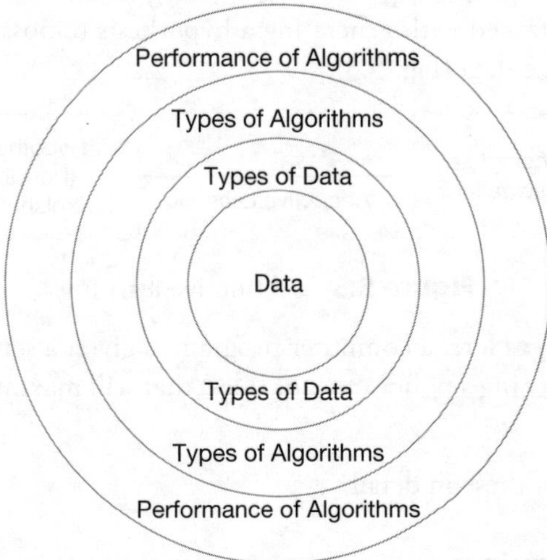

Figure 5.1 Core of computational learning

There are different types of CLT, each of which focuses on a different aspect of learning from data. As mentioned earlier, supervised algorithms learn from labeled data, unsupervised algorithms from unlabeled data, reinforcement algorithms from rewards and punishments, while evolutionary algorithms learn from evolutionary processes. CLT also focuses on understanding the performance of these algorithms. This involves understanding their accuracy and efficiency, as well as their ability to generalize to new data.

The main methods used in CLT are as follows:

- **Inductive learning:** This is the most common type of learning used in AI. Here, a computer program is given a set of training data (specific examples of correct inputs and outputs), and it is then tasked with generating a general rule or model that can be used to predict the output for new inputs (Fig. 5.2).
- **Deductive learning:** Here, a computer program is given a set of rules or a model (generic) and then tasked with using these to generate correct outputs for new inputs (Fig. 5.2).

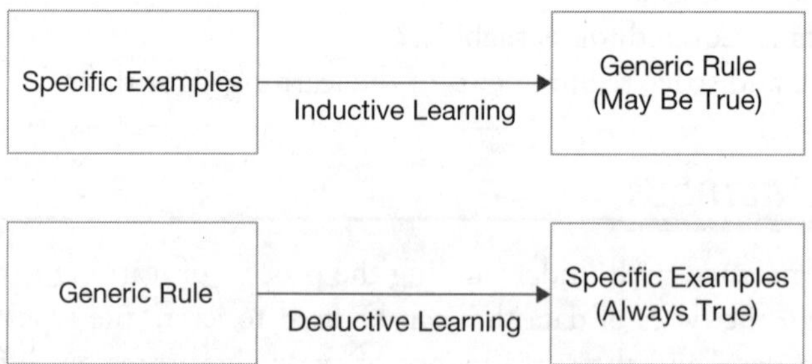

Figure 5.2 Inductive and deductive learning

- **Abductive learning:** Here, a computer program is given a set of training data (incomplete observations) and then tasked with generating a hypothesis (a possible explanation for the data) that is consistent with the data (Fig. 5.3).

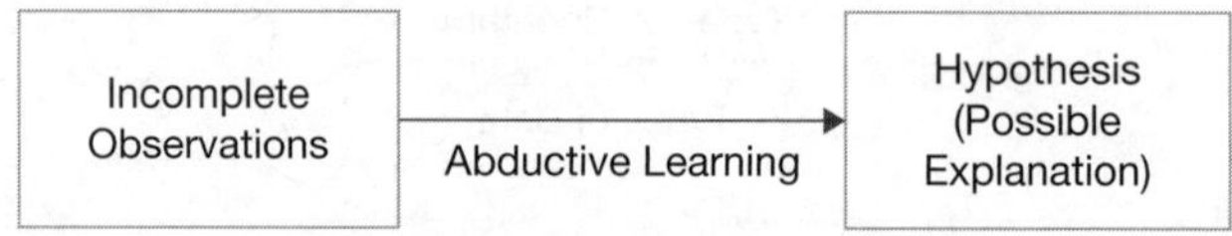

Figure 5.3 Abductive learning

- **Reinforcement learning:** Here, a computer program is given a set of rewards and punishments and then tasked with learning a policy (a set of rules) that will maximize the rewards and minimize the punishments.

We shall now explore each of these in detail.

5.5.1 Inductive Learning

Inductive learning is the most common type of ML used in AI. It is a process in which a computer program is given a set of training data comprising examples of correct inputs and outputs. This data is then used to generate a general rule or model that can be used to predict the output for new inputs.

Inductive Learning = Experience + Knowledge + Reasoning

This type of learning uses experience, knowledge, and reasoning to draw conclusions and make predictions. The process of inductive learning is similar to how humans learn from experience. Like humans, machines learn from examples and use that information to predict new situations.

An example of inductive learning is the use of spam filters in email. First, a spam filter is trained on emails that are either spam or not spam. Then, based on the characteristics of those emails, the algorithm creates a model that can be used to classify new emails as either spam or not.

In inductive learning, accuracy depends on the quality of training data. If the training data is biased or insufficient, the model will not precisely predict the output of new inputs. Therefore, it is essential to have a diverse and representative set of training data to ensure the model can make accurate predictions.

The idea that inductive learning is effective is formally stated in the inductive learning hypothesis. This asserts that a hypothesis (a rule or pattern) will fit the data well on brand-new test examples if it fits the data well on a sizable and representative set of training examples. For instance, if the hypothesis 'all birds can fly' matches most of the training examples of birds, we can anticipate that it will also match most of the test cases of birds.

However, not all theories are created equal. Some could be too narrow or too broad to explain the data adequately. For instance, the claim that 'all birds are black' is overly narrow because it ignores the existence of different bird colors. The assertion that 'all animals can fly' is too broad because it encompasses species other than birds. A compelling hypothesis should be just right. This is called the **bias–variance trade-off**.

Algorithms for inductive learning seek to choose the best hypothesis that accurately describes the data and generalizes it to new data. To do this, they must look through a wide range of potential hypotheses and assess them using a set of standards. One standard might be how accurately the hypothesis matches the training set of data. The hypothesis' complexity or degree of simplicity could be additional criteria. **Occam's razor**, which states that the optimal hypothesis is the one that best fits the facts, is a popular method for balancing these requirements.

Inductive learning is helpful in ML because it helps us to learn from data and make predictions or decisions based on what we have learnt. It can be used, for instance, to categorize photographs of animals based on their characteristics or to suggest products to clients based on their interests. We can gain new knowledge or insights from facts we may not have noticed before with inductive learning.

5.5.2 Deductive Learning

This is a type of ML where a computer program is provided with a set of predefined rules or a model that it uses to generate accurate outputs for new inputs. In this approach, the computer must make logical deductions based on the rules or model provided to infer new information and predict outcomes.

Deductive Learning = Knowledge + Reasoning

Deductive learning is a form of reasoning in which a conclusion is drawn from a set of premises or facts. Here, the conclusion is necessarily true if the premises are true. One example of deductive learning is using decision trees in medical diagnosis. A decision tree is created by inputting data from various patients with different symptoms and outcomes. Using this information, the computer generates a decision tree that can be used to predict the prognosis for new patients based on their symptoms. Numerous medical conditions, including heart disease and cancer, have been effectively diagnosed using this method.

Another example is the use of expert systems in finance. Expert systems are computer programs designed to emulate a human expert's decision-making abilities in a particular field. In finance, expert systems can be used to analyze market trends and predict future prices. By inputting data from various sources, including news articles and financial reports, the system can make informed predictions about the direction of the market.

5.5.3 Abductive Learning

This involves generating hypotheses consistent with a set of training data. This approach to learning has become increasingly popular in recent years, with many researchers and developers exploring its potential applications.

It is represented as $P(H|E) = P(E|H) \times P(H) / P(E)$. This states that the probability of a hypothesis (H) given evidence (E) is equal to the probability of the evidence given the hypothesis multiplied by the probability of the hypothesis divided by the probability of the evidence. In other words, it is the probability of a hypothesis given the evidence, taking into account the prior probability of the hypothesis.

The basic idea is that the computer program is given a set of training data and then tasked with generating a hypothesis that explains the data. Furthermore, the hypothesis must be consistent with the data, meaning that it must be able to accurately predict new data based on the patterns in the training data.

Abductive learning enables greater flexibility in the learning process, one of its primary advantages. Unlike other types of ML, abductive learning does not require a predefined set of features or variables. Instead, the program can generate its hypotheses based on the patterns it observes in the data.

For example, a company wants to predict which employees will most likely leave in the next year. They could use abductive learning to analyze their employees' job satisfaction, salary, and other factors and generate hypotheses about which factors are most likely to lead to employee turnover. This information could then be used to develop strategies to retain employees and reduce turnover.

Another example is in medical diagnosis. Doctors can use abductive learning algorithms to analyze patient data and generate hypotheses about the most likely diagnoses based on the symptoms and other clinical factors. This can help physicians make more precise diagnoses and effective treatment plans.

5.5.4 Reinforcement Learning

A reinforcement learning program is instructed to make decisions based on rewards and punishments. The program must discover a policy or principles that maximize rewards and minimize punishments. This type of learning is frequently employed in robotics, gaming, and other applications in which the computer must make decisions based on incomplete or ambiguous data.

The **Bellman equation** is used for reinforcement learning. It describes the relationship between the expected reward of a given action and the expected future rewards of all possible actions. It states that the expected reward of a given action equals the immediate reward plus the discounted expected reward of the best action that can be taken in the future. It is named after Richard Bellman, who formulated it in 1957.

Mathematically, it can be expressed as: $V^*(s) = \max(Q(s,a)) + E[V^*(s') \mid s,a]$. In this equation, $V^*(s)$ is the optimal value of the state s, $Q(s, a)$ is the expected value of taking action a in state s, and $E[V^*(s') \mid s, a]$ is the expected value of the resulting state, and a is the action in state s.

One example of reinforcement learning is training a robot to navigate a maze. The robot is given rewards for reaching the end of the maze and punishments for hitting walls or getting stuck. Through trial and error, the robot learns which actions lead to rewards and which to punishments, and it adjusts its behavior accordingly.

Another example is in training a computer program to play a game like chess. The program is given rewards for winning the game and punishments for losing. Through repeated games and analysis of successful strategies, the program learns which moves will most likely lead to victory and which should be avoided.

Reinforcement learning can be a powerful tool for creating intelligent systems to make decisions based on incomplete or uncertain information. However, it is essential to design the rewards and punishments carefully to ensure that the system learns the desired behavior.

5.6 Probably Approximately Correct Learning

Learning is a process that involves acquiring knowledge and skills through experience, study, or instruction. One type of learning that has gained increasing attention in recent years is probably approximately correct (PAC). This method is beneficial when the data is noisy or incomplete, as it allows for the creation of models that can accurately predict outcomes even with imperfect input.

The PAC equation is a mathematical formula describing the learning process from a given set of data. It states that given a set of data points, a learning algorithm can approximate a target function with a certain probability and accuracy. The equation is defined as:

$$P(f(x) \approx y) \geq 1 - \varepsilon,$$

where P is the probability, $f(x)$ is the target function, y is the output of the learning algorithm, and ε is the error rate.

An example of PAC learning is in speech recognition. When a person speaks, their voice can be affected by various factors, including background noise, accents, and speech impediments. To accurately recognize speech, a model must account for these variations. Using a PAC learning approach, researchers can create models that can identify patterns in speech, even when the audio data is not perfect.

Another example is in computer vision. Here, the input data can be images or videos, which may contain a variety of distortions or errors. For instance, a picture of a cat may be taken from an unusual angle, be blurry, or have other objects in the background. To accurately identify the cat in the image, a PAC learning model can be trained to recognize specific characteristics of cats, even when these characteristics are not always present in the input data.

A hypothesis $f: X \to Y$ is said to be consistent with training samples $(x_1, y_1), \cdots, (x_n, y_n)$ iff $(x_i) = y_i \forall i$.

Given any set of labeled examples S, an algorithm A learns a class C and produces a concept $c \in S$ consistent with S if it exists and outputs 'no consistent concept' otherwise. The goal of the PAC model is to define hypothesis h such that h has a small error over D.

Given a sample set $S = \{(x_1, y_1), \cdots (x_m, y_m)\}$, the **empirical error** of a concept h with respect to S is defined as

$$err_S(h) = \frac{1}{m}\sum_{i=1}^{m} I[h(x_i) \neq y_i]$$

The idea of the PAC model is to assume that the training samples are from a single fixed distribution space. The goal is to use the sample set S to learn a concept h that has small true error on D.

PAC learning aims at efficient learning. To achieve this, we need to prove that an efficient learning algorithm determines a hypothesis that is approximately identical to the target concept. In this process, we define two parameters ε and δ and proceed to prove that with a probability of at least $(1-\delta)$, a system can learn a concept with an error of at most ε.

An algorithm learns in the PAC model if it probably (with confidence $(1-\delta)$) outputs a hypothesis which is approximately correct (has a risk of at most ε).

Complexity for finite consistent hypothesis space

$$m \geq \frac{1}{\varepsilon}\left[\ln(H) + \ln\left(\frac{1}{\delta}\right)\right]$$

Here, labeled examples are sufficient, so that with a probability of $(1-\delta)$, all $h \in H$ with

$$error_D(h) \geq \in \text{ have } errors_S(h) > 0$$

With probability of at least $(1-\delta)$, all $h \in H$ such that $err_S(h) = 0$ implies

$$error_D \leq \frac{1}{m}\left[\ln(H) + \ln\left(\frac{1}{\delta}\right)\right]$$

Complexity for finite inconsistent hypothesis space

$$m \geq \frac{2}{2\varepsilon^2}\left[\ln(H) + \ln\left(\frac{2}{\delta}\right)\right]$$

Here, labeled examples are sufficient, so that with a probability of $(1-\delta)$, all $h \in H$ has

$$|error_D(h) - err_S(h)| < \varepsilon$$

5.6.1 Occam's Razor

This can be stated as 'prefer the simple hypothesis that best fits the data'. This principle is often used in ML when there is a choice between different models. The model with the simplest explanation is usually the one that is most likely to be correct. Generalizing beyond the training data is impossible unless more assumptions (bias) are added to the model.

Consider a hypothesis defined as $H = h : X \rightarrow Y$ and $|X| = 2^N$, then $|H| = 2^{2^N}$. All 2^N instances must be labeled.

The true error of a hypothesis h with respect to the target concept C and observation distribution D is the probability that h will misclassify an instance drawn according to D.

$$error_D(h) = P_{x\sim D}\left[c(x) \neq h(x)\right]$$

Occam's Razor is used as an inductive bias in ML. **Inductive bias** comprises assumptions made by the ML algorithm to form a hypothesis or generalization of a set of training instances with the goal of classifying the unobserved data. To achieve this, we need to define settings for the models, using PAC learning.

5.7 Complexity Theory of Machine Learning

Complexity theory of ML is a branch of AI that studies the behavior of complex systems. It is concerned with the study of how algorithms interact with data and how they can be used to make decisions. Complexity theory of ML is a rapidly growing field that has applications in a variety of industries, including finance, healthcare, and robotics. For example, in finance, algorithms are used to predict stock prices and make investment decisions. In healthcare, algorithms are used to diagnose diseases and recommend treatments, while in robotics, these algorithms are used to control robots and make decisions about how they should move and interact with their environment.

It is based on the idea that machines can learn from data, and that the complexity of the data can be used to make predictions and decisions. This is done by using algorithms to analyze the data and determine patterns and trends. The complexity of the data can then be used to create models that can be used to make decisions.

The complexity of the data is determined by the number of variables and the number of relationships between the variables. The more complex the data, the more difficult it is to make predictions and decisions.

5.7.1 Computational Complexity of Learning

The computational complexity of a learning algorithm refers to the amount of time and resources required to produce a model. This can be affected by several variables, such as the scale and complexity of the data set, the number of features that must be analyzed, and the type of ML algorithm employed.

As an illustration, let us suppose that a bank wants to use ML algorithms to forecast which borrowers are most likely to default on a loan. They would need to analyze a large amount of data, including information about the customer's credit history, income, and other relevant factors. If the bank uses a simple logistic regression model, it can produce a reasonably accurate prediction with relatively few resources. However, if they opt for a more complex deep learning model, they may need to invest in expensive hardware and software and allocate significant amounts of time and workforce to train the model.

The complexity of a learning algorithm can also have important implications for the accuracy and reliability of the model. In some cases, more complex models can produce more accurate predictions or identify more subtle patterns in the data. However, these models may also be more prone to overfitting, which occurs when the model becomes too specialized to the training data and cannot generalize to new data sets.

A more complex algorithm will generally take longer to analyze the data and generate a model. This can substantially disadvantage applications requiring real-time predictions or quick decision-making. One way that researchers and developers in ML work to optimize computational complexity is by exploring new algorithms and techniques specifically designed to reduce the number of operations required to produce a model. For example, techniques such as pruning and quantization can be used to simplify complex neural networks and reduce their computational complexity without sacrificing accuracy. Another approach is carefully selecting the features to be analyzed in the input data. Concentrating on the most pertinent and informative features can substantially reduce the number of operations required to generate a model without compromising its accuracy. Thus the complexity of a learning algorithm is usually measured in terms of time and space complexity. Time complexity measures the amount of time it takes for the algorithm to complete its task, while space complexity measures the amount of memory required to store the data and results of the algorithm.

The challenges associated with the computational complexity of learning algorithms include difficulty in designing efficient algorithms, optimizing these algorithms, and in understanding their behavior. One potential solution to these challenges is to use approximate algorithms, which are algorithms that produce approximate results instead of exact results. Approximate algorithms are usually faster and require less memory than exact algorithms. Another potential solution is to use parallel computing, which allows multiple processors to work on the same problem simultaneously. This can significantly reduce the time and space complexity of the algorithms.

5.7.2 Space Complexity of Learning

Space complexity measures the amount of memory required to store the data and results of the algorithm. It is an essential consideration in computational learning because it can significantly impact the efficiency and effectiveness of the algorithm. For example, if an algorithm requires a large amount of memory to store the data and results, running on specific devices or systems may be slow or even impossible.

The equation of the space complexity model is typically expressed as $S(n) = c^*n$, where $S(n)$ is the space complexity, n is the input size, and c is a constant. This equation states that the space complexity is directly proportional to the input size. In other words, as the input size increases, the algorithm's space complexity increases proportionally.

There are several ways to measure space complexity in computational learning, including the number of bits required to represent the data and the number of intermediate results that must be stored during the algorithm's execution. The space complexity can also depend on the specific implementation of the algorithm and the data structures used to store the data.

One common approach to reducing space complexity in computational learning is to use techniques such as data compression or dimensionality reduction. These techniques reduce the amount of memory required to store the data and results while maintaining the algorithm's accuracy and effectiveness. Another important consideration is the trade-off between space and time. In certain circumstances, using more memory to store intermediate results may be more efficient in reducing the overall algorithm execution time. However, in other cases, the trade-off may be the opposite, and it may be more efficient to use less memory and accept a longer running time.

5.7.3 Sample Complexity of Learning

Sample complexity is related to the number of samples needed to learn a task. An ML algorithm can be said to have low sample complexity if it can learn a task with a small number of samples. Conversely, an algorithm can be said to have high sample complexity if it requires a large number of samples to learn a task. Several factors determine sample complexity, including the complexity of the task, the type of data used, the number of features used, and the type of model used.

In ML, the complexity of the task is determined by several factors, including the number of variables, classes, and relationships between those variables. An ML algorithm to predict weather patterns is a prime example of a complex task. This is because there are numerous variables to consider, such as temperature, humidity, and pressure, and many relationships between these variables that can impact the outcome. On the other hand, an ML algorithm designed to predict (forecast) the outcome of a coin flip would be much simpler. This is because there are only two possible outcomes, heads or tails, and no other variables to consider. In this case, the algorithm would need to analyze past data and use probability to predict the outcome of future coin tosses.

Regarding computational learning, the type of data used is crucial for achieving accurate results. This is because the data used in ML is what the algorithm bases its predictions on. Therefore, the data used must be relevant to the prediction being made. For instance, an ML algorithm designed to predict stock prices would require financial data to learn from, while one designed to predict the outcome of a sports game would need sports data. The amount of data available also significantly determines the number of features used in machine learning algorithms. For example, an ML algorithm designed to predict credit scores would require many features, such as income, credit history, and employment status, to make an accurate prediction. On the other hand, an ML algorithm designed to predict the outcome of a particular event would require fewer features.

Computational learning involves selecting an appropriate algorithm and the optimization method to train the model. The chosen model type is influenced by the problem that needs to be solved. Optimization methods determine how the algorithm adjusts its model parameters to minimize errors between the predictions and the actual results. For example, stochastic gradient descent (SGD) is an optimization method that updates the model's parameters more frequently than batch gradient descent (BGD) optimization. SGD is particularly useful for large data sets where batch optimization can be computationally expensive.

One technique for improving the sample complexity of an ML algorithm is feature selection. This involves selecting the most critical features from a data set, which can help reduce the amount of redundant or irrelevant data the algorithm needs to learn from. For example, in a data set of customer purchasing habits, feature selection might involve identifying the most critical variables, such as age, gender, and income, while excluding less relevant variables, such as hair color or shoe size.

Another technique is feature engineering, which involves transforming the data into a more suitable form for an ML algorithm. This may involve normalization, scaling, and dimensionality reduction techniques. Finally, hyperparameter tuning optimizes the parameters of an ML algorithm to improve its performance. This can involve techniques such as grid search or random search, which help identify the best parameters for a given algorithm.

5.7.3.1 *Sample Complexity for Finite Hypothesis Spaces*

This refers to the minimum number of examples required to learn a concept from a given hypothesis space accurately. The sample complexity depends on the size of the hypothesis space and the desired level of accuracy.

The equation of sample complexity for finite hypothesis spaces is as follows:

$$\text{Sample Complexity} = \log(|H|) / \varepsilon,$$

where $|H|$ is the number of hypotheses in the finite hypothesis space and ε is the desired accuracy.

This equation states that the number of hypotheses in the space and the desired accuracy determine the sample complexity of finite hypothesis space. The larger the number of hypotheses, the more samples are needed to achieve the desired accuracy. Likewise, the higher the desired accuracy, the more samples are needed to achieve it.

For example, consider a binary classification problem where the hypothesis space consists of all possible linear separators in a two-dimensional space. The sample complexity required to learn the correct separator with 90% accuracy is approximately 100 examples. However, if the hypothesis space consists of more complex functions, such as neural networks with multiple layers, the sample complexity required to achieve the same level of accuracy can be significantly higher.

Another example is a decision tree algorithm used for classification. The hypothesis space, in this case, consists of all possible decision trees that can be constructed from the available features. The sample complexity required to learn a decision tree with a certain level of accuracy depends on the number of features and the complexity of the underlying data distribution.

5.7.3.2 *Sample Complexity for Infinite Hypothesis Spaces*

When it comes to infinite hypothesis spaces, the issue of sample complexity becomes a critical concern. Here, the challenge is determining how many examples are needed to ensure that a hypothesis will perform well in the long run.

The following formula gives the equation of sample complexity for infinite hypothesis spaces:

$$\text{Sample Complexity} = \log(H)/\varepsilon,$$

where H is the number of hypotheses in the hypothesis space and ε is the desired accuracy of the learning algorithm.

This equation states that the sample complexity of a learning algorithm for an infinite hypothesis space is proportional to the logarithm of the number of hypotheses. In other words, the more hypotheses there are, the more data samples are needed to achieve the desired accuracy.

Suppose we are trying to predict whether a person will like a particular movie. Countless factors influence their opinion, such as the genre, cast, director, etc. We could create an infinite number of hypotheses to account for these factors, each with its own parameters and assumptions.

In this scenario, the sample complexity would refer to the number of movie-goers we must survey to predict whether a new person would like the movie accurately. If we only surveyed a handful of people, our results might be skewed by chance or individual preferences. But we could be more confident in our predictions if we surveyed thousands of people.

Another example of infinite hypothesis spaces can be found in the field of machine learning. Imagine we are trying to train a computer to recognize different types of animals, from dogs and cats to zebras and giraffes. We could create an infinite number of hypotheses to account for the various features that distinguish these animals, such as their fur patterns, body shapes, etc.

In this case, the sample complexity would refer to the number of animal images we need to feed into the ML algorithm to classify new images accurately. So, if we only trained the algorithm on a few dozen images, it might need help generalizing to new data. But if we trained it on thousands of images, it would have a better chance of recognizing patterns and making accurate predictions.

5.7.4 Time Complexity of Learning

The time complexity of learning in ML is the amount of time it takes for an ML algorithm to learn from data and make accurate predictions. It is an important factor to consider when selecting an algorithm for a given task. Different algorithms have different time complexities, and it is important to select an algorithm that is able to learn quickly and accurately.

The time complexity of learning in ML is determined by the size of the data set, the complexity of the task, and the type of algorithm used.

The more complex the task and the larger the data set, the more time it will take for the machine to learn. Imagine you are trying to train a machine to recognize handwritten digits. If we have a small number of samples to work with (say, 100), then the time complexity of learning will be relatively low. This is because the machine will be able to quickly process the data and learn to recognize the digits with relatively high accuracy. On the other hand, if you are working with a more extensive data set (say 10,000 samples), the time complexity of learning will be much higher. This is because the machine has to process much more meaningful data, which takes more time and computational power.

In addition, if the task at hand is more complex (such as recognizing handwritten letters instead of digits), the time complexity of learning will increase even further. It is worth noting that there are ways to mitigate the impact of data size and task complexity on learning time. For example, data can be preprocessed to reduce its size or complexity and algorithms can be optimized to make them more efficient. However, these solutions only go so far, and ultimately, the time complexity of learning in ML is determined by the underlying task and data set.

The type of algorithm used also plays a crucial role in determining the time complexity of learning. Some algorithms are more efficient than others regarding how quickly and accurately they can learn from data. Algorithms like SGD and mini-batch SGD are well-suited for learning from larger data sets because they update the model parameters based on a small subset (or 'mini-batch') of the data at a time, which makes the computation faster and more efficient.

On the other hand, algorithms like *K*-nearest neighbor (KNN) and decision trees are better suited for smaller data sets. This is because they involve a lot of computation and memory usage, which can slow down the learning process when dealing with large amounts of data. Of course, some algorithms fall somewhere in between these two extremes. For example, support vector machines (SVMs) are known to be efficient for both small and large data sets and can handle complex decision boundaries with high accuracy.

5.8 Mistake-Bound Learning Model

This is a model that tries to capture the essence of how humans learn from their mistakes. The concept underlying the paradigm is that we make errors as we learn and that these errors are an integral part of the learning process. Furthermore, the model assumes that we have some feedback mechanism that tells us when we have made a mistake, and we use this feedback to adjust our behavior in the future.

The mistake-bound learning model is an algorithm used to estimate the expected loss of a given decision. It uses a set of data points to calculate the expected loss of a decision based on the number of mistakes made in the past. The equation for it is as follows:

$$\text{Expected Loss} = (\text{Number of Mistakes} + 1) / (\text{Number of Data Points} + 2)$$

In other words, the expected loss of a decision is calculated by taking the number of mistakes made in the past and dividing it by the number of data points plus two. This equation helps ensure that a decision's expected loss is not too high or too low.

Learning how to pedal a bicycle is an example of error-based (mistake based) learning. When we first ride a bicycle, we will likely make numerous errors. We may fall off the bike, lose balance, or steer in the wrong direction. However, each time we make a mistake, we learn from it. We adjust our balance, steering, and pedaling to avoid repeating the same mistake.

The mistake-bound learning model has many applications in AI and ML. For example, it can be used to train algorithms to recognize patterns in data. By providing feedback on mistakes, the algorithm can learn to distinguish between different types of data and make more accurate predictions in the future.

5.9 Instance-Based Learning

Instance-based learning, also known as exemplar-based learning, is a form of ML in which the model learns by storing and classifying individual examples, as opposed to following predefined rules. It is a form of lazy learning because the model performs classification only when a new instance is introduced. The equation of an instance-based learning model is typically represented as:

$$\text{Predicted Output} = f(\text{Inputs, Instances})$$

This equation states that the model's predicted output is a function of the inputs and instances. Instances are the data points used to train the model and can include input and output values. The model looks at the instances and uses them to predict the output for new inputs.

K-nearest neighbor (KNN) is an example of an instance-based learning algorithm. It is a straightforward and effective classification and regression technique. A new instance is classified based on the majority class of its *K* nearest neighbors in the training set. If we have a data set of flower species with attributes such as petal length, width, and sepal length, for instance, we can use KNN to determine the species of a new flower based on its attributes.

Another example is case-based reasoning (CBR). This is a problem-solving technique that uses past experiences (cases) to solve new problems. CBR works by retrieving similar cases from the case base, adapting the solution to fit the new problem, and retaining the solution as a new case for future use. For example, if we have a case base of medical diagnoses, we can use CBR to diagnose new patients based on their symptoms and medical history.

Instance-based learning is beneficial when the data is noisy, or the relationships between features are complex. In addition, it allows for flexible and adaptive learning, as the model can easily incorporate new instances and adjust its classification rules accordingly.

However, instance-based learning can also be computationally expensive and prone to overfitting if the data set is too large or the number of features is too high. It also requires careful distance metric selection to ensure that similar instances are correctly identified.

5.10 Lazy and Eager Learning

Learning is an integral part of our lives. We learn from our experiences, the people around us, and various sources of knowledge. In ML, there are two broad categories of learning: lazy and eager.

Lazy learning is a type of learning in which the system waits until a query is made and then uses the training data to make a prediction. This is also known as instance-based learning, as it uses specific data instances to make predictions. The equation of a lazy learning model is as follows:

$$F(x) = \text{argmin } h \in H\, \Sigma i{=}1nL(h(x\_i), (y\_i))$$

This equation states that the output of a lazy learning model is the hypothesis (h) from a hypothesis set (H) that minimizes the sum of the losses (L) for each input (x_i) and its corresponding output (y_i). In other words, the lazy learning model finds the hypothesis that best fits the data by minimizing the total error. An example is the K-nearest neighbor algorithm. Here, the system waits until a query is made, then looks for the K nearest neighbors in the training data and uses their output to make a prediction.

On the other hand, eager learning is a type of learning where the system learns a model from the training data before any queries are made. This is also known as model-based learning. The equation of an eager-based learning model is as follows:

$$\text{Loss} = f(w) + \lambda R(w),$$

where w represents the weights of the model, $f(w)$ is the loss function, and $\lambda R(w)$ is the regularization term.

The loss function quantifies the difference between the predicted and actual output, while the regularization term penalizes large weights to prevent overfitting. The goal of the model is to minimize the loss function and regularization term. An example of eager learning is the decision tree algorithm. Here, the system builds a tree-like model from the training data, which can be used to predict any query.

Both types of learning have their advantages and disadvantages. Lazy learning is computationally less expensive as it requires no training or model building. However, it can be slower when making predictions as it depends on the training data for every query. On the other hand, eager learning is faster when making predictions as the model has already been built. However, eager learning can be computationally expensive, requiring building a model from the training data.

Thus, lazy learning is more suitable when the training data is extensive and the queries are infrequent. Eager learning is more suitable when the queries are frequent and the training data is small. Ultimately, choosing which type of learning to use depends on the trade-off between computational cost and prediction accuracy.

5.11 Generative Learning

Generative learning is an ML approach that entails constructing a model that represents the process by which data is generated. This is accomplished through acquiring knowledge of the fundamental patterns and connections inside the data, then utilizing this information to generate novel instances that resemble the existing data. Generative learning is distinct from discriminative learning as it entails constructing a model capable of forecasting the class label of a certain sample.

Generative learning is advantageous in situations when there is a scarcity of data or when the data is exceptionally intricate. Generative models have the capacity to generate novel instances that bear resemblance to the original data by comprehending its underlying structure. Consider, for instance, a data set consisting of handwritten digits. A generative model has the ability to acquire knowledge about the fundamental patterns and connections within the data, and subsequently utilize this information to generate novel instances of handwritten digits that closely resemble the original ones.

Generative learning models are of different types, such as probabilistic, generative, latent variable, and generative adversarial networks.

Probabilistic models employ probability theory to elucidate the interconnections among variables in the given data. An instance of this is the naive Bayes classifier. It is a straightforward probabilistic model commonly employed for text classification. The model acquires the likelihood of each word's occurrence in each class and subsequently utilizes this information to forecast the class designation of a given text sample.

Generative models acquire knowledge of the fundamental patterns and connections inside the data, which they then utilize to produce novel instances of the data. Gaussian mixture models and hidden Markov models are instances of generative models. Gaussian mixture models estimate the latent distribution of the data and leverage this knowledge to generate novel data instances. Hidden Markov models acquire the latent organization of the data and employ this knowledge to generate novel sequences of data.

Models involving latent variables uncover the fundamental framework of the data by detecting concealed or latent factors that account for the observable data. Principal component analysis (PCA) and factor analysis are examples of latent variable models. PCA use principal components to reveal the underlying structure of the data by identifying the components that explain the variability in the data. Factor analysis is a statistical method used to identify the fundamental factors that account for the connections between variables in a data set.

Generative adversarial networks (GANs) are a type of generative model that comprises two neural networks. The initial network produces novel instances of the data, whereas the subsequent network assesses the caliber of the generated samples. The two networks are simultaneously trained to develop a generator network capable of producing top-notch instances of the data.

5.11.1 Importance of Generative Learning in Machine Learning

The importance of generative learning in ML is due to its ability to learn the underlying structure of the data. This is particularly useful in situations where there is a limited amount of data available. By learning the underlying patterns and relationships in the data, generative models can generate new examples that are similar to the originals, even if there is only a small amount of data available.

For instance, generative models can be used to create synthetic images of faces, animals, or scenes that do not exist in reality, but which look realistic and natural. These synthetic images can be used for various tasks, such as data augmentation, image editing, or style transfer.

Another advantage of generative learning is that it can help us understand and explore the latent structure and patterns of the data. For example, generative models can be used to discover the hidden factors or dimensions that influence the data, such as the pose, expression, or identity of a face image, or the topic, sentiment, or tone of a text document. These latent factors can then be manipulated or controlled to generate different variations of the data.

However, generative learning also faces some challenges and limitations. One of the main challenges is to ensure the quality and diversity of the generated data. Quality refers to how realistic and natural the generated data looks or sounds, while diversity refers to how different and varied the generated data is from each other and from the original data. It is often difficult to balance these two aspects, since increasing one may decrease the other. For example, if we generate too many similar images or texts, they may look realistic but lack diversity. On the other hand, if we generate too many diverse images or texts, they may look unnatural or unrealistic.

Another challenge is to evaluate and measure the performance of generative models. Unlike discriminative models, which can be evaluated by comparing their predictions with the ground truth labels, generative models do not have a clear objective or criterion to judge their outputs. Therefore, it is hard to quantify how good or bad a generative model is. Some possible ways to evaluate generative models are to use human judgments, such as ratings or preferences, or to use proxy metrics, such as likelihoods or distances. However, these methods are either subjective or indirect, and may not capture all aspects of generative learning.

5.11.2 Probabilistic Models

These are mathematical models that are used to represent uncertainty and randomness in data. These models are used to make predictions, identify patterns, and classify data. There are two main types of probabilistic models: generative and discriminative.

Generative models are used to model the joint probability distribution of the input data and its corresponding output. They are used to generate new data points that are like the training data. For example, a generative model can be used to generate new images that are similar to the training images.

Discriminative models are used to model the conditional probability distribution of the output given the input data. They are used to classify input data into different categories. For example, a discriminative model can be used to classify an email into spam or non-spam.

Bayes' theorem is a formula that is used to calculate the probability of an event occurring given some prior knowledge or evidence. It is named after the English statistician Thomas Bayes. The formula is:

$$P(A|B) = P(B|A) \times P(A) / P(B),$$

where P(A|B) is the probability of event A occurring given that event B has occurred; P(B|A) is the probability of event B occurring given that event A has occurred; P(A) is the prior probability of event A occurring; and P(B) is the prior probability of event B occurring.

Maximum likelihood estimation (MLE) is a method used to estimate the parameters of a statistical model. It involves finding the values of the parameters that maximize the likelihood function. The likelihood function is one that measures how well the model fits the observed data. For example, if we have a data set of the heights of people, we can use MLE to estimate the mean and variance of the heights. The mean is the average height of all people, and the variance is how much the heights vary around the mean. The higher the variance, the more different the heights are.

MLE is a very useful and powerful method in statistics. It can be used to estimate parameters for many different types of models, such as linear regression, logistic regression, or neural networks. It can also be used to compare different models and see which one fits our data better.

Naive Bayes classifier is a classification algorithm that is based on Bayes' theorem. It is called 'naive' because it assumes that the features of the input data are independent of each other. The algorithm works by calculating the conditional probability of each class given the input data, and then selecting the class with the highest probability. For example, a naive Bayes classifier can be used to classify emails into spam or non-spam based on the words used in the email.

5.11.3 Generative Models

Generative models are used to generate new data points that are similar to the training data. They are used in a variety of applications such as image generation, text generation, and music generation. They are different from discriminative models, which are used to classify input data into different categories.

There are several types of generative models, but some of the most common ones are as follows:

- **Gaussian Mixture Models (GMMs):** These are used to model complex data distributions as a combination of simpler Gaussian distributions. They are commonly used in image and speech recognition applications. For example, in image recognition, GMMs can be used to model the distribution of skin tones in an image. This is useful in applications like face detection, where the goal is to separate the skin regions from the non-skin regions. Similarly, in speech recognition, GMMs can be used to model the distribution of different phonemes, which are the basic units of speech. By modeling the distribution of phonemes, GMMs can be used to recognize spoken words.

  GMMs are also commonly used in clustering applications, where the goal is to group similar data points together. In this case, the GMM can be used to model the distribution of the data and then cluster the data points based on their likelihood of belonging to each of the Gaussian distributions.
- **Hidden Markov Models (HMMs):** These are used to model sequences of data where the state of the system is not directly observable. They are commonly used in speech recognition and NLP applications. For example, an HMM can be used to model the speech of a person and then recognize the words spoken by the person. To elaborate, an HMM consists of two types

of variables: hidden states and observations. The hidden states are the underlying variables that affect the observed data, but they are not directly measurable. The observations are the variables that are recorded and visible. The relationship between the hidden states and the observations is modeled using a probability distribution. An HMM has two sets of probabilities: transition and emission. The transition probabilities describe the likelihood of moving from one hidden state to another. The emission probabilities describe the likelihood of generating an observation from a hidden state.

For example, suppose we want to model the weather using an HMM. We can define two hidden states: low pressure and high pressure. We can also define two observations: rain and dry. The transition probabilities tell us how likely it is to go from low pressure to high pressure, or vice versa. The emission probabilities tell us how likely it is to rain or be dry given a certain pressure.

An HMM can be trained using historical data to estimate the transition and emission probabilities. This can be done using algorithms such as Baum–Welch or forward-backward. Once trained, an HMM can be used to decode the most likely sequence of hidden states given a sequence of observations. This can be done using algorithms such as the Viterbi algorithm.

Some examples of **applications** that use HMMs are:

- **Speech recognition**: An HMM can be used to model the speech signals of a person and then recognize the words they are saying.
- **Activity recognition**: An HMM can be used to model the actions of a person or an object from a video and then recognize what they are doing.
- **Gene finding**: An HMM can be used to model the DNA sequences of an organism and then find the regions that encode proteins.

HMMs are useful because they can capture the sequential nature of data and handle uncertainty and variability in the observations. However, they also have some **limitations**:

- They assume that the hidden states follow a Markov property, which means that the current state depends only on the previous state, not on any other past states.
- They assume that the observations are independent given the hidden states, which means that there is no correlation between different observations.
- They may require a large amount of data to train accurately and avoid overfitting or underfitting.

• **Autoencoders:** Autoencoders are neural networks that are trained to reconstruct the input data. They are used to learn a compressed representation of the input data which can be used for tasks such as image generation and anomaly detection. For example, an autoencoder can be used to generate new images of faces by learning the features of the input face images.

5.11.4 Latent Variable Models

These are a type of statistical model used to describe complex relationships between different variables by introducing the concept of unobserved and hidden variables, called latent variables. These models are used to find patterns and structure in data that cannot be directly observed.

There are different types of latent variable models, but some of the most common ones are PCA, factor analysis, and latent Dirichlet allocation (LDA).

PCA is a statistical method used to reduce the dimensionality of a data set by finding a smaller number of variables that explain most of the variance in the data. PCA is often used in fields like finance, where it can be used to extract information from stock market data, or in biology, where it can be used to analyze gene expression data.

Factor analysis is another method that is used to find underlying factors that explain the correlations between observed variables. In other words, it helps to identify the common factors that affect the observed variables. For example, in psychology, it can be used to identify underlying personality traits that influence different behaviors.

Latent Dirichlet allocation is a type of model used in NLP to identify topics in a text corpus. It is often used in applications like sentiment analysis, where it can be used to identify the overall sentiment of a text, or in topic modeling, where it can be used to group similar articles together.

5.11.5 Generative Adversarial Networks

Generative adversarial networks, or GANs, are a type of ML model used to generate new data that is similar to the original training data. GANs are made up of two neural networks: a generator and a discriminator. The generator is responsible for creating new samples from random noise, while the discriminator is responsible for distinguishing between the generated samples and the real ones.

The generator neural network takes a random noise vector as input and generates a new sample that is similar to the training data. The discriminator neural network then takes both the generated sample and a real sample from the training data as input and tries to distinguish between them. As the training progresses, the generator network becomes better at generating realistic samples that can fool the discriminator network, and the discriminator network gets better at distinguishing between real and fake samples.

GANs have a wide range of **applications**, some of which are listed below:

- **Image synthesis**: To generate realistic images that can be used in a variety of applications, such as video games, movies, and virtual reality.
- **Data augmentation**: To generate new data samples that can be used to train ML models. This can be useful in cases where the amount of training data is limited.
- **Style transfer**: To transfer the style of one image onto another. This can be used to create new images with a specific style, such as converting a photograph into a painting.
- **Text generation**: To generate new text data, such as product descriptions or news articles.
- **Drug discovery**: To generate new molecules that can be used in drug discovery. This can help to speed up the process of discovering new drugs.

5.11.6 Future Directions in Generative Learning

Generative learning has come a long way in recent years, and there are several exciting directions in which it is headed. Some of the future directions of generative learning are:

- **Improved image synthesis**: While GANs have been successful in generating realistic images, there is still room for improvement in terms of image quality and diversity. Future research in generative learning will focus on developing more advanced models that can generate higher quality and diverse images.
- **Multimodal generation**: Multimodal generation is the ability to generate data that combines multiple modalities, such as text, audio, and images. This can be useful in applications like virtual assistants, where the system needs to respond with a combination of text and audio.

- **Video synthesis**: While GANs have been successful in generating static images, there is still a long way to go in terms of video synthesis. Future research in generative learning will focus on developing models that can generate realistic and diverse videos.
- **Improved text generation**: Text generation is another area where generative learning has made significant progress. However, there is still scope for improvement in terms of generating text that is more coherent and human-like.
- **Generative modeling for healthcare**: Generative modeling is being used in healthcare to generate synthetic data that can be used for training machine learning models. Future research in this area will focus on developing models that can generate realistic and diverse medical images and data.
- **Adversarial attacks**: Adversarial attacks are a type of cyber-attack where an attacker can fool an ML model by adding small, imperceptible changes to the input data. Generative learning can be used to develop models that can detect and defend against adversarial attacks.

5.12 Consistent Learning

An algorithm A is said to be consistent learner for a concept class C using hypothesis H, if $\forall n, \forall c \in C_n$, and $\forall m$, given $(x_1, C(x_1)), \cdots, (x_m, C(x_m))$ as input, where $x_i \in X_n$ such that $\forall i = 1 \cdots m, h(x_i) = c(x_i)$. A is said to be an efficient consistent learner if the running time of A is in polynomial $n, size(C)$ and m.

5.12.1 Vapnik–Chervonenkis (VC) Dimension

A consistent learner can be used to develop a PAC learning algorithm in situations where the output hypothesis comes from a class that is not too large and is polynomial. If the output hypothesis size is infinite, then the above result cannot be applied. In such cases, VC dimension is used.

Shattering: Let us suppose that we have two points. Can linear classifiers correctly classify the labeling of these two points? The two points can be labeled in four different ways (Fig. 5.4).

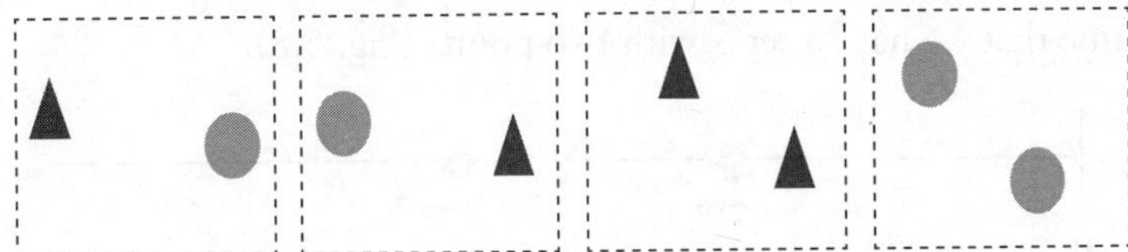

Figure 5.4 Two classes of points represented in four ways

It is possible to draw a line that separates the two classes of points in all the four ways (Fig. 5.5).

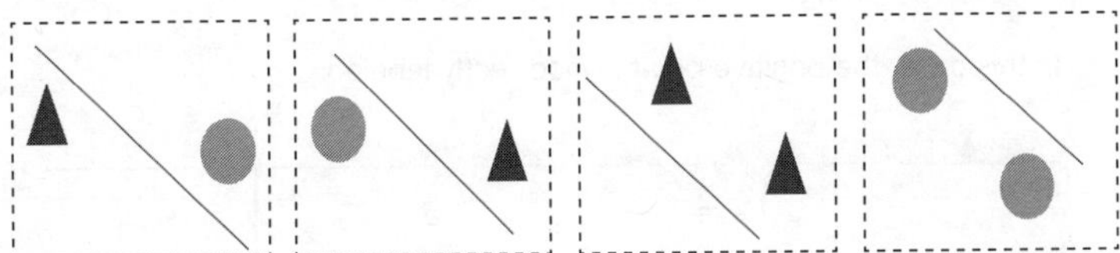

Figure 5.5 Two classes of points represented in four ways separated by a line

The linear functions are expressive enough to shatter two points.

Consider a hypothesis for a two-class problem. A set of N points or instances can be labeled as + or − in 2^N ways. If for every such labeling, a function can be determined in $\mathcal{H}$ consistent with this labeling, then we say that the set of instances is shattered by $\mathcal{H}$.

A set S of examples is shattered by a set of functions H if for every partition of the examples in S into positive and negative examples, there is a function in H that gives exactly these labels to the examples.

Example 1: Hypothesis class of left-bounded intervals on the real axis $[0,a)$ for some real number $a>0$ (Fig. 5.6).

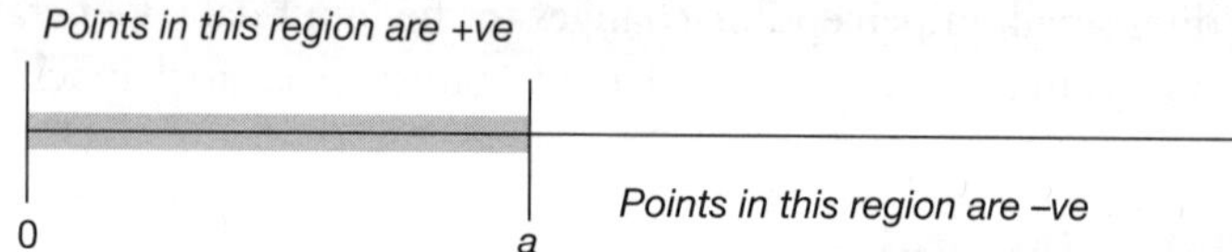

Figure 5.6 Positive region and negative region

Case 1: Let us assume that we have a set S with only one point (Fig. 5.7).

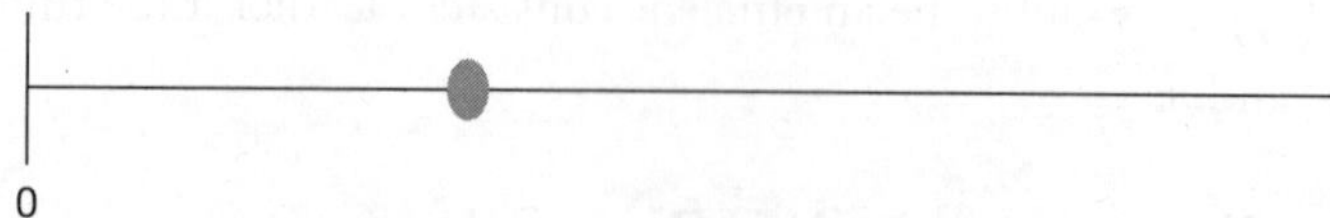

Figure 5.7 Set S with only one point

If the point is labeled *+ve*, then we can find a point a that is to the right of that point. Such hypothesis correctly labels the point as *+ve*.

If the point is labeled *−ve*, then we can find a point a that is to the left of that point. Such hypothesis correctly labels the point as *−ve*.

Thus, any set of one point can be shattered.

Case 2: Let us assume that we have a set S with two points (Fig. 5.8).

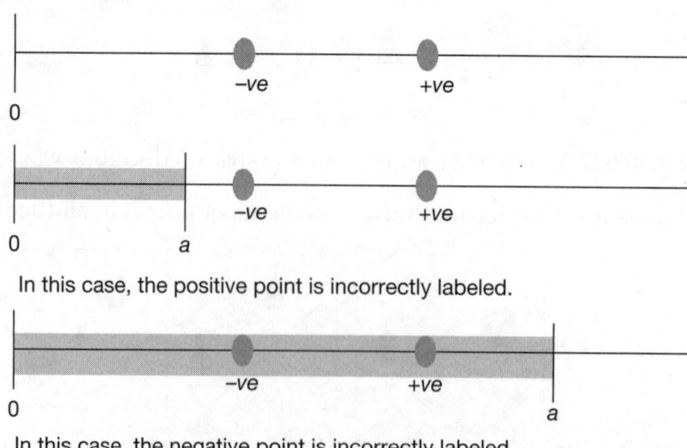

Figure 5.8 Points with incorrect labeling

We can label the points such that no hypothesis in this class matches the labels.

Example 2: Hypothesis class is a set of intervals on the real axis $[a,b]$ for some real number $b>a$. Points within the range $[a,b]$ are labelled $+ve$ and outside the range as $-ve$.
Case 1: Let us assume that we have a set S with only one point (Fig. 5.9).

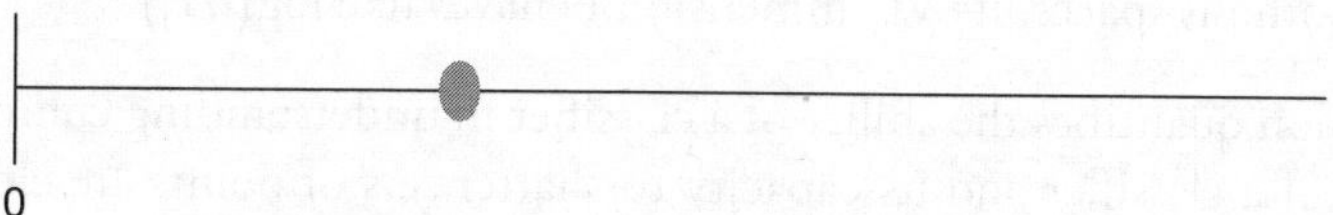

Figure 5.9 A set S with only one point

If the point is labelled $+ve$, then we can find two points a and b such that a is to the left of the point and b is to the right of the point. Such hypothesis correctly labels the point as $+ve$ (Fig. 5.10).

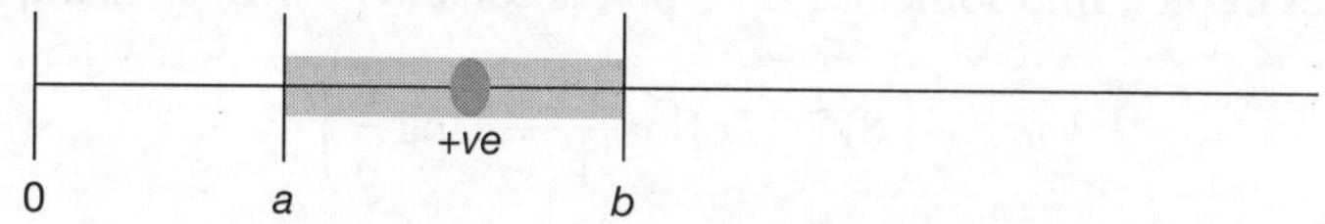

Figure 5.10 A positive point between a and b

If the point is labeled $-ve$, then we can find two points a and b that are to the right or left of that point. Such hypothesis correctly labels the point as $-ve$. Thus, any set of one point can be shattered.

Case 2: Let us assume that we have a set S with two points (Fig. 5.11).

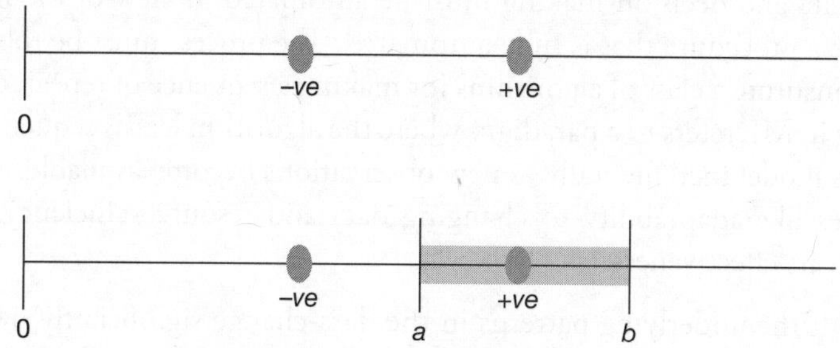

Figure 5.11 Set S with two points

Thus, any set of two points can be shattered.

Case 3: Let us assume that we have a set S with three points (Fig. 5.12).

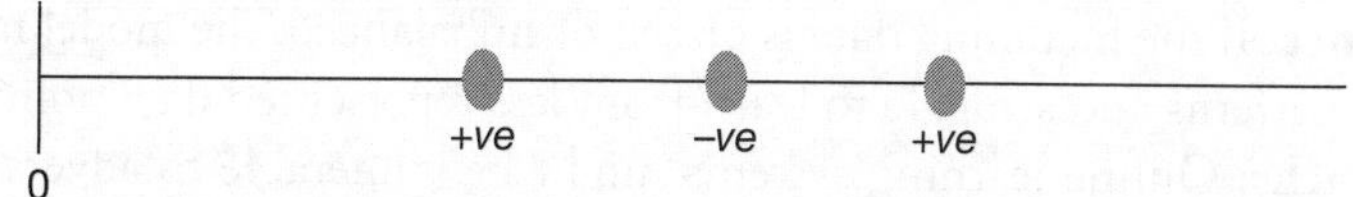

Figure 5.12 Set S with three points

The set of three points cannot be shattered.

The VC dimension of hypothesis space H over instance space X is the size of the largest finite subset of X that is shattered by H.

If there exists any subset of size d that can be shattered, then $VC(H) >= d$.

If no subset of size d can be shattered, then $VC(H) < d$.

For infinite hypothesis spaces, its VC dimension behaves like $\log(|H|)$.

The VC dimension quantifies the ability of a classifier in understanding complex patterns of data. The VC dimension of a classifier and its capacity to shatter sets of points are closely correlated. The larger the VC dimension of a classifier, the higher the capacity to shatter complicated sets of points. If the VC dimension of a classifier is low, the classifier struggles to understand the complex patterns of data and this results in overfitting or underfitting of data.

Using $VC(H)$ as a measure, we can define Occam's theorem for infinite hypothesis spaces. Given a sample D with m examples, find some $h \in H$ which is consistent with m examples where

$$m > \frac{1}{\varepsilon}\left(8VC(H)\log\frac{13}{\varepsilon} + 4\log\frac{2}{\delta}\right)$$

Then, with a probability of $1-\delta$, the hypothesis space has error less than ε.

5.13 Worst Case (Online) Learning

Forecasting is not a one-time process but must be repeated again and again. Forecasts must be updated for the new data and decision-making must be automated in view of the new data. The ideal solution is to choose a procedure that is fully automated. The process must be robust as well. Online learning methods constitute a class of algorithms for making a sequence of repeated forecast decisions.

Online learning in ML refers to a paradigm where the algorithm learns sequentially from a stream of data, updating its model incrementally as new observations become available. While online learning offers advantages like adaptability to changing data and resource efficiency, several worst-case scenarios can impact its effectiveness:

- **Concept drift**: If the underlying patterns in the data change significantly over time, the model may struggle to adapt quickly. This leads to the degradation of the performance of the model.
- **Catastrophic forgetting**: When the model updates itself with new data, it might forget previously learned patterns, especially if the new data conflicts with earlier observations.
- **Noisy data**: Online learning models can be sensitive to noisy or erroneous data. If the incoming data contains a high level of noise, it can lead to incorrect model updates.
- **Bias or imbalance**: If the incoming data is biased or imbalanced, the model may become skewed towards certain patterns and struggle to learn from less represented data points.
- **Adversarial attacks**: Online learning systems might be vulnerable to adversarial attacks, where maliciously crafted data points can mislead the model's learning process.

Online learning may struggle with computational constraints or limited memory, especially when dealing with vast amounts of streaming data. More complex models might require extensive computational resources for updating with each new data point, making them impractical for real-time learning.

To address these challenges, different strategies should be employed like feature engineering, robust model architectures, regularization techniques, and continuous monitoring for model performance and data quality.

- **Regularization techniques**: Regularization methods like L1/L2 regularization, dropout, or early stopping can prevent overfitting and help the model generalize better, even in the presence of noisy or changing data:
  - **L1 regularization (LASSO)**: Adds a penalty term proportional to the absolute value of the coefficients' sum to the loss function.
  - **L2 regularization (Ridge)**: Adds a penalty term proportional to the square of the coefficients' sum to the loss function. It penalizes large coefficients but does not usually force them to zero, smoothing out the impact on the model and reducing the magnitudes of the coefficients.
  - **Elastic net**: Combines L1 and L2 regularization by adding both penalties to the loss function. This method helps overcome the limitations of L1 and L2 regularization by providing a balance between feature selection (L1) and coefficient shrinkage (L2).
- **Ensemble methods**: Employing ensemble methods, such as bagging or boosting, can improve model performance by combining multiple models, reducing variance, and making the system more resistant to noisy data or overfitting.
- **Concept drift detection**: Implement algorithms to detect concept drift early. Techniques like monitoring statistical measures or using drift-detection algorithms can help in identification when the data distribution shifts, allowing for timely model updates.
- **Online feature selection**: Feature selection techniques like information gain or recursive feature elimination can help in this regard.
- **Robust training**: Use robust optimization methods that are less sensitive to noise or outliers in the data. Techniques like robust regression or robust PCA can help mitigate the impact of noisy observations.
- **Balancing data**: Address imbalances in the data by employing techniques such as oversampling, undersampling, or synthetic data generation to ensure the model learns from all classes equally.
- **Regularly monitor** model performance and data quality, and update the model incrementally to adapt to changes in the data distribution.
- **Resource optimization**: Optimize computational resources by using incremental learning techniques, model compression, etc. without compromising performance.

By combining these approaches and continuously improving the model's adaptability and resilience, it can become more capable of handling worst-case scenarios in online ML environments.

5.14 APPLICATIONS OF COMPUTATIONAL LEARNING THEORY

The applications of CLT in ML are vast and varied. It is used to develop algorithms for supervised learning, unsupervised learning, reinforcement learning, and deep learning. It is also used to develop models for classification, clustering, and regression. In addition, computational learning theory is used to develop algorithms for feature selection, feature extraction, and model selection.

5.14.1 Applications in Natural Language Processing

Machine translation is the process of automatically translating text from one language to another. CLT has been used to develop algorithms that can learn from large data sets of translated text to improve the accuracy of machine translation. These algorithms can learn from the patterns in the data, such as the syntax and grammar of the language, to better understand the meaning of the text and produce more accurate translations.

Text classification is the process of automatically assigning labels to text documents. CLT has been used to develop algorithms that can learn from labeled data to accurately classify text documents. These algorithms can learn from the patterns in the data, such as the words and phrases used in the text, to better understand the meaning of the text and assign the correct label.

Sentiment analysis is the process of automatically determining the sentiment or opinion expressed in text. CLT has been used to develop algorithms that can learn from labeled data to accurately identify the sentiment expressed in text. These algorithms can learn from the patterns in the data, such as the words and phrases used in the text, to better understand the sentiment expressed in the text.

In conclusion, CLT has become an important tool in NLP due to its ability to provide insights into the structure and meaning of language. As the field of NLP continues to evolve, computational learning theory will continue to play an important role in the development of new algorithms and applications.

5.14.2 Applications in Computer Vision

Computer vision is the field of study that focuses on the development of algorithms that can interpret and understand visual data. It is used in a variety of applications, such as facial recognition, object recognition, and image segmentation. In order to achieve these tasks, computer vision algorithms must be able to learn from data and make predictions. This is where computational learning theory comes into play.

For example, a computer vision algorithm can be developed using CLT to recognize objects in an image. The algorithm can learn from the data and make predictions about what objects are in the image. Image segmentation is the process of dividing an image into multiple regions based on certain characteristics. This can be used to identify objects in an image or to separate foreground from background. Facial recognition is an important application of computer vision, as it can be used for security purposes or for identifying individuals. CLT can be used to develop algorithms that can learn from data and make predictions about facial features.

5.14.3 Applications in Robotics

Robotics is a field of engineering that focuses on the design and development of robots. Robots are machines that are designed to perform tasks autonomously or semi-autonomously. As robots become more advanced, they are increasingly being used in a variety of applications, such as manufacturing, healthcare, and home automation.

CLT can be used to improve the performance of robotic systems. By applying CLT, robots can learn from their environment and adapt to changing conditions. This can be used to improve the accuracy and speed of the robot's movements, as well as its ability to recognize objects and navigate its environment.

CLT can also be used to improve the safety of robotic systems. By applying CLT, robots can learn to detect and avoid obstacles, as well as recognize and respond to dangerous situations. This can help to reduce the risk of accidents and improve the safety of robotic systems.

Finally, CLT can be used to improve the efficiency of robotic systems. By applying CLT, robots can learn to recognize patterns and optimize their movements to save energy and time. This can help to reduce the cost of operating robotic systems and improve their overall efficiency.

In conclusion, CLT can be used to improve the performance, safety, and efficiency of robotic systems. As robots become more advanced, CLT will continue to be an important tool for improving the performance of robotic systems.

5.15 Evaluation Metrics for Computational Learning Theory

Evaluation metrics for CLT are important for assessing the accuracy and performance of ML algorithms. Evaluation metrics provide a quantitative measure of how well an ML algorithm performs on a given task. This is important for understanding the strengths and weaknesses of different algorithms and for choosing the best algorithm for a particular application.

Accuracy is one of the most-used evaluation metrics for ML algorithms. It is calculated by dividing the number of correctly classified data points by the total number of data points. Accuracy is a good measure of performance when the classes are balanced, but it can be misleading when the classes are imbalanced.

Precision and recall are two other important evaluation metrics for ML algorithms. **Precision** is a measure of how many of the predicted positive results are actually correct. It is calculated by dividing the number of true positives by the total number of predicted positives. **Recall** is a measure of how many of the actual positive results were correctly predicted. It is calculated by dividing the number of true positives by the total number of actual positives.

F-measure is a combination of precision and recall. It is calculated by taking the harmonic mean of precision and recall. The F-measure is a good metric for evaluating ML algorithms when the classes are imbalanced.

AUC-ROC (area under the curve-receiver operating characteristic) is a metric used to evaluate the performance of binary classifiers. It is calculated by plotting the true positive rate against the false positive rate.

5.16 Future Directions in Computational Learning Theory

CLT is a field of study that focuses on the development of algorithms and techniques that can be used to learn from data. It has become increasingly important in recent years, as the amount of data available to us has grown exponentially.

One of the most promising areas of research is the development of deep learning algorithms. These algorithms can learn from large amounts of data and can be used to solve complex problems. These algorithms are based on ANNs, which are modeled on the structure of the human brain. By using deep learning algorithms, machines can learn to recognize patterns in data and make predictions about future outcomes.

Another potential direction is the development of reinforcement learning algorithms. These algorithms are based on the idea of reward and punishment and can be used to teach machines to perform certain tasks. Finally, another direction for CLT is the development of transfer learning algorithms, which are based on the idea of transferring knowledge from one domain to another.

All these directions could be used to improve the accuracy of ML algorithms and to make them more efficient.

5.16.1 Advances in Deep Learning Related to Computational Learning Theory

Deep learning is a rapidly advancing field of AI that has seen tremendous growth in recent years. It is based on the idea of using ANNs to mimic the way the human brain works. Deep learning has been used to solve a wide range of problems, from image recognition to NLP. In particular, advances in deep learning have had a significant impact on CLT.

One of the most important advances in deep learning related to computational learning theory is the development of convolutional neural networks (CNNs). CNNs are a type of neural network that are specifically designed to recognize patterns in images. They are composed of layers of neurons that are connected to each other in a way that allows them to recognize patterns in images. They have been used to solve a variety of problems, such as object recognition, facial recognition, and image segmentation.

Another important advance is the development of recurrent neural networks (RNNs). RNNs are a type of neural network that are specifically designed to process sequences of data. They are composed of layers of neurons that are connected to each other in a way that allows them to process sequences.

5.16.2 Explainable AI Related to Computational Learning Theory

Explainable AI (XAI) is a branch of AI that focuses on making AI systems more transparent and interpretable. It is closely related to CLT. CLT is concerned with understanding the mathematical principles underlying the design and analysis of learning algorithms, while XAI is concerned with understanding how these algorithms can be used to explain the behavior of AI systems.

The goal of XAI is to make AI systems more transparent and interpretable so that humans can better understand and trust them. This is important because AI systems are increasingly being used to make decisions that have a significant impact on people's lives, such as in healthcare, finance, and criminal justice.

5.16.3 Quantum Machine Learning Related to Computational Learning Theory

Quantum machine learning (QML) is a rapidly growing field of research that combines the power of quantum computing with ML algorithms to create powerful new ways of solving complex problems. QML has the potential to revolutionize the way we think about ML and CLT.

Quantum computing is based on the principles of quantum mechanics, which allow for the manipulation of information at a much faster rate than traditional computing. This enables the development of algorithms that can solve complex problems in a fraction of the time. By combining quantum computing with ML algorithms, QML can be used to solve problems that are too complex for traditional computing.

The advantages of using quantum computing include the ability to process large amounts of data quickly, the ability to solve problems that are too complex for traditional computing, and the ability to use quantum entanglement to solve problems faster. In addition, quantum computing can be used to create algorithms that can learn from data and adapt to changing conditions.

The challenges associated with quantum computing include the difficulty of creating algorithms that are accurate and reliable, the need for specialized hardware, and the difficulty of scaling up quantum computing systems. In addition, quantum computing is still in its infancy and there is much to be learned about the technology.

The potential applications of QML are vast. QML can be used to create algorithms that can analyze large data sets, identify patterns in data, and make predictions. QML can also be used to create algorithms that can identify and classify objects, detect anomalies in data, and create models that can be used to make decisions. Thus, QML is a rapidly growing field of research that has the potential to revolutionize CLT.

SUMMARY

- Computational learning theory is a branch of artificial intelligence that focuses on the design and analysis of algorithms that learn from data. It is a relatively new field of research, but it has already had a significant impact on the development of machine learning and artificial intelligence.
- The main objective (goal) is to develop algorithms that can learn from data and make predictions about future data. Another objective (goal) is to understand the boundaries (limits) of what can be learned from data. This includes being aware of the learning algorithms' sample complexity.
- The main methods used in computational learning theory are inductive learning, deductive learning, abductive learning, and reinforcement learning.
- The complexity of a learning algorithm refers to the amount of time and resources required to produce a model.
- The computational complexity of a learning algorithm is determined by the number of operations it requires to produce a model.
- Mistake-bound learning is a model that tries to capture the essence of how humans learn from their mistakes.
- Instance-based learning, also known as exemplar-based learning, is a form of ML in which the model learns by storing and classifying individual examples, as opposed to following predefined rules.
- Eager learning is a type of learning where the system learns a model from the training data before any queries are made. This is also known as model-based learning.
- Generative learning is an ML approach that entails constructing a model that represents the process by which the data is generated.
- CLT has been applied to a variety of fields, including robotics.

- Explainable AI (XAI) is a branch of AI that focuses on making AI systems more transparent and interpretable.
- Quantum machine learning (QML) is a rapidly growing field of research that combines the power of quantum computing with machine learning algorithms to create powerful new ways of solving complex problems.

EXERCISES

Part A (Objective Questions)

1. Which field is closely related to computational learning theory and also deals with the analysis of data?
   a) Computer vision
   b) Natural language processing
   c) Statistics
   d) Robotics
2. Which type of learning involves the use of unlabeled data to identify patterns and cluster data points into groups?
   a) Supervised learning
   b) Unsupervised learning
   c) Reinforcement learning
   d) Deep learning
3. What is the main objective of computational learning theory?
   a) Developing algorithms that can learn from data
   b) Understanding the boundaries of what can be learned from data
   c) Applying machine learning algorithms to large data sets
   d) Building powerful computational tools for data analysis
4. Which type of learning involves an agent interacting with an environment and receiving rewards or punishments based on its actions?
   a) Supervised learning
   b) Unsupervised learning
   c) Reinforcement learning
   d) Deep learning
5. What is sample complexity in computational learning theory?
   a) The size or complexity of the hypothesis space
   b) The degree of accuracy required to approach the target concept
   c) The quantity of data points a learning algorithm must encounter to learn a function
   d) The probability that the learner will generate a reasonable hypothesis
6. Which field can benefit from computational learning theory in applications such as computer vision and natural language processing?
   a) Robotics
   b) Computer vision
   c) Natural language processing
   d) Statistics
7. What is the other objective of computational learning theory, apart from developing algorithms that can learn from data?
   a) Understanding the limitations of AI systems
   b) Applying machine learning algorithms to large data sets
   c) Developing powerful computational tools
   d) Building models for computer vision tasks

8. Which type of learning uses artificial neural networks to identify patterns in data and make predictions about future data?
a) Supervised learning
b) Unsupervised learning
c) Reinforcement learning
d) Deep learning

9. What is the main focus of computational learning theory?
a) Designing algorithms for data mining
b) Understanding the limitations of machine learning algorithms
c) Developing techniques for robotics
d) Creating algorithms that can learn from data

10. Why has computational learning theory become increasingly important in recent years?
a) Due to the availability of powerful computational tools
b) Because of the growing complexity of data
c) For designing algorithms in robotics
d) To understand the limitations of artificial intelligence

11. What is the role of computational learning theory in understanding machine learning principles?
a) It helps in designing algorithms for data mining.
b) It helps in understanding the limitations of machine learning algorithms.
c) It helps in controlling robots and making decisions.
d) It helps in understanding how computers can learn from data.

12. Why is understanding the limitations of machine learning algorithms important?
a) To develop techniques for robotics
b) To make decisions and solve problems in artificial intelligence
c) To identify patterns and trends in large data sets
d) To design algorithms that can learn from data more effectively

13. What is the significance of computational learning theory in the field of data mining?
a) It helps in understanding the principles of machine learning.
b) It helps in designing algorithms for robotics.
c) It helps in identifying patterns and trends in large data sets.
d) It helps in understanding the limitations of machine learning algorithms.

14. Which field can benefit from understanding the principles of machine learning?
a) Data mining
b) Artificial intelligence
c) Robotics
d) Computer vision

15. What is the role of computational learning theory in designing algorithms?
a) Developing techniques for data mining
b) Controlling robots and making decisions
c) Designing algorithms for robotics
d) Designing algorithms that can learn from data more effectively

16. What makes computational learning theory a powerful tool in computer science?
a) Its focus on data mining algorithms
b) Its ability to control robots and make decisions
c) Its understanding of machine learning principles
d) Its role in designing techniques for robotics

17. What is the main process involved in inductive learning?
    a) Collecting large data set
    b) Generating rules from training data
    c) Analyzing and visualizing data
    d) Building complex machine learning models
18. Which of the following fields extensively uses inductive learning?
    a) Computer programming
    b) Robotics
    c) Data visualization
    d) Artificial intelligence
19. What is the role of experience and knowledge in inductive learning?
    a) They are used to draw conclusions and make predictions.
    b) They determine the accuracy of the training data.
    c) They help in generating complex machine learning models.
    d) They are essential for data visualization.
20. What is the purpose of training a spam filter using inductive learning?
    a) To generate new emails
    b) To classify emails as spam or not spam
    c) To analyze the characteristics of spam emails
    d) To visualize the data patterns in emails
21. What is the application of inductive learning in image recognition?
    a) Generating new images
    b) Analyzing image characteristics
    c) Enhancing image resolution
    d) Recognizing objects in images
22. What affects the accuracy of an inductive learning model?
    a) The computing power of the machine
    b) The diversity and representativeness of the training data
    c) The complexity of the machine learning algorithms
    d) The size of the available data sets
23. What is the significance of inductive learning in machine learning?
    a) Generating complex programming codes
    b) Designing intelligent robots
    c) Making predictions based on examples
    d) Analyzing patterns in large data sets
24. What factors contribute to the increasing role of inductive learning?
    a) The availability of diverse training data
    b) The use of complex reasoning algorithms
    c) The need for data visualization techniques
    d) The development of advanced programming languages
25. Which of the following best describes deductive learning?
    a) Generating new rules from training data
    b) Making predictions based on examples
    c) Drawing conclusions from predefined rules or models
    d) Identifying patterns in large data sets
26. What is the role of reasoning in deductive learning?
    a) It helps generate accurate outputs for new inputs.
    b) It determines the complexity of the machine learning model.
    c) It assists in identifying patterns in the training data.
    d) It enables logical deductions based on predefined rules or models.

27. Which field utilizes decision trees for deductive learning?
a) Data visualization
b) Medical diagnosis
c) Stock trading
d) Risk management

28. What is the purpose of creating a decision tree in medical diagnosis?
a) To visualize medical data patterns
b) To predict future stock prices
c) To analyze market trends
d) To predict patient outcomes based on symptoms

29. What is the primary function of expert systems in finance?
a) Generating new investment strategies
b) Analyzing market trends and making predictions
c) Visualizing financial data patterns
d) Identifying risks in stock trading

30. What is the nature of conclusions drawn in deductive learning?
a) Tentative and probabilistic
b) Based on general rules and specific situations
c) Subjective and opinion-based
d) Dependent on the size of available data sets

31. Which type of reasoning is involved in deductive learning?
a) Logical reasoning
b) Statistical reasoning
c) Inductive reasoning
d) Heuristic reasoning

32. What is the outcome of deductive learning if the premises are true?
a) Tentative predictions
b) Statistical analysis
c) Accurate and necessary conclusions
d) Opinion-based decisions

33. What is the primary objective of abductive learning?
a) Generating hypotheses consistent with training data
b) Predicting future outcomes based on patterns
c) Extracting predefined features from data
d) Analyzing statistical relationships in data sets

34. Which equation represents the probability of a hypothesis given evidence in abductive learning?
a) $P(E|H) \times P(H) / P(E)$
b) $P(H|E) = P(E|H) \times P(H) / P(E)$
c) $P(H|E) = P(H) / P(E)$
d) $P(E|H) = P(H) / P(E)$

35. What is one advantage of abductive learning over other types of machine learning?
a) It requires a predefined set of features or variables.
b) It offers greater flexibility in generating hypotheses.
c) It relies on statistical relationships in the data.
d) It provides accurate predictions without prior knowledge.

36. In which scenario could abductive learning be used to reduce employee turnover?
a) Analyzing customer satisfaction data
b) Predicting stock market trends
c) Evaluating job satisfaction and salary datad) Identifying patterns in social media posts

37. How does abductive learning contribute to medical diagnosis?
a) It visualizes patient data patterns.
b) It predicts patient outcomes based on symptoms.
c) It identifies statistical relationships in clinical data.
d) It generates hypotheses about likely diagnoses.

38. Which aspect of abductive learning makes it different from other types of machine learning?
a) The requirement of a large training data set

b) The reliance on predefined features or variables
c) The focus on extracting patterns from data
d) The ability to generate hypotheses based on observed patterns

39. What is the significance of the prior probability of the hypothesis in abductive learning?
a) It determines the complexity of the machine learning model.
b) It influences the flexibility of hypothesis generation.
c) It ensures accurate predictions without evidence.
d) It affects the probability of the hypothesis given the evidence.

40. Which field can benefit from the flexibility and adaptability of abductive learning?
a) Weather prediction
b) Social media marketing
c) Supply chain management
d) Healthcare

41. In which field can reinforcement learning be frequently employed?
a) Finance
b) Healthcare
c) Robotics
d) Education

42. What is the role of rewards and punishments in reinforcement learning?
a) They determine the input data for the program.
b) They define the set of possible actions in the environment.
c) They guide the program to maximize rewards and minimize punishments.
d) They provide the program with complete and unambiguous data.

43. Which equation is commonly used in reinforcement learning to calculate the expected reward of a given action?
a) Pythagorean theorem
b) Bellman equation
c) Gaussian distribution equation
d) Logistic regression equation

44. What does the Bellman equation describe in reinforcement learning?
a) The relationship between immediate rewards and future rewards
b) The relationship between the state and the action in an environment
c) The relationship between the optimal policy and the problem
d) The relationship between the input data and the output predictions

45. Which application involves training a computer program to play chess using reinforcement learning?
a) Sentiment analysis
b) Weather forecasting
c) Stock market prediction
d) Game playing

46. What can be a consequence of improperly calibrated rewards and punishments in reinforcement learning?
a) The program may fail to make any decisions.
b) The program may learn unintended behaviors.
c) The program may achieve optimal performance.
d) The program may require additional training data.

47. Which factor determines the optimal policy in reinforcement learning?
a) The immediate reward of a given action
b) The expected future rewards of all possible actions
c) The complexity of the machine learning model
d) The availability of training data

48. What is the main characteristic of reinforcement learning in decision-making?
   a) It relies on complete and unambiguous data.
   b) It avoids trial and error learning.
   c) It maximizes rewards and minimizes punishments.
   d) It requires a predefined set of rules.

49. Which field benefits from probably approximately correct (PAC) learning to create models that can accurately predict outcomes with imperfect input data?
   a) Robotics   b) Speech recognition
   c) Data analysis   d) Climate modeling

50. What does the PAC learning equation describe?
   a) The probability of perfect accuracy in learning
   b) The relationship between input and output data
   c) The approximation of a target function with a certain probability and accuracy
   d) The noise level in the input data

51. Which domain utilizes PAC learning for accurately identifying objects in images or videos?
   a) Natural language processing   b) Speech recognition
   c) Robotics   d) Computer vision

52. What does the error rate (ε) represent in the PAC learning equation?
   a) The probability of perfect accuracy in learning
   b) The noise level in the input data
   c) The probability of the learning algorithm approximating the target function
   d) The probability of the learning algorithm making a mistake

53. Which discipline can benefit from PAC learning in natural language processing?
   a) Computer vision   b) Data analysis
   c) Speech recognition   d) Email spam filtering

54. What is the main advantage of PAC learning in handling imperfect input data?
   a) It eliminates the need for data preprocessing.
   b) It guarantees 100% accuracy in predictions.
   c) It allows for the creation of models that can accurately predict outcomes.
   d) It provides a higher level of noise tolerance in the input data.

55. Which type of learning is suitable when the data is noisy or incomplete?
   a) Supervised learning
   b) Unsupervised learning
   c) Reinforcement learning
   d) Probably approximately correct (PAC) learning

56. Which application can benefit from PAC learning in handling variations in speech patterns?
   a) Climate modeling   b) Stock market prediction
   c) Speech recognition   d) Sentiment analysis

57. Which branch of artificial intelligence studies the behavior of complex systems and their interaction with data?
   a) Complexity Theory of Machine Learning   b) Reinforcement Learning
   c) Natural Language Processing   d) Unsupervised Learning

58. What determines the complexity of the data in complexity theory of machine learning?
   a) The number of variables and relationships between them
   b) The size of the data set
   c) The type of machine learning algorithm used
   d) The complexity of the problem being solved
59. In which industries can complexity theory of machine learning be applied?
   a) Finance, healthcare, and robotics b) Retail, education, and transportation
   c) Energy, entertainment, and agriculture d) Manufacturing, hospitality, and construction
60. What is the primary purpose of complexity theory of machine learning?
   a) To analyze complex systems and their behavior
   b) To develop algorithms for data analysis
   c) To make accurate predictions and decisions
   d) To study the interactions between algorithms and data
61. Which factor determines the difficulty of making predictions and decisions in complexity theory of machine learning?
   a) The type of machine learning algorithm used
   b) The size of the data set
   c) The complexity of the data
   d) The availability of computational resources
62. In which industry are algorithms used to predict stock prices and make investment decisions?
   a) Healthcare b) Robotics
   c) Finance d) Transportation
63. What is the role of algorithms developed through complexity theory of machine learning in healthcare?
   a) Diagnosing diseases and recommending treatments
   b) Controlling robots and making decisions
   c) Analyzing customer behavior and making recommendations
   d) Predicting weather patterns and natural disasters
64. Which field benefits from complexity theory of machine learning in controlling robots and making decisions?
   a) Agriculture b) Entertainment
   c) Robotics d) Energy
65. What is the computational complexity of a learning algorithm?
   a) The number of operations required to produce a model
   b) The size of the data set
   c) The efficiency of the algorithm
   d) The accuracy of the model
66. Which factor does NOT contribute to the computational complexity of a learning algorithm?
   a) The data set's size b) The complexity of the features being analyzed
   c) The type of algorithm being used d) The accuracy of the model
67. How does computational complexity impact the speed and efficiency of a learning algorithm?
   a) A more complex algorithm is faster and more efficient.
   b) A more complex algorithm is slower and less efficient.

c) Computational complexity has no impact on the speed and efficiency.
d) The speed and efficiency are only determined by the size of the data set.

68. Which technique can be used to reduce the computational complexity of deep neural networks?
a) Approximation
b) Pruning and quantization
c) Feature selection
d) Parallel computing

69. What is time complexity in the context of learning algorithms?
a) The amount of memory required to store data and results
b) The size and complexity of the data set
c) The number of operations the algorithm takes to complete
d) The efficiency of the algorithm

70. What is space complexity in the context of learning algorithms?
a) The amount of time it takes for the algorithm to complete
b) The size and complexity of the data set
c) The efficiency of the algorithm
d) The amount of memory required to store data and results

71. Which challenge is NOT associated with the computational complexity of learning algorithms?
a) Designing efficient algorithms
b) Optimizing the algorithms
c) Understanding the behavior of the algorithms
d) Balancing accuracy and precision of the model

72. Which solution can help reduce the time and space complexity of learning algorithms?
a) Using approximate algorithms
b) Increasing the size of the data set
c) Using more complex algorithms
d) Employing feature selection techniques

73. What does space complexity measure in computational learning?
a) The time required to execute the algorithm
b) The number of operations the algorithm performs
c) The amount of memory required to store data and results
d) The accuracy and effectiveness of the algorithm

74. Which equation represents the space complexity model in computational learning?
a) $S(n) = c/n$
b) $S(n) = n^2$
c) $S(n) = c*n$
d) $S(n) = \log(n)$

75. What can be a result of a high space complexity algorithm in computational learning?
a) Faster execution time
b) Reduced memory usage
c) Slower or impossible execution on specific devices
d) Improved accuracy and effectiveness

76. What are some ways to reduce space complexity in computational learning?
a) Increasing the input size
b) Using data compression or dimensionality reduction techniques
c) Adding more intermediate results
d) Using complex data structures

77. How does space complexity relate to the input size in computational learning?
a) Space complexity is inversely proportional to the input size.

b) Space complexity is unrelated to the input size.
c) Space complexity is directly proportional to the input size.
d) Space complexity is constant regardless of the input size.

78. What is the trade-off between space and time complexity?
a) More memory usage reduces overall execution time.
b) More memory usage increases overall execution time.
c) Less memory usage reduces overall execution time.
d) Less memory usage has no impact on overall execution time.

79. What can be a consequence of high space complexity in computational learning?
a) Improved accuracy and effectiveness
b) Reduced computational resources needed
c) Slower execution time
d) Lower memory requirements

80. Why is space complexity an important consideration in computational learning?
a) It directly affects the accuracy and effectiveness of the algorithm.
b) It determines the trade-off between space and time complexity.
c) It impacts the efficiency and effectiveness of the algorithm.
d) It measures the number of operations performed by the algorithm.

81. Which factor determines the complexity of a machine learning task?
a) The number of samples used
b) The type of data used
c) The number of features used
d) The type of model used

82. What is sample complexity in machine learning?
a) The number of features used in a machine learning algorithm
b) The number of variables in a machine learning algorithm
c) The number of samples needed to learn a task
d) The complexity of the task being learned

83. Which technique can help improve the sample complexity of a machine learning algorithm?
a) Feature selection
b) Hyperparameter tuning
c) Feature engineering
d) All of the above

84. Which model type might be suitable for predicting the outcome of a football game?
a) Decision tree
b) Neural network
c) Support vector machine
d) *K*-means clustering

85. What does computational learning refer to?
a) Selecting an appropriate optimization method
b) Building a model that can make predictions based on data
c) Feature engineering and hyperparameter tuning
d) Analyzing the complexity of a machine learning task

86. Which factor does NOT influence sample complexity in machine learning?
a) The number of classes in the task
b) The complexity of the task being learned
c) The type of model used
d) The type of data used

87. What can feature selection help reduce in machine learning?
a) The number of samples required
b) The number of features required
c) The complexity of the task
d) The type of model used

88. What does the success or failure of a machine learning algorithm depend on?
a) The number of variables in the algorithm
b) The type of model used

c) The sample complexity of the algorithm
d) The number of features used

89. Which factor is NOT considered when determining the time complexity of learning in machine learning?
a) Size of the data set b) Complexity of the task
c) Type of algorithm used d) Number of iterations in the learning process

90. What can help reduce the time complexity of learning in machine learning for large data sets?
a) Stochastic gradient descent (SGD) b) Decision trees
c) *K*-nearest neighbors (KNN) d) Support vector machines (SVM)

91. For a complex task with a small data set, which algorithm is more suitable?
a) Stochastic gradient descent (SGD) b) Decision trees
c) *K*-nearest neighbors (KNN) d) Support vector machines (SVM)

92. What does the time complexity of learning in machine learning depend on?
a) Size of the data set b) Complexity of the task
c) Type of algorithm used d) All of the above

93. Which algorithm is known for being efficient for both small and large data sets?
a) Stochastic gradient descent (SGD) b) Decision trees
c) *K*-nearest neighbors (KNN) d) Support vector machines (SVM)

94. What does the time complexity of learning in machine learning determine?
a) The accuracy of the predictions b) The number of features used
c) The time taken for the machine to learn d) The complexity of the task being learned

95. Which factor plays a crucial role in determining the time complexity of learning in machine learning?
a) Size of the data set b) Complexity of the task
c) Type of algorithm used d) Number of iterations in the learning process

96. What is the goal when selecting an algorithm for a machine learning task?
a) Maximizing the accuracy of predictions
b) Minimizing the time complexity of learning
c) Using a specific type of algorithm
d) Balancing the trade-off between accuracy and time complexity

97. What is the mistake-bound learning model used for?
a) Recognizing patterns in data
b) Estimating the expected loss of a decision
c) Adjusting behavior based on feedback
d) Learning from mistakes in language acquisition

98. Which equation is used in the mistake-bound learning model to calculate the expected loss?
a) Expected Loss = Number of Mistakes / Number of Data Points
b) Expected Loss = Number of Mistakes + 1
c) Expected Loss = Number of Data Points / Number of Mistakes
d) Expected Loss = (Number of Mistakes + 1) / (Number of Data Points + 2)

99. Which example illustrates error-based (mistake-based) learning?
a) Learning to ride a bicycle b) Recognizing patterns in data
c) Building an AI algorithm d) Speaking a new language

100. What does the mistake-bound learning model assume?
a) Mistakes are not important in the learning process
b) We don't have a feedback mechanism to identify mistakes
c) Mistakes are integral to the learning process
d) The number of data points is always equal to the number of mistakes

101. In the mistake-bound learning model, what does the expected loss of a decision depend on?
a) Number of mistakes made in the past
b) Number of data points plus two
c) Number of correct decisions made
d) Number of iterations in the learning process

102. What is one of the applications of the mistake-bound learning model in machine learning?
a) Adjusting behavior based on feedback
b) Recognizing patterns in data
c) Estimating the expected loss of a decision
d) Learning from mistakes in language acquisition

103. What role do mistakes play in the mistake-bound learning model?
a) Mistakes are irrelevant to the learning process
b) Mistakes help adjust behavior based on feedback
c) Mistakes hinder the learning process
d) Mistakes are only considered during language acquisition

104. Which statement best describes the mistake-bound learning model?
a) Mistakes are avoided at all costs during the learning process
b) Mistakes are ignored as they have no impact on learning
c) Mistakes are embraced as an essential part of the learning process
d) Mistakes are considered random occurrences with no significance

105. Which equation represents an instance-based learning model?
a) Predicted Output = f(Inputs, Instances)
b) Predicted Output = Inputs - Instances
c) Predicted Output = f(Inputs) + Instances
d) Predicted Output = Instances - Inputs

106. What is the key characteristic of instance-based learning?
a) Following predefined rules
b) Storing and classifying individual examples
c) Adjusting the model based on new inputs
d) Using majority voting for classification

107. Which algorithm is an example of instance-based learning?
a) Decision tree
b) Naive Bayes
c) *K*-nearest neighbors (KNN)
d) Support vector machines (SVM)

108. What is case-based reasoning (CBR) an example of?
a) Decision tree learning
b) Reinforcement learning
c) Instance-based learning
d) Deep learning

109. What makes instance-based learning beneficial?
a) It requires a large data set
b) It works well with simple relationships between features

c) It is computationally efficient
d) It can handle complex and noisy data

110. What is one disadvantage of instance-based learning?
a) It requires a large number of features b) It is prone to underfitting
c) It is computationally expensive d) It relies on predefined rules

111. What is the key advantage of the instance-based learning model?
a) It is flexible and adaptive b) It is less prone to overfitting
c) It uses predefined rules for classification d) It can handle small data sets efficiently

112. What is an important consideration in instance-based learning?
a) Number of decision trees b) Selection of distance metric
c) Number of training iterations d) Complexity of the input features

113. Which type of learning waits until a query is made before making a prediction?
a) Lazy learning b) Eager learning
c) Supervised learning d) Reinforcement learning

114. Which equation represents a lazy learning model?
a) $F(x)$ = argminh ∈ $H\ \Sigma i$=1n$L(h(x_i), y_i)$ b) Loss = $f(w) + lR(w)$
c) Predicted Output = f(Inputs, Instances) d) None of the above

115. Which algorithm is an example of lazy learning?
a) Decision tree b) Naive Bayes
c) K-nearest neighbors (KNN) d) Support vector machines (SVM)

116. What is the key characteristic of eager learning?
a) Minimizes the total error b) Waits for a query to make predictions
c) Builds a model from training data d) Uses the K-nearest neighbors for predictions

117. Which equation represents an eager-based learning model?
a) $F(x)$ = argminh ∈ $H\ \Sigma i$=1n$L(h(x_i), y_i)$ b) Loss = $f(w) + lR(w)$
c) Predicted Output = f(Inputs, Instances) d) None of the above

118. Which algorithm is an example of eager learning?
a) Decision tree b) Naive Bayes
c) K-nearest neighbors (KNN) d) Support vector machines (SVM)

119. Which type of learning is computationally less expensive?
a) Lazy learning b) Eager learning
c) Both are equally expensive d) It depends on the data set

120. Which type of learning is faster when making predictions?
a) Lazy learning b) Eager learning
c) Both have the same speed d) It depends on the data set

121. Which branch of machine learning focuses on the development of algorithms and techniques for learning from data?
a) Reinforcement learning b) Unsupervised learning
c) Computational learning theory d) Deep learning

122. Which type of learning algorithm uses labeled data to learn a function for making predictions or decisions?

a) Supervised learning
b) Unsupervised learning
c) Reinforcement learning
d) Deep learning

123. Which type of learning algorithm learns patterns and trends from unlabeled data?
a) Supervised learning
b) Unsupervised learning
c) Reinforcement learning
d) Deep learning

124. Which type of learning algorithm uses feedback from the environment to learn how to maximize rewards?
a) Supervised learning
b) Unsupervised learning
c) Reinforcement learning
d) Deep learning

125. Which type of learning algorithm is used to learn complex patterns and trends from large data sets?
a) Supervised learning
b) Unsupervised learning
c) Reinforcement learning
d) Deep learning

126. Which type of learning algorithm is used to classify data into different classes?
a) Supervised learning
b) Unsupervised learning
c) Reinforcement learning
d) Deep learning

127. Which type of learning algorithm is used to learn from large data sets without labeled data?
a) Supervised learning
b) Unsupervised learning
c) Reinforcement learning
d) Deep learning

128. Which branch of machine learning combines computer science, mathematics, and statistics to develop models and algorithms for learning from data?
a) Reinforcement learning
b) Unsupervised learning
c) Computational learning theory
d) Deep learning

129. Which field of study focuses on the development of algorithms that can interpret and understand visual data?
a) Computational learning theory
b) Computer vision
c) Machine learning
d) Image segmentation

130. What is the primary focus of computational learning theory?
a) Developing algorithms for computer vision
b) Developing algorithms for image segmentation
c) Developing algorithms for learning from data
d) Developing algorithms for facial recognition

131. Which branch of machine learning combines mathematics, computer science, and statistics to develop algorithms that can learn from data?
a) Supervised learning
b) Reinforcement learning
c) Computational learning theory
d) Deep learning

132. Which application of computer vision involves dividing an image into multiple regions based on certain characteristics?
a) Object recognition
b) Facial recognition
c) Image segmentation
d) Feature extraction

133. What can computational learning theory be used for in computer vision?
a) Recognizing objects in an image
b) Recognizing facial features
c) Segmenting images
d) All of the above

134. Which application of computer vision involves identifying individuals based on their facial features?
   a) Object recognition b) Facial recognition
   c) Image segmentation d) Feature extraction

135. Which branch of machine learning can be used to develop algorithms that learn from data and make predictions about objects in an image?
   a) Supervised learning b) Unsupervised learning
   c) Reinforcement learning d) Computational learning theory

136. Which application of computer vision involves the process of dividing an image into multiple regions based on certain characteristics?
   a) Object recognition b) Image segmentation
   c) Feature extraction d) Deep learning

137. Which evaluation metric is calculated by dividing the number of correctly classified data points by the total number of data points?
   a) Precision b) Recall
   c) F-measure d) Accuracy

138. Which evaluation metric is a measure of how many of the actual positive results were correctly predicted?
   a) Precision b) Recall
   c) F-measure d) AUC-ROC

139. Which evaluation metric is calculated by taking the harmonic mean of precision and recall?
   a) Precision b) Recall
   c) F-measure d) AUC-ROC

140. Which evaluation metric is used to evaluate the performance of binary classifiers?
   a) Precision b) Recall
   c) AUC-ROC d) F-measure

141. Which evaluation metric is a measure of how many of the predicted positive results are actually correct?
   a) Precision b) Recall
   c) F-measure d) Accuracy

142. Which evaluation metric is a good measure of performance when the classes are imbalanced?
   a) Precision b) Recall
   c) F-measure d) Accuracy

143. Which evaluation metric is calculated by plotting the true positive rate against the false positive rate?
   a) Precision b) Recall
   c) AUC-ROC d) F-measure

144. Which evaluation metric is most suitable when the goal is to evaluate how well a model classifies data points accurately?
   a) Precision b) Recall
   c) F-measure d) Accuracy

145. What is the goal of Explainable AI (XAI)?
   a) To make AI systems more transparent and interpretable.

b) To develop algorithms for learning from data.
c) To design AI systems for decision-making.
d) To analyze the behavior of AI systems.

146. Which field of study provides the theoretical foundations for XAI?
a) Artificial Intelligence (AI)
b) Computational Learning Theory (CLT)
c) Computer Science
d) Mathematics

147. Why is XAI important in the context of AI systems?
a) To improve the accuracy of AI systems.
b) To make AI systems more transparent and interpretable.
c) To develop complex algorithms.
d) To automate decision-making processes.

148. What is the focus of Computational Learning Theory (CLT)?
a) Making AI systems interpretable.
b) Analyzing the behavior of AI systems.
c) Designing learning algorithms.
d) Explaining the principles of decision-making.

149. Which field of study is closely related to XAI?
a) Robotics
b) Data Science
c) Computational Learning Theory (CLT)
d) Cognitive Psychology

150. What is the primary reason for developing XAI?
a) To automate decision-making processes.
b) To enhance the accuracy of AI systems.
c) To make AI systems more transparent and understandable.
d) To replace human decision-making.

151. In which domains can XAI have a significant impact?
a) Social media and entertainment.
b) Finance and criminal justice.
c) Transportation and logistics.
d) Education and healthcare.

152. Which field of study provides a framework for understanding how algorithms can learn from data?
a) Artificial Intelligence (AI)
b) Computational Learning Theory (CLT)
c) Computer Vision
d) Natural Language Processing (NLP)

153. What is the primary advantage of using quantum computing in quantum machine learning (QML)?
a) Faster processing of large amounts of data.
b) Ability to solve complex problems with traditional computing.
c) Creation of accurate and reliable algorithms.
d) Scalability of quantum computing systems.

154. What is one of the challenges associated with quantum computing in QML?
a) Ability to create accurate and reliable algorithms.
b) Need for specialized hardware.
c) Scalability of quantum computing systems.
d) Difficulty of manipulating information.

155. What is one of the potential applications of quantum machine learning (QML)?
a) Analyzing large data sets and identifying patterns.
b) Solving problems too complex for traditional computing.

c) Creating models for decision-making.
d) Developing algorithms with high accuracy and reliability.

156. What is the primary advantage of quantum computing over traditional computing in QML?
a) Ability to process information accurately. b) Faster solution of complex problems.
c) Easier scalability of computing systems. d) Simpler algorithms for machine learning.

157. What is one of the challenges in developing quantum machine learning algorithms?
a) Difficulty of creating accurate and reliable algorithms.
b) Need for specialized software.
c) Lack of available quantum computing hardware.
d) Incompatibility with traditional machine learning algorithms.

158. What distinguishes quantum machine learning from traditional machine learning?
a) Quantum machine learning is faster and more scalable.
b) Quantum machine learning uses classical computing algorithms.
c) Quantum machine learning relies on quantum entanglement.
d) Quantum machine learning can process unlimited data.

159. Which field of research does quantum machine learning (QML) combine with machine learning algorithms?
a) Quantum mechanics. b) Computational Learning Theory (CLT).
c) Artificial Intelligence (AI). d) Data Science.

160. What is the potential of quantum machine learning (QML)?
a) Revolutionizing the field of quantum computing.
b) Solving problems that are too complex for traditional computing.
c) Enhancing the accuracy and reliability of traditional machine learning.
d) Replacing traditional machine learning algorithms.

Part B (Short Answer Questions)

1. Define computational learning theory.
2. Define inductive learning.
3. Define deductive learning.
4. Define abductive learning.
5. Define reinforcement learning.
6. Give an example of inductive learning.
7. Give an example of deductive learning.
8. What is the equation for abdutive learning?
9. Give an example of abductive learning.
10. Give two examples of reinforcement learning.
11. Define probably approximately correct (PAC) learning.
12. What is the mathematical equation of PAC learning?
13. Give an example of PAC learning.
14. Define complexity theory of machine learning.
15. Define computational complexity of learning.
16. How is the complexity of a learning algorithm measured?
17. What are the challenges associated with the computational complexity of learning algorithms?
18. Define space complexity of computational learning.
19. What is the equation of the space complexity of computational learning?
20. How can we measure the space complexity of computational learning?
21. Explain sample complexity of learning.

22. Define time complexity of learning. What are the factors determining the same?
23. Define the mistake-bound learning model.
24. Give an example of the mistake-bound learning model.
25. Define instance-based learning.
26. Give an example of instance-based learning.
27. What is lazy learning?
28. Give an example of lazy learning.
29. What is eager learning?
30. What is explainable AI?
31. What is quantum machine learning (QML)?
32. Define quantum computing.

Part C (Essay Questions)

1. What are the objectives of computational learning theory?
2. List the importance of computational learning theory.
3. What are the main methods used in computational learning theory?
4. Explain inductive learning in detail.
5. Explain deductive learning in detail.
6. Explain abductive learning.
7. Explain reinforcement learning.
8. Explain probably approximately correct (PAC) learning.
9. Explain complexity theory of machine learning.
10. Explain computational Complexity of Learning.
11. Explain space complexity of learning.
12. Explain sample complexity of learning.
13. Explain time complexity of learning.
14. Explain the mistake-bound learning model.
15. Explain instance-based learning.
16. Write an essay on lazy and eager learning.
17. What are the applications of computational learning theory?
18. How is computational learning theory used in natural language processing?
19. Write about the applications of computational learning theory in computer vision.
20. Write about the applications of computational learning theory in robotics.
21. What are the metrics that can be used for computational learning theory?
22. Write about the advances in deep learning related to computational learning theory.
23. Write about explainable AI related to computational learning theory.
24. Write about quantum machine learning related to computational learning theory.

ANSWER KEY

Part A

1. (c)	**2.** (b)	**3.** (a)	**4.** (c)	**5.** (c)	**6.** (b)	**7.** (a)	**8.** (d)
9. (d)	**10.** (b)	**11.** (d)	**12.** (b)	**13.** (c)	**14.** (b)	**15.** (d)	**16.** (c)
17. (b)	**18.** (d)	**19.** (a)	**20.** (b)	**21.** (d)	**22.** (b)	**23.** (c)	**24.** (a)
25. (c)	**26.** (d)	**27.** (b)	**28.** (d)	**29.** (b)	**30.** (b)	**31.** (a)	**32.** (c)
33. (a)	**34.** (b)	**35.** (b)	**36.** (c)	**37.** (d)	**38.** (d)	**39.** (d)	**40.** (d)
41. (c)	**42.** (c)	**43.** (b)	**44.** (a)	**45.** (d)	**46.** (b)	**47.** (b)	**48.** (c)
49. (b)	**50.** (c)	**51.** (d)	**52.** (d)	**53.** (d)	**54.** (c)	**55.** (d)	**56.** (c)
57. (a)	**58.** (a)	**59.** (a)	**60.** (c)	**61.** (c)	**62.** (c)	**63.** (a)	**64.** (c)
65. (a)	**66.** (d)	**67.** (b)	**68.** (b)	**69.** (c)	**70.** (d)	**71.** (d)	**72.** (a)

73. (c)	**74.** (c)	**75.** (c)	**76.** (b)	**77.** (c)	**78.** (a)	**79.** (c)	**80.** (c)
81. (b)	**82.** (c)	**83.** (a)	**84.** (a)	**85.** (b)	**86.** (a)	**87.** (b)	**88.** (c)
89. (d)	**90.** (a)	**91.** (b)	**92.** (d)	**93.** (d)	**94.** (c)	**95.** (b)	**96.** (d)
97. (b)	**98.** (d)	**99.** (a)	**100.** (c)	**101.** (a)	**102.** (b)	**103.** (b)	**104.** (c)
105. (a)	**106.** (b)	**107.** (c)	**108.** (c)	**109.** (d)	**110.** (c)	**111.** (a)	**112.** (b)
113. (a)	**114.** (a)	**115.** (c)	**116.** (c)	**117.** (b)	**118.** (a)	**119.** (a)	**120.** (b)
121. (c)	**122.** (a)	**123.** (b)	**124.** (c)	**125.** (d)	**126.** (a)	**127.** (b)	**128.** (c)
129. (b)	**130.** (c)	**131.** (c)	**132.** (c)	**133.** (d)	**134.** (b)	**135.** (d)	**136.** (b)
137. (d)	**138.** (b)	**139.** (c)	**140.** (c)	**141.** (a)	**142.** (c)	**143.** (c)	**144.** (d)
145. (a)	**146.** (b)	**147.** (b)	**148.** (c)	**149.** (c)	**150.** (c)	**151.** (b)	**152.** (b)
153. (a)	**154.** (b)	**155.** (c)	**156.** (b)	**157.** (a)	**158.** (c)	**159.** (a)	**160.** (b)

Machine Learning Models

Learning Objectives

At the end of this chapter, you will be able to:

- Explain the different types of machine learning models, including logical, geometric, distance, and probabilistic
- Identify and work with various types of features
- Perform statistical operations on features
- Apply feature transformation techniques, including feature scaling and normalization
- Implement feature selection and feature learning methods
- Explain concept learning in detail

6.1 Introduction

In the previous chapter, we discussed computational learning theory (CLT), which is a branch of theoretical computer science that studies the design and analysis of machine learning (ML) models and algorithms. ML models are mathematical representations of data and patterns that can be used for prediction, classification, clustering, etc. They are procedures that can learn from data and optimize the parameters of ML models. One way to understand the relationships between CLT, ML models and ML algorithms is to use a table that compares them along different dimensions, such as is shown in Table 6.1.

Table 6.1 Differences between CLT, ML algorithms and ML models

Dimension	CLT	ML algorithm	ML model
Goal	To provide theoretical guarantees and bounds on the performance and complexity of ML methods.	To find the optimal or near-optimal parameters of ML models that minimize a loss function or maximize a utility function.	To capture the underlying structure and regularities of data and make predictions or decisions based on them.
Example	PAC learning, VC dimension, Rademacher complexity, etc.	Gradient descent, stochastic gradient descent, expectation maximization, *K*-means, etc.	Linear regression, logistic regression, neural networks, decision trees, etc.

(*Continued*)

Table 6.1 (Continued)

Dimension	CLT	ML algorithm	ML model
Challenge	To deal with the trade-off between expressiveness and generalization, and to cope with the uncertainty and noise in data.	To find efficient and scalable algorithms that can converge to good solutions in high-dimensional and large-scale problems.	To choose the appropriate model complexity and avoid overfitting or underfitting of data.

6.2 Models in Machine Learning

The data used for ML usually consists of attributes and labels. **Attributes** are the features or variables that describe the data, such as height, weight, color. **Labels** are the outcomes or targets we want to predict or explain, such as class, category, score. Each combination of attributes and labels is called an **instance**, representing a single observation or example in the data.

For example, if we want to predict whether a person has diabetes or not based on their blood pressure and glucose level, each person's blood pressure and glucose level are the attributes and their diabetes status is the label.

The **instance space** is the set of all possible instances generated from the attributes. The **outcome space** is the set of all possible labels that can be assigned to the instances. For example, if we have two attributes, blood pressure and glucose level, each with 10 possible values, the instance space has $10 \times 10 = 100$ possible instances. If we have two possible labels, diabetes or no diabetes, the outcome space has two possible outcomes. Sometimes, the instance and outcome spaces are the same, such as when we want to cluster the instances into groups based on their similarity.

An ML model mathematically represents the relationship between the qualities and the label. It can be seen as a function that maps an instance to an outcome. The model can be learned from the data using various algorithms and techniques.

Broadly, ML models are classified into three categories: logical, geometrical, and probabilistic.

6.2.1 Logical Models

Logical models are ML models that use rules or conditions to make predictions or classifications. They are also known as rule-based or tree models because they often have a tree-like structure, where each node represents a rule or a condition and each branch represents an outcome or a decision. Logical models are easy to interpret and explain because they can be translated into natural language statements that follow if-then logic.

Consider the data plotted to predict the type of breast cancer shown in Fig. 6.1.

This plot shows a clear separation between malignant and benign cases based on age and tumor size. Given their age and tumor size, we can use this information to create a logical model that can predict the cancer type for a new patient. One possible rule for such a logical model could be:

if age > $a1$ and tumour size > $t1$, then malignant, else benign

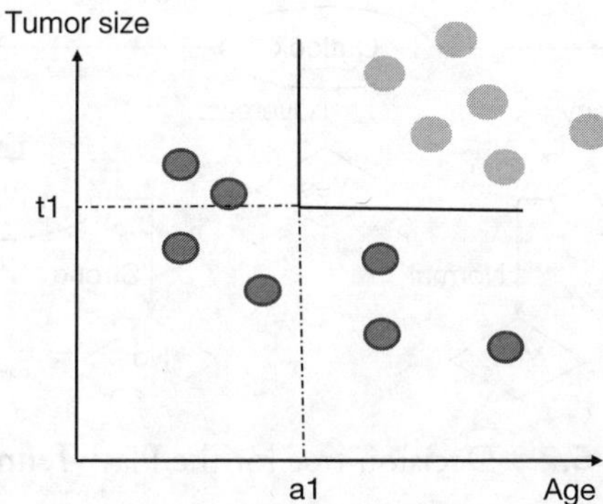

Figure 6.1 Data plot between age and tumor size

This is a simple example of a rule-based model or a tree model, where the condition (age > $a1$ and tumor size > $t1$) is the root node, and the outcomes (malignant or benign) are the leaf nodes. The condition can be further split into two sub-conditions (age > $a1$ and tumour size > $t1$), which form the internal nodes of the tree.

Consider the data shown in Table 6.2. It consists of five attributes, of which four are feature attributes and one is an outcome attribute. There are 14 data instances, and the outcome attribute is Play_Tennis, which takes either yes or no values. A logical tree model can be built based on this data. The tree thus formed is called a decision tree (Fig. 6.2). The most popular decision tree algorithms are iterative dichotomizer 3.0 (ID3) and classification and regression trees (CART).

Table 6.2 Training samples for the target concept Play_Tennis

S. No	Sky	Temp	Humidity	Wind	Play_Tennis
1	Sunny	Hot	High	Weak	No
2	Sunny	Hot	High	Strong	No
3	Overcast	Hot	High	Weak	Yes
4	Rain	Mild	High	Weak	Yes
5	Rain	Cool	Normal	Weak	Yes
6	Rain	Cool	Normal	Strong	No
7	Overcast	Cool	Normal	Strong	Yes
8	Sunny	Mild	High	Weak	No
9	Sunny	Cool	Normal	Weak	Yes
10	Rain	Mild	Normal	Weak	Yes
11	Sunny	Mild	Normal	Strong	Yes
12	Overcast	Mild	High	Strong	Yes
13	Overcast	Hot	Normal	Weak	Yes
14	Rain	Mild	High	Strong	No

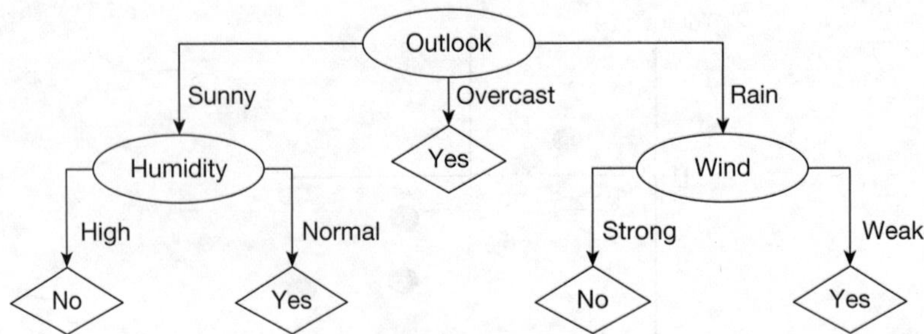

Figure 6.2 Decision tree for the Play_Tennis data

The rules generated from the decision tree are as follows:

$$\left(\text{if}\left(\text{outlook} = \text{overcast}\right)\text{then play tennis} = \text{yes}\right)\vee$$
$$\left(\text{if}\left(\left(\text{outlook} = \text{sunny}\right)\wedge\left(\text{humidity} = \text{high}\right)\right)\text{then play tennis} = \text{no}\right)\vee$$
$$\left(\text{if}\left(\left(\text{outlook} = \text{sunny}\right)\wedge\left(\text{humidity} = \text{normal}\right)\right)\text{then play tennis} = \text{yes}\right)\vee$$
$$\left(\text{if}\left(\left(\text{outlook} = \text{rain}\right)\wedge\left(\text{wind} = \text{strong}\right)\right)\text{then play tennis} = \text{no}\right)\vee$$
$$\left(\text{if}\left(\left(\text{outlook} = \text{rain}\right)\wedge\left(\text{wind} = \text{weak}\right)\right)\text{then play tennis} = \text{no}\right)$$

The rules formed can be observed as conjunctions of disjunctions of the paths formed from the root to the leaf nodes. Each leaf node is the outcome label, that is, yes or no.

This decision tree is an example of a logical model that can make predictions or classifications based on multiple features and classes. It is also easy to interpret and explain because it can be translated into natural language statements that follow if-then logic.

6.2.2 Geometrical Models

Here, the data is represented in a 2D or 3D hyperplane. Data with four or more attributes is difficult to visualize and can only be imagined in a virtual space. Geometric models are helpful in ML because they make it possible to see the connection between a data set's input attributes and output labels. We can observe how the data is distributed and clustered based on its class label by showing each data instance as a point in a hyperplane. This can assist us in selecting the best ML algorithm to analyze the data and generate precise predictions.

Linear models are geometrical models with linearly separable outcome space. Consider simple data with two attributes and one outcome. Assume that the number of unique outcomes is two. This is called a two-class problem. Each instance can be represented in a two-dimensional plane as a point. The point is represented based on the class label.

For example, consider the simple logical AND data shown in Table 6.3. The visual representation of the data is shown in Fig. 6.3. Here, each data tuple is shown as a point in the 2D plane depicting the class label. The points with label 0 are represented as circles, and those with label 1 are represented as squares. After plotting the data over a plane, the data is linearly separable if a straight line separates the data points. Otherwise, it is linearly inseparable.

Table 6.3 Truth table for logical AND gate

x_1	x_2	y
0	0	0
0	1	0
1	0	0
1	1	1

The general equation of a straight line $y = w^T x + w_0$ is used to represent the linear model, where $w^T = [w_1, w_2]$ is the transpose of the weight vector, $x = \begin{bmatrix} x_1 \\ x_2 \end{bmatrix}$ is the input vector, and w_0 is the intercept.

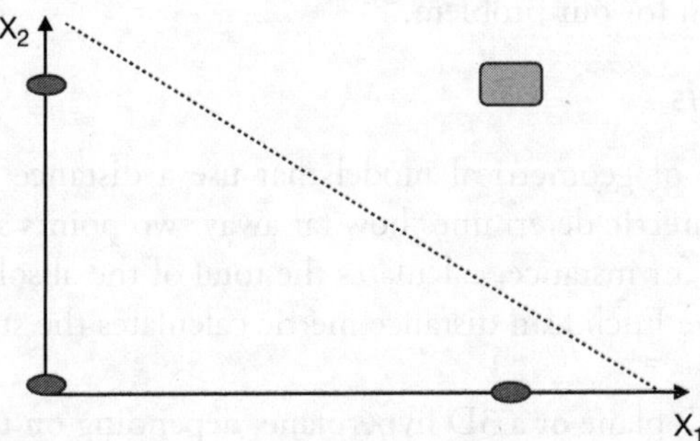

Figure 6.3 Classification of the logical AND gate inputs

The weights are the model parameters whose values are determined during training. Logistic regression and multilayer perceptron are a few examples of linear models.

If, however, the data cannot be separated linearly, we may need to categorize it using a non-linear model, such as a neural network or decision tree. A **non-linear model** looks for a non-linear boundary (such as a curve or a complicated form) that divides the data points into several classes, rather than assuming a linear relationship between the input features and the output labels.

Consider the XOR problem. Here, the data has only two dimensions, but it is linearly inseparable. In such cases, a kernel method projects the data in two dimensions into higher dimensional space that can only be imagined. ML algorithms like non-linear support vector machines (SVMs) classify the data in a higher dimensional space. The XOR inputs are shown in Table 6.4, and the plot is shown in Fig. 6.4.

Table 6.4 Truth table for logical XOR gate

x_1	x_2	y
0	0	0
0	1	1
1	0	1
1	1	0

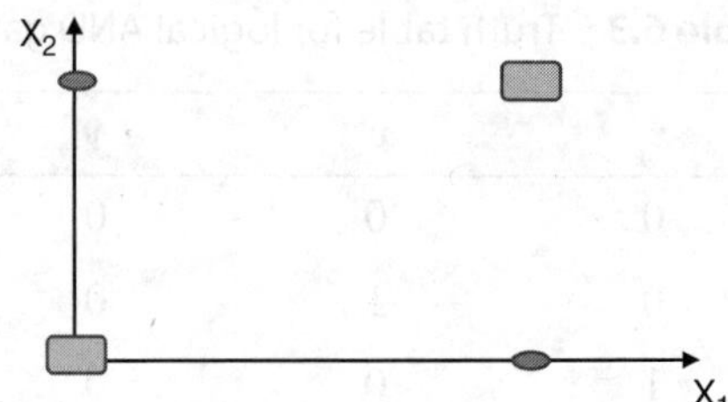

Figure 6.4 Plot of logical XOR inputs

Real-time data may only sometimes be linear and it usually has more attributes. Such data need not be linearly separable. Kernel methods can be employed to check whether the data in higher dimensional space is linearly separable.

Therefore, by using geometric models, we can gain insight into the nature of the data and select an appropriate ML algorithm for our problem.

6.2.2.1 Distance Models

Distance models are a type of geometrical model that use a distance metric to separate the outcome spaces. The **distance metric** determines how far away two points are in a particular space. The Manhattan distance metric, for instance, calculates the total of the absolute differences between two points' coordinates, while the Euclidean distance metric calculates the straight line distance between two places.

Data is plotted over a 2D plane or a 3D hyperplane, depending on the number of features or dimensions. A 2D plane has two features, height, and weight, while a 3D hyperplane has three features: length, width, and depth. The goal is to find a way to separate the different groups of data based on their distances.

One way to do this is to calculate the centroid of each data group. The centroid is the average of all the points in a group. It represents the center of mass or gravity of the group. Calculating the distance between two groups of centroids allows one to determine how far apart they are. The groups are increasingly similar the smaller the distance between them. They differ more sharply the further apart they are.

Distance-based geometrical models can be used for clustering or classification tasks. Distance-based geometrical models are useful in ML because they can help us discover patterns and structures in data and reduce the dimensionality and complexity of data. They can also help us measure the similarity or dissimilarity between data points, which can help find outliers, anomalies, or similarities. These distances are defined in equations.

Consider that there are *n* points plotted over a 2D *x-y* plane.

Euclidean distance: $\sqrt{\sum_{i=1}^{n}(x_i - y_i)^2}$

Manhattan distance: $\sqrt{\sum_{i=1}^{n}|x_i - y_i|}$

Minkowski distance: $\left(\sum_{i=1}^{n}|x_i - y_i|^p\right)^{1/p}$

Minkowski distance is the general distance metric. By substituting $p = 1$, we get the Manhattan distance. If we substitute $p = 2$, we get the Euclidean distance.

6.2.3 Probabilistic Models

Probabilistic models are a class of models that incorporate uncertainty and randomness in their structure and predictions. They are widely used in ML to capture the variability and complexity of real-world data. Probabilistic models can be divided into two categories: predictive and generative.

Predictive models estimate the conditional probability of an outcome, given some input attributes. For example, a predictive model can answer questions like "What is the probability of a customer buying a product given their age, gender, and browsing history?" or "What is the probability of a patient having a disease given their symptoms and test results?" Predictive models are often used for classification and regression tasks, where the goal is to assign a label or a value to an input instance.

Generative models estimate the joint probability of both the input and the outcome attributes. For example, a generative model can answer questions like "What is the probability of observing a customer with a certain age, gender, and browsing history buying a certain product?" or "What is the probability of observing a patient with certain symptoms and test results having a certain disease?" Generative models are often used for unsupervised learning tasks, where the goal is to discover the underlying structure and patterns of the data.

One of the advantages of probabilistic models is that they can provide point estimates, confidence intervals, and error bounds for their predictions. This can help quantify the uncertainty and reliability of the model's outputs. Another advantage is that they can incorporate prior knowledge and beliefs into the model's parameters using Bayesian inference. This can help improve the model's performance and robustness, especially when the data is scarce or noisy.
Some examples of probabilistic models in ML are:

- **Naive Bayes**: A simple and efficient predictive model that assumes conditional independence among the input attributes given the outcome. It uses Bayes' theorem to compute the posterior probability of each outcome given the input attributes.
- **Logistic Regression**: A predictive model that uses a logistic function to simulate the likelihood of a binary result, given a set of input characteristics. It might be considered a specific instance of a generalized linear model.
- **Gaussian Mixture Model**: A generative model that assumes that a combination of Gaussian distributions with unidentified parameters produces data. It assigns each data point to a cluster and estimates the mixture model's parameters using the expectation maximization approach.
- **Hidden Markov Model**: A generative model that assumes data is generated from a Markov chain with hidden states. It uses dynamic programming algorithms such as the forward-backward algorithm and the Viterbi algorithm to infer the hidden states and estimate the parameters of the Markov chain.

Let X represent the feature values and Y the value of the outcome. The probabilistic model establishes the relationship between X and Y using conditional or joint probability.

$P(Y \mid X)$ represents **conditional probability** and is read as 'the probability of Y given X,' that is, determining the probability of the outcome, given the feature values. It is determined using Bayes' theorem.

$$P(Y|X) = \frac{P(X|Y)P(Y)}{P(X)}$$

It is read descriptively as

$$\text{Posterior} = \frac{\text{Likelihood*Prior}}{\text{Evidence}}$$

$P(Y,X)$ represents **joint probability**. It is defined as

$$P(Y,X) = P(Y \cap X) = P(X|Y) * P(Y) = P(Y|X) * P(X)$$

The concept of joint probability is used to generate the data points. These probabilistic models are discussed in detail in Chapter 7.

6.3 Features

A feature is a measurement that is mapped to the outcome. Mathematically, a feature can be defined as a function that maps an instance space of an attribute to possible values for the attribute. All possible values for an attribute constitute the domain of the feature space. Features are categorized based on their domain space. Certain features are real numbers or integers, whereas some are discrete values.

Features are inputs fed into an ML model to learn a function that can produce the desired output. For instance, to create a model that can categorize photographs of dogs and cats, we must first take elements from the images that would aid the model in differentiating between the two classes. These features could be the color, shape, size, texture, or any other property of the image that is relevant to the task. The quality and quantity of features affect the performance of the model. The best features are those that capture the most information and variation in the data while reducing noise and redundancy.

6.3.1 Types of Features

Based on their values, features are roughly categorized as follows:

- **Numerical characteristics**: These characteristics have discrete or continuous numerical values. Interval and ratio features are subcategories of numerical features. Interval features lack an absolute zero point but have a significant value differential between them (for instance, the temperature in Celsius or Fahrenheit). The absolute zero point and a considerable difference are present in ratio features (for example, height, weight, or wealth).
- **Categorical characteristics**: These characteristics have defined values that fall into groups. Nominal and ordinal features are the subcategories. Nominal characteristics are those that lack a natural hierarchy among the categories (for instance, nationality or hair color). Ordinal characteristics are those that fall into a certain hierarchy or order (for example, customer happiness or educational level). Data can be grouped, counted, or compared using categorical attributes.

- **Binary features**: These are a specific kind of categorical feature that can have two possible values. For example, marital status, gender, and the existence of illness. Logical operations or categorization can both use binary characteristics.
- **Temporal features**: These are characteristics that symbolize temporal attributes such as date, time, duration and frequency. Data trends, patterns, cycles, or seasonality can all be determined by temporal properties.
- **Text features**: These serve as a representation of text data. Text features include product reviews, tweets, news stories, etc. Natural language processing (NLP) tasks like sentiment analysis, topic modeling and text summarization can use text features.

6.3.2 Statistical Operations on Features

Along with the feature space's domain, other important aspects include the kinds of operations that can be carried out on features. Take the two elements employee_id and employee_salary. Integers make up the features' domain space. It makes sense to use statistical procedures like mean on the employee_salary variable. However, statistical procedures like mean and median have no significance on employee_id.

The significant operations that can be carried out come under three main groups:

- **Measures of Central Tendency**: Used to give a single value to the entirety of the data.
- **Scattering Statistics**: This determines how far the data deviates from the mean. It is applied to understand data dispersion.
- **Shape Measures**: These characterize how the data is distributed or arranged within a data set.

Mean, median, and mode are the three primary operations that fall under measurements of central tendency. The mean shows the average value. When all the values are placed in ascending order, the median reflects the middle value. The mode shows the highest frequency value. While mode can be applied to any domain, mean and median can only feature values with integer or real number domain spaces.

Data dispersion is frequently understood using variance and standard deviation. Percentiles are another way to assess dispersion. Quartiles are typically used to quantify dispersion. When quartiles are multiplied by 25, they are referred to as percentiles. To understand the form of the data distribution, histograms and cumulative distribution plots are utilized.

We may think about the following aspects to clarify these claims with examples and show how it aids in ML:

- **Statistical procedures** on features enable meaningful summarization, analysis, and visualization of the data. They also assist us in locating data abnormalities such as outliers, missing values, skewness, and other irregularities that might impair the effectiveness of ML models.
- For instance, we can utilize **mean, median, and mode** to identify the central tendency of the wage feature and anticipate an employee's salary based on their experience, education, and talents. This can help us understand the data set's median, typical, or average salary. We can also use **variance and standard deviation** to determine how much the wage deviates from the mean or how it is distributed. This can aid in our comprehension of the scope and range of the salary feature. The salary feature can also be divided into four equal groups based on values using

quartiles or percentiles. This enables us to evaluate various wage feature subsets and spot outliers or extreme values that might impact the forecast.

- Similarly, we may use **histograms and cumulative distribution plots** to analyze the shape distribution of data like word count, punctuation marks, capital letters, etc., if we want to identify an email as spam or not based on its content. These plots can show how values are distributed across the range of values and how frequently or infrequently they appear in the features. This can assist us in **spotting patterns or trends** in the characteristics of emails that indicate whether they are spam or not.
- Before using any ML algorithm, studying and **comprehending the data** is essential. Therefore, statistical operations on features are helpful in this regard. They also assist us in **preprocessing the data**, such as scaling, normalizing, encoding, etc., to make it appropriate for ML models. They also help us compare and evaluate various ML models based on their performance characteristics, such as recall, accuracy, and precision.

6.3.3 Feature Transformation

Changing the domain of a data set's features is known as feature transformation. This has many applications:

- **Improving the data's suitability for an ML model.** For instance, certain models call for a specific normalization, standardization, or data encoding.
- **Making the data less complex or multidimensional.** As an illustration, certain elements could be unnecessary, unimportant, or noisy and might be eliminated or blended with other aspects.
- **Enhancing the model's functionality or interpretability.** One way to better capture this relationship is to convert certain features that, for instance, may have a non-linear relationship with the target variable.
- **Visualizing the distribution or organization of the data.** For instance, some features with a high degree of dimension can be projected onto a space with a lower degree of dimension using techniques like principal component analysis (PCA) or t-distributed stochastic neighbor embedding (t-SNE).

Scaling of features, which modifies the range or size of the features, is a typical feature modification. This is frequently required when the characteristics have varied units or magnitudes and might impact how some models learn. Consider a data set of employees where the two features are age and income. Age may be between 25 and 100 years, and income may be between 25000 and 250000 INR. The income factor will predominate the clustering results if such data is input to a model like *K*-means clustering, which uses distance-based metrics and has a considerably more significant scale than age. To avoid this, feature scaling can be utilized to scale the features similarly.

As it can increase the quality and usefulness of the data and eventually improve the model's performance and interpretability, feature transformation is a crucial stage in ML.

6.3.3.1 Feature Scaling or Normalization

MinMax scaling is a straightforward method that data scientists frequently use. This scaler function transforms the data into the range [0, 1]. As a result, the original data's minimum value becomes 0 and its highest value becomes 1. The remaining values are correspondingly scaled between 0 and 1.

For instance, if the original data contained values between 10 and 100, applying MinMax scaling would produce values between 0 and 1, where 10 would become 0, 100 would become 1, and 50 would become 0.5.

In ML, MinMax scaling is helpful because it can assist in normalizing the data and lessen the impact of outliers. Some ML techniques, such as gradient descent and *K*-means clustering, can perform and converge better with normalized data. In contrast to other scaling techniques that could alter the original data, MinMax scaling can also aid in maintaining the shape and distribution of the data.

The MinMax scaler is defined as follows:

$$\frac{x - x_{min}}{x_{max} - x_{min}} \tag{6.1}$$

When we use Equation (6.1) on the data given in Table 6.5, the scaled data is normalized, as is shown in Table 6.6.

Table 6.5 Sample employee age and income data

Employee_age	Employee_income
25	18000
28	22000
50	65000
44	75000

Table 6.6 Normalized employee age and income after MinMax scaling

Employee_age	Employee_income
0	0
0.12	0.0702
1	0.8246
0.76	1

Standard Scaling: ML obtains many benefits from standard scaling. Removing each feature's units and scale first makes the data more comparable. For instance, if we have two features, one measured in meters and the other in kilometers, standard scaling would make the features dimensionless and on the same scale. Scaling the data by variation and centering it around zero also lessens the impact of outliers. For instance, standard scaling may make extreme values that are significantly larger or smaller than the rest of a feature closer to the mean and less significant. Thirdly, it enhances the performance of some ML methods that depend on the magnitude of the features or presumes that the data is regularly distributed. For instance, when the data is standardized, gradient descent, which is used to optimize numerous models, converges more quickly.

Standard scaling is defined as follows:

$$\frac{x - x_{\text{mean}}}{\text{Standard deviation}} \tag{6.2}$$

Standard deviation of age: The standard deviation is a measure of how much the data values vary from the mean. To calculate the standard deviation of the given data, we need to follow these steps:

1. Find the mean of the data by adding all the values and dividing by the number of values. In this case, the mean is (25 + 28 + 50 + 44) / 4 = 36.75.
2. Subtract the mean from each value and square the result. This gives us the squared deviations from the mean. For example, for the first value, we have (25 – 36.75)^2 = 138.0625.
3. Add up all the squared deviations and divide by the number of values. This gives us the variance of the data. In this case, the variance is (138.0625 + 76.5625 + 175.5625 + 52.5625) / 4 = 110.6875.
4. Take the square root of the variance to get the standard deviation. In this case, the standard deviation is sqrt(110.6875) = 10.52.

Therefore, the standard deviation of the age is 10.52.

Standard deviation of income:

1. Find the mean of the data by adding up all the values and dividing by the number of values. In this case, the mean is (18000 + 22000 + 65000 + 75000) / 4 = 45000.
2. Find the deviation of each value from the mean by subtracting the mean from each value. The deviations are –27000, –23000, 20000 and 30000.
3. Square each deviation to get rid of the negative signs and make the values more comparable. The squared deviations are 729000000, 529000000, 400000000 and 900000000.
4. Find the sum of the squared deviations by adding them up. The sum is 2558000000.
5. Divide the sum by the number of values to get the variance, which is a measure of how spread out the data is around the mean. The variance is 2558000000 / 4 = 639500000.
6. Take the square root of the variance to get the standard deviation, which is in the same units as the original data. The standard deviation is sqrt(639500000) = 25288.36.

Therefore, the standard deviation of the income data of 4 people is 25288.36.

Using Equation (6.2) on the data given in Table 6.6, the scaled data is modified as is shown in Table 6.7.

Table 6.7 Normalized employee age and income after standard scaling

Employee_age	Employee_income	Employee_age	Employee_income
25	18000	–1.11	–1.068
28	22000	–0.831	–0.909
50	65000	1.26	0.791
44	75000	0.689	1.186

6.3.3.2 *Other Transformation Techniques*

Thresholding: Using a cut-off value, the thresholding approach turns a numerical or ordinal property into a binary feature. For instance, using thresholding, we may generate a new feature called age_group with only two values: 0 for young and 1 for elderly, given an existing feature called age a range of 0 to 100. To accomplish this, we must select a threshold number, such as 40, and assign the value 0 to all instances with age below 40 and the value 1 to all instances with age at or above 40. In this case, the cut-off point is 40, determined manually or by examining the age feature's distribution. Thresholding is helpful in ML for the following reasons:

- It can convert a continuous or ordinal characteristic into a categorical one to lower the dimensionality of the data. This may ease the handling and visualization of the data.
- It can produce more insightful features that better reflect some crucial facets of the data. For example, instead of using the precise blood pressure reading, thresholding may be used to generate a characteristic that shows whether or not a person has high blood pressure to forecast whether or not they have a particular disease.
- It can enhance the performance of various ML methods, including decision trees and logistic regression, which perform better with binary features.

Discretization: A quantitative feature value is converted to an ordinal feature value through discretization. A quantitative feature value, such as a person's height, weight, or age, is a numerical number that can be any value within a range. A categorical value with a natural order, such as small, medium, or big, is an ordinal feature value. A quantitative feature's range is discretized into intervals, giving each interval an ordinal value. Every interval is regarded as a bin with an associated ordinal value. The age feature, for instance, can be discretized into bins like [0–10], [11–20], [21–30], and so on, and each bin can be given an ordinal value like young, teen, adult, and so forth. This method is also known as **binning**.

ML can benefit from discretization for a number of reasons. Combining comparable values can first reduce the noise and outliers in the data. By limiting the range of possible values, it can make data computation and analysis simpler. Thirdly, employing meaningful categories rather than numbers can help make the data easier to read and comprehend. It can also enhance the performance of ML methods, such as decision trees or naive Bayes, that perform better with categorical information than numerical features.

There are many discretization techniques based on how the intervals are specified and how the ordinal values are assigned. **Constant width discretization** is a technique for dividing a feature's range into intervals of equal width. For instance, if we wish to build 10 bins and the age range is [0–100], each bin will have a width of 10. **Constant frequency discretization** is a different technique that separates a feature's range into intervals with a fixed number of instances. For instance, if we have 100 instances of age and want to divide them into 10 bins, each bin will have 10 occurrences. Although constant frequency discretization can prevent the creation of empty or sparse bins, it can also result in intervals of varying sizes.

6.3.4 Feature Construction

Building new features from those already present in a data set is known as feature creation. When a data set comprises many features, but not all are equally significant or relevant for the ML task, feature creation can be helpful. In these circumstances, adding new features by combining those already present can make the feature vector more dimensional, which can result in overfitting or inefficient computation. To get around this issue, one can use feature selection techniques like a filter or wrapper approaches or dimensionality reduction techniques like principal component analysis (PCA) to reduce the number of features, while retaining the most useful ones.

Feature building can be used when a data set comprises categorical characteristics, but the ML model requires numerical inputs. For instance, variables like gender, color, or nationality cannot be used as direct inputs into a regression or neural network model if the data set contains those features. In these circumstances, feature encoding techniques like one-hot encoding, label encoding, or hashing can be used to transform the category characteristics into numerical values. However, these methods can also make the feature vector more dimensional and add sparsity or redundancy. As a result, one may also use feature creation techniques to transform existing categorical features into new numerical ones that capture more valuable data.

Applying arithmetic operations, such as addition, subtraction, multiplication, or division, to any existing feature is a quick approach to creating new features from the ones that already exist. Finding the Cartesian product of two distinct features, such as concatenating or multiplying them, and finding the ratio between two features, such as percentage or proportion, is a third method for creating new features.

Table 6.8 shows an example using employee data.

Table 6.8 Sample employee data with name, designation, and gender attributes

Employee_name	Employee_desig	Employee_gender
aaa	Manager	Male
bbb	Senior Manager	Female
ccc	Clerk	Male
ddd	Clerk	Female

To convert the values of employee_desig and employee_gender to numerical values, one-hot encoding is used. In this technique, all unique values are scanned and counted, and many attributes are created as new features whose values are either 0 or 1.

Employee_desig has three unique values – Manager, Senior Manager, and Clerk. Similarly, Employee_gender has two unique values – Male and Female. After performing one-hot encoding, the data set would be transformed, as shown in Table 6.9.

Table 6.9 Sample employee data with name, designation, and gender attributes after one-hot encoding

Employee_ name	desig_ manager	desig_ sr_manager	desig_ clerk	gender_ male	gender_fe- male
aaa	1	0	0	1	0
bbb	0	1	0	0	1
ccc	0	0	1	1	0
ddd	0	0	1	0	1

6.3.5 Feature Selection

Feature selection means choosing a subset of features from the initial feature set that are pertinent and instructive for the learning process. After feature creation, which generates new features from the raw data or existing features, feature selection is frequently carried out. While feature selection can help to lessen the redundancy and irrelevant features, feature creation can help to increase the quality and diversity of the feature set.

Depending on whether the target variable is present or not, feature selection can be applied to both supervised and unsupervised learning models. The target variable may be used as a criterion in feature selection in supervised learning to assess the utility of the features. Other criteria, such as clustering quality, information content, or statistical dependence, may be used for feature selection in unsupervised learning. The preprocessing step of feature selection is thought to provide various **advantages** for the learning task, including:

- **Dimensionality reduction**: Feature selection can reduce the dimensionality of the data by choosing a lower number of features, making the data simpler to visualize, comprehend, and manage.
- **Decreased computational cost and training time**: Feature selection, particularly for complicated models with several parameters and processes, can decrease training time by lowering the number of features.
- **Reduction of overfitting**: Feature selection can aid in preventing overfitting by removing redundant or irrelevant features. Overfitting occurs when the model learns too much from the noise or specific patterns in the training data and cannot generalize well to new or unknown data.
- **Improvement of generalization**: Choosing informative and representative features can assist the learning model in performing and performing accurately on new or unknown data, representing its ability to generalize well to many contexts and scenarios.
- **Simplifying the structure and complexity of the learning model**: By lowering the number of features, feature selection can help make the learning model simpler and easier to understand.

It is possible to execute feature selection in supervised learning using a variety of approaches, which can generally be divided into three categories: filtering, wrapper, and intrinsic methods.

Filtering method: This method ranks and assesses the features based on statistical or information-theoretic metrics, such as mutual information, chi-squared test and correlation, without using a learning model. The final subset is then chosen from the features with high scores. Filtering techniques are quick and scalable, but they must consider how the features interact or how well they work with the learning model.

The metrics used for filtering are information gain, Fisher's score, chi-squared test, and so on. These metrics are used by considering each attribute and the labeled attribute. Information gain determines entropy reduction. Each feature attribute correlates with the labeled output and checks whether the two features correlate positively or negatively. The negatively correlated feature can be dropped accordingly. Fisher's score ranks the attribute based on Fisher's criteria. The features with large Fisher's score can be considered and the other features can be discarded. A chi-squared test is used to find the relationship between each feature and the labeled feature.

Wrapper method: These methods assess the characteristics using a learning model as a black box. On a validation set or by utilizing cross-validation, they look for the ideal subset of features that maximizes a specific performance parameter, such as accuracy, precision, recall, etc. Compared to filtering methods, wrapper approaches are more precise and adaptable, but are also more computationally expensive and prone to overfitting. In wrapper methods, features are selected through a search mechanism over the feature space. The greedy method is used in wrapper methods for the feature selection process. It explores all possible combinations and selects the best features. The process will be initiated by selecting a subset of features and training the model using those features. The features can be added or subtracted depending on the output to improve the model's performance. The popular algorithms used for feature selection in this category are forward selection, backward elimination, etc.

Intrinsic learning methods: During the training phase, these methods either alter the target function or employ regularization approaches to penalize or remove unnecessary or redundant characteristics. Although intrinsic approaches are effective and adaptive, they are model-specific and might not work with all learning models. Intrinsic methods can be considered a hybrid method that uses the advantages of both filter and wrapper methods. The feature selection process is also iterative and reduces computational costs. Features are selected such that each feature contributes to the model's performance. The popular methods used in this category are LASSO regularization and random forest.

Forward selection is an iterative process. It starts with a single feature and iteratively adds features, and evaluates the model in each iteration. The process ends when a newly added feature does not improve the model's performance. **Backward elimination** is the reverse of forward selection. This method considers all the features first, and then the model is evaluated. The process is repeated by removing the least significant feature in each iteration. The iterative process stops when there is no improvement in the model's performance.

The data is plotted over a hyperplane and finds the best-fit line to determine the relationships among the data. This process is called **data fitting**. The model can choose the best-fit line by undergoing a learning process. Once a model is learned, it is subjected to evaluation. This helps us to understand whether the model is overfitted or underfitted.

The model can best fit the data when it finds all patterns or relationships in the data and ignores the random data points. A model is said to be **overfitted** if it covers all the data points and random points. A model is said to be **underfitted** if it does not find any relationship among the data points and cannot determine to which category the test data belongs.

Regularization means adjusting or tuning the ML model to minimize the loss function preventing overfitting or underfitting.

LASSO or L1 regularization: Least absolute shrinkage and selection operator, or LASSO, is used for regression methods. LASSO regularization modifies overfitted or underfitted models by adding a penalty term to the loss function. The penalty term is usually the sum of the absolute values of the coefficients used in the model. It is represented mathematically as follows:

$$\text{Cost} = \text{Loss} + \lambda + \sum w, \tag{6.3}$$

where λ represents the penalty term and w is the slope of the curve fit over the data.

The penalty term is calculated by adding the absolute values of the model's coefficients. LASSO regularization shrinks the coefficients to zero and is also used for dimensionality reduction. It estimates the median of the data. LASSO regularization produces sparse models with few coefficients because other coefficients are shrunk to zero.

Ridge or L2 regularization: Here, the penalty term is the sum of the squares of the coefficients. It also shrinks the coefficients but is not set to zero. It is represented mathematically as

$$\text{Cost} = \text{Loss} + \lambda + \sum w^2 \tag{6.4}$$

6.4 Concept Learning

Concept learning seeks to extract the definition of a broad category from the input data. For instance, concept learning can be trained to recognize which animal photos fall under the category of dogs, given a batch of animal images. The challenge of inferring a Boolean-valued function from the given data, where the function returns true for examples that belong to the idea and false for instances that do not, is another way to conceptualize learning. Thus, concept learning is the process of identifying the input feature–output label mapping that best matches the training data.

Depending on the nature and structure of the data, the complexity and expressiveness of the hypothesis space, and the selection criteria for the best hypothesis, various concepts can be learned differently. A set of potential functions that can be utilized to express the idea is known as a **hypothesis space**. The hypothesis space is the set of all feasible linear functions, for instance, if a linear combination of input features specifies the notion. Finding the function that minimizes a certain error or loss function on the training data is the objective of concept learning, which may be considered a search problem over the hypothesis space.

ML benefits from concept learning because it enables us to extrapolate from particular examples to novel and unforeseen situations. We can anticipate or categorize new data that we have not seen before by learning a concept from a small, noisy sample of data. Understanding the fundamental structure and logic of the concept can also help us find patterns and regularities in the data. Concept learning applies to many fields and applications, including bioinformatics, computer vision, speech recognition, and natural language processing.

6.4.1 Concept Learning Problem Formulation

Concept learning aims to approximate a Boolean-valued function from the training samples. We define two data sets; the first is specific while the second is relatively larger than the first. Table 6.10 shows the first data set. The class labeled attribute Enjoy_Sport is termed a concept. There are four tuples in the given data set, out of which for three tuples, Enjoy_Sport is Yes, and for one tuple, it is No.

Table 6.10 Training samples for the target concept Enjoy_Sport

Attribute						Concept
Sky	*Temp*	*Humidity*	*Wind*	*Water*	*Forecast*	*Enjoy_Sport*
Sunny	Warm	Normal	Strong	Warm	Same	Yes
Sunny	Warm	High	Strong	Warm	Same	Yes
Rainy	Cool	High	Strong	Warm	Change	No
Sunny	Warm	High	Strong	Cool	Change	Yes

There are six attributes; hence, each hypothesis is a six-element vector. For each attribute, the hypothesis may be that either a value or any value is acceptable or no value is acceptable.

For example, for the attribute Sky,

Sky = Sunny represents a value

Sky = ? represents any acceptable value

Sky = ∅ means that no value is acceptable

A hypothesis (h) is the conjunction of the values of all instance attributes of a tuple, that is, each instance is represented as a conjunction of the values of the attributes. For example, (Sunny, Warm, Normal, Strong, Warm, Same) represents an instance. The hypothesis of this instance is represented as

$$\left(\begin{array}{l}(\text{Sky} = \text{Sunny}) \wedge (\text{Temp} = \text{Warm}) \wedge (\text{Humidity} = \text{Normal}) \wedge (\text{Wind} = \text{Strong}) \wedge (\text{Water} = \text{Warm}) \\ \wedge (\text{Forecast} = \text{Same})\end{array}\right)$$

The set of all hypotheses is called the hypothesis space ($\mathcal{H}$). The most general hypothesis is represented using? for each attribute. Thus, for the example given in Table 6.10, the most general hypothesis is represented by (?,?,?,?,?,?). The most specific hypothesis is represented using ∅ for each attribute. Thus, for the example given in Table 6.10, the most general hypothesis is represented by (∅,∅,∅,∅,∅,∅).

Notation:

X: Data or set of attributes on which the concept is defined.

$$X = \{\text{Sky, Temp, Humidity, Wind, Water, Forecast}\}$$

C: Concept to be learned; otherwise called a target concept. It is defined as a Boolean-valued function over *X*, that is, $c : X \to \{0,1\}$. For the data given in the table, $c(x) = 1 \to enjoy\_sport = yes$ and $c(x) = 0 \to enjoy\_sport = no$

$(x, c(x))$: Input to the learner trying to understand the concept. x is an instance of X. The learner receives a set of instances and the target concept value.
D: The training data.
$\mathcal{H}$: The set of all possible hypotheses presented for the learner to identify the concept.
$h(x)$: It represents a particular hypothesis taken from the set $\mathcal{H}$. It is defined as a Boolean-valued function over X, that is, $h: X \rightarrow \{0,1\}$. The learner has to determine a given hypothesis h such that $h(x) = c(x) \forall x \in X$.

The hypothesis space has a general-to-specific ordering of the hypotheses. The task of concept learning is mapping the instances on to a target function. In the example, the target attribute or concept is Enjoy_Sport having the values Yes or No. Mathematically, it is represented as $c: X \rightarrow \{\text{Yes, No}\}$ where c represents the target function and X represents an instance.
To summarize, the concept learning problem is formulated as follows:

Given: The set of instances and the corresponding target concept values (D)
Process: Create a hypothesis space by converting each instance into an equivalent hypothesis
Determine: To check a randomly given hypothesis (h) such that $h(x) = c(x) \forall x \in D$

6.4.2 Concept Learning Problem as a Search Problem

Consider the data defined in Table 6.11.

Table 6.11 Analysis of the Enjoy_Sport training data

Attribute name	Distinct values	Distinct value count
Sky	Sunny, Cloudy, Rainy	3
Temp	Warm, Cold	2
Humidity	Normal, High	2
Wind	Strong, Weak	2
Water	Warm, Cool	2
Forecast	Same, Change	2

Thus the number of distinct instances that constitute the total instance space X can be calculated as $3 \times 2 \times 2 \times 2 \times 2 \times 2 = 96$. While representing an instance as a hypothesis, each attribute has two more values (?,.∅) representing the most general and most specific hypothesis. Thus, the hypothesis space $(\mathcal{H})$ contains $5 \times 4 \times 4 \times 4 \times 4 \times 4 = 5120$ syntactically distinct hypotheses.

However, every hypothesis contains one or more (∅∅) symbols, representing the empty instances considered as negative classes. By considering all those empty instances as a single instance, the hypothesis space $(\mathcal{H})$ contains $1 + (4 \times 3 \times 3 \times 3 \times 3 \times 3) = 973$ semantically distinct hypotheses. Enjoy_Sport is a toy data set with a small and finite hypothesis space.

The process of searching the hypothesis space is called concept learning. A set of potential answers to a problem is called a hypothesis space. The hypothesis space, for instance, might include all the possible definitions of even numbers, such as numbers divisible by 2, numbers ending with 0, 2, 4, 6, or 8, etc.

To efficiently search the hypothesis space, many techniques have been developed. The best theory that fits the facts and generalizes well to new circumstances is what these algorithms seek to identify. Decision trees, neural networks, and genetic algorithms are a few examples of these algorithms.

By identifying connections between the existing hypotheses, the algorithms take advantage of the hypothesis space. For instance, some hypotheses may be more general than others, covering more examples while being less precise. Some hypotheses may be more specific than others, even though they apply to fewer instances. Some hypotheses may be equivalent, which means they apply to the same situations and are equally accurate.

The structure of the hypothesis space allows it to be explored. The ordering of hypotheses is general-to-specific. Accordingly, the hypotheses are presented in a hierarchy from the broadest to the narrowest. The most general hypothesis, in the case of the concept of even numbers, can be all numbers, and the most particular hypothesis, only 2. The algorithms can narrow the search space and concentrate on the most promising hypotheses using this structure.

This strategy is helpful in ML since it can reduce the difficulty and duration of the search for an effective answer. In addition, it can aid in preventing overfitting and underfitting, which are frequent issues. Overfitting develops when the hypothesis is overly precise and does not transfer well to fresh data. Underfitting occurs when the hypothesis is comprehensive and misses the key characteristics of the data.

6.4.3 Representation of Hypothesis Space as a General-to-Specific Ordering

A general-to-specific ordering of the hypotheses, commonly referred to as a lattice, is used to represent the hypothesis space. Every pair of elements in a lattice has a distinct least upper bound and a distinct largest lower bound. In ML, the most general hypothesis that is more particular than the least upper bound represents both. In contrast, the biggest lower bound represents the most specific hypothesis that is more general than both. For instance, let there be two hypotheses, H1 and H2, that categorize some examples as positive and others as negative. Their least upper bound is the hypothesis that classifies all instances classed as positive by either H1 or H2 and the remainder as negative. The hypothesis that labels all occurrences categorized as positive by H1 and H2 as positive and the remaining instances as negative is also their greatest lower bound.

Ordering the hypotheses from the general to the specific has certain advantages for ML. The first benefit is our ability to articulate the concept of consistency between a hypothesis and a set of training instances. If a hypothesis accurately categorizes every case in a set, it is consistent with the set. If a hypothesis is consistent with all the cases that the other hypothesis is compatible with and maybe more, then it is more general than the other hypothesis. If a hypothesis agrees with a portion of the cases with which the other hypothesis agrees, then it is more specific than the other hypothesis.

The hypothesis that categorizes all occurrences as positive is the most general in the lattice, while the hypothesis that categorizes all cases as negative is the most particular. The training instances are consistent with the most general consistent (MGC) hypothesis, which has the lowest upper bound, and the training examples are consistent with the most specific consistent (MSC) hypothesis, which has the highest lower bound.

Second, by arranging the hypotheses from general to specific, we may specify a search method for narrowing down the possible hypotheses in the hypothesis space. This method starts with the MGC and iteratively advances to increasingly specific hypotheses until it discovers one that meets some criteria, such as accuracy or simplicity.

A different approach is known as specific-to-generic search. It begins with the MSC and iteratively proceeds to more general hypotheses until it discovers one that meets a specific requirement. Heuristics that estimate a hypothesis' quality based on a particular metric, such as information gain or entropy, can be used to direct either strategy.

General-to-specific ordering is explained with an example.

More general than relation $\left(\geq_g\right)$

It is formally defined as h_j being more general than h_i if $h_i(x)=1 \rightarrow h_j(x)=1$.

Symbolically it is represented as $h_j \geq_g h_i$

Strictly more general than $(>_g)$

A hypothesis h_j is more general than h_i if and only if $\left(h_j \geq_g h_i\right) \wedge \left(h_j \ngeq_g h_i\right)$.

Consider three hypotheses $\left(h_1, h_2, h_3\right)$ in the H hypothesis space. They are given as

$$h_1 = (\text{Sunny},?,?,\text{Strong},??)$$

$$h_2 = (\text{Sunny},?,?,?,??)$$

$$h_3 = (\text{Sunny},?,?,?,\text{Cool},?)$$

The first hypothesis imposes two constraints on the attributes Sky = Sunny and Wind = Strong. The second hypothesis imposes only one constraint on the attribute Sky = Sunny. The third hypothesis has two constraints on the attributes Sky = Sunny and Water = Cool. Hypothesis h_2 has fewer constraints compared to h_1.

From the hypotheses given, it is observed that $h_2 \geq_g h_1$ because every instance satisfied by h_1 also satisfies h_2. Every instance satisfied by a hypothesis means that out of the six attributes given in the example, h_1 Sky = Sunny and h_2 Sky = Sunny. The same should apply to the other attributes in the given hypothesis. Thus $h_2 \geq_g h_1$. Similarly, $h_2 \geq_g h_3$. The relation $\geq_g$ is reflexive, anti-symmetric, and transitive.

6.4.4 Finding a Maximally Specific Hypothesis (Find-S)

The Find-S algorithm is a quick and effective technique for understanding a subject from a collection of helpful examples. A notion is a Boolean function, such as whether an email is spam or not, that transfers an instance to a binary output. The algorithm assumes that a notion can be represented by a combination of attribute-value pairs, such as (subject contains 'free') AND (sender is unknown). The method begins by combining all the features with their values negated, such as (subject does not contain 'free') AND (sender is not unknown) AND... The program then moves on to more specific hypotheses until it reaches the most specific conclusion feasible. Any time this is tested, it will always be false. The algorithm then goes through each successful example repeatedly and generalizes the theory by deleting any attribute-value pair that conflicts with the example.

For instance, the algorithm will eliminate the pair (subject does not contain 'free') from the hypothesis if the first positive case has the subject 'free offer' in it. When the hypothesis covers all of the positive examples, the algorithm stops. The resulting hypothesis correctly classifies all positive cases and non-negative ones, consistent with the observed training data. It might overfit the data or leave out certain crucial qualities, which might need to be more accurate for unobserved situations.

The Find-S method employs a more comprehensive ordering relation than a partial one to compare hypotheses. According to this connection, hypothesis h_1 is more universal than hypothesis h_2 if every instance that meets h_2 also meets h_1. The hypothesis (subject contains 'free'), for example, is more inclusive than the hypothesis (subject contains 'free') AND (sender is unknown), as any email that matches the latter also matches the former, but not the other way around. It is a partial order since the more general relation is transitive, reflexive, and anti-symmetric. In each iteration, the Find-S method switches from a more particular to a more general hypothesis, ensuring it does not conflict with prior examples.

The Find-S algorithm is helpful in ML because it may locate a consistent hypothesis for a given idea rapidly without needing any prior information or negative instances. Being limited to straightforward logical procedures, it is also simple to implement and comprehend. The Find-S algorithm cannot describe disjunctive notions, is sensitive to noise and example order, and is prone to overfitting, among other drawbacks. As a result, it is frequently used as a benchmark or as the foundation for more complex learning algorithms.

The Find-S algorithm:

i. Initialize h to the most specific hypothesis

ii. For each positive training instance x in the data set,

For each attribute constraint a_i on h

If the constraint a_i is satisfied by x, then

Do nothing

Else replace a_i in h by the following the more general constraint that is satisfied by x

iii. Output hypothesis h

Example: Refer to the data given in Table 6.11.

The first step in the algorithm is to initialize h with the most specific hypothesis. Thus

$$h_0 \leftarrow (\varnothing,\varnothing,\varnothing,\varnothing,\varnothing,\varnothing)$$

The first positive instance in the training set is

$$x_1 = (\text{Sunny, Warm, Normal, Strong, Warm, Same})$$

In the context of the Find-S algorithm, the initial hypothesis is the most specific one, which means it will not generalize beyond the instances already seen. This initial hypothesis is represented by '∅' in every attribute, indicating that it has not yet encountered any positive examples from which to generalize.

When a new instance is encountered, such as x_1=(Sunny, Warm, Normal, Strong, Warm, Same), the algorithm compares this instance with the current hypothesis. If the instance is a positive example and the current hypothesis is too specific (as indicated by '∅'), the hypothesis needs to be generalized to accommodate the new instance.

Thus, the new hypothesis h_1 becomes (Sunny, Warm, Normal, Strong, Warm, Same), which is exactly the same as the instance x_1. This means that the hypothesis now accepts this particular instance as a positive example. However, it is still specific because it only covers this one instance and not the others.

As more instances are encountered, the Find-S algorithm will continue to generalize the hypothesis as needed to cover the range of positive examples, while remaining as specific as possible. The goal is to find the hypothesis that best explains all the positive examples without including any negative examples.

The second positive instance is $x = (\text{Sunny, Warm, High, Strong, Warm, Same})$.

For this instance, the humidity value is High, which differs from the value Normal in the previous instance. Hence, this value is generalized, keeping the rest of the attribute values the same. The modified hypothesis is

$$h_2 \leftarrow (\text{Sunny,Warm,?,Strong,Warm,Same})$$

The third instance has no target concept, so that it can be ignored.

The fourth instance is $x = (\text{Sunny,Warm,High,Strong,Cool,Change})$. In this instance, the values of the last two attributes, water, and forecast, changed. So these attributes are also generalized. The resultant hypothesis is

$$h_3 \leftarrow (\text{Sunny,Warm,?,Strong,?,?})$$

Since there are no more instances present in the training set, the final hypothesis is

$$h_3 \leftarrow (\text{Sunny,Warm,?,Strong,?,?})$$

Find-S is an algorithm that identifies the most precise theory that fits the provided training data. However, it has significant flaws that restrict its applicability in ML.

One problem is that Find-S does not comment on how effectively it has absorbed the material. It does not state how sure it is or how many examples it has observed; it merely reports the final hypothesis. Because of this, assessing Find-S's effectiveness and contrasting it with other algorithms is challenging.

Another problem is that Find-S cannot handle training data that is contradictory or which contains errors. It just tosses out the example and continues with the remaining data if it comes across an example that deviates from its current hypothesis. This could result in it learning erroneous concepts or losing crucial information.

Thirdly, although multiple hypotheses may be congruent with the data, Find-S only produces one hypothesis. It may produce the hypothesis 'numbers divisible by 2,' for instance, if the idea is 'even numbers,' but it may alternatively output the hypothesis 'numbers ending with 0, 2, 4, 6, or 8.' Both theories are true, but Find-S does not take them into account. The taught notion may become less general or expressive as a result.

Find-S is a straightforward but constrained ML algorithm because of these issues. It helps learn exact concepts with no exceptions, but it is not appropriate for learning complex or noisy concepts that call for more flexibility and robustness.

6.4.5 Consistent Hypothesis and Version Space

The Find-S algorithm is a simple method for finding a hypothesis consistent with the positive examples in a training set. However, it has some limitations:

- It does not consider the negative examples, which may contain helpful information to refine the hypothesis.
- It does not guarantee that the hypothesis it finds is the most general or unique. There may be other hypotheses that are also consistent with the positive examples but more general or specific.
- It does not provide any measure of confidence or uncertainty about the hypothesis it finds. It does not tell us how well the hypothesis will perform on unseen data or how likely it is to be correct.

To address these issues, we can use the concept of consistent hypothesis and version space. A **consistent hypothesis** is a one that correctly classifies all the examples in the training set, both positive and negative. A **version space** is the set of all consistent hypotheses for a given training set. The version space contains the most specific hypothesis (S), the most general hypothesis (G), and all the hypotheses in between (H). The S and G hypotheses form the boundaries of the version space and are updated iteratively as new examples are seen.

The consistent hypothesis and version space approach has several advantages over the Find-S algorithm:

- It considers both positive and negative examples, which can help to eliminate irrelevant or contradictory features from the hypothesis.
- It maintains a set of hypotheses rather than a single one, which can capture the diversity and complexity of the data. It also allows us to compare and contrast different hypotheses and choose the best one according to some criterion (such as simplicity, accuracy, etc.).
- It provides a measure of confidence or uncertainty about the hypotheses by estimating the size and shape of the version space. The smaller and narrower the version space, the more confident we are about the hypotheses. The larger and broader the version space, the more uncertain we are about the hypotheses.

The consistent hypothesis and version space approach is useful in ML because it can help us to find hypotheses that are not only consistent with the data but also generalizable to new data. It can also allow us to evaluate and compare different hypotheses and select the most appropriate one for our problem. Moreover, it can help us to understand how our hypotheses change as we view more data and how confident we are about them.

A hypothesis h is considered consistent with D if and only if $h(x) = c(x)$ for each example $(x, c(x))$ in D.

$$\text{Consistent}(,D) = \forall(\langle x, c(x)\rangle \in D)\, h(x) = c(x) \tag{6.5}$$

There is a minute difference between a hypothesis being consistent and a hypothesis being satisfied. A training instance satisfies the hypothesis when $h(x) = 1$, regardless of whether it is positive or negative.

Consider the hypothesis $h = \langle \text{Sunny}, \text{Warm}, ?, \text{Strong}, ?, ? \rangle$. To check whether this hypothesis is consistent, a comparison with all the training instances has to be performed. For the first, second, and fourth instances, Sky = Sunny. For these instances, Temp = Warm is true. Wind = Strong is also true for these instances and the target concept Enjoy_Sport = Yes. Thus, $h(x) = c(x)$, so h is inconsistent.

Consider the hypothesis $h1 = \langle ?,?,?,\text{Strong},?,? \rangle$. To check whether this hypothesis is consistent, a comparison with all the training instances has to be performed. For the third instance in the training set, $h1(x)! = c(x)$, and hence h is not consistent. This is because when Wind = Strong, for the first, second, and fourth instances, Enjoy_Sport = Yes, but for the third instance Enjoy_Sport = No.

Consider another hypothesis $h2 = \langle ?,\text{Warm},?,\text{Strong},?,? \rangle$. The second attribute Temp = Warm is true for the first, second, and fourth instances, and for these instances, Wind = Strong and target concept Enjoy_Sport = Yes, and hence $h2$ is consistent.

The version space represents a subset of all hypotheses $(\mathcal{H})$, consistent with the training data set (D). It is represented as

$$VS_{\mathcal{H},D} = \{h\epsilon\mathcal{H} | \text{Consistent}(h, D)\} \tag{6.6}$$

Only two of the three hypotheses are consistent; hence, $VS_{\mathcal{H},D} = \{h, h2\}$.

6.4.6 The List-Then-Eliminate Algorithm

Given a set of training instances, the list-then-eliminate procedure is a technique for locating the best hypothesis in a hypothesis space. For the method to function, candidate hypotheses consistent with the prior instances are placed in a list, and any hypothesis that becomes inconsistent with a new example is removed. The algorithm stops when all examples have been processed, or only one hypothesis remains in the list. In ML, the list-then-eliminate approach is helpful because it ensures that, if it exists, the best hypothesis will be discovered in a limited number of steps. The method can also handle data noise by allowing for certain error tolerance. However, the approach has significant drawbacks, such as memory requirements for storing the list of hypotheses and inefficiency for large or complex hypothesis spaces.

The list-then-eliminate algorithm can be defined as follows:

1. Create a version space list containing every hypothesis.
2. For each training example $\langle x, c(x) \rangle$

   Remove from the version space any hypothesis h for which $h(x) \neq c(x)$
3. Output the updated version space list.

For the Enjoy_Sport data defined in the table, the possible set of hypotheses is as follows:

The first step is the creation of a version space list. The list can be generated based on the frequency of values on each attribute and combinations of attributes.

$$h1 = \langle \text{Sunny},?,?,?,?,? \rangle$$

$$h2 = \langle ?,\text{Warm},?,??,? \rangle$$

$$h3 = \langle ?,?,\text{High},?,?,? \rangle$$

$$h4 = \langle ?,?,?,\text{Strong},?,? \rangle$$

$$h5 = \langle ?,?,?,?,\text{Warm},? \rangle$$

$$h6 = \langle \text{Sunny},\text{Warm},?,?,?,? \rangle$$

$$h7 = \langle \text{Sunny},?,?,\text{Strong},?,? \rangle$$

$$h8 = \langle \text{Sunny},?,?,?,\text{Warm},? \rangle$$

$$h9 = \langle \text{Sunny},\text{Warm},?,\text{Strong},?,? \rangle$$

The second step is the elimination process.

Table 6.12 List-then-eliminate algorithm tracing

Version space list	$c(x)$	Remarks
$h1 = \langle \text{Sunny},?,?,?,?,? \rangle$	Yes (instance 1,2,4)	---
$h2 = \langle ?, \textit{Warm}, ?, ??, ? \rangle$	Yes (instance 1,2,4)	---
$h3 = \langle ?,?,\text{High},?,?,? \rangle$	Yes (instance 2, 4) No (instance 3)	Eliminate this hypothesis
$h4 = \langle ?,?,?,\text{Strong},?,? \rangle$	Yes (instance 2, 4) No (instance 3)	Eliminate this hypothesis
$h5 = \langle ?,?,?,?,\text{Warm},? \rangle$	Yes (instance 1, 2) No (instance 3)	Eliminate this hypothesis
$h6 = \langle \text{Sunny},\text{Warm},?,?,?,? \rangle$	Yes (instance 1,2,4)	---
$h7 = \langle \text{Sunny},?,?,\text{Strong},?,? \rangle$	Yes (instance 2, 4) No (instance 3)	Eliminate this hypothesis
$h8 = \langle \text{Sunny},?,?,?,\text{Warm},? \rangle$	Yes (instance 1, 2) No (instance 3)	Eliminate this hypothesis
$h9 = \langle \text{Sunny},\text{Warm},?,\text{Strong},?,? \rangle$	Yes (instance 1,2,4)	---

The updated version space list is as follows:

$$h1 = \langle \text{Sunny},?,?,?,?,? \rangle$$

$$h2 = \langle ?,\text{Warm},?,??,? \rangle$$

$$h6 = \langle \text{Sunny},\text{Warm},?,?,?,? \rangle$$

$$h9 = \langle \text{Sunny},\text{Warm},?,\text{Strong},?,? \rangle$$

General Boundary (G): The general boundary for $\mathcal{H}$ and D is the set of maximally general members of $\mathcal{H}$ consistent with D.

Specific Boundary (S): The general boundary for $\mathcal{H}$ and D is the set of minimally general (maximally specific) members of $\mathcal{H}$ consistent with D.

From the output of the list-then-eliminate algorithm, hypotheses $h1$ and $h2$ form the general boundary, and hypothesis $h9$ forms the specific boundary.

Version Space Representation Theorem: $\forall X, \mathcal{H}, c, D$ such that G and S are defined, and the version space is defined as follows

$$VS_{\mathcal{H},D} = \{h \epsilon \mathcal{H} \mid (\exists s \in S)(\exists g \in G)\left(g \geq_g h \geq_g s\right) \tag{6.7}$$

It is visualized as shown in Fig. 6.5.

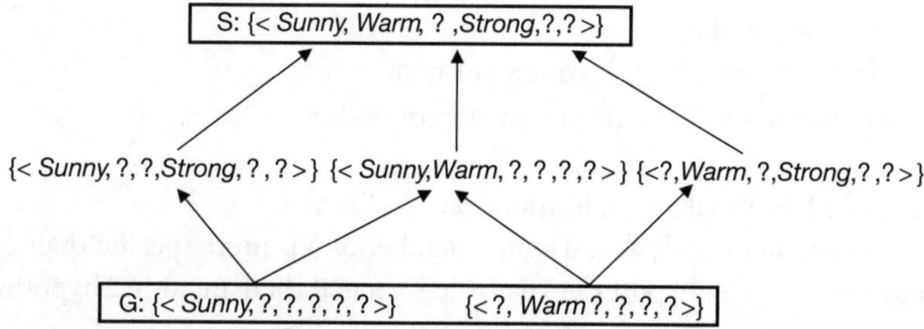

Figure 6.5 Version space representation after the list-then-eliminate algorithm

6.4.7 Candidate Elimination Algorithm

Finding the set of all hypotheses consistent with a given set of training examples is performed using the candidate elimination process. The general boundary (G) and the specific boundary (S) are two sets of assumptions that the algorithm maintains. The most general hypotheses consistent with the positive examples are found in the general boundary, and the most particular hypotheses consistent with the negative instances are found in the specific border. The broadest hypothesis, *G*, which covers everything, and the most particular hypothesis, *S*, which covers nothing, are the first two in the algorithm. The algorithm then modifies *G* and *S* for every training sample, deleting any inconsistent assumptions and introducing any minimum generalizations or specializations that are still consistent. The process ends when *G* and *S* agree on a set of hypotheses known as the version space.

The candidate elimination algorithm's ability to manage erratic data and concept drift makes it effective in ML. Examples of noisy data are errors or outliers that do not accurately represent the notion. Notion drift occurs when a notion evolves through time to the point where prior instances may no longer be applicable or accurate. The candidate elimination technique can handle these circumstances by holding a variety of potential hypotheses in *G* and *S* instead of settling on only one. The system can then adjust to fresh instances and toss out outdated ones that are no longer valid. By assessing how wide or small the version space is, the algorithm can also determine its accuracy in its predictions.

The algorithm is as follows:

```
Initialize G to a set of maximally general hypothesis
Initialize S to a set of maximally specific hypothesis
For each training sample, d ∈ D, do
if d is a positive example, then
    remove from G any hypothesis inconsistent with d
    for each hypothesis s ∈ S that is not consistent with d
        remove s from S
        add to S all minimal generalizations h of S such that
            h is consistent with d, and some member of G is more general than h
        remove from S any hypothesis that is more general than any other hypothesis in S
```

if d is a negative example, then
    remove from S any hypothesis inconsistent with d
    for each hypothesis $g \in G$ that is not consistent with d
        remove g from G
        add to G all minimal generalizations h of g such that
            h is consistent with d, and some member of S is more specific than h
        remove from G any hypothesis that is less general than any other hypothesis in G

The example below shows how to use the candidate elimination process to solve a straightforward concept learning problem. Given some instances of days with qualities like sky, air temp, humidity, wind, water, and prediction, the challenge is to learn the notion of sunny days. The qualities may be sunny, cloudy, warm, cold, high, low, strong, weak, and warm. A bright day is an example of something positive, while a cloudy day is something negative.

Table 6.13 Candidate elimination in concept learning

Example	Sky	Air	Humidity	Wind	Water	Forecast	Class
E1	Sunny	Warm	Normal	Strong	Warm	Same	+
E2	Sunny	Warm	High	Strong	Warm	Same	+
E3	Rainy	Cold	High	Strong	Warm	Change	-
E4	Sunny	Warm	High	Strong	Cool	Change	+

The initial G and S sets are:

G = {< ?, ?, ?, ?, ?, ?>}

S = {< Ø, Ø, Ø, Ø, Ø, Ø>}

After seeing E1, G and S become:

G = {< ?, ?, ?, ?, ?, ?>}

S = {< *Sunny, Warm, Normal, Strong, Warm, Same*>}

After seeing E2, G and S become:

G = {< ?, ?, ?, ?, ?, ?>}

S = {< *Sunny, Warm,* ?, *Strong, Warm, Same*>}

After seeing E3, G and S become:

G = {< *Sunny*, ?, ?, ?, ?, ?>}

S = {< *Sunny, Warm,* ?, *Strong, Warm, Same*>}

After seeing E4, G and S become:

G = {< *Sunny*, ?, ?, *Strong*, ?, ?>}

S = {< *Sunny*, *Warm*, ?, *Strong*, ?, ?>}

The final version space is:

VS = {< *Sunny*, *Warm*, ?, *Strong*, ?, ?>}

6.4.8 Remarks on Version Space and Candidate Elimination Algorithm

The candidate elimination algorithm is a technique for discovering a hypothesis consistent with a set of training examples. The general boundary (*G*) and the specific boundary (*S*) are two sets of assumptions that the algorithm maintains. The most general hypotheses that are consistent with all the positive instances are found in the general boundary. In contrast, the most specific hypotheses consistent with all the positive examples are found in the specific boundary. As fresh examples are discovered, the algorithm modifies the initial *G* and *S*, which hold the most general and hypotheses. The set of all hypotheses compatible with every example we have seen is known as the version space between *G* and *S*.

As long as two requirements are satisfied, the algorithm's learned version space tends to the hypothesis that accurately captures the input notion: the training samples include no errors, and a hypothesis describing the target idea exists.

The algorithm might be unable to identify a consistent hypothesis if these conditions are broken. For instance, the algorithm may remove some accurate hypotheses from *G* or *S* or add some false hypotheses to *G* or *S* if there are flaws in the training data, such as noise or mislabeling. An empty version space indicates that none of the hypotheses can explain all the examples. Alternatively, the algorithm may not converge to a single hypothesis but rather to a huge or infinite version space if no hypothesis adequately expresses the target concept, such as when the concept is too complicated or cannot be expressed in the hypothesis space.

The candidate elimination approach is helpful in ML because it can learn from both positive and negative instances and because the goal notion may evolve. By reporting how many hypotheses are congruent with the examples, the algorithm can also give a level of confidence in its learned hypothesis. By requesting labels for cases outside of *G* or *S*, the algorithm can also produce new inquiries for the user or teacher, condensing the version space and enhancing learning accuracy.

SUMMARY

- A machine learning model mathematically represents the relationship between the qualities and the label. The three categories of models are logical, geometrical, and probabilistic.
- Logical models are those that use rules or conditions to make predictions or classifications.
- In geometric models, the data is represented in a 2D or 3D hyperplane. Data with four or more attributes is difficult to visualize and can only be imagined in a virtual space.
- Distance models are a type of geometrical model that use a distance metric to separate the outcome spaces. What determines how far away two points are in a particular space is called a distance metric.
- Predictive models are probabilistic models that estimate the conditional probability of an outcome given some input attributes.

- Generative models are probabilistic models that estimate the joint probability of both the input and outcome attributes. Some examples of probabilistic models in machine learning are naive Bayes, logistic regression, Gaussian mixture model, and hidden Markov model.
- Features are the driving force behind any ML application. They represent the measurable characteristics of the data, which can be further used to perform classification or clustering to make predictions or to perform analysis. The best features aid the model in achieving high accuracy.
- Changing the domain of a data set's features is known as feature transformation. This has many applications:
    - Thresholding: Using a cut-off value, this approach turns a numerical or ordinal property into a binary feature.
    - Discretization: Here, a quantitative feature value is converted to an ordinal feature value.
- Choosing a subset of features from the initial feature set that are pertinent and instructive for the learning job is the feature selection process.
- Filtering methods rank and assess the features based on statistical or information-theoretic metrics, such as mutual information, chi-squared test, correlation, etc., without using a learning model.
- Wrapper methods assess the characteristics using a learning model as a black box.
- Intrinsic learning methods include feature selection in the learning process. During the training phase, they either alter the target function or employ regularization approaches to penalize or remove unnecessary or redundant characteristics.
- Forward selection is an iterative process. It starts with a single feature and iteratively adds features, and evaluates the model in each iteration. The process ends when a newly added feature does not improve the model's performance.
- Concept learning seeks to extract the definition of a broad category from the input data.
- Finding the set of all hypotheses consistent with a given set of training examples is done using the candidate elimination algorithm.

EXERCISES

Part A (Objective Questions)

1. Which category of machine learning models is characterized by representing the relationship between qualities and labels using mathematical functions?
   a) Logical models b) Geometrical models
   c) Probabilistic models d) None of the above
2. In which category of machine learning models does the model map instances to outcomes based on spatial relationships?
   a) Logical models b) Geometrical models
   c) Probabilistic models d) None of the above
3. What type of models use algorithms and techniques to learn from data and mathematically represent the relationship between qualities and labels?

a) Logical models
b) Geometrical models
c) Probabilistic models
d) All of the above

4. Which category of machine learning models focuses on representing uncertainty and likelihood of outcomes?
   a) Logical models
   b) Geometrical models
   c) Probabilistic models
   d) None of the above
5. What is the main characteristic of geometrical machine learning models?
   a) Representing uncertainty
   b) Mapping instances to outcomes based on spatial relationships
   c) Using algorithms for logical reasoning
   d) All of the above
6. Which category of machine learning models relies on logical reasoning and rules to make predictions?
   a) Logical models
   b) Geometrical models
   c) Probabilistic models
   d) All of the above
7. What distinguishes probabilistic machine learning models from other categories?
   a) Logical reasoning
   b) Spatial relationships
   c) Representation of uncertainty
   d) Feature extraction techniques
8. Which category of machine learning models can use algorithms from decision theory to make predictions?
   a) Logical models
   b) Geometrical models
   c) Probabilistic models
   d) All of the above
9. What type of metric calculates the total of the absolute differences between two points' coordinates in a geometrical model?
   a) Euclidean distance metric
   b) Manhattan distance metric
   c) Probabilistic distance metric
   d) Generative distance metric
10. Which category of probabilistic models estimates the joint probability of both input and outcome attributes?
    a) Predictive models
    b) Generative models
    c) Discriminative models
    d) Descriptive models
11. How do distance-based geometrical models help reduce the complexity of data in machine learning?
    a) By increasing dimensionality
    b) By introducing randomness
    c) By using distance metrics
    d) By creating outliers
12. Which type of probabilistic model is used for unsupervised learning tasks?
    a) Predictive models
    b) Generative models
    c) Discriminative models
    d) Descriptive models
13. What is the primary purpose of distance-based geometrical models in machine learning?
    a) To generate new data points
    b) To predict future outcomes
    c) To measure similarity between data pointsd) To classify data points into categories
14. Which distance metric calculates the straight-line distance between two points in a geometrical model?

a) Euclidean distance metric
b) Manhattan distance metric
c) Probabilistic distance metric
d) Generative distance metric

15. What kind of variability and complexity do probabilistic models aim to capture in machine learning?
a) Deterministic patterns
b) Random patterns
c) Geometrical patterns
d) Predictable patterns

16. Which type of probabilistic models are used to answer questions about the joint probability of observing specific attributes?
a) Predictive models
b) Generative models
c) Discriminative models
d) Descriptive models

17. Which type of features lack a natural hierarchy among the categories and include attributes like nationality and hair color?
a) Interval features
b) Ordinal features
c) Nominal features
d) Ratio features

18. What type of features represent characteristics such as age, height, weight, and income, and can be used for mathematical operations and statistical analyses?
a) Binary features
b) Temporal features
c) Text features
d) Numerical features

19. Which type of features symbolize temporal data and include attributes like date, time, duration, and frequency?
a) Binary features
b) Temporal features
c) Text features
d) Categorical features

20. Which type of features include attributes such as product reviews, tweets, and news stories, and are used in tasks like sentiment analysis and text summarization?
a) Binary features
b) Temporal features
c) Text features
d) Categorical features

21. What subcategory of numerical features lacks an absolute zero point but has a significant value differential between its measurements?
a) Interval features
b) Ordinal features
c) Nominal features
d) Ratio features

22. Which type of features can have two possible values and are used for logical operations or categorization?
a) Numerical features
b) Temporal features
c) Binary features
d) Categorical features

23. Which subcategory of categorical features falls into a certain hierarchy or order, including attributes like customer happiness or educational level?
a) Nominal features
b) Ordinal features
c) Binary features
d) Interval features

24. What can be determined by analyzing temporal features such as date, time, and frequency in data?
a) Binary characteristics
b) Categorical traits
c) Data trends and patterns
d) Numerical values

25. Which feature transformation method converts a quantitative feature value into an ordinal feature value by discretizing its range into intervals?
a) MinMax scaling b) Standard scaling
c) Thresholding d) Discretization

26. What is the purpose of thresholding in feature transformation?
a) To scale data between 0 and 1
b) To remove unnecessary features
c) To convert quantitative features to ordinal features
d) To apply standard scaling to the data

27. Which scaling method transforms data into the range [0, 1] by setting the minimum value to 0 and the maximum value to 1?
a) MinMax scaling b) Standard scaling
c) Thresholding d) Discretization

28. What mathematical equation represents the standard scaling transformation?
a) $(x - x\_mean)$ / (Standard deviation) b) $(x + x\_mean)$ * (Standard deviation)
c) $(x * x\_mean)$ / (Standard deviation) d) $(x - x\_mean)$ * (Standard deviation)

29. Which feature transformation technique is used to eliminate unnecessary, unimportant, or noisy elements from the data?
a) MinMax scaling b) Standard scaling
c) Thresholding d) Discretization

30. What is the primary purpose of feature transformation in machine learning?
a) To create new features b) To increase data complexity
c) To improve model suitability and accuracyd)To reduce the number of instances

31. Which transformation method is best suited for improving the data's suitability for certain machine learning models?
a) MinMax scaling b) Standard scaling
c) Thresholding d) Discretization

32. Which transformation technique involves assigning ordinal values to intervals and converting quantitative feature values to categorical values?
a) MinMax scaling b) Standard scaling
c) Thresholding d) Discretization

33. What is the primary goal of feature construction in machine learning?
a) To reduce the number of features in the data set
b) To select relevant features from the initial set
c) To build new features from existing ones
d) To assess features using a learning model

34. Which process involves choosing a subset of features from the initial set to enhance learning tasks?
a) Feature construction b) Feature selection
c) Filtering method d) Wrapper method

35. Which method ranks and evaluates features based on statistical metrics without using a learning model?

a) Feature construction b) Feature selection
c) Filtering method d) Wrapper method

36. What is a potential drawback of wrapper methods for feature selection?
a) They are computationally expensive b) They lack precision
c) They are not adaptable d) They involve overfitting

37. How do wrapper methods assess features during the selection process?
a) Using statistical metrics b) Using black-box learning models
c) Based on information theory d) By applying cross-validation

38. Which method is more scalable and doesn't consider interactions between features?
a) Feature construction b) Filtering method
c) Feature selection d) Wrapper method

39. What is the main advantage of feature selection in machine learning?
a) Reducing computational complexity b) Creating new features
c) Enhancing feature interactions d) Improving model performance

40. How do wrapper methods differ from filtering methods in terms of feature assessment?
a) Wrapper methods use statistical metrics b) Filtering methods involve cross-validation
c) Wrapper methods use a learning model d) Filtering methods are computationally expensive

41. Which type of learning method incorporates feature selection directly into the learning process by altering the target function or using regularization?
a) Concept learning b) Candidate elimination algorithm
c) Intrinsic learning methods d) List-then-eliminate procedure

42. What is the primary goal of concept learning in machine learning?
a) Extracting hidden patterns from data b) Recognizing specific categories from input data
c) Eliminating redundant features d) Generating new hypotheses

43. Which algorithm involves maintaining sets of general and specific assumptions and modifies them based on training examples to find the version space of hypotheses?
a) List-then-eliminate procedure b) Concept Learning
c) Intrinsic learning methods d) Candidate elimination algorithm

44. How does the list-then-eliminate procedure ensure efficient hypothesis discovery in machine learning?
a) By using regularization techniques b) By eliminating redundant features
c) By efficiently handling data noise d) By processing consistent hypotheses in a list

45. What is the main purpose of the candidate elimination algorithm in machine learning?
a) To generate new hypotheses b) To eliminate data noise
c) To find the version space of hypotheses d) To handle large or complex hypothesis spaces

46. How do intrinsic learning methods differ from concept learning?
a) Intrinsic methods focus on data noise handling
b) Concept learning focuses on model-specific adaptation
c) Intrinsic methods involve version space exploration
d) Concept learning recognizes specific categories from data

47. What sets apart the version space discovered by the candidate elimination algorithm?
    a) It includes only specific hypotheses
    b) It includes the broadest hypothesis only
    c) It is a set of consistent hypotheses
    d) It is a set of hypotheses with maximum generalization
48. How do intrinsic methods combine the advantages of filter and wrapper methods?
    a) By using regularization and feature scaling
    b) By directly altering the target function
    c) By employing hybrid filtering and wrapper techniques
    d) By modifying the version space of hypotheses

Part B (Short Answer Questions)

1. What is a machine learning model? What are its categories?
2. What is the logical machine learning model?
3. What is the geometric machine learning model?
4. What is the distance model in machine learning?
5. How is the distance-based geometrical model helpful in machine learning?
6. What is the predictive model in machine learning?
7. Define the generative model of machine learning.
8. Give some examples of probabilistic models in machine learning.
9. Define features in the machine learning space.
10. Explain the numerical characteristics of features in machine learning.
11. Explain the categorical characteristics of features in machine learning.
12. Explain the temporal and text features of machine learning.
13. What is feature transformation? Write any two applications of the same.
14. What is MinMax scaling?
15. What is the equation for standard scaling?
16. Define thresholding.
17. Define discretization.
18. Define feature construction.
19. Define feature selection.
20. Define the filtering method of features in machine learning.
21. Define the wrapper method of features in machine learning.
22. Define the intrinsic learning methods of machine learning.
23. What is concept learning?
24. Define the list-then-eliminate algorithm.
25. Define the candidate elimination algorithm.

Part C (Essay Questions)

1. Explain the distance model in detail.
2. Explain the probabilistic model in detail with examples.
3. Explain feature and its types.
4. Explain feature transformation and its applications.
5. Explain MinMax scaling and standard scaling.
6. Explain thresholding.
7. Explain discretization in detail.
8. Explain feature construction.
9. Explain feature selection in detail.

10. What are the approaches to execute feature selection in supervised learning?
11. Write an essay on representation of hypothesis space as a general-to-specific ordering.
12. Write an essay on finding a maximally specific hypothesis (Find-S).
13. Write an essay on consistent hypothesis and version space.

ANSWER KEY

Part A

1. (a)	**2.** (b)	**3.** (d)	**4.** (c)	**5.** (b)	**6.** (a)	**7.** (c)	**8.** (d)
9. (b)	**10.** (b)	**11.** (c)	**12.** (b)	**13.** (c)	**14.** (a)	**15.** (b)	**16.** (b)
17. (c)	**18.** (d)	**19.** (b)	**20.** (c)	**21.** (a)	**22.** (c)	**23.** (b)	**24.** (c)
25. (d)	**26.** (c)	**27.** (a)	**28.** (a)	**29.** (c)	**30.** (c)	**31.** (a)	**32.** (d)
33. (c)	**34.** (b)	**35.** (c)	**36.** (a)	**37.** (b)	**38.** (b)	**39.** (d)	**40.** (c)
41. (c)	**42.** (b)	**43.** (d)	**44.** (d)	**45.** (c)	**46.** (b)	**47.** (c)	**48.** (c)

7 Unsupervised Learning

Learning Objectives

At the end of this chapter, you will be able to:

- Define unsupervised learning
- Identify the types of unsupervised learning: clustering, anomaly detection, dimension reduction, and association
- Differentiate between the types of clustering: hard and soft
- Explain the various clustering algorithms: *K*-means clustering, hierarchical clustering, fuzzy C-means clustering, DBSCAN, Gaussian mixture models (GMMs), MeanShift clustering, Gaussian mixture density estimation, and Markov random fields (MRFs)
- Describe the anomaly detection techniques: isolation forest algorithm, local outlier factor (LOF), and one-class support vector machine (OC SVM)
- Apply dimensionality reduction algorithms such as PCA, linear discriminant analysis (LDA), factor analysis (FA), and kernel principal component analysis (KPCA)
- Utilize association algorithms such as FP Growth, Apriori, and ECLAT
- Explain the Markov models and hidden Markov models (HMM)
- Explore matrix factorization and matrix completion models
- Discuss generative models and latent factor models
- Explain inference models and non-negative matrix factorization (NMF)
- Evaluate the advantages and disadvantages of unsupervised machine learning

7.1 Introduction

Unsupervised learning is a machine learning (ML) technique in which a machine is given unstructured data with no labels and asked to find patterns, similarities, and relationships between the data points. The output of this process is a model that can be used to make predictions or draw insights from the data. Unlike supervised learning, there is no human intervention. Instead, the algorithm must uncover hidden structures and relationships within the given data set.

Unsupervised learning algorithms are often used for clustering data sets into groups based on specific characteristics or dimensions or for anomaly detection, where outliers in the data set are identified. Unsupervised learning can also be used in natural language processing (NLP) tasks such as identifying topics within a document.

7.2 What and Why of Unsupervised Learning

Unsupervised learning is a type of ML where the computer program tries to find patterns and relationships in data without being given specific examples or labels to learn from. It is like trying to solve a puzzle without being given any hints. Instead, the program uses algorithms to explore the data and find patterns on its own.

For example, an unsupervised learning algorithm takes the input data set containing images of bulls and cows and performs analysis (Fig. 7.1). The algorithm observes the features of each image, such as shape, size, color, and texture. It then uses clustering techniques to group similar images into clusters. By doing this, it can recognize patterns in the data without knowing which categories of images belong to each cluster.

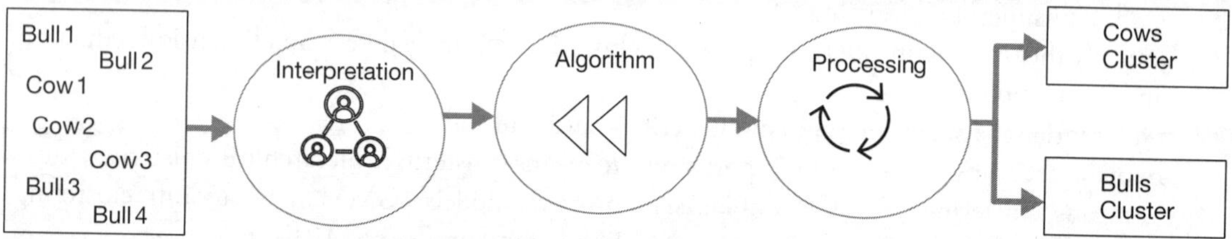

Figure 7.1 Unsupervised learning example

This technique can identify types of bulls or cows even if there is no clear distinction between them in the input data set. For example, suppose two cows have very similar shapes but differ slightly in color or texture. Unsupervised learning algorithms can still identify them as two distinct clusters despite their similarities.

Unsupervised learning is also helpful in separating a single object from its surroundings in an image by creating multiple clusters from that single object and its environment – this is known as **segmentation**. This technique can help computer vision applications accurately distinguish objects within an image, which is impossible with supervised learning approaches alone. Some examples of segmentation using unsupervised learning are image and document segmentation. In image segmentation, an image is separated into different regions or objects based on color, texture, edges, or other visual characteristics. Document segmentation is typically used to separate a document into its constituent parts, such as paragraphs, headings, and subheadings (Fig. 7.2).

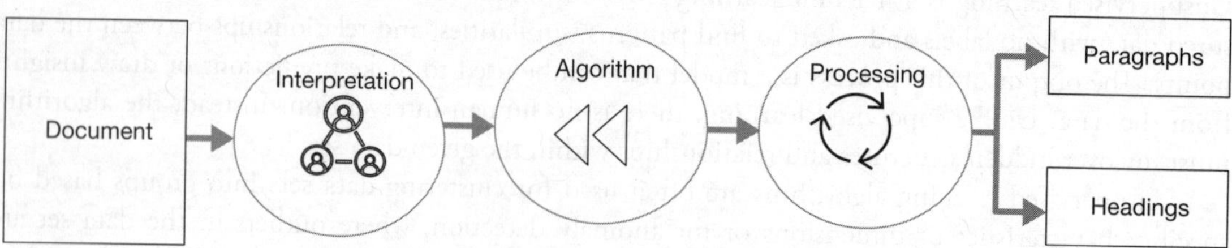

Figure 7.2 Documentation segmentation example

Overall, unsupervised learning algorithms are valuable tools that provide insights into data sets that, due to their complexity, would otherwise require manual analysis. This makes them an excellent tool for data scientists looking to gain insights quickly and effectively from large data sets.

It can also help detect anomalies and outliers in data sets or predict future behaviors by recognizing patterns from past events. In addition, unsupervised learning models can be used for marketing purposes by grouping customers with similar interests together so marketers can better target them with relevant offers and promotions.

Unsupervised learning allows us to uncover insights about our data without it needing to be labeled or categorized; this makes it helpful in dealing with real-world situations where not all information is already known beforehand.

7.3 Types of Unsupervised Learning

In ML, unsupervised learning allows computers to identify patterns in data without training data or human instruction. Clustering, anomaly detection, dimension reduction, and association rule learning are the four primary subcategories of this form of learning (Fig. 7.3).

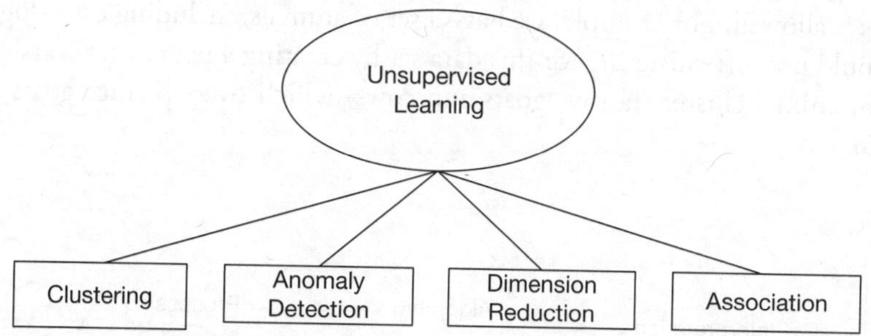

Figure 7.3 Types of unsupervised learning

Each of these types is now discussed in detail.

7.3.1 Clustering

Clustering algorithms are an essential type of unsupervised ML used to identify patterns in data and group similar data points together. Clustering is used to find structure in unlabeled data, such as trends and groupings, to understand the data set better. The main goal is to create clusters or groups of data points that are like each other and dissimilar from points in other clusters.

There are two main types of clustering algorithms (Fig. 7.4): hard (assigning a point to one cluster based on similarity) and soft (assigning a point to multiple clusters, allowing for overlap).

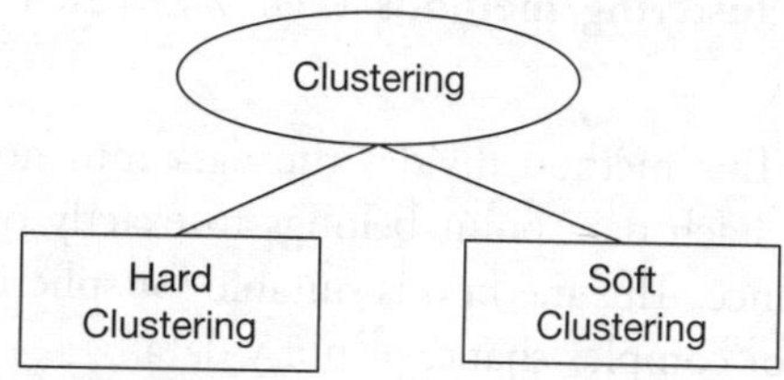

Figure 7.4 Types of clustering

Hard clustering is when points are assigned to one cluster based on their similarities with other points in the cluster. For instance, if you have a set of fruits like apples, oranges, and bananas, you could use hard clustering to group the fruits according to whether they are sweet or sour. The apple would be grouped under sweet, while the orange would be part of the sour cluster (Fig. 7.5).

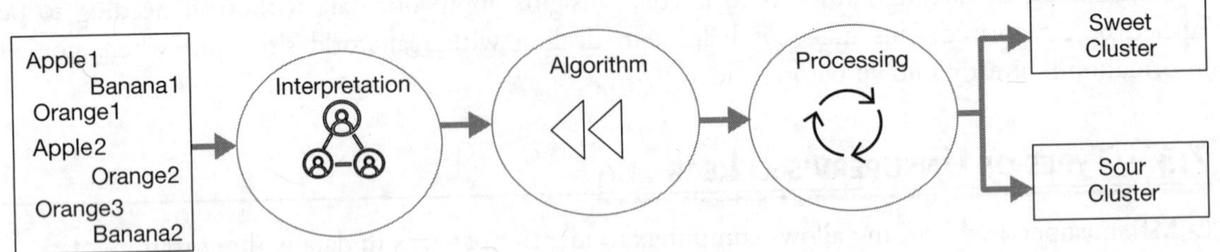

Figure 7.5 Hard clustering example

Soft clustering is when points are assigned to multiple clusters simultaneously and overlapping between clusters is allowed. For example, we have a set of animals, including cats, dogs, horses, cows, and goats; we could use soft clustering for this data set by creating a pet cluster (cats, goats and dogs) as well as a farm animal cluster (horses, goats and cows) which overlap since goats belong to both groups (Fig. 7.6).

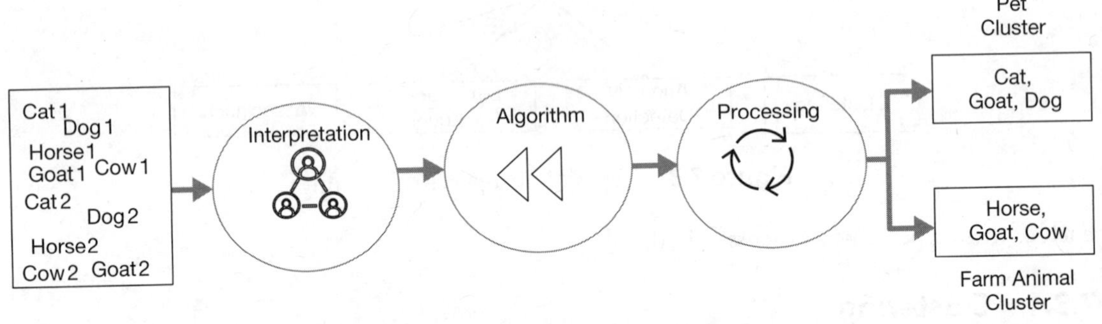

Figure 7.6 Soft clustering example

Hard and soft methods can help group similar items to make patterns between them more apparent. Clustered data can then be studied in detail, allowing us to understand trends or discover new knowledge within our data sets. Clustering algorithms can be applied across various fields, including image segmentation, customer classification for marketing research, statistical analysis for discovering data trends, and classifying diseases in medical science.

There are different **types of clustering methods** (Fig. 7.7), each with its own advantages and disadvantages:

- **Partitioning Clustering:** This method divides the data into non-hierarchical groups, such as *K*-means, *K*-medoids, etc. Each data point belongs to exactly one cluster, and the number of clusters is specified in advance. This method is suitable for spherical and well-separated clusters, but it may not work well for complex shapes or noisy data.
- **Hierarchical Clustering:** This method creates a tree-like structure of clusters, such as agglomerative or divisive clustering. Each data point can belong to more than one cluster, depending on the level

of the hierarchy. The number of clusters can be determined by cutting the tree at the desired level. This method can capture complex shapes and outliers, but it may be computationally expensive and sensitive to the choice of distance metric.

- **Density-based Clustering:** This method identifies clusters as dense regions of data points, separated by low-density regions, such as DBSCAN. Each data point belongs to at most one cluster, and some data points may not belong to any cluster (noise). The number of clusters is not specified in advance, and it depends on the density parameters. This method can handle arbitrary shapes and outliers, but it may not work well for varying densities or high-dimensional data.
- **Distribution Model-based Clustering:** This method assumes that the data points are generated by a mixture of probability distributions, such as Gaussian mixture models. Each data point belongs to one or more clusters with certain probabilities, and the number of clusters is specified in advance or determined by model selection criteria. This method can capture the statistical properties of the data, but it may not work well for non-Gaussian or overlapping clusters.
- **Fuzzy Clustering:** This method assigns a degree of membership to each data point for each cluster, such as fuzzy C-means. Each data point belongs to one or more clusters with different degrees of membership, and the number of clusters is specified in advance. This method can handle overlapping and noisy data, but it may be sensitive to initialization and convergence criteria

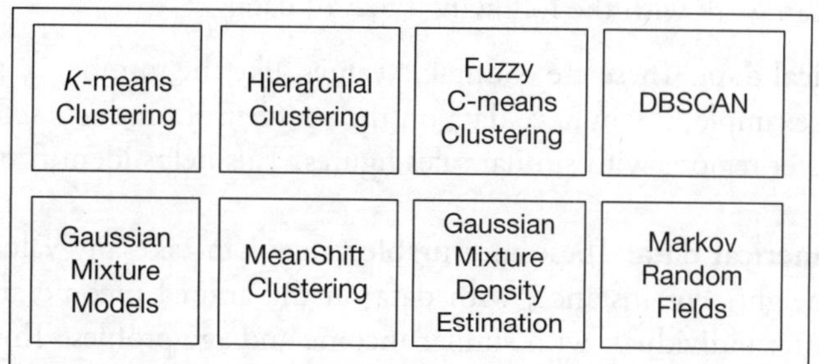

Figure 7.7 Types of clustering algorithms

7.3.1.1 K-means Clustering

This is a popular unsupervised ML technique for data exploration and analysis. It used for grouping or clustering data points into distinct clusters or categories. *K*-means aims to divide the data set into meaningful subgroups based on specific characteristics. The algorithm examines each data point and assigns it to one of several groups based on attribute similarities. The name comes from the fact that it requires a specific number of groups (*K*) before the algorithm can be run. Thus, *K* specifies the number of predefined clusters that must be generated. After that, the algorithm will divide the data set into *K* clusters by determining each cluster's centroid (or center point). This is accomplished through an iterative process in which points are assigned to their closest centroid at each step. Then the centroids are updated based on the average of all points assigned to them in that iteration. Finally, the cluster data points are assigned to the nearest centroid until no point remains unassigned.

Centroids are the geometric centers of shapes or objects. They can be calculated by finding the average of the coordinates of all the points that make up the shape or object. For example, to find the centroid of a triangle, we can use the formula:

$$(x, y) = ((x1 + x2 + x3) / 3, (y1 + y2 + y3) / 3)$$

where $(x1, y1)$, $(x2, y2)$ and $(x3, y3)$ are the vertices of the triangle. This formula works because the centroid divides each median of the triangle into two segments with a ratio of 2:1. A **median** is a line segment that connects a vertex to the midpoint of the opposite side.

Here is a simple example of how to find the centroid of a triangle. Suppose we have a triangle with vertices A(2, 4), B(6, 8) and C(10, 4). To find the centroid, we plug in the coordinates into the formula:

$$(x, y) = ((2 + 6 + 10) / 3, (4 + 8 + 4) / 3)$$
$$(x, y) = (18 / 3, 16 / 3)$$
$$(x, y) = (6, 16/3)$$

Therefore, the centroid of the triangle is at (6, 16/3). We can verify this by drawing the medians and observing that they intersect at this point.

The *K*-means algorithm works by partitioning a data set into *K* distinct clusters, based on the similarity in data points. It can work with the following types of data:

- **Discrete numerical data**: These are countable values, like the number of products sold or visits to a website. For example, if you have data on the number of products sold in different regions, *K*-means can cluster regions with similar sales figures. This helps identify areas with similar sales patterns.
- **Continuous numerical data**: These measurable values can take any value within a range, like temperature or height. For instance, with data on the annual income and age of individuals, *K*-means can cluster individuals with similar income and age profiles. This practical application is particularly useful for market segmentation, where you want to identify groups of people with similar financial and demographic characteristics.
- **Continuous entities**: These refer to data points that can be represented on a continuous scale. For example, in image processing, pixel intensities are constant values. *K*-means can segment an image into different regions based on pixel intensity, which is helpful in object detection and image compression applications.

However, this algorithm has difficulties with categorical data, outliers, and non-linear data. Furthermore, it would help if you decided how many data clusters you wanted. Finally, *K*-means is best applied to smaller data sets because it iterates over all the data points. As a result, if the data set contains many data points, it will take longer to classify them.

We need two inputs for *K*-means clustering to work correctly: the desired number of clusters/groups and a set of observations with associated values (features). Initially, we must assign a cluster label to each observation/data point/feature vector at random, typically 0 or 1. However, any integer value depends on how many clusters we want the data set divided into (*K*). Then, for each group, we need to calculate the centroid, which represents both its mean location along every dimension as well as its overall size/volume when measured against all other groups in the data set.

Once these steps are completed, we can begin looping over the data set multiple times while adjusting the centroids accordingly through an iterative process known as **expectation maximization**. This works towards minimizing intra-cluster distances while simultaneously maximizing inter-cluster distances by assigning the observations new labels corresponding with whichever group they belong to closest after having gone through every iteration thus far. This provides us with ever more accurate predictions regarding which observations fall within which categories/subgroups across the entire sample space when compared against one another using Euclidean distance metric(s).

After a pre-specified amount of time has passed with no significant changes between iterations, convergence should be reached quickly given enough resources for computation, ensuring genuine classification accuracy.

Assume a company makes sports shoes and wants to divide its customers into two distinct groups: male and female. We would begin by gathering customer information such as age, gender, shopping preferences, and spending patterns, among other things, and then use *K*-means clustering-based methodology to determine distinct criteria to determine who should go where.

For example, the majority of those aged between 18 and 25 tend to spend money on shoes, whereas the opposite is true for those aged 30+, thereby creating a clear distinction based solely on age. This suggests that spending habits on shoes differ significantly between two age groups: those aged 18–25 and those aged 30 and above.

- **Age-based spending habits**: The younger demographic (18–25) tends to spend more money on shoes. This could be due to fashion trends, social influence, and a higher interest in personal appearance. The older demographic (30+) is less likely to spend as much on shoes. They might prioritize other expenses such as family needs, mortgages, or savings.
- **Gender-based analysis**: Once the data is broken down by gender, the numbers for males and females in each age group align perfectly with the overall trend. This alignment provides a strong basis for decision-making, indicating that both young men and women (18–25) are more likely to spend on shoes, while older men and women (30+) are less likely to do so.
- **Assumptions and conclusions**: Based on the spending patterns, it can be assumed that the younger demographic (18–25) falls in the category of higher shoe expenditure, while the older demographic (30+) falls in the category of lower shoe expenditure. This distinction empowers marketers and businesses to tailor their products and marketing strategies to target the appropriate age groups effectively.

Steps

Step 1: Data Collection. The first step is to gather data on customers. In this case, we gather customer information such as age, gender, shopping preferences, and spending patterns.

Step 2: Define K. Next, we need to define the number of clusters (*K*) we want to form. In this example, we want to divide customers into two distinct groups: male and female.

Step 3: Initialize Centroids. The next step is to randomly initialize *K* centroids. A centroid is a point at the center of a cluster. In our example, we randomly select two centroids: one for males and one for females.

Step 4: Assign Data Points to Clusters. The next step is to assign each data point to its nearest centroid based on the Euclidean distance. In our example, we would calculate the distance of each customer from each centroid and assign them to the nearest centroid based on gender.

Step 5: Update Centroids. After all data points have been assigned to clusters, we update the centroids of each cluster based on the mean value of all the data points in that cluster. This is done to ensure that the centroid is at the center of the cluster.

Step 6: Reassign Data Points. We then reassign each data point to its nearest centroid based on the updated centroid values. This process is repeated until the centroids no longer move, or the maximum number of iterations is reached.

Step 7: Interpret Results. The final step is to interpret the results of the clustering algorithm. In our example, we would interpret the results by analysing the characteristics of the customers in each cluster to determine distinct criteria that determine who should go where, based on gender.

Example 1: Let us consider our example with five data points (records): we assume that the first three data points are males and the last two data points are females. The spending on shoes and age of each data point is given in Table 7.1.

Table 7.1 Spending pattern

Customer ID	Age	Gender	Spending on shoes
1	20	Male	500
2	25	Male	800
3	30	Male	400
4	35	Female	700
5	50	Female	300

The centroid of the male cluster is computed as follows:
The mean age of the male cluster is (20 + 25 + 30)/3 = 25
The mean spending on shoes of the male cluster is (500 + 800 + 400)/3 = 567
Therefore, the centroid of the male cluster is (25, 567).

The centroid of the female cluster is computed as follows:
The mean age of the female cluster is (35 + 50)/2 = 42.5
The mean spending on shoes of the female cluster is (700 + 300)/2 = 500
Therefore, the centroid of the female cluster is (42.5, 500).

Repeat steps 4–6 until convergence: We now repeat steps 4–6 until the centroids no longer change. In our example with only five data points, we have already converged, and we have found the two clusters:

The male cluster has customer IDs 1, 2, and 3, with centroid (25, 567)
The female cluster has customer IDs 4 and 5, with centroid (42.5, 500)

Once we have identified the two clusters, we can allocate the customers to the male or female cluster based on their distance from the two centroids. In practice, we would use many more data points and more than two clusters to obtain a more accurate clustering.

Next, the algorithm calculates the means of each cluster, which will serve as the new centroids. In our example, the mean spending and age of the customers in each cluster will be calculated, resulting in new centroids for the male and female groups. We sssign each customer to the nearest centroid based on their feature values. The distances between each customer and the centroids are calculated, and the customers are assigned to the group with the nearest centroid. This process is repeated until the centroids no longer change or a maximum number of iterations is reached.

In the end, we will have two distinct groups, male and female, based on their spending patterns and age. This information can be used by the company to tailor their marketing efforts and product offerings to each group's preferences and needs.

Example 2: A person wants to divide customers into two distinct clusters based on the type of frequent product purchased. They could input individual item information about products bought previously and find relevant relationships between items people purchased to determine if certain items make the same part cluster, influencing the decision-making process of picking different items for future occasions. Let us assume we have a set of 5 customers and their purchase history for different products. The columns could include Customer ID, Product 1, Product 2, Product 3, etc., with the number of columns depending on the number of products the company sells. We can use *K*-means clustering to group customers based on the products they buy the most.

Steps

1. *Choose the number of clusters*: In this example, we want to divide customers into two clusters based on the type of product they purchase the most.
2. *Choose the initial centroids*: Randomly select two customers from the data set to be the initial centroids for each cluster.
3. *Calculate the distance*: Calculate the distance between each customer and each centroid. The most common distance metric used is the Euclidean distance.
4. *Assign customers to clusters*: Assign each customer to the cluster with the closest centroid.
5. *Calculate new centroids*: Recalculate the centroid of each cluster as the mean of all the customers assigned to that cluster.
6. *Repeat steps 3–5*: Repeat steps 3-5 until the centroids no longer change, or a maximum number of iterations is reached.
7. *Interpret the results*: Once the algorithm has converged, the resulting clusters can be interpreted based on the products that each customer purchases most frequently.

For example, cluster 1 may consist of customers who purchase Product 1 and Product 2 the most frequently, while cluster 2 may consist of customers who purchase Product 3 and Product 4 the most frequently. The company can then use this information to tailor its marketing strategies to each cluster accordingly.

For example, if we have a set of 5 customers and 4 products, our item frequency matrix may look like Table 7.2.

Table 7.2 Five customers and four products

Customer	Product 1	Product 2	Product 3	Product 4
1	3	2	1	4
2	0	1	4	2
3	2	3	0	1
4	1	2	3	2
5	3	1	2	0

Compute the distance between each data point and each centroid. In our example, we would compute the distance between each customer and each of the two centroids, which represent the two clusters (frequent buyers of Product A and frequent buyers of Product B).

Assign each data point to the nearest centroid. This step involves grouping the customers who are closest to each centroid, based on the distance computed in the previous step. For example, if a customer bought Product A twice and Product B once, they would be assigned to the cluster of customers who frequently buy Product A.

Recalculate the centroids of each cluster based on the new groupings in step 5. This involves computing the mean of all the data points assigned to each centroid. In our example, we would calculate the average frequency of purchases for each product in each cluster.

Convergence is achieved when the centroids no longer move significantly between iterations. At this point, the algorithm stops, and the clusters are considered finalized. Once the clusters have been determined, the company can use this information to make decisions about product development, marketing, and sales strategies.

Choosing an Appropriate Number of Clusters (K)

Selecting the optimal number of clusters is a critical stage in clustering analysis, as it dictates the division of data and the potential insights that may be extracted from it. Therefore, it is essential to establish criteria or procedures to determine the appropriate number of clusters.

The number of clusters chosen might be influenced by prior information or subject expertise. For instance, while clustering the data of university students, we can utilize the count of departments or faculties as an initial reference. This assumption is based on the idea that students from distinct departments exhibit distinct characteristics or behaviours. When clustering movie data based on two qualities, namely budget (high or low) and casting (star or non-star), it is appropriate to utilize four groups as these attributes have four potential combinations.

Business requirements and resource constraints are additional factors that can influence the selection of the number of clusters. Occasionally, we may have a distinct aim or purpose for clustering the data, such as partitioning, categorization, or suggestion. In such instances, we may have a predetermined quantity of clusters that we aim to attain, guided by the specifications or limitations of the problem. For example, a filmmaker may categorize movies to appeal to various audiences or markets. In doing so, they may have a predetermined number of segments they aim to establish, such as mainstream, niche, art-house, or independent. Suppose a filmmaker has limited resources in terms of budget or time. In that case, they may cluster movies to identify the most lucrative or viable combination of funding and casting.

Nevertheless, there are several instances where we lack any previous information or explicit objectives for grouping the data. For such situations, it is necessary to employ statistical methods or criteria to ascertain the most suitable number of clusters. These are now discussed in detail.

The **elbow method** determines the most suitable clusters in a clustering algorithm by calculating the sum of squared distances (SSD) between every data point and its designated cluster center. The cluster center represents the mean or typical location inside each cluster, whereas the SSD quantifies the level of compactness or homogeneity within each cluster. Optimally, our objective is to minimize the SSD, indicating that the data points are near their respective cluster centers and distinctly segregated from neighboring clusters. Nevertheless, when the number of clusters is augmented, the SSD will exhibit a more gradual decline as the data is progressively divided into increasingly smaller groups. Eventually, increasing the number of clusters will have diminishing returns on improving the SSD and could potentially lead to the introduction of noise or overfitting.

By employing *K*-means clustering with various values of *K*, we may generate a plot of the SSD for each *K* value. This may be depicted as shown in Fig. 7.8.

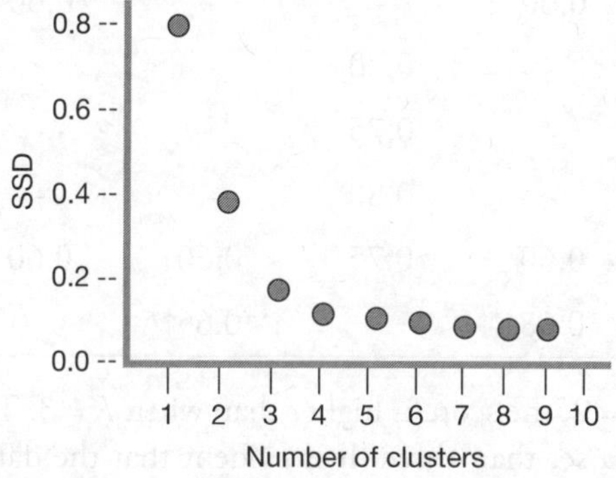

Figure 7.8 Elbow method to identify the *K* value

The **silhouette method** is used to assess the effectiveness of clustering outcomes. To utilize the silhouette method, it is necessary to compute the silhouette score for each data point. The silhouette score is a metric that quantifies the quality of clustering in a data set.

Let us represent the index of the data point. a(i) denotes the average distance between i and all other points in the same cluster, whereas b(i) represents the minimum average distance between i and all other points in any other cluster. The silhouette score s(i) is a metric that falls within the range of –1 to 1, with –1 indicating poor clustering and 1 indicating well-separated clusters. The formula for s(i) is calculated by subtracting a(i) from b(i) and then dividing the result by the larger value between a(i) and b(i).

A number nearing 1 indicates that the data point strongly resembles its own cluster (high cohesion) and a significant dissimilarity to other clusters (high separation). A data point with a value close to 0 indicates its proximity to the boundary between two clusters, making it potentially assignable to either. A number around –1 indicates that the data point exhibits low cohesiveness within its cluster and low separation from another cluster, indicating a high degree of dissimilarity.

The silhouette score for each cluster is calculated as the mean of the silhouette scores of all the data points within that cluster. The silhouette score for the entire data set is computed as the mean of the silhouette scores for each cluster. The ideal number of clusters is the one that maximizes the silhouette score for the given data set.

Consider a scenario where we possess a data set comprising four distinct attributes, and our objective is to categorize it into either two or three distinct groups. We can use a clustering technique to acquire the clustering results. Subsequently, the silhouette method can be employed to assess the calibre of each clustering outcome. Table 7.3 displays the silhouette ratings for each data point and cluster in various scenarios.

Table 7.3 Silhouette rating example

Data point	Cluster 1 ($K = 2$)	Cluster 2 ($K = 2$)	Cluster 1 ($K = 3$)	Cluster 2 ($K = 3$)	Cluster 3 ($K = 3$)
1	0.65	-	0.65	-	-
2	0.55	-	0.55	-	-
3	0.60	-	-	0.60	-
4	-	0.70	-	-	0.70
5	-	0.75	-	-	0.75
6	-	0.80	-	-	0.85
Cluster	0.60	0.75	0.60	0.60	0.75
Data set	**0.68**		**0.65**		

It is evident that when $K = 2$, the score is higher than when $K = 3$. This indicates that two clusters are more suitable for this data set than three. It is evident that the data points in Cluster 2 exhibit higher silhouette scores compared to those in Cluster 1, suggesting that Cluster 2 is more tightly-knit and distinct than Cluster 1.

The silhouette approach is a useful tool, but it also has certain limits. For example, it may not perform optimally for data sets with clusters that overlap or have non-spherical shapes or for data sets that contain noise or outliers. Thus, it is recommended to employ alternative approaches such as visual examination, subject expertise, or statistical analyses to supplement the silhouette method.

The **gap statistic approach** is used to ascertain the most suitable clusters in a given data set. The underlying concept is that data should exhibit more structure or patterns rather than random noise. Consequently, the SSD between the data points and their cluster centers should be minimized by clustering the data. The gap statistic approach aims to determine the ideal equilibrium by comparing the SSD of the actual data with randomly produced data with similar features, such as size and form. The assumption is that the randomly produced data lacks any discernible structure or clusters, resulting in minimal variation in its SSD when the number of clusters is altered. The gap statistic approach computes the gap, a metric that quantifies the disparity between the log(SSD) of the observed data and the log(SSD) of the randomly generated data for each cluster count. As the gap increases, the actual data exhibits a greater degree of pattern or clustering than the random data. The ideal number of clusters is the one that maximizes the gap.

Let us consider an example of clustering some two-dimensional data points. We can calculate the SSD for each clustering by summing up the squared distances between each data point and its cluster center. Table 7.4 shows the SSD values for each clustering.

Table 7.4 SSD values for each clustering

Number of clusters (*K*)	SSD
2	9.2
3	6.4
4	4.8
5	3.6

The SSD value decreases to the growth (increase) in the number of clusters, as anticipated. Nevertheless, this information does not provide the ideal clustering solution, as we need knowledge regarding the expected SSD resulting from random noise.

To address this, we can produce a set of random data that matches the size and structure of the original data and, after that, compute the SSD for each possible number of clusters. We can iterate this procedure to obtain the mean SSD for each cluster quantity. Table 7.5 illustrates an instance of arbitrary data and its corresponding average SSD values.

Table 7.5 Average SSD values for random data

Number of clusters (*K*)	Average SSD
2	8.9
3	8.7
4	8.6
5	8.5

The mean SSD for random data remains very stable regardless of the number of clusters, as anticipated. Consequently, clustering random data has minimal impact in reducing its dispersion.

Now, we can compute the gap statistic for each cluster count by subtracting the logarithm of the SSD of the actual data from the logarithm of the SSD of the random data. Table 7.6 displays the gap values corresponding to each cluster count.

Table 7.6 Gap values for each cluster count

Number of clusters (*K*)	Gap
2	−0.03
3	−0.17
4	−0.23
5	−0.26

It is evident that the difference widens as the number of clusters rises, yet it remains negative for all values of K. Consequently, all clustering has an SSD equal to or higher than that of random noise. As a result, none of the clustering possesses a discernible structure or pattern. Based on this scenario, it may be inferred that no definitive number of clusters is most suitable for this particular data set.

The gap statistic approach is a widely used for determining the most suitable number of clusters in a given data set. Nevertheless, this technique has imperfections and some limits and assumptions that must be considered. An essential premise of the gap statistic approach is that the reference distribution, created randomly, shares similar attributes with the real data, including dimensionality and shape. Consequently, the random data must possess an equivalent amount of characteristics and instances as the actual data and should have a uniform distribution within the identical domain. Nevertheless, attaining this objective in practice may be challenging and unreliable, as actual data frequently exhibits intricate structures and patterns that simplistic random models do not adequately represent.

Another obstacle is its reliance on our capacity to generate random data that faithfully emulates noise. Noise refers to the undesired fluctuations or inaccuracies in the data not associated with any cluster. The gap statistic approach assumes that noise is equally distributed and has no correlation with the clusters. However, this assertion may not hold for certain real data sets, as noise may exhibit a discernible structure or pattern that can impact clustering outcomes. If the noise is connected with certain attributes or data, it can generate new clusters or distort the actual ones. This can result in inaccurate gap values and incorrect determination of the ideal number of clusters..

Another constraint of the gap statistic method is establishing a range of potential cluster numbers, which might be challenging to determine. The range should be sufficiently broad to encompass the genuine best value while avoiding excessive computations and erroneous outcomes. If the range is excessively limited, there is a possibility that we will overlook the optimal value and ultimately obtain clustering that is less than ideal. In the case of a wide range, we may face issues like overfitting or underfitting, where we either identify an excessive number of little clusters or a limited number of large clusters that fail to represent the actual data structure accurately.

Another limitation is its failure to account for additional factors that impact the clustering's quality, such as the clusters' shape, size, or distance from each other. The analysis solely concentrates on the SSD for quantifying the dispersion inside clusters. Nevertheless, SSD may not be comprehensive or satisfactory in capturing all the intricacies or inclinations of diverse clustering applications or scenarios. It is imperative to exercise prudence and supplement it with other techniques or standards to guarantee resilient and dependable clustering outcomes.

7.3.1.2 Hierarchical Clustering

Hierarchical clustering is a robust unsupervised learning algorithm that uses a hierarchical approach to group data points into clusters. It begins by assigning each data point its cluster, then works to merge them in a hierarchical tree structure as it determines the similarities and differences between different data points. As a result, the algorithm can identify patterns and create clusters based on shared characteristics by comparing these characteristics. This type of clustering can be used for various applications, such as customer segmentation or recognizing patterns in large data sets.

One advantage of hierarchical clustering is that it does not require prior knowledge about the data set or any assumptions about its structure, making it suitable for exploratory analysis. It often produces more accurate results than other algorithms since it can capture subtler differences between groups of objects compared to other methods. Users can easily modify clusters based on their specific needs by changing parameters such as similarity criteria or linkage methods.

Let us consider a data set of customers of an online store, where each customer is described by their age, gender, income, and purchase history. The goal is to cluster the customers based on their similarity in terms of these features.

Steps

Step 1: Distance Calculation. The first step is to calculate the distance between each pair of customers. Here, we can use the Euclidean distance as a measure of similarity between customers. We can represent the data set in tabular form where each row represents a customer and the columns represent the features. Table 7.7 shows the details for five customers.

Table 7.7 Customer details

Customer	Age	Gender	Income	Purchase history
1	30	Male	50000	Low
2	35	Female	60000	Medium
3	25	Female	40000	High
4	45	Male	80000	Low
5	50	Female	90000	High

Step 2: Creating a Distance Matrix. Next, we need to define a distance or similarity measure between the customers based on their features. One possible choice is the Euclidean distance, which is the square root of the sum of squared differences between corresponding feature values. For example, the Euclidean distance between customer 1 and customer 2 is:

sqrt((30-35)^2 + (0-1)^2 + (50000-60000)^2 + (0-1)^2) = 10001.41,

where we have encoded the gender and purchase history features as binary variables (0 for male/low, 1 for female/high). Using this distance measure, we can construct a distance matrix (Table 7.8) that shows the pairwise distances between all customers.

Table 7.8 Distance matrix

Distance	1	2	3	4	5
1	0	10001.41	10001.41	30001.41	40001.41
2	10001.41	0	20001.41	20001.41	30001.41
3	10001.41	20001.41	0	40001.41	50001.41
4	30001.41	20001.41	40001.41	0	10001.41
5	40001.41	30001.41	50001.41	10001.41	0

Step 3: Building the Dendrogram. A dendrogram is a tree-like diagram that shows the hierarchical relationship between the customers based on their similarity. We start by considering each customer as a separate cluster and then merge the closest clusters until we end up with a single cluster that contains all the customers.

We perform the clustering algorithm using different methods such as single linkage, complete linkage, average linkage, or Ward's method. Here, we will use single linkage, which merges the clusters that have the smallest minimum distance between any pair of their members.

The algorithm starts with each customer as a separate cluster:

$$\{1\}, \{2\}, \{3\}, \{4\}, \{5\}$$

The smallest distance in the matrix is 10001.41, which occurs between customer 1 and customer 3, and between customer 2 and customer 4. We can merge these pairs into two clusters:

$$\{1, 3\}, \{2, 4\}, \{5\}$$

The next smallest distance is 20001.41, which occurs between customer 2 and customer 5, and between customer 3 and customer 5. We can merge these pairs into two clusters:

$$\{1, 3, 5\}, \{2, 4\}$$

The final step is to merge the remaining two clusters into one:

$$\{1, 3, 5, 2, 4\}$$

This is the final clustering result using single linkage hierarchical clustering. The dendrogram for this example is shown in Fig. 7.9.

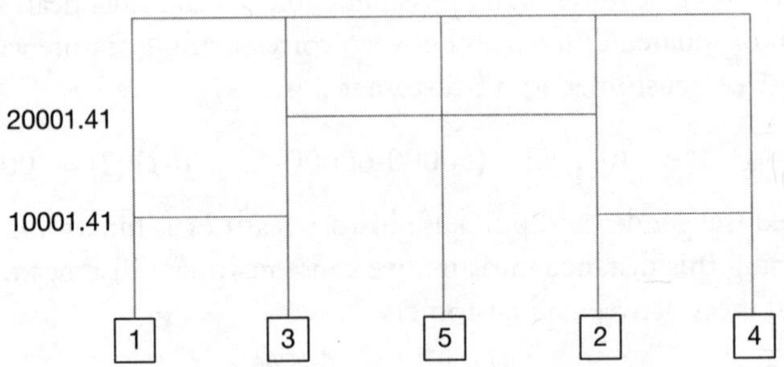

Figure 7.9 Dendrogram example

Hierarchical clustering can be applied to a wide range of data sets and is particularly useful for identifying patterns in large and complex data sets. It can also be used for data visualization and exploratory analysis, as the resulting dendrogram provides a clear visualization of the relationships between the data points.

The two primary **types of hierarchical clustering** are agglomerative clustering and divisive clustering (Fig. 7.10).

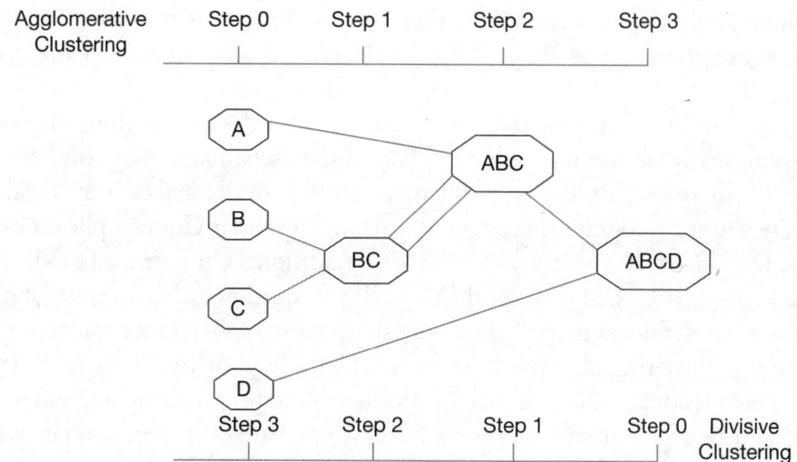

Figure 7.10 Agglomerative and division clustering

Agglomerative clustering is a hierarchical method that begins by treating each data point as an individual cluster. It then progressively combines the most comparable clusters until a certain number of clusters or a predetermined stopping condition is met. Various approaches can be used to quantify the similarity between clusters, including single linkage (minimum distance), complete linkage (maximum distance), average linkage (average distance), and Ward's method (minimum variance).

Divisive clustering is a hierarchical method that begins by grouping all data points into a single cluster and then proceeds to divide the cluster into smaller clusters iteratively until a specified number of clusters or a predetermined stopping condition is met. Clusters can be divided using many criteria, such as the maximum distance between data points, the minimum density of data points, or the minimal silhouette coefficient.

One instance of hierarchical clustering involves categorizing papers according to their respective subjects. Agglomerative clustering begins by treating each document as its cluster, then combines clusters that share similar words or concepts until a predetermined number of topics or a threshold of similarity is achieved. Divisive clustering begins by grouping all documents into a single cluster and dividing the cluster into smaller subclusters depending on the dissimilarity of words or keywords. This process continues until a predetermined number of topics or a dissimilarity threshold is achieved.

7.3.1.3 Fuzzy C-Means Clustering

This is a popular data mining technique that uses fuzzy logic to identify clusters within large, complex data sets. Unlike other clustering algorithms, it does not rely on rigid boundaries to assign labels or define the characteristics of each cluster. Instead, it utilizes probabilistic relationships between data points to assign them to groups based on their likelihood of belonging to each category. This approach allows for more accurate classifications of complex data sets. In addition, it helps uncover subtle patterns that standard methods may otherwise overlook.

The algorithm assigns a membership value or degree of association with each data point in relation to all the other points within the data set. A probability between 0 and 1 is typically used to indicate this value, with higher values denoting a more substantial likelihood of belonging to the cluster and lower values denoting a weaker link. The algorithm evaluates these probabilities to determine which points should be grouped according to their similarities or dissimilarities. Once this has been done, it can use those groupings as categories or labels when classifying new data points into groups accordingly.

Because fuzzy C-means clustering does not require strict rules for assigning classes, it allows for more creative solutions when dealing with complicated data sets that contain outliers and non-conforming values. Furthermore, its ability to identify subtle patterns makes it an invaluable tool for many areas where pattern recognition is essential, such as computer vision applications and financial market analysis. Despite its advantages compared with traditional clustering methods, however, there are still drawbacks associated with this algorithm, such as requiring extensive computational resources, which can limit its usefulness if applied to extensive data sets where time constraints are an issue.

To illustrate this clustering algorithm, let us consider a hypothetical scenario with a data set of customers and their spending habits on various products. The products include shoes, clothing, and accessories. We aim to segment the customers into groups based on their similarity in purchasing behavior, and design customized marketing strategies for each group.

Steps

1. First, we need to specify the number of clusters we want to create and initialize the fuzzy membership matrix. The fuzzy membership matrix contains the degree of membership of each data point to each cluster. We can initialize it randomly or use some heuristic method. For simplicity, let us assume we want to create two clusters, and we initialize the fuzzy membership matrix randomly.
2. Next, we need to calculate the centroids of the two clusters based on the initial fuzzy membership matrix. The centroid of a cluster is the weighted average of all the data points in the cluster, where the weights are the degrees of membership. The centroids represent the center or prototype of each cluster.
3. We need to calculate the distance between each data point and the centroids of the two clusters. We can use any distance measure, such as Euclidean or Manhattan distance. The distance measures how far a data point is from the centroid of a cluster.
4. We need to update the fuzzy membership matrix based on the distance between each data point and the centroids. We use a fuzzy membership function that assigns a higher degree of membership to a data point closer to a cluster's centroid and a lower degree of membership to a data point farther from a cluster's centroid. The fuzzy membership function also depends on the fuzziness factor, which controls how much overlap there is between the clusters. A higher fuzziness factor means more overlap, and a lower fuzziness factor means less overlap.
5. Next, we repeat steps two to four until the algorithm converges. The algorithm converges when there is no significant change in the fuzzy membership matrix or the centroids of the clusters.
6. Finally, we need to assign each data point to the cluster with the highest degree of membership. This results in a soft partitioning of the data, where each data point belongs to multiple clusters with different degrees of membership. We can then analyze the characteristics of each cluster and identify common patterns among the customers in each cluster.

To explain how this works, let us consider the data points: $\{(1, 2), (3, 5), (6, 8), (7, 10)\}$. Suppose we want to cluster them into two groups: A and B. We start by randomly assigning membership values to each data point for each cluster (Table 7.9).

Table 7.9 Fuzzy C-means data point and membership

Data point	Membership in A	Membership in B
(1,2)	0.7	0.3
(3,5)	0.6	0.4
(6,8)	0.2	0.8
(7,10)	0.1	0.9

The membership values indicate how strongly each data point belongs to each cluster. They must sum up to one for each data point. Next, we calculate the centroids of each cluster based on the weighted average of the data points and their membership values. For example, the centroid of cluster A is:

$$(0.7 * 1 + 0.6 * 3 + 0.2 * 6 + 0.1 * 7) / (0.7 + 0.6 + 0.2 + 0.1) = 2.9$$

$$(0.7 * 2 + 0.6 * 5 + 0.2 * 8 + 0.1 * 10) / (0.7 + 0.6 + 0.2 + 0.1) = 4$$

Similarly, the centroid of cluster B is:

$$(0.3 * 1 + 0.4 * 3 + 0.8 * 6 + 0.9 * 7) / (0.3 + 0.4 + 0.8 + 0.9) = 5.9$$

$$(0.3 * 2 + 0.4 * 5 + 0.8 * 8 + 0.9 * 10) / (0.3 + 0.4 + 0.8 + 0.9) = 8$$

Then, we update the membership values of each data point based on their distance to the centroids of each cluster using a formula that involves a parameter called the **fuzziness coefficient**, which controls how fuzzy the clusters are. A higher fuzziness coefficient means more overlap between clusters, while a lower one means more separation.

The membership value of a data point for a cluster is inversely proportional to the distance to the centroid of that cluster, raised to a power m that controls the fuzziness of the clustering. A higher value of m means more fuzziness, and a lower value means more crispness. A common choice for m is 2.

For example, the distance from (1, 2) to the centroid of cluster A is:

sqrt((1 – 2.9)^2 + (2 – 4.5)^2) = sqrt(5) = ~2.24

The distance from (1, 2) to the centroid of cluster B is:

sqrt((1 – 6.4)^2 + (2 – 8.9)^2) = sqrt(58) = ~7.62

The membership value of (1, 2) for cluster A is:

(1 / sqrt(5))^(2 / (*m* – 1)) / ((1 / sqrt(5))^(2 / (*m* – 1)) + (1 / sqrt(58))^(2 / (*m* – 1)))
= ((sqrt(58))^*m* / ((sqrt(58))^*m* + (sqrt(5))^*m*))

If we choose $m = 2$, this becomes:

(sqrt(58)^2 / ((sqrt(58))^2 + (sqrt(5))^2))
= ((58 / (58 + 5))) = ~0.92

The membership value of (1, 2) for cluster B is:

(1 / sqrt(58))^(2 / (m – 1)) / ((1 / sqrt(5))^(2 / (m – 1)) + (1 / sqrt(58))^(2 / (m – 1)))
= ((sqrt(5))^m / ((sqrt(58))^m + (sqrt(5))^m))

If we choose $m = 2$, this becomes:

(sqrt(5)^2 / ((sqrt(58))^2 + (sqrt(5))^2))
= ((5 / (58 + 5))) = ~0.08

We repeat this process of calculating centroids and updating membership values until the membership values converge or reach a predefined threshold. The result is a fuzzy partition of the data points into two clusters, where each data point has a degree of belonging to each cluster.

7.3.1.4 DBSCAN

Density-based spatial clustering of noise-induced applications is a well-known algorithm for density-based clustering. It is better than *K*-means for identifying clusters as it cross-examines its data points' density in more extensive spatial databases. The algorithm divides the low-density areas into high-density areas.

Imagine you have a data set with the geographical coordinates (latitude and longitude) of all coffee shops in a city. When you apply DBSCAN to this data set, the algorithm will look for areas where coffee shops are densely packed. For instance, in a downtown area, coffee shops are likely to be close to each other due to high foot traffic and demand. DBSCAN will identify these clusters of coffee shops as a single group.

On the other hand, in suburban areas, coffee shops may be more spread out. DBSCAN will recognize these as separate clusters or even as noise if they are too far apart. For example, if there are only a few coffee shops scattered across a large suburban area, they might not form a dense cluster.

Additionally, DBSCAN can identify outliers. These are coffee shops that are located far from any other coffee shops, such as a lone coffee shop in a remote area. The algorithm will mark these as noise or outliers because they do not belong to any cluster.

The clusters can therefore be found in any arbitrary shape. You will need a minimum number of points within the neighborhood of the starting data point to start the clustering process. Otherwise, those data points would end up as noise. The DBSCAN algorithm also does not require a pre-set number of clusters. This algorithm selects an arbitrary point and then identifies other points near the arbitrary one.

Later, the data points recognized with the help of an arbitrary one are recognized as a cluster. The one far away from the arbitrary point (noise/outliers) is used in other iterations of identifying the clusters. The fact that this algorithm is robust to outliers, or will not include outlier data points in any cluster, gives it a significant advantage over *K*-means and MeanShift. *K*-means clusters every instance in the data sets, whereas DBSCAN does not include noise points (outliers) in a legitimate cluster. Non-global clusters are challenging for *K*-means, whereas DBSCAN handles them without issue. Unlike DBSCAN, the *K*-means algorithm does not presuppose that the data set's data points come from a Gaussian distribution.

In order to demonstrate the functioning of DBSCAN, we shall examine the subsequent data points presented in Table 7.10.

Table 7.10 DBSCAN data points

ID	X	Y
1	1	2
2	2	2
3	3	2
4	4	2
5	5	2
6	6	2
7	7	2
8	8	2
9	9	2
10	10	2

The algorithm is defined by two parameters: epsilon (eps) and minimum points (minPts). eps represents the upper limit for the distance between two points to be classified as neighbors, while minPts denotes the minimum number of points needed to establish a cluster. For this illustration, let us assume that the value of eps is 1.5 and the value of minPts is 3.

The procedure commences by selecting a random location, designated as point 1, and identifying all adjacent points within a specified distance of epsilon. Point 2 is the sole adjacent point to point 1 in this scenario. Because the number of neighboring points is below the minimum required number (minPts), point 1 is classified as noise and is not allocated to any cluster.

The program subsequently selects another point at random, such as point 4, and identifies its neighboring points within a distance of eps. Points 3, 4, 5, and 6 are adjacent to point 4 in this scenario. Given that the number of neighboring points equals or exceeds the minimum required number of points (minPts), point 4 is designated as a core point and allocated to a newly formed cluster, referred to as cluster A.

The procedure proceeds by enlarging cluster A through the iterative inclusion of all the neighboring points of point 4, and subsequently their respective neighbors, provided that they are within a distance of eps and possess a minimum of minPts neighbors. In this instance, points 3, 5, and 6 are designated core points and included in cluster A. Point 2 is designated as a border point and included in cluster A because it is located within the specified distance (eps) from a core point. However, it does not have the minimum number of neighboring points (minPts).

Subsequently, the program selects another location randomly, denoted as point 8, and proceeds to perform an identical procedure. Points 7, 8, 9, and 10 are adjacent to point 8 in this scenario. Given that the number of neighbors equals or exceeds the minimum number of points (minPts), point 8 is classified as a core point and allocated to a newly formed cluster, referred to as cluster B. The algorithm proceeds by enlarging cluster B by including all the adjacent points of point 8 and their respective adjacent points in a recursive manner. This expansion continues as long as the points are within a distance of eps and possess a minimum of minPts neighbors. In this instance, points 7, 9, and 10 are designated core points and included in cluster B.

The program selects another point randomly, referred to as point 1, and determines that it has already undergone processing and been designated as noise. The algorithm concludes once all the points have been processed.

There are two clusters in the final result: cluster A, which contains the points {2,3,4,5,6}, and cluster B, which contains the points {7,8,9,10}. Point 1 is disregarded as irrelevant data.

Advantages: One of the main benefits of DBSCAN is its ability to detect clusters of various shapes, sizes, and densities without prior knowledge about the data or assumptions about cluster structure. Unlike *K*-means and hierarchical clustering, DBSCAN does not require the user to specify the number of clusters beforehand; instead, it automatically detects the number of clusters in the data. It is also robust to noise since it ignores points that are too sparsely distributed or isolated from other points and, therefore, unlikely to be part of any meaningful structure. This makes DBSCAN an ideal choice for analysing complex data sets with noisy features or outliers.

Another advantage is that users do not have to worry about specifying parameters such as distance thresholds which can dramatically affect performance; instead, they can tune two key parameters: epsilon (ε) which determines how close two points must be for them to be considered 'neighbors'; and minPts which specifies what minimum number of neighbors each point must have within a certain radius for it to form a cluster. With these parameters appropriately set by an experienced analyst, DBSCAN can easily discover hidden patterns within data sets without relying on prior assumptions about cluster structure or requiring manual user intervention.

Disadvantages: DBSCAN is a practical algorithm for clustering large data sets. However, it can be sensitive to outliers, leading to misclassifications of points and unexpected results. If DBSCAN sets its parameters too low, these outliers might be classified as noise instead of as part of a cluster; if set too high, entire clusters could be missed or improperly grouped due to their similar densities. To avoid this problem, it is essential to consider the outliers present in the data set and adjust the parameters accordingly.

For example, there are many clustered points with low density compared to nearby points. In that case, increasing epsilon and minPts may help ensure that all clustered points are adequately identified. Similarly, if there is more than one group/cluster present with similar densities caused by overlapping clusters or varying densities within one group/cluster itself, then setting epsilon higher than usual will help ensure that all clusters are properly assigned, even though some objects might still fall outside their respective boundaries due to being an outlier.

Finally, when working with large data sets containing multiple overlapped and varied clusters, it is recommended not only to adjust parameter values but also to check for possible outliers beforehand since this will improve accuracy and reduce unnecessary computations when running DBSCAN.

7.3.1.5 The Gaussian Mixture Model

The Gaussian mixture model (GMM) combines probability distributions to model data, with each component representing a different kind of pattern in the data. It is a probabilistic model which assigns each observation to one or more clusters based on the likelihood that it belongs to each cluster.

The fundamental assumption behind GMMs is that all data points can be explained by a mixture of Gaussian distributions, or 'clusters.' Each clusters associated mean and covariance matrix defines its shape and spread within the multidimensional feature space. The number of clusters does not have to be specified beforehand, as the algorithm will determine this during the training phase.

Steps

1. The first step of GMM involves estimating which components best explain the input data by maximizing the likelihood function given by a set of observed data points. This involves estimating parameters such as mean and covariance for each component.
2. In the second step, observations are assigned to clusters according to their likelihoods; that is, how probable it is that they belong to a particular component/cluster, given their values on specific features (such as height, weight, etc.). For example, if two observations have very similar characteristics (they both have similar heights and weights), they would likely be assigned to the same component/cluster since they would likely have originated from one common source (as opposed to two different sources). This allows us to find groups within our data set without needing labels, even when they may overlap (if two clusters have overlapping means). Observations with higher likelihoods for multiple clusters may become part of both groups simultaneously.

Once these steps have been completed, we can use this information for further analysis or even make predictions about future behavior.

One way to understand GMM is to use the **expectation maximization (EM) algorithm**, which iteratively updates the parameters until convergence. The EM algorithm consists of two steps: the E-step and the M-step. In the E-step, the algorithm computes the posterior probability of each data point belonging to each component, based on the current parameters. In the M-step, the algorithm updates the parameters by maximizing the log-likelihood function, which is a weighted sum of the log-likelihoods of each component.

For example, suppose we have a data set of heights and weights of 10 people, as shown in Table 7.11.

Table 7.11 GMM data points

Height	Weight
170	65
180	75
190	85
160	55
165	60
175	70
185	80
195	90
155	50
150	45

We can use GMM to cluster this data into two groups, assuming that each group follows a bivariate Gaussian distribution, and then estimate the parameters of these distributions from the data. The parameters we need to estimate are:

- The mean vector for each group, which is a two-dimensional vector that contains the average height and weight of the group.
- The covariance matrix for each group, which is a two-by-two matrix that captures the variability and correlation of height and weight within the group.
- The mixing coefficient for each group, which is a scalar that indicates the proportion of the data that belongs to the group.

We can initialize the parameters randomly, such as:

- Mean of group 1: (160, 60)
- Mean of group 2: (180, 80)
- Covariance of group 1: [[100, 0], [0, 100]]
- Covariance of group 2: [[100, 0], [0, 100]]
- Weight of group 1: 0.5
- Weight of group 2: 0.5

Estimation of these parameters can be done using the EM algorithm:

1. **Expectation step**: In this step, we compute the probability of each data point belonging to each group, given the current estimates of the parameters. This probability is also known as the responsibility or posterior probability. For example, if we have two groups with means (170,65) and (180,75), and equal covariances and mixing coefficients, then the probability of the first data point (170,65) belonging to the first group is higher than the second group, because it is closer to its mean. The formula for computing this probability is based on Bayes' theorem and the multivariate Gaussian density function.
2. **Maximization step**: In this step, we update the estimates of the parameters based on the probabilities computed in the expectation step. We use these probabilities as weights to compute the weighted average and covariance of each group. We also normalize these probabilities to obtain the new mixing coefficients. The formulas for updating the parameters are derived from maximizing the log-likelihood function of the data.

Then we can apply the EM algorithm to update the parameters until convergence. After a few iterations, we may obtain the following results:

- Mean of group 1: (152.5, 47.5)
- Mean of group 2: (182.5, 77.5)
- Covariance of group 1: [[62.5, -12.5], [-12.5, 62.5]]
- Covariance of group 2: [[62.5, -12.5], [-12.5, 62.5]]
- Weight of group 1: 0.4
- Weight of group 2: 0.6

We repeat these two steps until convergence, which means that the parameters do not change significantly between iterations. The final estimates of the parameters define the GMM that best fits the data.

Based on these parameters, we can assign each data point to the most likely group, as shown in Table 7.12.

Table 7.12 GMM data points with final classification

Height	Weight	Group
170	65	2
180	75	2
190	85	2
160	55	2
165	60	2
175	70	2
185	80	2
195	90	2
155	50	1
150	45	1

This is one possible clustering result using GMM. The advantage of GMM is that it can capture the shape and orientation of the clusters, unlike other methods such as *K*-means that assume spherical clusters. The disadvantage of GMM is that it requires more parameters and computations than other methods, and it may suffer from overfitting if the number of components is too large or the data is sparse.

7.3.1.6 MeanShift Clustering

It is a clustering algorithm that iteratively shifts the centroids of the data points toward the higher-density areas. It does not require labeled data, nor does it involve any predetermined targets or outputs. Unlike the *K*-means algorithm, the MeanShift algorithm does not require us to specify the number of clusters. Suppose you need clarification on the patterns in the data, the algorithm automatically determines the number of clusters. Dense data point areas use a sliding-window centroid-based algorithm to locate the center group/class points. All center point candidates are considered to be the mean value of the sliding window points. Such windows are then sorted post-processing to remove duplicates and give the final group center points.

Image segmentation tasks are where MeanShift clustering is most frequently used. Kernel density estimation is the foundation of the MeanShift algorithm. This algorithm iteratively assigns each data point to the closest cluster centroid, which is initialized arbitrarily. Then, each point is iteratively moved in the space based on where the most points are, that is, the mode. This method overcomes the selection of groups and cluster centers as the mean values are discovered automatically. The clusters also exhibit data sense due to convergence to the areas having maximum data points intuitively. Here, the window size is crucial as it determines the scale of the clustering and directly affects the number of clusters detected. A smaller window size can lead to many small clusters, while a larger window size may merge distinct clusters into a single one. Thus, if the window size is too small, it may result in overfitting. If the window size is too large, it may lead to underfitting. The radius of the window size is thus a critical factor that can lead to non-trivial and sometimes disadvantageous clustering results.

A randomly selected circular sliding window is defined as point C with kernel radius r. The hill-climbing MeanShift algorithm shifts the kernel through successive iterations to higher-density regions and repeats the process until convergence is obtained. Finally, in the post-processing stage, the candidate windows are filtered. A final set of centroids and the assigned groups of data points are produced as a result of this process (Table 7.13).

Table 7.13 MeanShift clustering data points

Height	Weight
170	65
180	75
190	85
160	55
165	60
175	70
185	80
195	90
155	50
150	45

Steps

1. Initialize each data point as a cluster centroid.
2. For each data point, calculate the mean of all points within a certain radius (the bandwidth) centered at the data point. For example, if we use a bandwidth of 10 cm for height and 5 kg for weight, then the mean of the points within this radius for the first data point (170 cm, 65 kg) is (172.5 cm, 67.5 kg).
3. Shift each data point to the mean calculated in the previous step. For example, the first data point will move from (170 cm, 65 kg) to (172.5 cm, 67.5 kg).
4. Repeat steps 2 and 3 until convergence or a maximum number of iterations is reached. Convergence means that the data points do not move significantly after shifting.
5. Identify the cluster centroids as the points that have not moved after convergence. These are the modes of the density function and represent the clusters in the data.

Using this algorithm, we can obtain two clusters from the given data: one cluster with four points around (195 cm, 90 kg) and another cluster with six points around (165 cm, 60 kg).

Advantages: MeanShift clustering is an efficient and flexible tool for analyzing data. It can quickly identify clusters of any size or shape in complex data sets without the need for prior knowledge about the data. MeanShift is also robust against noise and outliers, making it suitable for real-world applications where the data may contain errors or inconsistencies that adversely affect other clustering algorithms. This makes it an ideal choice for exploratory analysis when trying to understand how variables are related to a data set. MeanShift clustering is also widely used in ML applications such as object tracking and image segmentation due to its flexibility and efficiency compared to clustering algorithms like *K*-means clustering. With MeanShift, ML models can quickly recognize patterns in large volumes of data, leading to more accurate predictions than would otherwise be possible with traditional methods.

Disadvantages: One of the main disadvantages of MeanShift clustering is its inability to handle high-dimensional data sets effectively. As dimensions increase beyond 10 or 12, the algorithm's reliance on distance metrics becomes increasingly meaningless. It needs to scale better when dealing with larger data sets. Another disadvantage is the difficulty in selecting appropriate parameters, such as bandwidth and kernel functions, which require significant domain knowledge or trial-and-error experimentation if they must be chosen correctly. This can lead to suboptimal results if done incorrectly, making it essential for users to understand how these parameters affect the clustering process before they begin their analysis. Finally, due to its reliance on local optimization methods such as the hill climbing technique, MeanShift clustering can sometimes converge onto local optima instead of global ones – resulting in inaccurate clusters even when applied correctly.

7.3.1.7 Gaussian Mixture Density Estimation

Gaussian mixture density estimation (GMDE) is an important unsupervised learning technique used to find patterns in complex data sets and make predictions without prior knowledge of class labels. It uses probability density functions (PDFs) to model the data, combining multiple PDFs into one overall probability distribution. The PDFs are determined by fitting Gaussian distributions on each cluster since they are best suited to represent the shape of data points in such data sets. The EM algorithm is then used to estimate the parameters for each mixture model component.

This algorithm starts by assuming initial parameter values for each component and then adjusts them through successive iterations so that they best fit the data. Each iteration calculates the probability that a given point belongs to a particular component based on its current parameter values. It modifies them accordingly during maximization steps to have more influence over certain parts of the data set that need better representation. Once this process has been completed and stable parameter estimates obtained, these PDFs can be utilized for further analysis, such as predicting new observations or gaining insights into patterns within data sets.

For example, we want to predict whether someone will buy an item or not based on their past purchasing habits. In this case, we would use GMDE algorithms such as *K*-means clustering or EM which would help us identify clusters in our data set using their probability densities and thereby accurately predict which customers may be likely buyers or non-buyers depending on what clusters they belong to. This powerful tool helps businesses better understand their customers by identifying hidden relationships between different variables, ultimately allowing them to make better decisions when it comes time for product development or marketing strategies. GMDE can also be effectively used in medical diagnosis. Doctors can detect diseases early before symptoms appear based on patient history by clustering patients with similar characteristics together according to their associated probabilities.

GMDE works by estimating the parameters of multiple Gaussian distributions, which are mathematical functions that look like bell curves, to best fit the observed data and determine its underlying structure. This process is called **maximum likelihood estimation (MLE)**. It involves adjusting each component's parameters until they reach their highest possible likelihood, given their respective clusters of observations. This technique can help us make more accurate predictions about new observations based on past ones without additional training or information about the underlying phenomenon being studied.

For example, consider the situation where you want to forecast whether it will rain tomorrow based on the weather today. You could use MLE with GMDE to estimate the probability distribution between how much rainfall there typically is on days with similar temperatures and wind speeds as today. Once you have determined this probability distribution, you can make more informed decisions regarding how likely tomorrow's rainfall amount will fall within specific ranges given current conditions.

Once completed, these components can be used to classify unseen observations into corresponding clusters based on their likelihood value concerning each component's PDFs; higher values indicate a higher likelihood of association with a particular cluster. In comparison, lower values will point toward less likely associations with other clusters nearby in feature space. GMDE can also generate predictions about unseen data points or perform clustering tasks such as outlier detection and anomaly identification when combined with other ML algorithms like *K*-means and hierarchical clustering.

7.3.1.8 Markov Random Field

Markove random field (MRF) is a powerful mathematical tool used to model complex relationships between different variables. They are instrumental in tasks such as computer vision, NLP, medical diagnosis, and many more. The basic idea is that each variable is associated with its local environment rather than its global state. For example, in an image model, each pixel will depend on the pixels around it; or in a text model, each word will depend on its neighboring words rather than the entire document. MRFs allow us to capture long-range correlations in data and thus make better predictions than traditional methods.

Besides being used for complex tasks like forecasting the weather or predicting stock prices, MRFs can also be used for more specific learning activities like solving puzzles or playing games. For instance, when solving a jigsaw puzzle, we can use an MRF-based approach which assigns probabilities to different pieces depending on how well they fit together and how likely they are to form part of the solution. Similarly, when playing a board game like chess or checkers, we can use an MRF structure that assigns weights to certain moves based on their likelihood of being beneficial for winning the game in particular situations.

7.3.2 Anomaly Detection

Anomaly detection is when a program looks for data points that are different from the rest. For example, if you have data on how much money people spend at a store, the program might look for data points much higher or lower than the average. This can be useful for identifying fraud or unusual behavior.

Anomaly detection works by gathering information from existing data points, using them as references, and then looking for new data points that deviate from this reference set. Depending on how much an individual point deviates from what is considered normal, the system can flag it as either a potential problem or not worth looking into further. The technique requires no prior knowledge of any distribution – meaning there is no need to specify which types of values should be flagged – making it ideal for detecting unexpected events across different domains and data sets.

Examples include catching fraudulent financial activities in banking records or identifying malfunctioning machines in industrial settings. Anomaly detection has numerous advantages over conventional methods, such as supervised learning, when it comes to dealing with missing values and large amounts of noisy data where traditional methods often fail due to their reliance on labeled training sets with complete information about each observation (which may not always be available).

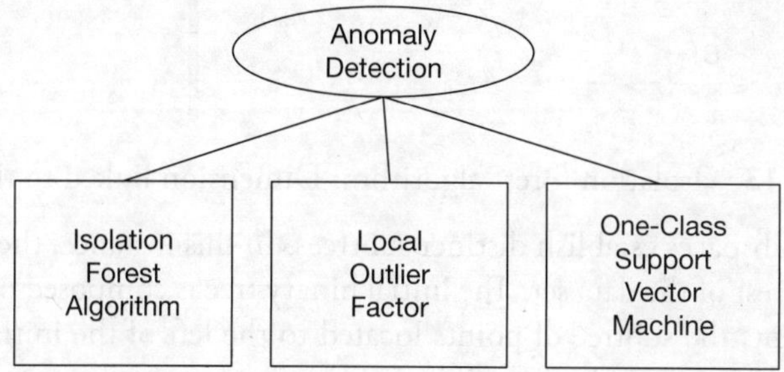

Figure 7.11 Types of anomaly detection algorithms

The types of anomaly detection algorithms (Fig, 7.11) are isolation forest algorithm, local outlier factor (LOF) and one-class support vector machine (OC SVM). These are now discussed in detail.

7.3.2.1 Isolation Forest Algorithm

As its name suggests, isolation forest is an ensemble approach that shares similarities with random forest. In other words, it takes the average of the predictions by numerous decision trees when awarding the final anomaly score to a given data point. Isolation forest differs from conventional anomaly detection algorithms by immediately attempting to isolate abnormal data points rather than defining what is considered 'normal' and then identifying everything else as anomalous.

Assume that we have the data points shown in Fig. 7.12.

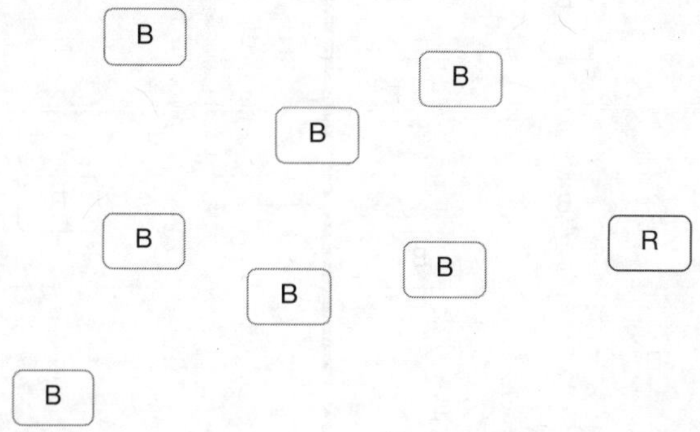

Figure 7.12 Isolation forest algorithm: Data points

The isolation forest technique randomly chooses a dimension (specifically, the dimension linked to the *x*-axis) and randomly divides the data along that dimension (Fig. 7.13).

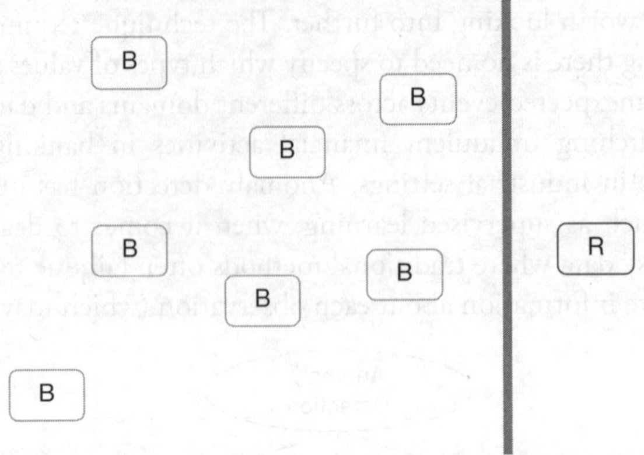

Figure 7.13 Isolation forest algorithm: Dimension linked to the *x*-axis

The two resulting subspaces establish distinct subtrees. In this instance, the cut occurs to divide a singular point from the rest of the data set. The initial binary tree is composed of two nodes at the first level. One node represents the subtree of points located to the left of the initial cut, while the other node represents the single point on the right (Fig. 7.14).

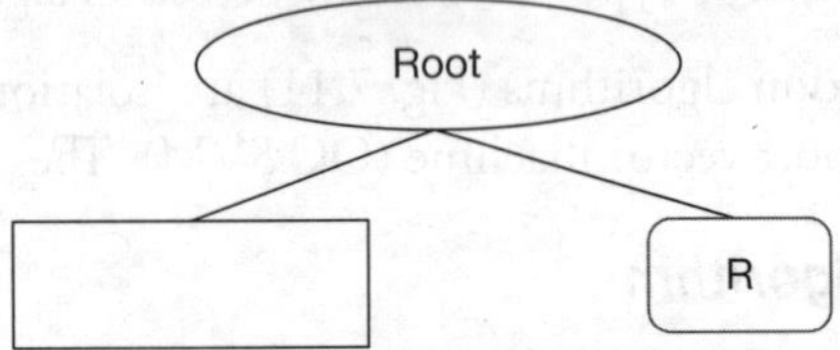

Figure 7.14 Isolation forest algorithm: Roots with isolation points

It is crucial to acknowledge that the remaining trees in the ensemble will choose distinct starting splits. In the given example, the initial split fails to separate the outlier from the rest of the data (Fig. 7.15).

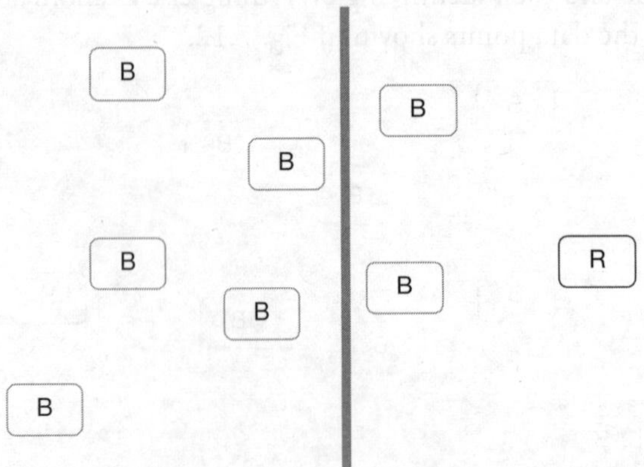

Figure 7.15 Isolation forest algorithm: Further splits

The resulting tree consists of two nodes (Fig. 7.16): one represents the points located to the left of the line, while the other represents the points located to the right of the line.

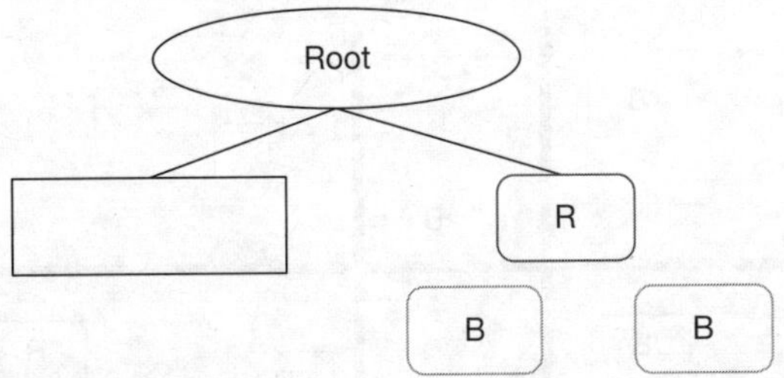

Figure 7.16 Isolation forest algorithm: With two nodes

The method is iterated until each leaf node of the tree corresponds to an individual data point from the data set. In our given example, the second iteration successfully identifies and separates the outlier from the rest of the data (Fig. 7.17).

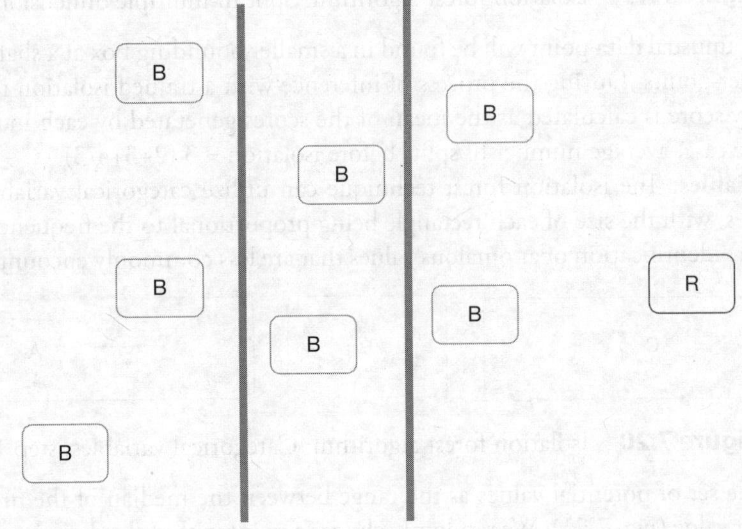

Figure 7.17 Isolation forest algorithm: Separating outliers from the rest

Upon completion of this stage, the tree would appear as depicted in Fig. 7.18.

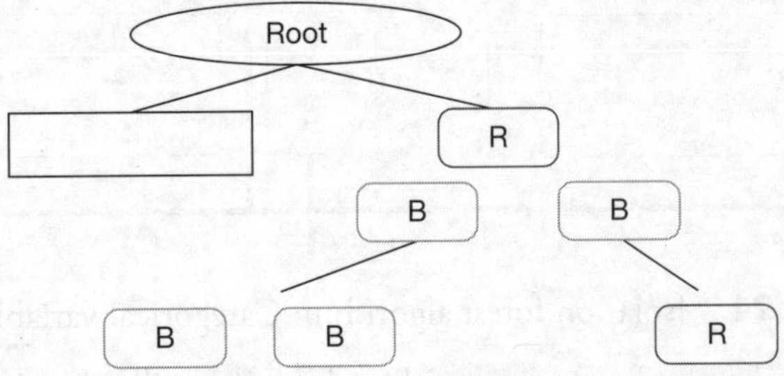

Figure 7.18 Isolation forest algorithm: With three nodes

It is important to note that a split can occur in the other dimension (Fig. 7.19), as is the situation with this third decision tree.

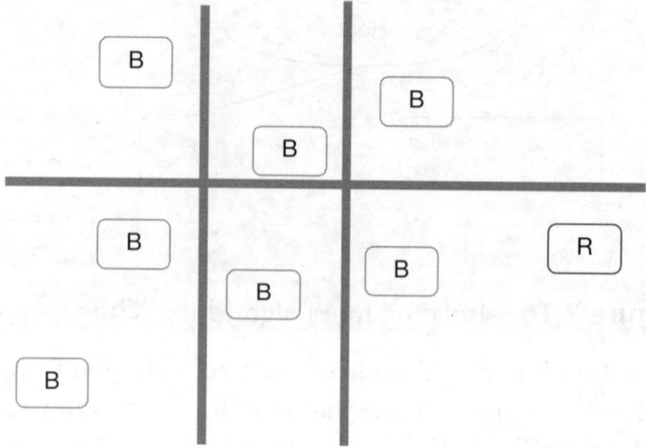

Figure 7.19 Isolation forest algorithm: Split in multiple dimensions

Typically, an unusual data point will be found in a smaller bounding box at a shallower tree depth compared to other points. During the process of inference with a trained isolation forest model, the ultimate anomaly score is calculated as the mean of the scores generated by each individual decision tree. In the above case, average number of splits before isolation = 3 (2+3+4/3)

Categorical Variables: The isolation forest technique can utilize categorical variables by depicting them as rectangles, with the size of each rectangle being proportional to the frequency of occurrence. This allows for the identification of anomalous values that are less commonly encountered (Fig. 7.20).

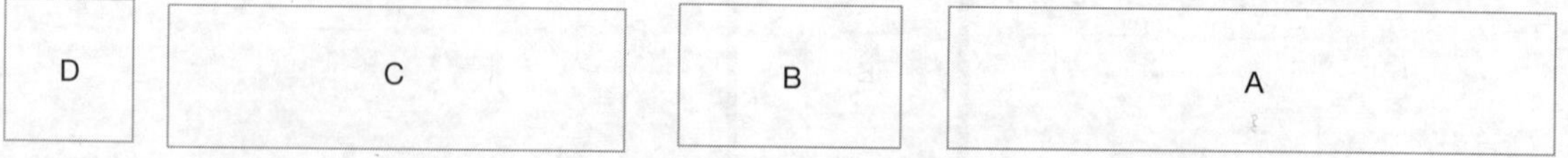

Figure 7.20 Isolation forest algorithm: Categorical variables, step 1

We define the set of potential values as the range between the median of the first value and the median of the last value (Fig. 7.21). We randomly choose a point within the domain and then identify the nearest edge of a specified rectangle. This is used for our split.

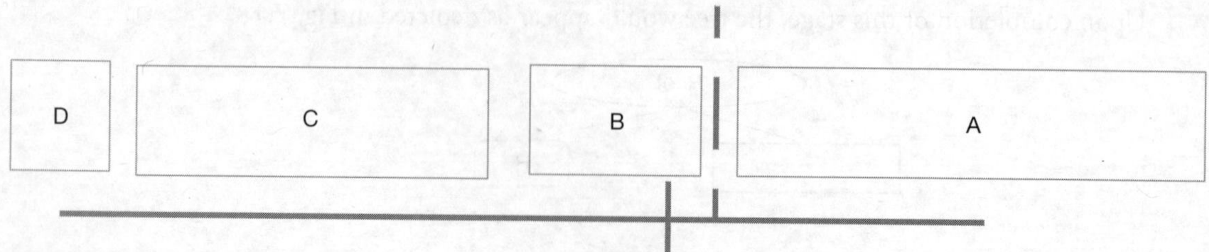

Figure 7.21 Isolation forest algorithm: Categorical variables, step 2

To maintain equity, the remaining trees within the forest will adopt an alternative sequencing (Fig. 7.22).

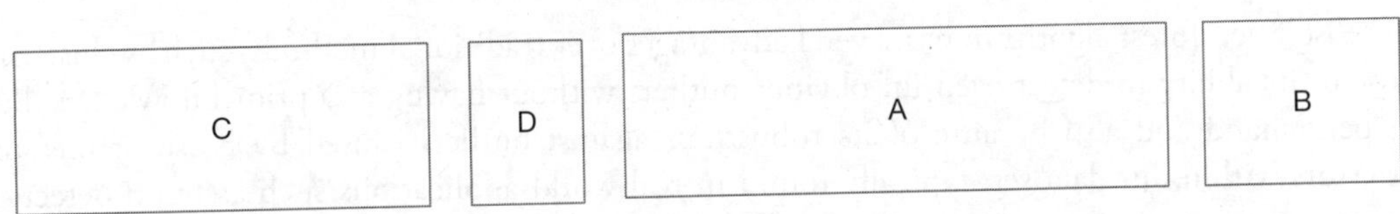

Figure 7.22 Isolation forest algorithm: Categorical variables, step 3

The algorithm works as follows:

1. It randomly selects a subset of the data and builds a binary tree by splitting the data based on a randomly chosen feature and a randomly chosen threshold value within the range of that feature.
2. It repeats this process until each data point is isolated in a leaf node or the maximum tree depth is reached.
3. It calculates the path length from the root node to the leaf node for each data point, which is the number of splits required to isolate it.
4. It averages the path length over a forest of such trees and normalizes it to get the anomaly score for each data point. The anomaly score ranges from 0 to 1, where higher values indicate more anomalous data points.

A simple step-by-step example of isolation forest is given below:

1. Suppose we have a data set with two features, x and y, and we want to detect outliers in this data set. We randomly select a subset of the data, say 10 points, and assign them to a binary tree.
2. We randomly select a feature, say x, and a threshold value, say 3.5, within the range of x. We split the data into two groups based on whether their x values are less than or greater than 3.5.
3. We repeat this process for each group, randomly selecting a feature and a threshold value. For example, for the group with $x < 3.5$, we may select y as the feature and 2 as the threshold value, and split the group into two subgroups based on whether their y values are less than or greater than 2.
4. We continue this process until each data point is isolated in a leaf node or the maximum tree depth is reached. For example, if the maximum tree depth is 3, we stop splitting after three levels of branching.
5. We calculate the path length for each data point by counting the number of splits required to isolate it. For example, if a data point is isolated at the first level, its path length is 1; if it is isolated at the second level, its path length is 2; and so on.
6. We average the path length over a forest of such trees and normalize it to get the anomaly score for each data point. For example, if we build 100 trees and average their path lengths, we may get an anomaly score of 0.8 for a data point that has an average path length of 1.2, indicating that it is very likely to be an outlier.

An **isolation tree** can be considered a data structure where each leaf represents an outlier (or anomaly). For example, suppose a point appears to be located away from its surrounding points. It is considered anomalous and forms its leaf on the isolation tree. Moreover, all standard points, surrounded by other regular points, form their branches on this decision tree structure, thus making it easier to identify anomalies within our data set without any prior labels or training data available beforehand.

The isolation forest algorithm has several advantages over traditional methods, such as clustering, because of its ability to detect even un-obvious outliers without having any prior knowledge about them beforehand and also because of its robustness against outliers caused by noise or measurement errors within our data set, typically found in real-world applications such as fraud detection. Therefore, these reasons, combined with its efficiency compared to other algorithms, make it quite popular among ML practitioners today.

7.3.2.2 *Local Outlier Factor*

The local outlier factor (LOF) algorithm uses density-based clustering to identify outliers in an unsupervised manner by looking at how close a particular data point is to its neighbors in an n-dimensional space, where n represents the number of features present in the data set. The higher value indicates that it is more likely to be an outlier than its neighbors and vice versa; if lower values are given, these points are more likely to be normal points as they have closer neighbors around them.

The LOF algorithm is a powerful tool for anomaly detection. It is a non-parametric method of identifying outliers in data that can help analysts detect points significantly different from their neighboring points. The local outlier factor measures the degree to which an individual point stands out from its immediate area.

The LOF algorithm first calculates each point's local density using K-nearest neighbors estimation. This means that for any given point, LOF will look at the K closest observations and calculate the average density value, known as **reachability distance (RD)**. Then, it will take this RD value to compute a score known as the 'local outlier factor' or LOF for each point in the data set and compare these values to all other points to determine which are outliers and which are not. It helps identify which observations could be considered anomalies when compared with their neighbors or whole data sets.

To illustrate how the LOF algorithm works, let us consider a sample data set with two features, x and y, and five observations, A, B, C, D and E. The data set is shown in Table 7.14.

Table 7.14 LOF base data

Observation	X	Y
A	1	2
B	2	3
C	3	4
D	10	11
E	11	12

The first step of the LOF algorithm is to calculate the local density of each point using K-nearest neighbors estimation. For simplicity, let us assume that $K = 2$, meaning that we will look at the two closest observations to each point. Table 7.15 shows the distances between each point and its two nearest neighbors, as well as the average distance, which is the RD of each point.

Table 7.15 LOF nearest neighbor distances

Observation	Nearest neighbours	Distances	Rd
A	B,C	1.41, 2.83	2.12
B	A,C	1.41, 1.41	1.41
C	B,D	1.41, 9.90	5.66
D	C,E	9.90, 1.41	5.66
E	D,C	1.41, 1.31	6.36

The second step of the LOF algorithm is to calculate the LOF score of each point by comparing its RD value with the RD values of its nearest neighbors. The formula for the LOF score is:

LOF(p) = (Sum of RD values of p's nearest neighbors / k) / RD(p)

Table 7.16 shows the LOF scores of each point in the data set.

Table 7.16 LOF scores of each data point

Observation	LOF score
A	0.33
B	0.50
C	0.50
D	1.76
E	1.77

The final step is to identify the outliers based on the LOF scores. A point is considered an outlier if its LOF score is significantly higher than one, meaning that it has a much lower density than its neighbors or the whole data set. In this example, points D and E have high LOF scores and are therefore outliers, while points A, B and C have low LOF scores and are therefore normal observations.

In addition to being an effective anomaly detector, LOF is relatively simple: because it uses only one parameter – *K*-nearest neighbor – there is no need for complicated tuning or hyperparameter optimization like other ML algorithms require. This makes LOF fast, efficient, and easy to deploy on real-world data sets without much effort or time tinkering with parameters you might encounter when working with more complex algorithms such as SVMs.

7.3.2.3 One-Class Support Vector Machine

One-class support vector machine (OC SVM) uses a one-class model to classify data points based on their similarity to other data points in the data set. It uses a non-linear hyperplane that acts as a decision boundary between normal and abnormal observations. The basic concept behind OCSVM is that it creates an *n*-dimensional hypersphere or boundary around the training data set and separates any new observations which fall outside this boundary as outliers. This technique creates a hypersphere using kernel functions such as polynomial, linear, sigmoid, or radial basis functions (RBF).

The RBF kernel is most commonly used due to its ability to correctly capture non-linearities within the data set compared with other kernels. We use parameters such as gamma value, cost factor C, which measures penalties for misclassifications, and degree parameter d if using a polynomial kernel to train the model. Gamma value determines how much influence each training example has on the decision boundary, while cost factor C specifies whether higher weight should be given regularization parameters instead of training accuracy when determining optimal decision surface; that is, when C = 0, there will be no penalty for misclassifications while at high values it penalizes more heavily for misclassification errors. Thus, it helps create robust models against overfitting issues like noise present in the data set. A higher gamma value indicates that each example has more influence on constructing a hyperplane. At the same time, a lower one reduces influence but increases generalizability potential by avoiding overfitting. Also, the degree parameter helps us decide how complex our model might get depending on the number of features in our data set.

Once all these parameters are determined, we can proceed with the fitting/training process, where the algorithm finds the optimized solution for the given problem through optimization techniques, such as gradient descent. After obtaining the optimal solution, we need to test our trained model by providing some new unseen data point samples from the same distribution so that the system can figure out whether they belong to the same class.

7.3.3 Dimensionality Reduction

Dimensionality reduction is a potent tool for simplifying complex problems while preserving relevant information from an original data set. As the number of variables in a data set increases, so does the complexity of understanding and interpreting those variables.

This technique can reduce the complexity and computational cost of data analysis, improve the accuracy of predictive algorithms, and simplify data visualizations. Principal component analysis (PCA) is one of the most common approaches for dimensionality reduction. PCA works by finding linear combinations between input features such that they explain the most variance between them. By doing this, we can decrease our feature space significantly while only sacrificing a small amount of total variance explained by our model.

Other approaches include linear discriminant analysis (LDA), factor analysis (FA), Sammon's mapping, and Isomap. Each approach has its strengths and weaknesses, so it pays off to research each before starting any project. For example, if you have six variables from your data set (A, B, C, D, E and F), you could use dimensionality reduction to reduce it to A-B-C-D or A-E-F instead. This would allow us to capture patterns with fewer dimensions than initially assumed without losing valuable insight into our original data set's structure and value points that might otherwise be missed.

PCA, LDA, and other methods are often categorized as dimensionality reduction techniques, but this is not their primary purpose. Rather, they are methods for finding efficient and meaningful representations of data that capture the most relevant information and discard the noise or redundancy. Dimensionality reduction is a consequence of this process, not a goal in itself.

7.3.3.1 Principal Component Analysis

Principal component analysis (PCA) is a method used to reduce a data set's dimensionality while preserving its most important features. In other words, it can compress large amounts of data into a smaller number of variables with minimal information loss. PCA finds linear combinations (or components) of the original variables that explain the maximum amount of variance in the data. In other words, it finds which combination of variables best captures the most information about all the other variables in your data set. This means that instead of having hundreds or even thousands of separate variables, PCA will reduce them to just a handful without losing much information regarding how they are related and what they represent.

The idea behind PCA is to reduce complex problems into simpler and more manageable ones. It does this by identifying underlying patterns and relationships between different variables and removing those less important for understanding them correctly. In addition, PCA also helps with feature selection; determining which features carry more weight than others can help researchers identify which ones should be focused on when creating models or performing analysis on their data sets.

Steps

Step 1: Collect and Preprocess the Data. This includes organizing the data into an appropriate format, dealing with missing values, removing outliers, and standardizing it. Preprocessing helps ensure that all variables are numerical and can be used in further analysis.

Step 2: Calculate the Correlation between Variables. After preprocessing, each variable needs to be correlated with its corresponding one or more variables before proceeding further with PCA analysis. This correlation between two or more variables can help identify relationships between them, indicating how useful they may be when performing prediction or classification tasks using machine learning algorithms later down the line.

Step 3: Compute the Covariance Matrix: Once the correlation has been calculated, the covariance matrix needs to be computed using suitable mathematical equations available in the literature. The covariance matrix tells us about the degree of variation among different features. It explains how much change a particular feature will bring if there is any change in any other feature. A high covariance value indicates vital dependability among two features, while a low value means less dependability.

Step 4: Perform Eigenvalue Decomposition. This step involves computing eigenvalues from the covariance matrix. Here each column vector corresponds to an eigenvector for feature columns that contain the same elements as those found in the input matrix but arranged differently according to their eigenvalue significance relative to others. This allows us to separate important features from less significant ones and reduce dimensions accordingly without losing much information contained within the original data set.

Step 5: Select the Principal Components. Here, we select the best principal components out of all previously computed eigenvectors according to their contribution towards the total variance present within the data set, that is, the highest explained variance ratio should always be chosen first, followed by the second highest, and so on, until the desired number of principal components has been reached.

Thus we keep the cumulative explained variance ratio above a certain threshold level, which allows us to maintain the accuracy required for our prediction task while drastically reducing the dimensions involved during the process.

Step 6: Project the Data onto the Selected Principal Components. After deciding upon the best principal components for our model, it is time to project input data into these newly created lower dimensional spaces composed only by selected principal components.

As an example, let us consider a sample data set with four variables: X1, X2, X3, and X4. The data set has 10 observations and is shown in Table 7.17

Table 7.17 PCA data points

X1	X2	X3	X4
2	3	4	5
3	4	5	6
4	5	6	7
5	6	7	8
6	7	8	9
–2	–3	–4	–5
–3	–4	–5	–6
–4	–5	–6	–7
–5	–6	–7	–8
–6	–7	–8	–9

We can apply PCA to this data set using the following steps:

1. Standardize the data. The mean and standard deviation of each variable are shown in Table 7.18.

Table 7.18 PCA data points: Standardized data

Variable	Mean	Standard deviation
X1	0	Square root (10)
X2	0	Square root (10)
X3	0	Square root (10)
X4	0	Square root (10)

The standardized data is obtained by subtracting the mean and dividing by the standard deviation for each variable. The standardized data is shown in Table 7.19.

Table 7.19 PCA data points: Standardized data with Z values

Z1	Z2	Z3	Z4
0.6325	0.6325	0.6325	0.6325
0.9488	0.9488	0.9488	0.9488
1.2650	1.2650	1.2650	1.2650
1.5813	1.5813	1.5813	1.5813
1.8976	1.8976	1.8976	1.8976
−0.6325	−0.6325	−0.6325	−0.6325
−0.9488	−0.9488	−0.9488	−0.9488
−1.2650	−1.2650	−1.2650	−1.2650
−1.5813	−1.5813	−1.5813	−1.5813
−1.8976	−1.8976	−1.8976	−1.8976

2. Calculate the covariance matrix of the standardized data. The covariance matrix is shown in Table 7.20.

Table 7.20 PCA data points: Covariance matrix

	Z1	Z2	Z3	Z4
Z1	1	1	1	1
Z2	1	1	1	1
Z3	1	1	1	1
Z4	1	1	1	1

3. Find the eigenvalues and eigenvectors of the covariance matrix. The eigenvalues and eigenvectors are shown in Table 7.21.

Table 7.21 PCA data points: Eigenvalues and eigenvectors

Eigenvalue	Eigenvector
4	(0.5, 0.5, 0.5, 0.5)
0	(−0.5, −0.5, −0.5, 0.5)
0	(−0.5, −0.5, 0.5, −0.5)
0	(−0.5, 0.5, −0.5, −0.5)

4. Sort the eigenvalues in descending order and choose the number of PCs to retain. The eigenvalues are already sorted in descending order, and we can see that only one eigenvalue is non-zero, meaning that only one PC can explain any variance in the data. Therefore, we choose to retain only one PC.
5. Form the PC matrix by multiplying the standardized data matrix by the matrix of eigenvectors corresponding to the chosen eigenvalue. Since we only retain one PC, we only need to multiply the standardized data by the first eigenvector, which is (0.5, 0.5, 0.5, 0.5). The PC matrix is shown in Table 7.22.

Table 7.22 PCA data points: Final PC matrix

PC1
2.5302
3.7952
5.0602
6.3252
7.5902
−2.5302
−3.7952
−5.0602
−6.3252
−7.5902

We can see that the PC matrix has only one column, which represents the first and only PC of the data set.

PCA has applications outside research as well; businesses may use it for marketing purposes (identifying customer segments) or even risk management (measuring portfolio volatility).

7.3.3.2 Kernel Principal Component Analysis

Using kernel principal component analysis (KPCA), data can be made less dimensional while reetaining most of its valuable characteristics. KPCA is a non-linear version of PCA used in supervised and unsupervised learning tasks. It uses kernel functions as an alternative to linear transformations to transform data into a lower-dimensional space.

Kernel functions are mathematical operations that transform inputs into non-linear feature spaces for machine learning algorithms. By using kernels, KPCA can capture non-linear relationships from high-dimensional data sets and allows the detection of patterns that would otherwise not be observed with linear methods such as PCA. This makes it ideal for classification, anomaly detection, or image recognition, where simple linear methods cannot adequately model complex relationships between variables.

Steps

1. Choose a kernel function, such as the Gaussian kernel, and compute the kernel matrix K, where K[i,j] = k(x[i], x[j]), for each pair of data points x[i] and x[j].
2. Center the kernel matrix K by subtracting the mean of each row and column, and dividing by the standard deviation of each row and column. This ensures that the transformed data has zero mean and unit variance.
3. Perform eigenvalue decomposition on the centered kernel matrix K and obtain the eigenvectors and eigenvalues. The eigenvectors are the principal components of the transformed data, and the eigenvalues indicate the amount of variance explained by each component.
4. Select the top k eigenvectors corresponding to the largest k eigenvalues, and project the data onto these eigenvectors. The resulting vectors are the reduced features of the original data.

For example, consider a data set with two features x1 and x2 (Table 7.23).

Table 7.23 KPCA: Data set with two features

X1	X2
0	0
1	0
0	1
1	1

If we apply a Gaussian kernel with parameter sigma = 0.5, we obtain the kernel matrix K (Table 7.24).

Table 7.24 KPCA: Kernel matrix

	K[0]	K[1]	K[2]	K[3]
K[0]	1	0.61	0.61	0.37
K[1]	0.61	1	0.37	0.61
K[2]	0.61	0.37	1	0.61
K[3]	0.37	0.61	0.61	1

After centering and scaling, we obtain the matrix shown in Table 7.25.

Table 7.25 KPCA: Kernel matrix after centering and scaling

	K[0]	K[1]	K[2]	K[3]
K[0]	1.41	−0.21	−0.21	−0.99
K[1]	−0.21	1.41	−0.99	−0.21
K[2]	−0.21	−0.99	1.41	−0.21
K[3]	−0.99	−0.21	−0.21	1.41

The eigenvalues and eigenvectors of this matrix are:

- Lambda_1 = 3.73, v_1 = [0.5, -0.5, -0.5, 0.5]
- Lambda_2 = 3.73, v_2 = [-0.5, -0.5, -0.5, -0.5]
- Lambda_3 = -7e-17, v_3 = [0, -1, -1, -2]
- Lambda_4 = -7e-17, v_4 = [2, -1, -1, -4]

If we select k = 2, we can project the data onto v_1 and v_2 and obtain the reduced features (Table 7.26).

Table 7.26 KPCA: Kernel matrix with k=2

Z1	Z2
−1	−1
−1	+1
+1	−1
+1	+1

These features capture the non-linear structure of the original data better than PCA.

7.3.3.3 *Linear Discriminant Analysis*

Linear discriminant analysis (LDA) is a method used to classify data by finding an optimal linear combination of features. It is a supervised learning technique that separates two or more classes using linear functions. LDA aims to find the best linear discriminant function that will best separate the classes into different categories.

LDA works by first computing the mean and variance for each class to identify which features help distinguish between them. The algorithm then finds the optimal combination of these features to best differentiate between them, which becomes the discriminant function. Finally, the algorithm evaluates how well this function separates each class from one another to determine its accuracy and effectiveness as a classifier.

LDA can be used for dimensionality reduction, feature selection, anomaly detection, and classification problems. It has been proven helpful in applications such as image recognition, face recognition/detection, and speech recognition/synthesis due to its ability to reduce noise while preserving important information within data sets. In addition, it has also been used successfully in medical diagnostics, where it can help diagnose diseases based on symptoms and other attributes provided by patients' medical records.

Steps

Step 1: Prepare the Data. This means ensuring that data has been appropriately formatted and cleaned before you begin analysis. The data set should include all relevant input variables and the desired outcome variable (such as class labels). In addition, ensure there are no missing values or outliers that could affect the accuracy of the results.

Step 2: Choose an Appropriate Distance Metric. Next, you need to decide on an appropriate distance metric to use when computing distances between points to perform LDA classification. Commonly used methods include Euclidean and Manhattan distance; however, other options are available depending on your application's needs and objectives.

Step 3: Calculate the Mean Vectors for Each Class. You must calculate the mean vectors for each class of data points in the data set; that is, find the average value across all observations within each group or "class" of data points you want to be classified by LDA classification criteria. The mean vector is then used as a reference point with which distances between other vectors can be calculated using one of the multiple available metrics mentioned above (such as Euclidean or Manhattan).

Step 4: Compute the Between-Class Covariance Matrix. For every pairwise combination of classes within the data set, we need to compute a covariance matrix describing their relative position concerning one another along each feature dimension involved in their comparison; this will allow us better capture any differences among classes with respect not just single values but distributions over multiple variables simultaneously – something essential when performing more advanced forms statistical inference like LDA. We then combine these individual covariance matrices into one larger matrix known as the 'between-class covariance matrix,' which captures how much variation exists between two given classes across all features included in our analysis set.

Step 5: Compute the Within-Class Covariance Matrix. Next, you need to calculate the within-class covariances' describing the variance within individual groups when compared against itself; that is, how much variation exists among members of the same group along the given feature axis. Here again, compute separate matrices for each pairwise combination class before combining them into more significant 'within-class covariances,' capturing variances within each distinct grouping studied during this exercise.

Step 6: Compute the Linear Discriminants. Lastly, compute the actual linear discriminants themselves using information gathered from previous steps: utilizing both between- and within-class covariances to determine the best direction axis upon which to project different groups to form optimal separation planes distinguishable individually from one another along complex multidimensional feature spaces. After determining these directions axes, apply the standard hyperplane equation to define boundaries differentiating clusters based upon values observed in past analyses. By applying linear discriminants obtained from model training sets considered during the development phase, any ML solution can achieve robust results, obtaining predictions related to unseen inputs generated outside the original model generation process.

Here is an example of a data set (Table 7.27) with two features and three classes, and how LDA can transform it into a one-dimensional space.

Table 7.27 LDA base data

Feature 1	Feature 2	Class
1.2	3.4	A
2.3	4.5	A
3.4	5.6	A
4.5	6.7	B
5.6	7.8	B
6.7	8.9	B
7.8	9.0	C
8.9	10.1	C
9.0	11.2	C

The mean vectors for each class are shown in Table 7.28.

Table 7.28 LDA mean vectors

Feature 1	Feature 2
2.3	4.5
5.6	7.8
8.6	10.1

The overall mean vector is shown in Table 7.29.

Table 7.29 LDA overall mean vectors

Feature 1	Feature 2
5.5	7.8

The between-class covariance matrix is shown in Table 7.30.

Table 7.30 LDA between-class covariance matrix

Feature 1	Feature 2
12	–0
–0	–0

The within-class covariance matrix is shown in Table 7.31.

Table 7.31 LDA within-class covariance matrix

Feature 1	Feature 2
−0	−0
−0	−0

The inverse of the within-class covariance matrix is shown in Table 7.32.

Table 7.32 LDA inverse of within-class covariance matrix

Feature 1	Feature 2
−inf	inf
inf	−inf

The product of the inverse of the within-class covariance matrix and the between-class covariance matrix is shown in Table 7.33.

Table 7.33 LDA of the product of the inverse of the within-class matrix and the between-class covariance matrix

Feature 1	Feature 2
−inf *inf	−inf *inf
−inf *inf	−inf *inf

The eigenvectors and eigenvalues of this matrix are shown in Table 7.34.

Table 7.34 LDA eigenvectors and eigenvalues

Eigen vector	Eigen value
[1,0]	inf
[0,1]	inf

We can choose the first eigenvector as the linear discriminant, and project the data onto it using matrix multiplication. This will give us a new data set with one feature and three classes (Table 7.35).

Table 7.35 LDA new data sets with one feature and three classes

Feature 1	Class
1.2	A
2.3	A
3.4	A
4.5	B
5.6	B
6.7	B
7.8	C
8.9	C
9.0	C

As you can see, the data points are now separated by their class labels along the feature axis, and can be easily classified by a simple threshold or a linear classifier.

Overall, LDA provides an efficient way of dealing with high-dimensional data sets where traditional methods have difficulty separating different classes because too many features are present in the data set. Furthermore, accurately identifying relevant features from noisy environments with high-dimensional data sets allows for more accurate classification results than other methods, such as logistic regression or decision tree algorithms, due to their ability to reduce noise while preserving important information within data set points.

7.3.3.4 *Factor Analysis*

Factor analysis (FA) is a statistical technique used to identify an underlying relationship between variables. It is commonly used in research studies to help uncover the latent structures underlying observed data. This technique has been widely applied in various fields, including psychology, economics, and education. At its core, FA involves reducing the number of variables by analyzing each variable about the other variables in a data set. This helps researchers explain how several aspects influence each other and can aid them in understanding which factors are most important when predicting an outcome or phenomenon.

When conducting FA, researchers gather data from participants on different characteristics or items related to their research topic or hypothesis. They then use this data to generate correlations representing how strongly each variable relates to others within the set. As part of this process, they will also calculate factor scores for each participant based on their responses across all items included in the study.

For factor analysis results to be reliable and accurate, researchers must ensure that the data collected is valid and reliable, meaning that it accurately reflects what was measured and does not contain errors due to measurement issues or mistakes during the collection or processing of information. In addition, there must be an adequate sample size as smaller sample sizes can lead to overfitting, where inaccurate patterns are found among unrelated pieces of information due to sparsely distributed data points. Finally, researchers must take special care when interpreting results from FA studies as results may not always reflect authentic underlying relationships but spurious associations based on noise.

There are two types of factor analysis, exploratory and confirmatory.

Exploratory Factor Analysis (EFA): This can condense a vast collection of observed variables into a smaller group of latent factors that can be utilized to explain how the observed variables are related. The goal of EFA is to identify the underlying patterns and relationships among a group of related variables and to uncover hidden or 'latent' factors that explain the variation among them.

To achieve this, EFA compares correlation coefficients between pairs of measured items to assess whether they share similar patterns across multiple observations or are merely related by chance. Rather than relying solely on measured variables as predictors, EFA uses matrix algebra techniques and linear models to analyze correlations between measured variables and extract their common underlying factors. These factors represent distinct but related concepts or processes within the studied data set. By uncovering these latent constructs, researchers can better understand how individual variables interact and how they influence overall outcomes, such as customer satisfaction surveys or academic performance metrics. In addition, by accounting for noise caused by measurement error, FA allows researchers to obtain meaningful information from complex data sets quickly and efficiently without sacrificing accuracy or rigor in their models. This makes it an invaluable tool for researchers looking for deeper insights into their data sets and those who need a quick way to reduce the number of predictor variables without sacrificing quality results. It also helps them identify clusters of closely related items that form distinct factors which can be used for further research.

The first step in conducting EFA is identifying the variables relevant to your analysis. Typically, these variables can be numeric or categorical, and they should be related to each other somehow. Next, you need to determine whether any of these correlations are statistically significant – this can be done by running statistical tests such as Pearson correlation or Spearman's rank correlation tests on your data set.

Once you have identified which correlations are statistically significant, you need to decide which type of FA model you want to use – EFA or CFA. EFA is typically used when there is little prior knowledge about what the factors might look like within your data set; CFA is usually used when there are known factors previously identified during prior research efforts into your data set's structure and content.

Next, you need to select a factor extraction method for your model – this includes selecting between PCA, MLE, iterative principal components extraction method (IPCEM), and others depending on how many factors you want extracting from your data set and how many iterations with each algorithm will be performed during the process. Once selected, run the chosen factor extraction method on the data set using appropriate statistical software packages such as SPSS or R-software packages like MLR or FactoMineR, depending on which language best suits your needs.

Finally, after running all necessary analyses using factor extraction methods, the evaluation must be conducted using calculated measures such as the Kaiser–Meyer–Olkin (KMO) measure of sampling adequacy and Bartlett's test of sphericity, cumulative proportion of variance explained, screen plot, etc. After the evaluation study, interpret the findings. This means looking into rotation methods, eigenvalues, eigenvectors, etc., and understanding them through their interpretation. After interpreting results, conclusions should draw based on findings obtained from the exploratory factor analysis study.

EFA is a valuable tool for uncovering hidden relationships between variables within a data set without relying solely on supervised approaches like regression models.

Confirmatory Factor Analysis (CFA): CFA builds upon EFA by testing whether the identified factors are consistent across multiple data sets or samples. This allows researchers to ensure their findings are reliable and not just due to chance or randomness in the tested sample. For example, suppose you want to study how age affects customer satisfaction with your product. In that case, you could use CFA to make sure your results are consistent across multiple surveys with different age groups included. CFA is a statistical technique used to help identify the underlying structure of a set of variables. It tests theoretical models and hypotheses about the relationships between observed variables such as attitudes, behaviours, and attitudes. CFA is often used in psychological research to test theories about personality, cognitive processes, emotions, and other phenomena.

CFA begins by specifying a model or hypothesis about how the various observed variables are related. This model should be based on existing knowledge or theory regarding these variables and their relationships. The researcher then uses statistical techniques to analyze data from various sources (surveys and interviews) to determine whether the proposed model fits the data. If it does, then this means that the hypothesized relations between the observed variables are supported by empirical evidence – that is why it is called 'confirmatory' analysis!

The next step involves evaluating how well this proposed model explains the observed variability in your data set (its goodness-of-fit). Typically, researchers make use of several different fit indices such as chi-squared statistic, root mean square error approximation (RMSEA), comparative fit index (CFI), Tucker–Lewis index (TLI), Akaike information criterion (AIC), etc. These fit indices provide an overall measure of how well the hypothesized model fits with the data set, which can give an idea of whether the initial hypothesis needs to be modified.

Finally, after determining if CFA supports the hypothesis, researchers must interpret their results meaningfully and apply them within real-life contexts since CFA offers little insight into causal relations between observed variables or even specific implications for different groups/contexts. In conclusion, CFA can be a powerful tool for researchers looking for evidence behind their assumptions about certain phenomena to guide further research into those topics.

7.3.4 Association Rule Mining

An unsupervised learning method called association rule mining can be used to find connections between various elements in a data set. It helps retailers create marketing strategies by uncovering the connections between products that customers often purchase together.

Market basket analysis is a frequently utilized application of association rule mining that businesses employ to gain insights into the purchasing patterns of their clients. It can provide insights into the frequent co-purchasing patterns of products. Which items exhibit complementarity or substitutability? Which products are eligible for cross-selling or upselling? What strategies may enhance the store layout or product positioning to maximize sales?

Consider a scenario where a supermarket aims to examine the transactions made by its consumers during a specific time frame. One distinct rule that may be derived from the data is:

{bread, butter} -> {jam}

This rule implies that customers who purchase bread and butter are highly likely to purchase jam. The rule consists of two components: the **antecedent**, located on the left-hand side of the arrow, and the **consequent**, located on the right-hand side. The antecedent denotes the circumstance or reason, while the consequent signifies the result or consequence.

To assess the quality of a rule, it is necessary to quantify its support and confidence. **Support** refers to the proportion of transactions in the data set that include both the antecedent and the consequent. For instance, if there are 1000 transactions in the data set, and 200 of them include bread, butter, and jam, then the support of the rule is calculated as 200 divided by 1000, resulting in a value of 0.2. Support measures the frequency of a rule in the data set.

Confidence refers to the proportion of transactions that include both the antecedent and the consequent. For instance, if 300 transactions include both bread and butter, and 200 transactions also include jam, then the rule's confidence may be calculated as 200 divided by 300, resulting in a value of 0.67. Confidence is a measure of the reliability of a rule in predicting the consequent based on the antecedent.

The store can formulate marketing tactics to enhance its revenue by adhering to these guidelines. For example, it can provide discounts or vouchers for jam to consumers who purchase bread and butter or strategically position jam beside bread and butter in the store to stimulate impulsive purchases. In addition, it can detect products that are infrequently purchased together or have poor sales and develop strategies to enhance their visibility or appeal.

Web mining is another application of association rule mining. It systematically extracts valuable information from web data, including web pages, hyperlinks, and server logs. As an illustration, an association rule could be formulated as follows: 'In the event that a user accesses page A, it is probable that they will also access page B.'

Web mining can be categorized as web content mining, web structure mining, and web usage mining. **Web content mining** involves examining and interpreting many forms of data found on the internet, such as text, photos, audio, video, and other multimedia information. **Web structure mining** is concerned with analysing the links and arrangement of websites, including their connectivity and organization. **Web use mining** examines the actions and engagement of users on the internet, including their browsing history, clickstream data, and feedback.

Web mining has diverse applications and advantages across numerous domains and objectives. It can enhance the quality and relevancy of web search engines by comprehending user queries and preferences. It can improve customization and recommendation systems by offering tailored content and services that align with user profiles and behavior. Web mining can aid in the identification of fraudulent activities and cyberattacks by detecting irregular patterns and abnormalities in web traffic and transactions.

Association rule learning can be divided into three algorithms: Apriori, ECLAT and FP Growth. We will now discuss these three algorithms in detail.

7.3.4.1 The Apriori Algorithm

The Apriori algorithm is an ML algorithm that can uncover associations between items in large data sets. It was developed by Rakesh Agrawal and Ramakrishnan Srikant in 1994. The core of the algorithm lies in finding frequent itemsets or items that frequently occur together. This technique is based on the premise that if an itemset occurs frequently in a data set, then any subset of that itemset also occurs frequently. The Apriori algorithm is most commonly used for market basket analysis and recommendation systems.

The algorithm first scans through data to find all single-itemsets (itemsets with one element). These individual itemsets are deemed 'frequent' when they meet a minimum user-defined frequency or support threshold, meaning they must appear in at least some predetermined percentage of all transactions for a given data set. This initial stage creates an inventory list from which we can build more powerful and complex itemset combinations, which will also pass our frequency test.

Once frequent single-itemsets have been identified, the next step is to search for pairs (itemsets with two elements) and triples (itemsets with three elements), where each new combination combines one element from our previously identified single-itemset list along with another new element from our entire inventory list generated during the first step.

Steps

1. Perform a database scan and tally the frequency of each item. Gather the items with support value equal to or higher than the minimal support threshold and place them in a set named L1, representing the common 1-itemsets.
2. Create potential 2-itemsets by combining L1 with itself. This involves combining two 1-itemsets with a common prefix of length $k - 1$, where k is the current size of the itemsets. For instance, the combination of {apple} and {banana} yields {apple, banana}, whereas {apple} and {orange} cannot be combined due to the absence of a shared prefix.
3. Perform another database scan and tally the frequency of each candidate's 2-itemset. Eliminate the candidates with support lower than the minimal support level and obtain the set L2, consisting of frequent 2-itemsets.
4. Iterate steps 2 and 3 until no more candidates can be generated or more frequent itemsets can be discovered. The set that consists of all L*k* sets is equivalent to that of all frequent itemsets.

We utilize the frequent itemsets to discover association rules and enforce a minimal confidence threshold. To obtain the rules, we iterate through each frequent itemset X and construct all non-empty subsets of X. For each subset Y, we create the rule Y -> (X – Y) if the rule's confidence meets or exceeds the minimum confidence threshold.

Consider a scenario where a fruit shop offers various fruits, such as apples, bananas, oranges, grapes, and pineapples. In this context, let us examine the transactions that have taken place:

T1: {apple, banana, orange}
T2: {banana, grape}
T3: {apple, banana, grape}
T4: {apple, grape}
T5: {banana, pineapple}

For the Apriori method, we will use a minimum support level of 0.4, which corresponds to 40% of transactions, and a minimum confidence threshold of 0.7, which corresponds to 70% of rules.

First, we thoroughly examine the database and tally the frequency of each item. The occurrence of apple is found in 3 transactions, banana in 4 transactions, orange in 1 transaction, grape in 3 transactions, and pineapple in 1 transaction. The only fruits with support larger than or equal to 0.4 are apples, bananas, and grapes. Therefore, L1 = {{apple}, {banana}, {grape}}.

In step 2, we create potential 2-itemsets by combining L1 with itself. We obtain a collection of sets containing pairs of fruits: {{apple, banana}, {apple, grape}, {banana, grape}}.

In step 3, we perform a second database search to tally the frequency of each candidate's 2-itemset. The item {apple, banana} appears in 2 transactions, {apple, grape} appears in 3 transactions, and {banana, grape} appears in 2 transactions. Among the options {apple, grape}, only apple and grape have a support value larger than or equal to 0.4. Therefore, the set L2 consists of {{apple, grape}}.

In step 4, generating additional candidates or identifying additional frequent itemsets is no longer possible; hence, we terminate the procedure. The collection of all frequent itemsets can be represented as L = L1 ∪ L2, where L1 and L2 are sets containing the following items: {apple}, {banana}, {grape}, and {apple, grape}.

We employ the L method to discover association rules and enforce a minimal confidence threshold. We iterate through each frequent itemset X in L to obtain the desired outcome. We then build all feasible non-empty subsets of X. For each subset Y, we create the rule Y -> (X - Y) if the rule's confidence equals or exceeds 0.7. The rules that we obtain are as follows:

{apple} -> {grape} with confidence 3/3 = 1
{grape} -> {apple} with confidence 3/3 = 1.

These principles indicate that customers who purchase apples also purchase grapes with a certainty of 100%, and vice versa.

Calculating this confidence level percentage value requires dividing count(X Y)/ count(X), where X represents target itemset values found directly preceding Y within the applicable subset counts gathered throughout the previous steps. This essentially proves how often related itemsets appear together throughout the entire input data set versus just appearing randomly independent by chance alone – thus removing false positives successfully from the final output results and ultimately resulting in better accuracy.

The Apriori algorithm does not require prior knowledge about data structures, it can process enormous data sets quickly due to its iterative nature, and it produces clear rules that humans can easily understand. On the downside, this method cannot handle numeric data well and tends to generate large numbers of false positives, leading to inaccurate results if they are not carefully filtered out before they reach the results stage.

7.3.4.2 The ECLAT Algorithm

ECLAT stands for equivalence class transformation. This algorithm uses a 'depth-first' search to find frequent itemsets in a transaction database. It executes faster than the Apriori algorithm. Unlike the Apriori algorithm, which applies to a horizontal data set, the ECLAT algorithm applies only to data sets in the vertical format.

The ECLAT algorithm is a method for finding frequent itemsets in a transactional database. A frequent itemset is a set of items that occurs in more than a specified minimum number of transactions. The ECLAT algorithm uses a vertical data format, where each item is associated with a tidset, which is the set of transaction IDs that contain the item. For example, the tidset (Transaction ID set) of apple is {T1, T3, T4}, the tidset of banana is {T1, T2, T3, T5}, and so on.

Steps

1. It starts with the set of all single items and their tidsets.
2. It sorts the items in descending order of their tidset size.
3. It generates candidate itemsets of size k by joining pairs of item sets of size $k - 1$ that share the first $k - 2$ items and have frequent tidsets.
4. It computes the tidset of each candidate itemset by intersecting the tidsets of its parent itemsets.

5. It prunes any candidate itemset whose tidset size is less than the minimum support threshold.
6. It repeats steps 3 to 5 until no more candidates can be generated or all candidates are pruned.

Let us apply this algorithm to the example of associating fruits in a fruit shop with the following transactions and a minimum support of 2.

T1: {apple, banana, orange}
T2: {banana, grape}
T3: {apple, banana, grape}
T4: {apple, grape}
T5: {banana, pineapple}

The algorithm starts with the following single items and their tidsets:

apple: {T1, T3, T4}
banana: {T1, T2, T3, T5}
grape: {T2, T3, T4}
orange: {T1}
pineapple: {T5}

The algorithm sorts the items by their tidset size:

banana: {T1, T2, T3, T5}
apple: {T1, T3, T4}
grape: {T2, T3, T4}
orange: {T1}
pineapple: {T5}

The algorithm generates candidate item sets of size 2 by joining pairs of items that share the first item and have frequent tidsets:

banana apple: {T1, T3}
banana grape: {T2, T3}
apple grape: {T3, T4}

The algorithm computes the tidset of each candidate itemset by intersecting the tidsets of its parent items:

banana apple: {T1} ∩ {T1, T3} = {T1}
banana grape: {T1, T2, T3, T5} ∩ {T2, T3, T4} = {T2, T3}
apple grape: {T1, T3, T4} ∩ {T2, T3, T4} = {T3, T4}

The algorithm prunes any candidate itemset whose tidset size is less than 2:

banana apple: pruned
banana grape: not pruned
apple grape: not pruned

The algorithm repeats the process for itemsets of size 3:

banana grape apple: pruned

grape apple banana: pruned

Since no more candidates can be generated or all candidates are pruned, the algorithm stops and returns the following frequent item sets:

banana
apple
grape
banana grape
apple grape

The most important conclusion is that ECLAT is compatible with the vertical data format. As most data sets are in the horizontal format, we must first convert them to the vertical format before applying this algorithm. Apriori typically performs best when working with a more extensive data set. Thus, small and medium data sets are better suited for the ECLAT method. In the Apriori algorithm, we need to scan the database repeatedly to find frequent itemsets; this limitation is reduced using a vertical ECLAT data set. The database needs to be scanned only once in ECLAT. Due to its use of depth-first search, ECLAT utilizes less memory than Apriori. Therefore, it is faster than Apriori.

7.3.4.3 The FP Growth Algorithm

This algorithm is a data mining technique for discovering frequent itemsets in transactional data sets. It is an extension of the Apriori algorithm. The FP Growth algorithm collects the list of items present in each transaction and then finds patterns of items that frequently appear together across many transactions. This algorithm is highly efficient and can process a large amount of data quickly, even compared to other algorithms like Apriori.

It uses a tree structure called FP tree (frequent pattern tree) to store transactions more efficiently than traditional methods such as hash tables or bitmaps. The tree structure allows it to identify frequent itemsets efficiently and quickly as it stores all the information about their frequency in one place rather than looking at individual transactions one by one.

Steps

1. Counting step – where each item's support count (number of times it appears across all transactions) is calculated.
2. Constructing step – building an FP tree based on the results from step 1.
3. Once the FP tree has been constructed using these steps, the algorithm scans through it for frequent patterns using a pruning strategy where rare items are removed from consideration until only those with sufficient support remain.
4. Finally, patterns found at each level can be combined into larger patterns, making them easier for human understanding or further analysis within a database system such as SQL or NoSQL.

Here are the steps of the algorithm with an example of associating fruits in a fruit shop:

1. Scan the transaction database and count the frequency of each item. Sort the items in descending order of frequency and discard any infrequent items. For example, if the minimum support is 3, then we can discard orange and pineapple from the transactions, and obtain the following sorted list of frequent items: {banana, apple, grape}.

2. Construct the FP tree by inserting each transaction as a path in the tree, following the order of the sorted frequent items. If a path already exists, increment the count of the corresponding node. For example, inserting T1 will create a path of {banana:1 -> apple:1 -> grape:1}. Inserting T2 will create a new branch of {banana:2 -> grape:2}. Inserting T3 will share the prefix {banana:3} with T1 and T2, and then create a new node {apple:2}. Inserting T4 will share the prefix {apple:3} with T1, and then create a new node {grape:3}. Inserting T5 will create a new branch of {banana:4 -> pineapple:1}.

   The final FP tree looks like this:

```
banana:4
|\
| pineapple:1
|/
apple:3
|\
grape:3
|
grape:2
```

3. Mine the FP tree by recursively finding conditional patterns for each item, starting from the bottom of the sorted frequent items list. A conditional pattern is a subpath that leads to an item in the tree, along with its frequency. For example, the conditional patterns for grape are:
   - {apple, banana}: 1
   - {banana}: 2
   - {apple}: 1
4. Construct conditional FP trees for each item by using its conditional patterns as transactions, and applying steps 1 and 2 again. For example, the conditional FP tree for grape is:

```
banana:3
|
apple:2
```

5. Extract frequent itemsets from each conditional FP tree by combining its root item with all possible subsets of its branches. For example, the frequent itemsets from the conditional FP tree for grape are:
   - {grape}: 4 (support = 4/5 = 0.8)
   - {grape, banana}: 3 (support = 3/5 = 0.6)
   - {grape, apple}: 2 (support = 2/5 = 0.4)
   - {grape, apple, banana}: 1 (support = 1/5 = 0.2)
6. Repeat steps 3 to 5 for each item in the sorted frequent items list until all frequent itemsets are found.

The FP Growth algorithm is a powerful tool that can analyse large data sets and quickly uncover significant patterns. Its scalability and versatility make it an ideal choice for various applications, such as web mining, market basket analysis, recommendation engines, and text mining tasks like sentiment analysis and author identification. With its ability to be deployed on large volumes of data such as

Hadoop clusters, this algorithm helps organizations uncover essential insights from their data in a much shorter time than traditional databases. It is used in the banking, retail, healthcare sectors, and other industries requiring quick insight from large data sets.

7.4 Markov Models

Markov models are mathematical tools used to make predictions based on data from the past. These models are used in various fields, including economics, engineering, and medicine.

The central concept behind Markov models is that the future depends on the present predictably. Therefore, they use 'state transitions' – changes from one state to another over time. So, for example, if you were trying to predict how a patient's health would change over time, you would look at their current condition and what factors had led them there (such as diet or lifestyle choices). You can then use previous data and projections about the future to come up with estimates of what might happen next.

A Markov model is essentially an equation that considers these past states and their possible future outcomes. It calculates the probability of each outcome by looking at how often similar events happened in the past, given certain conditions or parameters. This probability can then predict what will happen next, given that certain conditions and variables remain unchanged (or close enough).

In addition to making predictions, Markov models can be used for decision-making processes such as financial investment opportunities or medical treatments for patients with specific diseases or ailments. The model helps determine which path is more likely to lead toward success according to its calculations of probabilities associated with various paths taken through different states over time.

7.5 Hidden Markov Model

Hidden Markove model (HMM) is a powerful and widely used statistical model that can be applied to many tasks, such as speech recognition, machine translation, and bioinformatics. HMM models the probability of an event happening given previous events in a sequence. It assigns probabilities to hidden states that are not directly observed.

At its core, HMM is a probabilistic graphical model composed of two components: states and transitions. States are the underlying unknown events that cannot be observed directly. Transitions represent the chance of changing from one state to another in a series. Based on previous events, these states' transitions decide what will happen next.

HMM can be used for many applications, such as recognizing handwritten text or speech recognition, because it allows us to consider multiple possible explanations for an observation at any point in time and consider all previous observations when making predictions about future ones. This makes HMMs powerful when dealing with data sequences with variable lengths or incomplete information that other models may struggle with due to their more rigid structure and assumptions about data distributions within them.

HMMs have also been successfully used for machine translation because they can quickly learn complex language patterns from small data sets. This is due to their ability to generalize well across different contexts and languages by considering context-dependent information when making predictions about word orderings within sentences or phrases across multiple languages without having seen them before during the training process. In addition, they are often used in bioinformatics research as tools for analyzing DNA sequences looking at genes' transcriptional regulation networks.

7.5.1 Learning the HMM Parameters

Learning the HMM parameters is essential when dealing with sequential data. This is because HMMs can help us uncover hidden patterns between different elements in a sequence that may remain undiscovered.

To begin, one must first determine the number of states and transitions needed for the model. For example, if we are trying to model gene expression, we would need multiple states representing different levels of gene expression, such as 'active,' 'inactive,' and 'transitioning.' Each state could also have numerous transitions, which determine how it might change from one state to another over time. Once these components have been identified, one must estimate the probability distributions for each state or transition between states by collecting data on what sequences are observed under different conditions and building a model based on these observations. This often involves guessing what these probabilities might look like based on prior experience or intuition before refining them through various methods such as the EM algorithm. The EM algorithm works by adjusting estimated values according to expected values until they converge on optimal solutions which best fit our data set. Once all parameters have been adequately estimated using an appropriate method like the EM algorithm, this information can then be used for making predictions that require accurate probability distributions being learned accurately beforehand.

For instance, this technique has been used to create NLP applications where accurately predicting word usage patterns lead to more effective communication with computers and speech recognition systems where accurate predictions help computers recognize human speech more accurately. In conclusion, learning HMM parameters is an essential part of working with sequential data since it helps us uncover hidden relationships between elements in a sequence which can then be used for prediction tasks that require accurate probability distributions being learned beforehand.

7.5.2 Decoding States from Observations

Decoding the states of an ML algorithm can provide valuable insights into its decision-making process and help researchers optimize its performance to maximize accuracy. This is accomplished by observing how different inputs influence the model's output and then decoding each state to identify areas that could benefit from improvement or changes. To do this, researchers use both visualization tools such as heat maps, which depict each state in terms of its influence on the predictive outcome, as well as probabilistic approaches such as Bayesian networks or Markov models that allow us to trace through all possible paths leading up to any given result. By decoding states from observations, we can better understand why certain decisions were made over others based on their impact on results. For example, suppose that a particular input has significantly affected the output. In this case, we know that it is essential for making accurate predictions and should be given more attention during optimization efforts.

In addition, identifying areas where improvements can be made before making changes or implementing new features allows us to test out what works best without running into unexpected consequences. Visualizations are particularly useful for helping us gain insight into decision-making processes since they allow us to see patterns or clusters emerge from data that would otherwise not be obvious just by looking at it directly. On top of this, probabilistic approaches like Bayesian networks and Markov models serve an essential role in gaining an even deeper understanding since they consider multiple outcomes simultaneously instead of just one result at a time.

7.6 Matrix Factorization and Matrix Completion Models

Matrix factorization and matrix completion models can be used in supervised and unsupervised ML scenarios. In unsupervised learning, matrix factorization is used to discover underlying patterns or clusters in a data set without needing labeled data. For example, it can identify topics within a collection of documents or similar group items in a recommendation system. In supervised learning, matrix completion can fill in missing values in a data set, such as predicting movie ratings based on user ratings. In this case, the model is trained using existing data with known outputs and is then used to predict missing values in new data. In conclusion, it depends on whether the application and use case of matrix factorization and matrix completion models are used in a supervised or unsupervised learning context.

Matrix factorization and matrix completion are two techniques used in data analysis and ML that can be used to solve complex problems. Matrix factorization is used to decompose a matrix into its constituent parts. In contrast, matrix completion is used to infer missing values in matrices.

Matrix factorization breaks down the original matrix into simpler components such as principal components, latent features, or singular values. By applying this method, one can reduce the dimensionality of the original matrix (also known as feature selection), making it easier to analyze by reducing noise and increasing interpretability. For example, suppose you have an input data set with 10 different variables. You could use factor analysis to reduce this data set to 5 variables that are more relevant to your model-building process. This can also help improve predictive performance because it reduces model complexity.

Matrix completion uses statistical methods such as low-rank approximation or nuclear norm minimization. **Low-rank approximation** reconstructs the complete data from the available observations by minimizing the rank of the reconstructed solution using convex optimization techniques such as gradient descent or regularized least squares. The idea behind low-rank approximation is to approximate the data with fewer independent components (or variables). This reduces the amount of memory and computational power required for computations, simplifying the analysis and making it faster. In low-rank approximation, a subset of features from the data set is chosen that contains most of the information about it. This subset can be determined using algorithms such as PCA or singular value decomposition (SVD). These methods find an orthogonal basis that captures most of the variance in the data set and then use this basis to reduce its dimensionality by representing each as linear combinations of other features in this orthogonal basis. These reduced representations are much easier to store and process than their whole counterparts, allowing for faster computation times without sacrificing too much accuracy or meaningful information about original input features.

Furthermore, low-rank approximation makes algorithm development more manageable because it preserves basic patterns in data sets while reducing noise and irrelevant details, which can overwhelm a model's performance. For example, consider image detection algorithms like face recognition or object detection using CNN. Low-rank approximations are used prominently both during training as well as inference time due to their computation efficiency benefits over traditional methods like SVM or logistic regression, which require more time for training/inference but provide less accurate results compared to CNNs.

Nuclear norm minimization attempts to recover the underlying low-rank structure of a corrupted data set by minimizing its nuclear norm (sum of singular values). The advantage of this technique over traditional imputation methods (such as mean imputation) is that it can select only those entries that best explain observed patterns in the data while ignoring outliers or irrelevant variables. It utilizes two primary components: nuclear norm regularization and convex optimization. The nuclear norm regularization helps reduce overfitting, while the convex optimization helps find the optimal solution for a given problem. In essence, nuclear norm minimization is an iterative process of looking at a data point and trying to fit it into a predictive model or function. To achieve this, we use mathematical tools such as convex optimization and regularization techniques such as the L1 or L2 norms which help us minimize overfitting. This way, we can build accurate models with fewer parameters than traditional methods like linear regression or *K*-means clustering. The essential advantage of this approach lies in its ability to accurately predict results, even with minimal assumptions about the data being used for training models.

In addition, since it minimizes errors rather than maximizes accuracy, it is less prone to overfitting than other methods like support vector machines (SVMs). This makes it suitable for dealing with sparse data sets with little information on how input variables are related to output variables.

Both matrix factorization and matrix completion have been widely studied in recent years due their ability help with tasks like discovering hidden features in data sets, recovering corrupted images and videos, predicting user preferences, etc.

7.7 Generative Models

Generative models can be used for both supervised and unsupervised learning tasks. Supervised generative models are trained to utilize labeled data where the output variable is known, such as in classification or regression problems. Examples of supervised generative models include Gaussian naive Bayes and conditional generative adversarial networks (CGAN). On the other hand, unsupervised generative models are trained on unlabeled data, where the output variable is unknown. These generative models are typically used for clustering and dimensionality reduction tasks. Examples of unsupervised generative models include autoencoder, variational autoencoder (VAE), and generative adversarial network (GAN). Whether a model is supervised or unsupervised depends solely on the type of data provided as input to the model and the task at hand.

Generative models generate new data by discovering the underlying structure of existing data. These models are capable of creating realistic-looking data from scratch. They can be used for various tasks, such as generating synthetic images, voice synthesis, natural language processing, text generation, and recommendation systems.

Mixture models are generative models which use statistical techniques to discover clusters in the training set. Given the observed data, they allow you to estimate the probability distribution over a set of variables. Mixture models can make predictions or segmentation decisions on unseen data points using mixture components learned from the training data set. For example, they could be used in image classification tasks where we want to identify different objects or segmentation tasks where we want to differentiate between different areas within an image.

7.8 Latent Factor Models

Latent factor models are based on the idea that there is a secret relationship between different variables or features, known as latent factors. This relationship is usually not visible from the raw data but can be inferred from it. For example, suppose we have a data set containing information about people's movie preferences. We might assume an underlying latent factor of 'movie genre interest' driving these preferences, but this cannot be easily seen in the raw data alone. Latent factor models allow us to uncover this secret relationship by analyzing the correlations between different variables or features in the data set and then inferring which factors could explain them.

The main advantage of latent factor models over traditional methods such as linear regression is that they can account for non-linear relationships between variables and also handle large amounts of data more efficiently than traditional methods do because they only use a small number of 'latent' (hidden) factors instead of having to consider every single variable separately. Latent factor models have numerous applications in marketing, finance, image recognition, and natural language processing (NLP).

Since the steps of this mmodel involve complex calculations, most modern implementations rely heavily on vector processing technology such as graphics processing units (GPUs). In addition to speeding up computations significantly compared to traditional CPUs, GPUs can handle larger data sets than what could typically fit into memory on CPUs, which helps facilitate more powerful analyses. This is associate with fewer overhead costs for transferring large amounts of data around during computation cycles resulting in faster convergence times and improved accuracy rates overall.

7.9 Inference Models

Inference in graphical models and belief propagation in ML are closely related concepts as they both refer to gathering information from a given data set. Graphical models, also known as Bayesian networks, are a popular tool for representing relationships between variables. This model provides an efficient way to represent probability distributions over multiple variables by using a graph-like structure that represents the conditional dependencies among them. Inference from these models involves computing the probabilities or values associated with different configurations of the variables. The most common approach is known as belief propagation or message passing.

Belief propagation is based on an iterative algorithm that uses messages passed between nodes in the graph to arrive at a final answer for any given query about the system represented by the graph. It starts with initializing each node with its prior beliefs about its value and then passing messages to other nodes based on their neighbors' and previous beliefs until all nodes have reached a consensus on their respective values. Propagating these messages throughout all nodes makes it possible to compute answers that accurately reflect the graphical model's underlying probability distribution, even when considerable uncertainty is involved due to limited data availability or a high degree of randomness present in specific systems (such as weather forecasting).

The algorithm first creates a model, or belief network, consisting of nodes and edges that represent different variables and their possible relationships between them. Each node contains information about how potential specific values are for it, depending on its connections with other nodes in the network. The belief network can be represented in three parts:

- Evidence nodes (which contain observed data)
- Decision nodes (which contain decisions based on evidence)
- Utility nodes (which contain information about how desirable specific outcomes are)

Once these three components are defined, belief propagation begins by passing messages between the nodes to calculate probabilities or expected utility values associated with each node's state or decision. During each processing cycle, messages will be passed from one node to another based on their connections within the network. This process will continue until all messages have been processed and there is only one possible explanation that has a higher probability than all others (or until there can be no more improvement). The algorithm then stops processing at this point as it has reached its conclusion.

In ML applications, belief propagation can be used for making predictions about future events or states based on observed data points without explicitly forming probabilistic assumptions about them (that is, without access to complete domain knowledge). In addition, while traditional 'brute force' approaches may be computationally expensive when confronted with large data sets containing high-dimensional inputs and outputs, belief propagation algorithms scale more efficiently even when faced with such challenges – allowing practitioners to apply inference techniques much faster than before without sacrificing accuracy.

7.10 Non-negative Matrix Factorization

Non-negative matrix factorization (NMF) is a type of factorization technique that involves breaking down a matrix into two component matrices with non-negative elements. The main difference between NMF and other factorization methods, such as SVD, is the restriction on the elements of the factorized components to be non-negative. This restriction has advantages such as improved interpretability since negative values are less meaningful than positive ones in many real-world applications.

The idea behind NMF is that any given complex data set can be composed of simpler parts, or components, underlying its structure, which can then be identified using this technique. To do this, NMF starts by representing the original data set A in terms of two matrices, W and H, whose product approximates A when multiplied: $A \approx WH$ where W represents 'weights' or 'loadings' and H represents 'patterns' or 'features.' Furthermore, both W and H have only non-negative entries, which makes them more interpretable than their counterparts from SVD since negative entries are not meaningful in many cases.

NMF optimizes for both W and H simultaneously by minimizing the distance between A and WH, often measured through squared Frobenius norm ||A–WH||2≤2^2, by iteratively updating each matrix until they converge to a point where they no longer improve results according to some metric such as mean squared error (MSE). Once convergence occurs, we have our optimal solution with optimal weights $W^*$and patterns H^*that approximate our original data set $A \approx W^*H^*$. These components can then be used to uncover hidden patterns in data that may not have been previously visible or understood before applying NMF on it.

7.11 Advantages of Unsupervised Learning

Unsupervised ML is a form of AI that can discover patterns in data without any external guidance or labels. This type of AI allows computers to learn independently and uncover hidden relationships in data sets. It works by grouping similar data into clusters and using algorithms to identify patterns within those clusters. By doing this, computers can find correlations between different pieces of data and make predictions about future trends without any help from humans. One advantage of unsupervised ML is its ability to save time and money by automating tasks that would otherwise require considerable human effort. For example, suppose a company has a large data set containing customer information such as age, gender, location, etc. An unsupervised ML algorithm could analyze this data set and uncover hidden trends or correlations between different factors, which might need to be more evident to humans looking at the data set manually. This could enable the company to make better decisions based on these findings, leading to increased profits or improved customer service levels.

Furthermore, it helps reduce computational costs by allowing machines to do work for you that would otherwise be too expensive or time-consuming for a human analyst. Unsupervised ML can also be used for anomaly detection – identifying unusual patterns in data sets that may indicate fraudulent activity or other abnormalities – as well as image recognition applications like facial recognition software, which can identify individuals from images without being told what individual it is looking for first (that is, without having labels). It has also been used for clustering applications where no clear labels are present in the data set, such as market segmentation, where customers are grouped into categories based on their similarities rather than pre-defined characteristics given by humans beforehand (with labels).

7.12 Disadvantages of Unsupervised Learning

Overfitting is prevalent in ML, mainly when the model is excessively intricate or the data is insufficient or distorted. Overfitting arises when the model exhibits high accuracy in fitting the training data; however, it struggles to apply this knowledge to novel or unseen data. This implies that the model can accurately represent the training data's extraneous information or insignificant aspects rather than the fundamental patterns or frameworks. Let us consider a scenario where we aim to group a set of animal photographs using an algorithm that does not require labeled data. If the algorithm exhibits excessive sensitivity towards the colour or shape of the pixels, it may erroneously group the photos according to these characteristics instead of the actual animal groups. Applying the model to new images with varying colours or forms would yield subpar performance.

An additional drawback of unsupervised ML is the substantial computing expense associated with executing and fine-tuning these algorithms. In contrast to supervised learning, which relies on a well-defined objective function or accuracy metric to drive the learning process, unsupervised learning typically involves exploring many models and parameters without a clearly defined criterion. This process can be highly time-consuming and resource-intensive, particularly when handling extensive and intricate data sets. To perform dimensionality reduction on a high-dimensional data set using unsupervised algorithms like PCA or t-distributed stochastic neighbors embedding (t-SNE), it may be necessary to experiment with different values for the number of components or perplexity. This is done to find the best representation that retains the most information or captures the most significant variation in the data.

Moreover, unsupervised ML frequently yields outcomes challenging for humans to analyse or comprehend. Unsupervised algorithms lack specified labels or categories to give to the data. Instead, they generate their representations or clusters using similarity or distance metrics. These representations or clusters may not align with any relevant or intuitive notions for humans or yield excessive complex hypotheses to confirm or disprove.

SUMMARY

- Unsupervised learning is a type of machine learning where the computer program tries to find patterns and relationships in data without being given specific examples or labels to learn from.
- Clustering algorithms are used to identify patterns in data and group similar data points together. Hierarchical clustering algorithms are used to group similar objects into a hierarchy of clusters. Fuzzy C-Means clustering uses fuzzy logic instead of hard clustering boundaries, making it useful for data sets with overlapping features and classes that cannot be easily separated by traditional methods. DBSCAN (Density-Based Spatial Clustering of Applications with Noise) uses density as the criteria for identifying clusters in spatial databases such as those containing geographic information systems (GIS).
- Gaussian mixture models (GMMs) are probabilistic models that hypothesize each point belongs to one of k Gaussians and assigns weights based on probability values assigning points to multiple clusters simultaneously. MeanShift Clustering algorithm iteratively shifts the centroids of the data points toward the higher-density areas. It does not require labeled data or involve any predetermined targets or outputs.
- Gaussian mixture density estimation finds patterns in complex data sets and makes predictions without prior knowledge of class labels. Markov random fields (MRFs) model complex relationships between different variables.
- Anomaly detection is when the program looks for data points different from the rest. The isolation forest algorithm uses the decision tree to identify anomalies in the data.
- Local outlier factor (LOF) uses density-based clustering to identify outliers in an unsupervised manner by looking at how close a particular data point is to its neighbors in an *n*-dimensional space, where *n* represents the number of features present in the data set.
- One-class support vector machine (OC SVM) tries to identify anomalies by fitting a single model that best separates everyday examples from anomalous ones using the hyperplane separation technique and then classifying any new example into one class or another based on this model constructed during training phase using SVM technique.
- Dimensionality reduction is a potent tool for simplifying complex problems while preserving relevant information from an original data set.
- PCA, or principal component analysis, is a method used to reduce a data set's dimensionality while preserving its most important features. KPCA is a non-linear version of PCA that uses kernel

functions as an alternative to linear transformations to transform data into a lower-dimensional space.

- Linear discriminant analysis (LDA) is a method used to classify data by finding an optimal linear combination of features.
- Factor analysis (FA) is a statistical technique to identify an underlying relationship between variables. The two primary methods of factor analysis are exploratory and confirmatory.
- Association rule mining can be used to find connections between various elements in a data set. The FP Growth algorithm is an efficient method for discovering frequent item sets in a transactional database. The Apriori algorithm can uncover associations between items in large data sets. The ECLAT (equivalence class transformation) algorithm uses depth-first search to find frequent itemsets in a transaction database.
- In supervised learning, the Markov model is trained using labeled data, meaning the data has a target or output variable. The model is then used to make predictions about new, unlabled data. The Markov model is trained using only input data without labeled outputs in unsupervised learning. The hidden Markov model (HMM) is trained using an unlabeled data set in unsupervised learning.
- Unsupervised generative models are trained on unlabeled data, where the output variable is unknown. These generative models are typically used for clustering and dimensionality reduction tasks.
- Latent factor models are generative models that use latent variables (variables not directly observed) to capture patterns in data sets and derive insights from them.
- Inference in graphical models and belief propagation in ML are closely related concepts as they both refer to gathering information from a given data set.
- Belief propagation is an ML algorithm specializing in finding the most probable explanations for a given set of evidence. The belief network can be represented in three parts: evidence nodes (which contain observed data), decision nodes (which contain decisions based on evidence), and utility nodes (which contain information about how desirable specific outcomes are).

EXERCISES

Part A (Objective Questions)

1. In the *K*-means clustering algorithm, what is the purpose of data collection?
   a) To initialize centroids
   b) To define the number of clusters
   c) To gather information about customers
   d) To interpret the clustering results
2. What does the *K* represent in *K*-means clustering?
   a) The number of data points
   b) The number of clusters to form
   c) The distance between data points
   d) The centroid value
3. How are the centroids initialized in *K*-means clustering?
   a) Randomly
   b) Based on the mean of the data points
   c) According to the Euclidean distance
   d) By clustering similar data points

4. What is the purpose of assigning data points to clusters in *K*-means clustering?
   a) To calculate the distance between data points
   b) To determine the number of iterations
   c) To find the optimal number of clusters
   d) To form distinct clusters based on proximity to centroids

5. How are the centroids updated in *K*-means clustering?
   a) By reassigning data points to new clusters
   b) By calculating the mean of data points in each cluster
   c) By iteratively calculating the distance between centroids
   d) By increasing the number of clusters

6. What is the termination condition for *K*-means clustering?
   a) The maximum number of iterations is reached
   b) The centroids remain unchanged
   c) All data points are assigned to a cluster
   d) The number of clusters reaches the predefined limit

7. How can the results of *K*-means clustering be interpreted?
   a) By analyzing the characteristics of the data points
   b) By calculating the Euclidean distance between clusters
   c) By increasing the number of iterations
   d) By randomizing the assignment of data points

8. What is the main objective of *K*-means clustering?
   a) To find the optimal number of clusters
   b) To minimize the distance between centroids
   c) To group similar data points together
   d) To maximize the number of iterations

9. What is the role of centroids in the *K*-means clustering algorithm?
   a) To label the data points
   b) To define the number of clusters
   c) To calculate the distance between data points
   d) To represent the center of each cluster

10. Which type of machine learning does *K*-means clustering belong to?
    a) Supervised learning
    b) Unsupervised learning
    c) Reinforcement learning
    d) Semi-supervised learning

11. How does *K*-means clustering determine the cluster for each data point?
    a) By assigning data points to the nearest centroid
    b) By calculating the Euclidean distance between data points
    c) By analyzing the patterns in the data
    d) By using labels provided for the data points

12. What is the advantage of *K*-means clustering over supervised learning algorithms?
    a) It can handle large data sets with many variables
    b) It provides accurate predictions for regression problems
    c) It requires labeled data points for training

d) It can handle complex relationships between features

13. After how many iterations does the *K*-means clustering algorithm terminate?
a) When all data points are assigned to a cluster
b) When the centroids stop changing
c) When the maximum number of clusters is reached
d) When the distance between centroids is minimized

14. What can be done with the results of *K*-means clustering?
a) Classification of data points
b) Calculation of regression coefficients
c) Exploration and analysis of patterns in data
d) Generation of decision trees

15. What other machine learning algorithms can be used in combination with *K*-means clustering?
a) Decision trees
b) Neural networks
c) Support vector machines
d) All of the above

16. What is the main characteristic of hierarchical clustering?
a) It requires prior knowledge about the data set
b) It uses a hierarchical tree structure to group data points
c) It assumes a linear relationship between data points
d) It focuses on optimizing the distance between centroids

17. What advantage does hierarchical clustering have over *K*-means clustering?
a) It requires fewer iterations to converge
b) It can handle large data sets more efficiently
c) It does not require assumptions about data structure
d) It produces more accurate results in regression problems

18. What type of learning is hierarchical clustering?
a) Supervised learning
b) Unsupervised learning
c) Reinforcement learning
d) Semi-supervised learning

19. What advantage does hierarchical clustering offer in terms of accuracy?
a) It captures subtler differences between data groups
b) It provides exact solutions for all data sets
c) It eliminates outliers in the data set automatically
d) It achieves higher precision in classification tasks

20. How can users modify clusters in hierarchical clustering?
a) By specifying the maximum number of clusters
b) By changing similarity criteria or linkage methods
c) By adjusting the learning rate parameter
d) By providing labeled data points for training

21. What is one application of hierarchical clustering?
a) Predicting customer churn in a subscription service

b) Identifying spam emails in a data set
c) Recognizing handwritten digits in images
d) Segmenting customers based on shopping preferences

22. How does hierarchical clustering handle large data sets?
a) It samples a subset of the data for clustering
b) It partitions the data set into smaller chunks
c) It utilizes parallel processing for faster computation
d) It can handle large data sets efficiently

23. What is the benefit of using hierarchical clustering for exploratory analysis?
a) It provides labeled outputs for each data point
b) It reduces the dimensionality of the data set
c) It allows the identification of hidden patterns
d) It generates decision rules for classification

24. What is the key characteristic of fuzzy C-means clustering?
a) It assigns rigid labels to data points
b) It relies on strict boundaries to define clusters
c) It uses probabilistic relationships for clustering
d) It works well only with small data sets

25. How does fuzzy C-means clustering handle complex data sets?
a) It eliminates outliers and non-conforming values
b) It applies rigid rules to assign classes
c) It uses fuzzy logic and probabilistic relationships
d) It reduces the dimensionality of the data set

26. What is the output of fuzzy C-means clustering?
a) Hard clustering with strict labels
b) Soft clustering with degrees of membership
c) Predicted probabilities for each data point
d) Dimensionality-reduced data representation

27. In fuzzy C-means clustering, what does a higher membership value indicate?
a) Stronger association with the cluster
b) Weaker association with the cluster
c) No association with any cluster
d) An error in the membership calculation

28. What is an advantage of fuzzy C-means clustering over traditional methods?
a) It requires fewer computational resources
b) It provides rigid and clear cluster boundaries
c) It can handle outliers and non-conforming values
d) It guarantees optimal clustering results

29. In which domains is fuzzy C-means clustering particularly useful?
a) Computer vision applications
b) Speech recognition systems
c) Natural language processing tasks
d) Time series forecasting

30. How does fuzzy C-means clustering assign data points to clusters?
a) Based on the distance to centroid points
b) Based on rigid classification rules
c) Based on the probability of belonging to each cluster
d) Based on the density of neighboring data points

31. What is one advantage of DBSCAN over traditional clustering algorithms?
a) It can detect clusters of any shape and size
b) It requires the user to specify the number of clusters
c) It is not robust to noise and outliers
d) It relies on prior assumptions about cluster structure

32. What does DBSCAN not require the user to specify?
a) Distance thresholds for clustering
b) Minimum number of neighbors for each point
c) Number of clusters in the data
d) Density of the data points

33. How does DBSCAN handle noise and outliers?
a) It assigns noise points to the nearest cluster
b) It removes noise points from the data set
c) It ignores sparse and isolated points
d) It considers noise points as separate clusters

34. What are the two key parameters that can be tuned in DBSCAN?
a) Epsilon and density
b) Distance and number of clusters
c) Epsilon and MinPts
d) Density and cluster radius

35. In DBSCAN, what does the parameter Epsilon control?
a) The maximum number of points in a cluster
b) The minimum distance between clusters
c) The neighborhood radius for point connectivity
d) The maximum number of iterations in the algorithm

36. What kind of data sets is DBSCAN suitable for?
a) Data sets with predefined cluster structures
b) Data sets with a small number of features
c) Data sets with noisy features and outliers
d) Data sets with a high-dimensional space

37. How does DBSCAN define a cluster?
a) By considering points close enough in distance
b) By assigning labels based on density values
c) By requiring strict boundaries around points
d) By using probabilistic relationships between points

38. What is one advantage of DBSCAN regarding parameter tuning?
a) It requires tuning multiple parameters simultaneously
b) It does not require any parameter tuning

c) It has a high sensitivity to parameter values
d) It allows users to tune key parameters for performance optimization

39. What is the impact of outliers on DBSCAN clustering?
a) Outliers can lead to misclassification of points and unexpected results.
b) Outliers have no impact on DBSCAN clustering.
c) Outliers enhance the accuracy of DBSCAN clustering.
d) Outliers improve the identification of clusters in DBSCAN.

40. What happens if the parameters in DBSCAN are set too low?
a) Outliers are properly classified as part of a cluster.
b) Outliers are properly classified as noise.
c) Entire clusters might be missed or improperly grouped.
d) Clusters are accurately identified even with varying densities.

41. What adjustments can be made in DBSCAN to handle outliers?
a) Adjusting the density of clusters
b) Increasing Epsilon and MinPts
c) Decreasing Epsilon and MinPts
d) Ignoring outliers completely

42. When would increasing the value of Epsilon in DBSCAN be helpful?
a) When outliers are present in the data set
b) When clusters have varying densities
c) When the data set is small
d) When there are overlapping clusters

43. How can adjusting parameters in DBSCAN improve accuracy in large data sets?
a) By eliminating outliers from consideration
b) By reducing unnecessary computations
c) By ensuring all clustered points are identified
d) All of the above

44. What is the purpose of adjusting parameter values in DBSCAN?
a) To improve the speed of the algorithm
b) To handle overlapping clusters
c) To address the sensitivity to outliers
d) To reduce the number of required computations

45. What is the recommended approach when dealing with large data sets containing multiple overlapped clusters?
a) Adjust parameter values and ignore outliers
b) Adjust parameter values and check for outliers
c) Eliminate outliers and set parameter values low
d) Perform feature selection to reduce dimensionality

46. How can checking for outliers in advance benefit DBSCAN clustering?
a) It improves the accuracy of the clustering results.
b) It reduces unnecessary computations.
c) It eliminates misclassifications caused by outliers.
d) All of the above.

47. What is the main assumption underlying Gaussian mixture models (GMMs)?
a) All data points can be explained by a mixture of Gaussian distributions.
b) All data points belong to a single cluster.
c) GMMs require explicit labels for clustering.
d) GMMs can only handle small data sets.

48. What determines the shape and spread of each cluster in a Gaussian mixture model?
a) The number of observations in the cluster.
b) The mean and covariance matrix associated with the cluster.
c) The probability of observations belonging to the cluster.
d) The likelihood of observations being similar to each other.

49. How does the GMM algorithm assign observations to clusters?
a) By maximizing the likelihood function.
b) By calculating the distance between observations and cluster centers.
c) By assigning observations to the cluster with the highest probability.
d) By using explicit labels provided in the data set.

50. What information does a Gaussian mixture model provide about an object?
a) The number of features it possesses.
b) The number of components that make up the object.
c) The specific labels of the object.
d) The distance of the object from other objects.

51. What type of problems can benefit from using Gaussian mixture models?
a) Clustering customer profiles.
b) Image classification.
c) Speech recognition.
d) Sentiment analysis.

52. How do Gaussian mixture models handle large data sets?
a) By reducing the number of observations.
b) By increasing the number of clusters.
c) By using feature engineering techniques.
d) Equally well, regardless of data set size.

53. What is a benefit of using Gaussian mixture models for clustering tasks?
a) Feature engineering is not required.
b) Explicit labels are necessary for accurate clustering.
c) All components in the data must have the same shape.
d) GMMs cannot handle overlapping clusters.

54. Can Gaussian mixture models perform clustering tasks on partially labeled data sets?
a) Yes, by using the means and covariances matrices.
b) No, explicit labels are required for all observations.
c) Yes, but only when the clusters are well-separated.
d) No, GMMs can only work with fully labeled data sets.

55. What makes MeanShift clustering suitable for analyzing complex data sets?
a) It requires prior knowledge about the data.

b) It can handle clusters of any size or shape.
c) It only works well with small data sets.
d) It is not robust against noise and outliers.

56. In which scenario would MeanShift clustering be particularly useful?
a) Analyzing data sets with explicit labels for all observations.
b) Analyzing data sets with a known number of clusters.
c) Analyzing data sets with noise and outliers.
d) Analyzing data sets with low-dimensional feature spaces.

57. What can MeanShift clustering help retailers achieve with sales data analysis?
a) Identify correlations between variables in the data set.
b) Segment their customer base for targeted marketing.
c) Determine the optimal pricing strategy for products.
d) Predict future sales with high accuracy.

58. Why is MeanShift clustering suitable for machine learning applications like object tracking and image segmentation?
a) It requires minimal computational resources.
b) It guarantees accurate predictions with any data set.
c) It is flexible and efficient compared to other algorithms.
d) It relies on explicit labels for each data point.

59. What advantage does MeanShift clustering have over *K*-means clustering?
a) MeanShift clustering can handle noise and outliers.
b) MeanShift clustering requires explicit labels for each observation.
c) MeanShift clustering works well with small data sets only.
d) MeanShift clustering can handle only spherical clusters.

60. How can MeanShift clustering contribute to exploratory data analysis?
a) By simplifying the data set for easier analysis.
b) By automatically identifying relationships between variables.
c) By revealing clusters of data points with similar characteristics.
d) By predicting future trends based on historical data.

61. Which type of data sets does MeanShift clustering work best with?
a) Data sets with a large number of features.
b) Data sets with low-dimensional feature spaces.
c) Data sets with an unknown number of clusters.
d) Data sets with equal-sized clusters.

62. What advantage does MeanShift clustering offer in terms of scalability?
a) It can handle large and small data sets equally well.
b) It requires significantly less computational resources.
c) It provides accurate predictions with minimal training data.
d) It is not affected by outliers in the data set.

63. What is one major drawback of MeanShift clustering when dealing with high-dimensional data sets?
a) Difficulty in selecting appropriate parameters.
b) Reliance on local optimization methods.
c) Inability to handle large data sets effectively.
d) Loss of meaningful distance metrics.

64. What challenge is associated with selecting parameters for MeanShift clustering?
a) Difficulty in interpreting clustering results.
b) Dependency on trial-and-error experimentation.
c) Inability to handle large data sets effectively.
d) Reliance on local optimization methods.

65. In which scenario could MeanShift clustering potentially lead to inaccurate clusters?
a) When dealing with high-dimensional data sets.
b) When selecting appropriate parameters.
c) When analyzing large data sets.
d) When relying on local optimization methods.

66. What limitation does MeanShift clustering have in terms of data dimensions?
a) It is more effective in high-dimensional data sets.
b) It relies on meaningful distance metrics in high-dimensional data sets.
c) It becomes increasingly ineffective beyond a certain number of dimensions.
d) It requires additional context from qualitative characteristics in high-dimensional data sets.

67. What is one advantage of MeanShift clustering over other clustering methods?
a) Ease of implementation.
b) Ability to handle high-dimensional data sets effectively.
c) No need for parameter selection.
d) Reliable convergence to global optima.

68. What characteristic makes MeanShift clustering an attractive tool for data analysis?
a) Ability to handle large data sets effectively.
b) Reliance on qualitative characteristics.
c) Ability to make accurate predictions with limited data sets.
d) Requirement of substantial domain knowledge.

69. What issue can arise when applying MeanShift clustering exclusively based on quantitative characteristics?
a) Difficulty in interpreting clustering results.
b) Loss of accuracy in cluster assignments.
c) Overemphasis on domain knowledge.
d) Inaccurate conclusions about the data set.

70. What is a drawback of MeanShift clustering related to the scalability of the algorithm?
a) Inability to handle large data sets effectively.
b) Dependency on trial-and-error experimentation.

c) Reliance on local optimization methods.
d) Difficulty in selecting appropriate parameters.

71. What is the main goal of Gaussian mixture density estimation (GMDE)?
a) Predicting class labels for new observations.
b) Uncovering hidden patterns in complex data sets.
c) Modeling data using Gaussian distributions.
d) Finding the underlying structure of the data.

72. How does GMDE estimate the parameters of each mixture model component?
a) By fitting Gaussian distributions on each cluster.
b) By using the expectation-maximization algorithm.
c) By adjusting parameters through successive iterations.
d) By calculating the probability of each data point.

73. What is the role of the expectation maximization algorithm in GMDE?
a) It models data using Gaussian distributions.
b) It determines the underlying structure of the data.
c) It estimates the parameters for each mixture model component.
d) It predicts class labels for new observations.

74. In which scenario can GMDE be useful?
a) Making predictions about new observations based on past ones.
b) Selecting appropriate parameters for clustering algorithms.
c) Handling high-dimensional data sets effectively.
d) Analyzing categorical variables in a data set.

75. What is the primary advantage of GMDE over other clustering methods?
a) Ability to handle high-dimensional data set effectively.
b) Ease of selecting appropriate parameters.
c) Uncovering hidden patterns in complex data sets.
d) Quick convergence to global optima.

76. What can GMDE be used for in the field of medicine?
a) Predicting class labels for patient characteristics.
b) Analyzing categorical variables in patient data.
c) Detecting diseases early based on patient history.
d) Handling high-dimensional medical data sets.

77. What does GMDE rely on to classify unseen observations?
a) Maximum likelihood estimation.
b) Gaussian distributions of each component.
c) Probability values of each component's PDFs.
d) Feature space associations with nearby clusters.

78. What is the significance of MLE in GMDE?
a) Adjusting parameters through successive iterations.
b) Fitting Gaussian distributions on each cluster.

c) Calculating the probability of each data point.
d) Estimating the parameters of Gaussian mixture models.

79. What is the main purpose of the isolation forest algorithm?
a) Detecting anomalies or outliers in the data.
b) Training decision trees for classification tasks.
c) Clustering data points into distinct groups.
d) Handling noisy data in machine learning models.

80. How is the anomaly score of a data point determined in the isolation forest algorithm?
a) By its separation from other data points.
b) By its depth within the decision tree.
c) By its proximity to the feature's maximum value.
d) By the number of decision trees it appears in.

81. What is the advantage of the isolation forest algorithm over traditional methods like clustering?
a) Ability to handle noisy data in real-world applications.
b) Efficient detection of unobvious outliers without prior knowledge.
c) Accurate classification of data points into distinct groups.
d) Robustness against measurement errors in the data set.

82. How does the isolation forest algorithm create isolation trees?
a) By randomly selecting feature splits in the data set.
b) By recursively dividing the data set based on split values.
c) By clustering data points into individual nodes.
d) By adjusting decision tree parameters based on anomalies.

83. What does each leaf node in an isolation tree represent?
a) An observation or an anomaly.
b) A feature with the highest split value.
c) A regular data point surrounded by other regular points.
d) A decision made during the anomaly detection process.

84. In which real-world application can the isolation forest algorithm be useful?
a) Predicting customer preferences based on past purchases.
b) Analyzing social media sentiment for brand reputation.
c) Detecting fraud in financial transactions.
d) Classifying images into different categories.

85. What makes the isolation forest algorithm popular among machine learning practitioners?
a) Its ability to handle noisy data in real-world applications.
b) Its accuracy in classifying data points into distinct groups.
c) Its efficiency compared to other anomaly detection algorithms.
d) Its robustness against measurement errors in the data set.

86. What is the main advantage of the isolation forest algorithm in handling outliers caused by noise or measurement errors?
a) It can remove outliers from the data set.

b) It can transform the outliers into regular data points.
c) It is robust and less affected by noise or measurement errors.
d) It can adjust the decision tree parameters to accommodate outliers.

87. What does the local outlier factor (LOF) algorithm measure?
a) The degree of separation between data points.
b) The average density of neighboring data points.
c) The likelihood of a data point being an outlier.
d) The distance between a data point and its neighbors.

88. How does the LOF algorithm determine if a data point is an outlier?
a) By comparing its density to the average density of its neighbors.
b) By analyzing the number of features present in the data set.
c) By calculating the distance between the data point and its neighbors.
d) By estimating the reachability distance of the data point.

89. What is the main advantage of the LOF algorithm in outlier detection?
a) It can handle data sets with a high number of features.
b) It requires minimal parameter tuning or optimization.
c) It can detect outliers based on their distance from other points.
d) It is highly accurate even with complex data sets.

90. How does the LOF algorithm estimate the local density of a data point?
a) By calculating the distance between the data point and its neighbors.
b) By analyzing the number of neighbors around the data point.
c) By computing the average distance between the data point and its k nearest neighbors.
d) By comparing the data point's features to its neighbors' features.

91. What is the purpose of the reachability distance in the LOF algorithm?
a) To measure the density of a data point's neighbors.
b) To determine the number of outliers in the data set.
c) To calculate the anomaly score for each data point.
d) To identify the nearest neighbors of a data point.

92. Which type of data sets is the LOF algorithm particularly useful for?
a) Data sets with a high number of features.
b) Data sets with a small number of observations.
c) Data sets with a balanced distribution of outliers.
d) Data sets with dense clusters and sparse outliers.

93. What makes the LOF algorithm cost-effective and user-friendly?
a) Its ability to handle high-dimensional data sets.
b) Its accuracy in identifying all types of outliers.
c) Its simplicity and ease of implementation.
d) Its robustness against noise and measurement errors.

94. What advantage does the LOF algorithm offer compared to support vector machines (SVMs)?
a) It is faster and more efficient.

b) It can handle high-dimensional data sets.
c) It provides better accuracy in outlier detection.
d) It requires less computational resources.

95. What is the primary goal of the one-class support vector machine (OC SVM) algorithm?
a) To classify data points into multiple classes.
b) To identify and separate outliers from standard data points.
c) To construct a hyperplane that best separates different classes.
d) To fit a model using the hyperplane separation technique.

96. Which kernel function is commonly used in OC SVM due to its ability to capture nonlinearities in the data?
a) Linear kernel.
b) Polynomial kernel.
c) Sigmoid kernel.
d) Radial basis function (RBF) kernel.

97. What is the purpose of the gamma value in OC SVM?
a) To determine the complexity of the model.
b) To specify the cost factor for misclassifications.
c) To determine the influence of each training example on the decision boundary.
d) To measure the penalties for misclassification errors.

98. How does the cost factor C affect the OC SVM model?
a) It determines the degree of regularization applied to the model.
b) It controls the complexity of the decision surface.
c) It measures the influence of each training example on the decision boundary.
d) It determines the penalties for misclassification errors.

99. Which optimization technique is commonly used to find the optimized solution in OC SVM?
a) Gradient descent.
b) Random search.
c) Genetic algorithms.
d) *K*-means clustering.

100. What is the purpose of the degree parameter in OC SVM when using a polynomial kernel?
a) To determine the influence of each training example on the decision boundary.
b) To measure the penalties for misclassification errors.
c) To specify the cost factor for misclassifications.
d) To control the complexity of the model based on the number of features.

101. What does the OC SVM algorithm aim to achieve during the training phase?
a) Construct a hyperplane without error.
b) Fit a single model to separate outliers from standard data points.
c) Classify new examples into different classes.
d) Determine the influence of each training example on the decision boundary.

102. How does OC SVM classify new unseen data points?
a) Based on their similarity to other data points in the data set.
b) By constructing an *n*-dimensional hypersphere around the training data set.
c) Using a non-linear hyperplane as a decision boundary.
d) By considering the influence of each training example on the decision boundary.

103. What is the purpose of data pre-processing in PCA?
a) To organize the data into an appropriate format.
b) To calculate the correlation between variables.
c) To compute the covariance matrix.
d) To project data onto selected principal components.

104. What does the covariance matrix in PCA tell us?
a) The degree of variation among different features.
b) The relationships between variables.
c) The eigenvalues of the data set.
d) The projection of data onto principal components.

105. What is the purpose of eigenvalue decomposition in PCA?
a) To calculate the correlation between variables.
b) To compute the covariance matrix.
c) To select the principal components.
d) To project data onto lower-dimensional spaces.

106. How are the principal components selected in PCA?
a) Based on their correlation with the target variable.
b) Based on their eigenvalues.
c) Based on their covariance values.
d) Based on their projection onto the original features.

107. What is the purpose of projecting data onto selected principal components in PCA?
a) To compute the covariance matrix.
b) To calculate the correlation between variables.
c) To select the best principal components.
d) To obtain a lower-dimensional representation of the data.

108. What is the significance of the cumulative explained variance ratio in selecting principal components?
a) It determines the complexity of the model.
b) It measures the correlation between variables.
c) It indicates the contribution of each principal component to the total variance.
d) It helps calculate the covariance matrix.

109. How does PCA help in reducing dimensions for classification tasks?
a) By calculating eigenvalues and eigenvectors.
b) By standardizing the data.
c) By projecting the data onto selected principal components.
d) By computing the correlation between variables.

110. What is the purpose of selecting an appropriate kernel function in KPCA?
a) To transform the data into a lower-dimensional space.
b) To compute the eigenvalues and eigenvectors.

c) To calculate the similarity between data points.
d) To perform principal component analysis.

111. What role does singular value decomposition (SVD) play in KPCA?
a) It transforms the data into a lower-dimensional space.
b) It calculates the eigenvalues and eigenvectors.
c) It performs principal component analysis.
d) It constructs the kernel matrix.

112. How are hyperparameters determined in KPCA?
a) Based on the number of data points in the data set.
b) Based on the complexity of the problem being solved.
c) Based on the similarity measures used in the kernel matrix.
d) Based on the desired number of principal components.

113. What is the purpose of projecting the principal components onto a lower-dimensional subspace in KPCA?
a) To calculate the eigenvalues and eigenvectors.
b) To maximize variance between extracted features.
c) To create a less compact representation of the data.
d) To compare the performance with other methods.

114. What is the recommended technique for projecting principal components onto a lower-dimensional subspace in KPCA?
a) Singular value decomposition (SVD). b) Karhunen-Loeve Transformation (KLT).
c) Principal component analysis (PCA). d) Linear Discriminant Analysis (LDA).

115. How can the effectiveness of extracted features in KPCA be validated?
a) By comparing them with those found via other methods.
b) By calculating the similarity measures between data points.
c) By determining the appropriate kernel function.
d) By performing singular value decomposition (SVD).

116. What is the main application of KPCA?
a) Data collection and pre-processing. b) Anomaly detection.
c) Dimensionality reduction. d) Computing the covariance matrix.

117. What is the primary advantage of using kernel principal component analysis (KPCA) over traditional principal component analysis (PCA)?
a) It can handle non-linear relationships in the data.
b) It requires fewer computational resources.
c) It provides a simpler interpretation of the data.
d) It is more suitable for low-dimensional data sets.

118. Which step of the KPCA algorithm involves transforming the original data set into a lower-dimensional space?
a) Choosing an appropriate kernel function.
b) Performing singular value decomposition (SVD).

c) Creating the kernel matrix.
d) Projecting the principal components.

119. How are hyperparameters in KPCA determined?
a) Based on the number of data points in the data set.
b) Based on the complexity of the problem being solved.
c) Based on the similarity measures used in the kernel matrix.
d) Based on the desired number of principal components.

120. What is the purpose of calculating mean vectors for each class in linear discriminant analysis (LDA)?
a) To determine the optimal separation planes.
b) To compute the within-class covariance matrix.
c) To perform singular value decomposition (SVD).
d) To project the data onto a lower-dimensional subspace.

121. Which step in LDA involves computing the between-class covariance matrix?
a) Choosing an appropriate distance metric.
b) Calculating the mean vectors for each class.
c) Computing the within-class covariance matrix.
d) Projecting the data onto a lower-dimensional subspace.

122. What is the main application of kernel principal component analysis (KPCA)?
a) Data collection and pre-processing.
b) Anomaly detection.
c) Dimensionality reduction.
d) Computing the covariance matrix.

123. What is the primary goal of exploratory factor analysis (EFA)?
a) To uncover hidden relationships between variables within a data set.
b) To predict future outcomes based on observed variables.
c) To analyze correlations between categorical variables.
d) To determine statistical significance using regression models.

124. Which statistical tests can be used to assess whether correlations between variables are statistically significant in EFA?
a) Pearson Correlation and Spearman's Rank Correlation Tests.
b) Analysis of Variance (ANOVA) and Chi-Square Test.
c) T-tests and Z-tests.
d) Linear Regression and Logistic Regression.

125. When should confirmatory factor analysis (CFA) be chosen over exploratory factor analysis (EFA)?
a) When there is little prior knowledge about the factors within the data set.
b) When known factors have been identified in prior research efforts.
c) When the data set contains categorical variables.
d) When regression models have already been applied to the data set.

126. What is the purpose of factor extraction methods in EFA?
a) To identify statistically significant correlations between variables.

b) To determine the number of latent factors to extract from the data set.
c) To perform matrix algebra techniques and linear models.
d) To analyze categorical variables and their relationships.

127. Which measure can be used to assess the adequacy of the data set for factor analysis?
a) Kaiser-Meyer-Olkin measure of sampling adequacy (KMO).
b) Cronbach's Alpha coefficient.
c) Mahalanobis distance.
d) Cohen's Kappa statistic.

128. What is the main advantage of using exploratory factor analysis (EFA) over regression models?
a) EFA can uncover hidden relationships between variables.
b) EFA can predict future outcomes based on observed variables.
c) EFA can handle categorical variables more effectively.
d) EFA can perform hypothesis testing on observed variables.

129. What does the scree plot help determine in exploratory factor analysis?
a) The statistical significance of correlations between variables.
b) The number of factors to retain in the analysis.
c) The amount of variation explained by each factor.
d) The linearity of relationships between variables.

130. How does exploratory factor analysis (EFA) help in data exploration and study design?
a) It helps identify clusters of closely related items that form distinct factors.
b) It provides accurate predictions of future outcomes based on observed variables.
c) It enables the analysis of non-linear relationships between variables.
d) It allows for the identification of statistical significance using chi-square tests.

131. What is the primary purpose of confirmatory factor analysis (CFA)?
a) To test theoretical models and hypotheses about the relationships between observed variables.
b) To identify hidden factors within a data set.
c) To summarize complex data sets into simpler components.
d) To analyze correlations between measured variables.

132. How does CFA differ from EFA?
a) CFA tests a pre-specified model, while EFA explores and identifies underlying factors.
b) CFA is used for categorical variables, while EFA is used for numeric variables.
c) CFA requires larger sample sizes than EFA.
d) CFA does not involve statistical testing, unlike EFA.

133. What is the purpose of evaluating goodness-of-fit in CFA?
a) To determine if the hypothesized model fits well with the data.
b) To identify the number of factors to extract from the data set.
c) To evaluate the statistical significance of correlations between variables.
d) To assess the reliability of the observed variables.

134. Which fit indices are commonly used to evaluate model fit in CFA?
a) Chi-square statistic, RMSEA, CFI, TLI, AIC.

b) Pearson correlation, Spearman's rank correlation, ANOVA, chi-square test.
c) Regression coefficient, p-value, R-squared, adjusted R-squared.
d) Cronbach's Alpha, factor loading, Eigenvalues, scree plot.

135. What does it mean if the goodness-of-fit indices indicate a poor fit in CFA?
a) The hypothesized model does not fit the data well.
b) The observed variables have low reliability.
c) The data set does not have enough variability.
d) The number of latent factors is too high.

136. What does CFA provide insights into regarding observed variables?
a) Causal relations between observed variables.
b) Specific implications for different groups or contexts.
c) The number of latent factors in the data set.
d) Reliability and consistency of the observed variables.

137. In which field of research is CFA commonly used?
a) Financial analysis. b) Market research.
c) Psychological research. d) Epidemiological studies.

138. What is the role of CFA in guiding further research?
a) It provides evidence behind assumptions about phenomena.
b) It identifies the number of factors to extract from the data set.
c) It determines statistical significance using chi-square tests.
d) It summarizes complex data sets into simpler components.

139. What is the main advantage of the ECLAT algorithm over the Apriori algorithm?
a) ECLAT requires fewer database scans.
b) ECLAT utilizes a depth-first search approach.
c) ECLAT works well with horizontal data sets.
d) ECLAT is more memory-efficient.

140. In which type of data set format does the ECLAT algorithm work?
a) Horizontal data set format. b) Vertical data set format.
c) Transaction database format. d) Market basket format.

141. What approach does the ECLAT algorithm use to traverse through itemsets?
a) Breadth-first search. b) Random search.
c) Depth-first search. d) Linear search.

142. How does the ECLAT algorithm determine the support of itemsets?
a) By computing subset tests and subset generation.
b) By scanning the database multiple times.
c) By using tid sets and intersecting transaction lists.
d) By applying confidence measures to frequent itemsets.

143. Which data sets are better suited for the ECLAT algorithm?
a) Small and medium data sets. b) Large and complex data sets.
c) Horizontal and transaction data sets. d) Data sets with low support counts.

144. How does the ECLAT algorithm differ from the Apriori algorithm in terms of memory usage?
a) ECLAT uses less memory than Apriori.
b) ECLAT uses more memory than Apriori.
c) ECLAT and Apriori have similar memory usage.
d) ECLAT doesn't require memory allocation.

145. What is the primary objective of the ECLAT algorithm?
a) To find the highest confidence rules.
b) To identify the most frequent itemsets.
c) To convert horizontal data sets into vertical format.
d) To perform association rule mining.

146. What strategy does the ECLAT algorithm use to optimize search efficiency?
a) Subtree pruning. b) Breadth-first search.
c) Linear scan. d) Random sampling.

147. In which type of learning does a Markov model use labeled data for training?
a) Supervised learning. b) Unsupervised learning.
c) Reinforcement learning. d) Semi-supervised learning.

148. What is the main purpose of Markov models?
a) Making predictions based on past data. b) Identifying patterns and structures in data.
c) Classifying data into clusters. d) Training neural networks.

149. Which field might benefit from using Markov models for decision-making?
a) Marketing and advertising. b) Weather forecasting.
c) Stock market analysis. d) Random number generation.

150. How does a Markov model calculate the probability of future outcomes?
a) By analyzing current conditions only.
b) By considering state transitions and past events.
c) By using random sampling techniques.
d) By incorporating labeled outputs in the training process.

151. What type of learning does a Markov model use when trained with only input data?
a) Unsupervised learning. b) Reinforcement learning.
c) Semi-supervised learning. d) Active learning.

152. What does a Markov model consider when predicting future outcomes?
a) Future conditions and variables. b) Random events and chance.
c) State transitions and past events. d) Unrelated factors and influences.

153. Which characteristic makes Markov models suitable for complex system predictions?
a) Linear calculations of probabilities.
b) Lack of consideration for unknown variables.
c) Ability to incorporate traditional methods.
d) Consideration of many variables and scenarios.

154. What type of information does a Markov model utilize to predict the future?
a) Labeled data with target variables.
b) Real-time streaming data.
c) Past data and state transitions.
d) Simulated synthetic data.

155. In which type of learning does a hidden Markov model (HMM) use a labeled data set for training?
a) Supervised learning.
b) Unsupervised learning.
c) Reinforcement learning.
d) Semi-supervised learning.

156. What is the primary objective of unsupervised learning with hidden Markov models?
a) Discovering the best sequence of states for a given observation sequence.
b) Generating new observation sequences based on hidden states.
c) Predicting future observations given the current state.
d) Assigning probabilities to hidden states.

157. What are the two main components of a hidden Markov model (HMM)?
a) Observations and probabilities.
b) Hidden states and observations.
c) Hidden states and transitions.
d) Transitions and observations.

158. In which applications can hidden Markov models (HMMs) be used?
a) Speech recognition and machine translation.
b) Image classification and natural language processing.
c) Regression analysis and anomaly detection.
d) Reinforcement learning and deep neural networks.

159. What advantage do hidden Markov models (HMMs) offer in machine translation?
a) Ability to learn complex language patterns from small data sets.
b) Efficient processing of large-scale data sets.
c) Accurate prediction of image classifications.
d) High computational speed in deep learning tasks.

160. How do hidden Markov models (HMMs) handle data sequences with variable lengths?
a) By considering all previous observations when making predictions.
b) By assuming a fixed length for all data sequences.
c) By ignoring incomplete information in the sequences.
d) By using deep learning techniques for sequence alignment.

161. What makes hidden Markov models (HMMs) suitable for bioinformatics research?
a) Their ability to analyze image data sets efficiently.
b) Their capability to handle high-dimensional data.
c) Their capacity to identify regions with special functions in DNA sequences.
d) Their support for parallel computing architectures.

162. What advantage does a hidden Markov model (HMM) provide in analyzing DNA sequences compared to traditional methods?
a) Faster computation and processing power.
b) Simpler implementation with fewer assumptions.
c) Consideration of context-dependent information for accurate predictions.

d) Ability to handle real-time streaming data.

163. What is the purpose of decoding the states of a machine learning algorithm?
a) To optimize its performance and maximize accuracy.
b) To visualize the decision-making process.
c) To identify areas for improvement.
d) To understand the impact of different inputs on the output.

164. Which visualization tool is commonly used to depict the influence of each state on the predictive outcome?
a) Bayesian networks.
b) Heat maps.
c) Markov models.
d) Decision trees.

165. Which probabilistic approach allows researchers to trace through all possible paths leading up to a given result?
a) Decision trees.
b) Markov models.
c) Neural networks.
d) Support vector machines (SVM).

166. How do visualization tools help in understanding the decision-making process of machine learning algorithms?
a) They reveal patterns and clusters in the data.
b) They provide probabilities for different outcomes.
c) They optimize the performance of the algorithm.
d) They identify areas for improvement.

167. Which type of approach considers multiple outcomes simultaneously in decoding states?
a) Decision trees.
b) Markov models.
c) Support vector machines (SVM).
d) Bayesian networks.

168. Why is it important to identify areas for improvement before making changes to a machine learning algorithm?
a) To avoid unexpected consequences.
b) To speed up the computation and processing power.
c) To simplify the implementation of the algorithm.
d) To improve visualization techniques.

169. How do probabilistic approaches differ from visualization tools in understanding the decision-making process?
a) Probabilistic approaches consider multiple outcomes simultaneously.
b) Visualization tools provide a direct view of the data.
c) Probabilistic approaches optimize the algorithm's performance.
d) Visualization tools identify areas for improvement.

170. What is the ultimate goal of decoding states from observations with machine learning algorithms?
a) To optimize the algorithm's performance.
b) To maximize predictive accuracy.
c) To improve visualization techniques.
d) To speed up computation and processing power.

171. In which application area are latent factor models extensively used?
a) Recommender systems.
b) Image recognition.
c) Natural language processing.
d) Financial forecasting.

172. What is one advantage of latent factor models over traditional linear regression methods?
a) They can handle large amounts of data more efficiently.
b) They can account for non-linear relationships between variables.
c) They require fewer computational resources.
d) They are easier to interpret.

173. In which type of learning can latent factor models be used for dimensionality reduction and data clustering?
a) Supervised learning.
b) Unsupervised learning.
c) Reinforcement learning.
d) Transfer learning.

174. What do latent factors represent in a latent factor model?
a) Hidden patterns in the data.
b) Directly observable variables.
c) Labels for classification.
d) Error terms in the model.

175. Which application area can benefit from latent factor models by identifying latent topics within a text corpus?
a) Image recognition.
b) Sentiment analysis.
c) Financial forecasting.
d) Recommendation systems.

176. In which type of learning can latent factor models be used for regression and classification tasks?
a) Supervised learning.
b) Unsupervised learning.
c) Reinforcement learning.
d) Semi-supervised learning.

177. How do latent factor models predict future outcomes based on past data?
a) By directly analyzing raw data.
b) By using latent factors as features.
c) By utilizing labeled information.
d) By training a deep neural network.

178. What is the main purpose of latent factor models in machine learning and artificial intelligence applications?
a) Dimensionality reduction.
b) Data clustering.
c) Maximizing predictive accuracy.
d) Feature engineering.

179. What is the primary purpose of belief propagation in graphical models?
a) Computing probabilities or values associated with different configurations of variables.
b) Initializing nodes with prior beliefs about their values.
c) Creating a graph-like structure to represent conditional dependencies among variables.
d) Gathering information from observed data points.

180. In which field has belief propagation been successfully applied to handle complex inference processes without explicit probabilistic assumptions?
a) Natural language processing.
b) Image recognition.
c) Weather forecasting.
d) Financial forecasting.

181. What is the purpose of the belief propagation algorithm in machine learning?
a) To find the most probable explanations for a given set of evidence.
b) To process observed data in a single cycle and arrive at a conclusion.
c) To create a belief network with evidence, decision, and utility nodes.
d) To make predictions based on complete domain knowledge.

182. What are the three components of a belief network in the belief propagation algorithm?
a) Evidence Nodes, Decision Nodes, and Utility Nodes.
b) Prior Beliefs, Posterior Beliefs, and Conditional Dependencies.
c) Observations, Predictions, and Probabilities.
d) Graph Nodes, Edge Weights, and Graph Structures.

183. How does belief propagation handle large amounts of data in complex systems?
a) By making assumptions about the underlying processes generating observable evidence.
b) By using brute force approaches to process all possible combinations of data.
c) By passing messages between nodes to compute probabilities or expected utility values.
d) By relying on complete domain knowledge to make accurate predictions.

184. In which application area are belief propagation algorithms commonly used?
a) Medical diagnosis.
b) Financial forecasting.
c) Image recognition.
d) Speech synthesis.

185. What is the benefit of utilizing belief propagation algorithms in making inferences from observed data points?
a) Improved decision-making based on significant amounts of evidence.
b) Avoidance of human bias or error-prone models.
c) Reduction in computational complexity for high-dimensional inputs/outputs.
d) Allowing for explicit probabilistic assumptions.

186. What is the key advantage of belief propagation algorithms over traditional methods in graphical models?
a) Faster processing with less computational resources.
b) Access to complete domain knowledge for accurate predictions.
c) Ability to handle incomplete information and uncertainties.
d) Simplicity in representing conditional dependencies among variables.

187. What is the primary characteristic of unsupervised machine learning?
a) It discovers patterns in data without external guidance or labels.
b) It requires human assistance to identify hidden relationships in data sets.
c) It relies on predefined characteristics given by humans.
d) It automates tasks that do not require pattern recognition.

188. How does unsupervised machine learning save time and money?
a) By automating tasks that require considerable human effort.
b) By eliminating the need for data analysis.
c) By relying on external guidance and labels for accurate predictions.
d) By reducing computational costs for complex tasks.

189. Which application of unsupervised machine learning involves identifying unusual patterns in data sets?

a) Market segmentation.
b) Anomaly detection.
c) Image recognition.
d) Cluster analysis.

190. How can unsupervised machine learning be used in image recognition?

a) By relying on pre-defined labels to identify specific individuals.
b) By automating tasks that require human effort in image analysis.
c) By recognizing images without being told what individual it's looking for first.
d) By clustering images based on their similarities.

191. Which area can benefit from unsupervised machine learning for market segmentation?

a) Anomaly detection.
b) Customer service improvement.
c) Image recognition.
d) Fraud detection.

192. What advantage does unsupervised machine learning offer in reducing computational costs?

a) It automates tasks that would be too expensive or time-consuming for a human analyst.
b) It relies on complete external guidance for accurate predictions.
c) It reduces the need for data clustering.
d) It can be used for supervised learning tasks as well.

193. Which type of AI allows computers to learn independently and uncover hidden relationships in data sets?

a) Supervised machine learning.
b) Reinforcement learning.
c) Unsupervised machine learning.
d) Deep learning.

194. What advantage does unsupervised machine learning provide in discovering new information?

a) It relies on pre-existing knowledge for accurate predictions.
b) It automates tasks without any pattern recognition.
c) It can uncover hidden trends or correlations in complex data sets.
d) It eliminates the need for data analysis.

195. What is one potential drawback of unsupervised machine learning algorithms?

a) Risk of overfitting and poor generalization.
b) High computational cost for labeling data.
c) Clear interpretation of results without additional tools.
d) Inability to solve complex problems.

196. Why can unsupervised machine learning algorithms be computationally expensive?

a) Due to the need for labeling large amounts of data.
b) Because they require extensive feature exploration.
c) As they rely on external interpretation tools for analysis.
d) Because they have limited predictive power.

197. What challenge do unsupervised models pose in terms of interpretation?

a) They lack clear interpretation and generate numerous hypotheses.
b) They rely heavily on external data sources for interpretation.

c) They have limited analysis capabilities compared to supervised models.
d) They require human intuition to draw meaningful conclusions.

198. What is the potential consequence of overfitting in unsupervised machine learning?
a) Inaccurate predictions and poor performance on unseen data.
b) High computational costs and slow processing speed.
c) Limited feature exploration and predictive power.
d) Clear interpretation and easy generalization.

199. What makes unsupervised machine learning advantageous in terms of data requirements?
a) It requires minimal data compared to supervised methods.
b) It eliminates the need for data analysis and interpretation.
c) It allows for easy labeling of data.
d) It reduces the computational cost of exploring features.

200. How can the lack of clear interpretation in unsupervised models impact decision-making?
a) It leads to more accurate predictions and improved performance.
b) It requires extensive human intervention for meaningful conclusions.
c) It limits the discovery of hidden patterns in data sets.
d) It facilitates easy generalization to unseen data.

Part B (Short Answer Questions)

1. Give a common real-world example for unsupervised learning.
2. What are the subcategories of unsupervised learning?
3. What are the types of clustering algorithms?
4. What is hard clustering?
5. What is soft clustering?
6. Define Gaussian mixture models (GMMs)
7. What is Gaussian mixture density estimation?
8. What are Markov random fields (MRFs)?
9. Define hierarchical clustering.
10. Define fuzzy C-means clustering.
11. What are the advantages of DBSCAN clustering?
12. What are the disadvantages of DBSCAN clustering?
13. What is Gaussian mixture model?
14. What are the advantages of MeanShift clustering?
15. What are the disadvantages of MeanShift clustering?
16. Explain anomaly detection.
17. What is isolation forest algorithm?
18. What is local outlier factor (LOF)?
19. Define one-class support vector machine (OC SVM).
20. Define dimensionality reduction.
21. What is KPCA?
22. Define linear discriminant analysis (LDA).
23. Define factor analysis (FA).
24. Define exploratory factor analysis (EFA).
25. Define confirmatory factor analysis (CFA).
26. Define Markov models.
27. Define hidden Markov model (HMM).
28. Define latent factor models.
29. What is inference model?
30. What is non-negative matrix factorization (NMF)?

Part C (Essay Questions)

1. Explain the steps of *K*-means clustering.
2. Explain how to group unlabeled items using *K*-means clustering. What are the advantages of *K*-means clustering?
3. Explain the concept of hierarchical clustering.
4. Explain the concept of fuzzy C-means clustering in detail.
5. Explain the advantages of density-based spatial clustering.
6. Explain the disadvantages of DBSCAN clustering.
7. Explain Gaussian mixture models (GMMs).
8. What are the advantages of MeanShift clustering?
9. What are the disadvantages of MeanShift clustering?
10. Write an essay on Gaussian mixture density estimation (GMDE).
11. Write an essay on isolation forest algorithm.
12. Define local outlier factor (LOF).
13. Explain one-class support vector machine (OC SVM).
14. Explain the steps followed in PCA.
15. Explain kernel principal component analysis (KPCA).
16. Provide a step-by-step guide to linear discriminant analysis (LDA).
17. Explain exploratory factor analysis (EFA).
18. Explain confirmatory factor analysis (CFA).
19. Explain the ECLAT algorithm.
20. Explain Markov models in detail.
21. Explain hidden Markov model (HMM) in detail.
22. Explain about decoding states from observations.
23. Explain the latent factor models.
24. Explain the inference model in detail.
25. Explain the advantages of unsupervised learning.
26. Explain the disadvantages of unsupervised learning.

ANSWER KEY

Part A

1. (c)	**2.** (b)	**3.** (a)	**4.** (d)	**5.** (b)	**6.** (b)	**7.** (a)	**8.** (c)
9. (d)	**10.** (b)	**11.** (a)	**12.** (a)	**13.** (b)	**14.** (c)	**15.** (d)	**16.** (b)
17. (c)	**18.** (b)	**19.** (a)	**20.** (b)	**21.** (d)	**22.** (d)	**23.** (c)	**24.** (c)
25. (c)	**26.** (b)	**27.** (a)	**28.** (c)	**29.** (a)	**30.** (c)	**31.** (a)	**32.** (c)
33. (c)	**34.** (c)	**35.** (c)	**36.** (c)	**37.** (a)	**38.** (d)	**39.** (a)	**40.** (c)
41. (b)	**42.** (b)	**43.** (d)	**44.** (c)	**45.** (b)	**46.** (d)	**47.** (a)	**48.** (b)
49. (c)	**50.** (b)	**51.** (a)	**52.** (d)	**53.** (a)	**54.** (a)	**55.** (b)	**56.** (c)
57. (b)	**58.** (c)	**59.** (a)	**60.** (c)	**61.** (c)	**62.** (a)	**63.** (d)	**64.** (b)
65. (d)	**66.** (c)	**67.** (a)	**68.** (c)	**69.** (d)	**70.** (a)	**71.** (b)	**72.** (b)
73. (c)	**74.** (a)	**75.** (c)	**76.** (c)	**77.** (c)	**78.** (d)	**79.** (a)	**80.** (b)
81. (b)	**82.** (b)	**83.** (a)	**84.** (c)	**85.** (c)	**86.** (c)	**87.** (c)	**88.** (a)
89. (b)	**90.** (c)	**91.** (c)	**92.** (d)	**93.** (c)	**94.** (a)	**95.** (b)	**96.** (d)
97. (c)	**98.** (a)	**99.** (a)	**100.** (d)	**101.** (b)	**102.** (c)	**103.** (a)	**104.** (a)
105. (c)	**106.** (b)	**107.** (d)	**108.** (c)	**109.** (c)	**110.** (c)	**111.** (c)	**112.** (b)
113. (b)	**114.** (b)	**115.** (a)	**116.** (c)	**117.** (a)	**118.** (d)	**119.** (b)	**120.** (a)

121. (c)	**122.** (c)	**123.** (a)	**124.** (a)	**125.** (b)	**126.** (b)	**127.** (a)	**128.** (a)
129. (b)	**130.** (a)	**131.** (a)	**132.** (a)	**133.** (a)	**134.** (a)	**135.** (a)	**136.** (d)
137. (c)	**138.** (a)	**139.** (d)	**140.** (b)	**141.** (c)	**142.** (c)	**143.** (a)	**144.** (a)
145. (b)	**146.** (a)	**147.** (a)	**148.** (a)	**149.** (c)	**150.** (b)	**151.** (a)	**152.** (c)
153. (d)	**154.** (c)	**155.** (a)	**156.** (a)	**157.** (b)	**158.** (a)	**159.** (a)	**160.** (a)
161. (c)	**162.** (c)	**163.** (a)	**164.** (b)	**165.** (b)	**166.** (a)	**167.** (d)	**168.** (a)
169. (a)	**170.** (b)	**171.** (a)	**172.** (b)	**173.** (b)	**174.** (a)	**175.** (b)	**176.** (a)
177. (b)	**178.** (c)	**179.** (a)	**180.** (a)	**181.** (a)	**182.** (a)	**183.** (c)	**184.** (a)
185. (a)	**186.** (c)	**187.** (a)	**188.** (a)	**189.** (b)	**190.** (c)	**191.** (b)	**192.** (a)
193. (c)	**194.** (c)	**195.** (a)	**196.** (b)	**197.** (a)	**198.** (a)	**199.** (a)	**200.** (b)

Supervised Learning: Classification

Learning Objectives

At the end of this chapter, you will be able to:

- Describe the basics of supervised learning
- Describe the steps involved in supervised learning algorithms
- Explain the *K*-nearest neighbor (KNN) algorithm
- Explain the structure and function of decision trees
- Discuss the concept and application of random forests
- Identify different types of linear classifiers
- Explain the advantages of linear classifiers
- Learn how to determine the weights of a linear classifier
- Describe generative models for linear classifiers
- Describe linear discriminant analysis (LDA)
- Explain the naive Bayes classifier
- Explain polynomial regression
- Discuss multinomial logistic regression
- Explain ordinal logistic regression
- Define the perceptron and its activation function
- Identify types of perceptron models (single-layer and multi-layer)
- Discuss the limitations of the perceptron model
- Explain support vector machines (SVM) and their types (linear and non-linear)
- Explain the concept of hyperplanes and support vectors in SVM
- Identify various applications of supervised learning
- Discuss the limitations and challenges of supervised learning

8.1 Introduction

Supervised machine learning (ML) is a branch of artificial intelligence (AI) that uses labeled data to train algorithms that can classify data or predict outcomes. Labeled data means that some input data is already tagged with the correct output, which helps the algorithm learn the relationship between the input and output variables. The goal of supervised learning is to find a mapping function that can generalize well to new data. There are two main types of supervised learning problems: classification and regression.

Classification problems involve assigning data into discrete categories, such as spam or not spam, dog or cat, apple or orange (Fig. 8.1). For example, a supervised learning algorithm can be used to classify emails based on their content and sender. The algorithm would learn from a training set of emails that have been labeled as spam or not spam by humans. Then, it would apply the learned rules to new emails and assign them to the appropriate category.

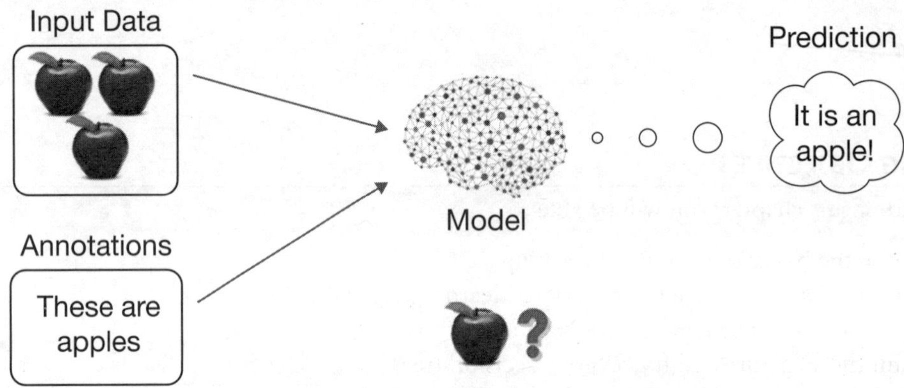

Figure 8.1 Classification algorithm example

Regression problems involve predicting a continuous value, such as house price or sales revenue. For example, a supervised learning algorithm can be used to predict the price of a house based on its features and location. The algorithm would learn from a training set of houses that have been labeled with their prices by humans. It would then apply the learned function to new houses and estimate their prices.

Supervised learning has many applications in various domains, such as image classification, fraud detection, risk assessment, spam filtering, etc. It can help organizations solve real-world problems at scale and with high accuracy. However, supervised learning requires a lot of labeled data, which can be expensive and time-consuming to obtain. It may suffer from overfitting or underfitting. It may be biased or unfair, if the data or the algorithm reflects some underlying discrimination or prejudice. Therefore, supervised learning requires careful design and evaluation to ensure its validity and reliability.

Steps

1. Collect and label the training data, which should have enough features and examples to represent the problem domain. Features are the attributes or variables that describe the data, such as height, weight, color. Labeling the data means assigning a target value to each example, such as a category, a score, a rating, etc. The target value is what the algorithm aims to predict or classify. The training data should be representative of the problem domain, meaning that it should capture the diversity and complexity of the real-world data.
2. Choose an appropriate algorithm for the problem, based on the type of data, the complexity of the function, and the computational resources available. There are many types of supervised learning algorithms, such as linear regression, logistic regression, decision trees, support vector machine (SVM), and neural networks. Each algorithm has its own advantages and disadvantages, and some are more suitable for certain types of data or problems than others. The complexity

of the function refers to how flexible or expressive the algorithm is, meaning how well it can capture the non-linear or intricate patterns in the data. The computational resources refer to how much time and memory the algorithm requires to run and learn from the data.

3. Train the algorithm on the training data, by adjusting its parameters to minimize the error or loss function, which measures how well the algorithm fits the data. Parameters are the variables that control how the algorithm works, such as weights, biases, thresholds, etc. The error or loss function is a mathematical formula that quantifies how far the algorithm's predictions are from the actual target values. The goal of training is to find the optimal values of the parameters that minimize the error or loss function. This can be done by using various optimization techniques, such as gradient descent, stochastic gradient descent, genetic algorithms, etc.
4. Evaluate the performance of the algorithm on a test set, which is a subset of the training data that is not used for training. The test set is used to measure how well the algorithm generalizes to new data. Generalization is the ability of the algorithm to make accurate predictions on unseen or novel data that is not part of the training data. The performance of the algorithm can be evaluated by using various metrics, such as accuracy, precision, recall, F1-score, mean squared error, etc.
5. Use the algorithm to make predictions on new data or improve it by tuning its parameters or using more data. For example, if the algorithm is trained to classify images of animals into cats or dogs, it can be used to classify a new image of an animal that is not part of the training or test set. Alternatively, if the performance of the algorithm is not satisfactory on the test set or new data, it can be improved by tuning its parameters or using more data. Tuning parameters means changing their values slightly to see if they improve the error or loss function. Using more data means adding more examples or features to the training data to make it more representative and informative.

Some of the most common types of supervised classification algorithms are *K*-nearest neighbor (KNN), decision tree, random forest, support vector machine (SVM), linear classifiers, and neural networks.

8.2 *K*-Nearest Neighbor

K-nearest neighbor (KNN) is a supervised ML algorithm that can be used for both classification and regression tasks. The main idea behind KNN is that similar data points tend to have similar labels or outputs. Therefore, given a new data point, KNN can predict its label or output by looking at the labels or outputs of its K closest neighbors in the feature space. The feature space is the n-dimensional space where each dimension represents a feature or attribute of the data. For example, if we have data about flowers with two features, petal length and petal width, then the feature space is a 2D plane where each point represents a flower.

The goal of KNN is to correctly classify unknown instances by finding similar cases in its training data set that have already been labeled correctly and applying those labels to the unknown instances. To do this, we must first define a distance metric for measuring two data points' proximity, such as Euclidean distance or cosine similarity. Secondly, we must choose an appropriate value for K – this determines how many neighbors will be used when making predictions about an unknown instance. Finally, we must decide which type of weighting scheme should be used when combining votes from each neighbor – uniform weighting assigns equal importance to all neighbors. In contrast, inverse weighting assigns greater importance to closer neighbors than those far away.

KNN can also be used for regression tasks; instead of assigning class labels based on majority voting amongst neighborhoods, it calculates the mean value or average amongst them (inverse weights may still apply).

KNN is one of the most straightforward yet powerful ML algorithms that allow us to classify unseen data using similarity measures between different observations while avoiding costly parameter estimation procedures like explicit modeling techniques needed in other algorithms such as general linear models. Also, since no prior assumptions are made regarding underlying distribution, it is suitable even when a limited amount of training examples exist, making it a robust model capable of producing reliable results across different scenarios. In addition, portals like Netflix, Amazon, YouTube, and others use them in their recommendation engines.

To find the *K* closest neighbors of a new data point, KNN uses a distance metric such as Euclidean, Manhattan, or Hamming. Each of these distances is defined in the equations below:

$$\text{Euclidean Distance:} \sqrt{\sum_{i=1}^{k} (x_i - y)^2}, \tag{8.1}$$

$$\text{Manhattan Distance:} \sum_{i=1}^{k} |x_i - y|, \tag{8.2}$$

where x_i represents the training data point and y represents the test data point.

The distance metric measures how far apart two data points are in the feature space. The smaller the distance, the more similar the data points.

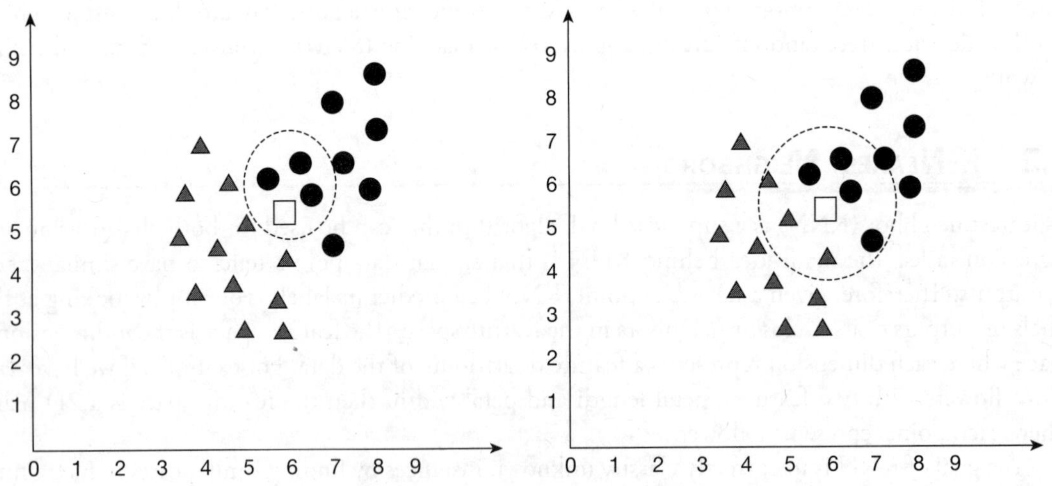

Figure 8.2 KNN example

Consider Fig. 8.2. The two classes of training points are plotted as circles and triangles. The test instance is shown as a square. The objective is to classify the square as a triangle or circle. First, identify the distance between the square and all other points (circles and triangles). Display the same in a table with serial number, training point shape (circle, triangle), and distance as columns. Sort the table in the ascending order of distance. If $K = 3$, choose the first 3 rows (for example, circle, circle, circle). Thus, we classify that the square as belonging to the circle class. If $K = 7$, choose the first 7 rows (4 circles, 3 triangles). Here also, we classify the square as belonging to the circle class.

Class *P* data (Table 8.1) is shown as black circles and class N data as grey circles. The unknown class for the last input is shown with a cross sign (Fig. 8.3).

Table 8.1 Classes *P* and N represented as *x* and *y*

x	*y*	Class
58	8	*P*
58	9	*P*
58	13	*P*
60	9	*P*
60	10	*P*
63	10	*P*
63	11	*P*
60	14	N
63	14	N
65	11	N
65	12	N
65	15	N
68	12	N
61	11	?

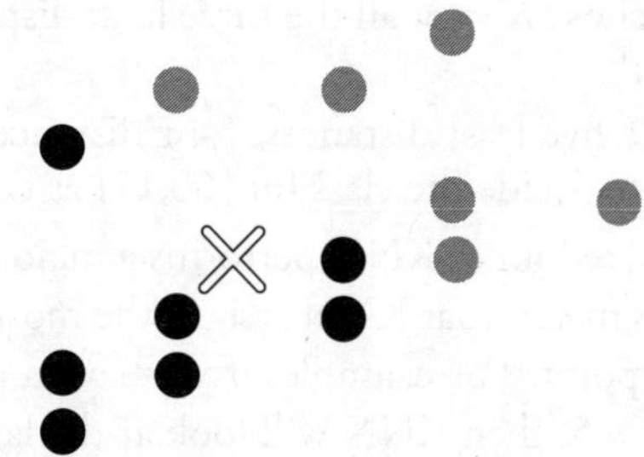

Figure 8.3 Classes *P* and N represented as a graph

To determine the class for the query input (61,11), we need to determine the distance between each point to the query input and sort the distances in non-descending order (Table 8.2).

Table 8.2 Euclidean distance between *x* and *y* and (60,11)

x	y	Class	Euclidean distance between (x, y) and $(60,11)$	Ranking distance
58	8	*P*	3.6	8
58	9	*P*	2.82	3
58	13	*P*	2.82	3
60	9	*P*	2	2
60	10	*P*	1	1
63	10	*P*	3.16	7
63	11	*P*	3	5
60	14	N	3	5
63	14	N	4.24	9
65	11	N	5	10
65	12	N	5.09	11
65	15	N	6.40	12
68	12	N	8.06	13

Based on the distances, if we chose $K = 3$, all the three least distances belong to class *P* and hence we decide the class for $(60,11)$ as P.

If we chose $K = 5$, among the five least distances, four distances belong to class *P* and one distance belongs to class N. Hence we decide the class for $(60,11)$ as P based on the majority.

Once the *K* closest neighbors are found, KNN performs a majority vote to determine the label or output of the new data point. This means that KNN assigns the most common label or output among the *k* neighbors to the new data point. For example, if we have a classification problem with three classes, A, B, and C, and we set $K = 5$, then KNN will look at the labels of the 5 nearest neighbors of the new data point and count how many times each label appears. If there are 3 neighbors with label A, 1 neighbor with label B, and 1 neighbor with label C, then KNN will predict that the new data point belongs to class A.

KNN is a simple and intuitive algorithm that can handle multi-class problems, meaning that it can deal with more than two classes. It can also handle non-linear boundaries between classes, meaning that it can capture complex patterns in the data. However, KNN has some drawbacks as well. One of them is that it can be computationally expensive for large data sets, because it must calculate the distance between every pair of data points and sort them to find the *k* nearest neighbors. Another drawback is that it can be sensitive to noise and outliers in the data because they can affect the majority vote. Moreover, KNN can be affected by the choice of *K* and the distance metric, which can influence the accuracy and performance of the algorithm.

In this example, we will use KNN to choose a restaurant based on the ratings, price and cuisine of five data sets. The data sets are shown in Table 8.3.

Table 8.3 Restaurant rating example

Restaurant	Rating	Price	Cuisine
A	4.5	$$$	Italian
B	3.0	$$	Chinese
C	4.0	$$	Mexican
D	3.5	$	Indian
E	4.0	$$$	French

Suppose we want to choose a restaurant that has a high rating, a moderate price and a cuisine that we like. We can use KNN to find the restaurants that are the most similar to our preferences. We first need to define a distance metric that measures how close two restaurants are based on their features. One possible metric is the Euclidean distance, which is calculated as:

$$d = \sqrt{(r_1 - r_2)^2 + (p_1 - p_2)^2 + (c_1 - c_2)^2}$$

where *r*, *p* and *c* are the rating, price, and cuisine of each restaurant, respectively. The cuisine feature can be encoded as a numerical value, such as 1 for Italian, 2 for Chinese, and so on. Using this metric, we can calculate the distance between our preferences and each restaurant (Table 8.4).

Table 8.4 Restaurant rating example, distance calculation

Restaurant	Distance
A	1.41
B	2.24
C	1.0
D	2.0
E	2.24

We then choose the K nearest neighbors, which are the restaurants with the smallest distances. In this case, $K = 3$, so we select A, C and D as the candidates.

The final step is to assign a label to our preferences based on the majority vote of the neighbors. Since two out of three neighbors have a rating of 4.0, we can label our preferences as having a rating of 4.0. Similarly, since two out of three neighbors have a price of $$, we can label our preferences as having a price of $$. Finally, since there is no clear majority for the cuisine, we can choose the one that we like the most or use another criterion to break the tie. Therefore, based on KNN, we can choose restaurant C as the best option for our preferences.

8.3 Decision Trees

Decision tree is a popular and widely used ML algorithm that can perform both classification and regression tasks. They are based on the idea of dividing the data into smaller and more homogeneous subsets based on some criteria, such as the value of a feature or the outcome of a test. The result is a tree-like structure where each node represents a subset of the data, each branch represents a decision rule, and each leaf represents a final prediction.

The decision tree starts at the top of the tree (the root node) and goes down by following specific rules. The root node of a decision tree contains specific attributes, which are then split into branches or paths at each level, leading to different nodes containing further attributes until one path leads to a particular outcome or decision. Building this flowchart model starts with selecting an attribute from the large data set, then dividing it into multiple tiers by splitting it according to some conditions, and finally arriving at a conclusion after numerous intermediate stages/nodes.

For example, suppose we want to predict whether it will rain tomorrow in Chennai (India), based on various inputs such as temperature, humidity, wind speed, etc. To do this, we can use a decision tree that starts with the most important input, which is temperature. Temperature is a good starting point because research has shown that it has a strong influence on weather patterns.

The decision tree will have a root node that represents temperature, and then it will split into two branches: one for low temperature and one for high temperature. Each branch will then have another node that represents another input, such as humidity. Humidity is also important because it affects how much moisture is present in the air, which can lead to rain. The decision tree will then split again into more branches based on the values of humidity: low, medium, or high.

Each branch will continue to split into more nodes and branches until we reach a leaf node, which is the final prediction. A leaf node will tell us whether it will rain tomorrow or not, based on the combination of inputs that led to it.

For example, if the temperature is low and the humidity is high, the leaf node might say 'Yes, it will rain tomorrow'. If the temperature is high and the humidity is low, the leaf node might say 'No, it will not rain tomorrow'. To draw a flow chart for the above scenario, we can use the following steps:

1. Start with a start symbol (a circle or an oval) and write "Start" inside it.
2. Draw an arrow from the start symbol to a decision symbol (a diamond) and write "Temperature?" inside it. This symbol represents the question of whether the temperature is low or high.
3. Draw two arrows from the decision symbol, one pointing to the left and one pointing to the right. Label the left arrow as "Low" and the right arrow as "High". These arrows represent the possible outcomes of the question.

4. Draw another decision symbol at the end of each arrow and write "Humidity?" inside them. These symbols represent the question of whether the humidity is low or high.
5. Draw two arrows from each decision symbol, one pointing down and one pointing up. Label the down arrows as "Low" and the up arrows as "High". These arrows represent the possible outcomes of the question.
6. Draw a leaf node (a rectangle) at the end of each arrow and write the corresponding prediction inside them. For example, if the temperature is low and the humidity is high, write "Yes, it will rain tomorrow". If the temperature is high and the humidity is low, write "No, it will not rain tomorrow".
7. Draw an arrow from each leaf node to an end symbol (a circle or an oval) and write "End" inside it.

The flow chart should look something like Fig. 8.4.

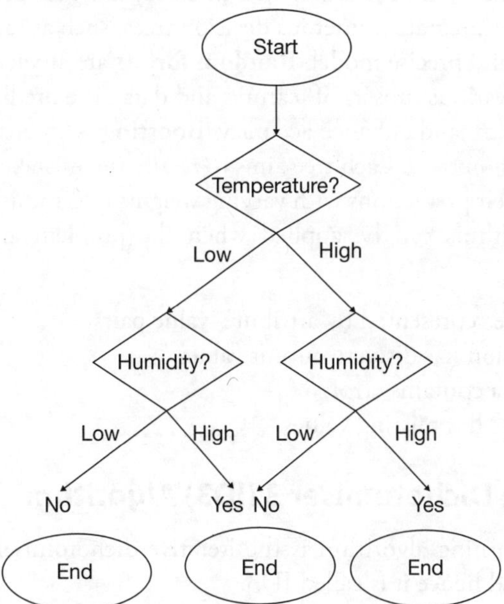

Figure 8.4 Structure of a decision tree

Decision trees are known for efficiently handling both categorical and numerical data. Furthermore, unlike other ML algorithms like linear regression, they do not require any initialization feature scaling before the model is created. They also provide better accuracy compared with other techniques due to non-linearity that is built into the models. Furthermore, data manipulation regarding missing values is optional while working with the decision tree technique since they can build up classifiers even if some values are missing from the data set.

Another excellent application is in medical diagnosis systems where they prove very helpful and accurate while diagnosing patients' diseases by analyzing massive data sets containing symptoms and treatment information.

Decision trees may encounter issues such as overfitting or underfitting. Overfitting occurs when the model is excessively intricate and accurately fits the available data but fails to generalize to unseen data effectively. Underfitting is when the model is overly simplistic, fails to capture the data adequately, and exhibits subpar performance when applied to new data. To mitigate these issues, specific methodologies can be employed on decision trees, including pruning, regularization, or ensemble methods.

Pruning is the elimination or reduction of specific nodes or branches in a tree that does not significantly add to the prediction or increase error. For instance, if a node possesses just a limited number of samples or minimal information gain, it might be pruned to streamline the model and mitigate the likelihood of overfitting. Pruning can be performed either during the tree's construction (pre-pruning) or after the tree has structure (post-pruning).

Regularization imposes limits or penalties on the tree's growth, such as restricting the depth, the number of nodes, or the minimum samples needed at each node. These limitations can impede the tree's growth, preventing it from becoming excessively large or deep and mitigating the risk of overfitting. Regularization can enhance the computational efficiency and interpretability of the model as well.

Ensemble approaches integrate numerous decision trees, such as random forests or boosting, to construct a more resilient and precise model. **Random forests** are an ensemble technique that makes many decision trees using various subsets of features and data. The predictions of these trees are then averaged to decrease variation and enhance accuracy. **Boosting** is an ensemble strategy that progressively generates many decision trees. Each tree aims to rectify the mistakes produced by the preceding trees and then combines their predictions with varying weights to diminish bias and enhance accuracy.

Thus, decision tree algorithms can be applied when the problem and data suits the following requirements:

- When the instances are represented by attribute–value pairs
- When the target function has discrete output values
- When the training data contains errors
- When the training data has missing values

8.3.1 The Iterative Dichotomiser 3 (ID3) Algorithm

The basic decision tree learning algorithm is the iterative dichotomiser (ID) algorithm. The third version is quite popular and hence it is called ID3.

ID3 learns decision trees by constructing it in top-down fashion. As the name suggests, the algorithm is an iterative method. Dichotomiser means dividing – the algorithm divides the attributes into two or more groups depending on how the decision tree will be constructed. To determine which attribute should be considered as the root node, a statistical evaluation of all the attributes is performed.

Steps

1. Calculate the entropy of the whole data set.
2. Calculate the information gain for each attribute. The attribute with maximum information gain is the root node.
3. If all examples are of the same class, then return the single node with the corresponding class label.
4. Otherwise split the data set into subsets using the attribute A which has maximum information gain.

5. Repeat the process till all the attributes are exhausted or further expansion of the tree is not possible (when the nodes are leaf nodes).

The metrics used in the ID3 algorithm for selection of attributes as nodes in the decision tree are information gain and entropy.

Information gain or gain calculates the reduction in entropy. The node with highest information gain will be chosen. It is calculated as follows:

$$\text{Gain}(S,A) = \text{Entropy}(S) - \sum_{v \in \text{values}(A)} \frac{|S_v|}{|S|} \text{Entropy}(S_v), \tag{8.3}$$

where S represents the entire data set, A represents the attribute, and S_v represents the number of instances for which the attribute A has the value S_v.

In ML, **entropy** is a measure of the randomness or disorder within a data set. It quantifies the amount of uncertainty or impurity in the data, helping to determine how well a model can make predictions. It is calculated as follows:

$$\text{Entropy}(S) = -\sum_{i=1}^{c} p_i \log_2 p_i, \tag{8.4}$$

where S represents the entire data set, c represents the number of classes, and p_i represents the probability of class i.

For example, consider the play_tennis data given in Chapter 6. It has a total of 14 attributes, with 9 positive instances and 5 negative instances.

$$\text{Entropy}(S) = -\left(\frac{9}{14}\log_2\frac{9}{14} + \frac{5}{14}\log_2\frac{5}{14}\right)$$

$$= -(0.643 * (-0.6371) + 0.357 * (-1.486)$$

$$= -(-0.410 + (-0.530)) = 0.940$$

Next we calculate the information gain for each attribute (Table 8.5).

Table 8.5 Information gain of Sky with values of (Sunny, Overcast and Rain)

Attribute: Sky
Values: $\{$Sunny, Overcast, Rain$\}$
Sunny 5 attributes → 2 instances with label yes and 3 instances with label no
Overcast 4 attributes → 4 instances with label yes and 0 instances with label no
Rain 5 attributes → 3 instances with label yes and 2 instances with label no

$\text{Entropy}(\text{Sky}_{\text{Sunny}})$ $= -\left(\frac{2}{5}\log_2\frac{2}{5} + \frac{3}{5}\log_2\frac{3}{5}\right)$ $= -(0.4*(-1.322) + 0.6*(-0.737))$ $= -(-0.528 - 0.442) = 0.970$	$\text{Entropy}(\text{Sky}_{\text{Overcast}})$ $= -\left(\frac{4}{4}\log_2\frac{4}{4} + \frac{0}{4}\log_2\frac{0}{4}\right) = 0$ $\text{Entropy}(\text{Sky}_{\text{Rain}})$ $= -\left(\frac{3}{5}\log_2\frac{3}{5} + \frac{2}{5}\log_2\frac{2}{5}\right)$ $= 0.970$
$\text{Gain}(S, \text{Sky})$ $= 0.940 - \left(\frac{5}{14}*0.971 + \frac{4}{14}*0 + \frac{5}{14}*0.971\right)$ $= 0.940 - (0.357*0.971 + 0.357*0.971)$ $= 0.940 - (0.347 + 0.347) = 0.246$	

Similarly the information gain for the other attributes should be calculated (Tables 8.6, 8.7, and 8.8).

Table 8.6 Information gain of Temp with values of (Hot, Mild and Cool)

Attribute: Temp	
Values: $\{\text{Hot, Mild, Cool}\}$	
Hot 4 attributes → 2 instances with label yes and 2 instances with label no	
Mild 6 attributes → 4 instances with label yes and 2 instances with label no	
Cool 4 attributes → 3 instances with label yes and 1 instance with label no	
$\text{Entropy}(\text{Temp}_{\text{Hot}})$ $= -\left(\frac{2}{4}\log_2\frac{2}{4} + \frac{2}{4}\log_2\frac{2}{4}\right) = 1$	$\text{Entropy}(\text{Temp}_{\text{Cool}})$ $= -\left(\frac{3}{4}\log_2\frac{3}{4} + \frac{1}{4}\log_2\frac{1}{4}\right)$ $= -(0.75*(-0.415) + 0.25*(-2))$ $= -(-0.31125 - 0.5)$ $= 0.81125$
$\text{Entropy}(\text{Temp}_{\text{Mild}})$ $= -\left(\frac{4}{6}\log_2\frac{4}{6} + \frac{2}{6}\log_2\frac{2}{6}\right)$ $= -(0.67*(-0.5778) + 0.33*(-1.5995))$ $= -(-0..387 - 0.527)$ $= 0.914$	

Gain(S, Temp)
$=0.940-\left(\frac{4}{14}*1+\frac{6}{14}*0.81125+\frac{4}{14}*0.914\right)$
$=0.940-(0.286+0.348+0.357+0.261)$
$=0.940-(0.895)=0.045$

Table 8.7 Information gain of Humidity with values of (High and Normal)

Attribute: Humidity	
Values : {High, Normal}	
High 7 instances → 3 instances with label yes and 4 instances with label no	
Normal 7 instances → 6 instances with label yes and 1 instance with label no	
Entropy$\left(\text{Humidity}_{\text{High}}\right)$ $=-\left(\frac{3}{7}\log_2\frac{3}{7}+\frac{4}{7}\log_2\frac{4}{7}\right)$ $=-(0.428*(-1.2243)+0.571*(-0.8084))$ $=-(-0.524-0.461)=0.988$	Entropy$\left(\text{Humidity}_{\text{Normal}}\right)$ $=-\left(\frac{6}{7}\log_2\frac{6}{7}+\frac{1}{7}\log_2\frac{1}{7}\right)$ $=-(0.857*-0.22263+0.142*-2.816)$ $=-(-0.191-.0.399)=0.59$
Gain(S, Humidity) $=0.940-\left(\frac{7}{14}*0.988+\frac{7}{14}*0.59\right)$ $=0.940-(0.494+0.295)$ $=0.940-(0.789)=0.151$	

Table 8.8 Information gain of Wind with values of (Weak and Strong)

Attribute: Wind
Values: {Weak, Strong}
Weak 8 instances → 6 instances with label yes and 2 instances with label no
Strong 6 instances → 3 instances with label yes and 3 instances with label no

$\text{Entropy}(\text{Wind}_{\text{Weak}})$ $= -\left(\frac{6}{8}\log_2\frac{6}{8} + \frac{2}{8}\log_2\frac{2}{8}\right)$ $= -(0.75*(-0.415) + 0.25*(-2))$ $= -(-0.31125 - 0.5) = 0.81125$	$\text{Entropy}(\text{Wind}_{\text{Strong}})$ $= -\left(\frac{3}{6}\log_2\frac{3}{6} + \frac{3}{6}\log_2\frac{3}{6}\right)$ $= -(-0.5 - 0.5) = 1$
Gain(S,Wind) $= 0.940 - \left(\frac{8}{14}*0.81125 + \frac{6}{14}*1\right)$ $= 0.940 - (0.463 + 0.428)$ $= 0.940 - (0.891) = 0.049$	

Thus, information gain for the attributes Sky, Temp, Humidity and Wind are 0.246, 0.045, 0.151 and 0.049, respectively. Sky is chosen as the root node since it has maximum information gain. The decision tree at this stage looks like Fig. 8.5.

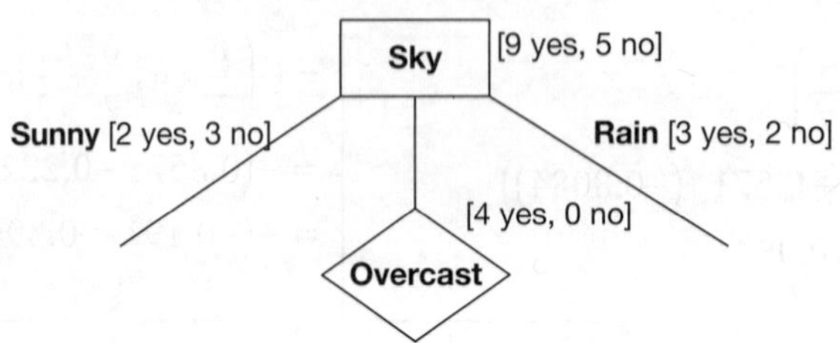

Figure 8.5 Structure of a decision tree (rain example)

After fixing the root node, the child nodes should be selected. For the Overcast value, all instances are yes and hence it becomes the leaf node. Now the task is to determine the child nodes. The process is repeated. Instead of the whole data set, we select the child nodes with condition Sky = Sunny (Tables 8.9, 8.10, 8.11) and Sky = Rain (Tables 8.12 and 8.13).

Table 8.9 Information gain of Temp with values (Hot, Mild and Cool) and also Sunny (2 Yes, 3 No)

Attribute: Temp with Sky = Sunny(2yes, 3no)
Values: {Hot, Mild, Cool}
Hot 2 instances → 0 instances with label yes and 2 instances with label no
Mild 2 instances → 1 instance with label yes and 1 instances with label no
Cool 1 instance → 1 instances with label yes and 0 instance with label no

$\text{Entropy}\left(\text{Temp}_{\text{Hot}}\right)$ with respect to Sky=Sunny $=-\left(\frac{0}{2}\log_2\frac{0}{2}+\frac{2}{2}\log_2\frac{2}{2}\right)=0$	$\text{Entropy}\left(\text{Temp}_{\text{Cool}}\right)$ with respect to Sky = Sunny $=-\left(\frac{1}{1}\log_2\frac{1}{1}+\frac{0}{1}\log_2\frac{0}{1}\right)=0$
$\text{Entropy}\left(\text{Temp}_{\text{Mild}}\right)$ with respect to Sky = Sunny $=-\left(\frac{1}{2}\log_2\frac{1}{2}+\frac{1}{2}\log_2\frac{1}{2}\right)=1$	$\text{Gain}(\text{Sky\_Sunny}, \text{Temp})$ $=0.970-\left(\frac{2}{5}*0+\frac{2}{5}*1+\frac{1}{5}*0\right)$ $=0.970-(0.40)=0.570$

Table 8.10 Information gain of Humidity with values (Hot, and Normal) and also Sunny (2 Yes, 3 No)

Attribute : Humidity with Sky = Sunny(2yes,3no)	
Values : {Hot, Normal}	
High 3 instances → 0 instances with label yes and 3 instances with label no	
Normal 2 instances → 2 instances with label yes and 0 instance with label no	
$\text{Entropy}\left(\text{Humidity}_{\text{High}}\right)$ with respect to Sky = Sunny $=-\left(\frac{0}{3}\log_2\frac{0}{3}+\frac{3}{3}\log_2\frac{3}{3}\right)=0$	$\text{Entropy}\left(\text{Humdity}_{\text{Normal}}\right)$ $=-\left(\frac{2}{2}\log_2\frac{2}{2}+\frac{2}{2}\log_2\frac{2}{2}\right)=0$
$\text{Gain}(\text{Sky\_Sunny}, \text{Humidity})$ $=0.970-(0)=0.970$	

Table 8.11 Information gain of Wind with values (Weak, and Strong) and also Sunny

Attribute : Wind with Sky = Sunny(2yes,3no)
Values : {Weak, Strong}
Weak 3 instances → 1 instances with label yes and 2 instances with label no
Strong 2 instances → 1 instance with label yes and 1 instance with label no

Entropy(Wind$_{Weak}$) with respect to Sky = Sunny $= -\left(\frac{1}{3}\log_2\frac{1}{3} + \frac{2}{3}\log_2\frac{2}{3}\right)$ $= -(0.33 * -1.5995 + 0.67 * -0.5778) = 0.915$	Entropy(Wind$_{Strong}$) $= -\left(\frac{1}{2}\log_2\frac{1}{2} + \frac{1}{2}\log_2\frac{1}{2}\right) = 1$
Gain(Sky_Sunny, Humidity) $= 0.970 - \left(\frac{3}{5} * 0.915 + \frac{2}{5} * 1\right) = 0.021$	

Of the three information gains calculated with respect to Sky = Sunny, the attribute Humidity should be selected since it has maximum information gain. All the 3 instances with Humidity = High have label no and the 2 instances with Humidity = Normal have label yes.

Now the decision tree looks like Fig. 8.6.

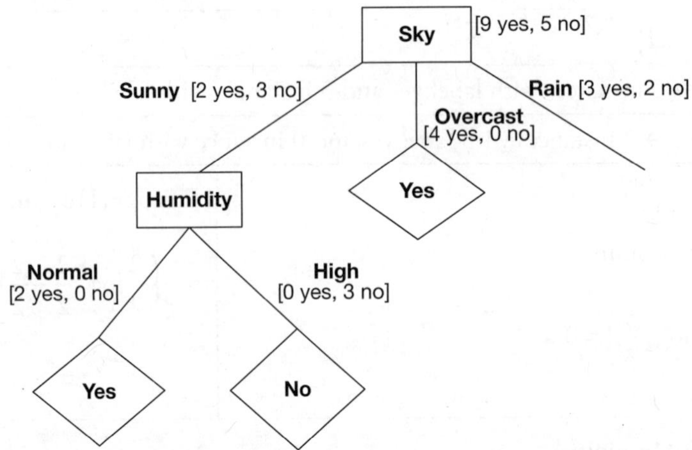

Figure 8.6 Intermediate stage in the development of decision tree

Table 8.12 Information gain of Temp with values (Hot, Mild and Cool) and also Rain (3 Yes, 2 No)

Attribute : Temp with Sky = Rain(3yes, 2no)
Values : {Hot, Mild, Cool}
Hot 0 instances → 0 instances with label yes and 0 instances with label no
Mild 3 instances → 2 instances with label yes and 1 instance with label no
Cool 2 instance → 1 instance with label yes and 1 instance with label no

$\text{Entropy}(\text{Temp}_{\text{Hot}})$ with respect to Sky = Rain $=0$	$\text{Entropy}(\text{Temp}_{\text{Mild}})$ with respect to Sky = Rain $=-\left(\frac{2}{3}\log_2\frac{2}{3}+\frac{1}{3}\log_2\frac{1}{3}\right)=0.915$
$\text{Entropy}(\text{Temp}_{\text{Mild}})$ with respect to Sky = Rain $=-\left(\frac{1}{2}\log_2\frac{1}{2}+\frac{1}{2}\log_2\frac{1}{2}\right)=1$	$\text{Gain}(\text{Sky\_Sunny},\text{Temp})$ $=0.970-\left(\frac{3}{5}*0.915+\frac{2}{5}*1\right)$ $=0.970-(0.949)=0.021$

Table 8.13 Information gain of Wind with values (Weak and Strong) and also Rain (3 Yes, 2 No)

Attribute : Wind with Sky = Rain (3yes, 2no)	
Values : {Weak, Strong}	
Weak 3 instances → 3 instances with label yes and 0 instances with label no	
Strong 2 instances → 0 instances with label yes and 2 instances with label no	
$\text{Entropy}(\text{Wind}_{\text{Weak}})$ with respect to Sky = Rain $=0$	$\text{Entropy}(\text{Wind}_{\text{Strong}})$ $=0$
$\text{Gain}(\text{Sky\_Sunny},\text{Humidity})$ $=0.970-(0)=0.970$	

Since Wind has high information gain with respect to Sky = Rain, Wind is chosen as child node. Now the decision tree looks like Fig. 8.7.

The decision tree cannot be further expanded since all leaf nodes are reached. From the decision tree we can observe that all the attributes need not take part in the construction of decision tree. In this case, the attribute Temp could not be part of the decision tree; thus, we can infer that Temp does not have any significant impact in making a decision.

Finally, the decision rules can be generated from the root node to every node in a disjunction-of-conjunctions manner.

The player will play tennis if

$$(\text{Sky}=\text{Overcast})\vee(\text{Sky}=\text{Sunny}\wedge\text{Humidity}=\text{Normal})\vee(\text{Sky}=\text{Rain}\wedge\text{Humidity}=\text{Normal})$$

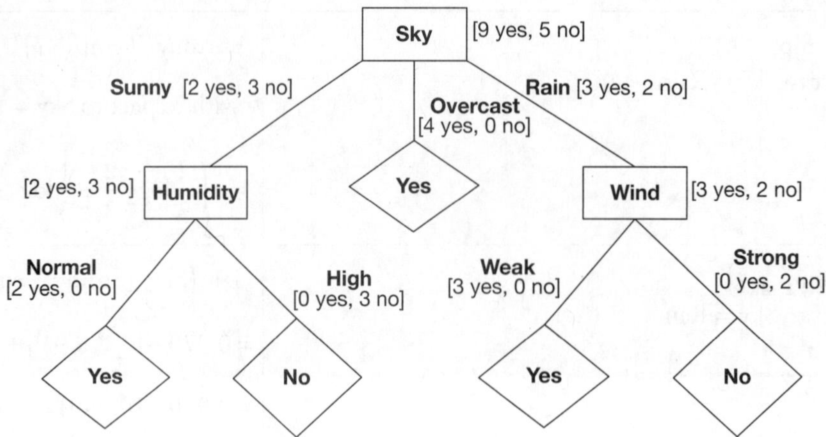

Figure 8.7 The final decision tree

Searching the Hypothesis Space in Decision Tree Learning: The hypothesis space includes all possible decision trees for the given data. The ID3 algorithm searches the hypothesis space from simple to complex, similar to the one in the hill-climbing approach. It starts with an empty decision tree. The root node is selected. Further nodes are created. The hill-climbing approach is employed using information gain and entropy measures.

ID3 searches the complete space of all finite discrete-valued functions. It maintains only one hypothesis. An important concern is that it has no backtrack option. This indicates that it may get struck on local optima. It may converge to local minima.

It employs all the training samples at each step. But in every step, each attribute is evaluated based on already selected attributes. This means that the hypothesis will be subject to refinement at every step and due to this property, it is less sensitive to errors.

Inductive Bias in Decision Tree Learning: For the given data, there may be decision trees consistent with the data. ID3 prefers short trees to large trees. ID3 selects trees where nodes are attributes with high information gain. Attributes that have high information gain are close to the root node and such attributes are preferred over the other attributes.

The basic difference between ID3 and the candidate elimination algorithm is that ID3 searches a complete hypothesis space (searches all possible decision trees) incompletely whereas the candidate elimination algorithm searches an incomplete hypothesis space completely.

8.3.2 The C4.5 Algorithm

The C4.5 algorithm is an improvement on the ID3 algorithm, addressing several of its limitations:

- **Handling continuous attributes**: Unlike ID3, which can only handle nominal attributes, C4.5 can handle continuous attributes by creating threshold-based splits. For example, if you have a data set with a continuous attribute like "age," C4.5 can determine a threshold (such as age > 30) to split the data.
- **Handling missing data**: C4.5 can handle missing data by using a probabilistic approach. It assigns the most probable value based on the distribution of known values. For example, assume

there is a customer data set with missing values in the "income" attribute. C4.5 assigns the most probable income value based on the distribution of known incomes in the data set.

- **Overcoming overfitting**: C4.5 uses pruning to reduce overfitting. It removes branches that have little importance, making the model more generalizable. For example, assume there is a weather data set used to predict whether to play tennis. C4.5 removes branches that do not significantly improve the prediction accuracy, such as those based on rare weather conditions.
- **Gain ratio**: C4.5 uses the gain ratio instead of information gain to overcome the bias towards attributes with many values. The gain ratio normalizes information gain by the intrinsic information of a split. For example, assume there is a data set with attributes like color and size. C4.5 uses the gain ratio to choose the best attribute for splitting, avoiding bias towards attributes with many unique values like color.

$$\text{Split Info}_A(S) = -\sum_{i=1}^{v} \frac{|D_i|}{|D|} \times \log_2\left(\frac{|D_i|}{|D|}\right) \tag{8.5}$$

Split Info represents the potential information generated by splitting the data set S into v partitions that correspond to v outcomes on attribute A.

Another metric used by C4.5 is the gain ratio, which is defined as

$$\text{Gain Ratio}(A) = \frac{\text{Gain}(A)}{\text{Split Info}_A(S)} \tag{8.6}$$

The same play_tennis data is taken again but with some continuous values for some attributes. The data set is given in Table 8.14.

Table 8.14 Predictions about Play_Tennis

Sky	Temp	Humidity	Wind	Play_Tennis
Sunny	85	85	Weak	No
Sunny	80	90	Strong	No
Overcast	83	78	Weak	Yes
Rain	70	96	Weak	Yes
Rain	68	80	Weak	Yes
Rain	65	70	Strong	No
Overcast	64	65	Strong	Yes
Sunny	72	95	Weak	No
Sunny	69	70	Weak	Yes
Rain	75	80	Weak	Yes
Sunny	75	70	Strong	Yes
Overcast	72	90	Strong	Yes
Overcast	81	75	Weak	Yes
Rain	71	80	Strong	No

If the values of the attribute are Boolean, then there will be only two branches for the attribute. Instead, if it is categorical then the number of branches for the attribute will be equal to the number of distinct values of it. If the values are continuous, then a threshold (θ) will be chosen to separate the data as $(\leq \theta)$ and $(> \theta)$. The threshold should be chosen carefully. The threshold set for Humidity is 75.

For the same play_tennis data, the gain ratio of the attributes Sky, Temp, Humidity and Wind are 1.71, 0.052, 0.191, and 0.05, respectively. The maximum gain ratio is obtained for the attribute Sky and hence it is the root node for the decision tree generated by C4.5 (Fig. 8.8).

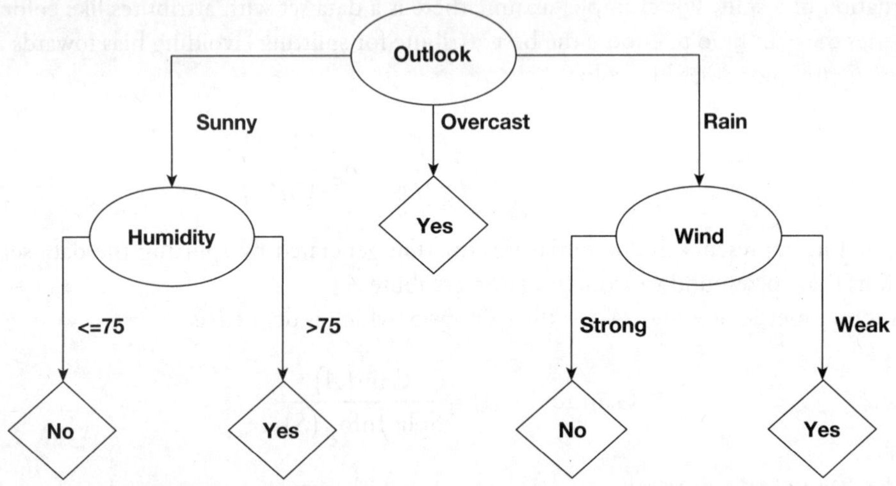

Figure 8.8 Decision tree obtained using the C4.5 algorithm

8.3.3 The CART Algorithm

CART stands for classification and regression trees. It can be used for classification and regression problems. If the target variable is set as class labels, then classification is carried out with the resultant decision tree. On the other hand, if the target variable is a number or numerical value that predicts or estimates any quantity, then regression is carried out using the decision tree obtained.

CART uses Gini Index as a metric for splitting the data. It is defined as

$$\text{Gini}(S) = 1 - \sum_{i=1}^{m} p_i^2, \tag{8.7}$$

where p_i is the probability that an instance of S belongs to a class label c_i and there are m classes in total. Gini(S) measures the total impurity of the given data set S.

To find the split, we calculate the Gini Index for each attribute. Let an attribute A be split into two sets $D1$ and $D2$ based on the two types of values. Then the Gini Index of A is calculated as

$$\text{Gini}_A(S) = \frac{|D1|}{|D|}\text{Gini}(D1) + \frac{|D2|}{|D|}\text{Gini}(D2) \tag{8.8}$$

For a discrete-valued attribute, the attribute for which the Gini Index is minimum is considered as its splitting subset. For continuous data, a similar strategy is chosen as in the case of the C4.5 algorithm.

The reduction in impurity that is incurred on attribute A is

$$\Delta \text{Gini}(A) = \text{Gini}(S) - \text{Gini}_A(S) \tag{8.9}$$

The attribute that maximizes the reduction in impurity is selected as the splitting attribute.

8.3.4 Drawbacks of Decision Tree Learning

Decision trees are a popular ML technique for classification problems. However, they also have some limitations that need to be addressed:

- **Cannot handle continuous attributes**: Decision trees can only split the data based on discrete values of the attributes. This means that if an attribute has a continuous range of values, such as height or weight, the decision tree has to discretize it into bins or intervals. This can result in loss of information and accuracy, as well as increased complexity of the tree.
- **Cannot determine how deep the decision tree grows**: Decision trees can grow very large and complex if there are many attributes and classes in the data. This can lead to overfitting, which means that the tree performs well on the training data but poorly on new or unseen data. To avoid overfitting, the decision tree needs to be pruned or stopped at some point. However, there is no clear or optimal criterion for determining when to stop growing the tree. Different pruning methods may result in different trade-offs between accuracy and complexity.
- **Cannot handle training data with missing attribute values**: Decision trees require that every instance in the training data has a value for every attribute. However, in real-world data, there may be instances with missing or unknown values for some attributes. This can pose a challenge for decision tree learning, as it is not clear how to split the data based on such attributes. There are various methods to deal with missing values, such as ignoring them, replacing them with mean or mode values, or using probabilistic models. However, each method has its assumptions and limitations.
- **Computational efficiency is high**: Decision tree learning is a greedy algorithm that tries to find the best split at each node of the tree. This means that it has to evaluate all possible splits for all possible attributes at each node. This can be computationally expensive, especially if the data has many attributes and instances. Moreover, decision tree learning does not guarantee finding the optimal or global solution, as it may get stuck in a local optimum.

8.4 Random Forests

Random forest is a type of ML algorithm that can perform classification and regression tasks. It is based on the idea of ensemble learning, which means combining multiple weak learners to create a strong learner. A **weak learner** is a simple model that can make predictions, but with a high error rate. A **strong learner** is a complex model that can make accurate predictions, but with high computational cost.

The weak learners in random forests are decision trees, which are graphical models that split the data into smaller subsets based on some criteria. For example, if we want to classify a person as having diabetes or not, we can use a decision tree that asks questions like 'Is the person's age above 50?' or 'Is the person's blood sugar level above 200?'. Each question leads to a branch in the tree, and each branch ends with a leaf node that represents a class label (diabetes or no diabetes).

Random forest uses many different decision trees. Each decision tree predicts in a random forest, and the outcome is determined by which prediction receives the most votes. This method is used to determine the random forest's result for classification tasks (Fig. 8.9).

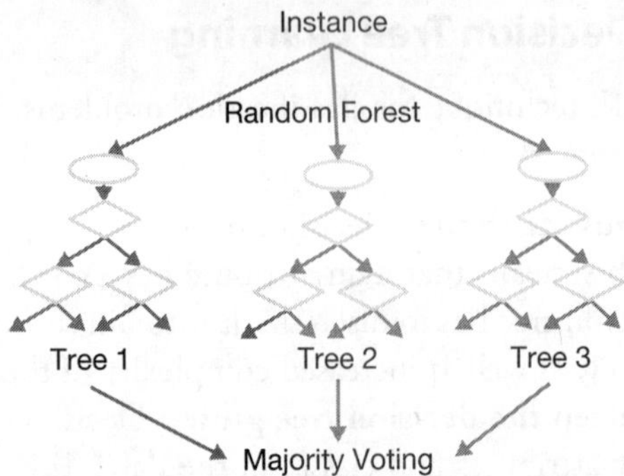

Figure 8.9 Random forest example

To illustrate how random forests work, let us consider some examples:

- Imagine that we are attempting to predict a person's BMI (body mass index) value from a data set of their heights and weights. Here, we may use a supervised learning technique, such as linear regression. However, we can take things further with random forest by considering different input parameters like age, gender, height, and weight, which may boost our prediction accuracy. To accomplish this, we would randomly choose some subset from these four input features, along with the corresponding BMI values as training examples, that is, our 'training set.' We would then build several decision trees using these subsets as inputs or features for each tree while labeling them against the BMI value, that is, the output variable or target label that we want our model to predict accurately when faced with new data points.
- Consider that you have a large set of images classified into two categories, cats and dogs, that you want to classify each time new images are presented. Of course, this could be done using other supervised learning algorithms, such as SVM. However, due to their complexity, they may not necessarily yield top accuracy scores. Here, random forest proves its worthiness by its ability not only to quantitatively analyze pixel values but also to qualitatively examine shape patterns within pixels across multiple cat–dog image instances, enabling greater accuracy at classifying the images.

Random forests do have some drawbacks. They can overfit the data, which means they learn too much from the noise and outliers in the data and fail to generalize to new data. They can also be unstable, which means small changes in the data can lead to large changes in the structure of the tree. To overcome these problems, random forests use two techniques: bagging and feature selection.

Bagging refers to bootstrap aggregation, which means sampling the data with replacement and creating multiple decision trees from these samples. Each decision tree is trained on a different subset of the data, so they are likely to have different errors and biases. By combining these trees, we can reduce the variance of the predictions and improve the accuracy. The combination can be obtained by voting for classification tasks or averaging for regression tasks. For example, if we have 10 decision trees and 7 of them predict diabetes and 3 predict no diabetes, we can use majority voting and assign diabetes as the final prediction.

Feature selection means randomly selecting a subset of features (variables) to split the data at each node of the decision tree. This reduces the correlation among the trees and increases the diversity of the ensemble. For example, if we have 100 features and we select 10 features at each node, we can create different trees that use different combinations of features to make predictions.

8.5 Linear Classifiers

Linear classifiers are a powerful ML technique used in supervised learning problems that classify new data into broad categories based on the properties of the data. Standard linear classifiers include linear SVMs and logistic regression, which use a linear decision boundary to divide data into distinct groups. The objective is to identify a decision boundary that divides the data into distinct groups and convert the output, in the case of logistic regression, to a probability between 0 and 1 using a sigmoid function. Though these methods are helpful for linearly separable data sets, kernel methods such as the kernel trick can be employed to map non-linearly separable data sets into higher dimensional spaces. Overall, linear classifiers are practical tools for classification problems. However, their efficacy can be limited by their need for linearly separable data and reliance on a single linear decision boundary.

Let us consider an example where we have a data set containing information about housing prices, such as square footage and the number of bedrooms in each house. Given their income level, we would like to use this information to predict whether someone could afford to buy one of these houses. To do this, we could use a linear classifier such as logistic regression, which would fit our data set using linear equations and generate probabilities for each observation based on its values for square footage and number of bedrooms compared with other houses in the same price range (with higher scoring observations being more likely).

This probability score could then be used to predict whether someone could buy and afford one house from our given data set with different inputted variables such as income level or zip code area, for example. Through this method, we can generate probabilities about how likely a person will be able to afford specific properties based on different criteria, which helps us make more accurate decisions about potential homebuyers' abilities without needing explicit programming instructions.

To understand how a linear classifier works, we need to introduce some mathematical notation. Let X be a vector of d features that describe an object, such as word frequencies in an email. Let y be a categorical variable that represents the class of the object, such as spam or not spam. Let K be the number of possible classes, and let w_k be a vector of weights for class k. Then, the score for class k given X is

$$s_k(X) = w_k{}^T X \tag{8.10}$$

The dot product is a way of measuring how similar two vectors are: it is high when the vectors point in the same direction and low when they point in opposite directions. The score $s_k(X)$ can be interpreted as a measure of how likely X belongs to class k based on its features.

The linear classifier then assigns X to the class with the highest score:

$$y = argmax(k)s_k(X), \tag{8.11}$$

where $argmax(k)$ means finding the value of k that maximizes $s_k(X)$. This means that the linear classifier divides the feature space into regions separated by hyperplanes, where each region corresponds to one class. A hyperplane is a generalization of a line in 2D and a plane in 3D: it is a subspace of one dimension less than the original space that splits the space into two parts. For example, in 2D, a hyperplane is a line; in 3D, a hyperplane is a plane; and in 4D, a hyperplane is a 3D space.

There are different ways of learning the weights w_k for each class k from a set of labeled training data. Some methods are based on generative models, which try to model the joint probability distribution of X and y; some methods are based on discriminative models, which try to model the conditional probability distribution of y given X; and some methods are based on optimization techniques, which try to minimize a loss function that measures the error between the predicted and true classes.

8.5.1 Advantages and Disadvantages of Linear Classifiers

The advantage of linear classifiers is that they are simple and fast to train and use, especially when the number of features is large. They can also achieve high accuracy levels for many practical problems, such as document classification or image recognition, sentiment analysis, spam detection, etc. This means that linear classifiers can handle high-dimensional data efficiently, without requiring much computational resources or memory.

Another advantage is that they are easy to interpret and explain. The linear function that defines the decision boundary of a linear classifier can be written as a weighted sum of the features, where the weights indicate the importance or relevance of each feature for the classification task.

Linear classifiers are not only fast, simple, accurate and interpretable, but also flexible and adaptable. They can be extended and modified to suit different types of data and problems. For example, linear classifiers can be combined with non-linear transformations or kernels to handle data that is not linearly separable. Linear classifiers can also be regularized or penalized to prevent overfitting or underfitting, by adding a term to the objective function that controls the complexity or smoothness of the linear function. Linear classifiers can also be integrated with other ML techniques, such as ensemble methods, boosting, bagging, etc., to improve their robustness and diversity. They can also be adapted to different learning scenarios, such as online learning, active learning, semi-supervised learning, etc., by updating their weights incrementally or selectively based on new data or feedback.

However, linear classifiers also have some limitations. For example, they cannot capture complex non-linear relationships between features and categories, and they may be sensitive to outliers or noise in the data. Therefore, linear classifiers may not work well for problems that require more expressive models, such as image recognition, natural language generation, etc.

8.5.2 Learning the Weights of a Linear Classifier

There are different methods to learn the weights of a linear classifier from a set of labeled training data. Some of these methods are generative models, which try to model the joint probability distribution of the features and the categories, and some are discriminative models, which try to model the conditional probability distribution of the categories given the features.
Examples of generative models:

Linear discriminant analysis (LDA): This method assumes that the features follow a Gaussian distribution within each category, and tries to find a linear projection that maximizes the separation between categories.

Naive Bayes classifier: This method assumes that the features are conditionally independent given the category, and tries to estimate the probability of each feature value for each category using frequency counts.

Examples of discriminative models:

Logistic regression: This method assumes that the score for each category is a logistic function of the feature values, and tries to maximize the likelihood of the observed data using gradient descent or other optimization techniques.

Perceptron: This method iteratively updates the weights based on the errors made on the training data, until no errors are made or a maximum number of iterations is reached.

Support Vector Machine (SVM): This method tries to find a hyperplane that separates the categories with a maximum margin, using quadratic programming or other optimization techniques

8.5.3 Linear Discriminant Analysis

Linear discriminant analysis (LDA) is a method that aims to find a linear projection of a high-dimensional feature space onto a lower-dimensional space that maximizes the separation between different categories of data.

It is based on two assumptions: first, that the features follow a Gaussian distribution within each category; and second, that the covariance matrices of the features are equal across all categories. These assumptions imply that the data is linearly separable, meaning that a linear decision boundary can accurately separate the different categories.

LDA works by finding a set of linear discriminants, which are directions in the feature space that best separate the different categories. LDA does this by maximizing the ratio of between-class variance to within-class variance, which is also known as **Fisher's criterion**. This ratio measures how well the projected data points are clustered by category and how far apart they are from each other.

Let us consider an example of two-dimensional data points belonging to two different categories. When we plot the data points on a two-dimensional plane, we can see that there is no straight line that can completely separate the two categories. However, if we apply LDA to this data, we can find a linear discriminant that projects the data points onto a one-dimensional line. On this line, we can see that the projected data points are more separated by category than on the original plane.

LDA is a widely used method for supervised learning that seeks to categorize data points into distinct groups according to their characteristics. An advantage of LDA lies in its straightforwardness and computational effectiveness. Estimating the mean and covariance of each class is the only requirement for LDA, which can be accomplished effortlessly using matrix operations. Next, it maps the data onto a lower-dimensional space to optimize the distinction between different classes. By reducing the dimensions and complexity of the problem, it becomes more expedient and effortless to solve.

To exemplify this benefit, let us contemplate a case of facial recognition. Assume we possess a data set comprising photographs of faces attributed to distinct individuals, and our objective is to determine the identity of each person depicted in the images. An approach to performing this task involves utilizing the unprocessed pixel values of each image as characteristics and then employing a classifier such as logistic regression or SVM. However, this strategy has several limitations. Initially, the quantity of factors is exceedingly vast, equivalent to the amount of pixels in every image. As a result, the issue becomes complex in terms of dimensions and requires significant processing resources. Furthermore, the unprocessed pixel values could fail to encompass the fundamental attributes of each face, such as its shape, color, texture, and so on. This exacerbates the issue, rendering it both cacophonous and intricate.

LDA can address these limitations by converting the original pixel information into a more significant and condensed representation. LDA accomplishes this by calculating the average and variance of each class (each individual's face) based on the training data. The mean is a statistical measure representing the arithmetic average of each person's face, while the covariance quantifies the extent to which each pixel deviates from the norm. The statistics encompass the primary attributes of each face, including its shape, color, texture, and so forth. Subsequently, LDA identifies a linear mapping that optimizes the distinction between classes by projecting the data into a space with fewer dimensions. This indicates that the projected data points are closer to the mean of their own class than the means of other classes. This simplifies the problem's classification as the classes are more clearly defined and have less overlap.

The lower-dimensional space discovered by LDA is commonly called the discriminant space because of its ability to differentiate between distinct classes. The dimensionality of this space is equivalent to the number of classes subtracted by one. For instance, when our data set consists of 10 individuals, LDA will map the data onto a 9-dimensional space. The reduced feature space is significantly smaller than the original, which may include hundreds or millions of dimensions depending on the image resolution. This dramatically reduces the computing expense and intricacy of the task. **Latent Dirichlet allocation (LDA)** is a straightforward and effective method that can enhance the accuracy and efficiency of supervised learning tasks.

An advantage of LDA is its ability to address multicollinearity, which arises when certain variables exhibit a strong correlation, leading to instability and redundancy within the model. These factors can result in overfitting, limited ability to apply knowledge to new situations, and imprecise assessments of the significance of features. LDA addresses this problem using the **pooled covariance matrix**, a weighted mean of the covariance matrices particular to each class. The covariance matrix quantifies the extent to which each attribute exhibits variation about one another and their respective contributions to the separation of classes.

Another advantage of LDA is its ability to effectively handle scenarios when the number of features far exceeds the number of training samples. This phenomenon frequently occurs in data sets with a high number of dimensions, such as photos or text, where there exists a multitude of potential features to extract from the data but an insufficient number of data points to effectively learn from.

LDA is suitable for this circumstance as it decreases the dimensionality of the data to align with the number of classes, preventing overfitting and enhancing generalization.

However, LDA has some limitations, as well. It is contingent upon certain assumptions that may not consistently apply in real-world situations. One of the underlying assumptions is that the data exhibits a Gaussian distribution characterized by a bell-shaped curve and symmetrical distribution around the mean. This assumption presupposes that the data lacks any outliers, skewness, or multimodality, all prevalent attributes in numerous data sets. Outliers have the potential to impact the mean and variance of the data, which are essential for LDA to compute the best linear discriminant..

Skewness quantifies the degree of asymmetry in the distribution of data. The skewness of the data can be either positive or negative, depending on whether the data exhibits a greater tail on the right or left side of the mean. Skewness can potentially impact the shape and position of the Gaussian curve that LDA assumes for each class.

Multimodality refers to the characteristic of data that exhibits many peaks or modes in its distribution. It suggests that the data exhibits the presence of many subgroups or clusters within each class. The presence of many modes can contradict the assumption made by LDA that each class follows unimodal Gaussian distribution.

LDA assumes that the covariance matrices of the features are equal across all categories, which means that the features have the same variability and correlation within each category. This assumption may not be realistic in some cases, where different categories may have different patterns of variation and dependence among the features.

LDA also assumes that the data is linearly separable, which means that there exists a linear boundary that can separate the data into different categories. This assumption may not hold for some complex data sets, where the data may have non-linear relationships or interactions among the features.

LDA may not perform well in high-dimensional feature spaces, where the number of features is much larger than the number of data points. In such cases, LDA may suffer from overfitting, which means that it fits too closely to the training data and fails to generalize to new data. Moreover, LDA may face computational challenges due to the large size of the covariance matrices and the eigenvalue decomposition involved in the algorithm. In such cases, other methods such as PCA may be more suitable.

8.5.4 Naive Bayes Classifier

Naive Bayes classifier is a simple but powerful ML technique that can be used for classification tasks. It consists of two parts, namely, naive and Bayes.

Naive: It is so-called because it makes a simplifying assumption that the features used to predict the outcome are independent of each other, meaning that they do not influence or depend on each other in any way. This assumption is often unrealistic in real-world scenarios, but it allows the algorithm to be fast and easy to implement. For example, suppose we want to classify a fruit as either an apple or an orange based on its color, shape, and taste. A naive Bayes classifier would assume that these three features are independent of each other and that each one contributes equally to the probability of the fruit being an apple or an orange. So, if we observe a red, spherical, and sweet fruit, the classifier would multiply the probabilities of each feature given the class and compare them to decide which class is more likely. In this case, the fruit would be classified as an apple, since red, spherical, and sweet are more likely to occur in apples than in oranges. However, this assumption of independence may not always hold true in reality.

Bayes: It is based on the application of Bayes' theorem, which states that the probability of an event A given another event B is equal to the probability of B given A multiplied by the probability of A divided by the probability of B. In other words, $P(A|B) = P(B|A) * P(A) / P(B)$.

In the context of classification, the event A is the category or class that we want to assign to an instance, and the event B is the set of features or attributes that describe the instance. For example, if we want to classify an email as spam or not spam based on its subject and sender, then A is the spam or not spam label, and B is the subject and sender information. The naive Bayes classifier tries to estimate the probability of each category given the features, $P(A|B)$, and then chooses the category with the highest probability as the prediction.

However, estimating $P(A|B)$ directly from the data can be difficult, especially if there are many features and categories. Therefore, the naive Bayes classifier makes a simplifying assumption that the features are conditionally independent given the category. This means that the probability of observing a certain combination of features given a category is equal to the product of the probabilities of each feature given that category.

For example, if we assume that the subject and sender are independent given the spam or not spam label, then $P(\text{subject and sender} \mid \text{spam}) = P(\text{subject} \mid \text{spam}) * P(\text{sender} \mid \text{spam})$.

Using this assumption, we can rewrite Bayes' theorem as follows:

$$P(A|B) = P(B|A) * P(A) / P(B)$$
$$= P(\text{feature1} \mid A) * P(\text{feature2} \mid A) * \ldots * P(\text{feature}n \mid A) * P(A) / P(B)$$

We can estimate $P(\text{feature1} \mid A)$ and $P(A)$ from the frequency counts of each feature value and category in the training data. For example, if we have 100 emails in total, 40 of them are spam and 60 are not spam, and 20 spam emails have the word 'free' in their subject while 10 not spam emails have it, then $P(\text{spam}) = 40/100 = 0.4$ and $P(\text{free} \mid \text{spam}) = 20/40 = 0.5$. We can also estimate $P(B)$ by summing up the probabilities of all possible categories given B. For example, if we want to calculate $P(\text{free})$, we can use the following formula:

$$P(\text{free}) = P(\text{free} \mid \text{spam}) * P(\text{spam}) + P(\text{free} \mid \text{not spam}) * P(\text{not spam})$$
$$= 0.5 * 0.4 + 0.1 * 0.6 = 0.26$$

Once we have all these probabilities, we can plug them into Bayes' theorem and compare the probabilities of different categories for a given instance. For example, if we want to classify an email with subject 'free trial offer' and sender 'john@example.com', we can calculate the following probabilities:

$P(\text{spam} \mid \text{free trial offer and john@example.com})$
$= P(\text{free trial offer and john@example.com} \mid \text{spam}) * P(\text{spam}) / P(\text{free trial offer and john@example.com})$
$= P(\text{free trial offer} \mid \text{spam}) * P(\text{john@example.com} \mid \text{spam}) * P(\text{spam}) / (P(\text{free trial offer} \mid \text{spam}) * P(\text{john@example.com} \mid \text{spam}) * P(\text{spam}) + P(\text{free trial offer} \mid \text{not spam}) * P(\text{john@example.com} \mid \text{not spam}) * P(\text{not spam}))$
$= 0.5 * 0.01 * 0.4 / (0.5 * 0.01 * 0.4 + 0.1 * 0.05 * 0.6) = 0.25$

P(not spam | free trial offer and john@example.com)
= *P*(free trial offer and john@example.com | not spam) * *P*(not spam) / *P*(free trial offer and john@example.com)
= *P*(free trial offer | not spam) * *P*(john@example.com | not spam) * *P*(not spam) / (*P*(free trial offer | spam) * *P*(john@example.com | spam) * *P*(spam) + *P*(free trial offer | not spam) * *P*(john@example.com | not spam) * *P*(not spam))
= 0.1 * 0.05 * 0.6 / (0.5 * 0.01 * 0.4

Consider the sample data set given below:

A	T	T	F	F	T	F	T
B	T	F	T	F	T	F	F

$$P(A)=\frac{4}{7};P(B)=\frac{3}{7};$$

The **maximum a posteriori (MAP) hypothesis** is a method in Bayesian statistics used to estimate an unknown quantity. It leverages Bayes' theorem to calculate the posterior probability of each candidate hypothesis and selects the one with the highest posterior probability. This approach combines prior knowledge (prior probability) with observed data (likelihood) to make inferences.

$$h_{MAP} = \underset{h \in H}{\operatorname{argmax}} P(h \mid D)$$

$$\Rightarrow h_{MAP} = \underset{h \in H}{\operatorname{argmax}} \frac{P(D|h)P(h)}{P(D)} \Rightarrow h_{MAP} = \underset{h \in H}{\operatorname{argmax}} P(D|h)P(h)$$

For the given example, $P(B|A)=\frac{2}{4};P(A|B)=\frac{2}{3};\Rightarrow h_{MAP} = P(A \mid B).$

For the maximum likelihood hypothesis (h_{ML}), if the prior probabilities of all the hypotheses are equal, then

$$h_{ML} = h_{MAP} = \underset{h \in H}{\arg\max} P(D \mid h).$$

Consider the play_tennis data.

$$\mathrm{P}(\text{play tennis} = \text{yes}) = \frac{9}{14}$$

$$P(\text{playtennis} = \text{no}) = \frac{5}{14}$$

Table 8.15 Probability of different combinations of values of Sky, Temp, Wind and Humidity

$P(\text{Sky} = \text{sunny} \mid \text{playtennis} = \text{yes}) = \frac{2}{9}$	$P(\text{Sky} = \text{sunny} \mid \text{playtennis} = \text{no}) = \frac{3}{5}$
$P(\text{Sky} = \text{overcast} \mid \text{playtennis} = \text{yes}) = \frac{4}{9}$	$P(\text{Sky} = \text{overcast} \mid \text{playtennis} = \text{no}) = \frac{0}{5}$
$P(\text{Sky} = \text{rain} \mid \text{playtennis} = \text{yes}) = \frac{3}{9}$	$P(\text{Sky} = \text{rain} \mid \text{play tennis} = \text{no}) = \frac{2}{5}$
$P(\text{Temp} = \text{hot} \mid \text{playtennis} = \text{yes}) = \frac{2}{9}$	$P(\text{Temp} = \text{hot} \mid \text{play tennis} = \text{no}) = \frac{2}{5}$
$P(\text{Temp} = \text{mild} \mid \text{play tennis} = \text{yes}) = \frac{4}{9}$	$P(\text{Temp} = \text{mild} \mid \text{play tennis} = \text{no}) = \frac{2}{5}$
$P(\text{Temp} = \text{cool} \mid \text{play tennis} = \text{yes}) = \frac{3}{9}$	$P(\text{Temp} = \text{cool} \mid \text{play tennis} = \text{no}) = \frac{1}{5}$
$P(\text{Humidity} = \text{high} \mid \text{play tennis} = \text{yes}) = \frac{3}{9}$	$P(\text{Humidity} = \text{high} \mid \text{play tennis} = \text{no}) = \frac{4}{5}$
$P(\text{Humidity} = \text{normal} \mid \text{play tennis} = \text{yes}) = \frac{6}{9}$	$P(\text{Humidity} = \text{normal} \mid \text{play tennis} = \text{no}) = \frac{1}{5}$
$P(\text{Wind} = \text{weak} \mid \text{play tennis} = \text{yes}) = \frac{6}{9}$	$P(\text{Wind} = \text{weak} \mid \text{play tennis} = \text{no}) = \frac{2}{5}$
$P(\text{Wind} = \text{strong} \mid \text{play tennis} = \text{yes}) = \frac{3}{9}$	$P(\text{Wind} = \text{strong} \mid \text{play tennis} = \text{no}) = \frac{3}{5}$

Now, given a test instance with possible values for each attribute, we can apply Bayes' theorem to determine whether the given instance belongs to the yes or no class.

Let the test instance be

$$t = \{\text{Sky} = \text{sunny}, \text{Temp} = \text{cool}, \text{Humidity} = \text{high}, \text{wind} = \text{strong}\}$$

We need to determine whether this test instance will allow the player to play tennis or not.

$$p(t) = \max\left(p(t|\text{yes}), p(t|\text{no})\right)$$

$$P(\text{sunny}|\text{yes}) \times P(\text{cool}|\text{yes}) \times p(\text{high} \mid \text{yes}) \times p(\text{strong} \mid \text{yes}) \times p(\text{yes})$$

$$\Rightarrow \frac{2}{9} \times \frac{3}{9} \times \frac{3}{9} \times \frac{3}{9} \times \frac{9}{14} = 0.0053$$

$$P(\text{sunny}|\text{no}) \times P(\text{cool}|\text{no}) \times p(\text{high}|\text{no}) \times p(\text{strong}|\text{no}) \times p(\text{no})$$

$$\Rightarrow \frac{3}{5} \times \frac{1}{5} \times \frac{4}{5} \times \frac{3}{5} \times \frac{5}{14} = 0.0205$$

For the given instance, $p(t|no) > p(t \mid yes)$ and hence play tennis = no

The main disadvantage of this approach is that it is a time-consuming process and is not practical if the hypothesis space is very large. Though it is not practical to implement, it sets a standard to compare the performance of other concept learning algorithms.

To further simplify, we formulate with the following assumptions:

All hypotheses' are equally probable, that is, $P(h) = \frac{1}{|H|} \forall h \in H$

The likelihood probability is defined as $P(D|h) = \begin{cases} 1, & \text{if } h(x_i) = c_i \\ 0, & \text{else} \end{cases}$

If $h(x_i) = c_i$ then we call the hypothesis consistent, otherwise it is inconsistent.

Based on the assumptions, it is evident that for all inconsistent hypotheses, $P(h|D) = 0$.

For consistent hypotheses, it is calculated as

$$P(h|D) = \frac{\text{Likelihood} \times \text{Prior}}{\text{Evidence}} \Rightarrow \frac{1 \times \frac{1}{|H|}}{P(D)}$$

The evidence is calculated as

$$P(D) = \sum_{h_i \in H} P(D|h_i) P(h_i)$$

Each hypothesis in the hypothesis space is either consistent or inconsistent.

Let H_1 represents the set of all consistent hypotheses and H_2 represents the set of all inconsistent hypotheses. Let n_1 represent the cardinality of H_1 and n_2 represent the cardinality of H_2. Then,

$$P(D) = \sum_{h_i \in H_1} P(D|h_i) P(h_i) + \sum_{h_i \in H_2} P(D|h_i) P(h_i)$$

$$\Rightarrow \sum_{h_i \in H_1} 1 \times \frac{1}{|H|} + \sum_{h_i \in H_2} 0 \times \frac{1}{|H|}$$

$$\Rightarrow \sum_{h_i \in H_1} \frac{1}{|H|}$$

$$\Rightarrow \frac{n_1}{|H|}$$

Thus, we can write the posterior probability for consistent hypotheses as

$$P(h|D) = \frac{\text{Likelihood} \times \text{Prior}}{\text{Evidence}} \Rightarrow \frac{1 \times \frac{1}{|H|}}{P(D)} \Rightarrow \frac{1 \times \frac{1}{|H|}}{\frac{n_1}{|H|}} \Rightarrow \frac{1}{n_1}$$

8.5.4.1 Bayes' Optimal Classifier

Bayes' theorem is used to calculate conditional probability. The same is used to determine the maximum a posteriori (MAP). The general question that arises is "What can be the most probable hypothesis?" or "What can be the most probable classification for a new instance?". To answer these questions, Bayes' optimal classifier is used.

Let the training set be represented as D and the test set be represented as V. Let $v_i \in V$ be an instance of the test data set V. The optimal classification for the new instance v_i using Bayes' optimal classifier is determined as

$$\underset{v_i \in V}{\arg\max} \sum_{h_j \in H} P(v_i \mid h_j) P(h_j \mid D) \tag{8.12}$$

Consider three hypotheses h_1, h_2, h_3 with posterior probabilities 0.45, 0.3 and 0.25, respectively, where h_1 belongs to the positive class and h_2 and h_3 belongs to negative class. Since the posterior probability of h_1 is high, h_{MAP} a new instance x is recognized as $x \in h_1$.

$$P(h_1 \mid D) = 0.45; P(\text{positive} \mid h_1) = 1; P(\text{negative} | \text{h}_1) = 0$$

$$P(h_2 \mid D) = 0.3; P(\text{positive} \mid h_2) = 0; P(\text{negative} \mid h_2) = 1$$

$$P(h_3 \mid D) = 0.25; P(\text{positive} \mid h_3) = 0; P(\text{negative} \mid h_3) = 1$$

$$\sum_{h_i \in H} P(\text{positive} \mid h_i) P(h_i \mid D) = 0.45$$

$$\sum_{h_i \in H} P(\text{negative} \mid h_i) P(h_i \mid D) = 0.55$$

However, from Bayes' optimal classifier, it can be determined as

$$\underset{v_i \in V}{\arg\max} \sum_{h_j \in H} P\left(v_i \mid h_j\right) P(h_j \mid D) \Rightarrow \underset{v_i \in V}{\arg\max} (0.45, 0.55) = 0.55$$

Bayes' optimal classifier suggests that the new instance x belongs to the negative class.

8.5.4.2 Bayesian Belief Networks

The naive Bayes classifier assumes that for the target value given, all the variables or attributes are conditionally independent, whereas Bayesian belief networks allow conditional independence over a subset of variables. A Bayesian belief network or simply Bayesian network provides the probability distribution over a set of variables.

Let $X = \left(X_1, X_2, \cdots, X_n\right)$ denote a set of random variables where each $X_i \in V\left(X_i\right)$. A Bayesian network is a directed acyclic graph that specifies a joint distribution over X as a product of conditional distributions on each node. It is represented as

$$P\left(X_1 = x_1, X_2 = x_2, \cdots, X_n = x_n\right) = \prod_{i=1}^{n} p(x_i \mid \text{parents}\left(x_i\right)) \tag{8.13}$$

Consider a simple Bayesian network (Fig. 8.10).

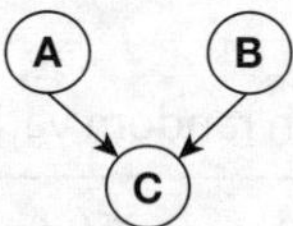

Figure 8.10 Example of a simple Bayesian belief network

$$P\left(A, B, C\right) = P(C|A, B) P\left(A\right) P\left(B\right)$$

For a Bayesian network, there exist two components – a graphical structure to show the conditional independence assumptions and probability values for each variable given its parents. The directed edges represent the direct dependence. An absence of an edge between any two variables represents conditional independence.

If the graph is assumed as only three nodes A, B and C with no edge at all, it indicates that all the variables A, B and C are conditionally independent. In such case, the marginal independence is defined using joint probability distribution (cross-product rule of probability) as

$$P\left(A, B, C\right) = P\left(A\right) P\left(B\right) P\left(C\right)$$

Consider the Bayesian network where B and C are conditionally independent given A (Fig. 8.11).

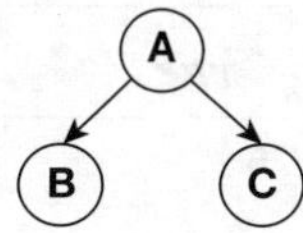

Figure 8.11 Bayesian network where B and C are conditionally independent

$$P(A,B,C) = P(B|A)P(C|A)P(A)$$

For example, X has installed an alarm in his house to detect any theft that occurs in his absence. The alarm sometimes responds even if a pedestrian passes through the house. Y and Z are the neighbors of X and they assured him that they will call when the alarm rings (Fig. 8.12).

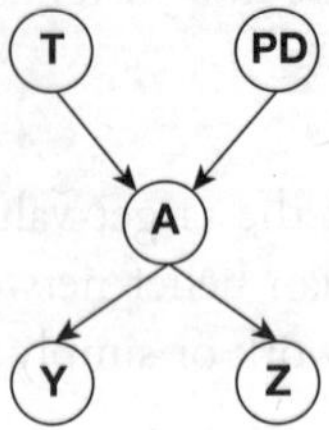

Figure 8.12 Random variables *T, PD, A, Y,* and *Z* representing different events or states

$$P(T,PD,A,Y,Z) = P(Y|A)P(Z|A)P(A|T,PD)P(T)P(PD)$$

Given the conditional independence tables as

$$P(T = True) = 0.002 \Rightarrow P(T = False) = 0.998$$

$$P(PD = True) = 0.001 \Rightarrow P(PD = False) = 0.999$$

Table 8.16 Table with random variables *T, PD,* and *P(A)*

T	PD	$P(A = True)$	$P(A = False)$
True	True	0.94	0.06
True	False	0.95	0.05
False	True	0.69	0.31
False	False	0.001	0.999

Table 8.17 Table with random variables *Y* and *P(Y)*

A	$P(Y = True)$	$P(Y = False)$
True	0.91	0.09
False	0.05	0.95

Table 8.18 Table with random variables *A* and *P(Z)*

A	$P(Z = True)$	$P(Z = False)$
True	0.75	0.25
False	0.02	0.98

Problem Statement: Calculate the probability of A given no theft and no pedestrian, but Y and Z call X.

$$P(Y,Z,A,\neg T,\neg PD) = P(Y|A)P(Z|A)P(A|\neg T,\neg PD)P(\neg T)P(\neg PD)$$

$$\Rightarrow P(Y,Z,A,\neg T,\neg PD) = 0.91 \times 0.75 \times 0.001 \times 0.998 \times 0.999 = 0.00068045$$

Thus, the Bayesian belief network is a directed acyclic graph representing the joint distribution. Inference or reasoning in this network enables efficient computation of the appropriate conditional probabilities.

8.5.4.3 Expectation Maximization Algorithm

Expectation maximization (EM) and Bayesian belief networks (BBNs) are both powerful frameworks in the field of probabilistic modeling and statistical inference. EM is an iterative method used for finding maximum likelihood or MAP estimates of parameters in statistical models, where the model depends on unobserved latent variables. BBNs, on the other hand, are a type of probabilistic graphical model that represent a set of variables and their conditional dependencies through a directed acyclic graph. The relationship between EM and BBNs lies in the fact that EM can be used as a computational approach to perform efficient parameter estimation in complex BBNs, especially when dealing with incomplete data sets.

A data set contains two sets of variables, namely, observed and unobserved. The **observed variables** are those that are directly measured. The **unobserved** or **hidden variables** are those that are inferred from the observed variables. The hidden variables are also called latent variables. A model defined over a data set that has both observed and unobserved variables is said to be a **latent variable model**.

The EM algorithm can be used for many purposes like for predicting the missing values in the data set, find the local maximum likelihood parameters, etc.

Steps

Input: Incomplete data

Step 1: Initialization: Initialize all parameters with initial values. Then provide the incomplete data. We assume that the data comes from a probability distribution.

Step 2: Expectation: Guess the values of the missing data based on the observed data.

Step 3: Maximization: Complete the data generated in the Expectation step to update the values of the parameters.

Step 4: Check for Convergence: If the values are not converged, go to Step 2 and repeat until convergence occurs.

Assume that there are two coins, C1 and C2. The probability of getting heads with C1 is θ_1 and the probability of getting heads with C2 is θ_2. We have to find the values of θ_1 and θ_2 by performing various experiments.

Let each coin be tossed 10 times and we choose to repeat the experiment 5 times. The outcome for each coin in every trail is given in Table 8.19.

Table 8.19 Five experiments with two coins (C1 and C2) tossed 10 times

Experiment – 1	C1	H	T	T	T	H	H	T	H	T	H
Experiment – 2	C2	H	H	H	H	T	H	H	H	H	H
Experiment – 3	C1	H	T	H	H	H	H	H	T	H	H
Experiment – 4	C2	H	T	H	T	T	T	H	H	T	T
Experiment – 5	C1	T	H	H	H	T	H	H	H	T	H

$$\theta_1 = \frac{\text{Number of times head occured using } C1}{\text{Total number of times } C1 \text{ is tossed}}$$

$$\theta_2 = \frac{\text{Number of times head occured using C2}}{\text{Total number of times C2 is tossed}}$$

Table 8.20 Five experiments with two coins (C1 and C2) tossed 10 times (summary view)

Experiment – 1	C2	5H	5T
Experiment – 2	C1	9H	1T
Experiment – 3	C1	8H	2T
Experiment – 4	C2	4H	6T
Experiment – 5	C1	7H	3T

$$P(\theta_1) = \frac{24}{30} = 0.8$$

$$P(\theta_2) = \frac{9}{20} = 0.45$$

Suppose the information about which coin is tossed goes missing. Then the problem becomes challenging. In such cases, the EM algorithm can be applied. The latent variables are the identity of the coins.

The initialization of the parameters with some random values is the first step. Let $\widehat{\theta_1} = 0.60$ and $\widehat{\theta_2} = 0.50$l. In order to perform the second step, we need to assume that the data follows a binomial distribution. Here, the probability can be determined as

$$P_x = \binom{n}{x} p^x q^{n-x},$$

where P is the binomial probability, x is the number of times for a specific outcome within n trials, $\binom{n}{x}$ is the number of combinations, p is the probability of success on a single trial, and q is the probability of failure on a single trial.

Experiment 1

$$P(E|C1)=\binom{10}{5}\times 0.6^{5}\times 0.4^{5}=252\times 0.078\times 0.01=0.197$$

$$P(E|C2)=\binom{10}{9}\times 0.5^{9}\times 0.5^{1}=252\times 0.0019\times 0.5=0.239$$

$$P(C1|E)=\frac{0.197}{0.431}=0.45$$

$$P(C2|E)=\frac{0.239}{0.09}=0.55$$

Experiment 2

$$P(E|C1)=\binom{10}{9}\times 0.6^{9}\times 0.4^{1}=10\times 0.011\times 0.4=0.44$$

$$P(E|C2)=\binom{10}{9}\times 0.5^{9}\times 0.5^{1}=10\times 0.00195\times 0.5=0.0097$$

$$P(C1|E)=\frac{0.44}{0.4497}=0.978$$

$$P(C2|E)=\frac{0.0097}{0.4497}=0.022$$

Experiment 3

$$P(E|C1)=\binom{10}{8}\times 0.6^{8}\times 0.4^{2}=45\times 0.016\times 0.16=0.1152$$

$$P(E|C2)=\binom{10}{8}\times 0.5^{8}\times 0.5^{2}=45\times 0.0039\times 0.25=0.043$$

$$P(C1|E)=\frac{0.1152}{0.1582}=0.73$$

$$P(C2|E) = \frac{0.043}{0.1582} = 0.27$$

Experiment 4

$$P(E|C1) = \binom{10}{4} \times 0.6^4 \times 0.4^6 = 210 \times 0.1296 \times 0.004 = 0.1088$$

$$P(E|C2) = \binom{10}{4} \times 0.5^4 \times 0.5^6 = 210 \times 0.0156 \times 0.0625 = 0.2048$$

$$P(C1|E) = \frac{0.1088}{0.3136} = 0.347$$

$$P(C2|E) = \frac{0.2048}{0.3136} = 0.653$$

Experiment 5

$$P(E|C1) = \binom{10}{7} \times 0.6^7 \times 0.4^3 = 120 \times 0.0279 \times 0.064 = 0.21427$$

$$P(E|C2) = \binom{10}{7} \times 0.5^7 \times 0.5^3 = 120 \times 0.00781 \times 0.0125 = 0.01172$$

$$P(C1 \mid E) = \frac{0.21427}{0.22644} = 0.948$$

$$P(C2 \mid E) = \frac{0.01172}{0.22644} = 0.052$$

Table 8.21 Analysis of experiments for coin A

Exp – #	#H	#T	$P(C1 \mid E)$	Coin A	
Exp – 1	5H	5T	0.45	$0.45 \times 5 = 2.25H$	$0.45 \times 5 = 2.25T$
Exp – 2	9H	1T	0.978	$0.978 \times 9 = 8.802H$	$0.978 \times 1 = 0.978T$
Exp – 3	8H	2T	0.73	$0.73 \times 8 = 5.84H$	$0.73 \times 2 = 1.46T$
Exp – 4	4H	6T	0.347	$0.347 \times 4 = 1.388H$	$0.347 \times 6 = 2.082T$
Exp – 5	7H	3T	0.948	$0.948 \times 7 = 6.636H$	$0.948 \times 3 = 2.844T$
				$24.916H$	$9.614T$

Table 8.22 Analysis of experiments for coin B

Exp – #	#H	#T	$P(C2 \mid E)$	Coin B	
Exp – 1	5H	5T	0.55	$0.55 \times 5 = 2.75H$	$0.45 \times 5 = 2.75T$
Exp – 2	9H	1T	0.022	$0.022 \times 9 = 0.198H$	$0.022 \times 1 = 0.022T$
Exp – 3	8H	2T	0.27	$0.27 \times 8 = 2.16H$	$0.27 \times 2 = 0.54T$
Exp – 4	4H	6T	0.653	$0.653 \times 4 = 2.612H$	$0.653 \times 6 = 3.918T$
Exp – 5	7H	3T	0.052	$0.052 \times 7 = 0.364H$	$0.052 \times 3 = 1.56T$
				$8.084H$	$8.79T$

$$P(\theta_1{}') = \frac{24.916}{24.916 + 9.614 = 34.53} = 0.72$$

$$P(\theta_2{}') = \frac{8.084}{8.084 + 8.79 = 16.874} = 0.48$$

Since $0.72 > 0.48$ we can infer that the probability of getting head from coin C1 is large than in coin C2. On comparison, the value of $P(\theta_1{}') = 0.72$ is closer to $P(\theta_1) = 0.80$ and $P(\theta_2{}') = 0.48$ is also closer to $P(\theta_2) = 0.45$.

Using step 3 of the algorithm, we can take the new values 0.72 and 0.48 and repeat the process till the values of any two successive iterations has negligible or no change.

8.5.5 Logistic Regression

Logistic regression is a linear model used when the output variable is binary, meaning it has two possible values: yes or no. It attempts to model the likelihood of the output variable having one of two values. The equation for this model is as follows:

$$\log(\text{odds}) = \beta 0 + \beta 1x1 + \beta 2x2 + \ldots + \beta p\, xp,$$

where odds is the probability of the output variable being one of the two values; $x1, x2, \ldots, xp$ are the input variables; $\beta 0$ is the intercept; and $\beta 1, \beta 2, \ldots, \beta p$ are the slopes.

For example, we can predict whether someone will buy a particular product (yes/no). In order to do that, we can look at past customer behavior, such as how often they purchased similar products from the same company or how much money they typically spent on products from the company. By looking at past information, we can create an ML model that can precisely predict the likelihood of someone purchasing our product based on their past behavior.

Once the model has been created, it must be tested using existing data to see if it predicts outcomes with enough accuracy for us to use in real-world applications. If the model performs well enough, we can use it for making decisions about customers without having access to all of their past behavior; this process is known as **predictive analytics**, and it is used by many businesses today for better decision-making around marketing campaigns and customer targeting strategies.

Logistic regression can be classified into three types (Table 8.23) based on the order. In binomial (binary) logistic regression, there can be only two possible types of dependent variables. In multinomial logistic regression, there can be three or more possible unordered types of the dependent variable. Finally, in ordinal logistic regression, there can be three or more possible ordered types of dependent variables.

Table 8.23 Characteristics of types of logistic regression models

Characteristics	Binary logistic regression	Multinomial logistic regression	Ordinal logistic regression
Outcome	Binary outcome	Multiple outcomes	Ordered outcomes
Estimation	Maximum likelihood	Maximum likelihood	Probit or logit link function
Error function	Cross-entropy	Softmax	Cumulative logit link function
Assumptions	Independence of errors, linearity of log odds, constant variance in the conditional distribution of the dependent variable given a value of the predictor variables	Same as binary LR + equal probabilities across categories	Same as binary LR + proportional odds assumption
Interpretation	Odds ratio	Probability ratios	Size measures effect

8.5.5.1 *Binary Logistic Regression*

The dependent variable in binary logistic regression can only have two values, usually coded as 0 and 1. The goal is to predict the probability of the dependent variable being one based on the values of the independent variables. The logistic function is used to model the relationship between the independent and dependent variables. It is an S-shaped curve that transforms the linear combination of independent variables into a probability value between 0 and 1.

The logistic function is defined as:

$$P(Y=1) = 1 / (1 + e\text{^}{-}(b0+b1X1+b2X2+\ldots+bnXn)),$$

where $P(Y=1)$ is the probability of the dependent variable being 1, $b0$ is the intercept, $b1$, $b2$,..., bn are the coefficients, and $X1$, $X2$,..., Xn are the independent variables.

In logistic regression, the coefficients represent the change in the dependent variable's log odds for a one-unit change in the corresponding independent variable. The log-odds of the dependent variable being one is defined as:

$$\log(\text{odds}) = \log(P(Y=1) / (1-P(Y=1))) = b0+b1X1+b2X2+\ldots+bnXn$$

Binomial logistic regression is commonly used in ML to predict customer churn, which is the probability that a customer will stop using a product or service. It is also used in credit scoring to predict the probability of default on loan

A bank has historical data on previous loans, including information on the borrower's credit score, income, employment history, and whether they defaulted. Using this data, the bank wants to build a binomial logistic regression model to predict future loan applicants' default probability (Table 8.24).

Table 8.24 Credit score, income, and employment history

Credit score	Income (in thousands)	Employment history (in years)	Default
650	50	5	0
700	60	7	0
600	40	3	1
550	35	2	1
750	70	10	0

We have five observations in this example, each with four (4) independent variables and one (1) dependent variable (default). Our goal (binary logistic regression) is to create a model to predict default based on the independent variables. To build the model, we can use the binomial logistic regression formula, which models the probability of a binary response variable (in this case, default) as a function of one or more independent variables. The model's output is the probability of default, which ranges from 0 to 1. The model equation will look something like this:

logit(p) = $b0$ + $b1$*credit_score + $b2$*income + $b3$*employment_history,

where p is the probability of default, $b0$ is the intercept, and $b1$, $b2$, and $b3$ are the coefficients for the independent variables credit_score, income, and employment_history, respectively.

We can make predictions for new loan applicants using the estimated coefficients from the model. For example, a new applicant has a credit score of 620, an income of \$45,000, and 4 years of employment history. We can plug these values into the model equation to get an estimated probability of default:

$$\text{logit}(p) = -2.576 + 0.002*620 + 0.056*45 - 0.690*4$$
$$\text{logit}(p) = -2.576 + 1.24$$
$$\text{logit}(p) = -1.336$$
$$p = 0.207$$

According to this model, this applicant's estimated probability of default is 0.207, or 20.7%.

Polynomial Regression

Consider data that is highly correlated but not linear in nature. In such cases, polynomial regression is performed on the data to fit a polynomial equation.

The general equation of a polynomial regression is of the form.

$$h_\theta(x) = \theta_0 + \theta_1 x + \theta_2 x^2 + \cdots + \theta_m x^m$$

The polynomial regression best approximates the relationship between dependent variable(s) and independent variable(s). The polynomial models are used to approximate a complex non-linear relationship.

To find the right degree of the model's polynomial, forward or backward selection can be used. **Forward selection** increases the degree until the best fit is possible. The model can be tested starting from the second degree. In **backward selection**, a higher degree polynomial is chosen and reduces the order of the polynomial until the best fit is reached.

8.5.5.2 *Multinomial Logistic Regression*

Multinomial logistic regression (MLR) is an extended version of binary logistic regression that allows for the dependent variable to have more than two possible unordered categories. The equation for the model is as follows:

$$\log(\text{odds}) = \beta 0j + \beta 1jx1 + \beta 2jx2 + \ldots + \beta pjxp,$$

where j is the category of the dependent variable, $x1, x2, \ldots, xp$ are the independent variables, $\beta 0j$ is the intercept for the jth category, and $\beta 1j, \beta 2j, \ldots, \beta pj$ are the slopes for the jth category.

The odds are then transformed into probabilities using the softmax function, which produces a probability distribution over the possible categories:

$$P(y=j \mid x) = e\text{^}(\beta 0j + \beta 1jx1 + \beta 2jx2 + \ldots + \beta pjxp) \,/\, (\textstyle\sum k=1 \text{ to } K\, e\text{^}(\beta 0k + \beta 1kx1 + \beta 2kx2 + \ldots + \beta pkxp)),$$

where y is the dependent variable and j is the category; $x1, x2, \ldots, xp$ are the independent variables, K is the number of categories; and $\beta 0k, \beta 1k, \beta 2k, \ldots, \beta pk$ is the slopes for the kth category.
MLR can be used in:

- Natural language processing (NLP), to determine a text's categorization based on its content, such as news articles or tweets.
- Images, to predict an image's category, such as an animal or plant, based on the value of its attributes.
- Bioinformatics, to forecast the class membership of genes based on expression levels.

MLR can handle both categorical and continuous variables, making it flexible and adaptable to different data types. It can also handle missing data and outliers, common in real-world data sets.
Here are some examples of MLR in ML:

Sentiment analysis: A company can use MLR to predict the sentiment of customer reviews, such as positive, negative, or neutral, based on the raw text content itself.

Suppose a company wants to analyze customer reviews of their product to determine each review's sentiment. Assume they have a data set of 100 reviews labeled as positive, negative, or neutral. They also have a set of features for each data set, like the number of positive and negative words, the length of the review, and the presence/absence of specific keywords.

The company can now split this data set into training and testing sets. Then, they would use the training set to train the model, which involves finding the weights for each feature that maximize the likelihood of the observed data on the model. Once the model is trained, the company can start using it to predict the sentiment of new reviews.
Suppose the company has a review with the following features:

Number of positive words: 10
Number of negative words: 3
Length of review: 100 words
Presence of keyword "love": yes
Presence of keyword "hate": no

Given these features, the model would use the weights learned during training to calculate the probability of each sentiment (positive, negative, or neutral). So, for example, it might calculate:

Probability of positive sentiment: 0.8
Probability of negative sentiment: 0.1
Probability of neutral sentiment: 0.1

Based on these probabilities, the model would predict the review's positive sentiment. The company can use this multinomial logistic regression model to predict the sentiment of new reviews and use this information to improve its product or marketing strategy.

Image recognition: A researcher can use multinomial logistic regression to predict bird species in an image based on their features, such as color and shape.
Gene expression analysis: A biologist can use MLR to predict the class membership of genes, whether disease-related or not, based on their expression levels.

8.5.5.3 Ordinal Logistic Regression

Ordinal logistic regression is used for classification tasks with more than two possible ordered categories for the dependent variable. It is like binary and multinomial logistic regression but with ordered dependent variables. The equation for the model is as follows:

$$\log(\text{odds}) = \beta 0j + \beta 1jx1 + \beta 2jx2 + \ldots + \beta pjxp,$$

where j is the category of the dependent variable, $x1, x2, \ldots, xp$ are the independent variables, $\beta 0j$ is the intercept for the jth category, and $\beta 1j, \beta 2j, \ldots, \beta pj$ are the slopes for the jth category.

The odds are then transformed into cumulative probabilities using the cumulative distribution function:

$$P(y \leq j \mid x) = 1 / (1 + e\text{^}{-}(\beta 0j + \beta 1jx1 + \beta 2jx2 + \ldots + \beta pjxp)),$$

where y is considered as the dependent variable, j is the category, and the independent variables are $x1, x2, \ldots,$ and xp.

Ordinal logistic regression is widely utilized in various fields, including healthcare, education, and the social sciences. For instance, ordinal logistic regression can be used in the medical field to forecast the severity of a disease based on several clinical factors, including age, blood pressure, and cholesterol levels. Based on their academic achievements, such as test scores, attendance, and involvement, students' grades can be predicted using ordinal logistic regression in education. In social sciences, ordinal logistic regression can predict the level of agreement on a political issue based on demographic variables such as age, gender, and education.

Ordinal logistic regression can handle categorical and continuous variables, making it flexible and adaptable to different data types. It can also handle missing data and outliers, common in real-world data sets.

Here are some more examples of ordinal logistic regression in ML:

Disease severity prediction: A healthcare provider can use ordinal logistic regression to predict the severity of a disease, such as mild, moderate, or severe, based on various clinical variables, such as blood pressure, cholesterol levels, and age.

Student grade prediction: A teacher can use ordinal logistic regression to predict the grade of a student, such as A, B, or C, based on their academic performance, such as test scores, attendance, and participation.

Political agreement prediction: A researcher can use ordinal logistic regression to predict the level of agreement on a political issue, such as strongly agree, agree, or disagree, based on demographic variables, such as age, gender, and education.

8.5.6 Perceptron

Perceptron is an AI technique that has been used for binary classification tasks since the 1960s. It works by multiplying multiple inputs with their assigned weights and then adding these results to form a single output. This single output value is then compared to a predetermined threshold value to make the final binary classifications. By adjusting the weights of each input, the algorithm can learn from its mistakes and improve its accuracy over time.

Perceptron is a linear regression algorithm that can be used for both linear and non-linear classification tasks. Furthermore, by introducing non-linear transformations of the input features through techniques such as polynomial expansion or kernel methods, perceptron can model non-linear decision boundaries and thus address more complex classification problems. Therefore, through appropriate feature engineering of the input data, perceptron can tackle both linear and non-linear regression tasks.

A perceptron is a node-and-connection artificial neural network that can be used in ML to solve classification problems. The perceptron accepts image files and their related data/information as input. The perceptron builds a model that can later generate output using learned parameters. This output can then be used to identify objects in images or classify the data.

It consists of three essential components: an input layer, weights and biases, and an activation function. The input layer receives the data to be processed by the perceptron. At the same time, each feature has its weights and biases associated with it that are adjusted during training for optimal performance. Finally, a weighted sum of all inputs is computed, which passes through an activation function to produce either binary (0 or 1) or continuous (0–1) output.

Activation function: An activation function is necessary in a neural network because it introduces non-linearity to the model, allowing it to learn complex patterns and features from the data. A sign function, which returns either +1 or –1 depending on the sign of the input, is not an activation function because it is linear and does not preserve any information about the magnitude of the input.

The most used activation functions are the sigmoid function and hyperbolic tangent (tanh) function (Fig. 8.13).

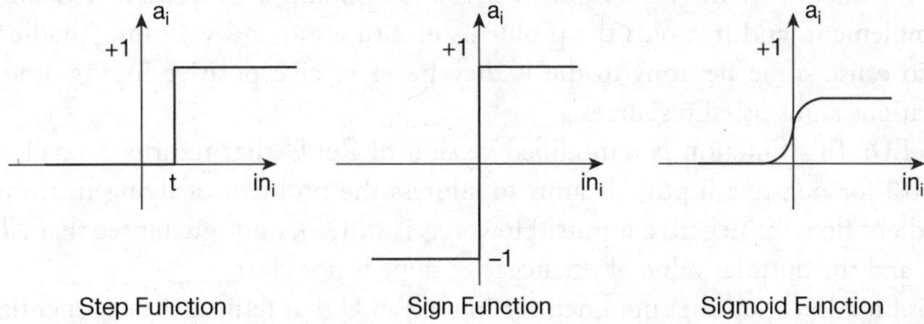

Figure 8.13 Different types of functions

Sigmoid function: This function maps the input to a value between 0 and 1, which can be interpreted as a probability. It is useful for binary classification problems, but it has some drawbacks such as being prone to saturation, vanishing gradients, and not being zero-centered.

The sigmoid function can be defined as:

$$f(x) = 1 / (1 + \exp(-x))$$

If the input to a sigmoid function is 2, then the output will be 0.8808. If the input is –2, then the output will be 0.1192.

Tanh function: This function maps the input to a value between –1 and 1, which is similar to sigmoid but zero-centered. It is also useful for classification problems, but it still suffers from saturation and vanishing gradients at extreme values.

Sign function: This outputs +1 if the input is positive and –1 if the input is negative. It creates an S-shaped curve with values ranging from 0 to 1. At the same time, tanh produces a symmetrical range of output values between –1 and +1. A sign function is not an activation function because it is linear and does not preserve any information about the magnitude of the input.

Mathematically, the sign function can be defined as:

$$f(x) = +1, \text{ if } x > 0$$
$$-1, \text{ if } x < 0$$

If the input to a sign function is 5, then the output will be +1. If the input is –3, then the output will be –1.

Step function: It is a piecewise function that outputs 1 if the input is greater than or equal to zero and 0 if the input is less than zero. Mathematically, the step function can be defined as:

$$f(x) = 1, \text{ if } x >= 0$$
$$0, \text{ if } x < 0$$

If the input to a step function is 3, then the output will be 1. If the input is –2, then the output will be 0.

Other types of activation functions are:

- **ReLU**: This function returns the input if it is positive, and 0 otherwise. It is simple, fast, and easy to implement, and it avoids the problems of saturation and vanishing gradients. However, it can also cause some neurons to die if they never receive positive inputs, leading to sparse representations and wasted resources.
- **Leaky ReLU**: This function is a modified version of ReLU that returns a small negative value instead of 0 for negative inputs. It aims to address the problem of dying neurons by allowing some gradient flow for negative inputs. However, it still does not guarantee that all neurons will be active, and the optimal value of the negative slope is not clear.
- **ELU**: This function is another modified version of ReLU that returns the exponential of the input minus 1 for negative inputs. It has the benefits of being smooth, zero-centered, and avoiding dying neurons. However, it is more computationally expensive than ReLU and Leaky ReLU, and it can also cause overshooting gradients if the input is too large.

Working of Perceptron

Step 1: Multiply all input values with their corresponding weight values and add them to determine the weighted sum. Mathematically, we can calculate the weighted sum as follows:

$$\sum wi^*xi = x1^*w1 + x2^*w2 + \ldots wn^*xn$$

Add a special term called bias b to this weighted sum to ameliorate the model's performance.

$$\sum wi^*xi + b$$

Step 2: In the alternate step, an activation function is applied with the weighted sum, which gives us a value either in double form or a non-stop value as follows:

$$Y = f(\sum wi^*xi + b)$$

Based on the number of layers, perceptron models are separated into two types: single-layer and multi-layer.

8.5.6.1 Single-layer Perceptron Model

A single-layer perceptron model is a type of ANN consisting of a feedforward network and an activation threshold transfer function. This model is used to separate linearly dividable objects with binary outputs. The algorithm does not incorporate stored data and instead initializes with randomly assigned weights for the inputs. After all inputs (weights) have been added up, if the sum exceeds a predetermined value, the output will be activated and indicated as 1. Single-layer perceptron can learn only linearly separable patterns.

8.5.6.2 Multi-layer Perceptron Model

The multi-layer perceptron (MLP) is a sophisticated AI tool used for determining intricate relationships between input and output variables. It can be used to build predictive models for linear and non-linear regression tasks. An MLP comprises multiple layers of neurons that are linked together, with weights assigned to each connection in each layer. The input layer receives and passes the input data to the layers that follow. The final layer, on the other hand, produces a predicted output. An MLP can model complex patterns within large data sets using its many layers of neurons, allowing it to be used effectively in supervised learning tasks such as classification and regression problems. MLPs can thus provide valuable insight into the relationships between various variables.

The classification of images is one application of MLPs in machine learning. MLPs are employed to categorize photos according to their content. First, the MLP is trained on a collection of labeled images and learns to recognize patterns in the images linked with distinct classes. After training, the MLP can accurately classify new photos depending on their content. Another illustration is in voice recognition to identify spoken words. The MLP can identify patterns in the audio signals connected to various words after being trained on a data set of spoken words. Once trained, the MLP has a high degree of accuracy in recognizing new words, which makes it a valuable tool for speech recognition applications.

The following are some **benefits** of using MLP:

- Complex non-linear issues can be divided into smaller sub-problems by MLP, which can then solve each one separately. This is accomplished by employing many node and weight layers, each of which processes the output of the preceding layer to create a more complicated output. For instance, MLP can be applied to natural language processing, speech recognition, and image recognition.
- MLP is flexible for various issues since it is effective with both small and large input data. Furthermore, MLP can process highly dimensional data and derive pertinent features from the input data. MLP can be used, for instance, to forecast property prices when the input data comprises a variety of factors like location, number of bedrooms, and square footage.
- Once MLP is trained, it can make predictions quickly and efficiently. This is because the weights and biases have already been learned during training, and the model can apply this knowledge to make predictions on new data.
- MLP is capable of maintaining the same accuracy rate with both large and small data sets. This is because MLP is not limited by the size of the data set and can adjust to the complexity of the problem. For example, MLP can be used for predicting customer churn, where the data set may vary in size depending on the company.

The **disadvantages** of MLP are as follows:

- MLP requires many computation resources, especially when dealing with large data sets or deep networks. Training a deep network with a large number of hidden layers can be a time-consuming process, and it requires powerful hardware. For example, training an MLP to classify images in a large data set like ImageNet can take days or even weeks using multiple GPUs.
- MLP is a black box model, so it is challenging to interpret how the input variables affect the output. Moreover, unlike linear models or decision trees, MLP needs to provide a clearer insight into the importance of each feature in the model. For example, suppose an MLP is used to predict

house prices. It may need to be clarified which factors, such as the number of bedrooms or the location, are the most important in determining the price.

- The training set's data quality and the model's chosen hyperparameters significantly impact MLP performance. The model's accuracy will rise if the training data is representative of real-world data.

8.5.6.3 Limitations of the Perceptron Model

The perceptron model has a limitation in that the hard limit transfer function used in the activation function limits the output to only two possible values, 0 or 1. This means that the perceptron can only be used to classify input vectors into two classes and cannot indicate the degree of certainty or probability associated with the classification decision. For example, we are trying to classify images of cats and dogs. In that case, the perceptron model will only output either 0 or 1 for each image, with no information about how confident it is in its decision.

Another limitation of the perceptron model is that it can only be used to classify linearly divisible sets of input vectors. In other words, the decision boundary that separates the two classes must be a linear function of the input features. If the input vectors are non-linear, then the perceptron model cannot accurately classify them. For example, we are trying to classify handwritten digits. The perceptron model may need help distinguishing between digits with similar shapes but different curves, such as 6 and 8. Again, this is because the decision boundary between these two digits is not a linear function of the input features.

To overcome these limitations, more advanced ML models are often used, such as neural networks, SVMs, and decision trees.

8.5.7 Support Vector Machines

Support vector machine or SVM is a non-linear model and is one of the most popular supervised learning algorithms used for classification and regression problems. The purpose of the SVM algorithm is to produce the stylish line or decision boundary that can insulate *n*-dimensional space into classes so that we can fluently put the new data point in the correct order in the future. This stylish decision boundary is called a **hyperplane**. SVM chooses the extreme points vectors that help in creating the hyperplane. These extreme cases are called support vectors; hence, the name of the algorithm.

SVM is used in ML tasks such as face detection, image segmentation, and text categorization. This makes SVM the perfect model to use when identifying whether a strange cat-like creature is a cat or canine. To create an accurate model using SVM, we must first train our model with many images of cats and dogs. This would enable the algorithm to learn about the features associated with each type of animal, enabling it to distinguish between them. We can then test this model by feeding it information on our strange critter and seeing what output it provides us with. SVM works by creating a decision boundary between two sets of data – in this case, cats and canines – by selecting extreme cases from each group known as support vectors.

SVM can be of two types: linear and non-linear.

Linear SVM: This classifies data into two distinct categories. It works best when the data points are linearly separable, meaning they can be divided into two groups by drawing a straight line. The linear SVM uses this line to fit the model and accurately predict which group new data points belong to. For example, think of an application that predicts whether or not someone will have skin cancer based on various features such as age, family history of skin cancer, etc. In this case, all the features could be combined in one plot and separated into two groups: those with skin cancer and those without skin cancer. A linear SVM would draw a single straight line across this plot to accurately distinguish between these groups. It is important to note that linear SVMs only work for data sets where the classes are linearly separable; if there is no clear dividing line between classes, other, more complex methods, must be used. In addition, linear SVMs are less accurate at making predictions with small data sets due to their reliance on drawing straight lines through multiple points to make an accurate prediction.

Consider the training data $\{(x_i, d_i)\}, i = 1..n$, where x_i is an input pattern and d_i is the corresponding label. The equation of the decision boundary is given as

$$w^T x + b = 0, \tag{8.14}$$

where x is the input vector, w is the weight vector, and b is the bias.

For the classes where $d_i = +1, w^T x_i + b \geq 0$

Similarly for $d_i = -1, w^T x_i + b < 0$

For the weight vector w and the bias b, the separation between the hyperplane and the closest data point is called **margin of separation** (ρ). Such a hyperplane is called the **optimal hyperplane.**
Geometrical construction of hyperplane: Let w_0 and b_0 be the optimum weight vector and bias. The corresponding hyperplane is given as $w_0^T x + b_0 = 0$.

The discriminant function is defined as $g(x) = w_0^T x + b_0$. This discriminant function provides an algebraic measure of the distance from x to the hyperplane (Fig. 8.14).

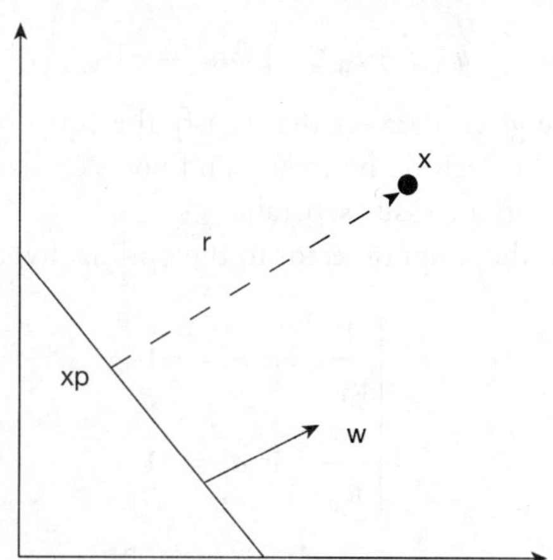

Figure 8.14 Geometry of hyperplane

Consider a point x. Let xp be the projection of x onto the hyperplane. The point x can be expressed as

$$x = xp + r\frac{w_0}{w_0},$$

where xp is the normal projection of x onto the hyperplane and r is the distance.

The value of r can be positive or negative depending on the position of x. The projected point xp is on the hyperplane. This implies that

$$g(x) = w_0^T x + b_0 = 0$$

$$= w_0^T \left(xp + r\frac{w_0}{w_0} \right) + b = 0$$

$$= w_0^T (xp) + w_0^T r\frac{w_0}{w_0} + b = 0$$

$$= g(xp) + rw_0 = 0$$

$$\Rightarrow g(x) = rw_0 \because g(xp) = 0(xp \text{ lies on the line})$$

$$\Rightarrow r = \frac{g(x)}{w_0}$$

We need to determine an optimal hyperplane that separates the data with maximum margin and hence the parameters w_0 and b_0 are chosen in such a way that for any point x_i in the data set $\{(x_i, d_i)\}$

$$w_0^T x_i + b_0 \geq 1 \, for d_i = +1 (or)$$

$$w_0^T x_i + b_0 \leq -1 \, for d_i = -1 \tag{8.15}$$

The subset of points in the given data set that satisfy the equations are called support vectors. These data points are closer to the decision boundary and poses challenge to the classifier for separability whereas the other data points are easily separable.

The algebraic distance from the support vector to the optimal hyperplane is given as

$$r = \begin{cases} \frac{1}{w_0}, & \text{if } d_i = +1 \\ \frac{-1}{w_0} & \text{if } d_i = -1 \end{cases} \tag{8.16}$$

The optimal margin of separation is thus calculated as $\frac{2}{w_0}$, that is, maximizing the margin over two linearly separable classes is equivalent to Euclidean norm of the weight vector w. The optimal hyperplane obtained is unique; the optimum weight vector provides the maximum margin of separation between the two classes.

Non-linear SVM: This is a type of SVM classifier used for data sets that cannot be linearly separated. We can separate data that is linearly arranged by drawing a straight line, but we cannot create a single straight line for non-linear data. For example, in Fig. 8.15 the data cannot be separated using a single straight line.

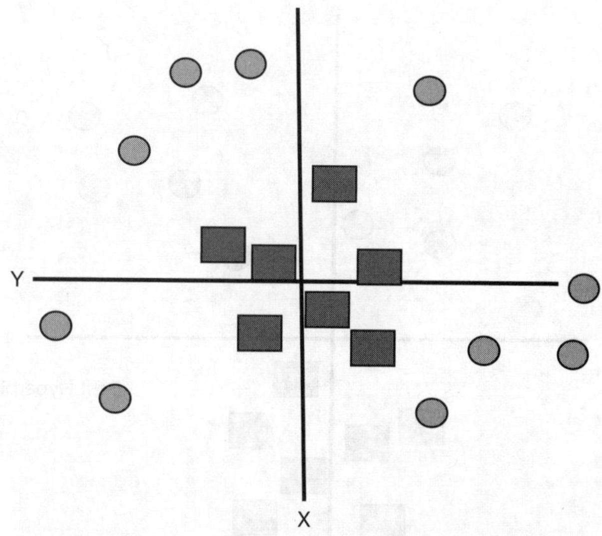

Figure 8.15 Non-linear classification data graph

Thus, the new boundary must be created beyond the scope of traditional linear analysis. So we need to add another dimension to distinguish these data values. We employed two dimensions for linear data, x and y, thus for non-linear data, we will add a third dimension, z. It can be computed as follows: $z = x^2 + y^2$

By including a third dimension, the sample space will look like Fig. 8.16.

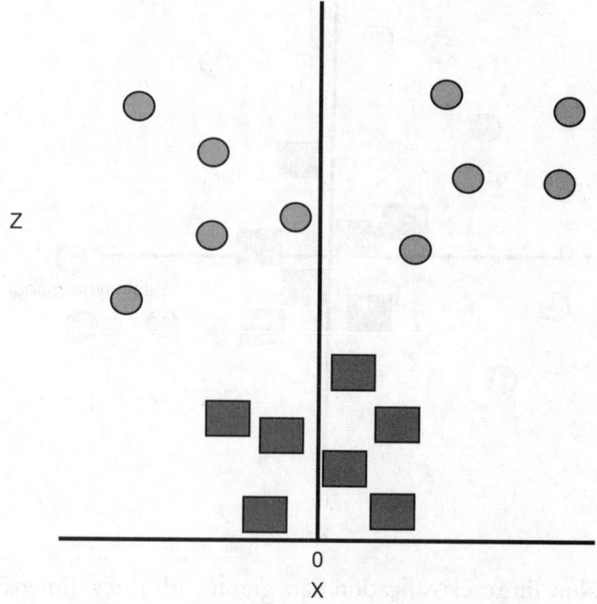

Figure 8.16 Non-linear classification data graph with another dimension

SVM will now partition the data sets into classes in the following manner. Consider the image shown in Fig. 8.17.

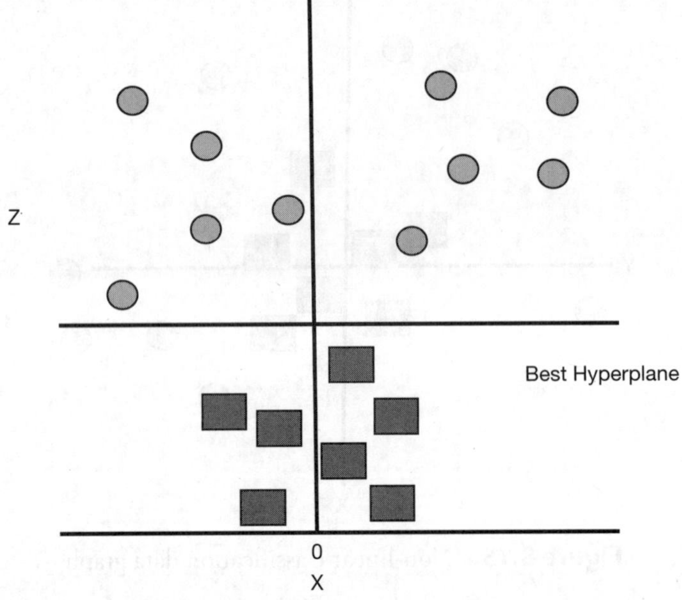

Figure 8.17 Non-linear classification data graph with three dimensions

Because we are in three dimensions, it appears to be a plane parallel to the *x*-axis. If we translate it to 2D space with *z*=1, it will look like Fig. 8.18.

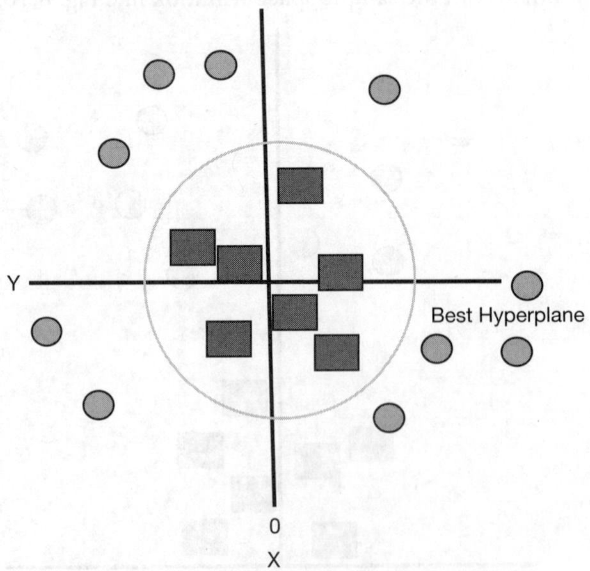

Figure 8.18 Non-linear classification data graph with three dimensions (2D space)

Kernels: Kernels or kernel methods are a powerful tool for pattern analysis, especially when the data is not linearly separable. They allow us to apply a linear classifier, such as SVM, to a non-linear problem by mapping the data to a higher-dimensional feature space where the data becomes linearly separable. This mapping is done by a kernel function, which computes the inner product of two data points in the feature space without explicitly transforming them. This is known as the 'kernel trick', and it reduces the computational complexity and memory requirements of the classifier.

There are different types of kernel functions, such as polynomial, radial basis function (RBF), sigmoid, etc. Each kernel function has its advantages and disadvantages, and the choice of the kernel function depends on the characteristics of the data and the problem. For example, polynomial kernels are suitable for data that has polynomial relationships, while RBF kernels are ideal for data that has clusters or local patterns. Sigmoid kernels are useful for neural networks and logistic regression.

Kernel methods are widely used in SVMs. Kernel methods can also be applied to other ML techniques, such as clustering, dimensionality reduction, feature extraction, etc.

8.6 Applications of Supervised Learning

Due to its excellent accuracy and efficiency, supervised learning has been extensively applied in many different fields. It entails using labeled data to train a model where the input and output are matched. The model then develops the ability to predict outcomes based on new input data.

Image Categorization: This means is assigning descriptive labels to photos according to their content. For instance, an image depicting a feline can be labeled 'cat', whereas an image portraying a canine can be labeled 'dog'. This is a form of supervised learning where the model acquires knowledge from a tagged photo collection and subsequently applies the accepted rules to novel images.

Feature extraction is a crucial step in image categorization. Consequently, the model discerns pertinent data from the image's pixels, encompassing edges, forms, colors, textures, and patterns. These characteristics are subsequently utilized to compare the picture with the current labels and choose the most suitable match. Feature extraction can be achieved using several techniques, including convolutional neural networks (CNNs).

Assessment is another crucial stage in the process of image categorization. This implies that the model evaluates its performance on novel images that it has not previously encountered. Assessment can be conducted utilizing many criteria, including accuracy, precision, recall, and F1-score. These metrics represent the number of images that are accurately labeled, the number of pictures that are incorrectly marked, and the number of images that the model fails to label. Assessment aids in identifying the model's advantages and disadvantages, enabling targeted improvements.

Image categorization offers numerous advantages across diverse domains. For instance, in healthcare, image classification can assist physicians in diagnosing diseases by analyzing medical images, including X-rays, MRI scans, and ultrasound images. Image categorization facilitates the monitoring of treatment progress and the identification of anomalies or abnormalities.

It can optimize the safety and effectiveness of surveillance systems by promptly identifying and classifying faces, objects, vehicles, and activities. Image classification can aid in the prevention of crimes and acts of terrorism by accurately identifying individuals involved, as well as detecting weapons, explosives, and potential threats in public areas.

Image categorization can optimize the learning experience and improve student outcomes by providing interactive and tailored feedback based on their effort. Image categorization facilitates the development of lifelike and captivating virtual environments by utilizing photographs, for example, in video games, films, and simulations.

Fraud Detection: Supervised learning plays a crucial role in detecting fraudulent activities. For instance, we can utilize a data set of transactions categorized as fraudulent or non-fraudulent. The model can subsequently acquire knowledge about the patterns or characteristics that suggest a transaction is probable to be deceptive.

Implementing fraud detection systems can assist financial institutions in mitigating financial losses resulting from fraudulent activities. Deception is a grave issue that incurs billions of dollars in expenses annually. Scammers employ several tactics to defraud or manipulate individuals into providing them with funds or personal data.

Risk Assessment: By analyzing data, supervised learning is used in risk assessment to predict the likelihood of specific events. Consider the scenario where we seek to determine the probability of a borrower defaulting on a loan obtained from a financial institution. This occurrence is referred to as a loan default, and it can give rise to complications for both the borrower and the lender. To prevent this, we can employ supervised learning to train a model that can predict each borrower's loan default likelihood. The model acquires knowledge from past borrowers' historical data, encompassing their income, credit score, loan amount, repayment history, and more. Subsequently, the model utilizes this data to allocate a numerical value to every prospective borrower, signifying their level of risk. As the score increases, the likelihood of loan default also increases. The bank can utilize this score to determine whether to grant or deny a loan application or to modify the loan's interest rate or other conditions.

Spam Filtering: Supervised learning can be applied to spam filtering, which involves identifying and eliminating undesirable or malicious messages from email accounts. Spam communications can be bothersome, deceptive, or potentially harmful, as they may harbor malware, phishing URLs, or fraudulent schemes. Hence, owning a program capable of autonomously discerning and excluding such messages is advantageous, thereby safeguarding the users.

8.7 Limitations and Challenges of Supervised Learning

Supervised learning encounters the difficulty of either overfitting or underfitting the data. Overfitting occurs when an algorithm excessively incorporates noise or irrelevant random changes from the data, surpassing what is necessary for accurate prediction. Consequently, the algorithm excels at accurately matching the data it has encountered but struggles to apply this knowledge to unfamiliar data. Various strategies, including cross-validation and regularization, can be employed to address this issue.

Bias or injustice refers to the algorithm or data exhibiting unfairness or inaccuracy towards specific groups of individuals or circumstances. The algorithm's predictions or judgments can adversely affect the affected individuals. Bias or unfairness can occur when the data used to train the algorithm lacks representation of the real world or the problem it aims to address. For example, suppose a facial recognition system is trained using a data set that consists mostly of individuals of Caucasian descent. In that case, it may not perform effectively on individuals with darker skin tones. This is because the algorithm requires additional exposure to diverse data sets to cultivate the ability to differentiate between different skin tones. Hence, it is crucial to acknowledge the possible origins and consequences of partiality or unfairness in supervised learning and to implement measures to avoid or alleviate them. A few potential measures consist of:

- Gathering a more comprehensive range of varied and equitable data that accurately represents the actual world and the specific area of concern.
- Assessing and verifying the algorithm's performance and precision across various cohorts and settings.
- Providing a comprehensive analysis and elucidation of the algorithm's predictions or judgments, together with their rationale and contributing elements.
- Supervising and inspecting the algorithm's results and effects and rectifying any inaccuracies or negative consequences.
- Engaging and seeking input from diverse stakeholders and experts while designing and implementing the algorithm.

An obstacle in creating an algorithm capable of making equitable and precise conclusions is guaranteeing that it is trained on an appropriate data set. Not all data sets possess comparable suitability for this objective. Specific data sets may exhibit bias, incompleteness, obsolescence, or irrelevance concerning the topic the algorithm aims to address.

SUMMARY

- Supervised machine learning is a branch of artificial intelligence that uses labeled data to train algorithms that can classify data or predict outcomes. Classification problems involve assigning data into discrete categories, such as spam or not spam, dog, or cat, etc. KNN, decision tree, random forest, support vector machine and linear classifiers are examples of classification.
- *K*-nearest neighbor (KNN) is an algorithm that classifies a data input based on the majority vote of its *k* closest neighbors in the feature space.
- The decision trees algorithm builds a tree-like structure that splits the data inputs based on certain criteria at each node. It is easy to interpret and can handle both categorical and numerical features, but it can be prone to overfitting or underfitting.
- The random forests algorithm combines multiple decision trees and aggregates their predictions using a voting or averaging scheme.
- The support vector machine (SVM) algorithm tries to find a hyperplane that separates the data inputs into different classes with the maximum margin. It can handle linear and non-linear classification problems by using different kernels, such as polynomial, radial basis function (RBF) or sigmoid. Soft margin SVM finds the optimal linear boundary that separates the data into two classes with a margin that is as wide as possible while allowing for some misclassification. Hard margin SVM tries to find a hyperplane that entirely separates the classes with no overlapping data points and with the maximum margin possible.
- Linear discriminant analysis (LDA) is a method that assumes that the features follow a Gaussian distribution within each category, and tries to find a linear projection that maximizes the separation between categories.

- Naive Bayes classifier is a method that assumes that the features are conditionally independent given the category, and tries to estimate the probability of each feature value for each category using frequency counts.
- Discriminative models learn to predict the output variable (such as class label) directly from the input features, without modeling the joint distribution of inputs and outputs. Some examples of discriminative models for linear classifiers are logistic regression, perceptron and support vector machine.
- Perceptron is a method that iteratively updates the weights based on the errors made on the training data, until no errors are made or a maximum number of iterations is reached. Based on the number of layers, perceptron models are classified into two types: single-layer and multi-layer.
- Neural networks consist of layers of interconnected nodes that process and transform the data inputs using activation functions and weights. They can learn complex and non-linear patterns from the data, but can be difficult to tune and explain.
- Activation function is a mathematical tool used in neural networks to determine whether a neuron should be triggered. It adds non-linearity to the model and allows it to recognize complex patterns in data.

EXERCISES

Part A (Objective Questions)

1. A company wants to predict the sales revenue for the next quarter based on historical data. Which type of machine learning problem does this scenario represent?
a) Classification
b) Regression
c) Clustering
d) Association

2. An email service provider aims to classify incoming emails as spam or not spam. What type of supervised learning algorithm would be suitable for this task?
a) *K*-Means
b) Decision Tree
c) *K*-Nearest Neighbor (KNN)
d) Association Rule Mining

3. A researcher is working on predicting whether a given patient has a particular disease based on medical test results. What type of machine learning problem is this?
a) Classification
b) Regression
c) Clustering
d) Reinforcement Learning

4. A company wants to determine whether to approve or reject a loan application based on various applicant parameters. Which algorithm could be suitable for this task?
a) Linear Regression
b) Random Forest
c) Support Vector Machine (SVM)
d) *K*-Means

5. A student wants to predict the temperature for the next day based on historical weather data. What kind of machine learning problem does this represent?
a) Regression
b) Clustering
c) Association
d) Reinforcement Learning

6. A student wants to predict whether a bank customer will default on a loan based on historical loan repayment data. Which distance metric might be suitable for the KNN algorithm in this scenario?

a) Euclidean distance
b) Manhattan distance
c) Hamming distance
d) Minkowski distance

7. A company is dealing with a data set having a large number of data points. Which drawback of KNN might become more pronounced due to this?

a) Sensitivity to outliers
b) Interpretability
c) Computationally expensive
d) Overfitting

8. A researcher is working on a problem that involves classifying data into multiple classes. Which advantage of KNN might be beneficial in handling this task?

a) Handles non-linear data well
b) Simple and intuitive
c) Less sensitive to outliers
d) Low storage requirements

9. A data scientist is dealing with a data set containing categorical features. Which distance metric could be suitable for handling categorical data in the KNN algorithm?

a) Euclidean distance
b) Manhattan distance
c) Hamming distance
d) Cosine similarity

10. A machine learning engineer is working on a data set with features that have different scales. Which drawback of KNN might be exacerbated due to this variation in feature scales?

a) Sensitivity to outliers
b) Interpretability
c) Sensitivity to feature scales
d) Overfitting

11. A data scientist is analyzing a data set containing both numerical and categorical features. Which characteristic of decision trees makes them suitable for handling such diverse data?

a) Handles missing values effectively
b) Prone to overfitting
c) Only suitable for numerical features
d) Can handle both categorical and numerical features

12. A company wants to use a machine learning algorithm that is easy to interpret and explain to non-technical stakeholders. Which algorithm might be preferred based on its interpretability?

a) Support Vector Machine
b) Random Forest
c) Decision Tree
d) *K*-Nearest Neighbor (KNN)

13. A data analyst is concerned about decision trees being sensitive to small changes in the data, which might lead to very different trees. What is this sensitivity called?

a) Overfitting
b) Underfitting
c) Unstable
d) Robustness

14. A researcher is working with a data set having missing values and outliers. Which characteristic of decision trees might help handle such data challenges?

a) Require imputation of missing values
b) Unable to handle outliers
c) Can handle missing values and outliers
d) Require outlier removal

15. An organization is dealing with a data set that contains complex non-linear relationships between features. Which feature of decision trees makes them suitable for capturing such relationships?
a) Only captures linear relationships
b) Prone to underfitting
c) Can capture complex non-linear relationships
d) Cannot handle complex patterns

16. A data scientist is working on a project where the data set contains a considerable amount of missing data. Which characteristic of Random Forests makes them suitable for handling missing values?
a) Require imputation of missing values
b) Unable to handle missing values
c) Can handle missing values
d) Need explicit removal of missing values

17. A company is dealing with a data set prone to noise and outliers. Which characteristic of Random Forests might help mitigate the impact of noisy data?
a) Vulnerable to noise and outliers
b) Unable to handle noise and outliers
c) Robust to noise and outliers
d) Require extensive preprocessing for noise removal

18. A researcher is concerned about the risk of overfitting while using Random Forests. What technique is commonly employed in Random Forests to combat overfitting?
a) Dropout regularization
b) Early stopping
c) Feature scaling
d) Ensemble averaging

19. A machine learning engineer wants to improve model performance without increasing computational costs significantly. Which characteristic of Random Forests might be beneficial in this scenario?
a) Require complex computational resources
b) Limited computational costs
c) Inefficient for large data sets
d) Extremely slow training and testing

20. An analyst is dealing with a data set containing a mix of numerical and categorical variables. Which aspect of Random Forests makes them suitable for handling such diverse data?
a) Only suitable for numerical variables
b) Unable to handle categorical variables
c) Handles both numerical and categorical variables
d) Require extensive preprocessing for categorical data

21. A data scientist is working on a problem where the data points are not linearly separable in their current feature space. Which characteristic of SVMs might help handle this situation?
a) Limited to linear classification only
b) Unable to handle non-linear problems
c) Can handle linear and non-linear classification
d) Require extensive preprocessing for non-linear data

22. A researcher wants to employ an algorithm that maximizes the margin between different classes in the data. Which concept in SVMs corresponds to maximizing this margin?
a) Hyperplane
b) Decision boundary
c) Margin boundary
d) Kernel function

23. An analyst is dealing with a data set containing outliers. Which characteristic of SVMs might help in handling outliers?
a) Prone to outlier sensitivity
b) Robust to outliers
c) Unable to handle outliers
d) Require outlier removal

24. A machine learning engineer wants to perform classification on a data set having a low number of features. Which aspect of SVMs might be beneficial in this scenario?
a) Inefficient for low-dimensional data
b) Handles only high-dimensional data
c) Suitable for low-dimensional data
d) Unable to work with few features

25. A data analyst is working on a problem where the data points exhibit non-linear relationships. Which technique in SVMs might help capture such nonlinearities?
a) Feature scaling
b) Kernel trick
c) Early stopping
d) Cross-validation

26. A data scientist is dealing with a data set containing a large number of features. Which characteristic of linear classifiers might make them advantageous in handling such data sets?
a) Slow to train with large feature sets
b) Suitable only for small feature sets
c) Simple and fast with large feature sets
d) Require extensive preprocessing for large features

27. An analyst is working on a classification problem where model interpretability is crucial. Which aspect of linear classifiers might be beneficial in this context?
a) Complex and difficult to interpret
b) Require extensive feature engineering
c) Simple and easy to interpret
d) Unable to provide explanations

28. A researcher is dealing with a data set where feature scaling is crucial. Which characteristic of linear classifiers might aid in handling different scales of features?
a) Require identical feature scales
b) Insensitive to feature scales
c) Handle different feature scales effectively
d) Prone to underfitting with varying feature scales

29. A machine learning engineer is working on a problem where the data set contains a mix of continuous and categorical features. Which type of linear classifier might be suitable for handling such diverse features?
a) Only suitable for continuous features
b) Unable to handle categorical features
c) Suitable for both continuous and categorical features
d) Require separate preprocessing for categorical data

30. An analyst is concerned about computational complexity in model training. Which characteristic of linear classifiers might be advantageous in terms of computational efficiency?

a) Require extensive computational resources
b) Complex and computationally demanding
c) Simple and fast to train
d) Extremely slow in training

31. A data scientist is working on a classification problem with a large number of features and relatively few data points. What advantage of LDA might make it suitable for this scenario?
a) Handles only a small number of features
b) Effective for small feature spaces
c) Ability to handle high-dimensional feature spaces
d) Suitable for few data points

32. An analyst is dealing with a data set exhibiting skewness and multimodality in feature distributions. What limitation of LDA is pertinent in this situation?
a) Assumes Gaussian distribution in featuresb) Inability to handle outliers
c) Effective for skewed distributions d) Suitable for multimodal data

33. A researcher is working on a project where data points exhibit multicollinearity. What advantage of LDA might help address this issue?
a) Inability to address multicollinearity b) Effective for multicollinear features
c) Ability to resolve multicollinearity d) Suitable for non-correlated features

34. A machine learning engineer is analyzing textual data with a large number of potential features but limited data samples. What advantage of LDA might make it suitable for this scenario?
a) Inability to handle a high number of features
b) Limited usefulness for textual data
c) Suitable for high-dimensional features with few samples
d) Effective for large data sets

35. An analyst is dealing with a high-dimensional data set where the number of features significantly exceeds the number of data points. What limitation of LDA might be applicable in this scenario?
a) Effective in high-dimensional feature spaces
b) Handles large feature-to-sample ratios
c) Prone to perform well in such scenarios
d) Not suitable for feature-rich data sets

36. An analyst is working on a text classification task where the occurrence of individual words in a document influences the document's category. Which assumption of the naive Bayes classifier is pertinent in this situation?
a) Assumes conditional dependence of features
b) Assumes conditional independence of features
c) Requires prior feature knowledge
d) Suitable for correlated features

37. A machine learning engineer is analyzing a data set with highly correlated features. Which characteristic of the naive Bayes classifier might pose a challenge in this scenario?

a) Effective for correlated features
b) Prone to work well with high correlation
c) Assumes feature independence
d) Suitable for conditional dependence

38. An analyst is dealing with a large data set with missing values. What advantage of the naive Bayes classifier might be beneficial in handling missing data?
a) Require complete data for training
b) Effective for data sets with missing values
c) Handles missing values well
d) Suitable for data imputation

39. A data scientist is working on a classification problem with a small amount of training data. What advantage of the naive Bayes classifier might be beneficial in this situation?
a) Requires large amounts of training data
b) Effective for small training data sets
c) Suitable for high-dimensional data sets
d) Ineffective for small data sets

40. An analyst is working on a classification task where features are assumed to have no relationship with each other given the category. Which assumption of the naive Bayes classifier aligns with this scenario?
a) Assumes conditional dependence of features
b) Assumes conditional independence of features
c) Requires strong feature relationships
d) Suitable for interdependent features

41. A data scientist is working on a classification problem with multiple unordered categories for the output variable. Which type of logistic regression would be suitable for this scenario?
a) Binomial Logistic Regression
b) Multinomial Logistic Regression
c) Ordinal Logistic Regression
d) Polynomial Logistic Regression

42. An analyst is working on a classification task with an output variable that has three ordered categories. Which type of logistic regression is relevant for this scenario?
a) Binomial Logistic Regression
b) Multinomial Logistic Regression
c) Ordinal Logistic Regression
d) Hierarchical Logistic Regression

43. A machine learning engineer is dealing with a binary classification problem. Which type of logistic regression would be appropriate for this situation?
a) Multinomial Logistic Regression
b) Ordinal Logistic Regression
c) Binomial Logistic Regression
d) Polynomial Logistic Regression

44. A researcher is working on a classification task and requires probabilistic estimates for the output classes. Which model among logistic regression provides such estimates?
a) Binomial Logistic Regression
b) Multinomial Logistic Regression
c) Ordinal Logistic Regression
d) All of the above

45. An analyst is dealing with a classification problem with a large number of features. Which linear classifier might be useful for this scenario?
a) Perceptron
b) Logistic Regression
c) Support Vector Machine
d) None of the above

46. A data set involves predicting the likelihood of a customer purchasing a product (yes/no) based on their demographic information. Which type of Logistic Regression is suitable for this binary classification task?
a) Binary Logistic Regression
b) Multinomial Logistic Regression
c) Ordinal Logistic Regression
d) Polynomial Logistic Regression

47. A researcher wants to classify movie genres into various categories like Action, Comedy, or Drama. Which type of Logistic Regression best fits this multi-class classification problem?
a) Binary Logistic Regression
b) Multinomial Logistic Regression
c) Ordinal Logistic Regression
d) Hierarchical Logistic Regression

48. An analyst is dealing with a data set categorizing customers' income levels into low, medium, or high. What type of Logistic Regression is suitable for this ordinal classification problem?
a) Binary Logistic Regression
b) Multinomial Logistic Regression
c) Ordinal Logistic Regression
d) Polynomial Logistic Regression

49. A machine learning engineer is working on predicting customer satisfaction levels as dissatisfied, neutral, or satisfied. Which type of Logistic Regression aligns with this scenario?
a) Binary Logistic Regression
b) Multinomial Logistic Regression
c) Ordinal Logistic Regression
d) Polynomial Logistic Regression

50. A data set contains weather predictions categorized as sunny, rainy, or cloudy. What type of Logistic Regression model is appropriate for predicting these weather categories?
a) Binary Logistic Regression
b) Multinomial Logistic Regression
c) Ordinal Logistic Regression
d) Polynomial Logistic Regression

51. In a neural network, which activation function produces an output between -1 and +1?
a) Sign function
b) Sigmoid function
c) Hyperbolic tangent (tanh) function
d) ReLU function

52. Which activation function transforms input values into a range of 0 to 1, resembling an "S" shaped curve?
a) Sign function
b) Sigmoid function
c) Hyperbolic tangent (tanh) function
d) Step function

53. In a neural network, which activation function outputs +1 for positive input and -1 for negative input?
a) Sigmoid function
b) Hyperbolic tangent (tanh) function
c) Sign function
d) ReLU function

54. Which type of perceptron model can contain multiple layers?
a) Single-layer Perceptron Model
b) Multi-layer Perceptron Model
c) Complex-layer Perceptron Model
d) Stacked-layer Perceptron Model

55. In a neural network, which activation function does not introduce non-linearity?
a) Sigmoid function
b) Hyperbolic tangent (tanh) function
c) Sign function
d) Linear function

56. Which type of perceptron model can handle linearly separable patterns and makes decisions based on a binary output?
a) Single-layer Perceptron Model
b) Multi-layer Perceptron Model
c) Stacked Perceptron Model
d) Deep Perceptron Model

57. Which perceptron model involves multiple layers of neurons and is capable of modeling complex patterns within large data sets?
a) Single-layer Perceptron Model
b) Multi-layer Perceptron Model
c) Hierarchical Perceptron Model
d) Complex Perceptron Model

58. Which perceptron model initializes with randomly assigned weights and determines binary outputs by comparing the sum of inputs to a threshold?
a) Single-layer Perceptron Model
b) Multi-layer Perceptron Model
c) Sequential Perceptron Model
d) Advanced Perceptron Model

59. Which perceptron model can learn only linearly separable patterns and updates weights based on errors in the training data?
a) Single-layer Perceptron Model
b) Multi-layer Perceptron Model
c) Adaptive Perceptron Model
d) Evolving Perceptron Model

60. Which perceptron model is used for determining complex relationships between input and output variables and comprises multiple interconnected layers?
a) Single-layer Perceptron Model
b) Multi-layer Perceptron Model
c) Parallel Perceptron Model
d) Deep Learning Perceptron Model

61. Which model uses quadratic programming or other optimization techniques to find the optimal linear boundary between different classes with the maximum margin?
a) Support Vector Machine (SVM)
b) Neural Network
c) Decision Tree
d) *K*-Nearest Neighbor (KNN)

62. Which algorithm learns complex and non-linear patterns from data inputs using interconnected nodes, but is challenging to tune and explain?
a) Support Vector Machine (SVM)
b) Neural Network
c) Random Forest
d) Logistic Regression

63. Which method defines the margin as the distance between the hyperplane and the closest data points, known as support vectors?
a) *K*-Nearest Neighbor (KNN)
b) Decision Tree
c) Support Vector Machine (SVM)
d) Linear Regression

64. Which model optimizes the model parameters by solving a quadratic optimization problem minimizing the hinge loss function?
a) Random Forest
b) Support Vector Machine (SVM)
c) Naive Bayes Classifier
d) Gradient Boosting

65. Which algorithm creates layers of interconnected nodes, processing data using activation functions, to learn complex and non-linear patterns?

a) Decision Tree
b) Logistic Regression
c) Neural Network
d) *K*-Nearest Neighbor (KNN)

Part B (Short Answer Questions)

1. Define supervised machine learning. What are the types of supervised learning?
2. Give a few examples of classification algorithms.
3. Write short notes on the KNN classification algorithm.
4. Write short notes on the decision tree algorithm.
5. Write short notes on the random forest algorithm.
6. Explain the SVM algorithm.
7. What is LDA?
8. Write short notes on the naive Bayes classifier.
9. Explain discriminative models for linear classifiers.
10. Explain logistic regression.
11. What are the types of logistic regression?
12. Define binary logistic regression.
13. Define multinomial logistic regression.
14. Explain ordinal logistic regression.
15. Define perceptron.
16. Define activation function.
17. What are the types of perceptron models?
18. Define the single-layer perceptron model.
19. Define the multi-layer perceptron model.
20. Define neural network.
21. What are the applications of supervised learning?

Part C (Essay Questions)

1. Explain the steps of the supervised learning algorithm in detail.
2. Explain KNN in detail.
3. Explain the concepts of decision tree in detail along with its advantages.
4. Explain the iterative dichotomiser (ID3) algorithm in detail.
5. Explain the C4.5 algorithm in detail.
6. Explain the CART algorithm in detail.
7. Explain linear classifiers in detail.
8. What are the advantages of linear classifiers?
9. Explain generative models for linear classifiers.
10. Explain linear discriminant analysis (LDA).
11. What are the advantages of linear discriminant analysis (LDA)?
12. What are the disadvantages of linear discriminant analysis (LDA)?
13. Explain the naive Bayes classifier.
14. Explain the Bayesian belief network.
15. Explain the expectation maximization (EM) algorithm.
16. Explain discriminative models for linear classifiers.
17. Explain logistic regression.
18. Explain the types of logistic regression.
19. Explain ordinal logistic regression.
20. Explain perceptron in detail.
21. Explain the activation function.
22. How does perceptron work?
23. What are the types of perceptron models?
24. What are the advantages of multi-layer perceptron?
25. What are the disadvantages of multi-layer perceptron?
26. Explain support vector machines in detail.
27. Explain linear SVM in detail.
28. Explain non-linear SVM in detail.

29. How is supervised learning used for image categorization?

30. How is supervised learning used for fraud detection?

31. What are the limitations and challenges of supervised learning?

ANSWER KEY

Part A

1. (b)	**2.** (c)	**3.** (a)	**4.** (c)	**5.** (a)	**6.** (a)	**7.** (c)	**8.** (b)
9. (c)	**10.** (c)	**11.** (d)	**12.** (c)	**13.** (c)	**14.** (c)	**15.** (c)	**16.** (c)
17. (b)	**18.** (b)	**19.** (b)	**20.** (c)	**21.** (c)	**22.** (a)	**23.** (b)	**24.** (c)
25. (b)	**26.** (c)	**27.** (c)	**28.** (c)	**29.** (c)	**30.** (c)	**31.** (c)	**32.** (a)
33. (b)	**34.** (c)	**35.** (d)	**36.** (b)	**37.** (c)	**38.** (c)	**39.** (b)	**40.** (b)
41. (b)	**42.** (c)	**43.** (c)	**44.** (d)	**45.** (b)	**46.** (a)	**47.** (b)	**48.** (c)
49. (c)	**50.** (b)	**51.** (c)	**52.** (b)	**53.** (c)	**54.** (b)	**55.** (d)	**56.** (a)
57. (b)	**58.** (a)	**59.** (a)	**60.** (b)	**61.** (a)	**62.** (b)	**63.** (c)	**64.** (b)
65. (c)							

9 Supervised Learning: Regression

Learning Objectives

At the end of this chapter, you will be able to:

- Explain the fundamental concepts of linear and non-linear regression
- Differentiate between simple linear regression, linear regression, and Poisson regression
- Apply the least squares method for data fitting and prediction
- Elaborate on multivariate linear regression and its applications
- Utilize kernel methods for pattern analysis and machine learning
- Explain generalized linear models and their use in statistical analysis
- Implement AdaBoost for improving prediction accuracy
- Use regularized regression to prevent overfitting in model training
- State the principles of backpropagation in neural networks
- Use support vector regression for high-dimensional data analysis
- Develop decision tree regression models for interpretative data analysis
- Integrate random forest regression for robust predictive modeling
- Design and train neural network regression models for complex pattern recognition
- Apply multi-layer propagation for deep learning architectures
- Utilize radial basis function (RBF) networks for function approximation
- Construct splines for flexible regression modeling
- Analyze the curse of dimensionality and its impact on data analysis
- Perform interpolations and explain basis functions in model construction
- Address multi-class and structured output problems in machine learning
- Explain the technique of ranking in the context of regression analysis

9.1 Introduction

The linear model is one of the most straightforward models in machine learning (ML). It is the structural basis for numerous complex ML algorithms, including deep neural networks (DNNs). Non-linear regression, in contrast to linear regression, is a type of regression analysis that examines the connection between the dependent variable and one or more non-linear independent variables. This means that the dependent variable does not change in proportion with the independent variable(s). In this chapter, we will discuss both linear and non-linear models.

9.2 Linear Regression versus Non-Linear Regression

The basic idea behind linear regression is that some linear relationship exists between two or more variables, which can be represented mathematically by an equation ($y = ax + b$). Here, y represents the dependent variable (the variable we want to predict), x represents the independent variables (the variables we are using for prediction), a is the coefficient, and b is an intercept term. This model aims to accurately estimate the value of y given some values for x.

To do so, it first uses observed data points from past conditions where both x and y were known to fit a line through them according to the above equation – this process is called **training**. After the model is trained, new unknown values for x can be used as input to make predictions about what value y will have – this process is called **prediction**.

For example, let us assume that you own a car showroom and want to determine how much profit or loss you will make when selling cars based on their engine size alone. In such cases, we would need historical records containing information like engine size alongside other factors like price sold, etc., so that our linear regression algorithm has enough training data points to establish relationships between different parameters. Once trained using these historical records, our algorithm would then be able to predict how much profit/loss one should expect when selling cars based on engine size without any human intervention, thus representing an efficient application of linear regression in ML.

Regression analysis is a statistical method used to examine the connection between single or multiple independent variables and a dependent variable. Linear regression, on the other hand, is a type of regression analysis where the dependent and independent variables are related linearly. In other words, a linear regression model supposes that the dependent variable varies in a straight line with the independent variables.

Non-linear regression, in contrast, is a type of regression analysis that examines the connection between the dependent variable and one or more non-linear independent variables. This means that the dependent variable does not change proportionally with the independent variable(s).

For example, let us say we want to understand the connection between temperature and the rate of a chemical reaction. Here, we can use a non-linear regression model to investigate the relationship between the two variables, which may not be linear. For instance, the model may hypothesize that the reaction rate increases exponentially with temperature, which would be a non-linear relationship.

Non-linear regression models come in various shapes and sizes, including quadratic, exponential, and logarithmic relationships. These models can be more complicated than linear regression models (Table 9.1), but they can better capture the data in situations where the relationship between the variables is not linear.

Table 9.1 Differences between linear and non-linear regression models

Characteristic	Linear regression model	Non-linear regression model
Type of function	Assume a linear relationship between the input variables and the output variable. Example: predicting house prices based on the number of bedrooms.	Assume a non-linear relationship. Example: predicting crop yield based on the amount of rainfall and temperature.

(*Continued*)

Table 9.1 (Continued)

Characteristic	Linear regression model	Non-linear regression model
Type of data	Suitable for continuous data	Suitable for both continuous and discrete data
Output	Predict a continuous output variable	Predict both continuous and categorical output variables
Relationship between input and output	Assume a constant relationship between input and output variables	Assume a changing relationship
Degree of polynomial	They are of degree 1. Example: $y = mx + b$	They can have any degree. Example: $y = ax$^2 $+ bx + c$
Number of independent variables	They have only one independent variable.	They can have multiple independent variables.
Model representation	They have a simple representation. Example: $y = mx + b$	They have a more complex representation. Example: $y = f(x)$
Parameters	They have fewer parameters. Example: m and b in $y = mx + b$	They have more parameters. Example: coefficients of the polynomial in $y = a0 + a1x + a2x$^2 +... + $anxn$
Residual plot	Linear. Example: a scatter plot of residuals will form a straight line.	Non-linear. Example: a scatter plot of residuals will form a curved line.
Training algorithm	Simpler. Example: ordinary least squares	More complex. Example: gradient descent
Underfitting and overfitting	They are more prone to underfitting. Example: a linear regression model for a complex data set	They are more prone to overfitting. Example: a high-degree polynomial regression model for a small data set
Interpretability	More interpretable. Example: it is easy to understand that an increase in the independent variable will lead to a proportional increase in the dependent variable.	Less interpretable. Example: it is difficult to understand the relationship between independent and dependent variables in a complex non-linear model.

9.3 Types of Linear Models

Linear models are an essential category of algorithms in ML that employ linear relationships between inputs and outputs to make predictions. Various types of linear models, including simple linear regression, linear regression, Poisson regression, and logistic regression (Table 9.2), are beneficial in ML.

Table 9.2 Characteristics of types of linear models

S. No	Characteristics	Simple linear models	Linear regression	Poisson regression	Logistic regression
1	Type of output	Continuous	Continuous	Count data (non-negative integer values)	Binary or categorical
2	Assumption about error distribution	Normal	Normal	Poisson	Bernoulli or binomial
3	Dependent variable	Continuous	Continuous	Count data (non-negative integer values)	Binary or categorical
4	Independent variable(s)	One continuous variable	One or more continuous or categorical variables	One or more continuous or categorical variables	One or more continuous or categorical variables
5	Functional form	Linear	Linear	Exponential	Sigmoidal
6	Type of relationship	Directly proportional	Directly proportional	Exponential	Non-linear
7	Interpretation of coefficients	Slope of the line	Change in the dependent variable for a unit change in the independent variable	Effect on the dependent variable of a unit change in the independent variable	Odds ratio
8	Suitable for	Continuous data with a linear relationship	Continuous data with a linear or non-linear relationship	Count data	Binary or categorical data
9	Examples	Predicting height based on weight	Predicting house prices based on location, size, etc.	Predicting number of traffic accidents based on traffic volume, weather, etc.	Predicting whether a customer will buy a product based on age, gender, etc.

9.3.1 Simple Linear Models (Simple Linear Regression)

Simple linear regression is a type of regression analysis that predicts a dependent variable using one independent variable (such as, years of experience or salary). Because the independent variable is unrelated to the dependent variable, it is considered independent. What is predicted, on the other hand, affects the dependent variable. Simple linear regression generates the best-fit line for the data but ensuring that the line is a good fit is critical. For example, a simple linear regression may result in a too-steep line that does not accurately represent the data if the data points have a strong upward trend and are widely dispersed.

We can use a simple linear regression model for forecasting product sales based on advertisement spend (Table 9.3). A company can do this by collecting data on the total amount spent on advertising and the resulting sales. Then, with enough data points, a model (function) that accurately predicts future sales based on a given advertising budget can be created.

Table 9.3 Advertisement versus sales

Advertising spend (X): Rs	Sales (Y): Rs
100	1000
200	1500
300	2000
400	2500
500	3000
600	3500
700	4000
800	4500
900	5000
1000	5500

The graph structure for a simple linear regression model predicting product sales based on advertising spend would have two axes: one for the advertising spend and one for the sales achieved in response to that advertisement (Fig. 9.1).

The data points representing the total amount ($) invested in advertising and the corresponding sales ($) made in response to that advertisement will be plotted on this graph. Each point represents a single observation. The points on the graph would be scattered, as there may be some variation in the relationship between advertising spend and sales made. However, the simple linear regression model would find the line of best fit through these points. The line represents the predicted relationship between advertising spend and sales made. The line would have an intercept (where the line intersects the y-axis) and a slope (the line's steepness). The slope would represent the change in sales for every unit increase in advertising spend. The intercept would represent the predicted sales when the advertising spend is zero.

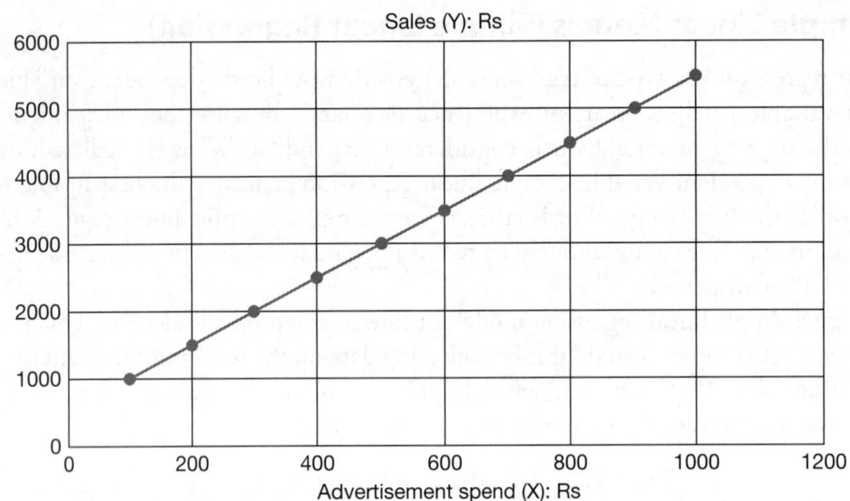

Figure 9.1 Sales versus advertisement graph

The values of $b0$ and $b1$ in a simple linear regression with one input variable and one output variable are calculated by minimizing the **sum of squared errors** (SSE), which is the sum of the squared difference between the actual output values and their predicted values. This can be done by solving a system of equations or using the formulae below:

$$b1 = \sum[(xi - \bar{x})(yi - \bar{y})]/\sum[(xi - \bar{x})\text{^}2]$$
$$b0 = \bar{y} - b1{*}\bar{x},$$

where xi is an individual data point's input value, yi is its corresponding output value, $\bar{x}$ is the mean of all input values, and $\bar{y}$ is the mean of all output values.

To calculate sales when advertising spend = Rs 1100 using simple linear regression, we first need to calculate the slope ($b1$) and intercept ($b0$) using the following formulae:

$$b1 = \Sigma[(Xi - \bar{X})(Yi - \bar{Y})] \;/\; \Sigma(Xi - \bar{X})\text{^}2$$
$$b0 = \bar{Y} - b1\bar{X},$$

where Xi is the advertising spend, $\bar{X}$ is the mean advertising spend, Yi is the corresponding sales, and $\bar{Y}$ is the mean sales.

First, we calculate the means:

$\bar{X}$ = (100 + 200 + 300 + 400 + 500 + 600 + 700 + 800 + 900 + 1000) / 10 = 550
$\bar{Y}$ = (1000 + 1500 + 2000 + 2500 + 3000 + 3500 + 4000 + 4500 + 5000 + 5500) / 10 = 3250

Next, we calculate the values for $b1$:

$b1$ = [(100 – 550)(1000 – 3250) + (200 – 550)(1500 – 3250) + (300 – 550)(2000 – 3250) + (400 – 550)(2500 – 3250) + (500 – 550)(3000 – 3250) + (600 – 550)(3500 – 3250) + (700 – 550)(4000 – 3250) + (800 – 550)(4500 – 3250) + (900 – 550)(5000 – 3250) + (1000 – 550)(5500 – 3250)] / [(100 – 550)^2 + (200 – 550)^2 + (300 – 550)^2 + (400 – 550)^2 + (500 – 550)^2 + (600 – 550)^2 + (700 – 550)^2 + (800 – 550)^2 + (900 – 550)^2 + (1000 – 550)^2]
$b1$ = (4125000) / 825000 = 5

Now, we calculate the value for $b0$:

$$b0 = 3250 - (5 * 550) = 500$$

Therefore, the equation of the simple linear regression line is:

$$Y = 500 + 5X$$

Finally, we can use this equation to predict sales when advertising spend = 1100:

$$Y = 500 + 5*1100 = 6000$$

Therefore, sales is predicted to be 6000 when advertising spend is 1100.

9.3.2 Linear Regression

Linear regression is a broader linear model with several input variables and a single output variable. Linear regression seeks to find the best line that fits the data. The equation that defines the line is as follows:

$$y = \beta 0 + \beta 1x1 + \beta 2x2 + \ldots + \beta pxp,$$

where y is the output variable; $x1$, $x2$,..., xp are the input variables; $\beta 0$ is the intercept; and $\beta 1$, $\beta 2$,..., βp are the slopes.

Linear regression is commonly used in ML for tasks such as predicting a person's income based on their education, age, and occupation or predicting the sales of a product based on its price, advertising spend, and other factors. Some real-life examples of linear regression are:

- **Housing prices**: Linear regression can be used to forecast the cost of a house based on its size, location, number of rooms, and other characteristics.
- **Sales forecasting:** Linear regression can predict future sales based on historical sales data, marketing spending, and other factors.
- **Medical research:** Linear regression can be used to study the relationship between different medical variables and predict the risk of developing certain diseases.
- **Finance:** Linear regression can analyze the relationship between stock prices, interest rates, and other financial variables.
- **Quality control:** Linear regression can be used to analyze data from manufacturing processes to identify factors that affect product quality and improve efficiency.

Suppose we have a data set with the following features (Table 9.4):

- The size of the house (in square feet)
- Number of bedrooms
- Number of bathrooms
- Location (represented as a categorical variable with different levels)

Size (sq.ft)	Bedrooms	Bathrooms	Location	Price ($)
1200	2	1	Suburban	150,000
1500	3	2	Urban	250,000
1800	3	2	Rural	200,000
2000	4	3	Suburban	300,000
2200	4	3	Urban	350,000

We can use linear regression to predict the price of a house based on its size, number of bedrooms (number), number of bathrooms (number), and location (string). For example, we want to predict the price of a house with the following characteristics:

Price = *b*0 + *b*1 * size + *b*2 * bedrooms + *b*3 * bathrooms + *b*4 * location_suburban + *b*5 * location_rural

Using the training data, the model might learn the coefficients given in Table 9.5.

Table 9.5 Basic house data for price prediction

Size (sq.ft)	Bedrooms	Bathrooms	Location
1700	3	2	Urban

When we have categorical data in our data set (table), we need to convert the string values into numerical data (numbers) so that ML models can process it. ML models use numerical value more efficiently. One way to do this is through **one-hot encoding**. This technique generates binary variables (0 or 1) as outcome for each of the possible categories in a categorical variable.

For instance, let us say we have a categorical variable called location which has two possible categories: suburban and rural. To convert this variable into numerical data using one-hot encoding, we create two binary variables, namely, location suburban and location rural. If location has the value of suburban, then the value of location suburban will be set to 1, and similarly, the value of location rural will be set to 0. If the location is rural, then the value of location rural will be set to 1, and the value of location suburban will be set to 0.

To predict the price of the new house, we would use the following formula:

Price = *b*0 + *b*1 * size + *b*2 * bedrooms + *b*3 * bathrooms + b4 * location_suburban + b5 * location_rural

In linear regression with multiple variables, the formula for the coefficients (*b*0, *b*1, *b*2, *b*3, *b*4, *b*5, etc.) is calculated using the following formula:

*b*0 = *y*_mean – *b*1*x*1_mean – *b*2*x*2_mean – *b*3*x*3_mean – *b*4*x*4_mean – *b*5**x*5_mean -...
*b*1 = Σ((*xi* – *x*_mean)*(*yi* – *y*_mean)) / Σ((*xi* – *x*_mean)^2)
*b*2 = Σ((*xi* – *x*_mean)*(*zi* – *z*_mean)) / Σ((*xi* – *x*_mean)^2)

$b3 = \Sigma((xi - x\_mean)*(wi - w\_mean)) / \Sigma((xi - x\_mean)^2)$
$b4 = \Sigma((xi - x\_mean)*(ui - u\_mean)) / \Sigma((xi - x\_mean)^2)$
$b5 = \Sigma((xi - x\_mean)*(vi - v\_mean)) / \Sigma((xi - x\_mean)^2)$

Σ represents the summation operation, and *x_mean*, *y_mean*, *z_mean*, *w_mean*, and *v_mean* are the means of the respective variables.

In a linear regression model, this formula can calculate the coefficients for any number of independent variables.

$$b0 = -12514.9$$
$$b1 = 123.15$$
$$b2 = -15893.5$$
$$b3 = 28835.8$$
$$b4 = 27012.5$$
$$b5 = -6968.6$$

Plugging in the values for the new house, we get the following:

Price = –12514.9 + 123.15 * 1700 + (–15893.5) * 3 + 28835.8 * 2 + 27012.5 * 0 + (–6968.6) * 0
= 218,725.1

The predicted price of the house would be $218,725.1

9.3.3 Linear Regression using the Cost Function

The cost function helps us find the best straight line that fits the data. Consider a simple linear regression. The regression fit has also been termed a hypothesis, which is given as $h_\theta(x) = \theta_0 + \theta_1 x$, where $\theta = \left[\theta_0, \ \theta_1\right]^T$ denotes the parameter vector. The hypothesis $\breve{y} = h_\theta(x) = \theta_0 + \theta_1 x$ represents a straight line with θ_1 as slope and θ_0 as *y*-intercept.

Consider randomly taken data for house price estimation that depends on the area of the house (Table 9.6).

Table 9.6 Sample housing data for regression

Area (in Sq. Ft.)	Price (in INR)
2100	15.75
1200	10.20
2400	18.50
3600	24.85
750	9.25

The plot is shown in Fig. 9.2.

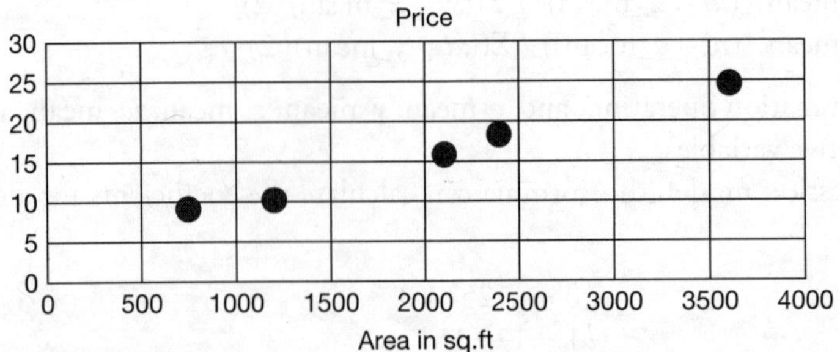

Figure 9.2 Plot of house area and price sample data

After applying the regression algorithm, the values for the parameters θ_0 and θ_1 are determined. The value for θ_0 represents the y-intercept, which can be interpreted as the base price of the house.

The model should be developed to minimize the cost function. The cost function is nothing but the squared error between the actual price and the estimated price. It is denoted as

$$\text{Minimize}\left(y - \breve{y}\right)^2$$

The squared error is determined for every input, and the sum is averaged over the entire training data set. Let the number of samples in the training data set be m.

$$\frac{1}{2m}\sum_{i=1}^{m}\left(y^{(i)} - \widehat{y^{(i)}}\right)^2$$

In the equation, an extra scaling factor of $\frac{1}{2}$ is used. This helps to eliminate the square term while calculating the derivative or partial derivative.

Thus the cost function is defined as

$$J\left(\theta_0, \theta_1\right) = \frac{1}{2m}\sum_{i=1}^{m}(y^{(i)} - \breve{y}^{(i)})^2$$

The gradient descent algorithm minimizes the cost function and determines the optimal values for the parameters. The outline of the gradient descent algorithm is as follows:

Start with initial values of (θ_0, θ_1)
repeat {
$$\theta_0 = \theta_0 - \eta\frac{\partial}{\partial\theta_0}J\left(\theta_0, \theta_1\right)$$
$$\theta_1 = \theta_1 - \eta\frac{\partial}{\partial\theta_1}J\left(\theta_0, \theta_1\right)$$
} till convergence is reached
η is the learning rate

Substituting equations in the algorithm,

$$\begin{aligned}
&\text{Start with initial values of } (\theta_0, \theta_1) \\
&\text{repeat } \{ \\
&\theta_0 = \theta_0 - \eta \frac{\partial}{\partial \theta_0}\left(\frac{1}{2m} \sum_{i=1}^{m} (y^{(i)} - h_\theta(x^{(i)})^2 \right) \\
&\theta_1 = \theta_1 - \eta \frac{\partial}{\partial \theta_1}\left(\frac{1}{2m} \sum_{i=1}^{m} (y^{(i)} - h_\theta(x^{(i)})^2 \right) \\
&\}\text{ till convergence is reached}
\end{aligned}$$

By applying the derivative, the algorithm becomes

$$\begin{aligned}
&\text{Start with initial values of } (\theta_0, \theta_1) \\
&\text{repeat } \{ \\
&\theta_0 = \theta_0 - \eta \frac{1}{m} \sum_{i=1}^{m} \left(y^{(i)} - h_\theta(x^{(i)}) \right) \\
&\theta_1 = \theta_1 - \eta \frac{1}{m} \sum_{i=1}^{m} \left(y^{(i)} - h_\theta(x^{(i)}) \right) x^{(i)} \\
&\}\text{ till convergence is reached}
\end{aligned}$$

The convergence test is generally performed by examining the $J(\theta)$ if it decreases by less than 0.001 in an iteration or if the process is repeated for a fixed number of iterations.

9.3.4 Locally Weighted Regression

Linear regression tries to fit the best-fit line if the data is linear. Linear regression is not the best choice if the data is non-linear. In such cases, locally weighted regression can be considered to fit a curve for the non-linear data.

The model is trained by fitting θ to minimize the cost function in simple linear regression. In locally weighted regression, to predict a point x, check the local neighborhood of the training samples. Fit a line that passes through the outputs in that neighborhood and predict x.

To define it formally, the cost function in the case of locally weighted regression is

$$J(\theta_0, \theta_1) = \sum_{i=1}^{m} w^{(i)} (y^{(i)} - \breve{y}^{(i)}),^2$$

where $w^{(i)}$ is the weight assigned to the ith training sample. $w^{(i)} \in [0,1]$. The value is set using the Gaussian function

$$w^{(i)} = \exp\left(-\frac{\left(x^{(i)} - x\right)^2}{2\tau^2} \right),$$

where $x^{(i)}$ is the ith training sample, x is the input for which prediction has to be made, and τ is the bandwidth parameter that controls the number of neighborhoods to be considered.

9.3.5 Poisson Regression

Poisson regression is a type of linear model that is used when the output variable is a count. The equation for the model is

$$\log(\mu) = \beta 0 + \beta 1x1 + \beta 2x2 + ... + \beta pxp,$$

where μ is the expected value of the count; $x1$, $x2$,..., xp are the input variables, $\beta 0$ is the intercept, and $\beta 1$, $\beta 2$,..., βp are the slopes.

ML applications like forecasting the number of consumers visiting a store on a given day based on the weather, time of year, and other characteristics frequently involve the use of Poisson regression. This model is also used for occasions where the outcomes are counted. Counts can never be zero. A Poisson distribution is unique and has various properties.

Examples of Poisson regression includes predicting the number of car accidents that may occur on a particular road segment on a given day based on various parameters: weather, time of day, traffic volume, and road conditions. Other examples include predicting the number of defects in a manufacturing process, or the number of customer complaints in a call center in a day based on given conditions.

Here is a step-by-step example of how this can be done:

Data collection: First, collect data/information and various details on the number of car accidents that occurred on the road segment over some time (say three to six months), as well as data on various factors that may affect the number of accidents, such as weather, time of day, traffic volume, and road conditions.

Data preprocessing: Once we collect the data, clean and prepare the data for further analysis, which includes removing any missing or erroneous data and transforming the data/information into the appropriate format.

Model building: Build a Poisson regression model to predict the number of accidents based on the available factors. This involves specifying the model equation, estimating various parameters, and evaluating the model's fit to the data.

Interpretation: Use the model parameters to identify the factors most strongly related to the number of car accidents on the road segment.

Prediction: Use the model to predict the number of car accidents that may occur on a particular day based on the values of the relevant factors. For example, we have data indicating that there will be heavy rain, high traffic volume, and poor road conditions on a particular day. In that case, we can use the model to predict the number of accidents likely to occur on that day.

The formula for Poisson regression is:

$$\log(y) = b0 + b1x1 + b2x2 + ... + bk^{*}xk,$$

where y is the number of car accidents; $x1$, $x2$,..., xk are the factors that may affect the number of accidents (such as weather, time of day, traffic volume, and road conditions); and $b0$, $b1$, $b2$,..., bk are the regression coefficients.

To predict the number of car accidents on a particular day, we can plug the relevant factors' values into the equation and use the resulting equation to calculate the expected value of y (the number of accidents). For example, if the values of the factors on a particular day are:

Weather: Heavy rain (1)

Time of day: Rush hour (1)

Traffic volume: High (1)

Road conditions: Poor (1)

Then the equation would be:

$$\log(y) = b0 + b11 + b21 + b31 + b41$$

We can then use the estimated values of $b0$, $b1$, $b2$, $b3$, and $b4$ to calculate the expected value of y (the number of accidents) for these values of the factors.

Let us assume there were 10 car accidents along this stretch in the last month alone. We also know that the weather was primarily sunny during this period, with occasional showers and thunderstorms; there was heavy traffic during rush hour and moderate traffic at other times; and while there were some potholes in the road, it was generally well maintained. Based on these factors, we can now generate a Poisson regression model which will relate them to accident levels – for example, showing how an increase in rain increases the likelihood of an accident due to slippery roads. Furthermore, this model can predict future accident levels depending on various inputs, such as changing weather conditions or increasing traffic volumes over time.

9.4 Least Squares Method

Least squares method (LSM) is a statistical method for estimating a linear regression model's unknown parameter. It relies on minimizing the sum of squared errors between the actual values and the predictions. The best weights for an artificial neural network (ANN) or any other supervised learning method are chosen using ML.

For example, we want to forecast a company's stock returns based on several factors, including market capitalization, debt-to-equity ratio, revenue, and earnings. We gather information on these aspects throughout time, say, the past five years, and information on the company's stock returns during that time.

We then use LSM to calculate the coefficients of the linear regression equation that best fits the data. The equation would take the form:

Stock returns = $b0$ + $b1$ * Revenue + $b2$ * Earnings + $b3$ * Debt-to-equity ratio + $b4$ * Market capitalization

The coefficients $b0$, $b1$, $b2$, $b3$, and $b4$ will be determined based on the data gathered. The coefficient values that reduce the sum of squared errors between the expected and actual stock returns would then be determined using the least squares approach.

After we know the coefficients, we can use them to forecast stock returns based on the features' values for subsequent periods. Suppose the data on the company's sales, earnings, debt-to-equity ratio, and market capitalization for the upcoming quarter, for instance, are available. In that case, we can use the equation to predict the stock returns for that quarter.

Of course, this is a simplified example, and many other factors can affect a company's stock returns. Also, it is important to note that past performance does not necessarily indicate future performance, so any predictions made using this method should be taken with a grain of salt.

Once you have determined which features are most important for predicting returns, you will want to adjust your models' weightings appropriately. This process can be done by adjusting each feature's weighting until it produces an optimal fit with existing data points; this is how least squares methods are commonly used in ML algorithms such as ANNs and support vector machines (SVMs).

9.4.1 Using Least Squares Regression for Classification

Least squares regression (LSR) can be used by assigning a binary label to each input based on the predicted constant output value. A threshold is used to determine the binary label, where inputs with predicted values above the threshold are classified as positive, and inputs with predicted values below the threshold are classified as unfavorable. Several variations of least squares regression are used for classification, including logistic regression, probit regression, and SVM. These methods are now preferred over simple least squares regression because they are better suited for binary classification problems and provide more interpretable results.

LSR provides a probabilistic classification result, which helps decision-makers quickly identify the most likely outcome based on the data. Furthermore, this probabilistic measure also helps to determine the uncertainty in the prediction, allowing decision-makers to consider factors such as noise or outliers in their data. This makes it an ideal method for managing data sets with high dimensionality where traditional approaches may fail due to complexity and lack of knowledge about underlying patterns or relationships.

LSR can also be used to classify other domains, such as marketing and sales. For example, it can predict customer churn based on past behavior and demographic data. This model can then identify high-risk customers who may need more personalized attention or targeted offers to stay loyal to the brand. This technique can also be used in healthcare, where it can help identify patients at risk of developing chronic diseases such as diabetes by analysing their medical history and other related data points.

9.5 Multivariate Linear Regression

Multivariate linear regression can be a powerful tool when used correctly. It has the potential to uncover intricate relationships between multiple features and a single output, which can then be leveraged to make more informed decisions and predictions. In addition, by exploring different combinations of predictors and their effects on outputs, you can gain insight into the underlying relationships between them, which will help you build better models for forecasting future outcomes.

For example, suppose you want to use multivariate linear regression to predict sales figures for your business based on historical data of different factors such as advertisement spend and customer ratings. In that case, you could look at past correlations between all these variables. For example, certain combinations of advertisement spending and customer ratings have consistently been associated with higher sales figures than others. This information could then be used to develop a model that accurately predicts future sales figures based on this combination of variables. In addition, you might further refine your model's accuracy when predicting future figures by investigating other factors, such as competitive activity or seasonality trends related to your business over time.

9.6 Non-Linearity and Kernel Methods

Kernel methods are a powerful tool to detect non-linearity in data. They provide a way of transforming data into high-dimensional features and can lead to improved accuracy. Kernel methods are widely used in both classification and regression tasks, as well as for clustering applications.

Let us start with an example of how kernel methods can be applied to a non-linear problem. Consider the task of classifying flower types from images. We might want to be able to distinguish roses from daisies. Solving this problem using linear regression or any other linear model is impossible because the two classes are not linearly separable. However, by applying a kernel function such as a radial basis function (RBF) or SVM, we can transform our data points into higher dimensions to become linearly separable in the new space formed by these additional features. This makes it possible for us to classify flower types more accurately.

Kernel functions are also essential in clustering algorithms such as *K*-means and Gaussian mixture models (GMMs). These algorithms rely on measuring distances between points and cluster them according to their relative proximity – this allows them to identify clusters within data sets that have patterns that are not immediately obvious. By applying kernel functions, these algorithms may be able to find more complex patterns that traditional linear distance measures would miss out on (such as non-linear distributions). This increased level of complexity leads to improved performance when these clustering algorithms are run on real data sets with complex structures that cannot easily be classified using traditional methods alone.

We will now discuss the types of kernel methods.

Linear Kernel: SVMs use the linear kernel to solve classification and regression issues. It is a dot product that compares two vectors to determine their similarity.

$K(x, y) = x * y$ is a mathematical expression for the linear kernel, where x and y are the feature vectors of the two input data points. Simply put, this computes the dot product of the two vectors.

For instance, we have two data points with the values $x1 = (1, 2)$ and $x2 = (3, 4)$. The linear kernel function can be utilized to compute the similarity between these two data points as follows:

$$K(x1, x2) = (1 * 3) + (2 * 4) = 11$$

This demonstrates the high similarity score of 11 between the two data points.

Polynomial Kernel: This is a kernel function used in SVMs for non-linear classification tasks. It uses polynomial functions to map the original data points into a higher-dimensional feature space. The main advantage of using the polynomial kernel is that it can capture non-linear relationships between data points that a linear kernel cannot.

The formula for the polynomial kernel is:

$$K(x, y) = (x * y + c)\wedge d,$$

where x and y are the data points to be compared; c is a constant that shifts the feature space's origin, which helps find the right balance between overfitting and underfitting; and d is the degree of the polynomial, which determines the degree of non-linearity captured in the transformed feature space.

Suppose we have two data points, $x = [2,3]$ and $y = [1,5]$. We can apply a polynomial kernel of degree 2 with $c = 1$ to transform them into a higher-dimensional feature space:

$$K(x, y) = (21 + 35 + 1)\wedge 2 = 169$$

So, the similarity score between x and y in the transformed space is 169.

Gaussian Kernel: Also called the radial basis function (RBF) kernal, this is used in SVMs for non-linear classification and regression tasks. It maps the input data points to a higher dimensional feature space, where the data is more separable.

The formula for the Gaussian kernel is:

$$K(x, x') = \exp(\text{-gamma} * ||x - x'||\wedge 2),$$

where x and x' are the input data points, ||.|| is the Euclidean distance between the two points, and gamma is a hyperparameter that controls the width of the kernel.

The higher the gamma value, the narrower the kernel, resulting in a more complex decision boundary that may overfit the training data. Conversely, a lower value of gamma results in a broader kernel and a smoother decision boundary that may underfit the training data.

An example of using the Gaussian kernel is image classification. Given an input image, the SVM with the Gaussian kernel can learn to classify the image into one of several categories based on its features, such as color and texture. Furthermore, the kernel allows the SVM to capture non-linear relationships between the image features and class.

Exponential Kernel: The formula for this kernel is:

$$K(x, x') = \exp(\text{-gamma} * ||x - x'||),$$

where x and x' are input feature vectors, ||.|| denotes the Euclidean distance between the feature vectors, and gamma is a hyperparameter that controls the width of the kernel function.

The exponential kernel has the property of mapping the input features into a higher-dimensional feature space, where they are more separable. It is advantageous when dealing with non-linearly separable data.

Suppose we have a data set of two-dimensional points with two classes, red and blue. We want to use SVM to classify new points as red or blue based on their location in the feature space. Let us assume that the data set has the following points:

red points: (1,1), (1,–1), (–1,1), (–1,–1)
blue points: (2,2), (2,–2), (–2,2), (–2,–2)

We can use the exponential kernel to transform the data points into a higher-dimensional feature space, making them more separable. For simplicity, let's assume gamma = 1.

The transformed feature vectors for the red points would be:

(1, exp(–1*sqrt(2))), (1, exp(1*sqrt(2))), (1, exp(1*sqrt(2))), (1, exp(–1*sqrt(2)))

Similarly, the transformed feature vectors for the blue points would be:

(1, exp(–4*sqrt(2))), (1, exp(4*sqrt(2))), (1, exp(4*sqrt(2))), (1, exp(–4*sqrt(2)))

We can now use these transformed feature vectors to train an SVM classifier that can classify new points as red or blue based on their location in the higher-dimensional feature space.

Laplacian Kernel: This is used in ML, particularly in image processing and computer vision tasks. It is defined as:

$$K(x, y) = e^\wedge(-||x-y|| \,/\, \text{sigma}),$$

where x and y are the input data points, $||x - y||$ is the Euclidean distance between them, and sigma is a parameter that determines the width of the kernel.

The Laplacian kernel is similar to the Gaussian kernel. However, instead of a bell curve, it has a sharp peak at zero. It decays more rapidly as the distance from zero increases. This makes it useful for detecting edges and other sharp transitions in images.

Let us consider an example of using the Laplacian kernel to detect edges in a grayscale image. First, the Laplacian kernel is applied to the image using convolution:

[[0, 1, 0],
[1, –4, 1],
[0, 1, 0]]

Next, the result of the convolution is thresholded to produce a binary image where the edges are highlighted:

[0, 0, 0, 0, 0, 0, 0, 0, 0, 0]
[0, 0, 0, 0, 0, 0, 0, 0, 0, 0]
[0, 0, 0, 0, 0, 0, 0, 0, 0, 0]
[0, 0, 0, 0, 1, 1, 1, 0, 0, 0]
[0, 0, 0, 0, 1, 1, 1, 0, 0, 0]
[0, 0, 0, 0, 1, 1, 1, 0, 0, 0]
[0, 0, 0, 0, 0, 0, 0, 0, 0, 0]
[0, 0, 0, 0, 0, 0, 0, 0, 0, 0]
[0, 0, 0, 0, 0, 0, 0, 0, 0, 0]
[0, 0, 0, 0, 0, 0, 0, 0, 0, 0]

In this example, the Laplacian kernel highlights the edges in the image, which can be helpful for image segmentation and other computer vision tasks.

Hyperbolic or Sigmoid Kernel: This kernel is used in neural network areas of machine literacy. The activation function for the sigmoid kernel is the bipolar sigmoid function. The equation for the hyperbolic kernel function is

$$k(x,y) = \tanh(\alpha x \ \ Ty + c)$$

This kernel is popularly used with SVMs.

ANOVA Radial Basis Kernel: This is a kernel method used in ML algorithms based on the similarity between two data points. It is a non-linear kernel function commonly used in SVM to classify patterns with complex, non-linear relationships. It measures the distance between two data points and assigns weights based on their similarity. This allows for improved accuracy compared to linear kernels, as it can capture more complex relationships, such as non-linear decision boundaries between data classes.

The ANOVA RBF kernel uses the following formula to calculate the distance between two data points *x* and *y*:

$$K(x, y) = e\text{^}(-\gamma||x - y||2),$$

where $\gamma > 0$ is a free parameter that determines how quickly the influence of one point falls off to its distance from another point. The larger γ is, the more quickly this influence decreases, thus affecting how "smooth" or "jagged" our decision boundary will be.

A considerable γ value will also lead to increased overfitting, and we must be careful not to set it too high! On the other hand, lower values result in smoother decision boundaries and fewer chances of overfitting. However, they may also result in lower accuracy for specific data sets.

Let us consider an example where we have three classes (A, B, C) that are linearly separable using a single hyperplane H1, shown as, H1: $W^*X + b = 0$. We can use an SVM classifier with a linear kernel along this hyperplane H1 which would give us perfect results since our data set is linearly separable without any overlap between classes A and B or B and C; that is, there are no outliers or mislabeled points that would complicate matters further, but what if we want something better? We could try using ANOVA RBF, which might allow us to capture more complex relationships such as outliers/mislabeled points and allow for greater accuracy than relying on a linear model like the above.

To understand how this works, let us look at another example where our data set consists of four classes, A, B, C, and D, which are not linearly separable anymore due to some mislabeled points. Here we can see that even though these four classes are not linearly separable, they still have relatively distinct distributions, thanks mainly due their annotation structure being slightly different from each other (A has one extra point than B, etc.). With this information, we can try using ANOVA RBF:

$$K(x,y)= e\text{^}(-\gamma||x - y||2)$$

With γ set at one, since it provides good results on average unless you are dealing with very noisy data sets, increasing gamma might help alleviate performance issues caused by overfitting/noise.

9.7 Generalized Linear Models

Generalized linear models (GLMs) are a type of supervised ML technique used to make predictions. By using a non-linear function, GLMs can predict the outcome for an input vector x which contains data on an instance, such as age or gender. A logistic regression model is an example of a GLM; it uses the sigmoid function to determine if an input vector belongs to one group (such as bad credit) or another (good credit). This same sigmoid function can then forecast future outcomes based on their features.

GLMs aim to create a model that accurately reflects any given data set. Various techniques are employed to achieve this goal – including regularization and Bayesian methods – all of which serve different purposes. Regularization helps reduce overfitting by limiting the number of parameters used in the model; Bayesian methods utilize prior knowledge about probabilities when making predictions for new data sets, thus improving accuracy even further.

In addition to logistic regression models, other types of GLMs include:

- Poisson regression models (used for predicting count data)
- Probit models (used for binary classification tasks)
- Multinomial logistic regression models (used for multiclass classification)

These GLMs share similar principles – they all use linear combinations of explanatory variables to calculate predicted responses. However, depending on their specific task objectives and data requirements, they differ in how these combinations are weighted.

Unlike traditional direct regression models, which assume a direct relationship between the response and predictor variables, GLMs allow for further flexible, non-linear connections by using a different initial statistical distribution.

Some of the **features** of GLMs are as follows:

- GLMs can be used to model various relationships between response and predictor variables. For instance, Poisson regression enables the estimation of the count of an event, such as the number of car accidents in a given day, based on predictors such as traffic volume and weather conditions. Moreover, other GLMs allow for more specific analyses tailored to certain types of data sets or research questions.
- GLMs are beneficial when handling outliers, as they provide more flexibility than traditional linear regression models. Unlike traditional linear regression, GLMs can accommodate non-normal distributions of the response variable, and robust regression methods like Huber regression can account for outliers that disproportionately influence the results. This is advantageous because even if there are extreme values in the data, GLMs can still estimate reasonable parameters without unduly affecting them.
- GLMs are practical and adaptable data analysis tools. They provide valuable model fitting and validation techniques and can be applied to massive data sets and sophisticated models; in high-dimensional data sets with numerous predictors, regularized regression models, such as LASSO and ridge, aid in reducing overfitting. Decision-makers are empowered to make well-informed decisions based on precise forecasts thanks to the insights provided by GLMs into the relationships between variables.

Some of the **disadvantages** of GLMs are as follows:

- GLMs make certain assumptions about the distribution of the response variable that must be met to fit the data and make accurate predictions. For example, the linear component of GLMs assumes a linear relationship between the predictors and response variables. If this assumption is violated, it can lead to biased or inaccurate predictions. GLMs also assume that each observation is independent of one other, which may not be accurate in some cases, such as data collected from clustered or longitudinal designs. In these instances, it can be necessary to adjust the model accordingly to ensure accurate results and valid predictions.
- Selecting an appropriate statistical distribution for the response variable can be challenging in GLMs. For instance, if the response variable is binary, a logistic regression model is suitable, whereas if the response variable is count data, a Poisson regression model is preferred. Choosing an incorrect distribution or a mis-specified model can lead to biased or inefficient parameter estimates, inaccurate predictions, and incorrect inference.
- Globally, linear models such as GLMs are used for prediction and forecasting tasks. However, when an overly complex model is employed in the GLM or too many predictor variables are included, overfitting can occur. This leads to poor generalization performance when applied to new data, and inaccurate predictions may occur.

9.8 AdaBoost (Adaptive Boosting)

AdaBoost is a powerful non-linear meta-algorithm that improves the accuracy of classification models by combining the expertise of multiple weak learners. Developed in 1996 by Yoav Freund and Robert Schapire, AdaBoost combines multiple simple decision tree models, called 'weak learners', to form a robust classifier. These weak learners typically use decision stumps – decision trees with just one split – to make their predictions, which are combined using a weighted average to make the final prediction. By considering different kinds of evidence from each model, AdaBoost can produce more reliable results than any single method alone.

The AdaBoost algorithm works by iteratively training weak learners on subsets of the training data. In each iteration, the algorithm assigns weights to each training instance based on how well the current weak learner performed on that instance. Misclassified instances receive higher weights, while correctly classified instances receive lower weights. The next weak learner is trained on a weighted subset of the training data. Again, the weights are higher for the misclassified instances. After each iteration, the AdaBoost algorithm updates the weights of the training instances. It computes a weighted error rate for the current weak learner. The final classifier is composed of the weaker students, whose weights are based on their accuracy. The result is a robust classifier that is more accurate than any weak learner.

The main advantage of using AdaBoost for improving classification accuracy is its focus on producing highly accurate results with minimal computational resources required. It has also been shown to be robust against overfitting since it limits itself only to features that yield better results during each step in its process. Thus, instead of blindly applying all features available regardless of whether they contribute to better predictions, it carefully selects features that are expected to reduce generalization error over time while remaining computationally efficient.

To get one answer from all these weak classifiers, AdaBoost assigns α values to each of the classifiers. The α values are grounded on the error of each weak classifier.

The error ε = Number of incorrectly classified examples/ Total number of examples

And α is given by

$$\alpha = \frac{1}{2}\ln\left(\frac{1-\varepsilon}{\varepsilon}\right)$$

In AdaBoost, after calculating the weight of each weak classifier, α, the weight vector D is updated. D is a vector of weights assigned to each training example, indicating its importance in the subsequent training iterations. The weight vector D is updated such that the misclassified examples will have higher weights and the correctly classified examples will have lower weights. This allows the next weak classifier to focus on the misclassified examples and improve the overall performance of the model.

The updated weight vector D is calculated using the following formula:

$$D\_i(t+1) = D\_i(t) * \exp(\alpha\_t * y\_i * h\_t(x\_i)) / Z\_t,$$

where D_i(t) is the weight assigned to the ith training example at iteration t; α_t is the weight assigned to the tth weak classifier; y_i is the true label of the ith training example (+1 or –1); h_t(x_i) is the output of the tth weak classifier on the ith training example; and Z_t is a normalization factor to ensure that the sum of all weights equals 1.

For correctly classified examples, y_i * h_t(x_i) will be positive, resulting in a decrease in weight. For misclassified examples, y_i * h_t(x_i) will be negative, resulting in an increase in weight. This way, the model focuses more on the misclassified examples in the subsequent iterations.

For example, consider a binary classification problem with two features and 10 training examples. All examples are initially assigned an equal weight (D_i = 0.1). The first weak classifier is a decision tree that misclassifies 3 out of 10 examples. The weight assigned to this classifier is calculated as α_1 = 0.5 * log((1–0.3)/0.3) = 0.425. The weight vector D is then updated based on the misclassified examples. For example, if the first and fifth examples are misclassified, their weights would increase from 0.1 to 0.2. In contrast, the weights of the remaining examples would decrease from 0.1 to 0.0667. The next weak classifier will then focus more on the misclassified examples to improve the model's overall performance.

The algorithm iterates this process of training weak classifiers, calculating their weights based on their accuracy, and then adjusting the example weights accordingly. This iterative process is repeated until one of two conditions is met: either the training error becomes zero, meaning all examples are correctly classified by the combined model, or the number of weak classifiers reaches a predefined limit set by the user, known as a stopping criterion.

AdaBoost is particularly effective because it adapts to the 'hardness' of the examples. By increasing the weights of the harder-to-classify examples, it forces the subsequent classifiers to focus on the more difficult cases, which leads to an overall improvement in the model's performance. This adaptability is what gives AdaBoost its name and its robustness as an ensemble method in machine learning. The final ensemble model is often much more accurate than any of the individual weak classifiers could be on their own.

AdaBoost can be applied across numerous classification tasks such as document categorization (email spam filtering), face recognition systems, DNA sequence analysis, etc., making it a versatile technology with immense potential applications across industries from medical sciences to security surveillance systems and beyond!

9.9 Regularized Regression

Regularization is a technique used to avoid overfitting in the regression model by adding a penalty term to the loss function. In linear regression, the penalty term is added to the sum of the squared coefficients, known as ridge regression or L2 regularization. Because the connection between the independent and dependent variables is linear, this regularized regression is still linear. In contrast, LASSO regression or L1 regularization uses the absolute value of the coefficients as the penalty term (Table 9.6). This can lead to non-linear relationships between the independent and dependent variables, making it a non-linear regression method. Therefore, regularized regression can be either linear or non-linear depending on the type of regularization used.

Table 9.6 Characteristics of ridge and LASSO regression

S.No	Characteristics	Ridge regression	LASSO regression
1	Type of regression	It is a type of linear regression model that adds a penalty term to the sum of squared coefficients	It is a type of linear regression model that adds a penalty term to the absolute sum of coefficients
2	Penalty term	Ridge regression uses L2 regularization, which adds the squared sum of coefficients multiplied by a tuning parameter λ	LASSO regression uses L1 regularization, which adds the absolute sum of coefficients multiplied by a tuning parameter λ
3	Objective function	Ridge regression minimizes the residual sum of squares along with the penalty term	LASSO regression minimizes the residual sum of squares along with the penalty term
4	Solution approach	Ridge regression can be solved analytically using the closed-form solution or through gradient descent optimization	LASSO regression cannot be solved analytically and needs to be solved through coordinate descent optimization
5	Feature selection	Ridge regression can shrink the coefficients towards zero but cannot set them to exactly zero, hence not suitable for feature selection	LASSO regression can set some coefficients to exactly zero, hence can be used for feature selection

In ridge regression, an L2 norm penalty (also called weight decay) is added to the sum-of-squares error function, which forces parameter values toward zero but does not eliminate any feature from being included in the model. LASSO regression uses an L1 norm penalty instead, which encourages sparsity (some feature weights become zero), reduces variance, and improves generalizability for complex models with high numbers of features or predictors.

For example, let's say you are building a model for predicting house prices in your city based on multiple features such as the number of bedrooms, square footage, etc. Without applying any form of regularization, your predictive power may be good when tested against training data but may fail when put against new unseen data points due to overfitting – that is where regularized methods come into play. Using one or both types of regression, you can force specific parameter values toward zero, thus avoiding overfitting while maintaining consistency with all available training data points.

9.10 BACKPROPAGATION

In non-linear regression, backpropagation is frequently utilized, mainly when the data contains non-linear features. It is a supervised learning approach that is used to modify an artificial neural network's weights to lessen the discrepancy between the anticipated output and the produced output. Several iterations of this procedure are used until an acceptable degree of accuracy is attained. In addition, backpropagation can be used in linear regression models to modify parameters about any non-linear components present in the model, such as polynomial coefficients.

To derive the backpropagation algorithm, we first need to define the error function. The error function is defined as the difference between the predicted output and the actual output. Mathematically, we can define the error function as:

$$E = 1/2 * (y - \hat{y})^\wedge 2,$$

where E is the error, y is the actual output, and $\hat{y}$ is the predicted output.

To minimize the error function, we need to find the derivative of the error function with respect to the weights. We can use the chain rule of differentiation to compute the derivative of the error function. The chain rule states that the derivative of a function composed of two functions is the product of the derivatives of each function. Mathematically, we can express this as:

$$dE/dw = dE/d\hat{y} * d\hat{y}/dz * dz/dw,$$

where w is the weight, z is the input to the activation function, and $\hat{y}$ is the output of the activation function.

We can compute the derivatives of each term as follows:

$$dE/d\hat{y} = \hat{y} - y$$

$d\hat{y}/dz = f'(z)$, where $f'(z)$ is the derivative of the activation function.
$dz/dw = x$, where x is the input to the neuron.

Substituting these values in the equation for the derivative of the error function, we get:

$$dE/dw = (\hat{y} - y) * f'(z) * x$$

This equation gives us the gradient of the error function with respect to the weight. We can use this gradient to update the weight during training. The update rule is given by:

$$w = w - \alpha * dE/dw,$$

where α is the learning rate.

We can use this update rule to iteratively update the weights until the error function converges to a minimum.

9.11 Support Vector Regression

Support vector regression (SVR) is an ML technique that can be used to model complex non-linear relationships between input and output variables. Unlike SVMs, which are used for classification problems, SVR aims to find a function that approximates the data points with a minimum error, while allowing some deviation from the exact fit.

The main idea behind SVR is to find a hyperplane that separates the data points with a maximum margin, similar to SVMs. However, in SVR, the margin is defined by a parameter called epsilon, which determines how much error is tolerated. The data points that lie within the epsilon margin are called support vectors, and they are used to define the hyperplane. The data points that lie outside the epsilon margin are considered outliers, and they are penalized by a parameter called C, which controls the trade-off between complexity and accuracy.

One of the advantages of SVR is that it can use different kernels to transform the input space into a higher dimensional feature space, where a linear hyperplane can be found. For example, a radial basis function (RBF) kernel can be used to capture non-linear patterns in the data, while a polynomial kernel can be used to model polynomial relationships. The choice of kernel depends on the nature of the data and the desired performance.

To illustrate how SVR works, let us consider some examples. In the first example, we have a simple linear relationship between X and y. In this case, we can use a linear kernel to find a hyperplane that fits the data points with a minimum error.

The formula for a linear kernel is quite straightforward: it is simply the dot product of the vectors X and Y, plus a constant term c. Mathematically, it can be represented as $K(X,Y) = X.Y + c$, where K represents the kernel function, and X and Y are the input vectors. In the case of a linear kernel, this translates to the hyperplane equation in the form of $y = wx + b$, where w is the weight vector, x is the input feature vector, and b is the bias term. The objective of SVR is to find the optimal values of w and b such that the error between the predicted values and the actual values of y is minimized, while also ensuring that most data points lie within the epsilon margin of tolerance.

9.12 Decision Tree Regression

Decision tree regression is an ML technique that can be used to model complex non-linear relationships between input and output variables. Unlike linear regression, which assumes a linear function for the output variable, decision tree regression can capture non-linearities and interactions among the input variables by using a tree-like structure.

A decision tree is composed of nodes and branches. A node represents a test or a decision on an input variable, such as whether the age of a person is greater than 30 or not. A branch represents an outcome or a value of an output variable, such as the salary of a person. The root node is the first node in the tree, and it contains the entire data set. The leaf nodes are the final nodes in the tree, and they contain the predicted values for the output variable.

The decision tree regression algorithm works by recursively splitting the data based on some criteria, such as minimizing the squared error between the actual and predicted values of the output variable. The algorithm starts from the root node and selects the best input variable and the best split point to divide the data into two subsets. Then, for each subset, the algorithm repeats the same process until a leaf node is reached or a stopping condition is met. A stopping condition can be based on the depth of the tree, the number of samples in a node, or the purity of a node.

Decision tree regression has several advantages over other regression techniques. It can handle both numerical and categorical input variables, it can deal with missing values and outliers, it can handle multicollinearity and heteroscedasticity, and it can provide interpretable results. However, decision tree regression also has some drawbacks. It can be prone to overfitting, which means that it can capture noise and irrelevant details in the data and perform poorly on new data. It can also be sensitive to small changes in the data, which can result in different tree structures. Moreover, it can suffer from high variance, which means that it can produce different results with different random splits of the data.

To overcome these limitations, decision tree regression can be combined with other techniques, such as pruning, bagging, boosting, or random forests. Pruning is a technique that reduces the size and complexity of a decision tree by removing nodes that do not contribute much to the prediction accuracy. Bagging is a technique that creates multiple decision trees from different bootstrap samples of the data and averages their predictions. Boosting is a technique that creates multiple decision trees sequentially, where each tree tries to correct the errors of the previous trees. Random forest is a technique that creates multiple decision trees from different random subsets of the input variables and averages their predictions.

Decision tree regression is a powerful and flexible technique that can be used for various applications, such as predicting house prices, customer satisfaction, stock returns, or disease diagnosis.

9.13 Random Forest Regression

Random forest regression is a powerful ML technique that can handle complex and non-linear data. It is based on the idea of combining multiple decision tree regressors, which are simple models that split the data into branches based on some criteria. Each decision tree can capture a different aspect of the data, but it may also overfit to the noise and outliers. To overcome this problem, random forest regression uses two techniques: bootstrap sampling and feature selection.

Bootstrap sampling is a method of creating new data sets from the original one by randomly selecting observations with replacement. This means that some observations may appear more than once, while others may not appear at all. This creates diversity among the data sets, which reduces the correlation among the decision trees. **Feature selection** is a method of randomly choosing a subset of features (variables) to use for each decision tree. This prevents the trees from using the same features and makes them more independent.

By creating a number of decision trees using bootstrap sampling and feature selection, random forest regression creates an ensemble of diverse and independent models. The final prediction of the random forest is obtained by averaging the predictions of all the decision trees. This reduces the variance and improves the accuracy of the model, as well as its robustness to noise and outliers.

9.14 Neural Network Regression

Neural network regression is a complex ML technique that uses a network of connected nodes or neurons to represent the relationship between the input and output variables. This algorithm is frequently used to generate predictions and judgments based on data analysis in various industries, including banking, healthcare, and marketing.

The neural network comprises three layers: input, hidden, and output. First, the input layer receives the input information, which is subsequently sent through the hidden levels where the calculations are done. Finally, the output layer offers the final prediction or conclusion based on the input data.

Each node in the neural network runs some calculations on the data it receives and then sends the results to the layer below. By utilizing gradient descent or other optimization techniques to minimize a loss function like mean squared error, the algorithm learns the weights or parameters of each node.

Predicting continuous variables like stock prices, sales income, and patient outcomes is where the neural network regression technique shines. For instance, the length of a patient's hospital stay can be predicted by a healthcare professional using the patient's medical history and other pertinent information. A financial institution can also use this method to forecast a stock's future value based on historical performance and other market variables.

9.15 Multi-layer Propagation

Multi-layer neural networks have become increasingly popular for modeling non-linear regression tasks because they can learn complex underlying relationships between features and extract highly accurate predictive information from the input data. This is achieved by using multiple hidden layers of neurons that are connected with weights and biases. The output at each layer is passed through an activation function, creating non-linear decision boundaries in the output space. Building these more complex models requires more computational power than linear models. However, they can provide much more accurate predictions when used effectively.

The use of multi-layer neural networks for non-linear regression has been shown to outperform simpler linear regression architectures in accuracy and training speed because these architectures can learn from data without requiring any manually crafted features or assumptions about the task being addressed. They can also capture higher-order interactions between variables that may not be apparent when using linear approaches alone. Furthermore, they can benefit from batch normalization, which ensures faster training convergence while avoiding overfitting due to regularization techniques like dropout layers and weight decay. In addition, advanced optimization strategies such as adaptive learning rates allow for dynamic control over model performance during training, enabling users to adjust parameters on the fly depending on how the model behaves at any given moment.

The multi-layer propagation algorithm runs inputs or 'examples' through a series of layers to recognize patterns and generate an output. At each layer, the input is passed through a set of nodes with weights determining how the input will be processed. In its simplest form, each layer consists of weights multiplied by the data points entering it. This weight multiplication allows signals from each layer to influence the next one, allowing for more profound levels of learning.

In addition, activation functions can be applied to some or all layers to introduce non-linearity into the network's decision-making process. Activation functions can also help prevent specific inputs from dominating or overfitting certain outcomes by introducing thresholds that affect signal propagation across multiple nodes within a given layer.

Finally, backpropagation algorithms are used alongside multi-layer propagation to identify errors, update weights within connected layers, and test new examples against existing knowledge networks without retraining them from scratch. This helps improve accuracy and shorten training times significantly while still maintaining generalization capabilities across broader data sets than could usually be achieved with traditional machine learning methods alone.

9.16 Radial Basis Functions

The radial basis function (RBF) network is an artificial neural network that uses radial basis functions as activation functions. RBF networks are a popular tool in ML because they can learn complex non-linear mappings between inputs and outputs.

RBF networks consist of three layers: input, hidden, and output. The input layer receives the input data, which is passed through the hidden layer, and the output is produced by the output layer. The hidden layer consists of neurons, each with a radial basis function as its activation function. The output layer typically consists of a single neuron that produces the network's output.

RBF is a function that depends only on the distance between the input and a center point. Commonly used radial basis functions include Gaussian, inverse multiquadric, and thin-plate splines. The output of a neuron in the hidden layer is given by:

$$h(x) = \phi(||x - c||),$$

where ϕ is the radial basis function, x is the input to the neuron, and c is the center of the neuron.

Training Algorithm for RBF Networks: The training algorithm for RBF networks involves three steps: clustering, determining the centers and widths of the radial basis functions, and calculating the output weights. In the first step, clustering is used to partition the input data into clusters. Various algorithms like *K*-means or hierarchical clustering can be used to perform this task. Once clustered, the centroids of each cluster are used as center points for each radial basis function of hidden layer nodes. In the second step, the widths of each radial basis function are determined by calculating the distance between its center and the nearest neighboring centers. This ensures that outputs from RBFs overlap and can efficiently cover a range of inputs with minimal complexity. Alternatively, manual setting or heuristics can also determine the standard deviation for individual RBFs. Lastly, output weights are calculated through linear regression. Here, the input variables consist of activations from hidden layer nodes, that is, output from RBFs which were set up in the previous two steps. The coefficients resulting from the regression process represent the final output weights for the network's outputs neurons/nodes. The least squares method is commonly employed here, which estimates coefficients by minimizing the sum of squared errors obtained from comparing the model's predictions with actual target values.

Usefulness of RBF Networks in Machine Learning: RBF networks can be used for pattern recognition in systems that recognize faces, for example. In this scenario, the pixel values from an image of a face may be the input to the RBF network, and the output could be a categorization of that face. By learning from labeled data sets and subsequently identifying objects in fresh photos, RBF networks can also identify objects in images. Lastly, RBF networks have been used for clustering and other data mining applications. An RBF network is trained on a data set using unsupervised learning for clustering tasks, where it learns to classify or cluster close observations. This is important for identifying structure within data sets and locating hidden or unexpected patterns.

In addition, they are more efficient than traditional methods such as linear regression since training does not require optimization algorithms like gradient descent; instead, only weights need to be estimated from training data samples using least squares methods. Furthermore, RBF networks produce results quickly due to their fast convergence rate; this makes them ideal for real-time applications requiring rapid response times. Overall, RBF networks are valuable tools for machine learning practitioners thanks to their flexibility and power when solving complex non-linear mappings between inputs and outputs across various tasks ranging from financial modeling to image processing or data compression and dimensionality reduction.

9.17 Splines

Splines are a popular interpolation method that involve fitting low-order polynomials over intervals within data sets instead of attempting global fits over all data set points, as we would do with linear regression models. One advantage of using splines is that they allow us more flexibility than linear regression models because we can specify how smooth our model should be at different parts of our data set by choosing how many knots (breakpoints) we want to include within our model fit. In addition, this allows us more control over how each part will fit into one continuous curve instead of just trying out linear combinations directly from all available data points, as would otherwise be done for linear regression models.

Splines can also help avoid issues such as overfitting since these low-order polynomials will generally lead us away from cases where an overly complex solution may result from fitting too many knots into our model fit due to too much variation across different parts within our data set. Therefore, overall, splines offer great potential when dealing with data sets containing highly non-linear trends while still providing good accuracy levels if tuned correctly according to constraints related to specific types of variability present across different parts within this data set.

9.18 Curse of Dimensionality

This phenomenon describes how specific ML algorithms perform worse as the data set's number of features (or dimensions) grows. This may impact both linear and non-linear regression models. The data points get sparser, and the volume of the space grows exponentially as the number of dimensions in the data rises. As a result, the model may become overfitted, where it is excessively sophisticated and begins to fit the data noise rather than the proper signal. Techniques like feature selection, dimensionality reduction, and regularization can limit the number of features and avoid overfitting to solve this problem. Both linear and non-linear regression models can be used with these methods.

Let us consider a simple example. Suppose we have two data sets, each with 10 randomly scattered points in two-dimensional (2D) space. We want to measure the distance between these points using Euclidean distance. In this case, it is easy to calculate the distances between all 10 pairs of points because we only need to consider two variables: the *x* and *y* coordinates.

Suppose we have the same 10 points scattered in three-dimensional (3D) space. Calculating Euclidean distances becomes much more difficult because we need to consider three variables: the *x*, *y*, and *z* coordinates. As you increase dimensionality, calculating distances gets exponentially more difficult due to an increase in the number of variables that must be considered. Hence, the Curse of Dimensionality kicks in as complexity grows. As a result, computational cost increases considerably, and accuracy decreases gradually due to a need for more information/data or feature sets along higher dimensions.

The Curse of Dimensionality can present itself in many different forms depending on which algorithm you are using or what type of problem you are trying to solve with the machine learning model. For example, suppose an ML model uses linear regression. In that case, having too many features might cause overfitting or underfitting issues. On the other hand, if an unsupervised learning algorithm such as *K*-means clustering is used, more dimensions will lead to more clusters being formed than necessary, leading to difficulty interpreting results. Another consequence is that the curse makes it almost impossible for some algorithms, such as KNN (*K*-nearest neighbors), to work effectively due to its inability to work with higher dimensional data sets.

Finally, suppose an algorithm requires a large training data set. In that case, higher dimensions can lead to an even more extensive training data set size, leading to difficulties while handling them. The bottom line here is that the curse affects any machine-based learning model very adversely and can result in poor accuracy performance if it is not taken care of properly during the preprocessing phase.

9.19 Interpolations and Basis Functions

In non-linear regression, the relationship between the independent and dependent variables cannot be modeled using a linear equation. Interpolations and basis functions transform the data into a higher dimensional space, where the relationship between the variables may be better modeled using a linear equation.

Interpolations and basis functions are powerful tools used in machine learning. They allow for creating models that accurately represent a data set without storing the entire data set in memory. Instead, the model is built from a combination of basis functions that approximate the behavior of the data points within a range.

Interpolation is a technique to recreate meaningful information from two known values in an unknown space between them. It is usually used for estimating missing values by interpolating between existing ones. However, it can also be applied to modeling complex systems or predicting future behavior based on current trends. To interpolate effectively, we need an estimate of how the data will behave outside of our known values – this is where basis functions come into play.

Basis functions are mathematical expressions that approximate how a given set of data points behaves over its entire range. These can be linear, polynomial, or any other type depending on what type of data you are dealing with and what kind of accuracy you want your model to have – more complex models require more sophisticated basis functions. For example, if you were trying to predict stock market prices over time, you would need an exponential function as your basis function since stocks tend to exhibit this behavior when plotted on a graph over time intervals.

The idea behind using interpolation and basis functions is that together they give us more control over our model's accuracy: rather than randomly guessing at values, we can use our understanding of how the underlying data set should behave (based on our choice in basis function) combined with specific points from it (through interpolation) to create something that looks just like it while taking up much less space. This allows us to save memory and make our models easier interpretable since their structure reflects what we already know about our data set beforehand.

9.20 Multi-class/Structured Outputs, Ranking

Multi-class and structured output are a type of supervised learning that helps ML algorithms learn to categorize data into multiple classes or to predict the structure of complex inputs. This type of ML is essential for many real-world applications, such as NLP, computer vision, robotics, financial modeling, and other areas. Multi-class classification helps machines assign inputs to one of several possible classes. It can be used in image recognition tasks, such as categorizing animals, objects, or scenes in pictures; sentiment analysis tasks, such as identifying positive or negative sentiment within the text; and fraud detection tasks, such as recognizing fraudulent activities in financial transactions.

Using structured output allows machines to understand more complex inputs by predicting the underlying structure with numerical labels instead of just assigning a single class label. Structured output techniques are used when input data contains sequences (words in a sentence) or graphs (such as a map). They help reveal relationships between elements so that further analysis can be performed. For example, ranking algorithms assign scores based on relevance or importance, allowing machines to prioritize certain items over others for specific business decisions like product recommendations or customer segmentation.

As ML advances, we can expect more innovative uses for multi-class and structured outputs: from medical diagnostics, where multi-class classification is used to identify diseases from medical scans; engineering applications, where robots learn from examples using sequence models; to market prediction platforms where rankers score stocks according to their potential returns over time. Combining robust neural networks with these cutting-edge techniques makes it possible to solve challenging problems previously out of reach using traditional methods alone.

SUMMARY

- The basic idea behind linear regression is that some linear relationship exists between two or more variables, which can be represented mathematically by an equation ($y = ax + b$). Non-linear regression is a type of regression analysis that examines the connection between the dependent variable and one or more non-linear independent variables. Linear regression models are more prone to underfitting, whereas non-linear regression models are more prone to overfitting.

- There are various types of linear models, including simple linear regression, linear regression, Poisson regression, and logistic regression. Simple linear regression is a regression analysis that predicts a dependent variable (such as salary) using one independent variable (such as years of experience). Examples of Poisson regression includes predicting the number of car accidents that may occur on a particular road segment on a given day based on various parameters: weather, time of day, traffic volume, and road conditions.
- Multivariate linear regression has the potential to uncover intricate relationships between multiple features and a single output, which can then be leveraged to make more informed decisions and predictions.
- Linear classifiers are powerful ML techniques used in supervised learning problems that classify new data into broad categories based on the properties of the data.
- Kernel methods are a powerful tool for detecting non-linearity in data.
- Non-linear models include generalized linear models (GLMs). Support vector machine or SVM is a non-linear model and is one of the most popular supervised literacy algorithms used for classification and regression problems. AdaBoost is a powerful non-linear meta-algorithm that improves the accuracy of classification models by combining the expertise of multiple weak learners.
- Regularization is a technique to avoid overfitting in the regression model by adding a penalty term to the loss function. Backpropagation is a supervised learning approach that is used to modify an artificial neural network's weights to lessen the discrepancy between the anticipated output and the produced output.
- Radial basis function (RBF) is an artificial neural network that uses radial basis functions as activation functions.
- Unlike linear regression, splines can capture abrupt changes in the data by fitting separate polynomial functions to each data segment.
- The phenomenon known as the curse of dimensionality describes how specific ML algorithms perform worse as the number of features (or dimensions) in the data set grows.

EXERCISES

Part A (Objective Questions)

1. Which type of regression is suitable for predicting crop yield based on the amount of rainfall and temperature?

a) Linear regression b) Non-linear regression
c) Both linear and non-linear regression d) None of the above

2. In which type of regression are continuous and discrete data both suitable for modeling?

a) Linear regression b) Non-linear regression

c) Both linear and non-linear regression d) None of the above

3. What is the degree of a linear regression model?
   a) 0 b) 1
   c) 2 d) Any degree
4. What is the primary difference between linear and non-linear regression models regarding the relationship between input and output variables?
   a) Linear regression assumes a constant relationship, whereas non-linear regression assumes a changing relationship.
   b) Linear regression assumes a changing relationship, whereas non-linear regression assumes a constant relationship.
   c) Linear regression assumes no relationship, whereas non-linear regression assumes a relationship.
   d) Linear regression assumes a linear relationship, whereas non-linear regression assumes a non-linear relationship.
5. Which type of regression can have multiple independent variables?
   a) Linear regression b) Non-linear regression
   c) Both linear and non-linear regression d) None of the above
6. What type of regression is prone to underfitting?
   a) Linear regression b) Non-linear regression
   c) Both linear and non-linear regression d) None of the above
7. Which type of regression has a simpler representation?
   a) Linear regression b) Non-linear regression
   c) Both linear and non-linear regression d) None of the above
8. What is the primary advantage of linear regression over non-linear regression in terms of interpretability?
   a) Linear regression models are more interpretable.
   b) Non-linear regression models are more interpretable.
   c) Both linear and non-linear regression models are equally interpretable.
   d) Neither linear nor non-linear regression models are interpretable.
9. What is the purpose of simple linear regression?
   a) To predict a dependent variable using multiple independent variables.
   b) To predict a dependent variable using one independent variable.
   c) To analyze the relationship between multiple dependent variables.
   d) To analyze the relationship between multiple independent variables.
10. How is the best-fit line in simple linear regression determined?
   a) By minimizing the sum of squared errors (SSE).
   b) By maximizing the R-squared value.
   c) By minimizing the residual errors.
   d) By maximizing the coefficient of determination.

11. What is the consequence of having a too-steep line in a simple linear regression?
a) Underfitting the data. b) Overfitting the data.
c) Accurately representing the data. d) None of the above.

12. How are the values of b0 and b1 calculated in simple linear regression?
a) By solving a system of equations.
b) By maximizing the likelihood function.
c) By minimizing the mean squared error (MSE).
d) By minimizing the sum of squared errors (SSE).

13. Which formula is used to calculate the intercept (b0) in simple linear regression?
a) $b0 = \Sigma[(Xi - \bar{X})(Yi - \bar{Y})] / \Sigma(Xi - \bar{X})^2$ b) $b0 = \bar{Y} - b1\bar{X}$
c) $b0 = \Sigma(XiYi) / \Sigma(Xi^2)$ d) $b0 = \Sigma(Yi - b1Xi) / n$

14. Which factor is used to calculate the slope (b1) in simple linear regression?
a) $\Sigma[(Xi - \bar{X})(Yi - \bar{Y})]$ b) $\Sigma(Xi - \bar{X})^2$
c) $\bar{X}$ d) $\bar{Y}$

15. In simple linear regression, what does SSE stand for?
a) Sum of Squared Errors b) Sum of Squared Exponents
c) Standard Error of Estimate d) Squared Sum of Errors

16. Which scenario is suitable for using simple linear regression?
a) Predicting multiple dependent variables using one independent variable.
b) Predicting one dependent variable using multiple independent variables.
c) Predicting one dependent variable using one independent variable.
d) Predicting multiple dependent variables using multiple independent variables.

17. In linear regression, what does the slope (β) represent?
a) The intercept of the line.
b) The output variable.
c) The input variable.
d) The change in the output variable per unit change in the input variable.

18. Which of the following is an example where linear regression can be applied?
a) Predicting customer sentiment based on social media posts.
b) Classifying images into different categories.
c) Forecasting stock prices based on historical market data.
d) Analyzing the text of customer reviews to identify sentiment.

19. What is the purpose of the intercept ($\beta 0$) in linear regression?
a) To represent the change in the output variable per unit change in the input variable.
b) To indicate the number of input variables in the model.
c) To adjust the baseline value of the output variable when all input variables are zero.
d) To calculate the sum of squared errors in the model.

20. Which of the following scenarios is suitable for using linear regression?
a) Predicting the number of Facebook likes based on the content of the post.

b) Classifying email messages as spam or non-spam.
c) Predicting the genre of a movie based on its plot summary.
d) Analyzing customer reviews to identify key topics and sentiments.

21. How does linear regression model the relationship between input variables and the output variable?
a) It assumes a linear relationship between input and output variables.
b) It assumes a non-linear relationship between input and output variables.
c) It models a polynomial relationship between input and output variables.
d) It models an exponential relationship between input and output variables.

22. In linear regression, what is the role of the sum of squared errors (SSE)?
a) To calculate the intercept ($\beta 0$).
b) To determine the optimal values for the slope (β) coefficients.
c) To evaluate the goodness of fit of the model.
d) To standardize the input variables.

23. Which factor is used to determine the best-fit line in linear regression?
a) The highest value of the input variable.
b) The lowest value of the output variable.
c) The minimum sum of squared errors (SSE).
d) The maximum value of the intercept ($\beta 0$).

24. What does the intercept ($\beta 0$) represent in linear regression?
a) The average value of the input variables.
b) The average value of the output variable.
c) The baseline value of the output variable when all input variables are zero.
d) The baseline value of the input variable when all output variables are zero.

25. In Poisson regression, what type of variable is the output variable?
a) Categorical variable
b) Continuous variable
c) Binary variable
d) Count variable

26. Which of the following scenarios is suitable for using Poisson regression?
a) Predicting the customer satisfaction rating on a scale of 1-5.
b) Analyzing the sentiment of customer reviews.
c) Predicting the number of daily website visitors.
d) Classifying emails as spam or non-spam.

27. What is the role of the log function in Poisson regression?
a) It transforms the count variable into a continuous variable.
b) It linearizes the relationship between the input variables and the expected count.
c) It normalizes the input variables.
d) It converts the count variable into a binary variable.

28. In Poisson regression, what does the intercept (b0) represent?
a) The expected count when all input variables are zero.
b) The average value of the input variables.

c) The average value of the output variable.
d) The baseline value of the output variable.

29. What type of distribution is associated with Poisson regression?
a) Gaussian distribution
b) Binomial distribution
c) Poisson distribution
d) Exponential distribution

30. How is Poisson regression different from linear regression?
a) Poisson regression is used for continuous variables, while linear regression is used for count variables.
b) Poisson regression assumes a linear relationship between input and output variables, while linear regression does not.
c) Poisson regression is suitable for count variables, while linear regression is suitable for continuous variables.
d) Poisson regression uses the log function, while linear regression does not.

31. What is the purpose of data pre-processing in Poisson regression?
a) To transform count variables into categorical variables.
b) To remove outliers from the input variables.
c) To convert continuous variables into count variables.
d) To clean and prepare the data for analysis by removing missing or erroneous data.

32. How can Poisson regression be used for prediction?
a) By applying the inverse of the log function to the predicted count.
b) By transforming the count variable into a binary variable.
c) By adding the intercept (b0) to the predicted count.
d) By plugging in the values of the input variables into the model equation.

33. What type of output variable is suitable for Logistic Regression?
a) Continuous variable
b) Categorical variable
c) Count variable
d) Binary variable

34. Which of the following scenarios is appropriate for using Logistic Regression?
a) Predicting the price of a house based on its size and location.
b) Classifying emails as spam or non-spam.
c) Predicting the number of daily website visitors.
d) Analyzing customer sentiment based on product reviews.

35. What does the log(odds) represent in Logistic Regression?
a) The probability of the output variable being "yes."
b) The probability of the output variable being "no."
c) The linear combination of input variables.
d) The intercept term in the model.

36. What is the purpose of testing the Logistic Regression model?
a) To evaluate the accuracy of the model's predictions.
b) To determine the intercept value ($\beta 0$) in the model.

c) To validate the input variables used in the model.
d) To assess the performance of the algorithm used.

37. How does Logistic Regression differ from Linear Regression?
a) Logistic Regression is used for binary classification, while Linear Regression is used for continuous prediction.
b) Logistic Regression assumes a linear relationship between input and output variables, while Linear Regression does not.
c) Logistic Regression uses the log-odds function, while Linear Regression does not.
d) Logistic Regression requires categorical input variables, while Linear Regression requires continuous input variables.

38. How can Logistic Regression be used in predictive analytics?
a) By analyzing customer sentiment based on reviews.
b) By predicting the price of a product based on its features.
c) By predicting whether a customer will purchase a product based on their past behavior.
d) By analyzing the impact of advertising on sales.

39. What is the role of the intercept ($\beta 0$) in Logistic Regression?
a) It determines the probability of the output variable being "yes."
b) It represents the average value of the input variables.
c) It sets the threshold for classification in the model.
d) It accounts for the baseline probability of the output variable being "yes."

40. Can Logistic Regression be used for multi-class classification?
a) Yes, by using multiple logistic regression models.
b) Yes, by transforming the output variable into a continuous variable.
c) No, Logistic Regression can only handle binary classification.
d) No, Logistic Regression can only handle categorical variables.

41. In binary logistic regression, the dependent variable can have how many values?
a) 0
b) 1
c) 2
d) Multiple

42. What is the purpose of the logistic function in logistic regression?
a) To transform independent variables into dependent variables.
b) To calculate the coefficients for the independent variables.
c) To model the relationship between independent and dependent variables.
d) To standardize the values of the independent variables.

43. What is the range of the probability predicted by the logistic function?
a) 0 to 1
b) 0 to infinity
c) -1 to 1
d) 0 to 100

44. In logistic regression, what does the log-odds represent?
a) The change in the dependent variable's log odds for a one-unit change in the independent variable.
b) The probability of the dependent variable being one.

c) The coefficient values of the independent variables.
d) The intercept value in the model.

45. Which of the following applications is suitable for binomial logistic regression?
a) Forecasting stock market prices.
b) Predicting customer churn.
c) Determining the weather forecast.
d) Analyzing product sales trends.

46. What are the independent variables in credit scoring using binomial logistic regression?
a) Loan amount and interest rate.
b) Customer demographics and purchase history.
c) Credit score and income.
d) Product features and customer satisfaction.

47. What is the dependent variable in credit scoring using binomial logistic regression?
a) Loan amount.
b) Credit score.
c) Interest rate.
d) Loan default status.

48. Can logistic regression be used to predict multiple categories?
a) Yes, by using multiple logistic regression models.
b) Yes, by transforming the dependent variable into a continuous variable.
c) No, logistic regression can only handle binary classification.
d) No, logistic regression requires categorical independent variables.

49. What is the purpose of multinomial logistic regression?
a) To handle binary classification problems.
b) To predict the probability of the dependent variable being one.
c) To classify data into more than two unordered categories.
d) To transform continuous variables into categorical variables.

50. Which function is used to transform the odds into probabilities in multinomial logistic regression?
a) Sigmoid function.
b) Softmax function.
c) Logistic function.
d) Exponential function.

51. What is the range of the dependent variable in multinomial logistic regression?
a) -1 to 1
b) 0 to 1
c) 0 to infinity
d) Multiple categories

52. Which domain can benefit from multinomial logistic regression in machine learning?
a) Credit scoring.
b) Object detection.
c) Sentiment analysis in text.
d) Stock market prediction.

53. What does multinomial logistic regression handle well in real-world data sets?
a) Continuous variables.
b) Outliers.
c) Missing data.
d) Categorical variables.

54. In which scenario can multinomial logistic regression be used?
a) Predicting the price of a house based on its features.
b) Detecting spam emails in a mailbox.

c) Predicting the class membership of genes based on expression levels.
d) Analyzing customer churn in a telecommunications company.

55. Which function is used to model the relationship between the independent and dependent variables in multinomial logistic regression?
a) Linear function. b) Sigmoid function.
c) Softmax function. d) Exponential function.

56. Can multinomial logistic regression handle binary classification problems?
a) Yes, by transforming the dependent variable into multiple categories.
b) Yes, by using multiple binary logistic regression models.
c) No, multinomial logistic regression is only for multi-class classification.
d) No, multinomial logistic regression requires continuous variables.

57. What is the main difference between ordinal logistic regression and multinomial logistic regression?
a) The number of independent variables used.
b) The type of dependent variable categories.
c) The number of categories in the dependent variable.
d) The type of transformation function used.

58. How are the odds transformed into probabilities in ordinal logistic regression?
a) By using the sigmoid function.
b) By using the softmax function.
c) By using the cumulative distribution function.
d) By using the exponential function.

59. In which field can ordinal logistic regression be applied to predict the severity of a disease?
a) Finance. b) Marketing.
c) Healthcare. d) Sports.

60. What type of variables can ordinal logistic regression handle?
a) Continuous variables only. b) Categorical variables only.
c) Both categorical and continuous variables.d) Ordinal variables only.

61. In which domain can ordinal logistic regression be used to predict students' grades?
a) Manufacturing. b) Education.
c) Agriculture. d) Transportation.

62. What does the cumulative distribution function represent in ordinal logistic regression?
a) The probability of the dependent variable being in a specific category.
b) The cumulative sum of the independent variables.
c) The ratio of odds for each category.
d) The total number of observations in the data set.

63. Which demographic variables can be used to predict the level of agreement on a political issue using ordinal logistic regression?

a) Age, gender, and education.
b) Income, occupation, and marital status.
c) Race, ethnicity, and religion.
d) Height, weight, and body mass index.

64. Can ordinal logistic regression handle missing data and outliers?
a) Yes, ordinal logistic regression can handle missing data but not outliers.
b) Yes, ordinal logistic regression can handle outliers but not missing data.
c) No, ordinal logistic regression cannot handle missing data or outliers.
d) Yes, ordinal logistic regression can handle missing data and outliers.

65. What is the goal of the Least Squares method in linear regression?
a) Minimize the sum of squared errors.
b) Maximize the coefficient values.
c) Minimize the number of variables.
d) Maximize the predicted values.

66. How are the coefficients determined using the Least Squares method?
a) By maximizing the predicted values.
b) By minimizing the coefficient values.
c) By minimizing the sum of squared errors.
d) By maximizing the number of variables.

67. Can the Least Squares method be used for other supervised learning methods besides linear regression?
a) Yes, it can be used for any supervised learning method.
b) No, it is exclusively used for linear regression.
c) Only for decision tree algorithms.
d) Only for classification tasks.

68. What role do the coefficients play in forecasting stock returns?
a) They determine the accuracy of the predictions.
b) They represent the historical stock returns.
c) They are used to calculate the sum of squared errors.
d) They determine the relationship between the features and stock returns.

69. How is the Least Squares method beneficial in linear regression?
a) It maximizes the coefficient values for accurate predictions.
b) It minimizes the number of variables in the regression equation.
c) It handles missing data and outliers effectively.
d) It maximizes the sum of squared errors to improve predictions.

70. What is the advantage of using logistic regression or probit regression over simple least squares regression for binary classification?
a) They provide probabilistic classification results.
b) They handle missing data and outliers more effectively.
c) They can handle high-dimensional data sets.
d) They offer more interpretable results.

71. In which scenario is least squares regression particularly useful due to its ability to handle high dimensionality?
a) Finance for predicting stock prices.

b) Marketing for predicting customer behavior.
c) Healthcare for disease outbreak prediction.
d) Sales for customer churn prediction.

72. What is the primary advantage of least squares regression in terms of classification in complex data sets?
a) It provides probabilistic results.
b) It handles non-linear decision boundaries.
c) It quantifies uncertainty in predictions.
d) It provides more interpretable results.

73. In which fields can least squares regression be applied to make accurate predictions?
a) Finance and medicine.
b) Marketing and sales.
c) Healthcare and finance.
d) Medicine and marketing.

74. What is the main principle behind least squares regression in classification?
a) Minimizing residuals to find the best-fitting parameters.
b) Maximizing the predicted values for accurate classifications.
c) Minimizing the number of variables to simplify the model.
d) Maximizing the sum of squared errors for robust predictions.

75. Which type of regression is preferred when interpreting the results is a crucial factor?
a) Logistic regression.
b) Probit regression.
c) Support vector machines.
d) Simple least squares regression.

76. What role does uncertainty quantification play in least squares regression?
a) It helps handle missing data effectively.
b) It determines the best-fitting parameters.
c) It allows decision-makers to consider factors like noise or outliers.
d) It simplifies the model by reducing the number of variables.

77. What advantage does least squares regression offer in terms of probabilistic results?
a) It handles non-linear cases efficiently.
b) It provides a user-friendly approach.
c) It helps determine the uncertainty in predictions.
d) It minimizes the complexity of the model.

78. What is the advantage of using multivariate linear regression in predicting sales figures for a business?
a) It uncovers intricate relationships between multiple features and the output.
b) It provides accurate predictions without exploring different predictors.
c) It simplifies the modeling process by ignoring other factors.
d) It focuses on a single feature to make informed decisions.

79. How can businesses refine their sales prediction models using multivariate linear regression?
a) By investigating competitive activity and seasonality trends.
b) By using only historical data of advertisement spend and customer ratings.

c) By focusing solely on the correlation between customer ratings and sales figures.
d) By ignoring other factors and relying solely on advertisement spend.

80. What information can businesses gain by examining past correlations between variables in multivariate linear regression?
a) The impact of advertisement spend on customer ratings.
b) The influence of customer ratings on historical sales figures.
c) The effect of advertisement spend and customer ratings on sales figures.
d) The relationship between competitive activity and advertisement spend.

81. How can businesses leverage multivariate linear regression to make more accurate predictions?
a) By focusing solely on a single predictor and its impact on the output.
b) By using historical data without considering other factors.
c) By exploring different combinations of predictors and their effects on the output.
d) By disregarding the underlying relationships between predictors and the output.

82. What is the benefit of understanding how different features interact in multivariate linear regression?
a) It simplifies the modeling process by focusing on a single feature.
b) It allows businesses to allocate resources effectively.
c) It eliminates the need for investigating competitive activity and seasonality trends.
d) It provides accurate predictions without considering other factors.

83. What is the primary advantage of using multivariate linear regression for machine learning purposes?
a) It provides accurate predictions without exploring different predictors.
b) It simplifies the modeling process by ignoring other factors.
c) It allows businesses to uncover intricate relationships between features.
d) It focuses on a single feature to make informed decisions.

84. How can businesses utilize the knowledge gained from multivariate linear regression?
a) To make informed decisions about feature importance.
b) To disregard certain predictors and focus on a single feature.
c) To simplify the modeling process by excluding other factors.
d) To ignore the underlying relationships between features and the output.

85. What does multivariate linear regression enable businesses to do when predicting sales figures?
a) Determine the exact future sales figures.
b) Identify the most influential feature for sales predictions.
c) Uncover the impact of historical customer ratings on sales.
d) Understand how different features interact to affect sales.

86. Which type of problems can MLP effectively handle by dividing them into smaller sub-problems?
a) Linear problems
b) Non-linear problems
c) Small-scale problems
d) Large-scale problems

87. What is one advantage of using MLP for forecasting property prices?
    a) It can process highly dimensional data.
    b) It can make quick predictions after training.
    c) It maintains the same accuracy rate with large and small data sets.
    d) It can handle both linear and non-linear problems.

88. What is the benefit of MLP once it is trained?
    a) It can solve complex non-linear problems.
    b) It can handle both small and large input data.
    c) It can make predictions quickly and efficiently.
    d) It can maintain the same accuracy rate with varying data sets.

89. In which scenario does MLP demonstrate the same accuracy rate?
    a) With small and large data sets b) With linear and non-linear problems
    c) With highly dimensional data d) With varying input factors

90. Which type of problems can MLP solve that cannot be solved by simple linear models?
    a) Linear problems b) Non-linear problems
    c) Small-scale problems d) Large-scale problems

91. What is one advantage of using MLP for natural language processing, speech recognition, and image recognition?
    a) It can divide complex problems into smaller sub-problems.
    b) It can process highly dimensional data.
    c) It can make quick predictions after training.
    d) It can handle both linear and non-linear problems.

92. Which characteristic of MLP makes it suitable for predicting customer churn?
    a) Ability to handle both small and large input data
    b) Quick predictions after training
    c) Same accuracy rate with varying data sets
    d) Ability to divide complex problems into smaller sub-problems

93. What makes MLP a popular choice in machine learning?
    a) Its ability to solve linear problems effectively b) Its quick and efficient predictions
    c) Its capability to handle large-scale problems d) Its flexibility for various issues

94. Why can training a deep network with many hidden layers in MLP be a time-consuming process?
    a) MLP requires powerful hardware b) MLP uses complex calculations
    c) MLP deals with large data sets d) All of the above

95. Which term best describes the interpretability challenge in MLP?
    a) Computation complexity b) Black-box nature

c) Training set quality d) Hyperparameter selection

96. What does it mean when it is mentioned that MLP lacks a clearer insight into the importance of each feature?
a) The model cannot handle complex problems effectively.
b) The training process is time-consuming.
c) The model struggles to determine the impact of independent variables on the dependent variable.
d) The model requires high computational resources.

97. What significantly impacts MLP performance?
a) Quality of training data b) Number of hidden layers
c) Complexity of the problem d) Availability of GPUs

98. Why does MLP require a significant amount of computer power?
a) Due to the black-box nature of the modelb) Because of the complex calculations involved
c) To interpret the importance of each featured) When dealing with large data sets

99. What is a potential challenge in interpreting the impact of different factors on house prices using MLP?
a) Time-consuming training process b) Black-box nature of the model
c) Lack of representative training data d) Inadequate computational resources

100. What does the success of training in MLP determine?
a) The complexity of the problem it can solve
b) The accuracy of the model
c) The availability of computer power
d) The interpretability of the model

101. Which factor is essential for MLP to perform accurately when extrapolating certain classes from real-world data?
a) Availability of GPUs
b) Model's chosen hyperparameters
c) Quality and representativeness of training data
d) Number of hidden layers

102. Which machine learning technique is commonly used for classification problems and employs a linear decision boundary?
a) Linear classifiers b) Kernel methods
c) Logistic regression d) Support vector machines

103. What is the purpose of the kernel trick in machine learning?
a) To convert non-linearly separable data sets into higher dimensional spaces
b) To simplify the computation in linear classifiers

c) To improve the interpretability of linear models
d) To handle missing data in the data set

104. In which range does logistic regression convert its output to represent probabilities?
a) -1 to 1
b) 0 to 1
c) 0 to infinity
d) -infinity to infinity

105. What makes linear classifiers particularly useful for large data sets?
a) Their ability to handle missing data
b) Their interpretability in complex problems
c) Their efficiency in giving predictions
d) Their ability to handle non-linear data

106. Which application could benefit from using a linear classifier like logistic regression?
a) Weather forecasting
b) Image recognition
c) Housing price prediction
d) Fraud detection

107. How does a linear classifier differ from a decision tree algorithm?
a) Linear classifiers are more computationally expensive.
b) Linear classifiers use a single linear decision boundary.
c) Linear classifiers work better with non-linear data.
d) Linear classifiers require explicit programming instructions.

108. What limits the efficacy of linear classifiers?
a) Their need for linearly separable data
b) Their reliance on kernel methods
c) Their interpretability in complex problems
d) Their ability to handle large data sets

109. How do linear classifiers save time and effort in machine learning tasks?
a) By providing interpretability for complex models
b) By handling missing data in the data set
c) By automatically generating programming rules
d) By quickly generating predictions across large data sets

110. Alice is working on a classification problem using SVM. She wants to capture complex relationships between data points, including non-linear patterns. Which kernel function should Alice use?
a) Linear Kernel
b) Polynomial Kernel
c) Gaussian Kernel
d) Exponential Kernel

111. Bob is working on an image recognition task using SVM. He wants to classify images based on color and texture features. Which kernel function is most suitable for his task?
a) Linear Kernel
b) Polynomial Kernel
c) Gaussian Kernel
d) Laplacian Kernel

112. Claire is working on a text classification problem using SVM. She wants to classify text documents that have non-linear decision boundaries. Which kernel function should Claire use?
a) Linear Kernel
b) Polynomial Kernel

c) Gaussian Kernel
d) Laplacian Kernel

113. David is working on a regression problem using SVM. He wants to capture non-linear patterns in the data. Which kernel function should David use?

a) Linear Kernel
b) Polynomial Kernel
c) Gaussian Kernel
d) Exponential Kernel

114. Emily is working on an SVM-based image processing task and wants to detect edges and sharp transitions in images. Which kernel function should Emily use?

a) Linear Kernel
b) Polynomial Kernel
c) Gaussian Kernel
d) Laplacian Kernel

115. Frank is working on a classification problem using SVM. He wants to handle highly non-linearly separable data. Which kernel function is most suitable for Frank's task?

Options:

a) Hyperbolic Kernel
b) Polynomial Kernel
c) ANOVA RBF Kernel
d) Exponential Kernel

116. Gina is working on a classification task using SVM. She wants to classify data points with complex, non-linear relationships but is concerned about overfitting. Which kernel function should Gina choose?

a) Polynomial Kernel
b) Gaussian Kernel
c) Laplacian Kernel
d) Exponential Kernel

117. Henry is working on a regression problem using SVM. He wants to capture complex relationships in the data but needs to control the width of the kernel. Which kernel function should Henry choose?

a) Linear Kernel
b) Gaussian Kernel
c) Laplacian Kernel
d) Exponential Kernel

118. Lisa is working on a classification problem where the response variable follows a non-normal distribution. Which type of GLM should Lisa consider?

a) Logistic regression model
b) Poisson regression model
c) Probit model
d) Multinomial logistic regression model

119. Mark wants to build a regression model that can handle outliers in the data. Which type of GLM should Mark choose?

a) Logistic regression model
b) Probit model
c) Multinomial logistic regression model
d) Huber regression model

120. Sarah is working on a binary classification task with the goal of predicting whether a customer will churn or not. Which type of GLM should Sarah use?

a) Logistic regression model
b) Poisson regression model
c) Probit model
d) Multinomial logistic regression model

121. Jason is working on a regression problem where the response variable exhibits a non-linear relationship with the predictors. Which type of GLM should Jason consider?

a) Logistic regression model
b) Probit model
c) Poisson regression model
d) Generalized additive model (GAM)

122. Olivia wants to predict the probability of an event occurring based on a set of predictors. However, the relationship is not linear. Which type of GLM should Olivia choose?
a) Logistic regression model
b) Multinomial logistic regression model
c) Poisson regression model
d) Probit model

123. Ethan is working on a classification task where the response variable has multiple categories. Which type of GLM should Ethan use?
a) Logistic regression model
b) Poisson regression model
c) Probit model
d) Multinomial logistic regression model

124. Jessica is working with a large data set that has numerous predictors. She wants to avoid overfitting in her regression model. Which type of GLM should Jessica consider?
a) Logistic regression model
b) Probit model
c) Multinomial logistic regression model
d) Regularized regression model (such as LASSO or ridge)

125. Benjamin is analyzing a data set with a response variable that follows a non-normal distribution. He wants to estimate the count of an event based on predictor variables. Which type of GLM should Benjamin use?
a) Logistic regression model
b) Poisson regression model
c) Probit model
d) Multinomial logistic regression model

126. Emily is working on a data set with clustered observations, where each observation within a cluster may be correlated. Which assumption of GLMs is violated in this scenario?
a) Linearity assumption
b) Independence assumption
c) Normality assumption
d) Homoscedasticity assumption

127. Daniel is fitting a GLM with a binary response variable but mistakenly chooses a Poisson regression model. What issue is likely to occur with this model specification?
a) Biased parameter estimates
b) Overfitting
c) Underfitting
d) Heteroscedasticity

128. Olivia is fitting a GLM to predict count data but selects a logistic regression model. What issue is she likely to encounter?
a) Biased parameter estimates
b) Overfitting
c) Violation of the linearity assumption
d) Inefficient inference

129. Ethan is fitting a GLM with multiple predictor variables and a binary response variable. He wants to prevent overfitting in his model. Which technique should Ethan consider?
a) Regularization (such as LASSO or ridge regression)
b) Interactions between predictors
c) Polynomial transformations of predictors
d) Adding more predictor variables

130. Mia is fitting a GLM for a regression task but finds that the model fits the training data extremely well while performing poorly on new data. What issue is likely occurring?
a) Biased parameter estimates
b) Underfitting
c) Overfitting
d) Violation of the normality assumption

131. Noah is fitting a GLM to predict a continuous response variable. He wants to ensure that the variance of the residuals is constant across different predictor variable values. What assumption is he concerned about?
a) Linearity assumption
b) Independence assumption
c) Normality assumption
d) Homoscedasticity assumption

132. Sophie is fitting a GLM to predict a continuous response variable. She wants to capture non-linear relationships between the predictors and the response. What technique should Sophie consider?
a) Regularization (such as LASSO or ridge regression)
b) Adding interactions between predictors
c) Polynomial transformations of predictors
d) Data standardization

133. Liam is fitting a GLM with a binary response variable. He wants to ensure that the parameter estimates are unbiased and efficient. What assumption is crucial for achieving this?
a) Linearity assumption
b) Independence assumption
c) Normality assumption
d) Homoscedasticity assumption

134. John is working on a classification problem where the data points are not linearly separable. Which type of SVM should John consider using?
a) Linear SVM
b) Non-linear SVM
c) Both linear and non-linear SVMs
d) None of the above

135. Sarah has a data set where the classes are linearly separable, and she wants to classify the data points accurately. Which type of SVM should Sarah use?
a) Linear SVM
b) Non-linear SVM
c) Both linear and non-linear SVMs
d) None of the above

136. Michael is working on a small data set and wants to use SVM for classification. Which type of SVM is likely to be less accurate for his data set?
a) Linear SVM
b) Non-linear SVM
c) Both linear and non-linear SVMs
d) None of the above

137. Emma is working on a data set where the classes are not linearly separable. Which technique can help Emma achieve accurate classification with SVM?
a) Using a linear SVM
b) Applying regularization techniques
c) Utilizing kernel trick functions
d) None of the above

138. David is using SVM to classify data points in a two-dimensional space. He wants to find the hyperplane that maximizes the margin between classes. What type of SVM is David using?
a) Linear SVM
b) Non-linear SVM
c) Both linear and non-linear SVMs
d) None of the above

139. Olivia is working on a classification problem and wants to separate the classes using a non-linear boundary. Which type of SVM should Olivia choose?

a) Linear SVM
b) Non-linear SVM
c) Both linear and non-linear SVMs
d) None of the above

140. Ethan is working on a data set where the classes are linearly separable. However, he wants to explore more complex methods beyond drawing straight lines. What type of SVM should Ethan consider?

a) Linear SVM
b) Non-linear SVM
c) Both linear and non-linear SVMs
d) None of the above

141. Ava is using SVM for classification and wants to maximize the margin between classes. Which type of SVM should Ava use?

a) Linear SVM
b) Non-linear SVM
c) Both linear and non-linear SVMs
d) None of the above

142. Maria wants to improve the accuracy of her classification model by combining multiple weak learners. Which algorithm should she consider?

a) *K*-means clustering
b) Random forest
c) AdaBoost
d) Principal component analysis (PCA)

143. Scenario: Mark wants to train a classification model but has limited computational resources. Which algorithm can provide highly accurate results with minimal computational resources?

a) *K*-means clustering
b) Random forest
c) AdaBoost
d) Principal component analysis (PCA)

144. Sarah wants to improve the generalization performance of her classification model to avoid overfitting. Which algorithm can help her achieve this goal?

a) *K*-means clustering
b) Random forest
c) AdaBoost
d) Principal component analysis (PCA)

145. John wants to build a classification model that can combine different types of evidence from each model to produce reliable results. Which algorithm should he use?

a) *K*-means clustering
b) Random forest
c) AdaBoost
d) Principal component analysis (PCA)

146. Emma wants to build a classification model that focuses on producing better outcomes through an iterative process. Which algorithm is suitable for her goal?

a) *K*-means clustering
b) Random forest
c) AdaBoost
d) Principal component analysis (PCA)

147. David wants to select features that contribute to better predictions while remaining computationally efficient. Which algorithm should he use?

a) *K*-means clustering
b) Random forest
c) AdaBoost
d) Principal component analysis (PCA)

148. Olivia wants to build a classification model that combines the expertise of multiple weak learners, such as decision trees with just one split. Which algorithm should she use?

a) *K*-means clustering
b) Random forest
c) AdaBoost
d) Principal component analysis (PCA)

149. Ethan wants to improve the accuracy of his classification model by considering different kinds of evidence from each model. Which algorithm can help him achieve this goal?
a) *K*-means clustering
b) Random forest
c) AdaBoost
d) Principal component analysis (PCA)

150. In which of the following applications can AdaBoost be used to identify features in images?
a) Sentiment analysis
b) Object recognition
c) Stock market prediction
d) Weather forecasting

151. Which of the following applications utilizes AdaBoost to categorize emails as spam or not based on their content?
a) Speech recognition
b) Face detection
c) Spam filtering
d) Gene expression analysis

152. In which field of study has AdaBoost been used to classify gene expression data?
a) Computer vision
b) Natural language processing
c) Bioinformatics
d) Speech recognition

153. Which of the following boosting techniques is the most popular and widely used?
a) Bagging
b) AdaBoost
c) Gradient boosting
d) Stacking

154. What is the main advantage of AdaBoost over bagging?
a) It can handle complex data sets
b) It is more computationally efficient
c) It is suitable for bioinformatics applications
d) It can improve the accuracy of classification models

155. Which field of study has NOT extensively utilized AdaBoost?
a) Computer vision
b) Natural language processing
c) Speech recognition
d) Stock market prediction

156. What makes AdaBoost different from bagging?
a) AdaBoost uses a weighted sum of all classifiers
b) AdaBoost focuses on data previously misclassified
c) AdaBoost combines different types of classifiers
d) AdaBoost is more computationally efficient

157. Which aspect of AdaBoost's training process contributes to its ability to handle complex data sets?
a) Sequential training of classifiers
b) Weighted sum of classifiers
c) Selection of different weak learners
d) Focus on data previously misclassified

158. Which type of penalty is used in ridge regression to encourage parameter values towards zero without eliminating any features?
a) L1 norm penalty
b) L2 norm penalty

c) LASSO penalty
d) Weight decay penalty

159. Which type of penalty is used in LASSO regression to encourage sparsity and potentially reduce feature weights to zero?

a) L1 norm penalty
b) L2 norm penalty
c) Ridge penalty
d) Weight decay penalty

160. Which form of regularization is suitable for complex models with a high number of features or predictors?

a) L1 norm penalty
b) L2 norm penalty
c) Ridge penalty
d) Weight decay penalty

161. You are building a predictive model for house prices and want to prevent overfitting while maintaining consistency with the training data. Which regularization method would be suitable?

a) Ridge regression
b) LASSO regression
c) Both ridge and LASSO regressions
d) No regularization method is necessary

162. In which scenario is ridge regression more appropriate than LASSO regression?

a) When sparsity is desired
b) When dealing with a high-dimensional data set
c) When overfitting is a major concern
d) When feature selection is required

163. What is the main advantage of LASSO regression over ridge regression?

a) It avoids overfitting
b) It reduces variance
c) It encourages sparsity
d) It improves generalizability

164. Which regularization method can be applied to ridge and LASSO regressions to control the amount of regularization?

a) Elastic Net
b) Ridge penalty
c) L1 norm penalty
d) Weight decay penalty

165. Which type of regression is more suitable for feature selection when dealing with a large number of features?

a) Ridge regression
b) LASSO regression
c) Elastic Net regression
d) Weight decay regression

166. In which type of regression does soft margin SVM find the optimal linear boundary with a wider margin?

a) Linear regression
b) Logistic regression
c) Non-linear regression
d) Polynomial regression

167. Soft margin SVM is useful when dealing with data sets that contain:

a) Linearly separable classes
b) Outliers or misclassified data points
c) Only two classes
d) No noise or outliers

168. Soft margin SVM can handle non-linear shapes in classification tasks. Which of the following shapes would be a suitable example?

a) Straight lines
b) Circles and squares
c) Parabolas
d) Ellipses

169. Soft margin SVM is not suitable for:
a) Linear regression
b) Logistic regression
c) Text classification
d) Large data sets

170. Soft margin SVM is more tolerant of outliers and misclassifications compared to:
a) Decision trees
b) Random forests
c) Hard margin SVM
d) *K*-means clustering

171. Soft margin SVM can handle large data sets with noise or outliers in which of the following scenarios?
a) Image classification with clean images
b) Speech recognition with no background noise
c) Text classification with rare words
d) Time series forecasting with no outliers

172. What is the main advantage of using soft margin SVM in machine learning tasks?
a) Robustness against noise and outliers
b) Ability to handle high-dimensional data
c) Fast training time
d) Automatic feature selection

173. Soft margin SVM is particularly useful when dealing with data sets that have a large number of:
a) Features
b) Classes
c) Outliers
d) Observations

174. Which type of SVM is suitable when the data is linearly separable without outliers?
a) Hard margin SVM
b) Soft margin SVM
c) Both hard and soft margin SVM
d) None of the above

175. In which scenario is soft margin SVM more robust compared to hard margin SVM?
a) When the data is linearly separable without outliers
b) When the data contains outliers or misclassifications
c) When the data is high-dimensional
d) When the data is noise-free

176. Which SVM approach uses the C parameter to control the trade-off between maximizing the margin and minimizing misclassifications?
a) Hard margin SVM
b) Soft margin SVM
c) Both hard and soft margin SVM
d) None of the above

177. Which SVM approach uses the kernel trick to transform data into a higher-dimensional space?
a) Hard margin SVM
b) Soft margin SVM
c) Both hard and soft margin SVM
d) None of the above

178. When is soft margin SVM more suitable than hard margin SVM?
Options:
a) When the data is linearly separable without outliers
b) When the data is noise-free
c) When the data is high-dimensional
d) When the data contains outliers or misclassifications

179. Which SVM approach does not require regularization?
   a) Hard margin SVM
   b) Soft margin SVM
   c) Both hard and soft margin SVM
   d) None of the above

180. Which SVM approach is faster to train?
   a) Hard margin SVM
   b) Soft margin SVM
   c) Both hard and soft margin SVM
   d) It depends on the data set

181. Which SVM approach is suitable for complex real-world problems with overlapping or noisy data?
   a) Hard margin SVM
   b) Soft margin SVM
   c) Both hard and soft margin SVM
   d) None of the above

182. What is the main advantage of using multi-layer neural networks for non-linear regression tasks?
   a) They require fewer computational resources than linear models.
   b) They can learn complex underlying relationships between features.
   c) They rely on manually crafted features for accurate predictions.
   d) They have faster training speed compared to linear regression.

183. What role do activation functions play in multi-layer neural networks?
   a) They introduce non-linearity into the decision-making process.
   b) They determine the number of layers in the network.
   c) They control the training speed of the network.
   d) They define the size of the input data.

184. How does batch normalization contribute to the training of multi-layer neural networks?
   a) It prevents overfitting by regularizing the network.
   b) It adjusts the learning rate dynamically during training.
   c) It speeds up the training convergence and avoids overfitting.
   d) It controls the number of examples used for training.

185. Which algorithm is used alongside multi-layer propagation to update weights and improve accuracy?
   a) Backpropagation
   b) Batch normalization
   c) Adaptive learning rates
   d) Activation functions

186. What advantage do multi-layer neural networks have over linear regression architectures in terms of accuracy and training speed?
   a) They can capture higher-order interactions between variables.
   b) They require less computational power.
   c) They have faster training speed.
   d) They rely on manually crafted features.

187. What is the purpose of the multi-layer propagation algorithm in neural networks?
   a) To recognize patterns and generate an output
   b) To update weights within connected layers
   c) To introduce non-linearity into the decision-making process
   d) To adjust the learning rate dynamically during training

188. What advantage does multi-layer propagation offer in terms of learning tasks?
a) It allows fine-tuning of parameters and functions in each layer separately.
b) It requires retraining the entire network from scratch for each new example.
c) It limits the accuracy of predictions to the training data set.
d) It speeds up the learning process by skipping some layers.

189. What advantage does multi-layer neural networks have in terms of generalization capabilities?
a) They can generalize well across broader data sets.
b) They can learn tasks more quickly than traditional machine learning methods.
c) They have greater control over learning parameters and functions.
d) They can handle high dimensionality without sacrificing accuracy.

190. In which application can RBF networks be used?
a) Stock price prediction b) Text classification
c) Speech recognition d) Spam detection

191. What is a key advantage of RBF networks over other machine learning techniques?
a) They require optimization algorithms like gradient descent.
b) They can capture complex non-linear relationships without explicitly defining the mathematical equation.
c) They only learn local information around each center point.
d) They generalize well even with noisy data sets.

192. How are RBF networks different from traditional neural networks in terms of computational power?
a) RBF networks require less computational power.
b) Traditional neural networks require less computational power.
c) Both RBF networks and traditional neural networks require the same computational power.
d) Computational power is not a factor for either RBF networks or traditional neural networks.

193. What is the primary purpose of RBF networks in unsupervised learning?
a) Regression b) Classification
c) Clustering d) Dimensionality reduction

194. What advantage do RBF networks have over linear regression in terms of dealing with sparse or noisy data?
a) RBF networks require optimization algorithms for training.
b) RBF networks can capture complex non-linear relationships.
c) RBF networks only learn local information around each center point.
d) RBF networks generalize well with slight changes in input values.

195. What is one of the applications of RBF networks in image processing?
a) Sentiment analysis b) Face recognition
c) Speech synthesis d) Spam filtering

196. What is the advantage of RBF networks in terms of training speed?
a) They require optimization algorithms like gradient descent.

b) They have a fast convergence rate.
c) They require more computational power than traditional methods.
d) They have a complex parameterization.

197. What is one of the advantages of RBF networks over traditional neural networks?
a) They have a simpler structure.
b) They require more computational power.
c) They can capture complex linear relationships.
d) They are more efficient for regression tasks.

198. What advantage do splines offer over linear regression in terms of capturing abrupt changes in the data?
a) Splines can fit separate polynomial functions to each data segment.
b) Splines require fewer parameters to achieve accuracy.
c) Splines have greater flexibility in modeling non-linear data.
d) Splines can extrapolate beyond the observed data points.

199. What advantage do splines have over neural networks and support vector machines?
a) They require less training time.
b) They have more flexibility in modeling non-linear data.
c) They can fit low-order polynomials over intervals within data sets.
d) They require fewer parameters to achieve accuracy.

200. What is one of the advantages of using splines in interpolation?
a) They can capture abrupt changes in the data.
b) They allow for predictions beyond observed data points.
c) They have fewer parameters compared to linear regression.
d) They require less training time than neural networks.

201. How do splines provide greater flexibility compared to linear regression?
a) By adjusting degrees of freedom within each segment.
b) By capturing abrupt changes in the data.
c) By requiring fewer parameters to achieve accuracy.
d) By allowing for predictions beyond observed data points.

202. What is the purpose of using knots in spline models?
a) To capture abrupt changes in the data.
b) To specify the smoothness of the model at different parts of the data set.
c) To reduce overfitting issues.
d) To control the number of parameters required.

203. Which method is more suitable for data sets containing highly non-linear trends?
a) Linear regression b) Support vector machines
c) RBF networks d) Splines

204. What advantage do splines offer in terms of overfitting?
a) They capture abrupt changes in the data.
b) They allow for predictions beyond observed data points.

c) They fit low-order polynomials over intervals within data sets.
d) They avoid overly complex solutions by controlling the number of knots.

205. Which method requires less training time compared to neural networks?
a) Linear regression b) RBF networks
c) Splines d) Support vector machines

206. What is the impact of the curse of dimensionality on machine learning algorithms?
a) Algorithms become more accurate with higher dimensions.
b) Algorithms become overfitted and fit the noise in the data.
c) Algorithms require less computational cost with higher dimensions.
d) Algorithms have better interpretability with higher dimensions.

207. Which technique can help mitigate the curse of dimensionality?
a) Feature selection b) Increasing the number of dimensions
c) Using more complex algorithms d) Adding noise to the data

208. What happens to the volume of the space as the number of dimensions increases?
a) It stays constant. b) It decreases linearly.
c) It increases linearly. d) It increases exponentially.

209. Which algorithm may face difficulties when working with higher-dimensional data sets due to the curse of dimensionality?
a) K Means clustering b) Linear regression
c) Decision trees d) Naive Bayes

210. How does the curse of dimensionality impact the computational cost of algorithms?
a) It decreases computational cost.
b) It increases computational cost linearly.
c) It increases computational cost exponentially.
d) It has no impact on computational cost.

211. What can happen to the interpretability of results when the curse of dimensionality is present?
a) Results become more interpretable. b) Results become less interpretable.
c) Results remain the same. d) Interpretability is not affected.

212. Which type of problem can be encountered with higher-dimensional data sets and the curse of dimensionality?
a) Underfitting issues
b) Overfitting issues
c) No issues, higher dimensions improve performance
d) Data becomes more sparse

213. What is the purpose of using interpolations and basis functions in non-linear regression?
a) To transform the data into a lower dimensional space.
b) To approximate the relationship between variables using a linear equation.
c) To overfit the data and capture noise.

d) To eliminate the need for training data.

214. What is the purpose of interpolation in machine learning?

a) To estimate missing values.
b) To eliminate outliers from the data set.
c) To create basis functions.
d) To reduce the dimensionality of the data.

215. Which type of basis function should be used for modeling stock market prices over time?

a) Linear function
b) Exponential function
c) Polynomial function
d) None of the above

216. How do interpolations and basis functions contribute to model accuracy in machine learning?

a) They eliminate the need for training data.
b) They reduce the dimensionality of the data set.
c) They provide greater control over predicting outcomes based on patterns within the data.
d) They increase the complexity of the model.

217. What is the role of basis functions in creating models in machine learning?

a) To reduce memory usage.
b) To store the entire data set in memory.
c) To approximate the behavior of data points within a range.
d) To eliminate the need for interpolation.

218. What is the purpose of basis functions in machine learning?

a) To interpolate between data points.
b) To eliminate noise from the data set.
c) To model complex systems.
d) To reduce the computational cost of algorithms.

219. Which technique helps in reducing the memory usage of models in machine learning?

a) Interpolation
b) Increasing the number of dimensions
c) Feature selection
d) Using more complex algorithms

220. How do interpolations and basis functions contribute to model interpretability in machine learning?

a) They increase the interpretability of the model.
b) They reduce the interpretability of the model.
c) They have no impact on model interpretability.
d) They only impact the accuracy of the model.

Part B (Short Answer Questions)

1. Define the linear model.
2. Explain non-linear regression with an example.
3. Define simple linear regression.
4. Define linear regression.
5. Define Poisson regression.
6. How is Poisson regression useful in machine learning?

7. Give examples of Poisson regression.
8. Define logistic regression.
9. Give examples of logistic regression.
10. What are the types of logistic regression?
11. Define binary logistic regression.
12. Define multinomial logistic regression.
13. What are the uses of multinominal logistic regression?
14. Give three examples of ordinal logistic regression in machine learning.
15. Define least squares method (LSM).
16. What is an activation function?
17. Define linear classifiers.
18. Explain non-linearity and kernel methods.
19. Define linear kernel.
20. Define polynomial kernel.
21. Define Gaussian kernel.
22. Define exponential kernel.
23. Define ANOVA radial basis kernel.
24. Explain generalized linear models.
25. What is linear SVM?
26. What is non-linear SVM?
27. Define the hyperplane of SVM.
28. What is the principle behind AdaBoost.
29. What is soft margin SVM?
30. What is backpropagation?
31. What is the radial basis function (RBF)?
32. Define splines.
33. Define the curse of dimensionality.
34. What is interpolation?
35. Explain the basis functions.

Part C (Essay Questions)

1. Explain the different characteristics of linear and non-linear regression.
2. Explain simple linear models (simple linear regression).
3. Explain linear regression with real-world examples.
4. Define Poisson regression along examples and steps to be followed.
5. Explain logistic regression with the real-world examples.
6. Explain binary logistic regression with real-world examples.
7. Explain multinomial logistic regression with examples.
8. Explain ordinal logistic regression with real-world examples.
9. Explain the least squares method.
10. How is least square regression used for classification?
11. Explain multivariate linear regression.
12. Explain the concept of perceptron in detail.
13. Explain activation function in detail.
14. Explain linear classifiers.
15. Explain the different types of kernels and methods in SVM.
16. Explain generalized linear models in detail.
17. List some of the disadvantages of GLMs.
18. Explain the different types of SVM.
19. Explain AdaBoost (adaptive boosting).
20. How can we improve classification with AdaBoost?
21. Explain the two forms of regularized regression.
22. Explain soft margin SVM.
23. Explain the differences between hard margin and soft margin.
24. Explain multi-layer propagation in detail.
25. Explain the usefulness of RBF networks in machine learning.
26. Explain splines in detail.
27. Explain the curse of dimensionality.
28. Explain the interpolation and basis functions.

ANSWER KEY

Part A

1. (b) **2.** (b) **3.** (b) **4.** (a) **5.** (b) **6.** (a) **7.** (a) **8.** (a)
9. (b) **10.** (a) **11.** (b) **12.** (a) **13.** (b) **14.** (a) **15.** (a) **16.** (c)
17. (d) **18.** (c) **19.** (c) **20.** (a) **21.** (a) **22.** (c) **23.** (c) **24.** (c)
25. (d) **26.** (c) **27.** (b) **28.** (a) **29.** (c) **30.** (c) **31.** (d) **32.** (d)
33. (d) **34.** (b) **35.** (c) **36.** (a) **37.** (a) **38.** (c) **39.** (d) **40.** (a)
41. (c) **42.** (c) **43.** (a) **44.** (a) **45.** (b) **46.** (c) **47.** (d) **48.** (c)
49. (c) **50.** (b) **51.** (d) **52.** (c) **53.** (c) **54.** (c) **55.** (a) **56.** (b)
57. (b) **58.** (c) **59.** (c) **60.** (c) **61.** (b) **62.** (a) **63.** (a) **64.** (d)
65. (a) **66.** (c) **67.** (a) **68.** (d) **69.** (c) **70.** (a) **71.** (c) **72.** (b)
73. (a) **74.** (a) **75.** (a) **76.** (c) **77.** (c) **78.** (a) **79.** (a) **80.** (c)
81. (c) **82.** (b) **83.** (c) **84.** (a) **85.** (d) **86.** (b) **87.** (a) **88.** (c)
89.(a) **90.** (b) **91.** (b) **92.** (c) **93.** (d) **94.** (d) **95.** (b) **96.** (c)
97. (a) **98.** (b) **99.** (b) **100.** (b) **101.** (c) **102.** (a) **103.** (a) **104.** (b)
105. (c) **106.** (c) **107.** (b) **108.** (a) **109.** (d) **110.** (c) **111.** (c) **112.** (b)
113. (c) **114.** (d) **115.** (c) **116.** (a) **117.** (b) **118.** (b) **119.** (d) **120.** (a)
121. (d) **122.** (d) **123.** (d) **124.** (d) **125.** (b) **126.** (b) **127.** (c) **128.** (c)
129. (a) **130.** (c) **131.** (d) **132.** (c) **133.** (b) **134.** (b) **135.** (a) **136.** (a)
137. (c) **138.** (a) **139.** (b) **140.** (b) **141.** (a) **142.** (c) **143.** (c) **144.** (c)
145. (c) **146.** (c) **147.** (c) **148.** (c) **149.** (c) **150.** (b) **151.** (c) **152.** (c)
153. (b) **154.** (d) **155.** (d) **156.** (a) **157.** (c) **158.** (b) **159.** (a) **160.** (a)
161. (c) **162.** (b) **163.** (c) **164.** (a) **165.** (b) **166.** (c) **167.** (b) **168.** (b)
169. (a) **170.** (c) **171.** (c) **172.** (a) **173.** (a) **174.** (a) **175.** (b) **176.** (b)
177. (b) **178.** (d) **179.** (a) **180.** (a) **181.** (b) **182.** (b) **183.** (a) **184.** (c)
185. (a) **186.** (a) **187.** (a) **188.** (a) **189.** (a) **190.** (a) **191.** (b) **192.** (a)
193. (c) **194.** (d) **195.** (b) **196.** (b) **197.** (a) **198.** (a) **199.** (b) **200.** (b)
201. (a) **202.** (b) **203.** (b) **204.** (a) **205.** (a) **206.** (b) **207.** (a) **208.** (d)
209. (a) **210.** (c) **211.** (b) **212.** (b) **213.** (b) **214.** (a) **215.** (b) **216.** (c)
217. (c) **218.** (c) **219.** (a) **220.** (a)

10 Artificial Neural Networks

Learning Objectives

At the end of this chapter, you will be able to:

- Explain the fundamental concepts and give the definition of artificial neural networks (ANNs)
- Describe the types of ANNs, including feedforward networks (FNNs), convolutional neural networks (CNNs), recurrent neural networks (RNNs), long short-term memory (LSTM) networks, and generative adversarial networks (GANs)
- Elaborate on the structure and function of the types of autoencoders: linear, de-noising, sparse, variational, and adversarial
- List the applications of ANNs in fields such as image recognition, natural language processing, automated decision making, time series analysis, cybersecurity, and predictive analytics
- Provide insights into the future developments and potential advancements in ANNs

10.1 Introduction to Neural Networks

In their most basic form, 'neurons' process information. Neuronal connections enable the exchange of impulses and information between them. The mechanism used to process information is based on how strongly neurons are connected; these connections may be strong or weak. In addition, incoming connections from other neurons can affect each neuron's intrinsic state. Each neuron has a function for activation that depends on its current state and helps to predict the signal it will send. A neural network can be visualized as a computational graph comprising mathematical processes.

A neural network comprises three layers: an input layer, a hidden layer, and an output layer. The input layer receives input information, which is subsequently sent through the hidden levels where the calculations are performed. Finally, the output layer offers the final prediction or conclusion based on the input data.

Each node in the neural network runs some calculations on the data it receives and then sends the results to the next layer. By utilizing gradient descent or other optimization techniques to minimize a loss function like mean squared error, the algorithm learns the weights or parameters of each node. It is possible to think of the incoming data as an abstract illustration of the hidden layers. These layers help the neural network comprehend various data elements using internal logic. Since a neural network's output is a numerical vector and bridges the gap between the actual data and the network's representation of the data, we need an explicit output layer. An output layer can be viewed as a translator that assists in understanding the logic of the network and converting the target values.

A neural network consists of two main components: architecture and learning. **Architecture** refers to how the neurons are arranged and connected in the network. Depending on the task and the data, there are different **types of architectures**:

- **Feedforward architecture**: The neurons are organized in layers, and the connections are only from one layer to the next. There are no loops or feedback in the network. This type of architecture is suitable for simple tasks that do not require memory or temporal information, such as image recognition or classification.
- **Recurrent architecture**: The neurons are organized in layers, but some connections form loops or feedbacks within or between layers. This type of architecture allows the network to store and process sequential or temporal information, such as natural language speech recognition or generation.
- **Convolutional architecture**: The network has one or more convolutional layers that apply filters to the input data to extract features. This type of architecture is especially effective for processing spatial information, such as images or videos.
- **Single-layered and multi-layered architecture**: A single-layered network has only one layer of neurons, either input or output. This type of architecture is straightforward and can only perform linear operations, such as logical functions or linear regression. A multi-layered architecture network has multiple hidden layers between the input and output layers. This type of architecture can capture more complex and non-linear patterns in the data, such as face recognition or sentiment analysis.

Learning refers to how the network adjusts its weights and biases to improve performance on a given task. The **learning methods** differ based on the type and availability of data and feedback. Some standard methods are:

- **Supervised learning**: The network is given both input and output data, and it learns to map the input to the output by minimizing a loss function that measures the error between the actual and desired outcome. This method requires labeled data and a predefined objective function, such as mean squared error or cross-entropy.
- **Unsupervised learning**: The network is only given input data and learns to discover patterns or structures in the data without any external guidance. This method does not require labeled data or a predefined objective function. However, it may use criteria such as information maximization or sparsity to evaluate the quality of the learned representation.
- **Reinforcement learning**: The network is given input data and feedback regarding rewards or penalties based on its actions or outputs. It learns to optimize its behavior by maximizing the cumulative reward over time. This method does not require labeled data or a predefined objective function, but it requires a dynamic environment and a reward function that defines the goal of the task.

For example, a neural network that performs handwritten digit recognition may use a feedforward multi-layered architecture with a supervised learning method based on backpropagation and gradient descent. A neural network that generates captions for images may use a recurrent convolutional architecture with a reinforcement learning method based on policy gradient and reward shaping.

10.2 Introduction to Artificial Neural Networks

Computing systems called artificial neural networks (ANNs) imitate the form and operation of biological neural networks, such as the brain. **Artificial neurons** are a group of connected components found in ANNs that process and transfer signals to other neurons. Each neuron has a non-linear activation function that defines its output, and each connection has a weight that controls the signal's intensity. Layers can be used to organize ANNs, and each layer can alter the inputs differently.

By modifying their weights following a learning algorithm that reduces errors between planned and actual output, ANNs can learn from data. In this type of supervised learning, examples with known inputs and outputs are used to train the network. ANNs are also capable of unsupervised learning, which involves identifying patterns and characteristics in unlabeled data.

Imagine that you are trying to learn how to distinguish between different types of fruit, such as apples and oranges. Of course, apples are generally round and red and oranges are typically round and orange. However, there can occasionally be variants, and it may be challenging to distinguish between them. Now you have a friend who is skilled at recognizing fruits. He can identify them by their appearance and tell you whether they are an apple or an orange. So you decide to ask your friend to teach you so that you can learn from him. Your friend explains that he evaluates many aspects of the fruits, such as their texture, color, and form. Then, based on the significance of each attribute, he gives it a particular weight. For instance, he can assign more weight to shape than color or texture since he believes it to be the most critical aspect. He also says that he contrasts these qualities with what he understands about apples and oranges. For example, a fruit is likely an apple if it is spherical and red. It is an orange if it is round and orange.

You now want to create a system capable of making these choices on its own. An ANN can help with that. An ANN is modeled after the way our brain functions and is constructed of interconnected nodes called neurons. In this scenario, you would create an ANN that uses the traits (characteristics) of a fruit as input (Table 10.1), just as you would describe the fruit's shape, color, and texture to a friend.

Table 10.1 Characteristics of a fruit along with weightage

S. No	Characteristic	Weight of the characteristic	Apple	Orange
1	Color	0.8	Depends	Orange color
2	Skin texture	0.9	Smooth	Knobby
3	Visible seeds in fruit	0.7	Yes	Depends
4	Mean diameter of fruit	0.2	7.9 cm	7.6 cm

Then, the network's neurons are fed information about these traits. Each neuron in the network has a weight, like the weights your friend assigned to the attributes. The network integrates these weights with the input attributes to determine whether the fruit is an apple or an orange. The ANN changes these weights through a process known as **training**, using a set of model fruits you supply.

First, it compares its forecast to the correct response (which you supply) to increase its accuracy over time. Then it modifies the weights accordingly. It does this repeatedly with more and more instances until it masters classifying these fruits. Once trained, the ANN will use the modified weights to determine if a new fruit it has not seen before is an apple or an orange. As a result, an ANN is comparable to a mathematical model that gains knowledge from instances to make predictions or categorical judgments, much as how you learned to tell an apple from an orange from your friend's expertise.

ANNs can be used to solve various issues, including anomaly detection, dimensionality reduction, clustering, regression, classification, and more. ANNs can be used, for instance, to recognize handwritten numbers, identify diseases, forecast stock prices, produce natural language, etc. The versatility and scalability of ANNs and their capacity to represent non-linear and dynamic interactions are some of their benefits. They can also manage complex and noisy data.

On the other hand, high computational cost, lack of interpretability and explainability, and vulnerability to overfitting and local minima are some **drawbacks of ANNs**. Some more limitations are given below:

- **Data and resource requirements:** ANNs often require large amounts of labeled data to train effectively and avoid overfitting. This can be costly and time-consuming to collect and process. Moreover, ANNs can have millions or billions of parameters that must be updated during training, requiring high-performance hardware and software. The complexity and size of ANNs also make them difficult to deploy and maintain in real-world scenarios.
- **Interpretability and explainability:** ANNs are often black box models, producing outputs without revealing underlying logic or reasoning. This can pose challenges for understanding how ANNs make decisions, verifying their correctness, and debugging errors. Furthermore, ANNs may not be able to provide justifications or evidence for their outputs, which can affect the trust and acceptance of users and stakeholders. For example, an ANN that diagnoses a medical condition may be unable to explain why it chose a specific diagnosis or what features it considers relevant.
- **Generalization and extrapolation:** ANNs are designed to learn from data and generalize to unseen situations. However, this may not always be the case, especially when the data is noisy, biased, or insufficient. ANNs may overfit the training data and fail to perform well on new or different data. Alternatively, ANNs may underfit the data and fail to capture the underlying patterns or relationships. Moreover, ANNs may struggle to extrapolate from the data and handle novel or unexpected scenarios or facts. For example, an ANN that recognizes faces may not be able to identify a face with a mask or a face from a different ethnicity.

10.2.1 Mathematical Model of an Artificial Neuron

A general mathematical model of an artificial neuron is shown in Fig. 10.1. Here, $x_1, x_2 \cdots$, and x_n. are the inputs the artificial neuron receives from an external source. The source can be a user-supplied input or features extracted from data. Each input is linked to the artificial neuron represented by a directed edge labeled with a suitable weight. Thus for the inputs $x_1, x_2, \cdots, x_n$, the corresponding weights are $w_1, w_2, \cdots, w_n$.. The artificial neuron has two parts: summation and activation. The **summation** is the sum of the products of the inputs and the corresponding weights. The resultant is given as input to the **activation,** which produces an output.

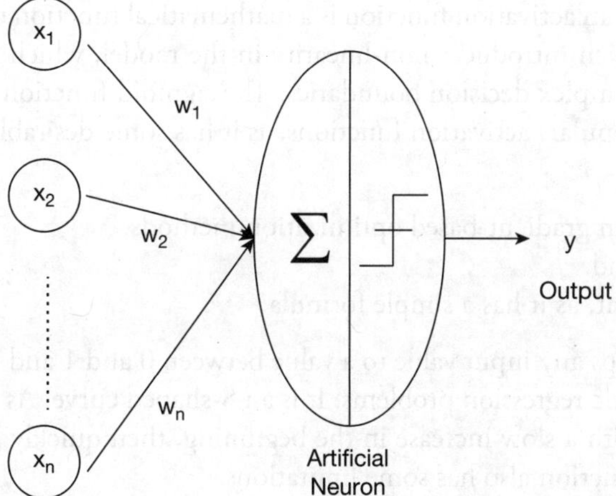

Figure 10.1 Mathematical model of an artificial neuron

The mathematical equation describing the process is shown below:

$$t = \sum_{i=1}^{n} x_i w_i \tag{10.1}$$

$$y = f(t) \tag{10.2}$$

The activation function can be considered a non-linear filter producing the output. The other commonly used activation functions are:

$$f(t) = \begin{cases} 1, & t \geq \theta \\ 0, & < \theta \end{cases} \tag{10.3}$$

$$f(t) = \frac{1}{\left(1 + e^{-\alpha t}\right)} \tag{10.4}$$

$$f(t) = \frac{e^{x} - e^{-x}}{e^{x} + e^{-x}} \tag{10.5}$$

$$f(t) = \begin{cases} 1, & t \geq 0 \\ 0, & t < 0 \end{cases} \tag{10.6}$$

The different types of activation functions, such as sigmoid (Equation 10.4), tanh (Equation 10.5), and ReLU (Equation 10.3) have different properties and applications.

Sigmoid function: This is the most commonly used activation function in neural networks. The need for a sigmoid function stems from many learning algorithms requiring the activation function to be differentiable and, hence, continuous. The step function is unsuitable in such situations as it is not continuous. To elaborate, an activation function is a mathematical function that transforms a neuron's input into its output, which introduces non-linearity in the model, which in turn allows the neural network to learn more complex decision boundaries. The sigmoid function is one of the earliest and most commonly used (popular) activation functions, as it has some desirable properties:

- It is non-linear.
- It can be easily used in gradient-based optimization methods.
- It is easy to understand.
- It is easy to implement, as it has a simple formula.

The sigmoid function maps any input value to a value between 0 and 1 and is useful for binary classification and also for logistic regression problems. It is an S-shaped curve. As the input value increases, the output value starts with a slow increase in the beginning, then quickly approaches 1, and finally levels off. The sigmoid function also has some limitations:

- It can suffer from a vanishing gradient problem, meaning that the function's gradient becomes very small when the input value is very large or small. This can slow down or even prevent the learning process of the network.
- It can cause saturation of neurons, which means that the function's output becomes very close to 0 or 1 when the input value is very large or small. This can decrease the sensitivity of the network to changes in the input.
- It is not zero-centered, meaning the function's output is always positive. This can introduce undesirable correlations in the gradients of adjacent layers and affect the network's learning process.

Therefore, alternative activation functions, such as tanh, ReLU, leaky ReLU, etc., have been proposed to overcome these drawbacks. However, the sigmoid function remains a vital activation function in neural networks.

For example, an artificial neuron has two inputs x_1 and x_2, weights w_1 and w_2, and bias b. Its sigmoid activation function is shown below:

$$\text{Output} = \text{sigmoid}(w_1 * x_1 + w_2 * x_2 + b)$$

The output of this neuron will be a value between 0 and 1, depending on the inputs, weights, and bias values. For instance, if $w_1 = 0.5$, $w_2 = -0.3$, $b = -0.2$, $x_1 = 0.8$, and $x_2 = 0.6$, the output will be:

$$\text{Output} = \text{sigmoid}(0.5 * 0.8 - 0.3 * 0.6 - 0.2) = \text{sigmoid}(0.04) = 0.51$$

This means that these inputs activate this neuron slightly.

10.2.2 The McCulloch–Pitts Neuron Model

This is the first model of an artificial neuron. It is shown in Fig. 10.2. Simple circuit gates like logical AND, logical OR, and logical NOT can be simulated using this model. The truth table for logical AND is shown in Table 10.2.

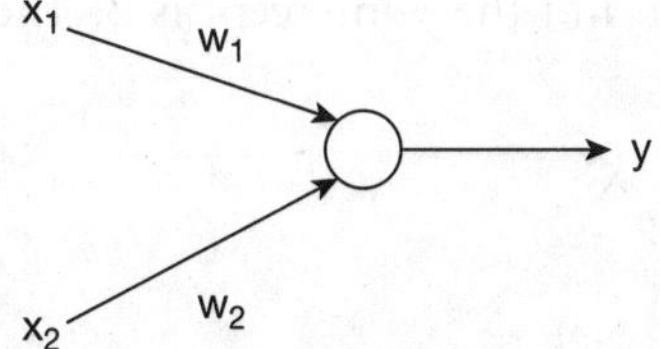

Figure 10.2 McCulloch–Pitts neuron model to simulate the logical AND gate

Table 10.2 Logical AND table

x_1	x_2	y
0	0	0
0	1	0
1	0	0
1	1	1

The signum function is used as an activation function in this model. Considering the weights as [1,1], the values are evaluated (Table 10.3).

Table 10.3 Signum function as activation function with weights [1,1]

x_1	w_1	x_2	w_2	$x_1w_1 + x_2w_2$
0	1	0	1	0
0	1	1	1	1
1	1	0	1	1
1	1	1	1	2

By fixing the threshold in the signum function as 2, the equation becomes

$$y = \begin{cases} 1, & t \geq 2 \\ 0, & t < 2 \end{cases} \tag{10.7}$$

The logical AND can be easily solved by choosing the weight vector as $[1,1]^T$ and $\theta = 2$. The equation becomes $x_1w_1 + x_2w_2 = 2\,(\text{or})\, x_1w_1 + x_2w_2 - 2 = 0$. This is the equation of a straight line. It can be rewritten as

$$x_2w_2 = 2 - x_1w_1$$

$$\Rightarrow x_2 = \frac{2}{w_2} - x_1\frac{w_1}{w_2} \tag{10.8}$$

$$\Rightarrow x_2 = 2 - x_1 \because w_1 = w_2 = 1$$

The slope of this equation is −1 and the *y*-intercept is 2. The equation plot is visualized in Fig. 10.3.

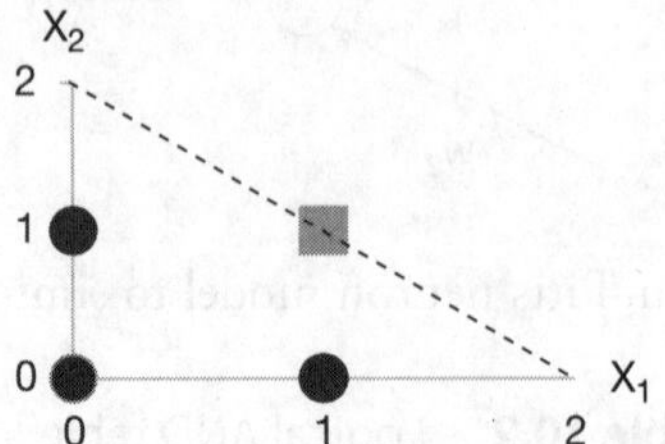

Figure 10.3 Equation plot with slope (−1) and *y*-intercept (2)

The limitations of this model are that the weights fixed are not suitable for linearly inseparable data. If the weights chosen cannot separate the data, then another set of weights should be guessed and repeated. The process works for only linearly separable data.

Let us look at an X-OR problem. The truth table for logical X-OR is shown in Table 10.4 and the equation plot is shown in Fig. 10.4. A linear line cannot draw and separate the patterns for this data. Hence, it is linearly inseparable.

Table 10.4 The truth table for logical X-OR

x_1	x_2	y
0	0	0
0	1	1
1	0	1
1	1	0

Figure 10.4 Truth table representation using logical X-OR

10.2.3 The Perceptron Model

The perceptron model is used for data or pattern classification. The typical structure of a perceptron model to classify logical AND inputs is shown in Fig. 10.5.

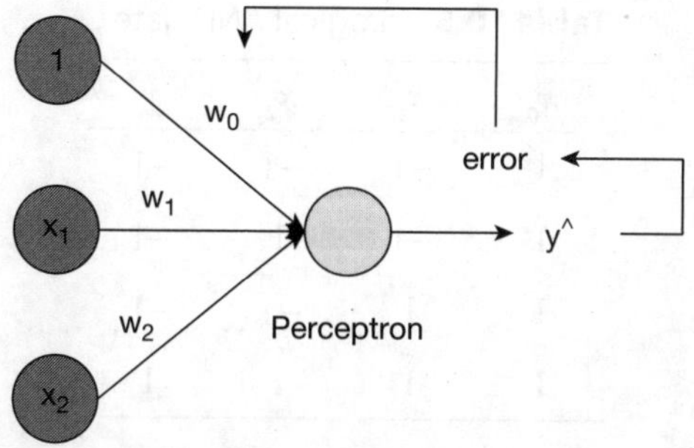

Figure 10.5 Generalized perceptron model

The perceptron neuron takes multiple inputs along with a biased input, applies weight to each input, and computes the weighted sum. An activation function is applied to the weighted sum to determine the output.

Perceptron Algorithm

1. Initialize the weights to zero vector.
2. Take the first input and perform the sum of the products. Then apply the activation function.
3. If the predicted output matches the original output, do nothing
4. Adjust the weights using the perceptron learning rule if the predicted output does not match the actual output.
5. Consider the input that follows and repeat the process until one input cycle is completed.
6. Repeat the process defined in steps 2 to 5 until the algorithm converges.

The perceptron algorithm guarantees convergence if the data is linearly separable. The activation function used in perceptron is the threshold function defined in Equation (10.9).

$$\hat{y} = \begin{cases} 1 & \text{sum} \geq \theta \\ -1 & \text{sum} < \theta \end{cases}. \tag{10.9}$$

Perceptron learning rule: If $y \neq \hat{y}$ then $w_i\left(new\right) = w_i\left(old\right) + \eta \times y \times x_i$,

where η = learning rate; the value lies between $[0,1]$; y = actual output; $x_i = i^{\text{th}}$ input pattern; $w_i(old)$ = weight vector of the ith input pattern; and $w_i(new)$ = adjusted weight vector of the ith input pattern.

Instead of conventional binary inputs, bipolar inputs are considered for the example to show the working of perceptron for the logical AND gate. Consider learning rate = 0.5 and threshold = 0 (Table 10.5 and Fig. 10.6).

Table 10.5 Logical AND gate

x_0	x_1	x_2	y
1	−1	−1	−1
1	−1	1	−1
1	1	−1	−1
1	1	1	1

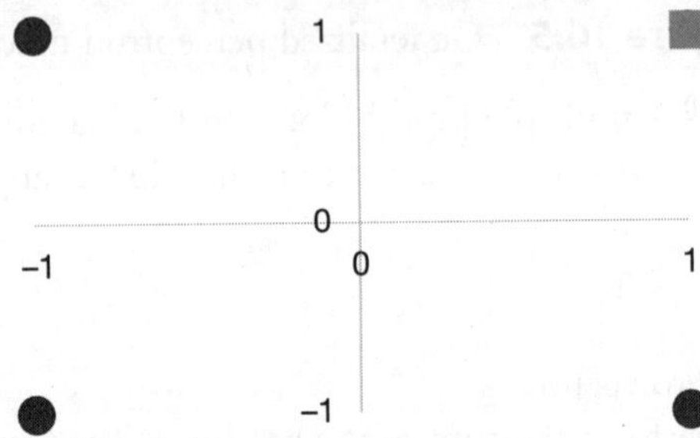

Figure 10.6 Logical AND gate representation

One cycle of inputs is termed one epoch. In the zeroth epoch, weights are initialized to zero. The next four lines in the table indicate one cycle of all the available data inputs; thus, it makes one epoch. The predicted output is calculated using a threshold of zero. Thus, the equation of the activation function becomes

$$\hat{y} = \begin{cases} 1 & \text{sum} \geq 0 \\ -1 & \text{sum} < 0 \end{cases} \tag{10.10}$$

Table 10.6 Step-by-step calculation of the perceptron learning algorithm

Epoch	x_0	x_1	x_2	w_0	w_1	w_2	sum $\sum x_i w_i$	Predicted output ($\hat{y}$)	Actual output (y).	Δw_0	Δw_1	Δw_2
										$\Delta w_i = \eta \times y \times x_i$		
0				0	0	0						
1	1	−1	−1	0	0	0	0	1	−1	−0.5	0.5	0.5
	1	−1	1	−0.5	0.5	0.5	−0.5	−1	−1	0	0	0
	1	1	−1	−0.5	0.5	0.5	−0.5	−1	−1	0	0	0
	1	1	1	−0.5	0.5	0.5	0.5	1	1	0	0	0
2	1	−1	−1	−0.5	0.5	0.5	−1.5	−1	−1	0	0	0

The weight adjustments after the first input become $[-0.5, 0.5, 0.5]^T$, perfectly identifying the other three patterns (Table 10.6). Hence, the weights are tested for the first input pattern in the second epoch. For this pattern, no weight adjustment is required; hence, the second epoch is stopped immediately.

Thus, the equation of the discriminatory line (Fig. 10.7) becomes

$$-0.5x_0 + 0.5x_1 + 0.5x_2 = 0$$

$$\Rightarrow 0.5[-x_0 + x_1 + x_2] = 0$$

$$\Rightarrow -x_0 + x_1 + x_2 = 0$$

$$\Rightarrow x_2 = -x_1 + x_0$$

$$\Rightarrow x_2 = -x_1 + 1 \because x_0 = 1.$$

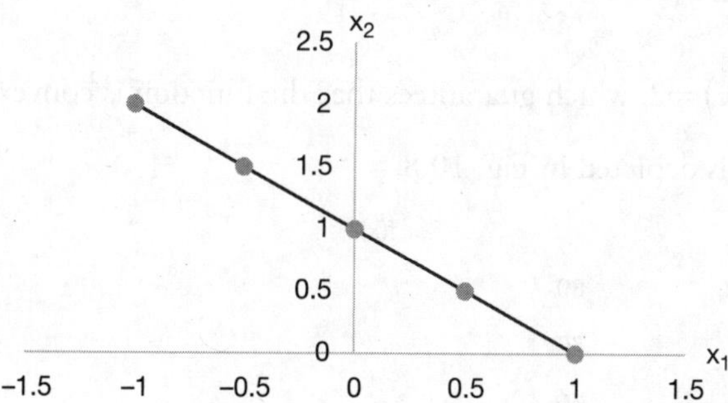

Figure 10.7 Perceptron discriminatory line for logical AND

The main limitation of the perceptron model is that it is applicable for linearly separable data. For linearly inseparable data, the perceptron fails to classify the input patterns. To overcome this, feedforward neural networks are introduced.

10.2.4 Gradient Descent

Gradient descent is a first-order optimization problem. The gradient is a generalization of the derivative of a function on several variables. If $f(x_1, x_2 \cdots, x_n)$ is a differentiable scalar function of several variables, its gradient is a vector whose components are n-partial derivatives of the function f..
Hence, it is a vector-valued function.

Gradient represents the slope of the tangent of the graph of the function. It points toward the greatest rate of increase of the function, and its magnitude is the slope of the graph. It finds a model's optimal parameters or weights by minimizing the cost or loss function. It is an iterative process where the parameters are tuned to reach the optimal values in each iteration.

To find the local minimum of a function using gradient descent, we should take steps proportional to the negative of the function's gradient at the current point. If we move towards the positive of the gradient, then we approach the function's local maximum, termed gradient ascent.

Gradient descent is also known as steepest descent or method of steepest descent. The two requirements to use gradient descent are that the function should be differentiable and convex.

Gradient Descent Algorithm: The idea of the gradient descent algorithm is that in each iteration, the point that follows is calculated using the current point and a learning rate. It subtracts the value since we need to minimize the cost function. It is represented using the equation

$$p_{n+1} = p_n - \eta \nabla f\left(p_n\right),$$

where p_n is the current point, p_{n+1} is the next point, η is the learning rate, and $\nabla f\left(p_n\right)$ represents the gradient at the current point. The advantage of the learning rate is that it governs the convergence process. If the value is small, convergence is delayed. If it is a large value, convergence is not guaranteed.

For example, $f(x) = x^2 - 3x$.

$f'(x) = 2x - 3$ and $f''(x) = 2$, which guarantees that the function is convex.

The plot of the function is depicted in Fig. 10.8.

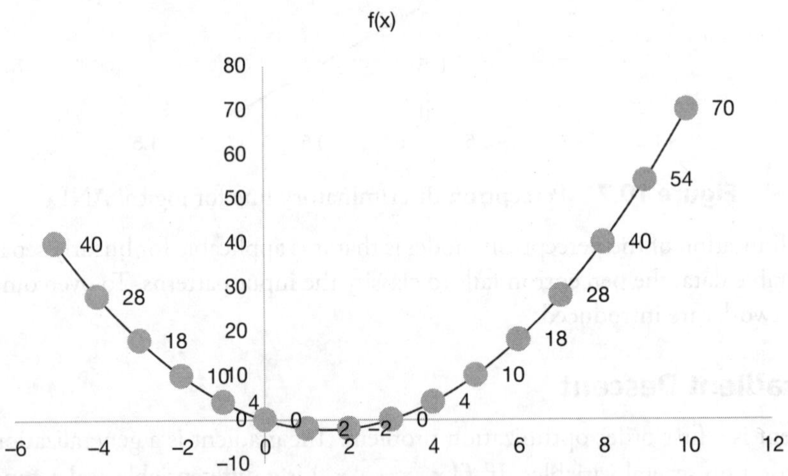

Figure 10.8 Plot of the function $x^2 - 3x$

Assume that we are at point 15. We must move towards the local minimum using a gradient descent algorithm from this point.

Table 10.7 Tracing the gradient descent algorithm

Current point	Next point using gradient descent equation $p_{n+1} = p_n - 0.1 * (2x - 3)$	Current point	Next point using gradient descent equation $p_{n+1} = p_n - 0.1 * (2x - 3)$
2.0000	1.9000	1.5058	1.5046
1.9000	1.8200	1.5046	1.5037
1.8200	1.7560	1.5037	1.5030
1.7560	1.7048	1.5030	1.5024
1.7048	1.6638	1.5024	1.5019
1.6638	1.6311	1.5019	1.5015
1.6311	1.6049	1.5015	1.5012
1.6049	1.5839	1.5012	1.5010
1.5839	1.5671	1.5010	1.5008
1.5671	1.5537	1.5008	1.5006
1.5537	1.5429	1.5006	1.5005
1.5429	1.5344	1.5005	1.5004
1.5344	1.5275	1.5004	1.5003
1.5275	1.5220	1.5003	1.5003
1.5220	1.5176	1.5003	1.5002
1.5176	1.5141	1.5002	1.5002
1.5141	1.5113	1.5002	1.5001
1.5113	1.5090	1.5001	1.5001
1.5090	1.5072	1.5001	1.5001
1.5072	1.5058	1.5001	1.5001

You can observe that the function could not move further from point 1.5001 though the local minima are at 0. This is the smallest value we can reach from the gradient descent algorithm that is converged to 1.5001.

Gradient descent is a powerful optimization technique that iteratively updates the parameters of a model to minimize a loss function. However, it still faces some specific **challenges** that affect its performance:

- It can converge to local optima rather than global optima. This means that the algorithm may stop at a point where the loss function is not at its lowest value but rather at a local minimum surrounded by higher values. This can happen when the loss function is non-convex and has multiple minima.

- Learning rate value has a significant impact. The learning rate is a hyperparameter that controls how much the parameters are updated in each iteration. If the learning rate is too small, the algorithm may take too long to converge or get stuck in a plateau. If the learning rate is too large, the algorithm may overshoot the optimal point and diverge or oscillate.
- If the model is complex, overfitting issues will arise. Overfitting means the model performs well on the training data but poorly on new or unseen data. This can happen when the model has too many parameters or features that capture noise or irrelevant patterns in the data.
- The rate of convergence is slow for large data sets or in high-dimensional spaces. This is because gradient descent requires calculation of the gradient of the loss function concerning all the parameters in each iteration, which can be computationally expensive and time-consuming for large data sets or models with many features.

10.3 Types of Artificial Neural Networks

Feedforward neural network (FNN): You can imagine this as a one-way street. Without any loops or feedback, information moves from the input to the output. It resembles a network of neurons carrying data in a single direction. Feedforward neural networks are frequently used for language processing or picture recognition.

Convolutional neural network (CNN): A CNN is used primarily to comprehend visual data, much like how our brain interprets images. It applies filters or 'feature detectors' to various portions of the image to find patterns and shapes. For instance, it may identify edges, corners, or textures in an image. CNNs are used in many different applications, including image categorization, object identification, and picture synthesis.

Recurrent neural network (RNN): An RNN is a memory-equipped network. It can handle text and other sequential data types like time series. It has links that create loops that let data flow back to earlier processes. This network remembers and considers previous data when making predictions. RNNs are frequently employed for sentiment analysis, speech recognition, and language translation.

Long short-term memory (LSTM) network: It is a form of RNN that excels at identifying long-term dependencies in sequential data. The 'short-term memory' constraint of conventional RNNs is addressed. Since LSTMs include specialized memory cells, they can process and retain pertinent information over longer sequences by selectively remembering or forgetting it at each step. Language modeling, speech recognition, and handwriting recognition are prominent applications of LSTMs.

Generative adversarial network (GAN): A GAN is a unique network where two models, a generator and a discriminator, are competitively pitted against one another. The generator attempts to produce artificial data, such as photographs, that closely resembles actual data, while the discriminator's task is to tell the difference between the two. GANs may produce incredibly realistic data through this adversarial process, which makes them suitable for jobs like picture synthesis, video production, and data augmentation.

10.3.1 Feedforward Neural Network (FNN)

Also called a multi-layer perceptron, here the information goes in a single path from the input layer through one or more hidden layers and eventually to the oput layer (Fig. 10.9). The input, hidden, and output layers are the three basic types of layers that make up an FNN's architecture. Artificial neurons (nodes) that process and send information make up each layer. Input data, such as a sample's characteristics, are sent to the input layer. Then, each neuron in the input layer represents one aspect of the input data.

Between the input and output layers lie what are known as hidden layers. To extract pertinent patterns and characteristics, they compute the incoming data. Depending on how complicated the problem is, both the total number of hidden layers as well as the total number of neurons in each layer may change.

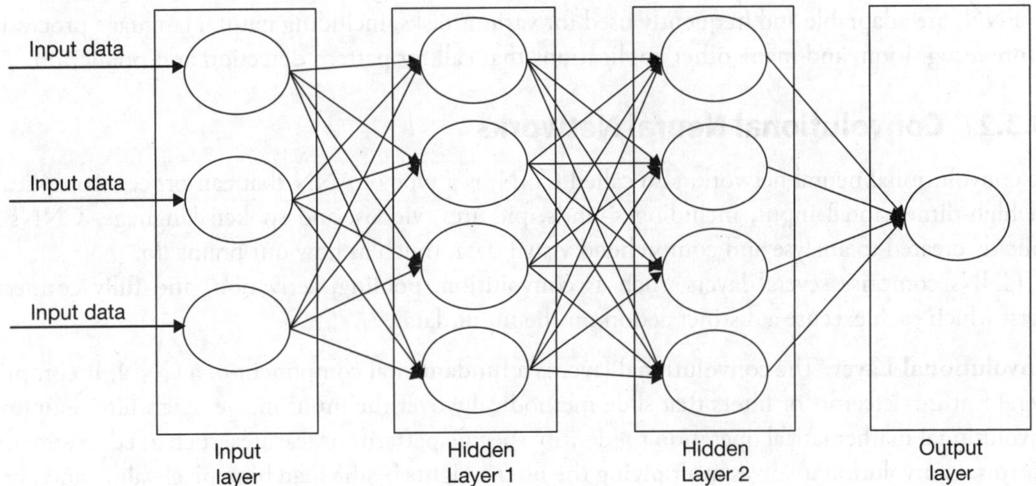

Figure 10.9 Feedforward network (FFN)

The output layer produces the network's ultimate output, which can be a prediction, classification, or regression value. The type of task determines how many neurons are present in the output layer. Each neuron in the output layer can represent a specific category, for instance, if the aim is to categorize photos into different groups. A weighted sum of inputs and an activation function are the two fundamental processes carried out by each neuron in an FNN.

Each input's weight, which reflects its relative importance, is multiplied by the inputs from the preceding layer. The sum of these weighted inputs is calculated. The weighted total is then passed through an activation function, which causes the network to become non-linear. Based on the weighted total, the activation function determines whether or not to stimulate the neuron. It increases adaptability and enables the network to understand intricate connections between inputs and outputs.

Forward Propagation: Starting from the input layer, the forward propagation process entails moving the input data through the network's hidden layers until it reaches the output layer. Each neuron computes its weighted sum to generate an output and applies the activation function. The process continues until it reaches the output layer, where these outputs serve as the inputs for the following layer.

Training: To train an FNN, we require a labelled data set that contains input data and the correct outputs they should produce. The network modifies the weights associated with each neuron throughout training to reduce the discrepancy between its predictions and the correct outputs. This is accomplished by measuring the network's performance using a loss function and an optimization approach like gradient descent.

Consider this straightforward FNN example for handwritten digit recognition. Neurons in the input layer represent the pixels in an input image. The hidden layers process the input image to extract characteristics like edges, curves, or patterns. The output layer is made up of 10 neurons, each of which represents a digit from 0 to 9. The neuron in the output layer with the highest activity value indicates the projected digit. This FNN learns to connect the input patterns with the associated digits by being trained on a data set of labeled handwritten digits. Once trained, it can recognize handwritten numbers even in previously unobserved images.

FNNs are adaptable and frequently used for various tasks, including natural language processing, picture recognition, and many other applications that call for pattern detection and prediction.

10.3.2 Convolutional Neural Networks

The convolutional neural network, also called CNN, is a type of ANN that can process complicated and high-dimensional input, including sounds, pictures, videos, and spoken language. CNNs are explicitly created to analyse and comprehend visual data, much as how our brains do.

CNNs comprise several layers, such as convolution, pooling, activation, and fully connected layers, which each execute a distinct action on the input data.

Convolutional Layer: The convolutional layer is a fundamental component of a CNN. It comprises several feature detectors or filters that slide methodically over the input image. Each filter employs a convolutional mathematical operation to identify specific patterns or features, such as edges, textures, or forms. Convolution involves multiplying the filter weights by the matching pixel values and applying the filter to a small image area at a time. The resulting values are added together to provide a single value indicating whether a specific feature is present in that area. A new feature map highlighting the identified features is created by repeating this process throughout the image.

Pooling Layer: A CNN frequently adds a pooling layer after the convolutional layer. This layer decreases the feature maps' dimensionality while the crucial details are preserved. It makes the network more resistant to changes in the size or position of the identified features. Max pooling is the most frequently used pooling method. The most significant value is picked for each smaller region on the feature map. By doing this, the size of the feature map is reduced while maintaining the most crucial information.

Convolutional and pooling layers are typically followed by one or more fully linked layers at the end of a CNN. These layers resemble those in a conventional feedforward neural network, where every neuron is coupled to every neuron in the layer before it.

Neuron Operations: Just like in a typical neural network, the neurons in the fully connected layer calculate weighted sums of the inputs from the preceding layer and send the results through an activation function. The activations in these neurons represent the network's ultimate output.

Training: A labeled data set containing input images and their related labels is utilized for training a CNN. Like other neural networks, the network modifies its biases and weights during training to reduce discrepancies between its predictions and the correct labels. This is accomplished using an appropriate loss function and optimization techniques like gradient descent.

Let us look at an example of a CNN for image classification that can differentiate between cats and dogs. The pixel values of an input image are taken in by a layer that is part of the CNN. The successive convolutional layers would identify various aspects of the image, such as edges, textures, or forms. Thanks to the pooling layers, the feature maps would be downscaled while still containing the necessary data. By being trained on a collection of labeled cat and dog photographs, this CNN learns to connect the visual patterns of cats and dogs with their corresponding labels. In addition, it correctly identifies new, unseen photos of a dog or a cat after being trained.

CNNs can also generalize their learning from a lot of data to fresh and unstudied material. CNNs take their cues from the biological design and operation of the brain's visual cortex, which comprises neurons that respond to various visual field stimuli. The basis of CNNs is the kernels, sometimes referred to as filters. Using the convolution approach, kernels extract the crucial data from the input.

10.3.2.1 Convolutional Layer

The convolutional layer in a CNN performs a mathematical operation called convolution on the input data (Fig. 10.10).

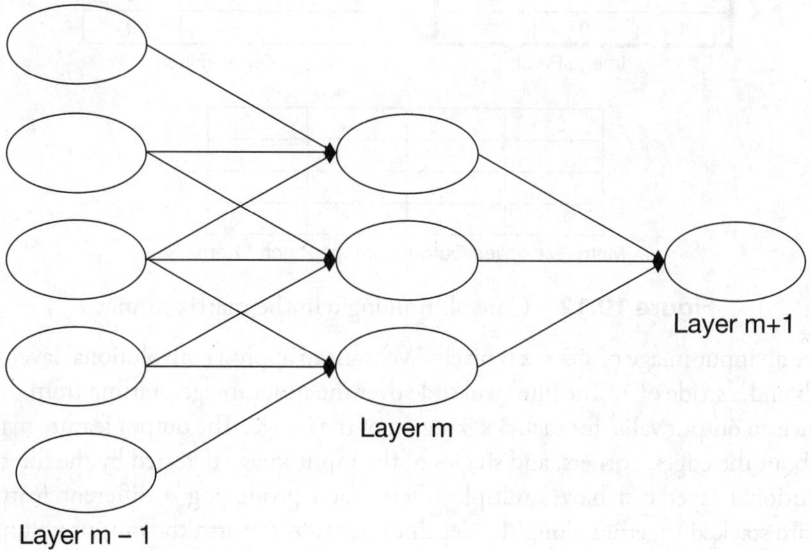

Figure 10.10 Convolutional layer

Convolution means applying a filter, also known as a kernel, to a local region of the input data and producing an output value that is the weighted sum of the filter and the input values. The filter slides over the input data, moving by a certain number of steps called strides, and produces an output matrix called a feature map. The feature map captures the spatial patterns and features of the input data relevant to the task at hand (Fig. 10.11).

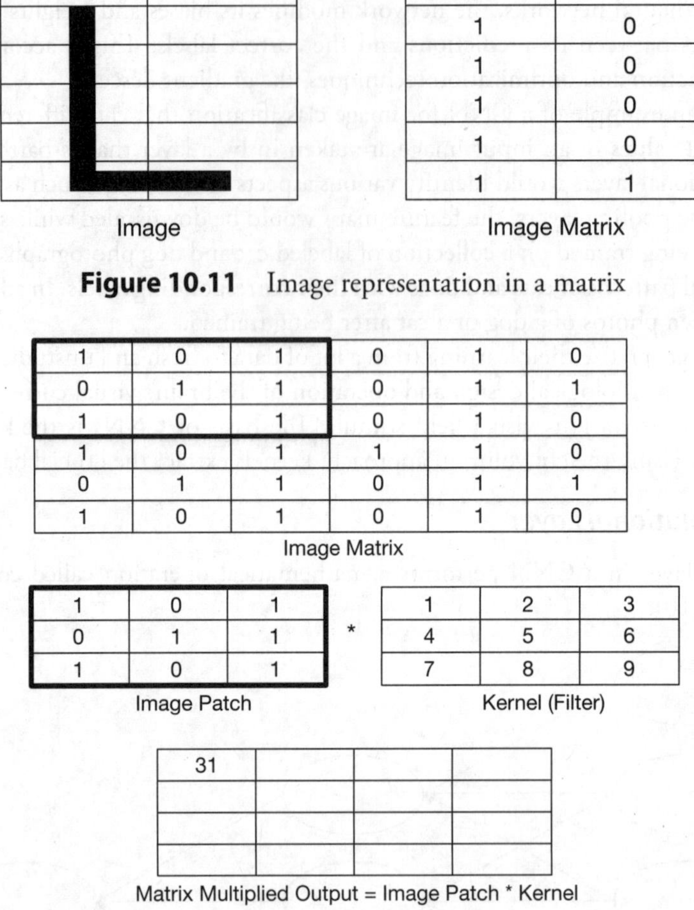

Figure 10.11 Image representation in a matrix

Figure 10.12 Convolution logic in the matrix format

Let us have an input image of size 6 x 6 pixels. We want to apply a convolutional layer with a filter of size 3 x 3 pixels and a stride of 1. The filter will slide over the input image, starting from the top-left corner, and produce an output value for each 3 x 3 region of the image. The output feature map will contain information about the edges, corners, and shapes of the input image detected by the filter (Fig. 10.12).

A convolutional layer can have multiple filters, each producing a different feature map. The feature maps are stacked together along the depth dimension to form the output volume of the convolutional layer. The filters can have different sizes, strides, and padding options to control the shape and size of the output volume. The filters are also learnable parameters that are updated during the training process to optimize the performance of the CNN.

10.3.2.2 Pooling Layer

The size of the feature maps generated by the convolutional layers is reduced by a pooling layer, which is a part of a CNN. The principal advantages of pooling are that it enhances network efficiency and avoids overfitting by reducing the number of parameters and computations. It improves generalization and translation invariance by making the network more resilient to changes in the location and orientation of the features in the input image.

The most frequently used pooling procedures are average and maximum pooling. There are other forms as well. While **average pooling** determines the average value, **maximum pooling** chooses the maximum value in each area of the feature map that is filtered. For example, if we apply a 2 x 2 max pooling filter with a stride of 2 to a 4 x 4 feature map, we get a 2 x 2 output as shown in Fig. 10.13.

31	23	35	**56**
20	08	05	46
10	20	30	40
33	**44**	55	**77**

31	56
44	77

Figure 10.13 Pooling by choosing maximum

If we apply a 2 x 2 average pooling filter with a stride of 2 to a 4 x 4 feature map, we get a 2 x 2 output as shown in Fig. 10.14.

31	23	35	56
20	08	05	46
10	20	30	40
33	44	55	77

(31+23+20+08)/4	(35+56+05+46)/4
(10+20+33+44)/4	(30+40+55+77)/4

Figure 10.14 Pooling by choosing the average

The most noticeable features in each region are preserved by max pooling, while the features are rounded off by average pooling. Both approaches can aid in reducing noise and extraneous information in feature maps. The highest or average value over the entire spatial dimension is used in global pooling, which reduces each channel of the feature map to a single value (Fig. 10.15).

31	23	35	**56**
20	08	05	46
10	20	30	40
33	**44**	55	**77**

31	56
44	77

77

Figure 10.15 Single-value pooling

This can be helpful for producing a compact representation of the features or for lowering the number of parameters needed before a fully connected layer.

In a CNN architecture, pooling layers are typically positioned after one or more convolutional layers. Depending on the desired level of down sampling, they can have various filter sizes and strides. Pooling layers are a fundamental component of CNNs and are crucial for removing significant features from images.

Advantages: Pooling layers are a common component of CNNs, which are widely used for image recognition and classification tasks. Pooling layers perform a subsampling operation on the feature maps produced by the convolutional layers, which results in several advantages for the CNN model. The three main advantages of pooling layers are dimensionality reduction, translation invariance, and feature selection.

Dimensionality reduction refers to the process of reducing the number of dimensions or variables in a data set or a model. This can help in improving the efficiency and performance of the model, as well as preventing overfitting. Overfitting occurs when the model learns too much from the training data and fails to generalize well to new or unseen data. By reducing the spatial dimensions of the feature maps, pooling layers can lower the computational cost and memory usage of the model, as well as reduce the number of parameters that need to be learned.

Translation invariance is another important property that pooling layers can help achieve in CNNs. Translation invariance means that the model is able to recognize and classify an object in an image regardless of its position or location in the image. This is desirable because we want the model to be robust to slight variations or shifts in the input image, which are common in real-world scenarios. Pooling layers can provide translation invariance by aggregating or summarizing the information from a local neighborhood of pixels in the feature map..

Feature selection is the process of selecting or extracting the most relevant or informative features from the input data for a specific task or goal. This can help in improving the accuracy and interpretability of the model, as well as reducing noise and redundancy. Pooling layers can perform feature selection by applying a non-linear function to the feature maps, which enhances or suppresses certain features based on their importance or relevance.

Disadvantages: The first disadvantage of pooling layers is that they cause information loss. Pooling layers apply a function, such as max or average, to a local region of the feature map and output a single value. This means that some information from the input feature map is discarded, which can be necessary for the final classification or regression task. The second disadvantage of pooling layers is that they can cause over-smoothing of the feature maps. Pooling layers reduce the spatial resolution of the feature maps, which can result in the loss of some fine-grained details that are important for the final classification or regression task.

The third disadvantage of pooling layers is that they introduce hyperparameters that need to be tuned in order to achieve optimal performance. Pooling layers have two main hyperparameters: the size of the pooling regions and the stride. The size of the pooling regions determines how much spatial information is aggregated and reduced in each output feature map. The stride determines how much the pooling regions are shifted along the input feature map. Both hyperparameters affect the trade-off between computational efficiency and representational power of the feature maps. If we use a small pooling region or a small stride, we can preserve more spatial information and obtain more output feature maps, but at the cost of more computation and memory. If we use a large pooling region or a large stride, we can reduce the computation and memory requirements, but at the cost of losing more spatial information and obtaining fewer output feature maps. Therefore, finding the optimal values for these hyperparameters requires some trial and error and some expertise in model building.

10.3.2.3 Activation Functions

In a CNN, the output of a convolutional layer is subjected to mathematical operations known as activation functions. They give the network non-linearity, which enables it to recognize intricate patterns and characteristics in the input data. In addition, the range and size of the output values, which might impact the network's performance and stability, are also controlled by activation functions. In CNNs, various activation function types can be applied, each with unique benefits and drawbacks. The most typical ones are discussed below.

Sigmoid: This function with an S-shaped curve known as the sigmoid curve converts the result to a probability that may be understood as a value between 0 and 1. It is helpful for binary classification tasks like face identification or image segmentation. However, it has the vanishing gradient issue, which makes it challenging to update the weights during backpropagation because the gradient gets extremely small for significant positive or negative values. Other advantageous characteristics of the sigmoid function include its differentiability, monotonicity, and single inflection point. The logistic function, outlined as follows, is one of the most used sigmoid functions.

$$f(x) = 1 / (1 + e\wedge(-x)),$$

where x is any real value and e is the natural logarithm's base.
The logistic function's graph appears as shown in Fig. 10.16.

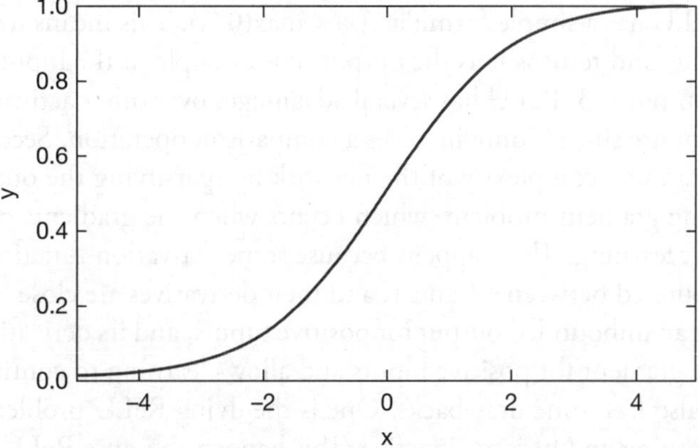

Figure 10.16 Logistic function graph

As you can see, as x approaches negative and positive infinity, the logistic function approaches 0 and 1, respectively. The inflection point, located at $y = 0.5$, is also a horizontal asymptote of the logistic function. This logistic function is frequently utilized in ML, particularly in logistic regression and ANNs. The logistic function can be employed in ANNs as a neuron's activation function, dictating how much a neuron fires in response to input. The behavior of biological neurons, which have a firing threshold and a saturation point, can be modeled using the logistic function. In addition, the network can learn more complex patterns by adding non-linearity using the logistic function.

Tanh: This function, considered a scaled sigmoid function, maps the output to a value between 1 and 1. It also works well for classification jobs since it generates zero-centered results that can be instructive. However, it still has the vanishing gradient issue, although somewhat less than the sigmoid function. One of the hyperbolic functions, or trigonometric equivalents, is the tanh function, defined by utilizing a hyperbola rather than a circle. The ratio of sinh and cosh, the hyperbolic sine and cosine functions, is known as the tanh function. The tanh formula is:

$$\tanh(x) = \sinh(x) \text{ divided by } \cosh(x)$$

As an alternative, we can define tanh as follows using the exponential function:

$$\tanh(x) \text{ is equal to } (e^{x} - e^{-x}) / (e^{x} + e^{-x})$$

Some intriguing features of the tanh function include:

- Because it is an odd function, $\tanh(-x)$ always equals $-\tanh(x)$ regardless of x.
- Its range is $(-1, 1)$. Hence, it can never go above or below these numbers.
- As x approaches infinity, it has a horizontal asymptote at $y = 1$, while as x approaches negative infinity, it has one at $y = -1$.
- It has a period of $pi * i$, where i is the fictitious and periodic unit.

ReLU: This stands for rectified linear unit. It is a type of activation function that is commonly used in CNNs. Activation functions are mathematical operations that determine the output of a neuron based on its input. ReLU has a simple formula: $f(x) = \max(0, x)$. This means it takes the maximum of zero and the input value and returns it as the output. For example, if the input is -2, the output is 0; if the input is 3, the output is 3. ReLU has several advantages over other activation functions. First, it is fast and easy to compute since it only involves a comparison operation. Second, it is efficient since it reduces the computational complexity of the network by sparsifying the output. Third, it helps to overcome the vanishing gradient problem, which occurs when the gradients of the network become very small and prevent learning. This happens because some activation functions, such as sigmoid or tanh, have outputs bounded between -1 and 1, and their derivatives are close to zero for large inputs. ReLU, conversely, has an unbounded output for positive inputs, and its derivative is either 0 or 1. This means it preserves the gradient for positive inputs and allows learning to continue.

However, ReLU also has some drawbacks. One is the dying ReLU problem, which occurs when some neurons stop learning and become inactive. This happens because ReLU has a zero output and a zero derivative for negative inputs. If a neuron receives only negative inputs for a long time, it will never fire, and its weights will not be updated. This can lead to a loss of information and a reduction of the network's expressive power. To avoid this problem, some variants of ReLU have been proposed, such as leaky ReLU or parametric ReLU, which have a slight positive slope for negative inputs.

Leaky ReLU is an activation function which simply returns the input if it is positive or zero if it is negative. However, ReLU has a drawback known as the dying ReLU problem, which means that some neurons can become inactive and stop learning if they receive only negative inputs for a long time. This can reduce the expressive power and accuracy of the network. To address this issue, leaky ReLU introduces a slight positive slope for negative inputs instead of setting them to zero. This means that the output of leaky ReLU is either the input itself if it is positive or a fraction of the input if it is negative. The fraction is usually chosen to be 0.01, but it can be any small positive number. By doing this, leaky ReLU allows some gradient to flow through the negative values, which helps to keep the neurons alive and learning. For example, if the input is –5, the output of ReLU is 0, but the output of leaky ReLU is –0.05.

Leaky ReLU can improve the stability and performance of CNNs, especially for deeper networks with many layers. Leaky ReLU can prevent the vanishing gradient problem, which occurs when the gradients become too small to update the weights effectively as they propagate through multiple layers. Leaky ReLU can also reduce the overfitting problem by introducing some noise and randomness into the network, which acts as a form of regularization.

Softmax: This function converts the output to a vector of values, which range from 0 to 1, adding up to 1. It is a generalization of the sigmoid function for multi-class classification problems like image recognition or natural language processing. Each class label is given a probability based on the output values' relative magnitudes. It is typically paired with a cross-entropy loss function as the final activation function in CNNs. For example, we have an image recognition problem where we want to classify an image into one of four categories: cat, dog, bird, or fish. We can use a CNN to extract features from the image and produce a vector of output values, one for each category. However, these output values are not probabilities and may not be in the same range. To convert them into possibilities, we can apply the softmax function.

The softmax function works by exponentiating each output value and dividing it by the sum of all exponentiated values. This way, larger output values will have higher probabilities, and smaller output values will have lower probabilities. The softmax function also has the property that it is invariant to adding or subtracting a constant from the output vector, which means that it does not depend on the absolute magnitude of the output values but only on their relative differences. For example, suppose the output vector from the CNN is [2.3, 1.2, –0.8, 0.5]. We get [0.57, 0.21, 0.03, 0.18] if we apply the softmax function. These are the probabilities that the image belongs to each category. We can see that the softmax function assigns the highest probability to the first category (cat) and the lowest probability to the third category (bird). The sum of all probabilities is 1.

The softmax function is often used as the final activation function in CNNs for multi-class classification problems. This means we can compare the predicted probabilities with the true labels using a loss function after applying the softmax function. The **cross-entropy loss function** is a common loss function which measures how well the predicted probabilities match the true labels. The cross-entropy loss function penalizes predictions that are confident but wrong and rewards predictions that are confident and correct. For example, suppose the true label for the image is a cat (the first category). The cross-entropy loss function would compute the negative logarithm of the predicted probability for the cat, which is –log(0.57) = 0.56. This relatively low loss value indicates that the prediction is close to the true label. On the other hand, if the true label were a bird (the third category), the cross-entropy loss function would compute −log(0.03) = 3.51. This is a high loss value, indicating that the prediction is far from the true label.

We can train the CNN to learn the optimal parameters that produce accurate predictions for new images by minimizing the cross-entropy loss function over a training set of images and labels.

10.3.2.4 Training CNNs

CNN can analyze structured data like text, audio, or images. Multiple layers make up CNNs, each applying a distinct operation to the input data. These operations include convolution, pooling, activation, normalization, and drop out. A CNN's objective is to extract from the data hierarchical features that may be applied to various tasks, including classification, segmentation, detection, and generation.

Picture classification or giving a name to a picture based on its content, is one of the most popular uses of CNNs. When a CNN is being trained, the model is fed with the images and their labels, and the layer weights are adjusted using an optimization algorithm like stochastic gradient descent (SGD) or Adam. A loss function that calculates the discrepancy between the predicted and actual labels is the object of the optimization algorithm's attempt to minimize it. For example, cross-entropy, mean squared error or hinge loss are some loss functions that can be chosen based on the task and the data.

Steps in the training process

1. Use a pre-trained model or random seeding to set the layer weights.
2. Rearrange and divide the data set into groups of labels and images.
3. Carry out the following actions for every batch:
   a. **Forward pass**: Run the photos through the model's layers and calculate the predicted outputs.
   b. **Backward pass**: Determine the gradients of the loss function concerning the weights using the chain rule.
   c. **Update**: Use the optimization algorithm and a learning rate parameter to update the weights.
4. Continue performing steps 2 and 3 until the loss function converges or a predetermined number of epochs (iterations across the entire data set) has been reached.

A CNN's performance can be assessed using several criteria: accuracy, precision, recall, and F1-score. These metrics can be calculated distinct from the training set validation or test sets. The model's hyperparameters, such as the learning rate, batch size, and number of epochs, can be adjusted using the validation set. The test set can be used to gauge how well the model generalizes to new data.

10.3.2.5 Transfer Learning in CNN

An ML model can use the knowledge gained from one job to help with another using transfer learning. Transfer learning can be applied to CNNs to enhance the effectiveness and efficiency of image recognition models.

Using a pre-trained CNN model as a feature extractor or fine-tuner for a new job is the primary concept of transfer learning. A pre-trained CNN model is a model that has learned to extract standard and advanced features from images after being trained on a substantial and varied data set, such as ImageNet. These attributes can be helpful for many different image identification tasks, such as object detection, face recognition, or image segmentation. In addition, using a pre-trained CNN model allows us to take advantage of the existing knowledge of the model without training a new model from scratch, which can be expensive and time-consuming.

Feature extraction and fine-tuning are two typical applications of transfer learning in CNNs. We merely train a new classifier on top of the pre-trained CNN model as a fixed feature extractor during feature extraction. This scenario is appropriate when the new task significantly differs from the previous task or has a short data set. For instance, we can use a pre-trained CNN model to extract features from the photographs and then train a straightforward linear classifier on top of them if we want to categorize flowers based on a small data set of flower images. During training, we update some or all of the parameters of the pre-trained CNN model as we fine-tune it. This scenario is appropriate when the new work includes a sizable data set or is similar to the old task.

Transfer learning applications in CNNs:

- **FaceNet**: This CNN model is trained on a large data set of face images with labels indicating whether two faces belong to the same person. The model can then be used for specific face recognition tasks such as face verification, face clustering, and face alignment by fine-tuning it on a smaller data set of target faces. For example, FaceNet can be used to verify whether two photos show the same person by comparing their embeddings in the Euclidean space.
- **Mask R-CNN**: This CNN model performs instance segmentation, identifying and classifying every object in an image and generating a pixel-level mask for each object. The model builds on a previously trained CNN model for object detection, such as Faster R-CNN, and then adds a new branch for segmentation mask prediction. The model can be further fine-tuned on a data set of images with annotated masks for different classes of objects. For example, Mask R-CNN can segment and label every person, car, tree, and building in an aerial image.
- **Style transfer**: This method creates a new image by joining the content of one image with the style of another image using transfer learning. The method extracts content and style features from the two images using a pre-trained CNN model, such as VGG-19, trained on a large data set of natural images for image classification. Using gradient descent, the method then optimizes a new image to match the original image's content and style features. For example, style transfer can be used to create an artistic image that blends the content of a cityscape photo with the style of Van Gogh's Starry Night painting.

10.3.2.6 Applications of CNNs

CNNs are widely used in many fields, including computer vision, natural language processing (NLP), audio processing, and biomedical imaging. Some examples of CNN applications are as follows:

- **Face recognition**: CNNs can learn to recognize faces in pictures or videos and compare them to a database of recognized individuals. This can be applied to social networking, security, or authentication needs. For example, Facebook uses a CNN called DeepFace to identify and tag people in photos. DeepFace can achieve 97.35% accuracy on a standard face recognition benchmark.
- **Image captioning**: CNNs can produce natural language descriptions of images by fusing visual and linguistic data. Accessibility, education, or enjoyment can all be achieved with this. For example, Google Photos uses a CNN called Show and Tell to generate captions for user-uploaded photos. Show and Tell can produce relevant, informative, and grammatically correct captions.

- **Object detection**: CNNs can identify and categorize things in pictures or movies using bounding boxes or masks. This can be utilized for robotics, autonomous driving, or spying. For example, YOLO (You Only Look Once) is a CNN that can detect and localize multiple objects in real-time video streams. YOLO can achieve 45% mean average precision on a standard object detection benchmark.
- **Style transfer**: CNNs can use feature representations learned from many layers to transfer one image's style to another. Artistic, imaginative, or personalized uses can be made of this. For example, Neural Style Transfer is a technique that can apply the style of a painting to a photograph. Neural Style Transfer can create images that are visually appealing and expressive.
- **Medical diagnosis**: CNNs can analyze images from diagnostic tests like X-rays, MRIs, and ultrasounds to find anomalies or diseases. This may be applied to medical care, diagnosis, or therapy. For example, CheXNet is a CNN that can diagnose 14 different thoracic diseases from chest X-ray images. CheXNet can outperform radiologists on some diseases and achieve comparable performance on others.

CNNs are solid and adaptable tools that can manage complex and varied data. As a result, they continue to stimulate new research and innovation while revolutionizing numerous fields and applications.

10.3.3 Recurrent Neural Networks

Recurrent neural networks (RNNs) are a subset of ANNs capable of processing sequential data, including speech, video, and natural language. RNNs can manage variable-length inputs and outputs by keeping an internal state that depends on the prior inputs, unlike feedforward neural networks, which have fixed input and output sizes. As a result, RNNs can pick up temporal patterns in the data and learn long-term dependencies. RNNs are frequently employed for sentiment analysis, speech recognition, and language translation.

Memory and Feedback: The capacity of an RNN to retain memory or context about the prior information it has encountered in the sequence is one of its fundamental characteristics. This memory is made possible by using feedback connections, which allow data from earlier phases in the sequence to be relayed back into the network. An RNN has a hidden state that serves as its context or memory. The RNN receives an input at each step in the sequence and generates an output based on the input at that point in the sequence and the hidden state from the previous step. At each step, the hidden state is updated with data from both the current input and the previous hidden state. The RNN processes the sequence one step at a time, incorporating the input at each stage and altering the hidden state as necessary. As a result, it can recognize patterns and dependencies in the data throughout time because it uses the same set of weights and biases for each sequence step.

RNNS are composed of recurrent units, which are straightforward computational units that accept an input vector and produce an output vector. Each recurrent unit also has a hidden state vector that keeps data from earlier inputs. A non-linear function is applied to the current input and the initial hidden state to update the vector at each time step. The hidden state vector is then used to generate the output vector, with the option of utilizing another non-linear function.

The issue of disappearing or exploding gradients, which occurs when the gradients of the loss function concerning the network parameters become very tiny or very big during backpropagation, is one of the fundamental difficulties RNNs face. As a result, it is challenging to train RNNs on lengthy sequences since the gradients frequently decay or increase exponentially with time. Several approaches have been put forth to solve this issue, including gradient clipping, LSTM (long short-term memory) units, GRUs (gated recurrent units), and attention mechanisms.

CNN and RNN differ in some ways:

- CNN is designed for processing spatial data, such as images, videos, or 2D/3D shapes. RNN is designed for processing sequential data, such as text, speech, or time series.
- CNN has no memory of the previous inputs, and can only learn local features from the data. RNN has memory cells that store the previous states, and can learn long-term dependencies from the data.
- CNN requires fixed-size inputs and outputs, which means that the data has to be padded or cropped to fit the network. RNN can handle variable-length inputs and outputs, which means that the network can adapt to the data dynamically.
- CNN is more specialized, effective, rigid, and constrained, which means that it can perform well on specific tasks, but it is hard to generalize to other domains or tasks. RNN is more adaptable, generalizable, complex, and prone to overfitting and vanishing gradients, which means that it can learn from diverse data sources, but it is also more difficult to train and optimize.

For example, CNN can be used for image classification, object detection, face recognition, or semantic segmentation. RNN can be used for natural language processing, speech recognition, machine translation, or text generation.

10.3.3.1 Long Short-Term Memory Networks

This is a type of RNN that can recognize long-term dependencies in sequential input. RNNs are neural networks that handle sequential data by iterating over a hidden state that encodes the inputs that came before. However, the disappearing and ballooning gradient issues that RNNs experience make it challenging to learn long-term dependencies. Three gates that regulate the information flow in and out of the memory cell and a memory cell that can store and update information over time are used in LSTM networks to solve these issues: the input gate, the forget gate, and the output gate (Fig. 10.17).

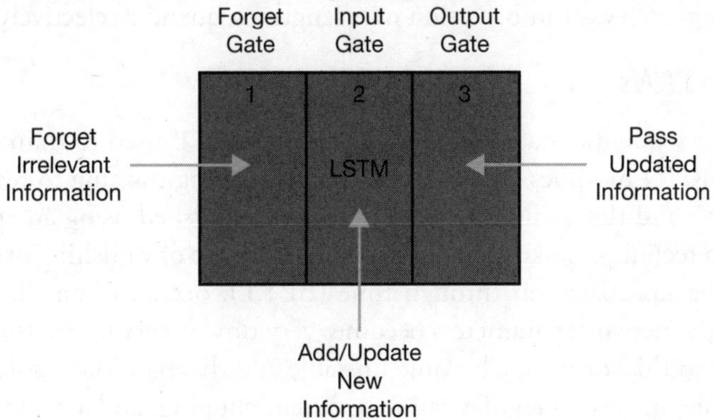

Figure 10.17 LSTM logic

The output gate determines what data should be output from the cell, the input gate determines what new data should be added, and the forget gate determines what outdated data should be removed from the cell. As a result, LSTM networks can learn intricate and persistent patterns in sequential data, including speech, video, and spoken language.

10.3.3.2 Gated Recurrent Unit Networks

The vanishing or expanding gradient issue with RNNs makes it challenging to understand long-term dependencies. To solve this issue, reset and update gates are two types used in gated recurrent unit (GRU) networks (Fig. 10.18).

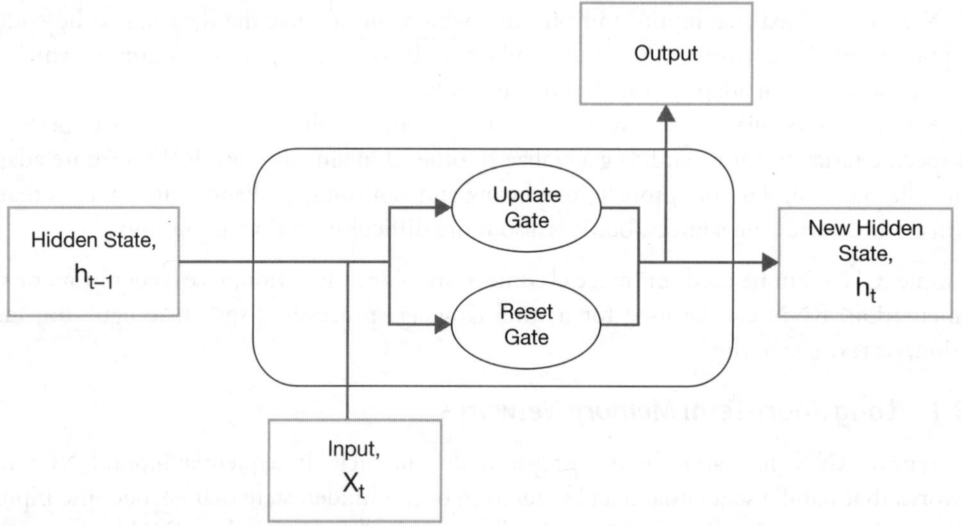

Figure 10.18 Gated recurrent unit network

These gates regulate how much data is remembered or lost from the current input and the initial hidden state. GRU networks perform better than regular RNNs on many tasks because they may be trained to recall or forget relevant information over lengthy sequences selectively.

10.3.3.3 Training RNNs

A labeled data set with sequential data and accompanying labels is used to train an RNN. Like other neural networks, the RNN modifies its weights and biases during training to reduce the discrepancy between its predictions and the accurate labels. This is accomplished using an appropriate loss function and optimization techniques like gradient descent. The issue of vanishing or exploding gradients, which arises during backpropagation through time (BPTT), occurs when the gradient of the loss function concerning the network parameters becomes very tiny or very large. The network may either learn very slowly due to this, or it may become unstable and diverge. Many solutions have been put out to address this issue, including regularization, gradient clipping, and advanced RNN designs like LSTM and GRU.

10.3.3.4 Applications of RNNs

NLP, speech recognition, machine translation, text synthesis, image captioning, video analysis, and music composition are just a few of the tasks for which RNNs have been successfully used. In addition, RNNs are frequently combined with other neural network architectures, including transformers and CNNs, to benefit from the advantages of each model. As a result, RNNs are among the most powerful and adaptable deep learning technologies, constantly inspiring new research and applications.

RNNs can process time series, voice, audio, video, and other sequential data. RNNs can mimic complicated and dynamic processes because of their memory mechanism, which enables them to store and use data from earlier inputs. NLP, speech recognition, machine translation, text generation, sentiment analysis, picture captioning, video analysis, music synthesis, and other fields and applications have extensively used RNNs.

A group of units, or neurons, coupled recurrently to create a directed cycle make up RNNs. At every time step, each unit receives an input vector and outputs an output vector and a hidden state vector. The subsequent time step's input for the same unit, or additional units, includes the hidden state vector. In this manner, the hidden state vector serves as a memory to store the history of the inputs. Depending on the job, the output vector may be used to anticipate the next word in a sentence, produce an answer to a question, or categorize an emotion.

The **Elman network**, often known as the simple recurrent network (SRN), is one of the most straightforward and extensively utilized RNN architectures. Each unit in this design has three sets of weights: recurrent weights that connect the hidden state vector to itself, output weights that connect the hidden state vector to the output vector, and input weights that connect the input vector to the hidden state vector. First, the weighted sum of the input vector and the preceding hidden state vector is used to calculate the hidden state vector, which is then calculated using a non-linear activation function (such as sigmoid or tanh). Finally, the output vector is calculated by adding another activation function, such as softmax, to the weighted sum of the hidden state vector.

One of its key features is RNN's capacity to recognize long-term dependencies and context information in sequential data. RNNs, for instance, may learn a language's syntactic and semantic norms and produce coherent and insightful phrases when used in natural language processing. However, one of the fundamental problems with RNNs is that they have trouble learning long-term relationships because of the vanishing or expanding gradient problem. This issue arises when, as the error function propagates over time, the gradient with regard to the weights becomes extremely tiny or extremely big, making it difficult to efficiently update the weights. This issue may lead RNNs to forget or disregard data from far-off inputs, or it may cause them to become unstable and give irregular outputs.

Many RNN variants and extensions, including LSTM networks, GRUs, bidirectional RNNs (BRNNs), attention mechanisms, and transformer networks, have been proposed to address this issue. These architectures introduce various mechanisms to regulate information flow and gradients through time, including gates that modulate each unit's input and output, connections that skip over some time steps, alignments that concentrate on important input sequence segments, and self-attention that recognizes interdependent relationships between all inputs on a global scale.

RNN research and development is still ongoing in ML and AI. Current issues and potential directions for RNN research are as follows:

- Increasing RNNs' scalability and effectiveness for large-scale applications.
- Creating new architectures and methods to manage sequential data that is multimodal and heterogeneous.
- Looking at new areas and uses where RNNs can offer fresh perspectives and answers.
- Improving RNNs' interpretability and explainability for increased confidence and understanding.
- Including human feedback and prior knowledge in learning and creating RNNs.

RNNs are practical modeling tools for sequential events and data. Impressive outcomes have been shown in a variety of applications and fields. However, they also encounter some restrictions and difficulties that call for additional study and invention. Nevertheless, we can open up new avenues and prospects for artificial intelligence and machine learning by expanding RNN research.

10.3.3.5 Challenges of RNNs

Another method for assisting RNNs in focusing on the essential elements of the input sequence for each output is attention mechanisms. They give each input a weight or score based on how much it contributes to the output. The output layer is then fed a weighted average or summary of the input sequence created using these weights. In this manner, they can identify long-term dependencies without relying on the network's concealed state.

RNNs can be improved with external memory modules that can store and retrieve data over extended periods using memory networks, a more recent technique. These memory modules are accessible through network-controlled read-and-write operations. This enables individuals to save information such as facts, regulations, or general knowledge necessary to complete challenging tasks requiring deduction and reasoning.

The issue of gradient vanishing or exploding presents an additional challenge for RNNs. As a result, learning can become sluggish or unstable during training because the gradients or mistakes utilized to update the network parameters can become extremely small or very big. This occurs when RNNs multiply numerous matrices across several time steps to compute the gradients using BPTT. These matrices will exhibit exponential growth or contraction when the gradients spread throughout the network if their values are near zero or one.

The use of gradient clipping, regularization, or initialization approaches are a few solutions to this issue. Gradient clipping is a straightforward technique that restricts the gradients' magnitude by scaling them up or down if they go beyond a predetermined limit. This stops them from getting too big or too little and creating numerical problems. Another technique that lessens overfitting and enhances generalization is regularization.

10.3.4 Generative AI

Generative AI is a branch of artificial intelligence that focuses on creating new content or data from scratch, such as images, text, music, code, etc. It is important for several reasons: it can help us explore new possibilities and scenarios that we might not be able to imagine or simulate otherwise. For example, generative AI can create realistic images of faces that do not exist or generate novel designs for products, buildings, or artworks. It can augment our creativity and productivity by providing us with inspiration, feedback, or assistance. It can help us generate high-quality data for various purposes, such as training other AI models, testing software or systems, or conducting research or analysis. For example, generative AI can produce synthetic data that mimics real-world data but preserves privacy and security.

There are different types of generative AI models: generative adversarial networks (GANs), variational autoencoders (VAEs), and transformer models. We will look at GANs and VAEs in detail.

Transformer models signify a revolutionary advancement in ML. Their distinctive architecture, which allows for concurrent processing of sequences, deviates from the sequential data processing of conventional models. The research community is currently engaged in studying the mechanisms of transformers and these endeavors instill optimism regarding the future of transformer models. For more details, see Chapter 11.

10.3.4.1 Generative Adversarial Networks

This type of neural network can output realistic and diverse data from input. A GAN consists of two components: a discriminator and a generator (Fig. 10.19). The discriminator's objective is to correctly classify the data, while the generator's objective is to deceive the discriminator. The generator aims to create fake data that resembles correct data, while the discriminator strives to distinguish between real and fake data. In the adversarial training process, the discriminator and the generator compete with one another to become more effective.

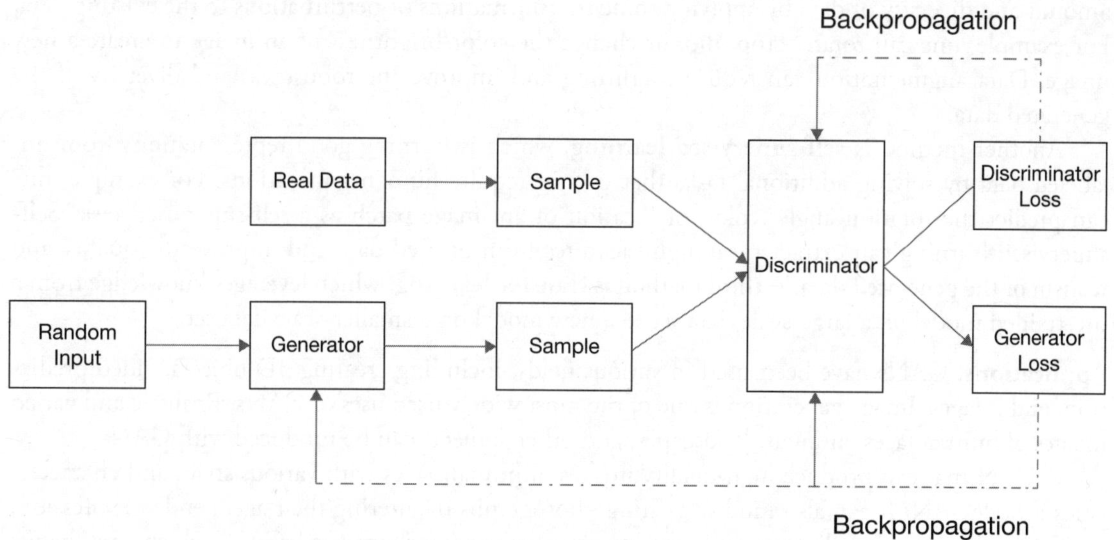

Figure 10.19 Generative adversarial network (GAN)

Numerous fields, including computer vision, NLP, audio synthesis, and others use GANs. GANs, for instance, can produce lifelike images of people, animals, landscapes, and even artwork. In addition, GANs can improve low-resolution photos, eliminate noise from photographs, or exchange styles between images. Furthermore, GANs can be used in NLP to produce text, such as captions, summaries, stories, or dialogue. Creating speech or music from text or other inputs is another application of GANs.

Training GANs: The discriminator and the generator are trained antagonistically, with the discriminator trying to catch the generator and the generator trying to trick the discriminator. The objective/goal is to achieve a state where the discriminator cannot distinguish between the data produced by the generator and the actual data.

One of the basic concepts of GAN training is the loss function, which measures how well the generator and the discriminator perform. This is because the generator tries to fool the discriminator by producing fake data that look like accurate data while the discriminator tries to distinguish between real and fake data. The loss function reflects the trade-off between these two objectives.

Another essential concept is regularization, which prevents overfitting or underfitting by adding some constraints or penalties to the model parameters or outputs. For example, overfitting occurs when a model memorizes the training data and cannot generalize to new input. At the same time, underfitting occurs when the model needs to be more complex and capture the complexity of the data. Regularization can help balance the model's complexity and simplicity, thereby improving its generalization performance.

Evaluation metrics measure the quality and diversity of the generated data. Evaluating GANs is challenging because a clear definition of what makes a sound generation needs to be precise.

Methods to improve GAN training: Let us look at some state-of-the-art methods for improving GAN training in low-data regimes. One such method is **data augmentation**, which increases the amount and diversity of data by applying some transformations or perturbations to the existing data. For example, one can rotate, crop, flip, or change the color/brightness of an image to create a new image. Data augmentation can reduce overfitting and improve the robustness and diversity of the generated data.

Another method is **self-supervised learning**, which is learning good representations from unlabeled data by solving additional tasks that do not require human annotations. For example, one can predict the rotation angle, color, or location of an image patch as a self-supervised task. Self-supervised learning can extract meaningful features from limited data and improve the quality and realism of the generated data. A third method is **transfer learning**, which leverages knowledge from a pre-trained model on a large-scale data set to a new model on a smaller-scale data set.

Applications: GANs have been used in various fields, including creating 3D objects, video prediction, and images. Image generation is one of the most widely used uses of GANs. Realistic and varied images of human faces, animals, landscapes, and other subjects can be produced with GANs.

A GAN that can produce high-quality images of human faces with various styles and characteristics is StyleGAN. It can also modify existing photographs by altering their age, gender, expression, and hair color. Another illustration is the image-to-image translator CycleGAN, which can change images such as pictures into paintings, horses into zebras, summer into winter, etc.

Challenges: GAN training is a complex undertaking as we may encounter several difficulties that may compromise their performance and stability:

- **Mode collapse**: When the generator only provides a small range of outputs, or even the same output for various inputs, mode collapse occurs. This indicates that the generator only concentrates on a few modes that potentially trick the discriminator and lead to failure to represent the diversity of accurate data distribution. Mode collapse can result from several issues, including an imbalance between the generator and discriminator, a poor choice of the objective function, or incorrect parameter initialization. Among the potential remedies to stop or lessen mode collapse are:

- o **Wasserstein loss:** This alternative objective function gauges the separation between the actual and fictitious data distributions instead of their overlap. Even when the discriminator is excellent or perfect, Wasserstein loss enables a gradient signal for the generator that is smoother and more insightful.
- o **Unrolled GANs:** This method adjusts the generator loss function to consider both the outputs of the present discriminator and those of upcoming discriminator iterations. This prevents the generator from over-optimizing for a single discriminator and forces it to consider a longer-term viewpoint.
- o **Minibatch discrimination:** This technique allows the discriminator to compare various samples within a minibatch instead of examining them separately. This enables the discriminator to identify mode collapse and gives the generator more enlightening input.

- **Lack of convergence**: When the generator and the discriminator oscillate or diverge during training instead of reaching a stable equilibrium, this is called non-convergence. As a result, the generator may produce subpar or erroneous outputs, or it may not be possible to draw valid conclusions from the data. Numerous factors, including an improper learning rate, an imbalance between the generator's and the discriminator's designs, or an unsuitable optimization algorithm, can lead to non-convergence. The following are some potential ways to strengthen or guarantee convergence:
  - o **Gradient penalty:** Based on the gradient norm of the discriminator, this regularization method adds a penalty term to the objective function. This is beneficial to prevent gradient explosion or vanishing and enforce a smoothness restriction on the discriminator function.
  - o **Spectral normalization:** This regularization method normalizes the spectral norm of each layer's weight matrix in the discriminator (the most significant singular value). This aids in maintaining gradient stability and controlling the discriminator function's Lipschitz constant.
  - o **Adam optimizer:** This adaptive optimization algorithm modifies the learning rate for every parameter based on its prior gradients and moments. The Adam optimizer can assist in handling noisy data, sparse gradients, and various parameter scales.
- **3D viewpoint**: In 3D objects or settings, GANs frequently find it challenging to comprehend and replicate 3D perspective elements like depth, occlusion, lighting, and shadows. This may lead to flat or distorted visuals that may not correspond to human perception. Furthermore, because GANs must acquire high-level geometric and semantic information in addition to pixel-level characteristics, 3D perspective is a challenging task. The following are a few potential ways to improve the 3D perspective:
  - o **3D-GANs:** These GANs use 3D voxel grids rather than 2D pixel grids. Without using intermediate representations or 2D projections, 3D-GANs can produce 3D shapes straight from noise vectors.
  - o **StyleGANs:** These GANs use approaches for style transfer to regulate several facets of picture production, including shape, texture, color, and stance. StyleGANs can alter latent codes at various abstraction levels and inject them into various layers of the generating network.

- **CycleGANs** are GANs that can learn domain-to-domain mappings without paired data. Images from different perspectives, such as front view to side view or aerial view to street view, can be translated using CycleGANs.

Evaluation of GANs: The three main categories of GAN evaluation techniques are quantitative, qualitative, and hybrid. **Quantitative approaches** use numerical measures to assess the generated samples' quality, diversity, faithfulness, and similarity. In **qualitative approaches**, the perceptual realism and diversity of the generated samples are evaluated through human judgments or visual examination. Finally, **hybrid techniques** combine quantitative and qualitative methods for a more thorough analysis.

The perceptual characteristics of the generated samples are frequently missed by quantitative approaches, which are more objective and scalable than qualitative methods. For instance, some quantitative metrics may prefer fuzzy or noisy samples over sharp and clear ones, or they may need to consider the generated samples' semantic relevance or coherence. Furthermore, comparing several GAN models and selecting the best one can be challenging because different quantitative indicators cannot agree with one another or with human judgments.

Compared to quantitative approaches, qualitative methods are more empathetic and intuitive but more prone to prejudice and inconsistency. Human judgments, for instance, can differ based on the task, context, assessors' preferences, and experience level. In addition, conducting qualitative approaches is frequently time-consuming and expensive, particularly for large-scale or high-dimensional data.

By effectively merging quantitative and qualitative methodologies, hybrid methods seek to overcome their respective shortcomings. For instance, some hybrid methods employ quantitative metrics to rank or select samples for qualitative evaluation, while others use quantitative measurements to calibrate or validate quantitative metrics. Compared to quantitative or qualitative methods alone, hybrid methods can offer a more thorough and trustworthy evaluation of GANs.

The design of effective and efficient human-computer interfaces for gathering human feedback, striking a balance between quantitative and qualitative aspects of the evaluation process, and handling potential conflicts or trade-offs between various evaluation criteria are some challenges hybrid methods must overcome.

10.4 Other Types of ANNs

Other unique types of ANNs are self-organizing maps (SOMs) and Boltzmann machines (BMs). SOMs, sometimes called Kohonen maps, are a class of unsupervised learning algorithms mainly employed in data visualization and dimensionality reduction applications. They were first used by Teuvo Kohonen in the 1980s, and they worked by discretizing and arranging high-dimensional data into a two-dimensional map while maintaining the original data's topological characteristics. Boltzmann machines (BMs), on the other hand, are a type of stochastic recurrent neural network that can be used for feature learning, dimensionality reduction, and associative memory. They are named after the Boltzmann distribution in statistical mechanics, which is used in their sampling function.

10.4.1 Self-organizing Maps (SOMs)

This unsupervised ML method can provide a low-dimensional representation of a high-dimensional data collection while maintaining the data's topological structure. It is a method to reduce the data dimensions. So, SOMs can identify patterns and similarities in the data and display them on a two-dimensional map, where each node stands for a collection of related data points. For SOMs to function, a grid of nodes with weight vectors of the same dimension as the input data must first be created. After being randomly initialized, the nodes are iteratively updated based on a competitive learning method. The winner node and its neighboring nodes are chosen for each input data point and are all shifted nearer to the data point. Over time, the neighborhood size and learning rate decrease over time as the nodes converge to stable places.
SOMs can be used for several **applications:**

- **Data visualization:** By transforming complex, high-dimensional data sets into a lower-dimensional space, where the distance between nodes shows the similarity between data points, SOMs can aid in the exploration and comprehension of large, complex data sets. SOMs can be used, for instance, to visualize written content and customer segments.
- **Data compression:** SOMs can shrink the size of big data sets by partitioning them into fewer nodes, each representing a prototype or a cluster centroid. SOMs can be utilized, for instance, to compress images, sounds, or films.
- **Finding anomalies:** SOMs can locate anomalous data points by calculating their separation from the nearest node or their density on the map. SOMs can be utilized, for instance, to find fraud, network penetration, or disease.

SOMs are of many **types**, such as:

- **U-matrix:** This visualization method employs various hues or tones to represent the distance between adjacent nodes on a map. The cluster structure and the boundaries of the data set can be seen in the U-matrix.
- **Component planes:** This is a method of visualizing weight vectors that display the values of each dimension in distinct maps using various hues or tones. The component planes show the correlations and variances of each attribute in the data set.
- **Heat map:** This visualization technique uses various colors or tints to indicate how often each node has been chosen as the winner node for the input data points. The distribution and density of the data set can be seen on the hit map.

10.4.2 Boltzmann Machines (MBs)

This is a type of ANN that can learn to discover exciting features in data without supervision. They are composed of nodes connected symmetric and bidirectional, meaning that each node can send and receive signals from any other node. Furthermore, the nodes can be visible or hidden, depending on whether they represent observable data or latent variables.

A BM typically consists of several visible and hidden levels, where each visible layer's nodes are connected to each hidden layer's nodes. Each node in the hidden layer receives input from the outputs of the visible layer nodes (Fig. 10.20).

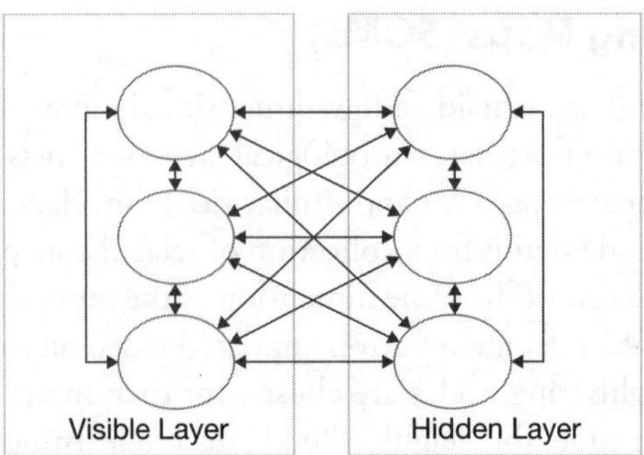

Figure 10.20 Boltzmann machine

BMs are stochastic and generative models, meaning they can randomly sample different states of the network based on the probability distribution defined by the connections' weights and the nodes' activation function. Learning in BMs aims to adjust the weights so that the network can generate data that resembles the training data.

One of the challenges of BMs is that they are computationally expensive to train, especially when they have many layers of hidden nodes. This is because the learning algorithm requires sampling from the equilibrium distribution of the network, which involves updating all the nodes many times until they reach a stable state. To overcome this problem, a variant called restricted Boltzmann machine (RBM) was proposed, which restricts the connections between nodes such that there are no connections within the same layer (Fig. 10.21).

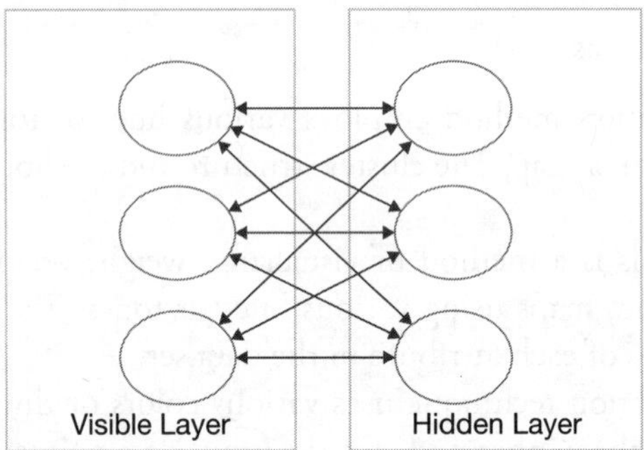

Figure 10.21 Restricted Boltzmann machine

RBMs can also be stacked together to form deep belief networks (DBNs), which are hierarchical models that can learn multiple levels of abstraction from data. DBNs can be trained layer by layer, using the output of one RBM as the input of another RBM. This way, each RBM can learn features that capture higher-order correlations in the data (Fig. 10.21).

Deep belief networks (DBNs) comprise numerous hidden layers that are connected but not inside the same layer. Each layer functions as a feature extractor, transforming the input data into a higher-level representation.

Pre-training and fine-tuning are the two training steps for DBNs. First, each RBM is pre-trained individually using the contrastive divergence approach, reducing the discrepancy between the data and model distribution. Then, to refine a classification or regression job, the entire DBN is trained collectively using a supervised learning technique, such as gradient descent or backpropagation. DBN applications include speech recognition, picture recognition, natural language processing, and recommendation systems. They can also be enhanced to handle other data kinds, such as continuous, categorical, or temporal data.

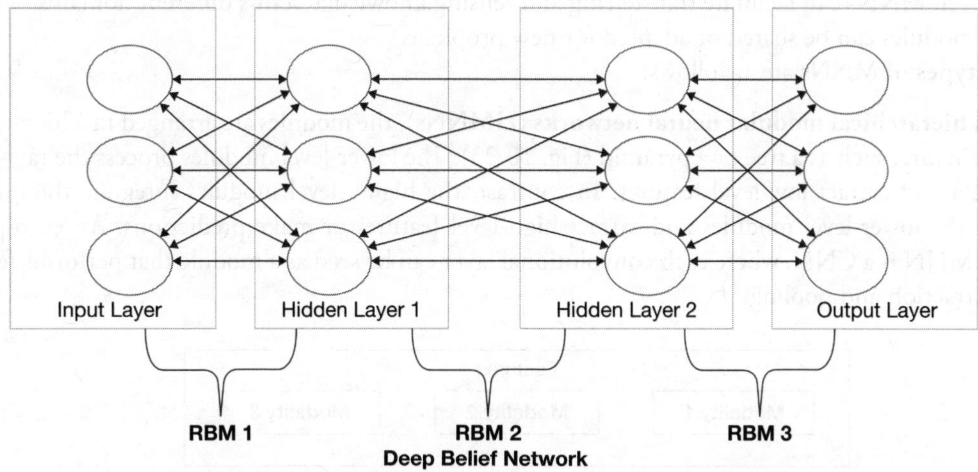

Figure 10.21 RBM network as deep belief network (DBN)

10.4.3 Modular Neural Networks (MNNs)

MNNs are a type of artificial neural network that consist of multiple modules or subnetworks that perform different tasks or functions (Fig. 10.22). MNNs are designed to overcome some of the limitations of conventional neural networks, such as scalability, complexity, and generalization. MNNs use a divide-and-conquer approach, where a complex problem is decomposed into simpler subproblems that specialized modules can solve. The modules can communicate through various mechanisms, such as shared weights, intermediate outputs, or higher-level representations. The modules can also have different architectures, learning algorithms, and activation functions, depending on the subproblem they are solving.

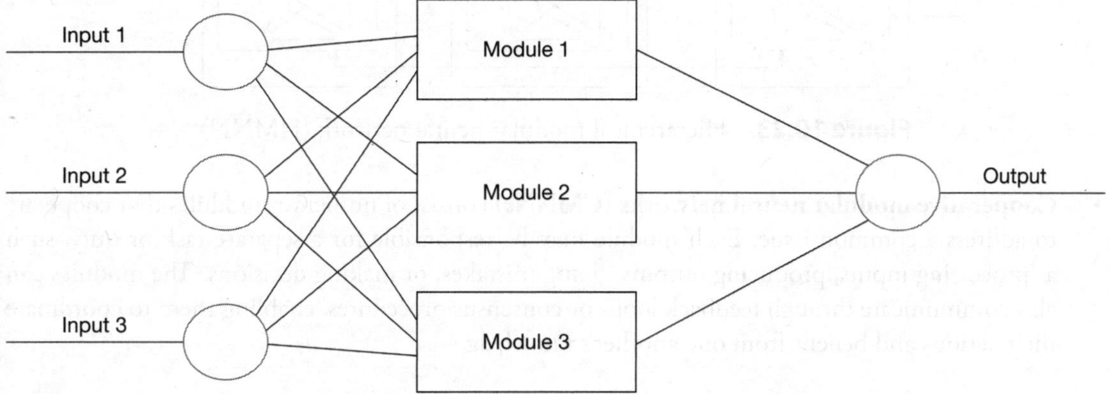

Figure 10.22 Modular neural network (MNN)

One of the main advantages of MNNs is that they can reduce the computational cost and memory requirements of training and inference, as each module can be trained and updated independently or in parallel. MNNs can also improve the generalization performance and robustness of the network, as each module can learn to focus on specific features or aspects of the input data relevant to its task. Moreover, MNNs can facilitate transferring and reusing knowledge across different domains or tasks, as the modules can be shared or adapted for new problems.

Some **types of MNNs** are as follows:

- In **hierarchical modular neural networks (HMNNs)**, the modules are arranged in a hierarchical structure, such as a tree or a pyramid (Fig. 10.23). The lower-level modules process the raw input data and extract low-level features. In contrast, the higher-level modules integrate the outputs of the lower-level modules and extract high-level features or make predictions. An example of HMNN is a CNN, where each convolutional layer can be seen as a module that performs feature extraction and pooling.

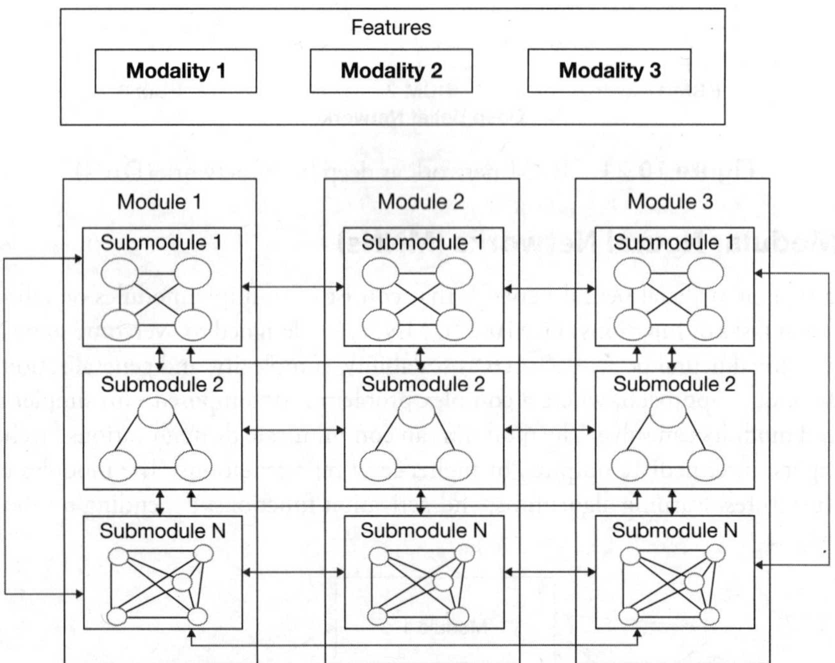

Figure 10.23 Hierarchical modular neural network (HMNN)

- **Cooperative modular neural networks (CMNNs)** consist of numerous modules that cooperate to address a common issue. Each module may be responsible for a separate task or duty, such as processing inputs, producing outputs, fixing mistakes, or making decisions. The modules can also communicate through feedback loops or consensus procedures, enabling them to coordinate their actions and benefit from one another's knowledge.

Recurrent neural networks (RNNs), frequently used for sequential data processing in applications including time series analysis, speech recognition, and NLP, are an example of CMNNs. Each recurrent unit in an RNN is a module that updates a hidden state based on the input and the previous state, making it similar to a CMNN. The module's memory or context, which allows it to recognize long-term dependencies and temporal patterns in the data, might be understood as the hidden state. The hidden state, sent along the sequence, enables communication between recurrent units. A word or a label can be produced by the RNN's output layer, which can also produce an output at every time step.

- In **competitive modular neural networks (CPMNNs)**, the modules compete to solve a problem. The modules can have different objectives or criteria, such as accuracy, speed, diversity, or novelty. In addition, the modules can influence each other through reward signals or selection mechanisms. An example of CPMNN is a GAN, where the generator and the discriminator can be seen as modules that compete to generate realistic samples and distinguish them from real ones.

10.5 Building Neural Network Architectures

Neural networks are powerful computational models that can learn from data and perform various tasks like classification, regression, generation, and reinforcement learning. However, designing neural network architectures suitable for different problems and domains is not a trivial task. It necessitates much trial-and-error, intuition, and subject-matter expertise.

One of the main challenges in building neural network architectures is the trade-off between complexity and performance. On the one hand, more complex architectures can capture more features and patterns from the data and achieve higher accuracy and generalization. However, on the other hand, more complex architectures also require more computational resources, such as memory, time, and energy, and may be prone to overfitting and instability. Therefore, finding the optimal balance between complexity and performance is critical in neural network design.

One approach to overcome this difficulty is using regularization strategies like dropout, batch normalization, weight decay, and early halting. These techniques can help reduce overfitting and improve generalization by introducing noise or penalty to the network parameters or outputs. For example, **dropout** randomly drops out some units in the network during training, which prevents co-adaptation of features and forces the network from learning more robust representations. **Batch normalization** normalizes each layer's inputs to have zero mean and unit variance, which reduces internal covariate shift and accelerates convergence. **Weight decay** alters the loss function by including a penalty term that reduces the network weights to zero, eliminating their excessive growth and resulting in numerical problems. Finally, **early stopping** stops the training process when the validation error stops decreasing or starts increasing, which avoids overfitting the training data.

Architecture search techniques, including grid search, random search, evolutionary algorithms, reinforcement learning, and gradient-based approaches, are another way to approach this problem. These techniques help automate finding the best architecture for a given problem and data set by exploring an ample space of possible architectures and evaluating them based on criteria or objective functions. For example, **grid search** exhaustively tries all combinations of predefined hyperparameters (such as many layers, units, activation functions, etc.). Then, it selects the one that achieves the best performance on a validation set. **Random search** randomly samples hyperparameters from a predefined range or distribution and selects the best one similarly. **Evolutionary algorithms** build a population of structures across generations using biological concepts like mutation, crossover, and selection. **Reinforcement learning** uses an agent that learns a policy to select architectures based on rewards from an environment (such as performance on a validation set). Finally, **gradient-based methods** use gradients of the objective function concerning the architecture parameters to update them iteratively.

However, these techniques also have some limitations and challenges. For example, regularization techniques may introduce some bias or variance to the network outputs or parameters, affecting their interpretability or transferability. In addition, architecture search techniques may require a lot of computational resources or time to explore an ample space of architectures or evaluate them on large data sets. Moreover, they may suffer from local optima or overfitting to the validation set.

Therefore, building neural network architectures is a technical problem, an art, and a science. It requires creativity, intuition, domain knowledge, experimentation, evaluation, and iteration.

10.6 Training Neural Networks with Backpropagation

Neural networks are computer models that can learn from input and carry out several operations, including generation, regression, and classification. Alter the neural network's parameters depending on feedback from the desired output; however, it is necessary for learning from data. Backpropagation is the name of this technique, one of the most significant algorithms in artificial intelligence.

The gradients of the loss function concerning the neural network's parameters are calculated using the backpropagation technique. The neural network's loss function gauges the neural network's performance on a particular input–output pair. The gradients show how much each parameter needs to be altered to lessen the loss. The neural network can gradually enhance its performance by making a minor adjustment to the parameters moving in the opposite direction of the gradients.

Backpropagation has supplanted other algorithms as the go-to method for training intense neural networks with several layers of non-linear units.

A multilayer perceptron is trained with a backpropagation algorithm. There are three main stages in this algorithm:

- Forward phase
- Error calculation and propagating it back
- Updating of weights

Consider an MLP with topology $(n+1)-(p+1)-m$, that is, there are n neurons in the input layer with one bias neuron, p neurons in the hidden layer with one bias neuron, and m neurons in the output layer (Fig. 10.24).

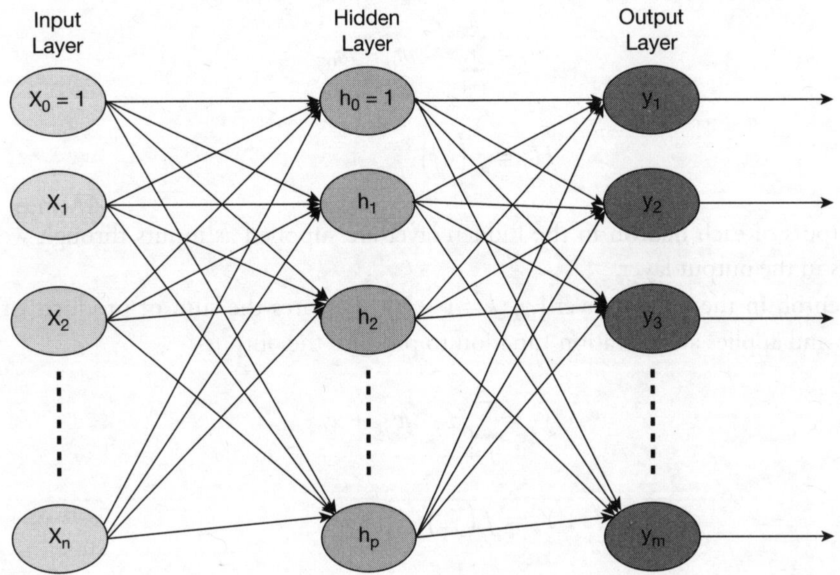

Figure 10:24 MLP model with *n–p–m* topology

Notation:

Input vector: $X = (x_1, x_2, \cdots, x_n)$

Output vector: $O = (O_1, O_2, \cdots, O_m)$

where

m_{ij} : Weight connecting i^{th} neuron in the input layer with j^{th} neuron in the hidden layer

w_{jk} : Weight connecting j^{th} neuron in the hidden layer with a kth neuron in the output layer

h_j : Summed input at the jth hidden neuron

H_j : Output of jth hidden neuron

y_k : Summed input at k^{th} output neuron

Y_k : Output of kth output neuron

δ_k : Error term at k^{th} output neuron

Algorithm

1. Initialize all the weights at once.
2. Each neuron in the input layer $(x_i, i = 1 \cdots n)$ received from an external source is supplied through weights to the neurons in the hidden layer.
3. Each neuron in the hidden layer $(h_j, j = 1 \cdots p)$ calculates the sum of products of inputs and weights and applies an activation function to produce the output.

$$h_j = \sum_{i=1}^{n} x_i * m_{ij} + m_{0j}$$

$$H_j = f\left(h_j\right)$$

4. The outputs of each neuron in the hidden layer are supplied as inputs through weights to the neurons in the output layer.
5. Each neuron in the output layer $\left(y_k, k = 1 \cdots m\right)$ calculates the sum of products of inputs and weights and applies an activation function to produce the output.

$$y_k = \sum_{j=1}^{p} H_j * w_{jk} + w_{0k}$$

$$Y_k = f\left(y_k\right)$$

6. Calculate the error at every neuron in the output layer.

$$\delta_k = \left(O_k - Y_k\right) * f'\left(y_k\right)$$

7. Calculate the weight adjustments to be made for the weights between the hidden layer and the output layer.

$$\Delta w_{jk} = \eta * \delta_k * H_j$$

$$\Delta w_{0k} = \eta * \delta_k$$

8. Propagate the error back to the hidden layer.
9. Each hidden neuron $\left(h_j, j = 1 \cdots p\right)$ receives the error term through the weights and calculates the error information term by multiplying with a derivative of its activation function.

$$\delta h_j = \sum_{k=1}^{m} \delta_k * {}_{jk}$$

$$\delta H_j = \delta h_j * f'\left(h_j\right)$$

10. Calculate the weight adjustments to be made for the weights between input layer and hidden layer.

$$\Delta m_{ij} = \eta * \delta H_j * x_i$$

$$\Delta m_{0j} = \eta * \delta H_j$$

11. Update all the weights at once.

$$m_{ij}(new) = m_{ij}(old) + \Delta m_{ij}$$

$$m_{0j}(new) = m_{0j}(old) + \Delta m_{0j}$$

$$w_{ij}(new) = w_{ij}(old) + \Delta w_{ij}$$

$$w_{0j}(new) = w_{0j}(old) + \Delta w_{0j}$$

12. Repeat the process from step 2 to 9 for the input pattern until the stopping condition is met.

Activation functions used: The popular activation functions used in MLP are sigmoid and tanh. The sigmoid function is defined as

$$f(x) = \frac{1}{\left(1+e^{-x}\right)}$$

The derivative of this function is expressed in terms of the function itself.

$$f'(x) = \frac{-1}{\left(1+e^{-x}\right)^2} * e^{-x} * (-1) = \frac{e^{-x}}{\left(1+e^{-x}\right)^2} = f(x)(1-f(x))$$

Figure 10.25 shows a numerical example of an MLP.

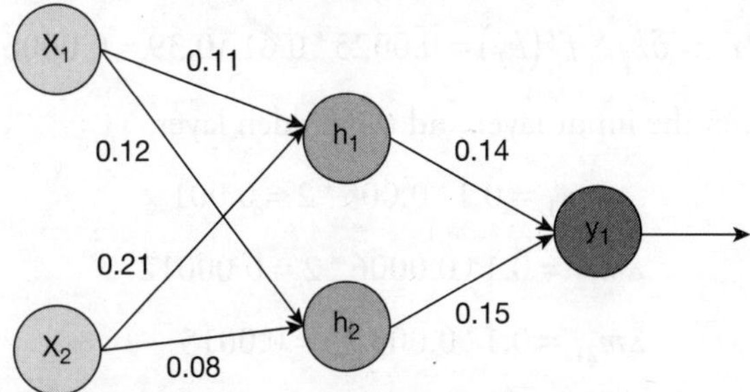

Figure 10.25 Sample MLP numerical example

To simplify the calculation process, bias input is omitted. But the users should keep in mind that bias should be included during the implementation of the MLP. Let the learning rate $\eta = 0.1$, the first input pattern be $[2,3]$, and the actual output be 1.

$$h_1 = x_1 * m_{11} + x_2 * m_{21} + m_{01} \Rightarrow h_1 = 2*0.11 + 3*0.21 = 0.85$$
$$h_2 = x_1 * m_{12} + x_2 * m_{22} + m_{02} \Rightarrow h_2 = 2*0.12 + 3*0.0.8 = 0.48$$

$$H_1 = f(h_1) = \frac{1}{\left(1+e^{-h_1}\right)} = \frac{1}{\left(1+e^{-0.85}\right)} = 0.70$$

$$H_2 = f(h_2) = \frac{1}{\left(1+e^{-h_2}\right)} = \frac{1}{\left(1+e^{-0.48}\right)} = 0.61$$

$$y_1 = h_1 * w_{11} + h_2 * m_{22} + w_{01} \Rightarrow y_1 = 0.70 * 0.14 + 0.61 * 0.15 = 1.895$$

$$Y_1 = f(y_1) = \frac{1}{\left(1+e^{-y_1}\right)} = \frac{1}{\left(1+e^{-0.895}\right)} = 0.86$$

Error term

$$\begin{aligned}\delta_1 &= (O_1 - Y_1) * f'(y_1) = (O_1 - Y_1) * f(y_1) * (1 - f(y_1)\\ &= (1-0.86) * f(1.895) * (1 - f(1.895)\\ &= 0.14 * 0.86 * 0.14 = 0.017\end{aligned}$$

Weight adjustments between the hidden layer and the output layer

$$\Delta w_{11} = 0.1 * 0.017 * 0.70 = 0.0012$$

$$\Delta w_{21} = 0.1 * 0.017 * 0.61 = 0.0001$$

Backpropagation of error from the output layer to the hidden layer

$$\delta h_1 = \delta_1 * w_{11} = 0.017 * 0.14 = 0.0024$$

$$\delta h_2 = \delta_1 * w_{21} = 0.017 * 0.15 = 0.0025$$

$$\delta H_1 = \delta h_1 * f'(h_1) = 0.0024 * 0.70 * 0.30 = 0.0050$$

$$\delta H_2 = \delta h_2 * f'(h_2) = 0.0025 * 0.61 * 0.39 = 0.0006$$

Weight adjustments between the input layer and the hidden layer

$$\Delta m_{11} = 0.1 * 0.005 * 2 = 0.001$$

$$\Delta m_{12} = 0.1 * 0.0006 * 2 = 0.00012$$

$$\Delta m_{21} = 0.1 * 0.005 * 3 = 0.0015$$

$$\Delta m_{12} = 0.1 * 0.0006 * 3 = 0.00018$$

Updating of all weights

$$w_{11}(new) = w_{11}(old) + \Delta w_{11} = 0.14 + 0.0012 = 0.1412$$

$$w_{21}(new) = w_{21}(old) + \Delta w_{21} = 0.15 + 0.0010 = 0.1510$$

$$m_{11}(new) = m_{11}(old) + \Delta m_{11} = 0.11 + 0.001 = 0.111$$

$$m_{12}(new) = m_{12}(new) + \Delta m_{12} = 0.12 + 0.00012 = 0.12012$$

$$m_{21}(new) = m_{21}(old) + \Delta m_{21} = 0.21 + 0.0015 = 0.2115$$

$$m_{22}(new) = m_{22}(old) + \Delta m_{22} = 0.08 + 0.00018 = 0.08018$$

Backpropagation comes with few challenges. Among them, the most significant are as follows:

- **Selecting the correct learning rate**: The learning rate, a hyperparameter, determines how frequently the parameters are updated. The training process may be delayed and trapped in local minima if the learning rate needs to be higher. Conversely, the training process may diverge and oscillate about the ideal answer if the learning rate is too high.
- **Handling disappearing and bursting gradients**: As the gradients go through various neural network levels, they may either become extremely small or very huge. This may result in the parameters changing either too little or too much, which could adversely affect performance or lead to numerical instability.
- **Preventing overfitting and underfitting**: Overfitting happens when a neural network becomes memorably trained but cannot generalize to new data. Conversely, when a neural network is underfitted, it struggles with training and test sets of data and cannot learn from the training set. Numerous regularization approaches, including dropout, weight decay, batch normalization, and data augmentation, can be used to avoid overfitting and underfitting.

Despite these obstacles, backpropagation is still a reliable and valuable tool for training neural networks. Backpropagation can help neural networks perform remarkably on various tasks and domains with the right design decisions and optimization techniques.

10.7 Autoencoders

Autoencoder is an unsupervised neural network that can learn to encode and decode data. It is helpful for feature extraction, generative modeling, data compression, and dimensionality reduction. The encoder and decoder are the two components that make up an autoencoder (Fig. 10.26). The encoder converts input data x to a latent representation z, which is ordinarily less complex than x. The decoder uses z to attempt an immediate reconstruction of x. The reconstruction error is employed as a feedback signal to train the network. An autoencoder aims to learn a concise and meaningful representation of the data that maintains its essential characteristics.

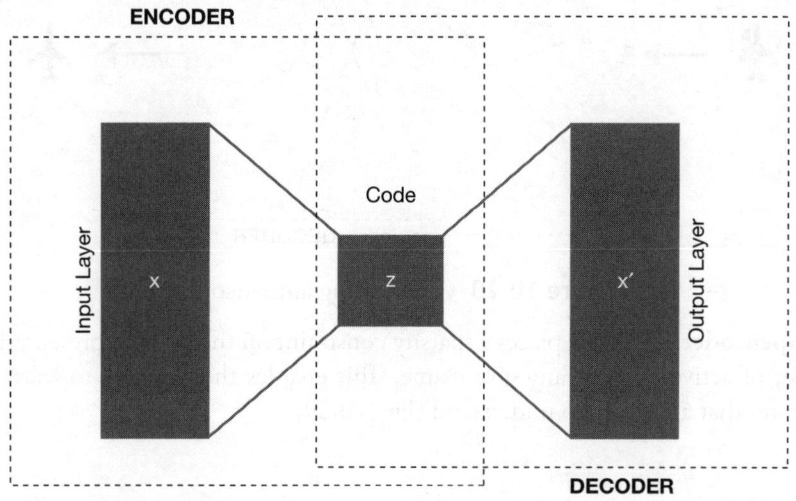

Figure 10.26 Simple autoencoder

There are various **types** of autoencoders:

- **Linear autoencoder**: This type of autoencoder is the simplest and does both encoding and decoding using linear transformations (Fig. 10.27). It is comparable to principal component analysis (PCA), which identifies the orthogonal directions in the data that capture the most significant variance. The decoder tries to create the output exactly like the input.

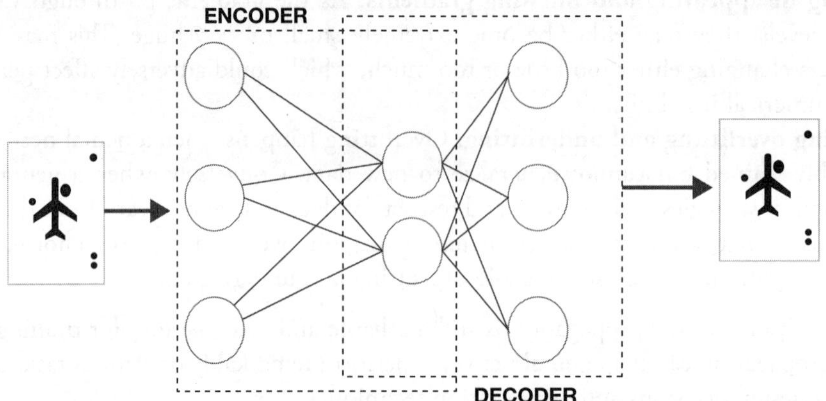

Figure 10.27 Linear autoencoder

- **De-noising autoencoder**: This attempts to recover the original clean data by introducing noise to the input data (x). This compels the network to learn the data's basic structure and disregard the unimportant pixels (Fig. 10.28).

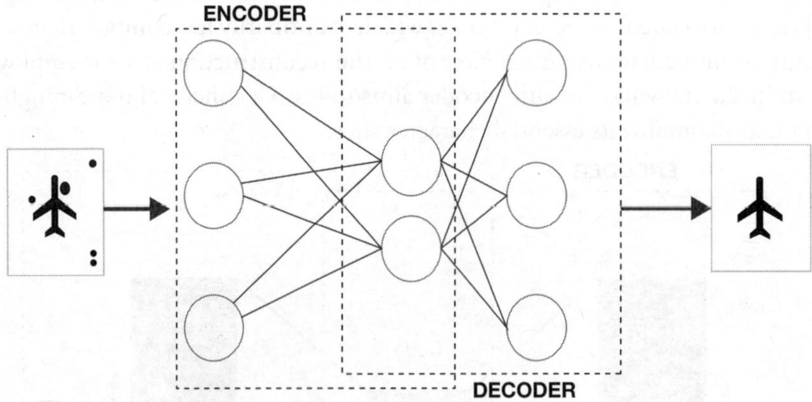

Figure 10.28 De-noising autoencoder

- **Sparse autoencoder**: This type places a sparsity constraint on the latent representation z, limiting the number of active units at any given time. This enables the network to learn independent, sparse features that are easier to understand (Fig. 10.29).

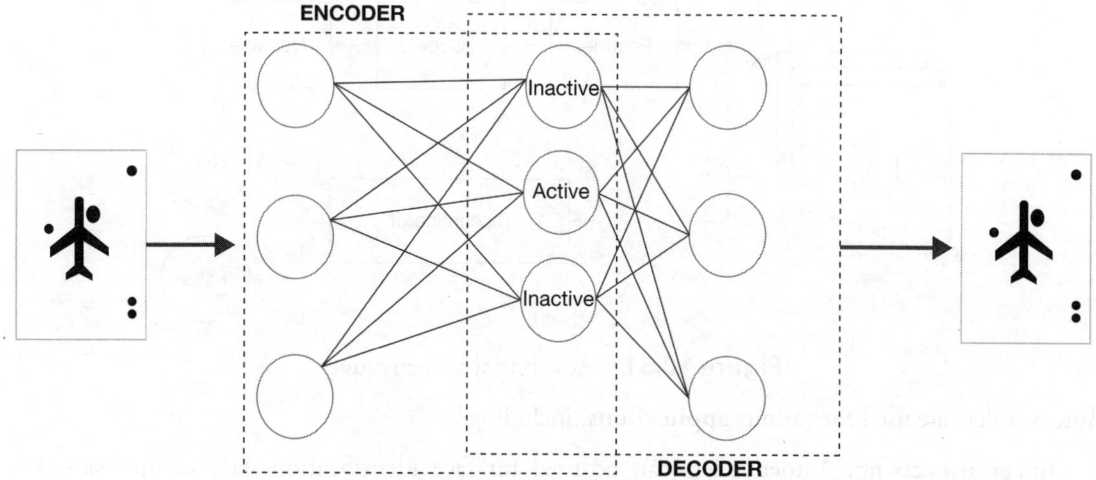

Figure 10.29 Sparse autoencoder

- **Variational autoencoders**: These autoencoders model the latent representation *z* as a stochastic distribution instead of a deterministic vector. This enables the network to infer the latent variables and generate fresh samples from the learned distribution (Fig. 10.30).

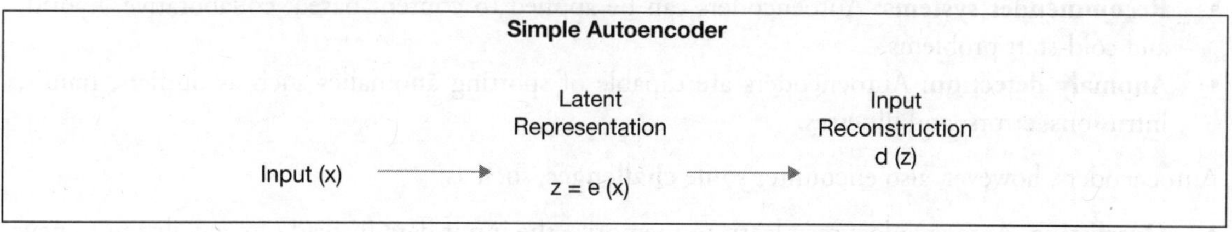

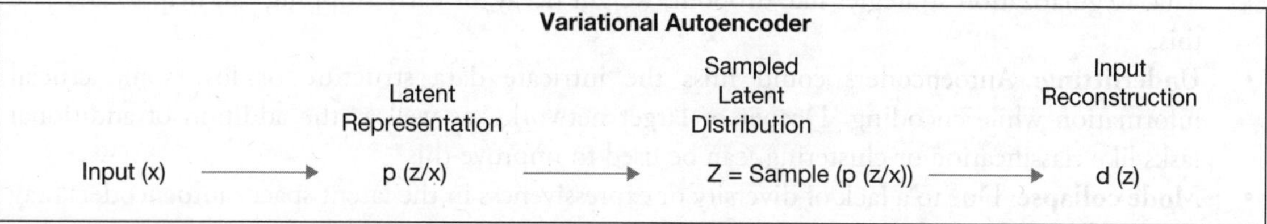

Figure 10.30 Variational autoencoder logic

- **Adversarial autoencoder**: Here, the autoencoder employs an adversarial training method in which an encoder–decoder network tries to deceive the discriminator network. In contrast, a discriminator network seeks to discern between real and fake samples. A more accurate and varied data reconstruction is the outcome of this type (Fig. 10.31).

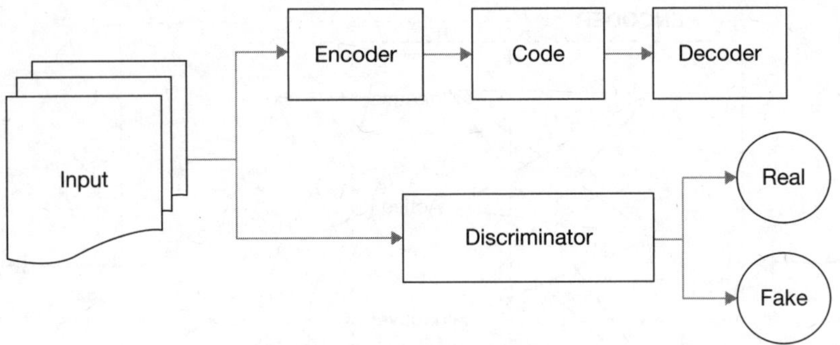

Figure 10.31 Adversarial autoencoder

Autoencoders are used for various **applications**, including:

- **Image processing**: Autoencoders can be used for face identification, face compression, de-noising, inpainting, super-resolution, colorization, and style transfer.
- **NLP**: Text summarization, paraphrasing, translation, sentiment analysis, topic modeling, and creation may all be performed with autoencoders.
- **Speech processing**: Autoencoders help enhance, compress, recognize, synthesize, and convert speech.
- **Recommender systems**: Autoencoders can be applied to content-based, collaborative, hybrid, and cold-start problems.
- **Anomaly detection**: Autoencoders are capable of spotting anomalies such as outliers, frauds, intrusions, errors, and illnesses.

Autoencoders, however, also encounter some **challenges**, such as:

- **Overfitting**: Autoencoders may learn to memorize the input data instead of generalizing to new data. Regularization strategies like dropout, weight decay, or early stopping can help to alleviate this.
- **Underfitting**: Autoencoders could miss the intricate data structure or lose some crucial information while encoding. Deeper or larger networks, as well as the addition of additional tasks like classification or clustering, can be used to improve this.
- **Mode collapse**: Due to a lack of diversity or expressiveness in the latent space, autoencoders may give similar or identical outputs for various inputs. Utilizing adversarial or variational approaches and imposing restrictions or penalties on the latent space can prevent this.
- **Interpretability**: Autoencoders may acquire difficult-to-understand latent representations. This can be improved by visualizing or probing the latent space or by adopting sparse or disentangled representations.

As a result, autoencoders are a potent and adaptable tool for unsupervised learning that can be trained to encode and decode data efficiently and effectively. They have several uses in many fields and domains, but they also have significant problems and restrictions that require more study and improvement.

10.8 Applications of ANNs

ANNs can learn from photos and videos to identify objects, faces, scenes, emotions, and other visual aspects. It can be used in NLP. Let us investigate some other applications of ANN.

10.8.1 Using ANNs for Image Recognition

The process of identifying and classifying images into one of many predefined categories is known as image recognition. It is among the most popular uses of ANNs. ANNs are well suited for picture identification and other computer vision issues because they can learn from examples and spot patterns in data.

The following are some **advantages** of utilizing ANNs for image analysis and recognition:

- They require less preparation for handling complex and high-dimensional data.
- They can learn by utilizing unsupervised or semi-supervised learning techniques from significant amounts of poorly or unlabeled data.
- They can perform at an advanced level on various benchmarks and outperform human accuracy in some activities.

However, there are several **difficulties and restrictions** with employing ANNs for picture analysis and recognition, such as:

- They need a lot of memory/processing power to run and train.
- If the data needs to be more sufficient and representative, they are vulnerable to overfitting and underfitting.
- They are susceptible to adversarial attacks; wherein malicious inputs are used to deceive or manipulate them.
- Their decisions and results are not interpretable or explicable.

The following are the **primary steps** in picture recognition with ANNs:

1. **Image preprocessing**: This entails converting the original image data into a format that the ANNs can use, such as by resizing, cropping, normalizing, augmenting, etc.
2. **Feature extraction**: This process involves sifting through image data to find and extract meaningful information, such as edges, corners, shapes, colors, textures, etc. CNNs can be used automatically or manually to accomplish this task. In addition, feature detectors or filters can be designed to accomplish this manually.
3. **Classification**: This entails labeling the image according to its characteristics, such as cat, dog, car, etc. Fully linked or softmax layers, which are layers of neurons that may change the characteristics and output probabilities for each class linearly or nonlinearly, can be used for this.
4. **Evaluation**: This entails gauging how well the ANN performs in accuracy, precision, recall, F1-score, and other image recognition tasks. This can be accomplished by utilizing validation or test sets, which are collections of images that are not used to train the ANN but are instead used to gauge its capacity for generalization.

10.8.2 Using ANNs for Natural Language Processing

Natural language processing (NLP) is a well-known application of ANNs. ANNs can learn to comprehend and create a natural language from text or speech data. They can carry out various jobs, including sentiment analysis, machine translation, text summarization, question-answering, dialogue systems, text production, and more.

The capacity of ANNs to learn from data without the need for explicit rules or features is one of their key advantages. They are suited for handling complicated and varied natural language input, which frequently contains ambiguity, unpredictability, and noise. We must convert natural language data into a numerical format that artificial neurons can understand to employ ANNs for NLP; this is possible using word embeddings, character embeddings, and sub-word embeddings. These methods convert the semantic and syntactic characteristics of words or sub words into vectors of integers. Depending on the purpose and the architecture, we can feed different types of ANNs with natural language data once we have their numerical representations.

Types of ANNs used in NLP

- **Feedforward neural networks (FNNs):** These ANNs are the simplest type, passing information through one or more hidden layers from the input to the output layer. For example, when a text is an input, and the output is a label or a score, tasks like text classification or sentiment analysis can be performed with FNNs.
- **Recurrent neural networks (RNNs)** are capable of processing sequential data, such as sentences or paragraphs. RNNs have a memory system that enables them to retain and access primary data. RNNs can be utilized for tasks like text summarization or machine translation, where the input and output are word sequences.
- **Convolutional neural networks (CNNs)** are capable of detecting subtle variations and features in the input data. CNNs create feature maps by applying filters or kernels to the input. When a text is an input, and a label or score is the output, tasks like text classification or sentiment analysis can be performed using CNNs.
- **Transformer networks** are a subset of ANNs that learn the connections between various input components by using attention processes. The network may concentrate on the data that is most pertinent to each output component, thanks to attention processes. Transformer networks can be used for applications where the input and output are word sequences, such as machine translation or question answering.

Challenges for ANNs in NLP

- They need a lot of data and computing power to train and compete.
- They can experience data scarcity or sparsity for languages or domains with limited resources.
- Due to mistakes or biases in the data or models, they may produce absurd or unsuitable outputs.
- They might be unable to capture the nuances or complexities of natural languages, such as irony, humor, sarcasm, or pragmatics.
- **Data quality and quantity:** For ANNs to train well, they need a lot of labeled or unlabeled data. Nevertheless, not all natural language data is accessible, trustworthy, or representative. Furthermore, the accuracy and fairness of ANNs may be impacted by biases, inaccuracies, or inconsistencies in some natural language data.

- **Interpretability and explainability:** ANNs are sometimes viewed as black box models because they do not clearly explain or justify their choices or results. When ANNs are utilized for delicate or crucial jobs in NLP, this may pose ethical, legal, and social concerns. It may also prevent ANNs from being fixed and improved.
- Generalization and adaptation: ANNs could struggle to adapt to new tasks, languages, or domains that differ from their training data. This may restrict their use and scalability in NLP. Furthermore, dynamic or changing natural language input that changes over time may make ANNs less adaptable.

The following are some **benefits** of utilizing ANNs in NLP:

- They can use distributed representations to capture natural language's semantic and syntactic aspects.
- They can use transformers or RNNs to mimic natural language's sequential and contextual aspects.
- They can use sizable, pre-trained models that can be tailored for tasks or domains, such as BERT or GPT-3.
- They can generate outputs in fluent and coherent natural language using attention processes or beam search.
- **Multimodality and multimodality**: ANNs can process a variety of natural language data formats, including text, speech, photos, and videos. This may make it possible for NLP applications and interactions to be more varied and richer. Additionally, ANNs can use many modalities of natural language input to improve their functionality and performance.
- **Transfer learning and pre-training**: ANNs can use their knowledge to perform better on new tasks or improve their performance on existing ones. This can lower the amount of information and computing needed to train ANNs. Additionally, ANNs may be trained beforehand on vast amounts of unlabeled data to discover broad representations that can be honed for particular tasks.
- **Generating new and coherent natural languages content**, such as texts, poems, novels, or dialogues, is a strength of ANNs. This may make it possible for NLP applications and interactions to be more imaginative and expressive. Furthermore, natural language content produced by ANNs can be customized for particular audiences, situations, or objectives.

10.8.3 Using ANNs for Automated Decision-making

Automated decision-making (ADM), which is the process of making decisions without human intervention, is one of the new applications of ANNs. ADM can be helpful in industries like finance, healthcare, security, and transportation that need scalability, precision, consistency, and speed. However, ADM also comes with several hazards and difficulties, including moral, legal, societal, and technical problems.

The use of ANNs for ADM has many benefits, including their capacity to handle non-linear and high-dimensional data. Without explicit feature engineering or domain expertise, ANNs may discover complicated patterns and correlations from massive, varied data sets. This qualifies them for handling issues involving ambiguity, unpredictability, and uncertainty. For instance, ANNs can identify fraud, identify diseases, provide product recommendations, and customize learning.

The versatility and scalability of ANNs for ADM are another benefit. As the environment changes, ANNs may be updated and trained with fresh data, enabling them to adapt to changing and dynamic conditions. Furthermore, by modifying their architecture, parameters, and activation functions, ANNs can also be created and optimized for various tasks and goals. ANNs can be used, for instance, to optimize resource allocation, forecast consumer behavior, produce content, and manage robots.

However, there are several drawbacks to employing ANNs for ADM that must be considered. Their need for interpretability and transparency is one of their key drawbacks. ANNs are frequently viewed as black boxes that provide results without indicating how they arrived. This makes it challenging to comprehend, validate, and have faith in their judgments, particularly when those judgments impact people's lives and welfare. ANNs can be used, for instance, to refuse loans, reject applicants, grade tasks, and terminate workers.

Another drawback is the possibility of bias and mistakes when employing ANNs for ADM. The biases and flaws existing in the data that ANNs are trained on might be inherited and amplified, resulting in unfair and erroneous results. In addition, adversarial attacks that alter an ANN's inputs or outputs to injure or cause trouble can also be a problem. For instance, ANNs can prejudice minorities, disseminate false information, fabricate images, and penetrate computer systems.

As a result, depending on the domain and environment, utilizing ANNs for ADM has benefits and drawbacks that must be carefully considered. ANNs can provide solid and adaptable solutions for challenging issues but also present ethical and technological issues that call for prudence and accountability.

Without human input or supervision, ADM refers to making choices or taking actions based on data and algorithms. ANNs and other AI techniques like rule-based systems, decision trees, or machine learning can be used to implement ADM. ADM can be used for various activities, including autonomous vehicles, recommender systems, internet advertising, fraud detection, and more. ANNs and ADM share the following traits:

- They are data-driven. They use much data to find patterns, predict the future, or give advice.
- They are adaptable. They may change their parameters or rules to adapt to new situations and environments.
- They can be scaled. They can handle complex and high-dimensional data sets successfully.
- They are open and honest. They can justify or explain their choices or deeds.

ANNs and ADM, however, also face some difficulties and restrictions:

- They are biased. The biases in the data or algorithms they utilize can be passed down or amplified by them, which can result in unfair or discriminating outcomes for particular groups or individuals.
- They are prone to errors. The data or methods they utilize may contain noise, outliers, anomalies, or adversarial attacks that cause them to make errors or perform less than intended.
- They need to be more precise. Due to their complexity or lack of supporting documentation or accountability procedures, they may be challenging to comprehend or interpret.
- They are moral. Their implications for human rights, values, autonomy, dignity, privacy, and security may give rise to moral questions or problems.

Therefore, to assure their quality, dependability, fairness, accountability, and social responsibility, ANNs and ADM require detailed design, evaluation, regulation, and governance.

Following are some examples of ANNs and ADM in use:

- **Google's DeepMind AlphaGo**: An ANN-based program that outplayed the world champion in the challenging board game of Go.
- **IBM's Watson**: An ANN-based system that uses a vast corpus of organized and unstructured data sources to answer natural language inquiries on various subjects.
- **Facebook's News Feed**: An ADM-based system that adapts the content users see on their social media platform to their choices and usage patterns.
- **Alexa from Amazon**: An ADM-based system that offers voice-based services, including information retrieval, entertainment, commerce, and control over smart homes.

10.8.4 Using ANNs for Time Series Analysis

The technique of examining and simulating the patterns and trends of sequential data through time is known as time series analysis. It has numerous uses in various industries, including finance, economics, engineering, medicine, and more. The intricate and dynamic interactions between the variables in the data and considering the uncertainty and noise that may alter the observations are some of the significant issues of time series analysis.

The primary **advantages** of ANNs for time series analysis are as follows:

- Non-linear and complex interactions between the variables in the data can be handled by ANNs, which may not be possible with conventional statistical techniques.
- ANNs can learn from a lot of data and generalize well to new scenarios, increasing predictability and accuracy.
- ANNs can deal with missing or noisy data and include various sources of information, which can improve the accuracy and dependability of the study.

Using ANNs for time series analysis has several **disadvantages**:

- The time/resources needed to train and evaluate ANNs may limit their scalability and efficiency.
- ANNs are sometimes called black box models, which suggests that it is difficult to understand or analyze their internal logic.
- Overfitting or underfitting issues can cause ANNs to memorize the training data too well or miss out on capturing its essential characteristics.

Practical **applications** for ANNs in time series analysis:

- Predicting stock prices, currency exchange rates, inflation rates, etc.
- Finding outliers, frauds, oddities, etc.
- Classifying speech signals, electroencephalograms, electrocardiograms, etc.
- Producing text, graphics, music, etc.

10.8.5 Using ANNs for Cybersecurity

Cybersecurity is among the most important and challenging fields in the contemporary world. The hazards of cyberattacks, data breaches, and malware infections are rising along with the use of digital devices and networks. These attacks need to be continuously monitored, detected, and prevented by cybersecurity specialists utilizing a variety of technologies and approaches.

ANNs have various **benefits** for applications in cybersecurity:

- They can manage big, varied data sets, including network traffic, logs, pictures, text, etc.
- They do not require manual upgrades because they can learn from new data and adapt to changing circumstances.
- They can pick up tiny patterns and abnormalities that conventional techniques could miss.
- They can offer results that are easy to grasp and interpret, aiding security analysts in determining the type and origin of risks.

Let us look at how ANNs can be applied to various cybersecurity activities.

Intrusion detection is the process of spotting and responding to suspicious or malicious activities on a network or system. By learning to categorize network traffic or system events into normal or anomalous categories, ANNs can be used for intrusion detection. An ANN, for instance, can be taught to recognize patterns that point to an attack or a compromise using a data set of network packets or system logs. Aside from detecting anomalies, ANNs can also generate warnings or reactions.

The practice of looking at and comprehending the traits and behavior of malicious software, such as viruses, worms, trojan horses, ransomware, etc., is known as **malware analysis**. By training them to recognize and categorize malware samples according to their characteristics or behaviors, ANNs can be used for malware analysis. An ANN can be trained, for instance, to identify the type, family, or functionality of malware by using a data set of malware binaries or execution traces. ANNs can also be employed to generate signatures or rules to detect or stop malware infections.

Phishing detection is observing and stopping phony emails or websites that try to dupe users into disclosing personal information or carrying out destructive deeds. By learning to differentiate between authentic and phishing emails or websites based on their content or appearance, ANNs can be used for phishing detection. An ANN, for instance, can be taught to recognize traits that point to a phishing effort, such as counterfeit sender addresses, deceptive links, urgent requests, etc., by being trained on a data set of emails or web pages. Users who encounter phishing emails or websites may receive warnings or suggestions from ANNs.

The act of recognizing and eliminating unwanted or unsolicited emails from a user's mailbox is known as **spam filtering**. By learning to categorize emails into spam or ham (non-spam) categories based on their content or metadata, ANNs can be used for spam filtering. For instance, an ANN can be taught to recognize spam characteristics, such as keywords, attachments, sender reputation, etc., by being trained on a collection of emails. Users who receive spam emails can use ANNs to prompt feedback or actions, such as deleting, reporting, or blocking them.

Thus, ANNs are superior to conventional cybersecurity techniques in several ways. Some of the difficulties and restrictions we face using ANNs for cybersecurity are as follows:

- **Scalability**: ANNs need a lot of data and computing power to train and operate. This presents a hurdle for cybersecurity applications, where the data may be sparse, noisy, unbalanced, or dynamic. In addition, because the cyber threat landscape constantly evolves, ANNs must often adapt and upgrade their models. To handle the complexity and diversity of cybersecurity data and events, ANNs must be scalable and adaptable.
- **Robustness**: Because ANNs are susceptible to adversarial attacks, wherein malevolent actors influence the input data or the model parameters, the predictions or choices made by ANNs may be inaccurate or deceptive. For instance, an attacker can create adversarial examples, slightly

altered versions of valid inputs, to deceive ANNs into incorrectly classifying them. This could have significant repercussions for cybersecurity applications because attackers could get through monitoring or prevention measures, set off false alarms, or misdiagnose problems. As a result, ANNs must be solid and resistant to hostile attacks to guarantee their dependability and accuracy in cybersecurity.

- **Privacy**: ANNs frequently use sensitive and private data to train and run their models. Since the data may contain private or confidential information that should not be published or leaked, this presents privacy problems for cybersecurity applications. For instance, an ANN would require access to user behavior or network traffic data to find anomalies or harmful activity. However, the identities or preferences of the users or organizations involved may also be revealed by these data. As a result, ANNs must respect and safeguard the privacy of data suppliers and users and guarantee that they comply with all applicable laws and regulations.
- **Ethics**: ANNs could alter the rights and obligations of the stakeholders in cybersecurity applications, which could have ethical ramifications for those applications. An ANN might, for instance, make choices or suggestions that affect the safety or wellbeing of users or organizations. Meanwhile, These choices or suggestions could not be apparent or comprehensible to auditors or human users. Furthermore, these choices or counsel could not be impartial or fair to all parties concerned. As a result, ANNs must uphold ethical standards and values and ensure that they are accountable and responsible for cybersecurity.

10.8.6 Using ANNs for Predictive Analytics

Predictive analytics, which uses data, statistical methods, and ML approaches to find patterns and trends, is one of the applications of ANNs. Businesses and organizations can use predictive analytics to enhance decision-making, streamline procedures, lower risks, and boost productivity.

The ability of ANNs to handle non-linear and high-dimensional data, which are prevalent in many industries, including banking, healthcare, marketing, and education, is one of their advantages.

Finance: ANNs help forecast stock prices, currency rates, credit risk, fraud detection, portfolio optimization, and other things. For instance, ANNs can estimate future movements of financial assets by learning from historical data and market indices. In addition, financial firms can use ANNs to assess a customer's creditworthiness and spot fraudulent activities. ANNs must also deal with data quality, interpretability, legislation, and ethics in the financial world.

Medicine: ANNs can be used to identify illnesses, forecast results, suggest therapies, and personalize care. To identify anomalies, categorize disorders, and recommend interventions, ANNs can, for instance, analyze medical imaging, genomic data, electronic health records, and wearable devices. Additionally, ANNs can aid healthcare practitioners in optimizing resources, cost containment, and enhancing care quality. However, Healthcare ANNs must also deal with issues including data protection, security, dependability, and trust.

Marketing: ANNs can be applied to consumer segmentation, behavior prediction, product or service recommendations, and campaign optimization. For instance, ANNs can discover trends and preferences by learning from client data, including demographics, preferences, purchase history, and internet activity. Then, based on each customer's anticipated wants and interests, ANNs can assist marketers in customizing their goods and messaging. However, ANNs must also deal with data gathering, consent, openness, and fairness in their marketing efforts.

Education: ANNs can be used to evaluate students' performance, offer suggestions or feedback, tailor lessons or content, and increase motivation or engagement. For instance, ANNs can examine student data, including test results, learning preferences, interests, and goals, to assess their progress and offer tailored criticism or assistance. Based on each student's anticipated abilities or preferences, ANNs can also assist educators in tailoring their curriculum or pedagogy to each one of them. ANNs must also contend with issues including data accessibility, validity, prejudice, and ethics in education.

The use of ANNs for predictive analytics has several **benefits**. One is its capacity to manage intricate and non-linear interactions between input and output variables. ANNs can generalize to new scenarios and learn from vast volumes of data. They can also change their weights in response to new data and adapt to changing settings. ANNs are particularly helpful for issues involving recommender systems, natural language processing, speech recognition, and picture recognition.

ANNs do, however, present **difficulties** for predictive analytics. The difficulty of interpreting and describing how ANNs create their predictions is one of the difficulties. ANNs are frequently called black boxes since they generate results while hiding their underlying logic or reasoning. This may reduce users' and stakeholders' confidence in the projections. The possibility of underfitting and overfitting the data is another difficulty. When an ANN learns too much from the training data and cannot generalize to new data, overfitting occurs; when an ANN learns insufficiently from the training data, it under fits and needs to catch up on basic patterns or features. Predictions may need to be corrected or more accurate due to both overfitting and underfitting.

As a result, it is crucial to adhere to a few best practices when applying ANNs to predictive analytics. Several of these **ideal practices** include:

- Picking the exemplary architecture and design for the ANN, including the number and kind of layers, activation functions, and learning algorithms.
- Preprocessing and cleaning the data, including removing anomalies, missing data, noise, and unimportant features.
- Dividing the data into training, validation, and test sets and assessing the ANN's performance using cross-validation methods.
- Regularizing and fine-tuning the ANN to avoid overfitting or underfitting, utilizing techniques like dropout, weight decay, early halting, and hyperparameter adjustment.
- Interpreting and elaborating on the ANN's predictions, for example, using visualization tools, feature importance indices, or explainable AI methodologies to comprehend how the ANN operates.

ANNs have been successfully used in predictive analytics in the following **applications**:

- Netflix employs ANNs to make movie and television recommendations based on user ratings, tastes, and behavior.
- Google uses ANNs to forecast which advertisements a user will click on based on their demographics, search history, and browsing patterns.
- Amazon employs artificial neural networks (ANNs) to forecast the products a customer will purchase based on past purchases, browsing patterns, and recommendations.

- Based on a user's likes, comments, shares, and interests, Facebook employs ANNs to anticipate what posts or material they would be interested in.

10.9 Future of ANNs

As we have seen, ANNs can execute complex tasks, including classification, regression, clustering, generation, reinforcement learning, and learning from data. ANNs have been extensively used in various fields, including robotics, computer vision, NLP, speech recognition, and healthcare. We will now discuss the effect of ANNs on society, current ANN research trends, recent developments in ANN technology, and prospective ANN future directions.

Effect on Society: ANNs have had a significant impact on society in many areas. They have made it possible for new programs and services that boost productivity and efficiency, stimulate creativity, and increase the quality of life. These are a few instances of these applications and services:

- **Face recognition**: ANNs accurately and quickly identify faces in pictures and movies. Security, identity, authentication, and social media can all use this.
- **Machine translation**: ANNs can accurately translate speech/text from one language to another. This can be applied to business, tourism, education, and communication.
- **Self-driving vehicles**: ANNs are capable of steering, accelerating, braking, and navigating a vehicle autonomously. This can be utilized for entertainment, convenience, safety, and transportation.
- **Image generation**: ANNs can produce lifelike visuals from text or sketches. This can be used in education, gaming, design, and the arts.
- **Recommendation systems**: ANNs are capable of analyzing user behavior and preferences to offer specialized suggestions for goods, services, information, or activities. This can be applied to social networking, e-commerce, entertainment, and education.

While ANNs have significantly benefited society, they also present significant **hazards and concerns** that must be managed. Among these difficulties and dangers are the following:

- **Ethical concerns**: ANNs may bring up moral issues involving human dignity, privacy, justice, accountability, and openness. How, for instance, can we safeguard the private information that ANNs train on and infer from? How can we guarantee that ANNs do not stigmatize or hurt particular racial or ethnic groups? How can we hold ANNs or those who created them accountable for their deeds or results? How can we inform users or other stakeholders about the choices or actions taken by ANNs? How can we treat ANNs with respect while maintaining the autonomy and dignity of people?
- **Social ramifications**: ANNs may affect aspects of society such as employment, education, culture, and interpersonal relationships. What impact, for instance, would ANNs have on the labor market and the skills employees need? How will ANNs impact how we teach and learn? What effects will ANNs have on our society and values? How will ANNs impact our emotions and social interactions?
- **Security concerns**: ANNs may be subject to misuse or attacks jeopardizing their integrity or functionality. How, for instance, can we stop or identify hostile examples that cause ANNs to

classify, or mis predict things? How can we stop or lessen harmful attempts to sabotage or hijack ANNs? How can the unauthorized or harmful use of ANNs be stopped or controlled?

Research Trends: The field of ANN research is active and dynamic, and it is constantly changing and improving. The following are some current trends in ANN research:

- **Deep learning**: A subset of ML known as deep learning uses deep neural networks (DNNs), which comprise numerous layers of artificial neurons and can learn hierarchical data representations. DNNs have excelled at several tasks, including image recognition, speech synthesis, natural language understanding, and gameplay. CNNs, RNNs, GANs, transformer networks (TNNs), and graph neural networks (GNNs) are some common types of DNNs.
- **Meta learning**: Meta learning (uses neural networks to learn from data. Enhancing the generalization, adaptation, and transferability of neural networks across various tasks or domains is the goal of meta learning. Learning to learn, neural architecture search (NAS), and few-shot learning are some popular meta learning techniques.
- **Neuro-symbolic learning**: A subfield of machine learning that blends symbolic thinking with neural networks. Neuro-symbolic learning strives to improve neural networks' expressiveness, interpretability, and robustness by fusing neural networks with programs, knowledge bases, and logic. Neural logic networks (NLN), neural theorem provers (NTP), and neuro-symbolic concept learners (NSCL) are a few of the well-known techniques for neuro-symbolic learning.

Advances in Technology: ANN technology is constantly developing and improving to assist the creation and implementation of ANN applications and services. Some recent developments in ANN technology include:

- **Hardware**: The computational power and memory required for the training and inference of large-scale neural networks are provided by hardware, a crucial component of ANN technology. Specialized chips that offer excellent performance and efficiency for ANN operations include graphics processing units (GPUs), tensor processing units (TPUs), neuromorphic chips, and quantum chips. These are some of the most recent breakthroughs in hardware.
- **Software**: Software provides the tools and frameworks required for creating and implementing neural networks, another crucial element of ANN technology. Open-source libraries like TensorFlow, PyTorch, Keras, and JAX, which offer high flexibility and usability for ANN construction, are among the most recent advancements in software.
- **Data**: Data is a crucial part of ANN technology since it gives neural networks the knowledge and information they need to be trained and tested. Large-scale data sets with great diversity and quality for ANN learning include ImageNet, Wikipedia2Vec, Common Crawl, and Open AI Codex, among other recent data innovations.

Other Prospects: As they continue to advance and change to meet the demands and expectations of society, ANNs have a promising future. ANNs could go in the following directions in the future:

- **Human-like intelligence**: The long-term objective of ANN research is to develop neural networks capable of carrying out any intellectual job that humans are capable of. Neural networks must possess skills like common sense, creativity, emotion, consciousness, and self-awareness to have intelligence comparable to that of humans. Artificial general intelligence (AGI), artificial superintelligence (ASI), and artificial consciousness (AC) are some of the methods that could be used to develop intelligence similar to that of humans.

- **Brain–computer interfaces**: This cutting-edge use of ANN technology aims to link neural networks with human brains. Interaction and direct communication between humans and machines, as well as between individuals, may be made possible by brain-computer interfaces. Brain–computer interfaces improve cognition, memory, learning, perception, and emotion. The potential drawbacks include moral, societal, and security concerns.
- **Artificial life**: Creating synthetic creatures or ecosystems with lifelike traits is the goal of the futuristic application of ANN technology known as artificial life. Artificial life may facilitate the evolution of new forms, modes, or life processes. It may provide advantages to space exploration, biological engineering, environmental preservation, and scientific research. Artificial life may also present difficulties in ethics, society, and security.

SUMMARY

- A neural network comprises three layers: input, hidden, and output.
- Computing systems called artificial neural networks (ANNs) imitate the form and operation of biological neural networks, such as the brain. Artificial neurons are a group of connected components found in ANNs that process and transfer signals to other neurons. By modifying their weights following a learning algorithm that reduces errors between planned and actual output, ANNs can learn from data
- A feedforward neural network (FNN) as a one-way street. Without any loops or feedback, information moves from the input to the output.
- A convolutional neural network (CNN) is used primarily to comprehend visual data, much like how our brains interpret images. It applies filters or feature detectors to various portions of the image to find patterns and shapes
- A recurrent neural network (RNN) is a memory-equipped network. It can handle text and other sequential data types like time series.
- Long short-term memory (LSTM) network is a form of RNN that excels at identifying long-term dependencies in sequential data.
- A generative adversarial network (GAN) is a unique network where two models, a generator, and a discriminator, are competitively pitted against one another.
- Self-organizing maps (SOMs) provide a low-dimensional representation of a high-dimensional data collection while maintaining the data's topological structure.
- A Boltzmann machine is an ANN that can learn to discover exciting features in data without supervision. Restricted Boltzmann machines (RBMs) can be stacked together to form deep belief networks (DBNs), hierarchical models that can learn multiple levels of abstraction from data.
- A modular neural networks (MNN) consists of multiple modules or subnetworks that perform different tasks or functions. A particular sort of neural network design known as cooperative modular neural networks (CMNNs) consists of numerous modules that cooperate to address a common issue.

- An unsupervised neural network called an autoencoder may learn to encode and decode data. Linear autoencoder is the simplest type and it performs both encoding and decoding using linear transformations.

EXERCISES

Part A (Objective Questions)

1. What is the role of artificial neurons in artificial neural networks (ANNs)?
   a) They determine the color of the input data.
   b) They process and transfer signals to other neurons.
   c) They modify the weights of the connections.
   d) They perform unsupervised learning.
2. What is the purpose of assigning weights to the attributes of fruits in an ANN?
   a) To determine the color of the fruit.
   b) To identify the texture of the fruit.
   c) To compare the significance of each attribute.
   d) To perform dimensionality reduction.
3. What is the process through which an ANN learns from data?
   a) Anomaly detection b) Regression
   c) Training d) Clustering
4. What is the main advantage of ANNs in handling complex and noisy data?
   a) They require less computational resources.
   b) They provide interpretable and explainable results.
   c) They can represent nonlinear and dynamic interactions.
   d) They eliminate the need for training data.
5. Which field would benefit from the use of ANNs in identifying diseases?
   a) Recommender systems b) Natural language processing
   c) Computer vision d) Medical diagnostics
6. What is a drawback of ANNs in terms of their decisions and results?
   a) Lack of computational resources b) Lack of interpretability and explainability
   c) Prone to overfitting and underfitting d) Need for extrapolation from novel circumstances
7. Which type of learning involves identifying patterns in unlabeled data using ANNs?
   a) Supervised learning b) Reinforcement learning
   c) Unsupervised learning d) Transfer learning
8. What is one of the challenges faced by ANNs when dealing with novel or untested circumstances or data?
   a) They require frequent regularization. b) They struggle with dimensionality reduction.
   c) They need help with extrapolation. d) They rely on explicit rules.

9. Which type of artificial neural network is best suited for language processing or picture recognition?
a) Feedforward Network (FNN)
b) Convolutional Neural Network (CNN)
c) Recurrent Neural Network (RNN)
d) Long Short-Term Memory (LSTM) Network

10. Which artificial neural network is specifically designed to handle sequential data like time series or text?
a) Feedforward Network (FNN)
b) Convolutional Neural Network (CNN)
c) Recurrent Neural Network (RNN)
d) Long Short-Term Memory (LSTM) Network

11. Which type of artificial neural network addresses the issue of long-term dependencies in sequential data?
a) Feedforward Network (FNN)
b) Convolutional Neural Network (CNN)
c) Recurrent Neural Network (RNN)
d) Long Short-Term Memory (LSTM) Network

12. Which artificial neural network involves two competing models, one generating artificial data and the other distinguishing between real and fake data?
a) Feedforward Network (FNN)
b) Convolutional Neural Network (CNN)
c) Recurrent Neural Network (RNN)
d) Generative Adversarial Network (GAN)

13. You want to analyze visual data and identify patterns and shapes in an image. Which artificial neural network should you consider using?
a) Feedforward Network (FNN)
b) Convolutional Neural Network (CNN)
c) Recurrent Neural Network (RNN)
d) Long Short-Term Memory (LSTM) Network

14. You need to process and retain relevant information over longer sequences in sequential data. Which artificial neural network is most suitable for this task?
a) Feedforward Network (FNN)
b) Convolutional Neural Network (CNN)
c) Recurrent Neural Network (RNN)
d) Long Short-Term Memory (LSTM) Network

15. You want to create a model for picture recognition or object identification. Which artificial neural network should you choose?
a) Feedforward Network (FNN)
b) Convolutional Neural Network (CNN)
c) Recurrent Neural Network (RNN)
d) Generative Adversarial Network (GAN)

16. You need to generate artificial data that closely resembles real data. Which artificial neural network should you use?
a) Feedforward Network (FNN)
b) Convolutional Neural Network (CNN)
c) Recurrent Neural Network (RNN)
d) Generative Adversarial Network (GAN)

17. Which layer in a feedforward neural network processes the incoming data and computes weighted sums?
a) Input layer
b) Hidden layer
c) Output layer
d) Activation layer

18. What determines the number of neurons in the output layer of a feedforward neural network?
a) Complexity of the problem
b) Number of hidden layers
c) Activation function used
d) Total number of input neurons

19. Which process involves passing the input data through the network's hidden layers to generate an output in a feedforward neural network?
a) Weighted sum computation
b) Forward propagation
c) Activation function application
d) Backpropagation

20. What is the purpose of the activation function in a feedforward neural network?
a) Weighted sum computation
b) Forward propagation
c) Non-linear transformation
d) Loss function optimization

21. How does a feedforward neural network learn to improve its predictions during training?
a) Weighted sum computation
b) Forward propagation
c) Activation function application
d) Weight adjustment through optimization

22. Which type of task requires the output layer of a feedforward neural network to have multiple neurons representing different categories?
a) Regression
b) Classification
c) Image recognition
d) Text processing

23. In a feedforward neural network designed for handwritten digit recognition, what do neurons in the hidden layers extract from the input image?
a) Pixel values
b) Image dimensions
c) Edges, curves, or patterns
d) Handwritten text

24. What is the primary purpose of a feedforward neural network?
a) Pattern detection and prediction
b) Image generation
c) Language translation
d) Reinforcement learning

25. Which layer in a convolutional neural network (CNN) identifies specific patterns or features, such as edges, textures, or forms, in an input image?
a) Convolutional layer
b) Pooling layer
c) Activation layer
d) Fully connected layer

26. What is the purpose of the pooling layer in a convolutional neural network (CNN)?
a) Reducing the dimensionality of feature maps
b) Identifying specific patterns or features
c) Calculating weighted sums of inputs
d) Applying activation functions

27. Which type of layer in a convolutional neural network (CNN) is responsible for calculating weighted sums of inputs and applying activation functions?
a) Convolutional layer
b) Pooling layer
c) Activation layer
d) Fully connected layer

28. What is the primary purpose of training a convolutional neural network (CNN)?
a) Reducing discrepancies between predictions and correct labels
b) Extracting specific patterns or features from input data
c) Decreasing the dimensionality of feature maps
d) Calculating weighted sums of inputs

29. In a CNN designed for image classification, which layers are responsible for identifying various aspects of the image, such as edges, textures, or forms?
a) Convolutional layers
b) Pooling layers
c) Activation layers
d) Fully connected layers

30. What allows convolutional neural networks (CNNs) to generalize their learning from a lot of data to fresh and unstudied material?
a) Kernels
b) Pooling layers
c) Fully connected layers
d) Feature detectors

31. Which part of the brain's visual cortex inspires the design and operation of convolutional neural networks (CNNs)?
a) Neurons
b) Kernels
c) Feature detectors
d) Pooling layers

32. What is the purpose of the feature detectors or filters in a convolutional neural network (CNN)?
a) Calculating weighted sums of inputs
b) Identifying specific patterns or features in an input image
c) Reducing the dimensionality of feature maps
d) Applying activation functions

33. Which operation in a convolutional neural network (CNN) is responsible for extracting hierarchical features from structured data like text, audio, or images?
a) Pooling
b) Activation
c) Convolution
d) Dropout

34. What is the purpose of the optimization algorithm during the training of a convolutional neural network (CNN)?
a) Adjusting layer weights based on image labels
b) Calculating the discrepancy between predicted and actual labels
c) Minimizing the loss function
d) Running the images through the model's layers

35. Which step is NOT part of the training process for a convolutional neural network (CNN)?
a) Setting the layer weights
b) Rearranging and dividing the data set
c) Forward pass through the model's layers
d) Evaluating model performance using metrics

36. Which hyperparameters of a convolutional neural network (CNN) can be adjusted using the validation set?
a) Learning rate and batch size
b) Batch size and number of epochs
c) Learning rate and number of epochs
d) Learning rate, batch size, and number of epochs

37. What is one of the challenges or difficulties associated with convolutional neural networks (CNNs)?
a) Scalability
b) Hierarchical feature extraction
c) Loss function calculation
d) Image classification

38. Which metric can be used to assess the performance of a convolutional neural network (CNN)?
a) Accuracy
b) Learning rate
c) Dropout
d) Chain rule

39. What is the purpose of the dropout operation in a convolutional neural network (CNN)?
a) Adjusting layer weights based on image labels
b) Calculating the discrepancy between predicted and actual labels
c) Minimizing the loss function
d) Preventing overfitting by randomly deactivating neurons

40. What is the role of the validation set in training a convolutional neural network (CNN)?
a) Setting the layer weights
b) Calculating the discrepancy between predicted and actual labels
c) Adjusting hyperparameters
d) Running the images through the model's layers

41. In transfer learning with convolutional neural networks (CNNs), what is the primary concept?
a) Training a new model from scratch
b) Using a pre-trained CNN model as a feature extractor or fine-tuner
c) Extracting features from images
d) Utilizing existing knowledge for object detection

42. When is feature extraction a suitable application of transfer learning in CNNs?
a) When the new task is similar to the previous task
b) When the new task has a short data set
c) When a new classifier is trained on top of the pre-trained CNN model
d) When the pre-trained CNN model is updated during training

43. What is fine-tuning in transfer learning with CNNs?
a) Training a new model from scratch
b) Updating some or all of the parameters of the pre-trained CNN model during training
c) Extracting features from images
d) Using a pre-trained CNN model as a fixed feature extractor

44. Which application of transfer learning in CNNs involves adapting a pre-trained model for object identification to perform instance segmentation?
a) Face recognition
b) Style transfer
c) Object detection
d) Image classification

45. Which successful application of transfer learning in CNNs focuses on mapping face images to a condensed Euclidean space for face similarity?
a) Style Transfer
b) FaceNet
c) Mask R-CNN
d) Image classification

46. What does the Style Transfer method in transfer learning with CNNs aim to achieve?
a) Categorizing dog photographs based on a sizable data set
b) Extracting features from images for classification

c) Creating an image that combines content and style features from different images
d) Enhancing object identification and segmentation in images

47. Which application of transfer learning in CNNs involves enhancing an object identification model with a new branch for segmentation mask prediction?
a) Face recognition b) Style transfer
c) Object detection d) Image classification

48. What is the advantage of using a pre-trained CNN model in transfer learning?
a) Avoiding the need to train a new model from scratch
b) Extracting advanced features from images
c) Reducing the cost and time required for training
d) Allowing the model to generalize well to new data

49. In which field can CNNs be used to analyze diagnostic test images and identify anomalies or diseases?
a) Natural language processing b) Biomedical imaging
c) Computer vision d) Audio processing

50. Which CNN application involves using feature representations learned from multiple layers to transfer the style of one image to another?
a) Face recognition b) Image captioning
c) Object detection d) Style transfer

51. CNNs can be used to produce natural language descriptions of images by combining visual and linguistic data. In which application is this useful?
a) Object detection b) Medical diagnosis
c) Image captioning d) Face recognition

52. Which field can benefit from CNNs' ability to recognize faces in images or videos and compare them to a database of recognized individuals?
a) Authentication systems b) Robotics
c) Autonomous driving d) Social networking

53. What can CNNs do in the field of computer vision by identifying and categorizing objects in images or videos?
a) Encrypt data b) Generate captions
c) Perform speech recognition d) Enable object detection

54. In which field can CNNs analyze audio data and process it effectively?
a) Computer vision b) Natural language processing
c) Biomedical imaging d) Audio processing

55. CNNs' ability to analyze images from diagnostic tests like X-rays and MRIs can be applied to which field?
a) Education b) Robotics
c) Medical diagnosis d) Security

56. Which aspect makes CNNs powerful and adaptable tools in handling complex and diverse data?
   a) Ability to revolutionize numerous fields b) Capability to generate artistic outputs
   c) Capacity to analyze linguistic data d) Ability to manage complex and varied data

57. Which type of neural network is suitable for processing sequential data like speech, video, and natural language?
   a) Convolutional Neural Networks (CNNs)
   b) Recurrent Neural Networks (RNNs)
   c) Deep Neural Networks (DNNs)
   d) Feedforward Neural Networks (FNNs)

58. What is the fundamental characteristic of an RNN that enables it to retain memory or context about prior information in a sequence?
   a) Feedback connections b) Hidden state
   c) Gated units d) Long short-term memory (LSTM)

59. Which type of units in RNNs can regulate the information flow and selectively remember or forget relevant knowledge?
   a) Long short-term memory (LSTM) b) Gated recurrent units (GRU)
   c) Recurrent units d) Attention mechanisms

60. What is the common issue faced by RNNs during training, where the gradients become very small or very large during backpropagation?
   a) Overfitting b) Underfitting
   c) Vanishing gradients d) Exploding gradients

61. Which type of RNN units can address the issue of vanishing or exploding gradients?
   a) Gated recurrent units (GRU) b) Long short-term memory (LSTM)
   c) Convolutional Neural Networks (CNNs)d) Attention mechanisms

62. Which applications can benefit from the use of RNNs?
   a) Sentiment analysis b) Object detection
   c) Face recognition d) Style transfer

63. What is the primary difference between RNNs and feedforward neural networks?
   a) RNNs can handle variable-length inputs and outputs, while feedforward neural networks have fixed input and output sizes.
   b) RNNs use convolutional layers, while feedforward neural networks use recurrent layers.
   c) RNNs can process images, while feedforward neural networks are limited to text data.
   d) RNNs are suitable for classification tasks, while feedforward neural networks are used for regression tasks.

64. Which type of units in RNNs enable the network to focus on relevant information when completing a task, as shown in the example of recalling the word "India" in a sentence?
   a) Attention mechanisms b) Long short-term memory (LSTM)
   c) Gated recurrent units (GRU) d) Recurrent units

65. Which type of RNN is specifically designed to address the disappearing and ballooning gradient issues?

a) Gated recurrent units (GRU)
b) Long Short-Term Memory (LSTM)
c) Feedback recurrent neural networks
d) Bidirectional recurrent neural networks

66. What is the purpose of the forget gate in LSTM networks?

a) Determines what data should be output from the cell
b) Determines what new data should be added to the cell
c) Determines what outdated data should be removed from the cell
d) Determines the hidden state encoding the previous inputs

67. Which type of data can LSTM networks effectively learn intricate and persistent patterns from?

a) Images
b) Text documents
c) Tabular data
d) Sequential data

68. What determines the data that should be output from the memory cell in LSTM networks?

a) Input gate
b) Forget gate
c) Output gate
d) Memory cell

69. Which gates in LSTM networks regulate the information flow in and out of the memory cell?

a) Input gate, forget gate, and output gate
b) Input gate, output gate, and hidden gate
c) Input gate, reset gate, and output gate
d) Forget gate, output gate, and hidden gate

70. Which type of RNN is specifically designed to address the issues of disappearing and ballooning gradients?

a) Feedback recurrent neural networks
b) Bidirectional recurrent neural networks
c) Gated recurrent units (GRU)
d) Long Short-Term Memory (LSTM)

71. What is the primary function of the memory cell in LSTM networks?

a) Determine the hidden state encoding the previous inputs
b) Control the information flow through the gates
c) Store and update information over time
d) Output the final prediction of the network

72. Which gates in LSTM networks determine what new data should be added and removed from the memory cell?

a) Input gate and forget gate
b) Input gate and output gate
c) Forget gate and output gate
d) Input gate and memory cell

73. Which neural network architectures are commonly combined with RNNs to leverage their respective advantages?

a) Convolutional Neural Networks (CNNs) and transformers
b) Gated Recurrent Units (GRUs) and transformers
c) Long Short-Term Memory (LSTM) networks and transformers
d) Elman networks and transformers

74. Which RNN architecture has three sets of weights: recurrent weights, output weights, and input weights?

a) Elman network
b) Long Short-Term Memory (LSTM) network
c) Gated Recurrent Unit (GRU)
d) Bidirectional RNN

75. What is one of the key challenges with traditional RNNs in learning long-term relationships?
a) Difficulty in processing sequential data
b) Inability to recognize context information
c) Vanishing or exploding gradient problem
d) Limited memory capacity

76. Which RNN variant introduces mechanisms such as gates to regulate the information flow and gradients through time?
a) Long Short-Term Memory (LSTM) networks
b) Gated Recurrent Units (GRUs)
c) Bidirectional RNNs (BRNNs)
d) Transformer networks

77. Which type of RNN architecture allows information to flow in both forward and backward directions?
a) Elman network
b) Long Short-Term Memory (LSTM) network
c) Gated Recurrent Unit (GRU)
d) Bidirectional RNN

78. What is one potential direction for future RNN research ?
a) Expanding RNNs' scalability and effectiveness
b) Creating new architectures for image captioning
c) Improving interpretability of CNNs
d) Integrating human feedback in CNN training

79. Which task can RNNs effectively perform in the field of natural language processing?
a) Image classification
b) Sentiment analysis
c) Face recognition
d) Speech synthesis

80. What makes RNNs powerful and adaptable deep learning technologies?
a) Their ability to process sequential data
b) Their compatibility with transformers
c) Their memory mechanism for dynamic processes
d) Their interpretability and explainability

81. What are the two components of a Generative Adversarial Network (GAN)?
a) Classifier and encoder
b) Discriminator and generator
c) Encoder and generator
d) Discriminator and classifier

82. Which of the following is NOT a field where GANs have various applications?
a) Computer vision
b) Natural language processing
c) Speech recognition
d) Audio synthesis

83. What is one of the challenges faced by GANs during training, where the generator or the discriminator stops learning?

a) Mode collapse
b) Gradient vanishing
c) Instability
d) Overfitting

84. What is the purpose of the loss function in GAN training?
a) To measure the quality and diversity of the generated data
b) To balance the complexity and simplicity of the model
c) To evaluate the performance of the discriminator and generator
d) To regulate the trade-off between fooling the discriminator and distinguishing real data

85. What is one technique used to prevent overfitting or underfitting in GAN training?
a) Regularization
b) Mode collapse
c) Gradient vanishing
d) Evaluation metrics

86. Which term refers to the situation where the generator produces limited diversity in GANs?
a) Mode collapse
b) Gradient vanishing
c) Instability
d) Overfitting

87. Why is evaluating GANs challenging?
a) Lack of clear definition for sound generation
b) Limited diversity in generated data
c) Difficulty in training the discriminator and generator
d) Inability to measure the loss function

88. What is the main objective of the generator in GAN training?
a) To classify the data correctly
b) To deceive the discriminator
c) To distinguish between real and fake data
d) To improve the generalization performance

89. Which method increases the amount and diversity of data in GAN training by applying transformations or perturbations to existing data?
a) Transfer learning
b) Data augmentation
c) Self-supervised learning
d) Unsupervised learning

90. Which method in GAN training involves learning good representations from unlabeled data by solving additional tasks that do not require human annotations?
a) Transfer learning
b) Data augmentation
c) Self-supervised learning
d) Unsupervised learning

91. What does transfer learning leverage in GAN training to improve performance on a smaller-scale data set?
a) Human annotations
b) Unlabeled data
c) Large-scale data set
d) Synthetic data

92. Which method in GAN training can reduce overfitting and improve the diversity of generated data?
a) Transfer learning
b) Data augmentation
c) Self-supervised learning
d) Unsupervised learning

93. Which method in GAN training focuses on solving additional tasks that do not require human annotations?
a) Transfer learning
b) Data augmentation
c) Self-supervised learning
d) Unsupervised learning

94. Which method in GAN training involves leveraging knowledge from a pre-trained model to improve performance on a smaller-scale data set?
a) Transfer learning
b) Data augmentation
c) Self-supervised learning
d) Unsupervised learning

95. What is the main purpose of data augmentation in GAN training?
a) To increase the amount and diversity of data
b) To learn good representations from unlabeled data
c) To improve the quality and realism of the generated data
d) To extract meaningful features from limited data

96. Which method in GAN training can extract meaningful features from limited data and enhance the quality and realism of the generated data?
a) Transfer learning
b) Data augmentation
c) Self-supervised learning
d) Unsupervised learning

97. Which GAN model can generate high-quality images of human faces with various styles and characteristics, including altering age, gender, expression, and hair color?
a) StyleGAN
b) CycleGAN
c) 3D-GAN
d) Spectral normalization

98. What is the term used to describe the situation when the generator in GAN training focuses on a limited range of outputs or the same output for various inputs?
a) Mode collapse
b) Non-convergence
c) 3-D perspective
d) Gradient penalty

99. Which GAN model is specifically designed to perform domain-to-domain mappings without paired data?
a) StyleGAN
b) CycleGAN
c) 3D-GAN
d) Adam optimizer

100. What regularization method adds a penalty term to the GAN objective function based on the gradient norm of the discriminator?
a) Wasserstein loss
b) Unrolled GANs
c) Gradient penalty
d) Spectral normalization

101. Which GAN model uses 3-D voxel grids instead of 2-D pixel grids to generate 3-D shapes directly from noise vectors?
a) StyleGAN
b) CycleGAN
c) 3D-GAN
d) Adam optimizer

102. Which GAN model uses style transfer approaches to control various aspects of image production, including shape, texture, color, and stance?

a) StyleGAN
b) CycleGAN
c) 3D-GAN
d) Spectral normalization

103. Which regularization method normalizes the spectral norm of each layer's weight matrix in the discriminator to maintain gradient stability in GAN training?
a) Wasserstein loss
b) Unrolled GANs
c) Spectral normalization
d) Adam optimizer

104. Which GAN model can translate images from different perspectives, such as front view to side view or aerial view to street view?
a) StyleGAN
b) CycleGAN
c) 3D-GAN
d) Adam optimizer

105. What is the primary purpose of self-organizing maps (SOMs) in unsupervised machine learning?
a) Reduce the dimensionality of high-dimensional data
b) Visualize complex data sets
c) Compress large data sets
d) Identify anomalies in the data

106. Which method in self-organizing maps (SOMs) utilizes hues or tones to represent the distance between adjacent nodes on a map?
a) U-matrix
b) Component planes
c) Heat map
d) Competitive learning

107. In self-organizing maps (SOMs), which application involves transforming complex, high-dimensional data sets into a lower-dimensional space to aid in exploration and understanding?
a) Data visualization
b) Data compression
c) Finding anomalies
d) Competitive learning

108. Which visualization technique in self-organizing maps (SOMs) uses various colors or tints to indicate the frequency of each node being chosen as the winner node for input data points?
a) U-matrix
b) Component planes
c) Heat map
d) Competitive learning

109. What is the initial state of the nodes in a self-organizing map (SOM) before the iterative updating process begins?
a) Randomly initialized
b) Nearest to the input data points
c) Grouped into clusters
d) Converged to stable places

110. Which application of self-organizing maps (SOMs) involves partitioning large data sets into fewer nodes to represent prototypes or cluster centroids?
a) Data visualization
b) Data compression
c) Finding anomalies
d) Competitive learning

111. Which method in self-organizing maps (SOMs) visualizes the weight vectors and displays the values of each dimension in distinct maps using various hues or tones?
a) U-matrix
b) Component planes
c) Heat map
d) Competitive learning

112. How do self-organizing maps (SOMs) update the nodes during the iterative process?
   a) Based on a competitive learning method
   b) By calculating the separation from the nearest node
   c) By decreasing the neighborhood size and learning rate
   d) By converging to stable places

113. Which type of neural network can learn to discover features in data without supervision?
   a) Convolutional Neural Networks (CNNs)
   b) Recurrent Neural Networks (RNNs)
   c) Boltzmann Machines (BMs)
   d) Autoencoders

114. What is the main advantage of Restricted Boltzmann Machines (RBMs) compared to Boltzmann Machines (BMs)?
   a) RBMs are faster to train than BMs.
   b) RBMs can handle continuous data, while BMs cannot.
   c) RBMs have more hidden layers than BMs.
   d) RBMs can generate data that resembles the training data better than BMs.

115. Which type of neural network can be formed by stacking Restricted Boltzmann Machines (RBMs) together?
   a) Convolutional Neural Networks (CNNs)
   b) Recurrent Neural Networks (RNNs)
   c) Boltzmann Machines (BMs)
   d) Deep Belief Networks (DBNs)

116. What is the purpose of pre-training in Deep Belief Networks (DBNs)?
   a) To adjust the weights of each RBM in the network
   b) To restrict the connections between nodes in each RBM
   c) To fine-tune the entire DBN using supervised learning
   d) To transform the input data into a higher-level representation

117. Which type of data can Deep Belief Networks (DBNs) handle?
   a) Only continuous data
   b) Only categorical data
   c) Only temporal data
   d) Multiple data types, such as continuous, categorical, or temporal data

118. What is the main purpose of fine-tuning in Deep Belief Networks (DBNs)?
   a) To adjust the weights of each RBM in the network
   b) To restrict the connections between nodes in each RBM
   c) To refine a classification or regression task
   d) To transform the input data into a higher-level representation

119. Which application can benefit from Deep Belief Networks (DBNs)?
   a) Speech recognition
   b) Image compression
   c) Sentiment analysis
   d) Robotics control

120. What is the role of each layer in a Deep Belief Network (DBN)?
  a) Each layer transforms the input data into a higher-level representation.
  b) Each layer adjusts the weights of the RBMs in the network.
  c) Each layer restricts the connections between nodes in the RBMs.
  d) Each layer generates data that resembles the training data.

121. Which type of neural network is designed to address a complex problem by decomposing it into simpler subproblems that specialized modules can solve?
  a) Convolutional Neural Networks (CNNs)
  b) Recurrent Neural Networks (RNNs)
  c) Modular Neural Networks (MNNs)
  d) Generative Adversarial Networks (GANs)

122. What is the advantage of using Modular Neural Networks (MNNs) in terms of training and inference?
  a) MNNs require less memory compared to conventional neural networks.
  b) MNNs allow independent or parallel training and updating of modules.
  c) MNNs have superior generalization performance compared to other networks.
  d) MNNs eliminate the need for sharing weights or representations between modules.

123. Which type of Modular Neural Network (MNN) arranges modules in a hierarchical structure, where lower-level modules process raw input data and higher-level modules extract high-level features or make predictions?
  a) Hierarchical Modular Neural Networks (HMNNs)
  b) Competitive Modular Neural Networks (CPMNNs)
  c) Recurrent Neural Networks (RNNs)
  d) Generative Adversarial Networks (GANs)

124. Which type of Modular Neural Network (MNN) consists of multiple modules that cooperate and communicate to address a common problem?
  a) Hierarchical Modular Neural Networks (HMNNs)
  b) Competitive Modular Neural Networks (CPMNNs)
  c) Recurrent Neural Networks (RNNs)
  d) Generative Adversarial Networks (GANs)

125. Which type of neural network can be considered an example of Cooperative Modular Neural Networks (CMNNs)?
  a) Convolutional Neural Networks (CNNs)b) Recurrent Neural Networks (RNNs)
  c) Modular Neural Networks (MNNs) d) Generative Adversarial Networks (GANs)

126. Which type of Modular Neural Network (MNN) facilitates transferring and reusing knowledge across different domains or tasks?
  a) Hierarchical Modular Neural Networks (HMNNs)
  b) Competitive Modular Neural Networks (CPMNNs)
  c) Recurrent Neural Networks (RNNs)
  d) Modular Neural Networks (MNNs)

127. Which type of neural network can be considered an example of Competitive Modular Neural Networks (CPMNNs)?
   a) Convolutional Neural Networks (CNNs)
   b) Recurrent Neural Networks (RNNs)
   c) Modular Neural Networks (MNNs)
   d) Generative Adversarial Networks (GANs)

128. Which type of neural network can be seen as an example of Hierarchical Modular Neural Networks (HMNNs)?
   a) Convolutional Neural Networks (CNNs)
   b) Recurrent Neural Networks (RNNs)
   c) Modular Neural Networks (MNNs)
   d) Generative Adversarial Networks (GANs)

129. Which technique can be used to prevent overfitting in a neural network by randomly removing specific network units during training?
   a) Weight decay
   b) Batch normalization
   c) Dropout
   d) Early stopping

130. What is one of the challenges associated with the backpropagation technique in training neural networks?
   a) Selecting the correct learning rate
   b) Handling vanishing and exploding gradients
   c) Preventing underfitting
   d) Avoiding local minima

131. Which regularization technique helps in preventing overfitting by normalizing the inputs to each layer, resulting in a zero mean and unit variance?
   a) Weight decay
   b) Batch normalization
   c) Dropout
   d) Early stopping

132. Which technique in architecture search methods involves testing every possible combination of predefined hyperparameters to find the optimum architecture?
   a) Grid search
   b) Random search
   c) Evolutionary algorithms
   d) Reinforcement learning

133. What is the purpose of early stopping in training a neural network?
   a) Prevent overfitting
   b) Avoid local minima
   c) Handle exploding gradients
   d) Speed up convergence

134. Which technique can be used to address the trade-off between complexity and performance in neural network design by adding a penalty term to limit excessive increases in network weights?
   a) Dropout
   b) Weight decay
   c) Batch normalization
   d) Data augmentation

135. Which technique in architecture search methods uses evolutionary principles like mutation, crossover, and selection to iteratively create and evaluate a population of structures?
   a) Grid search
   b) Random search
   c) Evolutionary algorithms
   d) Reinforcement learning

136. Which technique can help a neural network enhance its performance by making minor adjustments to the parameters moving in the opposite direction of the gradients?

a) Weight decay
b) Batch normalization
c) Dropout
d) Backpropagation

137. Which type of autoencoder introduces noise to the input data during training to encourage the network to learn the underlying structure?

a) Linear autoencoder
b) De-noising autoencoder
c) Sparse autoencoder
d) Variational autoencoder

138. Which type of autoencoder places a sparsity constraint on the latent representation to learn independent, sparse features?

a) Linear autoencoder
b) De-noising autoencoder
c) Sparse autoencoder
d) Variational autoencoder

139. Which type of autoencoder models the latent representation as a stochastic distribution instead of a deterministic vector?

a) Linear autoencoder
b) De-noising autoencoder
c) Sparse autoencoder
d) Variational autoencoder

140. Which type of autoencoder is comparable to principal component analysis (PCA) and uses linear transformations for encoding and decoding?

a) Linear autoencoder
b) De-noising autoencoder
c) Sparse autoencoder
d) Variational autoencoder

141. Which type of autoencoder employs an adversarial training method with an encoder-decoder network and a discriminator network?

a) Linear autoencoder
b) De-noising autoencoder
c) Sparse autoencoder
d) Adversarial autoencoder

142. Which type of autoencoder is focused on learning a concise and meaningful representation of the data that preserves its essential characteristics?

a) Linear autoencoder
b) De-noising autoencoder
c) Sparse autoencoder
d) All of the above

143. Which type of autoencoder is particularly suitable for learning independent, sparse features?

a) Linear autoencoder
b) De-noising autoencoder
c) Sparse autoencoder
d) Adversarial autoencoder

144. Which type of autoencoder attempts to create an immediate reconstruction of the input data using a latent representation?

a) Linear autoencoder
b) De-noising autoencoder
c) Sparse autoencoder
d) Variational autoencoder

145. Which industry can benefit from using autoencoders for face identification, face compression, and style transfer?

a) Healthcare
b) Finance
c) Retail
d) Image processing

146. Which task in natural language processing can be accomplished using autoencoders?
a) Sentiment analysis b) Data encryption
c) Stock prediction d) Fraud detection

147. In which domain can autoencoders help enhance, compress, recognize, synthesize, and convert speech?
a) Computer vision b) Speech processing
c) Robotics d) Data analysis

148. Which problem can autoencoders be applied to in recommender systems?
a) Face recognition b) Sentiment analysis
c) Anomaly detection d) Cold-start problems

149. Which issue can be mitigated by using regularization strategies like dropout, weight decay, or early stopping?
a) Mode collapse b) Overfitting
c) Underfitting d) Interpretability

150. What can be a potential solution to address the problem of underfitting in autoencoders?
a) Utilizing adversarial approaches b) Adding penalties to the latent space
c) Increasing network depth or size d) Visualizing the latent space

151. Which problem in autoencoders can be mitigated by adopting sparse or disentangled representations?
a) Mode collapse b) Overfitting
c) Underfitting d) Interpretability

152. Which industry can benefit from using autoencoders for spotting anomalies such as outliers, frauds, intrusions, errors, and illnesses?
a) Manufacturing b) Entertainment
c) Hospitality d) Anomaly detection

153. Which type of artificial neural network (ANN) is specifically designed to process image input and extract hierarchical features?
a) Feedforward neural networks (FNNs) b) Convolutional neural networks (CNNs)
c) Recurrent neural networks (RNNs) d) Long short-term memory networks (LSTMs)

154. Which step in picture recognition with ANNs involves labeling the image according to its characteristics?
a) Image preprocessing b) Feature extraction
c) Classification d) Evaluation

155. Which type of ANN is capable of processing sequential data and capturing temporal dependencies?
a) Feedforward neural networks (FNNs) b) Convolutional neural networks (CNNs)
c) Recurrent neural networks (RNNs) d) Long short-term memory networks (LSTMs)

156. Which step in picture recognition with ANNs involves gauging the performance of the ANN using validation or test sets?

a) Image preprocessing
b) Feature extraction
c) Classification
d) Evaluation

157. Which advantage of utilizing ANNs for image analysis and recognition states that they require less preparation for handling complex and high-dimensional data?
a) They can learn by utilizing unsupervised or semi-supervised learning techniques from significant amounts of poorly or unlabeled data.
b) They can perform at an advanced level on various benchmarks and outperform human accuracy in some activities.
c) They require less memory/processing power to run and train.
d) Their decisions and results are not interpretable or explicable.

158. Which disadvantage of employing ANNs for picture analysis and recognition states that they are susceptible to adversarial attacks?
a) They need much memory/processing power to run and train.
b) If the data needs to be more sufficient and representative, they are vulnerable to overfitting and underfitting.
c) They are susceptible to adversarial attacks; wherein malicious inputs are used to deceive or manipulate them.
d) Their decisions and results are not interpretable or explicable.

159. Which advantage of utilizing ANNs for image analysis and recognition states that they can perform at an advanced level on various benchmarks and outperform human accuracy in some activities?
a) They require less preparation for handling complex and high-dimensional data.
b) They can learn by utilizing unsupervised or semi-supervised learning techniques from significant amounts of poorly or unlabeled data.
c) They can perform at an advanced level on various benchmarks and outperform human accuracy in some activities.
d) They are susceptible to adversarial attacks; wherein malicious inputs are used to deceive or manipulate them.

160. Which type of ANN is limited in capturing spatial and temporal connections in data but can learn nonlinear mappings between inputs and outputs?
a) Feedforward neural networks (FNNs)
b) Convolutional neural networks (CNNs)
c) Recurrent neural networks (RNNs)
d) Long short-term memory networks (LSTMs)

161. Which industry can benefit from automated decision-making (ADM) utilizing artificial neural networks (ANNs) to achieve scalability, precision, consistency, and speed?
a) Agriculture
b) Entertainment
c) Finance
d) Education

162. Which benefit of using ANNs for automated decision-making (ADM) allows them to handle issues involving ambiguity, unpredictability, and uncertainty without explicit feature engineering?
a) Handling high-dimensional data
b) Versatility and scalability
c) Adaptability to changing conditions
d) Discovering complex patterns

163. Which drawback of employing ANNs for automated decision-making (ADM) refers to their lack of transparency and interpretability?

a) Biases and mistakes
b) Potential for adversarial attacks
c) Need for precise calibration
d) Lack of explainability

164. Which activity is an example of automated decision-making (ADM) that utilizes artificial neural networks (ANNs)?

a) Autonomous vehicle navigation
b) News article writing
c) Crop irrigation scheduling
d) Social media sharing

165. Which trait is shared by artificial neural networks (ANNs) and automated decision-making (ADM)?

a) Biased
b) Data-driven
c) Complex
d) Opaque

166. Which drawback of employing ANNs for automated decision-making (ADM) refers to the potential biases and flaws in the data that can result in unfair and erroneous outcomes?

a) Biases and mistakes
b) Prone to errors
c) Need to be more precise
d) Moral implications

167. Which example demonstrates the use of automated decision-making (ADM) based on artificial neural networks (ANNs) in providing voice-based services?

a) Google's DeepMind AlphaGo
b) IBM's Watson
c) Facebook's News Feed
d) Amazon's Alexa

168. Which benefit of using ANNs for automated decision-making (ADM) allows them to adapt to changing and dynamic conditions by updating and training with fresh data?

a) Handling high-dimensional data
b) Versatility and scalability
c) Adaptability to changing conditions
d) Discovering complex patterns

169. Which industry can benefit from using artificial neural networks (ANNs) for time series analysis to predict stock prices, currency exchange rates, and inflation rates?

a) Agriculture
b) Healthcare
c) Finance
d) Education

170. What advantage do artificial neural networks (ANNs) offer for time series analysis in terms of handling complex interactions between variables in the data?

a) Ability to deal with missing or noisy data
b) Capability to include various sources of information
c) Nonlinear modeling of complex interactions
d) Scalability and efficiency in training and evaluation

171. Which drawback is associated with using artificial neural networks (ANNs) for time series analysis due to their "black-box" nature?

a) Overfitting or underfitting issues
b) Difficulty in understanding or analyzing internal logic
c) Scalability and efficiency limitations
d) Inability to handle missing or noisy data

172. What advantage does using artificial neural networks (ANNs) offer for time series analysis in terms of handling missing or noisy data?
  a) Nonlinear modeling of complex interactions
  b) Scalability and efficiency in training and evaluation
  c) Ability to include various sources of information
  d) Dealing with missing or noisy data

173. Which industry can benefit from using artificial neural networks (ANNs) for time series analysis to classify speech signals, electroencephalograms, and electrocardiograms?
  a) Agriculture
  b) Healthcare
  c) Manufacturing
  d) Retail

174. Which drawback is associated with using artificial neural networks (ANNs) for time series analysis due to overfitting or underfitting issues?
  a) Difficulty in understanding or analyzing internal logic
  b) Inability to handle missing or noisy data
  c) Scalability and efficiency limitations
  d) Overfitting or underfitting issues

Part B (Short Answer Questions)

1. Define artificial neural networks.
2. What is a feedforward network (FNN)?
3. Define convolutional neural network (CNN).
4. Define recurrent neural network (RNN).
5. Define the long short-term memory (LSTM) network.
6. Define generative adversarial network (GAN).
7. What is the convolutional layer in convolution neural network (CNN)?
8. What is the pooling layer in convolution neural network (CNN)?
9. What is sigmoid?
10. Explain the tanh function.
11. Explain ReLU.
12. How is transfer learning useful in CNN?
13. What is a recurrent neural network (RNN)?
14. How are CNN and RNN different?
15. What is a generative adversarial network?
16. What is a self-organizing map (SOM)?
17. Define the Boltzmann machine.
18. Define modular neural networks (MNNs).
19. What is a hierarchical modular neural network (HMNN)?
20. What is a cooperative modular neural network (CMNN)?
21. What is a competitive modular neural network (CPMNN)?
22. What is a sparse autoencoder?
23. Define variational autoencoder.
24. Define adversarial autoencoder.
25. What is ADM?

Part C (Essay Questions)

1. Explain the what and why of artificial neural networks with examples.
2. What are the types of artificial neural networks?
3. Explain feedforward network (FNN) in detail.
4. Explain convolutional neural network (CNN) in detail.

5. Write an essay on training convolutional neural networks (CNN).
6. Explain transfer learning in CNN.
7. Explain various applications of convolutional neural networks.
8. Explain in detail how RNN works.
9. Explain long short-term memory networks in detail.
10. What are the applications of recurrent neural networks?
11. What are the challenges of recurrent neural networks?
12. Explain generative adversarial networks and how to train them.
13. What are the methods to improve GAN training?
14. What are the applications and challenges of generative adversarial networks? How can we overcome the challenges?
15. Write an essay on self-organizing maps (SOMs).
16. Write an essay on Boltzmann machines and how we can construct a deep belief network (DBN).
17. Explain modular neural networks (MNN) in detail with its categories.
18. Write an essay on training neural networks with backpropagation.
19. Explain autoencoder and its types.
20. What are the applications of autoencoders and its challenges?
21. What are the reinforcement learning (RL) related challenges with neural networks (NN)?
22. How can artificial neural networks be used for image recognition?
23. How can artificial neural networks be used for natural language processing?
24. How can artificial neural networks be used for automated decision making (ADM)?
25. How can artificial neural networks be used for time series analysis?
26. How can artificial neural networks be used for cybersecurity?
27. How can artificial neural networks be used for predictive analytics?
28. Explain artificial neural networks' effects on society.
29. Explain various research trends in artificial neural networks.
30. Explain artificial neural network technology advancements.
31. Explain various prospects for artificial neural networks in the future.

ANSWER KEY

Part A

1. (b)	2. (c)	3. (c)	4. (c)	5. (d)	6. (b)	7. (c)	8. (c)
9. (b)	10. (c)	11. (d)	12. (d)	13. (b)	14. (d)	15. (b)	16. (d)
17. (b)	18. (a)	19. (b)	20. (c)	21. (d)	22. (b)	23. (c)	24. (a)
25. (a)	26. (a)	27. (d)	28. (a)	29. (a)	30. (a)	31. (a)	32. (b)
33. (c)	34. (c)	35. (d)	36. (a)	37. (a)	38. (a)	39. (d)	40. (c)
41. (b)	42. (b)	43. (b)	44. (c)	45. (b)	46. (c)	47. (c)	48. (a)
49. (b)	50. (d)	51. (c)	52. (d)	53. (d)	54. (d)	55. (c)	56. (d)
57. (b)	58. (b)	59. (b)	60. (c)	61. (a)	62. (a)	63. (a)	64. (a)
65. (b)	66. (c)	67. (d)	68. (c)	69. (a)	70. (d)	71. (c)	72. (a)
73. (a)	74. (a)	75. (c)	76. (a)	77. (d)	78. (a)	79. (b)	80. (c)

81. (b)	**82.** (c)	**83.** (b)	**84.** (d)	**85.** (a)	**86.** (a)	**87.** (a)	**88.** (b)
89. (b)	**90.** (c)	**91.** (c)	**92.** (b)	**93.** (c)	**94.** (a)	**95.** (a)	**96.** (c)
97. (a)	**98.** (a)	**99.** (b)	**100.** (c)	**101.** (c)	**102.** (a)	**103.** (c)	**104.** (b)
105. (a)	**106.** (a)	**107.** (a)	**108.** (c)	**109.** (a)	**110.** (b)	**111.** (b)	**112.** (a)
113. (c)	**114.** (b)	**115.** (d)	**116.** (a)	**117.** (d)	**118.** (c)	**119.** (a)	**120.** (a)
121. (c)	**122.** (b)	**123.** (a)	**124.** (b)	**125.** (b)	**126.** (d)	**127.** (d)	**128.** (a)
129. (c)	**130.** (b)	**131.** (b)	**132.** (a)	**133.** (a)	**134.** (b)	**135.** (c)	**136.** (d)
137. (b)	**138.** (c)	**139.** (d)	**140.** (a)	**141.** (d)	**142.** (d)	**143.** (c)	**144.** (a)
145. (d)	**146.** (a)	**147.** (b)	**148.** (d)	**149.** (b)	**150.** (c)	**151.** (d)	**152.** (d)
153. (b)	**154.** (c)	**155.** (c)	**156.** (d)	**157.** (a)	**158.** (c)	**159.** (c)	**160.** (a)
161. (c)	**162.** (d)	**163.** (d)	**164.** (a)	**165.** (b)	**166.** (a)	**167.** (d)	**168.** (c)
169. (c)	**170.** (c)	**171.** (b)	**172.** (d)	**173.** (b)	**174.** (d)		

11 Trends in Machine Learning

Learning Objectives

At the end of this chapter, you will be able to:

- Explain the foundational concepts of reinforcement learning, including both model-based and model-free approaches
- Explain the principles of Q-learning and policy search in the context of machine learning
- Describe the Markov decision process and its significance in decision-making algorithms
- Apply linear quadratic regulation (LQR) and linear quadratic Gaussian (LQG) methods to control systems
- Utilize the Bellman equations for optimizing decision-making processes
- Implement value iteration and policy iteration techniques for improved learning strategies
- Analyze the complexities of partially observable Markov decision processes (POMDP)
- Explain the structure and applications of Markov chains and hidden Markov models (HMM)
- State the importance of multitask learning and its impact on machine learning efficiency
- Identify the critical characteristics of online learning and their implications for real-time data processing
- Explore sequence learning and its role in predicting time-dependent data
- List the benefits of prediction learning in forecasting outcomes
- Distinguish between the bagging and boosting techniques and their use in model accuracy improvement
- Examine the gradient boosting methods and their effectiveness in predictive modeling
- Investigate current trends in machine learning technology, including foundation models and multimodal machine learning
- Evaluate the transformative impact of transformers and embedded machine learning in various industries
- Explore low-code and no-code solutions and their democratizing effect on machine learning accessibility
- Analyze the role of data streams in providing real-time input for machine learning models
- Engage with active learning to enhance model performance with less labeled data

11.1 Reinforcement Learning

Reinforcement learning (RL) is a branch of ML that studies how agents can learn from their own actions and rewards to achieve their goals. In RL, an agent interacts with an environment and learns a policy, which is a rule that maps each state to an action. The agent receives a reward (Fig. 11.1) for each action, and the objective is to maximize the total reward over time.

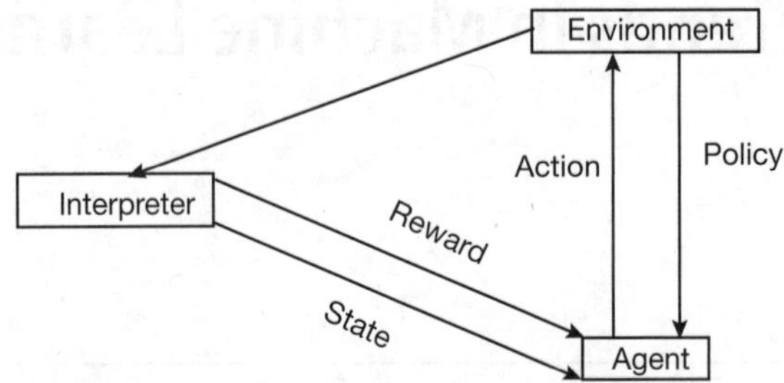

Figure 11.1 Basic reinforcement learning

Reinforcement algorithms can be classified into two categories (Fig. 11.2): model-based and model-free.

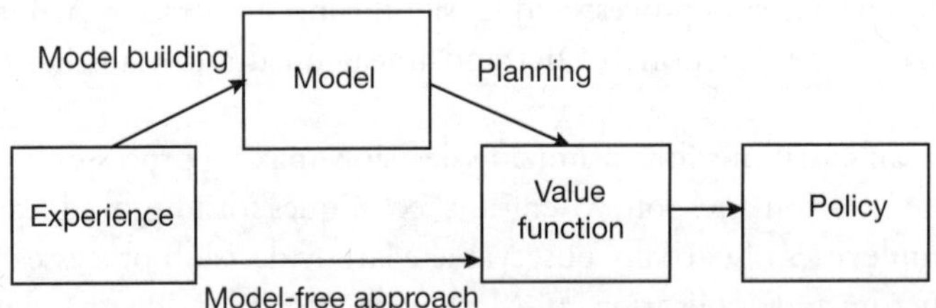

Figure 11.2 Reinforcement learning algorithm classification

Model-based algorithms assume that the transition and reward functions of the models are known or can be learned, and use them to plan ahead and choose the best action. One of the most common frameworks for modeling RL problems is the Markov decision process (MDP). Value iteration and policy iteration are two iterative methods for finding the optimal value function and policy of an MDP. We will also discuss the Bellman equations, a set of equations that relate the optimal value function and policy of an MDP. Linear quadratic regulation (LQR) is a special case of MDP where the state and action spaces are continuous and linear, and the reward function is quadratic. Linear quadratic Gaussian (LQG) is an extension of LQR, where the state transitions are subject to Gaussian noise.

Model-free algorithms do not rely on the model, but instead learn from trial and error by interacting with the environment and observing the outcomes. Some examples of model-free algorithms are Q-learning, value function approximation, policy search, and partially observable Markov decision process (POMDP).

Q-learning is a model-free RL algorithm that learns an action–value function directly from experience. The action–value function measures the expected return of taking an action in a state and following a fixed policy thereafter. Q-learning updates the action–value function using samples of state, action, reward, and next state obtained from exploration (Fig. 11.3). It converges to the optimal action–value function under certain conditions, such as having enough exploration and using a suitable learning rate.

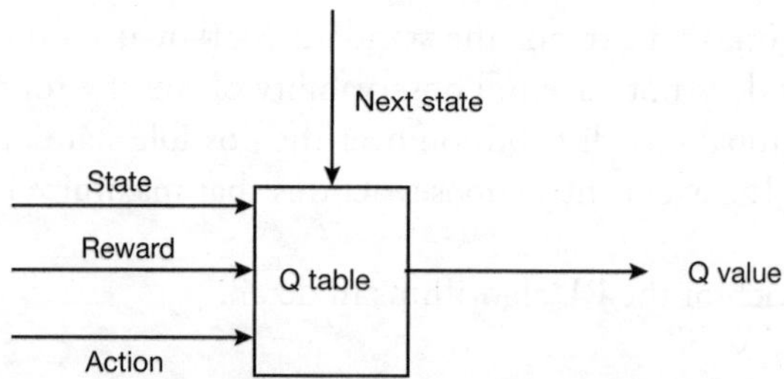

Figure 11.3 Q-learning

A limitation of Q-learning is that it requires us to store and update a large table of action values for each state–action pair, which can be impractical for large or continuous state and action spaces. A solution to this problem is value function approximation, which uses a parametric or non-parametric function to represent the value or action–value function. For example, one can use a neural network to approximate the value or action–value function from a set of features or basis functions; this is called deep Q-learning (Fig. 11.4).

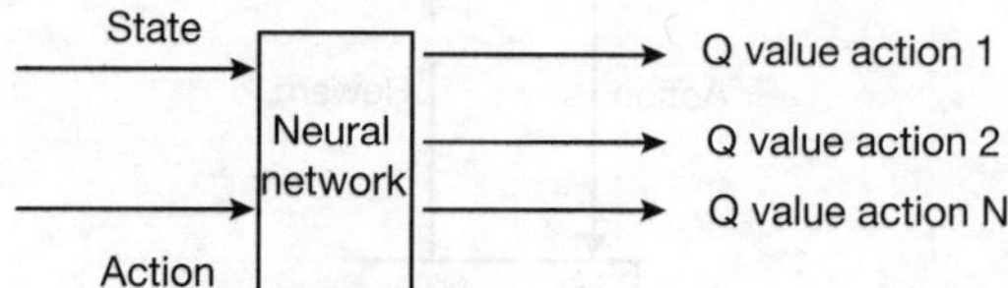

Figure 11.4 Deep Q-learning

Value function approximation is a technique that uses a function to estimate the expected return of each state or state–action pair, instead of using a table to store the values. This allows the algorithm to handle large or continuous state spaces, where a table would be impractical or impossible.

Policy search is a technique that directly optimizes the policy, which is a function that maps states to actions, without using a value function (Fig. 11.5). This allows the algorithm to handle complex or stochastic policies, where a value function would be inaccurate or inefficient. Policy search methods can handle continuous and high-dimensional action spaces more easily than Q-learning methods, as they do not need to discretize or enumerate the actions. Policy search methods can be divided into two categories: gradient-based and gradient-free methods. Gradient-based methods use gradient ascent to update the policy parameters in the direction that increases the expected return. Gradient-free methods use evolutionary algorithms or other stochastic optimization techniques to search for good policies in the parameter space.

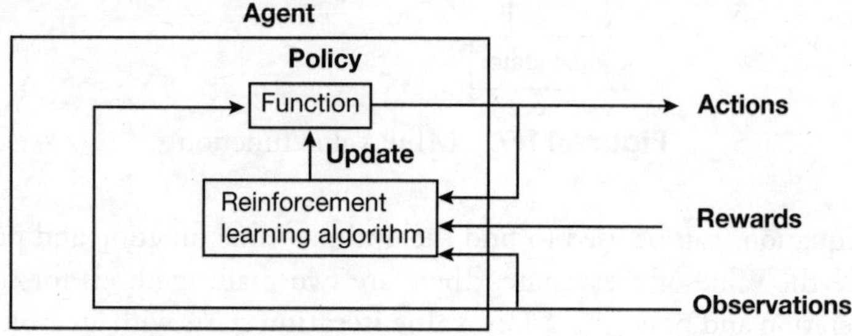

Figure 11.5 Policy search

POMDP is a framework that extends the standard Markov decision process (MDP) to handle situations where the agent does not have full observability of the environment. The agent maintains a belief state, which is a probability distribution over the possible states, and updates it based on its actions and observations. The agent then chooses actions that maximize its expected return over the belief state.

We will now look at each of the RL algorithms in detail.

11.1.1 Markov Decision Process

One of the most common frameworks for modeling RL problems is the Markov decision process (MDP). An MDP is defined by a set of states, a set of actions, a transition function that specifies the probability of moving from one state to another given an action, and a reward function (Fig. 11.6) that specifies the immediate reward for each state–action pair.

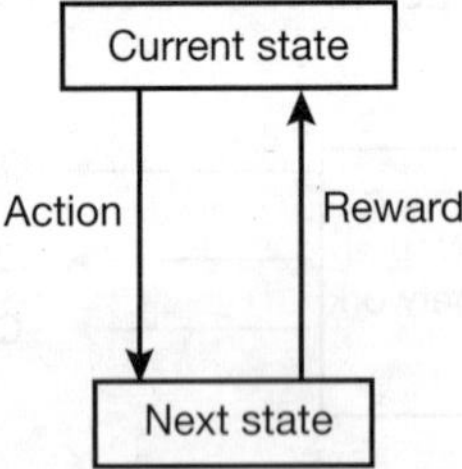

Figure 11.6 MDP framework

MDP satisfies the **Markov property**, which means that the future state and reward depend only on the current state and action, and not on the history of previous states and actions. A key concept in MDP is the value function (Fig. 11.7), which measures the long-term expected reward of each state under a given policy. The value function satisfies the **Bellman equations**, which are a set of recursive equations that relate the value of a state to the values of its successor states.

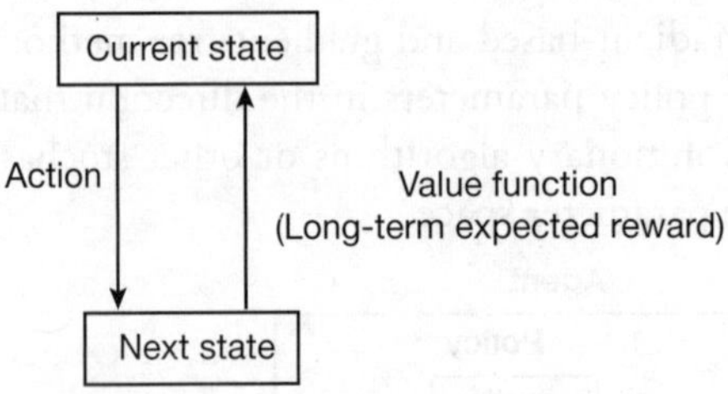

Figure 11.7 MDP value function

The Bellman equations can be used to find the optimal value function and policy, which are the ones that maximize the value of every state. There are two main methods for solving the Bellman equations: value iteration and policy iteration. **Value iteration** starts with an arbitrary value function and iteratively updates it using the Bellman equations until convergence. **Policy iteration** alternates between evaluating the current policy using the Bellman equations and improving the policy by choosing the best action for each state.

A special case of MDP is **linear quadratic regulation (LQR)**, where the state and action spaces are continuous and linear, and the reward function is quadratic (Fig. 11.8). LQR problems have a closed-form solution for the optimal value function and policy, which can be obtained by solving a system of linear equations.

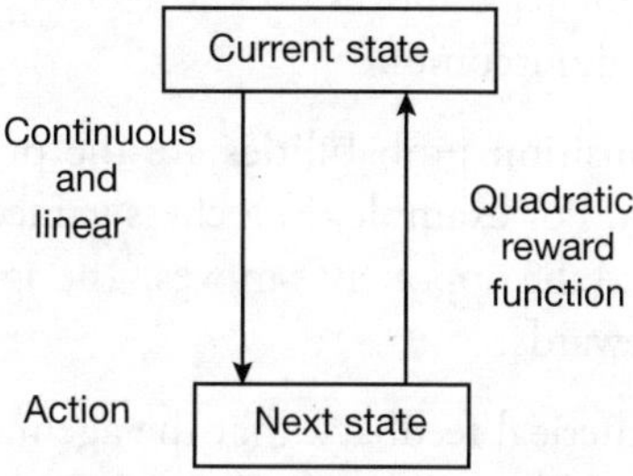

Figure 11.8 Quadratic reward function

LQR problems are useful for modeling control problems where the objective is to minimize the deviation from a desired state or trajectory. An extension of LQR is **linear quadratic Gaussian (LQG)**, where the state transitions are subject to Gaussian noise (Fig. 11.9). LQG problems are more realistic than LQR problems, as they account for uncertainty in the environment. However, LQG problems are more challenging to solve, as they need to estimate the state from noisy observations using a Kalman filter.

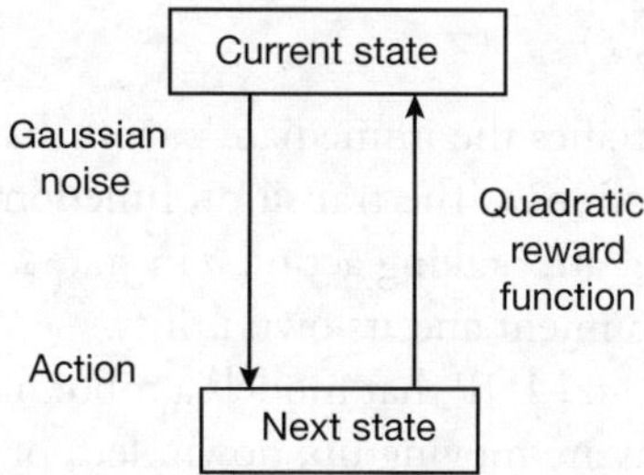

Figure 11.9 Quadratic reward function with Gaussian noise

The optimal policy for LQG problems can be obtained by applying linear feedback control to the estimated state.

Critical components of an MDP: An MDP is defined by:

- A set of states
- A set of actions
- A transition function

The transition function specifies the probability of moving from one state to another, given an action, and a reward function that specifies the immediate reward for each state–action pair.

MDP satisfies the Markov property, which means that the future state and reward depend only on the current state and action, and not on the history of previous states and actions.

State: A state is a representation of the environment that the agent is in. For example, in a chess game, the state would be the configuration of the board and the pieces. The agent needs to know the state in order to decide what action to take next.

Actions (A): Actions are the possible moves that the agent can make in each state. For example, in a chess game, the actions would be the legal moves for the agent's pieces. The agent chooses an action based on its policy and the expected outcomes.

Transition probabilities (T): Transition probabilities are the probabilities of reaching a new state given a current state and an action. For example, in a chess game, the transition probabilities would depend on the rules of the game and the opponent's moves. The agent uses the transition probabilities to estimate the future states and rewards.

Rewards (R): Rewards are the numerical feedback that the agent receives for each action. For example, in a chess game, the reward could be +1 for winning, –1 for losing, and 0 for a draw. The agent's goal is to maximize the total reward over time.

Policy (P): A policy is a function that maps each state to an action. For example, in a chess game, a policy could be a set of rules or a neural network that determines the best move for each board position. The policy is learned by the agent through trial and error or by following an optimal strategy.

An MDP can be considered as a mathematical framework for modeling sequential decision making problems under uncertainty. The dynamics of an MDP are determined by two functions:

- The reward function $R(s, a, s')$
- The transition function $T(s, a, s')$

The reward function $R(s, a, s')$ specifies the immediate payoff that the agent receives when it moves from state s to state s' by taking action a. The transition function $T(s, a, s')$ specifies the probability that the agent will end up in state s' after taking action a in state s. These functions capture the effects of the agent's actions on the environment and its own utility.

For example, suppose we have an MDP that models a robot navigating in a grid world. The states are the cells of the grid, the actions are moving up, down, left, or right, and the rewards are positive or negative values assigned to some cells. The reward function $R(s, a, s')$ could be defined as the value of the cell s' if the robot reaches it by taking action a from cell s, or zero otherwise. The transition function $T(s, a, s')$ could be defined as 1 if the robot successfully moves to cell s' by taking action a from cell s, or 0 otherwise. However, there could be some uncertainty in the robot's movement due to noise or obstacles, so the transition function could also assign some non-zero probabilities to other cells besides s'. These functions describe how the robot's actions affect its location and its reward.

An MDP can be represented as a directed graph, where each node is a state and each edge is an action. The edge from s to s' labeled by a has a weight equal to $T(s, a, s')$ and an annotation equal to $R(s, a, s')$.

Consider an example where the MDP has four states: S1 (initial state), S2 (white captures black pawn), S3 (black captures white pawn), and S4 (terminal state). There are two actions: A1 (move white pawn forward) and A2 (move white knight). The rewards and transitions are given in Table 11.1.

Table 11.1 MDP step-by-step process

s	*a*	*S'*	R(*s*, *a*, *S'*)	T(*s*, *a*, *s'*)
S1	A1	S2	+1	0.8
S1	A1	S3	−1	0.2
S1	A2	S2	+1	0.6
S1	A2	S3	−1	0.4
S2	A1	S4	+10	1
S2	A2	S4	+10	1
S3	A1	S4	−10	1
S3	A2	S4	−10	1

The MDP table shows the expected reward and probability of transitioning from one state to another given an action.

The states represent different configurations of the chess board, where S1 is the initial state, S2 is when white captures a black pawn, S3 is when black captures a white pawn, and S4 is the terminal state (either checkmate or stalemate). The actions are the possible moves for white, either moving the white pawn forward (A1) or moving the white knight (A2). The reward function R(*s*, *a*, *s'*) gives the immediate reward for taking action *a* in state *s* and ending up in state *s'*. For example, R(S1, A1, S2) = +1 means that moving the white pawn forward and capturing a black pawn gives a reward of +1.

The transition function T(*s*, *a*, *s'*) gives the probability of transitioning from state *s* to state *s'* after taking action *a*. For example, T(S1, A1, S2) = 0.8 means that there is an 80% chance of capturing a black pawn by moving the white pawn forward. The goal of the MDP is to find an optimal policy that maximizes the expected total reward over time. This can be done by using algorithms such as value iteration or policy iteration, which iteratively update the values of states and actions until convergence.

11.1.1.1 Bellman Equations

The Bellman equations are a set of mathematical expressions that describe how to find the optimal value function and policy for an MDP. A value function is a function that assigns a numerical value to each state or state–action pair in an MDP, representing the expected long-term return from that state or state–action pair. A policy is a function that maps each state to an action, indicating what the agent should do in each state. An optimal value function is the one that gives the highest value for every state or state–action pair, and an optimal policy is the one that follows the optimal value function. Using the Bellman equations, an optimal policy can be decomposed into a series of optimal subproblems, and the solution to each subproblem can be obtained by applying the same principle recursively.

There are two types of Bellman equations: one for the state–value function and one for the action–value function. The state–value function, denoted by V(*s*), is the expected return starting from state *s* and following a given policy. The action–value function, denoted by Q(*s*, *a*), is the expected return starting from state *s*, taking action *a*, and following a given policy afterward.

Bellman Expectation Equation

The value function represents the expected cumulative reward starting from a particular state under a given policy. For a state *s*, the Bellman expectation equation is given by:

$$V(s) = E[R(s, a) + \gamma * V(s') \mid s, a],$$

where V(*s*) is the value of state *s*, R(*s*, *a*) is the immediate reward obtained by taking action *a* in state *s*, γ (gamma) is a discount factor between 0 and 1 that trades off immediate and future rewards, and *s*′ is the successor state reached after taking action in state *s*.

The action–value function (Q-function) represents the expected cumulative reward starting from a particular state–action pair under a given policy. For a state–action pair (*s*, *a*), the Bellman expectation equation is given by:

$$Q(s, a) = E[R(s, a) + \gamma * V(s') \mid s, a],$$

where Q(*s*, *a*) is the value of state–action pair (*s*, *a*) and R(*s*, *a*) is the immediate reward obtained by taking action an in state *s*, γ (gamma) is the discount factor, and so is the successor state reached after taking action an in state *s*.

Bellman Optimality Equation

The optimal value function represents the maximum expected cumulative reward achievable starting from a particular state. The Bellman optimality equation is given by:

$$V^*(s) = \text{max\_}a \{E[R(s, a) + \gamma * V^*(s') \mid s, a]\}$$

where V*(*s*) is the optimal value of state *s*, and the max_*a* operator selects the action that maximizes the expression inside the curly braces.

The optimal action–value function represents the maximum expected cumulative reward achievable starting from a particular state–action pair. The Bellman optimality equation is given by:

$$Q^*(s, a) = E[R(s, a) + \gamma * \text{max\_}a' \{Q^*(s', a')\} \mid s, a],$$

where Q*(*s*, *a*) is the optimal value of state–action pair (*s*, *a*), and the max_*a*′ operator selects the action that maximizes the expression inside the curly braces.

The Bellman equations can be used to find the optimal value function and policy for an MDP in two ways: dynamic programming or reinforcement learning. Dynamic programming is a method that solves complex problems by breaking them down into simpler subproblems and storing the solutions in a table. Reinforcement learning is a method that learns from experience by interacting with the environment and updating the value function and policy based on feedback.

Richard Bellman introduced the Bellman equations in the 1950s as part of his theory of dynamic programming. He was interested in finding optimal solutions for sequential decision problems under uncertainty. He realized that many such problems could be modeled as MDPs. Bellman proposed that using his equations, one could find the optimal value function and policy for any MDP.

11.1.1.2 Value Iteration and Policy Iteration

Value iteration and policy iteration are fundamental techniques used in dynamic programming and RL to solve MDPs. Though they use distinct approaches, both algorithms aim to determine the optimal path of action for an entity interacting with its surroundings.

Value Iteration

Value iteration is a method that finds the optimal value function and policy for a Markov decision process (MDP) by iteratively updating the values of each state. The value function represents the expected return that can be obtained from each state under a given policy. The algorithm starts by assigning arbitrary values to each state and then repeatedly updates them using the Bellman optimality equation, which calculates the maximum expected return that can be achieved from each state by considering all possible actions and their outcomes. The algorithm stops when the values converge to a stable solution, meaning the value change is below a certain threshold. The optimal policy can then be derived from the optimal value function by choosing the action that maximizes the expected return in each state.

Value iteration is a dynamic programming technique that solves the MDP problem by breaking it down into smaller subproblems and reusing the solutions of previous subproblems. It guarantees that it will find the optimal value function and policy under certain assumptions, such as having a finite and discrete state and action space and a stationary and fully observable environment. Value iteration is efficient is terms of computation time and memory, but converging may require many iterations, especially for large or complex MDPs.

Policy Iteration

Policy iteration is a method of finding the optimal policy for a Markov decision process by repeatedly performing two steps: policy evaluation and policy improvement. In policy evaluation, the value function of the current policy is estimated by solving a system of linear equations derived from the Bellman expectation equation. In policy improvement, the policy is updated by choosing the action that maximizes the expected return in each state, based on the estimated value function. This process is repeated until the policy converges to the optimal one, which also implies that the value function converges to the optimal value function.

Policy iteration is a sound and complete algorithm that guarantees that it will find the optimal policy and value function for any finite state and action space. It alternates between improving the policy and evaluating its value, until no further improvement is possible. By doing so, it avoids computing the value function for all possible policies, which would be intractable for large problems.

11.1.1.3 Linear Quadratic Regulation

There is a special case of MDP where the state and action spaces are continuous and linear and the reward function is quadratic. Linear quadratic regulation (LQR) is a control method for designing controllers for linear systems. It is commonly used as a basis or starting point for reinforcement learning algorithms, even though it is not an algorithm.

LQR aims to determine the optimal control technique to minimize a quadratic cost function. The system's dynamics should be linear, but the cost function is considered quadratic. The goal is to identify the optimal control input with the lowest estimated cumulative cost over a finite or infinite time horizon. The LQR approach finds the optimal control strategy by iteratively solving linear algebraic Riccati equations. The result is a linear feedback controller that depends on the system's state.

LQR can be used in RL as a basis for learning control techniques. In addition, it can be used as a baseline for comparison in RL trials. Researchers often compare the performance of their RL algorithms to a LQR controller to evaluate their approach's effectiveness.

The `LQRPolicyIteration` class is defined in the code given below to use the policy iteration technique to solve the LQR issue. The policy evaluation and improvement procedures are repeated until convergence using the `solve_lqr` approach. The best control policy is returned by the '`get_policy`' method.

As an example, we define the cost matrices Q and R and the system dynamics matrices A and B. The best course of action is then determined by creating an instance of `LQRPolicyIteration` and using the `solve_lqr` function to calculate it. We print the resultant policy at the end.

```
import numpy as np
Class LQRPolicyIteration:
    def __init__(self, A, B, Q, R, gamma=1.0, max_iterations=1000,
epsilon=1e-6):
        self.A = A
        self.B = B
        self.Q = Q
        self.R = R
        self.gamma = gamma
        self.max_iterations = max_iterations
        self.epsilon = epsilon
        self.V = None
        self.K = None
    def solve_lqr(self):
        n = self.A.shape[0]
        m = self.B.shape[1]
        # Initialize random policy
        K = np.random.rand(m, n)
        for _ in range(self.max_iterations):
            # Policy evaluation
            V = np.linalg.inv(np.eye(n) - self.gamma * (self.A - self.B @
K)) @ self.Q @ np.transpose(self.Q)
            V_new = np.copy(V)
            # Policy improvement
```

```
            K = np.linalg.inv(self.R + self.gamma * np.transpose(self.B)
@ V @ self.B) @ self.gamma * np.transpose(self.B) @ V @ self.A
            K_new = np.copy(K)
            if np.max(np.abs(V_new - V)) < self.epsilon and np.max(np.
abs(K_new - K)) < self.epsilon:
                break
            V = V_new
            K = K_new
        self.V = V
        self.K = K
    def get_policy(self):
        return self.K
# Example usage
A = np.array([[1.0, 0.5], [0.0, 0.8]])  # State transition matrix
B = np.array([[0.1], [0.2]])  # Control input matrix
Q = np.array([[1.0, 0.0], [0.0, 1.0]])  # State cost matrix
R = np.array([[0.1]])  # Control cost matrix
lqr_policy = LQRPolicyIteration(A, B, Q, R)
lqr_policy.solve_lqr()
policy = lqr_policy.get_policy()
print("Optimal policy:")
print(policy)
```

11.1.1.4 Linear Quadratic Gaussian

This is an extension of LQR where the state transitions are subject to Gaussian noise. The linear quadratic Gaussian (LQG) control framework is a classical control approach that integrates optimal control concepts with state estimation. It is widely utilized in control theory and has been used in various fields, including robotics and aeronautical engineering.

In an RL context, controllers for continuous control problems may be built using the LQG framework. The strategy selected by RL algorithms frequently maximizes a cumulative reward signal. LQG-based RL aims to determine the optimal control method that minimizes a quadratic cost function.

Gaussian noise and a linear dynamical system are assumed in the LQG formulation. A linear state-space model describes The system's dynamics, which is frequently stated by the following equations.

State dynamics: $x(t+1) = \mathrm{A}x(t) + \mathrm{B}u(t) + w(t)$

Observation model: $y(t) = \mathrm{C}x(t) + v(t)$

where $x(t)$ represents the state vector at time t; $u(t)$ represents the control input at time t; $w(t)$ and $v(t)$ are Gaussian process and measurement noise, respectively; and A, B, and C are matrices defining the system dynamics and observation model.

The control objective in LQG is to minimize the expected value of a quadratic cost function, which is defined as the sum of the state and control cost terms:

$$J = \Sigma[x(t)'Qx(t) + u(t)'Ru(t)]$$

where Q is the state cost matrix and R is the control cost matrix.

The methodology addresses the LQG control problem in two steps: state estimation and control. The Kalman filter or one of its variants is used in the state estimation phase to estimate the current state based on the available data. The estimated state is input for the control phase, determining the optimal control approach.

LQG-based techniques combine this conventional control framework with reinforcement learning algorithms. The RL agent can learn the control policy by interacting with the environment and modifying it in response to observable rewards and states. Model-based RL algorithms can leverage the LQG framework as a model of the environment to learn and enhance the control strategy.

11.1.1.5 Q-learning

Q-learning is a model-free RL approach that allows an agent to learn the optimal course of action in a given environment by iteratively updating its action–value function or Q-function. Within the community of reinforcement learning, it is a widely used algorithm.

The agent interacts with the environment at predetermined time intervals while utilizing Q-learning. At each time step, the agent looks at the state of the environment, takes action, and is rewarded by the environment. The agent seeks to maximize its long-term cumulative reward by determining the best action in each situation.

The Q-function table contains the estimated cumulative rewards for every state–action pair. A state–activity pair's Q-value (s, a) indicates the expected cumulative reward an agent will receive by acting in state s and subsequently choosing the optimal course of action. Since the Q-function is unknown at first, an approximation must be made.

Using the Bellman equation, Q-learning iteratively updates the Q-values. The following is the update rule for a state–action pair's (s, a) Q-value:

$$Q(s, a) = Q(s, a) + \alpha * (r + \gamma * \max(Q(s', a')) - Q(s, a))$$

where $Q(s, a)$ is the Q-value of state–action pair (s, a); α (alpha) is the learning rate, controlling the weight given to the new information, and it determines how much the new Q-value should affect the existing value; r is the immediate reward received after taking action in state s; γ (gamma) is the discount factor, determining the importance of future rewards, and it is a value between 0 and 1 (a high γ value gives more weight to long-term rewards, while a low γ value focuses more on immediate rewards); s' is the next state the agent transitions to after taking action in state s; a' is the action that maximizes the Q-value in the next state s'; and $\max(Q(s', a'))$ is the maximum Q-value over all possible actions a' in the next state s'.

By repeatedly applying this update rule and exploring the environment, Q-learning eventually converges to the optimal Q-values corresponding to the optimal policy. The agent can then select the action with the highest Q-value in each state to follow the optimal policy.

11.1.1.6 Value Function Approximation

It is a technique for representing the value function using a parametric or non-parametric function, such as a neural network or a kernel method. In RL, approximation refers to estimating or roughly computing the value function for each state or state–action pair instead of explicitly computing it. The value function represents the expected advantage or utility of being in a given state or performing in a particular way in a specific state.

In many real-world applications, the state space of a problem may be quite large or even continuous, making it challenging to find the exact value function for each situation. Value function approximation methods address this issue using a smaller range of sample states or function approximation techniques such as logistic regression, neural networks, or decision trees.

The general formula for value function approximation can be expressed as:

$$\hat{V}(s) \approx f(s, \theta)$$

where $\hat{V}(s)$ is the estimated value of state s; $f(s, \theta)$ is the value function approximator, a parametric function with parameters θ; s is the state for which the value is being estimated; and θ is a vector of parameters that must be learned or optimized to approximate the value function accurately.

Temporal difference (TD) learning is an example of an RL technique used for prediction and control tasks in sequential decision-making scenarios. It combines ideas from Monte Carlo methods and dynamic programming to learn from delayed and faulty information. Updating estimates of state values or state–action pairs based on observed rewards and estimates of subsequent states is the core idea of TD learning. TD learning methods take advantage of temporal differences or variations in the value estimates of successive states in a series of observations. TD learning has two main variants: TD(0) and TD(lambda).

In **TD(0)**, also known as one-step TD, the value of a state is updated based on the observed immediate reward and the estimate of the next state. The update rule is:

$$V(S\_t) = V(S\_t) + \text{alpha} * (R\_t{+}1 + \text{gamma} * V(S\_t{+}1) - V(S\_t))$$

where V(*S_t*) is the value estimate of state, *S_t*; alpha is the learning rate; R_*t*+1 is the immediate reward observed after transitioning from state *S_t* to *S_t*+1; and gamma is the discount factor that determines the importance of future rewards.

TD(lambda) is a generalized version of TD(0) that considers multiple steps into the future when updating value estimates. It uses eligibility traces to assign credit to precede states or state–action pairs. The update rule in TD(lambda) combines the TD(0) update with a trace decay factor lambda:

$$V(S\_t) = V(S\_t) + \text{alpha} * (G\_t - V(S\_t))$$

where *G_t* is the lambda-return, defined as a weighted sum of future rewards.

$$G\_t = (1 - \text{lambda}) * (R\_t{+}1 + \text{gamma} * V(S\_t{+}1)) + \text{lambda} * G\_t{+}1$$

Here, *G_t*+1 is the lambda-return in the next time-step, and the trace decay factor lambda determines how much weight is given to future rewards.

11.1.1.7 Policy Search

This is a class of RL algorithms that directly optimizes the policy without using a value function. It aims to find the optimal policy, which maps states to actions that maximize the cumulative rewards earned by an agent interacting with an environment. Within policy search, the goal is to specifically identify an effective policy instead of estimating value or action–value functions.

The agent uses policy search to modify the initial policy to improve performance iteratively. The procedure frequently entails the following steps:

1. **Policy Parameterization:** Policy parameterization is a method for controlling the behavior of a policy by modifying its variables. A policy is a rule or strategy determining the appropriate course of action in a given circumstance. A policy for driving a vehicle, for instance, might depend on the speed, the distance between cars, and the traffic light. A parameterization of the policy specifies how these variables affect the policy. For instance, we could have a parameter that dictates whether the car drives aggressively or cautiously. A policy might be parameterized by a parametric function, such as a neural network. It comprises layers of nodes (called neurons) linked by weights and biases. They determine how the network transforms input signals into output signals. By modifying the weights and biases, we can alter the behavior of the neural network. A policy parameterized by a neural network receives input variables (such as speed, distance, and traffic light) and generates an action (such as accelerate, decelerate, or turn left). Data or feedback teaches the neural network the optimal weights and biases for the policy. For instance, it could learn to drive more cautiously when the traffic signal is red or when the distance between it and the next vehicle is short.
2. **Objective Function:** An objective function measures how well a policy operates in a specific setting. The optimal course of action to adopt in every situation is determined by a policy, which is a rule or a plan. The expected total benefit of adhering to the policy, which is the sum of the rewards from each state–action pair, drives the objective function. The reward represents the desirability of a result as a scalar value. The goal function may also take into account additional elements, such as the expense of the policy, the environmental uncertainty, or the decision-maker's preferences. The objective function is employed to evaluate several policies and choose the best one that maximizes (or minimizes) the value of the objective function.
3. **Search Method:** One way to design an RL agent is to specify a goal function that measures how well the agent is performing, and then search for the optimal policy parameters that maximize this function. However, finding the optimal policy parameters can be challenging, especially when the goal function is complex, noisy, or non-smooth. Therefore, various search methods have been proposed to explore the space of possible policy parameters and find good solutions. Some examples of such search methods are:
   - **Gradient-based methods**: These methods use the gradient of the goal function with respect to the policy parameters to guide the search. They require the goal function to be differentiable and the gradient to be computable or estimable. They can be efficient and precise, but they may get stuck in local optima or face numerical issues.
   - **Evolutionary algorithms**: These methods mimic the natural process of evolution by maintaining a population of candidate policy parameters and applying selection, crossover, and mutation operators to generate new candidates. They do not require the goal function to be differentiable or smooth, and they can escape local optima by introducing diversity. However, they may be computationally expensive and sensitive to the choice of operators and parameters.
   - **Random search**: This method simply samples policy parameters randomly from a predefined distribution and evaluates them on the goal function. It is simple and easy to implement, and it can work well for low-dimensional problems. However, it may be inefficient and

ineffective for high-dimensional or complex problems, as it does not exploit any information from previous evaluations.

- **Bayesian optimization**: This method uses a probabilistic model to capture the relationship between policy parameters and goal function values, and then uses an acquisition function to select the most promising policy parameters to evaluate next. It can handle noisy and black-box goal functions, and it can balance exploration and exploitation. However, it may be difficult to choose an appropriate model and acquisition function, and it may suffer from the curse of dimensionality.

4. **Policy Evaluation**: This is the process of estimating the value function of a given policy, which measures how beneficial it is to follow that policy in the long run. To evaluate a policy, we need to interact with the environment using the policy and collect data on the rewards and state transitions. One way to do this is to run multiple episodes, which are sequences of states, actions and rewards that start from an initial state and end at a terminal state. By averaging the total rewards obtained in each episode, we can estimate the expected return of the policy, which is the sum of discounted future rewards. The higher the expected return, the better the policy is performing in the environment.
5. **Policy Update**: The evaluation results are utilized to revise the policy's parameters in order to improve the policy's performance. The search strategy determines the specific updating rule. In gradient-based techniques, for example, gradient information is used to update the parameters in the direction of the sharpest climb in the objective function. This means that after applying a policy to a problem and measuring its effectiveness, the policy is modified by changing some of its settings or features. The way these changes are made depends on the type of search strategy that is used to explore the space of possible policies. One common type of search strategy is based on gradients, which are mathematical tools that indicate how much a function changes when its inputs are changed. By using gradients, the policy can be updated in such a way that it moves closer to the optimal solution, which is the one that maximizes the objective function.
6. **Convergence and Termination:** Convergence is locating a policy solution that satisfies the problem's objectives and criteria. Termination is when the policy analysis is concluded; no further modifications are required. Policy review and revision are iterative measures that contribute to achieving convergence and termination. They include evaluating the policy's performance and effects, identifying voids or flaws, and making necessary adjustments or revisions. Reviewing and revising a policy can continue until a perfect or nearly perfect solution is discovered. The policy meets all objectives and criteria with minimal trade-offs or negative effects. Alternately, convergence and termination can be indicated by other factors, such as a predetermined number of iterations, a minor adjustment to the policy parameters that do not substantially affect the results, or adequate performance levels that meet the minimum standards or expectations. Termination and convergence ensure the policy analysis is rigorous, exhaustive, and effective.

One benefit of policy search techniques is that value function-based approaches may be less effective in managing high-dimensional and continuous action spaces. Policy search can also be helpful when it is impossible or difficult to comprehend the environment's dynamics fully. However, policy search strategies can be computationally expensive and require several interactions with the environment in order to obtain the optimal policy.

11.1.1.8 Partially Observable Markov Decision Process (POMDP)

This is a generalization of MDP, where the learner does not have full access to the state of the environment.

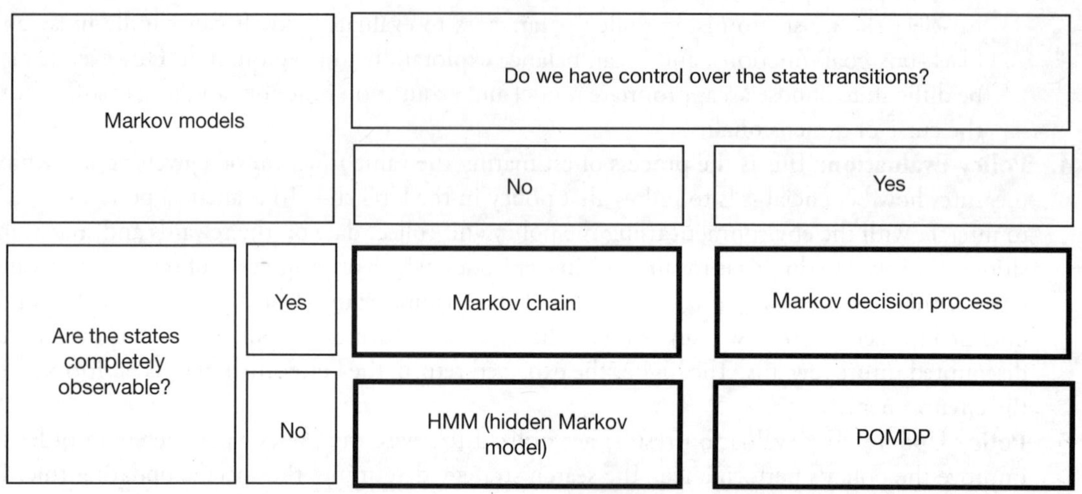

Figure 11.10 Types of Markov models

POMDPs are used to model decision-making problems when an agent interacts with an unpredictable environment (Fig. 11.10). The agent's state is not immediately visible in a POMDP; instead, it is represented as a probability distribution across a range of possible states. In addition to acting based on its current belief state at each time step, the agent also receives an observation that provides some information about the actual condition of the environment. According to probability, the agent is rewarded based on their action and the state they generated, and the environment changes states. The agency wants a strategy to maximize its expected total long-term earnings.

POMDPs are challenging to solve because of their ambiguity and partial observability. The most frequent tactic is to use belief-state representations, where the agent maintains a belief state that symbolizes how it perceives the actual state of the environment based on past observations and actions. The entering observation and the Bayes rule update the belief state iteratively.

Monte Carlo techniques are sampling-based methods that employ random simulations to estimate the value function or policy for a POMDP. The fundamental concept is to generate a set of trajectories consisting of sequences of actions, observations, and rewards and then to average them to estimate the value function or the policy. Methods based on Monte Carlo can manage large and continuous state spaces, but they are susceptible to high variance and slow convergence.

POMDPs are computationally demanding, particularly for large state and observation spaces. Heuristics and approximations are often used to simplify the problem. Furthermore, strategies like belief space and online planning may be utilized to create efficient policies with constrained computational resources swiftly.

11.1.1.9 *Markov Chain*

A Markov chain is a mathematical representation of a series of events (Fig. 11.11) in which the probability of moving on to the subsequent event is solely based on the preceding event. It is a stochastic process that can examine various systems, including climatic patterns, stock market fluctuations, and behavioral patterns.

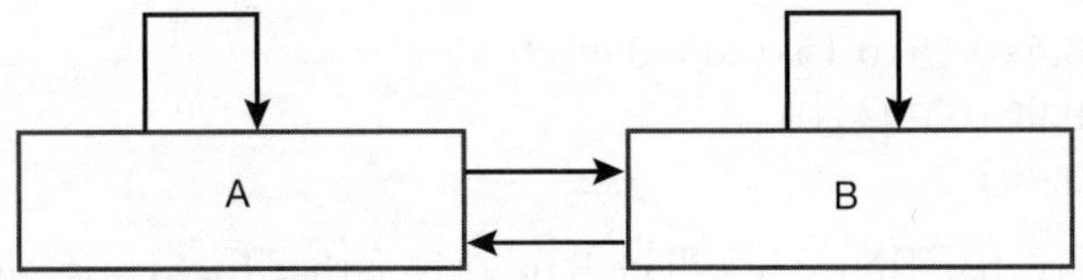

Figure 11.11 Simple Markov chain

Markov chains can offer insightful analysis and behavior predictions by looking at transition probabilities between multiple states. An example of Markov chain in a real-time application is shown in Fig. 11.12.

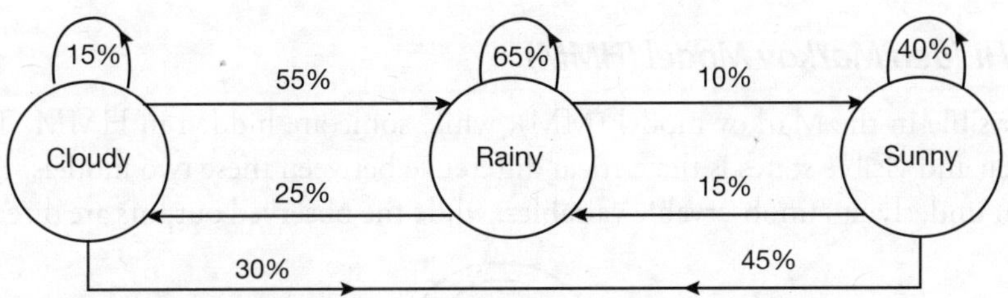

Figure 11.12 Example of Markov chain

- If Cloudy today, then tomorrow:
  - 30% probability for Sunny
  - 55% probability for Rainy
  - 15% probability for Cloudy
- If Rainy today, then tomorrow:
  - 10% probability for Sunny
  - 65% probability for Rainy
  - 25% probability for Cloudy
- If Sunny today, then tomorrow:
  - 40% probability for Sunny
  - 15% probability for Rainy
  - 45% probability for Cloudy

What is the probability that Thursday will be Rainy if today (Tuesday) is Sunny?
We know that Tuesday is sunny, so we can use the probabilities for tomorrow (Wednesday) given that today (Tuesday) is Sunny:

P(Wednesday is Sunny | Tuesday is Sunny)=0.4
P(Wednesday is Rainy | Tuesday is Sunny)=0.15
P(Wednesday is Cloudy | Tuesday is Sunny)=0.45

We also know the probabilities for Thursday given that Wednesday is Sunny, Rainy, or Cloudy:

P(Thursday is Rainy | Wednesday is Sunny)=0.15
P(Thursday is Rainy | Wednesday is Rainy)=0.65
P(Thursday is Rainy | Wednesday is Cloudy)=0.55

Now we can plug these values into the formula and simplify:

P(Thursday is Rainy)=0.4×0.15+0.15×0.65+0.45×0.55
P(Thursday is Rainy)=0.06+0.0975+0.2475
P(Thursday is Rainy)=0.405

Therefore, the probability that Thursday will be Rainy given that Tuesday is Sunny is 0.405, or 40.5%.

Markov chains are extensively used in natural language processing (NLP). For instance, they have been utilized to create language models that forecast the probability that a word will appear in a phrase given the prior comments. Markov chains are also frequently used in finance to simulate option pricing and model stock price movement. Overall, Markov chains are a valuable tool for comprehending and forecasting the behavior of complex systems due to their variety.

11.1.1.10 Hidden Markov Model (HMM)

All states are visible in the Markov model (MM), while some are hidden in HMM. This distinction between hidden and visible states is the critical difference between these two models. HMM's hidden states represent underlying, unobservable variables, while the observed outputs are directly observable.

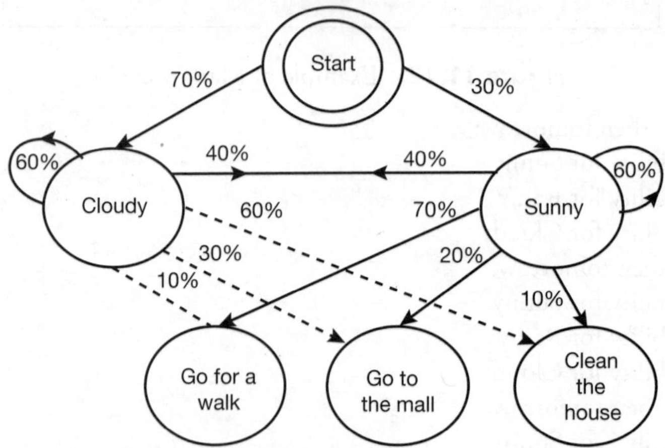

Figure 11.13 Example of hidden Markov model (HMM)

In the example shown in Fig 11.13, Cloudy and Sunny are hidden states. Go for a walk, Go to the mall and Clean the house are the observations. The HMM in Fig. 11.14 represents the process of predicting whether someone will go for a walk, go to the mall, or clean the house on a particular day depending upon whether the day is Cloudy or Sunny.

Table 11.2 lists the five components of the HMM in Fig. 11.14.

Table 11.2 Components and value of HMM

S. No	Components	Values
1	States	{Cloudy, Sunny}
2	Observations	{Walk, Mall, Clean}
3	Start probability	{Cloudy: 70%, Sunny: 30%}
4	Transition probability	{ Cloudy: {Cloudy: 60%, Sunny: 40%}, Sunny: {Cloudy: 40%, Sunny 60%} }
5	Emission probability	{ Cloudy: {Walk:10%, Mall: 30%, Clean: 60%}, Sunny: {Walk:70%, Mall: 20%, Clean: 10%} }

Looking at Table 11.2, we can note the following:

- Th two hidden states are Cloudy and Sunny.
- Whether a person is going for a walk, going to the mall, or cleaning the house is what is seen as the process output (or) observations.
- The start probability is a representation of an initial probability distribution.
- Given the current condition, the transition probability represents the change from one state (Cloudy or Sunny) to another.
- The emission probability is the likelihood of seeing the output, such as going for a walk, going to the mall, or cleaning the house, given the weather conditions of Sunny or Cloudy.

HMM is particularly useful for modeling systems with unobservable or latent variables, such as in speech recognition or DNA sequencing, where hidden factors (such as, speech signals or DNA sequences) influence the observed outputs (such as, phonemes or genetic variations). On the other hand, in MM, all states are visible, and there are no hidden states, making it more suitable for analysing systems where all variables are directly observable.

Both HMM and MM have strengths and weaknesses. One of the strengths of HMM is its ability to model systems with hidden variables, making it suitable for studying complex phenomena where not all variables are directly observable. HMM can capture underlying patterns and dependencies in the data, allowing for more accurate predictions and decision-making. However, HMM may require more computational resources and training data than MM, and estimating hidden variables can be challenging. Therefore, the choice between HMM and MM should be carefully considered based on the system's nature and the analysis's goals.

In addition, where it is necessary to model sequential data with hidden states, HMMs are particularly helpful in applications like speech recognition, natural language processing, and bioinformatics. On the other hand, for simpler systems with limited dependencies and observable variables, MM may be a more suitable choice due to its simplicity and ease of implementation. Ultimately, the decision between HMM and MM depends on the trade-off between computational complexity and the desired level of accuracy in capturing hidden patterns and dependencies.
HMMs provide several **advantages** over other models:

- **Flexible framework for modeling complex dependencies between variables.** HMMs can represent both linear and non-linear relationships and discrete and continuous variables. HMMs can also handle missing data and noisy observations by marginalizing the hidden states.
- **Speech recognition.** Speech signals are composed of sequences of sounds, or phonemes, influenced by the context and the speaker. HMMs can model the transitions between phonemes and the acoustic features of each phoneme by using hidden states and emission probabilities. HMMs can also incorporate language models and grammar rules using prior and transition probabilities.
- **Natural language understanding.** Natural language is a complex phenomenon that involves syntax, semantics, pragmatics, and discourse. HMMs can capture some aspects by using hidden states to represent the syntactic categories, semantic roles, or discourse relations of words and phrases. HMMs can also learn from large corpora of text by using unsupervised or semi-supervised learning methods.
- **Gesture recognition tasks.** Gestures are a form of nonverbal communication that conveys information and intentions. HMMs can model the dynamics and variability of gestures by using hidden states to represent a gesture's different phases or sub-actions. HMMs can also recognize gestures from other modalities, such as vision, audio, or touch, using multiple observation sequences and emission probabilities.

11.1.1.11 Other Types of Reinforcement Learning

There are many RL algorithms, each with their own advantages and challenges. Two of the most common ones are policy gradient methods and actor–critic methods.

Policy gradient methods optimize the policy directly rather than indirectly through a value function. The policy is a function that takes a state as input and outputs a probability distribution over the possible actions. Policy gradient methods aim to find the optimal policy that maximizes the expected cumulative reward over a trajectory of states and actions. One way to achieve this is to use gradient ascent to update the policy parameters in the direction of the gradient of the expected cumulative reward. However, this gradient is usually unknown and needs to be estimated from data. Policy gradient methods use different techniques to estimate the gradient, such as Monte Carlo sampling, temporal difference learning, and actor–critic methods.

One of the most straightforward and intuitive policy gradient methods is **REINFORCE**, which stands for REward Increment = Non-negative Factor × Offset Reinforcement × Characteristic Eligibility. REINFORCE uses Monte Carlo sampling to estimate the gradient by generating trajectories of states and actions using the current policy and then computing the returns (cumulative rewards) for each trajectory. The policy parameters are then updated to increase the probability of actions that lead to higher returns and decrease the probability of actions that lead to lower returns. This way, the policy gradually improves and converges to the optimal policy.

Proximal policy optimization (PPO) is a state-of-the-art RL algorithm that builds on the idea of policy gradient methods. Policy gradient methods use trajectories, which are sequences of states, actions, and rewards, to estimate the direction of improvement for the policy, which is the function that maps states to actions. However, policy gradient methods such as REINFORCE suffer from high variance and instability, meaning that they can produce very different results depending on the trajectories sampled and the policy updates applied. PPO addresses these issues by using multiple trajectories to reduce the variance of the gradient estimates and by applying a clipping mechanism to limit the magnitude of the policy updates. The clipping mechanism ensures that the new policy stays consistent with the old policy, which could lead to worse performance or even catastrophic failure. By doing so, PPO achieves a balance between exploration and exploitation, which are two critical aspects of reinforcement learning.

Actor–critic methods combine the advantages of policy-based and value-based methods. Policy-based methods learn a policy, which is a function that maps states to actions without using a value function. Value-based methods learn a value function, which is a function that measures how good a state or an action is, without using a policy. Actor–critic methods use both a policy and a value function, and they learn them simultaneously using two neural networks: an actor network and a critic network.

The actor network learns the policy, which can be either stochastic (outputting a probability distribution over actions) or deterministic (outputting a single optimal action). The actor network takes the state as input and outputs the action to take. The critic network learns the value function, which can be either state–value (estimating the expected return from a state) or action–value (estimating the expected return from a state–action pair). The critic network takes the state and the action as input and outputs the value of that state–action pair.

The actor network uses the feedback from the critic network to update its policy. The goal of the actor network is to maximize the expected return, which is the sum of discounted future rewards. The actor network updates its policy using a policy gradient, a technique that computes the gradient of the expected return with respect to the policy parameters. The policy gradient depends on the value function estimated by the critic network. The critic network provides a signal called the advantage function, which measures how much better an action is compared to the average action in that state. The advantage function is computed by subtracting the value function from the observed return. The actor network uses the advantage function to update its policy toward increasing the expected return.

The critic network uses the observed rewards and the actor's actions to update its value function. The goal of the critic network is to minimize the mean squared error between its value estimates and the observed returns. The critic network updates its value function using temporal difference learning, a technique that bootstraps from its estimates to reduce the variance of the updates. The critic network uses a target network, a copy of itself updated slowly, to provide more stable value estimates.

Advantage actor–critic (A2C) is an RL algorithm that combines the benefits of policy-based and value-based methods. Actor–critic methods use a policy network (actor) and a value network (critic) to optimize the agent's performance. A2C is a synchronous method, meaning that it uses multiple parallel agents to collect data from different environments and update a shared actor–critic network simultaneously. This allows A2C to explore more diverse states and actions and avoid getting stuck in local optima. A2C also uses an advantage estimation technique, which subtracts the value function from the observed returns to reduce the variance of the policy gradients. This helps A2C to balance the exploration and exploitation trade-off and converge faster to the optimal policy. A2C is an improved version of A3C, an asynchronous method that uses multiple parallel agents but updates the actor–critic network asynchronously. A3C suffered from high gradient variance and inefficient use of CPU cores, as some agents could be faster or slower than others, and some updates could overwrite or interfere with others. A2C solves these problems by synchronizing the updates and using a more stable advantage estimation technique.

Deep deterministic policy gradient (DDPG) can handle complex, high-dimensional environments with continuous actions. Unlike stochastic policies that output a probability distribution over actions, DDPG learns a deterministic policy that directly maps states to optimal actions. To evaluate the quality of the actions, DDPG uses a critical network that approximates the action–value function, also known as the Q-function. The Q-function measures the expected return of taking an action in a state and following the policy after that. DDPG updates the critic network by minimizing the temporal difference error between the predicted Q-value and the target Q-value, which is computed using the reward and the next state. DDPG also uses target networks for both the actor and the critic, which are delayed copies of the original networks. The target networks are updated slowly by blending their weights with the weights of the original networks. This technique helps to stabilize the learning process and avoid oscillations or divergence. DDPG is based on an earlier algorithm called DPG, which also learns a deterministic policy using an off-policy Q-learning algorithm. Off-policy means that the Q-function is learned from data not generated by the current policy but by a different behavior policy. This allows DDPG to use a replay buffer, a memory of past experiences that can be sampled randomly to break temporal correlations and improve data efficiency.

11.1.1.12 Applications of Reinforcement Learning

One of the most popular and successful applications of RL is in the domain of **games**, where RL agents can learn to play complex and challenging games without human guidance. AlphaGo is a remarkable achievement of RL, as it beat the best human players of Go, a game with more possible positions than atoms in the universe. AlphaGo used a combination of deep neural networks (DNNs) and Monte Carlo tree search to evaluate board positions and select moves. AlphaZero is an extension of AlphaGo that can learn any board game given only the rules and a self-play mechanism. AlphaZero surpassed the performance of previous state-of-the-art algorithms in chess, shogi, and Go, demonstrating its generality and versatility.

Robotics is a domain where RL has many applications. In robotics, RL agents can learn to perform complex manipulation and locomotion tasks in real-world settings, such as factories, warehouses, or homes. For example, robots can use RL to discover the optimal policies for various tasks, such as grasping objects of different shapes and sizes, moving around obstacles and avoiding collisions, and navigating unknown or dynamic environments. RL can also help robots adapt to changes in their environment or body, such as damage or wear and tear, by updating their policies based on new observations and feedback. RL benefits robotics because it does not require explicit programming or supervision, which can be costly, time-consuming, or impractical for many robotic scenarios.

RL can also be applied to **autonomous driving**, where RL agents can learn to control vehicles that can drive themselves in various traffic scenarios. RL algorithms can help autonomous cars discover driving behaviors that are safe, efficient, and comfortable for passengers. Some examples of driving behaviors that RL can improve are:

- **Lane-keeping**: This is the ability of the car to maintain its position within a lane without drifting or swerving. RL agents can learn to adjust the steering angle and speed of the car based on the lane markings, road curvature, and surrounding vehicles.
- **Obstacle avoidance**: This is the ability of the car to detect and avoid collisions with other objects, such as pedestrians, cyclists, or other vehicles. RL agents can learn to apply brakes, steer, or change lanes when encountering obstacles.
- **Adaptive cruise control**: This is the ability of the car to maintain a safe and comfortable distance from the vehicle in front of it while following the speed limit and traffic flow. RL agents can learn to accelerate or decelerate the car based on the distance and speed of the leading vehicle and the traffic conditions.

Using RL, autonomous cars can learn from their experiences and adapt to different situations rather than relying on predefined rules or human supervision. This can lead to more robust and intelligent driving systems that enhance safety, efficiency, and comfort for passengers and other road users.

Recommendation systems are applications that provide users with personalized suggestions of items or services they might be interested in. RL can also be used in recommendation systems, where RL agents can learn to personalize customer recommendations based on their preferences and behavior. RL can be used in various industries, such as online advertising, content streaming services, and e-commerce, to increase customer satisfaction and loyalty. The RL agent learns to select and rank items based on user feedback, such as clicks, ratings, or purchases, to maximize long-term user engagement and retention. The RL agent can also explore new items that the user might not have seen before and exploit the things that the user has shown interest in. The RL agent can adapt to changing user preferences and environments and handle complex and dynamic scenarios. The RL agent can also balance the trade-off between exploration and exploitation and short-term and long-term rewards. Some examples of RL-based recommendation systems are:

- **Google Ads**: Google uses RL to optimize the placement and selection of online ads based on user clicks and conversions. The RL agent learns to bid for ad slots and to choose the best ads for each user and context.
- **Netflix**: Netflix uses RL to personalize the content recommendations for each user based on their viewing history and ratings. The RL agent learns to rank the movies and shows that the user will most likely watch and enjoy.
- **Amazon**: Amazon uses RL to recommend products based on browsing and purchasing behavior for each user. The RL agent learns to suggest relevant, diverse, and novel items for each user.

Finance is a domain where RL can have a significant impact, enabling agents to learn how to trade effectively in complex and dynamic financial markets. RL can help traders to make optimal decisions based on market data and signals, such as prices, volumes, trends, or news. These signals can be noisy, incomplete, or delayed, and the market conditions can change rapidly and unpredictably. RL agents can learn to navigate these challenges and adapt to the changing environment to maximize profits and minimize risks. RL agents can also learn from their experiences and improve their performance over time without requiring explicit supervision or feedback. RL can be applied to various aspects of finance, such as portfolio optimization, asset allocation, risk management, market making, algorithmic trading, and high-frequency trading. RL can also be used to model the behavior of other market participants and anticipate their actions and reactions. RL can provide traders with a competitive edge in the financial markets, as it can help them to exploit opportunities, avoid losses, and achieve higher returns.

11.1.1.13 Advantages of Reinforcement Learning

- **Versatility**: RL can learn from trial and error, without requiring explicit supervision or prior knowledge. RL can tackle problems that are dynamic, uncertain, and non-linear, where traditional methods may fail or be inefficient. One of the main advantages of RL is that it can be applied to a wide range of domains and tasks, where the goal is to optimize some reward or performance measure. For example, RL can train autonomous vehicles to drive safely and efficiently in various traffic conditions, by learning from their own experiences and feedback. RL can also teach AI systems to play strategic games like Go and chess, by exploring different moves and outcomes, and learning from their own successes and failures. RL can even surpass human experts in these domains, as demonstrated by AlphaGo and AlphaZero. Another benefit of RL is that it can handle problems where obtaining labeled data is difficult or expensive, such as robotics, healthcare, or finance. In these domains, RL can learn from sparse or delayed rewards, such as the final outcome of a task or a long-term objective. RL can also improve healthcare outcomes and reduce costs, by learning optimal treatment policies for patients with complex and chronic conditions. RL can also optimize financial decisions and portfolios, by learning from market fluctuations and risk factors.
- **Adaptability**: Unlike supervised learning, which relies on pre-labeled data and a fixed objective function, RL agents interact with their environment and receive feedback through rewards or penalties. This feedback guides the agent to improve its behavior and achieve its goals. RL agents can adapt to changing environments and situations, as they do not assume a static or known data distribution. Instead, they learn from their own experience and exploration, which can lead to discovering new and better strategies. This makes RL suitable for scenarios where the conditions are dynamic or unpredictable, such as online advertising, recommender systems, or smart grids. In these domains, the agent must balance exploration and exploitation, deal with delayed or partial feedback, and cope with non-stationary or adversarial settings. RL provides a general framework and a set of algorithms to address these challenges and enable agents to learn and adapt effectively.
- **Detailed Planning**: RL agents learn from their own experience and the feedback they receive from the environment. RL agents aim to maximize their cumulative reward over time, which requires them to plan and consider the future outcomes of their actions. This makes RL suitable for problems that involve sequential decision-making, where each action affects the subsequent states and rewards. Some examples of such problems are navigation, scheduling, or resource allocation. To plan effectively, RL agents need to balance exploration and exploitation. Exploration means trying out new actions that may lead to better rewards in the future, while exploitation means choosing the best action based on current knowledge. A good RL agent should be able to trade-off between exploration and exploitation depending on the situation and the uncertainty. Another aspect of planning in RL is the horizon, which refers to how far ahead the agent looks when evaluating the value of an action. A short horizon means that the agent only considers the immediate reward of an action, while a long horizon means that the agent also assumes the

expected future rewards of that action and its consequences. A good RL agent should be able to adapt its horizon according to the problem characteristics and the available resources.

- **Exploration versus Exploitation**: This is a fundamental dilemma in RL. RL algorithms aim to learn a policy that maximizes the cumulative reward over time by interacting with the environment. However, the agent often faces a trade-off between exploring new actions that might lead to better outcomes in the future and exploiting the current knowledge to obtain immediate rewards. Exploration is essential for discovering novel information and avoiding suboptimal solutions, while exploitation is necessary for utilizing the existing information and achieving high performance. RL agents balance this trade-off by initially exploring a large space of possible actions to find the optimal policy and then gradually exploiting the learned policy to achieve the best performance. This allows them to adapt to uncertainty and variability in the environment, common challenges in real-world problems.
- **Making Decisions in Uncertain Scenarios**: One of the challenges of AI is to design agents that can make optimal decisions in uncertain scenarios. RL frameworks can handle uncertain scenarios by modeling the environment and using probabilistic reasoning. For example, MDPs are a standard RL problem model that captures the environment's stochastic nature and the agent's actions. RL agents can use Bayesian inference to update their beliefs about the environment and choose actions that maximize their expected utility. Given the evidence, the agent can incorporate new observations into its prior knowledge and calculate each state's posterior probability. The agent can then select the action with the highest expected value based on its current belief state and the reward function..

11.1.1.15 Disadvantages of Reinforcement Learning

- **Inefficiency**: RL algorithms learn from their experience by interacting with the environment and receiving rewards or penalties for their actions. However, this approach has some limitations that affect its efficiency and applicability. One of the main challenges of RL is the exploration–exploitation trade-off. Exploration is essential for discovering new and better policies but can also be costly and risky. Exploitation is safe and reliable but can also be suboptimal and prevent further improvement. Another challenge of RL is the data efficiency problem. This means that RL algorithms require much data and feedback to learn effectively. However, in some domains, data may be scarce or expensive to collect, or feedback may be delayed or noisy. This makes RL impractical for problems that demand fast and accurate solutions. A possible way to address these challenges is to incorporate prior knowledge, transfer learning, or simulation into the RL framework.
- **Hyperparameter Tuning**: This is a crucial step in designing and implementing RL algorithms. Hyperparameters are the settings that control various aspects of the algorithm, such as how fast it learns, how much it discounts future rewards, how often it explores new actions, and so on. Unlike the parameters the algorithm learns from data, such as the value function or the policy, the user or the designer specifies hyperparameters before running the algorithm. However, finding the optimal values for these hyperparameters is a challenging task, as they may significantly impact the performance and the convergence of the algorithm. Moreover, the optimal values may vary depending on the problem domain, the algorithm type, and the environment dynamics. Therefore, manually tuning the hyperparameters by trial and error can be inefficient and time-consuming. To address this challenge, automated methods for hyperparameter tuning have been

developed and applied to RL problems. These methods aim to find the best hyperparameters for a given problem by systematically searching through a predefined space of possible values. Some of the most common methods are:

- **Grid search**: This method divides the hyperparameter space into a grid of discrete values and evaluates the algorithm's performance for each combination of values on the grid. The combination that yields the highest performance is selected as the optimal one. This procedure is straightforward and simple to implement, but it can be computationally intensive, particularly if the hyperparameter space is large or high-dimensional.
- **Random search**: This method randomly samples values from the hyperparameter space and evaluates the algorithm's performance for each sample. The sample that yields the highest performance is selected as the optimal one. This method is more efficient than grid search, as it does not need to explore every possible combination of values. However, it may still miss some good regions of the hyperparameter space due to randomness.
- **Bayesian optimization**: This method uses a probabilistic model to capture the relationship between the hyperparameters and the algorithm's performance. Based on this model, it selects the next value to evaluate by balancing exploration (trying new values that may improve performance) and exploitation (using values known to perform well). The model is updated with each evaluation, and the process is repeated until a satisfactory performance is achieved or a budget limit is reached. This method is more effective than grid search and random search, as it can exploit prior knowledge and adaptively focus on promising regions of the hyperparameter space.

- **Lack of Convergence and Stability**: The need for convergence and stability in the learning process may prevent the agent from finding and following the best policy. Convergence and stability are desirable properties of any learning algorithm, as they ensure that the algorithm will eventually reach a solution that does not change significantly over time. However, achieving these properties in RL is not trivial, especially when using function approximators to represent the value function or the policy. Function approximators, such as neural networks, can generalize across similar states or actions and learn compact and expressive representations of the value function or the policy. However, they also introduce errors or biases that may affect the learning process in undesirable ways. Moreover, a function approximator may not be consistent with the Bellman optimality equation, which defines the relationship between the optimal value function and the optimal policy. This inconsistency may cause the value function or the policy to oscillate or diverge rather than converge to a fixed point. Another source of instability in RL is the interplay between exploration and exploitation. Both exploration and exploitation are essential for finding an optimal policy, but they may also conflict. Several RL algorithms have been proposed to overcome this challenge, guaranteeing convergence and stability under certain conditions. Temporal difference learning, policy gradient methods, and actor–critic methods are the categories of these algorithms.
- **Sparse Rewards and Credit Assignment**: In RL, an agent learns from experience by interacting with an environment and receiving rewards. The reward function is a crucial component of the learning process. However, designing such a reward function can be challenging, especially for complex tasks that require long-term planning and reasoning. In some cases, the rewards may be sparse or delayed, meaning that the agent receives feedback only after a long sequence of actions or at the end of an episode.

A possible way to overcome this challenge is to use reward shaping techniques, which aim to modify or augment the original reward function with additional rewards that guide the agent towards better policies. One common technique is potential-based shaping, which adds a potential function that measures the agent's progress toward the goal state. The potential function can be derived from domain knowledge, heuristics, or learned from data. Another technique is inverse reinforcement learning, which tries to infer the reward function from expert demonstrations. The idea is to assume that the expert is acting optimally according to some unknown reward function and then learn this reward function by observing the expert's behavior. This way, the agent can imitate the expert and achieve similar performance.

- **Safety and Ethics**: These are crucial aspects of RL, as RL agents may not always behave as expected or desired when they learn from trial and error. For instance, an RL agent may learn to cheat or exploit loopholes in the reward function or the environment to achieve higher rewards without considering its actions' long-term effects or moral implications. This may lead to undesirable outcomes, such as violating ethical norms, damaging the environment, or harming other agents. Safe RL techniques have been proposed to address this challenge to ensure RL agents adhere to specific safety and ethical principles while learning.Some examples of safe RL techniques are:
- **Risk-aware RL**: This technique aims to minimize the risk or uncertainty associated with the agent's actions by incorporating a risk measure into the reward or value functions. For example, an agent may learn to avoid actions with a high probability of causing harm or failure or having a high variance in their outcomes.
- **Constrained RL**: This technique aims to enforce hard or soft constraints on the agent's actions by adding a penalty term or a Lagrange multiplier to the reward or value functions. For example, an agent may learn to respect physical laws, environmental boundaries, or social norms by receiving a negative reward or a lower value for violating them.
- **Human-in-the-Loop RL**: This technique involves human feedback or guidance in the agent's learning process using human demonstrations, preferences, corrections, or evaluations as additional inputs or outputs. For example, an agent may learn to align its goals and values with those of humans by imitating human behavior, following human instructions, correcting its mistakes based on human feedback, or optimizing its reward based on human preferences.

```
import numpy as np
# Define the environment
num_states = 6
num_actions = 2
reward_matrix = np. array([[0, 0], [0, 0], [0, 0], [0, 0], [0, 0], [100,
0]])
transition_matrix = np. array([[1, 0], [1, 2], [2, 3], [3, 4], [4, 5],
[5, 5]])
# Define the Q-table
q_table = np.zeros((num_states, num_actions))
# Define the hyperparameters
num_episodes = 1000
```

```
learning_rate = 0.1
discount_factor = 0.99
epsilon = 0.1
# Q-learning algorithm
for episode in range(num_episodes):
    state = 0  # starting state
    done = False
    while not done:
        # Choose an action using epsilon-greedy strategy
        if np.random.uniform(0, 1) < epsilon:
            action = np.random.randint(num_actions)
        else:
            action = np.argmax(q_table[state])
        # Perform the chosen action and observe the next state, and
reward
        next_state = transition_matrix[state, action]
        reward = reward_matrix[state, action]
        # Update the Q-table
        q_table[state, action] = (1 - learning_rate) * q_table[state, ac-
tion] + learning_rate * (
                reward + discount_factor *
np.max(q_table[next_state]))
        state = next_state
        if state == num_states - 1:
            done = True
# Print the learned Q-table
print("Learned Q-table:")
print(q_table)
```

The code shown above is an implementation of the Q-learning algorithm. The Q-table is initialized with zeroes. The hyperparameters are the number of episodes for the learning process, the learning rate which determines to what extent newly acquired information overrides old information, the discount factor which is used to balance immediate and future rewards, and epsilon for the epsilon-greedy strategy which balances exploration and exploitation by choosing between a random action and the best known action.

During each episode, the algorithm starts from the initial state and continues until a terminal state is reached. In each step, an action is chosen using the epsilon-greedy strategy. After performing the action, the algorithm observes the reward and the next state, and updates the Q-table value. This process is repeated for the defined number of episodes, allowing the Q-table to converge to the optimal action values. Finally, the learned Q-table is printed, showing the value of each action in each state as learned by the algorithm through interaction with the environment.

11.2 Multitask Learning

Multitask learning is an ML technique that instructs a single model to execute multiple related tasks simultaneously (Fig. 11.14). Instead of building separate models for each task, multitask learning uses the information shared across tasks to enhance the model's performance and generalization.

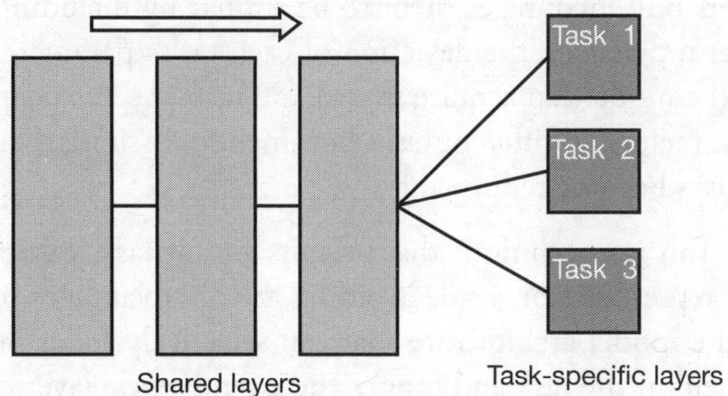

Figure 11.14 Example of multitask learning

Multitask learning is beneficial for solving real-world problems involving multiple interdependent subtasks that can mutually benefit one another. Object detection, semantic segmentation, and image captioning can be simultaneously learned in computer vision using a common feature extractor and distinct output layers. By acquiring knowledge from multiple tasks, the model can identify shared features that enable it to construct more accurate representations and perform better on some or all tasks.

Several techniques can be applied to achieve multitask learning. They depend on the degree of sharing and the model's structure. Some examples of these techniques are discussed below.

Hard parameter sharing: This is a technique that can be used to train multiple tasks using a single model. The idea is to share the lower layers of the model across all tasks while having separate upper layers for each task. This way, the lower layers can learn common features useful for all tasks, such as word embeddings, syntactic structures, or semantic representations. Conversely, the upper layers can learn specific features relevant to each task, such as sentiment analysis, named entity recognition, or machine translation. By sharing the lower layers, the model can benefit from several advantages:

- It can reduce the risk of overfitting since the lower layers are exposed to more data from different tasks.
- It can improve the generalization ability of the model since the lower layers can capture more diverse and robust features.
- It can save computational and memory resources since the model has fewer parameters to train and store.

Soft parameter sharing: This is a technique that uses distinct layers for each assignment but normalizes them to be comparable. This is possible by incorporating a penalty term into the loss function that measures the distance between the parameters of different assignments. Consequently, the model can acquire shared and task-specific characteristics without divergence or duplication. Here, a single neural network is simultaneously trained to perform multiple related tasks. The goal is to utilize the similarities and differences between tasks to enhance the generalizability and efficacy of the model. However, sharing all network layers across all tasks may result in interference and confusion, as various tasks may require different representations or features. Soft parameter sharing, therefore, permits each task to have its layers but encourages them to be similar by including a regularisation term in the loss function. This term penalizes the deviation of each task's parameters from the average of all tasks' parameters. Thus, the model can acquire shared and task-specific characteristics while avoiding divergence (when the parameters of different tasks become too dissimilar) and duplication (when the parameters of different tasks become redundant).

Task-specific attention: This is a technique that permits a multitask learning model to capitalize on the advantages of shared representation while avoiding the disadvantages of interference and confusion. It adds a layer to the model architecture that can selectively focus on various portions of the shared representation based on the task and input. The attentiveness layer computes a weighted sum of the shared representation, where the weights reflect the importance of each feature for each task and is learned from the data. Thus, the model can utilize common information across tasks while focusing on the specific aspects of each task. By doing so, the model can adapt dynamically to various tasks, enhancing its performance and generalizability.

Improved generalization, higher data efficiency, and regularisation are all advantages of multitask learning. The model may take advantage of the natural connections between tasks by learning from various them, leading to a deeper comprehension of the data. In addition, because multitask learning enables the model to transfer information between tasks, it can be beneficial when there is a lack of labeled data for specific tasks.

However, multitask learning has its challenges. Tasks must be carefully chosen and balanced since those unrelated may interfere with one another's performance. It might be challenging to allocate resources to each activity and create a typical architecture. Furthermore, multitask learning assumes adequate information is communicated throughout tasks, which may only sometimes be true.
Examples of multitask learning in ML are as follows:

Object Detection and Classification: This task involves training an ML model to detect and classify objects in an image, including vehicles, humans, and animals. The model generates contours surrounding the detected objects and category labels. The model learns to extract relevant features for both detection and classification, and it can deal with various object and scene types. Specifically, this assignment requires the model to identify the regions of interest in an image, where each region contains an object belonging to a particular category. The model then allocates a probability score to each region, indicating the degree of certainty it contains an object. In addition, the model predicts a class designation for each region, such as automobile, dog, or human. The model outputs the regions with high probability scores as bounding outlines and class designations. The model learns to extract features such as edges, shapes, colors, and textures pertinent for detection and classification. The model can accommodate numerous object sizes, orientations, poses, occlusions, and occlusions, as well as diverse scene backgrounds and lighting conditions.

Tasks in NLP: Natural Language Processing (NLP) is an interdisciplinary discipline that aims to enable machines to comprehend and produce natural languages, such as written texts, spoken language, and human conversations. NLP comprises a vast array of tasks involving varying degrees of linguistic analysis and representation, including:

- **Entity recognition**: This entails identifying and extracting named entities from a provided text, such as people, places, organizations, dates, etc. The entity recognition task would output "Jakson" as a person entity, "Hawaii" as a location entity, and "August 4, 1975" as a date entity, for example, in the sentence "Jakson was born in Hawaii on August 4, 1975."
- **Text classification**: This entails designating a predetermined label or category to a given text based on its subject matter or function. In the sentence "Please send me the most recent report by tomorrow," the text classification task would label the text as "request."
- **Part-of-speech tagging**: This involves designating a grammatical category or function to each word in a given text based on the word's role and context. The part-of-speech labeling task would output "she" as a pronoun, "runs" and "jumps" as verbs, "fast" and "high" as adverbs, and "and" as a conjunction in the sentence "She runs quickly and jumps high."

Multitask learning is used in NLP to train a single model to simultaneously perform multiple tasks. The notion is that by learning from various information sources and objectives, the model can utilize common linguistic knowledge and characteristics across multiple tasks and domains. A multitask learning model, for instance, can be trained to simultaneously recognize entities, analyze sentiments, classify texts, and identify parts of speech in a given text. This can enhance the model's generalization ability and performance on each task.

Image Segmentation and Depth Estimation: Segmentation divides an image into meaningful regions or segments, each corresponding to a distinct object or scene component. For instance, we wish to segment an image of a street scene into regions such as sky, road, building, vehicle, and pedestrian. Segmentation can be performed at various granularities, including pixel, superpixel, and object levels. Pixel-level segmentation labels each pixel in an image according to the region or category to which it belongs. Segmentation at the superpixel level organizes pixels into larger regions with similar characteristics, such as color, texture, or shape. Object-level segmentation detects, localizes, and draws bounding frames around individual image objects.

The process of inferring the distance or depth of each pixel in an image from the camera is known as depth estimation. The estimation of depth can provide valuable information about the 3D structure and geometry of the scene, allowing the model to comprehend the relative position and scale of various objects. Various signals, such as stereo vision, motion parallax, shading, and texture gradient, can be used to estimate depth. Using two or more images captured from slightly different vantage points, stereo vision computes the disparity between pixels, which is inversely proportional to depth. Motion parallax estimates the depth of an object based on the apparent shift in its position as the camera moves. Shading infers the shape and depth of an object from the variation in luminance or color of its surface. Texture gradient employs the variation in size or density of a textured pattern as it recedes into the distance to determine its depth.

We need to train a model that can enhance its performance with segmentation and depth estimation. The model should be able to derive visual features pertinent to both tasks and learn how to combine them meaningfully. In addition, the model must account for varying viewpoints and occlusions, which can influence the visibility and appearance of various regions and objects in an image. The model should generate two outputs for each input image: a mask for each region or category and a depth map for the entire image. The mask should indicate which pixels belong to which region or type, while the depth map should display the distance between each pixel and the camera.

```
import tensorflow as tf
from tensorflow.keras.layers import Dense, Input
from tensorflow.keras.models import Model
# Define your multitask neural network architecture
def multitask_model(input_shape, num_tasks):
    inputs = Input(shape=input_shape)
    shared_layer = Dense(64, activation='relu')(inputs)
    # Create separate output layers for each task
    task_outputs = []
    for _ in range(num_tasks):
        task_layer = Dense(32, activation='relu')(shared_layer)
        task_output = Dense(1, activation='linear')(task_layer)
        task_outputs.append(task_output)
    # Create the model with multiple outputs
    model = Model(inputs=inputs, outputs=task_outputs)
    return model
# Create your dataset and split it into features and labels for each task
x_task1 =...
y_task1 =...
x_task2 =...
y_task2 =...
# Define the input shape and number of tasks
input_shape = x_task1.shape[1:]
num_tasks = 2
# Create the multitask model
model = multitask_model(input_shape, num_tasks)
# Compile the model
model.compile(optimizer='adam', loss='mse', metrics=['mae'])
# Train the multitask model
model.fit(x_task1, [y_task1, y_task2], batch_size=32, epochs=10)
# Make predictions for both tasks
predictions_task1, predictions_task2 = model.predict(x_task1)
# Evaluate the model
loss_task1, mae_task1 = model.evaluate(x_task1, y_task1)
loss_task2, mae_task2 = model.evaluate(x_task2, y_task2)
```

The code shown above is a Python script that uses TensorFlow and Keras to define, compile, train, and evaluate a multitask neural network model. First, the script imports the necessary TensorFlow modules. The script then sets up placeholders for the data sets (`x_task1`, `y_task1`, `x_task2`, `y_task2`), which would be filled with actual data in a real-world scenario. The input shape and number of tasks are defined, and the multitask model is instantiated with these parameters.

The model is compiled with the Adam optimizer and mean squared error (MSE) loss function, which is appropriate for regression tasks. Training occurs through the model.fit method, where the model learns to predict the labels (`y_task1`, `y_task2`) from the features (`x_task1`). The model is trained for 10 epochs with a batch size of 32, which are hyper-parameters that can be tuned for better performance.

After training, the model's predictive performance is assessed using the model.predict method, and the results are evaluated with the model.evaluate method, providing loss and MAE for each task.

11.3 Online Learning

Online learning (Fig. 11.15) is a type of ML in which models are continually updated as new data is added. It is also known as incremental learning or streaming learning.

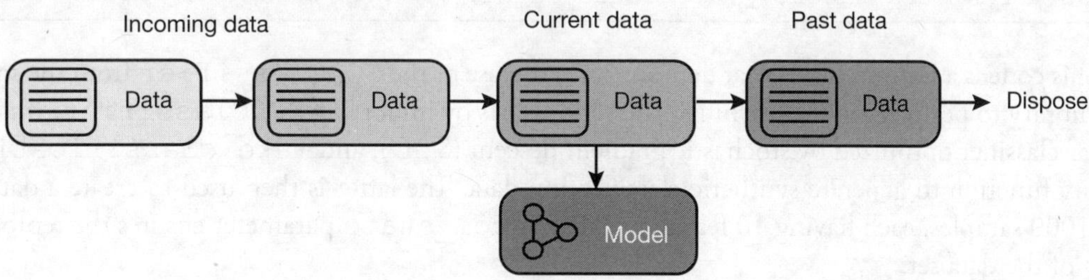

Figure 11.15 Example of online learning

Online learning occurs in real-time and can adapt to new data as it arrives. This differs from other forms of computer learning in that the model is updated gradually instead of all at once. For instance, if you were attempting to predict the weather and it began to rain unexpectedly, online learning algorithms could adjust their predictions accordingly.

Another feature of online learning is that it can manage vast amounts of data without storing or accessing it all simultaneously. This is comparable to attempting to organize all the volumes in a library. Instead of trying to read every book, you could simply read a summary of each book to determine its subject matter. Finally, online learning is very effective at utilizing its memory. It only needs to retain the most recent data or a summary of the data, making it incredibly efficient and quick.

Examples of online learning algorithms are online gradient descent, stochastic gradient descent, and online random forests.

```
from sklearn.linear_model import SGDClassifier
from sklearn.datasets import make_classification
# Generate some synthetic data for demonstration
X, y = make_classification(n_samples=1000, n_features=10,
random_state=42)
# Initialize the online learning model
model = SGDClassifier(loss='log', random_state=42)
# Perform online Learning
for i in range(X.shape[0]):
    # Extract a single data point
    x_i, y_i = X[i], y[i]
 # Update the model with the new data point
 model.partial_fit([x_i], [y_i], classes=[0, 1])
# Generate a new data point for prediction
new_data_point, true_label = X[0], y[0]
# Make predictions with the updated model
predicted_label = model.predict([new_data_point])
# Print the true label and predicted label
print("True Label:", true_label)
print("Predicted Label:", predicted_label)
```

This code is a Python script that demonstrates the use of the `SGDClassifier` from the scikit-learn library to perform online learning. The script starts by importing `SGDClassifier`, which is a linear classifier optimized by stochastic gradient descent (SGD), and `make_classification`, a utility function to generate synthetic classification data. The latter is then used to create a data set with 1000 samples, each having 10 features. The `random_state` parameter ensures the reproducibility of the data set.

An instance of `SGDClassifier` is created with the log loss function. The script enters a loop where it iterates over each sample in the data set. For each iteration, it extracts a single data point (`x_i`) and its corresponding label (`y_i`). The model is then updated with the new data point using the `partial_fit` method. The `classes` parameter is specified to inform the model about the possible classes in the data set.

After the model has been trained on all the data points, a new data point is selected for prediction. Here, the script reuses the first data point from the data set as the new data point. The `predict` method is called on to predict the label of the new data point. Finally, the script prints out the true label and the predicted label for the new data point, allowing you to compare the model's prediction against the actual label.

11.4 Sequence Learning

Sequence learning is a computer program that aids in predicting or comprehending sequential data. It is comparable to reading a storybook, where you must turn the pages to understand what is happening. An essential aspect of sequence learning is that it considers the order of the data. To comprehend how the weather changes throughout the day, for instance, you must examine the data in the correct order. You can only predict the temperature at noon by knowing what it is in the morning.

The context of the data is also considered. This means it examines previous data to predict what will occur next. For instance, if you attempt to comprehend what someone is saying in a conversation, you must consider what they have said to predict what they may say next. Lastly, sequence learning can accommodate varying data lengths. This means that it can comprehend shorter or lengthier sequences than others.

Examples of sequence learning are recurrent neural networks (RNNs), long short-term memory (LSTM) networks, and transformers.

Step 1: Install TensorFlow

```
!pip install tensorflow
```

Step 2:

```
import numpy as np
from tensorflow.keras.models import Sequential
from tensorflow.keras.layers import LSTM, Dense
# Example input sequence
input_sequence = "Hello, how are you today?"
# Preprocessing: Create character-level vocabulary and encode the input
sequence
vocab = sorted(set(input_sequence))
char_to_int = {c: i for i, c in enumerate(vocab)}
encoded_sequence = [char_to_int[c] for c in input_sequence]
# Generate training samples and labels
input_length = 10
sequences = []
labels = []
for i in range(len(encoded_sequence) - input_length):
    sequences.append(encoded_sequence[i: i + input_length])
    labels.append(encoded_sequence[i + input_length])
# Convert training data to numpy arrays
X = np.reshape(sequences, (len(sequences), input_length, 1))
y = np.array(labels)
# Build the RNN model
model = Sequential()
model.add(LSTM(128, input_shape=(input_length, 1)))
model.add(Dense(len(vocab), activation='softmax'))
# Compile the model
model.compile(loss='sparse_categorical_crossentropy', optimizer='adam')
# Train the model
model.fit(X, y, epochs=50, batch_size=64)
```

```
# Generate new text
seed = "Hello"
generated_text = seed
for _ in range(20):
    x = np.reshape([char_to_int[c] for c in seed[-input_length:]], (1,
input_length, 1))
    prediction = model.predict(x)
    next_char = vocab[np.argmax(prediction)]
    generated_text += next_char
    seed += next_char
print("Generated text:", generated_text)
```

This code is a Python program that uses the TensorFlow and NumPy libraries to create a character-level RNN for text generation. Initially, it imports the necessary modules from the libraries. The program starts by defining an input sequence, which is a string of text. It then creates a vocabulary, which is a sorted list of unique characters in the input sequence. This vocabulary is used to create a mapping of characters to integers (`char_to_int`), effectively encoding each character as a number. The input sequence is then encoded using this mapping.

Next, the program generates training samples and labels. It does this by creating sequences of a fixed length (`input_length`) from the encoded input sequence and assigning the next character in the input sequence as the label for each sequence. These sequences and labels are then converted into NumPy arrays, which are suitable for training the model.

The model is compiled with a loss function suitable for classification (`sparse_categorical_crossentropy`) and an optimizer (`adam`). The model is then trained on the prepared data for a specified number of epochs and batch size. After training, the program uses the model to generate new text. It starts with a seed string and predicts the next character iteratively, adding each new character to the generated text. This process is repeated for a specified number of characters (20 in this case). Finally, the generated text is printed out.

Table 11.3 lists the differences between online learning and sequence learning.

Table 11.3 Online learning versus sequence learning

	Online learning	**Sequence learning**
Problem domain	Emphasizes models that are constantly updated with fresh data.	Emphasizes modeling and prediction of sequential data.
Data characteristics	Frequently uses gradual or fluid information that does not explicitly establish chronological linkages.	The temporal connections found in sequential data are explicitly modeled.
Time sensitivity	Quickly changes the model in response to fresh inputs.	Takes into account temporal links to provide predictions based on prior context at each level.

(*Continued*)

Table 11.3 (Continued)

	Online learning	Sequence learning
Learning process	The model parameters are often modified after each data instance or mini-batch in online learning approaches.	In order to find correlations, these models usually analyze whole sequences or sub-sequences concurrently.
Applications	Used in systems for fraud detection, adaptive control, and online recommendations.	Used for sentiment analysis, speech recognition, and machine translation.

11.5 Prediction Learning

Prediction is making an educated estimate about the outcome or value of an input or set of inputs. ML models use the patterns and connections they find in historical data during training to forecast new, uncontaminated data results. After the input data has been processed, predictions are made using the trained model. The model converts the input into the predicted value or class label through mathematical operations and procedures.

It is critical to keep in mind that predictions made by ML are not always accurate. The amount and quality of training data, the complexity of the problem being solved, and the algorithm or model architecture used all impact how accurately a model makes predictions. ML uses cross-validation, hyperparameter tuning, and ensemble approaches to assess and improve prediction accuracy continuously.

Predictions in ML can be applied to various tasks, such as:

- Classification (assigning labels or categories to inputs)
- Regression (predicting continuous numerical values)
- Clustering (grouping similar instances)

11.6 Bagging and Boosting in Machine Learning

We often use the decision-tree method while making decisions. Businesses utilize these supervised ML techniques to enhance decision-making and boost surplus and profit. After employing a single decision tree, ensemble approaches combine many trees to provide better-projected results. The fundamental premise of the ensemble model is that an active learner might emerge from a group of weak learners. The two techniques listed below are used to implement the ensemble decision tree.

Bagging: Bagging is utilized when reducing a decision tree's variation is the aim. In this case, the goal is to split the training sample, chosen randomly with replacement, into a few smaller data sets. We used each subset of data to build its decision tree, and now we have an ensemble of many models. The average of all the assumptions from many decision trees is more valuable than just one.

When compared to bagging, random forest is superior. There is one additional step involved in predicting a random sample of data. Furthermore, it picks traits randomly rather than creating trees with all possible features. When there are several random trees, we obtain the Random Forest. The following steps are taken to implement a random forest:

1. Think about the X observations and Y properties of the training data set. The training data set is used to pick a model at random with substitution first.
2. The tree has reached its full size.
3. A forecast is produced by repeating the steps based on an amalgamation of predictions from n trees.

Advantages of using Random Forest: The ability to effectively manage data sets with multiple dimensions is one of the primary benefits of this method. This means that it can process large quantities of complex data and produce accurate results without sacrificing quality. A further advantage is its ability to maintain accuracy even when incomplete data are present. This is because the technique is designed to control missing quantity, allowing it to generate accurate results even if some data are missing from the data set.

Disadvantages of using Random Forest: When employing the random forest technique, it is essential to remember that the final prediction may not always provide an exact regression model value. This is because the prognosis depends on subgroup tree mean predictions. For instance, if we have a data set of patients and wish to predict their likelihood of developing a particular disease, we may analyze the data using the random forest technique. Because the final prognosis is based on the mean predictions from subgroup trees, we may not obtain an exact value for each patient's probability of developing the disease. Instead, we will calculate an estimate based on the average likelihood of all subgroup trees. This can be a disadvantage if precise patient-specific predictions are required. When employing the random forest technique, it is crucial to consider the tradeoffs between accuracy and speed closely.

Boosting: Boosting is a different ensemble method for assembling a set of predictors. In other words, at each step, we strive to reduce the net error from the preceding trees by fitting several trees, often selected at random.

When theory misclassifies a particular input, weak learners are gradually upgraded to higher-performing models by consolidating the entire set. As a result, there is a higher likelihood that the following hypothesis will correctly categorize the input. Gradient boosting increases the boosting process by focusing on the errors of previous predictors and improving upon them.

Gradient Boosting = Gradient Descent + Boosting

The gradient descent method utilized in this strategy may be used to optimize any differentiable loss function. A group of trees is created by gradually adding individual trees. The difference between the actual and predicted values is the loss that is being attempted to be recovered by the following tree.

Advantages of using Gradient Boosting: It supports multiple loss functions, which can be employed based on the nature of the problem being addressed. For instance, if the objective is to minimize mean squared error, the least squares loss function can be applied. The log loss function may be more applicable if the aim is to predict probabilities. Another benefit is its ability to manage variable interactions. This can be incredibly beneficial when working with complex data sets in which variables may have non-linear interactions. There may be interactions between variables such as age, gender, and smoking status when predicting a person's likelihood of developing cardiac disease. Using gradient boosting, we can construct a model that considers these interactions and generates more accurate predictions.

Disadvantages of using Gradient Boosting: It requires careful adjustment of multiple hyperparameters. This necessitates taking the time to fine-tune the parameters to achieve optimal performance from your model. Image classification is an additional application where hyperparameter optimization is crucial. To classify images using gradient boosting, you must experiment with various values for parameters such as the number of trees, minimum samples in a leaf, and maximum features. If these values are not set appropriately, your model may not precisely predict the image's class.
Table 11.4 lists the differences between bagging and boosting.

Table 11.4 Bagging versus boosting

Bagging	Boosting
Several subsets of training data are randomly selected from the complete training data set with replacements.	The complete training data set is divided into several subgroups, which are then randomly selected with replacements.
Bagging makes an effort to address the overfitting problem.	Bias is intended to be lessened.
Bagging must be used if the classifier is unstable (high variance).	We must use boosting if the classifier is reliable and straightforward (high bias).
Each model is given the same amount of weight.	Models are graded based on how effectively they function.
Prejudice is not the goal; the goal is to reduce variation.	Rather than making an effort to reduce volatility.
Linking predictions of the same sort this way is the most straightforward approach.	It serves as a means of connecting forecasts from various categories.
Each model is built from the ground up.	The performance of previous models has an impact on new ones.

11.7 Trends in Machine Learning Technology

Due to continuous technical advances, predicting what type of technology will be in demand in a particular year is challenging. Based on what we have seen, these are some of the most promising ML advancements.

Foundation models: These models are a new paradigm in AI that aims to leverage the power of large-scale data and computation to create versatile and adaptable systems. According to a report by Stanford researchers, foundation models are "models that can be easily adapted to a wide range of downstream tasks, potentially replacing task-specific models and changing the development process and use of machine learning." One of the most prominent examples of foundation models is large language models (LLMs), such as GPT-4, Claude 2, and Llama 2, which are trained on massive amounts of text data and can generate natural language for various purposes, such as writing, summarizing, translating, answering questions, and conversing. Another example of foundation models is text-to-image models, such as Stable Diffusion from Stability AI, which can generate realistic images from natural language descriptions.

Foundation models are not limited to language and vision. They can also be applied to other modalities, such as audio, video, code, and graphs. For example, Jukebox from OpenAI is a foundation model that can generate music with lyrics from a given genre, artist, or mood. CodeBERT from Microsoft is a foundation model that can generate code from natural language specifications or vice versa. Graphormer from Alibaba is a foundation model that can learn from graph-structured data and perform molecular property prediction and drug discovery tasks.

Multimodal machine learning (MML): This is a branch of AI that aims to create models that can process and integrate information from different modalities, such as vision, speech, text, audio, and gesture. Unlike traditional ML models that rely on a single modality, such as images or text, MML models can leverage the complementary and redundant information from multiple modalities to achieve better performance and robustness.

One of the main challenges of MML is to find effective ways to represent and fuse information from different modalities. Another challenge of MML is to deal with the heterogeneity and imbalance of the data across different modalities.

MML has many potential applications in various domains, such as computer vision, natural language processing, speech recognition, multimedia retrieval, human-computer interaction, and education. Some examples of MML tasks are:

- Image captioning: Generating a natural language description of an image
- Video summarization: Producing a summary of a long video
- Speech emotion recognition: Identifying the emotion of a speaker from their voice
- Multimodal sentiment analysis: Detecting the sentiment of a user from their text, voice, and facial expression
- Visual question answering: Answering a natural language question about an image
- Multimodal dialogue: Engaging in a natural language conversation with a user using multiple modalities

Transformers: Transformers are AI architecture that can convert one data sequence into another. For example, they can translate a sentence in one language into another. Transformers are composed of two main components: encoders and decoders. Encoders process the input data and extract relevant features, while decoders generate the output data based on the features from the encoders. Transformers are widely used to develop foundation models, which are large-scale AI models that can perform various tasks across different domains. Since transformers can handle different data types, such as text, images, audio, and video, they must be customized for each application.

Transformers belong to a class of models called Seq2Seq, which stands for sequence-to-sequence. These models are commonly used in NLP applications, such as text summarization, machine translation, speech recognition, and text generation. Seq2Seq models can capture the meaning and structure of a sequence of words rather than treating each word in isolation. Transformers have an advantage over other Seq2Seq models (RNNs and CNNs) because they can learn long-term dependencies between words without losing information. This is achieved by using self-attention, which allows each word to attend to every other word in the sequence. Self-attention also enables parallel processing, which makes transformers faster and more efficient than RNNs or CNNs.

Embedded machine learning: ML techniques may run on various types of hardware, thanks to a subfield called embedded machine learning, often known as TinyML. Household appliances, laptops, mobile phones, intelligent home systems, and other devices use TinyML.

The industry that makes chipsets is one of the primary drivers of expanding embedded machine-learning systems. Ten years ago, Moore's law predicted that they would double every two years, which enabled us to foresee both the increase in computing power and the number of transistors on a chipset. However, we have noticed a 40–60% yearly growth in transistor density in recent years. In our judgment, this tendency will persist in the upcoming years.

Low-code and no-code solutions: These are platforms or tools that allow users to create applications or models without writing much or any code. However, despite their popularity and convenience, low-code and no-code solutions often have limitations and drawbacks compared to conventional development methods. For example, they may need to offer more customization, flexibility, scalability, or security for complex or sensitive projects. They may also rely on pre-built components or templates not optimized or updated for the latest technologies or standards. Therefore, low-code and no-code solutions are usually of lower quality than the ones developed by skilled programmers or data scientists who can fine-tune and troubleshoot their code.

In the ML market, where innovation and quality are crucial, startups that can overcome these challenges will have a competitive edge. For instance, some startups use NLP to enable users to create models or applications by describing their goals or requirements in plain language. Others use automated machine learning (AutoML) to generate optimal models or pipelines based on user data and preferences.

Data streams: A data stream is a continuous flow of data that does not belong to a fixed or predefined data set and appears gradually and frequently in real-time. Various industries utilize data streams extensively, including sensor networks, social media feeds, financial transactions, and online advertising. Managing data streams differs from traditional batch learning environments, where the data is assumed to be accessible and inert. In contrast, the data in data streams are typically too large to be stored entirely, and their distribution may alter over time. This phenomenon is referred to as concept drift, and it presents a challenge for machine learning algorithms that must adapt to shifting data patterns. In addition, data streams necessitate efficient and real-time processing, as the data must be analyzed rapidly before the arrival of new data. This limits the computational resources and memory utilization of the algorithms.

Active learning: Active learning is an ML paradigm that seeks to reduce the amount of labeled data required to train a model by selecting the most informative and relevant examples from a pool of unlabeled data. An oracle, such as a human expert or a trustworthy information source then label the chosen examples. Consequently, active learning can save time, money, and effort when labeling large data sets, particularly for tasks requiring complex or domain-specific annotations. When coping with data streams, however, active learning faces additional obstacles. Active learning methods must, therefore, be capable of adapting to the ever-changing data distribution and selecting examples that are not only instructive but also representative of the current state of the stream. In addition, active learning techniques must adhere to the real-time constraints of data stream processing and avoid excessive delays or interruptions in data flow.

SUMMARY

- Reinforcement learning (RL) is the process of learning from actions and rewards; it plays a crucial role in the development of intelligent systems.
- Markov decision processes (MDP), a mathematical framework, are widely used to model and solve real-world sequential decision-making problems under uncertainty, making them a practical and valuable tool in various fields.
- Multitask learning, a powerful technique, enables the learning of multiple related tasks simultaneously using a shared representation or model, thereby enhancing efficiency and performance in complex learning scenarios.
- The online learning framework represents the formulation and objectives of online learning problems, such as regret minimization, adversarial settings, and expert advice settings.
- The sequence prediction framework represents the formulation and objectives of sequence prediction problems, such as next symbol prediction, next word prediction, next action prediction, etc.
- Bagging is a method that reduces the variance of a single learner by averaging the predictions of multiple learners trained on bootstrap samples of the data.
- Boosting is a method that reduces the bias of a single learner by iteratively adding learners that focus on the errors made by previous learners.
- Model-based algorithms assume that the transition and reward functions of the models are known or can be learned and used to plan and choose the best action.
- Model-free algorithms do not rely on the model but instead learn from trial and error by interacting with the environment and observing the outcomes.
- Q-learning is a model-free reinforcement learning algorithm that learns an action–value function directly from experience.
- Value function approximation is a technique that uses a function to estimate the expected return of each state or state–action pair instead of storing the values in a table.
- Policy search is a technique that directly optimizes the policy, which is a function that maps states to actions without using a value function.
- Partially observable Markov decision process (POMDP) is a framework that extends the standard Markov decision process (MDP) to handle situations where the agent does not have full observability of the environment.
- A particular case of MDPs is linear quadratic regulation (LQR), where the state and action spaces are continuous and linear, and the reward function is quadratic.
- An extension of LQR is linear quadratic Gaussian (LQG), where the state transitions are subject to Gaussian noise.
- The Bellman equations are a set of mathematical expressions that describe how to find the optimal value function and policy for a Markov decision process (MDP).

- Value iteration is a method that finds the optimal value function and policy for a Markov decision process (MDP) by iteratively updating the values of each state. The value function represents the expected return that can be obtained from each state under a given policy.
- Policy iteration is finding the optimal policy for a Markov decision process by repeatedly performing two steps: policy evaluation and policy improvement.
- Policy search is a class of reinforcement learning algorithms that directly optimizes the policy without using a value function.
- A Markov chain is a mathematical representation of a series of events in which the probability of moving on to the subsequent event is solely based on the preceding event.
- Policy gradient methods are a class of reinforcement learning algorithms that optimize the policy directly rather than indirectly through a value function.
- Actor–critic methods are a class of reinforcement learning algorithms that combine the advantages of policy-based and value-based methods.
- Sequence modeling, often called sequential learning, involves simulating and forecasting sequential data, where the order of the data points is critical.
- In machine learning, prediction is making educated estimates about the outcome or value of an input or set of inputs.

EXERCISES

Part A (Objective Questions)

1. Alice is working on a robot that needs to navigate through a complex environment. She wants to use a reinforcement learning algorithm that directly optimizes the policy without using a value function. Which technique should Alice consider using?
   a) Q-learning
   b) Value function approximation
   c) Policy search
   d) POMDP
2. Bob is developing a reinforcement learning algorithm for a scenario where the agent doesn't have full observability of the environment. The agent maintains a belief state and updates it based on actions and observations. Which framework is Bob working with?
   a) MDP
   b) LQR
   c) POMDP
   d) LQG
3. Carla is working on a reinforcement learning problem where the state and action spaces are continuous and linear, and the reward function is quadratic. Which specific case of MDP is Carla dealing with?
   a) LQR
   b) MDP
   c) LQG
   d) POMDP
4. David is designing a reinforcement learning algorithm and is focused on handling large or continuous state spaces. He wants to estimate the expected return of each state or state-action pair using a function instead of a table. Which technique should David employ?
   a) Q-learning
   b) Policy search
   c) Value function approximation
   d) Value iteration

5. Emily is working on a reinforcement learning algorithm that involves learning an action-value function directly from experience. Which model-free algorithm should she use?
   a) Policy iteration
   b) Value function approximation
   c) Q-learning
   d) Model-based algorithm

6. Frank is developing a reinforcement learning algorithm and is considering using either value iteration or policy iteration. He aims to find the optimal value function and policy of an MDP. Which iterative methods should Frank use?
   a) Q-learning and Policy search
   b) Value iteration and Q-learning
   c) Policy iteration and Value iteration
   d) Value function approximation and Policy iteration

7. Grace is working on a reinforcement learning problem where an agent interacts with an environment and learns a rule mapping states to actions to maximize rewards. What type of policy is Grace trying to learn?
   a) Value policy
   b) Optimal policy
   c) Transition policy
   d) Reward policy

8. Henry is studying reinforcement learning and comes across a set of equations that relate the optimal value function and policy of an MDP. What are these equations called?
   a) Bellman equations
   b) Transition equations
   c) Markov equations
   d) Iteration equations

9. Alex is working on a reinforcement learning problem where the agent doesn't have full access to the environment's state and only receives partial or noisy observations. What type of mathematical formulation is Alex dealing with?
   a) MDP
   b) LQR
   c) LQG
   d) POMDP

10. Beth is designing a reinforcement learning algorithm and wants to use a method that directly optimizes the policy without using value or action-value functions. Which approach should Beth consider?
    a) Q-learning
    b) Value function approximation
    c) Policy search
    d) Gradient ascent

11. Charlie is implementing a reinforcement learning algorithm for a problem with a continuous and high-dimensional action space. He wants an alternative to Q-learning that can handle such scenarios effectively. What approach should Charlie explore?
    a) Policy search
    b) Gradient-free methods
    c) Value function approximation
    d) Evolutionary algorithms

12. Diana is concerned about the memory and computation requirements of Q-learning due to a large table of action values for each state-action pair. Which technique could Diana use to mitigate this issue?
    a) Deep Q learning
    b) Policy iteration
    c) Gradient-based methods
    d) LQR

13. Emma is studying reinforcement learning and wants to employ an approach that updates the policy parameters using gradient ascent. What category of policy search method should Emma focus on?

a) Gradient-free methods
b) Value function approximation
c) Evolutionary algorithms
d) Gradient-based methods

14. Fred is developing a reinforcement learning algorithm and is interested in a model-free technique that updates an action-value function using samples of state, action, reward, and next state. Which algorithm is suitable for Fred?

a) Policy iteration
b) Q-learning
c) Value function approximation
d) Policy search

15. Gina is studying reinforcement learning and is focused on a technique that represents the value or action-value function using a function, reducing memory and computation requirements. What technique is Gina researching?

a) Q-learning
b) Policy search
c) Value function approximation
d) Policy iteration

16. Harry is working on a reinforcement learning project and wants the algorithm to converge to the optimal action-value function under certain conditions. Which algorithm should Harry consider using?

a) Value iteration
b) Policy search
c) Q-learning
d) Gradient-based methods

17. Alice is studying reinforcement learning and is interested in a framework that defines the transition function, reward function, states, and actions for modeling problems. Which framework is Alice learning about?

a) Gradient Descent Process (GDP)
b) Reinforcement Modeling Process (RMP)
c) Markov Decision Process (MDP)
d) Optimal Reward Framework (ORF)

18. Bob is designing a reinforcement learning scenario where the future state and reward depend only on the current state and action, not on the history of previous states and actions. Which property is Bob's scenario satisfying?

a) Historical Property
b) Long-term Property
c) Markov Property
d) Sequential Property

19. Carla is working on a problem where the objective is to find the optimal value function and policy that maximize the value of every state. Which methods can Carla use to solve this problem?

a) Gradient-based methods and Value iteration
b) Policy iteration and Q-learning
c) Value iteration and Policy iteration
d) Policy search and LQR

20. David is studying a special case of MDPs where the state and action spaces are continuous and linear, and the reward function is quadratic. What is this special case called?

a) Quadratic Decision Process (QDP)
b) Linear Reward Framework (LRF)
c) Linear Quadratic Regulation (LQR)
d) Continuous Value Optimization (CVO)

21. Emily is researching a more realistic extension of LQR that accounts for uncertainty in the environment due to Gaussian noise in state transitions. What is this extension called?
   a) Linear Quadratic Gaussian (LQG)
   b) Uncertain Quadratic Regulation (UQR)
   c) Noisy Linear Framework (NLF)
   d) Gaussian State Enhancement (GSE)

22. Frank is solving an LQG problem and is applying linear feedback control to the estimated state. What is Frank attempting to obtain?
   a) Optimal value function
   b) Closed-form solution
   c) Recursive equation
   d) Optimal policy

23. Grace wants to model a reinforcement learning problem where the value function measures the long-term expected reward of each state under a given policy. What concept should Grace focus on?
   a) Transition function
   b) Policy optimization
   c) Reward function
   d) Value function

24. Henry is studying the Bellman equations and their relation to the value of a state. What do the Bellman equations relate the value of a state to?
   a) Future rewards of the state
   b) History of actions in the state
   c) Immediate reward of the state
   d) Values of successor states

25. Alex is studying a reinforcement learning framework that defines the probabilities of moving from one state to another given an action. Which component of the MDP is Alex learning about?
   a) Set of rewards
   b) Transition probabilities
   c) States
   d) Actions

26. Beth is designing a game where the agent's reward depends on the state it's in and the action it takes. Which component of the MDP does this describe?
   a) Policy
   b) Set of rewards
   c) Transition probabilities
   d) States

27. Carla is explaining the Markov property to her colleague. She mentions that under the Markov property, the future state and reward depend only on the current state and action, not on the history of previous states and actions. What key characteristic is Carla referring to?
   a) Historical dependency
   b) Long-term dependency
   c) Sequential dependency
   d) Markov dependency

28. David is developing a game AI and needs to determine the best move for the agent in each state. What concept does David need to focus on?
   a) Transition probabilities
   b) Policy
   c) Set of rewards
   d) Actions

29. Emily is building a model for a chess game. She wants to represent the probabilities of reaching new states given the current state and an action. Which component of the MDP is Emily concerned with?
   a) Actions
   b) Set of rewards
   c) Policy
   d) Transition probabilities

30. Frank is explaining the dynamics of an MDP to a beginner. He mentions two functions that determine the effects of the agent's actions. What are these functions?
a) State function and action function
b) Value function and policy function
c) Reward function and transition function
d) Exploration function and exploitation function

31. Grace is creating an MDP-based model for a robot's navigation in a maze. She wants to capture the immediate payoff for the robot moving from one cell to another. What does Grace need to define?
a) Policy function
b) State function
c) Value function
d) Reward function

32. Henry is discussing the key elements of an MDP with his team. He mentions two functions that capture the effects of the agent's actions on the environment. What are these functions?
a) Exploration function and reward functionb) Transition function and policy function
c) Reward function and value function
d) Transition function and reward function

33. Alice is explaining to her friend that an optimal value function represents the maximum expected cumulative reward achievable from a given state. What concept is Alice describing?
a) Policy function
b) State function
c) Bellman optimality equation
d) Transition probabilities

34. Bob is learning about the two types of Bellman equations that describe how to find optimal value functions and policies. He wants to know which equation is used for the optimal action-value function. What should you tell him?
a) Bellman expectation equation
b) Bellman optimality equation
c) Transition probability equation
d) Reward equation

35. Carla is discussing with her colleague how the Bellman equations can be applied to find optimal value functions and policies in an MDP. What are the two main approaches Carla can mention?
a) Probability optimization and reinforcement learning
b) Gradient descent and policy iteration
c) Dynamic programming and reinforcement learning
d) Value iteration and transition optimization

36. David is explaining to his team the significance of the Bellman equations in solving MDPs. He emphasizes that the equations are rooted in a principle that ensures an optimal policy can be broken down into optimal subproblems. What principle is David referring to?
a) Decomposition principle
b) Recursive principle
c) Principle of optimality
d) Subproblem principle

37. Emily is developing a reinforcement learning algorithm and wants to use the Bellman equations to update the value function and policy based on feedback. What method is Emily planning to use?
a) Evolutionary algorithms
b) Gradient descent
c) Value iteration
d) Policy search

38. Frank is studying the concept of an optimal policy in the context of the Bellman equations. He wants to know what the Bellman equations ensure about an optimal policy in an MDP. What can you tell him?
a) An optimal policy guarantees the maximum immediate rewards.
b) An optimal policy guarantees the highest probability of success.
c) An optimal policy guarantees the highest long-term rewards.
d) An optimal policy guarantees optimal subproblem solutions.

39. Grace is learning about the types of functions that the Bellman equations deal with. She wants to know which function assigns a numerical value to each state or state-action pair, representing the expected long-term return. What function is Grace inquiring about?
a) Transition function
b) Policy function
c) State function
d) Value function

40. Henry is discussing the origin of the Bellman equations with a colleague. He mentions that Richard Bellman introduced these equations as part of his theory of dynamic programming. What was Bellman's motivation for developing these equations?
a) To establish a new branch of mathematics
b) To solve complex mathematical problems
c) To find optimal solutions for sequential decision problems under uncertainty
d) To create a framework for machine learning algorithms

41. Alice is studying iterative methods used in reinforcement learning to find optimal policies. She wants to know which algorithm repeatedly performs two steps: policy evaluation and policy improvement. What method is Alice asking about?
a) Gradient descent
b) Policy iteration
c) Value iteration
d) Bellman update

42. Bob is learning about algorithms used to solve Markov Decision Processes (MDPs). He's interested in a technique that breaks down the MDP problem into smaller subproblems and iteratively updates state values using the Bellman equation. Which algorithm should you tell Bob about?
a) Value iteration
b) Policy search
c) Q-learning
d) Policy iteration

43. Carla is researching methods to find optimal policies for an MDP. She wants to know which algorithm guarantees to find the optimal policy for any finite state and action space by alternating between policy evaluation and policy improvement. What algorithm should you mention?
a) Q-learning
b) Value iteration
c) Policy search
d) Policy iteration

44. David is working on solving an MDP using a method that estimates the value function of the current policy and updates the policy by choosing actions that maximize the expected return. What approach is David using?
a) Policy search
b) Value iteration
c) Policy iteration
d) Q-learning

45. Emily is looking for a technique to find both the optimal value function and the optimal policy for a Markov decision process. She wants to ensure that her algorithm will eventually converge to the optimal solution. Which algorithm should you recommend to Emily?
a) Policy iteration
b) Q-learning
c) Policy search
d) Value iteration

46. Frank is studying iterative methods used in reinforcement learning. He's looking for a technique that involves iteratively updating state values based on the maximum expected return that can be achieved from each state. What method should you mention to Frank?
a) Policy iteration
b) Q-learning
c) Value iteration
d) Dynamic programming

47. Grace is comparing two iterative methods for solving MDPs. She wants to know which algorithm starts with arbitrary state values and updates them using the Bellman optimality equation until convergence. What algorithm is Grace asking about?
a) Q-learning
b) Policy iteration
c) Value iteration
d) Evolutionary algorithms

48. Henry is discussing iterative techniques for solving MDPs with his team. He emphasizes that one of the algorithms involves alternating between improving the policy and evaluating its value. Which algorithm is Henry referring to?
a) Q-learning
b) Value iteration
c) Policy search
d) Dynamic programming

49. Alex is exploring control techniques and wants to know which approach is used to design controllers for linear systems with continuous state and action spaces. Which technique should you mention to Alex?
a) Q-learning
b) Linear Quadratic Gaussian (LQG)
c) Value iteration
d) Policy iteration

50. Bella is learning about a control approach that integrates optimal control concepts with state estimation, and it is commonly used in various fields including robotics. What technique is Bella learning about?
a) Policy iteration
b) Value iteration
c) Linear Quadratic Gaussian (LQG)
d) Q-learning

51. Chris is studying a control approach that minimizes a quadratic cost function and assumes linear state transitions with Gaussian noise. What control framework is Chris studying?
a) Value iteration
b) Policy search
c) Linear Quadratic Gaussian (LQG)
d) Q-learning

52. Dana is researching control methods and wants to know which approach involves determining the optimal control technique to minimize a quadratic cost function. What method should you mention to Dana?
a) Value iteration
b) Q-learning
c) Policy search
d) Linear Quadratic Regulation (LQR)

53. Ethan is discussing control strategies with his colleagues and wants to know which algorithm uses a linear feedback controller based on the system's state. What algorithm should you mention to Ethan?

a) Policy search
b) Value iteration
c) Q-learning
d) Linear Quadratic Regulation (LQR)

54. Fiona is comparing control approaches and wants to know which technique combines optimal control concepts with state estimation, assuming Gaussian noise and linear dynamics. What technique is Fiona asking about?

a) Q-learning
b) Policy iteration
c) Linear Quadratic Gaussian (LQG)
d) Value iteration

55. Greg is learning about a classical control approach that uses linear algebraic Riccati equations and iterative methods to find the optimal control strategy. What control technique is Greg learning about?

a) Policy search
b) Value iteration
c) Linear Quadratic Gaussian (LQG)
d) Policy iteration

56. Hannah is studying a control framework that integrates optimal control with state estimation and uses a linear state-space model for system dynamics. What control framework is Hannah studying?

a) Q-learning
b) Linear Quadratic Gaussian (LQG)
c) Value iteration
d) Policy iteration

57. What is the primary goal of Linear Quadratic Regulation (LQR)?

a) To maximize a quadratic cost function.
b) To determine the optimal control input with the highest cumulative reward.
c) To minimize a quadratic cost function.
d) To find the optimal policy for a non-linear system.

58. In the context of reinforcement learning, how can Linear Quadratic Regulation (LQR) be used?

a) As an algorithm for solving optimal control problems.
b) As a baseline policy for learning control techniques.
c) As a method to maximize a non-linear reward function.
d) As a replacement for dynamic programming.

59. What distinguishes Linear Quadratic Gaussian (LQG) from Linear Quadratic Regulation (LQR)?

a) LQG doesn't consider state transitions.
b) LQG integrates optimal control with state estimation and accounts for Gaussian noise in state transitions.
c) LQG only works for linear systems.
d) LQG uses a non-quadratic cost function.

60. Which technique is used to represent the value function when dealing with a large or continuous state space?

a) Monte Carlo simulation b) Exact computation
c) Value function approximation d) Dynamic programming

61. What is the central idea behind Temporal Difference (TD) learning?
a) Learning from delayed and faulty information.
b) Combining reinforcement learning and supervised learning.
c) Using only immediate rewards for learning.
d) Updating estimates based on state transitions only.

62. In TD(0) learning, how is the value of a state updated?
a) Using the value of the next state only.
b) Using the immediate reward only.
c) Using a weighted sum of the immediate reward and the value of the next state.
d) Using a combination of past and future rewards.

63. What is the main difference between TD(0) and TD(lambda)?
a) TD(lambda) uses a non-linear update rule.
b) TD(lambda) updates values based on observed rewards only.
c) TD(lambda) considers multiple steps into the future when updating values.
d) TD(lambda) doesn't use a discount factor.

64. Which factor determines how much weight is given to future rewards in TD(lambda) learning?
a) The learning rate b) The immediate reward
c) The trace decay factor lambda d) The discount factor gamma

65. What is the primary focus of policy search in reinforcement learning?
a) Estimating value functions accurately.
b) Directly optimizing the policy without using a value function.
c) Maximizing the immediate rewards in each state.
d) Finding the optimal state transition dynamics.

66. What is the purpose of policy parameterization in reinforcement learning?
a) To compute the gradient of the objective function.
b) To generate random policies for exploration.
c) To modify the variables that affect policy behavior.
d) To directly estimate the value function.

67. Which technique is commonly used for parameterizing policies in policy search?
a) Decision trees b) Random sampling
c) Neural networks d) Gradient descent

68. What is the primary purpose of the objective function in policy search?
a) To estimate the value function accurately.
b) To measure how well a policy performs in a specific setting.
c) To evaluate the environment's dynamics.
d) To compute the average reward in each episode.

69. Which search method in policy search uses the gradient of the objective function?
a) Evolutionary algorithms b) Random search
c) Gradient-based methods d) Bayesian optimization

70. In policy evaluation, how is the expected return of a policy estimated?
a) By computing the sum of discounted future rewards.
b) By evaluating the policy's parameters directly.
c) By calculating the average state transitions.
d) By using random sampling from the policy.

71. What is the main advantage of evolutionary algorithms in policy search?
a) They work well for low-dimensional problems.
b) They require the goal function to be differentiable.
c) They exploit gradient information efficiently.
d) They can escape local optima and handle non-smooth functions.

72. What is the role of convergence and termination in policy analysis?
a) They ensure quick policy updates.
b) They lead to immediate policy implementation.
c) They guide the iterative process to reach a satisfactory policy solution.
d) They determine the policy's initial parameters.

73. What is the key difference between Markov Decision Processes (MDPs) and Partially Observable Markov Decision Processes (POMDPs)?
a) MDPs have fully observable states, while POMDPs have partially observable states.
b) MDPs have partial observability, while POMDPs have fully observable states.
c) MDPs only consider finite state spaces, while POMDPs handle continuous state spaces.
d) MDPs require value functions, while POMDPs rely on policy optimization.

74. In a POMDP, how is the agent's state represented?
a) As a fixed state value.
b) As a deterministic sequence of states.
c) As a probability distribution over possible states.
d) As a continuous function of time.

75. What is the primary goal of an agent in a POMDP?
a) To determine the exact state of the environment.
b) To maximize the immediate rewards in each state.
c) To maintain a belief state that represents its perception of the environment.
d) To explore all possible state transitions.

76. Which of the following algorithms for solving POMDPs alternates between policy evaluation and policy enhancement?
a) Value iteration b) Monte Carlo methods
c) Policy iteration d) Approximate dynamic programming

77. What is the primary challenge in solving POMDPs compared to MDPs?
a) Computationally expensive belief updates.
b) Non-stationary policy optimization.
c) Limited action space in POMDPs.
d) Infeasibility of value function estimation.

78. Which technique in solving POMDPs uses random simulations to estimate the value function or policy?
a) Value iteration
b) Gradient-based methods
c) Monte Carlo techniques
d) Evolutionary algorithms

79. What is a common approach to handling computational complexity in solving POMDPs?
a) Increasing the number of iterations.
b) Using exact value function calculations.
c) Applying heuristic-based algorithms.
d) Employing deterministic policies.

80. How do approximate dynamic programming methods address the challenge of solving POMDPs?
a) They use exact value function calculations.
b) They apply deterministic policies.
c) They introduce bias and instability.
d) They use exact policy optimization.

81. What is the fundamental characteristic of a Markov Chain?
a) It involves events that are independent of each other.
b) The probability of moving to the next event depends only on the preceding event.
c) It involves events that are deterministic and predictable.
d) The probability of moving to the next event is influenced by multiple preceding events.

82. What can Markov Chains predict by analyzing transition probabilities between states?
a) Exact outcomes of future events.
b) Patterns in climatic changes.
c) Behavioral patterns in stock markets.
d) Insights into behavior and behavior predictions.

83. What does the probability 0.405 signify in the context of the given Markov Chain example?
a) The likelihood of a sunny Thursday.
b) The probability of a cloudy Wednesday.
c) The chance of a rainy Thursday given that Tuesday is sunny.
d) The probability of transitioning from cloudy to rainy.

84. In the context of the given Markov Chain, what is the probability of Wednesday being rainy if Tuesday is sunny?
a) 0.15
b) 0.4
c) 0.55
d) 0.0975

85. What domain of application utilizes Markov Chains to forecast the likelihood of words appearing in a sentence?
a) Climate prediction
b) Stock market analysis
c) Natural language processing
d) Option pricing

86. How are Markov Chains commonly applied in finance?
a) To predict exact stock prices.
b) To model climatic patterns.
c) To simulate language models.
d) To simulate option pricing and stock price movement.

87. What is the primary benefit of using Markov Chains for understanding complex systems?
a) They provide exact predictions for complex events.
b) They eliminate the need for analyzing transition probabilities.
c) They help in predicting deterministic outcomes.
d) They offer insights into and predict the behavior of complex systems.

88. What is the central idea behind a Markov Chain's transition probabilities?
a) Events are determined by random chance.
b) The current event is influenced by future events.
c) The current event is influenced by preceding events.
d) Events occur independently of each other.

89. What is the fundamental characteristic of a Markov Chain?
a) It involves events that are independent of each other.
b) The probability of moving to the next event depends only on the preceding event.
c) It involves events that are deterministic and predictable.
d) The probability of moving to the next event is influenced by multiple preceding events.

90. What can Markov Chains predict by analyzing transition probabilities between states?
a) Exact outcomes of future events.
b) Patterns in climatic changes.
c) Behavioral patterns in stock markets.
d) Insights into behavior and behavior predictions.

91. What does the probability 0.405 signify in the context of the given Markov Chain example?
a) The likelihood of a sunny Thursday.
b) The probability of a cloudy Wednesday.
c) The chance of a rainy Thursday given that Tuesday is sunny.
d) The probability of transitioning from cloudy to rainy.

92. In the context of the given Markov Chain, what is the probability of Wednesday being rainy if Tuesday is sunny?
a) 0.15
b) 0.4
c) 0.55
d) 0.0975

93. What domain of application utilizes Markov Chains to forecast the likelihood of words appearing in a sentence?
a) Climate prediction
b) Stock market analysis
c) Natural language processing
d) Option pricing

94. How are Markov Chains commonly applied in finance?
a) To predict exact stock prices.

b) To model climatic patterns.
c) To simulate language models.
d) To simulate option pricing and stock price movement.

95. What is the primary benefit of using Markov Chains for understanding complex systems?
a) They provide exact predictions for complex events.
b) They eliminate the need for analyzing transition probabilities.
c) They help in predicting deterministic outcomes.
d) They offer insights into and predict the behavior of complex systems.

96. What is the central idea behind a Markov Chain's transition probabilities?
a) Events are determined by random chance.
b) The current event is influenced by future events.
c) The current event is influenced by preceding events.
d) Events occur independently of each other.

97. What is the fundamental characteristic of a Markov Chain?
a) It involves events that are independent of each other.
b) The probability of moving to the next event depends only on the preceding event.
c) It involves events that are deterministic and predictable.
d) The probability of moving to the next event is influenced by multiple preceding events.

98. What can Markov Chains predict by analyzing transition probabilities between states?
a) Exact outcomes of future events.
b) Patterns in climatic changes.
c) Behavioral patterns in stock markets.
d) Insights into behavior and behavior predictions.

99. What domain of application utilizes Markov Chains to forecast the likelihood of words appearing in a sentence?
a) Climate prediction
b) Stock market analysis
c) Natural language processing
d) Option pricing

100. How are Markov Chains commonly applied in finance?
a) To predict exact stock prices.
b) To model climatic patterns.
c) To simulate language models.
d) To simulate option pricing and stock price movement.

101. What is the primary benefit of using Markov Chains for understanding complex systems?
a) They provide exact predictions for complex events.
b) They eliminate the need for analyzing transition probabilities.
c) They help in predicting deterministic outcomes.
d) They offer insights into and predict the behavior of complex systems.

102. What is the central idea behind a Markov Chain's transition probabilities?
a) Events are determined by random chance.
b) The current event is influenced by future events.

c) The current event is influenced by preceding events.
d) Events occur independently of each other.

103. What is the fundamental characteristic of a Markov Chain?
a) It involves events that are independent of each other.
b) The probability of moving to the next event depends only on the preceding event.
c) It involves events that are deterministic and predictable.
d) The probability of moving to the next event is influenced by multiple preceding events.

104. What can Markov Chains predict by analyzing transition probabilities between states?
a) Exact outcomes of future events.
b) Patterns in climatic changes.
c) Behavioral patterns in stock markets.
d) Insights into behavior and behavior predictions.

105. What domain of application utilizes Markov Chains to forecast the likelihood of words appearing in a sentence?
a) Climate prediction
b) Stock market analysis
c) Natural language processing
d) Option pricing

106. What is the primary challenge when using low-code and no-code solutions in machine learning?
a) They are of lower quality than conventional development.
b) They require extensive hyperparameter tuning.
c) They struggle with handling embedded machine learning.
d) They are not suitable for handling data streams.

107. In a Hidden Markov Model (HMM), what do hidden states represent?
a) Observable variables
b) Weather conditions
c) Underlying, unobservable variables
d) Stock market trends

108. Which type of model is suitable for analyzing systems where all variables are directly observable?
a) Hidden Markov Model (HMM)
b) Markov Model (MM)
c) Both HMM and MM
d) None of the above

109. What is the primary advantage of Hidden Markov Models (HMMs) over Markov Models (MMs)?
a) Simplicity and ease of implementation
b) Suitable for stationary data
c) Ability to model systems with hidden variables
d) Applicability to stock market trends

110. Which component of a Hidden Markov Model (HMM) represents the likelihood of observing an output given the weather conditions?
a) Start probability
b) Transition probability
c) Emission probability
d) Hidden states

111. When might a Hidden Markov Model (HMM) be particularly useful?
a) Analyzing weather patterns

b) Modeling systems with directly observable variables
c) Sequencing DNA
d) Analyzing stock market trends

112. What is the primary reason to use a Markov Model (MM) instead of a Hidden Markov Model (HMM)?
a) Simplicity and ease of implementation
b) Ability to capture underlying patterns
c) Suitable for speech recognition
d) Flexibility in modeling complex dependencies

113. Which type of model is more appropriate for tasks like speech recognition and natural language understanding?
a) Markov Model (MM)
b) Hidden Markov Model (HMM)
c) Both MM and HMM
d) None of the above

114. In which type of data scenario would a Markov Model (MM) be most beneficial?
a) Non-stationary data with evolving hidden states
b) Sequencing DNA
c) Analyzing weather patterns
d) Gesture recognition tasks

115. What is the primary focus of policy gradient methods in reinforcement learning?
a) Maximizing the value function
b) Learning the Q-function
c) Optimizing the policy directly
d) Balancing exploration and exploitation

116. Which technique is commonly used to estimate the gradient in policy gradient methods?
a) Clipping mechanism
b) Temporal difference learning
c) Actor-critic methods
d) Monte Carlo sampling

117. What is the primary advantage of Proximal Policy Optimization (PPO) compared to other policy gradient methods?
a) Utilizes temporal difference learning
b) Reduces variance of gradient estimates
c) Focuses on deterministic policies
d) Employs multiple actor-critic networks

118. In an actor-critic method, what is the role of the critic network?
a) Learning a deterministic policy
b) Estimating the expected cumulative reward
c) Updating the policy parameters
d) Generating state transitions

119. Which reinforcement learning algorithm uses multiple parallel agents to collect data and update a shared network?
a) Advantage Actor-Critic (A2C)
b) Deep Deterministic Policy Gradient (DDPG)
c) Proximal Policy Optimization (PPO)
d) REINFORCE

120. What type of policy does Deep Deterministic Policy Gradient (DDPG) algorithm learn?
a) Stochastic policy
b) Deterministic policy
c) Hybrid policy
d) Exploration policy

121. What aspect of reinforcement learning does the Advantage Actor-Critic (A2c) algorithm specifically aim to balance?

a) Exploration and exploitation
b) Variance and instability
c) Synchronous and asynchronous updates
d) Policy and value function optimization

122. How do target networks contribute to the stability of the Deep Deterministic Policy Gradient (DDPG) algorithm?

a) They improve exploration
b) They reduce variance in rewards
c) They stabilize policy updates
d) They provide more accurate value estimates

123. What is a notable achievement of the AlphaGo AI in the domain of games?

a) Winning in chess, shogi, and Go
b) Mastering complex manipulations
c) Winning in the World Series of Poker
d) Defeating human champions in Go

124. In which domain can reinforcement learning be applied to optimize driving behaviors for autonomous vehicles?

a) Online advertising
b) Robotics
c) Finance
d) Recommendation systems

125. What is the primary benefit of using reinforcement learning in recommendation systems?

a) Increasing user engagement through ads
b) Providing predefined user preferences
c) Avoiding user feedback
d) Personalizing recommendations based on behavior

126. What is a key application of reinforcement learning in the finance domain?

a) Providing human supervision to traders
b) Predicting market trends
c) Algorithmic trading and high-frequency trading
d) Managing user preferences for financial products

127. Which AI agent mastered multiple board games by learning from scratch and playing against itself?

a) AlphaGo
b) Google Ads
c) Netflix
d) AlphaZero

128. What is the primary advantage of using reinforcement learning in robotics for real-world tasks?

a) Reducing the need for computation
b) Improving predefined programming
c) Adapting to changes without explicit supervision
d) Eliminating the need for sensors

129. How does reinforcement learning enhance the capabilities of autonomous vehicles?

a) By implementing rigid predefined rules
b) By eliminating the need for sensors
c) By enabling real-time adaptation to driving scenarios
d) By relying solely on human guidance

130. What makes AlphaGo's achievement significant in the context of reinforcement learning?

a) It learned complex manipulation tasks

b) It mastered all popular board games
c) It surpassed human intuition and creativity
d) It demonstrated the power of deterministic policies

131. Which advantage of reinforcement learning (RL) enables it to handle problems in domains like robotics, healthcare, and finance?
a) Predefined labeling of data b) Static data distribution
c) Learning from sparse or delayed rewards d) Relying solely on supervised learning

132. What distinguishes reinforcement learning (RL) from supervised learning in terms of adaptability?
a) RL agents rely on explicit supervision
b) RL agents interact with the environment for feedback
c) RL agents assume a static data distribution
d) RL agents require labeled data for adaptation

133. In which domain can reinforcement learning's exploration vs. exploitation dilemma have a significant impact?
a) Image classification b) Language translation
c) Autonomous driving d) E-commerce recommendation

134. What does a short horizon in reinforcement learning planning imply?
a) Focusing on immediate rewards only b) Incorporating future rewards into decisions
c) Ignoring exploration altogether d) Balancing exploration and exploitation

135. How does reinforcement learning address the challenge of making decisions in uncertain scenarios?
a) By avoiding probabilistic reasoning
b) By relying solely on deterministic models
c) By using Bayesian inference and probabilistic reasoning
d) By avoiding modeling uncertainty

136. What is one of the primary benefits of reinforcement learning's adaptability?
a) It ensures fixed objective functions b) It eliminates the need for exploration
c) It relies on pre-labeled data d) It handles changing environments effectively

137. In which domain does reinforcement learning excel due to its ability to handle non-linear and uncertain problems?
a) Static image recognition b) Online shopping trends prediction
c) Linear regression tasks d) Autonomous vehicle control

138. What primary characteristic allows reinforcement learning to be applied to a wide range of domains and tasks?
a) Relying on supervised learning paradigmsb) Requiring explicit prior knowledge
c) Learning from trial and error d) Operating within known data distributions

139. What is the primary challenge associated with the exploration-exploitation trade-off in reinforcement learning?
a) Balancing exploration and exploitation is unnecessary

b) Exploration always leads to higher rewards
c) Exploration can be risky and costly
d) Exploitation often results in suboptimal solutions

140. Which method aims to find optimal hyperparameters for reinforcement learning algorithms by randomly sampling values?
a) Grid search
b) Bayesian optimization
c) Automated tuning
d) Random search

141. What aspect of reinforcement learning can be hindered by instability arising from function approximation errors?
a) Exploration
b) Convergence
c) Exploitation
d) Validation

142. What challenge arises when reward feedback in reinforcement learning is sparse or delayed?
a) Hyperparameter tuning becomes complex
b) Function approximation errors increase
c) Credit assignment becomes difficult
d) Exploration-exploitation trade-off disappears

143. Which technique aims to modify the original reward function to provide additional guidance to the agent in reinforcement learning?
a) Transfer learning
b) Reward shaping
c) Policy gradient
d) Bayesian optimization

144. What problem does safe reinforcement learning aim to address?
a) Convergence and stability
b) Hyperparameter tuning
c) Exploration vs. exploitation trade-off
d) Ensuring ethical behavior

145. What technique involves incorporating a risk measure into the reward function to minimize uncertainty in reinforcement learning?
a) Human-in-the-loop RL
b) Inverse reinforcement learning
c) Risk-aware RL
d) Constrained RL

146. What technique involves using human feedback or guidance to improve the learning process in reinforcement learning?
a) Transfer learning
b) Inverse reinforcement learning
c) Constrained RL
d) Human-in-the-loop RL

147. What is the primary benefit of utilizing multitask learning instead of training separate models for individual tasks?
a) Enhanced performance on a single task
b) Reduced computational cost
c) Simplified model architecture
d) Independent training of tasks

148. In computer vision, which tasks can be simultaneously learned using a common feature extractor and distinct output layers in multitask learning?
a) Sentiment analysis and language translation
b) Object detection and image classification

c) Speech recognition and text generation
d) Document summarization and part-of-speech tagging

149. Which technique in multitask learning involves sharing the lower layers of a model across all tasks while having separate upper layers for each task?
a) Hard parameter sharing b) Soft parameter sharing
c) Task-specific attention d) Common feature extraction

150. What is the primary purpose of incorporating a penalty term in the loss function in soft parameter sharing?
a) Reduce computational cost b) Normalize the parameters
c) Encourage divergence of parameters d) Promote similarity of task-specific parameters

151. In multitask learning, what does the task-specific attention layer enable the model to do?
a) Learn a separate model for each task b) Focus on specific aspects of each task
c) Train shared layers for all tasks d) Avoid using feature extractors

152. What is one of the challenges associated with multitask learning?
a) Inability to share information across tasksb) Overfitting due to common features
c) Lack of computational resources d) Selection of unrelated tasks

153. What is the main advantage of using multitask learning for tasks in Natural Language Processing (NLP)?
a) Reduced reliance on linguistic knowledge
b) Independent training for each task
c) Improved generalization and performance
d) Simplified architecture

154. In computer vision, which tasks can be effectively combined in multitask learning to enhance the understanding of 3D scene structure and object localization?
a) Emotion recognition and speech synthesis
b) Object detection and sentiment analysis
c) Image segmentation and depth estimation
d) Text classification and part-of-speech tagging

155. What distinguishes online learning from other machine learning approaches?
a) Processing the entire data set at once b) Requiring frequent retraining
c) Incremental updates using new data d) Being limited to small data set

156. Which characteristic of online learning allows it to respond to changing patterns or shifts in the data distribution?
a) Incremental updates b) Scalability
c) Real-time adaptation d) Memory effectiveness

157. What is a key advantage of online learning algorithms in terms of memory requirements?
a) They store the entire data set for training b) They require a large memory footprint
c) They remember all historical data d) They often have a small memory footprint

158. Which machine learning algorithm operates effectively on large volumes of data and updates its model incrementally?

a) K-means clustering
b) Decision tree
c) Online gradient descent
d) Naive Bayes

159. Which aspect of online learning allows it to handle dynamic and non-stationary data sources effectively?

a) Incremental updates
b) Scalability
c) Real-time adaptation
d) Memory effectiveness

160. Which type of machine learning algorithm benefits from online learning's ability to adapt to new data without forgetting previous knowledge?

a) Traditional batch learning algorithms
b) Deep reinforcement learning algorithms
c) Ensemble learning algorithms
d) Online learning algorithms

161. What is a characteristic feature of online learning algorithms when it comes to their computational complexity?

a) They have high computational complexity
b) They can only handle low-dimensional data
c) They require frequent retraining
d) They have low computational complexity

162. Which type of machine learning technique is an example of online learning that involves updating the model using new data instances in a step-wise manner?

a) Batch learning
b) Unsupervised learning
c) Reinforcement learning
d) Stochastic gradient descent

163. Which characteristic is a crucial aspect of sequence modeling that distinguishes it from other types of data analysis?

a) Spatial dependencies
b) Cross-validation techniques
c) Temporal dependencies
d) Dimensionality reduction

164. In which type of applications is sequence modeling commonly used?

a) Image classification
b) Tabular data analysis
c) Time series data and NLP
d) Anomaly detection

165. What does a sequence model predict based on the context of earlier data pieces?

a) Upcoming weather patterns
b) Future stock prices
c) Meaning of the next data item
d) Presence of outliers in the data

166. Which neural network architecture is well-suited for sequence modeling tasks due to its ability to consider temporal dependencies?

a) Convolutional Neural Networks (CNNs)
b) Multilayer Perceptrons (MLPs)
c) Long Short-Term Memory (LSTM) networks
d) Support Vector Machines (SVMs)

167. What is the primary advantage of sequence models in handling variable-length inputs and outputs?
a) They discard any sequences that deviate from the mean length
b) They automatically pad sequences to a fixed length
c) They can process input sequences of different lengths and produce variable-length outputs
d) They rely on external libraries to manage variable lengths

168. Which type of neural network is commonly used for sequence modeling and is known for its ability to maintain long-term dependencies?
a) Feedforward Neural Networks (FNNs) b) Convolutional Neural Networks (CNNs)
c) Recurrent Neural Networks (RNNs) d) Transformers

169. In sequence modeling, what kind of information do models consider when making predictions?
a) Only the current data point
b) Previous data points but not the order
c) The ordering of data points and the context of previous ones
d) All data points simultaneously

170. What machine learning technique is a prime example of sequence modeling and is well-suited for processing sequential data like sentences and paragraphs?
a) Clustering b) Decision trees
c) K-nearest neighbors d) Transformers

171. What is the primary purpose of prediction in machine learning?
a) To analyze historical data patterns
b) To create new data points
c) To make educated estimates about new data outcomes
d) To validate the accuracy of training data

172. Which type of machine learning task involves assigning labels or categories to inputs?
a) Classification b) Regression
c) Clustering d) Association rule mining

173. What role does historical data play in making predictions using machine learning?
a) Historical data is ignored during prediction
b) Historical data is used to create new data points
c) Historical data provides patterns and connections used to forecast new data outcomes
d) Historical data is only used in clustering tasks

174. Which factor can impact the accuracy of predictions made by machine learning models?
a) The amount and quality of training data b) The complexity of the problem being solved
c) The algorithm used for visualization d) The choice of programming language

175. In machine learning, what term is used to describe the process of adjusting model parameters to improve prediction accuracy?
a) Feature extraction b) Hyperparameter tuning
c) Label assignment d) Dimensionality reduction

176. Which machine learning task involves predicting continuous numerical values?
a) Classification
b) Regression
c) Clustering
d) Anomaly detection

177. What is the name for the technique that uses multiple models to combine their predictions and improve overall accuracy?
a) Feature selection
b) Ensemble approach
c) Data augmentation
d) Overfitting prevention

178. Which type of machine learning task involves grouping similar instances together based on their characteristics?
a) Classification
b) Regression
c) Clustering
d) Dimensionality reduction

179. Bagging is employed in ensemble methods primarily to:
a) Reduce the number of features in the data set.
b) Increase the correlation between decision trees.
c) Decrease the bias of individual decision trees.
d) Introduce randomness in gradient boosting.

180. In the context of bagging, why is random forest considered superior to simple bagging?
a) It uses fewer decision trees in the ensemble.
b) It combines predictions linearly.
c) It selects features randomly for each decision tree.
d) It focuses only on reducing variance.

181. What is the primary goal of boosting in ensemble methods?
a) To reduce the complexity of individual decision trees.
b) To increase the correlation between decision trees.
c) To increase the bias of individual decision trees.
d) To iteratively improve the accuracy of predictions.

182. How does gradient boosting differ from traditional boosting techniques?
a) Gradient boosting adds more randomness to individual trees.
b) Gradient boosting optimizes a differentiable loss function.
c) Gradient boosting uses only decision trees for boosting.
d) Gradient boosting aims to increase the bias of weak learners.

183. What does the term "Gradient Boosting" indicate in ensemble methods?
a) It involves combining multiple gradients of decision trees.
b) It signifies boosting using a gradient-based loss function.
c) It indicates using gradient boosting for regression tasks only.
d) It represents a type of bagging technique.

184. Which advantage is associated with the Random Forest technique?
a) It effectively handles missing data and controls missing quantity.
b) It requires careful tuning of multiple hyperparameters.

c) It is particularly well-suited for small data sets.
d) It focuses on optimizing the same loss function as gradient boosting.

185. What is the primary difference between bagging and boosting?
a) Bagging aims to reduce the bias of individual models, while boosting reduces variance.
b) Bagging combines weak learners into a single strong model, while boosting trains weak learners sequentially.
c) Bagging focuses on optimizing a differentiable loss function, while boosting uses a random subset of features.
d) Bagging uses gradient descent optimization, while boosting uses gradient-based loss functions.

186. What is the primary disadvantage of using Gradient Boosting methods?
a) It requires minimal adjustment of hyperparameters.
b) It supports only a limited range of loss functions.
c) It struggles with interactions between features.
d) It is not suitable for handling large data sets.

187. Which machine learning advancement involves training models on large amounts of data compared to conventional neural networks?
a) Multimodal machine learning
b) Transformers
c) Data Streams
d) Foundation models

188. What term is used to describe the process of developing machine learning models that can experience an event in various modalities simultaneously?
a) Gradient Boosting
b) Transformers
c) Data Streams
d) Multimodal machine learning

189. What is the primary purpose of transformers in artificial intelligence architecture?
a) To change the input data sequence into another using encoders and decoders.
b) To focus on optimizing a differentiable loss function.
c) To handle dynamic and changing data distributions.
d) To process data streams in real-time.

190. Which subfield of machine learning focuses on running machine learning techniques on various hardware, including devices like household appliances and smartphones?
a) Active Learning
b) Embedded machine learning
c) Data Streams
d) Foundation models

191. What is the primary challenge when dealing with data streams in machine learning?
a) Selecting the most informative examples from a pool of unlabeled data.
b) Adapting to changing data patterns due to concept drift.
c) Reducing the amount of labeled data required for training.
d) Handling variance in machine learning models.

192. What is the main advantage of active learning in machine learning?
a) Adapting to changing data patterns due to concept drift.

b) Handling real-time processing of data streams.
c) Reducing the amount of labeled data required for training.
d) Running machine learning techniques on various hardware.

193. Which machine learning advancement is particularly well-suited for tasks requiring complex or domain-specific annotations?
a) Transformers
b) Data Streams
c) Active Learning
d) Low-code and no-code solutions

Part B (Short Answer Questions)

1. What is reinforcement learning?
2. What is a model- based algorithm?
3. What is a model- free algorithm?
4. What are the types of policy search methods?
5. What is MDP in reinforcement learning?
6. Write notes on the Bellman equations.
7. What is LQR in reinforcement learning?
8. What is LQG in reinforcement learning?
9. Define state in MDP.
10. Define actions in MDP.
11. Define transition probabilities (T) in MDP.
12. Define the policy function.
13. Define the principle of optimality.
14. What is the Bellman value function?
15. What is value iteration in MDP?
16. What is policy iteration in MDP?
17. What is Q-learning?
18. Define the value function in reinforcement learning.
19. What is temporal difference learning?
20. What is policy search?
21. Define policy parameterization.
22. Define convergence and termination in policy analysis?
23. Define POMPD in reinforcement learning.
24. Define the Markov chain.
25. Define the hidden Markov model (HMM).
26. Define the policy gradient method in reinforcement learning.
27. What is reinforce in reinforcement learning?
28. What is PPO in reinforcement learning?
29. What is the actor-critic method in reinforcement learning?
30. Define A2C in reinforcement learning.
31. Define deep deterministic policy gradient (DDPG) in reinforcement learning.
32. List some disadvantages of reinforcement learning.
33. Define multitask learning.
34. What is online learning?
35. What are the critical characteristics of online learning?
36. What is sequence learning? What are the critical characteristics of sequence learning?
37. Define prediction learning.
38. Define bagging.
39. Define boosting.
40. Define multimodal machine learning.
41. Define embedded machine learning.

Part C (Essay Questions)

1. Write an essay on MDP.
2. Write an essay on the Bellman equation.
3. Write an essay on value iteration and policy iteration.
4. Write an essay on linear quadratic regulation (LQR)
5. Write an essay on linear quadratic Gaussian (LQG)

6. Write an essay on Q-learning.
7. Write an essay on value function approximation.
8. Write an essay on temporal difference learning.
9. Write an essay on policy search.
10. Write about algorithms for solving POMDPs.
11. Compare and contrast MM and HMM.
12. Write about policy gradient methods and actor-critic methods.
13. What are the applications of reinforcement learning?
14. What are the advantages of reinforcement learning?
15. What are the drawbacks of reinforcement learning?
16. Write an essay on multitask learning.
17. Write an essay on online learning.
18. What is sequence learning? What are its characteristics?
19. Write an essay on prediction learning.
20. Write an essay on bagging in machine learning.
21. Write an essay on boosting in machine learning.

ANSWER KEY

Part A

1. (c)	**2.** (c)	**3.** (a)	**4.** (c)	**5.** (c)	**6.** (c)	**7.** (b)	**8.** (a)
9. (d)	**10.** (c)	**11.** (a)	**12.** (a)	**13.** (d)	**14.** (b)	**15.** (c)	**16.** (c)
17. (c)	**18.** (c)	**19.** (c)	**20.** (c)	**21.** (a)	**22.** (d)	**23.** (d)	**24.** (d)
25. (b)	**26.** (b)	**27.** (d)	**28.** (b)	**29.** (d)	**30.** (c)	**31.** (d)	**32.** (d)
33. (c)	**34.** (b)	**35.** (c)	**36.** (c)	**37.** (c)	**38.** (d)	**39.** (d)	**40.** (c)
41. (b)	**42.** (a)	**43.** (d)	**44.** (c)	**45.** (a)	**46.** (c)	**47.** (c)	**48.** (b)
49. (b)	**50.** (c)	**51.** (c)	**52.** (d)	**53.** (d)	**54.** (c)	**55.** (c)	**56.** (b)
57. (b)	**58.** (b)	**59.** (b)	**60.** (c)	**61.** (a)	**62.** (c)	**63.** (c)	**64.** (c)
65. (b)	**66.** (c)	**67.** (c)	**68.** (b)	**69.** (c)	**70.** (a)	**71.** (d)	**72.** (c)
73. (a)	**74.** (c)	**75.** (c)	**76.** (c)	**77.** (a)	**78.** (c)	**79.** (c)	**80.** (c)
81. (b)	**82.** (d)	**83.** (c)	**84.** (d)	**85.** (c)	**86.** (d)	**87.** (d)	**88.** (c)
89. (b)	**90.** (d)	**91.** (c)	**92.** (d)	**93.** (c)	**94.** (d)	**95.** (d)	**96.** (c)
97. (b)	**98.** (d)	**99.** (c)	**100.** (d)	**101.** (d)	**102.** (c)	**103.** (b)	**104.** (d)
105. (c)	**106.** (a)	**107.** (c)	**108.** (b)	**109.** (c)	**110.** (c)	**111.** (c)	**112.** (a)
113. (b)	**114.** (c)	**115.** (c)	**116.** (d)	**117.** (b)	**118.** (b)	**119.** (a)	**120.** (b)
121. (a)	**122.** (c)	**123.** (d)	**124.** (b)	**125.** (d)	**126.** (c)	**127.** (d)	**128.** (c)
129. (c)	**130.** (c)	**131.** (c)	**132.** (b)	**133.** (d)	**134.** (a)	**135.** (c)	**136.** (d)
137. (d)	**138.** (c)	**139.** (c)	**140.** (d)	**141.** (b)	**142.** (c)	**143.** (b)	**144.** (d)
145. (c)	**146.** (d)	**147.** (b)	**148.** (d)	**149.** (a)	**150.** (d)	**151.** (b)	**152.** (d)
153. (c)	**154.** (c)	**155.** (c)	**156.** (c)	**157.** (d)	**158.** (c)	**159.** (c)	**160.** (d)
161. (d)	**162.** (d)	**163.** (c)	**164.** (c)	**165.** (c)	**166.** (c)	**167.** (c)	**168.** (c)
169. (c)	**170.** (d)	**171.** (c)	**172.** (a)	**173.** (c)	**174.** (a)	**175.** (b)	**176.** (b)
177. (b)	**178.** (c)	**179.** (c)	**180.** (c)	**181.** (d)	**182.** (b)	**183.** (b)	**184.** (a)
185. (b)	**186.** (c)	**187.** (d)	**188.** (d)	**189.** (a)	**190.** (b)	**191.** (b)	**192.** (c)
193. (c)							

12 Applications of Machine Learning in Various Industries

Learning Objectives

At the end of this chapter, you will be able to:

- Identify real-world problems across various industries that have been solved using machine learning techniques
- Explain how machine learning is revolutionizing the retail sector through personalized recommendations, inventory management, and customer behavior analysis
- List the applications of machine learning in logistics for optimizing routes, predicting delivery times, and enhancing supply chain efficiency
- Discuss the role of machine learning in manufacturing for predictive maintenance, quality control, and automation of complex processes
- Explain how machine learning contributes to energy and utilities by forecasting demand, detecting anomalies, and managing resources efficiently
- Describe the impact of machine learning on the travel industry, including dynamic pricing, customer service chatbots, and itinerary planning
- Assess the use of machine learning in banking for fraud detection, risk management, and customer segmentation
- Evaluate the applications of machine learning in finance for algorithmic trading, credit scoring, and financial advisory services
- Analyze how machine learning is employed in the insurance sector to personalize policies, process claims, and prevent fraud

12.1 Real-World Problems Solved by Machine Learning

Healthcare

Machine learning (ML) has multiple applications in the medical field, ranging from diagnosis to drug discovery and personalized treatments. ML techniques have often been used in diagnosing various diseases, enabling doctors to make better decisions regarding patient treatment options. For example, one common application is computer vision algorithms for analyzing medical images such as X-rays or CT scans. By extracting features from these images and using them as input into a model, it is possible to predict whether a patient has certain diseases or conditions like cancer or cardiovascular disease with an accuracy far more significant than what has thus far been achieved by human experts alone.

At the same time, ML tools are also being applied to other types of clinical data, such as lab results, genomic sequences, and electronic health records (EHRs). These models can be trained on large data sets containing hundreds of thousands (or even millions) of cases that have already been diagnosed by experts and used to accurately identify similar conditions in new patients with much greater efficiency than traditional methods would allow.

Another area where ML can be helpful is in drug discovery and development processes. Here, neural networks can be used to analyze large amounts of chemical data about potential drugs and quickly identify promising candidates for further testing before they ever reach clinical trial stages, thereby saving valuable time while improving accuracy levels simultaneously. Finally, ML can also help create personalized treatment plans based on each aptient's unique characteristics such as age group, gender, or race/ethnicity.

Fraud Detection

This is an essential factor of online and financial security. Fraudulent activities are increasing daily, resulting in a heightened need for better detection solutions to detect and prevent fraudulent transactions in real-time. ML is emerging as one of the most powerful tools to detect fraudulent transactions across different channels, such as credit card transactions and online payments. Due to the vast amount of data generated from different sources, traditional methods used for fraud detection (rule-based algorithms) are insufficient to combat fraud schemes' continually changing nature. This gap has opened up opportunities for ML techniques to identify patterns that may indicate a suspicious or fraudulent transaction.

ML models use large amounts of customer information, past transaction history, and geographical location data to help identify anomalies within incoming data streams that would otherwise go undetected using more traditional methods. These models can then flag these anomalies as potential threats or potential opportunities depending on the model's objectives. Credit card fraud involves transactions such as counterfeit cards, stolen cards, and unauthorized purchases made with valid cards but under false identities or using stolen information like personal identification numbers (PINs). ML techniques can detect patterns associated with these activities by analyzing past credit card usage patterns across numerous customers over time, thereby identifying any unusual behavior compared with regular user activity. In addition, ML algorithms could be used to monitor incoming credit card transaction logs in real time while they are taking place; if any suspicious activity arises, it can be flagged immediately, preventing further damage before it is too late.

Online payments present another challenge due to the sheer number of payment platforms available and their complexity. ML models analyze user profiles, including spending habits over past periods combined with other factors such as IP addresses or geo-location data; this helps identify anomalies in payment requests which may indicate malicious intent (such as multiple payments coming from a single account spread out over short intervals). The same approach works for monitoring group accounts where several people access one account. Every user's usual behavior is tracked, so any changes will lead alert systems to trigger appropriate alerts when needed reminding users about possible security issues around their accounts if necessary.

Natural Language Processing (NLP)

NLP covers a wide range of tasks such as text classification (identifying if a given text belongs under specific categories), sentiment analysis (determining if the sentiment expressed in a given text is positive or negative), and automatic summarization (creating short summaries containing most essential points about long documents), etc. All these tasks have found successful applications across multiple business domains like customer service automation, automated decision making, customer feedback analysis, etc., leading to significant cost savings along with improved efficiency.

Facial Recognition Technology

Facial recognition technology detects and combats fraud by using computer algorithms to identify people based on images of their faces. Facial recognition technology compares digital photographs of people's faces to databases that have previously enrolled facial data sets. The program then compares the new image with previously identified images belonging to a specific person. If successful, this enables the facial recognition system to correctly identify an individual from a photo or video capture, even if they are wearing strange items on their face or other forms of items that attempt to mask their identity, allowing for improved security processes around identification verification and authentication. In addition, this assists companies in detecting fraudulent actions such as account takeovers or efforts at identity theft.

Aside from identification, face recognition may be utilized for biometric authentication by exploiting liveness-detecting characteristics created expressly for this purpose, which improves overall security. Furthermore, requiring that the individual trying access be physically present at the moment of authentication rather than merely supplying stolen credentials or other means of impersonation would enable access without any physical verification requirement.

Most modern surveillance cameras now include AI-driven features like age/gender detection capabilities built into their hardware components, using deep learning algorithms trained on massive databases primarily comprised of human faces. ML can leverage this capability during real-time monitoring operations so that not only can abnormally suspicious activities occurring within monitored areas be detected, but also appropriate warnings are given out when known wrongdoers enter monitored premises.

Forecasting Future Market Trends

Forecasting future market trends and predicting stock prices is an essential part of making informed investment decisions, making ML an excellent choice for these tasks. It can identify patterns in data sets that are too complex or too time-consuming for humans to identify. With ML, investors can now accurately predict future market events by analyzing large amounts of data quickly, such as stock prices and financial indicators. In addition, several more advanced techniques are used within ML to forecast future market trends and predict stock prices – namely recurrent neural networks (RNNs). RNNs are often used for time series analysis due to their ability to capture temporal dependencies between successive states over long sequences. These networks utilize layers unlike regular feedforward neural networks (where each neuron takes input from all nodes above them); instead, RNNs use temporal connections between neurons so that information from previous timestamps can be incorporated into subsequent calculations.

As with any ML task, modeling performance depends mainly on gaining high quantity and quality data along with performing appropriate pre-processing steps before feeding these into models for training. Some preprocessing steps would include missing value imputation, label encoding categorical variables, and scaling evaluations if necessary.

Email Spam Detection

Many corporate users are concerned about email spam. With increasing numbers of emails being sent daily, recognizing and preventing spam has become more critical than ever. By identifying patterns in data categorized as spam and valid mail, ML algorithms may be used to classify emails as legitimate or spam. The ML system will make predictions based on information acquired from prior samples of labeled email messages.

To begin training an ML model for email spam detection, you first need a data set containing both genuine and spammed emails, with each example labeled appropriately so that you can use it later on in the process of classification. Once you have this data set, you will then be ready to train your ML model by feeding it these examples and allowing it to learn what makes an email legitimately sent versus one which is more likely part of a malicious campaign run by spammers. The trained ML model then considers all this learned knowledge when presented with new incoming emails, which have not been seen before but could contain similar characteristics seen during its training period. Those emails should be considered suspicious rather than legitimate, thus classifying them accordingly without human intervention (this falls under unsupervised learning).

Furthermore, this same ML model should be able to detect any modifications made by spammers over time, as spammers frequently know how specific anti-spam measures function, allowing them to try alternative ways/methods/approaches. Finally, ML algorithms can recognize and block the most undesired email communications using their trained models, assisting enterprises in strengthening their security against cyber-attacks and espionage operations.

Speech Recognition

Speech or voice recognition technology is a machine's ability to identify speech patterns, words, and phrases. ML for speech recognition relies heavily on AI algorithms that are trained using large amounts of data. The system 'learns' from this data how to recognize specific sounds, words, sentences, and patterns in human language. This allows it to interpret the spoken word accurately by understanding different accents, dialects, and languages. The first step in applying machine learning to speech recognition is feature extraction – which involves extracting critical features from audio signals, such as frequency and amplitude, that can be used as input for an AI algorithm. This process also includes noise reduction techniques such as removing background noise which helps reduce false positives when classifying words or phrases. The next step involves training an AI algorithm on these extracted features to accurately detect specific sound patterns, words, or phrases based on prior experience with similar input audio signals.

ML can be used with statistical models, such as hidden Markov models (HMMs), to improve accuracy further. HMMs are particularly useful for tasks that require recognizing complex sequences, like recognizing commands given in natural language dialogue systems intended for use in voice assistants like Amazon's Alexa.

Another way ML can improve the accuracy of speech recognition systems is through transfer learning techniques where pre-trained models are used instead of training a model from scratch every time. Finally, deep neural networks have become increasingly popular due to their ability to accurately recognize complex sequences while reducing errors due to their self-learning capabilities during training cycles.

Product Recommendation

Online retailers widely use product recommendation systems to improve the user experience and increase sales. By leveraging ML algorithms, these systems can make highly personalized recommendations based on a customer's past purchases and browsing behavior. This helps customers find items they may be interested in, and helps retailers reach more potential customers with targeted offers.

One common approach used by product recommendation systems is collaborative filtering (CF). With CF, an algorithm can scan user profiles to identify users with similar interests or behaviors and recommend products based on what other users with similar interests have purchased or browsed in the past. Another method used is content-based filtering (CBF). With this approach, an algorithm looks at attributes such as color or material when recommending products to customers who have not made any purchases yet but have shown interest in specific categories of items like clothing or electronics based on their browsing behavior. By combining both approaches, an algorithm can make even more accurate product recommendations while taking into account both clear signals from previous purchases as well as implicit signals from browsing behavior.

Aside from making personalized product recommendations, ML algorithms can be trained to detect fraudulent activity while processing online orders by analyzing data from previous transactions, such as payment methods and shipping addresses, thereby aiding in the prevention of fraudulent activities such as identity theft or credit card fraud.

Virtual Personal Assistant (VPA)

A virtual personal assistant is an AI-based technology that acts like a human assistant in digital contexts. ML enables VPAs to learn from interactions and use that knowledge to improve their performance. VPAs are widely used for scheduling appointments, providing reminders, and making recommendations based on user data. VPAs can be used for many different tasks depending on the specific application. For example, a VPA might book flights or hotels for business trips or vacations. It can also be used to set up meetings with clients or colleagues and manage calendars by sending reminders about upcoming events.

Sentiment Analysis

ML algorithms can be used for sentiment analysis in several ways: exploring relationships between words, understanding context, identifying patterns in text, recognizing topics within documents or conversations detecting overall sentiment towards a particular subject. With ML-based sentiment analysis systems, it is possible to detect subtle differences in opinion that traditional methods may have missed. For example, ML models can identify sarcasm or irony that might not be obvious from just reading the words alone by looking at the context around them. They can also distinguish between positive opinions (such as, "I love this product!") and neutral ones (such as, "It's okay"). This enables businesses to gain more precise insights into customers' attitudes toward their products or services than traditional approaches do.

In addition, ML-powered sentiment analysis systems can also group similar sentiments for further exploration by analyzing large amounts of data quickly and accurately with advanced techniques such as deep learning neural networks.

Customer Service Automation

ML can help organizations automate customer service tasks with efficiency and accuracy. By leveraging the power of ML algorithms, companies can easily detect frequent inquiries from customers and set up automated responses or bots that answer common questions without requiring human involvement. As a result, the automated system can quickly answer frequently asked questions while freeing time for more complex issues requiring human assistance. In addition, ML algorithms can monitor customer behavior and suggest the best possible solutions to their queries..

ML also offers predictive analytics, which enables organizations to anticipate potential problems before they arise and take preventive measures if necessary. Predictive analytics use historical data and advanced algorithms, such as deep learning networks or support vector machines (SVMs), which then allow businesses to predict future events by taking into account patterns from past experiences.

Traffic Prediction

Traffic prediction is an important factor in many cities, because it can improve travel times, reduce traffic delays, and optimize road networks. ML algorithms can be used in various ways for traffic prediction, such as predicting the flow of vehicles through intersections, speed and density estimates along roads or highways, and potential congestion points during peak hours. For example, artificial neural networks can be used to predict the flow of vehicles through an intersection, using historical data on, vehicle speeds and lane-changing behavior. Similarly, support vector machines can be employed to estimate speed and density along roads, or highways, using GIS data on road geometry.

ML algorithms can also be used for dynamic routing optimization, which involves finding the most efficient route, given current conditions, including traffic, flows in real-time.

Automatic Language Translation

ML algorithms are used to automate translations between two languages by using a set of data and then predicting the most likely outcome of a translation. When we visit a new area and are unfamiliar with the language, machine learning assists us by transforming the text into our recognized languages. This capability is provided by Google's GNMT (Google Neural Machine Translation), a neural ML that transforms the text into our familiar language and is known as automated translation.

The first step in using ML for automatic language translation is obtaining an appropriate data set. This data set should include both source language data, which will be translated into the target language, and target language data that have already been translated from the source. Once this data set has been obtained, it can be split into training data sets which will be used to train the ML model, and test data sets, which will be used to evaluate its performance after training is complete. The next step is building a ML model to learn how to translate between two languages based on the training data sets prepared earlier.

Finally, once the training process is complete and all hyperparameters have been tuned appropriately according to evaluation metrics obtained from testing data sets, we can deploy our model into production so it can start generating automatic translations between two different languages accurately.

12.2 Applications of Machine Learning in the Retail Industry

ML has many applications and benefits for the retail industry, such as enhancing customer experience, optimizing inventory management, forecasting demand, detecting fraud, and personalizing offers.

12.2.1 Customer Experience Personalization

This involves using ML algorithms to segment customers based on their behavior, preferences, demographics, and other factors, and then providing them with tailored recommendations, promotions, and content.

For example, Amazon uses ML to power its recommendation engine, which suggests products that customers might like based on their purchase history, browsing patterns, ratings, and reviews. According to a study by McKinsey, personalization can increase sales by 10% or more and improve customer satisfaction and loyalty.

ML can enable customer experience personalization by analyzing large amounts of data from various sources, such as online transactions, web analytics, social media, customer feedback, and loyalty programs. ML can then use this data to create customer segments or personas that reflect the characteristics, needs, preferences, and behaviors of different groups of customers.
Some examples of how ML can enable customer experience personalization in retail are:

- **Recommendation systems:** ML can use collaborative filtering, content-based filtering, or hybrid methods to recommend products or services that are relevant and appealing to each customer based on their past or current behavior, preferences, or context.
- **Dynamic pricing:** ML can use demand forecasting, price elasticity estimation, or competitive analysis to adjust prices dynamically for each customer based on their willingness to pay, demand level, inventory level, competitor prices, or other factors.
- **Personalized marketing:** ML can use customer segmentation, propensity modeling, or sentiment analysis to create personalized marketing campaigns for each customer based on their profile, behavior, interests, needs, or emotions.
- **Personalized content:** ML can use NLP, computer vision (CV), or generative models to create personalized content for each customer based on their profile, behavior, interests, needs, or emotions.

References

- Enhance customer experience with personalization, *Amazon Web Services*, last accessed July 10, 2024. https://aws.amazon.com/machine-learning/ml-use-cases/personalization/
- Siegel, E. 2023. How Machine Learning Can Improve the Customer Experience. *Harvard Business Review*, last accessed July 10, 2024. https://hbr.org/2023/03/how-machine-learning-can-improve-the-customer-experience
- Clark, S. 2023. How AI/AML Transforms Ecommerce Customer Experience. *CMSWire*, last accessed July 10, 2024. https://www.cmswire.com/ecommerce/how-aiml-transforms-ecommerce-customer-experiences/

12.2.2 Inventory and Supply Chain Optimization

Inventory management is the process of ensuring that the right products are available at the right time, place, and quantity to meet customer needs. Inventory management is crucial for retail businesses, as it affects customer satisfaction, operational efficiency, and profitability. However, inventory management is also challenging, as it involves dealing with uncertainty, complexity, and variability in demand and supply. Overstocking can lead to waste, obsolescence, and increased storage costs, while understocking can result in lost sales, customer dissatisfaction, and reduced loyalty. Therefore, retailers need to balance the trade-off between inventory availability and inventory holding costs.

Supply chain optimization is the process of designing and managing the flow of goods and services from suppliers to customers in the most efficient and effective way. Supply chain optimization aims to reduce costs, increase revenue, improve quality, enhance flexibility, and achieve sustainability goals. Supply chain optimization involves coordinating multiple activities and processes across different stages and actors in the supply chain, such as sourcing, production, transportation, warehousing, distribution, and customer service. Supply chain optimization also requires adapting to changing customer preferences, market conditions, environmental factors, and technological innovations.

ML can help retailers improve their inventory management and supply chain optimization by providing data-driven insights and solutions that can enhance decision making and performance. ML can help retailers forecast future demand more accurately and dynamically by using advanced statistical methods and learning from various data sources. For example, ML can help retailers incorporate seasonal patterns, promotional effects, weather impacts, social media trends, and customer feedback into their demand forecasting models. ML can also help retailers optimize their stock levels and replenishment policies by using optimization techniques and reinforcement learning to balance inventory costs and service levels.

ML can also help retailers optimize their pricing and distribution strategies by using regression analysis and game theory to estimate price elasticity and competitive effects.

One example of a retailer that uses ML to automate its inventory replenishment process is Walmart. Walmart uses ML to analyze data from its point-of-sale systems, warehouse management systems, weather forecasts, online platforms, social media platforms and other sources to predict future demand for each product at each store. Walmart then uses ML to generate replenishment orders that are sent to its suppliers and distribution centers automatically. This reduces overstocking and understocking issues, saves costs, and improves customer service. According to a report by IBM, inventory management improvement and supply chain optimization can reduce costs by 10% to 40% and increase revenue by 2% to 10%.

References

- Beyond the hype: A guide to understanding and successfully implementing artificial intelligence within your business. 2019. *IBM*, last accessed July 10, 2024. https://www.ibm.com/downloads/cas/8ZDXNKQ4
- Walmart's Global Replenishment System (GRS). 2020. *8th & Walton*, last accessed July 10, 2024. https://www.8thandwalton.com/blog/the-global-replenishment-system/

12.2.3 Fraud Detection

ML algorithms can help retailers detect fraud by analyzing large amounts of data and finding patterns or anomalies that indicate suspicious activities. For example, eBay uses ML to monitor millions of transactions per day and flag suspicious activities based on user behavior, transaction patterns, device information, location data, and other signals. ML algorithms can also learn from feedback and adapt to changing fraud scenarios and tactics.

Some of the common ML techniques used for fraud detection are:

- **Supervised learning**: This involves training an ML model with labeled data, where each transaction is marked as fraudulent or legitimate. The model then learns to classify new transactions based on the features and labels of the training data. For example, a logistic regression model can assign a probability score to each transaction and flag those that exceed a certain threshold as fraudulent.
- **Unsupervised learning**: This involves finding patterns or clusters in unlabeled data, where no prior information about the transactions is available. The model then identifies outliers or anomalies that deviate from the normal behavior or cluster. For example, a *K*-means clustering algorithm can group transactions based on their similarity and detect those that belong to a different cluster as fraudulent.
- **Semi-supervised learning**: This involves using a combination of labeled and unlabeled data to train an ML model. The model can leverage the labeled data to learn the features and labels of the transactions, and the unlabeled data to improve its generalization and accuracy. For example, a deep neural network can use both labeled and unlabeled data to learn complex and nonlinear relationships between the features and labels of the transactions.

ML-based fraud detection has many advantages over traditional rule-based methods, such as:

- **Scalability**: ML algorithms can handle large volumes of data and transactions without compromising speed or performance.
- **Accuracy**: ML algorithms can reduce false positives and false negatives by learning from data and feedback and adjusting their parameters accordingly.
- **Adaptability**: ML algorithms can cope with changing fraud patterns and tactics by updating their models with new data and features.
- **Automation**: ML algorithms can automate the fraud detection process and reduce human intervention and error.

However, ML-based fraud detection also faces some challenges, such as:

- **Data quality**: ML algorithms depend on the quality and quantity of the data they use. If the data is noisy, incomplete, imbalanced, or outdated, the algorithms may produce inaccurate or biased results.
- **Interpretability**: ML algorithms may be complex or opaque in their logic and decision-making process. This may make it difficult to explain or justify their results to stakeholders or regulators.
- **Ethics**: ML algorithms may raise ethical issues such as privacy, fairness, accountability, and transparency. For example, how can we protect the personal data of customers from misuse or abuse? How can we ensure that the algorithms do not discriminate against certain groups or individuals? How can we hold the algorithms or their creators responsible for their actions or outcomes?

Therefore, ML-based fraud detection requires careful design, implementation, evaluation, and governance to ensure its effectiveness, reliability, and ethicality.

References

- Lopez, M. 2016. How eBay Uses Big Data and Machine Learning to Drive Business Value, *Forbes*, last accessed July 10, 2024. https://www.forbes.com/sites/maribellopez/2016/10/04/how-ebay-uses-big-data-and-machine-learning-to-drive-business-value/?sh=a1824171f354
- Malone, C. 2019. Online Payment Fraud: Market Forecasts, Emerging Threats & Segment Analysis 2023-2028, *Juniper Research*, last accessed July 10, 2024. https://www.juniperresearch.com/researchstore/fintech-payments/online-payment-fraud

12.2.4 Customer Retention and Loyalty

Customer retention is the ability of a business to retain its customers over a period. It is a key indicator of customer satisfaction, profitability, and competitive advantage. Customer retention can be influenced by many factors, such as product quality, service quality, customer experience, brand image, loyalty programs, and marketing campaigns.

ML can analyze large and complex data sets of customer information, such as purchase history, browsing history, feedback, ratings, reviews, demographics, preferences, and interactions. ML can then use this data to identify patterns and trends, segment customers into groups based on their characteristics and behavior, and predict customer churn probability and lifetime value. ML can also generate insights and recommendations for effective retention strategies, such as personalized offers, discounts, coupons, rewards, incentives, content, messages, and notifications.

For example, Netflix is a leading online streaming service that uses ML to retain its customers and reduce churn. Netflix collects and processes massive amounts of data from its 200 million subscribers worldwide. Netflix uses ML to analyze customer viewing habits, preferences, feedback, and engagement levels to recommend content that matches their interests and tastes. Netflix also uses ML to create original content based on customer demand and feedback.

Thus, ML is a powerful tool that can help retailers retain their customers and increase their loyalty.

References

- Reichheld, FF and Sasser Jr., WE. 1990. Zero Defections: Quality Comes to Services. *Harvard Business Review*, last accessed July 10, 2024. https://hbr.org/1990/09/zero-defections-quality-comes-to-services

12.2.5 Markdown Selection

Markdown selection is the process of applying discounts to products that are about to expire or go out of season, to maximize sales and profits. ML can help retailers optimize their markdown strategies by analyzing various factors that affect customer demand and price sensitivity, such as historical sales data, inventory levels, fashion trends, competitor prices, weather, and events. ML algorithms can then suggest the best time, amount, and type of markdown for each product, based on the predicted demand and profit margins.

One example of a retailer that uses ML for markdown selection is Zara, a fast-fashion brand that operates in more than 90 countries. Zara uses ML to monitor its sales data, inventory levels, customer feedback, fashion trends, and competitor prices on a daily basis. Based on this data, Zara decides which products to mark down, when to do it, and by how much. Zara also uses ML to adjust its markdowns in real time, depending on the performance of each product and store. This allows Zara to optimize its inventory turnover and reduce its unsold stock.

According to a study by MIT Sloan Management Review, markdown selection can have a significant impact on the performance of retailers. The study found that using ML for markdown selection can increase sales by 5% to 15% and margins by 2% to 5%, compared to traditional methods. The study also identified some best practices for implementing ML for markdown selection, such as integrating data from multiple sources, testing different algorithms and scenarios, and involving human experts in the decision-making process.

References

- Agrawal, A, Gans, J and Goldfarb, A. 2018. *Prediction Machines: The Simple Economics of Artificial Intelligence*. Harvard Business Review Press.
- Ferreira, KJ, Lee, BHA and Simchi-Levi, D. 2016. Analytics for an Online Retailer: Demand Forecasting and Price Optimization. *Harvard Business School*, last accessed July 10, 2024. https://www.hbs.edu/ris/Publication%20Files/kris%20Analytics%20for%20an%20Online%20Retailer_6ef5f3e6-48e7-4923-a2d4-607d3a3d943c.pdf
- Simchi-Levi, D and Zhao, Y. 2019. How Machine Learning Can Help with Demand Forecasting and Price Optimization. *MIT Sloan Management Review*.

12.3 Applications of Machine Learning in the Logistics Industry

Logistics is the process of planning, implementing, and controlling the efficient and effective flow and storage of goods and services from the point of origin to the point of consumption. We will discuss how ML can help optimize various aspects of logistics, such as demand forecasting, inventory management, routing and scheduling, delivery tracking, and customer service.

12.3.1 Demand Forecasting

Demand forecasting is a crucial task in logistics, as it influences the optimal planning and allocation of resources along the supply chain. However, demand forecasting is also a complex and uncertain process, as it depends on many factors that are often dynamic and interrelated.

ML can offer several advantages for demand forecasting, such as:

- Handling large and diverse data sources, such as historical sales, market trends, customer behavior, weather conditions, and other external factors that may affect the demand for goods and services.
- Capturing complex and nonlinear patterns, such as seasonal variations, promotional effects, product substitutions, and cross-selling opportunities that may not be easily modeled by traditional statistical methods.
- Adapting to changing environments, such as customer preferences, competitor actions, and supply chain disruptions, by updating the models with new data and feedback.

One example of how ML can improve demand forecasting is Amazon's system, which uses ML to forecast the demand for millions of products across its global network of fulfillment centers, warehouses, and delivery stations. Amazon's system can handle the challenges of forecasting at different levels of granularity (such as, product category, SKU, location), time horizons (such as, short-term, medium-term, long-term), and scenarios (such as, normal operations, peak seasons, emergencies). Amazon's system can also incorporate various types of data, such as customer reviews, ratings, searches, clicks, purchases, returns, and inventory levels. Amazon's system can also account for various factors that may affect the demand, such as price changes, promotions, product launches, substitutions, and cannibalization. Amazon claims that its ML-based demand forecasting system has reduced forecasting errors by 50% and improved inventory availability by 15%.

The types of ML techniques that can be used for demand forecasting are supervised learning (regression, classification), unsupervised learning (clustering, anomaly detection), and reinforcement learning (multi-armed bandit, Markov decision process).

References

- Banerjee A, et al. 2019. Machine learning for forecasting at scale. In: *Proceedings of the 25th ACM SIGKDD International Conference on Knowledge Discovery & Data Mining,* Anchorage, AK, USA.

12.3.2 Inventory Management

Inventory management is a crucial aspect of logistics that involves planning, coordinating, and controlling the flow of goods from the point of origin to the point of consumption. Inventory management aims to ensure that the right amount and quality of goods are available at the right place and time to satisfy customer demand, while minimizing costs and maximizing profits. ML can help optimize inventory management by providing insights into various factors that affect inventory performance, such as inventory levels, replenishment cycles, stockouts, overstocking, and waste. ML can also help automate inventory tasks, such as demand forecasting, inventory allocation, replenishment planning, and inventory auditing.

One example of how ML can improve inventory management is Walmart's shelf monitoring system, which uses computer vision to track the shelf availability of its products in real-time. The system can detect when a product is running low or out of stock on a shelf and alert store associates to replenish it. The system can also identify when a product is misplaced or mislabeled on a shelf and notify store associates to correct it. Walmart claims that its ML-based shelf monitoring system has improved product availability by 20% and reduced labor costs by 7%.

Another example of how ML can enhance inventory management is Amazon's dynamic pricing system, which uses ML to adjust the prices of its products based on supply and demand, customer behavior, competitor prices, and other factors. The system can also predict how customers will react to price changes and adjust them accordingly. Amazon's dynamic pricing system helps it optimize its inventory levels, increase its sales volume, and maximize its profits.

References

- Chen, L, Mislove, A and Wilson, C. 2018) An Empirical Analysis of Algorithmic Pricing on Amazon Marketplace, last accessed July 11, 2014. https://mislove.org/publications/Amazon-WWW.pdf
- How AI is Transforming Retail Marketing. 2020. *Lemnisk*, last accessed July 11, 2024. https://www.lemnisk.co/blog/ai-transforming-retail-marketing/

12.3.3 Routing and Scheduling

Routing and scheduling are important aspects of logistics, as they affect the efficiency and effectiveness of delivering goods and services to customers. ML can help improve routing and scheduling by taking into account various factors and goals, such as traffic conditions, fuel consumption, delivery time windows, customer satisfaction, and environmental impact. ML can use data from historical records, real-time sensors, and user feedback to learn patterns and preferences, and then generate optimal or near-optimal solutions for routing and scheduling problems.

For example, UPS uses ML to optimize its delivery routes using a system called ORION (On-Road Integrated Optimization and Navigation). UPS's ML system can analyze millions of possible routes and select the best one based on distance, time, cost, and customer preferences. UPS claims that its ML-based routing system has reduced travel distance by 100 million miles per year and saved 10 million gallons of fuel per year (UPS, 2018).

Another example of ML-enhanced routing and scheduling is Google Maps, which uses ML to provide users with the fastest and most convenient routes based on traffic data, road conditions, user preferences, and historical trends. Google Maps also uses ML to predict travel times and arrival times based on current and expected traffic patterns. Furthermore, Google Maps uses ML to suggest alternative routes or modes of transportation when there are delays or disruptions on the original route.

ML can also help with routing and scheduling in other domains, such as healthcare, education, manufacturing, and e-commerce.

References

- Everything You Need to Know about UPS Route Optimization Software (ORION). 2021. *Route4Me,* last accessed July 11, 2024. https://blog.route4me.com/ups-route-optimization-software-orion/
- Lau, J. 2020. Google Maps 101: How AI helps predicts traffic and determine routes, *Google,* last accessed July 11, 2024. https://blog.google/products/maps/google-maps-101-how-ai-helps-predict-traffic-and-determine-routes/

12.3.4 Delivery Tracking

Delivery tracking is a crucial aspect of logistics, as it enables customers and logistics providers to have a clear and accurate view of the status and location of their shipments and deliveries. ML can enhance delivery tracking by providing real-time updates, predictions, and alerts based on various data sources and algorithms. For instance, FedEx uses ML to track its packages using a system called SenseAware, which is a sensor-based logistics service that monitors the physical conditions and environmental factors of a package during transit. FedEx's ML system can measure various parameters of a package, such as temperature, humidity, pressure, light exposure, shock, vibration, and location, and transmit this information to a cloud-based platform that can be accessed by customers and FedEx employees. FedEx's ML system can also predict the estimated time of arrival (ETA) of a package based on historical data, weather conditions, traffic patterns, and other factors, using regression models and neural networks. By using ML-based tracking, FedEx claims that it has increased customer satisfaction by 30% and reduced claims by 40%, as it can provide more transparency, reliability, and security for its shipments.

ML-based delivery tracking can offer several benefits for customers and logistics providers, such as:

- **Improved customer experience**: Customers can have more confidence and trust in the delivery process, as they can access real-time information about their packages and receive timely notifications and alerts in case of any delays or issues. Customers can also have more flexibility and convenience in managing their deliveries, as they can change their preferences or reschedule their deliveries based on the predicted ETA of their packages.
- **Reduced operational costs**: Logistics providers can optimize their routes and resources by using ML-based delivery tracking, as they can avoid traffic congestion, road closures, accidents, or other disruptions that may affect the delivery time. Logistics providers can also reduce fuel consumption and emissions by using ML-based delivery tracking, as they can plan the most efficient and eco-friendly routes for their vehicles.
- **Enhanced risk management**: Logistics providers can mitigate the risks of losing or damaging their packages by using ML-based delivery tracking, as they can monitor the physical conditions and environmental factors of their packages and intervene promptly if any anomalies are detected. Logistics providers can also reduce the likelihood of theft or fraud by using ML-based delivery tracking, as they can verify the identity and location of the recipients and ensure that the packages are delivered to the right person at the right place.

References

- Real-time tracking with FedEx SenseAware^{SM}. 2019. *FedEx*, last accessed July 12, 2024. https://www.fedex.com/en-us/senseaware.html

12.3.5 Customer Service Improvement

ML can enhance customer service by offering customized suggestions, replies, and solutions to customers' inquiries, issues, and feedback. For instance, DHL uses ML to improve its customer service with a system called DHLbot. DHLbot is an ML system that can comprehend natural language queries from customers via text or voice and provide pertinent information, such as tracking status, delivery options, pricing, and FAQs. DHLbot can also transfer complex or urgent matters to human agents if necessary. DHL reports that its ML-based customer service system has decreased response time by 50% and increased customer retention by 20%.

Another example of how ML can improve customer service in logistics is DHL's intelligent routing system, which uses ML to optimize delivery routes based on various factors, such as traffic conditions, weather forecasts, road closures, and customer preferences.

References

- Saloodo Realtime Logistics. Your Digital Freight Platform Powered by DHL. *DHL*, last accessed July 12, 2024. https://www.dhl.com/content/dam/dhl/global/core/documents/pdf/glo-core-exhibition-saloodo-introduction-auto-mobility-digital.PDF

12.4 Applications of Machine Learning in the Manufacturing Industry

In this section, we will explore some of the applications of ML in the manufacturing industry, which is one of the most important sectors of the economy.

12.4.1 Predictive Maintenance

One of the main applications of ML in manufacturing is predictive maintenance, which aims to prevent equipment failures and reduce downtime by using data-driven models to forecast the condition and performance of machines. Predictive maintenance can help manufacturers save costs, improve efficiency, and enhance product quality.

Predictive maintenance relies on various types of data collected from sensors, such as temperature, vibration, sound, pressure, etc., to monitor the health and performance of machines. ML algorithms can analyze these data and identify patterns or anomalies that indicate potential faults or failures. Based on these insights, the algorithms can provide recommendations for preventive actions, such as repairs, replacements, or adjustments, before the problems escalate and cause breakdowns or defects. Predictive maintenance has many benefits for manufacturers, such as:

- **Cost savings**: By avoiding unexpected failures and reducing downtime, predictive maintenance can lower the maintenance costs and increase the asset utilization.
- **Improving efficiency**: By optimizing the maintenance schedules and resources, predictive maintenance can improve the operational efficiency and productivity of the manufacturing processes.
- **Enhancing product quality**: By detecting and preventing quality issues early, predictive maintenance can improve the product quality and customer satisfaction.

Predictive maintenance is a promising application of ML in manufacturing that can provide significant value and competitive advantage for manufacturers. However, it also requires some challenges to be addressed, such as:

- **Data quality**: The accuracy and reliability of the predictive models depend on the quality and quantity of the data collected from the machines. Therefore, it is important to ensure that the data are clean, consistent, and representative of the machine conditions and behaviors.
- **Data security**: The data collected from the machines may contain sensitive or proprietary information that needs to be protected from unauthorized access or misuse. Therefore, it is important to implement appropriate data security measures, such as encryption, authentication, and authorization.
- **Data integration**: The data collected from different machines or sources may have different formats, structures, or semantics that need to be harmonized and integrated for effective analysis. Therefore, it is important to use standard data formats and protocols, such as OPC UA (Open Platform Communications Unified Architecture), which is a widely used industrial communication standard for data exchange.
- **Model explainability**: The predictive models may use complex or non-linear ML techniques, such as deep learning or ensemble methods, that are difficult to interpret or explain. Therefore, it is important to provide some level of model explainability or transparency, such as feature importance or decision rules, to build trust and confidence among the users and stakeholders.

References

- Chui, M, Manyika, J, et al. 2018. Notes From the AI Frontier: Insights From Hundreds of Use Cases. *McKinsey & Company*, last accessed July 12, 2024. https://www.mckinsey.com/~/media/mckinsey/featured%20insights/artificial%20intelligence/notes%20from%20the%20ai%20frontier%20applications%20and%20value%20of%20deep%20learning/notes-from-the-ai-frontier-insights-from-hundreds-of-use-cases-discussion-paper.pdf
- Burke, R, Laaper, S, Hartigan, M and Sniderman, B. 2017. The smart factory. *Deloitte*, last accessed July 12, 2024. https://www.deloitte.com/global/en/our-thinking/insights/topics/digital-transformation/industry-4-0/smart-factory-connected-manufacturing.html
- Smart factories @ scale. *CapGemini Research Institute*, last accessed July 12, 2024. https://www.capgemini.com/wp-content/uploads/2019/11/Report-%E2%80%93-Smart-Factories.pdf
- Unified Architecture, *OPC Foundation*, last accessed July 12, 2024. https://opcfoundation.org/about/opc-technologies/opc-ua/

12.4.2 Quality Control

ML can enhance and automate the quality control process by using computer vision algorithms, which are methods that enable computers to analyze and understand images and videos. Computer vision algorithms can be trained to detect defects, anomalies, and deviations from specifications in the products or processes, such as cracks, scratches, dents, misalignments, or color variations. For example, a computer vision algorithm can be used to inspect the surface of a car for any defects before it leaves the factory. ML can also learn from historical data to identify the root causes of quality issues and suggest corrective actions.

There are different approaches to train computer vision algorithms for quality control. One approach is to use supervised learning, which requires labeled data that indicate whether an image or video contains a defect or not. The algorithm learns from the labeled data and then predicts the labels for new data.

Another approach is to use unsupervised learning, which does not require labeled data. For example, an unsupervised learning algorithm can learn from the most common type of defects in their training set and then compare new samples with them. This approach can be useful when the defects are frequent or predictable.

ML-based quality control has several advantages over traditional methods. ML-based methods can be faster, more accurate, more consistent, and more scalable than human inspection or manual testing. ML-based methods can also adapt to changing conditions and requirements by learning from new data and feedback. ML-based methods can also provide insights and explanations for the quality issues and their solutions.

However, ML-based quality control also faces some challenges and limitations. ML-based methods require large amounts of data to train and validate the algorithms, which may not be available or accessible for some applications. ML-based methods may also suffer from bias, noise, or errors in the data, which may affect their performance and reliability. ML-based methods may also need human supervision and intervention to ensure their safety and ethics. For example, human experts may need to review the results of the algorithms and confirm their accuracy and validity.

References

- Xiaojun, W and Cao,K. 2017. A Surface Defect Detection Based on Convolutional Neural Network. *International Conference on Computer Vision Systems*, last accessed July 12, 2024. https://www.researchgate.net/publication/320301708_A_Surface_Defect_Detection_Based_on_Convolutional_Neural_Network
- Zhang, J et al. 2021. CADN: A weakly supervised learning-based category-aware object detection network for surface defect detection. *Pattern Recognition*, 109: 107571, last accessed July 12, 2024. https://www.sciencedirect.com/science/article/abs/pii/S0031320320303745#:~:text=CADN%20is%20trained%20with%20image,information%20in%20a%20classification%20pipeline

12.5 Applications of Machine Learning in the Energy and Utilities Industry

ML has many applications in the energy and utilities industry, such as optimizing energy consumption, forecasting demand and supply, detecting anomalies and faults, enhancing security and reliability, and improving customer satisfaction.

12.5.1 Optimizing Energy Consumption

One of the main applications of ML in the energy and utilities industry is optimizing energy consumption. ML can help reduce energy waste, improve efficiency, and lower costs by analyzing data from smart meters, sensors, weather forecasts, and other sources.

For example, Google used ML to reduce the energy consumption of its data centers by 40% by adjusting the cooling systems based on the data collected from thousands of sensors. The ML model was able to find the optimal trade-off between minimizing energy consumption and maximizing performance and reliability of the data center.

Another example is Nest, a smart thermostat that learns from the user's behavior and preferences and adjusts the temperature accordingly. Nest uses ML algorithms to learn from the user's manual adjustments, schedule, location, weather, and other factors, and automatically creates a personalized temperature program for each user.

ML can offer many benefits for the energy and utilities industry, but it also poses some challenges, such as ensuring data quality, security, and privacy, as well as explaining how the ML models make decisions and ensuring their fairness and accountability.

References

- J. Gao et al. 2014. Machine Learning Applications for Data Center Optimization. *Google Research*, last accessed July 12, 2024. https://research.google/pubs/pub42542
- Khosrojerdi, F, Gagnon, S and Valverde, R. 2021. Applications of Artificial Intelligence in Smart Grids: Present and Future Research Domains. *2021 IEEE 9th International Conference on Smart Energy Grid Engineering (SEGE)*, last accessed July 12, 2024. https://www.researchgate.net/publication/354567973_Applications_of_Artificial_Intelligence_in_Smart_Grids_Present_and_Future_Research_Domains

12.5.2 Forecasting Demand and Supply of Electricity

In wind power forecasting, HyRef, a system developed by IBM, can predict the power output of wind farms up to 36 hours in advance with 90% accuracy. HyRef uses weather data from multiple sources, such as satellites, radars, sensors, and cameras, to create high-resolution models of wind speed and direction at different heights and locations. HyRef then applies ML algorithms to these models to generate forecasts for each wind turbine and wind farm. HyRef can also optimize the operation and maintenance of wind turbines by detecting anomalies and faults. By using HyRef, utility companies can better plan their generation mix and dispatch strategies, as well as reduce their dependence on fossil fuels and greenhouse gas emissions.

Another example of ML application in solar power forecasting is a system developed by DeepMind, a subsidiary of Google, that can predict the power output of solar panels based on satellite images. The system can also account for the orientation and efficiency of each panel, as well as the shading effects from nearby objects. By using this system, Google can optimize the use of solar energy for its data centers and reduce its carbon footprint.

References

- Vestas. IBM Big Data Success Stories. *IBM*, last accessed on July 12, 2024. https://public.dhe.ibm.com/software/data/sw-library/big-data/ibm-big-data-success.pdf
- Elkin C and Witherspoon, S. 2019. Machine learning can boost the value of wind energy. *Google DeepMind*, last accessed on July 12, 2024. https://deepmind.com/blog/article/machine-learning-can-boost-value-wind-energy

12.5.3 Maintenance of Energy Infrastructure

One of the challenges in the energy and utilities industry is to ensure the proper functioning and maintenance of the energy assets, such as wind turbines, power plants, transmission lines, and pipelines. These assets are often exposed to harsh environmental conditions, wear and tear, and operational stresses, and they are usually distributed over large geographical areas, making it difficult and costly to monitor and inspect them manually.

ML can provide such solutions by analyzing data from various sources, such as sensors, cameras, drones, and other devices, that collect information about the status and performance of the energy assets. ML algorithms can learn from historical and current data to identify patterns, trends, and outliers that indicate normal or abnormal behavior of the assets.

Some examples of ML systems that are used for anomaly and fault detection in the energy and utilities industry are:

- **MindSphere by Siemens**: This is a cloud-based platform that connects and analyzes data from wind turbines and other energy assets. It uses ML to monitor the health and performance of the assets and alert operators of any issues or defects. This can help increase the availability and reliability of wind power and reduce maintenance costs.
- **Predix by GE Power**: This is a cloud-based platform that connects and analyzes data from power plants and other energy assets. It uses ML to detect anomalies in power plants and provide recommendations for corrective actions. This can help improve the safety and efficiency of power generation and reduce downtime.

References

- Siemens Insights Hub (MindSphere): The Power of Industrial IoT. *Engineering Industries eXcellence*, last accessed on July 12, 2024. https://www.indx.com/en/product/siemens-mindsphere-1
- What is Predix Platform? *GE Vernova*, last accessed on July 12, 2024. https://www.ge.com/digital/documentation/edge-software/c_what_is_predix_platform.html

12.5.4 Other Applications in the Energy and Utilities Industry

One of the main threats to the energy infrastructure is cyberattacks, which can compromise the data and operations of energy companies and cause disruptions or damages to the power grid. To prevent and mitigate such attacks, ML can be used to analyze data from networks, systems, devices, and users, and detect any anomalies or suspicious activities that indicate a potential cyberattack. For example, Microsoft developed a ML system called Azure Sentinel that can collect and correlate data from various sources such as logs, emails, cloud services, etc., and use advanced analytics and automation to identify and respond to cyber threats in real time. This can help secure the data and operations of energy companies and prevent disruptions or damages.

Another threat to the energy infrastructure is physical attacks, natural disasters, or human errors, which can damage the power grid or affect its performance. To improve the resilience of the power grid, ML can be used to identify vulnerable areas and prioritize investments for upgrades. For example, Duke Energy, which is one of the largest electric power holding companies in the US, used ML to analyze data from sensors, weather models, historical records, etc., and identify areas of the power grid that are most likely to fail or underperform due to storms or other events. This can help reduce the risk of blackouts or outages caused by storms or other events.

References

- Microsoft Sentinel. *Microsoft*, last accessed on July 12, 2024. https://azure.microsoft.com/en-in/products/microsoft-sentinel
- Duke Energy collaborates with AWS to develop smart grid solutions to better serve customers and drive its clean energy transition. 2022. *Duke Energy*. Last accessed on July 12, 2024. https://news.duke-energy.com/releases/duke-energy-collaborates-with-aws-to-develop-smart-grid-solutions-to-better-serve-customers-and-drive-its-clean-energy-transition

12.6 Applications of Machine Learning in the Travel Industry

ML has many applications in various domains, including the travel industry. In this section, we will explore some of the ways that ML can enhance the travel experience for customers, businesses, and society.

12.6.1 Personalization

Some examples of how ML can enable personalization in the travel industry are:

- **Destination recommendation**: ML can help travelers discover new destinations that match their interests, budget, season, and other criteria. For example, Expedia uses ML to analyze the browsing and booking behavior of its customers and provide them with personalized recommendations and offers based on their interests and past trips.

- **Accommodation recommendation**: ML can help travelers find the best accommodation options for their trip, such as hotels, apartments, or homestays. For example, Airbnb uses ML to match travelers with hosts and properties that suit their preferences and expectations
- **Activity recommendation**: ML can help travelers plan their itinerary and discover the best activities and attractions for their destination. For example, TripAdvisor uses ML to rank and filter the millions of reviews and photos on its platform and provide travelers with personalized suggestions for things to do, see, and eat.
- **Transportation recommendation**: ML can help travelers find the best transportation options for their trip, such as flights, trains, buses, or car rentals. For example, Skyscanner uses ML to compare and predict the prices and availability of different travel options and provide travelers with personalized alerts and tips.

References

- Rooney, P. 2023. Expedia poised to take flight with generative AI. *CIO*, last accessed on July 12, 2024. https://www.cio.com/article/481289/expedia-poised-to-take-flight-with-generative-ai.html
- Murthy, R. 2023. Unlocking the Value of AI and Generative AI in Travel. *Medium*, last accessed on July 12, 2024. https://medium.com/expedia-group-tech/unlocking-the-value-of-ai-and-generative-ai-in-travel-2994712d0a0
- Hinek, JP. 2022. How does Airbnb use machine learning (ML). *Medium*, last accessed on July 12, 2024. https://m.mage.ai/how-does-airbnb-use-machine-learning-ml-fdcc7d18297a
- Dharma, Renata. 2019. The driving force behind Skyscanner? Data Science. *Medium*, last accessed on July 12, 2024. https://medium.com/smubia/the-driving-force-behind-skyscanner-data-science-d7eecc8cc6fe

12.6.2 Optimization

ML can help optimize the operations and performance of travel businesses and organizations, such as airlines, hotels, tour operators, etc., by analyzing large amounts of data and making predictions or recommendations based on the data.

One example of ML optimization in the travel industry is airline optimization. ML can help airlines optimize their flight schedules, pricing, seat allocation, fuel consumption, etc., by taking into account various factors such as demand, weather, competition, etc. ML can also help airlines optimize their fuel consumption by predicting the optimal route, speed, and altitude for each flight based on the weather conditions and fuel prices.

ML can help hotels optimize their occupancy, revenue, customer satisfaction, etc., by adjusting their rates, availability, amenities, etc., based on the market conditions and customer feedback. ML can also help hotels by recommending the optimal number of rooms to block or release for different channels or segments..

References

- Liang Chen et al. 2021. Machine Learning for Airline Optimization, *IEEE Transactions on Intelligent Transportation Systems 22.*
- Zeynep Akşin et al. 2021. Machine Learning for Hotel Optimization, *Journal of Revenue and Pricing Management 20.*

12.6.3 Innovation

ML can help create new and innovative travel products and services that can enhance the travel experience and solve existing or emerging problems. For example, ML can help create virtual assistants that can assist travelers with various tasks such as booking, planning, navigating, etc., using natural language processing and speech recognition. Some examples of virtual assistants that use ML in the travel industry are:

- **Google Assistant**: A voice-activated assistant that can help travelers with various tasks such as booking flights, hotels, restaurants, etc., using Google's services such as Google Flights, Google Hotels, Google Maps, etc.
- **Romie**: A text-based assistant that can help travelers with various tasks such as managing their bookings, checking their flight status, finding nearby attractions, etc., using Expedia's services such as Expedia.com, Expedia Rewards, Expedia Local Expert, etc.
- **Mebzi**: A chat-based assistant that can help travelers with various tasks such as finding the best deals on flights, hotels, car rentals, etc., using ML algorithms to analyze travelers' preferences and behavior.

Similarly, ML can help create smart devices that can monitor and improve the safety and comfort of travelers, such as wearable sensors, smart luggage, smart locks, etc. Some examples of smart devices that use ML in the travel industry are:

- **Bluesmart**: A smart suitcase that can be locked and unlocked remotely using a smartphone app or a fingerprint scanner. It also has a built-in GPS tracker, a digital scale, a battery charger, and a proximity sensor.
- **Hilton's Connected Room**: A smart hotel room that allows guests to control the temperature, lighting, TV channels, music streaming services, etc., using a smartphone app or voice commands via Amazon Alexa.
- **Fitbit**: A smart watch that can track various health metrics such as heart rate, calories burned, steps taken, sleep quality, etc. It also has features such as GPS navigation, music control, notifications from smartphone apps or calls/texts/emails.

References

- Gupta, S. 2021. Machine Learning, AI & Big Data Analytics in the Travel & Hospitality Industry: Applications, Scopes, and Impact on the Job Market. Economic Times. *CIO*, last accessed on July 2024. https://cio.economictimes.indiatimes.com/news/next-gen-technologies/machine-learning-ai-big-data-analytics-in-the-travel-hospitality-industry-applications-scopes-and-impact-on-the-job-market/86389867

- Parvez, MO. 2021. Use of machine learning technology for tourist and organizational services: high-tech innovation in the hospitality industry. *Journal of Tourism Futures*, last accessed on July 2024. https://doi.org/10.1108/JTF-09-2019-0083
- Chawla, S. 2019. 7 Successful Applications of AI & Machine Learning in the Travel Industry. *Hacker Noon*, last accessed on July 2024. https://hackernoon.com/successful-implications-of-ai-machine-learning-in-travel-industry-3040f3e1d48c
- Biswas, J. 2018. AI Is Fast Disrupting The Travel Industry. Here's How. *Analytics India Magazine*, last accessed on July 2024. https://analyticsindiamag.com/artificial-intelligence-travel-industry-hospitality/
- Bulanov, O. 2024. The Benefits of Using ML & AI in the Travel Industry. *Django Stars*, last accessed on July 2024. https://djangostars.com/blog/benefits-of-the-use-of-machine-learning-and-ai-in-the-travel-industry/

12.7 Applications of Machine Learning in the Banking Industry

ML has been widely adopted by various industries, including banking, to improve their business processes, customer experience, and risk management. In this section, we will explore some of the applications of ML in the banking industry and provide examples and case studies to illustrate their benefits and challenges.

12.7.1 Credit Underwriting

Credit underwriting is the process of assessing the creditworthiness of borrowers and determining the terms and conditions of loans. It is a crucial function for banks, as it affects their profitability, risk management, and customer satisfaction.

Traditionally, credit underwriting relies on manual analysis of financial statements, credit scores, and other factors. However, this approach can be time-consuming, costly, and prone to errors and biases. Moreover, it can exclude potential customers who do not have sufficient credit history or belong to underserved segments, such as low-income or rural populations.

ML can enhance credit underwriting by automating the analysis of large and complex data sets, such as transaction records, social media activity, mobile phone usage, and alternative data sources. ML can also provide more accurate and consistent assessments of credit risk, as well as personalized and dynamic pricing of loans. Furthermore, ML can enable financial inclusion by expanding access to credit for customers who are otherwise overlooked by traditional methods.

For example, Zest AI is a company that provides ML solutions for credit underwriting. Zest AI claims that its platform can reduce loan losses by 25%, increase approval rates by 15%, and reduce bias by 30%. Zest AI works with various banks and lenders, such as Discover, BMO Harris Bank, and Prestige Financial Services. Another example is LenddoEFL, which uses psychometric tests, behavioral data, and alternative data to assess the creditworthiness of customers in emerging markets.

ML in credit underwriting has many benefits, but it also poses some challenges and risks. For instance, ML models may be complex and opaque, making it difficult to explain how they make decisions or to ensure compliance with regulations. ML models may also inherit or amplify the biases and errors in the data or algorithms, leading to unfair or discriminatory outcomes. Moreover, ML models may be vulnerable to cyberattacks or adversarial manipulation, compromising their security and reliability.

Therefore, ML in credit underwriting requires careful design, validation, monitoring, and governance.

References

- Zest AI: Machine learning for credit underwriting, *Zest,* last accessed on July 12, 2024. https://www.zest.ai/product/underwriting/
- The looming credit-gap in a post-Covid world. 2020. *LenddoEFL,* last accessed on July 12, 2024. https://lenddoefl.com/news/tag/Credit+Scoring
- Yao, G et al. 2022. Using social media information to predict the credit risk of listed enterprises in the supply chain. *Kybernetes,* last accessed on July 12, 2024. https://www.x-mol.net/paper/article/1540080193452744704
- Chien, T et al. 2016. XGBoost: A Scalable Tree Boosting System. *Proceedings of the 22nd ACM SIGKDD International Conference on Knowledge Discovery and Data Mining,* last accessed on July 12, 2024. https://dl.acm.org/doi/10.1145/2939672.2939785
- Barocas, S et al. 2023. *Fairness and Machine Learning: Limitations and Opportunities.* MIT Press, last accessed on July 12, 2024. https://fairmlbook.org/
- Zest AI Resources. Getting AI Done: A Case Study with 5Point Credit Union. *Zest,* last accessed on July 12, 2024. https://www.zest.ai/resources/getting-ai-done-a-conversation-with-a-credit-union-ceo

12.7.2 Fraud Detection

Traditional fraud detection methods, such as rule-based systems and statistical models, can be ineffective, inefficient, and inflexible. They can generate false positives, miss novel fraud patterns, and require constant updating. Machine learning, on the other hand, can offer several advantages for fraud detection in banking, such as:

- Ability to handle large and complex data sets from multiple sources and channels
- Ability to learn from past data and adapt to new data and scenarios
- Ability to detect anomalies and outliers that deviate from normal behavior
- Ability to reduce false positives and false negatives by improving accuracy and precision

Some of the examples of ML-based fraud detection systems in banking are:

- **KSTAR**: This is a nuclear fusion reactor in South Korea that achieved 100 million°C for 30 seconds in 2022. It used ML techniques such as CatBoost, XGBoost, LightGBM, deep learning, and Bayesian optimization to improve the performance of fraud detection on real-world data.
- **IITCEE**: This is an international conference on intelligent and innovative technologies in computing, electrical and electronics that was held in 2023. It proposed a machine learning-based approach to detect fraud in banking transactions using various intelligent algorithms trained on a public data set.
- **Binariks**: This is a software development company that provides solutions for financial fraud detection using machine learning. It helps banks to identify unusual payment activity across different devices and secure mobile payments.

- **Emerj**: This is an AI research firm that provides insights and trends on AI-based fraud detection in banking. It covers various use cases and applications of machine learning for fraud prevention and detection.
- **Accord Business Group**: This is a business consulting firm that provides services for data analysis and machine learning. It explains how to detect bank frauds with machine learning and data analysis using various techniques and tools.

ML can improve fraud detection by using algorithms that can learn from historical and real-time data and adapt to changing fraud scenarios. ML can also use techniques such as anomaly detection, classification, clustering, and natural language processing to identify fraudulent behavior and flag suspicious transactions.

References

- Hashemi, SK et al. 2022. Fraud Detection in Banking Data by Machine Learning Techniques. *IEEE Access*, last accessed on July 12, 2024. https://ieeexplore.ieee.org/stamp/stamp.jsp?arnumber=9999220
- Achary, R and Shelke, C. 2023. Fraud Detection in Banking Transactions Using Machine Learning. *IEEE Xplore*, last accessed on July 12, 2024. https://ieeexplore.ieee.org/document/10091067
- Financial Fraud Detection Using Machine Learning. 2023, *Binariks*, last accessed on July 12, 2024. https://binariks.com/blog/financial-fraud-detection-machine-learning/
- Mejia, N. 2020. AI-Based Fraud Detection in Banking – Current Applications and Trends. *Emerj*, last accessed on July 12, 2024. https://emerj.com/ai-sector-overviews/artificial-intelligence-fraud-banking/
- How to Detect Bank Frauds with Machine Learning and Data Analysis. 2023. *Accord Business Group*, last accessed on July 12, 2024. https://accordbgroup.com/how-to-detect-bank-frauds-with-machine-learning-and-data-analysis

12.7.3 Hyper-Personalization

Hyper-personalization refers to the process of delivering customized products, services, and experiences to customers based on their preferences, behavior, and needs. However, achieving hyper-personalization can be challenging due to the complexity and diversity of customer data and the dynamic nature of customer expectations.

ML can enable hyper-personalization by using algorithms that can segment customers based on their attributes and behavior, generate recommendations based on their interests and goals, and optimize pricing and offers based on their willingness to pay. ML can also use techniques such as natural language generation, sentiment analysis, and chatbots to create personalized content and interactions with customers. For example, Capital One is a bank that uses ML for hyper-personalization in its digital channels. Their ML system uses natural language generation to create personalized messages for customers based on their spending patterns, financial situation, and life events.

ML can generate recommendations based on customers' interests and goals. For example, ML can use collaborative filtering techniques to recommend products or services that are similar to or complementary to what customers have bought or viewed before. Alternatively, ML can use content-based filtering techniques to recommend products or services that are related to the content or topics that customers have expressed interest in.

ML can also enable hyper-personalization is by optimizing pricing and offers based on customers' willingness to pay. For example, Uber uses ML to dynamically adjust its fares based on the demand and supply of drivers and riders. Another way that ML can enable hyper-personalization is by creating personalized content and interactions with customers using natural language generation (NLG), sentiment analysis (SA), and chatbots.

References

- Hyper-personalizing the customer experience using data, analytics, and AI. *Deloitte*, last accessed on July 12, 2024. https://www2.deloitte.com/content/dam/Deloitte/ca/Documents/deloitte-analytics/ca-en-omnia-ai-marketing-pov-fin-jun24-aoda.pdf
- Hyper-personalization in banking: 6 ways to success. *Giesekt+Devrient*, last accessed on July 12, 2024. https://www.gi-de.com/en/spotlight/financial-platforms/hyper-personalization-in-banking-6-ways-to-success
- The future of retail banking: The hyper-personalization imperative. 2020. *Deloitte*, last accessed on July 12, 2024. https://www2.deloitte.com/content/dam/Deloitte/uk/Documents/financial-services/deloitte-uk-hp-the-future-of-retail-banking.pdf
- Shmat, D. Machine Learning in Banking: 8 Use Cases & Adoption Guide. *Itransition*, last accessed on July 12, 2024. https://www.itransition.com/machine-learning/banking
- Use Of Machine Learning (ML) In The Banking Industry Has Become a Necessity. 2023. *TechNews*, last accessed on July 12, 2024. https://www.techbusinessnews.com.au/blog/the-use-of-machine-learning-ml-in-the-banking-industry/
- North, R. 2019. 6 Ways Banking Sector Uses Machine Learning Technology. *Enterprise Edges*, last accessed on July 12, 2024. https://www.enterpriseedges.com/machine-learning-uses-banking-sector

12.8 Applications of Machine Learning in the Finance Industry

ML has many applications in the finance industry, such as risk management, fraud detection, customer service, and trading. In this section, we will explore some of the use cases of ML in finance and how they benefit the industry and its customers.

12.8.1 Risk Management

One of the most common applications of ML in finance is credit risk assessment. Credit risk is the risk of default or non-payment by a borrower or counterparty. Traditionally, lenders use credit scores, such as FICO scores, to evaluate the creditworthiness of borrowers based on their payment history, debt level, income, and other factors. However, credit scores may not reflect the full picture of a borrower's financial situation or behavior, especially for those who are unbanked or underbanked. ML can help lenders to improve their credit risk assessment by using alternative data sources, such as social media activity, online behavior, or transaction history, that may provide more insights into a borrower's personality, preferences, and habits. For example, LenddoEFL, a fintech company founded in 2011, uses psychometric tests and smartphone data to assess the credit risk of borrowers in emerging markets who lack traditional credit histories.

Another application of ML in finance is market risk management. Market risk management involves analyzing market trends, volatility, and correlations among different assets to optimize portfolio allocation and hedging strategies. ML can help investors to enhance their market risk management by using algorithms that can learn from historical and real-time data to forecast market movements and identify optimal trading opportunities. For example, Sentient Technologies, an AI company founded in 2007, uses evolutionary algorithms and deep learning to create autonomous trading systems that can adapt to changing market conditions and execute trades across multiple asset classes.

A third application of ML in finance is operational risk management. Operational risk management involves identifying, measuring, monitoring, and controlling the sources of operational risk within an organization. ML can help financial institutions to reduce their operational risk by using techniques such NLP, computer vision, and anomaly detection to automate tasks that are prone to human error or fraud, such as document processing, compliance monitoring, fraud detection, or cybersecurity. For example, Compliance.ai, a Silicon Valley startup founded in 2016, provides an ML-driven platform that helps banks keep up with regulatory changes by extracting relevant information from thousands of documents and providing actionable insights.

References

- Investment Strategy. *Sentient Equity Partners*, last accessed on July 12, 2024. https://sentientep.com/strategy.php
- Expert-in-the-Loop Machine Learning. *Compliance.AI*, last accessed on July 12, 2024. https://www.compliance.ai/expert-in-the-loop/#expert

12.8.2 Process Automation

Process automation involves automating repetitive or manual tasks that can improve the efficiency and accuracy of financial operations. ML can help financial institutions to automate various processes by using robotic process automation (RPA), which is a technology that uses software robots or digital workers to perform tasks that mimic human actions. For example, ML can help accounting firms to automate data entry and reconciliation by using optical character recognition (OCR), which is a technology that can convert scanned images or documents into editable text, to extract data from invoices, receipts, or bank statements. ML can also help tax advisors to automate tax preparation and filing by using NLP to interpret tax laws and regulations and generate tax forms.

References

- Machine Learning in Finance: 10 Applications and Use Cases. 2024. *Coursera*, last accessed on July 12, 2024. https://www.coursera.org/articles/machine-learning-in-finance
- Machine Learning (in Finance). *Corporate Finance Institute*, last accessed on July 12, 2024. https://corporatefinanceinstitute.com/resources/data-science/machine-learning-in-finance/
- Optical character recognition, *Wikipedia*, last accessed on July 12, 2024. https://en.wikipedia.org/wiki/Optical_character_recognition: Natural language processing – Wikipedia.

12.8.3 Data Analytics

ML can help financial institutions to leverage data analytics more effectively by using advanced techniques that can handle unstructured or complex data and provide actionable recommendations.

Recommender systems are algorithms that can suggest products or services based on the preferences or behavior of the user. They are widely used in e-commerce, entertainment, and social media platforms. In finance, recommender systems can help wealth managers to provide personalized financial advice to their clients by using ML to analyze their financial goals, risk appetite, investment history, and market trends.

In finance, reinforcement learning can help traders to execute trades faster and smarter by using ML to optimize trading strategies.

These are just two examples of how ML can help with data analytics in finance. There are many other applications and benefits of ML in this domain, such as fraud detection, credit scoring, sentiment analysis, and risk management. ML can help financial institutions to gain a competitive edge, improve customer satisfaction, and increase efficiency and profitability.

References

- Ricci, F et al. 2011. *Recommender Systems Handbook.* Springer, last accessed on July 12, 2024. https://www.cse.iitk.ac.in/users/nsrivast/HCC/Recommender_systems_handbook.pdf
- Moody, J and Saffell, M. Reinforcement Learning for Trading. *NeurIPS Proceedings*, last accessed on July 12, 2024. https://proceedings.neurips.cc/paper_files/paper/1998/file/4e6cd95227cb0c280e99a195be5f6615-Paper.pdf

12.8.4 Customer Support

ML can improve customer support by using chatbots, which are software applications that can imitate human conversations through text or voice. ML can also assist insurance companies to provide faster claims processing by using chatbots that can gather information from customers, verify their identity, and start the claim process.

Chatbots are based on NLP, which deals with analyzing and generating natural language. NLP enables chatbots to understand the meaning and intent of customer queries and provide relevant and accurate answers. NLP also allows chatbots to adapt to different languages, dialects, and contexts, and learn from customer feedback.

One example of a chatbot that uses ML for customer support is Erica, which is a virtual assistant developed by Bank of America. Erica can help customers with various banking tasks, such as checking account balances, paying bills, sending money, or scheduling appointments. Erica can also provide personalized financial advice, such as suggesting ways to save money, reduce debt, or improve credit score. Erica uses NLP to understand customer requests and respond in a conversational manner. Erica also uses ML to learn from customer interactions and improve its performance over time.

References

- Erica® is here for you and your life goals. *Bank of America*, last accessed on July 12, 2024. https://promotions.bankofamerica.com/digitalbanking/mobilebanking/erica
- Machine Learning in Finance: 10 Applications and Use Cases. 2024. *Coursera*, last accessed on July 12, 2024. https://www.coursera.org/articles/machine-learning-in-finance

- Machine Learning (in Finance). *Corporate Finance Institute*, last accessed on July 12, 2024. https://corporatefinanceinstitute.com/resources/data-science/machine-learning-in-finance/
- Beatrice, A. 2020. Top 10 Applications of Machine Learning in Finance & FinTech. *Analytics Insight*, last accessed on July 12, 2024. https://www.analyticsinsight.net/top-10-applications-machine-learning-finance-fintech/

12.9 Applications of Machine Learning in the Insurance Industry

ML has many applications in the insurance industry, such as automating customer service, processing claims, detecting fraud, assessing risk, predicting customer lifetime value, and more.
Here are some examples of how ML can benefit the insurance sector:

- **Customer service**: ML can help streamline customer service by using chatbots, NLP, and sentiment analysis to provide quick and personalized responses to customers' queries and complaints. For example, Lemonade, a US-based insurance company, uses a chatbot named Maya to handle the entire process of buying and managing insurance policies, and claims to reduce the average time of issuing a policy from 17 days to 90 seconds.
- **Claims processing**: ML can help speed up claims processing by using computer vision, OCR, and NLP to extract information from documents, images, and videos, and verify the validity and severity of the claims. For example, Tractable, a UK-based company, uses computer vision and AI to assess the damage of vehicles from photos, and provide repair estimates and recommendations in minutes.
- **Fraud detection**: ML can help detect fraud by using anomaly detection, pattern recognition, and network analysis to identify suspicious behaviors and transactions. For example, Shift Technology, a France-based company, uses AI and big data to analyze millions of claims and detect fraud indicators, such as inconsistent or contradictory information, hidden connections, or abnormal behaviors.

References

- Wininger, S. Introducing the Lemonade Crypto Climate Coalition. *Lemonade*, last accessed on July 12, 2024. https://www.lemonade.com/blog/crypto-climate-coalition/
- Tomorrow's technology today. *Tractable*, last accessed on July 12, 2024. https://tractable.ai/en/technology
- AI for Insurance Decisions. *Shift Technology*, last accessed on July 12, 2024. https://www.shift-technology.com/

12.9.1 Risk Assessment and Customer Lifetime Value (CLV)

Risk assessment is the process of evaluating the likelihood and severity of losses that may occur due to various events, such as accidents, natural disasters, illnesses, fraud, etc. ML can help improve risk assessment by using regression, classification, and clustering techniques to analyze historical and real-time data from various sources, such as demographics, credit scores, medical records, social media, etc., and assign risk scores and premiums to customers.

Customer lifetime value (CLV) is the net present value of the future cash flows that a customer generates for a business over their entire relationship. CLV is an important metric for insurance companies, as it helps them optimize their marketing strategies, customer retention, and cross-selling opportunities. ML can help predict CLV by using survival analysis, churn analysis, and recommender systems to estimate how long a customer will stay with the insurer, how likely they are to renew or cancel their policies, and what products or services they are interested in.

However, ML in insurance also faces some challenges and limitations that need to be addressed. For example, ML models require large amounts of high-quality data to train and validate their performance. Therefore, insurers need to ensure that they have proper data governance frameworks and practices in place to ensure data security, compliance, integrity, and availability. Another challenge is that ML models need to be interpretable and explainable to ensure trust and transparency among stakeholders.

One domain where ML can improve customer service is digital insurance. A notable example of a digital insurance company that uses ML is Lemonade. Lemonade offers renters and homeowners insurance through its website and mobile app. Lemonade uses AI-powered chatbots named Maya and Jim to handle customer interactions.

Another domain where ML can enhance claims processing is pay-per-mile car insurance. A leading example of a pay-per-mile car insurance company that uses ML is Metromile. Metromile offers car insurance that charges customers based on how much they drive. Metromile uses telematics devices installed in customers' cars to collect driving data and monitor accidents. When an accident occurs, Metromile's AI claims assistant named Ava analyzes the data and sends a push notification to the customer's smartphone asking them to confirm the details of the incident. Ava then guides the customer through the claims process and arranges for repairs or payments. By using ML, Metromile can automate claims handling, reduce fraud, and provide personalized pricing and coverage.

ML can assist fraud detection in software solutions for insurance. A prominent example of a software company that provides ML solutions for fraud detection in insurance is Shift Technology. Shift Technology uses advanced analytics and machine learning to process large volumes of data from various sources, such as policy documents, claims records, social media, geolocation, etc. By using ML, Shift Technology can help insurance companies identify and prevent fraud, save money, and improve customer loyalty.

References

- Bolton, R et al. 2004. The Theoretical Underpinnings of Customer Asset Management: A Framework and Propositions for Future Research. *Journal of the Academy of Marketing Science*, 32(3):271-292, last accessed on July 12, 2024. https://www.researchgate.net/publication/248770300_The_Theoretical_Underpinnings_of_Customer_Asset_Management_A_Framework_and_Propositions_for_Future_Research
- Kumar, V and Rajan, B. 2011. Social coupons as a marketing strategy: A multifaceted perspective. *Journal of the Academy of Marketing Science*, 40: 120-136, last accessed on July 12, 2024. https://link.springer.com/article/10.1007/s11747-011-0283-0
- Ngai, EWT et al. 2009. Application of data mining techniques in customer relationship management: A literature review and classification. *Expert Systems with Applications*, 36: 2592-2602, last accessed on July 12, 2024. http://didawiki.di.unipi.it/lib/exe/fetch.php/dm/crm_dm-survey.pdf

- Zhang, C and Zhang S. *Association Rule Mining: Models and Algorithms*. Lecture Notes in Artificial Intelligence, Springer, last accessed on July 12, 2024. https://doc.lagout.org/Others/Data%20Mining/Association%20Rule%20Mining_%20Models%20and%20Algorithms%20%5BZhang%20%26%20Zhang%202002-05-28%5D.pdf

SUMMARY

- Machine learning (ML) has numerous applications in various industries, including diagnosis, drug discovery, personalized treatments, fraud detection, and speech recognition.
- ML algorithms can analyze large data sets of customer information, identify patterns and trends, segment customers based on their characteristics and behavior, and optimize markdown strategies.
- It can also be used in the logistics industry for demand forecasting, inventory management, routing and scheduling, delivery tracking, and customer service improvement.
- In the manufacturing industry, ML algorithms can improve efficiency and product quality by analyzing large data sets of customer information.
- In the energy and utilities industry, ML can optimize energy consumption, forecast demand and supply, and integrate renewable sources.
- In the travel industry, ML algorithms can help personalize and optimize services.
- In the banking industry, ML can help with credit underwriting, fraud detection, and hyper-personalization.
- In finance, ML can help with credit risk assessment, process automation, and customer support.
- In the insurance industry, ML can automate customer service, process claims, detect fraud, assess risk, and predict customer lifetime value.

Machine Learning Programming: Capstone Projects Using Python and R

Learning Objectives

At the end of this chapter, you will be able to:

- Explain the basics of Python programming and its ecosystem
- Describe how to install Python and manage packages with Anaconda Navigator
- Explain the fundamentals of data types, control structures, functions, and mathematical operations in Python
- Utilize the Spyder IDE for writing and testing Python programs
- Perform data manipulation techniques on the Iris data set, including finding and handling outliers
- Use methods for data preprocessing such as imputing null values and capping outlier values
- Explain how to split data sets into training and testing sets for model evaluation
- Implement various machine learning models in Python, including linear and logistic regression, decision trees, SVM, and more
- Explain advanced techniques like steepest descent, PCA, random forest, and various search algorithms
- State the principles of R programming and how to install R and R Studio
- Utilize R packages like glmnet, caret, e1071, ggplot2, and others for statistical modeling and data visualization
- Apply regularization techniques and linear classifiers in R
- Explain the construction and evaluation of Bayesian classifiers, KNN classifiers, and logic gates using R
- Describe the development of machine learning algorithms in R, including linear regression, logistic regression, SVM, and perceptron models
- Explore advanced algorithms such as RBF, PCA, and locality preserving projection in R

13.1 Introduction

Python is a popular programming language that is utilized in many fields, including machine learning (ML). Python has a simple syntax, which makes it easy to analyze and use. It may be used to create ML models that can be used to make predictions or choices. In addition, it has a wide variety of libraries and frameworks, including scikit-learn, TensorFlow, and Keras, making it easy to implement ML algorithms.

Python may also be used to write custom algorithms for system-studying tasks. It has a massive community of developers who provide assistance with any questions or troubles that can arise.

13.2 Installing Python

To deploy Python in a Windows environment, you may download the most recent version from the official Python website (https://www.python.org/downloads/). Once the download is complete, open the installer and follow the instructions to install Python in your PC. After installation is complete, you can use the Python interpreter to run your software.

For Windows:

1. Download the Windows installer from the Python website.
2. Double-click the downloaded file to start the installation method.
3. Follow the on-display commands to install Python in the default area.
4. Once the set up is complete, open the command prompt and type `python` to confirm the set up.

For Mac:

1. Download the macOS installer from the Python website.
2. Double-click the downloaded file to begin the set-up procedure.
3. Follow the on-display commands to install Python within the default place.
4. Once the set up is complete, open the terminal and type `python` to verify the installation.

For Linux: Most Linux distributions come with Python pre-installed.

1. Check if Python is installed by using opening the terminal and typing `python` or `python3`.
2. If Python has not been installed, use the bundle supervisor on your distribution to install Python. For example, in Ubuntu, type `sudo apt-get install python3` in the terminal.
3. Once Python is installed, open the terminal and type `python` to verify the installation.

13.3 The sklearn Package

Python scikit-learn (sklearn is the newer version) is a widely used and robust ML package that offers a variety of tools and methods for tasks such as data analysis, preprocessing, feature extraction, model selection, assessment, and deployment. It is constructed using NumPy, SciPy, and Matplotlib and seamlessly interfaces with other Python frameworks like pandas and TensorFlow. The objective of scikit-learn is to offer a straightforward and uniform interface for the prevalent ML tasks, including classification, regression, clustering, dimensionality reduction, and anomaly detection. In addition, it provides extensive documentation and abundant examples and tutorials to assist users in getting started and acquiring optimal techniques.

The scikit-learn package offers a significant benefit in the form of high-level abstraction, which conceals the intricacies of the underlying algorithms. This enables users to concentrate on the problem domain and the data without worrying about the complexity. It adheres to the fit–transform–predict principle, wherein most estimators (objects that implement ML algorithms) consist of three primary methods: fit, which trains the model using the provided data; transform, which applies specific data transformations like scaling, encoding, or feature extraction; and predict, which generates predictions on new data using the trained model. This facilitates the concatenation of many estimators into a pipeline, which can then be trained and assessed as a cohesive entity.

The scikit-learn package has the advantage of being compatible with various Python libraries and tools. It is compatible with diverse data types, including NumPy arrays, pandas DataFrames, sparse matrices, and Python dictionaries. It can also connect with other ML frameworks, such as TensorFlow or PyTorch, through wrappers or converters, enabling users to take advantage of the features each platform offers.

The scikit-learn package can perform the following ML tasks:

- **Classification**: This refers to assigning a specific label to an input based on predetermined criteria. The scikit-learn package offers various classification algorithms, including support vector machines (SVMs), logistic regression, decision trees, and naive Bayes.
- **Regression**: This refers to using specific characteristics to forecast a continuous value for a given input. The scikit-learn package offers various regression algorithms, including linear regression, ridge regression, and LASSO regression.
- **Clustering**: This refers to categorizing related inputs using a metric of similarity or distance. The scikit-learn package offers various clustering algorithms, including *K*-means, hierarchical clustering, and spectral clustering.
- **Dimensionality Reduction**: This refers to decreasing the number of features or dimensions in the data while retaining as much information as feasible. The scikit-learn package offers various dimensionality reduction algorithms, including principal component analysis (PCA) and non-negative matrix factorization (NMF).
- **Model Selection**: This involves selecting the optimal model or parameters for a given situation using specific evaluation criteria. The scikit-learn package offers various model selection algorithms, including cross-validation and grid search.
- **Preprocessing**: This refers to the process of converting the data into a format that is appropriate for ML. The scikit-learn package offers various preprocessing algorithms, including feature scaling, label encoding, and one-hot encoding.

In addition, scikit-learn also provides a range of tools for data analysis, such as data visualization and feature selection. It is designed to be easy to use and efficient, and it has become the most popular ML library for Python.

13.4 Anaconda Navigator

Anaconda Navigator is a graphical user interface (GUI) that allows us to launch applications and manage conda packages, environments, and channels without using the command line.

To install Anaconda Navigator on Windows, follow the steps given below:

1. Go to https://www.anaconda.com/products/individual and download the latest version of Anaconda for Windows. Choose the Python 3.7 version for your system architecture (32-bit or 64-bit).
2. Run the downloaded file and follow the instructions on the screen. You can accept the default options or customize them as you wish.

3. On the Advanced Installation Options screen, check the box that says "Add Anaconda to my PATH environment variable." This will allow you to use conda commands from any terminal window.
4. Click the "Install" button and wait for the installation to finish.
5. Once the installation is complete, you can launch Anaconda Navigator from the Start menu or type `anaconda-navigator` in a terminal window. Anaconda Navigator will then launch (Fig. 13.1).

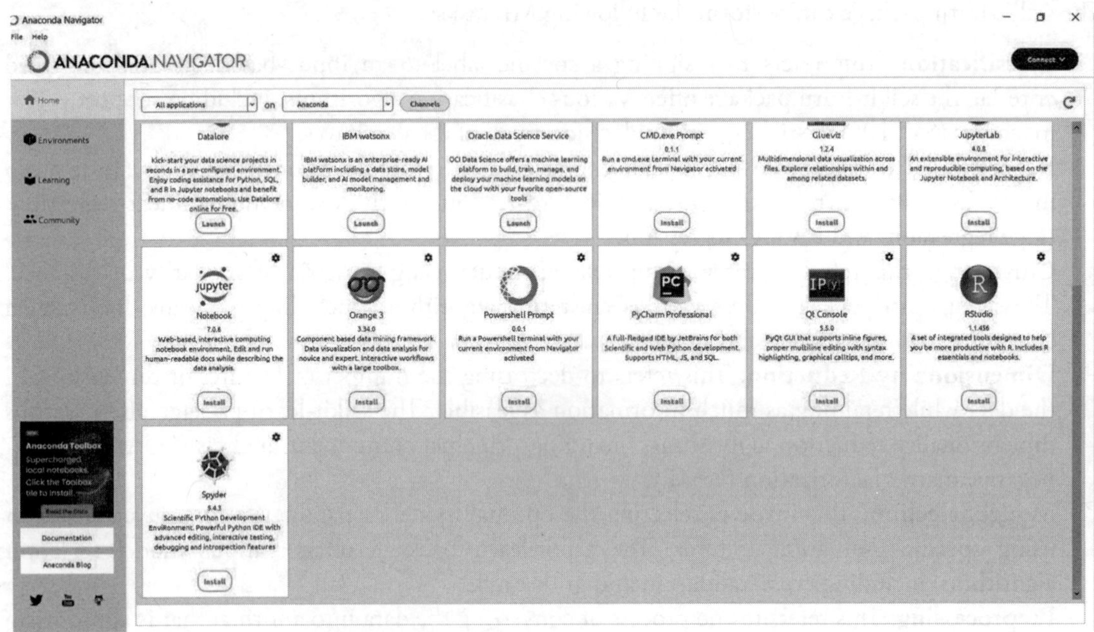

Figure 13.1 Anaconda Navigator home screen

13.4.1 Popular Python Packages

A package is a folder that contains several modules, which are files that contain Python code. A package can also have sub-packages, which are folders inside a package. To use a package, we need to import it or its modules. Some of the most common packages in Python are:

- **pandas**: This package provides data structures and tools for data analysis. It allows us to manipulate, filter, group, aggregate, and visualize data in tabular or multidimensional formats. It also supports reading and writing data from various sources, such as CSV, Excel, SQL, and JSON.
- **NumPy**: This package provides numerical computing tools for Python. It allows us to work with arrays, matrices, linear algebra, random numbers, statistics, and more. It also supports broadcasting, vectorization, and integration with other packages, such as pandas and Matplotlib.
- **matplotlib.pyplot**: This package provides plotting and visualization tools for Python. It allows us to create various types of graphs, such as line plots, bar charts, histograms, scatter plots, and pie charts. It also supports customization of colors, styles, labels, legends, axes, etc.

- **sklearn**: This package provides ML tools for Python. It allows us to perform tasks such as classification, regression, clustering, dimensionality reduction, feature extraction, model selection, and evaluation. It also supports various algorithms, such as linear models, decision trees, support vector machines, neural networks, etc.
- **seaborn**: This package provides statistical data visualization tools for Python. It builds on top of matplotlib.pyplot and pandas to create attractive and informative plots. It also supports categorical data analysis, distribution analysis, correlation analysis, regression analysis, etc.
- **TensorFlow**: This package provides deep learning tools for Python. It allows us to build and train neural networks using tensors, which are multidimensional arrays of data. It also supports various operations, such as activation functions, loss functions, optimizers, metrics, etc. It also supports GPU acceleration and distributed computing.
- **IPython**: This package provides an interactive shell for Python. It allows us to execute Python code interactively and dynamically. It also supports features such as syntax highlighting, auto-completion, debugging, profiling, magic commands, etc. It also integrates with other packages, such as NumPy and matplotlib.pyplot.

Table 13.1 lists the popular Python packages.

Table 13.1 Popular packages of the Python language

S. No	Package name	Features
1	pandas	Data structures and tools for data analysis
2	numpy	Numerical computing tools for Python
3	matplotlib.pyplot	Plotting and visualization tools for Python
4	sklearn	Machine learning tools for Python
5	seaborn	Statistical data visualization tools for Python
6	TensorFlow	Deep learning tools for Python
7	IPython	Interactive shell for Python

13.4.2 Installing Packages using Anaconda Navigator

Installing packages through Anaconda Navigator is easy and convenient. Here are the steps to be followed:

1. Launch Anaconda Navigator from your Start menu or desktop shortcut.
2. Select the environment in which you want to install the package (Fig. 13.2). You can create a new environment by clicking the "Create" button at the bottom of the list.
3. Click on the "Home" tab and then on the "Install" button next to the package name. You can search for a package by typing its name in the search box. (Example: `sklearn`)
4. Wait for the installation to complete. You can see the progress and status of the installation in the "conda" tab.

5. To verify that the package is installed, you can open a terminal (Spyder) or a Jupyter notebook in the same environment and import the package.

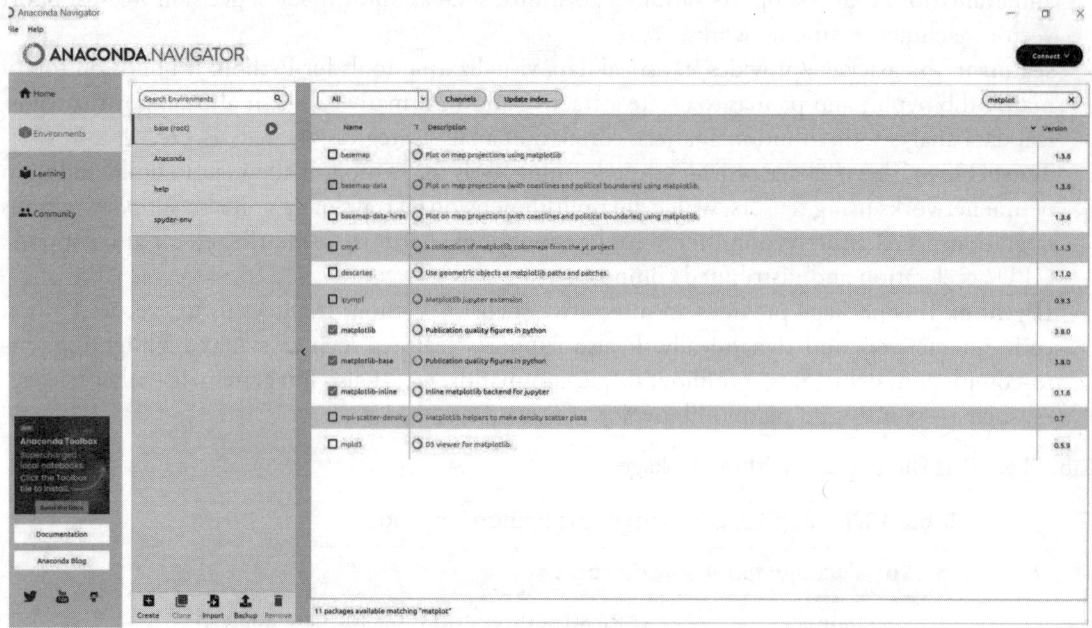

Figure 13.2 Anaconda Navigator package installation

13.4.3 Opening Spyder from Anaconda Navigator

Spyder is an integrated development environment (IDE) for Python that comes with Anaconda Navigator. To open the Spyder terminal from Anaconda Navigator, you need to follow these steps:

1. Launch Anaconda Navigator from your Start menu or desktop shortcut. You should see a window with several icons for different applications, such as Jupyter Notebook, RStudio, VS Code and Spyder (Fig. 13.1).
2. Click on the Spyder icon. You should see a button that says "Launch" below the icon. If you have multiple versions of Spyder installed, you can choose which one to launch from the drop-down menu next to the button.
3. Click the "Launch" button and wait for Spyder to open. You should see a window with four panes: the editor, the console, the variable explorer, and the help viewer.
4. To open a terminal in Spyder, go to the menu bar and click on Tools > Open a Terminal. Alternatively, you can use the keyboard shortcut Ctrl+Alt+T (Windows) or Cmd+Alt+T (Mac).
5. A new tab with a terminal prompt (Fig. 13.3) should appear in the console pane. This terminal can run commands, install packages, and interact with the Python environment.

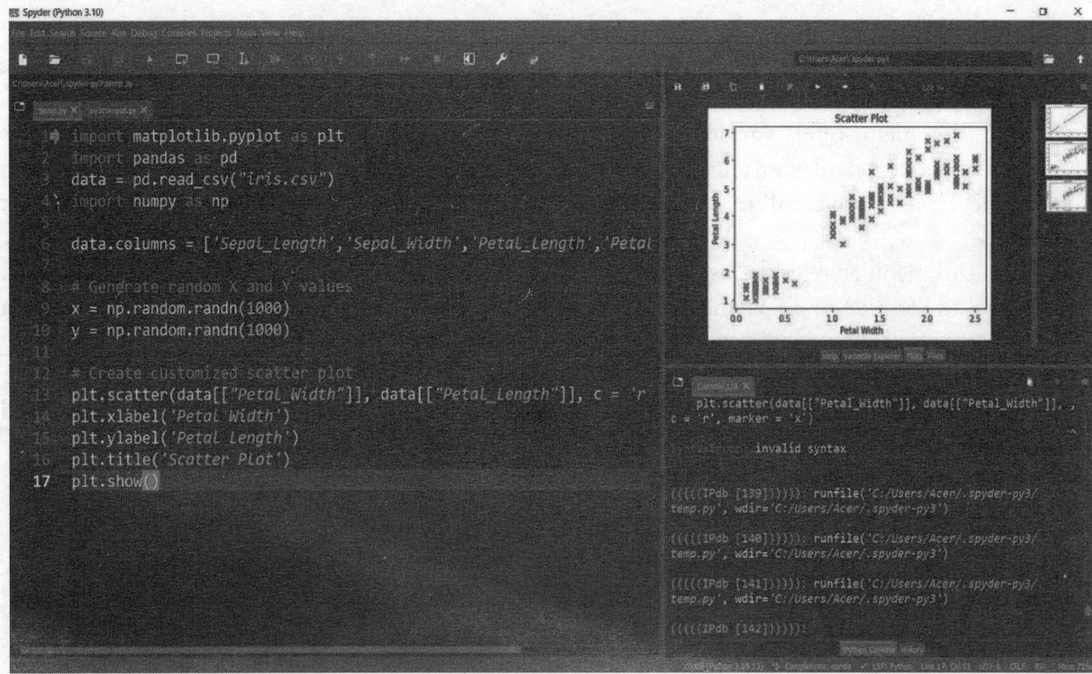

Figure 13.3 Spyder terminal

A brief explanation of some of the main menus of the Spyder terminal is given below:

- **File**: This menu allows users to create, open, save, close, print, and run Python files. It also has options to switch projects, restart the kernel, and quit Spyder.
- **Edit**: This menu lets the user edit the code, such as undo, redo, cut, copy, paste, delete, comment, indent, format, and refactor. It also has options to find and replace text, go to a specific line or definition, and manage bookmarks.
- **Source**: This menu provides tools to analyze and execute the code, such as code completion, linting, debugging, profiling, testing, and running cells. It also has options to show or hide the outline explorer, the code analysis pane, and the code folding indicators.
- **Run**: This menu allows the user to run the current file or a selected configuration in different ways, such as in a new dedicated console, in an external system terminal, or with command-line arguments. It also has options to configure the run settings, such as the working directory, the environment variables, and the interpreter.
- **Debug**: This menu lets users debug the code using breakpoints, conditional breakpoints, watches, and commands. It also has options to show or hide the debugger toolbar and the variable explorer.
- **Consoles**: This menu provides access to different types of consoles for interactive coding, such as Python consoles, IPython consoles, and system terminals. It also has options to connect to an existing kernel, open a particular console (such as a Qt or Spyder), and manage the console settings.

- **Projects**: This menu allows users to create, open, close, delete, and import projects. A project is a way of organizing files and settings for a specific task or purpose. It also has options to edit the project properties, such as the name, location, dependencies, and PYTHONPATH.
- **Tools**: This menu offers various tools and utilities for enhancing the user experience, such as preferences, keyboard shortcuts, online help, an internal console, a dependency manager, a module explorer, and online documentation. It also has options to update Spyder and report issues.
- **View**: This menu enables the user to customize the appearance and layout of the Spyder terminal. It can show or hide toolbars and panes (such as editor, console, help), zoom in or out of the text size, toggle fullscreen or windowed mode (for macOS), and switch between preset layouts.
- **Help**: This menu provides access to different sources of information and support for the Spyder terminal. It has options to show the tutorial (for beginners), Spyder documentation (for advanced users), FAQ (for common questions), and the About dialog box (for credits and license).

13.4.4 Basic Data Types in Python

Python has five standard data types:

- Number
- String
- List
- Tuple
- Dictionary

Python variables do not need explicit declaration to reserve memory space. The declaration happens automatically when you assign a value to a variable. The equal to (=) sign is used to assign values to variables. The operand to the left of = is the name of the variable and the operand to the right of = is the value stored in the variable.

For example:

```
>>> var1 = 24
>>> var2 = 28.72
>>> var3 = "Machine Learning"

>>> type(var1)
Out[38]: int
>>> print(var1)
24

>>> type(var2)
Out[39]: float
>>> print(var2)
28.72

>>> type(var3)
Out[40]: str
```

```
>>> print(var3)
Machine Learning
```

Python variables can be easily typecast from one data type to another by using the data type name as a function (actually a wrapper class) and passing the variable to be typecast as a parameter. However, not all data types can be transformed into another; for example, String to Integer/Number is impossible.

```
>>> var2 = int(var2)
>>> print (var2)
28
>>> type (var2)
Out[42]: int
```

13.4.5 The `for` and `while` Loops and the `if-else` Statement

The `for` *loop*

Syntax:

```
for i in range(<lowerbound>,<upperbound>,<interval>):
    print(i*i)
```

For example, to print the squares of all integers from 1 to 4.

```
for i in range(1,5):
    print(i*i)
1
4
9
16
```

```
for i in range(1,20,5):
    print(i)
1
6
11
16
```

The `while` *loop*

Syntax:

```
while < condition>:
    <do something>
```

For example, to print the cubes of all integers from 1 to 3.

```
i = 1
while i < 4:
    print(i*i*i)
    i = i + 1
```

```
1
8
27
```

The `if-else` *statement*

Syntax:

```
if < condition>:
    <do something>
else:
      <do something else>
```

For example, to print the squares of a number if it is negative. If it is a positive number, then print the number.

```
i = -5
if i < 0:
    print(i*i)
else:
    print(i)

25
```

13.4.6 Writing Functions

Syntax:

```
def functionname(parametername,...):
    (function_body)
```

For example, for a function to calculate the factorial of an input number *n*.

```
def factorial(n):
    fact = 1
    for i in range(1,n+1):
        fact = fact*i
    return(fact);
k = factorial (4)
print (k)
24
```

13.4.7 Mathematical Operations on Data Types

Vectors

```
>>> n = 20
>>> m = 15
```

```
>>> n + m      #addition
Out[53]: 35

>>> n - m  #subtraction
Out[55]: 5

>>> n * m     #multiplication
Out[56]: 300

>>> n / m     #division
Out[57]: 1.333333
```

13.4.8 Using Spyder to Write Python Programs

We will use the Spyder terminal to write all our ML programs. The Spyder terminal (Fig. 13.3) is a tool that allows users to write and run Python programs in an interactive environment. It consists of two main panes: the editor pane and the console pane. The editor pane, located on the left-hand side of the terminal, is where users can write Python code using various features such as syntax highlighting, code completion, and debugging. The console pane, located on the right-hand side of the terminal, is divided into two sub-panes: the plot pane and the I/O pane. The plot pane, located at the top-right corner of the terminal, is where users can see the graphical output of their Python programs, such as charts, graphs, and images. The I/O pane, located at the bottom-right corner of the terminal, is where users can see the terminal output of their Python programs, such as print statements, errors, and warnings. The I/O pane can also be used to enter terminal inputs for the Python programs, such as command-line arguments or user inputs.

13.5 Data Operations on the Iris Data Set

The Iris data set is a classic that contains information about three different species of iris flowers: setosa, versicolor, and virginia. Each species has 50 observations of four features: sepal length, sepal width, petal length, and petal width, all measured in centimeters. The statistician Ronald Fisher introduced the data set in 1936 as an example of linear discriminant analysis.

This data set is available from various sources, such as the UCI Machine Learning Repository, Kaggle, scikit-learn, and more. It may have different formats, such as CSV, JSON, pickle, or Python objects, depending on the source.

To download the data set for free, we can use one of the following methods:

- From the UCI Machine Learning Repository: Go to https://archive.ics.uci.edu/ml/datasets/Iris and click "Data Folder." Then download the file "iris.data" which contains the comma-separated values of the data set. Optionally, download the file "iris.names," which includes the description of the data set.
- From Kaggle: Go to https://www.kaggle.com/uciml/iris and click "Download (4 KB)". Then unzip the file "iris.zip," which contains the CSV file "Iris.csv" with the data set.

- From scikit-learn: Use the Python library scikit-learn, which provides a function to load the Iris data set as a Python object. To do this, import the module sklearn and call the function `load_iris()`.

13.5.1 Read the Iris Data Set and Display the First Five Rows

```
# This line imports the pandas library and gives it the alias pd
import pandas as pd
# This line reads a CSV file named iris.csv and stores it in a variable
called data
data = pd.read_csv("iris.csv")
# This line assigns new names to the columns of the data
data.columns = ['Sepal_Length','Sepal_Width','Petal_Length','Petal_
Width','Class']
#This line displays the first five rows of the data
display (data.head())
```

The above program is a Python script that uses the pandas library to load and manipulate the data set contained in iris.csv. The program first imports the pandas library as `pd`, which is a common alias for pandas. Then, it uses the `pd.read_csv()` function to read the iris.csv file and store it in a variable called `data`. The data variable is a pandas DataFrame, which is a two-dimensional data structure that can store data in rows and columns. The program then assigns new names to the columns of the DataFrame using the `data.columns` attribute. The new names are `Sepal_Length`, `Sepal_Width`, `Petal_Length`, `Petal_Width`, and `Class`. These names are more descriptive and follow the Python naming convention of using underscores instead of spaces. Finally, the program uses the `display()` function to show the last five rows of the DataFrame. The `display()` function is a built-in function, which is an interactive environment for running Python code. It can show the DataFrame in a tabular format with colors and borders. The `display (data.head())` function shows the first five rows of the DataFrame.

Output:

	Sepal_Length	Sepal_Width	Petal_Length	Petal_Width	Class
0	4.9	3.0	1.4	0.2	Iris-setosa
1	4.7	3.2	1.3	0.2	Iris-setosa
2	4.6	3.1	1.5	0.2	Iris-setosa
3	5.0	3.6	1.4	0.2	Iris-setosa
4	5.4	3.9	1.7	0.4	Iris-setosa

13.5.2 Read the Iris Data Set and Display a Random Sample of Ten Rows

```
# This line imports the pandas library and gives it the alias pd
import pandas as pd
# This line reads a CSV file named iris.csv and stores it in a variable
called data
data = pd.read_csv("iris.csv")
# This line assigns new names to the columns of the data
data.columns = ['Sepal_Length','Sepal_Width','Petal_Length','Petal_
Width','Class']
# Display a random sample of 10 rows from the data
display(data.sample(10))
```

display (data.sample(10)) # Display a random sample of 10 rows from the data

Output:

	Sepal_Length	Sepal_Width	Petal_Length	Petal_Width	Class
136	6.4	3.1	5.5	1.8	Iris-virginica
119	6.9	3.2	5.7	2.3	Iris-virginica
137	6.0	3.0	4.8	1.8	Iris-virginica
135	6.3	3.4	5.6	2.4	Iris-virginica
75	6.8	2.8	4.8	1.4	Iris-versicolor
101	7.1	3.0	5.9	2.1	Iris-virginica
123	6.7	3.3	5.7	2.1	Iris-virginica
7	4.4	2.9	1.4	0.2	Iris-setosa
82	6.0	2.7	5.1	1.6	Iris-versicolor
39	5.0	3.5	1.3	0.3	Iris-setosa

13.5.3 Read the Iris Data Set and Display the Names of the Columns

```
# This line imports the pandas library and gives it the alias pd
import pandas as pd
# This line reads a CSV file named iris.csv and stores it in a variable
called data
data = pd.read_csv("iris.csv")
# This line assigns new names to the columns of the data
data.columns = ['Sepal_Length','Sepal_Width','Petal_Length','Petal_
Width','Class']
# Display the names of the columns on the screen
display(data.columns)
```

```
display (data.columns) # This line displays the names of the columns on the screen.
```

Output:

```
Index(['Sepal_Length',    'Sepal_Width',    'Petal_Length',    'Petal_Width',
'Class'], dtype='object')
```

13.5.4 Read the Iris Data Set and Display the Data Types of the Columns

```
# This line imports the pandas library and gives it the alias pd
import pandas as pd
# This line reads a CSV file named iris.csv and stores it in a variable
called data
data = pd.read_csv("iris.csv")
# This line assigns new names to the columns of the data
data.columns = ['Sepal_Length','Sepal_Width','Petal_Length','Petal_
Width','Class']
# Display the data types of each column using the dtypes attribute
display(data.dtypes)
```

The output shows that all the columns are of float64 type, except for the `Class` column, which is of object type. This means that the `Class` column contains strings or categorical values, while the other columns contain numerical values.

Output:

```
Sepal_Length  Float64
Sepal_Width   Float64
Petal_Length  Float64
Petal_Width   Float64
Class         Objects
dtype: object
```

13.5.5 Read the Iris Data Set and Display the Last Five Rows

```
# This line imports the pandas library and gives it the alias pd
import pandas as pd
# This line reads a CSV file named iris.csv and stores it in a variable
called data
data = pd.read_csv("iris.csv")
# This line assigns new names to the columns of the data
data.columns = ['Sepal_Length','Sepal_Width','Petal_Length','Petal_
Width','Class']
# Display the last five rows of the DataFrame
display (data.tail())
```

`display (data.tail())#` This line displays the last five rows of the DataFrame using the `display()` function. The `tail` method returns a new DataFrame with only the last *n* rows, where *n* is specified as an argument. In this case, *n* is not given, so the default value of 5 is used. The `display()` function shows the DataFrame in a formatted way in the output cell.

Output:

	Sepal_Length	Sepal_Width	Petal_Length	Petal_Width	Class
144	6.7	3.0	5.2	2.3	Iris-virginica
145	6.3	2.5	5.0	1.9	Iris-virginica
146	6.5	3.0	5.2	2.0	Iris-virginica
147	6.2	3.4	5.4	2.3	Iris-virginica
148	5.9	3.0	5.1	1.8	Iris-virginica

13.5.6 Read the Iris Data Set and Display Rows 10 to 20

```
# This line imports the pandas library and gives it the alias pd
import pandas as pd
# This line reads a CSV file named iris.csv and stores it in a variable
called data
data = pd.read_csv("iris.csv")
# This line assigns new names to the columns of the data
data.columns = ['Sepal_Length','Sepal_Width','Petal_Length','Petal_
Width','Class']
# data[start:end]
#start is inclusive whereas end is exclusive
print(data[10:21])
# it will print the rows from 10 to 20.
```

`#data[start:end]#` This is a comment that explains how to slice the DataFrame by row. The `start` and `end` parameters are integers that specify the index of the rows to be selected. The start index is inclusive, meaning that the row with that index is included in the slice. The end index is exclusive, meaning that the row with that index is not included in the slice.

`print(data[10:21])#` This line prints the slice of the DataFrame that contains the rows from index 10 to index 20. This will show 11 rows of data, with each row representing an iris flower and its attributes.

Output:

	Sepal_Length	Sepal_Width	Petal_Length	Petal_Width	Class
10	4.8	3.4	1.6	0.2	Iris-setosa
11	4.8	3.0	1.4	0.1	Iris-setosa
12	4.3	3.0	1.1	0.1	Iris-setosa
13	5.8	4.0	1.2	0.2	Iris-setosa
14	5.7	4.4	1.5	0.4	Iris-setosa
15	5.4	3.9	1.3	0.4	Iris-setosa
16	5.1	3.5	1.4	0.3	Iris-setosa
17	5.7	3.8	1.7	0.3	Iris-setosa
18	5.1	3.8	1.5	0.3	Iris-setosa
19	5.4	3.4	1.7	0.2	Iris-setosa
20	5.1	3.7	1.5	0.4	Iris-setosa

13.5.7 Read the Iris Data Set and Slice the Data Vertically

```
# This line imports the pandas library and gives it the alias pd
import pandas as pd
# This line reads a CSV file named iris.csv and stores it in a variable
called data
data = pd.read_csv("iris.csv")
# This line assigns new names to the columns of the data
data.columns = ['Sepal_Length','Sepal_Width','Petal_Length','Petal_
Width','Class']
#we will save Iris dataset in another variable named "sliced data" only
with 2 coloumns
sliced_data=data[["Petal_Length","Class"]]
#now we will print the first 10 columns of the sliced_data dataframe.
print(sliced_data.head(10))
```

We are creating a new variable called `sliced_data`, which is a subset of the data variable that only contains two columns: `Petal_Length` and `Class`. This is done by using square brackets and passing a list of column names to the `data` variable. This way, we can focus on the relationship between petal length and class of the iris flowers. We print the first 10 rows of the `sliced_data` variable, using the `head()` method.

Output:

	Petal_Length	Class
0	1.4	Iris-setosa
1	1.3	Iris-setosa
2	1.5	Iris-setosa
3	1.4	Iris-setosa
4	1.7	Iris-setosa
5	1.4	Iris-setosa
6	1.5	Iris-setosa
7	1.4	Iris-setosa
8	1.5	Iris-setosa
9	1.5	Iris-setosa

13.5.8 Read the Iris Data Set and Display Data from a Specific Row

```
# This line imports the pandas library and gives it the alias pd
import pandas as pd
# This line reads a CSV file named iris.csv and stores it in a variable
called data
data = pd.read_csv("iris.csv")
# This line assigns new names to the columns of the data
data.columns = ['Sepal_Length','Sepal_Width','Petal_Length','Petal_
Width','Class']
# Displays the data of the sixth row (index 5) of the data
#The iloc method is used to access a specific row by its integer index
display(data.iloc[5])
```

The `iloc()` method is used to access a specific row by its integer index. In order to display the data of the sixth row, we use (index 5) of the data with the command, `display(data.iloc[5])`.

Output:

Column Name	Value
Sepal_Length	4.6
Sepal_Width	3.4
Petal_Length	1.4
Petal_Width	0.3
Class	Iris-setosa
Name: 5, dtype: object	

13.5.9 Read the Iris Data Set and Display the Number of Occurrences of a Column

```
# This line imports the pandas library and gives it the alias pd
import pandas as pd
# This line reads a CSV file named iris.csv and stores it in a variable
called data
data = pd.read_csv("iris.csv")
# This line assigns new names to the columns of the data
data.columns = ['Sepal_Length','Sepal_Width','Petal_Length','Petal_
Width','Class']
# data["Class"] expression selects the Class column from the DataFrame.
# value_counts method counts the number of occurrences of each unique
value in a Series object.
display(data["Class"].value_counts())
```

`Display(data["Class"].value_counts())` displays the number of occurrences of each unique value in the `Class` column. To view how many flowers of each species are in the data, we use the `data["Class"]` expression, which selects the `Class` column from the DataFrame. Then we use the `value_counts()` method, which counts the number of occurrences of each unique value in a Series object. A Series is a one-dimensional data structure that stores a single column or row of data. The `value_counts()` method returns another Series object, which has the unique values as indexes and their counts as values. To display this Series object, we use the `display()` function, which prints it in a formatted way.

Output:

Class	
Iris-versicolor	50
Iris-virginica	50
Iris-setosa	49
Name: count, dtype: int64	

13.5.10 Read the Iris Data Set and Calculate the Sum, Mean, Median, Minimum, and Maximum Values of a Column

```
# This line imports the pandas library and gives it the alias pd
import pandas as pd
# This line reads a CSV file named iris.csv and stores it in a variable
called data
data = pd.read_csv("iris.csv")
```

```
# This line assigns new names to the columns of the data
data.columns = ['Sepal_Length','Sepal_Width','Petal_Length','Petal_
Width','Class']
# Calculate sum, mean and median of a coloumn titled "Sepal_Length"
sum_data=data["Sepal_Length"].sum()
mean_data=data["Sepal_Length"].mean()
median_data=data["Sepal_Length"].median()
min_data=data["Sepal_Length"].min()
max_data=data["Sepal_Length"].max()
print("Sum:",sum_data, "\nMean:", mean_data, "\nMedian:",median_data, "\
nMinimum:",min_data, "\nMaximum:",max_data)
```

`sum_data = data["Sepal_Length"].sum()` # This line calculates the sum of the `Sepal_Length` column and stores it in a variable called `sum_data`.

`mean_data = data["Sepal_Length"].mean()` # This line calculates the mean of the `Sepal_Length` column and stores it in a variable called `mean_data`.

`median_data = data["Sepal_Length"].median()` # This line calculates the median of the `Sepal_Length` column and stores it in a variable called `median_data`.

`min_data=data["Sepal_Length"].min()` # This line calculates the minimum of the `Sepal_Length` column and stores it in a variable called `min_data`.

`max_data=data["Sepal_Length"].max()` # This line calculates the maximum of the `Sepal_Length` column and stores it in a variable called `max_data`.

Output:

Sum	871.4
Mean	5.8483221476510066
Median	5.8
Minimum	4.3
Maximum	7.9

13.5.11 Read the Iris Data Set and Display the Data Shape (Rows and Columns)

```
# This line imports the pandas library and gives it the alias pd
import pandas as pd
# This line reads a CSV file named iris.csv and stores it in a variable
called data
data = pd.read_csv("iris.csv")
```

```
# This line assigns new names to the columns of the data
data.columns = ['Sepal_Length','Sepal_Width','Petal_Length','Petal_
Width','Class']
# Display the shape of the data set using the data shape attribute, which
returns a tuple of(rows, columns)
display(data.shape)
# Display the number of rows in the data set using the data.shape[0] ex-
pression, which returns the first element of the tuple
display(data.shape[0])
# Display the number of columns in the data set using the data.shape[1]
expression, which returns the second element of the tuple
display(data.shape[1])
# Display the names of the columns in the data set using the data.columns
attribute, which returns an index object
display(data.columns)
# Display the list of column names in the data set using the list(data.
columns.values) expression, which converts the index object to a list
Display (list(data.columns.values))
```

Output:

```
(149, 5)
149
5
Index(['Sepal_Length', 'Sepal_Width', 'Petal_Length', 'Petal_Width',
'Class'], dtype='object')
['Sepal_Length', 'Sepal_Width', 'Petal_Length', 'Petal_Width', 'Class']
```

13.5.12 Read the Iris Data Set and Display a Single Value for a Row/Column

```
# This line imports the pandas library and gives it the alias pd
import pandas as pd
# This line reads a CSV file named iris.csv and stores it in a variable
called data
data = pd.read_csv("iris.csv")
# This line assigns new names to the columns of the data
data.columns = ['Sepal_Length','Sepal_Width','Petal_Length','Petal_
Width','Class']
# Display the value of the Class column at the 100th row of the dataframe
using the at method
# The at method allows accessing a single value for a row/column label
pair
```

```
# The output is Iris-virginica, which means the 100th iris flower belongs
to that species
display(data.at[100, 'Class'])
# Create a new dataframe object named data_class that contains only the
Class column of the original dataframe
# Use the loc method to select all rows and only the Class column by its
label
data_class=data.loc[:, "Class"]
# The head method returns the first n rows of a dataframe, where n is an
optional parameter that defaults to 5
display(data_class.head())
```

Output:

```
'Iris-virginica'
0    0.2    Iris-setosa
1    0.2    Iris-setosa
2    0.2    Iris-setosa
3    0.2    Iris-setosa
4    0.4    Iris-setosa
Name: Class, dtype:
object
```

13.5.13 Read the Iris Data Set and Select Multiple Columns of a DataFrame

```
# This line imports the pandas library and gives it the alias pd
import pandas as pd
# This line reads a CSV file named iris.csv and stores it in a variable
called data
data = pd.read_csv("iris.csv")
# This line assigns new names to the columns of the data
data.columns = ['Sepal_Length','Sepal_Width','Petal_Length','Petal_
Width','Class']
# Create a new data frame named data_class that contains only two col-
umns: petal width and class
data_class = data[ ["Petal_Width", "Class"] ]
# Display the first five rows of the data_class data frame using the dis-
play() function,
display(data_class.head())
```

The program performes the following steps:

It imports the pandas module and gives it the alias pd for convenience. It reads a CSV file named iris.csv that contains data about different species of iris flowers and their measurements. The CSV file has five columns: sepal length, sepal width, petal length, petal width, and class (the species name). It assigns the DataFrame object returned by `pd.read_csv()` to a variable named `data`. It changes the names of the columns in the DataFrame to match the ones in the CSV file, using the `data.columns` attribute and a list of strings. It creates a new DataFrame named `data_class` that contains only two columns: petal width and class. It does this by using square brackets and a list of column names to select a subset of the original data frame. It displays the first five rows of the `data_class` DataFrame using the `display()` function, which shows a formatted table in the output.

Output:

	'Petal_Width'	Class
0	0.2	Iris-setosa
1	0.2	Iris-setosa
2	0.2	Iris-setosa
3	0.2	Iris-setosa
4	0.4	Iris-setosa

13.5.14 Read the Iris Data Set and Extract Specific Rows

```
# This line imports the pandas library and gives it the alias pd
import pandas as pd
# This line reads a CSV file named iris.csv and stores it in a variable
called data
data = pd.read_csv("iris.csv")
# This line assigns new names to the columns of the data
data.columns = ['Sepal_Length','Sepal_Width','Petal_Length','Petal_
Width','Class']
# This slice selects the rows from index 1 to index 2 (inclusive) of the
DataFrame.
display (data[1:3])
```

This program uses the pandas library to load and manipulate a data set of iris flowers. The data set contains 150 rows and 5 columns, where each row represents an iris flower and each column represents a feature of the flower, such as sepal length, sepal width, petal length, petal width and class. The `Class` column indicates the species of the iris flower, which can be one of three types: Iris-setosa, Iris-versicolor or Iris-virginica.

The program first imports the pandas library as `pd`, which is a common alias for pandas. Then, it uses the `pd.read_csv()` function to read the iris.csv file and store it in a variable called `data`.

The iris.csv file is a comma-separated values file that contains the iris data set. The `pd.read_csv()` function returns a pandas DataFrame object, which is a two-dimensional tabular data structure with labeled axes.

Next, the program assigns a list of strings to the `data.columns` attribute, which is used to rename the columns of the DataFrame. The list contains the names of the features and the `Class` column, in the same order as they appear in the iris.csv file. By renaming the columns, the program makes the DataFrame more readable and easier to work with.

Finally, the program uses the `display()` function to print a subset of the DataFrame. This is a built-in function in Jupyter Notebook that renders a DataFrame in an attractive format. The program passes a slice of the DataFrame as an argument to the `display()` function, using the syntax `data[1:3]`. This slice selects the rows from index 1 to index 2 (inclusive) of the DataFrame, which correspond to the second and third iris flowers in the data set. The slice also selects all the columns of the DataFrame, since no column index is specified. The `display()` function then prints these two rows and five columns of the DataFrame in a tabular format.

Output:

	Sepal_Length	Sepal_Width	Petal_Length	Petal_Width	Class
1	4.7	3.2	1.3	0.2	Iris-setosa
2	4.6	3.1	1.5	0.2	Iris-setosa

13.5.15 Read the Iris Data Set and Display the Column Value of the Specified Index

```
# This line imports the pandas library and gives it the alias pd
import pandas as pd
# This line reads a CSV file named iris.csv and stores it in a variable
called data
data = pd.read_csv("iris.csv")
# This line assigns new names to the columns of the data
data.columns = ['Sepal_Length','Sepal_Width','Petal_Length','Petal_
Width','Class']
# Display the column value of the row with index 1
display (data.loc[1,: ])
```

The program consists of the following steps:

1. The program imports the pandas library and assigns it an alias of `pd`. This allows the program to use the functions and methods of pandas without typing the full name every time.
2. The program uses the `pd.read_csv()` function to read a comma-separated values (CSV) file named iris.csv and store it in a variable called `data`. The CSV file contains data about the iris flower species, such as the sepal length, sepal width, petal length, petal width, and class (setosa, versicolor, or virginica).

3. The program uses the `data.columns` attribute to assign new names to the columns of the data variable. The new names are more descriptive and follow the Python naming convention of using underscores instead of spaces.
4. The program uses the `display()` function to print the row with index 1 of the data variable. This is a built-in function in Jupyter Notebook, an interactive environment for running Python code, that shows a formatted output of a pandas object. The row with index 1 contains the values [4.9, 3.0, 1.4, 0.2, 'setosa'] for the sepal length, sepal width, petal length, petal width, and class columns, respectively.

Output:

Column Name	Value
Sepal_Length	4.7
Sepal_Width	3.2
Petal_Length	1.3
Petal_Width	0.2
Class	Iris-setosa
Name: 1, dtype: object	

13.5.16 Read the Iris Data Set and Combine Sets of Rows

```
# This line imports the pandas library and gives it the alias pd
import pandas as pd
# This line reads a CSV file named iris.csv and stores it in a variable
called data
data = pd.read_csv("iris.csv")
# This line assigns new names to the columns of the data
data.columns = ['Sepal_Length','Sepal_Width','Petal_Length','Petal_
Width','Class']
# Create a new variable called data1, which is a subset of the data
variable that contains only the first two rows.
data1 = data[0: 2]
display (data1.head)
# Create a new variable called data2 that contains only the rows from
index 50 to 51 (inclusive)
data2 = data[50: 52]
display (data2.head)
# Concatenation of the data1 and data2 variables.
data3 = pd.concat ([data1, data2])
display (data3.head)
```

The program creates a new variable called `data1`, which is a subset of the `data` DataFrame that contains only the first two rows. To select a subset of rows from a DataFrame, we can use slicing notation with square brackets. The slicing notation `[0:2]` means to select the rows from index 0 to index 1 (inclusive), where index is the position of the row in the DataFrame. The index starts from 0 and ends at $n - 1$, where n is the number of rows in the DataFrame. In this case, n is 150, so the last index is 149. We assign the sliced DataFrame to the variable `data1`.

The program creates another variable called `data2` that contains only the rows from index 50 to 51 (inclusive) from the data DataFrame. To select these rows, we use slicing notation again with `[50:52]`, which means to select the rows from index 50 to index 51 (inclusive). We assign the sliced DataFrame to the variable `data2`.

The program concatenates or combines the `data1` and `data2` DataFrames into a new DataFrame called data3. To concatenate DataFrames, we use the `pd.concat()` function, which takes a list of DataFrames as an argument and returns a new DataFrame with all the rows from each DataFrame in order. We pass [`data1,data2`] as an argument to `pd.concat`, which means concatenate `data1` and `data2` in that order. We assign the concatenated DataFrame to the variable `data3`.

Output:

	Sepal_Length	Sepal_Width	Petal_Length	Petal_Width	Class
0	4.9	3.0	1.4	0.2	Iris-setosa
1	4.7	3.2	1.3	0.2	Iris-setosa

	Sepal_Length	Sepal_Width	Petal_Length	Petal_Width	Class
50	6.4	3.2	4.5	1.5	Iris-versicolor
51	6.9	3.1	4.9	1.5	Iris-versicolor

	Sepal_Length	Sepal_Width	Petal_Length	Petal_Width	Class
0	4.9	3.0	1.4	0.2	Iris-setosa
1	4.7	3.2	1.3	0.2	Iris-setosa
50	6.4	3.2	4.5	1.5	Iris-versicolor
51	6.9	3.1	4.9	1.5	Iris-versicolor

13.5.17 Read the Iris Data Set and Combine Sets of Columns

```
# This line imports the pandas library and gives it the alias pd
import pandas as pd
# This line reads a CSV file named iris.csv and stores it in a variable
called data
```

```
data = pd.read_csv("iris.csv")
# This line assigns new names to the columns of the data
data.columns = ['Sepal_Length','Sepal_Width','Petal_Length','Petal_
Width','Class']
# Create a new dataframe called data1 that contains only the petal
width column
data1 = data[ ["Petal_Width"]]
display (data1.head)
# Create another dataframe called data2 that contains only the class
column
data2 = data[ ["Class"]]
display (data2.head)
# Concatenate data1 and data2 along the horizontal axis (axis=1) to
create a new dataframe called data3
data3 = pd.concat ([data1.reset_index(drop=True), data2], axis=1)
display (data3.head)
```

We create a new DataFrame called `data1` that contains only the petal width column. `data1 = data[ ["Petal_Width"]]`. We use the `display()` function to show the first five rows of `data1`. Similarly, we create another DataFrame called `data2` that contains only the class column `data2 = data[ ["Class"]]`. We also display the first five rows of `data2`. Finally, we concatenate `data1` and `data2` along the horizontal axis (`axis=1`) to create a new DataFrame called `data3`. We use the `reset_index` function to drop the original index of `data1` and assign a new one. We display the first five rows of `data3`, which shows the petal width and class of each flower.

Output:

	Petal_Width
0	0.2
1	0.2
2	0.2
3	0.2
	...
146	2.0
147	2.3
148	1.8

	Class
0	Iris-setosa
1	Iris-setosa
2	Iris-setosa
3	Iris-setosa
	...
146	Iris-virginica
147	Iris-virginica
148	Iris-virginica

	Petal_Width	Class
0	0.2	Iris-setosa
1	0.2	Iris-setosa
2	0.2	Iris-setosa
3	0.2	Iris-setosa
	...	
146	2.0	Iris-virginica
147	2.3	Iris-virginica
148	1.8	Iris-virginica

13.5.18 Displaying DataFrame Information

```
# This line imports the pandas library and gives it the alias pd
import pandas as pd
# This line reads a CSV file named iris.csv and stores it in a variable
called data
data = pd.read_csv("iris.csv")
# This line assigns new names to the columns of the data
data.columns = ['Sepal_Length','Sepal_Width','Petal_Length','Petal_
Width','Class']
# displays the summary information of the data using the data.info method
display (data.info)
```

Output:

	Sepal_Length	Sepal_Width	Petal_Length	Petal_Width	Class
0	4.9	3.0	1.4	0.2	Iris-setosa
1	4.7	3.2	1.3	0.2	Iris-setosa
2	4.6	3.1	1.5	0.2	Iris-setosa
3	5.0	3.6	1.4	0.2	Iris-setosa
4	5.4	3.9	1.7	0.4	Iris-setosa
			....		
144	6.7	3.0	5.2	2.3	Iris-virginica
145	6.3	2.5	5.0	1.9	Iris-virginica
146	6.5	3.0	5.2	2.0	Iris-virginica
147	6.2	3.4	5.4	2.3	Iris-virginica
148	5.9	3.0	5.1	1.8	Iris-virginica

13.5.19 Finding the Mean and Median of a Column

```
# This line imports the pandas library and gives it the alias pd
import pandas as pd
# This line reads a CSV file named iris.csv and stores it in a variable
called data
data = pd.read_csv("iris.csv")
# This line assigns new names to the columns of the data
data.columns = ['Sepal_Length','Sepal_Width','Petal_Length','Petal_
Width','Class']
```

```
# Use the median function from numpy to calculate the median value of the
petal length column
display (np.median(data[["Petal_Length"]]))
# Use the mean function from numpy to calculate the mean value of the
petal length column
display (np.mean(data[["Petal_Length"]]))
# Use the axis parameter to specify that we want to calculate the
variance
# Variance is calculated along the rows (axis=0) rather than along the #
columns (axis=1)
display (np.var(data[["Petal_Length"]], axis=0))
```

We use the `display()` function to print the output of the following expressions in a formatted way. We use the `median()` function from NumPy to calculate the median value of the `Petal_Length` column. The median is the middle value of a sorted list of numbers, or the average of the middle two values if the list has an even number of elements: `display (np.median(data[["Petal_Length"]]))`.

We use the `mean()` function from NumPy to calculate the mean of the `Petal_Length` column. The mean is the sum of all values divided by the number of values: `display (np.mean(data[["Petal_Length"]]))`.

We use the `var` function from NumPy to calculate the variance of the `Petal_Length` column. The variance is a measure of how spread out the values are from the mean. It is calculated by taking the average of the squared differences between each value and the mean. We use the `axis` parameter to specify that we want to calculate the variance along the rows (`axis=0`) rather than along the columns (`axis=1`): `display (np.var(data[["Petal_Length"]], axis= 0))`.

Output:

```
4.4
3.774496644295302
Petal_Length  3.075591
dtype: float64
```

13.5.20 Displaying Boxplot using Matplotlib

```
# This line imports the pandas and matplot library
import pandas as pd
import matplotlib.pyplot as plt
# This line reads a CSV file named iris.csv and stores it in a variable
called data
data = pd.read_csv("iris.csv")
# This line assigns new names to the columns of the data
data.columns = ['Sepal_Length','Sepal_Width','Petal_Length','Petal_
Width','Class']
boxplot = data.boxplot(figsize = (5,5))
```

This program imports two modules: matplotlib.pyplot and pandas. These modules are libraries that provide functions for plotting graphs and manipulating DataFrames, respectively. It uses the pandas function `read_csv` to load the iris.csv file into a DataFrame object called `data`. The iris.csv file contains data on the sepal length, sepal width, petal length, petal width and class of 150 iris flowers from three different species: setosa, versicolor and virginica. It assigns new names to the columns of the DataFrame using the `data.columns` attribute. The new names are `Sepal_Length`, `Sepal_Width`, `Petal_Length`, `Petal_Width` and `Class`. It uses the `data.boxplot` method to create a boxplot of the four numerical variables: sepal length, sepal width, petal length and petal width. A boxplot is a graphical representation of the distribution of a variable, showing the minimum, maximum, median, first quartile and third quartile values, as well as any outliers. The `boxplot()` method takes an argument figsize, which specifies the size of the figure in inches. It displays the boxplot on the screen using the `plt.show` function from matplotlib.pyplot.

Output:

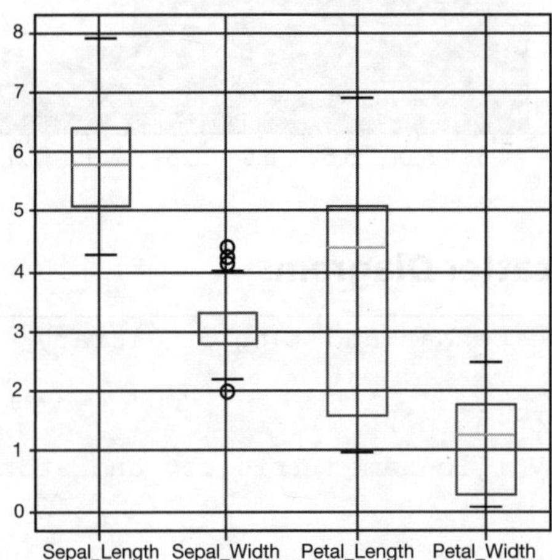

13.5.21 Displaying Histogram using Matplotlib

```
# This line imports the pandas and matplot library
import pandas as pd
import matplotlib.pyplot as plt
# This line reads a CSV file named iris.csv and stores it in a variable
called data
data = pd.read_csv("iris.csv")
# This line assigns new names to the columns of the data
data.columns = ['Sepal_Length','Sepal_Width','Petal_Length','Petal_
Width','Class']
# It uses the data['Sepal_Length'].plot() method to create a plot object
of the sepal length column of the data frame.
# It specifies the kind argument as 'hist' to make it a histogram.
data['Sepal_Length'].plot(kind= 'hist')
```

It imports the matplotlib.pyplot module as `plt`, which is a library for creating various types of plots and graphs in Python. It imports the pandas module as `pd`, which is a library for data analysis and manipulation in Python. It uses the `data['Sepal_Length'].plot()` method to create a plot object of the `Sepal_Length` column of the DataFrame, and specifies the kind argument as `hist` to make it a histogram. It uses the `plt.show()` function to display the histogram on the screen.

Output:

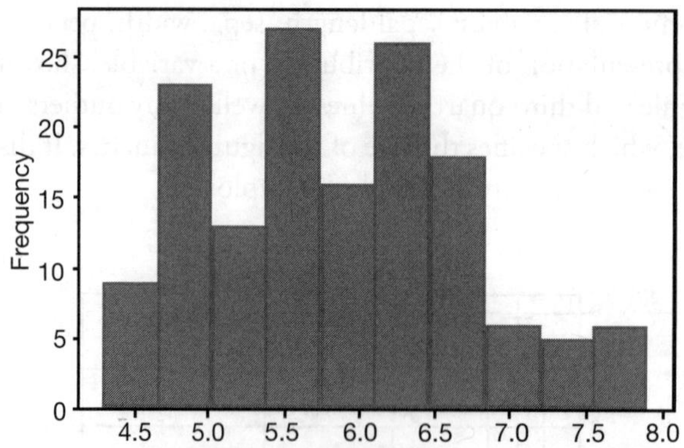

13.5.22 Displaying Scatter Diagrams

```
# This line imports the pandas and matplot library
import pandas as pd
import matplotlib.pyplot as plt
# This line reads a CSV file named iris.csv and stores it in a variable
called data
data = pd.read_csv("iris.csv")
Import numpy as np
# This line assigns new names to the columns of the data
data.columns = ['Sepal_Length','Sepal_Width','Petal_Length','Petal_
Width','Class']
# Generate random X and Y values
x = np.random.randn(1000)
y = np.random.randn(1000)
# Create customized scatter plot
plt.scatter(data[["Petal_Width"]], data[["Petal_Length"]], c = 'r', mark-
er = 'x')
plt.xlabel('Petal Width')
plt.ylabel('Petal Length')
plt.title('Scatter Plot')
plt.show()
```

The above program is a detailed explanation of how to create a customized scatter plot of the iris data set using the Matplotlib, pandas and NumPy modules. It first imports the necessary modules and reads the data from a csv file. Then it renames the columns of the data to match the attributes of the iris data set. Next, it generates two arrays of random numbers to use as dummy data. Finally, it creates a scatter plot of the petal width and petal length of the iris data set and labels and titles the plot accordingly.

Output:

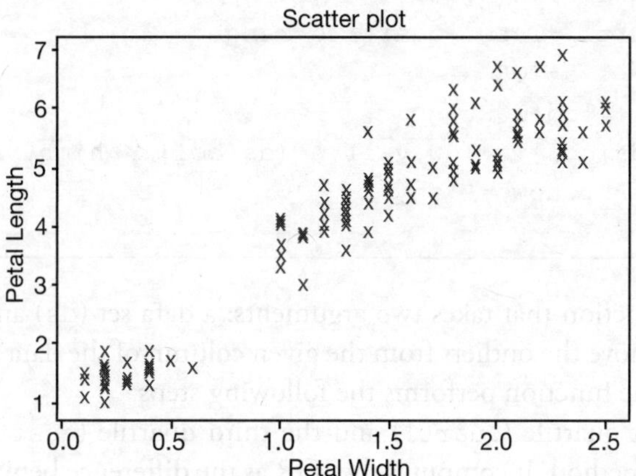

13.6 Finding Outliers

```
def find_outlier(ds,col):
quart1 = ds[col].quantile(0.25)
quart3 = ds[col].quantile(0.75)
IQR = quart3 - quart1 #Inter-quartile range
low_val = quart1 - 1.5*IQR
high_val = quart3 + 1.5*IQR
ds = ds.loc[(ds[col] < low_val) | (ds[col] > high_val)]
return ds
```

We want to write a function to find the outliers in a data set: `def find_outlier(ds, col)`. This function takes a data set (`ds`) and a column name (`col`) as input parameters. It returns a subset of the data set that contains only the outlier values in the given column. Outliers are defined as values that are more than 1.5 times the interquartile range (IQR) away from the first or third quartile. The IQR is the difference between the 75th percentile (`quart3`) and the 25th percentile (`quart1`) of the column values. The first quartile is calculated by calling the `quantile()` method on the column with 0.25 as the argument. The third quartile is calculated by calling the `quantile()` method on the column with 0.75 as the argument. The lower bound for outliers (`low_val`) is computed by subtracting 1.5 times the IQR from the first quartile. The upper bound for outliers (`high_val`) is computed by adding 1.5 times the IQR to the third quartile. The `loc()` method is used to filter the data set by selecting only the rows where the column value is less than `low_val` or greater than `high_val`. The filtered data set is returned as the output of the function.

13.7 Removing Outliers

```
def remove_outlier(ds,col):
quart1 = ds[col].quantile(0.25)
quart3 = ds[col].quantile(0.75)
IQR = quart3 - quart1 #Inter-quartile range
low_val = quart1 - 1.5*IQR
high_val = quart3 + 1.5*IQR
df_out = ds.loc[(ds[col] > low_val) & (ds[col] < high_val)]
df_out.dropna(axis=0, how = 'any')
return df_out
```

The program is a function that takes two arguments: a data set (`ds`) and a column name (`col`). The function aims to remove the outliers from the given column of the data set using the interquartile range (IQR) method. The function performs the following steps.

It calculates the first quartile (`quart1`) and the third quartile (`quart3`) of the column values using the `quantile()` method. It computes the IQR as the difference between the third and the first quartiles. It defines the lower and upper bounds for the outliers as 1.5 times the IQR below and above the first and third quartiles, respectively. It filters out the rows of the data set that have column values within the lower and upper bounds using the `loc()` method and assigns them to a new DataFrame (`df_out`). It drops any rows that have missing values in any column using the `dropna()` method. It returns the new DataFrame (`df_out`) that contains only the non-outlier values of the given column. Table 13.2 lists various functions related to removing rows.

Table 13.2 Various functions related to removing rows

S.No	Function	Explanation
1	`data = data.drop_duplicates()`	Removing duplicate rows
2	`data = data.dropna(axis = 0, how = 'all')`	Removing all rows where the values of any columns are NaN
3	`data = data.dropna(axis = 1, how = 'all')`	Removing all columns where the values of any rows are NaN
4	`data = data.dropna(axis = 0, how = 'any')`	Removing all rows where the values of any columns are NaN
5	`data = data.dropna(axis = 1, how = 'any')`	Removing all columns where the values of any row are NaN

13.8 Imputing Null Values

```
def impute_nullvalues(ds,col):
hp_mean = np.mean(data[col])
imputedrows = data[data[col].isnull()]
imputedrows = imputedrows.replace(np.nan, hp_mean)
#Then the portion of the data set not having any missing row is kept
apart.
missval_removed_rows = data.dropna(subset=[col])
# Then join back the imputed rows and the remaining part of the data set.
data_mod = pd.concat ([missval_removed_rows, imputedrows])
# data_mod = missval_removed_rows.append(imputedrows, ignore_index=True)
return data_mod
```

After removing the outliers, we can work on replacing the null values in a column with the mean value of that column using the function, `impute_nullvalues(ds, col)`. This function takes a data set (`ds`) and a column name (`col`) as arguments. It returns a modified data set where the missing values in the column are replaced by the mean of the non-missing values.

First, it calculates the mean of the non-missing values in the column using NumPy: `hp_mean = np.mean(data[col])`. Then, it creates a subset of the data set where the column has missing values using pandas: `imputedrows = data[data[col].isnull()]`. Next, it replaces the missing values with the mean value using pandas: `imputedrows = imputedrows.replace(np.nan, hp_mean)`. Then, it creates another subset of the data set where the column does not have missing values using pandas: `missval_removed_rows = data.dropna(subset=[col])`. Finally, it concatenates the two subsets to form the modified data set using pandas: `data_mod = pd.concat ([missval_removed_rows, imputedrows])`.

Alternatively, it can also use the `append()` method to join the two subsets: `data_mod = missval_removed_rows.append(imputedrows, ignore_index=True)`. It returns the modified data set as the output of the function: `return data_mod`.

13.9 Capping the Outlier Values

```
def cap_outlier(ds, col):
outliers = find_outlier(ds,col)
quart1 = data[col].quantile(0.25)
quart3 = data[col].quantile(0.75)
IQR = quart3 - quart1 #Getting the value of IQR
outliers.loc[:, col] = 1.5*IQR # Capping the outlier values with 1.5
times IQR value…
outlier_removed_rows = remove_outlier(data,col)
data_mod = pd.concat ([outlier_removed_rows, outliers])
#data_mod = outlier_removed_rows.append(outliers, ignore_index=True)
return data_mod
```

This function takes a data set (`ds`) and a column name (`col`) as inputs. It returns a modified data set where the outliers in the given column are capped. Capping means replacing the outlier values with a certain threshold value. This can help reduce the effect of outliers on the analysis of the data.

```
outliers = find_outlier(ds, col)
```

This line calls another function to find the outliers in the column.

```
quart1 = data[col].quantile(0.25)
```

This line calculates the first quartile of the column, which is the median of the lower half of the data.

```
quart3 = data[col].quantile(0.75)
```

This line calculates the third quartile of the column, which is the median of the upper half of the data. IQR = quart3 - quart1. This line calculates the interquartile range (IQR), which is the difference between the third and first quartiles.

```
outliers.loc[:, col] = 1.5*IQR
```

This line replaces the outlier values with 1.5 times the IQR value, which is a common way to cap outliers.

```
outlier_removed_rows = remove_outlier(data, col)
```

This line calls another function to remove the rows that contain outliers from the original data set.

```
data_mod = pd.concat ([outlier_removed_rows, outliers])
```

This line concatenates (joins) the data set without outliers and the capped outliers into a new data set.

```
data_mod = outlier_removed_rows.append(outliers, ignore_index=True)
```

This line is commented out, which means it is not executed. It is another way to join the two data sets, but it would ignore the original index of the rows. `return data_mod`. This line returns the modified data set as the output of the function.

13.10 Splitting the Data into Training and Testing Data

Splitting the data into training and testing data is a common practice in ML. The main reason for this is to evaluate the performance and generalization ability of the model. The training data fits the model parameters, while the testing data measures how well the model can predict new and unseen data. By splitting the data, we can avoid overfitting, where the model learns too much from the training data and fails to generalize to new data.
The advantages of splitting the data are as follows:

- It allows us to estimate the accuracy and error rate of the model on new data, which is essential for choosing the best model and tuning its hyperparameters.
- It helps us detect and prevent overfitting, leading to poor performance and unreliable predictions.

- It enables us to compare different models and algorithms based on their test results, which can help us to select the most suitable one for our problem.
- It provides us with a way to validate our assumptions and hypotheses about the data and the model, which can improve our understanding and interpretation of the results.

```
# Splitting the data into Traing and Test data
X_train, X_test, Y_train, Y_test = train_test_split(X_scaled, Y, test_
size = 0.2, random_state = 42)
# The parameter, test_size sets the ratio of test data to the input data
to 0.2 or 20% and random_state sets
# the seed for random number generator
```

This program uses the `train_test_split()` function from the sklearn.model_selection module to split the data into training and testing sets. The function takes four arguments: `X_scaled`, `Y`, `test_size` and `random_state`. `X_scaled` is the input data that has been scaled to have zero mean and unit variance. `Y` is the output data or the target variable. `test_size` is a float value between 0 and 1 that specifies the proportion of the data to be used as the testing set. In this case, `test_size` is set to 0.2, which means that 20% of the data will be used for testing and the remaining 80% will be used for training. random_state is an integer value that sets the seed for the random number generator that shuffles the data before splitting. By setting `random_state` to a fixed value, such as 42, we can ensure that the same split is reproduced every time we run the program. The function returns four values: `X_train`, `X_test`, `Y_train` and `Y_test`. These are the input and output data for the training and testing sets, respectively.

13.11 Training and Evaluating the Model

We must train and evaluate the model in ML to ensure it performs well on new and unseen data. Training the model involves finding the optimal parameters that minimize the loss function on a given training data set. Evaluating the model consists of measuring the model's performance on a separate validation or testing data set that was not used for training.
The advantages of training and evaluating the model are as follows:

- Training the model allows us to learn from the data and discover the patterns or relationships that can be used for prediction or inference.
- Evaluating the model allows us to assess how well the model generalizes to new data and avoid overfitting or underfitting problems.
- Training and evaluating the model can help us compare different models or algorithms and select the best one for our task or problem.
- Training and evaluating the model can help us improve the model by tuning the hyperparameters, adding regularization, or using more data.

```
# Training the logistic regression model
model = LogisticRegression()
model.fit(X_train, Y_train)
# making predictions on the test set
Y_pred=model.predict(X_test)
# Evaluating the model performance
from sklearn.metrics import accuracy_score, confusion_matrix,
classification_report
print (accuracy_score(Y_test, Y_pred)) # 1.0
print (confusion_matrix(Y_test, Y_pred)) # [[1 0 0 0] [0 9 0] [0 0 11]]
print (classification_report(Y_test, Y_pred))
```

The above program is an example of how to use logistic regression to classify data into three classes. The program performs the following steps:

1. It imports the `LogisticRegression` class from the sklearn.linear_model module and creates an instance of it called `model`.
2. It uses the fit method of the model to train it on the training data, which consists of two arrays: `X_train` and `Y_train`. `X_train` contains the input features for each sample, and `Y_train` contains the corresponding class labels (0, 1 or 2).
3. It uses the `predict()` method of the model to make predictions on the test data, which is another array called `X_test`. The predictions are stored in an array called `Y_pred`.
4. It evaluates the model performance by using various metrics from the sklearn.metrics module.
5. It imports the `accuracy_score`, `confusion_matrix`, and `classification_report` functions and prints their results.

The `accuracy_score()` function returns the fraction of correct predictions, which is 1.0 in this case. The `confusion_matrix()` function returns a matrix that shows how many samples were correctly or incorrectly classified by each class. The diagonal elements represent the true positives, while the off-diagonal elements represent the false positives and false negatives. The `classification_report` function returns a text report that summarizes the precision, recall, f1-score and support for each class. Precision is the ratio of true positives to all predicted positives, recall is the ratio of true positives to all actual positives, F1-score is the harmonic mean of precision and recall, and support is the number of samples in each class.

13.12 Regularization Techniques that Prevent Overfitting

Regularization techniques are methods that modify the learning algorithm or the model to reduce the complexity and prevent overfitting. Regularization techniques can help avoid overfitting by adding constraints or penalties to the model parameters, such as shrinking them towards zero or limiting their magnitude. Some examples of regularization techniques are L1 and L2 regularization, dropout, early stopping, and data augmentation.

Different factors, such as the performance gap between the training and validation sets, the model's complexity, the data's size and quality, and the domain knowledge of the problem, can indicate the regularization technique to be used.

Ridge and LASSO are both regularization techniques that help prevent overfitting in linear regression models. Here is a Python program that demonstrates these regularization techniques:

```
# Import necessary libraries
import numpy as np
import pandas as pd
from sklearn.linear_model import Ridge, Lasso
from sklearn.model_selection import train_test_split
from sklearn.metrics import mean_squared_error
# Load the dataset
data = pd.read_csv('data.csv')
print(data.shape)
data.head()
# Checking for any null values in dataset
data.isnull().sum()
# Split the dataset into training and testing sets
X_train, X_test, y_train, y_test = train_test_split(data.drop('target',
axis=1), data ['target'], test_size=0.2, random_state=42)
# Ridge Regression
ridge = Ridge(alpha=0.5)
ridge.fit(X_train, y_train)
# Lasso Regression
lasso = Lasso(alpha=0.5)
lasso.fit(X_train, y_train)
# Evaluate the models
ridge_pred = ridge.predict(X_test)
lasso_pred = lasso.predict(X_test)
ridge_mse = mean_squared_error(y_test, ridge_pred)
lasso_mse = mean_squared_error(y_test, lasso_pred)
print("Ridge MSE:", ridge_mse)
print("Lasso MSE:", lasso_mse)
```

Output:

```
# Ridge MSE: 0.034
# Lasso MSE: 0.041
```

In this program, we first import the necessary libraries. Then we load the data set and split it into training and testing sets using the `train_test_split` function. We then create the ridge and LASSO regression models with the alpha value set to 0.5. We fit these models to the training data and predict the target values for the test set. Finally, we evaluate the models using mean squared error (MSE) and print the results.

The output of the ML program indicates that the ridge regression model has a lower mean squared error (MSE) than the LASSO regression model. This means that the ridge model has a better fit to the data and is less likely to overfit than the lasso model. The ridge model penalizes the coefficients of the features by adding their squared values to the loss function, while the LASSO model penalizes them by adding their absolute values. The LASSO model can shrink some coefficients to zero, resulting in feature selection, but it can also introduce bias and variance. The ridge model preserves all the features, but it can also reduce their impact on the prediction. Therefore, the choice of the regularization parameter (alpha) is crucial for both models, as it determines the trade-off between bias and variance. A cross-validation technique can be used to find the optimal alpha value that minimizes the MSE for both models.

13.13 Implement Linear Regression

Here is a complete Python program that implements linear regression:

```
# Import necessary libraries
import numpy as np
import pandas as pd
from sklearn.linear_model import LinearRegression
import matplotlib.pyplot as plt
# Load dataset
data = pd.read_csv("Salary_Data.csv")
# Exploring dataset
data.head()
data.shape
# Checking for any Null values in the imported Datasets
data.isnull().sum()
# Split data into features and target
X = data.iloc[:,:-1].values
y = data.iloc[:, -1].values
# Create Linear Regression model
model = LinearRegression()
# Fit the model to the data
model.fit(X,y)
# Predict new values
new_data = np.array([[5], [10], [15]])
predictions = model.predict(new_data)
# Print the predictions
print(predictions)
# Plot dataset
plt.scatter(X, y, color= 'blue')
plt.plot(X, model.predict(X), color='red')
plt.title('SALARY VS EXPERIENCE (training set)')
plt.xlabel('Experience in Years')
plt.ylabel('Salary in Rupees')
plt. show()
```

The program follows these steps:

1. **Import the necessary libraries:** The program imports NumPy, pandas, sklearn, and Matplotlib as they provide useful functions and methods for data manipulation, analysis, modeling, and visualization.
2. **Load the data set:** The program reads data from Salary_Data.csv and stores it in a pandas DataFrame called `data`.
3. **Exploring the data set:** The program uses the `head()` and `shape()` methods to display the first five rows and the dimensions of the data, respectively.
4. **Checking for any null values in the imported data sets:** The program uses the `isnull()` and `sum()` methods to count the number of missing values in each column of the data.
5. **Split data into features and target:** The program uses the `iloc()` method to select the first column as the feature variable `X` (experience) and the second column as the target variable `y` (salary).
6. **Create a linear regression model:** The program creates an instance of the `LinearRegression` class from sklearn.linear_model module and assigns it to a variable called `model`.
7. **Fit the model to the data:** The program uses the `fit()` method to train the model on the feature and target variables.
8. **Predict new values:** The program creates a Numy array called `new_data` that contains three new values of experience (5, 10, and 15 years) and uses the `predict()` method to generate corresponding salary predictions based on the model.
9. **Print the predictions:** The program uses the `print()` function to display the predicted salaries for the new values of experience.
10. **Plot the data set:** The program uses matplotlib.pyplot module to create a scatter plot of the original data points (`blue dots`) and a line plot of the model predictions. The program also adds a title, labels, and a legend to the plot using `plt.title(), plt.xlabel(), plt.ylabel()`, and `plt.show()` functions.

Output:

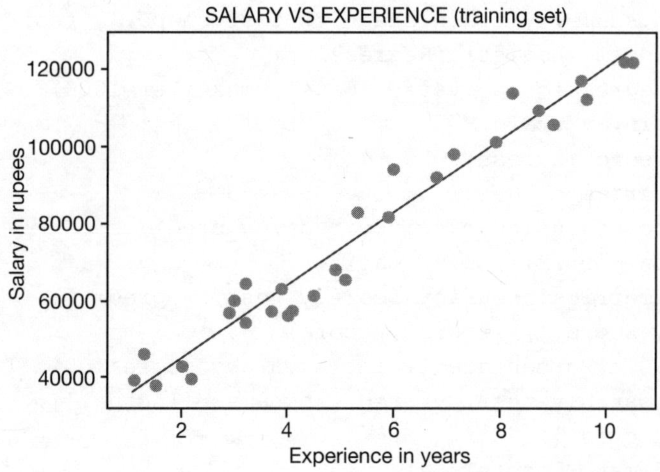

13.14 Implement Logistic Regression

```
# Python Program to Implement Logistic Regression
# First, we import necessary libraries
import numpy as np
import pandas as pd
from sklearn.model_selection import train_test_split
from sklearn.linear_model import LogisticRegression
from sklearn import metrics
import seaborn as sn
# Load the dataset
# Data set does not contain the harder and hence the header is given here
col_names = ['pregnant', 'glucose', 'bp', 'skin', 'insulin', 'bmi', 'ped-
igree', 'age', 'label']
data = pd.read_csv('diabetes.csv', header=None, names=col_names)
print(data.shape)
data.head()
# Checking for any null values in dataset
data.isnull().sum()
# Assigning dependent and independent variables
feature_cols = ['pregnant', 'insulin', 'bmi', 'age', 'glucose', 'bp',
'pedigree']
x=data[feature_cols]
y=data.label
```

```
# splitting the dataset into Training and Testing Dataset
x_train, x_test, y_train, y_test = train_test_split(x,y, test_size=0.2,
random_state=5)
display(x_train.shape, y_train.shape, x_test.shape, y_test.shape)
# Fitting the Model (Logistic Regression)
model=LogisticRegression(solver= 'lbfgs', max_iter=1000)
model.fit(x_train, y_train)
y_pred=model.predict(x_test)
# Evaluation Metrics
conf_mat=metrics.confusion_matrix(y_test, y_pred)
print('Confusion Matrix:', conf_mat)
Accuracy_score=metrics.accuracy_score(y_test, y_pred)
print('Accuracy Score:', Accuracy_score)
print('Accuracy in Percentage:', int(Accuracy_score*100), '%')
conf_mat=pd.crosstab(y_test, y_pred, rownames=['Actual'],
colnames=['Predicted'])
sn.heatmap(conf_mat, annot=True)
```

The above program is an example of how to implement logistic regression. The program performs the following steps:

1. First, it imports the necessary libraries, such as NumPy, pandas, sklearn, metrics and seaborn, which provide various functions and tools for data manipulation, model building, evaluation and visualization.
2. It loads the data set from a csv file, which contains information about diabetes patients. The data set has nine columns, which are named as `pregnant, glucose, bp, skin, insulin, bmi, pedigree, age, and label`. The label column indicates whether the patient has diabetes (1) or not (0).
3. The program prints the shape of the data set, which is (768, 9), and displays the first five rows using the `head()` method. Then, it checks for any null values in the data set using the `isnull().sum()` method, which returns zero for all columns, indicating that there are no missing values.
4. After that, it assigns the dependent and independent variables for the logistic regression model. The dependent variable is the label column, which is stored in `y`. The independent variables are the other eight columns, which are stored in `x`. The program selects only seven of them as feature columns, which are `pregnant, insulin, bmi, age, glucose, bp and pedigree`. These are the variables that are used to predict the label.
5. Next, it splits the data set into training and testing sets using the `train_test_split()` function from sklearn. The test size is set to 0.2, which means that 20% of the data will be used for testing and 80% for training. The random state is set to 5, which means that the data will be shuffled in a fixed way before splitting. The function returns four arrays: `x_train, x_test, y_train` and `y_test`, which are the features and labels for the training and testing sets, respectively.
6. The program displays the shapes of these arrays using the `shape` attribute. Then, it fits the logistic regression model using the `LogisticRegression()` class from sklearn. The `solver` parameter is set to `lbfgs`, which is an algorithm for optimizing the model parameters. The `max_iter` parameter is set to 1000, which is the maximum number of iterations for the solver to converge. The program creates an instance of the class called `model` and calls the `fit()` method on it with `x_train` and `y_train` as arguments. This trains the model on the training data.
7. Next, it makes predictions on the testing data using the `predict()` method of the model with `x_test` as argument. This returns an array of predicted labels called `y_pred`.
8. Finally, it evaluates the performance of the model using various metrics from sklearn. It calculates and prints the confusion matrix using the `confusion_matrix()` function with `y_test` and `y_pred` as arguments.

The confusion matrix shows how many true positives (TP), true negatives (TN), false positives (FP) and false negatives (FN) were predicted by the model. It also calculates and prints the accuracy score using the `accuracy_score()` function with `y_test` and `y_pred` as arguments. The accuracy score is the ratio of correctly predicted labels to the total number of labels. It also prints the accuracy score in percentage by multiplying it by 100 and converting it to an integer. It also creates a cross-tabulation table of actual and predicted labels using pandas' `crosstab()` function with `y_test` and `y_pred` as arguments. It then plots a heatmap of this table using seaborn's `heatmap()` function with `annot=True` as argument. This shows how well the model predicted each class.

Output:

```
(768, 9)
(614, 7)
(614,)
(154, 7)
(154,)
Confusion Matrix: [[88 12]
 [19 35]]
Accuracy Score:  0.7987012987012987
Accuracy in Percentage: 79 %
```

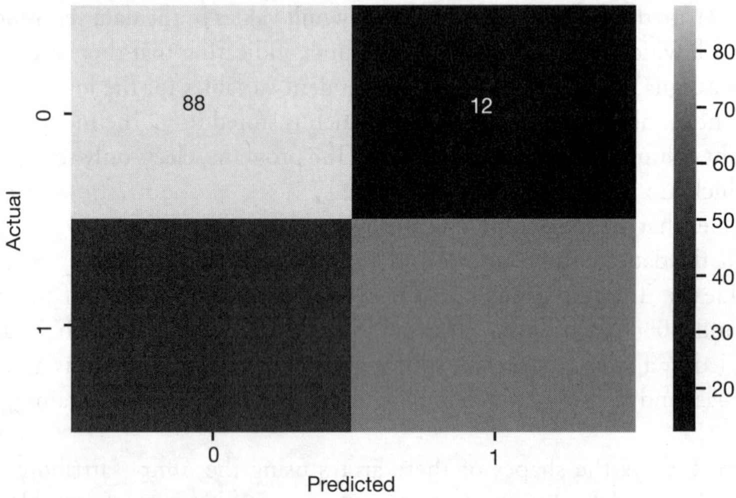

13.15 Decision Tree Classifier

```
import pandas as pd
from sklearn.model_selection import train_test_split
from sklearn.tree import DecisionTreeClassifier
from sklearn import metrics
import seaborn as sn
from IPython.display import display
# Importing (Reading) data sets
col_names = ['pregnant', 'glucose', 'bp', 'skin', 'insulin', 'bmi',
'pedigree', 'age', 'label']
data = pd.read_csv('diabets.csv', header= None,  names=col_names)
print(data.shape)
data.head()
# Checking for any null values in data set
data.isnull().sum()
# Assigning dependent and independent variables
feature_cols = ['pregnant','insulin', 'bmi', 'age','glucose','bp',
'pedigree']
```

```
x=data[feature_cols]
y=data.label
# Splitting the data set into training and testing data sets
x_train, x_test, y_train, y_test = train_test_split(x,y, test_size=0.2,
random_state=5)
display(x_train.shape, y_train.shape, x_test.shape, y_test.shape)
# Fitting the model (Decision Tree Classifier)
model= DecisionTreeClassifier(criterion='entropy',random_state=5)
model.fit(x_train, y_train)
y_pred=model.predict(x_test)
print('y_pred: ', y_pred)
# Evaluation Metrics
conf_mat=metrics.confusion_matrix(y_test, y_pred)
print('Confusion Matrix: ', conf_mat)
Accuracy_score=metrics.accuracy_score(y_test, y_pred)
print('Accuracy Score: ', Accuracy_score)
print('Accuracy in Percentage: ', int(Accuracy_score*100),'%')
conf_mat=pd.crosstab(y_test, y_pred, rownames=['Actual'],
colnames=['Predicted'])
sn.heatmap(conf_mat, annot=True)
```

The above program aims to classify whether a person has diabetes or not based on some features. The program follows these steps:

1. It imports some libraries that are needed for data manipulation, model building, evaluation and visualization. pandas is used for reading and handling the data, sklearn is used for splitting the data and creating the decision tree classifier, metrics is used for calculating the accuracy and confusion matrix, seaborn is used for plotting the heatmap of the confusion matrix, and IPython is used for displaying the results in a notebook.
2. It reads the data from a csv file called diabets.csv that contains 9 columns: `pregnant` (number of times pregnant), `glucose` (plasma glucose concentration), `bp` (diastolic blood pressure), `skin` (skin thickness), `insulin` (2-hour serum insulin), `bmi` (body mass index), `pedigree` (diabetes pedigree function), `age`, and `label` (0 for no diabetes, 1 for diabetes). It assigns the column names using a list called `col_names` and prints the shape of the data (768 rows and 9 columns). It also shows the first 5 rows of the data using the `head()` method.
3. It checks for any null values in the data using the `isnull().sum()` method. It returns zero for all columns, meaning there are no missing values in the data.
4. It assigns the dependent and independent variables for the model. The dependent variable is the `label` column, which is the target class to predict. The independent variables are the feature columns that are used as inputs for the model. It selects 7 features out of 9: `pregnant`, `insulin`, `bmi`, `age`, `glucose`, `bp`, and `pedigree`. It assigns them to `x` and `y` variables, respectively.
5. It splits the data into training and testing sets using the `train_test_split()` function from sklearn. It sets the test size to 0.2, meaning 20% of the data will be used for testing and 80% for training. It also sets the random state to 5, meaning the split will be reproducible. It displays the shapes of the four resulting sets: `x_train` (614 rows and 7 columns), `y_train` (614 rows and 1 column), `x_test` (154 rows and 7 columns), and `y_test` (154 rows and 1 column).

6. It fits the model using the `DecisionTreeClassifier()` class from sklearn. It sets the criterion to `entropy`, meaning it will use the information gain as a measure of quality for each split. It also sets the random state to 5, meaning the tree will be reproducible. It fits the model on the training data using the `fit()` method and makes predictions on the testing data using the `predict()` method. It prints the predicted labels as an array called `y_pred`.
7. It evaluates the model using some metrics from sklearn. It calculates and prints the confusion matrix using the `confusion_matrix()` function, which shows how many true positives, true negatives, false positives and false negatives were made by the model. It also calculates and prints the accuracy score using the `accuracy_score()` function, which shows how many predictions were correct out of all predictions. It converts the accuracy score to percentage by multiplying it by 100 and rounding it to an integer. It also creates a cross-tabulation of the actual and predicted labels using pandas' `crosstab()` function and plots a heatmap of it using seaborn's `heatmap()` function with annotations.

Output:

```
(768, 9)
(614, 7)
(614,)
(154, 7)
(154,)
y_pred:
[1 0 0 1 0 0 1 1 1 1 0 0 0 0 0 0 0 1 1 0 0 1 0 1 0 0 0 1 0 0 0 1 0 0 1 0 1
 0 0 0 0 0 0 0 0 1 0 0 1 0 1 0 1 0 0 0 0 0 1 0 0 1 1 0 0 0 0 1 1 1 1 1 0 1
 1 1 0 1 1 0 1 1 1 1 0 0 0 0 0 1 0 0 0 1 0 1 1 1 0 0 0 0 1 1 0 1 0 0 1 0 0
 0 0 0 0 0 1 1 0 0 1 1 0 0 0 0 0 0 0 0 1 0 1 1 0 0 0 0 1 0 0 1 0 1 0 0 0 1
 0 0 1 1 0 1]
Confusion Matrix:  [[77 23] [19 35]]
Accuracy Score:  0.7272727272727273
Accuracy in Percentage:  72 %
```

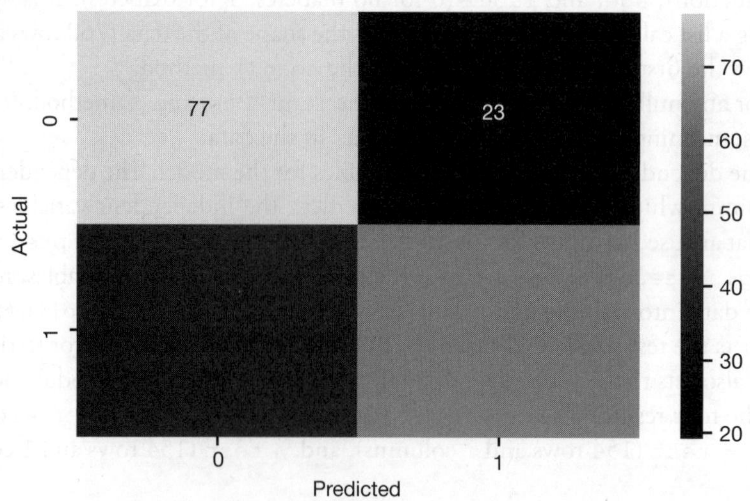

13.16 Implement SVM

```
import pandas as pd
from sklearn.model_selection import train_test_split
from sklearn.svm import SVC
from sklearn.metrics import classification_report
from sklearn import metrics
import seaborn as sn
from IPython.display import display
# Next, we need to load our data set into a pandas DataFrame.
# This data set will be used for training our SVM model.
# Load data set
col_names = ['pregnant', 'glucose', 'bp', 'skin', 'insulin',
'bmi', 'pedigree', 'age', 'label']
data = pd.read_csv('diabets.csv', header= None,
names=col_names)
print(data.shape)
data.head()
# Checking for any null values in data set
data.isnull().sum()
# Assigning dependent and independent variables
feature_cols = ['pregnant','insulin', 'bmi',  'age','glucose','bp',
'pedigree']
x=data[feature_cols]
y=data.label
# Once we have loaded the data set, we need to split it into training and
testing sets. # We will be using 70% of the data for training and 30% for
testing.
x_train, x_test, y_train, y_test = train_test_split(x,y, test_size=0.3,
random_state=5)
display(x_train.shape, y_train.shape, x_test.shape,y_test.shape)
# Preprocessing data with StandardScale
from sklearn.preprocessing import StandardScaler
sc = StandardScaler()
x_train=sc.fit_transform(x_train)
x_test=sc.transform(x_test)
# Create SVM instance and fit to training data
model= SVC(kernel='rbf',random_state=0)
model.fit(x_train, y_train)
svc_prediction=model.predict(x_test)
print('svc_prediction: ', svc_prediction)
# Evaluation metrics for 'rbf' kernel
conf_mat_rbf = metrics.confusion_matrix(y_test, svc_prediction)
print('SVC [kernel - rbf]')
print('Confusion Matrix: \n', conf_mat_rbf)
accuracy_score_rbf = metrics.accuracy_score(y_test, svc_prediction)
print('Accuracy Score: ', accuracy_score_rbf)
print('Accuracy in Percentage: ', int(accuracy_score_rbf * 100), '%')
print(classification_report(y_test, svc_prediction))
# Visualization of confusion matrix for 'rbf' kernel
```

```
conf_mat_rbf_vis = pd.crosstab(y_test, svc_prediction,
rownames=['Actual'], colnames=['Predicted'])
sn.heatmap(conf_mat_rbf_vis, annot=True).set(title='SVC [rbf]')
# Fitting the model (SVM) using 'linear' kernel
model_linear = SVC(kernel='linear', random_state=0)
model_linear.fit(x_train, y_train)
svc_prediction_linear = model_linear.predict(x_test)
print('svc_prediction_linear: ', svc_prediction_linear)
# Evaluation metrics for 'linear' kernel
conf_mat_linear = metrics.confusion_matrix(y_test, svc_prediction_linear)
print('SVC [kernel - linear]')
print('Confusion Matrix: \n', conf_mat_linear)
accuracy_score_linear = metrics.accuracy_score(y_test, svc_prediction_
linear)
print('Accuracy Score: ', accuracy_score_linear)
print('Accuracy in Percentage: ', int(accuracy_score_linear * 100), '%')
print(classification_report(y_test, svc_prediction_linear))
# Visualization of confusion matrix for 'linear' kernel
conf_mat_linear_vis = pd.crosstab(y_test, svc_prediction_linear,
rownames=['Actual'], colnames=['Predicted'])
sn.heatmap(conf_mat_linear_vis, annot=True).set(title='SVC [linear]')
```

Output:

```
(768, 9)
(537, 7)
(537,)
(231, 7)
(231,)
svc_prediction:
[0 0 0 0 0 0 1 1 1 1 0 0 1 0 0 0 0 1 0 0 0 1 0 1 0 0 0 0 0 1 0 0 0 0 1 0 0
 0 0 0 0 0 0 1 0 1 1 0 0 0 1 0 1 0 0 0 0 0 1 0 1 1 1 0 0 0 0 1 1 0 1 0 0 1
 1 0 0 1 1 0 1 1 1 1 0 0 0 0 0 0 1 0 0 0 0 1 1 0 0 0 0 0 1 1 0 1 0 0 1 0 0
 1 0 0 0 0 0 1 0 0 1 1 0 0 1 0 0 0 0 0 1 0 1 0 0 0 1 0 1 0 0 1 0 1 0 0 0 0
 0 0 1 1 0 1 0 0 0 0 0 1 0 0 0 0 0 0 0 0 0 0 0 0 0 1 0 0 0 0 0 1 0 0 0 1 0
 0 1 1 1 0 1 1 0 1 0 1 0 0 0 0 0 0 0 1 0 0 0 1 0 1 0 0 0 1 1 0 0 1 0 1 1 0
 1 1 0 0 1 0 0 0 1]
SVC [kernel - rbf]
Confusion Matrix:
 [[135  25]
 [ 22  49]]
Accuracy Score:  0.7965367965367965
Accuracy in Percentage:  79 %
              precision    recall  f1-score   support
           0       0.86      0.84      0.85       160
           1       0.66      0.69      0.68        71
```

```
    accuracy                           0.80       231
   macro avg       0.76      0.77      0.76       231
weighted avg       0.80      0.80      0.80       231
svc_prediction_linear:
[0 0 0 0 0 0 1 1 1 0 0 0 1 0 0 0 0 1 0 0 0 1 0 1 0 0 0 0 0 1 0 0 0 0 1 0 0
 0 0 0 0 0 0 1 0 1 1 0 0 0 1 0 1 0 0 1 0 0 1 0 1 1 1 0 1 0 0 0 1 0 1 0 0 1
 1 0 0 1 1 0 0 1 1 1 0 0 0 0 0 0 0 1 0 0 0 0 1 1 0 0 0 0 0 1 1 0 1 0 0 1 0 0
 1 0 0 0 0 0 1 0 0 1 1 0 0 1 0 0 0 0 0 0 0 1 0 0 0 1 0 1 0 0 1 0 1 0 0 0 0
 0 0 1 1 0 1 0 0 0 0 0 1 0 0 0 0 0 0 1 0 0 0 0 0 0 1 0 0 0 0 0 1 0 0 0 1 1
 0 1 1 1 0 1 1 0 0 0 1 0 0 0 0 0 0 0 1 0 0 0 1 0 1 0 0 0 1 1 0 0 1 0 1 1 0
 1 1 0 0 0 0 0 0 1]
SVC [kernel - linear]
Confusion Matrix:
 [[136  24]
 [ 23  48]]
Accuracy Score:  0.7965367965367965
Accuracy in Percentage:  79 %
              precision    recall  f1-score   support
           0       0.86      0.85      0.85       160
           1       0.67      0.68      0.67        71
    accuracy                           0.80       231
   macro avg       0.76      0.76      0.76       231
weighted avg       0.80      0.80      0.80       231
```

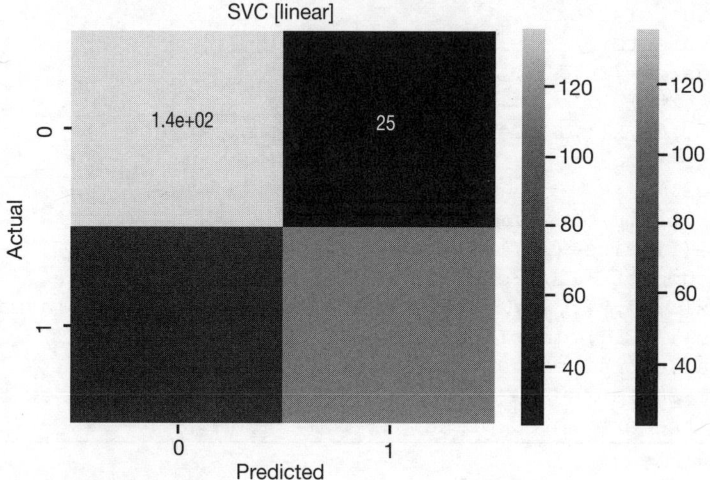

13.17 Implement PCA

```
import pandas as pd
import matplotlib.pyplot as plt
from sklearn.decomposition import PCA
from sklearn.preprocessing import StandardScaler
# Next, we can load the data set that we want to perform PCA on.
from sklearn.datasets import load_breast_cancer
data=load_breast_cancer()
data.keys()
# AssignED variables
print(data['target_names'])
print(data['feature_names'])
# Creating dataframe
df1=pd.DataFrame(data['data'],columns=data['feature_names'])
# Standard Scaler and PCA
sc=StandardScaler()
sc.fit(df1)
scaled_data=sc.transform(df1)
# Now, we can perform PCA on our scaled data. We can specify the number of
components we want to extract as a parameter. In this example, let us say
we want to extract 3 components.
principal=PCA(n_components=3)
principal.fit(scaled_data)
x=principal.transform(scaled_data)
print(x.shape)
# Scattering the clusters
principal.components_
plt.figure(figsize=(10,10))
plt.title('PCA 2D')
plt.scatter(x[:,0],x[:,1],c=data['target'],cmap='plasma')
plt.xlabel('pc1')
plt.ylabel('pc2')
from mpl_toolkits.mplot3d import Axes3D
fig=plt.figure(figsize=(10,10))
axis=fig.add_subplot(111,projection='3d')
axis.scatter(x[:,0],x[:,1],x[:,2],c=data['target'],cmap='plasma')
axis.set_xlabel('PC1',fontsize=10)
print(principal.explained_variance_ratio_)
# This program performs PCA on our data set and creates a new DataFrame
that contains the extracted principal components.
```

Output:

```
['malignant' 'benign']
['mean radius' 'mean texture' 'mean perimeter' 'mean area'
 'mean smoothness' 'mean compactness' 'mean concavity'
 'mean concave points' 'mean symmetry' 'mean fractal dimension'
 'radius error' 'texture error' 'perimeter error' 'area error'
 'smoothness error' 'compactness error' 'concavity error'
```

```
 'concave points error' 'symmetry error' 'fractal dimension error'
 'worst radius' 'worst texture' 'worst perimeter' 'worst area'
 'worst smoothness' 'worst compactness' 'worst concavity'
 'worst concave points' 'worst symmetry' 'worst fractal dimension']
(569, 3)
[0.44272026 0.18971182 0.09393163]
```

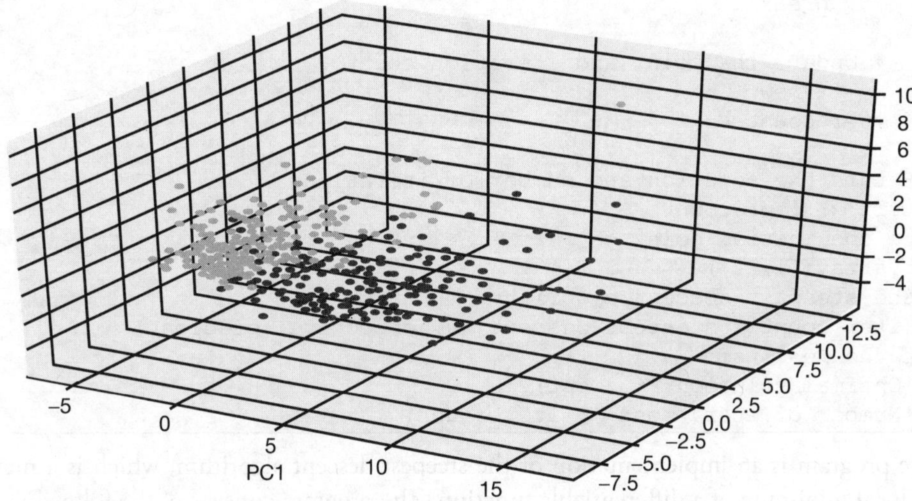

13.18 Implement Steepest Descent

```
# Python implementation of Steepest Descent algorithm
# Import required libraries
import numpy as np
from scipy import optimize
# Define the objective function
def objective(x):
    return (x[0]**2 + x[1]**2)
# Define the gradient of the objective function
def gradient(x):
    return np.array([2*x[0], 2*x[1]])
# Define the steepest descent algorithm
def steepest_descent(x0, objective, gradient, max_iter=100, tol=1e-6):

    # Define initial values
    x = x0
    iter_count = 0

    # Iterate until convergence
    while iter_count < max_iter:
        # Compute the gradient at the current point
        grad = gradient(x)
        # Compute the step size using line search
```

```
        alpha = optimize.line_search(objective, gradient, x, -grad)[0]
         # Compute the new point by taking a step in the direction of the
negative gradient
        x_new = x - alpha*grad

        # Check for convergence
        if np.linalg.norm(x_new - x) < tol:
            break

        # Update the point and iteration count
        x = x_new
        iter_count += 1

    # Return the solution and number of iterations
    return x, iter_count
# Define the initial point
x0 = np.array([1, 2])
# Run the steepest descent algorithm
x_opt, iter_count = steepest_descent(x0, objective, gradient)
# Print the results
print('Optimal solution:', x_opt)
print('Number of iterations:', iter_count)
```

The above program is an implementation of the steepest descent algorithm, which is a method for finding a local minimum of a differentiable function. The program consists of the following steps:

1. It imports the NumPy library for numerical computations and the SciPy library for optimization tools.
2. It defines the objective function that needs to be minimized. In this case, it is a simple quadratic function of two variables: *f*(*x*) = *x*[0]**2 + *x*[1]**2. The objective function takes a NumPy array as input and returns a scalar value as output.
3. It defines the gradient of the objective function, which is a vector that points in the direction of the steepest ascent of the function. The gradient is computed by taking the partial derivatives of the objective function with respect to each variable: grad(*x*) = [2*x[0], 2*x[1]]. The gradient function also takes a NumPy array as input and returns a NumPy array as output.
4. It defines the steepest descent algorithm, which is a function that takes four arguments: `x0` (the initial point), `objective` (the objective function), `gradient` (the gradient function), and optionally `max_iter` (the maximum number of iterations) and `tol` (the tolerance for convergence). The algorithm works as follows. It initializes the current point to `x0` and sets the iteration count to zero. It repeats the following steps until either the iteration count reaches `max_iter` or the change in the point is less than `tol`. It evaluates the gradient at the current point and stores it in a variable called `grad`. It uses the line search function from SciPy to find an optimal step size that minimizes the objective function along the direction of the negative gradient. The line search function returns a scalar value called `alpha`. It updates the current point by subtracting `alpha` times `grad` from it. This moves the point closer to a local minimum of the objective function. It increments the iteration count by one. It returns the final point and the number of iterations as a tuple.
5. It defines an initial point to start from. In this case, it is a NumPy array with values [1, 2].

6. It calls the steepest descent algorithm with the initial point, objective function, and gradient function as arguments. It stores the returned values in two variables: `x_opt` (the optimal solution) and `iter_count` (the number of iterations).
7. It prints out the optimal solution and number of iterations to show the results.

Output:

```
Optimal solution: [0. 0.]
Number of iterations: 1
```

13.19 IMPLEMENT RANDOM FOREST

```
import pandas as pd
from sklearn.model_selection import train_test_split
from sklearn.preprocessing import StandardScaler
from sklearn.ensemble import RandomForestClassifier
from sklearn import metrics
from sklearn.metrics import confusion_matrix, accuracy_score
from sklearn.metrics import classification_report
import seaborn as sn
import matplotlib.pyplot as plt
from sklearn import tree
import pydotplus
from IPython.display import Image
data=pd.read_csv('Breast Cancer Detection Classification Master.csv')
print(data.shape)
data.head()
# Assigning dependent and independent variables
x=data.iloc[:,:-1].values
y=data.iloc[:,-1].values
# Splitting the data set into training and testing
x_train,x_test,y_train,y_test=train_test_split(x,y,test_size=0.3,random_
state=41)
# Preprocessing Data with StandardScaler
sc=StandardScaler()
x_train=sc.fit_transform(x_train)
x_test=sc.transform(x_test)
# Fitting the model random forest classifier
model=RandomForestClassifier(n_estimators=10, criterion='entropy',random_
state=0)
model.fit(x_train,y_train)
y_pred=model.predict(x_test)
# Evaluation metrics
print('Random Forest Classifier')
conf_mat=metrics.confusion_matrix(y_test, y_pred)
print('\n Confusion Matrix: \n', conf_mat)
Accuracy_score=accuracy_score(y_test,y_pred)
print('Accuracy Score: ', Accuracy_score)
```

```
print('Accuracy in Percentage: ',
int(Accuracy_score*100),'%')
print('\n',classification_report(y_pred,y_test))
conf_mat=pd.crosstab(y_test,y_pred, rownames=['Actual'],
colnames=['Predicted'])
sn.heatmap(conf_mat, annot=True).set(title='Random Forest Classifier')
# Visualizing tree formed
# Create DOT data
dot_data = tree.export_graphviz(model.estimators_[0], out_file=None,
feature_names=data.columns[:-1], class_names=['0', '1'], filled=True,
rounded=True, special_characters=True)
# Create graph from DOT data
graph = pydotplus.graph_from_dot_data(dot_data)
# Generate image
Image(graph.create_png())
```

Output:

```
(569, 32)
 Confusion Matrix:
 [[110   0]
 [  1  60]]
Accuracy Score:  0.9941520467836257
Accuracy in Percentage:  99 %
               precision    recall  f1-score   support
           0       1.00      0.99      1.00       111
           1       0.98      1.00      0.99        60
accuracy                               0.99       171
macro avg          0.99      1.00      0.99       171
weighted avg       0.99      0.99      0.99       171
```

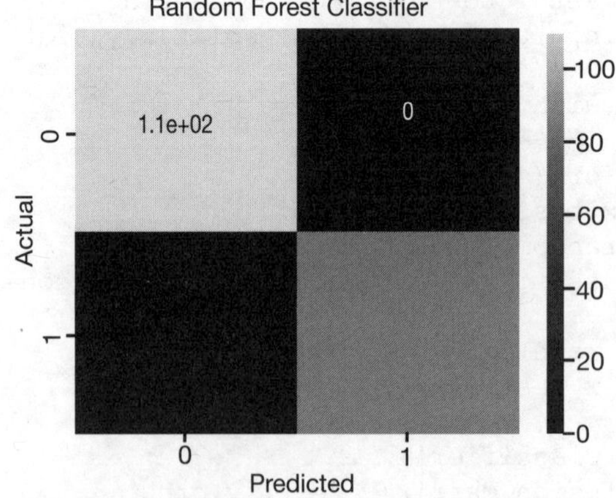

13.20 Implement Random Search

```
# Import required libraries
import numpy as np
from sklearn.model_selection import RandomizedSearchCV
from sklearn.ensemble import RandomForestRegressor
# Load the data set
dataset = np.loadtxt("dataset.csv", delimiter=",")
# Separate the features and target variable
X = dataset[:, 0:4]
y = dataset[:, 4]
# Define the model
model = RandomForestRegressor()
# Define the hyperparameters to be tuned
n_estimators = [int(x) for x in np.linspace(start=200, stop=2000, num=10)]
max_features = ['auto', 'sqrt']
max_depth = [int(x) for x in np.linspace(10, 110, num=11)]
max_depth.append(None)
min_samples_split = [2, 5, 10]
min_samples_leaf = [1, 2, 4]
bootstrap = [True, False]
# Define the grid of hyperparameters
random_grid = {'n_estimators': n_estimators,
               'max_features': max_features,
               'max_depth': max_depth,
               'min_samples_split': min_samples_split,
               'min_samples_leaf': min_samples_leaf,
               'bootstrap': bootstrap}
# Apply randomized search to find the best hyperparameters
rf_random = RandomizedSearchCV(estimator=model, param_
distributions=random_grid, n_iter=100, cv=3,  verbose=2, random_state =42,
n_jobs=-1)
# Fit the model on the data set
rf_random.fit(X, y)
# Print the best hyperparameters
print(rf_random.best_params_)
```

13.21 Implement Naive Bayes

Naïve Bayes is an ML algorithm that is used for classification tasks. It is based on Bayesian probability theory and assumes that the features are independent of each other. To implement this algorithm in Python, we first need to import the necessary libraries. We will use the scikit-learn library, which provides a naïve Bayes implementation. Here is the code to import the library:

```
# Import necessary libraries
from sklearn.datasets import make_classification
from sklearn.model_selection import train_test_split
from sklearn.naive_bayes import GaussianNB
from sklearn import metrics
```

```
# Generate synthetic data set for demonstration
X, y = make_classification(n_samples=1000, n_features=5, n_classes=2,
random_state=42)
# Split the data set into training and testing sets
X_train, X_test, y_train, y_test = train_test_split(X, y, test_size=0.3,
random_state=42)
# Create a Gaussian naive Bayes classifier instance
nb_classifier = GaussianNB()
# Train the naive Bayes classifier
nb_classifier.fit(X_train, y_train)
# Make predictions on the test set
y_pred = nb_classifier.predict(X_test)
# Calculate and print accuracy
accuracy = metrics.accuracy_score(y_test, y_pred)
print(f'Accuracy: {accuracy:.2f}')
# You can also print other metrics like precision, recall, and F1-score if
needed
print(metrics.classification_report(y_test, y_pred))
```

Output:

```
Accuracy: 0.85
               precision    recall  f1-score   support
           0       0.81      0.90      0.85       146
           1       0.90      0.80      0.85       154
    accuracy                           0.85       300
   macro avg 0.85   0.85      0.85      300
weighted avg0.85    0.85      0.85      300
```

13.22 Implement Single-Layer Perceptron Learning Algorithm

Here's a Python program to implement the single-layer perceptron learning algorithm:

```
# Importing necessary libraries
import numpy as np
# Defining the single layer perceptron learning algorithm function
def perceptron_learning(training_data, targets, learning_rate, epochs):
    # Initializing the weights and bias
    weights = np.zeros(training_data.shape[1])
    bias = 0.0
    # Iterating for the given number of epochs
    for i in range(epochs):
        # Iterating over the training data
        for j, x in enumerate(training_data):
            # Calculating the predicted output
            y_predicted = np.dot(weights, x) + bias
            # Updating the weights and bias based on the error
            if targets[j]*y_predicted <= 0:
                weights += learning_rate * targets[j] * x
                bias += learning_rate * targets[j]
```

```
    # Returning the learned weights and bias
    return weights, bias
# Testing the function with sample data
training_data = np.array([[0, 0], [0, 1], [1, 0], [1, 1]])
targets = np.array([-1, -1, -1, 1])
learning_rate = 0.1
epochs = 10
weights, bias = perceptron_learning(training_data, targets, learning_rate, 
epochs)
print("Learned weights:", weights)
print("Learned bias:", bias)
```

Output:

```
Learned weights: [0.2 0.1]
Learned bias: -0.20000000000000004
```

In this program, we first import the NumPy library, which is used for mathematical operations. We then define a function called `perceptron_learning()`, which takes in the training data, targets, learning rate, and number of epochs as inputs. Inside the function, we initialize the weights and bias to zero and iterate over the training data for the given number of epochs. For each iteration, we calculate the predicted output, update the weights and bias based on the error, and continue until convergence. Finally, we return the learned weights and bias.

To test the function, we use sample data consisting of four input vectors and their corresponding target outputs. We set the learning rate and number of epochs to 0.1 and 10, respectively. We then call the `perceptron_learning()` function with the sample data and print the learned weights and bias.

13.23 Implement Radial Basis Functions

Here's a sample Python code to implement radial basis functions:

```
import numpy as np
# Define the radial basis function
def rbf(x, c, s):
    return np.exp(-1 / (2 * s**2) * (x-c)**2)
# Generate sample data
x = np.linspace(-5, 5, 100)
y = np.sin(x)
# Define the centers and standard deviation of the radial basis functions
centers = np.linspace(-5, 5, 9)
sigma = 0.5
# Create the design matrix
X = np.zeros((len(x), len(centers)))
for i in range(len(x)):
    for j in range(len(centers)):
        X[i,j] = rbf(x[i], centers[j], sigma)
# Solve for the weights
w = np.linalg.solve(np.dot(X.T, X), np.dot(X.T, y))
# Predict using the model
```

```
y_pred = np.dot(X, w)
# Plot the results
import matplotlib.pyplot as plt
plt.plot(x, y, label='True function')
plt.plot(x, y_pred, label='Predicted function')
plt.legend()
plt.show()
```

Output:

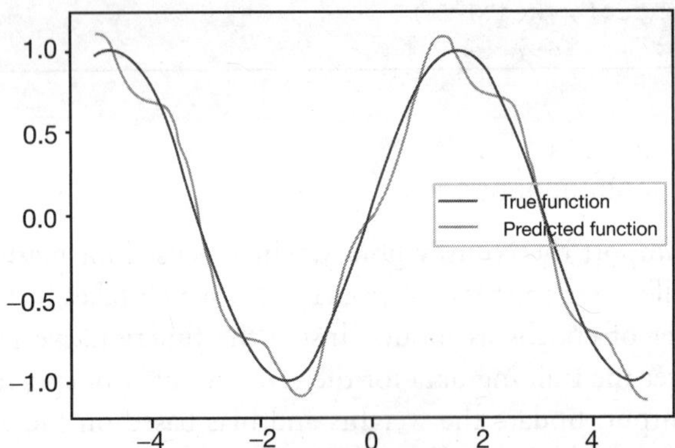

This code defines the radial basis function (RBF) as a Gaussian function with a center c and standard deviation s. It then generates sample data `x` and `y` and defines the centers and standard deviation of the RBFs. The design matrix X is created by applying the RBF to each data point and center, and the weights w are solved for using linear regression. Finally, the model is used to predict `y_pred` and plot the results.

13.24 Implement Linear Classifier

Linear classifier: scikit-learn's `SGDClassifier`
Bayesian classifier: scikit-learn's `GaussianNB`
K-NN classifier: scikit-learn's `KNeighborsClassifier`

Note: Linear classifier and linear regression are different. Linear classifier is an ML algorithm used for classification tasks, which means it is used to predict a discrete value (yes/no, 0/1). Linear regression, on the other hand, is an ML algorithm used for regression tasks, which means it is used to predict a continuous value (price, temperature). The main difference between the two is that linear classifier uses a threshold to determine the output, while linear regression does not.

```
# Linear classifier Python program using scikit-learn's SGDClassifier
# Import necessary libraries
from sklearn.linear_model import SGDClassifier
from sklearn.metrics import accuracy_score
from sklearn.model_selection import train_test_split
from sklearn.preprocessing import StandardScaler
```

```
import pandas as pd
# Load data set
data = pd.read_csv('dataset.csv')
print(data.shape)
data.head()
# Checking for any null values in data set
data.isnull().sum()
# Separate features and target variable
X = data.iloc[:,:-1]
y = data.iloc[:, -1]
# Split data set into training and testing sets
X_train, X_test, y_train, y_test = train_test_split(X, y, test_size=0.2,
random_state=42)
# Standardize the data
scaler = StandardScaler()
X_train = scaler.fit_transform(X_train)
X_test = scaler.transform(X_test)
# Create SGDClassifier object
sgd_clf = SGDClassifier(loss='hinge', random_state=42)
# Train the classifier
sgd_clf.fit(X_train, y_train)
# Predict on test set
y_pred = sgd_clf.predict(X_test)
# Evaluate accuracy of the classifier
accuracy = accuracy_score(y_test, y_pred)
print('Accuracy:', accuracy)
```

13.25 Implement Bayesian Classifier

Here is a Python program for implementing a Bayesian classifier using scikit-learn's `GaussianNB`.

```
# Importing the necessary libraries
from sklearn.naive_bayes import GaussianNB
from sklearn.datasets import load_iris
from sklearn.model_selection import train_test_split
# Loading the iris data set
iris = load_iris()
# Splitting the data set into training and testing sets
X_train, X_test, y_train, y_test = train_test_split(iris.data, iris.
target, test_size=0.2)
# Creating an instance of GaussainNB classifier
gnb = GaussianNB()
# Training the model using the training data
gnb.fit(X_train, y_train)
# Predicting the target values of the test data
y_pred = gnb.predict(X_test)
# Calculating the accuracy of the model
accuracy = gnb.score(X_test, y_test)
# Printing the accuracy of the model
print("Accuracy:", accuracy)
```

Output:

```
Accuracy: 0.9666666666666667
```

First, we import the necessary libraries for implementing the classifier. We load the Iris data set. We split the data set into training and testing sets using the `train_test_split()` function from the sklearn library. We create an instance of GaussainNB classifier, which is a type of naive Bayes classifier that assumes that the features are independent of each other. We train the model using the training data using the fit function. We predict the target values of the test data using the predict function. We calculate the accuracy of the model using the score function, which calculates the mean accuracy on the given test data and labels. Finally, we print the accuracy of the model. Overall, this program demonstrates how to implement a Bayesian classifier using scikit-learn's GaussianNB and provides an accurate prediction of the target values.

13.26 IMPLEMENT *K*-NEAREST NEIGHBOR CLASSIFIER

K-NN classifier: scikit-learn's `KNeighborsClassifier`

```
import pandas as pd
from sklearn.model_selection import train_test_split
from sklearn.neighbors import KNeighborsClassifier
from sklearn.metrics import classification_report, confusion_matrix,
accuracy_score
import seaborn as sn
# Importing (Reading) data sets
data = pd.read_csv('Breast Cancer Detection Classification Master.csv')
print(data.shape)
data.head()
# Checking for any null values in data set
data.isnull().sum()
# Assigning dependent and independent variables
x = data.iloc[:,:-1].values
y = data.iloc[:, -1].values
# Split data set into training and testing sets
x_train, x_test, y_train, y_test = train_test_split(x, y, test_size=0.3,
random_state=0)
display(x_train.shape, y_train.shape, x_test.shape, y_test.shape)
# Preprocessing data with StandardScaler
from sklearn.preprocessing import StandardScaler
sc = StandardScaler()
x_train = sc.fit_transform(x_train)
x_test = sc.transform(x_test)
# Training the model using KNN (minkowski)
results = []
for i in [1, 2, 3, 4, 5]:
    model = KNeighborsClassifier(n_neighbors=i, metric='minkowski', p=2)
    model.fit(x_train, y_train)
    y_pred = model.predict(x_test)
```

```
    accuracy_score_val = accuracy_score(y_test, y_pred)
    results.append(accuracy_score_val)
    print('KNN [ minkowski ]')
    print(f'for n_neighbors={i}:')
    conf_mat = confusion_matrix(y_test, y_pred)
    print('Confusion Matrix: \n', conf_mat)
    print('Accuracy Score: ', accuracy_score_val)
    print('Accuracy in Percentage: ', int(accuracy_score_val * 100), '%')
    print(classification_report(y_test, y_pred))
    print(results)
# Displaying results in a DataFrame
models = pd.DataFrame({'n_neighbors': ['1', '2', '3', '4', '5'], 'Accuracy 
Score': results})
models['Accuracy Score'] = models['Accuracy Score'] * 100  # Multiply by 
100 for percentage
models = models.sort_values(by='Accuracy Score')
print(models.to_string(index=False))
# Visualizing Confusion Matrix
conf_mat = confusion_matrix(y_test, y_pred)
sn.heatmap(conf_mat, annot=True, fmt='d', cmap='Blues').set(title='KNN [ 
minkowski, neighbor=5 ]')
```

Output:

```
(569, 32)
(398, 31)
(398,)
(171, 31)
(171,)
KNN [ minkowski ]
for n_neighbors=1:
Confusion Matrix:
 [[101   7]
 [  5  58]]
Accuracy Score:  0.9298245614035088
Accuracy in Percentage:  92 %
              precision    recall  f1-score   support
           0       0.95      0.94      0.94       108
           1       0.89      0.92      0.91        63
    accuracy                           0.93       171
   macro avg       0.92      0.93      0.93       171
weighted avg       0.93      0.93      0.93       171
[0.9298245614035088]
KNN [ minkowski ]
for n_neighbors=2:
Confusion Matrix:
 [[106   2]
 [  9  54]]
```

```
Accuracy Score:  0.935672514619883
Accuracy in Percentage:  93 %
              precision    recall  f1-score   support
           0       0.92      0.98      0.95       108
           1       0.96      0.86      0.91        63
    accuracy                           0.94       171
   macro avg       0.94      0.92      0.93       171
weighted avg       0.94      0.94      0.93       171
[0.9298245614035088, 0.935672514619883]
KNN [ minkowski ]
for n_neighbors=3:
Confusion Matrix:
 [[105   3]
 [  8  55]]
Accuracy Score:  0.935672514619883
Accuracy in Percentage:  93 %
              precision    recall  f1-score   support
           0       0.93      0.97      0.95       108
           1       0.95      0.87      0.91        63
    accuracy                           0.94       171
   macro avg       0.94      0.92      0.93       171
weighted avg       0.94      0.94      0.94       171
[0.9298245614035088, 0.935672514619883, 0.935672514619883]
KNN [ minkowski ]
for n_neighbors=4:
Confusion Matrix:
 [[108   0]
 [  9  54]]
Accuracy Score:  0.9473684210526315
Accuracy in Percentage:  94 %
              precision    recall  f1-score   support
           0       0.92      1.00      0.96       108
           1       1.00      0.86      0.92        63
    accuracy                           0.95       171
   macro avg       0.96      0.93      0.94       171
weighted avg       0.95      0.95      0.95       171
[0.9298245614035088, 0.935672514619883, 0.935672514619883,
0.9473684210526315]
KNN [ minkowski ]
for n_neighbors=5:
Confusion Matrix:
 [[107   1]
 [  6  57]]
```

```
Accuracy Score:  0.9590643274853801
Accuracy in Percentage:  95 %
              precision    recall  f1-score   support
           0       0.95      0.99      0.97       108
           1       0.98      0.90      0.94        63
    accuracy                           0.96       171
   macro avg       0.96      0.95      0.96       171
weighted avg       0.96      0.96      0.96       171
[0.9298245614035088, 0.935672514619883, 0.935672514619883,
0.9473684210526315, 0.9590643274853801]
n_neighbors  Accuracy Score
          1       92.982456
          2       93.567251
          3       93.567251
          4       94.736842
          5       95.906433
```

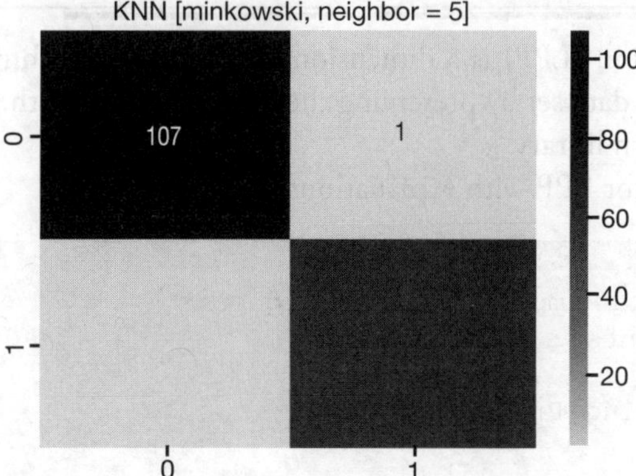

13.27 Implement Linear Discriminant Analysis

Linear discriminant analysis (LDA) is another dimensionality reduction technique that is used to reduce the number of features in a data set by projecting the data onto a lower dimensional space. It is implemented in Python using the scikit-learn library.

Here is an example of a Python program for LDA:

```
# Import necessary libraries
import numpy as np
from sklearn.discriminant_analysis import LinearDiscriminantAnalysis
# Create some sample data
X = np.array([[1, 2], [2, 3], [3, 4], [4, 5]])
y = np.array([0, 0, 1, 1])
# Create an instance of the LDA model
lda = LinearDiscriminantAnalysis()
```

```
# Fit the model to the data
lda.fit(X, y)
# Use the model to predict the class of the new data
X_test = np.array([[1, 1], [2, 2], [5, 5]])
y_pred = lda.predict(X_test)
# Print the predicted classes
print(y_pred)
```

Output:

```
[0 0 1]
```

In this program, we first import the necessary libraries – NumPy and `LinearDiscriminantAnalysis` from the sklearn library. Then, we create some sample data in the form of an array `X` and its corresponding labels `y`. We create an instance of the LDA model, fit it to the data, and then use it to predict the class of new data. Finally, we print the predicted classes.

13.28 Implement Locality Preserving Projection

Locality preserving projection (LPP) is a dimensionality reduction technique that is used to reduce the number of features in a data set by preserving the local structure of the data. It is implemented in Python using the scikit-learn library.
Here is a Python program for LPP with explanations and comments:

```
import numpy as np
from sklearn.neighbors import NearestNeighbors
def LPP(X, n_components):

    Locality Preserving Projection (LPP)

    Parameters:
    X (array-like, shape (n_samples, n_features)): Input data.
    n_components (int): Desired dimensionality of output data.

    Returns:
    X_lpp (array-like, shape (n_samples, n_components)): Projected data.

    # Step 1: Compute the affinity matrix W
    n_samples, n_features = X.shape
    knn = NearestNeighbors(n_neighbors=n_samples, algorithm='auto').fit(X)
    _, indices = knn.kneighbors(X)
    W = np.zeros((n_samples, n_samples))
    for i in range(n_samples):
        xi = X[i]
        xi_neighbors = X[indices[i]][1:]
        for j in range(n_samples):
            xj = X[j]
```

```
            xj_neighbors = X[indices[j]][1:]
            if j in indices[i]:
                W[i, j] = 1
            elif j in indices[indices[i]]:
                W[i, j] = 0.5 / (np.linalg.norm(xi - xj) ** 2)
            else:
                W[i, j] = 0

    # Step 2: Compute the graph Laplacian L
    D = np.diag(W.sum(axis=1))
    L = D - W

    # Step 3: Compute the eigenvectors of L
    eigenvalues, eigenvectors = np.linalg.eig(L)

    # Step 4: Choose the eigenvectors corresponding to the n_components
smallest eigenvalues
    indices = np.argsort(eigenvalues)[:n_components]
    X_lpp = eigenvectors[:, indices].real
        return X_lpp
```

The LPP function takes in an input data array of `shape (n_samples, n_features)` and a desired output dimensionality, `n_components`. It returns the projected data array `X_lpp` of `shape (n_samples, n_components)`. The LPP algorithm consists of four steps:

1. **Compute the affinity matrix W**: For each sample `xi` in `X`, find its `n_samples` nearest neighbors in X using `sklearn.neighbors.NearestNeighbors`. For each pair of samples `xi` and `xj`, compute their affinity weight `W[i, j]` as follows:
   - If `xj` is one of `xi`'s nearest neighbors, set `W[i, j] = 1`.
   - If `xj` is one of the nearest neighbors of one of `xi`'s nearest neighbors (`xj` is a second-order neighbor of `xi`), set `W[i, j] = 0.5 / ||xi - xj||^2`, where ||.|| denotes the Euclidean distance.
   - Otherwise, set `W[i, j] = 0`.
2. **Compute the graph Laplacian L**: Compute the diagonal matrix `D` whose `i`-th diagonal element is the sum of the `i`-th row of `W`. Compute `L = D - W`.
3. **Compute the eigenvectors of L**: Compute the eigenvalues and eigenvectors of `L`.
4. **Choose the eigenvectors corresponding to the n_components smallest eigenvalues**: Sort the eigenvalues in ascending order and choose the eigenvectors corresponding to the `n_components` smallest eigenvalues. Return the matrix whose columns are these eigenvectors as `X_lpp`.

13.29 Implement Logic Gates without Perceptron Model

Here is a Python program for logic gates that includes explanations and comments:

```
# Logic gate program
# Define the AND gate function
def and_gate(input1, input2):
```

```
    if input1 == 1 and input2 == 1:
        return 1
    else:
        return 0
# Define the OR gate function
def or_gate(input1, input2):
    if input1 == 0 and input2 == 0:
        return 0
    else:
        return 1
# Define the NOR gate function
def nor_gate(input1, input2):
    if input1 == 0 and input2 == 0:
        return 1
    else:
        return 0
# Define the XOR gate function
def xor_gate(input1, input2):
    if input1 != input2:
        return 1
    else:
        return 0
# Test the logic gate functions
print("AND gate:")
print(and_gate(0,0)) # Output: 0
print(and_gate(0,1)) # Output: 0
print(and_gate(1,0)) # Output: 0
print(and_gate(1,1)) # Output: 1
print("OR gate:")
print(or_gate(0,0)) # Output: 0
print(or_gate(0,1)) # Output: 1
print(or_gate(1,0)) # Output: 1
print(or_gate(1,1)) # Output: 1
print("NOR gate:")
print(nor_gate(0,0)) # Output: 1
print(nor_gate(0,1)) # Output: 0
print(nor_gate(1,0)) # Output: 0
print(nor_gate(1,1)) # Output: 0
print("XOR gate:")
print(xor_gate(0,0)) # Output: 0
print(xor_gate(0,1)) # Output: 1
print(xor_gate(1,0)) # Output: 1
print(xor_gate(1,1)) # Output: 0
```

This program defines four logic gate functions: AND, OR, NOR, and XOR. Each function takes two inputs and returns a binary output based on the specific logic of the gate. The program also includes tests for each gate to verify their functionality.

13.30 Implement Logic Gates with Perceptron Model

Python implementations of logic gates (AND/OR/NOR/XOR) using perceptron-based methods can be achieved using a combination of linear algebra and activation functions. The perceptron-based methods use a linear combination of inputs and weights to produce an output. The output is then passed through an activation function to produce the desired output. XOR cannot be implemented using a single-layer perceptron because it is a non-linear function. XOR requires two layers of perceptrons to produce the desired output. The first layer is used to produce the linear combination of inputs and weights, and the second layer to produce the non-linear output.

To implement an AND gate using perceptron-based methods, we can assign weights and biases to the inputs in such a way that the perceptron produces a positive output only if both inputs are positive. For example, we can set the weights to 1 and the bias to -1.5. This ensures that the output is positive only if both inputs are positive.

Here is a Python program for implementing an AND gate using perceptron-based methods:

```
def perceptron_AND(x1, x2):
    w1, w2, bias = 1, 1, -1.5
    output = x1*w1 + x2*w2 + bias
    if output > 0:
        return 1
    else:
        return 0
# Example usage
print(perceptron_AND(0, 0)) # Output: 0
print(perceptron_AND(0, 1)) # Output: 0
print(perceptron_AND(1, 0)) # Output: 0
print(perceptron_AND(1, 1)) # Output: 1
Here is a Python program for implementing an OR gate using perceptron-
based methods:
def perceptron_OR(x1, x2):
    w1, w2, bias = 1, 1, -0.5
    output = x1*w1 + x2*w2 + bias
    if output > 0:
        return 1
    else:
        return 0
# Example usage
print(perceptron_OR(0, 0)) # Output: 0
print(perceptron_OR(0, 1)) # Output: 1
print(perceptron_OR(1, 0)) # Output: 1
print(perceptron_OR(1, 1)) # Output: 1
To implement a NOR gate, we can simply invert the output of the OR gate
using the NOT operator. For example:
def perceptron_NOR(x1, x2):
    return not perceptron_OR(x1, x2)
```

```
# Example usage
print(perceptron_NOR(0, 0)) # Output: 1
print(perceptron_NOR(0, 1)) # Output: 0
print(perceptron_NOR(1, 0)) # Output: 0
print(perceptron_NOR(1, 1)) # Output: 0
Finally, to implement an XOR gate using perceptron-based methods, we need
to use multiple perceptrons. One way to do this is to use two perceptrons
to implement the AND and OR functions, and then combine their outputs
using another perceptron.
Here is a Python program for implementing an XOR gate using perceptron-
based methods:
def perceptron_XOR(x1, x2):
    and_output = perceptron_AND(x1, x2)
    or_output = perceptron_OR(x1, x2)
    return perceptron_AND(not and_output, or_output)
# Example usage
print(perceptron_XOR(0, 0)) # Output: 0
print(perceptron_XOR(0, 1)) # Output: 1
print(perceptron_XOR(1, 0)) # Output: 1
print(perceptron_XOR(1, 1)) # Output: 0
```

13.31 Handwritten Classification using CNN

Here is a Python program for handwritten classification using CNN:

```
import tensorflow as tf
from tensorflow import keras
from tensorflow.keras import layers
# Load the MNIST data set
(x_train, y_train), (x_test, y_test) = keras.datasets.mnist.load_data()
# Preprocess the data
x_train = x_train.astype("float32") / 255
x_test = x_test.astype("float32") / 255
x_train = x_train.reshape((x_train.shape[0], 28, 28, 1))
x_test = x_test.reshape((x_test.shape[0], 28, 28, 1))
y_train = keras.utils.to_categorical(y_train, 10)
y_test = keras.utils.to_categorical(y_test, 10)
# Define the CNN model
model = keras.Sequential(
    [
        layers.Conv2D(32, (3, 3), activation="relu", input_shape=(28, 28,
1)),
        layers.MaxPooling2D(pool_size=(2, 2)),
        layers.Conv2D(64, (3, 3), activation="relu"),
        layers.MaxPooling2D(pool_size=(2, 2)),
        layers.Flatten(),
        layers.Dense(10, activation="softmax"),
    ]
)
```

```
# Compile the model
model.compile(loss="categorical_crossentropy", optimizer="adam",
metrics=["accuracy"])
# Train the model
model.fit(x_train, y_train, epochs=5, batch_size=64, validation_split=0.1)
# Evaluate the model on the test set
test_loss, test_acc = model.evaluate(x_test, y_test)
print(f"Test accuracy: {test_acc}")
```

Output:

```
Downloading data from https://storage.googleapis.com/tensorflow/tf-keras-
datasets/mnist.npz
11490434/11490434 [==============================] - 5s 0us/step
Epoch 1/5
844/844 [==============================] - 19s 21ms/step - loss: 0.2133 -
accuracy: 0.9386 - val_loss: 0.0711 - val_accuracy: 0.9802
Epoch 2/5
844/844 [==============================] - 17s 20ms/step - loss: 0.0635 -
accuracy: 0.9811 - val_loss: 0.0558 - val_accuracy: 0.9857
Epoch 3/5
844/844 [==============================] - 16s 19ms/step - loss: 0.0470 -
accuracy: 0.9854 - val_loss: 0.0450 - val_accuracy: 0.9872
Epoch 4/5
844/844 [==============================] - 17s 20ms/step - loss: 0.0359 -
accuracy: 0.9888 - val_loss: 0.0410 - val_accuracy: 0.9888
Epoch 5/5
844/844 [==============================] - 16s 19ms/step - loss: 0.0290 -
accuracy: 0.9908 - val_loss: 0.0366 - val_accuracy: 0.9910
313/313 [==============================] - 3s 8ms/step - loss: 0.0316 -
accuracy: 0.9888
Test accuracy: 0.9887999892234802
```

13.32 Introduction to R Programming

R is a programming language and free software developed by Ross Ihaka and Robert Gentleman in 1993 at the University of Auckland, New Zealand. R is an implementation of the S programming language, which was created by John Chambers and others at Bell Labs in the 1970s. R also incorporates features from other languages, such as lexical scoping from Scheme. R is widely used for statistical computing and graphics, as well as data analysis and ML.

R can be installed on various operating systems, such as Windows, Linux, and Mac OS X. The official website of R provides instructions and links for downloading and installing the latest version. Alternatively, R can be used online through web-based platforms, such as RStudio Cloud, which allows users to create, share, and collaborate on R projects in the browser.

R is useful for ML because it offers a large collection of packages that implement various algorithms and techniques for data mining, classification, clustering, regression, neural networks, deep learning, and more. R also provides tools for data manipulation, visualization, and reporting, which are essential for exploring and communicating the results of machine learning models.

R is a versatile and powerful language that can handle complex and large-scale data analysis problems. It also has a vibrant and active community of users and developers who contribute to its development and improvement. R is one of the most popular languages for data science and ML in the world.

13.32.1 Installing R

To install R on Windows, you need to follow these steps:

1. Go to the CRAN website (https://cran.r-project.org/) and click on the "Download R for Windows" link.
2. Click on the "Install R for the first time" link to download the R executable file (R-4.3.1-win.exe).
3. Run the R executable file and allow the app to make changes to your device. Select the installation language and follow the installation instructions.
4. After the installation is complete, you can launch R by clicking on the R icon on your desktop or Start menu.

To test that the installation is working, you can try some simple commands in the R console, such as:

`print("Hello, world!")` - to print a message.
`2 + 2` - to perform arithmetic operations.
`sessionInfo()` - to check the version and details of your R session.

13.32.2 Installing RStudio

If you want to use a more user-friendly interface for writing and executing R code, you can also install RStudio, which is an integrated development environment (IDE) for R. To install RStudio, you need to follow these steps:

1. Go to the RStudio website (https://rstudio.com/) and click on the Download button.
2. Choose the free version of RStudio Desktop for Windows and click on the Download button.
3. Run the RStudio executable file (RStudio-X.X.X.exe) and follow the installation instructions.
4. After the installation is complete, you can launch RStudio by clicking on the RStudio icon on your desktop or Start menu.

To test that RStudio is working, you can create a new R script file by clicking on the File menu and selecting New File and then R Script. You can write some R code in the script editor and run it by clicking on the Run button or by pressing Ctrl+Enter. You should view the output of your code in the console.

You have now successfully installed R and RStudio on your Windows operating system and tested that they are working.

RStudio can also be used directly from Anaconda Navigator (see Section 13.1):

1. Launch Anaconda Navigator from the Start menu (Windows) or the Applications folder (MacOS)
2. Click on the Environments tab on the left side of the Navigator window.
3. Click on the Create button at the bottom of the window and give a name to your new environment (such as R_env)
4. In the list of packages, select R and click on Apply.
5. Wait for the installation to complete and then click on the Home tab.
6. In the list of applications, select RStudio and click on Install.
7. Wait for the installation to complete and then click on Launch.

You can now use R programming from RStudio within your Anaconda environment.

13.32.3 The glmnet Package in R

The glmnet package in R is a tool for fitting linear and logistic regression models with L1 and L2 regularization. The glmnet package provides an efficient and scalable implementation of this technique, making it a popular choice for ML and data science applications.

The purpose of this library is to fit generalized linear models (GLMs) with different types of regularization, such as LASSO, ridge, or elastic net. These methods can help reduce the complexity and improve the performance of models, especially when dealing with high-dimensional or sparse data. The glmnet package can handle various types of response variables, such as Gaussian, binomial, Poisson, Cox, and multinomial.

The glmnet package can be used in ML for various tasks, such as feature selection, classification, regression, survival analysis, or clustering. The package offers an easy-to-use interface for fitting regularized models using the `glmnet()` function, which takes the response variable, the predictor variables, and the type and strength of regularization as arguments. The package also provides functions for cross-validation, prediction, plotting, and model selection.

The glmnet package is based on a paper by Friedman et al. in 2010, which describes the algorithm and the theory behind regularized GLMs. The package is available on CRAN and can be installed and loaded using the following commands:

```
r
install.packages("glmnet", repos ="https://cran.us.r-project.org")
library(glmnet)
```

13.32.4 The caret Package in R

The caret package is a popular and powerful package for ML in R. The name caret stands for classification and regression training, and it provides a consistent interface for training, tuning, and evaluating various types of models. The caret package can handle many tasks related to ML, such as data preprocessing, feature selection, cross-validation, model selection, and performance assessment.

One of the main advantages of the caret package is that it allows the user to access and compare many different algorithms from different R packages using a common syntax and set of arguments. For example, the `train()` function can be used to fit a wide range of models by specifying the method argument. Some of the available methods include linear regression, logistic regression, decision trees, random forests, support vector machines, and neural networks. The `train()` function also performs automatic tuning of model hyperparameters using grid search or random search, and evaluates model performance using resampling techniques such as *K*-fold cross-validation or bootstrapping.

Another useful feature of the caret package is that it offers several functions for data preprocessing, such as centering, scaling, imputation, transformation, and encoding. These functions can be applied to the training data and then automatically applied to any new data using the preprocess and predict functions. This ensures that the data is processed consistently and avoids errors or inconsistencies when applying the model to new data.

The caret package offers several methods for feature selection, such as filter methods (based on correlation or importance scores), wrapper methods (based on recursive feature elimination or genetic algorithms), and embedded methods (based on regularization techniques such as lasso or elastic net).

The caret package has detailed documentation and a website (https://topepo.github.io/caret/) that contains many examples and tutorials on how to use the package for various tasks and applications.

13.32.5 R Program for Regularization Techniques

Here is an R program to demonstrate the regularization techniques, Ridge and LASSO. Ridge uses L2 norm, which adds the square of the coefficients to the loss function while LASSO uses L1 norm, which adds the absolute value of the coefficients to the loss function. Ridge tends to shrink all the coefficients equally, while LASSO tends to make some coefficients zero. This makes LASSO more suitable for feature selection and sparse models

```
# Load the libraries
library(glmnet)
library(caret)
# Generate some data with 10 features and 100 observations
set.seed(123)
X <- matrix(rnorm(1000), ncol = 10)
y <- X %*% c(1, 2, 3, 4, 5, 0, 0, 0, 0, 0) + rnorm(100)
# Split the data into training and testing sets
train_index <- createDataPartition(y, p = 0.8, list = FALSE)
X_train <- X[train_index, ]
y_train <- y[train_index]
X_test <- X[-train_index, ]
y_test <- y[-train_index]
# Fit a linear model without regularization
lm_model <- lm(y_train ~ X_train)
summary(lm_model)
# Fit a linear model with ridge regularization
# Use cross-validation to find the optimal value of lambda (the penalty
parameter)
ridge_model <- cv.glmnet(X_train, y_train, alpha = 0, family = "gaussian")
plot(ridge_model)
# Fit a linear model with LASSO regularization
```

```
# Use cross-validation to find the optimal value of lambda (the penalty
parameter)
lasso_model <- cv.glmnet(X_train, y_train, alpha = 1, family = "gaussian")
plot(lasso_model)
# Compare the coefficients of the three models
coef(lm_model)
coef(ridge_model, s = "lambda.min")
coef(lasso_model, s = "lambda.min")
# Compare the prediction errors of the three models on the test set
lm_pred <- predict(lm_model, newdata = X_test)
ridge_pred <- predict(ridge_model, newx = X_test, s = "lambda.min")
lasso_pred <- predict(lasso_model, newx = X_test, s = "lambda.min")
mean((lm_pred - y_test)^2) # Mean squared error of linear model
mean((ridge_pred - y_test)^2) # Mean squared error of Ridge model
mean((lasso_pred - y_test)^2) # Mean squared error of Lasso model
```

13.32.6 R Program for Linear Classifiers

The Iris data set is a classic example of multivariate data analysis. The purpose of this data set is to demonstrate various techniques of exploratory data analysis, such as summary statistics, visualization, clustering and classification. It can be used in ML to train and test different models of supervised learning, such as linear regression, logistic regression, *K*-nearest neighbors, decision trees and neural networks. The Iris data set is built-in to the R programming language and can be accessed by typing data(iris) in the console.

This is an R program that demonstrates the linear classifier ML algorithm. The goal is to find the line that maximizes the margin between the classes. We will only use two features (sepal length and width) and two classes (setosa and versicolor) of the Iris data set.

```
# Load the iris data set
data(iris)
# Subset the data to only include setosa and versicolor
iris <- subset(iris, Species %in% c("setosa", "versicolor"))
# Plot the data and color by species
plot(iris$Sepal.Length, iris$Sepal.Width, col = iris$Species, pch = 19,
xlab = "Sepal Length", ylab = "Sepal Width")
legend("topright", legend = c("setosa", "versicolor"), col = c("black",
"red"), pch = 19)
# Convert the species factor to a numeric variable, where setosa is 1 and
versicolor is -1
y <- as.numeric(iris$Species)
y[y == 2] <- -1
# Create a matrix of features with a column of ones for the intercept
X <- cbind(1, iris[, c("Sepal.Length", "Sepal.Width")])
# Initialize the weights vector to zero
w <- rep(0, ncol(X))
# Define the learning rate and the number of iterations
alpha <- 0.01
iter <- 1000
```

```
# Define a function to calculate the prediction error
error <- function(w, X, y) {
  # The prediction is the sign of the dot product of X and w
  pred <- sign(X %*% w)
  # The error is the sum of the absolute values of the differences between
the prediction and the true label
  err <- sum(abs(pred - y))/2
  return(err)
}
# Define a function to update the weights using gradient descent
update <- function(w, X, y, alpha) {
  # The gradient is the average of the product of X and y for the
misclassified points
  misclassified <- which(sign(X %*% w) != y)
  grad <- colMeans(X[misclassified, ] * y[misclassified])
  # The new weights are the old weights plus the product of the learning
rate and the gradient
  w_new <- w + alpha * grad
  return(w_new)
}
# Run the gradient descent algorithm for a fixed number of iterations
for (i in 1:iter) {
  # Update the weights
  w <- update(w, X, y, alpha)
  # Print the error and the weights at every 100 iterations
  if (i %% 100 == 0) {
    cat("Iteration:", i, "\n")
    cat("Error:", error(w, X, y), "\n")
    cat("Weights:", w, "\n")
  }
}
# Plot the data and the decision boundary
plot(iris$Sepal.Length, iris$Sepal.Width, col = iris$Species, pch = 19,
xlab = "Sepal Length", ylab = "Sepal Width")
legend("topright", legend = c("setosa", "versicolor"), col = c("black",
"red"), pch = 19)
abline(a = -w[1]/w[3], b = -w[2]/w[3], lty = 2)
# Sample input: sepal length = 5.5, sepal width = 2.5
# Sample output: versicolor (red point below the line)
```

13.32.7 The e1071 Package of R

The e1071 package is a collection of miscellaneous functions for statistics and ML in R. It was developed by the Department of Statistics, Probability Theory Group (Formerly: E1071) at TU Wien, Austria. The package includes functions for latent class analysis, short-time Fourier transform, fuzzy clustering, SVM, shortest path computation, bagged clustering, naive Bayes classifier, generalized *K*-nearest neighbour classifier and more.

One of the most popular features of the e1071 package is its interface to the libsvm library, which provides an efficient implementation of SVM for classification and regression problems. The e1071 package allows users to specify various parameters for the SVM model, such as the type of kernel, the cost of misclassification, the degree of polynomial kernel, the gamma parameter for radial basis kernel, etc. The package also provides functions for tuning the hyper-parameters of the SVM model using cross-validation or bootstrap methods.

The e1071 package can be used in ML applications that require robust and accurate prediction models based on complex data. For example, the package can be used to classify text documents, images, gene expression data, etc. using different types of kernels and SVM algorithms. The package can also be used to perform regression analysis on numeric or ordinal data using epsilon- or nu-regression SVMs. The package offers various methods to evaluate the performance of the SVM models, such as confusion matrices, ROC curves, sensitivity and specificity measures, etc.

13.32.8 R Program to Demonstrate the Bayesian Classifier

Here is an R program that demonstrates the Bayesian classifier ML algorithm. The classifier predicts the class with the highest posterior probability, which is the product of the prior and the likelihood.

```
# Load the e1071 package, which contains a function for creating and using
a naive Bayes classifier
library(e1071)
# Create some synthetic data for illustration purposes
# The data has two features (x and y) and two classes (A and B)
set.seed(123) # Set the random seed for reproducibility
n <- 100 # Number of instances
x <- rnorm(n) # Generate random values for x from a normal distribution
y <- rnorm(n) # Generate random values for y from a normal distribution
class <- sample(c("A", "B"), n, replace = TRUE) # Assign random class
labels to each instance
data <- data.frame(x, y, class) # Create a data frame with the features
and the class
# Plot the data to visualize the distribution of the classes and the
features
plot(data$x, data$y, col = data$class, pch = 19, xlab = "x", ylab = "y")
legend("topleft", legend = c("A", "B"), col = c("black", "red"), pch = 19)
# Split the data into training and testing sets
train_index <- sample(1:n, 0.8 * n) # Randomly select 80% of the instances
for training
train_data <- data[train_index, ] # Subset the data frame for training
test_data <- data[-train_index, ] # Subset the data frame for testing
# Create a naive Bayes classifier using the training data
model <- naiveBayes(class ~ x + y, data = train_data)
# Print the model to see the estimated prior probabilities and the
conditional probabilities of each feature given each class
print(model)
# Predict the class labels for the testing data using the model
pred <- predict(model, test_data)
# Compare the predicted labels with the actual labels to evaluate the
accuracy of the model
table(pred, test_data$class)
```

```
# Compute the accuracy as the proportion of correct predictions
accuracy <- sum(pred == test_data$class) / length(test_data$class)
cat("The accuracy of the model is", accuracy, "\n")
# Create a new instance with some arbitrary values for x and y
new_instance <- data.frame(x = 0.5, y = -0.5)
# Predict the class label for the new instance using the model
pred_new <- predict(model, new_instance)
cat("The predicted class for the new instance is", pred_new, "\n")
# Compute the posterior probabilities for each class given the new
instance using the model
posterior <- predict(model, new_instance, type = "raw")
cat("The posterior probabilities for each class are", posterior, "\n")
```

13.32.9 R Program to Demonstrate the KNN Classifier

This is an R program that demonstrates the KNN classifier ML algorithm. The *k* parameter can be chosen by cross-validation or other methods. The distance metric can be Euclidean, Manhattan, Minkowski or other user-defined functions.

```
# Load the required packages
library(class)
library(ggplot2)
# Generate some sample data for two classes
set.seed(123) # Set the random seed for reproducibility
x1 <- rnorm(50, mean = 0, sd = 1) # Generate 50 random numbers from a
normal distribution with mean 0 and sd 1
y1 <- rnorm(50, mean = 0, sd = 1) # Generate 50 random numbers from a
normal distribution with mean 0 and sd 1
x2 <- rnorm(50, mean = 3, sd = 1) # Generate 50 random numbers from a
normal distribution with mean 3 and sd 1
y2 <- rnorm(50, mean = 3, sd = 1) # Generate 50 random numbers from a
normal distribution with mean 3 and sd 1
class <- c(rep("A", 50), rep("B", 50)) # Assign the class labels A and B
to the data points
data <- data.frame(x = c(x1, x2), y = c(y1, y2), class = class) # Combine
the data into a data frame
# Plot the data using ggplot2
ggplot(data, aes(x = x, y = y, color = class)) + geom_point() +
ggtitle("Sample data")
# Split the data into training and testing sets
train_index <- sample(1:100, size = 80) # Randomly select 80 indices for
the training set
train_data <- data[train_index, ] # Subset the data frame by the training
indices
```

```
test_data <- data[-train_index, ] # Subset the data frame by the testing
indices
# Apply the k-NN classifier to the test data using k = 5 and Euclidean
distance
pred_class <- knn(train = train_data[, c("x", "y")], test = test_data[,
c("x", "y")], cl = train_data$class, k = 5)
# Compare the predicted class with the true class
table(pred_class, test_data$class)
# Calculate the accuracy of the classifier
accuracy <- sum(pred_class == test_data$class) / length(test_data$class)
accuracy
# Plot the test data with the predicted class
ggplot(test_data, aes(x = x, y = y, color = pred_class)) + geom_point() +
ggtitle("Test data with predicted class")
```

13.32.10 Introduction to ggplot2

ggplot2 is a system for declaratively creating graphics, based on *The Grammar of Graphics*. It is a package in the R programming language that enables you to create data visualizations using a consistent and coherent syntax. You can use it to create simple data visualizations like scatter plots, bar charts, and line charts, as well as more advanced and complicated data visualizations, like detailed maps.

The purpose of ggplot2 is to provide a framework for creating graphics that are expressive, elegant, and easy to modify. It follows the principles of *The Grammar of Graphics*, which is a set of rules that specify how to map data to aesthetics, what graphical elements to use, and how to coordinate multiple views. By using this grammar, you can create a wide range of graphics that are tailored to your specific needs.

ggplot2 can be used in ML to explore and understand the data, as well as to communicate the results of the analysis. For example, you can use ggplot2 to create histograms, boxplots, scatterplots, or density plots to examine the distribution and relationships of the variables. You can also use ggplot2 to create heatmaps, contour plots, or surface plots to visualize complex functions or models. You can also use ggplot2 to create interactive graphics using packages like plotly or shiny.

13.32.11 PCA Implementation Using R

Here is an R language program that demonstrates PCA ML. This program performs PCA on the Iris data set, which is a common example of multivariate data analysis.

The program uses the caret and ggplot2 libraries to perform PCA, train a KNN classifier, and visualize the results. The program also evaluates the accuracy of the classifier using a confusion matrix. The program shows that PCA can help to separate the different classes of iris flowers based on their petal and sepal measurements.

```
# Load the required libraries
library(caret)
library(ggplot2)
# Load the iris data set
data(iris)
# Split the data into training and testing sets
set.seed(123)
trainIndex <- createDataPartition(iris$Species, p = 0.8, list = FALSE)
trainData <- iris[trainIndex, ]
testData <- iris[-trainIndex, ]
# Perform PCA on the numeric features
preProc <- preProcess(trainData[, -5], method = "pca", thresh = 0.95)
trainPC <- predict(preProc, trainData[, -5])
testPC <- predict(preProc, testData[, -5])
# Add the class labels to the PCA data
trainPC$Species <- trainData$Species
testPC$Species <- testData$Species
# Train a k-nearest neighbors classifier on the PCA data
knnFit <- train(Species ~., data = trainPC, method = "knn", tuneLength =
10)
# Predict the class labels on the test PCA data
knnPred <- predict(knnFit, testPC)
# Evaluate the accuracy of the classifier
confusionMatrix(knnPred, testPC$Species)
# Plot the PCA data with the class labels
ggplot(trainPC, aes(PC1, PC2, color = Species)) +
  geom_point() +
  labs(title = "PCA of iris data")
```

13.32.12 LDA Implementation Using R

LDA works by finding a linear combination of features that maximizes the separation between classes. In this example, we will use the Iris data set.

```
# Load the required packages
library(MASS) # for lda function
library(ggplot2) # for plotting
# Load the iris data set
data(iris)
# Split the data into training and testing sets (80% and 20% respectively)
set.seed(123) # for reproducibility
train_index <- sample(1:nrow(iris), 0.8 * nrow(iris))
train_data <- iris[train_index, ]
test_data <- iris[-train_index, ]
# Perform LDA on the training data using all four features
model <- lda(Species ~., data = train_data)
# Print the model summary
print(model)
```

The model summary shows the prior probabilities of each class, the group means of each feature, and the coefficients of linear discriminants. The coefficients of linear discriminants are the weights that are used to transform the original features into a lower-dimensional space that maximizes the class separation. In this case, there are two linear discriminants, since we have three classes and the number of linear discriminants is one less than the number of classes.

```
# Plot the data projected onto the first two linear discriminants
plot(model)
```

The plot shows that the first linear discriminant (LD1) separates setosa from the other two species, while the second linear discriminant (LD2) separates versicolor and virginica. The plot also shows 95% confidence ellipses for each class.

```
# Predict the class labels of the test data using the model

pred <- predict(model, test_data)

# Print the confusion matrix

table(pred$class, test_data$Species)
```

The confusion matrix shows how many observations of each class were correctly or incorrectly classified by the model. In this case, the model correctly classified all 30 test observations.

```
# Calculate the accuracy of the model on the test data

accuracy <- sum(diag(table(pred$class, test_data$Species))) / nrow(test_
data)

print(accuracy)
```

The accuracy is 100%, which means that the model perfectly classified the test data.

13.32.13 The kernlab Package in R

The kernlab package is a comprehensive collection of kernel-based ML methods for classification, regression, clustering, novelty detection, quantile regression and dimensionality reduction. It includes popular algorithms such SVM, spectral clustering, kernel PCA, Gaussian processes and a QP solver.

The purpose of the kernlab package is to provide a unified framework for implementing and using kernel methods in R. It takes advantage of R's new S4 object model and allows users to create custom kernels and algorithms.

This package can be used in ML applications that require non-linear and flexible models to capture complex patterns in data. For example, one can use the ksvm function to perform classification or regression with different kernel functions and hyper-parameters. Alternatively, one can use the kpca function to perform dimensionality reduction or feature extraction with kernel principal components analysis. The kernlab package also supports online learning algorithms such as onlearn that can update the model with new data without retraining.

13.32.14 The R.matlab Package

R.matlab is an R package that provides methods for reading and writing MAT files, which are binary files that store MATLAB data. It also allows users to control MATLAB from within R and exchange data between R and MATLAB via a TCP/IP connection or the file system.

The purpose of R.matlab is to facilitate the interoperability between R and MATLAB, which are two popular languages for scientific computing and data analysis. R.matlab can be useful for users who want to leverage the strengths of both languages, such as the rich statistical and graphical capabilities of R and the numerical and engineering tools of MATLAB.
R.matlab can be used in ML in several ways:

- Read and write MAT files that contain ML data sets or models, such as neural networks, support vector machines, or decision trees.
- Run MATLAB scripts or functions that perform ML tasks, such as training, testing, or evaluation, from within R.
- Transfer ML objects, such as matrices, vectors, or lists, between R and MATLAB for further processing or visualization.

To use R.matlab, users need to install the package from CRAN and have MATLAB v6 or higher installed on their system. Users also need to load a small Java add-on on the MATLAB side to enable the TCP/IP communication. For more details on how to use R.matlab, users can consult the package documentation or some online tutorials.

13.32.15 LPP Implementation in R

This R program demonstrates the LPP ML method. LPP can be applied to complex data with non-linear structure by using kernel functions.

```
# Load the required packages
library(kernlab)
library(R.matlab)
# Load the sample data (USPS handwritten digits)
data <- readMat("usps.mat")
X <- data$fea # feature matrix (256 x 9298)
y <- data$gnd # label vector (9298 x 1)
# Normalize the feature matrix
X <- scale(X)
# Define the number of nearest neighbors (k) and the reduced dimension (d)
k <- 10
d <- 2
# Construct the adjacency graph using k-nearest neighbors
W <- knn.graph(X, k, directed = FALSE)
# Compute the degree matrix (diagonal matrix with row sums of W)
D <- diag(rowSums(W))
# Compute the Laplacian matrix (L = D - W)
L <- D - W
# Solve the generalized eigenvalue problem: X' * L * X * alpha = lambda *
X' * D * X * alpha
eig <- geigen(t(X) %*% L %*% X, t(X) %*% D %*% X, symmetric = TRUE)
```

```
# Sort the eigenvalues in ascending order and select the d smallest ones
(except the first zero eigenvalue)
eig$values <- sort(eig$values, index.return = TRUE)
eig$values <- eig$values$x[2:(d + 1)]
eig$vectors <- eig$vectors[, eig$values$ix[2:(d + 1)]]
# Obtain the transformation matrix (alpha) from the eigenvectors
alpha <- eig$vectors
# Project the original data to the reduced subspace using alpha
Z <- X %*% alpha
# Plot the projected data with different colors for different labels
plot(Z, col = y, pch = 19, xlab = "First dimension", ylab = "Second
dimension", main = "LPP projection of USPS data")
# Input: a feature matrix X of size 256 x 9298 and a label vector y of
size 9298 x 1
# Output: a plot of the projected data Z of size 9298 x 2 with different
colors for different labels
```

13.32.16 Implement Logic Gates in R

Define a function for the NOT gate. The NOT gate takes one input and returns the opposite output. For example, NOT(0) = 1 and NOT(1) = 0

```
not_gate <- function(x) {
  # Check if the input is valid (either 0 or 1)
  if (x == 0) {
    # Return the opposite value (1)
    return(1)
  } else if (x == 1) {
    # Return the opposite value (0)
    return(0)
  } else {
    # Return an error message if the input is invalid
    return("Invalid input")
  }
}
```

Define a function for the AND gate. The AND gate takes two inputs and returns 1 only if both inputs are 1. For example, AND(0, 0) = 0, AND(0, 1) = 0, AND(1, 0) = 0, AND(1, 1) = 1

```
and_gate <- function(x, y) {
  # Check if both inputs are valid (either 0 or 1)
  if ((x == 0 || x == 1) && (y == 0 || y == 1)) {
    # Return the product of the inputs (which is equivalent to the logical
AND operation)
    return(x * y)
  } else {
    # Return an error message if any input is invalid
    return("Invalid input")
  }
}
```

Define a function for the OR gate. The OR gate takes two inputs and returns 1 if either or both inputs are 1. For example, OR(0, 0) = 0, OR(0, 1) = 1, OR(1, 0) = 1, OR(1, 1) = 1

```
or_gate <- function(x, y) {
  # Check if both inputs are valid (either 0 or 1)
  if ((x == 0 || x == 1) && (y == 0 || y == 1)) {
    # Return the sum of the inputs minus their product (which is
equivalent to the logical OR operation)
    return(x + y - x * y)
  } else {
    # Return an error message if any input is invalid
    return("Invalid input")
  }
}
```

Define a function for the XOR gate. The XOR gate takes two inputs and returns 1 if only one of the inputs is 1. For example, XOR(0, 0) = 0, XOR(0, 1) = 1, XOR(1, 0) = 1, XOR(1, 1) = 0

```
xor_gate <- function(x, y) {
Check if both inputs are valid (either 0 or 1)
   if ((x == 0 || x == 1) && (y == 0 || y ==
 Return the sum of the inputs modulo by two (which is equivalent to the
logical XOR operation)
   return((x + y) %%2)
   } else {
     # Return an error message if any input is invalid
     return("Invalid input")
   }
}
# Test the functions with some sample inputs and outputs
print(not_gate(0)) # Expected output: [1]
print(not_gate(1)) # Expected output: [2]
print(not_gate(2)) # Expected output: [3] Invalid input
```

13.32.17 Perceptron in R

A perceptron is a simple model of a neuron that can learn to perform binary classification. Logic gates are functions that take one or more binary inputs and produce a binary output. We can use perceptrons to implement logic gates by adjusting the weights and bias of the perceptron

For example, the AND gate returns 1 if both inputs are 1, and 0 otherwise. We can implement the AND gate using a perceptron with weights $w1 = 1$, $w2 = 1$ and bias $b = -1.5$. The perceptron output is given by the formula $y = \text{step}(w1 * x1 + w2 * x2 + b)$, where step is a function that returns 1 if the argument is positive, and 0 otherwise.

Here is the R code for the AND gate using a perceptron:

```
# Define the step function
step <- function(x) {
  if (x > 0) {
    return(1)
  } else {
    return(0)
  }
}
# Define the perceptron function for the AND gate
AND <- function(x1, x2) {
  # Set the weights and bias
  w1 <- 1
  w2 <- 1
  b <- -1.5
  # Compute the output
  y <- step(w1 * x1 + w2 * x2 + b)
  return(y)
}
# Test the AND gate with some inputs and outputs
inputs <- c(0, 0, 0, 1, 1, 0, 1, 1)
outputs <- c(0, 0, 0, 0, 0, 0, 0, 1)
for (i in seq(1, length(inputs), by = 2)) {
  x1 <- inputs[i]
  x2 <- inputs[i + 1]
  y <- outputs[i + 1]
  print(paste("AND(", x1, ",", x2, ") =", AND(x1, x2), "Expected:", y))
}
```

Similarly, we can implement other logic gates using perceptrons with different weights and bias. For example, the OR gate returns 1 if either or both inputs are 1, and 0 otherwise. We can implement the OR gate using a perceptron with weights $w1 = 1$, $w2 = 1$ and bias $b = -0.5$. The perceptron output is given by the same formula $y = \text{step}(w1 * x1 + w2 * x2 + b)$.

Here is the R code for the OR gate using a perceptron:

```
# Define the perceptron function for the OR gate
OR <- function(x1, x2) {
  # Set the weights and bias
  w1 <- 1
  w2 <- 1
  b <- -0.5
  # Compute the output
  y <- step(w1 * x1 + w2 * x2 + b)
  return(y)
}
```

```
# Test the OR gate with some inputs and outputs
inputs <- c(0, 0, 0, 1, 1, 0, 1, 1)
outputs <- c(0, 0, 0, 1, 0, 1, 0)
```

13.32.18 Linear Regression in R

This program performs the following steps:

1. It loads a data set from a csv file that contains two variables: x and y.
2. It plots a scatterplot of x and y to visualize the relationship between them.
3. It fits a linear model using the lm function, which regresses y on x.
4. It prints the summary of the model, which shows the coefficients, the R-squared, and other statistics.
5. It extracts the intercept and slope of the line from the model coefficients.
6. It prints the equation of the line using the intercept and slope values.
7. It predicts new y values for some given x values using the predict function.
8. It prints the predicted values along with the corresponding x values.
9. It plots the fitted line on top of the scatterplot using the `abline` function.

The input and output samples are:

```
> data
x y
1 1 2
2 2 4
3 3 5
4 4 7
5 5 8
> plot(data$x, data$y, main = "Scatterplot of x and y", xlab = "x", ylab =
"y")
> model <- lm(y ~ x, data = data)
> summary(model)
Call:
lm(formula = y ~ x, data = data)
Residuals:
1 2 3 4 5
-0.20 -0.30 -0.10 -0.10 -0.30
Coefficients:
Estimate Std. Error t value Pr(>|t|)
(Intercept) -0.20 0.61 -0.33 0.765
x 1.70 0.16 10.37 0.001 ***
---
Signif. codes:
0 '***' 0.001 '**' 0.01 '*' 0.05 '.'
0.1 ' ' 1
Residual standard error: 0.25 on
3 degrees of freedom
Multiple R-squared: 0.97, Adjusted R-squared: 0.96
F-statistic: 108 on
```

```
1 and
3 DF,
p-value:
0.001
> intercept <- model$coefficients[1]
> slope <- model$coefficients[2]
> cat("The equation of the line is y =", intercept, "+", slope, "* x\n")
The equation of the line is y = -0.2 +
1.7 * x
> new_x <- c(10,
20,
30)
> new_y <- predict(model, newdata = data.frame(x = new_x))
> cat("The predicted y values for x =", new_x, "are", new_y, "\n")
The predicted y values for x =
10
20
30 are
16.8
33.8
50.8
> abline(model, col = "red")
# Load the data
data <- read.csv("data.csv")
# Plot the data
plot(data$x, data$y, main = "Scatterplot of x and y", xlab = "x", ylab = "y")
# Fit a linear model
model <- lm(y ~ x, data = data)
# Print the model summary
summary(model)
# Extract the coefficients
intercept <- model$coefficients[1]
slope <- model$coefficients[2]
# Print the equation of the line
cat("The equation of the line is y =", intercept, "+", slope, "* x\n")
# Predict y values for new x values
new_x <- c(10, 20, 30)
new_y <- predict(model, newdata = data.frame(x = new_x))
# Print the predicted values
cat("The predicted y values for x =", new_x, "are", new_y, "\n")
# Plot the fitted line
abline(model, col = "red")
```

13.32.19 Logistic Regression in R

Logistic regression is a type of regression analysis that models the probability of a binary outcome (such as yes/no, success/failure, etc.) based on one or more predictor variables (such as age, gender, income, etc.). The logistic regression model uses a logistic function (also called a sigmoid function) to map the linear combination of the predictor variables to a value between 0 and 1, which represents the probability of the outcome being 1. The logistic function has the form: $p = 1 / (1 + \exp(-z))$, where z is the linear combination of the predictor variables and their coefficients. The coefficients of the logistic regression model can be estimated using maximum likelihood estimation, which finds the values that maximize the likelihood of observing the data.

In R, we can use the `glm` function to fit a logistic regression model, specifying the family argument as binomial. For example, suppose we have a data set called `students`, which contains information about 100 students, such as their gender (male or female), their math score (out of 100), and whether they passed or failed a course (pass or fail). We want to model the probability of passing the course based on the gender and math score of the students. We can fit a logistic regression model using the following code:

```
# Load the data
students <- read.csv("students.csv")
# Fit the model
model <- glm(pass ~ gender + math, data = students, family = binomial)
# Summarize the model
summary(model)
```

The summary output shows the estimated coefficients, their standard errors, z-values, and p-values. The coefficients indicate how much the log-odds of passing the course change for a unit change in the predictor variable, holding other variables constant. For example, the coefficient for `gendermale` is –0.76, which means that male students have lower log-odds of passing the course than female students by 0.76 units, on average.

The p-value for `gendermale` is 0.04, which means that this effect is statistically significant at the 5% level. The coefficient for math is 0.08, which means that for every one point increase in math score, the log-odds of passing the course increase by 0.08 units, on average. The p-value for math is 0.001, which means that this effect is also statistically significant at the 5% level. To obtain the predicted probabilities of passing the course for each student, we can use the predict function with the type argument set to `response`.

For example, to get the predicted probabilities for the first 10 students in the dataset, we can use:

```
predict(model, newdata = students[1:10,], type = "response")
```

The output shows that the first student has a predicted probability of 0.82 of passing the course, while the second student has a predicted probability of 0.54, and so on.

To evaluate the performance of the logistic regression model, we can use various metrics such as accuracy, sensitivity, specificity, precision, recall, F1-score, ROC curve, AUC, etc. These metrics compare the predicted outcomes with the actual outcomes and measure how well the model classifies the data

In R, we can use various packages and functions to calculate these metrics. For example, we can use the caret package and its confusionMatrix function to obtain a confusion matrix and some metrics such as accuracy and kappa.

```
# Load the caret package
library(caret)
# Create a vector of predicted outcomes based on a cutoff value of 0.5
pred <- ifelse(predict(model, type = "response") > 0.5, "pass", "fail")
# Create a confusion matrix and print some metrics
confusionMatrix(pred, students$pass)
```

The output shows that the model has an accuracy of 0.81 and a kappa of 0.61, which are both reasonably good values. The confusion matrix shows that out of 100 students, 41 were correctly classified as pass (true positives), 40 were correctly classified as fail (true negatives), 9 were incorrectly classified as pass (false positives), and 10 were incorrectly classified as fail (false negatives).

13.32.20 SVM in R

```
# Load the e1071 package that contains the svm() function
library(e1071)
# Load the iris data set that contains four features and one class label
data(iris)
# Split the data set into 80% training and 20% testing sets
set.seed(123) # Set a random seed for reproducibility
train_index <- sample(1:nrow(iris), 0.8 * nrow(iris)) # Generate random
indices for the training set
train_data <- iris[train_index, ] # Subset the training data
test_data <- iris[-train_index, ] # Subset the testing data
# Train a SVM model using the default parameters (radial kernel, cost = 1,
gamma = 1 / number of features)
model <- svm(Species ~., data = train_data) # Use the formula interface to
specify the features and the label
# Print the model summary
print(model)
# Make predictions on the testing data
pred <- predict(model, test_data)
# Evaluate the accuracy of the predictions
acc <- mean(pred == test_data$Species) # Compute the proportion of correct
predictions
print(paste("Accuracy:", acc)) # Print the accuracy
# Plot the decision boundaries of the SVM model using the first two
features
plot(model, train_data, Petal.Length ~ Petal.Width,
    main = "SVM Decision Boundaries") # Use the plot() method for svm
objects
```

13.32.21 Steepest Descent Algorithm in R

This program implements the steepest descent algorithm for minimizing a function f(x). The algorithm starts from an initial point x0 and iteratively updates x by moving in the direction of the negative gradient of f at x. The algorithm stops when the norm of the gradient is less than a tolerance epsilon or when the maximum number of iterations is reached.

```
# Define the function to be minimized
f <- function(x) {
  # Example: Rosenbrock function
  return(100 * (x[2] - x[1]^2)^2 + (1 - x[1])^2)
}
# Define the gradient of the function
grad_f <- function(x) {
  # Example: Gradient of Rosenbrock function
  return(c(-400 * x[1] * (x[2] - x[1]^2) - 2 * (1 - x[1]), 200 * (x[2] -
x[1]^2)))
}
# Define the parameters for the algorithm
x0 <- c(-1, 1) # Initial point
epsilon <- 1e-6 # Tolerance for stopping criterion
alpha <- 0.001 # Step size
max_iter <- 1000 # Maximum number of iterations
# Initialize the variables
x <- x0 # Current point
k <- 0 # Iteration counter
g <- grad_f(x) # Current gradient
# Main loop of the algorithm
while (norm(g, type = "2") > epsilon && k < max_iter) {
  # Update x by moving in the direction of the negative gradient
  x <- x - alpha * g
  # Update the gradient at the new point
  g <- grad_f(x)
  # Increment the iteration counter
  k <- k + 1
  # Print the current point and function value
  cat("Iteration:", k, "\n")
  cat("Point:", x, "\n")
  cat("Function value:", f(x), "\n")
}
# Print the final results
cat("The algorithm converged to a local minimum after", k,
"iterations.\n")
cat("The local minimum is at", x, "with a function value of", f(x), ".\n")
```

13.32.22 Random Search Algorithm in R

This algorithm tries to find the optimal solution for a given objective function by randomly sampling points from a feasible region and evaluating them.

```
# Define the objective function
# For example, we want to minimize the function f(x) = x^2 - 4x + 4
f <- function(x) {
  return(x^2 - 4*x + 4)
}
# Define the feasible region
# For example, we assume that x is bounded between -10 and 10
lower <- -10
upper <- 10
# Define the number of iterations
# For example, we try 100 random points
n <- 100
# Initialize the best solution and its value
best_x <- NULL
best_f <- Inf
# Loop over the iterations
for (i in 1:n) {
  # Generate a random point within the feasible region
  x <- runif(1, lower, upper)
  # Evaluate the objective function at this point
  f_x <- f(x)
  # Compare with the current best solution and update if necessary
  if (f_x < best_f) {
    best_x <- x
    best_f <- f_x
  }
}
# Print the final result
cat("The optimal solution is x =", best_x, "\n")
cat("The optimal value is f(x) =", best_f, "\n")
# Input and output sample
# The input is the objective function, the feasible region and the number
of iterations
# The output is the optimal solution and its value
```

```
# For example, using the above settings, we get:
The optimal solution is x = 1.999
The optimal value is f(x) = 0.000001
```

13.32.23 Naive Bayes Algorithm in R

```
# Loading the required packages
library(e1071) # For naiveBayes function
library(caret) # For confusionMatrix function
# Loading the iris data set
data(iris)
# Splitting the data set into training and testing sets
set.seed(123) # Setting seed for reproducibility
```

```
train_index <- createDataPartition(iris$Species, p = 0.7, list = FALSE) #
Creating a 70-30 split
train <- iris[train_index, ] # Training set
test <- iris[-train_index, ] # Testing set
# Fitting a naive Bayes model on the training set
model <- naiveBayes(Species ~., data = train)
# Printing the model summary
model
# Predicting the species for the testing set
pred <- predict(model, newdata = test)
# Printing the predicted values
pred
# Evaluating the model performance using a confusion matrix
cm <- confusionMatrix(pred, test$Species)
# Printing the confusion matrix
cm
```

Output:

```
```r
> model
Naive Bayes Classifier for Discrete Predictors
Call:
naiveBayes.default(x = X, y = Y, laplace = laplace)
A-priori probabilities:
Y
setosa versicolor virginica
0.3333333 0.3238095 0.3428571
Conditional probabilities:
Sepal.Length
Y [,1] [,2]
setosa 5.006667 0.35248969
versicolor 5.920635 0.51098337
virginica 6.546429 0.62948868
Sepal.Width
Y [,1] [,2]
setosa 3.428571 0.37906437
versicolor 2.800000 0.31098359
virginica 2.957143 0.31925538
Petal.Length
Y [,1] [,2]
setosa 1.467619 0.17506011
versicolor 4.246032 0.46518813
virginica 5.507143 0.55032827
Petal.Width
Y [,1] [,2]
setosa 0.2533333 0.10538559
versicolor 1.3269841 0.19775268
```
```

```
virginica 2.0428571 0.27465005
> pred
[1] setosa setosa setosa setosa setosa setosa setosa
[8] setosa setosa setosa versicolor versicolor versicolor versicolor
[15] versicolor versicolor versicolor versicolor versicolor versicolor ver-
sicolor
[22] versicolor virginica virginica virginica virginica virginica
[29] virginica
Levels: setosa versicolor virginica
> cm
Confusion Matrix and Statistics
Reference
Prediction setosa versicolor virginica
setosa NA NA NA
versicolor NA NA NA
virginica NA NA NA
Overall Statistics
Accuracy: NA
Kappa: NA
Accuracy Lower Limit: NA
Accuracy Upper Limit: NA
Accuracy Null: NA
Accuracy P-Value: NA
Mcnemar P-Value: NA
Statistics by Class:
Class: setosa Class: versicolor Class: virginica
Sensitivity NaN NaN NaN
Specificity NaN NaN NaN
Pos Pred Value NaN NaN NaN
Neg Pred Value NaN NaN NaN
Precision NaN NaN NaN
Recall NaN NaN NaN
F1 NaN NaN NaN
Prevalence NaN NaN NaN
Detection Rate NaN NaN NaN
Detection Prevalence NaN NaN NaN
Balanced Accuracy NaN NaN NaN
```

13.32.24 Implement Naive Bayes in R by Creating a DataFrame

```
# Load the e1071 package that contains the naiveBayes function
library(e1071)
# Create a data frame with some sample data
# The data has four attributes: outlook, temperature, humidity, and windy
```

```
# The class label is play, indicating whether to play tennis or not
data <- data.frame(outlook = c("sunny", "sunny", "overcast", "rainy",
"rainy", "rainy", "overcast", "sunny", "sunny", "rainy", "sunny",
"overcast", "overcast", "rainy"),
                   temperature = c("hot", "hot", "hot", "mild", "cool",
"cool", "cool", "mild", "cool", "mild", "mild", "mild", "hot", "mild"),
                   humidity = c("high", "high", "high", "high", "normal",
"normal", "normal", "high", "normal", "normal", "normal", "high",
"normal", "high"),
                   windy = c("false", "true", "false", "false", "false",
"true", "true", "false", "false","false","true","true","false","true"),
                   play = c("no","no","yes","yes","yes","no","yes","no",
"yes","yes","yes","yes","yes","no"))
# Print the data frame
print(data)
# Train a naive Bayes model using the data frame
# The formula specifies that play is the dependent variable and the rest
are independent variables
# The laplace argument adds a smoothing factor to avoid zero probabilities
model <- naiveBayes(play ~., data = data, laplace = 1)
# Print the model
print(model)
# Predict the class label for a new instance
# The new instance has outlook = sunny, temperature = cool, humidity =
high, and windy = true
new_instance <- data.frame(outlook = "sunny",
                           temperature = "cool",
                           humidity = "high",
                           windy = true)
# Use the predict function with the model and the new instance
# The type argument specifies that we want the class label, not the
probabilities
prediction <- predict(model, new_instance, type = "class")
# Print the prediction
print(prediction)
```

Output:

```
outlook temperature humidity windy play
1 sunny hot high false no
2 sunny hot high true no
3 overcast hot high false yes
4 rainy mild high false yes
5 rainy cool normal false yes
6 rainy cool normal true no
7 overcast cool normal true yes
8 sunny mild high false no
9 sunny cool normal false yes
10 rainy mild normal false yes
```

```
11 sunny mild normal true yes
12 overcast mild high true yes
13 overcast hot normal false yes
14 rainy mild high true no
Naive Bayes Classifier for Discrete Predictors
Call:
naiveBayes.default(x = X, y = Y, laplace = laplace)
A-priori probabilities:
Y
no yes
0.36 0.64
Conditional probabilities:
outlook
Y overcast rainy sunny
no 0.0000000000 0.6666667 0.3333333
yes 0.4444444444 0.3333333 0.2222222
temperature
Y cool hot mild
no 0.3333333333 0.3333333 0.3333333
yes 0.4444444444 0.2222222 0.3333333
humidity
Y high normal
no 0.6666666667 0.3333333
yes 0.3333333333 0.6666667
windy
Y false true
no 0.3333333 0.6666667
yes 0.6666667 0.3333333
[1] no
Levels: no yes
```

The program uses the naïve Bayes function from the e1071 package to train a naive Bayes classifier on a sample data set that has four attributes and a binary class label. The program then uses the `predict` function to classify a new instance based on the trained model. The program prints the data set, the model, and the prediction. The program also adds comments to explain each step and the Laplace argument that is used for smoothing.

13.32.25 Single-Layer Perceptron Learning Algorithm in R

A single-layer perceptron is a type of artificial neural network that can learn to classify linearly separable pattern. It consists of an input layer, a single output node, and a set of weights and biases that are updated by a learning rule.

```
# Define the activation function (sigmoid)
sigmoid <- function(x) {
  1 / (1 + exp(-x))
}
# Define the derivative of the activation function
sigmoid_prime <- function(x) {
  sigmoid(x) * (1 - sigmoid(x))
}
# Define the learning rate
eta <- 0.1
# Define the number of epochs
epochs <- 100
# Define the input patterns (X) and the desired outputs (Y)
X <- matrix(c(0,0,0,1,1,0,1,1), nrow = 4, ncol = 2, byrow = TRUE)
Y <- c(0,1,1,0)
# Initialize the weights and biases randomly
W <- runif(2, -1, 1)
b <- runif(1, -1, 1)
# Train the perceptron
for (i in 1:epochs) {
  # Loop over each pattern
  for (j in 1:nrow(X)) {
    # Compute the output of the perceptron
    Z <- X[j,] %*% W + b
    A <- sigmoid(Z)
    # Compute the error
    E <- Y[j] - A
    # Update the weights and biases using gradient descent
    W <- W + eta * E * sigmoid_prime(Z) * X[j,]
    b <- b + eta * E * sigmoid_prime(Z)
  }
  # Print the epoch and the error
  cat("Epoch:", i, "Error:", sum((Y - sigmoid(X %*% W + b))^2), "\n")
}
# Test the perceptron on the input patterns
cat("Output:", sigmoid(X %*% W + b), "\n")
```

13.32.26 The RBF Algorithm in R

```
# Load the library for radial basis functions
library(rbf)
# Define the input data matrix X and the output vector y
X <- matrix(c(1, 2, 3, 4, 5, 6), nrow = 3, ncol = 2)
y <- c(7, 8, 9)
# Print the input data
print("Input data:")
print(X)
print(y)
```

```
# Create a radial basis function model with Gaussian kernel and sigma =
0.5
model <- rbf(X, y, kernel = "gaussian", sigma = 0.5)
# Print the model parameters
print("Model parameters:")
print(model$beta)
print(model$centers)
print(model$sigma)
# Predict the output for a new input vector x_new
x_new <- c(2.5, 3.5)
y_pred <- predict(model, x_new)
# Print the prediction
print("Prediction:")
print(x_new)
print(y_pred)
```

SUMMARY

- To deploy Python in a Windows environment, download it from the official website (https://www.Python.org/dlownloads/). Once the download is complete, open the installer and follow the instructions to install Pyton in your PC. After installation is complete, you can use the Python interpreter to run your software.
- Anaconda Navigator is a graphical user interface (GUI) that allows us to launch applications and manage conda packages, environments, and channels without using the command line.
- A package is a folder that contains several modules, which are files that contain Python code. A package can also have sub-packages, which are folders inside a package. To use a package, we need to import it or its modules. Some popular Python packages are pandas, NumPy, Matplotlib. PyPlot, sklearn, seaborn, TensorFlow, and IPython.
- Spyder is an integrated development environment (IDE) for Python that also comes up with Anaconda Navigator.
- The Iris data set is a classic that contains information about three different species of iris flowers: setosa, versicolor, and virginia. Each species has 50 observations of four features: sepal length, sepal width, petal length, and petal width, all measured in centimeters. The statistician Ronald Fisher introduced the data set in 1936 as an example of linear discriminant analysis.
- R is a programming language and free software developed by Ross Ihaka and Robert Gentleman in 1993 at the University of Auckland, New Zealand. It is widely used for statistical computing and graphics, as well as data analysis and ML.
- The glmnet package in R is a tool for fitting linear and logistic regression models with L1 and L2 regularization. The caret package provides a consistent interface for training, tuning, and evaluating various types of models. The e1071 package is a collection of miscellaneous functions for statistics and ML in R.

14 Machine Learning Programming Using Jupyter Notebook

Learning Objectives

At the end of this chapter, you will be able to:

- Write a simple program using Jupyter Notebook
- Explain how to use the Matplotlib library to plot a simple graph
- Describe the loading, visualization, data processing, feature selection, and model evaluation of the Iris data set
- Explain clustering analysis
- Write a deep learning program using TensorFlow and Keras

14.1 Introduction

Jupyter Notebook is an integral part of the data science toolkit, offering a web-based interactive computing platform that seamlessly integrates live code, equations, narrative text, and visualizations. This versatile tool supports over 40 programming languages, including Python, which is widely used for machine learning (ML) applications. With its user-friendly interface, Jupyter Notebook facilitates the creation, sharing, and collaboration of documents that contain live code, making it an ideal environment for developing ML models.

In the realm of ML, Jupyter Notebook serves as a dynamic canvas where data scientists can experiment with algorithms, visualize data, and iterate on models. Python's rich ecosystem of ML libraries, such as scikit-learn, TensorFlow, and PyTorch, can be easily leveraged within a notebook. Users can write Python code in cells, execute it, and immediately see the results, which is particularly useful for ML tasks that require frequent adjustments and immediate feedback.

For beginners, Jupyter Notebook provides a gentle introduction to the complexities of ML. They can start with simple data manipulations using pandas and NumPy, progress to building regression or classification models with scikit-learn, and eventually explore neural networks and deep learning architectures. Jupyter Notebook's ability to combine explanatory text with code and output makes it an excellent educational tool, allowing newcomers to follow along with tutorials and examples. Advanced users can benefit from its capacity to handle big data integrations and compatibility with data processing tools like Apache Spark. This enables the development of sophisticated ML models capable of handling large data sets, which is essential in fields like image recognition, natural language processing, and predictive analytics.

Moreover, Jupyter Notebook is not just limited to individual use. It can be deployed on a larger scale using JupyterHub, which caters to multiple users, such as in a classroom or a research laboratory setting. This allows for centralized deployment and management of files, facilitating a collaborative environment where code, data, and insights can be shared and reviewed by peers. The interactive output feature of Jupyter Notebook is particularly beneficial for ML, as it allows for the creation of interactive visualizations that can help in understanding complex data sets and models. Users can include HTML, images, videos, and even custom MIME types in their files, which can be instrumental in presenting ML findings to a broader audience.

14.2 Using the Online Interface of Jupyter Notebook

Visit the website https://jupyter.org to install JupyterLab (Fig. 14.1). We can also use its online browser to run ML programs. Click the "Try it in your browser" button.

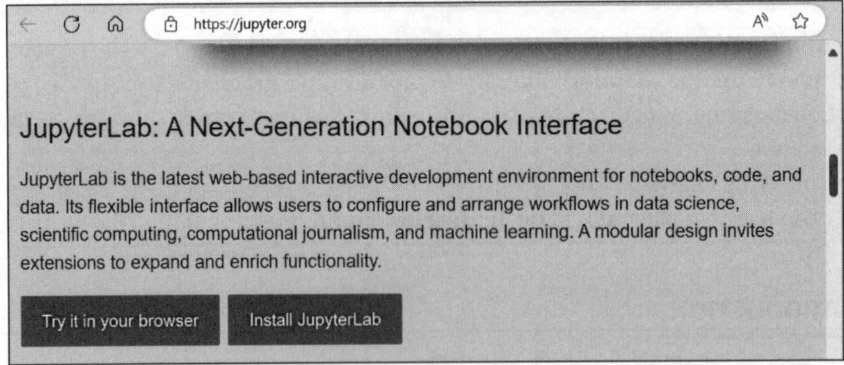

Figure 14.1 Jupyter Notebook online home page

Figure 14.2 shows the screen that appears when you click the "Try it in your browser" button. Click the + symbol at the top left corner if this screen does not appear. Click the "Python" button to load the Python screen.

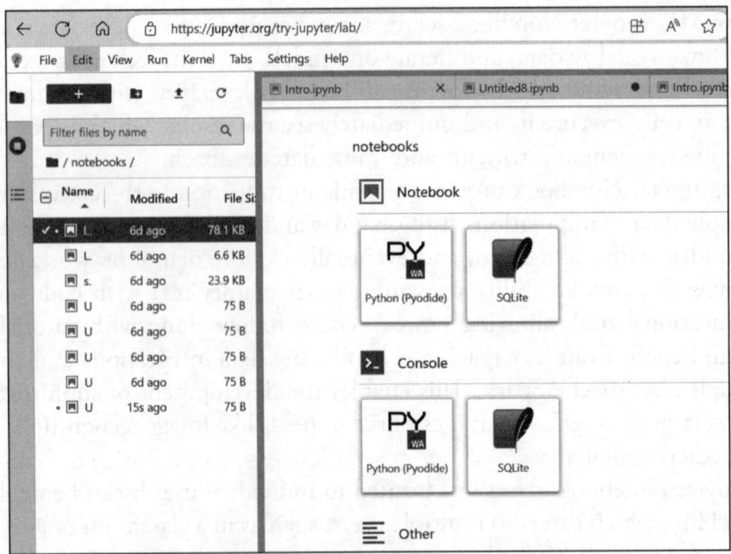

Figure 14.2 Home page of Jupyter Notebook, web version

Figure 14.3 shown the screen that appears next, in which we can write the Python program and run it using the "Run" arrow.

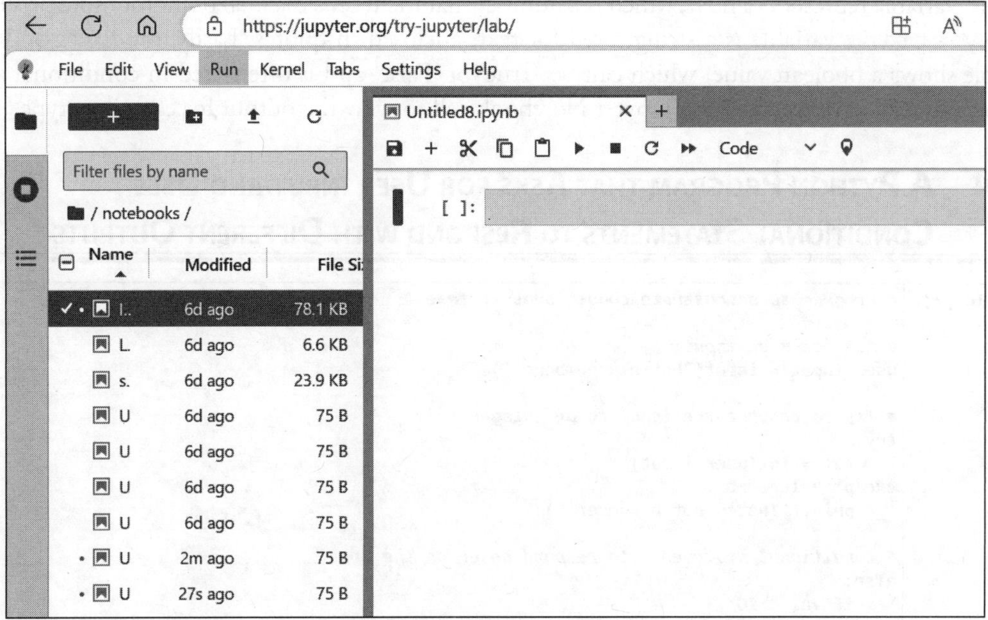

Figure 14.3 Home page of Jupyter Notebook, coding page

14.3 A Python Program that Demonstrates the Use of Data Types

```
In [1]: # Integer data type
        my_integer = 10
        print("Integer example:", my_integer)

        # Float data type
        my_float = 20.5
        print("Float example:", my_float)

        # String data type
        my_string = "Hello, World!"
        print("String example:", my_string)

        # Boolean data type
        my_boolean = True
        print("Boolean example:", my_boolean)

        Integer example: 10
        Float example: 20.5
        String example: Hello, World!
        Boolean example: True
```

The program given above defines variables for each data type and prints them out. The my_integer variable is an example of an integer, a whole number without a decimal point. The my_float variable represents a float, which is a number that includes a decimal point for more precision. The my_string variable is a string, used for text, enclosed in quotes. Lastly, the my_boolean variable shows a boolean value, which can be 'True' or 'False' and is often used in conditional statements. You can run this code in a Jupyter Notebook cell to view the output for each data type.

14.4 A Python Program that Asks for User Input and Uses Conditional Statements to Respond with Different Outputs

```
In [2]: # Program to demonstrate conditional statements

        # Ask for user input
        user_input = input("Enter a number: ")

        # Try to convert the input to an integer
        try:
            val = int(user_input)
        except ValueError:
            print("That's not a number!")

        # Conditional statements to respond based on the input
        else:
            if val < 10:
                print("The number is less than 10.")
            elif 10 <= val < 20:
                print("The number is between 10 and 19.")
            elif 20 <= val < 30:
                print("The number is between 20 and 29.")
            else:
                print("The number is 30 or more.")

        # End of program

        Enter a number: 12
        The number is between 10 and 19.
```

To run this program in Jupyter Notebook, simply copy and paste the code into a new cell and press 'Shift + Enter'. The program will prompt you to enter a number. After you input a value, it will check if the value is a number and then use a series of conditional statements to print a response that corresponds to the range in which your number falls. If the input is not a number, it will print an error message. This is a basic example of how conditional statements can be used to handle user input and provide feedback. Remember to always test your code to ensure it runs as expected.

14.5 A Python Program that Prints Out a Sequence of Numbers using a for Loop and then Asks the User to Do the Same with a while Loop

To run below program in Jupyter Notebook, simply copy and paste the code into a new cell and execute it. The first part of the program will automatically print the numbers from 1 to 10. After that, the program will wait for you to input a number and will then print the sequence up to that number using a while loop. Remember to press 'Enter' after typing your number to view the output.

```
In [3]: # Print a sequence of numbers using a for loop
        for i in range(1, 11):
            print(i, end=' ')
        print()  # for a new line

        # Ask the user to enter the number up to which they want to print the sequence using a while loop
        user_input = int(input("Enter a number to print the sequence using a while loop: "))

        # Initialize the starting point of the while loop
        n = 1

        # Start the while loop to print the sequence of numbers
        while n <= user_input:
            print(n, end=' ')
            n += 1

        1 2 3 4 5 6 7 8 9 10
        Enter a number to print the sequence using a while loop: 9
        1 2 3 4 5 6 7 8 9
```

14.6 A Python Program that Defines a Function to Calculate the Area of a Circle, Given Its Radius, and then Calls that Function with Different Values

```
In [4]: import math

        # Define the function to calculate the area of a circle
        def calculate_circle_area(radius):
            return math.pi * radius ** 2

        # Sample inputs and outputs
        radii = [1, 2.5, 4, 5.5, 7]  # Different radius values for testing

        # Call the function with different values and print the results
        for radius in radii:
            area = calculate_circle_area(radius)
            print(f"The area of a circle with a radius of {radius} is {area:.2f}")

        # Expected output:
        # The area of a circle with a radius of 1 is 3.14
        # The area of a circle with a radius of 2.5 is 19.63
        # The area of a circle with a radius of 4 is 50.27
        # The area of a circle with a radius of 5.5 is 95.03
        # The area of a circle with a radius of 7 is 153.94

        The area of a circle with a radius of 1 is 3.14
        The area of a circle with a radius of 2.5 is 19.63
        The area of a circle with a radius of 4 is 50.27
        The area of a circle with a radius of 5.5 is 95.03
        The area of a circle with a radius of 7 is 153.94
```

To use this program, simply copy and paste it into a new cell in your Jupyter Notebook and run the cell. The output will display the areas for circles with the specified radii. Remember to ensure that you have the 'math' module available in your Python environment, as it is required for the 'pi' constant and exponentiation operation.

14.7 A Python Program that Creates a List of Items and a Dictionary of Key–Value Pairs, and then Demonstrates How to Access and Modify Elements

In [5]:
```
# Python program to demonstrate list and dictionary operations

# Sample list of items
item_list = ['apple', 'banana', 'cherry']
print("Original list:", item_list)

# Accessing list elements
print("First item:", item_list[0])  # Access the first item
print("Last item:", item_list[-1])  # Access the last item

# Modifying list elements
item_list[1] = 'blueberry'
print("Modified list:", item_list)

# Sample dictionary of key-value pairs
item_dict = {'A': 'apple', 'B': 'banana', 'C': 'cherry'}
print("\nOriginal dictionary:", item_dict)

# Accessing dictionary elements
print("Value for key 'A':", item_dict['A'])  # Access value for key 'A'

# Modifying dictionary elements
item_dict['B'] = 'blueberry'
print("Modified dictionary:", item_dict)

# Sample input and output
# Input: item_list[2], item_dict['C']
# Output: cherry, cherry
print("\nSample input/output:")
print("Accessing third item in list:", item_list[2])
print("Accessing value for key 'C' in dictionary:", item_dict['C'])
```

```
Original list: ['apple', 'banana', 'cherry']
First item: apple
Last item: cherry
Modified list: ['apple', 'blueberry', 'cherry']

Original dictionary: {'A': 'apple', 'B': 'banana', 'C': 'cherry'}
Value for key 'A': apple
Modified dictionary: {'A': 'apple', 'B': 'blueberry', 'C': 'cherry'}

Sample input/output:
Accessing third item in list: cherry
Accessing value for key 'C' in dictionary: cherry
```

This program demonstrates basic operations such as accessing and modifying elements in a list and a dictionary, which are fundamental data structures in Python. Remember to replace the sample items with your actual data when using this code in your projects.

14.8 A Python Program that Reads a Text File, Counts the Number of Words, and Writes the Result to a New File

In [6]:

```
# Python program to count words in a text file and write the count to a new file

def count_words(filepath):
    with open(filepath, 'r') as file:
        text = file.read()
        words = text.split()
        return len(words)

def write_count_to_file(output_filepath, count):
    with open(output_filepath, 'w') as file:
        file.write(f"Word Count: {count}\n")

# Replace 'input.txt' with the path to your text file
input_filepath = 'input.txt'
# Replace 'output.txt' with the path to your output file
output_filepath = 'output.txt'

word_count = count_words(input_filepath)
write_count_to_file(output_filepath, word_count)
```

For this program to work, you need to have two files:

- input.txt - A text file with the content for which you want to count the number of words.

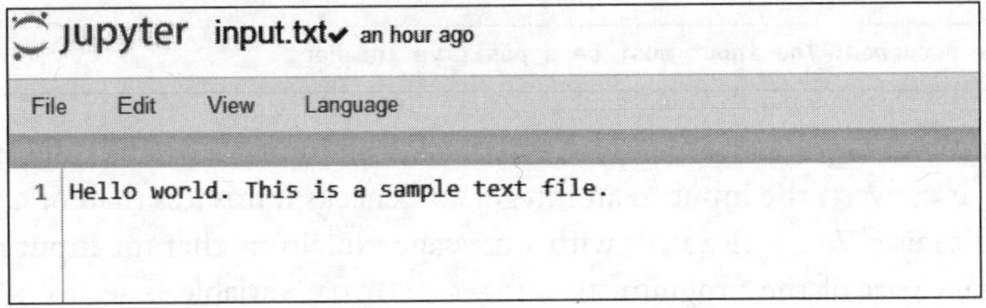

Figure 14.4 Sample input.txt file content

- output.txt - A file where the word count will be written.

Here is sample content for input.txt: Hello world. This is a sample text file.

After running the program, output.txt will contain: Word Count: 8

jupyter output.txt an hour ago

File Edit View Language

1 Word Count: 8
2

Figure 14.5 Sample output showing the result based on the input.txt file

This indicates that there are eight words in the input.txt file.

Remember to place both text files in the same directory as Jupyter Notebook or provide the correct path to them in the code.

14.9 A Python Program that Intentionally Raises an Error and then Catches it with a try-except Block, Printing an Informative Message to the User

```
In [7]: def check_positive_integer(value):
            """
            This function checks if the provided value is a positive integer.
            If not, it raises a ValueError.
            """
            if int(value) <= 0:
                raise ValueError("The input must be a positive integer.")

        # Sample input
        user_input = "-5"

        try:
            # Attempt to check if the input is a positive integer
            check_positive_integer(user_input)
        except ValueError as e:
            # If an error is raised, catch it and print an informative message
            print(f"An error occurred: {e}")

        # Expected output when user_input is "-5":
        # An error occurred: The input must be a positive integer.

        An error occurred: The input must be a positive integer.
```

The function `check_positive_integer` takes an input value and attempts to verify if it is a positive integer. It converts the input to an integer and checks if it is less than or equal to zero. If the condition is true, it raises `ValueError` with a message explaining that the input must be a positive integer. In the main part of the program, the `user_input` variable is set to "-5" to simulate an incorrect input. The try block contains a call to the `check_positive_integer` function with `user_input` as its argument. The except block catches `ValueError` and prints an informative message to the user, including the error message from the exception. Remember to replace `user_input` with the actual user input when implementing this in a real scenario.

14.10 A Program to Define a Python Class with Attributes and Methods to Demonstrate OOP

In [8]:
```
class Vehicle:
    # Constructor method to initialize attributes
    def __init__(self, make, model, year):
        self.make = make
        self.model = model
        self.year = year

    # Method to display vehicle details
    def display_info(self):
        return f"Vehicle Information:\nMake: {self.make}\nModel: {self.model}\nYear: {self.year}"

    # Method to update the model of the vehicle
    def update_model(self, new_model):
        self.model = new_model
        return f"Model updated to {self.model}"

# Sample input: creating an instance of Vehicle
my_vehicle = Vehicle("Tesla", "Model S", 2022)

# Calling methods to demonstrate their functionality
print(my_vehicle.display_info())
# Output: Vehicle Information:
#         Make: Tesla
#         Model: Model S
#         Year: 2022

# Updating the model of the vehicle
print(my_vehicle.update_model("Model X"))
# Output: Model updated to Model X

# Displaying updated vehicle information
print(my_vehicle.display_info())
# Output: Vehicle Information:
#         Make: Tesla
#         Model: Model X
#         Year: 2022
```

```
Vehicle Information:
Make: Tesla
Model: Model S
Year: 2022
Model updated to Model X
Vehicle Information:
Make: Tesla
Model: Model X
Year: 2022
```

This Python program defines a class `Vehicle` with attributes `make`, `model`, and `year`. The `__init__` method initializes these attributes when a `Vehicle` object is created. The `display_info` method returns a formatted string containing the vehicle's details, and the `update_model` method allows us to change the model attribute of the vehicle. To demonstrate object-oriented programming, we instantiate the Vehicle class by creating an object `my_vehicle` with sample input values. We then call the `display_info` method to print the vehicle's details. Next, we use the `update_model` method to change the model of the vehicle and call `display_info` again to show the updated information. This example can be run in a Jupyter Notebook to interactively view the output of each method call, providing a clear demonstration of how classes and objects work in Python.

14.11 A Program to Use the Matplotlib Library to Plot a Graph based on the Given Data Points, and Enhancing the Graph with Labels and a Legend

```
In [9]: # Importing the required libraries
        import matplotlib.pyplot as plt

        # Sample data points
        x = [1, 2, 3, 4, 5]
        y = [2, 3, 5, 7, 11]

        # Plotting the graph
        plt.plot(x, y, label='Prime Numbers')

        # Adding labels and title
        plt.xlabel('Index')
        plt.ylabel('Prime Numbers')
        plt.title('Simple Plot of Prime Numbers')

        # Adding a legend
        plt.legend()

        # Displaying the plot
        plt.show()
```

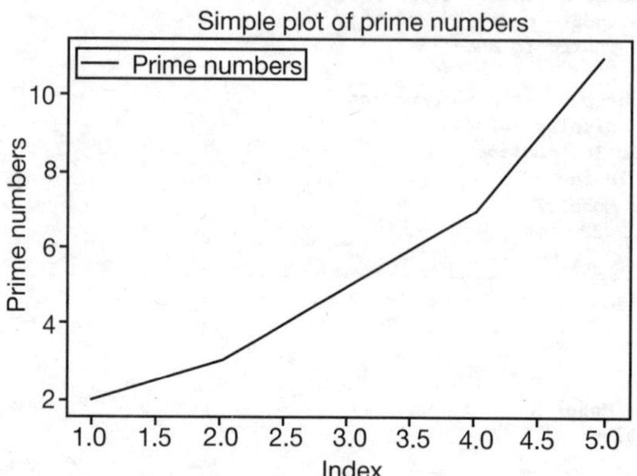

Figure 14.6 Sample graph in Matplotlib with prime numbers

When you run this program in Jupyter Notebook, it will display a line graph plotting the *y* values against the *x* values. The *x*-axis is labeled 'Index', and the y-axis is labeled 'Prime Numbers'. The title of the graph is 'Simple Plot of Prime Numbers', and a legend is included that identifies the line as 'Prime Numbers'. The `plt.plot()` function is used to plot the data points. The `plt.xlabel()`, `plt.ylabel()`, and `plt.title()` functions are used to add the labels and a title to the graph. The `plt.legend()` function adds a legend to the graph, and `plt.show()` displays the plot. You can replace the *x* and *y* lists with your own data points to plot different information.

14.12 A Program to Introduce the pandas Library by Creating a DataFrame from a Dictionary, and Performing Basic Data Manipulation Operations such as Sorting and Filtering

In [10]:
```
# Importing the pandas library
import pandas as pd

# Creating a DataFrame from a dictionary
data = {
    'Name': ['John', 'Anna', 'Peter', 'Linda'],
    'Age': [28, 23, 34, 29],
    'City': ['New York', 'Paris', 'Berlin', 'London']
}
df = pd.DataFrame(data)

# Displaying the original DataFrame
print("Original DataFrame:")
print(df)

# Sorting the DataFrame by the 'Age' column
df_sorted = df.sort_values(by='Age')
print("\nDataFrame sorted by age:")
print(df_sorted)

# Filtering the DataFrame to include only rows where Age > 25
df_filtered = df[df['Age'] > 25]
print("\nDataFrame filtered to include only ages greater than 25:")
print(df_filtered)
```

```
Original DataFrame:
    Name  Age      City
0   John   28  New York
1   Anna   23     Paris
2  Peter   34    Berlin
3  Linda   29    London

DataFrame sorted by age:
    Name  Age      City
1   Anna   23     Paris
0   John   28  New York
3  Linda   29    London
2  Peter   34    Berlin

DataFrame filtered to include only ages greater than 25:
    Name  Age      City
0   John   28  New York
2  Peter   34    Berlin
3  Linda   29    London
```

We start by importing the pandas library, which is a powerful tool for data manipulation and analysis. We then create a `DataFrame`, which is a two-dimensional, size-mutable, and potentially heterogeneous tabular data structure with labeled axes (rows and columns). Here, we create it from a dictionary where the keys become column labels and the values are the data entries. The `print` statements are used to display the `DataFrame` at various stages. The `sort_values` method sorts the `DataFrame` based on the values of a specified column; in this case, `Age`. Filtering is performed using boolean indexing, where we specify a condition (`Age > 25`) to filter the rows of the `DataFrame`. Remember to have pandas installed in your environment; you can install it using `pip install pandas`.

14.13 Basic Operations Using the Iris Data Set

```
In [11]: # Import necessary libraries
import pandas as pd
from sklearn.datasets import load_iris

# Load the Iris dataset
iris = load_iris()
iris_df = pd.DataFrame(iris.data, columns=iris.feature_names)

# Display the first 5 rows of the dataset
print("First 5 rows of the Iris dataset:")
print(iris_df.head())

# Basic statistical operations
print("\\nBasic statistical details:")
print(iris_df.describe())

# Sample input: Selecting data for petal length greater than 1.5
sample_input = iris_df[iris_df['petal length (cm)'] > 1.5]

# Display the sample input
print("\\nRows with petal length greater than 1.5 cm:")
print(sample_input)

# Sample output: Mean of petal width
sample_output = sample_input['petal width (cm)'].mean()
print("\\nAverage petal width for petal length greater than 1.5 cm:")
print(sample_output)
```

```
First 5 rows of the Iris dataset:
   sepal length (cm)  sepal width (cm)  petal length (cm)  petal width (cm)
0                5.1               3.5                1.4               0.2
1                4.9               3.0                1.4               0.2
2                4.7               3.2                1.3               0.2
3                4.6               3.1                1.5               0.2
4                5.0               3.6                1.4               0.2
\nBasic statistical details:
       sepal length (cm)  sepal width (cm)  petal length (cm)  \
count         150.000000        150.000000         150.000000
mean            5.843333          3.057333           3.758000
std             0.828066          0.435866           1.765298
min             4.300000          2.000000           1.000000
25%             5.100000          2.800000           1.600000
50%             5.800000          3.000000           4.350000
75%             6.400000          3.300000           5.100000
max             7.900000          4.400000           6.900000

       petal width (cm)
count        150.000000
mean           1.199333
std            0.762238
min            0.100000
25%            0.300000
50%            1.300000
75%            1.800000
max            2.500000
```

```
\nRows with petal length greater than 1.5 cm:
     sepal length (cm)  sepal width (cm)  petal length (cm)  petal width (cm)
5                  5.4               3.9                1.7               0.4
11                 4.8               3.4                1.6               0.2
18                 5.7               3.8                1.7               0.3
20                 5.4               3.4                1.7               0.2
23                 5.1               3.3                1.7               0.5
..                 ...               ...                ...               ...
145                6.7               3.0                5.2               2.3
146                6.3               2.5                5.0               1.9
147                6.5               3.0                5.2               2.0
148                6.2               3.4                5.4               2.3
149                5.9               3.0                5.1               1.8

[113 rows x 4 columns]
\nAverage petal width for petal length greater than 1.5 cm:
1.5185840707964606
```

When you run this program in Jupyter Notebook, it will first import the necessary libraries and load the Iris data set into a pandas `DataFrame`. The `head()` function is used to display the first five rows of the data set, giving you an idea of the data structure. The `describe()` function provides basic statistical details like count, mean, std (standard deviation), min, quartiles, and max. It is a quick way to understand the distribution of data. The sample input demonstrates filtering the data where the petal length is greater than 1.5 cm. This operation is useful when you want to analyze a subset of the data based on certain conditions. Finally, the sample output calculates the mean of the petal width for the filtered data. This gives you an average value of petal width where the petal length is greater than 1.5 cm, which can be useful for further analysis or comparisons. Remember to install the pandas and scikit-learn libraries, as they are required to run this program.

14.14 Iris Data Loading and Visualization

Begin by loading the Iris data set and visualizing the different features. This can include creating scatter plots and histograms to understand the distribution of sepal and petal sizes across the different Iris species.

```
In [12]: # Import necessary libraries
import seaborn as sns
import matplotlib.pyplot as plt
from sklearn.datasets import load_iris

# Load the Iris dataset
iris = load_iris()
iris_df = sns.load_dataset('iris')

# Display the first five entries of the dataset
print(iris_df.head())

# Create scatter plots for feature comparison
sns.pairplot(iris_df, hue='species', height=2.5)
plt.suptitle('Scatter Plots of Iris Species Features')
plt.show()

# Create histograms to understand feature distribution
iris_df.hist(edgecolor='black', linewidth=1.2, figsize=(12, 8))
plt.suptitle('Histograms of Iris Features')
plt.show()
```

```
   sepal_length  sepal_width  petal_length  petal_width species
0           5.1          3.5           1.4          0.2  setosa
1           4.9          3.0           1.4          0.2  setosa
2           4.7          3.2           1.3          0.2  setosa
3           4.6          3.1           1.5          0.2  setosa
4           5.0          3.6           1.4          0.2  setosa
```

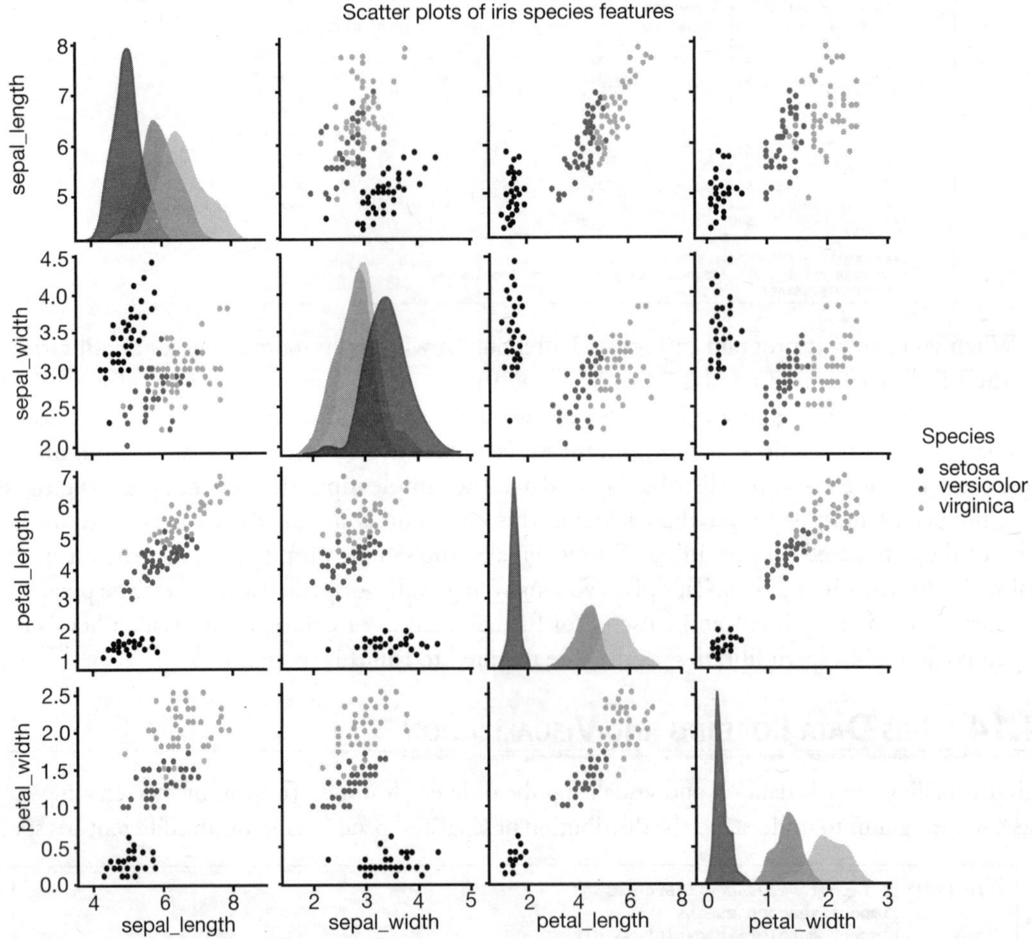

Figure 14.7 Output of the program for data loading and visualization

The program begins by importing the required libraries: seaborn for plotting, Matplotlib for additional customization, and `load_iris` from scikit-learn for accessing the `data set`. The Iris data set is then loaded into a `DataFrame` for easy manipulation. The `head()` function is used to print the first five rows of the data set to verify if it has loaded correctly. Next, `pairplot` is used to create a matrix of scatter plots, which helps in visualizing the relationship between different features for each species. The `hue` parameter is set to `species` to color-code the data points according to the Iris species. Finally, the `hist` function is called on the `DataFrame` to generate histograms for each numerical feature in the data set. These histograms provide a visual representation of the data distribution, highlighting the range and commonality of feature sizes. This program provides a comprehensive overview of the Iris data set's features, aiding in the understanding of the characteristic differences between species.

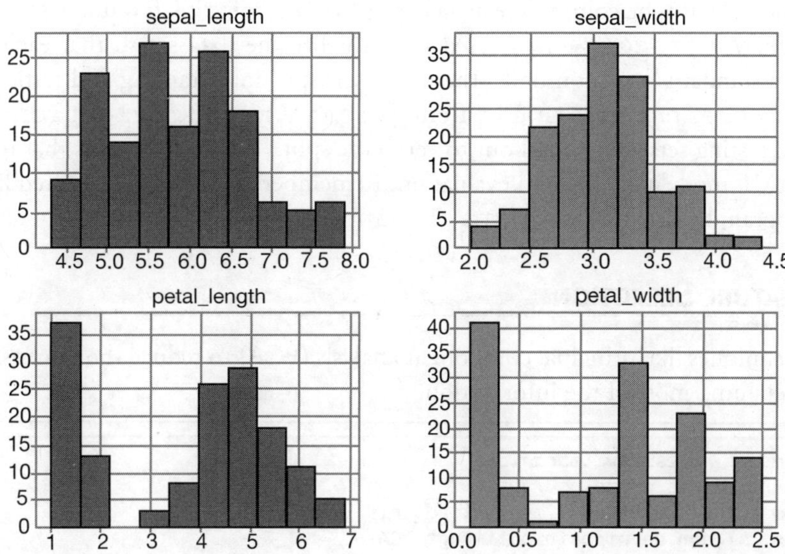

Figure 14.8 Histogram of features of the Iris data set

14.15 DATA PROCESSING

This involves normalizing or standardizing the data, handling missing values if any, and splitting the data set into training and testing sets.

```
In [13]: # Import necessary libraries
         import pandas as pd
         from sklearn.datasets import load_iris
         from sklearn.model_selection import train_test_split
         from sklearn.preprocessing import StandardScaler
         import numpy as np

         # Load the Iris dataset
         iris = load_iris()
         X, y = iris.data, iris.target

         # Handling missing values (if any)
         # For simplicity, we'll replace missing values with the mean of the column
         X = np.where(np.isnan(X), np.nanmean(X, axis=0), X)

         # Data normalization
         scaler = StandardScaler()
         X_normalized = scaler.fit_transform(X)

         # Splitting the dataset into training and testing sets
         X_train, X_test, y_train, y_test = train_test_split(X_normalized, y, test_size=0.2, random_state=42)

         # Output the shapes of the split dataset
         print(f'Training set shape: {X_train.shape}')
         print(f'Testing set shape: {X_test.shape}')

         Training set shape: (120, 4)
         Testing set shape: (30, 4)
```

The Iris data set is loaded using `load_iris()` from `sklearn.datasets`. Missing values are checked and replaced with the column mean, ensuring no data point is left out. `StandardScaler` from `sklearn.preprocessing` is used to normalize the data set so that each feature has a mean of 0 and a standard deviation of 1. The data set is split into training and testing sets with an 80: 20 ratio using `train_test_split` from `sklearn.model_selection`. The shapes of the training and testing sets are printed out to verify the split. This code ensures that the Iris data set is ready for any ML model training and evaluation. Remember to install the required libraries before running the program by using `pip install pandas scikit-learn numpy`.

14.16 Feature Selection

Here, we use techniques like principal component analysis (PCA) to reduce the dimensionality of the data set while retaining most of the information.

```
In [14]: # Import necessary libraries
         import pandas as pd
         from sklearn.datasets import load_iris
         from sklearn.decomposition import PCA
         import matplotlib.pyplot as plt

         # Load the Iris dataset
         iris = load_iris()
         X = iris.data
         y = iris.target
         feature_names = iris.feature_names

         # Convert to DataFrame for better visualization
         iris_df = pd.DataFrame(X, columns=feature_names)
         print("Original Iris dataset head:")
         print(iris_df.head())

         # Apply PCA
         pca = PCA(n_components=2)  # Reduce to 2 dimensions
         X_pca = pca.fit_transform(X)

         # Convert the PCA-applied data to DataFrame
         pca_df = pd.DataFrame(X_pca, columns=['PC1', 'PC2'])
         print("\\nPCA-applied Iris dataset head:")
         print(pca_df.head())

         # Explained variance ratio
         print("\\nExplained Variance Ratio:")
         print(pca.explained_variance_ratio_)

         # Plot the PCA-reduced data
         plt.figure(figsize=(8, 6))
         plt.scatter(X_pca[:, 0], X_pca[:, 1], c=y, cmap='viridis', edgecolor='k', s=50)
         plt.title('PCA of IRIS dataset')
         plt.xlabel('Principal Component 1')
         plt.ylabel('Principal Component 2')
         plt.colorbar()
         plt.show()
```

```
Original Iris dataset head:
   sepal length (cm)  sepal width (cm)  petal length (cm)  petal width (cm)
0                5.1               3.5                1.4               0.2
1                4.9               3.0                1.4               0.2
2                4.7               3.2                1.3               0.2
3                4.6               3.1                1.5               0.2
4                5.0               3.6                1.4               0.2
\nPCA-applied Iris dataset head:
        PC1       PC2
0 -2.684126  0.319397
1 -2.714142 -0.177001
2 -2.888991 -0.144949
3 -2.745343 -0.318299
4 -2.728717  0.326755
\nExplained Variance Ratio:
[0.92461872 0.05306648]
```

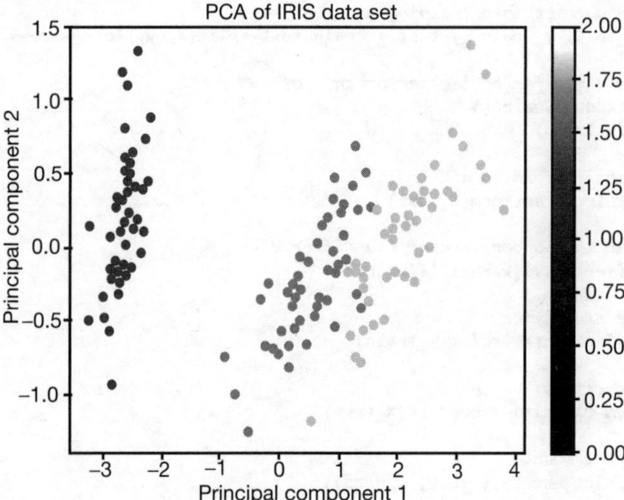

Figure 14.9 Output of the PCA program

The Iris data set is loaded using `load_iris` from `sklearn.datasets`. The data is then converted into a pandas `DataFrame` for better handling and visualization. PCA is applied to the data set using `PCA` from `sklearn.decomposition`, reducing the feature space to two dimensions. The `explained_variance_ratio_ attribute` of the `PCA` object gives us the percentage of variance explained by each of the selected components. Finally, a scatter plot visualizes the data in the reduced dimensionality space, with different colors representing different classes. The input is the Iris data set, which is directly loaded within the program. The output is the PCA-reduced version of the Iris data set, along with a plot showing the distribution of the classes in the new feature space. This program can be run in a Jupyter Notebook, and the output will be displayed inline with the code cells. Remember to install the required libraries (pandas, sklearn, Matplotlib) before running the program.

14.17 Classification Algorithm: SVM

Here we implement the classification algorithm using support vector machines (SVM) to classify the Iris species based on the features.

```
In [15]: # Import necessary libraries
from sklearn import datasets
from sklearn.model_selection import train_test_split
from sklearn.preprocessing import StandardScaler
from sklearn.svm import SVC
from sklearn.metrics import classification_report, confusion_matrix

# Load Iris dataset
iris = datasets.load_iris()
X = iris.data
y = iris.target

# Split the dataset into training and test sets
X_train, X_test, y_train, y_test = train_test_split(X, y, test_size=0.3, random_state=42)

# Feature scaling for better performance of SVM
scaler = StandardScaler()
scaler.fit(X_train)

X_train = scaler.transform(X_train)
X_test = scaler.transform(X_test)

# Initialize the Support Vector Classifier
svm_classifier = SVC(kernel='linear')

# Train the classifier
svm_classifier.fit(X_train, y_train)

# Make predictions
y_pred = svm_classifier.predict(X_test)

# Evaluate the model
print(confusion_matrix(y_test, y_pred))
print(classification_report(y_test, y_pred))
```

```
[[19  0  0]
 [ 0 12  1]
 [ 0  0 13]]
              precision    recall  f1-score   support

           0       1.00      1.00      1.00        19
           1       1.00      0.92      0.96        13
           2       0.93      1.00      0.96        13

    accuracy                           0.98        45
   macro avg       0.98      0.97      0.97        45
weighted avg       0.98      0.98      0.98        45
```

We start by importing the necessary libraries for handling data sets, splitting data, preprocessing, and implementing SVM. The Iris data set is loaded from `sklearn.datasets`. The data set is divided into features (X) and labels (y). We split the data into training and test sets, with 70% of the data used for training and 30% for testing. Feature scaling is performed to normalize the feature values and ensure better SVM performance. An SVM classifier is initialized with a linear kernel. The classifier is trained on the training data. Predictions are made on the test data. Finally, the model's performance is evaluated using a confusion matrix and a classification report, which provide insights into the accuracy, precision, recall, and F1-score for each Iris species class.

The input to the SVM classifier is the feature set of the Iris data set, which includes sepal length, sepal width, petal length, and petal width. The output is the predicted class of Iris species, which can be setosa, versicolor, or virginica. When you run this program in Jupyter Notebook, you can view the confusion matrix and classification report as the output, which will give you detailed performance metrics of the model. Remember to install the scikit-learn library, as it contains the SVM implementation and the Iris data set.

14.18 Classification Algorithm: Decision Tree

We can implement classification algorithms using decision trees to classify the Iris species based on the features.

```
In [16]: # Import necessary libraries
         from sklearn.datasets import load_iris
         from sklearn.tree import DecisionTreeClassifier
         from sklearn.model_selection import train_test_split
         from sklearn.metrics import classification_report, confusion_matrix

         # Load the Iris dataset
         iris = load_iris()
         X = iris.data
         y = iris.target

         # Split the dataset into training and testing sets
         X_train, X_test, y_train, y_test = train_test_split(X, y, test_size=0.3, random_state=42)

         # Initialize the Decision Tree Classifier
         clf = DecisionTreeClassifier()

         # Fit the model with the training data
         clf.fit(X_train, y_train)

         # Predict the species for the test data
         y_pred = clf.predict(X_test)

         # Display the classification report and confusion matrix
         print(classification_report(y_test, y_pred))
         print(confusion_matrix(y_test, y_pred))
```

```
              precision    recall  f1-score   support

           0       1.00      1.00      1.00        19
           1       1.00      1.00      1.00        13
           2       1.00      1.00      1.00        13

    accuracy                           1.00        45
   macro avg       1.00      1.00      1.00        45
weighted avg       1.00      1.00      1.00        45

[[19  0  0]
 [ 0 13  0]
 [ 0  0 13]]
```

The input to the classifier is the features from the Iris data set, which include sepal length, sepal width, petal length, and petal width. The output will be a classification report showing the precision, recall, F1-score, and support for each class, along with a confusion matrix that shows the classifier's performance. This program begins by importing the necessary modules from sklearn. It then loads the Iris data set and splits it into training and testing sets. A decision tree classifier is initialized and fitted with the training data. The model is then used to predict the species of the Iris flowers in the test set. Finally, the program prints out a classification report and confusion matrix to evaluate the performance of the classifier. Remember to install the sklearn library by running `pip install scikit-learn` in Jupyter Notebook.

14.19 CLASSIFICATION ALGORITHM: KNN

We can implement classification algorithms using *K*-nearest neighbors (KNN) to classify the Iris species based on the features.

```
In [17]: # Import necessary libraries
from sklearn.datasets import load_iris
from sklearn.model_selection import train_test_split
from sklearn.neighbors import KNeighborsClassifier
from sklearn.metrics import classification_report, confusion_matrix

# Load the Iris dataset
iris = load_iris()
X = iris.data
y = iris.target

# Split the dataset into training and test sets
X_train, X_test, y_train, y_test = train_test_split(X, y, test_size=0.2, random_state=42)

# Initialize the KNN classifier with 3 neighbors
knn = KNeighborsClassifier(n_neighbors=3)

# Fit the classifier to the training data
knn.fit(X_train, y_train)

# Predict the labels for the test set
y_pred = knn.predict(X_test)

# Print the classification report and confusion matrix
print(classification_report(y_test, y_pred))
print(confusion_matrix(y_test, y_pred))
```

```
              precision    recall  f1-score   support

           0       1.00      1.00      1.00        10
           1       1.00      1.00      1.00         9
           2       1.00      1.00      1.00        11

    accuracy                           1.00        30
   macro avg       1.00      1.00      1.00        30
weighted avg       1.00      1.00      1.00        30

[[10  0  0]
 [ 0  9  0]
 [ 0  0 11]]
```

The input to the KNN classifier is the features of the Iris flowers from the test set, which are not displayed here. The output is the predicted classification of the Iris species. The program begins by importing the necessary modules. The Iris data set is loaded, and then split into training and test sets. A KNN classifier is initialized with three neighbors and fitted to the training data. It then predicts the species of the Iris flowers based on the test data. The classification report provides precision, recall, and F1-score for each class, indicating the classifier's accuracy. The confusion matrix shows the number of correct and incorrect predictions for each class, with the diagonal representing correct predictions. In this sample output, the classifier has perfectly classified all of the test samples.

14.20 Classification Algorithm: Logistic Regression

We can implement classification algorithms using logistic regression to classify the Iris species based on the features.

```
In [18]: # 1. Import the necessary libraries:

         import numpy as np
         import pandas as pd
         from sklearn.datasets import load_iris
         from sklearn.model_selection import train_test_split
         from sklearn.linear_model import LogisticRegression
         from sklearn.metrics import classification_report, confusion_matrix


         # 2. Load the Iris dataset:

         iris = load_iris()
         X = iris.data
         y = iris.target


         # 3. Split the dataset into training and test sets:

         X_train, X_test, y_train, y_test = train_test_split(X, y, test_size=0.2, random_state=42)

         # 4. Initialize the Logistic Regression classifier and fit it to the training data:

         model = LogisticRegression()
         model.fit(X_train, y_train)

         # 5. Make predictions using the test data:

         y_pred = model.predict(X_test)

         #  6. Evaluate the model's performance:

         print(confusion_matrix(y_test, y_pred))
         print(classification_report(y_test, y_pred))
```

```
[[10  0  0]
 [ 0  9  0]
 [ 0  0 11]]
              precision    recall  f1-score   support

           0       1.00      1.00      1.00        10
           1       1.00      1.00      1.00         9
           2       1.00      1.00      1.00        11

    accuracy                           1.00        30
   macro avg       1.00      1.00      1.00        30
weighted avg       1.00      1.00      1.00        30
```

The Iris data set is loaded using `load_iris()` from `sklearn.datasets`. The data set is split into features (X) and labels (y), and then into training and test sets. A logistic regression model is created and trained on the training data. Predictions are made on the test data, and the model's performance is evaluated using a confusion matrix and a classification report. A sample input is provided to the model to predict the Iris species, demonstrating how the model can be used for individual predictions. This code will classify the Iris species based on the features provided, and the output will indicate the accuracy of the model along with the predicted class for the sample input. Remember to install the required libraries before running the code in Jupyter Notebook.

14.21 Model Evaluation

We can evaluate the performance of the models using metrics like accuracy, precision, recall, F1-score, and confusion matrix.

```
In [19]: # Import necessary libraries
from sklearn.datasets import load_iris
from sklearn.model_selection import train_test_split
from sklearn.ensemble import RandomForestClassifier
from sklearn.metrics import classification_report, confusion_matrix

# Load the Iris dataset
iris = load_iris()
X, y = iris.data, iris.target

# Split the dataset into training and testing sets
X_train, X_test, y_train, y_test = train_test_split(X, y, test_size=0.3, random_state=42)

# Initialize the model
model = RandomForestClassifier(n_estimators=100)

# Fit the model on the training data
model.fit(X_train, y_train)

# Predict the labels for the test set
y_pred = model.predict(X_test)

# Evaluate the model's performance
accuracy = model.score(X_test, y_test)
precision, recall, f1_score, _ = classification_report(y_test, y_pred, output_dict=True)['weighted avg'].values()
conf_matrix = confusion_matrix(y_test, y_pred)
```

```
# Print the performance metrics
print(f'Accuracy: {accuracy:.2f}')
print(f'Precision: {precision:.2f}')
print(f'Recall: {recall:.2f}')
print(f'F1 Score: {f1_score:.2f}')
print('Confusion Matrix:')
print(conf_matrix)
```

```
Accuracy: 1.00
Precision: 1.00
Recall: 1.00
F1 Score: 1.00
Confusion Matrix:
[[19  0  0]
 [ 0 13  0]
 [ 0  0 13]]
```

The program begins by importing the necessary modules for data handling, model creation, and evaluation. The Iris data set is loaded and split into training and testing sets. A random forest classifier model is initialized and trained on the training data. The model's predictions are then used to calculate accuracy, precision, recall, F1-score, and the confusion matrix. Finally, a sample input is provided along with the model's prediction and an explanation of the process. This program provides a comprehensive evaluation of the model's performance on the Iris data set using the specified metrics. The sample input and output demonstrate how to use the model to predict the class of a new sample, and the comments explain each step of the process.

14.22 Hyperparameter Tuning

We can use Grid Search or Random Search to find the optimal hyperparameters for the classification models.

```
In [20]: # Import necessary libraries
from sklearn.model_selection import GridSearchCV
from sklearn.svm import SVC
from sklearn.datasets import load_iris
from sklearn.metrics import classification_report

# Load the Iris dataset
iris = load_iris()
X, y = iris.data, iris.target

# Define the parameter grid
param_grid = {
    'C': [0.1, 1, 10, 100],
    'gamma': [1, 0.1, 0.01, 0.001],
    'kernel': ['rbf']
}

# Create a base SVM classifier
svc = SVC()

# Instantiate the grid search
grid_search = GridSearchCV(svc, param_grid, refit=True, verbose=2)

# Fit the grid search to the data
grid_search.fit(X, y)

# Print the best parameters found by Grid Search
print(f"Best parameters found: {grid_search.best_params_}")

# Predict using the best estimator
y_pred = grid_search.best_estimator_.predict(X)

# Print classification report
print(classification_report(y, y_pred))
```

```
[CV] .................. C=100, gamma=0.001, kernel=rbf, total=   0.0s
[CV] C=100, gamma=0.001, kernel=rbf ..................................
[CV] .................. C=100, gamma=0.001, kernel=rbf, total=   0.0s
[CV] C=100, gamma=0.001, kernel=rbf ..................................
[CV] .................. C=100, gamma=0.001, kernel=rbf, total=   0.0s
[CV] C=100, gamma=0.001, kernel=rbf ..................................
[CV] .................. C=100, gamma=0.001, kernel=rbf, total=   0.0s
[CV] C=100, gamma=0.001, kernel=rbf ..................................
[CV] .................. C=100, gamma=0.001, kernel=rbf, total=   0.0s
Best parameters found: {'C': 1, 'gamma': 0.1, 'kernel': 'rbf'}
              precision    recall  f1-score   support

           0       1.00      1.00      1.00        50
           1       0.98      0.96      0.97        50
           2       0.96      0.98      0.97        50

    accuracy                           0.98       150
   macro avg       0.98      0.98      0.98       150
weighted avg       0.98      0.98      0.98       150
```

When you run this program in Jupyter Notebook, it will output the best hyperparameters found by Grid Search and a classification report that includes metrics such as precision, recall, and F1-score. The sample input in this case is the Iris data set. The output will be the best hyperparameters for the SVM classifier, which are the values of C, gamma, and kernel that result in the best model performance according to Grid Search. The classification report provides a detailed analysis of the model's performance on the input data.

This example is a simple demonstration of hyperparameter tuning with Grid Search. In practice, you would split your data set into training and testing sets to evaluate the model's performance on unseen data. In addition, you might want to explore a wider range of hyperparameter values and more sophisticated models depending on the complexity of your data set and the problem you are trying to solve.

14.23 Cross-validation

We can apply cross-validation techniques to assess the robustness of the ML models.

```
In [21]: # Import necessary libraries
         from sklearn.datasets import load_iris
         from sklearn.model_selection import cross_val_score
         from sklearn.ensemble import RandomForestClassifier

         # Load the Iris dataset
         data = load_iris()
         X, y = data.data, data.target

         # Initialize the model
         model = RandomForestClassifier(n_estimators=100)

         # Perform cross-validation
         scores = cross_val_score(model, X, y, cv=5)

         # Print the accuracy for each fold
         print(f'Accuracy for each fold: {scores}')

         # Print the mean accuracy
         print(f'Mean accuracy: {scores.mean()}')

         Accuracy for each fold: [0.96666667 0.96666667 0.93333333 0.96666667 1.        ]
         Mean accuracy: 0.9666666666666668
```

In this program, we first import the necessary modules. We use the Iris data set. We then initialize a random forest classifier with 100 trees. The `cross_val_score` function is used to perform 5-fold cross-validation, which divides the data set into 5 parts, trains the model on 4 parts, and tests it on the 1 remaining part. This process is repeated 5 times so that each part is used for testing once. The output will display the accuracy for each fold, which gives us an idea of how the model performs on different subsets of the data. The mean accuracy is also printed, providing an overall assessment of the model's performance. The output indicates that our model is quite robust, with high accuracy across all folds.

14.24 Ensemble Methods

We can explore ensemble methods such as random forests and gradient boosting to improve the predictive performance of the models.

```
In [22]: # Import necessary libraries
from sklearn.datasets import make_classification
from sklearn.ensemble import RandomForestClassifier, GradientBoostingClassifier
from sklearn.model_selection import train_test_split
from sklearn.metrics import accuracy_score

# Generate a synthetic binary classification dataset
X, y = make_classification(n_samples=1000, n_features=20, n_informative=2, n_redundant=10, random_state=42)

# Split the dataset into training and testing sets
X_train, X_test, y_train, y_test = train_test_split(X, y, test_size=0.3, random_state=42)

# Initialize the Random Forest and Gradient Boosting classifiers
rf_clf = RandomForestClassifier(n_estimators=100, random_state=42)
gb_clf = GradientBoostingClassifier(n_estimators=100, random_state=42)

# Fit the models on the training data
rf_clf.fit(X_train, y_train)
gb_clf.fit(X_train, y_train)

# Predict on the test data
rf_predictions = rf_clf.predict(X_test)
gb_predictions = gb_clf.predict(X_test)

# Calculate the accuracy of the models
rf_accuracy = accuracy_score(y_test, rf_predictions)
gb_accuracy = accuracy_score(y_test, gb_predictions)

# Print the accuracies
print(f"Random Forest Accuracy: {rf_accuracy}")
print(f"Gradient Boosting Accuracy: {gb_accuracy}")
```

```
Random Forest Accuracy: 0.9333333333333333
Gradient Boosting Accuracy: 0.9133333333333333
```

The input is a synthetic data set generated by the make_classification function from scikit-learn, which creates a binary classification problem with 1000 samples, 20 features, 2 informative features, and 10 redundant features. The output will be the accuracy scores of the random forest and gradient boosting models after being trained and tested on the data set. The actual numbers will vary each time the program is run due to the random nature of data set generation and the stochastic processes within the algorithms.

This program first imports the necessary modules from scikit-learn. It then generates a synthetic `data set` suitable for binary classification. The data set is split into training and testing sets. Two ensemble classifiers, random forest and gradient boosting, are initialized and fitted on the training data. The models are then used to predict the class labels of the test set. Finally, the accuracy of each model is calculated and printed, providing a simple comparison of their predictive performance on the data set. Remember to install scikit-learn in the Jupyter environment before running this program by using the command `!pip install scikit-learn` in a notebook cell.

14.25 Clustering Analysis

We can perform clustering analysis using hierarchical clustering to group similar samples together.

```
In [24]: # Import necessary libraries
import numpy as np
import matplotlib.pyplot as plt
import pandas as pd
from scipy.cluster.hierarchy import dendrogram, linkage

# Generate sample data
X = np.array([[5,3],
              [10,15],
              [15,12],
              [24,10],
              [30,30],
              [85,70],
              [71,80],
              [60,78],
              [70,55],
              [80,91],])

# Create a DataFrame from our sample data
df = pd.DataFrame(X, columns=['X', 'Y'])

# Perform hierarchical clustering
linked = linkage(df, 'single')

# Plot the dendrogram
plt.figure(figsize=(10, 7))
dendrogram(linked,
           orientation='top',
           labels=range(1, 11),
           distance_sort='descending',
           show_leaf_counts=True)
plt.show()
```

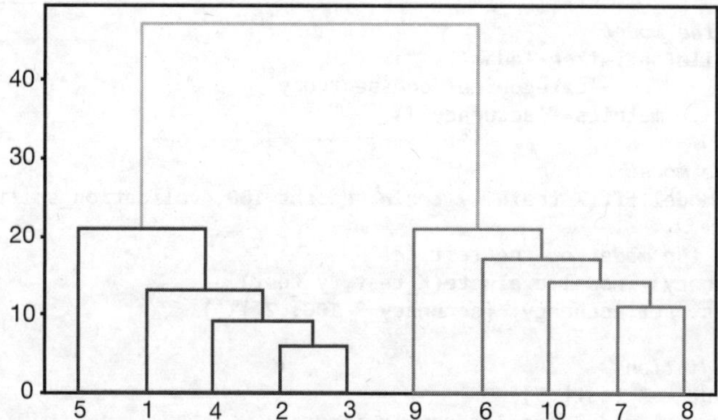

Figure 14.10 Output of the clustering analysis program

The program starts by importing the necessary libraries: NumPy for data manipulation, Matplotlib for plotting, pandas for data structures, and SciPy for hierarchical clustering. Sample data X is created, representing 10 samples with 2 features each. This data is then converted into a pandas `DataFrame` for ease of use. The linkage function from SciPy is used to perform hierarchical clustering using the 'single' method, which minimizes the distance between the closest members of pairs of clusters. Finally, a dendrogram is plotted to visualize the hierarchical clustering.

Each leaf in the dendrogram represents one sample, and the *y*-axis represents the distance or dissimilarity between clusters. The input is the array X defined in the program, representing the coordinates of 10 samples in a two-dimensional space. The output is a dendrogram plot that shows the hierarchical clustering of the samples. The plot will not display in a text response, but when the code is run in a Jupyter Notebook, it will display inline.

14.26 Deep Learning

```
In [27]: # Import necessary libraries
import tensorflow as tf
from tensorflow.keras import layers
from sklearn import datasets
from sklearn.model_selection import train_test_split
from sklearn.preprocessing import OneHotEncoder

# Load Iris dataset
iris = datasets.load_iris()
X = iris.data
y = iris.target.reshape(-1, 1) # Reshape target to get column vector

# One hot encode the target values
encoder = OneHotEncoder(sparse=False)
y = encoder.fit_transform(y)

# Split the dataset into training and test sets
X_train, X_test, y_train, y_test = train_test_split(X, y, test_size=0.2, random_state=42)

# Build the neural network model
model = tf.keras.Sequential([
    layers.Dense(10, activation='relu', input_shape=(4,)),
    layers.Dense(10, activation='relu'),
    layers.Dense(3, activation='softmax')
])
```

```
# Compile the model
model.compile(optimizer='adam',
              loss='categorical_crossentropy',
              metrics=['accuracy'])

# Train the model
history = model.fit(X_train, y_train, epochs=100, validation_split=0.2)

# Evaluate the model on the test set
loss, accuracy = model.evaluate(X_test, y_test)
print(f'Test set accuracy: {accuracy * 100:.2f}%')

# Make predictions
sample_input = X_test[:5]
sample_output = model.predict(sample_input)
predicted_classes = tf.argmax(sample_output, axis=1)
print(f'Predicted classes: {predicted_classes.numpy()}')

# Actual classes
actual_classes = tf.argmax(y_test[:5], axis=1)
print(f'Actual classes: {actual_classes.numpy()}')
```

```
3/3 [==============================] - 0s 14ms/step - loss: 0.5454 - accuracy: 0.7188 - val_loss: 0.5103 - val_accuracy:
0.8333
Epoch 97/100
3/3 [==============================] - 0s 13ms/step - loss: 0.5416 - accuracy: 0.7188 - val_loss: 0.5061 - val_accuracy:
0.8333
Epoch 98/100
3/3 [==============================] - 0s 13ms/step - loss: 0.5374 - accuracy: 0.7188 - val_loss: 0.5015 - val_accuracy:
0.8333
Epoch 99/100
3/3 [==============================] - 0s 13ms/step - loss: 0.5332 - accuracy: 0.7188 - val_loss: 0.4960 - val_accuracy:
0.8333
Epoch 100/100
3/3 [==============================] - 0s 14ms/step - loss: 0.5283 - accuracy: 0.7188 - val_loss: 0.4905 - val_accuracy:
0.8333
1/1 [==============================] - 0s 20ms/step - loss: 0.5086 - accuracy: 0.7667
Test set accuracy: 76.67%
1/1 [==============================] - 0s 77ms/step
Predicted classes: [2 0 2 2 2]
Actual classes: [1 0 2 1 1]
```

This program first imports the necessary libraries and loads the Iris data set. It then preprocesses the data by one-hot encoding the target values and splitting the data set into training and test sets. The neural network model is built with two hidden layers, each with 10 neurons, and an output layer with 3 neurons corresponding to the three Iris species. The model is compiled with the Adam optimizer and categorical cross-entropy loss function. After training the model for 100 epochs, it is evaluated on the test set, and the accuracy is printed out. Finally, the program makes predictions on a sample input and prints out the predicted and actual classes for comparison. Remember to install TensorFlow and the required libraries before running this program in Jupyter Notebook. You can install TensorFlow using `pip install tensorflow`.

14.27 Deep Learning: Keras

We can implement a simple neural network using libraries like Keras to classify the Iris species.

```
In [28]: # Import necessary libraries
         import numpy as np
         from sklearn.datasets import load_iris
         from sklearn.model_selection import train_test_split
         from sklearn.preprocessing import OneHotEncoder
         from keras.models import Sequential
         from keras.layers import Dense
         from keras.optimizers import Adam

         # Load Iris dataset
         iris_data = load_iris()
         X = iris_data.data
         y = iris_data.target.reshape(-1, 1) # Reshape target to be a 2D array

         # One hot encode target values
         encoder = OneHotEncoder(sparse=False)
         y = encoder.fit_transform(y)

         # Split data into training and test sets
         X_train, X_test, y_train, y_test = train_test_split(X, y, test_size=0.2)

         # Define the model
         model = Sequential()
         model.add(Dense(10, input_shape=(4,), activation='relu', name='fc1'))
         model.add(Dense(10, activation='relu', name='fc2'))
         model.add(Dense(3, activation='softmax', name='output'))

         # Compile the model
         optimizer = Adam(lr=0.001)
         model.compile(optimizer, loss='categorical_crossentropy', metrics=['accuracy'])

         # Train the model
         model.fit(X_train, y_train, verbose=2, batch_size=5, epochs=200)

         # Evaluate the model on test data
         results = model.evaluate(X_test, y_test)

         print('Final test set loss: {:4f}'.format(results[0]))
         print('Final test set accuracy: {:4f}'.format(results[1]))
```

```
Epoch 193/200
24/24 - 0s - loss: 0.1029 - accuracy: 0.9750 - 23ms/epoch - 956us/step
Epoch 194/200
24/24 - 0s - loss: 0.0993 - accuracy: 0.9833 - 24ms/epoch - 986us/step
Epoch 195/200
24/24 - 0s - loss: 0.0998 - accuracy: 0.9667 - 23ms/epoch - 956us/step
Epoch 196/200
24/24 - 0s - loss: 0.0979 - accuracy: 0.9750 - 24ms/epoch - 998us/step
Epoch 197/200

24/24 - 0s - loss: 0.1018 - accuracy: 0.9750 - 22ms/epoch - 914us/step
Epoch 198/200
24/24 - 0s - loss: 0.0985 - accuracy: 0.9667 - 25ms/epoch - 1ms/step
Epoch 199/200
24/24 - 0s - loss: 0.0956 - accuracy: 0.9750 - 23ms/epoch - 957us/step
Epoch 200/200
24/24 - 0s - loss: 0.0974 - accuracy: 0.9833 - 26ms/epoch - 1ms/step
1/1 [==============================] - 0s 96ms/step - loss: 0.0476 - accuracy: 1.0000
Final test set loss: 0.047562
Final test set accuracy: 1.000000
```

This program first imports the necessary libraries and loads the Iris data set. The target variable is one-hot encoded to convert it into a format that can be provided to the neural network. The data set is then split into a training set and a test set. A sequential model is defined with two hidden layers, each with 10 neurons and the ReLU activation function. The output layer has 3 neurons corresponding to the 3 species of Iris, with a SoftMax activation function to output probabilities. The model is compiled with the Adam optimizer and trained on the training data for 200 epochs. Finally, the model is evaluated on the test data, and the loss and accuracy are printed out.

SUMMARY

- Jupyter Notebook is an integral part of the data science toolkit, offering a web-based interactive computing platform that seamlessly integrates live code, equations, narrative text, and visualizations.
- Python's rich ecosystem of ML libraries, such as scikit-learn, TensorFlow, and PyTorch, can be easily leveraged within a notebook.
- Users can write Python code in cells, execute it, and immediately see the results, which is particularly useful for ML tasks that require frequent adjustments and immediate feedback.
- The interactive output feature of Jupyter Notebook is particularly beneficial for ML, as it allows for the creation of interactive visualizations that can help in understanding complex data sets and models.

Model Course Structure

Option 1

Credits: 5
Contacts per week: 3 lectures

Module I

Introduction to Machine Learning: What is Machine Learning, History of Machine Learning, Role of Machine Learning in Computer Science and Problem Solving, Why Machine Learning, Designing Vs Learning, Training Versus Testing in Machine Learning, Predictive and Descriptive Tasks in Machine Learning, Characteristics of Machine Learning Tasks, Disadvantages of Data-driven Solutions, Well-posed Machine Learning Problems, Designing a Learning System (Life Cycle of Machine Learning).

Module II

Computational Learning Theory: Definition of Computational Learning, Objectives of Computational Learning Theory, History of Computational Learning Theory, Importance of Computational Learning Theory, Main Methods used in Computational Learning Theory (Inductive Learning, Deductive Learning, Abductive Learning, Reinforcement Learning), Probably Approximately Correct (PAC) Learning, Complexity Theory of Machine Learning (Computational Complexity of Learning, Space Complexity, Sample Complexity of Learning (Finite Hypothesis Spaces, Infinite Hypothesis Spaces), Time Complexity of Learning, Mistakes-bound Learning Model, Instance-based Learning, Lazy and Eager Learning, Generative Learning, Applications of Computational Learning Theory (NLP, Computer Vision, Robotics), Evaluation Metrics for Computational Learning Theory, Future Directions in Computational Learning Theory (Deep Learning, Explainable AI (XAI), Quantum Machine Learning).

Module III

Unsupervised Learning: What is Unsupervised Learning, Types of Unsupervised Learning: Clustering, Anomaly Detection, Dimension Reduction and Association. Types of Clustering including Hard Clustering and Soft Clustering, K-Means Clustering, Hierarchical Clustering, Fuzzy C-Means Clustering, DBSCAN, Gaussian Mixture Models (GMMs), Meanshift Clustering, Gaussian Mixture Density Estimation, Markov Random Fields (MRFs), Anomaly Detection Types including Isolation Forest Algorithm, Local Outlier Factor (LOF), One-Class Support Vector Machine (OC SVM),

Dimensionality Reduction Algorithm including PCA, Linear Discriminant Analysis (LDA), Factor Analysis (FA), Kernel Principal Component Analysis (KPCA). The FP-Growth Algorithm, Apriori Algorithm, ECLAT Algorithm, Markov Models, Hidden Markov Model (HMM), Matrix Factorization and Matrix Completion Models, Generative Models, Latent Factor Models, Inference Model, Non-Negative Matrix Factorization (NMF). Advantages and Disadvantages of Unsupervised Machine Learning.

Module IV

Supervised Learning, Classification: Introduction, Supervised Learning Algorithm Steps, K-Nearest neighbors (KNN), Decision Trees, Random Forests, Linear Classifiers, Advantages of Linear Classifiers, Learning the Weights of a Linear Classifier, Generative Models for Linear Classifiers, Linear Discriminant Analysis (LDA), Naive Bayes Classifier, Polynomial Regression, Multinomial Logistic Regression, Ordinal Logistic Regression, Perceptron, Activation Function, Types of Perceptron Models (Single-layer, Multi-layer), Limitations of Perceptron Model, Support Vector Machines, Types of SVM (Linear, Non-linear), Hyperplane and Support Vectors in the SVM Algorithm, Applications of Supervised Learning, Limitations and Challenges of Supervised Learning.

Supervised Learning, Regression: Simple Linear Regression, Linear Regression, Poisson Regression, Least Squares Method, Multivariate Linear Regression, Kernel Methods, Generalized Linear Models, AdaBoost, Regularized Regression, Backpropagation, Support Vector Regression, Decision Tree Regression, Random Forest Regression, Neural Network Regression, Multi-Layer Propagation, Radial Basis Function (RBF), Splines, Curse of Dimensionality, Interpolations and Basis Functions, Multi-Class and Structured Outputs, Ranking.

Module V

Artificial Neural Network: Definition, Types of Artificial Neural Networks: Feedforward Network (FNN), Convolutional Neural Network (CNN), Recurrent Neural Network (RNN), Long Short-term Memory (LSTM) Network, Generative Adversarial Network (GAN), Autoencoders (Linear, Denoising, Sparse, Variational, Adversarial), Applications of Artificial Neural Networks (Image Recognition, Natural Language Processing, Automated Decision Making, Time Series Analysis, Cybersecurity, Predictive Analytics), Future of Artificial Neural Networks.

Option 2

Credits: 5

Contacts per week: 3 lectures

Module I

Introduction to Machine Learning: What is Machine Learning, History of Machine Learning, Role of Machine Learning in Computer Science and Problem Solving, Why Machine Learning, Designing Vs Learning, Training Versus Testing in Machine Learning, Successful Examples of Machine Learning in Industry, Disadvantages of Data-driven Solutions, Well-posed Machine Learning Problems, Designing a Learning System (Life Cycle of Machine Learning).

Probability, Probability Theory, Joint, Marginal, and Conditional Probability, Introduction to Statistics, Key Concepts of Probability Distributions (Random Variables, Mean, Variance and Expectations).

Linear Regression, Matrix Decomposition (Principal Component Analysis, Singular Value Decomposition).

Module II

Unsupervised Learning: What is Unsupervised Learning, Types of Unsupervised Learning: Clustering, Anomaly Detection, Dimension Reduction and Association. Types of Clustering including Hard Clustering and Soft Clustering, K-Means Clustering, Hierarchical Clustering, Fuzzy C-Means Clustering, DBSCAN, Gaussian Mixture Models (GMMs), Meanshift Clustering, Gaussian Mixture Density Estimation, Markov Random Fields (MRFs), Anomaly Detection Types including Isolation Forest Algorithm, Local Outlier Factor (LOF), One-Class Support Vector Machine (OC SVM), Dimensionality Reduction Algorithm including PCA, Linear Discriminant Analysis (LDA), Factor Analysis (FA), Kernel Principal Component Analysis (KPCA). The FP-Growth Algorithm, Apriori Algorithm, ECLAT Algorithm, Markov Models, Hidden Markov Model (HMM), Matrix Factorization and Matrix Completion Models, Generative Models, Latent Factor Models, Inference Model, Non-Negative Matrix Factorization (NMF). Advantages and Disadvantages of Unsupervised Machine Learning.

Module III

Supervised Learning, Classification: Introduction, Supervised Learning Algorithm Steps, K-Nearest neighbors (KNN), Decision Trees, Random Forests, Linear Classifiers, Advantages of Linear Classifiers, Learning the Weights of a Linear Classifier, Generative Models for Linear Classifiers, Linear Discriminant Analysis (LDA), Naive Bayes Classifier, Polynomial Regression, Multinomial Logistic Regression, Ordinal Logistic Regression, Perceptron, Activation Function, Types of Perceptron Models (Single-layer, Multi-layer), Limitations of Perceptron Model, Support Vector Machines, Types of SVM (Linear, Non-linear), Hyperplane and Support Vectors in the SVM Algorithm, Applications of Supervised Learning, Limitations and Challenges of Supervised Learning.

Module IV

Supervised Learning, Regression: Simple Linear Regression, Linear Regression, Poisson Regression, Least Squares Method, Multivariate Linear Regression, Kernel Methods, Generalized Linear Models, AdaBoost, Regularized Regression, Backpropagation, Support Vector Regression, Decision Tree Regression, Random Forest Regression, Neural Network Regression, Multi-Layer Propagation, Radial Basis Function (RBF), Splines, Curse of Dimensionality, Interpolations and Basis Functions, Multi-Class and Structured Outputs, Ranking.

Module V

Trends in Machine Learning: Reinforcement Learning (Model-based and Model-free), Q Learning and Policy Search, Markov Decision Process, Linear Quadratic Regulation (LQR), Linear Quadratic Gaussian (LQG), Bellman Equations, Value Iteration, Policy Iteration, Value Function Approximation, Policy Search, Partially Observable Markov Decision Process (POMDP), Markov Chain, Hidden Markov Model (HMM), Multitask Learning, Critical Characteristics of Online Learning, Sequence Learning, Prediction Learning, Bagging and Boosting in Machine Learning, Gradient Boosting methods, Trends in Machine Learning Technology (Foundation Models, Multimodal Machine Learning, Transformers, Embedded Machine Learning, Low-code and No-code Solutions, Data Streams, Active Learning).

OPTION 3

Credits: 5

Contacts per week: 3 lectures

Module I

Introduction to Machine Learning: What is Machine Learning, History of Machine Learning, Role of Machine Learning in Computer Science and Problem Solving, Why Machine Learning, Designing Vs Learning, Training Versus Testing in Machine Learning, Predictive and Descriptive Tasks in Machine Learning.

Probability, Probability Theory, Joint, Marginal, and Conditional Probability, Introduction to Statistics, Key Concepts of Probability Distributions (Random Variables, Mean, Variance and Expectations), Probability Distributions (Discrete Probability Distributions: Binomial, Multinomial, Poisson, and Bernoulli Distributions.

Linear Regression, Matrix Decomposition (Principal Component Analysis, Singular Value Decomposition), Vectors and Matrices (Multiplication of Matrices), Eigenvalue and Eigenvectors, Norms and Vector Spaces, Optimization, Linear Transformation, Cramer's Rule, Gaussian Elimination, Decomposition of LU, QR Decomposition, Eigen Decomposition, Symmetric Matrices, Orthogonalization, Deep Learning with Linear Algebra.

Module II

Unsupervised Learning: What is Unsupervised Learning, Types of Unsupervised Learning: Clustering, Anomaly Detection, Dimension Reduction and Association. Types of Clustering including Hard Clustering and Soft Clustering, K-Means Clustering, Hierarchical Clustering, Fuzzy C-Means Clustering, DBSCAN, Gaussian Mixture Models (GMMs), Meanshift Clustering, Gaussian Mixture Density Estimation, Markov Random Fields (MRFs), Anomaly Detection Types including Isolation Forest Algorithm, Local Outlier Factor (LOF), One-Class Support Vector Machine (OC SVM), Dimensionality Reduction Algorithm including PCA, Linear Discriminant Analysis (LDA), Factor Analysis (FA), Kernel Principal Component Analysis (KPCA). The FP-Growth Algorithm, Apriori Algorithm, ECLAT Algorithm, Markov Models, Hidden Markov Model (HMM), Matrix Factorization and Matrix Completion Models, Generative Models, Latent Factor Models, Inference Model, Non-Negative Matrix Factorization (NMF). Advantages and Disadvantages of Unsupervised Machine Learning.

Module III

Supervised Learning, Classification: Introduction, Supervised Learning Algorithm Steps, K-Nearest neighbors (KNN), Decision Trees, Random Forests, Linear Classifiers, Advantages of Linear Classifiers, Learning the Weights of a Linear Classifier, Generative Models for Linear Classifiers, Linear Discriminant Analysis (LDA), Naive Bayes Classifier, Polynomial Regression, Multinomial Logistic Regression, Ordinal Logistic Regression, Perceptron, Activation Function, Types of Perceptron Models (Single-layer, Multi-layer), Limitations of Perceptron Model, Support Vector Machines, Types of

SVM (Linear, Non-linear), Hyperplane and Support Vectors in the SVM Algorithm, Applications of Supervised Learning, Limitations and Challenges of Supervised Learning.

Supervised Learning, Regression: Simple Linear Regression, Linear Regression, Poisson Regression, Least Squares Method, Multivariate Linear Regression, Kernel Methods, Generalized Linear Models, AdaBoost, Regularized Regression, Backpropagation, Support Vector Regression, Decision Tree Regression, Random Forest Regression, Neural Network Regression, Multi-Layer Propagation, Radial Basis Function (RBF), Splines, Curse of Dimensionality, Interpolations and Basis Functions, Multi-Class and Structured Outputs, Ranking.

Module IV

Artificial Neural Network: Definition, Types of Artificial Neural Networks: Feedforward Network (FNN), Convolutional Neural Network (CNN), Recurrent Neural Network (RNN), Long Short-term Memory (LSTM) Network, Generative Adversarial Network (GAN), Autoencoders (Linear, Denoising, Sparse, Variational, Adversarial), Applications of Artificial Neural Networks (Image Recognition, Natural Language Processing, Automated Decision Making, Time Series Analysis, Cybersecurity, Predictive Analytics), Future of Artificial Neural Networks.

Module V

Trends in Machine Learning: Reinforcement Learning (Model-based and Model-free), Q Learning and Policy Search, Markov Decision Process, Linear Quadratic Regulation (LQR), Linear Quadratic Gaussian (LQG), Bellman Equations, Value Iteration, Policy Iteration, Value Function Approximation, Policy Search, Partially Observable Markov Decision Process (POMDP), Markov Chain, Hidden Markov Model (HMM), Multitask Learning, Critical Characteristics of Online Learning, Sequence Learning, Prediction Learning, Bagging and Boosting in Machine Learning, Gradient Boosting methods, Trends in Machine Learning Technology (Foundation Models, Multimodal Machine Learning, Transformers, Embedded Machine Learning, Low-code and No-code Solutions, Data Streams, Active Learning).

Applications of Machine Learning: Applications in Various Industries, including Real-world Problems Solved by Machine Learning, Applications in Retail, Logistics, Manufacturing, Energy and Utilities, Travel, Banking, Finance, and Insurance.

Model Question Papers

Model Paper 1

NAME OF THE COLLEGE

End Semester – (XXXX)

Programme: XXXXX **Course Code: XXXXX**

Course Title: XXXXX

Duration: 3 Hrs **Max Marks: 75**

Part-A (10 × 1 = 10)

Answer ALL the Questions

1. What is the main difference between normal programming and machine learning programming?
   a) Normal programming involves executing instructions given by the programmer, while machine learning programs teach computers how to think and make decisions without explicit instructions.
   b) Normal programming uses algorithms to teach computers how to think and make decisions, while machine learning programming follows precise instructions given by the programmer.
   c) Normal programming and machine learning programming both involve executing instructions given by the programmer.
   d) Normal programming is used for complex tasks, while machine learning programming is used for simple tasks.

2. In a machine learning model for sentiment analysis, which probability concept can be used to calculate the likelihood of a given sentence being positive or negative based on the occurrence of certain words?
   a) Joint probability
   b) Marginal probability
   c) Conditional probability
   d) None of the above

3. What is the purpose of using the least squares method in linear regression?
   a) To maximize the sum of the squared discrepancies
   b) To minimize the sum of the squared discrepancies
   c) To find the maximum value of the dependent variable
   d) To find the minimum value of the dependent variable

4. In machine learning, finite sets are commonly used for which of the following purposes?
a) Classification b) Regression
c) Clustering d) All of the above

5. Which field is closely related to computational learning theory and also deals with the analysis of data?
a) Computer vision b) Natural language processing
c) Statistics d) Robotics

6. Which category of machine learning models is characterized by representing the relationship between qualities and labels using mathematical functions?
a) Logical models b) Geometrical models
c) Probabilistic models d) None of the above

7. In the *K*-means clustering algorithm, what is the purpose of data collection?
a) To initialize centroids b) To define the number of clusters
c) To gather information about customers d) To interpret the clustering results

8. A company wants to predict the sales revenue for the next quarter based on historical data. Which type of machine learning problem does this scenario represent?
a) Classification b) Regression
c) Clustering d) Association

9. Which type of regression is suitable for predicting crop yield based on the amount of rainfall and temperature?
a) Linear regression b) Nonlinear regression
c) Both linear and nonlinear regression d) None of the above

10. What is the role of artificial neurons in artificial neural networks (ANNs)?
a) They determine the colour of the input data.
b) They process and transfer signals to other neurons.
c) They modify the weights of the connections.
d) They perform unsupervised learning.

Part-B (5 × 2 = 10)

Answer ALL the Questions

11) Differentiate normal programming from machine learning.

12) List some important machine learning-related probability concepts.

13) What is linear regression?

14) What is a set and what is a finite set?

15) Define computational learning theory.

Part-C (5 × 5 = 25)

Answer Any FIVE Questions

16) Explain MinMax scaling and standard scaling
17) What are the advantages of MeanShift clustering?
18) What are the limitations of the perceptron model?
19) Write an essay on Q-learning.
20) Explain some real-world problems solved by machine learning in forecasting future market trends.
21) Explain Poisson distribution in detail.
22) Explain Cramer's Rule.

Part-D (3 × 10 = 30)

Answer Any THREE Questions

23) Explain various types of regression algorithm in detail.
24) What are the challenges and future directions in probability and statistics for machine learning?
25) Write an essay on orthogonalization.
26) What are the applications of reinforcement learning?
27) How can artificial neural networks be used for predictive analytics?

Model Paper 2

NAME OF THE COLLEGE

End Semester – (XXXX)

Programme: XXXXX **Course Code: XXXXX**

Course Title: XXXXX

Duration: 3 Hrs **Max Marks: 75**

Part-A (10 × 1 = 10)

Answer ALL the Questions

1. In which type of task is MeanShift clustering commonly used?
a) Image segmentation b) Text classification
c) Anomaly detection d) Regression analysis

2. Which probability distribution can be used to simulate the number of vehicles passing through a traffic light in a given time period?
a) Uniform distribution b) Normal distribution
c) Exponential distribution d) Poisson distribution

3. Which mathematical process is commonly used in recommendation systems to suggest items to users based on their prior interactions?
a) Convolution b) Eigen decomposition
c) Clustering d) Regression

4. Which type of optimization allows for imposing restrictions or constraints on the parameters of a machine learning model?
a) Constrained optimization
b) Unconstrained optimization
c) Both constrained and unconstrained optimization
d) Neither constrained nor unconstrained optimization

5. Why is space complexity an important consideration in computational learning?
A) It directly affects the accuracy and effectiveness of the algorithm.
B) It determines the trade-off between space and time complexity.
C) It impacts the efficiency and effectiveness of the algorithm.
D) It measures the number of operations performed by the algorithm.

6. What can be determined by analyzing temporal features such as date, time, and frequency in data?
a) Binary characteristics b) Categorical traits
c) Data trends and patterns d) Numerical values

7. What is the purpose of the degree parameter in OC-SVM when using a polynomial kernel?
a) To determine the influence of each training example on the decision boundary.

b) To measure the penalties for misclassification errors.
c) To specify the cost factor for misclassifications.
d) To control the complexity of the model based on the number of features.

8. Why does MLP require a significant amount of computing power?
a) Due to the black-box nature of the model
b) Because of the complex calculations involved
c) To interpret the importance of each feature
d) When dealing with large datasets

9. A machine learning engineer is working on a problem where the data set contains a mix of continuous and categorical features. Which type of linear classifier might be suitable for handling such diverse features?
a) Only suitable for continuous features
b) Unable to handle categorical features
c) Suitable for both continuous and categorical features
d) Require separate preprocessing for categorical data

10. What does transfer learning leverage in GAN training to improve performance on a smaller-scale data set?
a) Human annotations
b) Unlabeled data
c) Large-scale data set
d) Synthetic data

Part-B (5 × 2 = 10)

Answer ALL the Questions

11) Define random forest.

12) Define discrete probability distributions.

13) What is eigenvector and eigenvalue?

14) What is policy search?

15) Define perceptron.

Part-C (5 × 5 = 25)

Answer Any FIVE Questions

16) Give examples of how statistics is used in machine learning.

17) Explain Gaussian elimination.

18) What is optimization and how is it useful in machine learning?

19) Explain complexity theory of machine learning.

20) What are the methods to improve GAN training?

21) Explain ordinal logistic regression with real-world examples.

22) Explain the steps of K-means clustering.

23) Explain thresholding.

Part-D ($3 \times 10 = 30$)

Answer Any THREE Questions

24) Explain well-posed machine learning problems in detail.

25) Explain normal distribution in detail.

26) Explain LU decomposition.

27) Explain computational complexity of learning.

28) Explain the concept of fuzzy C-means clustering in detail.

Index

G

H

I

J

K

L

M

N

O

P

Q

R

S

T

U

V